T0391949

The Law of Rescission

The Law of Rescission

Third Edition

DOMINIC O'SULLIVAN KC
STEVEN ELLIOTT KC
RAFAL ZAKRZEWSKI

OXFORD
UNIVERSITY PRESS

Great Clarendon Street, Oxford, OX2 6DP,
United Kingdom

Oxford University Press is a department of the University of Oxford.
It furthers the University's objective of excellence in research, scholarship,
and education by publishing worldwide. Oxford is a registered trade mark of
Oxford University Press in the UK and in certain other countries

© Dominic O'Sullivan, Steven Elliott, Rafal Zakrzewski 2023

The moral rights of the authors have been asserted

First Edition published in 2008
Second Edition published in 2014
Third Edition published in 2023

All rights reserved. No part of this publication may be reproduced, stored in
a retrieval system, or transmitted, in any form or by any means, without the
prior permission in writing of Oxford University Press, or as expressly permitted
by law, by licence or under terms agreed with the appropriate reprographics
rights organization. Enquiries concerning reproduction outside the scope of the
above should be sent to the Rights Department, Oxford University Press, at the
address above

You must not circulate this work in any other form
and you must impose this same condition on any acquirer

Public sector information reproduced under Open Government Licence v3.0
(http://www.nationalarchives.gov.uk/doc/open-government-licence/open-government-licence.htm)

Published in the United States of America by Oxford University Press
198 Madison Avenue, New York, NY 10016, United States of America

British Library Cataloguing in Publication Data
Data available

Library of Congress Control Number: 2022933258

ISBN 978-0-19-885228-5

DOI: 10.1093/law/9780198852285.001.0001

Printed and bound in the UK by
TJ Books Limited

Links to third party websites are provided by Oxford in good faith and
for information only. Oxford disclaims any responsibility for the materials
contained in any third party website referenced in this work.

Preface to the First Edition

England has never had a book on the law of rescission. In the wider common law world only two books have ever been written, both by chance in 1916.[1] The treatments of rescission in standard texts on contract, restitution, and equity rarely stray beyond the landmark decisions of the highest appellate courts. There are few areas of contract law that have remained as unexplored.

Rescission is complex not least because it straddles the jurisdictional divide between the common law and equity and because it can involve both personal and proprietary rights. Some of the most fundamental problems to which these dualities give rise have never been resolved. Parallel and inconsistent lines of authority have been decided in apparent ignorance one of the other, the cases never having been collected together and analysed systematically. This book does not answer all of the questions that must be asked, but we hope that it goes some way towards ordering the subject.

What follows only attempts to state the law in England and Wales. The law of rescission is still largely uniform across the Commonwealth, however, and reference is made to cases decided in Australia, Canada, New Zealand, and elsewhere. This is particularly so in respect of cases deciding points not yet considered in England, and where there are material divergences between the principal Commonwealth jurisdictions.

This book has had a long gestation and in that time we have incurred many debts. John McGhee QC has given his time generously as a reviewer and his comments have always been thoughtful. We also thank for reviewing drafts and for discussing ideas Dr Johann Dieckmann, Dr James Edelman, Dr Laurence Emmett, Anthony de Garr Robinson QC, Robert Hill, Dr Ben Kremer, Dr Eva Micheler, and Edwin Peel. Thanks are also due to the late Professor Peter Birks, who supervised the doctoral thesis that formed the germ of this book and encouraged its publication.

Our gratitude further extends to the editorial and production teams at Oxford University Press, who have done their job with care and tolerance for our failings. Sarah O'Sullivan has also applied her editorial skills and we are grateful for the considerable time she has given us.

For funding the project at various stages we acknowledge the generosity of the Commonwealth Scholarship and Fellowship Commission and the British Academy.

---

[1] CB Morison, *Rescission of Contracts: A Treatise on the Principles Governing the Rescission, Discharge, Avoidance and Dissolution of Contracts* (1916) (New Zealand); HC Black, *A Treatise on the Rescission of Contracts and Cancellation of Written Instruments* (1916) (USA).

Our greatest debt, however, is to Sarah, Eva, and Kirstyn. We have all written this book alongside busy practices with the consequence that it has consumed evenings, weekends, and holidays that should have been spent with them. Their patience and support has carried us along.

Dominic O'Sullivan
Steven Elliott
Rafal Zakrzewski
3 August 2007

Preface to the Second Edition

We have been surprised and delighted by the generous reception the first edition of this book received in England and Wales and elsewhere. We are grateful to all of the reviewers who took the time to consider the book. We have also been pleased that professional colleagues and, evidently, a number of judges have found the book useful.

As with the first edition, this book only attempts to state the law in England and Wales, but developments and divergences elsewhere in the Commonwealth are also taken into account. In consequence the process of revision has been much greater than it might otherwise have been. We hope this effort enhances the value of the book.

Since the first edition there have been many important and fascinating new cases touching aspects of the law of rescission. To name just two, in *Pitt v Holt* [2013] 2 AC 108 the Supreme Court comprehensively addressed the rescission of mistaken gifts and other gratuitous transactions. The solution their Lordships adopted is consistent with that advanced in the first edition of this book, but the case has nonetheless led us to make substantial revisions to Chapter 29. In *Independent Trustee Services Ltd v GP Noble Trustees Ltd* [2013] Ch 91 the Court of Appeal considered the retrospective effect of rescission. That case will be considered by the Supreme Court but regrettably it has not been possible to delay publication of this edition.

There has also been an outpouring of scholarly work reappraising aspects of the subject. Most important for our purposes has been Birke Häcker's insightful thesis *Consequences of Impaired Consent Transfers* (2009) and her associated articles. Other new monographs we have found particularly valuable include Matthew Conaglen's *Fiduciary Loyalty* (2010) and Andrew Lodder, *Enrichment in the Law of Unjust Enrichment and Restitution* (2012), each of these the result of doctoral work as well. The American Law Institute's *Third Restatement of Restitution and Unjust Enrichment* (2011) has also been thought-provoking.

We would like to record our gratitude to the editorial and production teams of Oxford University Press for their patience, help, and support in bringing this book to publication. We are also grateful to Nicholas Derrington and Caitlin McKenna for valuable research assistance, to Warren Swain for his comments on Chapter 3, and to Andrew Kull for corresponding with us on points concerning the law in the United States of America.

Our greatest debt continues to be to Sarah, Eva, and Kirstyn.

Dominic O'Sullivan
Steven Elliott
Rafal Zakrzewski
3 August 2014

Preface to this Edition

As the years go by our debts mount. We thank Divya Behl for assisting in the research for this edition. We also thank the editorial team at Oxford University Press and now also the production team at Newgen KnowledgeWorks for their careful work and tolerance for our failings. The reviewers who considered the second edition also have our gratitude.

Our greatest debt continues to be to Sarah, Eva, and Kirstyn.

Dominic O'Sullivan KC
Steven Elliott KC
Rafal Zakrzewski
21 January 2023

Contents

Table of Cases	xxiii
Table of Legislation	lxxv

I. INTRODUCTION

1. Core Distinctions

A. Introduction	1.01
B. Termination *Ab Initio* and *De Futuro*	1.06
(1) Nature and basis of the distinction	1.07
(2) Termination *ab initio*: effects on contractual rights and obligations	1.14
(3) Termination *de futuro*: effects on contractual rights and obligations	1.20
(4) Termination *ab initio* and *de futuro*: rights to restitution	1.23
(5) Terminology	1.31
C. Void and Voidable Contracts	1.35
(1) Void and voidable contracts	1.36
(2) Contracts valid until rescinded and contracts ineffective until ratified	1.39
(3) Transfer of title	1.45
(4) Recovery of benefits	1.49
D. Rescission and Transactions Ineffective in Equity	1.57
(1) Introduction	1.57
(2) Where the claimant is not a party to the impugned transaction	1.67
(3) Where the claimant is a party to the impugned transaction	1.70
(4) Bribes	1.87
(5) Apparent gifts made ineffective by resulting trust	1.90
(6) Other ineffective transactions	1.91

2. Rescission and Independent Claims

A. Introduction	2.01
B. Damages	2.03
C. Equitable Compensation	2.10
D. Disgorgement of Profits	2.14
(1) Distinction between profit-based remedies and rescission	2.16
(2) Proprietary relief absent rescission	2.24
(3) Personal accountability for profits absent rescission	2.27

3. Historical Foundations

A. Introduction	3.01
B. The Common Law	3.04
(1) The effect of fraud on contract	3.05
(2) The effect of fraud on title	3.06
(3) Rescission as a condition to restitution	3.16
(4) Termination *de futuro* and *ab initio*	3.30
(5) Role of the forms of action	3.33

xii CONTENTS

C. Equity	3.34
(1) Introduction	3.34
(2) Orders effecting rescission	3.37
(3) The effect of fraud on contract	3.40
(4) The effect of fraud on title	3.42
(5) Rescission by election	3.53
D. The Special Case of Insurance	3.55
(1) Special relationship between common law and equity	3.56
(2) Chancery courts' policy of limited interference	3.59
(3) Change from 'void' to 'voidable'	3.63

II. GROUNDS

4. Misrepresentation	
A. Introduction	4.01
B. Types of Misrepresentation: Fraudulent, Negligent, Innocent	4.04
(1) Nature of fraudulent misrepresentation	4.05
(2) Importance of the distinction outside law of rescission	4.09
(3) Importance in relation to rescission	4.10
(4) Special vulnerability of contracts to rescission for fraud	4.13
C. Representation	4.17
(1) Representations of existing fact and of law	4.17
(2) Representation may be a contractual term	4.20
(3) Representation may be express or implied	4.26
(4) Passing on information generally not a representation	4.28
(5) Silence generally not a representation	4.29
(6) Sources of implied representations	4.32
(7) Determining what was represented (expressly and impliedly)	4.39
(8) What are not representations	4.44
(9) Materiality of the representation	4.62
D. Representation must be Made by the Representor to the Representee	4.74
(1) Those by whom the representation may be made	4.74
(2) Those to whom the representation must be made	4.76
E. Representation must be False	4.81
(1) Substantial correctness sufficient	4.83
(2) Representation must be false at the time of reliance	4.88
(3) Continuing representations and changes of circumstances	4.90
F. Representation must be Relied On	4.100
(1) Reliance and inducement: a question of causation	4.100
(2) Ambiguous statements or conduct	4.103
(3) Causation: fraudulent misrepresentation	4.104
(4) Causation: non-fraudulent misrepresentation	4.105
(5) Presumption of reliance and onus of proof	4.110
(6) Examples of non-reliance on a false representation	4.114
(7) Opportunity to discover truth does not disprove reliance	4.119
(8) Subsequent transactions	4.121
5. Non-Disclosure	
A. Introduction	5.01

B. No General Duty of Disclosure — 5.02
   (1) Exceptional cases where non-disclosure permits rescission — 5.04
C. Course of Dealings where Disclosure is Required — 5.10
   (1) Misrepresentation by silence — 5.10
   (2) Unilateral mistake — 5.11
D. Relationships where Disclosure is Required — 5.12
   (1) Fiduciary relationships — 5.12
   (2) Family arrangements — 5.14
   (3) Relationships of trust and confidence — 5.21
E. Transactions where Disclosure is Required — 5.24
   (1) Insurance — 5.24
   (2) Guarantees and suretyship — 5.41
   (3) Prospective partnerships — 5.58
   (4) Compromises — 5.59
   (5) Sales of land — 5.65

6. Duress and Undue Influence
A. Introduction — 6.01
B. Duress — 6.05
   (1) Introduction — 6.05
   (2) First requirement: illegitimate pressure — 6.09
   (3) Second requirement: coercion in the sense of no practical choice or alternative — 6.46
   (4) Third requirement: causation — 6.61
C. Undue Influence — 6.75
   (1) Introduction — 6.75
   (2) Two ways of proving undue influence — 6.76
   (3) Actual undue influence: undue influence proved directly — 6.80
   (4) Presumed undue influence: undue influence proved with the assistance of a presumption — 6.94
   (5) Severable transactions — 6.120

7. Mistake, Impaired Capacity, and Unconscionable Bargains
A. Introduction — 7.01
B. Mistake — 7.02
   (1) Common mistake — 7.07
   (2) Unilateral mistake — 7.12
   (3) Special doctrines of rescission for mistake — 7.27
C. Impaired Capacity: Mental Infirmity and Intoxication — 7.41
   (1) Mental infirmity — 7.45
   (2) Drunkenness or intoxication — 7.65
D. Unconscionable Bargains: Exploitation — 7.69
   (1) First requirement: serious disadvantage relative to the counterparty — 7.75
   (2) Second requirement: weakness exploited in morally culpable manner — 7.80
   (3) Third requirement: transaction overreaching and oppressive — 7.89
   (4) Possible defence: counterparty shows that transaction was fair, just, and reasonable — 7.93
   (5) Role of independent advice — 7.97
   (6) Other Commonwealth jurisdictions — 7.103

xiv CONTENTS

8. Conflict of Interest
  A. Introduction — 8.01
  B. Transactions with Fiduciaries — 8.03
    (1) Nature and basis of the fair-dealing rule — 8.05
    (2) Scope of the fair-dealing rule — 8.11
    (3) Compliance with the fair-dealing rule — 8.17
  C. Double Employment — 8.34
    (1) Consent to adverse duty or interest — 8.38
    (2) Disclosure and advice — 8.42
    (3) Substantive fairness — 8.45
    (4) Implication of counterparty — 8.46
  D. Bribery — 8.49
    (1) Rescission at law and in equity — 8.51
    (2) Elements of bribery — 8.52
    (3) Implication of counterparty — 8.61
  E. Causation Irrelevant — 8.72

9. Third Party Wrongdoing
  A. Introduction — 9.01
  B. Contracts — 9.03
    (1) The basic rule precluding rescission — 9.03
    (2) Agency — 9.04
    (3) Knowledge of misconduct — 9.05
    (4) Relationship with unilateral mistake — 9.06
  C. Surety Contracts — 9.07
    (1) Constructive notice — 9.08
    (2) Circumstances in which special measures must be taken — 9.14
    (3) Special measures that immunize the security — 9.18
  D. Gratuitous Dispositions — 9.21

III. RESCISSION BY ELECTION AND BY COURT ORDER

10. Common Law, Equity, and Fusion
  A. Introduction — 10.01
  B. Persistence of the Distinction between Rescission at Law and in Equity — 10.03
    (1) Absence of fusion — 10.03
    (2) The principle that rules of equity prevail — 10.10
    (3) Reform — 10.15
  C. Overview of the Distinctions between Rescission at Law and in Equity — 10.20
    (1) Introduction — 10.20
    (2) Grounds for rescission — 10.23
    (3) Bars to rescission — 10.30
    (4) Differences between rescinding at law and in equity — 10.34
    (5) Interaction between the common law and equitable doctrines — 10.39

11. Electing to Rescind
  A. Introduction — 11.01
  B. How an Election to Rescind is Made — 11.03

(1) Communicating an unequivocal intention to disaffirm	11.03
(2) Conduct must be unequivocal	11.15
(3) Disaffirming by pleading	11.19
(4) The need for communication	11.30
(5) Rescission as a defence	11.41
(6) Need for a tender or return of benefits at the time of electing	11.48
(7) Special requirements when defending a call on shares	11.50
C. Transactions Voidable at Law	11.53
(1) Election effects rescission	11.53
(2) Election to rescind irrevocable	11.57
D. Transactions Voidable only in Equity	11.59
(1) Summary	11.59
(2) Historical context	11.62
(3) The 'rescission by election' line of authority	11.67
(4) The 'rescission by court order' line of authority	11.85
(5) Other common law jurisdictions	11.97
(6) Conclusions	11.107
(7) Whether election to rescind is irrevocable	11.113
12. Extinction of the Contract	
A. Introduction	12.01
B. Rescission at Common Law	12.04
C. Rescission in Equity	12.07
(1) Contract set aside by court order	12.07
(2) Contract set aside by election?	12.11
(3) Discretion to grant rescission	12.22

IV. *RESTITUTIO IN INTEGRUM*

13. General Principles of *Restitutio in Integrum*	
A. Objective	13.01
B. Judicial Discretion	13.07
C. Heretical Approaches	13.14
D. Retrospective Effects	13.26
(1) Introduction	13.26
(2) Contractual rights	13.27
(3) Property rights	13.29
(4) Fiscal consequences	13.32
(5) Contribution under the Marine Insurance Act 1906	13.33
(6) Interest and income	13.34
E. Other Cases	13.35
(1) Replacement contracts	13.35
(2) Contract terminated by agreement	13.36
14. Mutual Restitution: Rescission at Law	
A. Introduction	14.01
B. Restitution of Benefits Transferred	14.02
(1) Nature of the right to restitution	14.02
(2) Restitution of property transferred	14.03
(3) Substitutive restitution of property transferred	14.29

(4) Restitution for money paid	14.36
(5) Restitution for services provided	14.41
C. Counter-restitution of Benefits Received	14.45
(1) Nature of the obligation to make counter-restitution	14.45
(2) The need for a return or tender of benefits received	14.52
(3) Security for counter-restitution	14.66
(4) Counter-restitution of property received	14.69
(5) Counter-restitution for money received	14.76
(6) Counter-restitution for services received	14.86

15. Mutual Restitution: Rescission in Equity

A. Introduction	15.01
B. Restitution of Benefits Transferred	15.03
(1) Nature of the right to restitution	15.03
(2) Restitution of property transferred	15.04
(3) Substitutive restitution of property transferred	15.14
(4) Restitution for money paid	15.33
(5) Restitution for services provided	15.39
C. Counter-restitution of Benefits Received	15.44
(1) Nature of the obligation to make counter-restitution	15.45
(2) Counter-restitution of property received	15.63
(3) Counter-restitution for money received	15.65
(4) Counter-restitution for services received	15.67
D. Equitable Rescission by Election	15.69
(1) Restitution	15.69
(2) Counter-restitution	15.73

16. Proprietary Claims

A. Introduction	16.01
B. Proprietary Claims upon Rescission at Law	16.02
(1) Property	16.02
(2) Money	16.05
(3) Tracing into substitutes	16.10
C. Proprietary Claims upon Equitable Rescission	16.12
(1) Title passes pending rescission	16.12
(2) Recovering title	16.19
(3) When does disaffirmation confer an equitable interest?	16.25
(4) Retrospective equitable title	16.41
(5) Proprietary claims in respect of money paid	16.45
(6) Nature of the proprietary interest arising upon equitable rescission	16.59

17. Financial Adjustments

A. Introduction	17.01
B. Restitution and Counter-restitution	17.02
(1) Benefits derived from land and chattels	17.03
(2) Joint acquisitions	17.14
(3) Interest	17.15
(4) Indemnity	17.23
(5) Offsetting equivalent benefits	17.30
C. Compensation	17.32
(1) Improvements and repairs	17.35

(2) Deterioration and depreciation	17.55
(3) Irrelevant detriments	17.61

18. *Restitutio in Integrum* Impossible

A. Basic Principles	18.01
(1) Purpose of the bar	18.03
(2) The role of fault	18.09
(3) The role of delay	18.12
B. The Bar at Law and in Equity	18.17
(1) The bar at law	18.18
(2) The bar in equity	18.27
(3) Persistence of the distinction	18.30
C. Where Counter-restitution Not Required	18.33
(1) Benefits obtained other than under the contract	18.34
(2) Defendant's fault	18.36
(3) Asset lost following tender	18.37
(4) Costless benefits	18.39
(5) Insurance fraud	18.40
(6) Benefits the defendant was bound to confer	18.43
(7) Worthless assets and services	18.46
(8) Set-off	18.47
D. Counter-restitution and Unavailable Assets	18.48
(1) Counter-restitution impossible	18.48
(2) Substitutive counter-restitution	18.52
(3) The future of substitutive counter-restitution	18.62
E. Counter-restitution: Miscellaneous Issues	18.77
(1) Possession, occupation, and use of asset	18.77
(2) Asset changed	18.85
(3) Asset depreciated owing to market decline	18.93
(4) Services	18.99
(5) Other intangible benefits	18.102
(6) Money	18.103
F. Prejudicial Change of Circumstances	18.106
(1) Unjustified prejudice	18.107
(2) Money committed to joint purposes	18.118
(3) Reversible change of circumstances	18.119
G. Miscellaneous Issues	18.121
(1) Date of assessment	18.121
(2) Onus of proof	18.124

19. Partial Rescission

A. Introduction	19.01
B. Partial Rescission	19.02
(1) Rationale	19.03
(2) Rule applies to bargains	19.05
(3) Unilateral dispositions	19.08
C. Adjustment of Insurance Contracts	19.09
D. Rescission Against Third Party Wrongdoers	19.10
E. Rescission on Terms	19.17
(1) *TSB Bank Plc v Camfield*	19.18

xviii CONTENTS

(2) Former exception in cases of mistaken dispositions of real property	19.22
F. Rescission on Terms Elsewhere in the Commonwealth	19.26
(1) Australia: *Vadasz v Pioneer Concrete*	19.26
(2) New Zealand	19.31
(3) Canada	19.32
(4) Hong Kong	19.33
G. Comment	19.34

V. THIRD PARTIES

20. Intervention of Third Party Rights

A. Introduction	20.01
B. Protection of Third Party Property Rights	20.06
(1) The bar at law	20.09
(2) The bar in equity	20.23
C. Protection of Other Third Party Rights	20.28
(1) Multilateral contracts	20.31
(2) Contracts relating to the subject matter of the voidable transaction	20.33
(3) The winding-up bar	20.36

21. Remote Recipients

A. Introduction	21.01
B. Remote Recipients Vulnerable to Rescission	21.03
(1) Volunteers	21.04
(2) Those taking with notice	21.08
(3) Assignee of a chose in action	21.22
(4) Crossed cheques	21.27
C. Nature of the Claim	21.29
(1) Basis of the claim against volunteers and those taking with notice	21.29
(2) Basis of the claim against assignees of a chose in action	21.31
(3) No new claim to rescind upon disposition to remote recipient	21.35
(4) Need to rescind original transaction	21.36
(5) Remote recipient in no better position than original transferee	21.37
D. Consequences of Recovery	21.40
(1) Avoidance of original contract	21.41
(2) No avoidance of contract with the remote recipient	21.42
(3) Restitution from the original transferee	21.43
(4) Counter-restitution to the original transferee	21.45
(5) Restitution from the remote recipient	21.48
(6) No counter-restitution to the remote recipient	21.50
(7) Remote recipient's rights against his transferor	21.54
E. Protection of Bona Fide Purchasers	21.55
(1) Common law and equitable doctrines of bona fide purchase	21.55
(2) Protection of purchaser of legal title	21.63
(3) Protection of purchaser of equitable title	21.64
(4) Onus of proof	21.71

22. Succeeding to Rights to Rescind

A. Introduction	22.01
B. Devolution on Death	22.05

(1) Heirs at law	22.05
(2) Beneficiary under a will	22.06
(3) Executors	22.07
C. Settlements	22.08
D. Assignment and Conveyance	22.09
(1) Assignment	22.09
(2) Second conveyance of same property	22.11

VI. OTHER BARS

23. Affirmation

A. Introduction	23.01
B. Nature and Justification	23.04
(1) Juristic nature	23.04
(2) Justification	23.10
C. Affirming Party must be Free from the Vitiating Factor	23.14
(1) Pressure and exploitation	23.14
(2) Misrepresentation, mistake, and non-disclosure	23.18
D. Need for Awareness of Right to Rescind	23.35
(1) Uncertainty as to whether electing party must know rights	23.35
(2) Awareness of rights required in England	23.40
(3) Awareness of rights not required in other parts of the Commonwealth	23.42
(4) Whether knowledge of right to rescind should be required	23.51
(5) What must be known	23.53
(6) Deliberately failing to inquire into rights	23.54
(7) Proving knowledge of rights	23.55
E. Communication	23.57
F. Unequivocal Words or Conduct	23.61
(1) General principle	23.61
(2) Application of the general principle	23.64
(3) Effect of reservation of rights	23.91
(4) Possibility of affirming after an election to rescind	23.97
G. Intention to Affirm is not Required	23.98
(1) General rule	23.98
(2) Where affirming conduct is not known to other party	23.101
(3) Relation to awareness of rights	23.102
H. Affirmation is Generally Irrevocable	23.103
(1) General rule	23.103
(2) Exception where subsequent discovery of new ground for rescission	23.104
I. Onus of Proof and Pleading	23.110
(1) Onus of proof	23.110
(2) Pleading	23.111

24. Delay and Estoppel

A. Introduction	24.01
B. The Different Doctrines Engaged by Delay	24.03
(1) Waiver by affirmation and by acquiescence	24.03
(2) Laches	24.14
(3) Statute of limitations applied directly	24.22
(4) Statute of limitations applied by analogy	24.25

xx CONTENTS

(5) Mere lapse of time	24.37
C. When Delay Bars Rescission	24.38
(1) Freedom from the vitiating factor	24.38
(2) Need for awareness of rights	24.57
(3) Unreasonable delay after emancipation from the vitiating factor	24.64
(4) What amounts to unreasonable delay	24.71
(5) The significance of prejudice	24.109
D. Estoppel	24.116

25. Bankruptcy and Winding Up

A. Introduction	25.01
B. Bankruptcy and Winding Up Generally	25.02
(1) No general bar to rescission	25.02
(2) Supervening bankruptcy: rescinding to assert a proprietary claim	25.04
(3) Supervening bankruptcy: rescinding to assert a personal claim	25.08
(4) Rescission as a defence against the trustee in bankruptcy	25.11
(5) Contracting with an undischarged bankrupt	25.12
(6) Whether right to rescind survives discharge from bankruptcy	25.17
(7) Winding up	25.18
C. Winding Up as a Bar to Shareholder's Rescission	25.21
(1) Introduction	25.21
(2) The bar	25.24
(3) Rationale	25.31
(4) Scope	25.42
(5) When winding up commences	25.62
(6) Operation of the bar before winding up	25.63
(7) Steps to be taken to prevent the bar operating	25.69
(8) Statutory exceptions	25.77

26. Contracting Out

A. Introduction	26.01
B. General Law	26.02
(1) Introduction	26.02
(2) Types of clauses	26.03
(3) Entire agreement clauses	26.04
(4) No representation clauses	26.06
(5) Non-reliance clauses	26.09
C. Misrepresentation Act 1967	26.12
(1) Section 3 of the Misrepresentation Act 1967	26.13
(2) Scope of section 3 of the Misrepresentation Act 1967	26.14
(3) Requirement of reasonableness	26.23
D. Consumer Protection Legislation	26.34

27. Bars for Non-Fraudulent Misrepresentation

A. Introduction	27.01
B. Transfer of Title to Real Property	27.05
(1) Nature of the bar	27.05
(2) Abolition of the bar in England and Wales	27.10
(3) Partial abolition of the bar in Australia	27.12
(4) Abolition of the bar in New Zealand	27.13
(5) Canada	27.14

(6) Hong Kong and Singapore	27.16
C. Transfer of Title to Personal Property	27.18
(1) Nature of the bar	27.18
(2) Abolition of the bar in England and Wales	27.28
(3) Australia	27.29
(4) New Zealand	27.31
(5) Canada	27.32
(6) Hong Kong and Singapore	27.34
D. Incorporation as a Contractual Term	27.36
(1) Nature of the bar	27.36
(2) Abolition of the bar in England and Wales	27.39
(3) Australia	27.40
(4) New Zealand	27.44
(5) Canada	27.45
(6) Hong Kong and Singapore	27.46
E. Contracts for the Sale of Goods	27.48
(1) Bar on rescinding all sales of goods	27.48
(2) Rescission barred when contractual right to reject is lost	27.54

28. Disproportionate Effect: Section 2(2) of the Misrepresentation Act 1967

A. Introduction	28.01
B. Conditions to the Exercise of the Power	28.06
C. Grounds on which the Power may be Exercised	28.10
D. Measure of Damages	28.15
(1) Consequential loss	28.22
(2) Two mistaken theories	28.25
E. Disproportionate Effect and the Fair-dealing Rule	28.36

VII. GIFTS AND DEEDS

29. Gifts and Deeds

A. Introduction	29.01
B. Gifts	29.02
(1) How gifts are made	29.02
(2) Void gifts	29.08
(3) Discretion to reject and to reclaim a gift	29.13
(4) Special vulnerability of gifts to rescission	29.15
(5) Significance of how the gift is made and what is given	29.24
(6) Gifts made by conduct	29.27
(7) Gifts made by deed	29.40
(8) Dispositions of another's assets: powers of appointment	29.52
(9) Gifts and theft	29.55
(10) Assimilation of gifts to disadvantageous contracts	29.56
C. Deeds	29.63
(1) Introduction	29.64
(2) Duress	29.68
(3) Fraud	29.72
(4) Cancellation of deeds	29.83

Index   633

Table of Cases

415703 BC Ltd v JEL Investments Ltd 2010 BCSC 202 ....18.100, 19.05

A Trust, The, Re [2009] JLR 447 ....29.46, 29.47
AAM Limited v Exotica Enterprise Limited [2019] NZHC 1482..........................23.36
Aaron's Reefs v Twiss [1896] AC 273 .... 4.42, 14.62, 23.28, 23.110, 24.04, 24.07, 24.71, 24.88
AB jnr v MB (unreported Grand Court, 13 August 2012)............................2.11, 24.14
Abacus Trust Co (Isle of Man) v Barr [2003] Ch 409 .... 1.60, 1.74, 29.54
Abbelby v Meyers (1867) LR 2 CP 651..3.27
Abbey National Bank plc v Stringer [2006] EWCA 338....................................6.100
Aberdeen Railway Co v Blaikie (1854) 1 Mac 461 ....8.04, 8.05, 8.11, 8.19
Abraham v Wingate Properties Ltd [1986] 1 WWR 568 (Man CA)...................4.24, 27.45
Abram Steamship Company Ltd v Westville Shipping Company Ltd 1922 SC 571;
 on appeal [1923] AC 773 .... 10.24, 11.04, 11.54, 11.67, 11.75, 11.76, 11.77, 11.79, 11.80,
             11.81, 11.82, 11.83, 11.104, 11.105, 11.107, 11.108, 12.04,
            15.63, 18.51, 18.121, 23.36, 23.41, 23.61, 23.66, 23.84
Abu Dhabi Investment Company v H Clarkson & Co Ltd [2007] EWHC 1267 ....4.90
Abu Dhabi National Tanker Co v Product Star Shipping Ltd (The Product Star) (No 2)
 [1993] 1 Lloyd's Rep 397 (CA) 6.38
AC v DC [2012] EWHC 2032 (Fam) 13.32
Academy of Health and Fitness Pty Ltd v Power [1973] VR 254..... 11.46, 11.47, 11.101, 12.07, 27.41
Achieve Goal Holdings Ltd v Zhong Xin Ore- Material Holding Company Ltd
 [2018] HKCFI 2718 ....1.08
Adam v Newbigging See Newbigging v Adam
Adam v Sworder (1863) 2 De GJ & S 44, 46 ER 291 ....17.12
Adam Opel GmbH and another v Mitras Automotive (UK) Ltd
 [2007] EWHC 3205 (QB) 6.07, 6.12, 6.26, 6.32, 6.51, 6.53, 6.56
Adare Finance DAC v Yellowstone Capital Management SA
 [2020] EWHC 2760 (Comm); [2021] 2 BCLC 140..............6.29, 6.38, 6.58, 7.75, 7.80, 7.89
Addenbrooke Pty Ltd v Duncan (No 2) (2017) 121 ACSR 406 (Full Fed Ct) 1.27, 1.53, 1.54
Addis v Campbell (1841) 4 Beav 401, 49 ER 394.... 3.40, 3.42, 16.42, 21.08, 21.37, 21.45, 21.52, 22.08
Addison v Ottawa Auto and Taxi Co (1913) 16 DLR 318
 (Ont SC (App Div)) 17.05, 17.30, 18.77, 18.88
Addlestone Linoleum Co, Re (1887) 37 ChD 191....................................25.49
Aequitas Ltd v AEFC [2001] NSWSC 14 .... 2.11, 2.12, 2.28
Aero-Gate Pte Ltd v Engen Marine Engineering Ltd [2013] 4 SLR 409 ....23.58
AG v Biphosphated Guano Co (1878) 11 ChD 327 (CA) 21.72
AG v Magdalen College Oxford (1854) 18 Beav 223, 52 ER 88........................3.52
AG v Ray (1874) 9 Ch App 397 ....27.19
AG v Vigor (1803) 8 Ves Jun 256, 32 ER 352 ....3.44
AG v Wilkins (1853) 17 Beav 285, 51 ER 1043 ....21.61
Agbeyegbe v Ikomi [1953] 1 WLR 263 (PC–Nigeria) 24.18
Agip SpA v Navigazione Alta Italia SpA (The Nai Genova and The Nai Superba)
 [1984] 1 Lloyd's Rep 353 (CA) 7.19
Agnew v Länsforsäkringsbolagens AB [2001] 1 AC 223 ....8.10
Agricultural and Rural Finance Pty Ltd v Gardiner (2008) 238 CLR 570 ....23.04, 23.08, 23.11, 24.03
Agricultural Land Management Ltd v Jackson (No 2) [2014] WASC 102.................17.34
Agripay Pty Ltd v Byrne [2011] 2 QdR 501 (CA) 29.59
Aguilar v Aguilar (1820) 5 Madd 414, 56 ER 953 ....15.60
AH McDonald and Company Pty Ltd v Wells (1931) 45 CLR 506...............1.19, 11.43, 12.06,
          18.01, 18.48, 18.72, 18.102, 19.03, 19.05
Ahuja Investments Limited v Victorygame Ltd [2020] EWHC 1153 (Ch) 4.121

xxiv TABLE OF CASES

Ahuja Investments Ltd v Victorygame Ltd [2021] EWHC 2382 (Ch) 4.104, 4.117
AIC Ltd v ITS Testing Services (UK) Ltd (The Kriti Palm) [2007] 1 All ER 667 (CA) 4.06
Akerhielm v De Mare [1959] AC 789 (PC–Eastern Africa) 4.05, 4.06
Akita Holdings Ltd v A- G of Turks and Caicos Islands [2019] AC 250 (PC—TCI). 2.27
Akron Securities Ltd v Iliffe (1997) 41 NSWLR 353 (CA). 13.32, 17.56, 18.35, 18.93, 27.29
Al Nehayan v Kent [2018] EWHC 333; (Comm); [2018] 1 CLC 216 . . . 6.03, 6.20, 6.44, 6.47, 6.63, 6.67
Alati v Kruger (1955) 94 CLR 216. . . . . 4.23, 4.24, 10.04, 10.45, 11.21, 11.56, 11.59, 11.97, 11.99,
                                               11.101, 11.112, 11.114, 12.04, 13.08, 14.27, 14.71, 15.12, 15.38,
                                               15.63, 15.69, 15.75, 15.76, 16.07, 16.13, 16.25, 16.60, 17.05,
                                               17.17, 17.18, 17.58, 18.01, 18.27, 18.32, 18.37, 18.38,
                                               18.54, 18.60, 18.77, 18.122, 18.123, 23.71, 24.115, 27.38
Aldrich v Norwich Union Life Ins Co Ltd [2000] Lloyd's Rep IR 1 (CA). 2.07, 2.09, 13.04
Alec Lobb (Garages) Ltd v Total Oil Great Britain Ltd [1983] 1 WLR 87;
    on appeal [1985] 1 WLR 173 (CA). 6.98, 6.100, 7.69, 7.70, 7.79,
                                               7.80, 7.81, 7.84, 7.89, 7.98, 7.102, 24.98, 29.60
Alev, The See Vantage Navigation Corporation v Suhail & Saud Bahwan Building
    Materials (The Alev)
Alexander v Rayson [1936] 1 KB 169 (CA) 14.27
Alexander v Webber [1922] 1 KB 642 . . . . 8.53, 8.54, 8.58
Alf Vaughan v Royscot Trust plc [1999] 1 All ER 856. . . . . 6.30, 6.40
Allason v Campbell (CA 26 Feb 1998) 18.45
Allcard v Skinner (1887) 36 ChD 145 (CA). 6.03, 6.83, 6.93, 6.96, 6.103, 6.107, 6.113, 6.114,
                                         6.115, 11.86, 11.90, 11.91, 11.107, 15.13, 16.42, 17.04,
                                   18.118, 22.06, 23.08, 23.09, 23.14, 23.54, 23.63, 23.103, 24.04,
                                 24.07, 24.08, 24.10, 24.25, 24.34, 24.35, 24.39, 24.44, 24.58,
                               24.65, 24.67, 24.71, 24.86, 24.119, 29.14, 29.36, 29.39
Allen v Flood [1898] AC 1 . . . . .6.38
Allen v Robles [1969] 1 WLR 1193 (CA) 24.68, 24.109, 24.111
Allen v Universal Automobile Insurance Co Ltd (1933) 45 Lloyd's LR 55 . . . . .4.83
Alliance & Leicester Building Society v Edgestop Ltd [1994] 2 All ER 38 .4.120
Allianz Australia Insurance Ltd v Rose Marie Lo-Guidice [2012] NSWSC 145 . . . . .1.98
Allied Irish Bank plc v Byrne [1995] 2 FLR 325 . . . . 11.80, 11.107, 19.18
Allied London Investments Ltd v Hambro Life Assurance plc [1985] 1 EGLR 45 . . . . .17.18
Allison v Clayhills (1907) 97 LT 709. . . . . 8.08, 8.12, 8.13, 8.15, 8.29, 8.30, 8.33
Alman v Associated Newspapers Ltd (ChD 20 June 1980) 18.105, 18.114, 20.31
Alsager v Parker (1842) 10 M & W 576, 152 ER 600. . . . . .3.37
Amadio Pty Ltd v Henderson (1998) 81 FCR 149 (Full Ct). 13.20, 18.35, 18.93
Amalgamated Investment & Property Co Ltd v John Walker & Sons Ltd
    [1977] 1 WLR 164 (CA). 7.07, 10.26
American Reserve Energy Corp v McDorman (2002) 117 ACWS (3d) 82
    (Nfld and Labrador CA) 16.15
American Sugar Refining Co v Fancher (1895) NE 206 (SCNY) 15.19, 16.07, 16.42, 25.07
AMP (UK) plc v Barker [2001] PLR 77 . . . . .29.44
Amsalem v Raivid [2008] EWHC 3028 (TCC). 6.07
Amuse Hong Kong Ltd v Chan Tin Kim [1994] HKCA 369 . . . . 11.105
Anangel Atlas Compania Naviera SA v Ishikawajima-Harima Heavy Industries Ltd
    [1990] 1 Lloyd's Rep 167 . . . . 8.51, 8.52, 8.54
Anderson v Costello (1871) 19 WR 628 (CP Ir) 14.61
Anderson v Fitzgerald (1853) 4 HLC 484, 10 ER 551 . . . . .4.63
Anderson v Mcpherson [No 2] [2012] WASC 19 . . . . .16.61
Anderson v Pacific Fire and Marine (1872) LR 7 CP 65 . . . . 4.48, 4.50
Anderson v Thornton (1853) 8 Exch 425, 155 ER 1415 . . . . 3.56, 3.63, 14.79, 14.80
Andrews v Mowbray (1807) Wils Ex 71, 159 ER 835 . . . . .8.28
Angel v Jay [1911] 1 KB 666. . . . . 7.28, 27.05, 27.07, 27.08, 27.21, 27.22
Anglesey v Annesley (1741) 1 Bro 289, 1 ER 573 . . . . .18.14
Anglo-Scottish Sugar Beet Corporation Ltd v Spalding Urban District Council [1937] 2 KB 607. .9.04

TABLE OF CASES

Angove's Pty Ltd v Bailey [2016] 1 WLR 3179 (Sup Ct) 1.52, 1.54, 1.92,
1.95, 1.97, 16.48, 16.58, 16.61, 16.70, 25.06

Angus v Clifford [1891] 2 Ch 449 (CA) 4.51

Anker-Petersen v Christensen [2002] WTLR 313 . . . . .29.44, 29.54

Annulment Funding Co Ltd v Cowey [2010] EWCA Civ 711;
[2010] BPIR 1304 . . . . .6.79, 6.85, 6.120, 9.07

Anon (1677) 1 Salk 126, 91 ER 119. . . . . .21.56

Anon (1695) B & M 468 . . . . .3.23

Anon (1697) B & M 469 . . . . .3.23

Anon (1704) 6 Mod 114, 87 ER 872 . . . . .3.05

Antclizo, The See Food Corporation of India v Antclizo Shipping Corporation (The Antclizo)

Antoine v Barclays Bank plc [2019] 1 WLR 1958 (CA) 1.60, 15.08

Antonio v Antonio [2010] EWHC 1199 (QB). 6.20, 6.64

ANZ Executors & Trustee Company Ltd v Qintex Australia (receivers and managers
appointed) [1991] 2 Qd R 360 (CA). 1.78

Aquatic Air Pty Limited v Siewart [2015] NSWSC 928 . . . . .23.43

Aquila Wsa Aviation Opportunities II Limited v Onur Air Tasimacilik AS
[2018] EWHC 519 (Comm) 4.07, 26.06, 26.11

Arboretum Devon (RLH) Ltd, Re [2021] EWHC 1047 (Ch) 26.11

Archbold v Scully (1861) 9 HLC 360, 11 ER 769. . . . . .24.08

Archer v Hudson (1844) 7 Beav 551, 50 ER 126, 49 ER 1180; aff'd
(1846) 15 LJ Ch 211 . . . . .6.103, 6.114, 9.04, 29.58

Ardmair Bay Holdings Ltd v Craig [2019] CSOH 58, [2020] SLT 549 . . . . .4.49

Argo Fund Ltd v Essar Steel Ltd [2005] EWHC 600 . . . . .4.124

Arkwright v Newbold (1887) 17 ChD 301 (CA). 4.35, 4.90

Armagas Ltd v Mundogas SA (The Ocean Frost) [1985] 1 Lloyd's Rep 1;
on appeal [1986] AC 717 (CA) 8.49, 8.52, 8.59, 8.61, 8.63, 8.65, 8.66, 8.67, 9.03, 9.04

Armitage v Nurse [1998] Ch 241 (CA) 4.05, 17.11

Armstrong v Jackson [1917] 2 KB 822 . . . . .2.08, 15.38, 17.04, 17.56, 18.02, 18.04, 18.09, 18.13,
18.85, 18.93, 18.95, 18.98, 18.117, 24.25, 24.27, 24.55, 24.90, 27.21, 27.24

Arnison v Smith (1875) 41 ChD 348 (CA) 4.104

Arrale v Costain Engineering Ltd [1976] 2 Lloyd's Rep 98 . . . . .7.85

Ashley's Case (1870) LR 9 Eq 263 . . . . .24.43, 24.88

Assicurazioni Generali v Arab Insurance Group
[2003] 1 All ER 140 (CA). 4.89, 4.90, 4.105, 4.117, 5.33

Associated Japanese Bank (International) Ltd v Credit du Nord SA
[1989] 1 WLR 255. . . . . .7.07, 7.09, 7.14, 10.26

Astley v Reynolds (1731) 2 Str 915, 93 ER 938 . . . . 6.21, 6.24, 6.56

Athenaeum Life Assurance Company Society v Pooley
(1858) 3 De G & J 294, 44 ER 1281 . . . . .21.23, 21.38

Athos, The See Telfair Shipping Corporation v Athos Shipping Co SA (The Athos)

Atlantic Baron, The See North Ocean Shipping Co Ltd v Hyundai Construction
Co Ltd (The Atlantic Baron)

Atlantic Lines and Navigation Co Inc v Hallam Ltd (The Lucy)
[1983] 1 Lloyd's Rep 188 (QB). 4.09, 4.35, 4.108, 11.80, 12.14,
15.67, 17.05, 18.100, 28.05, 28.08, 28.12, 28.13

Atlas Express Ltd v Kafco (Importers and Distributors) Ltd [1989] QB 833 . . . . 6.38, 6.51, 6.70

Attorney-General v Blake [2001] 1 AC 268 . . . . .17.07

Attorney-General of New South Wales v Peters (1924) 34 CLR 146 . . . . .4.117

Attorney-General for Hong Kong v Reid [1994] 1 AC 324 (PC–NZ) 8.49

Attwood v Small (1838) 6 Cl & Fin 232, 7 ER 684 . . . . 3.42, 4.66, 4.100, 4.118,
4.120, 14.33, 16.42, 18.86, 21.04

Australand Corporation (Qld) Pty Ltd v Johnson [2007] QCA 302 . . . . .15.51

Australia Estates Pty Ltd v Cairns City Council [2005] QCA 328 . . . . 7.10, 7.32

Australian Slate Quarries Ltd, Re (1930) 31 St Rep NSW 1 . . . . .14.36, 15.34, 15.36, 16.56

Australian Annuities Pty Ltd v Rowley Super Find Pty Ltd [2015] VSCA 9 . . . . .1.27

Avon County Council v Howlett [1983] 1 WLR 605 (CA) 24.121
Avon Finance Co Ltd v Bridger [1985] 2 All ER 281 (CA)............................. 6.100, 9.08
Avon Insurance v Swire [2000] 1 All ER 573 ....4.84
Avonwick Holdings Ltd v Azitio Holdings Ltd [2020] EWHC 1844 (Comm) 4.108
Avrora Fine Arts Investment Ltd v Christie, Manson & Woods Ltd
 [2012] PNLR 35 .... 4.53, 26.25, 26.26
Awaroa Holdings Ltd v Commercial Securities and Finance Ltd [1976] 1 NZLR 19 .... 4.74, 5.10
Axa General Insurance v Gottlieb [2005] 1 Lloyd's Rep IR 369............................11.41
AXA Sun Life Services plc v Campbell Martin Ltd
 [2011] 2 Lloyd's Rep 1 (CA)........................... 26.03, 26.05, 26.07, 26.19, 26.20, 26.29
Ayerst v C & K (Construction) Ltd [1976] AC 167......................................25.18
Ayres v Hazelgrove (QB 9 Feb 1984) 7.47, 7.64
Azevedo v IMCOPA–Importacao, Exportaacao e Industria de Oleos Ltda
 [2014] 1 BCLC 72 (CA) 8.57

B, Re [2009] 1 AC 11 (HL)..4.07
B & S Contracts and Design Ltd v Victor Green Publications Ltd [1984] ICR 419..... 6.12, 6.13, 6.32
B2C2 Ltd v Quoine Pte Ltd [2019] 4 SLR 17 ....7.24
Babcock v Lawson (1879) 4 QBD 394; on appeal (1880) 5 QBD 284 (CA) 20.11, 21.06, 21.58
Baburin v Baburin (No 2) [1991] 2 Qd R 240 (Full Ct) 18.16, 24.84, 24.114
Backhouse v Backhouse [1978] 1 WLR 243.................................... 7.78, 7.87, 7.89
Baden v Société Generale pour Favoriser le Developpement du Commerce et
 de l'Industrie en France SA [1993] 1 WLR 509.....................................7.62
Baghbadrani v Commercial Union Insurance Co plc [2000] 1 Lloyd's Rep IR 94 ..... 13.28, 23.65, 24.94
Baglehole v Walters (1811) 3 Camp 154, 170 ER 1338 ....4.38
Bailey v Barclays Bank plc [2014] EWHC 2882 (QB)....................................4.124
Bainbridge v Bainbridge [2016] WTLR 898 (Ch)................................. 16.41, 16.56
Bainbridge v Bainbridge [2016] WTLR 943 .... 13.32, 19.08, 20.01
Bainbrigge v Browne (1881) 18 ChD 188..................... 3.50, 6.103, 9.03, 9.05, 16.12, 21.04,
                21.71, 29.20, 29.50, 29.51, 29.58
Baird v BCE Holdings Pty Ltd (1996) 40 NSWLR 374..............7.10, 11.113, 13.32, 27.08, 27.09,
               27.12, 27.22, 27.24, 27.29, 29.56
Baker v LSREF III Wight Ltd [2016] 2 WLUK 408; [2016] BPIR 509........................5.57
Baker v Monk (1864) 4 De GJ & S 388, 46 ER 968 .... 7.75, 7.87, 7.99
Baldwyn v Smith [1900] 1 Ch 588.. 7.48, 29.21, 29.61
Balfour v Hollandia Raventhorpe NL (1978) 18 SASR 240 .... 17.56, 18.93
Ballantyne v Raphael (1889) 15 VLR 538..................................... 15.63, 20.31
Baltic Shipping Company v Dillon (1992) 176 CLR 344 .... 1.20, 1.51
Banco Santander SA v Banque Paribas [2000] EWCA Civ 57..............................21.22
Bank Belge pour l'Etranger v Hambrouck [1921] 1 KB 321 (CA)............... 16.08, 16.09, 29.31
Bank Leumi le Israel BM v British National Insurance Co Ltd [1988] 1 Lloyd's Rep 71...........4.57
Bank Leumi (UK) plc v Wachner [2011] EWHC 656 (Comm) 26.07
Bank Melli Iran v Samadi-Rad (ChD 9 February 1994)...................................19.18
Bank Negara Indonesia 1946 v Taylor [1995] CLC 255 ....28.07
Bank of America v Arnell [1999] Lloyd's Rep Bank 399......................... 1.93, 29.32, 29.39
Bank of China (Hong Kong) Ltd v Wong Kam Ho Trust [2014] 1 HKLRD 41 ....6.100
Bank of Credit and Commerce International v Aboody
 [1990] 1 QB 923 (CA) 6.02, 6.77, 6.85, 6.87, 6.89, 6.93, 6.109, 8.04, 8.08, 8.26, 9.04
Bank of Credit and Commerce International SA v Ali (No 1)
 [1999] 1 ICR 1068; on appeal [2000] 1 ICR 1410 (CA); on appeal
 [2002] 1 AC 251 .... 5.16, 5.59, 5.60, 5.62, 5.63, 5.64, 7.38
Bank of Hindustan, Re (1873) LR 16 Eq 417.................................. 18.50, 18.51, 22.12
Bank of Ireland v Pexxnet Ltd [2010] EWHC 1872 (Comm) 1.94
Bank of Montreal v Collum (2004) 29 BCLR (4th) 18 (BCCA) 5.52, 5.54, 5.55, 29.62
Bank of Montreal v Murphy (1985) 6 BCLR (2d) 169 (BCCA)....................... 15.24, 19.32
Bank of Montreal v Stuart [1911] AC 120 (PC–Canada)....................... 6.80, 6.85, 6.103

TABLE OF CASES xxvii

Bank of Scotland v Bennett [1997] 1 FLR 801 . . . . .6.85
Bank of Scotland v Hussain [2010] EWHC 2812 (Ch) 20.27
Bank of Tokyo-Mitsubishi UFJ Ltd v Baskan Gida Sanayi Ve Pazarlama AS
    [2009] EWHC 1276 (Ch) 4.91
Bank Tejarat v Hong Kong and Shanghai Bank
    [1995] 1 Lloyd's Rep 239 . . . . .16.07, 16.23, 16.44, 16.45, 16.51, 16.65, 16.66
Banks v Insurance Company of the West Indies (Cayman) Ltd
    [2016] (2) CILR 442 (CA) 5.26, 5.28
Banning v Wright [1972] 1 WLR 972 (HL) 23.05, 24.03
Banque Belge pour l'Etranger v Hambrouck [1921] 1 KB 321 (CA) 1.96, 16.08, 16.09, 29.31
Banque Financière de la Cité SA v Westgate Insurance Co Ltd [1991] 2 AC 249 . . . . .10.27
Banque Keyser Ullmann SA v Skandia (UK) Insurance Co Ltd [1900] 1 QB 665 (CA);
    aff'd [1991] 2 AC 249 . . . . .4.29, 4.30, 5.02, 5.03, 5.11, 5.26, 5.31, 10.27
Bantic v Boss Properties Pty [2000] VSC 121 . . . . .27.43
Banwaitt v Dewji [2014] EWCA Civ 67; [2013] EWHC 879 (QB) 13.05, 23.18, 24.07
Barber v Imperio Reinsurance Co (UK) Ltd (CA 15 July 1993) 23.93
Barclays Bank v Metcalfe & Mansfield [2011] ONSC 5008 . . . . .7.36
Barclays Bank v Svizera Holdings BV [2014] EWHC 1020 (Comm) 26.11
Barclays Bank Ltd v Quistclose Investments Ltd [1970] AC 567 . . . . .1.92
Barclays Bank Ltd v WJ Simms Son & Cooke (Southern) Ltd
    [1980] 1 QB 677 . . . . .1.46, 1.51, 1.55, 7.05, 14.39, 29.23
Barclays Bank Plc v Borkhatria [2018] EWHC 1326 (Comm) 5.47, 6.38
Barclays Bank plc v Boulter [1999] 1 WLR 1919 (HL) 3.50, 3.51, 9.14, 9.19,
                                                                    16.12, 21.30, 21.71, 21.72, 21.73
Barclays Bank plc v Caplan [1998] 1 FLR 532 . . . . .6.120, 19.06
Barclays Bank plc v O'Brien [1994] 1 AC 180, [1993] QB 109 (CA) 6.77, 6.80, 6.86,
            6.97, 6.98, 6.100, 6.103, 9.05, 9.07, 9.08, 9.09, 9.12, 9.13, 9.14, 9.17, 9.18, 11.86
Barclays Bank plc v Schwartz, The Times 2 Aug 1995 (CA) .7.01, 7.41, 7.43, 7.75
Barings plc v Coopers & Lybrand [2002] 1 Lloyd's Rep PN 395 . . . . 4.07, 4.08, 4.54
Barker v Vansommer (1782) 1 Bro CC 149, 28 ER 1046 . . . . 18.59, 18.75
Barker v Walters (1844) 8 Beav 92, 50 ER 36 . . . . 3.55, 3.57, 15.60, 15.66, 18.40
Barker and Owen v Richardson (1827) 1 Y&J 362, 148 ER 710 . . . . .29.84
Barnesly v Powel (1749) 1 Ves Sen 284, 27 ER 1034 . . . . 3.43, 29.84
Barnsley v Noble [2014] EWHC 2657 (Ch) [202], on appeal
    [2017] Ch 191 (CA) 4.49, 4.53, 4.57
Barrett & Sinclair v McCormack [1999] VUCA 11 . . . . .1.86
Barron v Willis [1900] 2 Ch 121 (CA), aff'd [1902] AC 271 . . . . 9.21, 19.08, 29.20, 29.50
Barry v Heider (1914) 19 CLR 197 . . . . .15.09
Barry v The Stoney Point Canning Co (1917) 55 SCR 51 . . . . 8.51, 8.54, 8.66
Bartholemew v Marwick (1864) 15 CB (NS) 711, 143 ER 964 . . . . 3.27, 14.35
Bartlett v Tuchin (1815) 6 Taunt 259, 128 ER 1034 . . . . .3.27
Barton v Armstrong [1976] AC 104 (PC–Australia) 4.104, 6.01, 6.13, 6.20, 6.27,
                                                                    6.31, 6.60, 6.63, 6.64, 6.66, 29.69, 29.70
Barton v County NatWest Ltd [1999] All ER (D) 782; on appeal
    [2002] 4 All ER 494n (CA) 4.05, 4.08, 4.30, 4.66, 4.100, 4.106, 4.112
Bassett v Nosworthy (1673) Rep Temp Finch 102, 23 ER 55 . . . . .21.61
Bate v Aviva Insurance UK Ltd [2014] EWCA Civ 334 . . . . 4.63, 4.112
Bateman v Overy [2014] EWHC 432 (Ch) 6.119
Bates v Graves (1793) 2 Ves Jun 288, 30 ER 637; 1 Ves Jun Supp 264,
    34 ER 781 . . . . 3.42, 3.43, 3.52, 22.05, 29.84
Bathurst Regional Council v Local Government Financial Service Pty Ltd (No 5)
    [2012] FCA 1200 . . . . .18.08, 24.65, 27.24, 27.29
Bawden v London, Edinburgh and Glasgow Assurance Co [1892] 2 QB 534 (CA) 4.114
Baytex Energy Ltd v Canada 2015 ABQB 278 . . . . .13.28
BCCI v Aboody See Bank of Credit and Commerce International SA v Aboody
BCCI v Ali See Bank of Credit and Commerce International SA v Ali

xxviii   TABLE OF CASES

Beach Petroleum NL v Kennedy (1999) 48 NSWLR 1 (CA) 8.33, 8.35
Beaney (Dec'd), Re [1978] 1 WLR 770 .... 1.47, 7.46, 7.52, 7.54, 7.58, 29.09, 29.21
Beattie v Lord Ebury (1872) 7 Ch App 777; on appeal (1874) LR 7 HL 102. .... 4.17, 4.57
Beckford v Wade (1805) 17 Ves Jun 87, 34 ER 34 .... 3.43
Behan v Obelon Pty Ltd (1985) 167 CLR 326 .... 5.49
Behan v Obelon Pty Ltd [1984] 2 NSWLR 637 .... 5.49
Behn v Burness (1863) 3 B & S 751, 122 ER 281 .... 4.10, 4.20, 4.24
Bell v Lever Bros Ltd [1932] AC 161. .... 1.36, 2.37, 4.29, 4.30, 5.03, 5.11, 10.24, 27.22
Bell v Robutka (1966) 55 DLR (2d) 436 (Alta CA) 17.65
Bell Group Ltd (in liq) v Westpac Banking Corporation (2008) 70 ACSR 1 .... 16.39
Bellamy v Sabine (1857) 1 De G & J 566, 44 ER 842; (1835) 2 Ph 425, 41 ER 1007;
     (1847) 2 Ph 446, 41 ER 1016 .... 3.42, 3.44, 15.38, 15.51, 20.27
Bendigo and Adelaide Bank Ltd v Williamson [2017] NSWSC 939. .... 21.31
Benedetti v Sawiris [2013] 3 WLR 351 (SC) 17.07, 17.08
Benham v United Guarantee and Life Insurance Co (1853) 7 Exch 744, 155 ER 1149. .... 4.57
Beningfield v Baxter (1886) 12 App Cas 167 (PC–Natal) 6.103
Bennett, ex p (1805) 10 Ves 381, 32 ER 893 .... 17.41, 17.42, 17.43, 17.59
Bennett v Francis (1801) 2 Bos & Pul 550, 126 ER 1433. .... 14.34, 20.13
Bennett v Vade (1742) 2 Atk 324, 26 ER 597 .... 3.44
Benson v Heathorn (1842) 1 Y & CCC 326, 62 ER 909 .... 8.19
Bentley v Craven (1853) 18 Beav 75, 52 ER 29 .... 2.38
Bentley v Vilmont (1887) LR 12 HL 471; (1887) 12 App Cas 471 .... 3.12, 11.31
Benyon v Fitch (1866) 35 Beav 570, 55 ER 1018 .... 3.38, 15.50, 15.51
Berger and Co Inc v Gill & Dufus SA [1984] 1 AC 382 .... 1.24
Bergmann v Daw [2010] QCA 143. .... 7.60
Berry v Armistead (1836) 2 Keen 221, 48 ER 613. .... 15.34, 16.56
Bertram and Sons v Lloyd (1904) 90 LT 357 (CA) 1.87
Bertrand v Racicot [1979] 1 SCR 441. .... 23.73
Bester v Perpetual Trustee Co Ltd [1970] 3 NSWLR 30. .... 24.35, 24.76, 24.79, 24.114
Betker v Williams (1991) 86 DLR (4th) 395 (BCCA). 7.34
Betsam Trust, Re [2009] WTLR 1489. .... 29.47
Bevan v Anderson and Peace River Sand & Gravel Co
     (1957) 12 DLR (2d) 69 (Alta SC) 11.104, 23.18, 23.24, 23.37, 27.32
Beynon v Cook (1874) 10 Ch App 389. .... 24.81, 24.82
BG plc v Nelson Group Services (Maintenance) Ltd [2002] EWCA 547 .... 4.53
BG v BF [2007] 3 SLR(R) 233 (CA) 5.20
Bikam OOD v Adria Cable Sarl [2012] EWHC 621 (Comm),
     [2013] EWHC 1985 (Comm) 4.24, 4.48, 26.03
Bill v Price (1686) 1 Vern 467, 23 ER 592. .... 3.38, 15.50, 18.59
Billage v Southee (1852) 9 Hare 534, 68 ER 623 .... 6.103, 15.51
Bingham v Bingham (1748) 1 Ves Sen 126, 27 ER 934, Ves Sen Supp 79, 28 ER 462 ... 5.14, 7.28, 7.39
Bisset v Wilkinson [1927] AC 177 (PC–NZ). 4.49, 4.50
Blachford, Re (1884) 27 ChD 676. .... 24.81
Black v Davies [2005] EWCA Civ 531 .... 17.19
Black v S Freedman & Co (1910) 12 CLR 105 .... 1.98
Black King Shipping Corporation v Mark Ranald Massie (The Litsion Pride)
     [1985] 1 Lloyd's Rep 513 .... 11.24, 11.41, 23.21, 23.22, 23.24, 23.28, 23.104, 23.105
Blackburn v Smith (1848) 2 Ex 783, 154 ER 707. .... 18.18, 18.23, 18.81
Blackburn Low & Co v Vigors (1887) 12 App Cas 531. .... 5.29
Blackham v Haythorpe (1917) 23 CLR 156. .... 8.22, 15.17
Blackie v Clarke (1852) 15 Beav 595, 51 ER 669 .... 29.58
Blackley Investments Pty Ltd v Burnie City Council (No 2) [2011] TASFC 6;
     (2011) 21 Tas R 98 (Full Ct). 5.03, 5.11, 7.21, 17.26, 17.61
Blackley Investments Pty Ltd v Burnie City Council (No 2)
     (2011) 21 Tas R 98 (Full Ct). 5.11, 7.21
Blacklocks v JB Developments (Godalming) Ltd [1982] 1 Ch 183. .... 22.02

TABLE OF CASES   xxix

Blackwell v Redman (1634) 1 Chan Rep 88, 22 ER 515 . . . . .3.37
Blake v Johnson (1700) Pre Ch 142, 24 ER 69 . . . . 3.42, 3.44, 3.46, 16.62, 22.06
Blake v Mowlatt (1856) 21 Beav 603, 52 ER 993 . . . . .3.44, 15.11, 17.56, 18.93
BLB Corporation v Jacobsen (1974) 48 ALJR 372 (HCA) 8.24
Bleasdale v Forster [2011] EWHC 596 (Ch) 4.66
Blomley v Ryan (1956) 99 CLR 362 . . . . 7.47, 7.66, 7.68, 7.75, 7.88, 7.89, 7.103
Bloomenthal v Ford [1897] AC 156 . . . . 4.47, 4.102
Bloomer v Spittle (1872) LR 13 Eq 427 . . . . 7.30, 11.92, 19.24
Bloor Street West Ltd v Moksha Yoga Studio [2013] ONSC 6501 . . . . .7.36
Blue Range Resources Corp, Re [2000] AJ 14 (Alta QB) 25.28, 25.39, 25.40
BM Auto Sales Pty Ltd v Budget Rent A Car System Pty Ltd (1976) 51 ALJR 254 . . . . .24.15
BP Oil International Ltd v Target Shipping Ltd [2012] 2 Lloyd's Rep 245,
    rev'd on a point [2013] 1 Lloyd's Rep 561 . . . . .7.13
Boardman v Phipps [1967] 2 AC 46 . . . . 2.17, 2.21, 8.34
Bodger v Nicholls (1873) 28 LT 441 . . . . .4.37
Bole's & British Land Co's Contract, Re (1902) 71 LJ Ch 130 . . . . .8.15
Bolkiah v KPMG [1999] 2 AC 222 . . . . .8.44
Bolton v Bishop of Carlisle (1793) 2 Hl Bl 259, 126 ER 540 . . . . .3.52
Bolton Metropolitan BC v Municipal Mutual Insurance Ltd [2006] 1 WLR 1492 (CA) 23.05, 23.07
Bolton Partners v Lambert (1889) 41 ChD 295 (CA) 1.40, 1.41
BOM v BOK [2018] SCA 83 . . . . .7.75
Bonhams 1793 Ltd v Cavazzoni [2014] EWHC 682 (QB) 26.02
Bonney v Ridgard (1784) 1 Cox 145, 29 ER 1101 . . . . .3.43
Booth v Warrington (1714) 4 Brown 164, 2 ER 111 . . . . .3.38, 15.34, 16.53, 29.27
Borland's Trustee v Steel Bros and Co [1901] 1 Ch 279 . . . . .14.22
Borrelli v Ting [2010] Bus LR 1718 . . . . .6.44
Borrelli v Ting [2010] UKPC 21 . . . . 6.13, 6.37, 6.43, 6.48, 26.01
Bosanquet v Dashwood (1734) Talb 38, 25 ER 648 . . . . 3.40, 15.37
Bostock v Blakeney (1789) 2 Bro CC 654, 29 ER 362 . . . . .1.63
Boston Deep Sea Fishing & Ice Co v Ansell (1888) 39 ChD 339 (CA) 3.30, 8.51
Bottin (International) Investments Ltd v Venson Group plc [2004] EWCA 1368 . . . . .26.11
Boulter v Stocks (1913) 47 SCR 440 . . . . 18.50, 23.18, 23.20, 23.104, 23.105
Boulting v ACTAT [1963] 2 QB 606 (CA) 8.39
Boustany v Pigott (1995) 69 P&CR 298 (PC–Antigua and Barbuda) 7.75, 7.78, 7.81,
                                                                                7.82, 7.87, 7.88, 7.89, 7.99, 7.102
Bouygues Offshore v Utisol Transport Contractors Ltd [1996] 2 Lloyd's Rep 153
    (SC South Africa) 18.04
Bowen v Evans (1844) 1 J & Lat 178; on appeal (1848) 2 HLC 257, 9 ER 1090 . . . . 3.42, 3.47
Boyd v Mayor of Wellington [1924] NZLR 1174 . . . . .15.09
Boyd & Forrest v The Glasgow Railway Company 1915 SC 20 (HL) 15.21, 15.40,
                                                                                18.56, 18.62, 18.99, 26.02
Boyns v Lackey (1958) SR (NSW) 395 . . . . .24.84
Boynton v Boynton (CA 19 June 1878) 29.86
Boynton v Monarch Life Insurance Co of New Zealand Ltd [1973] 1 NZLR 606 . . . . .11.04
Boyson v Thomas Cole (1817) 6 M & S 14, 105 ER 1148 . . . . .3.09
BP Exploration Co (Libya) Ltd v Hunt (No 2) [1979] 1 WLR 783 .17.18, 17.21
Bradbury v Anderton (1834) 1 CM&R 486, 149 ER 1099 . . . . .14.34
Bradford Third Equitable Benefit Building Society v Borders [1941] 2 All ER 205 (HL) 4.08, 9.04
Braut v Stec (2005) 51 BCLR (4th) 15 (BCCA) 7.103
Bray v Ford [1896] AC 44 . . . . 8.05, 8.11
Brennan v Bolt Burdon [2005] QB 303 (CA) 4.19, 7.09, 7.38
Breskvar v Wall (1971) 126 CLR 376 . . . . 1.47, 15.09, 16.25
Brickenden v London Loan and Savings Co [1934] 3 DLR 465 (PC–Canada) 8.72
Bridgeman v Green (1755) 2 Ves Sen 627, 28 ER 399; aff'd (1755) Wilm 58,
    97 ER 22 (HL) 3.38, 3.42, 6.85, 6.110, 9.21, 15.34, 15.37, 16.56, 21.04, 29.20, 29.50

xxx TABLE OF CASES

Bridgewater v Leahy (Qld CA, 14 March 1997); on appeal
(1998) 194 CLR 457 . . . . 7.73, 13.19, 15.46, 19.29, 22.06
Briess v Woolley [1954] AC 333 . . . . 4.88, 4.90, 4.116, 9.04
Bright v Eynon (1757) 1 Burr 390, 97 ER 365 . . . . 3.37, 29.84
Brindley (Dec'd), Re [2018] EWHC 157 (Ch) 6.87, 6.100, 6.115, 6.117
Brinsmead v Harrison (1871) LR 6 HL 584 . . . . 3.09, 14.29
Bristol and West Building Society v Mothew [1998] Ch 1 (CA) 2.11, 2.13, 3.50, 4.09, 8.04,
8.11, 8.18, 8.21, 8.24, 8.26, 8.34, 8.36, 8.41, 8.42, 8.45, 13.29, 13.30,
14.16, 15.19, 16.12, 16.34, 16.41, 16.42, 16.44, 16.56, 16.66, 23.04
Brit Syndicates Ltd v Grant Thornton [2006] EWHC 341 (Comm) 1.14, 1.16, 12.05, 13.27
Brit UW Ltd v F & B Trenchless Solutions Ltd [2016] Lloyd's Rep IR 69 . . . . .5.28
British Airways Board v Taylor [1976] 1 All ER 65 (HL) 4.17, 4.44, 4.61
British & Commonwealth Holdings plc v Quadrex Holdings Inc [1995] CLR 1169 (CA) 28.10
British Equitable Insurance Company v The Great Western Railway Company
(1869) 38 LJ Ch 132 (NS) 3.55, 3.57, 3.58, 3.62, 15.66
British Nuclear Group Sellafield Ltd v Gemeinschaftskernkraftwerk Grohnde GmbH
[2007] EWHC 2245 (Ch) 4.40
Brocklehurst's Dec'd, Re the Estate v Roberts [1978] Ch 14 . . . . .29.50
Brocklehurst's Estate, Re [1978] Ch 14 (CA) 6.88, 6.97, 6.101, 6.119
Bromley v Holland (1802) 7 Ves Jun 3, 32 ER 2 . . . . 3.40, 15.37
Bromley v Smith (1859) 26 Beav 644, 53 ER 1047 . . . . .17.63
Brook v Hook (1871) LR 6 Exch 89 . . . . .1.41
Brook v Wheaton Pacific Pontiac Buick GMC Ltd (2000) 76 BCLR (3d) 246 (CA) 18.88
Brooke v Lord Mostyn (1864) 2 De GJ & Sm 373, 46 ER 419; on appeal (1866) LR 4 HL 304 . . . . . .5.59
Brooking v Maudslay Son & Field (1888) 38 Ch 363 . . . . .3.60
Brooks v Bernstein [1909] 1 KB 98 . . . . .1.20
Brooks v Burns Philp Trustee Co Ltd (1969) 121 CLR 432 . . . . .1.62
Broome v Cassell [1972] AC 1027 . . . . .18.42
Broome v Speak [1903] 1 Ch 586 (CA) 25.29
Brophy v North American Life Assurance Co (1902) 32 SCR 261 . . . . .18.40
Brotherton v Aseguradora Colseguros SA [2003] 2 All ER (Comm) 298 (CA) 5.26, 10.18,
10.29, 11.80, 11.82, 11.83, 11.84, 11.107, 12.14
Brown v InnovatorOne plc [2012] EWHC 1321 (Comm) 4.49, 4.76, 4.101, 26.18
Brown v Langwoods Photo Store Ltd [1991] 1 NZLR 173 (CA) 1.08
Brown v McLintock (1873) LR 6 HL 456 . . . . .24.96
Brown v Norman 65 Miss 369, 4 So 293 (1888) 14.64, 14.65, 15.60
Brown v Raphael [1958] Ch 636 (CA) 4.50, 4.53, 4.54
Brown v Smitt (1924) 34 CLR 160 . . . . 2.17, 12.23, 13.02, 13.10, 15.46, 17.05, 17.33, 17.39,
17.42, 17.45, 17.49, 17.51, 17.52, 17.53, 18.77, 23.36, 23.61, 23.65, 23.66, 23.87
Brown v Stephenson [2013] EWHC 2531 (Ch) 6.110
Brown v Techdata Corp Inc 238 Ga 622, 234 SE 2d 787 (1977) 14.64
Brown & Doherty Ltd v Whangarei County Council [1990] 2 NZLR 63 . . . . .14.44
Brown Jenkinson & Co Ltd v Percy Dalton (London) Ltd [1957] 2 QB 621 . . . . .4.08
Browne v Mitton (1714) 4 Bro CC 167, 2 ER 114 . . . . 3.42, 22.08
Brownlie v Campbell (1880) 5 App Cas 925 (HL) 4.90, 7.28, 7.35, 27.05
Brusewitz v Brown (1923) NZLR 1106 . . . . .29.14
BSkyB Ltd, Sky Subscribers Services Ltd v HP Enterprise Services UK Ltd, Electronic
Data systems LLC [2010] EWHC 86 (TCC) 4.60, 4.84, 26.05
Buckland v Farmar and Moody [1979] 1 WLR 221 (CA) 1.09, 1.31
Buckland v Johnson (1854) 15 CB 145, 139 ER 375 . . . . 3.09, 14.29
Bulfield v Fournier (1894) 11 TLR 62 . . . . 8.57, 8.58
Bullock v Lloyds Bank Ltd [1955] Ch 317 . . . . 6.93, 9.21, 24.60, 24.62, 24.79, 29.20
Burger King v King Franchises [2013] EWHC 1761 (Comm) 6.38, 6.43, 6.70
Burin Peninsula Community Business Development Corporation v Grandy [2010] NLCA 69 . . . . . . .6.72
Burland v Earle [1902] AC 83 (PC–Canada) 2.28, 2.37, 2.39
Burmah Oil Co v Governor of the Bank of England, The Times 4 July 1981 . . . . .7.79

TABLE OF CASES   xxxi

Bustfree Pty Ltd v Llewellyn [2013] QCA 103..24.98
Butler v Croft (1973) 27 P & Cr 1 ....18.38, 24.115
Butler and Baker's case (1591) 3 Co Rep 25, 76 ER 684 ....14.74, 29.13
BV Nederlandse Industrie Van Eiprodukten v Rembrandt Enterprises Inc
   [2019] 1 All ER (Comm) 543; on appeal [2019] 3 WLR 1113 (CA)......................18.44
BV Nederlandse Industrie Van Eiprodukten v Rembrandt Enterprises
   [2020] QB 551 (CA)............................4.64, 4.66, 4.104, 4.105, 4.106, 13.35
Byne v Potter (1800) 5 Ves Jun 609, 31 ER 765 ....3.40
Byne v Vivian (1800) 5 Ves Jun 604, 31 ER 762....................................3.40, 15.37
Byrnes v Kendle (2011) 243 CLR 253..24.10

C21 London Estates Ltd v Maurice Macneill Iona Ltd [2017] EWHC 998 (Ch)................4.58
Cadence Asset Management Pty Ltd v Concept Sports Ltd (2005) 55 ACSR 145 (FCA);
   on appeal (2005) 147 FCR 434 (Full Ct) 18.61, 25.29, 25.38, 25.49, 25.50
Caldicott v Richards [2020] EWHC 767 (Ch)...........................15.46, 16.41, 17.04
Caldicott v Richards [2020] WTLR 823...2.18
Callaghan and Hedges t/a Stage 3 Discotheque v Syndicate 1049
   [2000] Lloyd's Rep IR 125 ....11.09, 23.62, 23.80, 24.101
Cambrian Mining Co, Re (1882) 48 LT 114..22.12
Camdex International v Bank of Zambia [1998] 1 QB 22 (CA) 22.10
Camerata Property Inc v Credit Suisse Securities (Europe) Ltd [2011] EWHC 479 (Comm)...... 26.26
Campbell v Back Office Investments Pty Ltd (2008) 66 ACSR 359 (NSWCA);
   on appeal (2009) 238 CLR 304 .... 18.38, 18.89, 18.94
Campbell v Hooper (1855) 3 Sm & Giff 153, 65 ER 603..................................7.47
Campbell v Fleming (1834) 1 Ad & E 40, 110 ER 1122....................1.32, 3.27, 3.28, 23.20,
                   23.22, 23.36, 23.41, 23.58, 23.104, 23.105
Campbell v Walker (1800) 5 Ves Jun 678, 31 ER 801 ....1.74, 24.65
Canadian Imperial Bank of Commerce v Melnitzer (1993) 1 ETR (2d) 1;
   aff'd (1997) 50 CBR (3d) 79 (Ont CA) 16.15, 16.50, 16.70
Canadian Indemnity Co v Johns-Manville Co [1990] 2 SCR 549...........................5.40
Cane v Allen (1814) 2 Dow 289, 3 ER 869 ....8.12, 8.13, 8.14, 8.32
Canham v Barry (1855) 15 CB 597, 139 ER 558 ....14.27, 29.79
Cantor Index Ltd v Shortall [2002] All ER (D) 161...6.66
Capcon Holdings plc v Edwards [2007] EWHC 2662 (Ch).......................... 11.43, 12.06,
                  18.89, 24.62, 24.118, 24.119
Cape Breton Company, Re (1885) 29 ChD 795 (CA); on appeal sub nom Cavendish
   Bentink v Fenn (1887) 12 App Cas 652 ....2.03, 2.11, 2.16, 2.28, 2.29,
     2.31, 2.32, 2.33, 2.34, 2.35, 2.36, 2.37, 2.38, 2.39, 18.48, 23.06, 23.86
Capel and Co v Sim's Ships Composition Company (1888) 58 LT (NS) 807....... 15.34, 15.63, 16.56
Car and Universal Finance Co Ltd v Caldwell [1963] 2 All ER 547;
   [1965] 1 QB 525 (CA) 10.05, 10.23, 11.05, 11.30, 11.31, 11.34, 11.35, 11.36,
          11.37, 11.38, 11.40, 11.80, 14.03, 16.02, 21.05, 21.09, 21.14,
           21.16, 21.48, 21.52, 21.57, 23.36, 23.41, 23.58, 23.61
Carbone v Metricon Homes Pty Ltd [2018] NSWCA 296................................1.31
Cargill v Bower (1878) 10 ChD 502 ....1.52, 4.42
Carillion Construction Ltd v Felix (UK) Ltd [2001] BLR 1....................6.07, 6.12, 6.58, 6.66
Carlill v Carbolic Smokeball [1893] 1 QB 256 (CA)......................................4.124
Carlish v Salt [1906] 1 Ch 335.. 4.29, 5.03, 17.62
Carter v Boehm (1766) 3 Burr 1909, 97 ER 1162; 1 Black W 593,
   96 ER 342...3.55, 3.56, 3.60, 3.63, 5.27, 10.23, 16.03
Carter v Golland [1937] 4 DLR 513 (Ont CA) 17.04, 18.60
Carter v Palmer (1837) 11 Bli NS 397, 6 ER 378 ....15.53
Cashin v Cashin [1938] 1 All ER 536 (PC–Canada)......................................5.15
Cassa di Risparmio della Repubblica di San Marino SpA v Barclays Bank Ltd
   [2011] 1 CLC 701 .... 4.49, 4.104, 26.04, 26.07, 26.11
Castle Phillips Finance v Piddington [1995] 1 FLR 783 (CA)............................19.21

TABLE OF CASES

Cavaleiro v Puget (1865) 4 F&F 537, 176 ER 680 ....14.27
Cave v Cave (1880) 15 ChD 639 ....3.47, 3.50, 16.12, 21.70
Cave v Holford (1798) 3 Ves 650, 30 ER 1203 ....3.42, 22.06
Cavendish v Geaves (1857) 24 Beav 163, 53 ER 319...21.22
Cavendish Bentink v Fenn *See* Cape Breton Company, Re
Cazenove v British Equitable Assurance Co (1859) 6 CB NS 437, 144 ER 527 ....4.81
CB v EB [2020] EWFC 72 ....5.20
CC Ltd v Apex Trust Ltd [2012] JLR 314 ....29.46
Cemp Properties (UK) Ltd v Dentsply Research Corporation [1991] 2 EGLR 197(CA)..........2.08
Cenk K, The [2012] 2 All ER (Comm) 855 ....6.44
Central Capital Corp (1996) 132 DLR (4th) 223 (Ont CA)....................................25.39
Central Estates (Belgravia) Ltd v Woolgar (No 2) [1972] 1 WLR 1048 ....23.92
Ceviz v Frawley [2021] EWHC 8 (Ch)...10.09
CH Offshore Limited v Internaves Consorcio Naviero SA [2021] 1 Lloyd's Rep 465............8.44
Chagos Islanders v Attorney-General [2003] EWHC 2222; on appeal
    [2004] EWCA 997 ....7.75, 7.78, 7.100
Champion v Rigby (1830) Tamlyn 421, 48 ER 168; 1 Russ & M 539, 39 ER 207;
    aff'd (1840) 9 LJ Ch (NS) 211 ....24.45, 24.49, 24.50, 24.58
Champtaloup v Thomas [1976] 2 NSWLR 264 (CA)........11.08, 23.61, 23.68, 23.92, 23.93, 23.99
Chancery Client Partners Ltd v MRC 957 Ltd [2016] Lloyd's Rep FC 578.................8.67, 9.03
Chandler v Webster [1904] 1 KB 493 (CA) 3.31
Chapman v Fraser BR Trin 33 Geo 3 (1793) 14.80, 18.40
Chapman v Greater Midland Insurance Pty Ltd
    [1981] 1 NSWLR 479.........................11.04, 11.21, 11.23, 11.29, 11.46
Chapman v Westpac New Zealand Limited [2018] NZHC 1986 ....5.51
Charles Hunt Ltd v Palmer [1931] 2 Ch 287 ....4.40
Charles Lloyd Property Group Pty Ltd v Buchanan [2013] VSC 148...................4.55, 5.10
Charter v Trevelyan (1835) 4 LJ Ch (NS) 209; (1839) 1 Beav 588, 48 ER 1069;
    (1844) 11 Cl & Fin 714, 8 ER 1273; (1846) 9 Beav 140, 50 ER 297 ....3.38, 3.42, 16.42,
                        21.04, 22.05, 24.10, 24.31, 24.43, 24.58, 24.96
Chartered Trust plc v Conloy (Romford County Court 22 May 1998) 11.38
Chartered Trust v Davies [1997] 2 EGLR 83 ....4.46
Chase v Spence [2006] AJ 733 (Alberta QB) 7.35
Chater v Mortgage Agency Services Number Two Ltd [2003] EWCA 490 (CA) 6.111
Cheese v Thomas [1994] 1 WLR 129 (CA) 2.08, 2.09, 6.03, 6.96, 6.100, 6.109,
                        11.86, 11.87, 11.107, 13.01, 13.09, 15.46, 17.05, 17.13, 17.14,
                        17.30, 17.50, 17.56, 18.27, 18.93, 18.94, 18.96, 18.118
Cheltenham Borough Council v Christine Susan Laird [2009] EWHC 1253 (QB) 4.82
Cherrington v Mayhew's Perma-Plants Ltd (1990) 71 DLR (4th) 371 (BCCA) 16.15
Chesterfield v Janssen *See* Earl of Chesterfield v Janssen
Chin (Dec'd), Re [2019] EWHC 523 (Ch) 6.100
China National Foreign Trade Transportation Corporation v Evlogia Shipping Co SA of
    Panama (The Mihalios Xilas) [1979] 1 WLR 1018 (HL) 23.57
Chint Australasia Pty Ltd v Cosmoluce Pty Ltd [2008] NSWSC 635....................18.102
Chwee Kin Keong v Digilandmall.com Pte Ltd [2005] 1 SLR 502(R) (CA)..........5.11, 7.11, 7.22
CIBC Mortgages plc v Pitt [1994] 1 AC 200 ....6.80, 6.85, 6.89, 6.93,
                        6.109, 8.05, 8.08, 8.17, 8.26, 9.16
Ciro Citterio Menswear plc, Re [2002] 1 BCLC 672..2.24
Citadel General Assurance Co v Johns-Manville Canada Inc [1983] 1 SCR 513 ....5.54
Citibank Ltd v Papandony [2002] NSWCA 375 ....1.46, 14.12
Citibank NA v Brown Shipley & Co Ltd [1991] 2 All ER 690 ....14.11, 14.12, 29.36
Citic Ka Wah Bank Ltd v Lau Kam Luen [2008] 2 HKLRD 167 ....19.33
Citicorp Australia Ltd v O'Brien (1996) 40 NSWLR 398.....................................8.33
Civil Service Co-operative Society v Blyth (1914) 17 CLR 601........................14.22, 14.72
Clare v Lamb (1875) LR 10 CP 334..14.26, 27.06
Clarion Ltd v National Provident Institution [2000] 1 WLR 1888 ....7.14

TABLE OF CASES   xxxiii

Clark v Cutland [2004] 1 WLR 783 (CA)...................................1.60, 1.78
Clark v Malpas (1862) 31 Beav 80, 54 ER 1067; aff'd (1862) 4 De GF & J 401,
    45 ER 1238.......................3.41, 3.42, 3.52, 7.75, 7.84, 7.89, 7.99, 15.07, 16.42, 22.05
Clark v Urquhart [1930] AC 28...25.29
Clark v Ward (1700) Prec Cha 150, 24 ER 72; on appeal (1706) 4 Bro PC 70, 2 ER 48......3.42, 22.05
Clark Boyce v Mouat [1994] 1 AC 428 (PC–NZ)..................8.24, 8.33, 8.36, 8.38, 8.39, 8.43
Clarke, Re [2019] EWHC 1193 (Ch)..29.42
Clarke v Dickson (1858) El Bl & El 148, 120 ER 463...........3.05, 3.41, 10.23, 13.01, 14.36, 14.59,
                    14.73, 18.03, 18.09, 18.14, 18.18, 18.23, 18.48, 18.54, 18.87
Clarke v Hart (1857) 6 HLC 633, 10 ER 1143................................24.09, 24.74
Clarke v Mackintosh (1862) 4 Giff 134, 66 ER 651...............................4.120
Clarke v Marlborough Fine Art (London) Ltd, The Times 5 July 2001.....................24.35
Clarkson v Barclays Private Bank and Trust (Isle of Man) Ltd [2007] WTLR 1703.......29.28, 29.47
Clarkson v Hanway (1723) 2 P Wms 203, 24 ER 700.................3.38, 3.42, 15.58, 15.65, 22.05
Classic International Pty Ltd v Lagos (2004) 60 NSWLR 241...........................15.10
Claughton v Price (1997) 30 HLR 396 (CA)............................15.37, 17.05, 17.30
Clavering v Clavering (1704) Prec Chan 235, 24 ER 114.............................3.52
Clay v Clay (2001) 202 CLR 410..1.74, 8.03
Cleaver v Schyde Investments Ltd [2011] 2 P & CR 21 (CA)...................4.93, 26.03, 26.29
Clef Aquitaine SARL v Laporte Materials (Barrow) Ltd [2001] QB 488 (CA)..................4.78
Clegg v Edmonson (1857) 8 De G M & G 787, 44 ER 593...............................24.74
Clinicare Ltd v Orchard [2004] EWHC 1694....................................4.33
Close v Phipps (1844) 7 Man & G 586, 135 ER 236................................6.24
Clough v London and North Western Railway Co (1871) LR 7 Ex 26........1.53, 3.51, 10.23, 11.03,
                11.04, 11.08, 11.19, 11.20, 11.28, 11.45, 11.46, 11.113, 14.03, 14.37,
                14.45, 14.47, 14.57, 14.62, 14.85, 16.02, 18.04, 18.14, 18.117, 20.13,
                23.04, 23.06, 23.18, 23.36, 23.41, 23.58, 23.61, 23.66, 23.74, 23.83,
                23.97, 23.99, 23.103, 24.04, 24.07, 24.39, 24.66, 24.109, 24.111
Cloutte v Storey [1910] 1 Ch 18....................................3.50, 16.12, 29.52
Clydebank Football Club Ltd v Steedman 2002 SLT 109..............................8.20
Co- Operative Bank Plc v Hayes Freehold Ltd [2017] EWHC 1820 (Ch)...............4.19, 4.118
Coaks v Boswell (1886) 11 App Cas 232.....................................4.117
Coastal Estates Pty Ltd v Melevende [1965] VR 433 (Full Ct)........10.23, 11.21, 11.28, 11.41, 11.56,
                11.113, 12.04, 12.06, 14.23, 14.36, 14.37, 14.38, 17.12, 18.83, 23.04,
                23.18, 23.20, 23.22, 23.37, 23.38, 23.39, 23.42, 23.43, 23.45, 23.46,
                23.48, 23.58, 23.61, 23.65, 23.66, 23.71, 23.83, 23.87, 23.103,
                23.104, 23.106, 23.110, 24.07, 24.71, 24.90, 24.109, 29.82
Cobbett v Brock (1855) 20 Beav 524, 52 ER 706................................9.05
Cochrane v Moore (1890) 25 QBD 57 (CA).........................1.46, 14.10, 29.06
Cockburn v GIO Finance Ltd (2001) 51 NSWLR 624 (CA)....2.01, 2.09, 11.101, 13.04, 15.09, 16.13
Cockell v Taylor (1852) 15 Beav 103, 51 ER 475.............21.24, 21.25, 21.33, 21.43, 21.46, 21.53
Cockerill v Westpac Banking Corporation (1996) 142 ALR 227 (FCA)..............11.04, 11.08,
                11.23, 11.101, 19.29, 23.14, 23.66, 23.110
Cocking v Pratt (1750) 1 Ves Sen 400, 27 ER 1105................................5.14, 7.39
Colchester Borough Council v Smith [1992] Ch 421 (CA)............................26.11
Coldunell Ltd v Gallon [1986] QB 1184 (CA)..............................6.100, 9.08
Cole v Pope (1898) 29 SCR 291.................................7.34, 7.37, 27.14
Cole v Trecothick (1804) 9 Ves 234, 32 ER 592.................................8.26
Coleby v Smith (1683) 1 Vern 205, 23 ER 416..............................3.42, 22.05
Coleman v Myers [1977] 2 NZLR 225 (CA)......................13.12, 17.16, 18.110, 18.111
Coles v Reynolds [2020] EWHC 2151 (Ch).................................6.103, 6.110
Coles v Trecothick (1804) 9 Ves 234, 32 ER 592....................8.08, 8.14, 8.25, 8.26, 8.27
Collins v Associated Greyhound Racecourses Ltd [1930] 1 Ch 1 (CA).......................4.80
Collins v Blantern (1765) 2 Wils KB 341, 95 ER 847.............................29.79
Collins v Howell-Jones [1981] EGD 207 (CA).............................26.14, 26.17
Collins by her next friend Poletti v May [2000] WASC 29...........................7.45, 7.61

xxxiv TABLE OF CASES

Collings v Lee [2001] 2 All ER 332 (CA) 1.79, 1.80, 1.81, 1.82, 16.12
Colonial Bank v European Grain and Shipping Ltd [1989] AC 1056 ....1.15
Colvin v Hartwell (1837) 5 Cl & Fin 484, 7 ER 488 ....15.48
Colyer v Finch (1856) 5 HLC 905, 10 ER 1159 ....21.61
Commercial Bank of Australia v Smith (1991) 102 ALR 453 .... 8.30, 8.40
Commercial Bank of Australia Ltd v Amadio (1983) 151 CLR 447,
       46 ALR 402 .... 4.36, 5.41, 5.44, 5.47, 5.49, 7.69, 7.70, 7.75,
                                                      7.81, 7.103, 11.48, 15.60, 19.27, 19.28, 19.44
Commercial Banking Co of Sydney v RH Brown and Co [1972] 2 Lloyd's Rep 360 (HCA) 4.76
Commission for New Towns v Cooper (GB) Ltd
       [1995] Ch 259 (CA) 4.112, 7.12, 7.14, 7.16, 7.19, 9.05
Commonwealth v Davis Samuel Pty Ltd (No 7) (2013) ACSR 258 (ACT Sup Ct)...... 1.78, 11.21, 11.25
Commonwealth Bank of Australia v Ridout Nominees Pty Ltd [2000] WASC 37 ....6.75
Commonwealth Homes and Investment Co Ltd v MacKellar (1939) 63 CLR 351 ....11.12
Commonwealth Homes & Investment Company Ltd v Smith (1937) 59 CLR 443 ....23.44
Commonwealth of Australia v Verwayen (1990) 170 CLR 394.................... 23.05, 23.08, 23.11,
                                                            23.42, 24.03, 24.118
Compagnia Seguros Imperio v Heath (REBX) [2001] 1 WLR 112 (CA)................... 2.11, 2.13
Compagnie Française des Chemins de Fer Paris-Orleans v Leeston Shipping
       Company Ltd [1919] Lloyd's Rep 235 .... 4.23, 15.34, 16.56, 18.27, 18.77, 27.21, 27.24, 27.38
Condogianis v Guardian Assurance Co Ltd [1921] 2 AC 125 (PC–Australia) 4.35
Conlon v Ozolins [1984] 1 NZLR 489 (CA) 7.33
Conlon v Simms [2008] 1 WLR 484 (CA) 5.04, 5.56, 5.58
Connop v Holmes (1835) 2 CM & R 719, 150 ER 304 .... 29.76, 29.79
Container Transport International Inc v Oceanus Mutual Underwriting
       Association (Bermuda) Ltd [1984] 1 Lloyd's Rep 476 ....5.30, 23.21, 23.24, 23.28
Contex Drouzhba Ltd v Wiseman [2008] BCC 301 (CA) 4.36
Continental Petroleum Products Ltd v Scotia DBG Investments Ltd [2016] JMSC Civ 219.......7.14
Conway v Prince Eze [2018] EWHC 29 (Ch), [2019] EWCA Civ 88 ....8.53, 8.59,
                                                            10.09, 10.18, 10.23, 11.95
Conway v Wade [1909] AC 506..6.14
Cook v Deeks [1916] 1 AC 554 (PC–Canada)................................... 2.28, 2.37, 2.39
Cook v Evatt (No 2) [1992] 1 NZLR 677 ....2.28
Cooke v Clayworth (1811) 18 Ves Jun 13, 34 ER 222 .... 3.40, 7.65, 7.68
Cooke v Munstone (1805) 1 Bos & Pul 351, 127 ER 499 ....3.24
Coomber, Re [1911] 1 Ch 723 (CA) 6.103, 6.117, 8.08
Cooper v National Provincial Bank Ltd [1946] KB 1 ....5.47
Cooper v Phibbs (1867) LR 2 HL 149...................... 2.37, 11.86, 11.107, 15.38, 17.05, 17.43
Cooper v Tamms [1988] 1 EGLR 257..4.114
Copping and Perball Pty Ltd v ANZ McCaughan Ltd (1997) 67 SASR 525 (Full Ct)...........28.21
Corbett v Barking, Havering and Brentwood Health Authority [1991] 2 QB 408 (CA) 17.18
Cornhill Insurance Company Ltd v L & B Assenheim (1937) 58 Lloyd's Rep 27 ....14.79
Cornish v Midland Bank plc [1985] 3 All ER 513 (CA) 6.100
Cory v Cory (1747) 1 Ves Sen 19, 27 ER 864 .... 7.65, 7.68
Cory v Eyre (1863) 1 De GJ & S 149, 46 ER 58...3.49
Cory v Patton (1872) LR 7 QB 304 ....5.32
Coupe v JM Coupe Publishing Ltd [1981] 1 NZLR 275 (CA)........................25.28, 25.57
Coutinho & Ferrostaal GmbH v Tracomex (Canada) Ltd [2015] BCSC 787 ....21.17, 23.112
Cowan de Groot Properties Ltd v Eagle Trust plc [1991] BCLC 1045 ....8.48
Cox v Prentice (1815) 3 M & S 344, 105 ER 641 .... 1.32, 10.24
Craig (Dec'd), Re [1971] Ch 95 .... 6.85, 6.100, 6.114, 29.18, 29.50
Craig v Lamoureux [1920] AC 349 (PC–Canada) 29.18
Craine v Colonial Mutual Fire Insurance Co (1920) 28 CLR 305.................... 23.11, 23.42,
                                                            23.85, 23.92, 23.93, 24.03
Cramaso LLP v Ogilvie-Grant [2014] AC 1093; 2 WLR 317 (SC) 4.77, 4.78, 4.90, 4.92
Craven-Ellis v Canons Ltd [1936] 2 KB 403 (CA)..1.55

TABLE OF CASES XXXV

Creative Technology Ltd v Huawei International Pte Ltd [2017] SGHC 201 .... 1.16, 4.54, 11.14
Credit Agricole Corporation and Investment Bank v Papadimitriou
    [2015] 1 WLR 4265 (PC—Gibraltar)...21.18, 21.72
Credit Lyonnais Bank Nederland v Export Credit Guarantee Department
    [1996] 1 Lloyd's Rep 200; on appeal [1998] 1 Lloyd's Rep 19 (CA);
    on appeal [2000] 1 AC 486.....................................5.43, 5.46, 5.47, 5.49
Credit Lyonnais Bank Nederland NV v Burch [1997] 1 All ER 144 (CA) 6.98, 6.100, 6.116, 6.117,
                7.70, 7.76, 7.79, 7.88, 7.89, 7.90, 7.97, 7.99, 7.101, 7.102, 9.05, 9.15, 29.20
Credit Suisse International v Stichting Vestia Groep [2014] EWHC 3103 (Comm) 26.11
Cremdean Properties Ltd v Nash (1977) 244 EG 547 (CA)...............26.06, 26.14, 26.15, 26.17
Cresendo Management Pty Ltd v Westpac Banking Corporation
    (1988) 19 NSWLR 40 (CA) 6.47, 6.66, 6.68
Cresswell v Potter [1978] 1 WLR 255n................7.77, 7.78, 7.87, 7.89, 7.93, 7.94, 7.97, 7.100
Crestsign Ltd v National Westminster Bank Plc [2015] 2 All ER (Comm) 133;
    appeal given on other grounds: [2015] EWCA Civ 986......................26.20, 26.26
Criterion Properties plc v Stratford UK Properties LLC [2004] 1 WLR 1846 (HL) 1.41, 1.77, 1.88
Crociani v Crociani (Royal Court of Jersey 11 September 2017) 20.01
Croft v Graham (1863) 2 De GJ & S 155, 46 ER 334 ....3.38, 15.50
Crosbie v Naidoo (2005) 216 ALR 105 (FCA)...............................25.34, 25.50
Crossman v Sheahan (2016) 115 ACSR 130 (NSWCA)...................................24.16
Crowden v Aldridge [1993] 1 WLR 433...5.16
Crown Holdings (London) Ltd (in liq), Re [2015] EWHC 1876 (Ch) 1.83, 1.85,
                        1.95, 4.36, 16.12, 16.70, 25.05, 25.07, 25.18
Crown Master International Trading Co Ltd v China Solar Energy Holdings Ltd
    [2015] 4 HKC 505................................. 16.13, 18.36, 18.93, 18.94, 20.05, 21.69
Crump v Wala [1994] 2 NZLR 331 ....23.36
Crystal Palace FC (2000) Ltd v Dowie [2007] EWHC 1392 (QB); [2007] IRLR 682 ......13.28, 20.35
CTN Cash and Carry Ltd v Gallaher Ltd [1994] 4 All ER 714 (CA)....6.03, 6.37, 6.40, 6.42, 6.54, 7.85
Cumming v Ince (1847) 11 QB 117, 116 ER 418...6.20
Cundy v Lindsay (1878) 3 App Cas 459 .... 1.46, 1.79, 14.12, 20.06, 21.05, 21.57, 25.57, 29.36
Curling v Marquis Townsend (1816) 19 Ves Jun 629, 34 ER 649.........................3.37
Curtis v Curtis [2011] EWCA Civ 1602..6.103
Curtis v The Chemical Cleaning and Dyeing Co Ltd [1951] 1 KB 805 (CA)........ 4.04, 4.35, 27.22
Curwen v Yan Yean Land Co Ltd (1891) 17 VLR 745 (Full Ct) 4.35, 19.11, 19.12, 19.16
Cutter v Powell (1795) 6 TR 320, 101 ER 573 ....3.25

D & C Builders Ltd v Rees [1966] 2 QB 617 (CA)...................................6.31, 6.36
D'Aranda v Houston (1834) 6 Car & P 511, 172 ER 1342...............................29.79
Da Costa v Scandret (1723) 2 P Wms 170, 24 ER 686.............................17.30, 18.40
Dabbs v Seaman (1925) 36 CLR 538...4.26
Dadourian v Simms [2009] 1 Lloyd's Rep 601 (CA)......................... 4.104, 4.106, 4.112
Daily Telegraph Newspaper Co v McLaughlin [1904] AC 776 (PC–Australia) 7.45
Dale v Spurrier (1802) 7 Ves Jun 232, 32 ER 94.......................................24.08
Daly, Re (1907) 39 SCR 122..1.74
Daly v The Sydney Stock Exchange Ltd (1986) 160 CLR 371 ....1.54, 1.71, 2.24, 11.27, 11.101,
                13.29, 15.19, 15.34, 16.13, 16.25, 16.27, 16.31, 16.33, 16.37,
                16.41, 16.42, 16.52, 16.53, 16.60, 21.04, 21.62, 21.63, 22.09
Daniel v Drew [2005] EWCA 507..6.41, 6.84, 6.87, 6.88
Daraydan Holdings Ltd v Solland International Ltd [2005] Ch 119...... 2.24, 8.49, 8.60, 16.55, 16.70
Darjan Estate Co plc v Hurley [2012] 1 WLR 1782.....................................6.86
David Securities Pty Ltd v Commonwealth Bank of Australia (1992) 175 CLR 353 ....1.55, 29.28
Davies v AIB Group (UK) plc [2012] EWHC (Ch) 2178......................... 6.81, 6.83, 6.92
Davies v London and Provincial Marine Insurance Company (1878) 8 ChD 469 ....4.30, 4.90
Davis v Duke of Marlborough (1819) 2 Swans 108, 36 ER 555 ....3.37
Davis v Morrison (1773) Lofft 185, 98 ER 99................................. 3.10, 3.11, 3.12
Dawes v Harness (1875) LR 10 CP 166....................... 11.23, 11.41, 11.45, 12.06, 29.82

xxxvi TABLE OF CASES

Dawson v Bell [2016] EWCA Civ 96; [2016] 2 BCLC 59 ....6.72
De Bernardy v Harding (1853) 8 Ex 822, 155 ER 1586.............................3.27, 14.43
De Bussche v Alt (1878) 8 ChD 286 (CA) 24.08, 24.09
De Costa v Scandret (1723) 2 P Wms 169, 24 ER 686.....................3.55, 3.57, 14.80, 15.66
De Ghetoff v The London Assurance Company (1720) 4 Brown's PC 525, 2 ER 295 ....3.56, 3.57
De Molestina v Ponton [2002] 1 Lloyd's Rep 271 .... 2.09, 13.04, 13.09, 13.14, 19.05, 19.21
De Symons v Minchwich (1796) 1 Esp 430, 170 ER 409 ....3.08, 14.34
Dean v Gibson [1958] VR 563...27.12
Debenham v Sawbridge [1905] 2 Ch 98..7.28
Debtor, Re A [1927] 2 Ch 367 (CA) 1.87, 8.55
Deepak Fertilisers and Petrochemicals Corporation v ICI Chemicals and
   Polymers Ltd [1999] 1 Lloyd's Rep 387 (CA)....................................26.04
Demagogue Pty Ltd v Ramensky (1992) 110 ALR 608 (Full FCA)..........................2.04
Demerara Bauxite Co Ltd v Hubbard [1923] AC 673
   (PC–British Guiana) 6.100, 8.13, 8.15, 8.22, 8.26, 8.28, 8.30, 8.32
Demetrios v Gikas Dry Cleaning Industries Pty Ltd (1991) 22 NSWLR 561 ....4.104
Demite Ltd v Protec Health Ltd [1998] BCC 638 ....8.20
Denton v Donner (1856) 23 Beav 285, 53 ER 112......................................1.74
Deposit and General Life Assurance Company Registered v Ayscough
   (1856) 6 El & Bl 761, 119 ER 1048.....................................3.41, 14.61, 14.62
Deputy Commissioner of Taxation (NSW) v Chamberlain (1990) 93 ALR 729................7.20
Derry v Peek (1889) 14 App Cas 337 ....3.35, 4.03, 4.05, 4.06, 4.08, 4.09, 4.11, 25.29
Desir v Alcide [2015] UKPC 24 ....6.85
Deutsche Bank AG v Sebastian Holdings Inc [2013] EWHC 3463 (Comm) 6.07
Deutsche Bank AG v Unitech Global Ltd (No 2) [2013] 2 Lloyd's Rep 629 ....5.41, 5.43, 5.45, 5.47
Deutsche Bank AG v Unitech Global Ltd [2013] EWCA Civ 1372.........................5.47
Deutsche Bank AG v Unitech Global Ltd [2016] 1 WLR 3598 (CA) 15.51, 15.55, 15.60
Deutsche Bank AG v Unitech Global Ltd [2017] EWHC 1381 (Comm).........19.05, 19.07, 19.40
Deutsche Bank (Suisse) SA v Khan [2013] EWHC 482 (Comm).............................7.15
Deutsche Morgan Grenfell Group plc v Inland Revenue [2007] 1 AC 558 ....1.52, 29.29
Devald v Zigeuner (1958) 16 DLR (2d) 285...7.30, 11.92
Dewar v Dewar [1975] 1 WLR 1532...29.13
Dhaliwal v Hussain [2017] EWHC 2655 (Ch) 4.39
Dhegetoft v The London Assurance (1728) Mos 84, 25 ER 285 ....3.56
Di Cenzo Construction Co Ltd v Glassico (1978) 90 DLR (3d) 127 (Ont CA) 7.34
Diamond v British Columbia Thoroughbred Breeders' Society
   (1965) 52 DLR (2d) 146 (BCSC)...27.60
Dickinson v Burrell (1866) 1 Eq Cas 337 ....16.42, 22.08
Dies v British and International Mining and Finance Corporation Ltd [1939] 1 KB 724 .... 1.20, 1.21
Dimmock v Hallett (1866) 2 Ch App 21 (CA)...4.46
Dimond v Lovell [2002] 1 AC 384 ....17.13
Dimsdale v Dimsdale (1856) 3 Drew 556, 61 ER 1015................................18.48, 18.50
Dimskal Shipping Co SA v International Transport Workers Federation
   (The Evia Luck) [1992] 2 AC 152 ....1.51, 6.31, 6.47, 6.66, 10.23, 14.07, 14.36
Diprose v Louth (No 1) (1990) SASR 438 ....29.32
Directors of the Central Railway of Venezuela v Kisch
   (1867) LR 2 HL 99 .... 4.119, 23.24, 23.30, 23.88, 24.43, 24.88
Dividend Fund Inc, Re (1974) VR 451..25.50
Dobell v Stevens (1825) 3 B&C 623, 107 ER 864......................................14.23
Doe d Archbishop of Berkley v Archbishop of York (1805) 6 East 86, 102 ER 1219..............3.52
Doe d Courtail v Thomas (1829) 9 B & C 288, 109 ER 107 ....3.52
Doe d Lewis v Bingham (1821) 4 B & Ald 672, 106 ER 1082............................3.52
Dold v Murphy [2020] NZLR 313 ....6.38
Doll v Howard (1897) 11 Man R 577 (CA) 20.31
Dominion Paper Box Co v Crown Tailoring Co (1918) 43 DLR 557 (Ont SC)................19.06
Dominion Royalty Corporation v Goffatt [1935] 1 DLR 780 (Ont CA); on appeal
   [1935] SCR 565; aff'd [1935] 4 DLR 736 (SCC)..............................18.01, 18.48

TABLE OF CASES xxxvii

Don Lodge Motel Ltd v Invercargill Licensing Trust [1970] NZLR 1105 . . . . 4.123, 19.06
Donau Pty Ltd v ACS AWD Shipbuilder Pty Ltd (2019) 101 NSWLR 679 (CA) 23.61
Donegal International Ltd v Republic of Zambia [2007] 1 Lloyd's Rep 397. . . . . 8.67, 9.05, 23.40, 26.11
Donnelly v Australia and New Zealand Banking Group Ltd [2014] NSWCA 145 . . . . 7.83, 19.26
Donovan v Fricker (1821) Jac 165, 37 ER 813 . . . . .3.38, 3.44, 15.37, 17.05
Dorotea Pty Ltd v Christos Doufas Nominees [1986] 2 Qd R 91 . . . . .26.11
Dougan v MacPherson [1902] AC 197 (HL Sc) 8.22, 8.25
Dowdle v Pay Now For Business Pty Ltd [2012] QSC 272 . . . . 19.28, 19.29, 29.59
Downs v Chappell [1996] 3 All ER 344; [1997] 1 WLR 426 (CA) 4.63, 4.100, 4.104
Doyle v Olby (Ironmongers) Ltd [1969] 2 QB 158 (CA) 4.09
Dr Compton's case 3.28
Drake Insurance plc v Provident Insurance plc [2003] Lloyd's Rep IR 781;
    on appeal [2004] QB 601; [2004] 1 Lloyd's Rep 268 (CA) 5.26, 10.09, 10.18, 10.29,
                                            11.10, 11.16, 11.17, 11.80, 11.81, 11.82, 11.84,
                                            11.107, 11.113, 12.14, 14.36, 19.06, 23.59, 23.103
Drew v Merry (1701) 1 Eq Ca Abr 176, 21 ER 969 . . . . 3.42, 22.06
DSND Subsea Ltd v Petroleum Geoservices ASA [2000] BLR 530. . . . . 6.07, 6.12, 6.29,
                                            6.38, 6.66, 6.70, 6.73, 23.14, 23.37
Dubai Aluminium v Salaam [2003] 2 AC 366 . . . . .9.04
Duffell v Wilson (1808) 1 Camp 401, 170 ER 999 . . . . 3.05, 3.63
Duke of Leeds v Earl of Amherst (1846) 2 Ph 117, 41 ER 886 . . . . .24.08
Duke of Sutherland v Heathcote [1891] 1 ChD 475 (CA) 15.51
Dunbar v Tredennick (1813) 2 Ball & Beatty 304 . . . . 3.38, 3.42, 15.10, 16.42, 21.08, 21.37, 21.44, 21.49
Dunbar Bank plc v Nadeem [1998] 3 All ER 876 (CA) 6.02, 6.93, 13.11,
                                            15.51, 16.62, 18.02, 18.48, 19.20, 20.08, 20.32
Duncan, Re [1899] 1 Ch 387 . . . . .16.08
Duncan v Worrall (1822) 10 Price 31, 147 ER 232 . . . . 3.55, 3.57, 3.60, 3.61, 14.80, 29.83
Dunhill v Burgin [2014] 1 WLR 933 (Sup Ct) 7.52, 7.63, 7.67
Dunne v English (1874) LR 18 Eq 524 . . . . .24.43
Duranty's case See Liverpool Borough Bank (Duranty's case), Re
Dusik v Newton (1985) 62 BCLR 1 (BCCA) 15.22
Dutch v Warren (1720) 1 Str 406, 93 ER 598 . . . . 3.23, 3.25, 3.27, 3.30, 11.47
Dyer v Tymewell (1689) 2 Vern 123, 23 ER 688 . . . . 3.38, 15.34, 16.56

EA Grimstead & Sons v McGarrigan [1999] EWCA (Civ) 3029
    (CA 27 Oct 1999) 4.41, 4.71, 4.103, 26.06, 26.10, 26.30
Eaglesfield v The Marquis of Londonderry (1876) 4 ChD 693 (CA) 4.17, 4.44
Earl of Ardglasse v Muschamp (1684) 1 Vern 237, 23 ER 438 . . . . 3.37, 3.38, 3.42, 16.42, 22.08
Earl of Aylesford v Morris (1873) 8 Ch App 484 (CA) 7.69, 7.75, 7.76, 7.93, 7.94, 7.97, 15.50
Earl of Beauchamp v Winn (1873) LR 6 HL 223 . . . . 2.37, 18.27, 24.59
Earl of Bristol v Wilsmore and Page (1823) B & C 514, 107 ER 190 . . . . 3.05, 3.08, 14.14
Earl of Chesterfield v Janssen (1750) 1 Atk 301, 26 ER 191; on appeal
    (1751) 2 Ves Sen 125, 28 ER 82 . . . . .3.35, 3.37, 3.38, 3.39, 3.42, 7.69, 15.50, 22.07
Earl of Deloraine v Browne (1792) 3 Bro CC 633, 29 ER 739 . . . . 24.10, 24.69
Earl of Illchester, ex p (1803) 7 Ves Jun 348, 32 ER 142 . . . . 3.42, 22.06
East Pine Management Ltd v Tawney Assets Limited and others
    [2014] BVIHCVAP 2012/0035 (ESCC CA, 24 March 2014) 4.100, 4.104
Eastern Services Ltd v No 68 Ltd [2006] 3 NZLR 335. . . . . 24.15, 24.16
Eastgate, Re [1905] 1 KB 465 . . . . 4.36, 11.05, 11.33, 11.34, 14.18, 21.05, 23.18, 24.39, 24.65, 25.04
Eco3 Capital Limited v Ludsin Overseas Ltd [2013] EWCA Civ 413 . . . . .4.08
Economides v Commercial Union Assurance plc
    [1998] QB 587 (CA) 4.49, 4.50, 4.55, 4.56, 5.29, 9.05
Eden v Ridsdale's Railway Lamp & Lighting Co (1889) 23 QBD 368 . . . . 8.54, 8.60
Edgar v Hector 1912 SC 348 . . . . .4.37
Edgington v Fitzmaurice (1885) 29 ChD 459 (CA) 4.06, 4.08, 4.13, 4.51, 4.60, 4.104
Edinburgh United Breweries Ltd v Molleson [1894] AC 90 (HL). 18.51

xxxviii TABLE OF CASES

Edwards v Ashik [2014] EWHC 2454 (Ch); leave to appeal refused
  [2014] EWCA Civ 1704 . . . . 4.104, 23.93
Edwards v Browne (1845) 2 Coll 100, 63 ER 654 . . . . 15.17, 15.18, 20.25
Edwards v Brown, Harries and Stephens (1831) 1 C & J 307, 148 ER 1436 . . . . 29.68, 29.76, 29.79
Edwards v Burt (1852) 2 De GM & G 55, 42 ER 791 . . . . 15.51, 17.63
Edwards v M'Leay (1815) Coop 311, 35 ER 568; on appeal
  (1818) 2 Swans 287, 36 ER 625 . . . . 7.28, 15.34, 15.63, 16.56, 17.39, 17.43, 17.49, 17.64, 27.05
Edwards v Meyrick (1842) 2 Hare 60, 67 ER 25 . . . . 8.07, 8.12, 8.28
Ehrensperger v Anderson (1848) 3 Ex 148, 154 ER 793 . . . . 1.32, 3.27
Ekins v Tresham (1675) 1 Lev 102, 83 ER 318 . . . . .14.23
El Ajou v Dollar Land Holdings plc [1993] 3 All ER 717 . . . . .1.71, 1.96, 2.24, 13.29, 15.19,
          16.07, 16.12, 16.33, 16.34, 16.41, 16.45, 16.51, 16.53, 16.60, 21.48
Eldan Services Ltd v Chandag Motors Ltd [1990] 3 All ER 459 . . . . .10.24, 16.05
Elder v Auerbach [1949] 2 All ER 692 (CA) 7.28, 27.05
Elder's Trustee and Executor Company Ltd v Commonwealth Homes and Investment
  Co Ltd (1941) 65 CLR 603 . . . . 23.20, 23.22, 23.31, 23.42, 23.44, 23.46,
          23.104, 23.105, 23.106, 23.107, 25.02, 25.28, 25.35, 25.67
Electricity Generation Corporation v Woodside Energy Ltd [2013] WASCA 36 . . . . .1.51
Ellis v Barker (1871) 7 Ch App 104 . . . . 6.93, 6.103
Ellis v Ellis (1909) 26 TLR 166 . . . . .29.56
Ellison v Lutre Pty Ltd (1999) 88 FCR 116 . . . . .23.44
Elston v King and Roscoe [2020] EWHC 55 (Ch) 7.38
Emanuel v Dane (1812) 3 Camp 299, 170 ER 1389 . . . . 3.08, 3.09, 14.14, 20.13
Emhill Pty Ltd v Bonsoc Pty Ltd (No 2) [2007] VSCA 108 . . . . 18.77, 19.02, 19.03
Empresa Cubana de Fletes v Lagonisi Shipping Co Ltd [1971] 1 QB 488 (CA) 11.37, 11.38
Englefeild v Englefeild (1687) 1 Vern 446, 23 ER 576 . . . . .3.38, 3.42, 15.37, 22.08
Enimont Overseas AG v RO Jugotnker Zadad (The Olib)
  [1991] 2 Lloyd's Rep 108 . . . . .1.51, 6.47, 6.48, 10.23, 14.07, 14.36
Ennis v Klassen (1990) 70 DLR (4th) 321 (Man CA) 27.22, 27.32, 27.60
Equiticorp Finance Ltd v Bank of New Zealand (1992) 29 NSWLR 260 .6.14
Equiticorp Industries Group Ltd v The Crown (No 47) [1998] 2 NZLR 481 . . . . .18.69, 18.76
Equuscorp Pty Ltd v Van der Ross [2005] VSC 110 . . . . .21.23, 21.46
Eric Gnapp Ltd v Petroleum Board [1949] 1 All ER 980 (CA) 6.54
Erlanger v The New Sombrero Phosphate Company
  (1878) 3 App Cas 1218 . . . . .2.13, 2.18, 2.21, 2.28, 2.29, 10.04, 11.09, 13.01, 13.08, 13.15,
          15.38, 15.63, 17.17, 17.33,18.01, 18.02, 18.03, 18.12, 18.13, 18.14,
          18.15, 18.24, 18.27, 18.55, 18.86, 18.95, 18.106, 18.107, 18.124,
          23.30, 23.66, 23.71, 23.80, 23.81, 23.110, 24.11, 24.16, 24.20,
          24.41, 24.43, 24.46, 24.50, 24.52, 24.53, 24.58, 24.65,
          24.71, 24.74, 24.87, 24.100, 24.101, 24.102, 24.103
Erlson Precision Holdings Ltd v Hampson Industries plc
  [2011] EWHC 1137 (Comm) 4.74, 4.94
Ernest v Vivian (1864) 33 LJ Ch (NS) 513 . . . . .3.50, 16.12, 21.70, 24.84
Espey v Lake (1852) 10 Hare 260, 68 ER 928 . . . . .3.37
Esquire (Electronics) Ltd v The Hong Kong And Shanghai Banking Corporation Ltd
  [2007] 3 HKLRD 439 . . . . .6.75
Esso Petroleum Co v Mardon [1976] 1 QB 801 (CA) 4.09, 4.54
Estate Properties Ltd v Wignall See Estate Realties Ltd v Wignall
Estate Realties Ltd v Wignall [1992] 2 NZLR 615 . . . . .2.21, 15.17, 15.19,
          16.13, 16.42, 16.52, 16.60, 16.65
ETC Corp v Title Guarantee & Trust Co 271 NY 124, 2 NE 2d 284, 3 NE 2d 471,
  105 ALR 999 (1936) 14.64
Evans v Bartlam [1937] AC 473 . . . . .23.40
Evans v Benson & Co [1961] WAR 12 . . . . .1.18, 23.71, 23.84, 23.105
Evans v Benyon (1887) 37 ChD 329 . . . . .24.58
Evans v Chesshire (1803) Ves Sen Supp 300, 28 ER 532 . . . . .3.37

TABLE OF CASES xxxix

Evans v Edmonds (1853) 13 CB 777, 138 ER 1407 . . . . .14.26, 29.79
Evans v European Bank Ltd (2004) 61 NSWLR 75 (CA) 1.98
Evans v Llewellin (1787) 1 Cox 333, 29 ER 1191 . . . . 3.38, 7.75, 7.84, 15.58, 15.65
Evans v Lloyd [2013] EWHC 1725 (Ch) 6.83, 6.97, 6.101, 6.108, 6.114,
6.117, 7.74, 7.78, 7.86, 29.16, 29.18, 29.40
Event Spaces Ltd v Gregg [2019] EWHC 3447 (Comm) 20.31
Evia Luck, The *See* Dimskal Shipping Co SA v International Transport Workers
Federation (The Evia Luck)
Experience Hendrix LLC v PPX Enterprises Inc [2003] 1 All ER (Comm) 830 . . . . .17.07
Eyre v Burmester (1862) 10 HLC 90, 11 ER 959 . . . . .3.49

F & B Transport Ltd v White Truck Sales Manitoba Ltd (1964) 47 DLR (2d) 419 (Man QB);
on appeal (1965) 49 DLR (2d) 670 (Man CA) 17.05, 17.35, 18.88
FAI General Insurance Company Ltd v Ocean Marine Mutual Protection and
Indemnity Association Ltd (1997) 41 NSWLR 559;
[1998] Lloyd's Rep IR 24 . . . . .1.14, 1.16, 12.05, 13.27
Fairbanks v Snow 13 NE 596 (1887) 14.07, 16.02, 29.70
Fairford Water Ski Club Ltd v Cohoon [2021] BCC 498 (CA) 8.20
Falck v Williams [1900] AC 176 . . . . .1.36
Far Eastern Shipping Co Public Ltd v Scales Trading Ltd
[2001] Lloyd's Rep Bank 29 (PC–NZ) 5.47, 5.51
Farah Constructions Pty Ltd v Say-Dee Pty Ltd [2007] HCA 22, 230 CLR 89 . . . . .8.22, 8.24
Farrar v Farrar's Ltd (1888) 40 ChD 395 (CA) 1.73
Farrer v Nightingale (1798) 2 Esp 639, 170 ER 481 . . . . .3.27
Farrington v Rowe McBride & Partners [1985] 1 NZLR 83 (CA) 8.34, 8.36
Feise v Parkinson (1812) 4 Taunt 640, 128 ER 482 . . . . 3.56, 3.63, 14.80
Fell v Whittaker (1871-72) LR 7 QB 120 . . . . .6.24
Fenton v Holloway (1815) 1 Stark 126, 171 ER 422 . . . . .7.65
Fenton v Kenny [1969] NZLR 552 . . . . .20.01, 23.91
Feret v Hill (1854) 15 CB 207, 139 ER 400 . . . . 14.24, 14.26, 14.27
Ferguson v Carrington (1829) 9 B & C 59, 109 ER 22 . . . . 3.05, 3.08, 3.09, 3.27, 14.34, 14.42, 20.13
Fermor's case (1601) 3 Co Rep 77a, 76 ER 800 . . . . .3.43
Ferris v Plaister (1994) 34 NSWLR 474 (NSWCA) 1.16
Feuer Leather Corp v Frank Johnstone & Sons [1981] Com LR 251 . . . . .21.74
Ffrench's Estate, Re (1887) 21 IR 283 . . . . .21.70
FHR European Ventures LLP v Mankarious [2015] AC 250 . . . . 1.78, 1.89, 2.14
Fibrosa Spolka Akcyjna v Fairburn Lawson Combe Barbour Ltd [1943] AC 32 . . . . .3.31
Field v Zien [1963] SCR 632 . . . . .27.45
Fielder v Smith [2005] All ER(D) 264 . . . . .6.106
Fielder v Starkin (1788) 1 H BL 17, 126 ER 11 . . . . 3.27, 14.54
Fineland Investments Ltd v Pritchard [2011] EWHC 113 (Ch) 7.61, 7.89
Finesky Holdings Pty Ltd v Minister of Transport for Western Australia [2002] WASCA 206 . . . . . 17.07
Fiona Trust v Privalov [2010] EWHC 3199 (Comm) 8.60
Fiona Trust & Holding Corporation v Privalov [2007] 1 All ER (Comm) 81;
[2007] 1 All ER (Comm) 891 (CA); [2007] 2 All ER (Comm)
1053 (HL) 1.16, 11.09, 23.18, 23.28, 23.34, 23.80, 24.39, 24.94, 24.101
First Conferences Ltd 2003 Employee Benefit Trust, In re [2010] JRC 055A 29.46
First Energy (UK) Ltd v Hungarian International Bank Ltd [1993] 2 Lloyd's Rep 194 (CA) 9.04
First Island Financial Services Ltd v Novastar Developments (Kelowna, Orchard Gardens)
Ltd (BCCA 5 December 2000) 16.13
First National Bank plc v Walker [2001] FLR 21 (CA) 23.89
First National Reinsurance Co Ltd v Greenfield
[1921] 2 KB 260 (CA) 11.50, 11.51, 11.52, 24.88, 25.74, 27.21, 27.24, 27.25
First Subsea Ltd v Balltec Ltd [2014] EWHC 866 (Ch) 24.33
First Tower Trustees Ltd v CDS (Superstores International) Ltd
[2019] 1 WLR 637 (CA) 26.11, 26.18, 26.20, 26.22, 26.29, 26.31

xl TABLE OF CASES

Fisher v Brooker [2009] 1 WLR 1764 (HL) 24.11, 24.15, 24.16, 24.18, 24.114
Fisher v Roberts (1890) 6 TLR 354 . . . . .21.28
Fitt v Cassanet (1842) 4 Man & G 898, 134 ER 369 . . . . 1.32, 3.27
Fitzgerald v Jacomb (1873) 4 AJR 189 (FC Sup Ct Vict) 5.47
Fitzroy v Cave [1905] 2 KB 364 (CA) 16.42, 22.11
Fitzroy Robinson Ltd v Mentmore Towers Ltd [2009] BLR 505 . . . . .4.93
Flack v Pattinson [2002] EWCA 1762 . . . . .4.120
Fleischhaker v Fort Garry Agencies Ltd (1957) 11 DLR (2d) 599 (Man CA) 15.22, 21.23
Fleming v Mair (1921) 58 DLR 318 (Sask CA) 18.49, 19.06
Fletcher v Krell (1873) 42 LJ QB 55 . . . . .4.30
Flight v Booth (1834) 1 Bing (NC) 370, 131 ER 1160 . . . . .14.23
Floods of Queensferry Ltd v Shand Construction Ltd (No 3) [2000] Building LR 81 . . . . . 28.08, 28.34
Flying Music Co Ltd v Theater Entertainment SA [2017] EWHC 3192 (QB) 6.38
Folkes v King [1923] 1 KB 282 (CA) 21.56, 21.59
Food Corporation of India v Antclizo Shipping Corporation (The Antclizo)
    [1987] 2 Lloyd's Rep 130 (CA) 7.12
FoodCo UK LLP (t/a Muffin Break) v Henry Boot Developments Ltd
    [2010] EWHC 358 (Ch) 4.28, 4.57, 26.02, 26.03, 26.11, 26.26, 26.28, 26.31
Ford by his Tutor Beatrice Ann Watkinson v Perpetual Trustees Victoria Ltd
    [2009] NSWCA 186 . . . . .7.45
Fordy v Harwood [1999] EWCA 1134 . . . . 4.46, 4.48
Forrester v Hodgson (1778) 3.25
Forsythe International (UK) Ltd v Silver Shipping Co Ltd (The Saetta) [1994] 1 WLR 1334 . . . . .21.74
Fortune Global Development Ltd v Shung Cheong Food Trading Ltd [2002] 2 HKLRD 447 . . . . .5.66
Forum Development Pte Ltd v Global Accent Trading Pte Ltd
    [1995] 1 SLR 474 (CA) 17.04, 17.24, 17.36, 17.62
Foskett v McKeown [2001] 1 AC 102 . . . . 1.63, 1.67
Foster v Action Aviation Ltd [2013] EWHC 2439 (Comm) 4.39, 4.57
Foster v Charles (1830) 7 Bing 105, 131 ER 40 . . . . .4.08
Fox v Mackreth (1788) 2 Bro CC 44, 29 ER 224; aff'd (1791) 4 Bro PC 258, 2 ER 175 . . . . .15.17
Fox v Wright (1821) 6 Madd 111, 56 ER 1034 . . . . .3.37
Francam v Foster (1693) Skinner 326, 90 ER 145 . . . . .3.23
Franks v Bolans (1868) 3 Chap App 717 . . . . .1.74
Frawley v Neill, The Times 5 Apr 1999 (CA) 24.15
Frazer v Walker [1967] 1 AC 569 (PC–NZ) 1.47, 15.09
Frederick E Rose (London) Ltd v William H Pim Jnr & Co Ltd
    [1953] 2 QB 450 (CA) 7.17, 27.22, 27.54
Freeman v Brown [2001] NSWSC 1028 . . . . 15.09, 17.30
Friends Provident Life Office v Hillier Parker May & Rowden (a firm) [1997] QB 85 (CA) 28.26
Frühling v Schroeder (1835) 2 Bing NC 77, 132 ER 31 . . . . .17.21
Fry v Lane (1888) 40 ChD 312 . . . . 7.75, 7.76, 7.77, 7.87, 7.88, 7.89,
    7.96, 7.97, 7.99, 17.63, 23.14, 24.44
Fuentes v Montis (1868) LR 3 CP 268 . . . . 21.56, 21.57, 21.59
Fuller v Happy Shopper Markets Ltd [2001] 2 Lloyd's Rep 49 . . . . .1.55
Fullwood v Hurley [1928] 1 KB 498 (CA) 8.18, 8.38
Fulton v Reay [1926] NZLR 195 . . . . 18.60, 18.76
Funding Corporation Block Discounting Ltd v Lexi Holdings plc [2011] EWHC 3101 (Ch) 20.07
Fysh v Page (1956) 96 CLR 233 . . . . .3.50, 16.12, 16.13, 18.16, 18.93,
    18.95, 24.17, 24.49, 24.51, 24.92, 24.114

G and C Kreglinger v New Patagonia Meat and Cold Storage Company Ltd [1914] AC 25 . . . . . .15.51
Galafassi v Kelly [2014] NSWCA 190 . . . . .11.08
Galle Gowns Ltd v Licenses & General Insurance Co Ltd (1933) 47 Lloyd's Rep 186 . . . . .4.35
Gallinar Holdings Pty Ltd v Riedel [2014] NSWSC 476 . . . . .7.20
Gamatronic (UK) Limited v Hamilton [2016] EWHC 2225 (QB),
    [2017] BCC 670 . . . . 15.50, 15.54, 18.33, 23.40, 23.79

TABLE OF CASES   xli

Gany Holdings (PTC) SA v Khan [2018] UKPC 21 (BVI)...............................13.30
Garcia v National Australia Bank Ltd (1998) 194 CLR 395.....................6.115, 9.09, 29.59
Gardiner v Gray (1815) 4 Camp 144, 171 ER 46..3.19
Garrard v Frankel (1862) 30 Beav 445, 54 ER 961...................7.30, 11.92, 19.24, 19.25
Garratt v Ikeda [2002] 1 NZLR 577 (CA) 1.07, 1.08
Gaydamak v Leviev [2012] EWHC 1740 (Ch) 9.04
Gearhart v Kraatz (1918) 40 DLR 26 (Sask SC (App Div)) 17.56, 18.09, 18.87
Geest plc v Fyffes plc [1999] 1 All ER 672 ....4.36
General Railway Syndicate, Whiteley's case, Re [1899] 1 Ch 770; on appeal
 [1900] 1 Ch 365 (CA)..25.72, 25.73, 25.75, 25.76
Georgallides v The Secretary of State for Business, Energy and Industrial Strategy
 [2021] 1 BCLC 177...4.74
George Wimpey UK Ltd v VI Components Ltd [2005] EWCA 77...........................7.19
Gerald Cooper Chemicals Ltd Re [1978] Ch 262 ....4.61
Gestmin SGPS S.A. v Credit Suisse (UK) Limited [2020] 1 CLC 428.......................4.26
GHLM Trading Ltd v Maroo [2012] EWHC 61 (Ch)...............................1.78, 13.16
Gibbon v Mitchell [1990] 1 WLR 1304 ....1.48, 11.86, 11.107, 13.32, 29.41, 29.42, 29.44, 29.46, 29.50
Gibbons v Caunt (1799) 4 Ves 840, 31 ER 435.....................................5.59, 7.38
Gibbons v Wright (1954) 91 CLR 423 ....7.52, 10.23, 16.03, 29.21, 29.61
Gibson v D'Este (1843) 2 Y & CCC 542, 63 ER 243 ....17.04, 17.05, 17.13, 17.16, 17.43, 17.64
Gibson v Goldsmid (1854) 5 De G M & G 757, 43 ER 1064........................15.48
Gibson v Jeyes (1801) 6 Ves 266, 31 ER 1044..........................8.03, 8.14, 8.26, 8.32
Gibson v National Cash Register Co 1925 SC 500 ....4.37
Giles v Edwards (1797) 7 TR 181, 101 ER 920.................................3.27, 3.28
Gill v McDowell [1903] 2 IR 463..4.37
Gillespie v Gillespie [2013] 2 QdR 440 (CA)................24.15, 24.16, 24.53, 24.62, 24.114
Gillette v Peppercorn (1840) 3 Beav 78, 49 ER 31 ....17.04, 18.50, 18.93
Gindis v Brisbourne (2000) 72 BCLR (3d) 19 (BCCA) 7.103
Giumelli v Giumelli (1999) 196 CLR 101...24.118
GL Baker Ltd v Medway Building and Supplies [1958] 1 WLR 1216 (CA) 21.72
Gladstone v Hadwen (1813) 1 M & S 517, 105 ER 193........................3.44, 14.33, 16.11
Glasson v Fuller [1922] SASR 148.................................24.09, 24.10, 24.11
Glennon v Federal Commissioner of Taxation (1927) 127 CLR 503 ....1.75
Glicksman v Lancashire and General Insurance Co [1925] 2 KB 593 (CA);
 on appeal [1927] AC 139..5.34
Global Currency Exchange Network Limited v Osage 1 Limited [2019] EWHC 1375 (Comm) 1.83
Global Currency Exchange Network Limited v Osage 1 Limited
 [2019] 1 WLR 5865 ....1.85, 16.07, 16.12, 16.51, 16.57
Global Flood Defence Systems Ltd v Johann Van Den Noort Beheer BV
 2016] EWHC 99 (IPEC) 4.42
Glubb, Re [1900] 1 ChD 354 (CA) 15.34, 16.56, 29.27, 29.31
Gluckstein v Barnes [1900] AC 240 ....2.37
GMAC Commercial Credit Development Ltd v Sandhu [2004] All ER (D) 589 ....26.10
Godbolt v Watts (1795) 2 Anst 543, 145 ER 961....................................15.60
Goddard-Watts v Goddard-Watts [2020] 4 WLR 51 (Fam) 5.20
Goff v Gauthier (1991) 62 P & CR 388...4.73
Gohil v Gohil (No 2) [2016] AC 849..5.20
Goldcorp Exchange, Re [1995] 1 AC 74 (PC–NZ)..................1.52, 10.24, 15.33, 16.05, 16.56
Goldrei, Foucard & Son v Sinclair and Russian Chamber of Commerce in London
 [1918] 1 KB 180 (CA)...............................2.03, 2.05, 2.06, 4.03, 9.04
Goldsmith v Rodger [1962] 2 Lloyd's Rep 249 (CA)..............4.33, 15.12, 27.05, 27.22, 27.53
Goldsworthy v Brickell [1987] 1 Ch 378 (CA) 6.98, 6.100, 6.103, 6.114, 10.07, 10.08,
            11.86, 11.87, 11.88, 11.107, 17.05, 23.06, 24.08, 24.10,
            24.15, 24.58, 24.59, 24.61, 24.92, 24.118, 29.50
Golightly v Reynolds (1772) Lofft 88, 98 ER 547.....................................3.12
Gollan v Nugent (1988) 166 CLR 18...14.25

xlii TABLE OF CASES

Gompertz v Denton (1832) 1 C & M 207, 149 ER 376 . . . . .3.27
Goodchild v Bradbury [2006] EWCA 1868. . . . . 6.03, 6.96, 6.100, 6.108, 6.113
Goodman v Pocock (1850) 15 QB 576, 117 ER 577 . . . . .3.25, 3.27
Goodwin v National Bank of Australasia Ltd (1968) 117 CLR 173. . . . . .5.44, 5.49
Goodwin v State Government Insurance Office (Qld) [1994] 2 QdR 15 . . . . .23.76
Goose v Wilson Sandford & Co [2001] Lloyd's Rep PN 189 (CA) 4.08
Gordon v Chief Commissioner of Metropolitan Police [1910] 2 KB 1080 (CA) 14.27
Gordon v Gordon (1816–21) 3 Swans 400, 36 ER 910 . . . . .5.59
Gordon v Holland (1913) 10 DLR 734 (PC–Canada) 1.67
Gordon v Martin (1732) Fitz 302, 94 ER 766. . . . . .3.24
Gordon v Selico Co Ltd [1986] EGLR 71 (CA) 4.38, 9.04
Gordon v Street [1899] 2 QB 641 (CA) 11.08, 11.41, 12.06, 29.82
Gore v Gibson (1845) 13 M & W 623, 153 ER 260 . . . . .7.66, 7.67, 10.23, 16.03
Gorjat v Gorjat [2010] EWHC 1537 (Ch) 6.108, 7.54
Goss v Chilcott [1996] AC 788 (PC–NZ). 1.26
Gosse v Tracy (1715) 1 P Wms 288, 23 ER 1053 . . . . .3.43
Gould v Cayuga County National Bank 86 NY 75 (1881) 11.64, 12.04, 14.64, 14.65
Gould v Okeden (1731) 4 Brown 198, 2 ER 135 . . . . 3.42, 16.42, 21.04
Gould v Vaggelas (1985) 157 CLR 215 . . . . 4.104, 4.111
Government of Spain v North of England SS Co Ltd (1938) 61 Lloyd's LR 44 . . . . .6.21
Government of Zanzibar v British Aerospace (Lancaster House) Ltd
[2000] 1 WLR 2333 . . . . .26.03, 26.04, 26.20, 26.28, 28.08, 28.09, 28.12
Govindram Seksaria v Radbone (1947) 50 BOMLR 561 (PC—India). 2.13
Graham v Freer (1980) 35 SASR 424 . . . . .27.50, 27.51
Graham v Johnson (1869) 8 Eq Cas 36. . . . . .21.23
Graham v Western Australian Insurance Company Ltd (1931) 40 Lloyd's Rep 64. . 11.41, 12.06, 14.79
Graiseley Properties Ltd v Barclays Bank plc [2013] EWCA Civ 1372. . . . . 4.36, 4.39, 4.124, 5.03
Grant v Gold Exploration and Development Syndicate Ltd [1900] 1 QB 233 (CA) 8.63
Grant v Imperial Trust Co [1935] 3 DLR 660 (SCC) 7.62
Grant v John Grant & Sons Pty Ltd (1954) 91 CLR 112 . . . . .5.64, 7.38
Grant Campbell & Co v Devon Lumber Co Ltd (1914) 7 OWN 209 (Ont SC (App Div)). 14.42
Gray v New Augarita Porcupine Mines Ltd [1952] 3 DLR 1 (PC). 2.27, 8.19, 8.20
Gray v Smith [2013] EWHC 4136 (Comm); [2014] 2 All ER (Comm) 359 . . . . 11.36, 11.40, 21.15, 21.21
Gray v Trick 243 Mich 388, 220 NW 741 (SC 1928). 15.16
Great Investments Ltd v Warner (2016) 243 FCR 516 (Full Ct) 1.27, 1.53, 1.78, 21.18
Great Peace, The See Great Peace Shipping Ltd v Tsavliris Salvage (International) Ltd
(The Great Peace)
Great Peace Shipping Ltd v Tsavliris Salvage (International) Ltd (The Great Peace)
[2003] QB 679 (CA) 1.36, 7.07, 7.08, 7.10, 7.11, 7.15,
7.16, 7.29, 7.30, 7.32, 7.37, 10.24, 10.26, 11.92, 19.25
Great Western Railway Co v London and County Banking Co Ltd [1901] AC 414 . . . . 21.28, 29.20
Greater Fredericton Airport Inc v NAV Canada [2008] NBCA 28; (2008) 280 DLR (4th) 405 . . . .6.27
Greater Pacific Investments Pty Ltd v Australian National Industries Ltd
(1996) 39 NSWLR 143 (CA) 1.71, 2.24, 3.50, 11.101, 13.29,
15.46, 16.12, 16.37, 16.41, 16.60, 18.11, 18.33, 18.104
Grecia Express, The See Strive Shipping Corporation v Hellenic Mutual War Risks
Association (The Grecia Express)
Green v Duckett (1883) 11 QBD 275 . . . . .6.24
Green Park Properties Ltd v Dorku Ltd [2001] 1 HKLRD 139; [2000] 4 HKC 538
Hong Kong CA) 4.26, 28.10, 28.12
Greencapital Aust Pty Ltd v Pasminco Cockle Creek Smelter Pty Ltd (subject to
Deed of Company Arrangement) (no 3) [2018] NSWSC 1956; rev'd on other
grounds [2019] NSWCA 53 . . . . .5.26
Greene King plc v Stanley [2001] EWCA 1966. . . . . .6.100
Greenridge Luton One Ltd v Kempton Investments Ltd [2016] EWHC 91 (Ch) 4.06
Greenslade v Dare (1855) 20 Beav 284, 52 ER 612 . . . . .7.62, 7.64

TABLE OF CASES xliii

Greenwood v Leather Shod Wheel Company [1900] 1 Ch 421 (CA)...................23.18, 25.29
Gregory v Gregory (1815) G Coop 201, 35 ER 530; aff'd (1821) Jac 631,
    37 ER 989...3.44, 24.04, 24.45, 24.113
Grenville v Da Costa (1797) Peake Add Cas 113, 97 ER 213.....................1.32, 3.27, 29.81
Gresley v Mousley (1859) 4 De G & J 78, 45 ER 31......................3.40, 3.42, 15.17, 16.25,
                    16.42, 20.26, 22.06, 24.10, 24.14, 24.43, 24.45, 24.49, 24.58
Griffith v Frapwel (1732) 1 Ves Sen 401, 27 ER 1105.................................5.14, 7.39
Grimaldi v Chameleon Mining NL (2012) 200 FCR 296 (Full Ct)..............1.58, 1.78, 16.70
Grimaldi v Chameleon Mining NL (No 2) (2012) 287 ALR 22 (FCA).........................2.26
Grimaldi v White (1802) 4 Esp 95, 170 ER 654..............................1.32, 3.28, 14.54
Grimoldby v Wells (1875) LR 10 CP 391..14.55, 14.62
Grist v Bailey [1967] Ch 532......................................7.07, 10.26, 19.25
Grogan v 'The Astor' Ltd (1925) 25 NSWLR 409.........................27.24, 27.25, 27.29
Gross v Lewis Hillman Ltd [1970] Ch 445 (CA).....................4.05, 4.42, 4.78, 22.12, 22.13
Grosvenor v Sherratt (1860) 28 Beav 659, 54 ER 520.....................................6.100
Grove v Perkins (1834) 6 Sin 576, 58 ER 510..5.59
Grundt v The Great Boulder Gold Mines Ltd (1937) 59 CLR 641...........................24.74
Grymes v Sanders 93 US 55, 62, 23 Led 798 (1876)....................................24.100
Guarantee Company of North America v Gordon Capital Corporation
    [1999] 3 SCR 423...1.08, 12.05
Guest v Beecroft (1957) 22 WWR 481 (BCSC)...18.90
Guinness plc v Saunders [1988] BCLC 607 (CA); on appeal
    [1990] 2 AC 663....................1.74, 2.22, 2.24, 8.19, 8.20, 15.67, 16.53, 18.43, 18.100
Gulf Azov Shipping Co Ltd v Idisi [2001] Lloyd's Rep 727...............................6.12
Gunatunga v DeAlwis (1996) 72 P & CR 161 (CA)..1.08
Gustav & Co Ltd v Macfield Ltd [2008] NZSC 47.......................................7.80
Gutnick v Indian Farmers Fertiliser Cooperative Ltd
    (2016) 49 VR 732 (CA)......................15.11, 15.63, 15.75, 15.76, 16.21, 16.25
Gwembe Valley Development Co v Koshy (No 3)
    [2004] 1 BCLC 131 (CA)..............2.10, 2.11, 2.17, 2.27, 8.09, 8.10, 8.20, 8.22, 8.72, 24.33

H, Re [1996] AC 563...4.07
Haas Timber & Trading Co Pty Ltd v Wade (1954) 94 CLR 593................11.52, 23.24, 23.28,
                    23.76, 23.88, 24.43, 24.65, 24.71, 24.90, 24.102, 24.105
Habib Bank Ltd v Habib Bank AG Zurich [1981] 1 WLR 1265 (CA).........................24.12
Habib Bank Ltd v Tufail [2006] EWCA Civ 374......................23.40, 24.48, 24.59, 24.61
Hackett v Crown Prosecution Service [2011] EWHC 1170 (Admin)........6.03, 6.100, 6.107, 6.117
Hagen v ICI Chemicals & Polymers Ltd (2002) IRLR 31..............................4.57, 4.84
Haines v Carter [2001] 2 NZLR 167 (CA); rev'd [2001] 3 NZLR 605 (PC— NZ)..............23.14
Haira v Burbery Mortgage Finance & Savings Ltd [1995] 3 NZLR 396 (CA)..............8.30, 8.40
Halifax Building Society v Thomas [1996] Ch 217 (CA)...........................2.24, 13.29,
                    15.19, 16.07, 16.41, 16.51, 23.36
Hall v Warren (1804) 9 Ves Jun 605, 32 ER 738.....................................7.56, 7.58
Halley v Law Society [2003] WTLR 845.............................1.83, 1.85, 1.86, 16.60
Hallows v Fernie (1868) 3 Ch App 467..4.43, 4.103
Halpern v Halpern (No 2) [2007] QB 88; [2008] QB 195 (CA)..................10.04, 10.12, 10.23,
                    11.55, 11.107, 12.04, 12.07, 13.16, 14.09, 14.45, 16.02,
                    18.01, 18.02, 18.05, 18.30, 18.32, 18.46, 18.101, 18.102
Hambrough v Mutual Life Insurance Co of New York (1895) 72 LT 140 (CA)..................4.63
Hamburg v Goldstein [2002] EWCA 122..7.74
Hamilton v Watson (1845) 12 Cl & F 109, 8 ER 1339 (HL Sc)............5.41, 5.42, 5.44, 5.45, 10.23
Hammond v Osborn [2002] EWCA Civ 885......................6.03, 6.96, 6.108, 6.110, 6.114,
                    6.115, 6.119, 29.27, 29.31, 29.32, 29.33, 29.39
Hancock Family Memorial Foundation Ltd v Porteous
    (2000) 22 WAR 198 (Full Ct)....................2.24, 11.26, 11.101, 16.37, 16.38, 16.52
Handcock v Berrey (1888) 57 LJ (Ch) 793..3.52

xliv TABLE OF CASES

Hanson v Keating (1844) 4 Hare 1, 67 ER 537 . . . . 13.01, 13.11, 15.48, 15.49, 19.17
Hanson v Lorenz & Jones (a firm) [1987] FTLR 23 (CA). 8.24, 8.33
Harbour Assurance Co (UK) v Kansa Ltd [1993] QB 701 . . . . .1.16
Hardie and Lane v Chilton [1928] 2 KB 306 . . . . .6.38
Hardoon v Belilios [1901] AC 118 . . . . .14.22
Hardy v Griffiths [2015] Ch 417 . . . . 26.22, 26.26, 26.29
Haringey LBC v Hines See London Borough of Haringey v Hines
Harmood v Oglander (1801) 6 Ves Jun 199, 31 ER 1010 . . . . 3.42, 22.06
Harriette N, The See Statoil ASA v Louis Dreyfus Energy Services LP ('The Harriette N')
Harrington v The Victoria Graving Dock Company (1878) 3 QBD 549 . . . . 8.55, 10.23
Harris v Digital Pulse Pty Ltd (2003) 56 NSWLR 298 (CA) 2.17
Harris v Oke (1759) 3.23
Harris v Pepperell (1867) LR 5 Eq 1 . . . . 7.30, 11.92, 19.24
Harrison v Guest (1860) 8 HLC 481, 11 ER 517 . . . . .7.84
Harrison v James (1862) 7 H & N 804, 158 ER 693 . . . . .3.27
Harrison v Owen (1738) 1 Atk 520, 26 ER 328 . . . . .3.52
Harry v Kreutziger (1978) 95 DLR (3d) 231 (BCCA). 7.103
Harsten Developments Ltd v Bleaken [2012] EWHC 2704 (Ch) 28.12
Hart v Burbidge [2013] EWHC 1628 (Ch) 6.75
Hart v Longfield (1703) 7 Mod 148, 87 ER 1156. . . . . .3.22
Hart v O'Connor [1985] AC 1000 (PC–NZ) 6.05, 6.54, 7.41, 7.47, 7.50, 7.61, 7.69, 7.79,
 7.80, 7.81, 7.85, 7.88, 10.23, 16.03, 29.16, 29.21, 29.56, 29.61
Hart v Swaine (1877) 7 ChD 42. . . . . 15.63, 17.49, 27.05
Hartelid v Sawyer & McClockin Real Estate Ltd [1977] 5 WWR 481. .4.120
Hartigan v International Society for Krishna Consciousness Ltd
 [2002] NSWSC 810 . . . . .15.17, 15.18, 15.25, 17.18
Harvard Nominees Pty Ltd v Tiller [2020] FCAFC 229. . . . . 10.04, 11.55, 11.101
Hassard v Smith (1872) IR 6 Eq 429 . . . . 7.56, 7.58, 7.61
Hastings-Bass (Dec'd), Re [1975] Ch 25. . . . . 29.52, 29.54
Hatch v Hatch (1804) 9 Ves 292, 32 ER 615 . . . . .8.08, 8.27, 24.44, 24.78
Hawes v Wyatt (1790) 2 Cox 263, 30 ER 122, (1790) 3 Bro CC 156,
 29 ER 463. . . . . 3.42, 3.52, 15.51, 20.06, 21.62, 21.63, 22.06, 22.08
Hawker Pacific Pty Ltd v Helicopter Charter Pty Ltd (1991) 22 NSWLR 298 (CA) 23.04, 23.14
Hawkins v Bone (1865) 4 F & F 311, 176 ER 578. . . . . 7.65, 7.67
Hayes v Ross (No 3) [1919] NZLR 786. . . . . .2.06, 17.05, 17.59, 17.62
Haynes v Hirst (1927) 27 NSW (SR) 480 . . . . .23.94
Haygarth v Wearing (1871) LR 12 Eq 320 . . . . .17.04
Hayne v Maltby (1789) 3 TR 438, 100 ER 665 . . . . .29.79
Head v Tattersall (1871) LR 7 Ex 7 . . . . .1.24
Heap v Motorists' Advisory Agency Ltd [1923] 1 KB 577 . . . . 21.17, 21.74
HEB Enterprises v Richards (unreported, Court of Appeal of the Cayman Islands,
 no. 20 of 2018, Rix, Martin and Moses JJA, 14 Nov 2019) 1.08
Hedley Byrne & Co Ltd v Heller & Partners Ltd [1964] AC 465 . . . . 4.09, 28.04
Heinl v Jyske Bank (Gibraltar) Ltd [1999] Lloyd's Rep Bank 511 (CA) 1.41, 1.44,
 1.63, 1.67, 1.78, 1.88, 29.20
Hely-Hutchinson v Brayhead Ltd [1968] 1 QB 549 (CA) 8.19, 8.20, 23.17
Henderson v Lacon (1867) LR 2 Eq 249. . . . . .25.70
Henderson v The Royal British Bank (1857) 7 El & Bl 356, 119 ER 1279. . . . . .25.32
Hennessy v Craigmyle & Co Ltd [1986] ICR 461 (CA) 6.46, 6.58, 6.72
Heperu Pty Ltd v Belle (2009) 76 NSWLR 230 (CA) 1.98
Heritage Travel and Tourism Ltd v Windhorst [2021] EWHC 2380 (Comm) 7.75
Herrod v Johnston (2013) 2 QdR 102 (CA). 24.15, 24.84, 24.105
Hewett v First Plus Financial Group plc [2010] EWCA Civ 312;
 [2010] 2 P & CR 22 (CA) 5.21, 5.22, 5.23, 6.85
Heyman v Darwins Ltd [1942] AC 356 . . . . 1.16, 1.20, 3.30
Heymann v European Central Railway Co (1868) LR 7 Eq 154 . . . . .24.90

Hick v Mors (1754) Amb 215, 27 ER 143; 3 Keny 117, 96 ER 1329 . . . . .3.42, 3.44, 15.51, 22.05

Highfield Property Investments Pty Ltd v Commercial and Residential
    Developments (SA) Pty Ltd [2012] SASC 165 . . . . .11.13

Highlands Insurance Co v Continental Insurance Co [1987] 1 Lloyd's Rep 109 . . . . .28.14

HIH Casualty & General Insurance v Chase Manhattan Bank
    [2003] 2 Lloyd's Rep 61 (HL). 4.13, 10.23, 26.02

Hill v Caillovel (1748) 1 Ves Sen 122, 27 ER 931. . . . . .21.32

Hill v Gray (1816) 1 Starke 435, 171 ER 521 . . . . 3.05, 3.27

Hill v Harris [1965] 1 QB 601 . . . . 7.28, 27.05

Hill v Langley (CA 29 January 1988) 1.70

Hill v Perrott (1810) 3 Taunt 274, 128 ER 109 . . . . 14.31, 14.35

Hilton v Barker Booth and Eastwood (a firm) [2005] 1 All ER 651 (HL) 8.43, 8.44

Hindle v Brown (1904) 20 TLR 385 . . . . .27.21

Hine v McCallum [1925] 2 DLR 403 (Man KB) 18.36

Hinton v Sparkes (1868) LR 3 CP 161 . . . . .1.20

Hitchens v Congreve (1831) 4 Sim 420, 58 ER 157. . . . . .2.35

Hoare v Bremridge (1872) 8 Ch App 22. . . . . 3.55, 3.58, 3.59, 3.63

Hoblyn v Hoblyn (1889) 41 ChD 200. . . . . .5.15

Hodges v Webb [1920] 2 Ch 70. . . . . .6.14

Hoffman v Cooke (1801) 5 Ves Jun 623, 31 ER 772 . . . . 3.40, 17.63

Hoffman, Re (ex p Worrell) v Schilling (1989) 85 ALR 145 (FCA); on appeal,
    (Full FCA, 14 August 1989). 4.36, 11.07, 23.29, 23.43, 23.46,
                                      23.51, 23.55, 23.66, 23.68, 23.76, 25.14

Hogan v Healy (1877) 11 IR Ex 119 . . . . . . .1.53, 14.47, 14.48, 14.57, 18.54, 18.102, 19.02, 19.03, 20.08

Hogan v Shee (1797) 2 Esp 522, 170 ER 441 . . . . .3.27

Hoghton v Hoghton (1852) 15 Beav 278, 51 ER 545. . . . . 5.15, 6.98

Holbrook v Sharpey (1812) 19 Ves Jun 131, 34 ER 467 . . . . 3.40, 15.37

Holder v Holder [1968] 1 Ch 353 (CA) 1.74, 17.44, 18.13, 18.113, 24.08, 24.59

Holland v Wiltshire (1954) 90 CLR 409. . . . . .1.18

Holliday v Lockwood [1917] 2 Ch 47. . . . . 4.121, 19.05

Hollis v Bulpett (1865) 13 WR 492, 12 LT 293. . . . . .15.59

Holmes v Burgess [1975] 2 NZLR 311 . . . . 27.41, 27.44, 27.48

Holman v Loynes (1854) 4 De GM & G 270, 43 ER 510. . . . . 8.12, 8.13

Holyoake v Candy [2017] EWHC 3397 (Ch) 6.07, 6.20, 6.39

Holz v Davis [2010] QSC 452 . . . . .7.70

Honeywell International Middle East Ltd v Meydan Group LLC [2014] EWHC 1344 (TCC). 8.50

Hop and Malt Exchange and Warehouse Company, Re, ex p Briggs
    (1866) LR 1 Eq Cas 483 . . . . 23.58, 23.88, 23.101

Hopkins v Tanqueray (1854) 15 CB 130, 139 ER 369. . . . . .4.10

Hornal v Neuberger Products Ltd [1957] 1 QB 247 (CA) 4.06

Horry v Tate & Lyle Refineries Ltd [1982] 2 Lloyd's Rep 416. . . . . 4.105, 6.100

Horsfall v Thomas (1862) 1 H & C 90, 158 ER 813 . . . . 4.38, 4.115

Horsler v Zorro [1975] 1 Ch 302. . . . . 1.08, 1.12, 1.31, 3.31, 11.27, 11.67, 11.77, 11.78,
                                  11.79, 11.81, 11.82, 11.83, 11.107, 11.108, 12.07

Horwood v Smith (1788) 2 TR 750, 100 ER 404 . . . . .3.12

Houghton v Houghton (1852) 15 Beav 278, 15 ER 545 . . . . 3.40, 3.52

Houldsworth v City of Glasgow Bank and liquidators
    (1880) 5 App Cas 317. . . . . .2.03, 3.41, 18.09, 25.27, 25.29, 25.48, 25.49, 25.50, 25.56

Houle v Knelsen Sand and Gravel Ltd [2015] ABQB 659 . . . . 7.35, 7.36, 27.14

Hovenden v Lord Annesley (1806) 2 Sch & Lef 607 . . . . . .3.43, 24.25, 24.29, 24.31, 24.54, 24.69, 24.108

Hovenden & Sons v Millhof (1900) 83 LT 41 (CA). 8.51, 8.55, 8.61

Howard v Howard-Lawson [2012] EWHC 3258 (Ch). 6.87

Howard-Jones v Tate [2012] 1 P & CR 11 (CA). 1.08

Howard Marine and Dredging Co Ltd v A Ogden & Sons (Excavations) Ltd
    [1978] QB 574 (CA). 26.15

Howell v Howell (1837) 2 My & Cr 478, 40 ER 722. . . . . .17.12

xlvi TABLE OF CASES

Howlett, Re [1949] Ch 767. . . . . .24.59
HP Mercantile Pty Ltd v Dierickx (2013) 306 ALR 53; [2013] NSWCA 479. . . . . .18.35, 19.05
HSBC Bank Plc v Brown [2015] EWHC 359 (Ch) 6.117
Hubbard v Glover (1812) 3 Camp 313, 170 ER 1394 . . . . .4.48
Hughes, ex p (1802) 6 Ves 617, 31 ER 1223 . . . . .17.40, 17.43
Hughes v Hughes [2005] EWHC 469. . . . . .6.101, 6.110
Hughes v Huppert [1991] 1 NZLR 474 . . . . .23.36
Hughes v Macpherson & UBC Home Loans Corporation Ltd
    [1999] EWCA Civ 1006 . . . . .15.56, 15.74, 21.39, 21.53
Huguenin v Baseley (1807) 14 Ves Jun 273, 33 ER 526. . . . . 3.44, 6.81, 6.98,
                                                       6.103, 6.115, 9.21, 21.04, 29.20, 29.56, 29.60
Hull and County Bank, Re (Burgess' case)
    (1880) 15 ChD 507 (CA) 20.36, 25.29, 25.36, 25.37, 25.38, 25.59, 25.60
Hulton v Hulton [1917] 1 KB 813 (CA) 13.01, 15.46, 15.50, 17.30, 17.31, 18.43, 18.102
Hummingbird Motors Ltd v Hobbs [1986] RTR 276 . . . . .4.53
Humphreys v Humphreys [2004] EWHC 2201 (Ch). 24.49, 24.65
Hungerfords v Walker (1989) 84 ALR 119 (HCA) 128 . . . . .13.03
Hunt v Hyde [1976] 2 NZLR 453 . . . . 1.08, 1.31, 3.30
Hunt v Silk (1804) 5 East 449, 102 ER 1142. . . . . .18.18, 18.23, 18.81, 18.101
Hunt v Optima (Cambridge) Ltd [2015] 1 WLR 1346 (CA) 4.22, 4.115
Hunter v Atkins (1834) 3 My & K 113, 40 ER 43. . . . . .8.27
Hunter BNZ Finance Ltd v CG Maloney (1988) 18 NSWLR 420 . . . . .9.21, 10.23, 11.21,
                                            14.03, 14.11, 14.13, 14.15, 14.29, 16.02, 16.44, 20.01,
                                                    20.13, 20.28, 20.31, 21.05, 21.28, 29.36
Hurst v Byrk [1999] Ch 1 (CA); on appeal
    [2002] 2 AC 185 . . . . .1.08, 1.15, 1.20, 1.22, 1.24, 1.31, 3.30, 12.05
Hurst v Green [2020] EWHC 344 (Ch) 6.108
Hurstanger Ltd v Wilson [2007] 1 WLR 2351; [2008] Bus LR 216 (CA) 2.11, 8.18, 8.38, 8.51, 8.57,
                                        10.06, 10.23, 11.86, 11.93, 11.95, 11.107, 12.17, 12.22, 28.36
Huyton SA v Distribuidora Internacional de Productos Agricolas SA de CV
    [2003] 2 Lloyd's Rep 780 (CA) 4.105, 7.14, 20.03, 20.16, 20.24, 28.07, 28.13
Huyton SA v Peter Cremer GmbH & Co [1999] 1 Lloyd's Rep 620 . . . .6.29, 6.48, 6.49, 6.58, 6.65, 6.67
Hyundai Heavy Industries Co Ltd v Papadopolous [1980] 1 WLR 1129 (HL) 1.20

Idemitsu Kosan Co Ltd v Sumitomo Corporation [2016] 2 CLC 297 . . . . 4.22, 4.24
IFE Fund SA v Goldman Sachs International [2007] 1 Lloyd's Rep 264;
    [2006] EWHC 2887 . . . . .4.39, 4.53, 26.14, 26.17
IGE USA Investments Limited v The Commissioner for Her Majesty's Revenue and
    Customs [2021] Ch 423 (CA), [2021] EWCA Civ 534. . . . . .10.09, 11.55, 11.68,
                                                    11.96, 11.111, 24.26, 24.27, 24.28, 24.36
IHC (a firm) v Amtrust Europe [2015] EWHC 257 (QB) 24.118
Impact Funding Solutions Ltd v Barrington Support Services Ltd [2017] AC 73 (Sup Ct) 26.18
Imageview Management Ltd v Jack [2009] Bus LR 1034 (CA) 8.54
Imperial Loan Co v Stone [1892] 1 QB 599 (CA) 7.48, 7.49, 7.51, 7.61, 10.23, 16.03, 29.21, 29.61
Imperial Mercantile Credit Association v Coleman (1871) 6 Ch App 556 . . . . .8.19
Imperial Ottoman Bank v Trustees, Executors and Securities Investment Corp
    [1895] WN 23, 13 R 287. . . . . .14.71, 15.38, 15.56, 23.82
Inche Noriah v Shaik Allie Bin Omar [1929] AC 127
    (PC–Straits Settlements) 6.100, 6.114, 6.117, 6.118, 29.50
Incledon v Watson (1862) 2 F & F 841, 175 ER 1312 . . . . .4.38
Independent Trustee Services Ltd v GP Noble Trustees Ltd [2013] Ch 91 (CA). 1.67, 1.69, 5.20,
            13.01, 13.27, 13.29, 13.30, 15.44, 15.63, 15.69, 15.76, 16.12, 16.25,
            16.29, 16.36, 16.41, 16.44, 16.51, 20.23, 21.06, 21.21, 21.61, 21.72
Indian Farmers Fertiliser Cooperative Ltd v Gutnick [2015] VSC 724 . . . . .15.11, 15.63
Industries and General Mortgage Co Ltd v Lewis [1949] 2 All ER 573 . . . . 8.51, 8.61
ING Bank NV v Ros Roca SA [2011] EWCA Civ 353 . . . . .4.29

TABLE OF CASES   xlvii

Ingram v IRC [1997] 4 All ER 395 (CA); on appeal [2000] 1 AC 293 . . . . 1.73, 1.74
Ingram v Little [1961] 1 QB 31 (CA) 1.46, 1.79, 14.12, 21.58, 29.36
Inntrepreneur Pub Co v East Crown Ltd [2000] 2 Lloyd's Rep 611 . . . . .26.04
Insurance Corporation of the Channel Islands Ltd v McHugh
    [1997] Lloyd's Rep IR 94 . . . . 11.09, 23.20, 23.22, 23.79, 24.101
Insurance Corporation of the Channel Islands Ltd v The Royal Hotel Ltd
    [1998] Lloyd's Rep IR 151 . . . . 11.11, 13.28, 23.20, 23.21, 23.22, 23.24,
                        23.28, 23.32, 23.40, 23.59, 23.62, 23.80, 23.100
Inter Export LLC v Townley [2018] EWCA Civ 2068 . . . . 4.58, 4.61, 4.90, 4.97
International Alpaca Management Pty Ltd v Ensor (1995) 133 ALR 561 (Full FCA) 21.17, 21.74
International Healthway Corp Ltd v The Enterprise Fund III Ltd [2018] SGHC 246 . . . . . 23.16, 23.58
International Society of Auctioneers and Valuers (Baillie's case), Re [1898] 1 Ch 110. . . . . .25.57
Intrawest Corp v No 2002 Taurus Ventures Ltd (2006) 54 BCLR (4th) 173 . . . . 7.35, 7.37, 27.14
Inverugie Investments Ltd v Hackett [1995] 1 WLR 713 (PC–Bermuda) 17.07
Investors Compensation Scheme Ltd v West Bromwich Building Society
    [1998] 1 WLR 896 (HL); further consideration [1999] 1 Lloyd's Rep PN 496 . . . . .3.50, 4.42,
                        15.46, 15.74, 16.12, 16.42, 17.17, 22.03, 22.09, 22.11
Involnert Management Inc v Aprilgrange Ltd [2015] 2 Lloyds Rep 289 . . . . 1.14, 1.16, 4.117,
                        23.40, 23.51, 23.56, 23.62, 23.83, 23.85, 23.104, 23.107
IRC v Spence (1941) 24 TC 312. . . . . .13.32
Ireland v Hart [1902] 1 Ch 552 . . . . .14.22
Irish National Insurance Company Ltd v Oman Insurance Company Ltd
    [1983] 2 Lloyd's Rep 453 . . . . .4.48
Iron Trades Mutual Insurance Co Ltd v Companhia de Seguros Imperio
    [1992] 1 Lloyd's Rep IR 213. . . . . 23.68, 23.85, 23.93, 24.68, 24.109, 24.111
Irons v Wang [2004] DCR 830 (DC–NZ) 14.07, 16.02
Irvani v Irvani [2000] 1 Lloyd's Rep 412 (CA). 6.101, 7.47, 7.65, 7.75, 7.92
Isaacs v Robertson [1985] AC 97 (PC—St Vincent & Grenadines) 1.60
Islington London Borough Council v Uckac [2006] 1 WLR 1303 (CA) 1.14, 11.95
Ivanof v Phillip M Levy Pty Ltd [1971] VR 167. . . . . .2.01, 2.06, 11.21, 11.38
Ivey v Genting Casinos UK Ltd [2018] AC 391 (Sup Ct) 4.05

Jacobus Marler Estates Ltd v Marler (1916) 114 LT 640n (HL) 2.28, 2.37, 2.39
JAD International Pty Ltd v International Trucks Australia Ltd
    (1994) 50 FCR 378 (Full Ct) 2.08, 11.101, 13.16, 15.63, 17.20, 17.45, 17.56, 18.16,
                        18.93, 18.95, 18.96, 23.18, 23.20, 23.26, 23.107, 24.51, 27.50, 27.56
Jaffray v Society of Lloyd's [2002] EWCA 1101. . . . . 4.05, 4.08, 4.27, 4.42
Jaggar v Lyttelton Marina Holdings Ltd (in rec) [2006] 2 NZLR 87 . . . . .23.62
Jaggard v Sawyer [1995] 1 WLR 269 (CA). 28.08, 28.31
James, ex p (1803) 8 Ves 337, 32 ER 385. . . . . 8.04, 8.14
James, ex p (1874) 9 Ch App 609. . . . . .25.10
James v Kerr (1880) 40 ChD 449. . . . . .7.75
Jams 2 Pty Ltd v Stubbings (No 4) [2019] VSC 482. . . . . 15.56, 19.29
Janus Nominees Ltd v Fairhall [2009] 3 NZLR 757 . . . . .7.23
Japan Leasing, In re [1999] BPIR 911 . . . . .1.92
Jarvis (Dec'd), Re [1958] 1 WLR 815 . . . . .24.74
Jarvis v Maguire (1961) 28 DLR (2d) 666 (BCCA) 2.03, 19.10
JEB Fasteners Ltd v Marks Bloom & Co [1983] 1 All ER 583 (CA). 4.106, 4.117
Jenkins v Morris (1880) 14 ChD 674 (CA) 7.55
Jennings v Broughton (1854) 5 De GM & G 126, 43 ER 818 . . . . 4.114, 4.118
Jennings v Cairns [2003] EWHC 1115 (Ch); on appeal [2003] EWCA 1935 . . . .2.13, 6.03, 6.96, 29.31
Jenys v Public Curator of Queensland (1953) 90 CLR 113. . . . . .29.42
Jerrard v Saunders (1794) 2 Ves Jun 454, 30 ER 721 . . . . .21.61
Jervis v Berridge (1873) 8 Ch App 351 . . . . .11.48, 14.52, 15.60, 20.25
JJ Harrison (Properties) Ltd v Harrison [2002] 1 BCLC 162 (CA). 1.76, 8.09, 8.22, 24.33
Joel v Law Union and Crown Insurance Co [1908] 2 KB 863 (CA) 5.29

TABLE OF CASES

Johnson v Agnew [1980] AC 367 . . . . .1.08, 1.12, 1.14, 1.15, 1.18, 1.20, 1.31,
3.30, 11.28, 11.78, 12.05, 13.27, 23.05, 23.11, 23.103
Johnson v Bones [1970] 1 NSWR 28 . . . . .8.24
Johnson v Credit Lyonnais Co (1877) 3 CPD 32 . . . . .21.56, 21.59
Johnson v EBS Pensioner Trustees Ltd (ChD 8 March 2001); on appeal
[2002] Lloyd's PN 309 (CA) 1.71, 8.16, 8.18, 8.23, 8.26, 8.36, 10.06, 10.08, 11.80, 11.86,
11.93, 11.94, 11.95, 11.107, 12.17, 12.22, 18.02, 18.116, 19.46
Johnson v McGrath (2005) 195 FLR 101 . . . . .25.49, 25.50, 25.51, 25.56
Johnson v Medlicott (1734) 2 Eq Cas Abr 186n, 22 ER 160 . . . . .7.68
Johnson v The King [1904] AC (PC–Sierra Leone) 17.19, 17.21
Jolly v Palmer [1985] 1 NZLR 658 . . . . .23.36
Jolly v Watson (unreported, High Court of Justice of the Isle of Man,
1 March 2012) 6.100, 18.69, 18.76
Jones v Dumbrell [1981] VR 199 . . . . .4.90
Jones v Gordon (1877) 2 App Cas 616 . . . . .21.16, 21.17
Jones v Morgan [2001] EWCA 995 . . . . 7.82, 7.91, 7.98
Jones v Moss [2007] NSWSC 969 . . . . .29.56
Jones v Ricketts (1862) 31 Beav 130, 54 ER 1087 . . . . .3.40
Jones v Stones [1999] 1 WLR 1739 (CA) 24.08, 24.12
Jones v Thomas (1837) 2 Y & C Ex 498, 160 ER 493 . . . . .8.12
Jonval Builders Pty Ltd v Commissioner for Fair Trading
(2020) 104 NSWLR 1 (CA) 2.04, 13.04, 17.43, 17.51, 18.91
Jonval Builders Pty Ltd v Comr for Fair Trading (2020) 383 ALR 334 (NSWCA) 10.04
Josife v Summertrot Holdings Ltd [2014] EWHC 996 (Ch) 7.63
Joy v Bannister (No 1) (1617) in Ritchie, Reports of Cases Decided by Francis Bacon
in the High Court of Chancery (1617–1621) (1932) 33 . . . . .3.42, 22.05
Joy v Bannister (No 2) (1617) in Ritchie, Reports of Cases Decided by Francis Bacon
in the High Court of Chancery (1617–1621) (1932) 36 . . . . .3.42, 21.04
JTC Employer Solutions Trustees Limited v Khadem [2021] EWHC 2929 (Ch) 29.42, 29.44
Jubilee Cotton Mills v Lewis [1924] AC 958 . . . . .2.37
Jurong Town Corp v Wishing Star Ltd [2005] 3 SLR 283 (Singapore CA) 4.104, 4.120, 23.58

K, Re [1988] Ch 310 . . . . .7.52
K v K [1976] 2 NZLR 31 . . . . .7.100
Kakavas v Crown Melbourne Ltd (2013) 250 CLR 392; 298 ALR 35 (HCA) 7.75, 7.82,
7.83, 7.103, 29.16
Kalls Enterprises Pty Ltd (in liq) v Baloglow (2007) 63 ACSR 557 (NSWCA) 1.78, 1.98
Kalsep Ltd v X-Flow BV, The Times 3 May 2001 . . . . 7.14, 7.88
Kammins Ballrooms Co Ltd v Zenith Investments (Torquay) Ltd
[1971] AC 850 . . . . 23.05, 23.07, 23.51, 23.55, 23.98, 24.08, 24.59, 24.118
Kanchenjunga, The See Motor Oil Hellas (Corinth) Refineries SA v Shipping
Corp of India (The Kanchenjunga)
Kanhaya Ltd v National Bank of India (1913) 29 TLR 314 (PC–India) 6.24, 6.56
Kang v Eau [2010] EWHC 1837 (QB) 11.114
Kapoor v National Westminster Bank plc [2010] EWHC 2986 (Ch) 9.20
Kasumu v Baba-Egbe [1956] AC 539 (PC-West Africa) 15.60
Kaufman v Gerson [1904] 1 KB 591 . . . . 6.12, 6.44, 6.84
Keates v Cadogan (1851) 10 CB 591, 138 ER 234 . . . . .4.30
Keatley v Churchman (1922) 65 DLR 357 (Alta SC (App Div)) 18.47
Kellogg Brown & Root Inc v Aerotech Herman Nelson Inc (2004) 238 DLR
(4th) 594 (Man CA) 17.07, 18.10, 18.46, 18.77, 18.78, 23.72, 24.71, 24.105
Kelly v Cooper [1993] AC 205 (PC–Bermuda) 8.41, 8.44
Kelowna Mountain Development Services Ltd, Re [2014] BCSC 1791 . . . . .7.11, 13.32
Kempson v Ashbee (1874) 10 Ch App 15 . . . . 6.103, 9.05, 23.37
Kennedy v Kennedy [2015] WTLR 837 . . . . 19.08, 29.42, 29.44
Kennedy v The Panama, New Zealand and Australian Royal Mail Co Ltd
(1867) LR 2 QB 580 . . . . .4.10, 7.35, 10.24, 14.59, 14.73, 27.19
Kenney v Browne (1796) 3 Ridg PC 462 . . . . .17.39, 17.40

TABLE OF CASES xlix

Kenny v Fenton [1971] NZLR 1 (CA) 18.11, 23.61, 23.66, 23.71, 23.91, 23.100, 23.103, 24.102
Kent v Freehold Land and Brickmaking Company (1867) LR 4 Eq 588 .... 15.34, 16.56, 25.62
Kesarmal v Valiappa Chettiar [1954] 1 WLR 380 (PC–Malaya).......................................6.12, 9.05
Kettlewell v Refuge Assurance Company [1908] 1 KB 545 (CA);
    aff'd [1909] AC 243...3.31, 3.63, 4.61, 14.36, 14.37, 14.77, 14.79
Khoury v Government Insurance Office (1984) 165 CLR 622 ....11.24, 23.07, 23.28,
                                                                                        23.42, 23.43, 23.46, 23.57, 24.109
Killick v Pountney [2000] WTLR 41 ....6.85
Killick v Roberts [1991] 1 WLR 1146 (CA)..1.26, 4.122, 13.31, 15.10
King v Hamlet (1834) 2 My & K 456, 39 ER 1018...18.14
King v Williamson (1994) 2 NZ ConvC 95 ....7.23
Kings North Trust Ltd v Bell [1986] 1 WLR 119 (CA)..9.08
Kings Security Systems Ltd v King [2021] EWHC 325 (Ch).......................................8.59, 18.120
Kingsford v Merry (1856) 11 Ex 577, 156 ER 960; rev'd on other grounds
    (1856) 1 H & N 503, 156 ER 1299...............14.03, 16.02, 20.14, 20.15, 21.05, 21.57, 21.58
Kingspan Environmental Ltd v Borealis A/S [2012] EWHC 1147 (Comm)..................4.106
Kingu v Walmar Ventures Ltd (1986) 10 BCLR (2d) 15 (BCCA) 7.37, 19.02, 19.05, 27.14
Kirwan v Cresvale Far East Ltd (2002) 44 ACSR 21 (NSWCA) 12.23, 13.10, 13.17
Kizbeau Pty Ltd v WG & B Pty Ltd (1995) 184 CLR 281 ....13.18
Kleinwort Benson Ltd v Lincoln City Council [1999] 2 AC 349...4.18, 4.19
Kleinwort Benson Ltd v Malaysia Mining Corp Berhad [1989] 1 WLR 379.....................4.58
Knights v Majoribanks (1849) 2 Mac & G 10, 42 ER 4...8.12
Knox v Gye (1872) LR 5 HL 656 ....24.25
Kolmar Group AG v Traxpo Enterprises Pvt Ltd [2011] 1 All ER (Comm) 46.............6.07, 6.26,
                                                                                        6.32, 6.53, 6.58, 6.67
Kosmar Villa Holidays plc v Trustees of Syndicate 1243 [2008] EWCA Civ 147;
    [2008] 2 All ER (Comm) 14 (CA)..23.11, 23.62, 24.73, 24.118, 24.120
Koutsonicolis v Principe (No 2) (1987) 48 SASR 328....13.32, 15.25, 17.08, 17.26, 23.18, 23.71, 24.39
Krakowski v Eurolynx Properties Ltd (1995) 183 CLR 563.......................4.40, 4.103, 9.04,
                                                                                        11.101, 11.114, 24.115, 27.12, 27.29
Krakowski v Trenorth Ltd (Vict SC 7 May 1996) 17.20
Kramer v Duggan (1955) St Rep (NSW) 385...27.29
Kramer v McMahon (1969) 89 WN (NSW) (Pt 1); [1970] NSWLR 194.........4.23, 11.101, 14.71,
                            15.34, 15.57, 15.61, 15.63, 15.75, 16.56, 17.04, 17.56, 18.38,
                            18.122, 23.61, 23.66, 23.71, 24.102, 24.115, 27.38, 27.42
Kregor v Hollins (1913) 109 LT 225 (CA) 8.18, 8.57, 8.60
Krell v Henry [1903] 2 KB 740 ....7.09
Kriti Palm, The See AIC Ltd v ITS Testing Services (UK) Ltd (The Kriti Palm)
Krypton Nominees Pty Ltd, Re [2013] VSC 446...4.117
KSH Farm Limited v KSH Plant Limited [2021] EWHC 1986 (Ch) 18.46
Kuek Siang Wei v Kuek Siew Chew [2015] 5 SLR 357 (CA)....................5.16, 5.17, 5.18, 5.19
Kuhlirz v Lambert Bros Ltd (1913) 108 LT 565..2.38
Kupchak v Dayson Holdings Co Ltd (1965) 53 DLR (2d) 482; (1965) 53 WWR 65 (BCCA) 2.13, 11.23,
                            15.14, 15.24, 15.25, 18.70, 18.110, 23.36, 23.61, 23.66, 23.71, 23.73, 23.110, 24.90
Kwei Tek Chao v British Traders and Shippers Ltd [1954] 2 QB 459 .... 1.24, 1.31
Kyle Bay Ltd (t/a Astons Nightclub) v Underwriters Subscribing Under Policy
    Number 019057/08/01 [2007] 1 CLC 164..4.48, 4.49

L'Estrange v F Graucob Ltd [1934] 2 KB 394 (CA)...27.22, 29.56
Lacey, ex p (1802) 6 Ves 626, 31 ER 1228.. 8.04, 8.14, 8.21
Laconia, The See Mardorf Peach & Co Ltd v Attica Sea Carriers Corporation
    of Liberia (The Laconia)
Lady Hudson's case (1704) 2 Eq Cas Abr 52, 22 ER 45 ....3.52
Ladywell Mining Company v Brookes (1887) 35 ChD 400 (CA) 2.28, 2.31, 2.32, 18.48
Lagunas Nitrate Company v Lagunas Syndicate [1899] 2 Ch 392 (CA)..... 11.09, 12.07, 12.23, 13.10,
                            13.13, 15.05, 15.17, 15.18, 15.38, 15.57, 17.04, 17.33, 17.43, 17.56,
                            18.09, 18.10, 18.13, 18.15, 18.86, 18.95, 18.96, 18.121, 23.73,
                            23.80, 23.108, 24.43, 24.46, 24.87, 24.92, 24.100, 24.101, 24.103

TABLE OF CASES

Lambert v MacKenzie [1949] OWN 758 (CA) 17.13, 17.42, 17.51
Lancashire Loans Ltd v Black [1934] 1 KB 380 (CA) 6.103
Land Enviro Corp Pty Ltd v HTT Huntley Heritage Pty Ltd
    [2012] NSWSC 382 . . . . .18.72, 23.13, 23.43, 24.12
Landers v Schmidt [1983] 1 Qd R 188 (Full Ct) 11.12
Langman v Handover (1929) 43 CLR 334 . . . . 15.48, 15.60
Langton v Langton [1995] 2 FLR 890 . . . . 6.85, 6.100, 7.74, 7.87, 17.30, 29.16, 29.40
Lansdown v Lansdown (1730) 2 Jac & W 205, 37 ER 695; Sel Cas T King 364,
    25 ER 441 . . . . 5.14, 7.28, 7.39
Larissa, The *See* Showa Oil Tanker Co Ltd of Japan v Maravan SA of Caracas (The Larissa)
Latec Investments Ltd v Hotel Terrigal Pty Ltd
    (1965) 113 CLR 265 . . . . 3.47, 3.50, 16.12, 16.17, 16.25, 16.60, 21.70
Latter v The Council of the Shire of Musswellbrook (1936) 56 CLR 422 . . . . .23.44
Laurence v Lexcourt Holdings Ltd [1978] 1 WLR 1128 (CA) 4.33, 4.40, 4.119, 7.07, 7.28, 27.05
Law v Law [1905] Ch 140 (CA) 23.20, 23.22, 23.100, 23.104, 23.106
Lawley v Hooper (1745) 3 Atk 278, 26 ER 962 . . . . .3.38, 15.50, 15.59, 15.65
Lawrence v Poorah [2008] UKPC 21 . . . . .7.73
Lawrie v Hwang [2012] QSC 422 . . . . 1.98, 6.75
Lawson (Inspector of Taxes) v Hosemaster Co Ltd [1966] 1 WLR 1300 . . . . .1.40
Lawton v Elmore (1858) 27 LR Exch (NS) 141 . . . . 14.55, 14.62
Lazarus Estates Ltd v Beasley [1956] 1 QB 702 (CA) 26.02
LCP Holding Ltd v Hombergh Holdings BV [2012] EWHC 3643 (QB) 6.07, 6.38
Leaf v International Galleries [1950] 2 KB 86 (CA) 23.25, 23.25, 24.37, 24.56,
                24.65, 24.75, 24.95, 24.97, 24.108, 27.22, 27.23, 27.37, 27.53, 27.54
Leask v Scott Brothers (1877) 2 QBD 376 (CA) 21.06
Leason Pty Ltd v Princes Farm Pty Ltd [1983] 2 NSWLR 381 . . . . 23.26, 27.29, 27.42, 27.50, 27.58
Lecky v Walter [1914] IR 378 . . . . 27.21, 27.24
Lee v Jones (1864) 17 CB (NS) 482, 141 ER 194 . . . . 5.41, 5.42, 5.44, 10.23
Lee v Soames (1888) 36 WR 884 . . . . .11.78
Lee Panavision Ltd v Lee Lighting Ltd [1992] BCLC 22 (CA) 8.20
Leech v Leech (1674) 2 Ch Rep 100, 21 ER 623 . . . . .3.52
Leeder v Stevens [2005] EWCA 50 . . . . 6.103, 6.107, 6.115
Leeds and Hanley Theatres of Varieties Ltd, Re [1902] 2 Ch 809 (CA) 2.11, 18.48
Leeds Bank, Re (1887) 56 LJ Ch 321 . . . . .4.105
Leeds City Brewery v Platts [1925] Ch 532 . . . . .17.11
Leeds City Council v Barclays Bank Plc [2021] QB 1027 . . . . 4.100, 4.115
Leeds Industrial Cooperative Society Ltd v Slack [1924] AC 851 . . . . .28.30
Legal and General Assurance Society Ltd v Drake Insurance Co Ltd
    [1992] QB 887 (CA) 893 . . . . .13.33
Legge v Croker (1811) 1 Ball & Beaty 506 . . . . 7.28, 27.05
Legh v Legh (1799) 1 B & P 447, 126 ER 1002 . . . . .29.84
Leibler v Air New Zealand Ltd [No 2] [1999] 1 VR 1 (CA) 7.21
Leighton's Conveyance, Re [1936] 1 All ER 667 . . . . .15.08
Leni Gas and Oil Investments Ltd v Malta Oil Pty Ltd
    [2014] EWHC 893 (Comm) 4.41, 4.104, 4.106
Leopardstown Club Ltd v Templeville Developments Ltd [2010] IEHC 152 . . . . .7.19
Lep Air Services Ltd v Rolloswin Investments Ltd [1973] AC 331 . . . . 1.18, 1.20
Lever Bros v Bell [1931] 1 KB 577 (CA) 27.22
Levett v Barclays Bank plc [1995] 1 WLR 1260 . . . . 5.44, 5.46, 5.53
Levison v Patent Steam Carpet Cleaning Co Ltd [1978] QB 69 . . . . .7.85
Lewis v Averay [1972] 1 QB 198 (CA) 1.48
Lewis v Hillman (1852) 3 HLC 606, 10 ER 239 . . . . 8.17, 8.18
Lewis v Howson [1928] 2 WWR 197 (Sask CA); on appeal [1929] SCR 174 . . . . .17.65
Lewisham LBC v Masterson (2000) 80 P & CR 117 (CA) 17.13
Leyland Daf Ltd v Automotive Products plc [1994] 1 BCLR 244 (CA) 6.38
LG Clarke, Re [1967] Ch 1121 (CA) 20.13

TABLE OF CASES   li

LHK Nominees Pty Ltd v Kenworthy [2001] WASC 205. . . . . .11.22, 16.38
Li Cho Kwan v Oliveiro Lana (unreported, High Court of Hong Kong Special
    Administrative Region, 23 March 2016) 11.10
Li San Ying v Bank of China (HK) Ltd (2004) 7 HKCFAR 579 . . . . .9.14
Liberian Insurance Agency Inc v Mosse [1977] 2 Lloyd's Rep 560 . . . . . . 24.68, 24.109, 24.110, 24.111
Liberty Mercian Ltd v Cuddy Civil Engineering Ltd [2013] EWHC 2688 (TCC);
    [2014] BLR 179. . . . . .7.19
Liberty Sky Investments Ltd v Goh Seng Heng [2019] SGHC 39 . . . . 18.48, 18.124, 12.08
Libyan Investment Authority v Goldman Sachs International
    [2016] EWHC 2530 (Ch). 6.86, 6.101
Lickbarrow v Mason (1787) 2 TR 63 100 ER 35 . . . . .21.56, 21.59
Liddle v Cree [2011] EWHC 3294 (Ch). 6.87, 7.80
Life Association of Scotland v Siddal, Cooper v Greene (1861) 3 De GF & J 58,
    45 ER 800. . . . . 8.39, 24.10, 24.48, 24.58, 24.69, 24.81
Liles v Terry [1895] 2 QB 679 . . . . .6.103, 29.20
Lim Lay Bee v Allgreen Properties Ltd [1999] 1 SLR 471 (CA). 1.08, 1.20
Limit No 2 Ltd v Axa Versicherung AG [2008] 2 CLC 673 (CA) 4.58, 4.60, 4.90,
                                         4.91, 4.97, 4.99, 4.121, 4.123
Lindon v Hooper (1776) 1 Cowp 414, 98 ER 1160 . . . . .3.25
Lindsay v O'Loughnane [2012] BCC 153 . . . . 4.36, 4.90
Lindsay Petroleum Co v Hurd (1874) LR 5 PC 221 (PC–Canada) 15.46, 15.50, 15.51, 15.63,
                     16.62, 18.13, 18.77, 23.110, 24.04, 24.15, 24.17,
               24.48, 24.49, 24.51, 24.53, 24.62, 24.100, 24.114
Lipkin Gorman v Karpnale [1991] 2 AC 548. . . . . 1.36, 15.31, 18.07, 18.106, 29.31
Lissenden v CAV Bosch Ltd [1940] AC 412 . . . . .23.04
Litson Pride, The See Black King Shipping Corporation v Massie (The Litson Pride)
Littlewoods Retail Ltd v HMRC [2014] EWHC 868 (Ch); [2014] STC 1761 . . . . .17.13
Littman v Aspen Oil (Broking) Ltd [2005] EWCA 1579 . . . . .7.19
Liverpool Borough Bank (Duranty's case), Re (1858) 26 Beav 268, 53 ER 901 . . . . 3.40, 9.03
Livesey v Jenkins [1985] 1 AC 424 . . . . .4.95, 5.19, 5.20, 5.59
Lloyd v Browning 2013] EWCA Civ 1637; [2014] 1 P&CR 11 . . . . .26.29, 26.31
Lloyd v Grace, Smith & Co [1912] AC 716 . . . . .8.66
Lloyd and Jobson v Spillett (1740) 2 Atk 148, 26 ER 493 . . . . .3.44
Lloyds Bank Ltd v Bundy [1975] QB 326 (CA). 6.23, 6.29, 6.38, 6.98, 6.100, 7.85
Lloyd's Bank Ltd, Re; Bomze and Lederman v Bomze [1931] 1 Ch 289. . . . . .6.100
Lloyds TSB Bank plc v Shorney, The Times 25 October 2001 . . . . .5.53
Lo Wo v Cheung Chan Ka [2001] HKCA 302. . . . . 7.70, 7.89
Load v Green (1846) 15 M & W 216, 153 ER 828 . . . . .3.02, 3.05, 3.06, 3.10, 3.12, 3.13, 3.14,
            3.16, 3.18, 3.40, 3.51, 10.23, 14.03, 14.04, 14.33, 16.02, 21.05, 21.57, 25.04
Lochmore Trust, In re the [2010] JRC 068, ...29.46
Locker and Woolf Ltd v Western Australian Insurance Co Ltd [1936] 1 KB 408 (CA) 5.28
Lodge v National Union Investment Company Ltd [1907] 1 Ch 300 . . . . .15.50, 15.60
Logicrose Ltd v Southend United Football Club Ltd [1988] 1 WLR 1256 . . . . .1.87, 8.49, 8.51,
              8.54, 8.62, 8.63, 8.68, 8.73, 9.05, 18.01, 18.34, 21.51, 29.20
Loizou v Derrimut Enterprises Pty Ltd [2004] VSC 176 . . . . .24.74
London Allied Holdings v Lee [2007] EWHC 2061 (Ch) 1.94, 2.01, 11.22, 11.25, 11.28
London and County General Agency Association, Hare's Case, Re (1869) 4 Ch App 503. . . . . . . .25.69
London and Leeds Bank, ex p Carling (1887) 56 LT (NS) 115 . . . . 25.02, 25.35, 25.66, 25.68, 25.72
London and Mediterranean Bank, Wright's case, Re (1871) 7 Ch App 55 . . . . .25.43
London and Provincial Electric Lighting and Power Generating Company Ltd,
    ex p Hale (1887) 55 LT (NS) 670. . . . . 23.104
London and Provincial Insurance Company v Seymour (1873) LR 17 Eq 85. . . . . .3.55
London Assurance v Mansel (1879) 11 ChD 363 . . . . .3.57, 3.58, 3.63, 4.63
London Borough of Haringey v Hines [2010] EWCA Civ 1111 . . . . 4.07, 4.122, 13.11
London General Omnibus Co Ltd v Holloway [1912] 2 KB 72 (CA). 5.44, 5.53
London Joint Stock Bank v Simmons [1892] AC 201. . . . . .21.16, 21.56

lii   TABLE OF CASES

Long v Lloyd [1958] 1 WLR 753 . . . . 27.05, 27.06, 27.22, 27.53, 27.54
Long v Long (1620) in J Ritchie, Reports of Cases Decided by Francis Bacon in the
    High Court of Chancery (1617–1621) (1932) 621 . . . . 3.42, 22.05
Longchamp v Kenny (1779) 1 Doug 137, 99 ER 91. . . . . .3.25
Longmate v Ledger (1860) 2 Giff 157, 66 ER 67 . . . . 7.75, 7.92, 7.99
Longstaff v Birtles [2002] 1 WLR 470 (CA). 2.10, 8.10, 8.15, 8.30
Lonhro plc v Fayed (No 2) [1992] 1 WLR 1 . . . . .11.59, 11.112
Lonrho plc v Fayed (No 2) [1992] 1 WLR 1 . . . . 2.24, 4.63, 4.67, 13.29, 13.30, 14.16, 15.19, 15.69,
                    16.12, 16.23, 16.25, 16.27, 16.31, 16.41, 16.44, 16.60, 16.63, 16.66
Lord Ward v Lulmey (1860) 5 H & N 87, 157 ER 1112. . . . . .3.52
Louth v Diprose (1992) 175 CLR 621 . . . . 6.85, 7.103, 29.14, 29.16, 29.18, 29.32, 29.40
Lovell v Hicks (1836) 2 Y&C Ex 46, 160 ER 306 . . . . .14.24
Lovesy v Smith, Re Lloyd's Bank Ltd [1931] 1 Ch 289 . . . . .6.103
Lowe v Lombank Ltd [1960] 1 WLR 196 (CA) 26.10
Lucas v Adams (1724) 9 Mod 118, 88 ER 352 . . . . .15.37
Lucks Ltd (Serpell's case), Re [1928] VLR 466. . . . . 24.18, 25.28, 25.34, 25.36, 25.47, 25.62
Lucy, The *See* Atlantic Lines and Navigation Co Inc v Hallam Ltd (The Lucy)
Lukacs v Wood (1978) 19 SASR 520. . . . . .7.32, 11.92, 15.09, 27.12
Lunn Poly Ltd v Liverpool & Lancashire Properties Ltd [2007] L & TR 6 (CA) 17.07
Lyde or Joyner v Lyde or Joyner (1616–1617) Reports of Cases Decided by
    Francis Bacon in the High Court of Chancery (1617–1621) (1932) 6 . . . . .3.42, 22.05
Lydney and Wigpool Iron Ore Company v Bird (1886) 33 ChD 85 (CA) 2.32
Lynch v DPP of Northern Ireland [1975] AC 653. . . . . .6.47
Lynde v Anglo-Italian Hemp Spinning Co [1896] 1 Ch 178 . . . . 9.04, 9.05
Lyon v Home (1868) LR 6 Eq 655 . . . . 6.85, 6.103
Lysney v Selby (1705) 2 Ld Raym 1118, 92 ER 230 . . . . .14.23

Mabanga v Ophir Energy plc [2012] EWHC 1589 (QB) 4.40
McAdam v Walker (1813) 1 Dow 148, 3 ER 654 . . . . .7.56
McAllister v Richmond Brewing Company (NSW) Pty Ltd
    (1942) 42 SR (NSW) 187 . . . . 2.04, 17.62, 17.64
McCall v Superior Court 36 P 2d 643 (1934). 11.65, 14.38
McCarthy v Kenny [1939] 3 DLR 556 (Ont SC) 15.24, 15.25, 17.04
McConnel v Wright [1903] 1 Ch 546 . . . . .25.29
McCormick v National Motor and Accident Insurance
    (1934) 49 Lloyd's Rep 362 (CA) 11.09, 23.80, 23.85, 24.65, 24.101
M'Culloch v Gregory (1855) 1 K & J 286, 69 ER 466 . . . . .27.05
McDonald v Dennys Lascelles Ltd (1933) 48 CLR 457 . . . . .1.07, 1.15, 1.20, 1.21, 3.30, 12.05
McDowall v Fraser (1779) 1 Doug KB 260, 99 ER 170. . . . . .4.62
MacFarlane v Heritage Corp (Australia) Pty Ltd [2003] QSC 353;
    aff'd [2004] QCA 183. . . . . 11.05, 11.21, 11.56, 14.14, 14.19, 15.74
McGowan v Blake 134 App Div 165, 118 NY Supp 905 (1909) 14.64
McGrath v Shah (1989) 57 P & CR 452 . . . . .26.14
McInerny v Lloyd's Bank Ltd [1974] 1 Lloyd's Rep 246 (CA) 4.78
McIntyre v Nemesis DBK Ltd [2009] NZCA 329 . . . . .6.50
McIvey v St Vincent's Hospital (Melbourne) Ltd [2005] VSCA 233. . . . . .7.60
Mackay v Wesley [2020] EWHC 1215 (Ch). 7.63, 19.08
Mackender v Feldia AG [1967] 2 QB 590 (CA). 1.14, 1.16, 12.05
McKenzie v McDonald [1927] VLR 134 . . . . .2.13, 2.18, 15.24, 15.25, 15.29, 18.70
MacKenzie v Royal Bank of Canada [1934] 1 AC 468 (PC–Canada). 5.50, 18.115,
                    18.115, 19.07, 19.40, 19.44, 19.46
McKeown v Boudard-Peveril Gear Co (1896) 65 LJ Ch 735 (CA) 4.35, 4.83
McKinnon v Brockington (1921) 60 DLR 303 (Man CA) 17.30, 18.88, 18.90
MacLeod v Kerr 1965 SC 253 . . . . .11.32
McMaster v Byrne [1952] 1 All ER 1362 (PC–Canada). 8.06, 8.13, 8.15, 8.23, 8.30, 8.72
Macmillan v Bishopsgate Investment Trust (No 3) [1995] 1 WLR 978 . . . . .21.68

TABLE OF CASES · liii

M'Millan v Sampson (1884) 10 VLR 74 . . . . 11.23, 12.06
McNally v GIO Finance Ltd (NSWSC 14 September 1994) 15.09
McNaught v Equitable Life Insurance 136 App Div 774, 777 (NY App Div, 1910). 23.94
MacPherson v European Strategic Board [1999] 2 BCLC 203 . . . . .23.17
McPherson v Watt (1877) 3 App Cas 254 (HL Sc) 8.04, 8.12, 8.13, 8.18, 8.21
McRae v Commonwealth Disposals Commission (1951) 84 CLR 377 . . . . 1.36, 7.09, 10.24
McWilliam v Norton Finance (UK) Limited [2015] 2 BCLC 730 (CA) 8.57
Magee v Pennine Insurance Co Ltd [1969] 2 QB 507 (CA) 7.07, 13.28
Magennis v MacCollough (c 1714–1727) Gilb Rep 235, 25 ER 163 . . . . .3.52
Magic Score Ltd v HSBC [2006] HKCU 1029 . . . . .19.16
Maguire v Makaronis (1998) 188 CLR 449 . . . . . . 1.71, 2.04, 2.17, 8.18, 8.39, 8.72, 11.101, 11.107, 12.07,
  15.08, 15.46, 15.53, 16.62, 17.16, 17.17, 17.20, 19.05, 19.29, 19.30, 19.38
Mahesan v Malaysia Government Officers' Co-operative Housing Society Ltd
  [1979] AC 374 (PC–Malaysia) 8.51, 10.23
Mahon v FBN Bank (UK) Ltd [2012] 2 BCLC 83 . . . . .9.17
Mahoney v Purnell [1996] 3 All ER 61 . . . . 2.13, 6.100, 6.107, 15.22, 15.23, 15.24, 15.25, 18.70
Mainstream Properties Ltd v Young [2005] All ER (D) 148 (CA). 4.19
Maitland v Irving (1846) 15 Sim 437, 60 ER 688 . . . . .29.58
Malik (Dec'd) v Shiekh [2018] 4 WLR 86 . . . . 6.97, 6.110
Manches v Trimborn (1946) 115 LJKB 305 . . . . 7.52, 7.66
Mander v Evans [2001] 1 WLR 2378 . . . . .25.17
Mangles v Dixon (1852) 3 HLC 702, 10 ER 278 . . . . 3.42, 21.22, 21.32
Manifest Shipping Co Ltd v Uni-Polaris Insurance Co Ltd (The Star Sea)
  [2003] 1 AC 469 . . . . .1.08, 1.09, 4.25, 5.25, 5.26, 5.32, 10.23, 11.41, 12.05, 13.27, 16.03
Mann v Paterson Constructions Pty Ltd (2019) 267 CLR 560. . . . . 1.08, 1.18, 1.30, 3.30
Manulife Bank of Canada v Conlin [1996] 3 SCR 415 . . . . .5.54
Marc Rich & Co AG v Portman [1997] 1 Lloyd's Rep 225 (CA) 5.30
Marcovitch v Liverpool Victoria Friendly Society (1912) 28 TLR 188 (CA). 4.30
Mardorf Peach & Co Ltd v Attica Sea Carriers Corporation of Liberia (The Laconia)
  [1977] AC 850. . . . . .11.38
Maredelanto Compania Naviera SA v Berghau-Handel GmbH (The Mihalis Angelos)
  [1971] 1 QB 164 (CA) 4.53
Marie Joseph, The See Pease v Gloahec
Markey v Coote (1876) Ir 10 CL 149 . . . . .18.82
Markovic v Coober Pedy Tours Pty Ltd South Australia [1994] SASC 4401 .2.01
Marks v Feldman (1869) LR 4 QB 481; on appeal (1870) LR 5 QB 275 (Ex) 14.32, 20.17, 20.21
Marks v GIO Australia Holdings Ltd (1998) 196 CLR 494 . . . . 2.09, 13.18
Marks & Spencer plc v Freshfields Bruckhaus Deringer [2004] 1 WLR 2331;
  on appeal [2004] EWCA Civ 741 . . . . .8.34
Maronis Holdings Ltd v Nippon Credit Australia Pty Ltd (2001) 38 ACSR 404 (NSWSC). 21.71
Marquis of Clanricarde v Henning (1861) 30 Beav 175, 54 ER 855 . . . . 8.26, 24.43, 24.45
Marini Ltd, Re [2004] BCC 172. . . . . .24.45
Marme Inversiones 2007 SL v Natwest Markets Plc [2019] EWHC 366 (Comm) 4.08, 4.26,
  4.36, 4.39, 4.74, 4.84, 4.100, 4.101, 4.102, 4.104,
  4.105, 4.106, 4.108, 4.115, 19.05, 23.40, 23.77
Marr v Tumulty 256 NY 15, 175 NE 356 (CA 1931) 18.34, 18.65, 18.75
Marriot v Marriot (1726) Gilb 204, 25 ER 142 . . . . .3.43
Marsden v Barclays Bank plc [2016] 2 Lloyd's Rep 420 (QB) 5.63
Marshall, Re [1920] 1 Ch 284 . . . . .7.58
Martin v Martin (Viner's Abridgment), 2 Eq Ca 475, 22 ER 404. . . . . .3.43
Martin v Savage and Turner (1672) in D Yale (ed), Lord Nottingham's 'Manual of
  Chancery Practice' and 'Prolegomena of Chancery and Equity' (1965) 265. . . . . .3.52
Maskell v Horner [1915] 3 KB 106 (CA) 6.21, 6.56, 6.70, 6.74
Mason v Ditchbourne and Sarson (1835) 1 M & Rob 460,
  174 ER 158. . . . . 29.74, 29.75, 29.76, 29.77, 29.78, 29.79
Mason v Gardiner (1793) 4 Bro CC 436, 29 ER 976 . . . . 3.40, 15.60

liv TABLE OF CASES

Mason v The State of New South Wales (1959) 102 CLR 108 ....6.12
Massey v Midland Bank plc [1995] 1 All ER 929 (CA).............................6.100, 9.15
Masterman-Lister v Brutton & Co [2002] EWCA Civ 1889 ....7.52
Masterman-Lister v Brutton & Co (Nos 1 and 2) [2002] 1 WLR 1511 (CA)...................7.45
Matchbet Ltd v Openbet Retail Ltd [2013] EWHC 3067 (Ch) 26.04
Mathewson's case (1597) 5 Co Rep 22b, 77 ER 84......................................3.37
Mathias v Yetts (1882) 46 LT 497 (CA)......................... 4.62, 4.63, 4.100, 4.111, 5.57
Matthew v Hanbury (1690) 2 Vern 188, 23 ER 723...........................3.42, 15.37, 22.07
Matthews v Baxter (1873) LR 8 Exch 132.....................7.65, 7.66, 10.23, 16.03, 23.15
Maturin v Tredennick (1864) 10 LT (NS) 331.....................14.71, 17.58, 18.37, 18.49, 19.06
May v Platt [1900] 1 Ch 616..7.30, 27.05
Mayfair Trading Co Pty Ltd v Dreyer (1958) 101 CLR 428 ....13.01, 15.49, 15.51, 15.60, 16.62
MBF Australia Ltd v Malouf [2008] NSWCA 214 ....1.46, 1.98, 11.25, 14.12, 14.13
MCC Proceeds Inc v Lehman Bros International (Europe) [1998] 4 All ER 675 (CA) 14.08, 14.17
MCI WorldCom International Inc v Primus Telecommunications Inc
    [2004] 2 All ER (Comm) 833 (CA)...................................4.40, 4.42, 4.47, 9.04
Mears Ltd v Shoreline Housing Partnership Ltd [2013] CP Rep 39 (CA) 26.05
Medina, The [1876] 1 P 272; aff'd [1876] 2 P 5 (CA)............................14.43, 18.100
Medsted Associates Limited v Canaccord Genuity Wealth (International) Limited
    [2019] 1 WLR 4481 (CA)..8.57
Meiklejohn v Campbell (1940) 56 TLR 663; on appeal (1940) 56 TLR 704 (CA)................3.37
Melbourne Banking Corporation Ltd v Brougham (1882) 8 App Cas 307 ....16.42, 22.11
Meldon v Lawless (1869) 18 WR 261 (CP Ir) 11.46, 14.61
Meluish v Milton (1876) 3 ChD 27 (CA) 4.90
Menegazzo v Pricewaterhousecoopers (A Firm) [2016] QSC 94 ....7.10
Mernda Developments Pty Ltd (in liq) v Alamanda Property Investments No 2 Pty Ltd
    (2011) 86 ACSR 277 (Vict CA)...16.70
Merrill Lynch International v Amorim Partners Ltd [2014] EWHC 74 (QB)...................7.12
Mersey Steel and Iron Co v Naylor Benzon & Co (1882) 9 QBD 648.........................1.31
Metal Constituents Ltd, Re (Lord Lurgan's case) [1902] 1 Ch 707 ....20.31
Metall und Rohstoff v Donaldson Lufkin & Jenrette Inc [1990] 1 QB 391 (CA).................6.31
Metropolitan Coal Consumer's Association (Karberg's case), Re
    [1892] 3 Ch 1 (CA)................... 9.05, 15.34, 15.63, 16.56, 17.17, 17.18
Meyer v Everth (1814) 4 Camp 22, 171 ER 8...3.19
Micarone v Perpetual Trustees [1999] SASC 265 (Full Ct) 19.29
Middlewood v Blakes (1797) 7 TR 162, 101 ER 911.....................................3.56
Midland Bank plc v Greene [1995] 1 FCR 374 ....18.27
Midland Bank plc v Greene [1995] 1 FLR 365....................15.46, 15.50, 15.53, 15.57
Midland Bank Trust Co Ltd v Green [1985] AC 513 ....21.10
Mihalis Angelos, The See Maredelanto Compania Naviera SA v Berghau-Handel
    GmbH (The Mihalis Angelos)
Mihalios Xilas, The See China National Foreign Trade Transport Corporation v
    Evlogia Shipping Co SA of Panama (The Mihalios Xilas)
Mihaljevic v Eiffel Tower Motors Pty Ltd and General Credits Ltd
    [1973] VR 545.........................4.23, 14.36, 15.36, 27.25, 27.29, 27.38, 27.41
Mildmay v Duckett (1678)..15.37
Miles v Wakefield Metropolitan DC [1987] AC 539....................................1.51
Mill v Hill (1852) 3 HLC 828, 10 ER 330 ....17.41, 17.42
Millar's Machinery Company Ltd v David Way and Son (1935) 15 Com Cas 204 ....1.24
Miller v Race (1758) 1 Burr 452, 97 ER 398...21.56
Milne v Durham Hosiery Mills Ltd [1925] 3 DLR 725 (Ont SC) 25.28, 25.58
Milroy v Lord (1862) 4 De GF & J 264, 45 ER 1185...........................14.22, 29.06, 29.07
Minder Music Ltd v Sharples [2015] EWHC 1454 (IPEC) 7.80
Ministry of Defence v Ashman [1993] 2 EGLR 102 (CA)...........................17.07, 17.08
Ministry of Defence v Thompson [1993] 2 EGLR 107 (CA) 17.07

TABLE OF CASES lv

Mir v Mir [2013] HKCA 144; [2012] 1 HKLRD 671 (High Court of HK SAR);
    appeal dismissed [2013] HKCA 144 .... 6.20, 24.99
Mirage Consulting Ltd v Astra Credit Union Ltd [2017] MBQB 63......... 19.02, 19.05, 20.31, 20.32
Mitchell v Homfray (1881) 8 QBD 587 .... 6.103, 23.08, 23.09
Mitchell v James [2001] All ER 116.. 7.91
Mitford v Featherstonaugh (1752) 2 Ves Sen 446, 28 ER 284 .... 15.37
Mixer's case (1859) 4 De G & J 575, 45 ER 223 .... 3.41, 18.14
Moffat v Moffat [1984] 1 NZLR 600 (CA) 7.100
Molloy v Mutual Reserve Life Insurance Co
    (1906) 94 LT 756 (CA)................... 24.25, 24.27, 24.28, 24.55, 24.63, 24.106, 24.107
Molotu Pty Ltd v Solar Power Ltd (1989) 6 BPR 13 .... 23.44
Molton v Camroux (1848) 2 Exch 487, 154 ER 584; aff'd (1849) 4 Exch 17,
    154 ER 1107.. 7.47, 7.61, 7.65, 7.66, 7.67, 10.23, 16.03
Monde Petroleum SA v WesternZagros Limited [2016] EWHC 1472 (Comm)
    upheld on appeal [2018] 2 All ER (Comm) 867 (CA) 4.102
Montgomery and Rennie v Continental Bags (NZ) Ltd
    [1974] NZLR 884 .... 7.32, 7.33, 27.08, 27.09, 27.13
Montesquieu v Sandys (1811) 18 Ves 302, 24 ER 331.............................. 8.12, 8.13
Moody v Condor Insurance Ltd [2006] 1 WLR 1847.............................. 19.07, 20.31
Moody v Cox [1917] 2 Ch 71 (CA)......................... 8.08, 8.22, 8.35, 8.36, 8.43
Moore v The National Mutual Life Association of Australasia Ltd
    [2011] NSWSC 416 .... 18.08, 23.62, 23.104, 23.105, 23.109
Moore Large & Co Ltd v Hermes Credit & Guarantee plc
    [2003] 1 Lloyd's Rep IR 315............. 23.37, 23.40, 23.51, 23.53, 23.55, 23.56, 23.79, 23.110
Morello Sdn Bhd v Jaques (International) Sdn Bhd [1995] 1 MLJ 577 (Fed Ct) 1.20
Morgan v Ashcroft [1938] 1 KB 49 (CA) 29.28
Morgan v Pooley [2010] EWHC 2447 (QB) 26.02, 26.06, 26.17, 26.25
Morley (t/a Morley Estates) v Royal Bank of Scotland Plc [2021] EWCA Civ 338 ..... 6.55, 6.60, 6.70
Morley v Elmaleh [2009] EWHC 1196 (Ch) 6.86, 6.99, 6.100, 6.101
Morley v Loughnan [1893] 1 Ch 736 .... 6.85, 6.103, 7.88, 29.27, 29.31, 29.32
Morris-Garner v One Step (Support) Ltd [2019] AC 649 .... 17.07
Morrison v Coast Finance Ltd (1965) 55 DLR (2d) 710 (BCCA) 7.103
Morrison v The Universal Marine Insurance Company (1873) LR 8 Ex 197........... 23.62, 24.119
Morse v Royal (1806) 12 Ves Jun 355, 33 ER 134 .... 1.74, 8.14
Mortgage Agency Services Number Two Ltd v Chater [2003] EWCA Civ 490............... 9.16
Mortgage Express Ltd v Bowerman & Partners (a firm) [1996] 2 All ER 836 (CA) 8.43, 8.44
Mortlock v Buller (1804) 10 Ves Jun 292, 32 ER 857 .... 18.03
Moses v Macferlan (1760) 2 Burr 1005, 97 ER 676 .... 3.23, 3.30
Moss v Mills and Boon (1805) 6 East 144, 102 ER 1242............................... 3.52
Mostyn v The West Mostyn Coal and Iron Co [1875] 1 CPD 145......................... 5.66
Motor Oil Hellas (Corinth) Refineries SA v Shipping Corp of India (The Kanchenjunga)
    [1990] 1 Lloyd's Rep 391 (HL).......... 23.04, 23.05, 23.40, 23.57, 24.03, 24.06, 24.118, 24.120
Mototrak Ltd v FCA Australia Pty Ltd [2018] EWHC 990 (Comm) 23.77
Motortrak Limited v FCA Australia PTY Ltd [2018] EWHC 1464 (Comm) 2.03
Moursi v Doherty [2019] EWHC 830 (Ch)... 6.117
Mount Morgan (West) Gold Mine Ltd, Re (1887) 56 LT 622 .... 4.26, 18.49, 19.06, 23.24, 24.43
Movitex Ltd v Bulfield [1988] BCLC 104.. 8.09
Moxon v Payne (1873) 8 Ch App 881.. 23.14, 23.37
Moyce v Newington (1878) 4 QBD 32 .... 11.05, 11.31, 11.37, 21.58
Mullens v Miller (1892) 22 ChD 194 .... 9.04
Multiservice Bookbinding v Marden [1979] Ch 84 .... 7.75, 7.76, 7.79, 7.81, 7.92, 7.99
Munchies Management Pty Ltd v Belpario (1988) 58 FCR 274 (Full Ct)................. 1.31, 2.04
Murad v Al-Saraj [2005] WTLR 1573 (CA) 2.17
Murad v Al-Saraj [2004] EWHC 1235 (Ch) 19.05
Murphy v Rayner [2011] EWHC 1 (Ch) 6.100, 6.115
Murray v Larsen [1953] 2 Lloyd's Rep 453..................................... 14.36, 14.70

lvi TABLE OF CASES

Murray v Mann (1848) 2 Ex 538, 154 ER 605 . . . . 3.27, 14.36, 14.37, 14.54, 14.69, 18.84
Murray v Palmer (1805) 2 Sch & Lef 474 . . . . .23.20
Museprime Properties Ltd v Adhill Properties Ltd [1990] 2 EGLR 196. .4.112
Mussen v Van Diemen's Land Co [1938] Ch 253 . . . . .1.31
Mutual Finance Ltd v John Wetton & Sons Ltd [1937] 2 KB 389 . . . . 6.44, 6.84
Mycock v Beatson (1879) 13 ChD 384 . . . . .16.48
Myddleton v Lord Kenyon (1794) 2 Ves 391, 30 ER 689 . . . . 19.02, 19.03

N & M Gangemi Nominees Pty Ltd v Hypax Pty Ltd [1997] FCA 1167. 18.124
Nab v Hills 92 Idaho 877, 452 P 2d 981 (1969) 14.65
Nadinic v Drinkwater (2017) 94 NSWLR 518 (CA). 4.07, 4.11, 10.04, 10.23,
11.101, 12.23, 13.18, 18.01
Nai Genova and Nai Superba, The *See* Agip SpA v Navigazione Alta Italia SpA
(The Nai Genova and The Nai Superba)
Naidoo v Naidu, The Times 1 November 2000 . . . . .6.93
Nash v De Freville [1900] 2 QB 72 . . . . 21.56, 21.59
Nash v Wooderson (1884) 52 LT 49 . . . . .4.03
Nasrulla v Rashid [2020] Ch 37 (CA). 1.47, 1.60, 1.81, 1.86, 1.95, 1.97, 1.99, 16.44
National Commercial Bank (Jamaica) Ltd v Hew
[2003] UKPC 51 . . . . 6.97, 6.100, 6.110, 17.16, 18.05, 19.05, 19.40
National Crime Agency v Robb [2015] Ch 520. . . . . .1.95, 1.96, 1.98, 16.07, 16.09,
16.12, 16.43, 16.51, 16.61, 16.62
National Crime Agency v Robb [2015] 3 WLR 23 . . . . .8.49
National Employers' Mutual General Insurance Association Ltd v Jones
[1990] 1 AC 24 (CA) 11.38, 11.40
National Merchant Buying Society Ltd v Bellamy [2012] EWHC 2563 (Ch) 6.40
National Motor Mail-Coach Company Ltd, Re [1908] 2 ChD 228. . . . . .25.77
National Patent Steam Fuel Co, ex p Worth (1859) 4 Drew 529, 62 ER 203. . . . . .4.80
National Provincial Bank Ltd v Ainsworth [1965] AC 1175 . . . . 3.50, 16.12
National Provincial Bank of England Ltd v Glanusk [1913] 3 KB 335 . . . . 5.47, 5.52
National Stadium Ltd (1923) 55 OLR 199 (Ont SC) 25.28, 25.69
National Westminster Bank plc v IRC [1995] 1 AC 111. . . . . .14.22
National Westminster Bank plc v Kotonou [2006] All ER (D) 325. . . . . .4.96
National Westminster Bank plc v Morgan [1985] AC 686. . . . . . . 6.100, 6.103, 6.107, 6.109, 6.111, 7.85
National Westminster Bank plc v Rabobank Nederland [2007] EWHC 1056 (Comm) 5.02
National Westminster Bank plc v Somer International (UK) Ltd [2002] QB 1286. . . . . 24.121
National Westminster Bank plc v Utrecht-America Finance Co [2001] 3 All ER 733 (CA) 26.30
National Westminster Bank plc v Waite [2006] EWHC 1287 . . . . .6.100
Neesom v Clarkson (1842) 2 Hare 163, 67 ER 68 . . . . 15.59, 15.65
Neill's case (1867) 15 WR 894 . . . . 24.102
Nelson v Rye [1996] 1 WLR 1378 . . . . 18.15, 18.117, 24.15, 24.16, 24.114
Nelthorpe v Dorrington (1685) 2 Lev 113, 83 ER 475 . . . . .3.52
Neste Oy v Lloyds Bank [1983] 2 Lloyd's Rep 658. . . . . .1.92
Neville v Snelling (1880) 15 ChD 679. . . . . .15.51
New Brunswick and Canada Railway and Land Co v Conybeare (1862) 9 HLC 711,
11 ER 907. . . . . 4.30, 4.49
New Sombrero Phosphate Company v Erlanger (1877) 5 ChD 73 (CA) 15.17, 15.38, 15.63
Newbigging v Adam (1886) 34 ChD 582 (CA);
aff'd (1888) 13 App Cas 308. . . . . .2.03, 2.04, 2.09, 2.17, 3.41, 4.11, 12.07, 13.01, 13.02, 13.25,
13.34, 15.34, 16.56, 17.17, 17.18, 17.23, 17.24, 17.25, 17.28, 17.36,
17.52, 17.56, 17.57, 17.62, 18.09, 18.89, 19.15, 19.36, 19.41, 19.42
Newfoundland Government v Newfoundland Railway Co (1888) 13 App Cas 199 . . . . .1.20
Newgate Stud Co v Penfold [2004] EWHC 2993 (Ch). 24.54
Newman v Pinto (1887) 57 LT 31 (CA) 4.26
Newton v Hunt (1833) 5 Sim 511, 58 ER 430. . . . . 3.38, 15.11
Newtons of Wembley Ltd v Williams [1965] 1 QB 560 (CA). 11.37, 11.38, 11.40, 14.14

TABLE OF CASES lvii

NGM Sustainable Developments Ltd v Wallis [2015] EWHC 2089 (Ch) 19.05
Nicholas v Thompson [1924] VLR 554 ....4.66, 11.20
Nichols v Jessup [1986] 1 NZLR 226 (CA)................................... 7.80, 7.81, 7.103
Niersmans v Pesticcio [2004] EWCA 372 .....6.03, 6.96, 6.104, 6.110, 6.115, 6.117, 7.58, 19.08, 29.51
Niramax Group Limited v Zurich Insurance plc [2020] EWHC 535 (Comm)..............5.28, 5.33
Niru Battery v Milestone Trading Ltd [2002] EWHC 1425; on appeal
    [2003] EWCA 1446 ....6.36
Nisbet and Potts' Contract, Re [1905] 1 Ch 391; on appeal [1906] 1 Ch 386 (CA)..............21.72
Noble v Adams (1816) 7 Taunt 59, 129 ER 24 .... 3.05, 3.08, 14.14
Nocton v Ashburton [1914] AC 932..4.119
Nolan v Minerva Trust Company Ltd [2014] 2 JLR 117; JRC 078A 1.86, 16.07, 16.13, 16.15, 16.68
Norman v Norman (No 2) (Practice Note) [2017] 1 WLR 2554............................5.20
Norreys v Zeffert [1939] 2 All ER 187 ....6.31
North v Ansell (1731) 2 P Wms 618, 24 ER 885 ....18.14
North & South Trust Co v Berkeley [1971] 1 WLR 470..............................8.36, 8.46
North British Insurance Co, The v Lloyd (1854) 10 Ex 523, 156 ER 545 ....5.42, 10.23
North Ocean Shipping Co Ltd v Hyundai Construction Co Ltd (The Atlantic Baron)
    [1979] QB 705.................................... 6.13, 6.22, 6.26, 6.29, 6.32, 6.46, 6.56, 6.73,
                          13.28, 23.14, 23.36, 23.41, 23.58, 23.77, 23.93, 23.99, 24.39
North Shore Ventures Ltd v Anstead Holdings Inc [2011] 1 All ER (Comm) 81 and
    [2012] Ch 31 (CA) 5.41, 5.42, 5.43, 5.45, 5.46, 5.47, 5.53, 5.56
North West Life Assurance Co of Canada v Shannon Height Developments Ltd
    (1987) 4 ACWS (3d) 246 (BCCA) 29.62
North-West Transportation Co Ltd v Beatty (1887) 12 App Cas 589 (PC–Canada) 8.19
Northcote Housing Association v Dixon (ChD 30 November 2001)............. 11.16, 15.10, 28.12
Northern & Central Gas Corp Ltd v Hillcrest Collieries Ltd (1975) 59 DLR (3d)
    533 (Alta SC)..27.32
Northern Bank Finance Corporation Ltd v Charlton [1979] IR 149 (SC)............. 13.08, 18.11,
                          18.89, 19.02, 19.13, 19.14, 19.15, 19.16, 20.01
Northern Rock Building Society v Archer [1999] Lloyd's Rep 32...........................6.100
Northumberland and Durham District Banking Co, Re, ex p Bigge (1858) 28 LJ Ch 50.........4.115
Northwestern Trust Co (McAskill's case), Re [1926] SCR 412 .... 25.28, 25.38, 25.57
Norton v Relly (1764) 2 Eden 286, 28 ER 908 ....6.85
Norway v Rowe (1812) 19 Ves Jun 144, 34 ER 472 ....15.38, 24.74
Norwich Peterborough Building Society v Steed [1993] Ch 116 (CA) 15.08
Norwich Union Fire Insurance Society Ltd v WHM Price Ltd
    [1934] AC 455 (PC–Australia) 1.46, 1.81, 14.39
Norwich Union Life Insurance Society v Qureshi [1999] Lloyd's Rep 263 ....7.75
Nosworthy v Instinctif Partners Ltd [2019] 2 WLUK 469................................7.75
Nottidge v Prince (1860) 2 Giff 246, 66 ER 103.................3.38, 3.42, 6.85, 15.13, 22.07, 29.36
Nottingham Patent Brick and Tile Co v Butler (1866) 16 QBD 778 (CA) 4.35
Novoship (UK) Ltd v Mikhaylyuk [2012] EWHC 3586 (Comm)......................8.52, 8.60
NRAM Ltd v Evans [2018] 1 WLR 639 (CA); leave to appeal refused
    [2018] 1 WLR 1563 (Sup Ct)...15.08
Nuneaton Borough AFC Ltd (No 2), Re [1991] BCC 44 ....8.20
Nutt v Easton [1899] 1 Ch 873..24.60
Nutt v Reed (1999) 96(42) LSG 44 (CA) 7.07, 10.26
Nwakobi, The Osha of Obosi v Nzekwu [1964] 1 WLR 1019 (PC–Nigeria) 24.15, 24.92
NZ Netherlands Society 'Oranje' Inc v Kuys [1973] 1 WLR 1126 (PC–NZ) 8.72
NZI Capital Corp Ltd v Poignmand (1997) ATPR 41–586 (FCA) 19.29

O'Connor v Hart [1983] NZLR 280 (CA); on appeal
    [1985] 1 NZLR 159 (PC) 11.101, 24.15, 24.44, 24.49, 24.53
O'Connor v SP Bray Ltd (1936) 36 St Rep (NSW) 248 .... 23.11, 23.18, 23.42, 23.92, 23.110, 24.09
O'Flaherty v McKinley [1953] 2 DLR 514, 30 MPR 172 (Nfld SC–Full Ct)...17.58, 18.37, 18.38, 18.87
O'Kane v Jones [2005] 1 Lloyd's Rep IR 174 ....4.122, 11.12, 13.33, 13.36, 23.79

lviii   TABLE OF CASES

O'Keefe v Taylor Estates Co Ltd [1916] St R Qd 301 (Full Ct)....................2.03, 11.41, 12.06
O'Neill v Ulster Bank Ltd [2016] BPIR 126 (NICA)..9.17
O'Rorke v Bolingbroke (1877) 2 App Cas 814....................................7.76, 7.92, 7.94
O'Sullivan v Management Agency and Music Ltd [1985] 1 QB 428 (CA)......2.21, 2.22, 2.23, 6.100,
            8.46, 9.05, 10.04, 11.86, 11.97, 11.107, 13.08, 13.16, 15.13, 15.21, 15.39, 15.67,
            15.68, 16.25, 17.19, 17.41, 18.01, 18.10, 18.27, 18.32, 18.67, 18.100, 18.102
Oakes v Turquand (1867) LR 2 HL 325 .... 3.41, 11.69, 11.73, 20.36, 24.90, 25.22, 25.24,
                    25.26, 25.27, 25.28, 25.29, 25.32, 25.33, 25.38, 25.41,
                    25.42, 25.45, 25.46, 25.51, 25.57, 25.58, 25.63, 25.78
Occidental Worldwide Investment Corp v Skibs A/S Avanti (The Siboen and the Sibotre)
      [1976] 1 Lloyd's Rep 293 .... 4.40, 4.90, 4.104, 6.22, 6.25, 6.26, 6.29, 6.46, 6.70,
                    11.10, 11.12, 13.28, 23.18, 23.20, 23.79, 23.93
Ocean Frost, The See Armagas v Mundogas SA (The Ocean Frost)
Odyssey Cinemas Ltd v Village Theatres Three Ltd [2010] NICA 25.........................28.12
Oelkers v Ellis [1914] 2 KB 139..........4.42, 15.63, 18.124, 24.25, 24.27, 24.55, 24.90, 24.93, 25.53
Official Receiver v Feldman (1972) 4 SASR 246 ....23.44
Ogilvie v Allen See Ogilvie v Littleboy
Ogilvie v Currie (1868) 37 LR Ch (NS) 541...........................23.30, 24.43, 24.88, 24.102
Ogilvie v Jeaffreson (1860) 2 Giff 353, 66 ER 147 ....21.61
Ogilvie v Littleboy (1897) 13 TLR 399 (CA); on appeal sub nom Ogilvie v Allen
      (1899) 15 TLR 294 (HL) 10.26, 29.14, 29.19, 29.30, 29.37, 29.42, 29.45, 29.46
Olfman v RBC Life Insurance Company [2013] MBQB 142..................................7.36
Olib, The See Enimont Overseas AG v RO Jugotnker Zadad (The Olib)
Oliver Ashworth (Holdings) Ltd v Ballard (Kent) Ltd
      [2000] Ch 12 (CA) 11.116, 23.04, 23.05, 23.40, 23.58, 23.92, 24.03, 24.109, 24.118
Olivine Capital Pte Ltd v Chia Chin Yan [2014] 2 SLR 1371 (CA) 5.11, 7.11, 7.22
Olympic Airways v Alysandratos [1999] VSC 244.......................................16.51
One Step (Support) Ltd v Morris- Garner [2019] AC 649.................................28.31
Ooregum Gold Mining of India v Roper [1892] AC 125...................................25.40
Orix Australia Corporation Ltd v M Wright Hotel Refrigeration Pty Ltd
      (2000) 15 FLR 267 ....14.11, 14.13, 14.15, 16.44, 29.36
Ormes v Beadle (1860) 2 Giff 166, 66 ER 70 .... 3.41, 15.39, 23.14, 23.36, 23.41, 24.100
Orr v Ford (1989) 167 CLR 316.....................24.08, 24.10, 24.12, 24.14, 24.15, 24.17, 24.114
OT Africa Line Ltd v Vickers plc [1996] 1 Lloyd's Rep 700 ....7.14
Overbrooke Estates Ltd v Glencombe Properties Ltd [1974] 1 WLR 1335 ....26.17
Overland Development Limited v Ronghuan Dong [2018] NZHC 2225 ....23.49, 23.70
Overseas Medical Supplies Ltd v Orient Transport Services Ltd
      [1999] 2 Lloyd's Rep 273 (CA) 26.25
Owen v Homan (1851) 3 Mac & G 378, 42 ER 307; on appeal
      (1853) 44 HLC 997, 10 ER 752 ....5.42, 9.05
Oxendale v Wetherell (1829) 9 B & C 385, 109 ER 143.................................3.27, 14.35

P v P (ancillary relief: consent order) [2004] 1 Fam 1.....................................5.20
P&O Nedlloyd BV v Arab Metals Co (No 2)
      [2007] 1 WLR 2288 (CA)..................................24.15, 24.25, 24.35, 24.37, 24.61
Padden v Bevan Ashford [2012] 1 WLR 1759 (CA)......................................9.19
Paget v Marshall (1884) 28 ChD 255 ....7.30, 11.92, 19.24
Paki v Attorney-General of New Zealand [2015] 1 NZLR 67 (NZSC).......................19.02
Pakistan International Airline Corp v Times Travel (UK) Ltd [2021] UKSC 40;
      [2021] 3 WLR 727 (Sup Ct)............................... 6.07, 6.26, 6.28, 6.29, 6.33, 6.37,
                    6.38, 6.40, 6.44, 6.58, 7.70, 7.79, 7.85
Pamamull v Albrizzi (Sales) Pty Ltd (No 2) [2011] VSCA 260 ....7.31
Pan Atlantic Insurance Co Ltd v Pine Top Insurance Co Ltd [1993] 1 Lloyd's Rep 496 (CA);
      on appeal [1995] 1 AC 501.. 4.66, 4.67, 4.105,
                    5.25, 5.28, 5.33, 10.27, 26.02
Pan Ocean Shipping Co Ltd v Creditcorp Ltd [1994] 1 WLR 161 (HL)......................1.51

TABLE OF CASES   lix

Panama and South Pacific Telegraph Company v India Rubber, Gutta Percha and
   Telegraph Works Company (1875) 10 Ch App 515 . . . . .1.87, 1.97, 8.49, 8.51, 8.56, 8.59
Pankhania v Hackney LBC [2002] EWHC 2441. . . . . .4.18, 28.08
Pao On v Lau Yiu Long [1980] AC 614 (PC–Hong Kong). 6.22, 6.25, 6.26, 6.46,
                                                                          6.55, 6.58, 6.66, 6.72, 6.73, 6.74
Papamichael v National Westminster Bank plc [2003] 1 Lloyd's Rep 341 . . . . .1.93
Papouis v Gibson-West [2004] EWHC 396. . . . . .6.93, 6.95
Paradise Motor Co Ltd, Re [1968] 1 WLR 1125 (CA) 15.63, 29.13
Paragon Finance plc v Staunton [2002] 2 All ER 248 (CA) 6.38
Parallel Media LLC v Chamberlain [2014] EWHC 214 (QB) 4.75
Parkdale, The [1897] P 53 (DC) 8.53
Parke v Wannell (1619) in J Ritchie, Reports of Cases Decided by Francis Bacon in the
   High Court of Chancery (1617–1621) (1932) 143 . . . . .3.52
Parker v Baltimore Paint and Chemical Corp 39 FDR 567 (Colo 1966) 15.60
Parker v McKenna (1874) 10 Ch App 96 . . . . .8.11
Parker v Patrick (1793) 5 TR 175, 101 ER 99 . . . . 3.10, 3.11, 3.12
Parker v Smallwood [1910] 1 Ch 777 . . . . .23.92
Partridge v Partridge [1894] 1 Ch 351 . . . . .24.11, 24.14
Pascoe v Turner [1979] 1 WLR 431 (CA). 29.07
Patel v Shah [2005] EWCA Civ 157 . . . . .24.15, 24.74
Pathania v Adedeji [2010] EWHC 3085 (QB). 6.103, 6.120
Paton v Rosesilver Group Corp [2017] EWCA Civ 158. . . . . .8.34, 8.41
Pauling's Settlement Trusts, Re [1964] Ch 303 (CA) 6.103, 24.58, 24.59
Paull v Paull [2018] EWHC 2520 (Ch). 6.110, 6.117
Pavey & Matthews Pty Ltd v Paul (1986) 162 CLR 221 . . . . 1.30, 1.36, 1.51
Pavlovic v Commonwealth Bank of Australia (1992) 56 SASR 587 . . . . .28.25
Pawson v Watson (1778) 2 Cowp 785, 98 ER 1361 . . . . 4.63, 4.83
Paxman v Union Assurance Society (1923) 39 TLR 424 . . . . .4.63
Payne v Bacomb (1781) 2 Dougl 651, 99 ER 412. . . . . .3.23
Payne v Rogers (1780) 1 Dougl 407, 99 ER 261 . . . . .29.84
Peacock v Evans (1809) 16 Ves Jun 513, 33 ER 1079. . . . . .3.38, 15.50
Peak Hotels and Resorts Limited v Tarek Investments Ltd [2015] EWHC 1997 (Ch) 15.51, 15.55
Peart Stevenson Associates Ltd v Holland [2008] EWHC 1868 (QB) 26.02
Pease v Gloahec (The Marie Joseph) (1866) LR 1 PC 219 . . . . 14.03, 16.02, 20.14, 21.05, 21.57
Pedashenko v Blacktown City Council (1996) 39 NSWLR 189 . . . . .8.18, 8.22, 15.17, 17.26
Peek v Gurney (1871) LR 13 Eq 79 (CA) 4.11
Peek v Gurney (1873) LR 6 HL 377. . . . . 2.05, 4.80, 24.43, 24.88, 25.51
Peekay Intermark Ltd and Harish Pawani v Australia and New Zealand Banking
   Group Ltd [2006] EWCA 386 . . . . 4.114, 4.118, 4.120, 26.02, 26.07, 26.11
Peer v Humphrey (1835) 2 AD & E 495, 111 ER 191 . . . . .3.05, 3.12
Pell Frischmann Engineering Ltd v Bow Valley Iran Ltd [2011] 1 WLR 2370 (PC–Jersey). 17.07
Peninsular and Oriental Steam Navigation Co v Johnson (1938) 60 CLR 189 . . . . .2.28
Pennell v Millar (1857) 23 Beav 172, 53 ER 68 . . . . 3.37, 3.40, 17.63
Pennington v Waine [2002] 1 WLR 2075 (CA). 29.06
Pennsylvania Shipping Co v Compagnie Nationale de Navigation
   [1936] 2 All ER 1167 (KB). 4.21, 27.36, 27.38, 27.45
Penson v Lee (1800) 2 Bos & Pul 330, 126 ER 1309 .3.56, 14.56, 14.79, 14.80
Pepper v Hart [1993] AC 593 . . . . .28.32
Percy Edwards (Ltd) v Vaughan (1910) 26 TLR 545 (CA). 21.10
Permanent Mortgages Pty Ltd v Vandenbergh (2010) 41 WAR 353. . . . . 5.22, 7.70, 7.73, 11.100, 15.53
Perpetual Trustees Australia Ltd v Heperu Pty Ltd
   (2009) 76 NSWLR 195 (CA). 1.46, 13.30, 14.11, 14.12, 14.15, 16.44
Perpetual Trustees Victoria Ltd v Burns [2015] WASC 234 . . . . 11.101, 15.56, 19.29
Perrott v Perrott (1811) 14 East 423, 104 ER 665 . . . . .3.37, 3.52
Perwaz v Perwaz [2018] UKUT 325 (TCC). 6.99
Pesticcio v Huet (2003) 73 BMLR 57 . . . . .7.58, 8.10, 15.19, 16.41, 29.38, 29.50

lx   TABLE OF CASES

Pesticcio v Huet [2003] EWHC 2293 (Ch) 6.103
Petrotrade Inc v Smith [2000] 1 Lloyd's Rep 486..........................8.51, 8.52, 8.54, 8.59, 8.65
Peyman v Lanjani [1985] Ch 457 (CA) 11.04, 11.113, 23.18, 23.35, 23.37, 23.39, 23.40, 23.41,
            23.51, 23.53, 23.58, 23.61, 23.62, 23.66, 23.78, 23.103, 23.110, 23.111, 24.03, 24.109
Phillips v Brooks Ltd [1919] 2 KB 243 ....1.48
Phillips v Phillips (1861) 4 De GF & J 208, 45 ER 1164 ....3.45, 3.47, 3.48, 3.49,
            3.50, 3.52, 21.32, 21.67, 21.68, 21.69, 22.06
Philpott v Superior Court 36 P 2d 635 (1934)..............................11.65, 12.04, 14.35
Phipps v Lovegrove (1873) LR 16 Eq Cas 80 ....21.22
Phosphate Sewage Company v Hartmont (1875) 5 ChD 394 (CA) 18.46
Photo Production Ltd v Securicor Transport Ltd [1980] AC 827...............1.15, 1.18, 1.20, 1.31
Pickering v Lord Stamford (1795) 2 Ves Jun 581, 30 ER 787 ....24.10
Pickett v Loggon (1807) 14 Ves Jun 215, 33 ER 503 ....3.38, 3.43, 15.58, 15.65, 24.100
Picturesque Atlas Publishing Co Ltd, The v Phillipson (1890) 16 VLR 675 (Full Ct)......14.61, 14.62
Pidcock v Bishop (1825) 3 B & C 605, 107 ER 857 ....5.42, 10.23
Pigot's case (1614) 11 Co Rep 26b, 77 ER 1177 ....1.26, 3.37
Pigott v Stratton (1859) 1 De GF & J 33, 45 ER 271.......................................4.41
Pilbrow v Pilbrow's Atmospheric Railway and Canal Propulsion Company
     (1948) 5 CB 440, 136 ER 950...29.81
Pilcher v Rawlins (1872) 7 Ch App 259 ....21.10, 21.56, 21.61, 21.66
Pilmore v Hood (1838) 5 Bing NC 97, 132 ER 1042.......................................4.78
Pisani v A-G for Gibraltar (1874) LR 5 PC 516 (Gibraltar) 8.04, 8.08, 8.26, 8.33
Pitt v Holt [2013] 2 AC 108 (SC); [2012] Ch 132...............7.05, 7.07, 9.21, 10.26, 13.32, 23.09,
            29.19, 29.22, 29.29, 29.30, 29.35, 29.37, 29.42, 29.43,
            29.44, 29.45, 29.46, 29.47, 29.52, 29.53, 29.54
Pitt v Smith (1811) 3 Camp 33, 170 ER 1296...7.65
Planche v Colburn (1831) 8 Bing 14, 131 ER 305 ....1.30, 3.27, 14.43
Plimer v Duke Group Ltd (in liq) (2001) 207 CLR 165 ....15.06
Plowright v Lambert (1885) 52 LT 646................................1.70, 3.42, 15.51, 22.07
Police v Dronjak [1990] 3 NZLR 75 ....29.55
Port Caledonia, The and The Anna [1903] P 184 ....14.43, 18.100
Porter v Latec Finance (Qld) Pty Ltd (1964) 111 CLR 177...........................1.46, 14.39
Portlock v Gardner (1842) 1 Hare 594, 66 ER 1168 ....3.43
Portman Building Society v Dusangh [2000] 2 All ER 221 (CA) 7.84, 7.86, 7.91
Portman Building Society v Hamlyn Taylor Neck (a firm) [1998] 4 All ER 202 (CA) 1.52, 15.35
Possfund Ltd v Diamond [1996] 1 WLR 1351..4.80
Potter v Dyer [2011] EWCA Civ 1417 ....11.03, 11.18, 19.20, 23.04, 23.58, 23.89
Pounds v Pounds [1994] 1 WLR 1535 (CA) 5.20
Powell v Edmunds (1810) 12 East 6, 104 ER 3..3.19
Powell v Powell [1900] 1 Ch 243 ....6.103, 6.117
Power v Wells (1778) 2 Cowp 818, 98 ER 1379 ....3.09, 3.20
Preda v Australian Imaging & Ultrasound Distributors Pty Ltd [2007] NSWSC 155 ....15.61
Premium Nafta Product Ltd v Fili Shipping Company Ltd [2007] 2 All ER (Comm) 1053 (HL) 1.16
Prendergast v Turton (1841) 1 Y & C 98, 62 ER 807; aff'd (1844) 13 LJ Ch 268.................24.74
President of India v La Pintada Compania Navigacion SA [1985] AC 104 ....17.19
Prest v Petrodel Resources Ltd [2013] 2 AC 415; [2013] 3 WLR 1 (SC).............1.09, 1.84, 26.02
Prickett v Badger (1856) 1 CB (NS) 296, 140 ER 123 ....14.43
Prime Sight Ltd v Lavarello [2014] 2 WLR 84 (PC) 26.07
Prince of Wales etc Association Company v Palmer (1858) 25 Beav 605, 53 ER 768.............3.55
Product Star, The See Abu Dhabi National Tanker Co v Product Star Shipping Ltd
     (The Product Star) (No 2)
Progress Bulk Carriers Ltd v Tube City IMS LLC [2012] EWHC 273 (Comm) 6.43
Property Alliance Group Ltd v Royal Bank of Scotland Plc [2018] 1 WLR 3529 ...... 4.26, 4.36, 4.39
Proprietary Mines Ltd v MacKay [1939] 3 DLR 215 (Ont CA);
     aff'd [1941] 1 DLR 240 (SCC)..................................2.11, 2.28, 18.01, 18.48
Prosser v Edmonds (1835) 1 Y & C Ex 481, 160 ER 196...................................22.11

Proudfoot v Montefiore (1867) LR 2 QB 511....................................5.29
Provident Finance Corporation Pty Ltd v Hammond [1978] VR 312.......................21.26
Prudential Assurance Co Ltd v HMRC [2019] AC 929 .... 17.19, 17.21, 17.22
PT Ltd v Spuds Surf Chatswood Pty Ltd [2013] NSWCA 446........................7.83
PT Royal Bali Leisure v Hutchinson & Co Trust Co Ltd [2004] EWHC 1014 (Ch) 11.93
Public Trustee v Chancellor of the Duchy of Lancaster [1927] 1 KB 516 (CA)................27.05
Public Trustee (WA) v Brumar Nominees Pty Ltd [2012] WASC 161 .... 7.53, 7.61
Pukallus v Cameron (1982) 180 CLR 477 ....7.31
Pulsford v Richards (1853) 17 Beav 87, 51 ER 965 .... 4.38, 4.100, 9.03
Purcell v M'Namara (1806) 14 Ves Jun 91, 33 ER 455 .... 24.44, 24.58
Pusey v Desbouvrie (1734) 3 P Wms 315, 24 ER 1081 ....5.59

QBE Insurance (Australia) Limited v Cape York Airlines Pty Ltd [2012] 1 QdR 158 (CA).......23.93
Queensland Mines Ltd v Hudson (1978) 52 ALJR 399 (PC)...............................8.34
Quest 4 Finance Ltd v Maxfield [2007] 2 CLC 706.....................................26.10
Quoine Pte Ltd v B2C2 Ltd [2020] SGCA(I) 2 .... 5.11, 7.22, 7.24, 7.25, 7.26
Qutb v Hussain [2005] EWHC 157 (Ch)..29.09

R v Attorney-General for England and Wales
    [2003] UKPC 22 (PC–NZ) 6.28, 6.30, 6.37, 6.40, 6.41, 6.75, 6.103
R v Barnard (1837) 7 C&P 784 ....4.26
R v Charles [1977] AC 177..4.36
R v Gomez [1993] AC 442...29.55
R v Hinks [2001] 2 AC 241................................ 1.46, 24.22, 29.06, 29.09, 29.13, 29.55
R v Lambie [1982] AC 449...4.36
R v Lawrence [1972] AC 626...29.55
R v Preddy [1996] AC 815...1.46, 16.45
R v Saddlers' Company (1863) 10 HLC 303, 11 ER 217 ....14.27
R (on the application of Steele) v Birmingham City Council [2005] EWCA Civ 1824...........25.17
Radcliffe v Price (1902) 18 TLR 446.......................................6.103
Radferry Pty Ltd v Starborne Holdings Pty Ltd (Full FCA 18 December 1998)........11.113, 23.97
Radford v Ferguson (1947) 50 WAR 14 ....21.28
Radin v Commonwealth Bank of Australia [1998] FCA 1361 ....5.47
Raiffeisen Bank International AG v Asia Coal Energy Ventures Ltd
    [2020] EWHC 2602 (Comm) 19.06
Raiffeisen Zentralbank Osterreich AG v The Royal Bank of Scotland plc
    [2011] 1 Lloyd's Rep 123 .... 4.30, 4.39, 4.40, 4.106, 4.108, 26.03, 26.06,
                                    26.07, 26.08, 26.17, 26.18, 26.21, 26.30
Railton v Mathews (1844) 10 Cl & Fin 934, 8 ER 993 (HL) 5.53
Ramphul v Toole (unreported CA, 17 March 1989)..............................28.07, 28.14
Ramsden v Hylton (1751) 2 Ves Sen 304, 28 ER 196...........................5.14, 7.39
Randall v Errington (1805) 10 Ves 423, 32 ER 909 ....8.18, 15.17
Randall v Randall [2004] EWHC 2258 (Ch)....................6.103, 6.114, 7.74, 29.16
Ratiu v Conway [2006] 1 All ER 571 (CA)..8.34
Rawlins v Wickham (1858) 1 Giff 355, 65 ER 954; (1858) 3 De G & J 304,
    42 ER 1285................15.34, 16.56, 17.24, 17.28, 18.124, 19.02, 23.24, 23.33, 24.43, 24.95
Ray v Sempers [1974] AC 370.. 4.36, 4.61, 4.90
Rayden v Edwardo Ltd [2008] EWHC 2689 (Comm) 18.89
RBC Properties Pte Ltd v Defu Furniture Pte Ltd [2014] SGCA 62 ..... 1.09, 1.31, 11.14, 13.02, 26.04
RBC Properties Pte Ltd v Defo Furniture Pte Ltd [2015] 1 SLR 997 (CA)......... 17.24, 28.10, 28.13
RE Jones Ltd v Waring and Gillow Ltd [1926] AC 670........................ 21.56, 21.59, 29.36
Read v Hutchinson (1813) 3 Camp 352, 170 ER 1408 ....3.08, 3.09, 3.27, 14.34, 14.42, 20.13
Readdy v Pendergast (1886) 55 LT 767 ....8.30
Reading v The King [1949] 2 KB 232 (CA); on appeal [1951] AC 507 ....8.53
Redgrave v Hurd (1881) 20 ChD 1 (CA) 2.07, 4.10, 4.69, 4.114, 4.118, 4.119, 4.120,
                                    7.04, 15.34, 16.56, 17.61, 23.24, 24.27, 27.02, 27.19

lxii TABLE OF CASES

Redican v Nesbit [1924] SCR 135; [1924] 1 DLR 536 (SCC) 7.34, 7.37, 18.10, 18.124,
20.01, 20.04, 27.06, 27.07, 27.08, 27.14
Rees v De Bernardy [1896] 2 Ch 437 . . . . .15.67, 18.36, 18.100, 24.62
Rees v Lines (1837) 8 Car & P 126, 173 ER 427 . . . . .3.24
Rees v Rees [2016] VSC 452. . . . . .7.10
Reese River Silver Mining Co Ltd v Smith (1869) LR 4 HL 64 . . . . .3.41, 3.53, 11.59, 11.67, 11.68,
11.69, 11.70, 11.71, 11.72, 11.76, 11.77, 11.79, 11.97, 11.98,
11.107, 11.108, 16.23, 25.29, 25.69, 25.70, 25.71
Regal (Hastings) Ltd v Gulliver [1967] 2 AC 134 . . . . .2.17
Rehman v Santander UK Plc [2018] EWHC 748 (QB) 4.28
Reinhard v Ondra LLP [2015] EWHC 1869 (Ch), [2016] 2 BCLC 571 . . . . .4.119
Renault UK Ltd v FleetPro Technical Services Ltd [2008] Bus LR D17 . . . . .4.76
Renner v Racz (1972) 22 DLR (3d) 443 (Alta SC (App Div)) 27.45
Resorts World at Sentosa Pte Ltd v Lee Fook Kheun [2018] SGHC 173 . . . . 7.66, 23.77
Reynell v Sprye (1852) 1 De GM & G 660, 42 ER 710. . . . . .4.10, 4.13, 4.38, 4.104, 4.119, 20.27
Rhodes v Bates (1865) 1 Ch App 252 . . . . .8.07
Rhodes v Macalister (1923) 29 Com Cas 19 (CA) 8.60
Rice v Rice (1853) 2 Drew 73, 61 ER 646 . . . . .21.68
Rich v Sydenham (1671) 1 Chan Ca 202, 22 ER 672. . . . . .15.47
Richard Brady Franks Ltd v Price (1937) 58 CLR 112 . . . . .1.78
Richards v HEB Enterprises Ltd (unreported, Grand Court of the Cayman Islands,
Civil Division, no G93 of 2016, Hon Justice Williams, 2 August 2018) 1.08
Richardson v Silvester (1873) LR 9 QB 34 . . . . 4.76, 4.79
Richmond Gate Property Co Ltd, Re [1965] 1 WLR 335. . . . . .1.51
Rick v Brandsema [2009] 1 SCR 295 (SCC). 5.20
Riddiford v Warren (1901) 20 NZLR 572 (CA). 27.48, 27.48
Rivaz v Gerussi Bros & Co (1880) 6 QBD 222 (CA). 14.80, 18.40
Riverlate Properties Ltd v Paul [1975] Ch 133 (CA). 7.12, 7.14, 7.30, 9.21, 11.92, 19.25, 29.19
Roadchef (Employee Benefits Trustees) Ltd v Hill
[2014] EWHC 109 (Ch). 21.10, 21.72, 29.52
Roberts v Roberts [1905] 1 Ch 705 (CA) 5.14, 7.39
Roberts v Rodney District Council [2001] 2 NZLR 402 . . . . .17.07
Roberts v Tunstall (1845) 4 Hare 257, 67 ER 645 . . . . 3.44, 24.04, 24.10, 24.11,
24.43, 24.45, 24.47, 24.49, 24.113
Roberts (A) & Co Ltd v Leicestershire County Council [1961] Ch 555. . . . . .7.19
Robeson v Waugh (1874) 2 R 63 . . . . .4.45
Robins v Incentive Dynamics Pty Ltd (2003) 175 FLR 286 (NSWCA) 1.58, 1.71, 2.24,
16.48, 16.52, 16.60, 16.69
Robinson v Abbott (1894) 20 VLR 146 (Full Ct). 24.58
Robinson v Ridley (1821) 6 Madd 2, 56 ER 988 . . . . .17.44
Robinson v Wall (1847) 2 Ph 372, 41 ER 986. . . . . .4.79
Roche v Sherrington [1982] 1 WLR 599, [1982] 2 All ER 426. . . . . 6.100, 6.103
Rogge v Rogge [2019] EWHC 1949 (Ch). 23.09, 29.19, 29.29, 29.42
Rolfe v Gregory (1865) 4 De GJ & S 576, 46 ER 1042 . . . . .24.50
Rolled Steel Products (Holdings) Ltd v British Steel Corporation
[1986] 1 Ch 246 (CA). 1.41, 1.67, 1.78, 1.88, 29.20
Romank v Achtem [2009] BCSC 1757 . . . . .7.34
Rookes v Barnard [1964] AC 1129 . . . . 6.06, 6.14
Root v Badley [1960] NZLR 756. . . . . .18.60, 18.77, 27.24, 27.31
Root v French (1835) 13 Wendell 570 (SCNY) 3.05, 3.11, 21.58, 21.59
Roper v Coombes (1827) 6 B & C 534, 108 ER 549. . . . . .3.27
Rose, Re, Midland Bank Executor and Trustee Co v Rose [1949] Ch 78 . . . . 14.22, 29.06
Rose, Re, Rose v IRC [1952] Ch 499 (CA) 14.22, 29.06
Rosenthal and Sons Ltd v Esmail [1965] 1 WLR 1117 . . . . .1.24
Rosetti Marketing Ltd v Diamond Sofa Co Ltd [2013] Bus LR 543 (CA) 8.38, 8.44
Ross River Ltd v Cambridge City Football Club Ltd [2008] 1 All ER 1004 . . . . . .8.49, 8.57, 8.63, 28.36

TABLE OF CASES lxiii

Ross River Ltd v Waveley Commercial Ltd [2012] EWHC 81 (Ch) 4.121
Ross River Ltd v Waveley Commercial Ltd [2008] 1 All ER 1004................. 4.66, 4.104, 4.108
Ross T Smyth & Co Ltd v TD Bailey Son & Co (1940) 164 LT 102 (HL) 24.04
Rowe v Oates (1905) 3 CLR 73 ....24.74
Roxborough v Rothmans of Pall Mall Australia (2001) 208 CLR 516 ....1.51
Royal Bank of Canada v Harowitz (1994) 17 OR (3d) 671...................................16.15
Royal Bank of Scotland v Etridge (No 2) [2002] 2 AC 773........ 4.46, 4.115, 4.117, 5.41, 5.43, 5.44,
5.46, 6.01, 6.03, 6.75, 6.76, 6.77, 6.78, 6.79, 6.80, 6.82, 6.83, 6.85, 6.87,
6.93, 6.94, 6.95, 6.97, 6.100, 6.102, 6.103, 6.104, 6.105, 6.106, 6.107,
6.108, 6.109, 6.111, 6.112, 6.113, 6.115, 6.117, 8.08, 9.03, 9.05, 9.13,
9.14, 9.15, 9.16, 9.17, 9.19, 9.20, 19.40, 21.72, 29.18, 29.20, 29.58
Royal Bank of Scotland plc v James O'Donnell and Ian McDonald [2014] CSIH 84; 2015 SC 258 .4.93
Royal Bank of Scotland plc v Chandra [2011] EWCA Civ 192 .... 4.49, 9.07
Royal Boskalis Westminster NV v Mountain [1999] QB 674 .... 6.12, 6.20, 6.23
Royal British Bank (Nicholl's case), Re (1859) 3 De G & J 387, 44 ER 1317...................18.61
Royal Brompton Hospital NHS Trust v Hammond [2002] 1 WLR 1397 (HL) 28.26
Royscott Trust Ltd v Rogerson [1991] 2 QB 297 (CA) 28.21
Ruby Consolidated Mining Company (Askew's case), Re (1874) 9 Ch App 664................25.46
Runciman v Walter Runciman [1992] BCLC 1084...11.93
Rushton v Worcester City Council [2002] HLR 9 (CA)....................................13.31
Russian (Vyksounsky) Ironworks Company, Re, (Whitehouse's case) [1867] LR 3 Eq 790..... 23.104
Russo v Beclar Pty Ltd (2011) 111 SASR 459 (Full Ct)........................ 23.58, 23.73, 23.84
RV Ward Ltd v Bignall [1967] 1 QB 534 (CA)..1.24
Ryan v Tiuta International Ltd [2014] 11 WLUK 703; [2015] BPIR 123 ....6.43

S-244 Holdings Ltd v Seymour Building Systems Ltd
(1994) 93 BCLR (2d) 34 (BCCA) 14.44, 18.100, 27.32, 27.60
S v S (ancillary relief: consent order) [2003] 1 Fam 1 ....5.20
S Pearson & Son Ltd v Dublin Corporation [1907] AC 351 (HL)...........................26.02
S Trust, In re [2011] JLR 375 .... 11.106, 29.46, 29.47
St Paul Fire and Marine Insurance Co (UK) Ltd v McConnell Dowell Constructors
[1995] 2 Lloyd's Rep 116 (CA) 4.112, 5.28, 5.33
Saetta, The See Forsythe International (UK) Ltd v Silver Shipping Co Ltd (The Saetta)
Salt v Stratstone Specialist Ltd [2015] EWCA Civ 745 [2016] RTR 17 (CA) 17.01, 17.05,
18.01, 18.77, 18.89, 18.93, 24.75, 24.95, 24.97, 28.08, 28.11
Salter v Bradshaw (1858) 26 Beav 161, 53 ER 858............................ 17.04, 24.31, 24.80
SAM Business Systems Ltd v Hedley & Co [2002] EWHC 2733....................26.06, 26.27
Samah v Shah Alam Properties Sdn Bhd [1999] MLJU 144 (CA) 1.08
Samson v Lockwood (1998) 40 OR (3d) 161 (CA for Ontario)..............................23.42
Samuel v Wadlow [2007] EWCA Civ 155 .... 4.123, 6.92, 13.28, 13.35, 24.59, 24.61, 24.62, 29.22
Santa Clara, The See Vitol SA v Norelf Ltd (The Santa Clara)
Sanwa Australia Finance Ltd v Finchill Pty Ltd [2001] NSWCA 466............. 14.11, 14.13, 14.15
Sargent v ASL Developments (1974) 131 CLR 634.... 11.08, 11.58, 11.116, 23.05, 23.07, 23.11, 23.18,
23.31, 23.42, 23.46, 23.48, 23.57, 23.60, 23.61, 23.92, 23.98
Sargent v Campbell [1972] Argus LR 708 .... 18.87, 23.36, 23.73
Satyam Computer Services Ltd v Unpaid Systems Ltd [2008] 1 All ER (Comm) 737,
[2008] EWCA Civ 487 ....5.63
Saunders v Anglia Building Society [1971] AC 1004 .... 1.36, 1.47, 29.56, 29.81
Savery v King (1856) 5 HLC 627, 10 ER 1046 ....8.26, 13.11, 18.58, 19.17, 20.32,
23.06, 23.14, 24.58, 24.65, 24.96
Say v Barwick (1812) 1 Ves & B 195, 35 ER 76...................................... 7.65, 7.68
Sayers v Burton (2009) 11 NZCPR 39 ....19.31
Scales Trading Ltd v Far Eastern Shipping Co Public Ltd [1999] 3 NZLR 26 (CA);
on appeal sub nom Far Eastern Shipping Co Public Ltd v Scales Trading
[2001] 1 NZLR 513 (PC) 5.44, 5.51, 19.31
Scarfe v Jardine (1882) 7 App Cas 345 .... 14.57, 23.06, 23.57, 23.61, 23.98

lxiv TABLE OF CASES

Scattergood v Sylvester (1850) 15 QB 506, 117 ER 551 . . . . .3.12
Scheuer v Bell [2004] VSC 71 . . . . 2.01, 11.101, 11.113, 20.32, 23.66, 23.97
Schmidt v Rosewood Trust Ltd [2003] 2 AC 709 (PC–Manx) 29.52
Schneider v Heath (1813) 3 Camp 506, 170 ER 1462 . . . . .4.38
Scholefield v Templer (1859) 4 De G & J 429, 45 ER 166 . . . . 9.21, 20.29, 29.20
Scholey v Central Railway Co of Venezuela (1868) LR 9 Eq 266, 39 LJ Ch 354. . . . . .23.76
Schulman v Hewson [2002] EWHC 855 (Ch). 24.15
Schwartz Family Co Pty Ltd v Capitol Carpets Pty Ltd [2019] NSWSC 238 . . . . 7.10, 7.21
Scott v Hanson (1829) 1 Russ & M 128, 39 ER 49 . . . . .4.46
Scott v Scott [1924] 1 IR 141 . . . . .21.70
Scott v Sebright (1886) 12 PD 21. . . . . 6.20, 6.62
Scottish Petroleum Company, Re (1882) 23 ChD 413 (CA) . . . 20.36, 25.29, 25.34, 25.69, 25.70, 25.72
Sea Star, The See Manifest Shipping Co Ltd v Uni-Polaris Insurance Co Ltd (The Sea Star)
Sears v Minco Plc [2016] EWHC 433 (Ch) 4.05, 4.117, 26.20
Seaton v Heath [1899] 1 QB 782 (CA) 3.58, 5.41, 5.42, 10.23
Secretary of State for Justice v Topland Group plc [2011] EWHC 983 (QB) 8.58
Seddon v North Eastern Salt Co Ltd [1905] 1 Ch 326; [1904–7] All ER Rep 817 . . . . . 4.83, 4.117, 7.37,
                              23.25, 23.25, 24.90, 27.02, 27.07, 27.09, 27.18, 27.20,
                              27.21, 27.22, 27.23, 27.24, 27.25, 27.26, 27.29, 27.56
Seiff v Fox [2005] 1 WLR 3811 . . . . 11.87, 11.94
Selsey v Rhoades (1824) 2 Sim & St 41, 57 ER 260 . . . . .8.27
Selway v Fogg (1839) 5 M & W 83, 151 ER 36 . . . . .3.27, 14.42, 14.43, 14.44
Sempra Metals Ltd v Inland Revenue Commissioners [2008] AC 561 . . . . . . .10.36, 17.13, 17.19, 17.21
Senanayake v Cheng [1966] AC 63 (PC–Singapore) 4.46, 11.09, 14.36, 15.36, 17.56, 18.89,
                              20.01, 20.03, 20.31, 23.66, 23.80, 24.101, 27.21, 27.22, 27.24, 27.25
Seneca Wire & Mfg Co v AB Leach & Co 247 NY 1, 159 NE 700 (CA 1928). 18.96
Senhouse v Christian (1795) 19 Ves Jun 157, 34 ER 476; 19 Beav 356, 52 ER 387. . . . . .24.74
Sgro v Australian Associated Motor Insurers Ltd (2015) 91 NSWLR 325 (CA) 4.07
Shackleton, Re (1875) 10 Ch App 446 . . . . 4.36, 4.61
Shaftsbury House (Developments) Ltd v Lee [2010] EWHC 1484 (Ch) 4.47, 26.20
Shalson v Russo [2005] Ch 281 . . . . 1.96, 2.24, 11.25, 11.59, 11.112, 13.29, 15.19, 15.69, 16.07,
                              16.09, 16.12, 16.25, 16.28, 16.29, 16.41, 16.45, 16.51, 16.70, 21.45, 25.18
Sharland v Sharland [2016] AC 871 . . . . .5.20
Sharpley v Louth and East Coast Railway Company (1876) 2 ChD 663 . . . . .24.88
Shaw v Applegate [1977] 1 WLR 970 (CA) 24.08
Shaw v Thackray (1853) 1 Sm & G 537, 65 ER 235. . . . . .7.65
Shaw v Woodcock (1827) 7 B & C 73, 108 ER 652 . . . . .6.24
Sheahan v Thompson (No 2) [2015] NSWSC 871 . . . . 11.100, 11.101
Sheffield Nickel and Silver Plating Company Ltd v Unwin
      (1877) 2 QBD 214 (CA) 18.03, 18.11, 18.48, 18.54, 18.89, 19.02, 19.03
Sheldon v RHM Outhwaite (Underwriting Agencies) Ltd [1996] AC 102 .24.54
Shepheard v Broome [1904] AC 342 . . . . .25.29
Sheppard v Shoolbred (1841) Car & M 61, 174 ER 409 . . . . 3.10, 3.11
Sherman dec'd, Re [1954] Ch 653 . . . . 1.74, 16.42, 22.06
Shields v Westpac Banking Corporation [2008] NSWCA 268 . . . . .1.98
Shill Properties Ltd v Bunch [2021] EWHC 2142 (Ch) 26.03
Ship v Crosskill (1870) LR 10 Eq 73 . . . . .4.88
Shipway v Broadwood [1899] 1 QB 369 (CA). 8.55, 8.56, 10.23
Shivas v Bank of New Zealand [1990] 2 NZLR 327 . . . . 5.51, 6.69
Shizelle, The [1992] 2 Lloyd's Rep 444 . . . . .21.55
Shogun Finance Ltd v Hudson [2004] 1 AC 919. . . . . 1.46, 1.79, 10.24, 14.12, 29.36
Shortt v MacLennan [1959] SCR 3 . . . . .7.34, 7.37, 23.73, 27.05, 27.14, 27.32
Showa Oil Tanker Co Ltd of Japan v Maravan SA of Caracas (The Larissa)
      [1983] 2 Lloyd's Rep 325 . . . . .4.105
Shuman v Coober Pedy Tours Pty Ltd (1994) 175 LSJS 159 . . . . .11.04, 11.101, 24.37, 24.56
SIB v Pantell SA [1992] 3 WLR 896 (CA). 18.69

TABLE OF CASES lxv

Sibbering v Earl of Balcarras (1850) 3 De G & SM 735, 64 ER 682 . . . . .24.31, 24.80, 24.81, 24.107
Sibley v Grosvenor (1916) 21 CLR 469. . . . . . . .2.03, 2.05, 2.06, 15.57, 17.05, 17.42, 17.43, 17.62, 19.10
Siboen, The and The Sibotre *See* Occidental Worldwide Investment Corp v
    Skibs A/S Avanti (The Siboen and Sibotre)
Sieff v Fox [2005] 1 WLR 3811 . . . . .1.60, 13.32, 29.41, 29.42, 29.44, 29.52, 29.53
Silkstone and Haigh Moor Coal Company v Edey [1900] 1 Ch 167. . . . . .17.16
Silver Queen Maritime Ltd v Persia Petroleum Services plc [2010] EWHC 2867 (QB). 5.59
Sim Poh Ping v Winsta Holdings Pte Ltd [2020] 1 SLR 1199. . . . . .17.34
Simmer v Copithorne [2018] ABQB 525. . . . . .11.04, 11.14
Simner v New India Assurance Co Ltd [1995] 1 Lloyd's Rep IR 240. . . . . .5.29
Simons v Zartom Investments Pty Ltd [1975] 2 NSWLR 30 . . . . .11.101, 27.42
Simpson v Moffat Communications Ltd [1983] BCJ No 2089 (BCCA). 7.103
Simpson v Simpson [1989] Fam Law 20 . . . . .6.100
Simpson v Walker (1831) 5 Sim 1, 58 ER 238 . . . . .3.42, 22.06
Sinclair v Brougham [1924] AC 398. . . . . 1.46, 14.39, 21.56
Sinclair Investments (UK) Ltd v Versailles Trade Finance Ltd [2012] Ch 453 (CA). 21.18
Singla v Bashir [2002] EWHC 883 . . . . 7.75, 7.82, 7.91
Six Continents Hotels Inc v Event Hotels GmbH [2006] EWHC 2317 . . . . 26.15, 26.28, 26.30
SK Shipping Europe Plc v Capital VLCC 3 Corp (The C Challenger) [2020]
    EWHC 3448 (Comm), [2021] 2 Lloyd's Rep 109; on appeal [2022]
    EWCA Civ 231, [2022] 1 Lloyd's Rep 521 (CA) 4.22, 4.108, 10.23, 11.96,
              23.05, 23.28, 23.40, 23.56, 23.58, 23.61, 23.62, 23.68, 23.85, 23.94, 23.95, 23.96,
              24.65, 28.03, 28.05, 28.11, 28.12, 28.13, 28.16, 28.22, 28.32, 28.33
Skeate v Beale (1840) 11 Ad & El 983, 113 ER 688 . . . . 6.21, 6.24
Skogan v Worthman [2010] MBQB 194 . . . . .7.36
Slater's Trusts, Re (1879) 11 ChD 227. . . . . 21.08, 21.25, 21.38
Slough Estates plc v Welwyn and Hatfield DC [1996] 2 PLR 50 . . . . .4.76
Small v Attwood (1832) You 407, 159 ER 1051 . . . . .3.42, 14.23, 14.33, 15.19, 16.11,
              16.42, 17.04, 17.43, 21.04, 21.48
Smith (Dec'd), Re [2015] 4 All ER 329 . . . . 7.52, 7.57
Smith v Chadwick (1882) 20 ChD 27 (CA); on appeal
    (1884) 9 App Cas 187 (HL) 4.08, 4.17, 4.44, 4.63, 4.66, 4.67, 4.103, 4.112, 4.117
Smith v Charlick (William) Ltd (1924) 34 CLR 38 . . . . 6.38, 6.54
Smith v Clay (1767) 3 Bro CC 646, 29 ER 743. . . . . .24.14
Smith v Cooper [2010] EWCA Civ 722; [2010] 2 FLR 1521 (CA) 6.107, 6.115, 6.117,
              6.118, 13.02, 17.14
Smith v Eric S Bush [1990] 1 AC 831 . . . . .4.120
Smith v Hughes (1871) LR 6 QB 597 (CA) 4.30, 5.03, 5.11, 7.12, 9.06
Smith v Kay (1859) 7 HLC 750, 11 ER 299. . . . . .4.66, 4.90, 4.104, 6.80, 6.85, 18.59
Smith v Land and House Property Corp (1884) 28 ChD 7 (CA) 4.46, 4.53, 4.112
Smith Kline & French Laboratories Ltd v Long [1989] 1 WLR 1 (CA) 4.61
Smith New Court Securities Ltd v Citibank NA *See* Smith New Court Securities Ltd v
    Scrimgeour Vickers (Asset Management) Ltd
Smith New Court Securities Ltd v Scrimgeour Vickers (Asset Management) Ltd
    [1994] 1 WLR 1271 (CA); on appeal sub nom Smith New Court Securities Ltd v
    Citibank NA [1997] AC 254 . . . . .2.08, 4.07, 15.16, 17.56, 18.53, 18.61, 18.64
Smithson v Hamilton [2008] 1 WLR 1453. . . . . .29.56
Society of Lloyds v Khan [1998] 3 FCR 93. . . . . 18.102, 20.31
Society of Lloyds v Leighs [1997] 6 Re LR 289 (CA). 18.102, 20.31, 20.32
Society of Lloyds v Lyons [1997] CLC 1398 (CA). 10.09, 11.80, 11.107
Soden v British and Commonwealth Holdings plc [1995] 1 BCLC 686 (CA);
    on appeal [1998] AC 298 . . . . 14.22, 25.28, 25.40, 25.49, 25.50, 25.56
Solle v Butcher [1950] 1 KB 671 (CA). 7.07, 7.29, 7.30, 10.26, 11.86, 11.92, 19.22, 19.24, 19.25, 27.22
Sollis v Leyshon [2018] EWHC 2853 (Ch) 6.117
Somes v British Empire Shipping Co (1860) 8 HLC 338, 11 ER 459. . . . . .6.24
Sons of Gwalia Ltd v Margaretic (2007) 231 CLR 160 . . . . 14.22, 14.72, 25.28, 25.34,
              25.38, 25.39, 25.50, 25.56, 25.78

lxvi   TABLE OF CASES

Sons of Gwalia Ltd v Margaretic (2005) 149 FCR 227 (Full Ct) 25.38, 25.39, 25.50, 25.56
Soper v Arnold (1887) 37 ChD 96 (CA). 27.05
South Australia Asset Management Corporation v York Montague [1997] AC 191 . . . . 2.08, 28.19
South Western General Property Co Ltd v Marton [1982] EGD 113. . . . . .26.15
South Western Mineral Water Company Ltd v Ashmore [1967] 1 WLR 1110 . . . . .15.51
Southern British National Trust Ltd v Pither (1936) 57 CLR 89 . . . . .21.24, 21.25, 21.33,
                                                                                              21.38, 25.21, 25.28, 25.38, 25.61
Southern Cross Mine Management Pty Ltd v Ensham Resources Pty Ltd
        [2005] QSC 233. . . . . .11.101, 21.71, 23.13, 23.31, 23.43, 23.105,
                                                                                  23.106, 23.109, 24.12, 24.39, 24.43, 24.100, 24.113
Southern Woollen-Mills, Re [1930] 1 NZLR 10 . . . . .24.88, 25.28, 25.69, 25.75
Special Trustees for Great Ormond Street Hospital for Children v Rushin
        [2003] All ER (D) 598 . . . . .7.46, 29.09, 29.21, 29.61
Spector v Ageda [1973] 1 Ch 30 . . . . 8.25, 8.26
Spence v Crawford [1939] 3 All ER 271 (HL Sc). 4.16, 10.04, 11.86, 11.87, 11.107, 12.23, 13.01,
                                                                          13.08, 13.10, 13.12, 13.13, 15.07, 15.11, 17.04, 17.27, 17.56,
                                                                          18.01, 18.04, 18.05, 18.07, 18.09, 18.10, 18.11, 18.33,
                                                                          18.39, 18.42, 18.108, 18.109, 18.110, 18.112, 18.120
Spencer v Handley and Burges (1842) 4 Man & G 414, 134 ER 169 . . . . 9.05, 29.79
Spice Girls Ltd v Aprilia World Services BV [2002] EWCA 15 . . . . . . .4.35, 4.40, 4.43, 4.93, 4.100, 9.04
Spriggs v Wessington Court Schools Ltd [2005] 1 Lloyd's Rep IR 474 . . . . . . 11.39, 23.21, 23.40, 23.59,
                                                                          23.62, 23.75, 23.76, 23.82, 23.85, 23.101, 23.105, 23.107, 24.68, 24.109, 24.111
Springwell Navigation Corp v JP Morgan [2008] EWHC 1186 (Comm);
        aff'd [2010] 2 CLC 705 (CA) 26.03, 26.07, 26.11, 26.17, 26.21
Spurrier v Elderton (1803) 4 Esp 1, 170 ER 717 . . . . .3.25
Stadium Finance Ltd v Robbins [1962] 2 QB 664 (CA) 21.74
Standard Chartered Bank v Ceylon Petroleum Corp [2011] EWHC 1785 (Comm) 26.29
Standard Chartered Bank v Pakistan National Shipping Corp (No 2)
        [2003] 1 AC 959 . . . . 4.104, 4.105, 4.120
Standing v Bowring (1885) 31 ChD 282 (CA). 14.74, 29.13, 29.14
Stapilton v Stapilton (1739) 1 Atk 2, 26 ER 1 . . . . .5.15
Stapleford Colliery Company, Re (1879) 14 ChD 432 . . . . .1.67
Star v O'Brien (1996) 22 ACSR 434 (NSWCA) 17.22
Statoil ASA v Louis Dreyfus Energy Services LP (The "Harriette N")
        [2009] 1 All ER (Comm) 1035 . . . . 7.12, 7.15
Statoil ASA v Louis Dreyfus Energy Services LP [2008] EWHC 2257 (Comm). 5.03
Steedman v Frigidaire Corporation [1933] 1 DLR 161 (PC–Canada) 11.24, 15.60, 18.78, 18.124
Stent v Bailis (1724) 2 P Wms 217, 24 ER 705 . . . . .3.37
Stephens v Lord Viscount Bateman (1778) 1 Bro CC 2, 28 ER 962. . . . . .5.14
Stepney v Biddulph (1865) 13 WR 576. . . . . .17.40
Steven v Bromley & Son [1919] 2 KB 722 (HL). 1.51
Stevenson v Mortimer (1778) 2 Cowp 805, 98 ER 1372. . . . . .3.25
Stevenson v Newnham (1853) 13 CB 285, 138 ER 1208 . . . . . . 3.41, 14.03, 14.31, 16.02, 20.11, 21.05, 21.57
Stewart v Complex 329 Ltd (1990) 109 NBR (2d) 117 . . . . 18.37, 20.08
Stewart v Kennedy (No 2) (1890) 15 App Cas 108 . . . . .7.35
Stewart Gill Ltd v Horatio Myer & Co Ltd [1992] 2 QB 600 (CA). 26.25, 26.27
Stirling Homes Corporation, in the Matter of 578 F 2d 206 (1978) (USCA 2d Cir) 25.39
Stocznia Gdanska SA v Latvian Shipping Co [1998] 1 WLR 574 (HL) 1.21, 1.31
Stoddart v Union Trust Ltd [1912] 1 KB 181 (CA) 21.23, 21.26, 21.36
Stone v City and County Bank Ltd (1877) 3 CPD 282 (CA) . . . 20.36, 25.27, 25.34, 25.46, 25.58, 25.60
Stone v Compton (1838) 5 Bing NC 142, 132 ER 1059. . . . . .9.05
Stone v Godfrey (1853) 1 Sm & G 590, 65 ER 258, aff'd 5 De GM & G 76, 43 ER 798. . . . . .5.14
Strait Colonies Pte Ltd v SMRT Alpha Pte Ltd [2018] SGCA 36. 23.50, 23.51,
                                                                                              23.51, 23.55, 23.58, 23.61
Street v Blay (1831) 2 B & AD 456, 109 ER 1212 . . . . 3.27, 11.47, 14.36, 14.37,
                                                                                              14.54, 14.69, 18.50, 18.54, 18.84

TABLE OF CASES lxvii

Streeter v Western Areas Exploration Pty Ltd
(2011) 278 ALR 291 (WACA) 24.17, 24.59, 24.74, 24.84, 24.100, 24.103, 24.114
Strive Shipping Corporation v Hellenic Mutual War Risks Association
(The Grecia Express) [2002] 2 Lloyd's Rep 88 . . . . 1.16, 5.26, 23.61, 23.68, 23.85, 23.93, 24.109
Strive Shipping Corporation v Hellenic Mutual War Risks Association
(The Grecia Express) [2002] Lloyd's Rep IR 669 . . . . .10.27, 10.29
Strode v Blackburne (1789) 3 Ves 222, 30 ER 979 . . . . .21.61
Strother v 3464920 Canada Inc [2007] 2 SCR 177 . . . . 8.34, 8.40, 8.44
Strover v Harrington [1988] Ch 390 . . . . .4.114, 4.119
Strutt v Smith (1834) 1 CM & R 312, 149 ER 1099 . . . . 3.08, 3.09, 3.27, 14.34, 20.13
Strydom v Vendside Ltd [2009] EWHC 2130 (QB) 7.70, 7.89, 7.92
Stuart v Wilkins (1788) 1 Doug 18, 99 ER 15 . . . . .3.19
Stump v Gaby (1852) 2 De M & G 623, 42 ER 1015 . . . . 3.45, 3.46, 16.42, 22.06, 29.81
Sturge v Starr (1833) 2 My & K 195, 39 ER 918 . . . . 9.03, 29.20
Sturge v Sturge (1849) 12 Beav 229, 50 ER 1049 . . . . .5.59
Sturgis v Champneys (1839) 5 My & Cr 97, 41 ER 308 . . . . .15.47
Sumpter v Hedges [1898] 1 QB 673 . . . . .1.30
Sutton (Dec'd), Re [2009] EWHC 2576 (Ch) 7.54
Sutton v Mishcon de Reya [2003] EWHC 3166 . . . . .6.85
Sutton v Sutton [2009] EWHC 2576 (Ch) 7.45, 7.46, 29.09, 29.10, 29.21
Svanosio v McNamara (1956) 96 CLR 186 . . . . .7.28, 7.31, 7.32, 7.33, 16.25, 27.06, 27.08, 27.12, 27.29
Svenska Handelsbanken v Sun Alliance and London Insurance plc
[1996] 1 Lloyd's Rep 519 . . . . 10.27, 23.77, 23.85, 23.93, 24.65, 24.73, 24.109, 24.111
Swift v Jewsbury See Swift v Winterbotham
Swift v Winterbotham (1873) LR 8 QB 244; on appeal sub nom Swift v Jewsbury
(1874) LR 9 QB 301 . . . . .4.76
Swinburne, Re [1926] Ch 38 . . . . .29.06
Swindle v Harrison [1997] 4 All ER 705 (CA) 2.10, 8.10, 8.18, 8.72
Swindle v Knibb (1929) 29 St Rep NSW 325 . . . . .1.20
Swordheath Properties Ltd v Tabet [1979] 1 WLR 285 (CA) 17.07
Sycamore Bidco Ltd v Breslin [2012] EWHC 3443 (Ch) 4.22
Sykes v Taylor-Rose [2004] EWCA 299 . . . . 4.53, 4.55, 4.56
Synergy Health (UK) Ltd v CGU Insurance plc [2011] Lloyd's Rep IR 500 . . . . .5.33
Sze Tu v Lowe (2014) 89 NSWLR 317 (CA) 1.98
Szep v Blanken [1969] SASR 65 . . . . .23.44

T & J Harrison v Knowles & Foster [1918] 1 KB 608 (CA) 27.22, 27.53
Taber v Paris Boutique & Bridal Inc [2010] ONCA 157 . . . . .6.27
Taberna Europe CDO II Plc v Selskabet [2017] QB 633 (CA) 4.80
Taheri v Vitek [2014] NSWCA 209; 87 NSWLR 403 (CA) 18.27, 19.06, 20.32
Tajik Aluminium Plant v Ermatov (No 3) [2006] EWHC 7 (Ch) 1.87, 1.88
Takhar v Gracefield Developments Limited [2020] AC 450 (Sup Ct) 4.13
Talbot v Von Boris [1911] 1 KB 854 (CA) 9.03, 9.05
Tamvaco v Simpson (1866) LR 1 CP 363 . . . . .6.21
Tapp v Galway (2007) 8 NZCPR 684 . . . . .23.70
Tate v Williamson (1866) 2 Ch App 55 . . . . .6.100, 6.117, 8.07, 17.12
Tawanui Developments Limited v DM Harnett [2009] NZHC 501 . . . . .23.36
Taylor v Ashton (1843) 11 M & W 401, 152 ER 86 . . . . .4.05
Taylor v Chester (1869) LR 4 QB 309 . . . . .14.27
Taylor v Johnson (1983) 151 CLR 422 . . . . 4.31, 5.11, 7.20, 7.32, 29.19
Taylor v Johnson (1882) 19 ChD 603 . . . . .6.103
Taylor v Motability Finance Ltd [2004] EWHC 2619 . . . . .1.30
Taylor v Schofield Peterson [1999] 3 NZLR 434 (CA) 8.40
Taylor v Walker [1958] 1 Ll L R 490 . . . . 8.52, 8.54, 8.56, 8.58, 8.61, 8.63
Telfair Shipping Corporation v Athos Shipping Co SA (The Athos)
[1981] 2 Lloyd's Rep 74; aff'd [1983] 1 Lloyd's Rep 127 (CA) 23.05, 24.109, 24.118
Tenax Steamship Co Ltd v The Brimness (owners) [1975] 1 QB 929 (CA) 11.37, 11.38

lxviii TABLE OF CASES

Tenji v Henneberry & Associates Pty Ltd (2000) 98 FCR 324 (Full Ct) 11.04, 11.48, 13.18, 15.60, 19.36, 23.13, 23.71, 24.12
Tennent v The City of Glasgow Bank and Liquidators (1879) 4 App Cas 615 (HL Sc) 20.01, 20.28, 20.36, 25.27, 25.34, 25.35, 25.36, 25.51, 25.63, 25.65, 25.67, 25.68
Thames Guarantee Ltd v Campbell [1985] QB 210 (CA) 18.03
Thames Trains Ltd v Adams [2006] EWHC 3291 . . . . .7.14
Thayer v Turner 49 Mass 550 (1844) 14.64, 14.65
Thomas v Arthur Hughes Pty Ltd [2015] NSWSC 1027 . . . . 11.100, 11.101, 16.21
Thomas v Beals 154 Mass 51, 27 NE 1004 (1891) 11.65, 12.04
Thomas v Powell (1794) 2 Cox 394, 30 ER 182 . . . . .27.05
Thomas Bates and Son Ltd v Wyndham's (Lingerie) Ltd [1981] 1 WLR 505 (CA) 7.19
Thomas Borthwick & Sons (Australasia) Ltd v South Otago Freezing Co Ltd
    [1978] 1 NZLR 538 (CA) 27.51
Thomas Witter Ltd v TBP Industries Ltd [1996] 2 All ER 573 . . . . 4.90, 4.102, 18.89, 18.124, 20.03, 20.04, 20.08, 26.06, 26.20, 26.27, 26.28, 28.08
Thompson v Foy [2009] EWHC 1076 (Ch) 6.86, 6.87, 6.91, 6.93, 6.100, 6.108
Thompson v Vincent [2001] 3 NZLR 355 . . . . .4.33
Thomson v Eastwood (1877) 2 App Cas 215 (HL Ir) 6.103, 8.08, 8.26
Thomson v Weems (1884) 9 App Cas 671 . . . . .4.40
Thornbridge Ltd v Barclays Bank Plc [2015] EWHC 3430 (QB) 26.20
Thorne v Kennedy (2017) 263 CLR 85 . . . . 6.103, 6.115
Thorne v Motor Trade Association [1937] AC 797 . . . . .6.44
Thorpe v Fasey [1949] 1 Ch 649 . . . . 18.49, 19.06
Thynn v Thynn (1684) 1 Vern 296, 23 ER 47 . . . . .3.43
Tigris International NV v China Southern Airlines Co Ltd [2014] EWCA Civ 1649 . . . . .8.49
Tilley v Bowman [1910] 1 KB 745 (CA) 21.05, 25.04
Times Travel (UK) Ltd v Pakistan International Airlines Corp [2017] EWHC 1367 (Ch) 6.44
Tiong Swee Eng v Yeo Khee Siang [2015] SGHC 116 . . . . .5.19, 5.20, 5.59, 28.13, 28.15, 28.16
Tiplady v Gold Coast Carlton (1984) 8 FCR 438 . . . . .23.44
Titan Steel Wheels Ltd v Royal Bank of Scotland [2010] 2 Lloyd's Rep 92 . . . . 26.20, 26.26
Tito v Waddell (No 2) [1977] Ch 106 . . . . 1.70, 1.72, 8.03, 8.09, 8.10, 24.33, 24.54
Tobacconists Ltd, Re [1931] NZLR 289 . . . . .25.57
Toksoz v Westpac Banking Corp (2012) 289 ALR 557 (NSWCA) 1.98
Toma v Olcorn [2019] VSCA 116 . . . . .7.21
Toner v Telford Homes Ltd [2021] EWHC 516 (QB) 26.03, 26.22
Toomey v Eagle Star Insurance Co Ltd (No 2) [1995] 2 Lloyd's Rep 88 . . . . 4.83, 26.02, 26.03
Tootal Clothing Ltd v Guinea Properties Management Ltd (1992) 64 P & CR 452 (CA) 1.36, 1.47
Tociapski v Tociapski [2013] EWHC 1770 (Ch) 6.108
Topham v Duke of Portland (1869) 5 Ch App 40 . . . . .29.52
Topham v Topham Group Ltd [2003] 1 BCLC 123 . . . . 7.29, 11.92, 19.25
Toronto Dominion Bank v Rooke (1983) 3 DLR (4th) 715 (BCCA) 5.43, 5.52, 5.55
Total Oil Great Britain Ltd v Thompson Garages (Biggin Hill) Ltd [1972] 1 QB 318 (CA) 1.24
Tottenham v Green (1863) 32 LJ Ch (NS) 201 . . . . 3.50, 16.12, 21.70
Toussaint v Martinnant (1787) 2 TR 100, 100 ER 55 . . . . .3.25
Towers v Barrett (1786) 1 TR 133, 99 ER 1014 . . . . 3.02, 3.18, 3.23, 3.24, 3.27, 3.28, 3.29
Toyota Finance Australia Ltd v Dennis (2002) 58 NSWLR 101 (CA) 14.18, 14.19
Tracy v Mandalay Pty Ltd (1953) 88 CLR 215 . . . . 2.11, 2.28, 2.32, 2.39
Tradax Export SA v European Grain & Shipping Ltd [1983] 2 Lloyd's Rep 100 . . . . .1.24
Trade Indemnity Co Ltd v Workington Harbour and Dock Board (No 1) [1937] AC 1 (HL) 5.48
Traditional Structures Ltd v HW Construction Ltd [2010] EWHC 1530 (TCC);
    [2010] CILL 2899 . . . . .7.19
Traill v Baring (1864) 4 De GJ & S 318, 46 ER 941 . . . . .3.35, 3.55, 3.58, 3.62, 4.90, 4.96
Trans-Canada Trading Co Ltd v M Loeb Ltd [1947] 2 DLR 849 (Ont HC) 18.58
Transvaal Lands Co v New Belgium (Transvaal) Land and Development Co
    [1914] 2 Ch 488 (CA) 8.19, 15.11, 15.63
Trasler v Purser (1848, VC) in Seton on Decrees (2nd edn, 1854) 302 . . . . .15.10

TABLE OF CASES lxix

Treadwell v Martin (1976) 67 DLR (3d) 493 (NBSC (App Div)). .15.22, 20.27
Trendtex Trading Corp v Credit Suisse [1982] 1 AC 679. . . . . .22.10, 22.14
Trevelyan v Charter (1846) 9 Beav 140, 50 ER 297 . . . . 15.10, 15.38, 20.25
Trevelyan v Charter (1835) 4 LJ (NS) 209; aff'd (1844) 11 Cl & Fin 714, 8 ER 1273 . . . . . . 15.17, 20.25, 21.04
Trevelyan v White (1839) 1 Beav 588, 48 ER 1069 . . . . .17.04, 17.42
Trevor v Whitworth (1887) 12 App Cas 409 . . . . .25.40
Trident Turboprop (Dublin) Ltd v First Flight Couriers Ltd [2008] 2 Lloyd's Rep 581;
    aff'd [2010] QB 86 (CA). 26.06, 26.32
Tri-star Customs and Forwarding Ltd v Denning [1999] 1 NZLR 33 (CA). 7.23
Tropical Traders Ltd v Goonan (1964) 111 CLR 41 . . . . .11.08, 23.61, 23.98, 23.103, 24.109
Trower v Newcome (1813) 3 Mer 704, 36 ER 270 . . . . .4.45
Truman (Ltd) v Attenborough *See* W Truman (Ltd) v Attenborough
Trustee of the Property of FC Jones & Sons (a firm) v Jones [1997] Ch 159 (CA). 16.09
Trustees of Beardsley Theobalds Retirement Benefit Scheme v Yardley
    [2011] EWHC 1380 (QB) 6.100
TSB Bank plc v Camfield [1995] 1 WLR 430 (CA) 9.01, 11.80, 11.93, 11.107, 13.11, 13.14,
                    19.04, 19.18, 19.20, 19.21, 19.26, 19.31, 19.33, 19.34, 19.35, 19.40, 28.12
Tudor Grange Holdings Ltd v Citibank [1992] Ch 53 . . . . .4.59
Tufton v Sperni [1952] 2 TLR 516 (CA). 6.98, 6.100, 6.107
Tuiara v Frost & Sutcliffe (a firm) [2003] 2 NZLR 833 . . . . 8.36, 8.40, 8.41
Turkey v Awadh [2005] EWCA 382 . . . . .6.111
Turner v Collins (1871) 7 Ch App 329 . . . . .24.62, 24.82, 24.86, 29.51
Turner v Green [1895] 2 Ch 205 . . . . 4.29, 5.03, 5.59
Turner v Harvey (1821) Jac 169, 37 ER 814 . . . . .4.30
Turner v Labafox International Pty Ltd (1974) 131 CLR 660 . . . . 23.42, 23.46, 23.48
Turner v Trelawney (1841) 12 Sim 49, 59 ER 1049 . . . . .8.46
Turner v Windever [2003] NSWSC 1147. . . . . .7.70
Turton v Benson (1718) 1 P Wms 496, 24 ER 488. . . . . 3.37, 3.42, 20.29, 21.23, 21.32, 21.33, 21.38
Tutt v Doyle (1997) 42 NSWLR 10 (CA) 3.50, 7.32, 11.92, 15.09, 16.12, 27.12
Twinsectra Ltd v Yardley [1999] Lloyd's Bank Rep 438 (CA); [2002] AC 164. . . . . 1.81, 1.92, 3.50,
                    13.29, 15.19, 16.12, 16.35, 16.36, 16.41, 16.42, 16.60, 21.04, 21.08, 21.62, 21.63
Twycross v Grant (1878) 4 CPD 40. . . . . .22.07
Tyrell, Re (1900) 82 LT 675 . . . . .7.28

UBS AG v Kommunale Wasserwerke Leipzig GmbH [2017] EWCA Civ 1567,
    [2017] 2 Lloyd's Rep 621 (CA) 8.67, 8.68, 8.69, 8.70, 8.73, 9.05, 11.95,
                    12.22, 18.108, 18.116, 19.05, 28.36
UCB Corporate Services Ltd v Thomason [2004] 2 All ER (Comm) 774;
    aff'd [2005] 1 All ER (Comm) 601 (CA) 4.105, 28.07, 28.13, 28.15, 28.16, 28.19, 28.23
UCB Corporate Services Ltd v Williams [2002] 3 FCR 448 (CA). .4.104, 6.89
UCB Group Ltd v Hedworth [2003] EWCA 1717 . . . . .6.89
Udell v Atherton (1861) 7 H & N 172, 158 ER 437 . . . . .18.84, 18.91
Ukraine v Law Debenture Trust Corp Plc [2019] QB 1121 (CA) 6.30
Union Bank of Australia Ltd v Puddy [1949] VLR 242 . . . . .5.44
United Australia v Barclays Bank Ltd [1941] AC 1 . . . . .14.29
United Enterprises v Freyer [2005] 1 Qd R 337. . . . . .13.32, 29.09
United Kingdom Ship Owning Company Ltd (Felgate's case), Re
    (1865) 2 De GJ & S 456, 46 ER 451 . . . . .9.03
United Pan-Europe Ltd v Deutsche Bank AG [2002] 2 BCLC 461 (CA) 2.17
United Ports and General Insurance Company (Back's case), Re (1874) 9 Ch App 392. . . . . .25.57
United Shoe Machinery Company of Canada v Brunet [1909] AC 330 (PC–Canada) . . . 11.03, 11.18,
                    11.41, 12.06, 19.02, 23.18, 23.36, 23.41, 23.89, 24.65, 29.82
United States of America v Macrae (1867) LR 3 HL 89 . . . . .13.09
United States Surgical Corp v Hospital Products International Pty Ltd
    [1983] 2 NSWLR 157 (CA) 21.71

lxx TABLE OF CASES

Universe Sentinel, The *See* Universe Tankships Inc of Monrovia v International
    Transport Workers Federation
Universe Tankships Inc of Monrovia v International Transport Workers Federation
    (The Universe Sentinel) [1983] 1 AC 366 . . . . 6.03, 6.12, 6.25, 6.26, 6.27, 6.28, 6.31, 6.37,
                                        6.38, 6.41, 6.44, 6.47, 6.48, 6.50, 6.71, 6.72, 14.07
University of Canterbury v Attorney-General [1995] 1 NZLR 78 . . . . .29.37
Urquhart v MacPherson (1878) 3 App Cas 831 (PC–Australia) 18.01, 18.04, 19.02, 19.06
USA v McRae (1867) LR 3 HL 79 . . . . .15.48
UTB LLC v Sheffield United Limited [2019] EWHC 2322 (Ch) 5.03, 7.12, 7.15

Vadasz v Pioneer Concrete (SA) Pty Ltd (1995) 184 CLR 102 . . . . .2.09, 13.19, 13.20, 13.21, 13.22,
                                18.116, 18.117, 18.120, 19.26, 19.27, 19.28, 19.29, 19.30, 19.31,
                                        19.34, 19.35, 19.36, 19.37, 19.38, 19.39, 19.41, 19.44
Vail v Reynolds 118 NY 297, 23 NE 301 (1890) 14.64
Vald Nielsen Holding A/ S v Baldorino [2019] EWHC 1926 (Comm) 4.74, 4.104
Vale v Armstrong [2004] EWHC 1160 . . . . .6.107, 6.109, 6.110, 6.117
Vale SA v Steinmetz [2020] EWHC Comm 3051 . . . . . . .16.12, 16.45, 16.48, 16.51, 16.61, 16.62, 16.70
Van der Merwe v Goldman [2016] 4 WLR 71 . . . . 7.05, 29.29, 29.42, 29.44, 29.56
Vane v Vane (1873) 8 Ch App 383 . . . . 16.42, 21.04, 24.96
Vantage Navigation Corporation v Suhail & Saud Bahwan Building Materials
    (The Alev) [1989] 1 Lloyd's Rep 138 . . . . 6.23, 6.31, 6.46, 6.56, 6.57
Vee Networks v Econet Wireless International Ltd [2005] 1 Lloyd's Rep 192 . . . . .1.16
Vernon v Bethell (1762) 2 Eden 110, 28 ER 838 . . . . .7.75
Versloot Dredging BV v HDI Gerling Industrie Versicherung AG
    [2017] AC 1 (Sup Ct) 4.104, 5.27, 5.32, 5.33
Vigers v Pike (1842) 8 Cl & F 562, 8 ER 220 . . . . .4.114, 18.86, 24.09, 24.58
Vimig Pty Ltd v Contract Tooling Pty Ltd (1987) 9 NSWLR 731 . . . . .27.22, 27.23, 27.24, 27.29
Viscount Clermount v Tasburgh (1819) 1 Jac & W 112, 37 ER 318 . . . . 3.40, 4.58
Vitek v Taheri [2013] NSWSC 589 . . . . .27.29
Vitek v Taheri (2014) 87 NSWLR 403 (CA) 19.06, 20.32
Vitol SA v Norelf Ltd (The Santa Clara) [1996] AC 800 . . . . .11.07
Vivendi SA v Richards [2013] BCC 771 . . . . .24.33
Vorley v Cooke (1857) 1 Giff 230, 65 ER 898 . . . . .3.41
Vyvyan v Vyvyan (1861) 30 Beav 165, 54 ER 813; aff'd 4 De G F & J 183, 45 ER 11 . . . . .24.58

W, Re [2001] Ch 609 (CA) 7.52
W Truman (Ltd) v Attenborough (1910) 26 TLR 601 . . . . 14.03, 14.14, 16.02, 20.15, 21.05, 21.57
Waddell v Blockley (1879) 4 QBD 678 (CA) 2.08
Wait, Re [1927] 1 Ch 606 (CA) 27.53
Wakefield v Newbon [1844] 6 QB 276, 115 ER 107 . . . . .6.24
Wakefield and Barnsley Banking Company v The Normanton Local Board
    (1881) 40 LT 697 . . . . .21.23, 23.28
Wales v Wadham [1977] 1 WLR 199 . . . . 4.58, 4.95, 4.116, 5.16, 5.19, 5.59, 5.60
Walker, Re [1905] 1 Ch 160 (CA) 7.58
Walker v Boyle [1982] 1 WLR 495 . . . . 26.03, 26.14, 26.29
Walker v Constable (1798) 1 B & P 306, 126 ER 919 . . . . .17.21
Walker v Galt 171 F 2d 613 (1948) 15.46
Wall v Cockerell (1863) 10 HLC 229, 11 ER 1013 . . . . .24.10, 24.43, 24.48, 24.53
Waller v Dalt (1676) Dickens 7, 21 ER 169 . . . . .15.52
Wallis Trading Inc v Air Tanzania Co Ltd [2020] EWHC 339 (Comm) .6.75
Waller v Waller (1619) in J Ritchie, Reports of Cases Decided by Francis Bacon in
    the High Court of Chancery (1617–1621) (1932) 156 . . . . .3.52
Wallwyn v Lee (1803) 9 Ves Jun 24, 32 ER 509 . . . . .21.61, 21.66
Walstab v Spottiswoode (1846) 15 M & W 501, 153 ER 947 . . . . 3.25, 3.27
Walters v Morgan (1861) 3 De GF & J 718, 45 ER 1056 . . . . .4.26
Wambo Coal Pty Ltd v Ariff (2007) 63 ACSR 429 (Sup Ct NSW) 1.93, 1.98
Wandinger v Lake (1977) 78 DLR (3d) 305 (Ont HC) 18.60

TABLE OF CASES   lxxi

Wang v Shao [2018] BCSC 377 . . . . .4.55
Ware & De Freville Ltd v Motor Trade Association [1921] 3 KB 40 (CA) .6.12
Warman International Ltd v Dwyer (1995) 182 CLR 544 . . . . .2.17
Waterloo Motors Ltd v Flood [1931] 1 DLR 762 (NBCA). 18.88
Waters Motors Pty Ltd v Cratchley (1964) 80 WN (NSW) 1165. . . . . .14.19, 17.29, 18.120,
                                                                       20.01, 20.26, 20.34
Waterview Property Limited v Gardner [2016] NZHC 2247 . . . . 4.59, 4.60
Watford Electronics Ltd v Sanderson CFL Ltd [2001] BLR 143;
    [2001] All ER (D) 290 . . . . .26.10, 26.20, 26.27, 26.31
Watkin v Watson-Smith, The Times 3 July 1986. . . . . 7.75, 7.87
Watson v Burton [1957] 1 WLR 19. . . . . .23.84, 24.102
Watson v Cullen (1886) 5 NZLR 17. . . . . 7.33, 27.12
Watson v Huber [2005] All ER (D) 156 . . . . .6.107
Watson v Massachusetts Mutual Life Insurance Co 140 F 2d 673 (DC Cir 1943);
    cert denied 322 US 746 (1944) 18.64
Watt v Westhoven [1933] VLR 458 (Full Ct). 27.48, 27.50, 27.51
Wauton v Coppard [1899] 1 ChD 92 . . . . .9.04
Way v Latilla [1937] 3 All ER 759 (HL) 15.43
Way's Trust, Re (1864) 2 De G J & S 365, 46 ER 416 . . . . .3.52
Weaver v Boroughs (1726) 1 Str 648, 93 ER 757 . . . . .3.23
Webb Distributors (Aust) Pty Ltd v Victoria
    (1993) 179 CLR 15 . . . . 25.28, 25.38, 25.40, 25.49, 25.50, 25.78
Webster v Havyn Pty Ltd [2004] NSWSC 227. . . . . .11.41
Weld v Petre [1929] 1 Ch 33 (CA). 24.08, 24.108, 24.114
Wells v Smith [1914] 3 KB 722 . . . . .4.114
Welven Ltd v Soar Group Ltd [2011] EWHC 3240 (Comm). 4.118
Wentworth v Rogers [2004] NSWCA 430 . . . . .21.72
West v National Motor and Accident Union Ltd [1955] 1 Lloyd's Rep 207 (CA) 11.41
West London Commercial Bank v Kitson (1884) 13 QBD 360 (CA). 4.13, 4.17
West Sussex Properties Ltd v Chichester District Council
    [2000] EWCA Civ 205 . . . . 11.24, 11.25, 12.23, 13.10, 16.56, 17.18
Westdeutsche Landesbank Girozentrale v Islington LBC [1996] AC 669;
    [1994] 1 WLR 938 (CA). 1.36, 1.46, 1.55, 1.93, 14.39, 16.56, 16.70, 17.18, 17.19, 29.32
Westdeutsche Landesbank Girozentrale v Islington LBC; Kleinwort Benson Ltd v
    Sandwell Borough Council [1994] 4 All ER 890. . . . . .17.18, 27.26
Western Bank of Scotland, The v Addie (1867) LR 1 Sc App 145 . . . . .13.01, 17.56, 18.01,
                                                                       18.02, 18.04, 18.87, 18.93
Westminster Bank Ltd v Lee [1956] 1 Ch 7 . . . . .21.70
Weston v Downes (1778) 1 Doug 23, 99 ER 19 . . . . 3.02, 3.18, 3.23, 3.24, 3.26, 3.28, 3.29
Westpac v Cockerill (1998) 152 ALR 267 (FCA) 6.40
Westpac Banking Corp v Markovic (1985) 82 FLR 7 .11.21, 16.07, 16.51, 25.15
Westpac Banking Corporation v Ollis [2007] NSWSC 956. . . . . .1.98
Westpac Banking Corporation v Robinson (1993) 30 NSWLR 668 (CA). 4.30, 5.03,
                                                                    5.11, 5.44, 5.47, 5.49, 5.50, 10.23
Westpac Securities Ltd v Dickie [1991] 1 NZLR 657 (CA) 5.51
Westpork Pty Ltd v Bio- Organics Pty Ltd [2018] WASC 291. . . . . .7.21
Westville Shipping Company Ltd v Abram Steamship Company Ltd 1922 SC 571
    See Abram Steamship Company Ltd v Westville Shipping Company Ltd
Whalley v Whalley (1821) 3 Bligh 1, 4 ER 506 . . . . .7.93
Wharton v May (1799) 5 Ves Jun 27, 31 ER 454 . . . . .15.51
Whelpdale's case (1604) 5 Co Rep 119a, 77 ER 239 . . . . 3.37, 10.23, 14.07, 29.68, 29.70
Whichcote v Lawrence (1798) 3 Ves 740, 30 ER 1248 . . . . .15.17
Whitbread v Watt [1901] 1 Ch 911 . . . . .15.56, 15.74
White v Garden (1851) 10 CB 919, 138 ER 364. . . . . .3.05, 3.11, 3.14, 3.41, 14.03, 14.19, 14.31,
                              16.02, 20.06, 20.10, 20.11, 20.12, 20.13, 21.05, 21.57, 21.58, 21.60, 21.63
White v Small (1682) 1 Chan Cas 103, 22 ER 867. . . . . 3.38, 3.42, 22.05

lxxii TABLE OF CASES

White and Carter (Councils) Ltd v McGregor [1962] AC 413 .... 7.79, 7.92
Whitehead Mann Ltd v Cheverny Consulting Ltd [2006] EWCA 1303...................... 26.04
Whitehorn Bros v Davison [1911] 1 KB 463 (CA) 14.03, 14.14, 16.02, 21.05, 21.09,
  21.10, 21.12, 21.13, 21.16, 21.18, 21.57, 21.71, 21.74
Whitmore v Francis (1820) 8 Price 616, 146 ER 1314 .... 15.60
Whittaker v Campbell [1984] 1 QB 318 (Div Ct) 1.46
Whittingham v Thornburgh (1690) 2 Vern 206, 23 ER 734; 2 Eq Ca Abr 635,
  22 ER 533.. 3.37, 3.55, 3.57, 15.66, 18.40
Whittington v Seale-Hayne (1900) 82 LT 49; [1900] WN 31......................... 17.25, 17.62
Whittle v Filaria Pty Ltd [2004] ACTSC 45 .... 18.85
Whurr v Devenish (1904) 20 TLR 385 .... 27.19, 27.53
Wickens v Cheval Property Developments Ltd [2010] EWHC 2249 (Ch) 26.02
Wiebe v Butchrt's Motors Ltd [1949] 4 DLR 838 (BCCA)........................... 17.30, 18.88
Wilde v Gibson (1848) 1 HLC 605, 9 ER 897...................................... 7.28, 27.05
Wilkinson v Brayfield (1693) 2 Vern 307, 23 ER 799, 1 Eq Ca Abr 258, 21 ER 1031........ 3.42, 22.06
William v Roffey Bros & Nicholls (Contractors) Ltd [1991] QB 1 .... 6.14, 6.34
William Pickersgill & Sons Ltd v London and Provincial Marine and
  General Insurance Company Ltd [1912] 3 KB 614.................................. 21.26
William Sindall plc v Cambridgeshire CC [1994] 1 WLR 1016 (CA) 2.08, 4.35, 7.07, 10.26,
  18.93, 18.96, 26.06, 26.17, 27.11, 28.12, 28.15, 28.17, 28.22, 28.25, 28.33, 28.34
Williams v Bayley (1886) LR 1 HL 200.................................. 6.20, 6.44, 6.72, 6.84
Williams v Central Bank of Nigeria [2014] AC 1189 .... 16.61
Williams v Central Bank of Nigeria [2014] UKSC 10; [2014] 2 WLR 355 (SC) 24.33, 24.36
Williams v Scott [1900] AC 499 (PC)... 1.74
Williams v Williams [2003] EWHC 742 .... 7.46, 7.52, 29.09, 29.21
Willis v Barron [1902] AC 271 .... 8.30, 8.40, 19.08
Willmott v Barber (1880) 15 ChD 96.. 24.08, 24.58
Wilson v Brisbane City Council [1931] St R Qd 360 ....14.36, 15.34, 15.36, 16.56, 17.04, 27.24, 27.29
Wilson v Duckett (1762) 3 Burr 1361, 97 ER 874 .... 3.56, 3.60, 14.80
Wilton v Farnworth (1948) 76 CLR 646.. 29.16, 29.56
Wiltrading (WA) Pty Ltd v Lumley General Insurance Ltd (2005) 30 WAR 290 (CA) 23.46, 24.03
Wiltshire v Cain (1958–60) 2 Barb LR 149 .... 7.48
Wiltshire v Marshall (1866) 14 LT 396... 7.75
Wing Hang Bank Ltd v Kwok Lai Sim [2009] 4 HKC 71 (CA) 9.20, 19.33
Winterbottom v Ingham (1845) 7 QB 611, 115 ER 620 .... 18.24, 18.82
Wintle v Nye [1959] 1 WLR 284 (HL) 6.103
WISE (Underwriting Agency) Ltd v Grupo Nacional Provincial SA
  [2004] 2 Lloyd's Rep 483 (CA) 5.30, 11.45, 23.68, 23.110
With v O'Flanagan [1936] Ch 575 (CA)............. 4.83, 4.90, 4.93, 4.97, 5.10, 14.36, 15.34, 15.36
Witten-Hannah v Davis [1995] 3 NZLR 141 (CA)................................... 8.30
Wood v Abrey (1818) 3 Madd 417, 56 ER 558................... 3.42, 7.75, 7.80, 7.92, 22.05
Wood v Commercial First Business Limited [2020] CTLC 1 .... 8.57, 8.63, 28.36
Wood v Commercial First Business Limited [2021] EWCA Civ 471,
  [2021] 3 WLR 395 (CA), [2022] Ch 123 (CA) 8.51, 8.52, 8.53, 10.09, 10.23
Wood v Commercial First Business Limited (Dissolved)
  [2021] EWHC 1403 (Ch)..................................... 13.13, 17.17, 17.18, 17.19
Woodland-Ferrari v UCL Retirement Scheme [2003] Ch 115 .... 25.17
Woodward v Aston (1672) 1 Ven 296, 86 ER 191 .... 3.52
Woolf v Woolf [2004] STC 1633 .... 29.41, 29.44
Woolwich Equitable Building Society v IRC (No 2) [1993] AC 70................. 6.23, 6.39, 17.21
Woolworths Ltd v Kelly (1991) 4 ACSR 431 (NSWCA)................................ 8.20
Worssam, Re (1882) 46 LT 584 .... 18.48
WPP Group plc v Reichmann [2000] All ER (D) 1409 .... 4.46, 4.99
Wright v Campbell (1861) 2 F & F 393, 175 ER 1111 .... 29.74, 29.77, 29.78
Wright v Carter [1903] 1 Ch 27 (CA)............. 6.103, 6.117, 8.26, 8.30, 8.31, 19.08, 29.18, 29.51
Wright v Lawes (1799) 4 Esp 82, 170 ER 649...................................... 3.10, 3.11

TABLE OF CASES lxxiii

Wright v National Westminster Bank plc [2014] EWHC 3158 (Ch) 13.32
Wright v Vanderplank (1855) 2 K & J 1, 69 ER 669; on appeal (1856) 8 De GM &
 G 133, 44 ER 340. . . . . 6.103, 23.06, 23.08, 23.09, 24.10, 24.78
Wright Prospecting Pty Ltd v Hancock Prospecting Pty Ltd [2013] WASC 248. . . . . 24.17, 24.74
Wright's case (1871) 12 Eq Cas 331. . . . . .3.41
Wyatt v Wyatt (1618–1620) in J Ritchie, Reports of Cases Decided by Francis Bacon
 in the High Court of Chancery (1617–1621) (1932) 126. 3.42, 3.52, 21.04
Wyndham v Chetwynd (1755) unreported, cited in (1757) 1 Burr 390, 397, 97 ER 365, 369; for
 subsequent proceedings; (1756) 1 Keny 253, 96 ER 984; (1757) 2 Keny 122,
 96 ER 121; 1 Bl W 95, 96 ER 53; 1 Burr 414, 97 ER 377 . . . . .29.84
Wythes v Labouchere (1859) 3 De G & J 593, 44 ER 1397 . . . . .5.47

Xie Li Xin v Thompson [2018] HKCFI 1096. . . . . 4.08, 4.30

Yang Foo-Oi by Leung Ping Chiu, Roy, her next friend v Wai Wai Chen and
 Timford Resources Limited (High Court of the HKSAR, 1739/2010,
 29 November 2016, Chan J) 5.16, 5.17, 5.18, 5.21
Yerkey v Jones (1939) 63 CLR 649 . . . . 6.103, 9.09, 29.59
York Buildings Co v Mackenzie (1795) 8 Bro PC 42, 3 ER 432 . . . . .17.04, 17.05, 17.18,
 17.35, 17.41, 20.26, 20.33
York Glass Co v Jubb (1925) 42 TLR 1 (CA) 7.61, 7.63
York Street Mezzanine Pty Ltd (in liq) v McEvoy (2007) 162 FCR 358 . . . . . . .1.09, 25.21, 25.29, 25.61
Yorkshire Bank plc v Tinsley [2004] EWCA 816. . . . . 4.123, 6.92, 13.35
Yost v International Securities Co (1918) 43 DLR 28 (Ont CA) 2.03, 2.05
Young v Billister (1860) 8 HLC 682, 11 ER 596. . . . . .14.32
YS GM Marfin II LLC v Lakhani [2020] EWHC 2629 (Comm). 6.03, 6.75, 6.81, 6.110
Yukos Hydrocarbons Investments Ltd v Georgiades [2020] EWHC 173 (Comm) 4.66, 5.63

Zachariadis v Allforks Australia Pty Ltd (2009) 26 VR 47 (CA) 5.49
Zamet v Hyman [1961] 1 WLR 1142 (CA) 6.98, 6.103, 6.114, 29.60
Zandfarid v Bank of Credit and Commerce International [1996] 1 WLR 1420 . . . . .25.07
Zien v Field (1963) 41 DLR (2d) 394 (BCCA). 4.23, 18.124, 27.37, 27.38, 27.45
Zucker v Straightlace Pty Ltd (1987) 11 NSWLR 87. . . . . .23.44, 23.99
Zurich Insurance v Hayward [2017] AC 142 (Sup Ct) 4.65, 4.66, 4.100, 4.102, 4.104, 4.114
ZX Group Pty Ltd v LPD Corporation Pty Ltd [2013] VSC 542 . . . . .23.68

Table of Legislation

UNITED KINGDOM

Statutes

Administration of Estates Act 1925
s 45 .... 22.05
Arbitration Act 1996
s 7 .... 1.16
s 49 .... 17.22
Bills of Exchange Act 1882
s 59 .... 21.56
s 81 .... 21.27
s 82 .... 21.28
s 90 .... 21.16
Carriage of Goods by Sea Act 1992
s 2(1)(a) 21.56
s 5(2).............................. 21.56
Cheques Act 1957
s 4 .... 21.28
Common Law Procedure Act 1852....3.02, 10.03
s 49 .... 3.09
s 55 .... 3.37
Common Law Procedure Act 1854 ...... 14.14
s 78 .... 14.14
s 83 .... 29.73
Companies Act 1862 ....11.74, 24.88, 25.21,
25.22, 25.23, 25.28, 25.32
s 25 .... 11.70, 11.71
s 35 .... 11.70, 11.71, 25.25
s 38 .... 25.43, 25.59
s 38(1)............................ 25.43
s 74 .... 25.43
s 75 .... 25.43
s 98 .... 11.70, 11.71
s 130 .... 25.63
Companies Act 1865
s 165 .... 2.30
Companies Act 1867
s 38 .... 25.29
Companies Act 1985 .... 8.20
s 111A............................ 25.50
s 317 .... 24.45
Companies Act 1989
s 131(1)........................... 25.50
Companies Act 2006.....8.20, 25.21, 25.23, 25.28
Pt 10, Ch 4 .... 23.17
s 40(1)............................. 1.78
s 41(2)............................. 1.78
s 46 .... 29.68
s 112(2)........................... 14.22

s 125 .... 25.25
s 177 .... 8.20, 23.17
s 177(2)............................ 8.20
s 177(2)(a) 8.20
s 177(6)(b) 8.20
s 178 .... 23.17
s 180 .... 8.20, 23.17
s 180(1)............................ 8.20
s 184 .... 8.20
s 185 .... 8.20
ss 188–210 .... 8.20
s 195(2)(c) 20.07
s 239 .... 23.17
s 554 .... 29.06
s 579(1)......................25.77, 25.78
s 579(2)......................25.77, 25.78
s 655 .... 25.50
ss 770–772 .... 29.06
Consumer Insurance (Disclosure and
Representations) Act 2012 ..... 5.24, 5.28,
5.30, 5.35, 5.36, 10.18, 10.22,
14.66, 15.66, 18.41
s 1 .... 5.35, 5.36, 14.82
ss 2–5 .... 14.82
s 2 .... 5.25, 5.35, 10.27
s 2(1)............................. 5.36
s 2(5)............................. 5.25
s 3 .... 5.35
s 4 .... 5.35
s 5 .... 5.35
s 6 .... 5.35
s 7 .... 5.35
s 8 .... 5.35
s 9 .... 5.35
s 10 .... 5.35
s 11 .... 5.25, 5.35, 10.27
s 12 .... 5.35
s 12(4)............................ 5.35
Sch 1 ....5.35, 10.27, 14.82, 19.09
Sch 1, para 2..................14.82, 14.83
Sch 1, para 5...................... 14.82
Sch 1, para 17..................... 14.81
Sch 2 .... 5.35
Consumer Rights
Act 2015.........17.05, 26.16, 26.34, 26.35
ss 20–22 ....27.28, 27.57
s 24(8)–(10)...................... 17.05
s 58(5)–(6)....................... 17.05
s 62 .... 26.35

lxxvi TABLE OF LEGISLATION

s 62(4) 26.35
s 62(5) 26.35
s 64(1) 26.35
s 64(2)–(5) 26.35
Sch 2 .... 26.35
Sch 4, para 1 .... 26.16
Consumer Rights Bill 2013
  Explanatory Notes 26.35
Contracts (Rights of Third Parties)
  Act 1999
  s 3(2) 20.31
Directors Liability Act 1890 .... 25.29
Factors Act 1889
  s 2 .... 11.36, 11.40, 16.67, 21.17, 21.74
  s 2(2) 11.36
  s 9 .... 11.40, 16.67
Financial Services Act 1986 .... 18.69
Financial Services and Markets
  Act 2000 .... 14.82
  s 90 .... 25.29
  s 90A 25.29
Gambling Act 2005
  s 334(1)(c) 1.36
  s 335 ....1.36
Gaming Act 1845
  s 18 ....1.36
Housing Act 1985
  Pt V 13.31
Inheritance Tax Act 1984
  s 150 .... 13.32
Insolvency Act 1986 .... 25.17, 25.23, 25.28
  s 74 .... 25.43
  s 74(1) 25.43, 25.59
  s 74(2) 25.43
  s 74(2)(f) 25.39, 25.78
  s 79 .... 25.43
  s 80 .... 25.43
  s 86 ....25.62, 25.63
  s 88 ....25.39, 25.55
  s 127 ....25.39, 25.55
  s 129(2) 25.62
  s 130(2) 25.19
  s 186 .... 25.78
  s 281 .... 25.17
  s 281(3) 25.17
  s 283(5) 25.04, 25.07, 25.09
  s 284 .... 25.12
  s 285(1) 25.07, 25.10
  s 285(2) 25.07, 25.10
  s 285(3) 25.09, 25.10
  s 306 .... 25.12
  s 307 .... 25.13, 25.15, 25.16
  s 345 .... 25.10
  s 382 .... 25.17
Insurance Act 2015 .... 4.87, 5.24, 5.30, 5.36, 10.18,
    10.22, 10.23, 14.79, 15.66, 18.41, 23.85

s 1 .... 14.84
ss 3–8 .... 10.27
s 3 ....5.38, 14.84
s 3(1) 5.36
s 3(3)(b) 5.36
s 3(3)(c) 4.84, 5.36
s 3(4) 5.36
s 3(5) 5.37
s 4 ....5.37
s 5 ....5.37
s 6 ....5.37
s 7(3) 4.63, 4.87, 5.37
s 7(5) 4.84, 4.87, 5.37
s 8 ....5.38
s 8(1) 5.38, 14.84
s 8(5) 5.38, 14.84
s 8(6) 5.38, 14.84
s 9 ....5.39
s 10 ....5.39
s 11 ....5.39
s 12 ....5.39
s 13 ....5.39
s 13A 5.39
s 14 ....5.36
s 14(1) 5.38
s 14(3) 5.25
ss 15–17 ....5.39
s 21(2) 4.63, 4.84, 5.28
s 21(3) 4.63
s 22 ....5.36
s 23 ....5.36
Sch 1 .... 5.38, 10.27, 19.09
  paras 2–5 ....5.38
  para 2 .... 14.84
  para 2(b) 5.39, 14.84
  para 3 ....5.39, 14.84
  para 4 ....5.39, 14.84
  para 4(3) 18.40
  para 5 .... 14.84
  para 8(b) 5.39, 14.84
  para 8(2) 18.40
  para 9(2) 5.39, 14.84
  para 12 .... 14.81
Joint Stock Banks Act 1844 .... 25.32
Judicature Act 1873 .... 10.03, 10.04
  s 25(1) 21.26
  s 25(11) 10.10, 12.07
Judicature Act 1875 .... 10.03, 10.04
Land Registration Act 1925 ....1.99
  s 82(1)(a) 15.08
  s 82(1)(b) 15.08
Land Registration Act 2002 .... 15.08
  s 27(2) 29.06
  s 58(1) 1.47
  s 65 .... 15.08
  s 96 .... 24.30

TABLE OF LEGISLATION   lxxvii

s 97 . . . . 24.30
s 108(2). 15.08
s 108(4). 15.08
Sch 4, para 1. . . . . 15.08
Sch 4, para 2. . . . . 15.08
Sch 4, para 2(a)(a). 15.08
Sch 4, para 2(b) 15.08
Sch 4, para 2(c) 15.08
Sch 4, para 3. . . . . 15.08
Sch 6. . . . . 24.30
Sch 8, para 1(1)(a). 15.08
Larceny Act 1861
  s 100 . . . . 3.12, 11.31
Larceny (England) Act 1827
  s 57 . . . . .3.12
Law of Property Act 1925
  s 1(6). 29.10
  s 40 . . . . .1.36
  s 52(1). 1.47, 29.06
  s 52(2). 29.06
  s 53 . . . . 29.06
  s 136 . . . . 22.10
  s 136(1). 21.26
  s 174 . . . . .7.76
  s 199 . . . . .9.11
Law of Property (Miscellaneous
    Provisions) Act 1989
  s 1 . . . . 29.68
  s 2 . . . . .1.47
  s 2(1). 1.36
Law Reform (Miscellaneous Provisions)
    Act 1970
  s 3(2). 29.14
Limitation Act 1623. . . . . 24.26, 24.31, 24.81, 24.82
Limitation Act 1939
  s 19(2). 24.33
Limitation Act 1980 . . . . 24.22, 24.27, 24.30
  s 2 . . . . 24.22, 24.27, 24.29
  s 3 . . . . 24.22
  s 5 . . . . 24.22
  s 15 . . . . 24.31, 24.81, 24.83
  s 15(1). 24.30
  s 21 . . . . 24.33
  s 32 . . . . 24.54
  s 36(1). 24.25, 24.26, 24.27, 24.30
  s 36(2). 24.09, 24.14
Marine Insurance Act 1906 . . . . 4.63, 4.87, 18.40
  s 17 . . . . .5.25, 5.32
  s 18 . . . . .5.28
  s 18(1). .5.29, 10.27
  s 18(2). .4.63, 5.28
  s 18(3). 5.30
  s 18(6). 5.28
  s 20 . . . . .4.84, 4.87
  s 20(2). .4.63, 4.87
  s 20(4). .4.84, 4.87

s 21 . . . . .5.32
s 33(3). 4.84
s 50(2). 21.26
s 80 . . . . 13.33
s 84 . . . . 14.81
s 84(1). 18.40
s 84(3)(a) 14.81, 18.40
Mental Capacity Act 2005 . . . . 7.57, 7.59
  s 7 . . . . .7.45
  ss 16–19 . . . . .7.58
  s 18(1)(f) 7.58
  s 20(1). 7.59
Mental Health Act 1983
  s 95 . . . . .7.58
  s 96 . . . . .7.58
  s 96(1)(h). 7.58
  s 99 . . . . .7.58
Merchant Shipping Act 1995
  s 16 . . . . 29.06
Misrepresentation Act 1967 . . . . 7.37, 10.33,
                                      27.02, 27.11
  s 1 . . . . 4.21, 4.23, 27.55
  s 1(1). 23.26
  s 1(1)(a) 27.39, 27.46, 27.47
  s 1(1)(b) 27.10, 27.11, 27.16, 27.13,
                           27.28, 27.34, 27.35, 27.56
  s 2 . . . . .2.07, 12.19
  s 2(1). 4.09, 4.106, 28.04, 28.07,
                                28.09, 28.20, 28.21
  s 2(2). 2.03, 4.09, 4.16, 4.69, 11.80,
                       12.14, 28.01, 28.03, 28.04, 28.05,
                       28.07, 28.08, 28.09, 28.10, 28.12,
                       28.15, 28.16, 28.19, 28.20, 28.21,
                       28.22, 28.23, 28.24, 28.25, 28.27,
                       28.30, 28.31, 28.33, 28.34, 28.36
  s 2(3). 28.20
  s 3 . . . . .26.12–26.24, 26.31, 26.32, 26.33
  s 4 . . . . 27.28
  s 4(1). 27.28
Partnership Act 1890
  s 41 . . . . 16.48
Powers of Criminal Courts (Sentencing)
    Act 2000
  s 148 . . . . 3.12, 11.31, 14.14
  s 149 . . . . .3.12
Real Property Limitation
    Act 1833. . . . . .24.26, 24.31, 24.81, 24.82
  ss 3–4 . . . . 24.81
Real Property Limitation Act 1874. . . . . . . 24.31
Restitution of Goods Stolen Act 1529 . . . . . .3.12
Sale of Goods Act 1893. . . . . .27.51, 27.54
  s 6 . . . . .7.09
Sale of Goods Act 1979. . . . . 27.54
  s 2(4). 21.07
  s 3 . . . . .7.45, 7.65
  s 17(1). 20.19

lxxviii TABLE OF LEGISLATION

s 23 . . . . 20.11, 21.07
s 24 . . . . 21.74
s 25 . . . . 11.40, 16.67, 21.74
s 35 . . . . 27.28, 27.57
s 35A 27.28, 27.57
s 36 . . . . 14.55, 14.62
s 48 . . . . .1.31
s 48(3) 1.24
s 48(4) 1.24
s 61(1) 21.07
s 61(3) 21.10
Sales of Reversions Act 1867 . . . . .7.76
Senior Courts Act 1981
s 35A 17.21
s 49 . . . . 10.10
s 49(1) 12.07
Statutes of Limitations 24.34
Stock Transfer Act 1963 . . . . 29.06
Theft Act 1968
s 32(3) 11.31
Sch 3, Pt 1 . . . . 11.31
Torts (Interference with Goods)
    Act 1977 . . . . 14.14
s 3 . . . . 14.14
s 3(2)(a) 6.56
s 3(2)(b) 6.56
Unfair Contract Terms Act 1977 . . . . 26.27
ss 2–7 . . . . 26.33
s 3(2)(b)(i) 26.19
s 8 . . . . 26.33
s 11 . . . . 26.31
s 11(1) 26.13, 26.24, 26.25
s 11(2) 26.25
s 13 . . . . 26.20
ss 16–21 . . . . 26.33
s 26 . . . . 26.32
s 27 . . . . 26.33
Sch 2 . . . . 26.25, 25.26
Uniformity of Process Act 1832 . . . . . 3.21, 10.03

STATUTORY INSTRUMENTS

Companies (Tables A–F) Regulations 1985, SI
    1985/805
Table A, regs 85–86 . . . . .8.20
Consumer Contracts (Information,
    Cancellation and Additional Payments)
    Regulations 2013, SI 2013/3134 . . . . . . .5.01
Consumer Protection (Amendment)
    Regulations 2014, SI 2014/870 . . . . 4.01,
                                      5.01, 6.01, 7.69
Consumer Protection from Unfair
    Trading Regulations 2008,
    SI 2008/1277 . . . . 4.01, 5.01, 7.69
reg 27E 4.01, 5.01, 6.01, 7.69
reg 27F 4.01, 5.01, 6.01, 7.69

Land Registration Rules 2003,
    SI 2003/1417
r 58 . . . . 29.06
Unfair Terms in Consumer
    Contracts Regulations 1999,
    SI 1999/2083 . . . . 26.34, 26.35

AUSTRALIA

Commonwealth

Australian Consumer Law 2011
s 4 . . . . .4.57
s 18 . . . . .4.57
s 20 . . . . 7.103
ss 20–22 . . . . 7.103
s 21 . . . . 7.103
s 22 . . . . 7.103
ss 237–39 . . . . .4.09
s 243 . . . . .4.09
Bankruptcy Act 1966 . . . . 25.14
s 58 . . . . 25.13, 25.16
s 58(1)(b) 25.15
Companies Code
s 360(1)(k) 25.50
Competition and Consumer Act 2010 . . . . 13.18
s 237 . . . . 19.36
Sch 2, s 243 . . . . 13.18, 15.74, 23.13, 23.44,
            23.71, 24.12, 25.78, 27.12, 27.30, 27.43
Corporations Act 2001
s 247E 25.50
s 468A 25.55
s 493A 25.55
s 515 . . . . 25.43
s 516 . . . . 25.43
ss 520–22 . . . . 25.43
s 527 . . . . 25.43
s 563A 25.39, 25.50, 25.78
s 601MB 25.29
s 728 . . . . 25.29
s 729 . . . . 25.29
s 737(1) 25.77, 25.78
s 925A 24.65, 25.29
s 1073 . . . . 23.44
s 1041H 25.29
s 1325 . . . . 25.29
s 1325(5) 25.78
Corporations Amendment
    (Sons of Gwalia) Act 2010 . . . . . 25.39, 25.50
Insurance Contracts Act 1984
s 9 . . . . 5.26, 5.30, 5.40, 10.18
s 21(2) 5.30
s 21A 5.40
s 22 . . . . .5.40
ss 28–33 . . . . 5.40, 10.18
s 31 . . . . .5.26
s 33A–D 5.40

TABLE OF LEGISLATION lxxix

Insurance Contract Regulations 2017
reg 7 ....5.40
reg 8 ....5.40
Securities and Investments Commission
Act 2001
regs 11–13 ....5.40
s 12DA 25.29
Trade Practices Act 1974 .... 13.18
s 51A..................................4.57
s 51AA, AB, AC..................... 7.103
s 52 ....4.57
s 87 .... 4.09, 13.18, 15.74, 23.13,
23.44, 23.71, 24.12, 27.43

Australian Capital Territory (ACT)

Civil Law (Wrongs) Act 2002
s 173(2)................. 27.12, 27.30, 27.43
s 175 .... 28.01
Sale of Goods Act 1954
s 62(1)............................. 27.50
s 62(2)............................. 27.50

New South Wales

Builders Licensing Act 1971 ....1.36
Conveyancing (Vendor Disclosure and
Warranty) Regulation 1986......... 23.44
Sale of Goods Act 1923
s 4(2).............................. 27.48
s 4(2A) 27.50
s 4(2A)(a).......................... 27.43
s 4(2A)(b) 27.30
s 28(1)........................21.17, 21.74
Workers Compensation Act 1926........ 23.44

Queensland

Succession Act 1981
s 49(1)............................. 22.06
s 66 .... 22.06

South Australia

Business Agents Act 1938
s 39 .... 23.44
Companies Act 1892
s 226 .... 23.44
Misrepresentation Act 1972
s 6(1)(a) 27.43
s 6(1)(b) 27.12, 27.30, 27.56
ss 7(3)–(5) 28.01
s 7(3)........................12.14, 28.05
s 7(4)............................. 28.03
s 7(5)........................12.14, 28.05

Victoria

Consumer Law and Fair Trading Act 2012
s 24 .... 27.30

s 24(2)............................. 27.43
s 26(1)(b) 11.38
Property Law Act 1958
s 134 .... 21.26

CANADA

New Brunswick

Law Reform Act 1993
s 6(1)..............................7.37
Law Reform Act 2011
s 6(1)............................. 27.14

GERMANY

BGB
art 142(I) 1.08

HONG KONG

Misrepresentation Ordinance
s 3(2)............................. 28.01

INDIA

Contracts Act 1872
s 19 ....1.08
s 19A.............................. 15.49
s 64 ....1.08, 14.45

MALAYSIA

Contracts Act 1950
s 19 ....1.08
s 20 .... 15.49
Specific Relief Act 1950
Chapter IV 'Rescission of Contracts' 1.08
s 34 ....1.08
s 37 .... 15.49

NEW ZEALAND

Contract and Commercial Law
Act 2017.....5.51, 7.23, 7.33, 11.102, 14.44,
23.70, 27.13, 27.31, 27.44, 27.49, 27.59
Pt 2, Subpart 2.......................7.10
Pt 2, Subpart 3.......................5.51
ss 24–32 ....7.33
s 24(1)..............................7.23
s 24(1)(a)(i) 7.23
s 24(1)(b) 7.23
s 24(1)(c) 7.23
s 24(3)..............................7.23
s 25 ....7.23
s 27 ....7.23
s 28 ..... 1.08, 7.23, 27.13, 27.31, 27.44, 27.59
s 31 ....7.23

lxxx TABLE OF LEGISLATION

s 32 .... 7.23
s 33 .... 1.08
s 37 ... 1.08, 11.102, 27.13, 27.31, 27.44, 27.59
s 38 .... 11.03, 23.36, 23.49
ss 40–47 .... 1.08
s 41 .... 11.03
s 41(1) 11.38
s 41(1)(b) 11.38
ss 42–49 .... 11.102
s 42 .... 27.13, 27.31, 27.44, 27.59
ss 43–49 .... 27.13, 27.31, 27.44, 27.59
s 45(d) 14.44
s 49 .... 1.08
s 200(2) 27.48
Contractual Mistakes Act 1977 ..... 7.10, 7.23, 7.33
Contractual Remedies Act 1979 .... 5.51,
               · 27.13, 27.59
s 7(3) 23.70
s 8 .... 11.38
s 9 .... 19.02
Insurance Law Reform Act 1977
ss 4–7 .... 5.26, 5.40
Sale of Goods Act 1895 .... 27.48
s 61(2) 27.48
Sale of Goods Act 1908
s 60(2) 27.48

SINGAPORE

Companies Act
s 76 .... 23.16

UNITED STATES OF AMERICA

California Civil Code 11.65
ss 1688–1691 .... 11.65
s 1691 .... 14.65
ss 3406–3408 .... 11.65
Uniform Commercial Code
Art 2–403(1) 21.07

Restatements

Restatement of Contracts
(Second) (1981) 15.11, 15.27
§ 372 .... 15.11

§ 380(1) 23.61
§ 380(2) 23.19, 23.61
§ 380(3) 15.38
§ 381(1) 24.65
§ 381(2) 23.19, 24.65
§ 381(3) 24.71
§ 382 .... 11.115
§ 384 .... 14.64
Restatement (First) of Restitution
(1937) 11.18, 11.115, 18.63, 18.66,
         23.89, 23.105, 23.108, 24.73, 24.92
§ 13 .... 18.97
§ 13 ill 16 .... 18.96
§ 65 .... 18.33
§ 65(d) 14.64
§ 65(4) 18.64
§ 66 .... 18.63
§ 66(3) 18.66
§ 68(2) 11.115, 23.97
§ 158 cmt c 17.40
§ 158 cmt d 17.40, 17.47
§ 163 .... 1.61
§ 166 .... 16.14
§ 167 .... 1.61
§ 260 .... 14.64
Restatement (Third) of Restitution
(2011) 1.10, 1.11, 1.12, 1.13, 1.27,
         2.05, 11.115, 14.64, 14.65,
         17.26, 18.03, 24.100
§ 2(2) 1.51
§ 13 cmt d 1.61
§ 37 .... 1.10, 1.31
§ 37(2) 1.10
§ 37 cmt e 27.06
§ 54 .... 1.10, 1.31, 11.115
§ 54(4) 1.10
§ 54(5) 14.65, 15.60
§ 54(6) 18.106, 23.89, 23.97,
         23.108, 24.92, 24.100
§ 54 cmt d 1.10
§ 54 cmt e 1.10
§ 54 cmt k 23.89, 23.97, 24.100
§ 55(1) 16.14
§ 55 cmt f 16.14
§ 70(2) 24.92

PART I

INTRODUCTION

1

Core Distinctions

A.	Introduction	1.01	(3) Transfer of title	1.45
B.	Termination *Ab Initio* and *De Futuro*	1.06	(4) Recovery of benefits	1.49
	(1) Nature and basis of the distinction	1.07	D. **Rescission and Transactions Ineffective in Equity**	1.57
	(2) Termination *ab initio*: effects on contractual rights and obligations	1.14	(1) Introduction	1.57
	(3) Termination *de futuro*: effects on contractual rights and obligations	1.20	(2) Where the claimant is not a party to the impugned transaction	1.67
	(4) Termination *ab initio* and *de futuro*: rights to restitution	1.23	(3) Where the claimant is a party to the impugned transaction	1.70
	(5) Terminology	1.31	(4) Bribes	1.87
C.	**Void and Voidable Contracts**	1.35	(5) Apparent gifts made ineffective by resulting trust	1.90
	(1) Void and voidable contracts	1.36	(6) Other ineffective transactions	1.91
	(2) Contracts valid until rescinded and contracts ineffective until ratified	1.39		

A. Introduction

This chapter is concerned to identify the concept of rescission. It does this by distinguishing **1.01** rescission from neighbouring concepts. In the course of the survey some frequent sources of confusion are clarified, and the shape of rescission outlined.

The term 'rescission' is often and confusingly used to describe two quite different ways in **1.02** which a contract may be brought to an end. One form of 'rescission' is founded on a defect in the formation of the contract, arising by reason of fraud, duress, undue influence, or other invalidating cause. The defect affects consent, and entitles one of the parties to extinguish the agreement as from the beginning, or *ab initio*.[1] But a contract may also be brought to an end by reason of the other party's later non-performance or defective performance, or because it has become frustrated: the contract was properly formed, but then not carried out in accordance with its terms. When a contract is 'rescinded' for breach or frustration in this way it is terminated only in respect of future rights and obligations, or *de futuro*.

This work is only concerned with 'rescission' in the first of these two senses of the word, and **1.03** uses the term to refer to terminating a contract *ab initio*, or the setting aside of a voidable gift. Terminating a contract *ab initio* is therefore a synonym for its rescission. The law regulating termination for breach or frustration is considered only in order to underline the distinctions between terminating a contract *ab initio* and *de futuro* (see Part B of this chapter).

---

[1] Gifts may also be rescinded. The rescission of gifts is governed by special rules and is discussed in Chap 29.

1.04 A contract that is valid until rescinded is called a voidable contract, and is to be distinguished from a void contract, which is an apparent contract that never comes into being. The chapter distinguishes voidable and void contracts, and then further distinguishes voidable contracts from contracts that are ineffective until ratified (see Part C of this chapter). These distinctions are important, for the law of rescission is concerned only with voidable contracts, and is not concerned with void contracts, or contracts that are ineffective until ratified.

1.05 Legal and beneficial title to property passes under a voidable contract, but may be regained upon rescission. Voidable gifts largely follow the same pattern. Transactions of this kind are to be differentiated from contracts and gifts where no beneficial title effectively passes, so that the transaction is made ineffective in equity as from the outset. This distinction is also considered (see Part D of this chapter), and is important because transactions that are ineffective in equity are, like void contracts, outside the scope of the law of rescission.

B. Termination *Ab Initio* and *De Futuro*

1.06 This section explains the distinction between terminating a contract *ab initio* and *de futuro*, and notes the confusing way in which the terms 'rescind' and 'rescission' are used to describe both of these modes of termination.

(1) Nature and basis of the distinction

1.07 Whereas rescinding a contract for fraud or other vitiating event terminates it *ab initio*, or from the beginning, when a contract is brought to an end for subsequent breach or frustration, it is terminated *de futuro*, or for the future. Sir Owen Dixon summarized the distinction in *McDonald v Dennys Lascelles Limited*:

> When one party to a simple contract, upon a breach by the other contracting party of a condition of the contract, elects to treat the contract as no longer binding upon him, the contract is not rescinded as from the beginning. Both parties are discharged from the further performance of the contract, but rights are not divested or discharged which have already been unconditionally acquired. Rights and obligations which arise from the partial execution of the contract and causes of action which have accrued from its breach likewise continue unaffected. When a contract is rescinded because of matters which affect its formation, as in the case of fraud, the parties are to be rehabilitated and restored, so far as may be, to the position they occupied before the contract was made. But when a contract, which is not void or voidable at law, or liable to be set aside in equity, is dissolved at the election of one party because the other has not observed an essential condition or has committed a breach going to its root, the contract is determined so far as it is executory only and the party in default is liable for damages for its breach.[2]

---

[2] (1933) 48 CLR 457, 476–77. It has been said that this passage provided the blueprint for what is now s 42 of the Contract and Commercial Law Act 2017 (NZ): *Garratt v Ikeda* [2002] 1 NZLR 577 (CA) [11].

In England this distinction was fully elaborated only in the second half of the twentieth **1.08** century.[3] Misconceptions that culminated in the decision in *Horsler v Zorro*[4] prompted some of the clearest extra-judicial explanations of the nature and basis of the distinction.[5] Eventually the law was definitively restated in *Johnson v Agnew*.[6] The divide between termination *ab initio* and *de futuro* is also recognized in Canada,[7] Singapore,[8] Hong Kong,[9] the Cayman Islands,[10] and Malaysia.[11] In New Zealand, on the other hand, it has been abolished by statute so far as rescission for misrepresentation or mistake is concerned.[12] German law does not recognize the same distinction.[13]

It is now accepted that it is the character of the event that confers the right to terminate **1.09** which is of decisive importance in explaining the entitlement to termination *ab initio* and *de futuro*. In the case of termination *ab initio* there is a defect in the formation of the contract, whereas termination *de futuro* involves a later, defective performance, or impossibility of performance. Hence, it is said, the contract in the former case can be undone from the start, whereas in the latter it can only be truncated for the future.[14] Indeed, according to Birke Häcker, whilst it may be usual to speak of a party rescinding his or her 'contract', it is

---

[3] See Chap 3, paras [3.30]–[3.31].

[4] [1975] 1 Ch 302; and see *Hurst v Bryk* [2002] 2 AC 185, 193. (But cf *Gunatunga v DeAlwis* (1996) 72 P & CR 161 (CA), described in *Howard-Jones v Tate* [2012] 1 P & CR 11 (CA) as having 'seriously questionable authority' (Lloyd LJ).)

[5] M Albery, 'Mr Cyprian Williams' Great Heresy' (1975) 91 LQR 337; F Dawson, 'Rescission and Damages' (1976) 39 MLR 214; AM Shea, 'Discharge for Performance of Contracts by Failure of Condition' (1979) 42 MLR 623, 630–31; and by way of background, S Williston, 'Repudiation of Contracts' (1901) 14 HLR 317, 421; PS Atiyah and GH Treitel, 'Misrepresentation Act 1967' (1967) 30 MLR 369, 370–71; WMC Gummow, (1976) 92 LQR 5. See also *Hunt v Hyde* [1976] 2 NZLR 453.

[6] [1980] AC 367, 397; *Hurst v Bryk* [2002] 2 AC 185, 193–94. In the insurance context, *Manifest Shipping Co Ltd v Uni-Polaris Insurance Co Ltd (The Star Sea)* [2003] 1 AC 469, 494. See also *Howard-Jones v Tate* [2012] 1 P & CR 11 (CA). For discussion of the 'rescission fallacy' in Australia, *Mann v Paterson Constructions Pty Ltd* (2019) 267 CLR 560 [7]–[9], [30], [51], [69], [180], [190] (*quantum meruit* in building contracts).

[7] *Guarantee Company of North America v Gordon Capital Corporation* [1999] 3 SCR 423, 439–41.

[8] *Lim Lay Bee v Allgreen Properties Ltd* [1999] 1 SLR 471 (CA) 483–84.

[9] *Achieve Goal Holdings Limited v Zhong Xin Ore-Material Holding Company Limited* [2018] HKCFI 2718 [299].

[10] *Richards v HEB Enterprises Ltd* (unreported, Grand Court of the Cayman Islands, Civil Division, no G93 of 2016, Hon Justice Williams, 2 August 2018) [63]–[69]; *HEB Enterprises v Richards* (unreported, Court of Appeal of the Cayman Islands, no. 20 of 2018, Rix, Martin and Moses JJA, 14 Nov 2019) [21] (where the distinction seems to be approved).

[11] *Samah v Shah Alam Properties Sdn Bhd* [1999] MLJU 144 (CA, Kuala Lumpur), citing Contracts Act 1950 (Malaysia), s 19; Specific Relief Act 1950 (Malaysia), Ch IV 'Rescission of Contracts'; cf Specific Relief Act 1950 (Malaysia), s 34, which prescribes the instances where a court may adjudge rescission, and draws no explicit distinction between termination *ab initio* and *de futuro*. See also Indian Contracts Act 1872, s 19, 64.

[12] Contract and Commercial Law Act 2017 (NZ), ss 28, 33, 37, 40–47, 49. But the Act does not alter the common law rule that accrued obligations remain following termination for breach: *Brown v Langwoods Photo Store Ltd* [1991] 1 NZLR 173 (CA) 176; *Garratt v Ikeda* [2002] 1 NZLR 577 (CA). See also *Hunt v Hyde* [1976] 2 NZLR 453, 457 (Casey J).

[13] R Zimmermann, 'Restitution after Termination for Breach of Contract in German Law' [1997] RLR 13. See also BGB article 142(I): 'If a transaction liable to be rescinded is rescinded, it is deemed to have been null and void from the outset' (discussed in Zimmermann, 13–14).

[14] M Albery, 'Mr Cyprian Williams' Great Heresy' (1975) 91 LQR 337, 337–38; E Peel, *Treitel: The Law of Contract* (15th edn, 2020) [9-097]; also *Buckland v Farmar and Moody* [1979] 1 WLR 221 (CA) 231–32, 237; and in the insurance context *Manifest Shipping Co Ltd v Uni-Polaris Insurance Co Ltd (The Star Sea)* [2003] 1 AC 469, 494–95. As to the relationship between defective consent and termination *ab initio*, S Worthington, 'The Proprietary Consequences of Rescission' [2002] 10 RLR 28, 29–30. See also *York Street Mezzanine Pty Ltd (in liq) v McEvoy* (2007) 162 FCR 358 [41] ('the right once exercised operates ab initio on the ground that the fraud or misrepresentation is an initial invalidating cause') (Finkelstein J, FCA); *Prest v Petrodel Resources Ltd* [2013] 2 AC 415 [18]; *RBC Properties Pte Ltd v Defu Furniture Pte Ltd* [2014] SGCA 62 [138].

6   I. INTRODUCTION

more accurate to say that the party entitled to rescind 'can revoke his or her defective consent to the agreement'.[15]

Contrast with the United States of America

1.10   The law in the United States has taken a different path. The *Third Restatement of Restitution* explains that 'rescission' as a remedy adapted to restoring both contracting parties to their pre-contractual position is available also for a subsequent repudiation or other material breach of contract.[16] In such cases the right is, however, both more restricted and more easily lost, than if it is based upon fraud, mistake, or other pre-contractual conduct affecting consent.[17] The remedy is, however, essentially the same in both types of case; in particular, in both cases rescission involves the mutual restitution *in specie* of property transferred, and mutual repayments of sums paid, so as to effect a restoration of the *status quo ante*.[18]

1.11   The justification for rescission is, however, said to be significantly different in the two fact patterns. Whereas rescission in cases of 'defective agreement', such as fraudulent misrepresentation, mistake, or undue influence, 'reverses a transfer that lacks an adequate legal basis and prevents the unjustified enrichment that would otherwise result on either side', the justification for rescission following defective performance 'is not the avoidance of unjust enrichment, but a concern with fairness to the injured party combined with remedial economy'.[19] 'Remedial economy' means the efficiency of restoring *in specie* benefits conferred under a contract, rather than incurring the time and effort to value expectation damages for breach.[20] A premise underpinning this distinction is that rescission and restitution for material breach is a remedy for breach of contract,[21] whereas rescission for a prior invalidating cause is not.

1.12   The position in the United States appears to be a further extension of the old cases that permitted 'rescission' and monetary restitution as a remedy for the other party's repudiation, at a time when no distinction was drawn between 'rescission' for pre-contractual fraud and for subsequent breach.[22] In English law this path forward, fostered by the line of

---

[15]   B Häcker, *Consequences of Impaired Consent Transfers* (2013) 21, fn 19, also pp 154, 163, 199; and cf PG Turner, 'Rescission of the Doctrine of Rescission for Fraud' (2016) 75 CLJ 206, 206–207 (right to rescind *ab initio* founded upon impairment of consent to be contractually bound).

[16]   *Restatement (Third) of Restitution* § 37 and § 54 (2011). Also, A Kull, 'Rescission and Restitution' (2006) 61 *The Business Lawyer* 569, 581–84 (discussing how the *Third Restatement of Restitution* breaks from the *Restatements of Contracts*, which are said to have confused the law in the United States by their failure to employ the term 'rescission' at all, or to properly describe it as a remedy for breach permitting restoration of both parties to the *status quo ante*).

[17]   *Restatement (Third) of Restitution* § 37 and § 54, esp § 37(2) (2011) (rescission for breach not available if defendant's only obligation is to pay money), vol 1, p 622 (no rescission for breach of executed conveyance of real property, but rescission permitted if transaction defective from inception, as for fraud or undue influence); § 54(4) (rescission for breach barred more easily than in cases of defective agreement, if counter-restitution is difficult); § 54 cmts. *d* and *e* (comparing rescission 'of defective agreements' and 'as a remedy for breach of contract', and identifying the more limited availability of the latter).

[18]   *Restatement (Third) of Restitution* § 37 and § 54 (2011).

[19]   *Restatement (Third) of Restitution* vol 2, pp 270, 271 (2011). The *Third Restatement* elsewhere observes that restitution following rescission is not always coincident with the reversal of an unjust enrichment: *Restatement (Third) of Restitution* vol 1, pp 6–7, 165–66, 607–08, vol 2 p 266 (2011). It is said that 'no issue of restitution' is presented by the avoidance of a wholly executory contract: *Restatement (Third) of Restitution* vol 1, p 167 (2011).

[20]   *Restatement (Third) of Restitution* vol 1, p 613; vol 2, pp 267, 271, 286, 324, col 1 (2011) Also, A Kull, 'Rescission and Restitution' (2006) 61 *The Business Lawyer* 569, 577 (remedial economy the 'primary justification' for rescission for breach).

[21]   *Restatement (Third) of Restitution* vol 1, pp 606–07, 613, vol 2 p 271 (2011).

[22]   Chap 3, para [3.27], also paras [3.30] and [3.31].

cases culminating in *Horsler v Zorro*,[23] was effectively blocked by the decision in *Johnson v Agnew*,[24] after which a sharp distinction is to be drawn between rescission *ab initio* for an initial invaliding cause, and termination *de futuro* for repudiation or other subsequent breach.[25] Precisely why the law in the United States has chosen its own importantly different path is unclear.[26] One reason may be that law in the United States never developed the distinction between terminating a contract *de futuro* for breach and erasing it *ab initio* for defective consent that came to be recognized in English law and elsewhere.[27]

The approach in the United States is unlikely to take hold in England, or in Commonwealth **1.13** jurisdictions where the English approach has taken root, for permitting rescission of a contract *ab initio* for its subsequent breach is at odds with the rationale underpinning the remedy as it is now conceived, which is that the contract can be unwound as from the beginning precisely because there was a defect in its formation.[28] The outcome achieved is also quite different from the basic objective of relief for breach of contract, which is to place the innocent party in the position that they would have occupied had the contract been performed, rather than in the position they were in before the contract was concluded (a point underlined in the *Third Restatement*[29]). The essentially bilateral concern of rescission is, also, at odds with the unilateral object of compensation for breach of contract, which focuses upon the position of the innocent party and not also on the position of the party in default.[30] Moreover, in those instances where restitution is permitted following termination for breach of contract, English law tends to view the right arising as founded upon the reversal of unjust enrichment.[31] For the *Third Restatement* the right is founded upon considerations of fairness to the injured party and remedial efficiency and not upon the reversal of unjust enrichment.[32] Also, the *Third Restatement* explicitly identifies rescission and restitution as remedies for breach of contract.[33] In English law, all rights to restitution in the nature of the old common counts arise independently of the terminated contract, and outside it, and cannot be characterized as remedies for breach.[34]

---

[23] [1975] 1 Ch 302; see M Albery, 'Mr Cyprian Williams' Great Heresy' (1975) 91 LQR 337.

[24] [1980] AC 367, 397.

[25] See further paras [1.07]–[1.09].

[26] For the development of the position in the United States described in the *Third Restatement of Restitution*, see A Kull, 'Rescission and Restitution' (2006) 61 *The Business Lawyer* 569; *Restatement (Third) of Restitution* vol 1, pp 606–09 (2011).

[27] See paras [1.07]–[1.09].

[28] See para [1.09].

[29] *Restatement (Third) of Restitution* vol 1, p 613, vol 2, p 271 (2011)—when rescission affords an alternative remedy for breach of a valid and enforceable contract it 'permits the injured party to make a fundamental election, choosing to go backward (to the status quo ante) instead of forward (by enforcement of the contractual exchange)'.

[30] See further Chap 13, paras [13.01]–[13.05]. Cf the right of a contracting party to terminate for breach and bring money had and received if there has been or if he can effect a total failure of consideration; as where the buyer of non-conforming goods rejects them and recovers the price paid, plus damages for breach (para [1.20]).

[31] See, eg, A Burrows, *A Restatement of the English Law of Unjust Enrichment* (2012) § 15 (and commentary thereto), 20–21, 86–92.

[32] Para [1.11].

[33] *Restatement (Third) of Restitution* vol 1, pp 606–608, 613, vol 2, p 271 (2011).

[34] In English law, breach of contract operates by permitting the contract to be terminated, and termination is a necessary condition for a claim to restitution for failure of consideration: but the right to restitution itself arises *ex contractu*, from the fact of an unjust or unjustified enrichment, and not from the breach itself. Also, A Burrows, *A Restatement of the English Law of Unjust Enrichment* (2012) § 15 (and commentary thereto), pp 20–21, 86–92, 166–67.

8   I. INTRODUCTION

(2) Termination ab initio: effects on contractual rights and obligations

1.14   A voidable contract is valid and effective until rescinded. When it is rescinded, 'the contract is treated in law as never having come into existence',[35] albeit the law recognizes that there once was a contract.[36] With certain narrow exceptions noted later, all rights and obligations existing by virtue of a contract at the moment of termination are dissolved. In order to identify these rights and obligations, it is necessary to distinguish contractual obligations that remain unperformed at the date of termination from those which have been performed. These are sometimes described as 'executory' obligations and 'executed' obligations.

1.15   Termination *ab initio* extinguishes all unperformed or executory obligations. In the case of obligations to be performed in the future this means the requirement to perform never arises. In the case of obligations the performance of which was overdue as at the date of termination, the defaulting party is released from the requirement to perform. This includes obligations that had unconditionally accrued, and which would have survived termination for breach, such as the obligation to pay a deposit.[37]

1.16   Termination *ab initio* likewise dissolves unperformed obligations intended to remain enforceable after the contract has been brought to an end, such as liquidated damages clauses, unless they can be construed as severable and unaffected by the vitiating factor. Arbitration clauses are the familiar example.[38] These are, however, unlike other terms in that the clause is itself a separate contract between the parties. There is Australian authority that exclusive jurisdiction clauses may also survive rescission *ab initio*,[39] and English support for this in the context of insurance.[40] Exclusive jurisdiction clauses are not, however, separate agreements like arbitration clauses, and the juristic basis for their survival is unclear. Mr Justice Colman expressed the view that an underwriter's contractual rights to investigate may also survive rescission of a policy of insurance.[41] This conclusion seems to have proceeded on

---

[35] *Johnson v Agnew* [1980] AC 367, 393; *Islington London Borough Council v Uckac* [2006] 1 WLR 1303 (CA) [26]; *Involnert Management Inc v Aprilgrange Limited* [2015] 2 Lloyds Rep 289 [175].

[36] *Mackender v Feldia AG* [1967] 2 QB 590 (CA) 603 (Diplock LJ); *FAI General Insurance Company Ltd v Ocean Marine Mutual Protection and Indemnity Association Ltd* (1997) 41 NSWLR 559, 563; [1998] Lloyd's Rep IR 24: 'The words are sufficient for most purposes but they cannot be taken literally. Neither rescission by a party or a judge's say so can turn back the clock to have that literal effect, and a contract avoided ab initio is not, in Newspeak, an uncontract... it remains that there was a contract' (exclusive jurisdiction clause surviving rescission); approved *Brit Syndicates Limited v Grant Thornton* [2006] EWHC 341 (Comm) [24].

[37] *McDonald v Dennys Lascelles Limited* (1933) 48 CLR 457, 476–77; *Johnson v Agnew* [1980] AC 367, 396–97; *Photo Production Ltd v Securicor Transport Ltd* [1980] AC 827, 844; *Colonial Bank v European Grain and Shipping Ltd* [1989] AC 1056, 1098–99; see also *Hurst v Bryk* [2002] 2 AC 185, 199–200.

[38] Arbitration Act 1996, s 7, following the approach in *Harbour Assurance Co (UK) v Kansa Ltd* [1993] QB 701 (jurisdiction existed where allegation that contract void *ab initio*), and moving beyond the position in *Heyman v Darwins Ltd* [1942] AC 356, 398 (suggesting arbitration clause dissolved). In Australia, *Ferris v Plaister* (1994) 34 NSWLR 474 (NSWCA) (arbitrator had jurisdiction where allegation that building contract rescinded for fraud). Cf where the arbitration agreement is independently void or voidable: *Vee Networks v Econet Wireless International Ltd* [2005] 1 Lloyd's Rep 192 [19]–[22]; *Fiona Trust & Holding Corporation v Privalov* [2007] 1 All ER (Comm) 81 [36]; [2007] 1 All ER (Comm) 891 (CA) [23]–[29]; *Premium Nafta Product Limited v Fili Shipping Company Limited* [2007] 2 All ER (Comm) 1053 (HL) [19], [35].

[39] *FAI General Insurance Company Ltd v Ocean Marine Mutual Protection and Indemnity Association Ltd* (1997) 41 NSWLR 559, 564, 567; [1998] Lloyd's Rep IR 24.

[40] *Mackender v Feldia AG* [1967] 2 QB 590 (CA); *Brit Syndicates Limited v Grant Thornton* [2006] EWHC 341 (Comm) [22]; *Involnert Management Inc v Aprilgrange Limited* [2015] 2 Lloyds Rep 289 [177]. For the argument that there exist further exceptions in the context of insurance, M Clarke, 'Rescission: a bridge too far for insurance good faith' [2012] LMCLQ 611, 612.

[41] *Strive Shipping Corporation v Hellenic Mutual War Risks Association (The Grecia Express)* [2002] 2 Lloyd's Rep 88, 163.

the footing that because rights of inspection survive termination for breach they ought equally to remain after rescission for non-disclosure.[42] However, the survival of contractual terms after termination is founded upon presumed intention, whereas their survival after rescission *ab initio* seems to be based on the idea that the obligation is severable and unaffected by the vitiating factor. Mr Justice Leggatt has since expressed the view that extension of the doctrine of separability to contractual rights of inspection is wrong in principle and unjustified as a matter of policy,[43] and it is suggested that this view is to be preferred. However similar reasoning has also been employed in Singapore, where Justice Chan Seng Onn has said *obiter* that a clause may survive rescission *ab initio* if it appears by clear language that this is what the parties intended.[44]

1.17 If property or money is conditionally transferred under a contract, such that there is upon termination *de futuro* a contractual obligation to return or repay it, termination *ab initio* dissolves that obligation.

1.18 On the other hand termination *ab initio* cannot terminate or dissolve contractual obligations that have already been performed, for following performance no obligation remains. Where a contractual obligation has been performed, termination *ab initio* takes effect by extinguishing the so-called secondary obligation to pay damages for any breach of that obligation.[45] Liability to pay damages for breach of contract is an obligation 'arising from the contract', which is the 'source' of that obligation.[46] Rescission of an agreement that has been performed extinguishes the contract from the start by dissolving any liability for breach.[47]

1.19 Equitable relief founded on the existence of contractual obligations, such as a claim for the specific performance of a contract, or an injunction to protect contractual rights, is likewise unavailable following rescission.[48]

(3) Termination de futuro: *effects on contractual rights and obligations*

1.20 A contract terminated by one party for the other's breach or repudiation, or terminated automatically by reason of frustrating events, is terminated *de futuro*, or for the future.[49] The prospective nature of termination *de futuro* means that although obligations that would have fallen due after the date of termination are extinguished, thus discharging the parties from the need to perform them, rights and obligations that have unconditionally accrued

---

[42] *Strive Shipping Corporation v Hellenic Mutual War Risks Association (The Grecia Express)* [2002] 2 Lloyd's Rep 88, 163.

[43] *Involnert Management Inc v Aprilgrange Limited* [2015] 2 Lloyd's Rep 289 [177]–[178].

[44] *Creative Technology Ltd v Huawei International Pte Ltd* [2017] SGHC 201 [293], [294] (limitation of liability clause did not survive rescission because intention to do so not expressed unequivocally).

[45] *Evans v Benson & Co* [1961] WAR 12, 17.

[46] *Lep Air Services Ltd v Rolloswin Investments Ltd* [1973] AC 331, 350; *Photo Production Ltd v Securicor Transport Ltd* [1980] AC 827, 845. In Australia, *Mann v Paterson Constructions Pty Ltd* (2019) 267 CLR 560 [12] (but cf at [194]–[197]).

[47] *Holland v Wiltshire* (1954) 90 CLR 409, 416, approved *Johnson v Agnew* [1980] AC 367, 397.

[48] Where rescission has become impossible, the vitiating conduct may still operate to bar a claim to specific performance: *AH McDonald and Company Pty Ltd v Wells* (1931) 45 CLR 506, 513.

[49] *McDonald v Dennys Lascelles Limited* (1933) 48 CLR 457, 476–78; *Heyman v Darwins Ltd* [1942] AC 356, 399; *Johnson v Agnew* [1980] AC 367, 397; *Photo Production Ltd v Securicor Transport Ltd* [1980] AC 827, 844; *Hurst v Bryk* [1999] Ch 1 (CA) 12, 21, 29; [2002] 2 AC 185, 193. For further discussion of the consequences of termination *de futuro*, E Peel, *Treitel: The Law of Contract* (15th edn, 2020) [18-016]–[18-024].

10   I. INTRODUCTION

prior to termination remain enforceable.[50] Unpaid deposits[51] and certain kinds of instalment payments[52] are the most common examples. Whether or not a right has unconditionally accrued depends upon a range of factors.[53] These include the nature of the obligation, what performance has been rendered by each party, and whether the party seeking to enforce the obligation is in breach. A central distinction is between payments on account of a lump sum price and for discrete items of performance. The question often turns on issues of construction and may be finely balanced.[54] Provisions intended to survive termination, such as liquidated damages clauses, likewise continue in force following termination *de futuro*.[55] In contrast, unconditionally accrued obligations dissolve upon termination *ab initio*, and provisions intended to survive termination will likewise dissolve, unless they fall within one of the exceptions considered earlier.

1.21   In some cases money and property will be conditionally transferred under a contract so that there is upon termination *de futuro* a contractual obligation to repay or return it.[56] These contractual rights are activated upon termination for breach. In contrast, termination *ab initio* dissolves them.

1.22   Rights to contractual damages survive termination for breach or frustration. Both parties remain liable to pay damages for any prior breaches, and where the contract is terminated for breach the defaulting party is also obliged to pay damages to compensate for the other party's loss of the bargain.[57] In contrast, all rights to damages for breach of contract are extinguished by termination *ab initio*.

(4) *Termination* ab initio *and* de futuro: *rights to restitution*

1.23   The rights to the restitution of benefits conferred under a contract terminated *ab initio* and *de futuro* are materially different. Property, money and services will each be considered separately.

---

[50]   *Lep Air Services Ltd v Rolloswin Investments Ltd* [1973] AC 331, 354–55; *Johnson v Agnew* [1980] AC 367, 397; *Photo Production Ltd v Securicor Transport Ltd* [1980] AC 827, 844, 849; *Hurst v Bryk* [2002] 2 AC 185, 193, 199. In Australia, *McDonald v Dennys Lascelles Limited* (1933) 48 CLR 457, 476–78. In Singapore, *Lim Lay Bee v Allgreen Properties Ltd* [1999] 1 SLR 471 (CA) 480–83.

[51]   *Hinton v Sparkes* (1868) LR 3 CP 161; cf in Malaysia, *Morello Sdn Bhd v Jaques (International) Sdn Bhd* [1995] 1 MLJ 577 (Fed Ct). A deposit paid by a rescinding vendor is repayable upon rescission *ab initio*: *Swindle v Knibb* (1929) 29 St Rep NSW 325, 328–29 (Harvey CJ, In Eq).

[52]   *Newfoundland Government v Newfoundland Railway Co* (1888) 13 App Cas 199, 207; *Brooks v Bernstein* [1909] 1 KB 98, 102 (instalment under a hire purchase contract).

[53]   *Dies v British and International Mining and Finance Corporation Limited* [1939] 1 KB 724, 743; *Baltic Shipping Company v Dillon* (1992) 176 CLR 344, 352–53, 391. See further J Beatson, *The Use and Abuse of Unjust Enrichment: Essays on the Law of Restitution* (1991) 45–77; E Peel, *Treitel: The Law of Contract* (15th edn, 2020) [21-005]–[21-017].

[54]   See for instance the disagreement in *Hyundai Heavy Industries Co Ltd v Papadopolous* [1980] 1 WLR 1129 (HL) 1137, 1142, 1150, 1152, 1153 (instalments under a ship-building contract), and the different analyses in *Hurst v Bryk* [1999] Ch 1; [2002] 2 AC 185 (partner's liabilities).

[55]   *Heyman v Darwins Ltd* [1942] AC 356, 374, 375, 398; *Hurst v Bryk* [1999] Ch 1, 22; also AM Shea, 'Discharge for Performance of Contracts by Failure of Condition' (1979) 42 MLR 623, 642–44.

[56]   *McDonald v Dennys Lascelles Limited* (1933) 48 CLR 457, 477; *Dies v British and International Mining and Finance Corporation Limited* [1939] 1 KB 724, 744; *Stocznia Gdanska SA v Latvian Shipping Co* [1998] 1 WLR 574 (HL) 589.

[57]   *Hurst v Bryk* [1999] Ch 1, 21–22; [2002] 2 AC 185, 193–94.

Property transferred

Title to property transferred or created[58] pursuant to a contract is generally not revested **1.24** upon termination for breach,[59] whereas this is a central effect of rescission. An exception is the purchaser who lawfully rejects non-conforming goods after title has passed to him; in that case title to the goods revests in the vendor upon the rejection.[60] However, although this situation resembles rescission, it differs insofar as termination is *de futuro* only, so that in addition to a right to recover the price paid,[61] the purchaser can claim damages for consequential losses caused by the seller's breach.[62]

Rationale

It is often said that title is revested upon rescission precisely because the contract is termin- **1.25** ated *ab initio*.[63] But this is not supported by the cases, and is difficult to reconcile with principle. That title to property is returned when a transaction is rescinded for fraud or other sufficient cause was clear from at least the seventeenth century in the courts of Chancery, and by the middle of the nineteenth at common law. At neither point had the law developed the concept of termination *ab initio*, or drawn a distinction with termination *de futuro*.[64] Nor is there support in modern authority for the proposition that title revests upon rescission because the contract is extinguished from the beginning.

The notion that title revests because the contract is extinguished *ab initio* is also difficult **1.26** to reconcile with principle, because it does not fit with various features of rescission. Title will revest upon rescission whether it initially passed by force of the contract, or by some collateral event, such as delivery or registration.[65] Rescission recovers title from a subsequent purchaser taking with notice of the relevant conduct, even though the contract with that subsequent purchaser remains in place and is enforceable.[66] Title to property gifted by delivery or other conduct is recoverable if the gift is induced by a relevant vitiating circumstance, notwithstanding that there is no contract to rescind.[67] Rescission is also available so as to revest or extinguish property even though the contract has been fully performed on both sides, so that there is in substance no contract left to be avoided.[68] Conversely, if some

---

[58] As in the case of a share issue or lease.

[59] *Total Oil Great Britain Ltd v Thompson Garages (Biggin Hill) Ltd* [1972] 1 QB 318 (CA) 324 (accepted repudiation of supply agreement did not extinguish demise of service station where agreement and demise part of one transaction); *Hurst v Bryk* [1999] Ch 1 (CA) 14, 26; also [2002] 2 AC 185, 199 (partner's interest in lease not divested upon his termination of the partnership agreement).

[60] *Kwei Tek Chao v British Traders and Shippers Ltd* [1954] 2 QB 459, 487; *Rosenthal and Sons Ltd v Esmail* [1965] 1 WLR 1117, 1131; *Berger and Co Inc v Gill & Dufus SA* [1984] 1 AC 382, 395; *Tradax Export SA v European Grain & Shipping Ltd* [1983] 2 Lloyd's Rep 100, 107. See also *Head v Tattersall* (1871) LR 7 Ex 7; JN Adams, 'Sale or Return Contracts: Shedding a Little Light' (1998) 61 MLR 432.

[61] *Kwei Tek Chao v British Traders and Shippers Ltd* [1954] 2 QB 459, 475.

[62] *Millar's Machinery Company Limited v David Way and Son* (1935) 15 Com Cas 204. See also Sale of Goods Act 1979 s 48(3), (4); *RV Ward Ltd v Bignall* [1967] 1 QB 534 (CA); M Kershaw, 'Seller and Buyer in Possession' in N Palmer and E McKendrick (eds), *Interests in Goods* (2nd edn, 1998) 329.

[63] This is, for instance, the premise of the argument in W Swadling, 'Rescission, Property, and the Common Law' (2005) 121 LQR 123. See also B Häcker, 'Rescission and Third Party Rights' [2006] 14 RLR 21, 23; B Häcker, 'Rescission of Contract and Revesting of Title: A Reply to Mr Swadling' [2006] 14 RLR 106; D Friedmann, 'Reversible Transfers—The Two Categories' [2003] 11 RLR 1, 3–5 (money). Also, DJ Meikle, 'Partial Rescission—Removing the Restitution from a Contractual Doctrine' (2003) 19 JCL 40, 56–57.

[64] See Chap 3, paras [3.15], [3.30]–[3.32], [3.38].

[65] See Chap 14, para [14.6] and Chap 15, para [15.5].

[66] See Chap 21, para [21.42].

[67] See Chap 29, paras [29.36]–[29.39]. Also, D Fox, *Property Rights in Money* (2008) [6.15]–[6.16].

[68] Eg *Killick v Roberts* [1991] 1 WLR 1146 (CA) 1150.

12 I. INTRODUCTION

exceptional event such as new legislation or the operation of the rule in *Pigot's* case caused a contract to become void, there is no reason to think that this would cause a revesting of title to property that has been transferred under the contract.[69]

1.27 Instead, title to property is recovered upon rescission because the fraud, undue influence, or other factor that makes the parties' contractual rights and obligations liable to be extinguished *ab initio* also, itself, renders defeasible title to any property that has been transferred pursuant to that contract.[70] The title is infected by the transferor's imperfect consent.[71] Extinction of the contract is simply a condition to the recovery of title, in that the law regards the contract's continuing existence as inconsistent with title revesting.[72] But it neither requires nor implies that title should revest.

1.28 The importance of drawing a distinction between the avoidance *ab initio* of contractual rights and obligations upon the rescission of a contract, and the revesting of title in assets transferred pursuant to it, has been underlined and explored in the important work of Birke Häcker.[73] More recently, Samuel Zogg has argued that the right to rescind involves two conceptually distinct powers, one *in personam* to avoid the contract, and a second *in rem* to revest ownership,[74] in the context of a wider argument that defective consent operates at three quite distinct levels, of property, contract, and unjust enrichment, and that there is no necessary correlation between its consequences at each level.[75]

---

[69] *Pigot's case* (1614) 11 Co Rep 26b, 27a; 77 ER 1177, 1178, explained A Beehag, 'Unilateral Alteration to Mortgage Documents' (1997) 8 J of Banking and Finance 289. Contrast money paid, which might be recoverable for a total failure of consideration: *Goss v Chilcott* [1996] AC 788 (PC—NZ).

[70] This view appears to be accepted in A Lodder, *Enrichment in the Law of Unjust Enrichment and Restitution* (2012) 132. Also, B Häcker, *Consequences of Impaired Consent Transfers* (2013) 211 ('the identical impairment was liable to infect both contract and conveyance'). Chap V of this work provides a sustained and comparative analysis of the point in the context of German law notions of the 'abstraction' between contract and conveyance. For the argument applied to personal rights to restitution following rescission, A Burrows, *A Restatement of the English Law of Unjust Enrichment* (2012) 162.

[71] Cf also, B Häcker, *Consequences of Impaired Consent Transfers* (2013) 154 arguing that the right to recover property on rescission 'is founded on the transferor's ability to revoke his defective consent to a conveyance either at common law or in equity', leading to a 'generalised power model' of proprietary claims upon rescission (163, 171, 199, 211); *Restatement (Third) of Restitution* (2011) vol 1, 164 'Where consent is defective for any of the reasons addressed in this Topic, the resulting transfer lacks an adequate legal basis. This means that it is ineffective to work a definitive alteration in property rights between the owner and transferee'; see also, vol 1, p 45.

[72] *Great Investments Ltd v Warner* (2016) 243 FCR 516 (Full Ct) [56], [57] (contract governs rights to property until set aside); *Addenbrooke Pty Ltd v Duncan (No 2)* (2017) 121 ACSR 406 (Full Fed Ct) [538], [539] (rescission necessary before constructive trust can arise because inconsistent with existence of the contract); cf *Australian Annuities Pty Ltd v Rowley Super Find Pty Ltd* [2015] VSCA 9 [128], [312] (rescission rule prevents double recovery—once upon proprietary restitutionary claim and a second time under the contract). But cf B Häcker, 'Rescission and Third Party Rights' [2006] RLR 1, 3–4; D Fox, *Property Rights in Money* (2008) [6.17]–[6.18]. Also, S Zogg, *Proprietary Consequences in Defective Transfers of Ownership* (2020) 117–18, 122, 477–78; Chap 20, paras [20.19]–[20.20].

[73] B Häcker, 'Rescission and Third Party Rights' [2006] 14 RLR 21, 23; B Häcker, 'Rescission of Contract and Revesting of Title: A Reply to Mr Swadling' [2006] 14 RLR 106; B Häcker, 'Proprietary Restitution after Impaired Consent Transfers: A Generalised Power Model' (2009) CLJ 324; B Häcker, *Consequences of Impaired Consent Transfers* (2013) 49–50, 125–59, 196–200, 211, 324–25. Cf A Lodder, *Enrichment in the Law of Unjust Enrichment and Restitution* (2012) 132. For the argument that rescission and restitution are wholly separate, N Tamblyn, 'Separating Recission and Restitution' (2016) 33 JCL 135.

[74] S Zogg, *Proprietary Consequences in Defective Transfers of Ownership* (2020) 139, 178–80, 211.

[75] S Zogg, *Proprietary Consequences in Defective Transfers of Ownership* (2020) chap 2 section 1, chap 4 sections 1.2 and 5, and chap 7, esp table 2 at p 540 (further developing ideas explained in S Zogg, *Effects of Mistake and other Defects on the Passage of Legal Title* (2019)).

Money paid

A personal claim to the recovery of money paid under a voidable contract always arises **1.29** upon rescission. On the other hand, it will generally only arise following the termination of a contract *de futuro* if the contract so provides, the consideration for the payment has totally failed, or if the parties' relationship is such that an equitable obligation to account arises, as upon the termination of a contract of agency or partnership.

Services rendered

A claim to payment in respect of services rendered also usually arises upon rescission, but **1.30** is rarely imposed following the termination of a contract *de futuro*. Unless the contract itself requires payment for work done prior to termination, a claim for a *quantum meruit* must be made out, and that is difficult where a contract is terminated for breach.[76] The rights of the service provider are generally to be found in the contract, not a restitutionary claim arising outside it.[77] A *quantum meruit* would appear to be confined to cases where the service provider has been wrongfully prevented from performing, or is in breach but the injured party has sufficiently accepted the benefit provided, or the case falls within another exceptional circumstance in which the law will permit recovery in restitution.[78]

(5) Terminology

The term 'rescission' is often used to refer both to the extinction of a voidable con- **1.31** tract *ab initio*, and to its termination *de futuro* for breach, particularly where the breach consists of a repudiation. This leads to confusion. Williston underlined the problem more than 100 years ago,[79] and his point has been repeated since.[80]

---

[76] For examples of successful claims: *Planche v Colburn* (1831) 8 Bing 14, 131 ER 305 (repudiation); *Pavey & Matthews Pty Ltd v Paul* (1986) 162 CLR 221 (contract unenforceable by statute). But cf where the party seeking payment on a *quantum meruit* is itself in breach: *Sumpter v Hedges* [1898] 1 QB 673 (builder's claim for payment of reasonable value of work carried out dismissed). See further, E Peel, *Treitel: The Law of Contract* (15th edn, 2020) [17-041]–[17-042], [17-1046], [17-1048], [22-032], [22-033].

[77] *Taylor v Motability Finance Ltd* [2004] EWHC 2619.

[78] E Peel, *Treitel: The Law of Contract* (15th edn, 2020) [22-032], [22-033]. For the position in Australia, *Mann v Paterson Constructions Pty Ltd* (2019) 267 CLR 560.

[79] '[W]ords have their importance. If wrongly used, wrong ideas are sure to follow, and wrong decisions follow wrong ideas. It is a source of serious confusion in the cases that a contract is frequently spoken of as 're-scinded'. . . when in truth one party to the contract has merely exercised his right to refuse to perform because of the wrongful conduct of the other party': S Williston, 'Repudiation of Contracts' (1901) 14 Harv LR 421, 425.

[80] *Mersey Steel and Iron Co v Naylor Benzon & Co* (1882) 9 QBD 648, 671 ('A fallacy may possibly lurk in use of the word "rescission" '); *Johnson v Agnew* [1980] AC 367, 392–93; *Hurst v Bryk* [2002] 2 AC 185, 194 ('The failure to distinguish between discharge by breach and rescission *ab initio* has led many courts astray and continues to do so'). Also, *Hunt v Hyde* [1976] 2 NZLR 453, 457. For other judicial discussion of the meaning of 'rescind', *Mussen v Van Diemen's Land Co* [1938] Ch 253, 260; *Horsler v Zorro* [1975] 1 Ch 302, 310–11; *Buckland v Farmar and Moody* [1979] 1 WLR 220 (CA) 231–32, 237; *Photo Production Ltd v Securicor Transport Ltd* [1980] AC 827, 844; *Munchies Management Pty Ltd v Belpario* (1988) 58 FCR 274, 287; *RBC Properties Pte Ltd v Defu Furniture Pte Ltd* [2014] SGCA 62 [138]; *Carbone v Metricon Homes Pty Ltd* [2018] NSWCA 296 [3], [39], [47]. For comment in the literature, A Bate, 'Rescission' [1955] Conv 116; M Albery, 'Mr Cyprian Williams' Great Heresy' (1975) 91 LQR 337, 342, 343, 351, 355–56; F Dawson, 'Rescission and Damages' (1976) 39 MLR 214, 217; AM Shea, 'Discharge for Performance of Contracts by Failure of Condition' (1979) 42 MLR 623, 626–30, 634; JD Heydon, MJ Leeming, and PG Turner, *Meagher Gummow and Lehane's Equity Doctrines and Remedies* (5th edn, 2015) [25-005]–[25-030]; E Peel, *Treitel: The Law of Contract* (15th edn, 2020) [9-096], [9-097].

14   I. INTRODUCTION

Although it has been said that 'rescission' should be reserved for termination *ab initio*,[81] it continues to be used indiscriminately.[82]

1.32   This current practice follows a long habit. The term 'rescission' has been used to describe the discharge of a contract for post-contractual breach, or for a pre-contractual misrepresentation, since at least 1800.[83] This was probably underpinned by the late arrival of the distinction between termination *de futuro* and *ab initio*. Further, as a matter of language, although the word 'rescission' and 'rescind' combine *re-* (back) and *scindere* ('to cut or tear asunder')[84] the combination can mean two different things. It may mean to cut *off*, and also to *annul* or *abrogate*.[85] The former connotes a prospective cutting off; the latter a retrospective annulment.

1.33   Even once confined to rescission *ab initio*, the terms 'rescind' and 'rescission' can refer to quite different things. The verb 'rescind' tends to connote the *action* of electing to reject a contract or gift. That is an empirical event, the subject of evidence. But 'rescind' as well as 'rescission' may also denote the legal *outcome* that may follow that action. In between these two meanings, the words may describe the phenomenon or process by which the outcome is achieved and a voidable transaction is undone. When used in that sense, 'rescission' describes the creation and extinction of rights and obligations in a manner adapted to annulling and reversing the legal relations that had formerly obtained, whilst the transaction was intact.[86]

1.34   In some cases the action of electing to rescind does not itself cause the legal process of rescission, while in others it does. Where it is important to separate the act of rescinding from the legal process of rescission, 'disaffirm' is better than 'rescind'.

---

[81]   PBH Birks, *Unjust Enrichment* (2nd edn, 2005) 299. Also, E Peel, *Treitel: The Law of Contract* (15th edn, 2020) [9-097], [18-001] preferring 'termination' to 'rescission' for cases of breach, and in this respect changing the nomenclature in earlier editions: eg GH Treitel, *The Law of Contract* (11th edn, 2003) 759–60.

[82]   Eg *Kwei Tek Chao v British Traders and Shippers Ltd* [1954] 2 QB 459, 480 (right to reject non-conforming goods 'a particular form of the right to rescind'); Sale of Goods Act 1979, s 48 ('rescission' by unpaid seller); *Stocznia Gdanska SA v Latvian Shipping Co* [1998] 1 WLR 574 (HL) ('rescission' for repudiation); *RBC Properties Pte Ltd v Defu Furniture Pte Ltd* [2014] SGCA 62 [138] (difference between 'rescission' for misrepresentation and for repudiation of a lease). See also A Kull, 'Restitution as a Remedy for Breach of Contract' (1994) 67 So Cal LR 1465, 1491 criticizing 'fastidious objection to' and 'exquisite correctness' in the use of the term rescind by American lawyers, and endorsing it as a term to describe any termination for breach leading to restitutionary claims, and reflected now in the *Restatement (Third) of Restitution* § 37 and § 54 (2011); discussed at paras [1.10]–[1.13].

[83]   Eg *Grimaldi v White* (1802) 4 Esp 95, 96; 170 ER 654, 654 ('rescind' for misrepresentation by non-disclosure); *Cox v Prentice* (1815) 3 M & S 344, 350; 105 ER 641, 643 ('rescind' for mistake); *Campbell v Fleming* (1834) 1 Ad & E 40, 42; 110 ER 1122, 1123 ('rescind' for fraud); *Grenville v Da Costa* (1797) Peake Add Cas 113, 114; 97 ER 213 ('rescind' for inability to perform); *Ehrensperger v Anderson* (1848) 3 Ex 148, 158; 154 ER 793, 158 ('rescind' for total refusal to perform). The use of 'rescind' to mean termination for repudiation, breach, or fraud is made explicit in *Fitt v Cassanet* (1842) 4 Man & G 898, 134 ER 369.

[84]   CT Onions (ed), *The Oxford Dictionary of English Etymology* (1966) 759 'rescind'; JA Simpson and ESC Weiner (eds), *The Oxford English Dictionary* (2nd edn, 1989) vol 13, 689 'rescission'.

[85]   *The Oxford Dictionary of English Etymology* (1966) 'rescind', 'rescission'. See also PBH Birks, *Unjust Enrichment* (2nd edn, 2005) 299: 'The Latin verb "scindere" was a strong word, with overtones of force, for "to cut" or "to cleave", and "rescindere" meant "to hack back" or "to hack down" and, by transference, "to cancel" or "to annul". It is not yet clear exactly how the word entered our law'; CB Morison, *Rescission of Contracts: A Treatise on the Principles Governing the Rescission, Discharge, Avoidance and Dissolution of Contracts* (1916) 10 'the word "rescission" is from the Latin *rescissio* (Fr *rescision*), *rescindere* meaning, primarily, to (physically) cut off, cut loose, cut or break down, to cut or tear open, and figuratively, in Roman law, to annul, abrogate, or repeal a law, decree, agreement, etc, and apparently, a personal status'.

[86]   See also PBH Birks, *Unjust Enrichment* (2nd edn, 2005) 299–300; R Zimmermann, 'Restitution after Termination for Breach of Contract in German Law' [1997] 5 RLR 13, 14; A Lodder, *Enrichment in the Law of Unjust Enrichment* (2012) 118.

C. Void and Voidable Contracts

Contracts that are valid until rescinded are conventionally called voidable contracts. The **1.35** discussion that follows distinguishes voidable contracts from contracts that are void from the start, and also distinguishes voidable contracts from contracts that are ineffective until ratified. It also considers the differences between the right to transfer and to recover benefits under void and voidable contracts.

(1) Void and voidable contracts

Void contracts

Although it is, if read literally, a contradiction in terms, the phrase 'void contract' is the con- **1.36** ventional label for the situation where two parties intend to agree and, as the case may be, to perform a legally binding contract, but no binding contract in fact comes into being. A variety of factors may have been responsible. There might have been insufficient consensus, as for example, where the parties were always at cross-purposes.[87] The contract might otherwise be void for mistake at common law,[88] as, for example, where its subject matter did not exist.[89] A plea of *non est factum* might be available to one party.[90] The agreement may have been *ultra vires* one of the parties,[91] or wholly void because prohibited by statute.[92] It is not the case that an agreement comes into being, but is unenforceable, as for lack of a statutory formality or other requirement.[93] No contract at all arises.

Voidable contracts

A void contract is quite different from a contract that is validly formed unless and until one **1.37** of the parties rescinds it *ab initio*. In that case the contract is binding until rescinded, and the right to rescind provides the only qualification to its enforceability. Contracts of this kind are usually described as 'voidable'. The contract is valid but is able to be made void by rescinding it.

Void and voidable instruments

Deeds and other instruments executed in order to transfer an interest in property or money, **1.38** as opposed to evidencing contractual rights and obligations, are also sometimes described as 'void'. When used in that context, the term void usually connotes that the instrument is of no force and effect: not in the sense that it fails to give rise to binding contractual obligations,

---

[87] *Falck v Williams* [1900] AC 176 (message confirming one charter understood as referring to another).

[88] *Bell v Lever Bros Ltd* [1932] AC 161; *Great Peace Shipping Ltd v Tsavliris Salvage (International) Ltd* [2003] QB 679 (CA).

[89] *McRae v Commonwealth Disposals Commission* (1951) 84 CLR 377 (salvage agreement for non-existent tanker).

[90] *Saunders v Anglia Building Society* [1971] AC 1004 (claim failed on facts).

[91] *Westdeutsche Landesbank Girozentrale v Islington LBC* [1996] AC 669 (swaps *ultra vires* local council).

[92] Eg oral contracts for the sale of land, under the Law of Property (Miscellaneous Provisions) Act 1989, s 2(1) (*Tootal Clothing Ltd v Guinea Properties Management Ltd* (1992) 64 P & CR 452 (CA) 455; but cf the Law of Property Act 1925, s 40), or gaming and wagering contracts under the former Gaming Act 1845, s 18 (*Lipkin Gorman v Karpnal* [1991] 2 AC 548, 577—however, s 18 of the Gaming Act 1845 was repealed by s 334(1)(c) of the Gambling Act 2005, and under s 335 the fact that a contract relates to gambling does not prevent its enforcement).

[93] Eg *Pavey & Matthews Pty v Paul* (1986) 162 CLR 221 (Builders Licensing Act 1971 (NSW)).

16   I. INTRODUCTION

but in the sense that it is not effective to transfer whatever interest is sought to be conveyed or assigned. It is 'void' in that it has no dispositive effect. This may be contrasted with an instrument that is effective to pass property rights, but subject to a right to regain those rights upon rescission. These are also sometimes described as 'voidable'. The main examples are deeds of gift vitiated by mistake or undue influence.[94]

(2) Contracts valid until rescinded and contracts ineffective until ratified

1.39   Sometimes a void contract may be made valid and binding by one party's election to ratify it. Most void contracts cannot be resuscitated in this way, and contracts that are void until ratified will for convenience be called 'ineffective' contracts. Bargains of this kind are sometimes called 'voidable' contracts, even though they are in substance the converse of a contract that is valid until rescinded. That difference is briefly considered next.

Contracts ineffective until ratified
1.40   A contract is ineffective until ratified where neither party is entitled or obliged under it unless and until the agreement is ratified, whereupon it becomes fully binding between the parties. This occurs when an agent concludes a bargain without having the actual or apparent authority of his principal to do so. The agreement is unenforceable until ratified by the principal, and the principal is the only party entitled to do so. Once ratified, the contract becomes binding as if the agent had actual authority as at the date he procured the agreement.[95] The ratification is effective retrospectively, and the contract is binding even if ratified after the other party has sought to withdraw,[96] and, apparently, such that title passing by force of the contract is deemed to have been conferred retrospectively.[97]

1.41   An agreement of this kind has variously been described as voidable not void,[98] not voidable,[99] as a transaction that is not a nullity,[100] and as one that is not the principal's contract and is not enforceable.[101] It has also been said that 'there is nothing to avoid or rescind' because no contract comes into existence,[102] but also that a transaction of this kind may be 'set aside'.[103]

Contrast with contracts valid until rescinded
1.42   Although it has been said that a contract that is ineffective until ratified is 'voidable' and may be 'set aside', it is 'voidable' only in the loose sense that one party has a choice to make

---

[94] The rescission of deeds of gift are attended by certain special rules, and these are separately considered in Chap 29.

[95] See further PG Watts and FMB Reynolds (eds), *Bowstead and Reynolds on Agency* (22nd edn, 2020) [2-047] (Article 13).

[96] *Bolton Partners v Lambert* (1889) 41 ChD 295 (CA).

[97] *Lawson (Inspector of Taxes) v Hosemaster Co Ltd* [1966] 1 WLR 1300, 1314 (transfer of shares).

[98] *Brook v Hook* (1871) LR 6 Exch 89, 99.

[99] *Heinl v Jyske Bank (Gibraltar) Ltd* [1999] Lloyd's Rep Bank 511 (CA) 521, 533; also *Brook v Hook* (1871) LR 6 Exch 89, 96.

[100] *Bolton Partners v Lambert* (1889) 41 ChD 295 (CA) 309 (Lindley LJ).

[101] *Rolled Steel Products (Holdings) Ltd v British Steel Corporation* [1986] 1 Ch 246 (CA) 299; *Criterion Properties plc v Stratford UK Properties LLC* [2004] 1 WLR 1846 (HL) 1856.

[102] *Heinl v Jyske Bank (Gibraltar) Ltd* [1999] Lloyd's Rep Bank 511 (CA) 521; see also 533.

[103] *Criterion Properties plc v Stratford UK Properties LLC* [2004] 1 WLR 1846 (HL) 1848.

it either binding or not binding. But that choice is largely the converse of the choice given to the party entitled to rescind. The choice of the party able to ratify is whether he will take steps to turn an ineffective transaction into a binding contract as from the beginning, or decline to ratify and so leave the agreement without force or effect. The choice of the party entitled to rescind is whether to take steps to extinguish and undo an otherwise valid and binding agreement as from the beginning, or instead to affirm and enforce his existing contractual rights.

In both contexts the party entitled enjoys a defence to claims upon the contract which may **1.43** be lost by his unilateral act: affirmation in the case of rescission, and ratification in the case of an agent's unauthorized agreement. But this apparent similarity is also founded on a fundamental difference. In the former case a defence exists because the contract can be set aside as from the beginning, and is lost by affirmation precisely because that extinguishes the entitlement to rescind. In the case of an unauthorized bargain, on the other hand, the contractual defence exists because the bargain is not binding when concluded, and is lost by ratification precisely because that makes it effective as from the beginning.

In addition, a contract valid until rescinded is capable of transferring property, and confers **1.44** a right to retain other benefits received under it unless and until it is set aside. A contract ineffective until ratified is incapable itself of transferring property rights, and confers no rights to retain benefits received unless and until it is ratified.[104]

(3) Transfer of title

Whereas no contractual rights or obligations arise where a contract is void, a voidable con- **1.45** tract is fully effective until rescinded. One consequence of this is that it is more difficult to transfer title to property where a contract is void than it is where the contract is merely voidable.

Title to property cannot pass pursuant to the terms of a void contract, for the law has de- **1.46** nuded those terms of legal force. The disponee must instead, if he is able, found title on acts done by the disponer when performing the apparent contract. Although legal title to money will generally pass where payment is made pursuant to a void contract,[105] property in chattels is transferred only if there is a delivery coupled with a sufficient intention that title will pass.[106] This latter requirement may not be satisfied in the case of some void contracts, and

---

[104] *Heinl v Jyske Bank (Gibraltar) Ltd* [1999] Lloyd's Rep Bank 511 (CA) 521.

[105] *Westdeutsche Landesbank Girozentrale v Islington LBC* [1996] AC 669, 689; *Sinclair v Brougham* [1924] AC 398, 418; *Barclays Bank Ltd v WJ Simms Son & Cooke (Southern) Ltd* [1980] 1 QB 677, 689. See also *Norwich Union Fire Insurance Society Ltd v WMH Price Ltd* [1934] AC 455 (PC—Aust); *Porter v Latec Finance (Qld) Pty Ltd* (1964) 111 CLR 177; D Fox, 'The Transfer of Legal Title to Money' [1996] RLR 60, 69–70. But no title passes where payments are made from one bank account to another. Rather, the payee comes to own title in a new asset, being the new or larger chose in action represented by the new or increased credit balance in his bank account: *R v Preddy* [1996] AC 815.

[106] *Cochrane v Moore* (1890) 25 QB 57 (CA), discussed F Pollock, 'Gifts of Chattels Without Delivery' (1890) 24 LQR 446, 446–51; see also *R v Hinks* [2001] 2 AC 241, 266; W Holdsworth, *A History of English Law* (A Goodhart et al, (eds)) (7th edn, 1956) vol 7, 503–09; and *Whittaker v Campbell* [1984] 1 QB 318 (Div Ct) 326–27 (no general principle of law that fraud vitiates consent); *Shogun Finance v Hudson* [2004] 1 AC 919 [6]–[8] (fraud does not itself negative contractual intention).

18   I. INTRODUCTION

is usually not satisfied where goods are delivered to a fraudster pretending to be someone else. In such a case it has been held that the contract is void and no title passes.[107]

1.47   On the other hand, a contract for the sale of land that is void for lack of writing will not prevent title to that land from passing upon conveyance,[108] and registration pursuant to a void contract will generally confer title to registered land.[109] But no title can pass if the estate is to be conveyed by deed rather than registration, and the instrument of conveyance is itself void. This is so, for example, when a deed of gift is executed by a donor of impaired mental capacity,[110] or where a plea of *non est factum* is available,[111] or where a conveyance of land is attempted other than by deed.[112]

1.48   There are not the same difficulties in transferring rights to assets under a voidable contract. The contract is valid until rescinded. Pending rescission it can transfer rights to money and to other assets as effectively as any other contract. So, for example, in cases where goods are delivered to a fraudster pretending to be someone else, and the fraud renders the contract voidable rather than void, title will generally pass.[113] Similarly, where an instrument of transfer is voidable, as in the case of a deed of gift vitiated by a serious unilateral mistake, the deed or other instrument is effective according to its terms unless and until set aside by the court.[114]

(4) Recovery of benefits

1.49   There are quite different rights to recover any benefits that may have been conferred in the course of performing void and voidable contracts. Of key importance is the general rule that a contract must first be brought to an end before the law will intervene and impose obligations to return benefits that were transferred pursuant to its terms.

1.50   The common law does not impose an obligation to repay sums paid under a contract unless and until the contract is terminated. The rule applies both to contracts that may be rescinded, and to those that may be terminated for breach or frustration.

---

[107] *Cundy v Lindsay* (1878) 3 App Cas 459, 466, 469, 471 (sale and delivery of handkerchiefs to fraudster); *Ingram v Little* [1961] 1 QB 31 (CA) (sale and delivery of car to fraudster). But cf C MacMillan 'Rogues, Swindlers and Cheats: The Development of Mistake of Identity in English Contract Law' [2005] 64 CLJ 711, 730, which may raise doubts as to whether *Cundy v Lindsay* offers reliable general guidance as to the intention necessary to pass title when chattels are delivered under a void contract. In Australia, *Citibank Ltd v Papandony* [2002] NSWCA 375 [64]–[65]; *MBF Australia Ltd v Malouf* [2008] NSWCA 214 [65]–[72]; *Perpetual Trustees Australia Ltd v Heperu Pty Ltd* (2009) 76 NSWLR 195 (CA) [71] (no title passes in cheques delivered by victim of fraud where no contract comes into being).

[108] *Tootal Clothing Ltd v Guinea Properties Management Ltd* (1992) 64 P & CR 452 (CA) 455; Law of Property (Miscellaneous Provisions) Act 1989, s 2.

[109] Land Registration Act 2002, s 58(1); *Nasrulla v Rashid* [2020] Ch 37 (CA) (forged transfer). In the Torrens system, *Fraser v Walker* [1967] 1 AC 569, *Breskvar v Wall* (1971) 126 CLR 376. See further E Cook and P O'Connor, 'Purchaser Liability to Third Parties in The English Land Registration System: A Comparative Perspective' (2004) 120 LQR 640.

[110] *Re Beaney Decd* [1978] 1 WLR 771 (deed of conveyance void); Chap 29, para [29.09].

[111] *Saunders v Anglia Building Society* [1971] AC 1004 (claim failed on the facts).

[112] Law of Property Act 1925, s 52(1).

[113] *Phillips v Brooks Ltd* [1919] 2 KB 243; *Lewis v Averay* [1972] 1 QB 198 (CA). See also D O'Sullivan, 'Distributing the Risk of Contract Fraud' (2001) 117 LQR 381.

[114] *Gibbon v Mitchell* [1990] 1 WLR 1304.

1. CORE DISTINCTIONS   19

Although probably first formulated for technical reasons peculiar to the forms of action, as **1.51**
a brake on claims in general assumpsit, and mainly in order to protect defendants,[115] the
agreed explanation for the rule today is that the contract governs the parties' rights until it
is brought to an end. The obligation to repay that the law imposes is inconsistent with the
terms of the contract, so it cannot arise until the contract is ended.[116] This thinking has
been described as an 'article of faith',[117] although one questioned by some scholars.[118] It also
applies to obligations imposed by the common law to make payment in respect of services
conferred under a contract,[119] and even if the contract is unenforceable.[120]

Despite having been developed by the old common law courts, the rule is now applied **1.52**
to claims to recover money paid under contracts that may be set aside in equity,[121] and is
treated as generally applicable when money is transferred under a voidable contract.[122]

---

[115] See Chap 3, para [3.25].

[116] *Barclays Bank Ltd v WJ Simms Son & Cooke (Southern) Ltd* [1980] 1 QB 677, 695; *Enimont Overseas AG v RO Jugotanker Zadar (The Olib)* [1991] 2 Lloyd's Rep 108, 118; *Dimskal Shipping Co SA v International Transport Workers Federation (The Evia Luck)* [1992] 2 AC 152, 165; *Pan Ocean Shipping Co Ltd v Creditcorp Ltd* [1994] 1 WLR 161 (HL) 164; SA Smith, 'Concurrent Liability in Contract and Unjust Enrichment: The Fundamental Breach Requirement' (1999) 115 LQR 245, 252–53 and J Beatson 'The Temptation of Elegance: Concurrence of Restitutionary and Contractual Claims' in W Swadling and G Jones (eds), *The Search for Principle: Essays in Honour of Lord Goff of Chieveley* (1999) 143, 147–50. Contrast *Miles v Wakefield Metropolitan DC* [1987] AC 539 (principle not applied). In Australia, *Baltic Shipping Company v Dillon* (1992) 176 CLR 344, 355–56; *Electricity Generation Corporation v Woodside Energy Ltd* [2013] WASCA 36 [33], [201]–[206] (point referred but not considered on appeal to the High Court, at (2014) 306 ALR 25 [32]); contrast *Roxborough v Rothmans of Pall Mall Australia* (2001) 208 CLR 516 (principle not applied) (discussed J Beatson and G Virgo, 'Contract, Unjust Enrichment and Unconscionability' (2002) 118 LQR 352; PBH Birks, 'Failure of Consideration and its Place on the Map' (2002) 2 OUCLJ 1; B Kremer, 'Restitution and Unconscientiousness: Another View' (2003) 119 LQR 188; P Jaffey, 'Failure of Consideration: Roxburgh v Rothmans' (2003) 66 MLR 284).

[117] SA Smith, 'Concurrent Liability in Contract and Unjust Enrichment: The Fundamental Breach Requirement' (1999) 115 LQR 245, 253.

[118] F Dawson, 'Rescission and Damages' (1976) 39 MLR 214, 219; SA Smith, 'Concurrent Liability in Contract and Unjust Enrichment: The Fundamental Breach Requirement' (1999) 115 LQR 245, 253–55; J Beatson 'The Temptation of Elegance: Concurrence of Restitutionary and Contractual Claims' in W Swadling and G Jones (eds), *The Search for Principle: Essays in Honour of Lord Goff of Chieveley* (1999) 143, 146, 151–57, 169; A Tettenborn, 'Subsisting Contracts and Failure of Consideration—A Little Scepticism' [2002] RLR 1. This discussion forms part of a wider literature concerning the relationship between rules of contract law and restitutionary obligations said to derive from unjust enrichment. Eg, S Stoljar, 'Contract, Gift and Quasi-Contract' (1959) 3 Sydney LR 33; SD Henderson, 'Promises Grounded in the Past: The Idea of Unjust Enrichment and the Law of Contracts' (1971) 57 Virginia LR 1115; JM Perillo, 'Restitution in a Contractual Context' (1973) 73 Columbia LR 1208; A Mead, 'Restitution Within Contract?' (1991) LS 172; K Barker, 'Unjust Enrichment: Containing the Beast' (1995) 15 OJLS 457, 459–63; D Nolan, 'The Classical Legacy and Modern English Contract Law' (1996) 59 MLR 603, 610–11; A Skelton, *Restitution and Contract* (1998); A Kull, 'Restitution as a Remedy for Breach of Contract' (1994) 67 So Cal LR 1465; A Kull, 'Restitution and the Non-Contractual Transfer' (1997) 11 JCL 93; *Restatement (Third) of Restitution* § 2(2), and cmt c, vol 1, pp 608–09 (2011). As to German law, R Zimmermann, 'Restitution after Termination for Breach of Contract in German Law' [1997] 5 RLR 13.

[119] *Steven v Bromley & Son* [1919] 2 KB 722 (HL) 730; *Re Richmond Gate Property Co Ltd* [1965] 1 WLR 335, 338, discussed KW Wedderburn, 'Contractual Rights Under Articles of Association—An Overlooked Principle Illustrated' (1965) 28 MLR 347–48; AT Denning, '*Quantum Meruit* and the Statute of Frauds' (1925) 41 LQR 79–80.

[120] *Pavey & Matthews Pty v Paul* (1986) 162 CLR 221, 234–35, 256 (contract unenforceable by statute to be terminated before *quantum meruit* could be claimed). The position is different if the statute also prohibits claims for a *quantum meruit.*

[121] *Cargill v Bower* (1878) LR 10 ChD 502, 517–18 'so long as the contract stands I could not direct the company to repay to the Plaintiff the money which, if the contract stands, are not properly repayable. He cannot have that money unless the contract is rescinded' (share issue under fraudulent prospectus); *Portman Building Society v Hamlyn Taylor Neck (a firm)* [1998] 4 All ER 202 (CA) 208.

[122] Eg *Re Goldcorp Exchange* [1995] 1 AC 74 (PC—NZ) 102; *Deutsche Morgan Grenfell v IRC* [2007] 1 AC 558 [84]–[85] (Lord Scott, dissenting, but not on this point); *Angove's Pty Ltd v Bailey* [2016] 1 WLR 3179 (Sup Ct) [31].

20   I. INTRODUCTION

1.53   The same logic should apply in relation to legal title to property that has passed pursuant to the terms of a voidable contract. Recovering legal title is inconsistent with the terms of the contract, and so can only occur after it is extinguished.[123]

1.54   The general rule is that the location of equitable title is also to be ascertained by reference to the contract so long as it stands.[124] But equitable title differs from legal title because an equitable proprietary interest may attach to money or property transferred under a voidable contract even though the contract is not extinguished at common law. It is sufficient if the transaction has been vitiated on grounds sufficient to generate a proprietary interest, the party asserting the interest elects to disaffirm the contract, and a court order for rescission remains available.[125]

1.55   The position is quite different where money is paid performing a void contract, and may be recovered because paid under a mistake, or because the consideration for it was absent or has failed. In such cases the payee is obliged to refund the sums paid as from the moment of receipt.[126] The position is the same where money is otherwise paid over in the mistaken belief that it was due, or by accident.[127] In both cases no demand is required before the common law imposes a debt in favour of the payer.[128] Similarly, if the provider of services under a void contract has a right to restitution in respect of work done, that right will also generally arise as from the time that the services were provided.[129] The position is quite different when benefits are transferred under a voidable contract. As has been seen, no right to restitution can arise unless and until the voidable contract is set aside, save insofar as an equitable proprietary interest may be crystallized when the innocent party elects to disaffirm the transaction.

1.56   The final principal difference between these two contexts is the fragility of the right to restitution. Personal restitutionary rights arising in the context of void contracts are lost *pro tanto* to the extent that the recipient enjoys a defence of change of position. There is no defence of this kind when benefits are conferred under a voidable contract. Instead, the right to restitution is lost entirely whenever any of the various bars to rescission are engaged. The

---

[123] *Hogan v Healy* (1877) 11 IR Ex 119, 121–22; see also *Clough v London and North Western Railway Co* (1871) LR 7 Ex 26, 34, 36 (recovery of title co-incident with extinction of contract). In Australia, *Great Investments Ltd v Warner* (2016) 243 FCR 516 (Full Ct) [56], [57] (contract governs rights to property until set aside); *Addenbrooke Pty Ltd v Duncan (No 2)* (2017) 121 ACSR 406 (Full Fed Ct) [538], [539] (rescission necessary before constructive trust can arise because inconsistent with existence of the contract); S Zogg, *Proprietary Consequences in Defective Transfers of Ownership* (2020) 117–18, 122 (contract provides basis for retention of ownership); also [1.27] above.

[124] *Daly v The Sydney Stock Exchange Limited* (1986) 160 CLR 371, 389; *Angove's Pty Ltd v Bailey* [2016] 1 WLR 3179 (Sup Ct) [31] ('the recipient having a contractual right to the money, it could not be unconscionable for them to receive it into their account'—rejecting the proposition that a constructive trust arose); *Addenbrooke Pty Ltd v Duncan (No 2)* (2017) 121 ACSR 406 (Full Fed Ct) [538], [539].

[125] See Chap 16, paras [16.21] and [16.22].

[126] *David Securities Pty Ltd v Commonwealth Bank of Australia* (1992) 175 CLR 353, 389 (payment under clause void for illegality); *Westdeutsche Landesbank Girozentrale v Islington LBC* [1996] AC 669, 717; [1994] 1 WLR 938 (CA) 943, 955 (contracts void as *ultra vires*). But cf where the factors causing the contract to be void also prevent any claim to restitution; as to which, E Peel, *Treitel: The Law of Contract* (15th edn, 2020) [22-026].

[127] *Barclays Bank Ltd v WJ Simms Son & Cooke (Southern) Ltd* [1980] 1 QB 677, 695; *David Securities Pty Ltd v Commonwealth Bank of Australia* (1992) 175 CLR 353, 389; *Fuller v Happy Shopper Markets Ltd* [2001] 2 Lloyd's Rep 49, 53–54.

[128] *Fuller v Happy Shopper Markets Ltd* [2001] 2 Lloyd's Rep 49, 54.

[129] *Craven-Ellis v Canons Ltd* [1936] 2 KB 403 (CA) 409–12.

right to restitution is therefore significantly more fragile where benefits are conferred under a voidable rather than a void contract.

D. Rescission and Transactions Ineffective in Equity

(1) Introduction

The general rule is that title to property passes under a voidable contract or gift and is recoverable if and when rescission occurs. In some circumstances, however, equity immediately fetches back beneficial title to assets transferred under a contract or gift, compelling the recipient to hold the title obtained on trust for the transferor as from the moment of its receipt. In cases of this kind equity makes the disposition of the asset ineffective as from the start. The transaction is not voidable, and the principles of rescission do not apply. A transaction may be ineffective in equity if the contract through which it was made is binding at law, or if the contract was wholly void at law. There is no symmetry between the incidence of void contracts and of transactions ineffective in equity.   **1.57**

The difference between voidable transactions and transactions ineffective in equity is one of practical importance. In the case of a voidable transaction, the availability of a proprietary claim is more fragile because it is subject to all of the bars to rescission, which do not inhibit the right to assert a proprietary interest when a transaction is ineffective in equity. Indeed, it has been said that requiring rescission is a means of ensuring that proper account is taken of the rights of third parties, and to prevent simultaneous recovery under the contract and by a proprietary remedy.[130]   **1.58**

Despite the practical importance of the distinction between a voidable transaction, and one rendered ineffective in equity from the outset, there is often some confusion as to which dispositions fall into which category of case. This is fuelled by the different senses in which the term 'voidable' is used.   **1.59**

Different meanings of 'voidable'
The labels 'void' and 'voidable' have well-established meanings in the law of contract, where they describe the status of a contract or purported contract.[131] Whilst it has been said, with some force, that the concepts of 'void' and 'voidable' belong to the realm of the law of contract,[132] they are also used to describe the status or effect in equity of a purported disposition of money or property, whether under a contract or not,[133] including by exercise of a   **1.60**

---

[130] *Robins v Incentive Dynamics Pty Ltd* (2003) 175 FLR 286 (NSWCA) 302–03 per Giles JA, referred to with approval *Grimaldi v Chameleon Mining NL* (2012) 200 FCR 296 (Full Ct) 365.

[131] See paras [1.36] and [1.37].

[132] *Antoine v Barclays Bank plc* [2019] 1 WLR 1958 (CA) 1975 [48], citing *Isaacs v Robertson* [1985] AC 97 (PC—St Vincent & Grenadines).

[133] *Sieff v Fox* [2005] 1 WLR 3811, 3837; *Clark v Cutland* [2004] 1 WLR 783 (CA) 792; *Nasrulla v Rashid* [2020] Ch 37 (CA) [58] (forged transfer of registered real property, imposition of a constructive trust 'engineer[ing] a replica of voidness', adopting language of S Gardner [2013] Conv 530). See also S Zogg, *Proprietary Consequences in Defective Transfers of Ownership* (2020) 129–30 (arguing that 'void' and 'voidable' may refer either to a contract or to a disposition of property, and supporting the view that a transfer of property may properly be described as 'void in equity').

22   I. INTRODUCTION

power of appointment.[134] The focus of the language is on the efficacy of a transfer of assets. In that context, the terms void and voidable have a less clearly defined meaning.

1.61   When employed with this focus on dispositions rather than agreements, the term voidable is sometimes used to describe transfers that are ineffective in equity as from the outset. This habit is evident in some cases concerned with the self-dealing rule.[135] American lawyers similarly speak of the rescission of voidable sales induced by fraud or other vitiating factors, even though (in contrast with English law) a constructive trust arises from the moment the sale is completed, so that the disposition is ineffective in equity as from the beginning.[136] When the term voidable is used in this sense, it focuses on legal rather than beneficial title.[137]

1.62   The fact that a transaction may be described as voidable therefore does not always provide reliable guidance as to whether the principles of rescission apply.[138] Those principles only apply where beneficial title passes pursuant to the transaction, but subject to an entitlement in the transferor to recover it by rescinding. The principles do not apply where beneficial title is immediately divested, such that the disposition is ineffective in equity from the start.

Rescission and the ratification of transactions ineffective in equity

1.63   In the case of some transactions that are ineffective in equity in the manner just described, the beneficial owner is permitted to ratify the transaction, and thereby pass equitable title to the recipient of the relevant asset. So, for example, a company may ratify an unauthorized transfer made by a director,[139] and in so doing will make effective the purported disposition of its assets. A *cestui que trust* is also given separate and specific rights of election against a defaulting trustee who has disposed of trust property without authority. These are conferred to ensure that the fiduciary cannot profit from his use of the trust property.[140]

1.64   Although transactions that are ineffective but that may be ratified are, confusingly, sometimes called voidable transactions, this is in fact the converse of rescission. The right is to elect to divest an existing beneficial interest, whereas rescission involves regaining a title lost or obtaining a new beneficial interest in traceable substitutes. The rules regulating the one species of transaction do not apply to the other. Likewise the rights of election of a *cestui que trust* are wholly inapposite outside the fiduciary context, and should be regarded as having limited if any relevance to the right to rescind.[141]

---

[134] *Abacus Trust Co (Isle of Man) v Barr* [2003] Ch 409, 419–20.

[135] See para [1.74].

[136] AW Scott and WA Fratcher, *The Law of Trusts* (5th edn, 2013) vol 1, [3.4.1], [4.6.1]–[4.6.4]; *Restatement (First) of Restitution* § 163 and § 167 (1937) (and commentary thereto). Also, *Restatement (Third) of Restitution* § 13 cmt d (2011).

[137] PBH Birks, *Unjust Enrichment* (2nd edn, 2005) 184.

[138] Cf *Brooks v Burns Philp Trustee Co Ltd* (1969) 121 CLR 432, 458 (Windeyer J).

[139] *Heinl v Jyske Bank (Gibraltar) Ltd* [1999] Lloyd's Rep Bank 511 (CA) 533 (Colman J); (cf 521–22 where Nourse LJ characterizes the issue as one of affirmation).

[140] *Bostock v Blakeney* (1789) 2 Bro CC 654, 656; 29 ER 362 (choice between personal claims); *Foskett v McKeown* [2001] 1 AC 102, 130–31 (right to proprietary claim to substitute).

[141] But cf RC Nolan, 'Dispositions Involving Fiduciaries: The Equity to Rescind and the Resulting Trust' in P Birks and R Rose (eds), *Restitution and Equity* (2000) chap 7.

Overview

This Part D outlines the main classes of case in which dispositions of money and property **1.65** are rendered ineffective in equity as from the start. These classes of case fall outside the scope of the law of rescission, and are treated here for the purpose of better defining the boundaries of the subject.

Transactions ineffective in equity are divided into five categories: **1.66**

1. contracts where the person claiming an interest is not a party;
2. contracts where he is a party to the impugned transaction;
3. contracts affected by bribery, which may fall into either of those two categories;
4. apparent gifts made ineffective by the imposition of a resulting trust; and
5. other cases.

(2) Where the claimant is not a party to the impugned transaction

Irrespective of the authority granted by the trust instrument, a trustee's title to the trust **1.67** estate confers a power to deal with the beneficiaries' property, and derives from his status as owner.[142] Where the disposition is unauthorized and a breach of trust, the beneficiary may assert his existing beneficial interest in the trust asset or its traceable proceeds in the hands of all recipients save a bona fide purchaser for value without notice, or one taking from him.[143] If the trustee sells, mortgages, lends, or otherwise disposes of the trust assets to a person who gives value, but takes with notice of the breach of trust, the disposition is ineffective in equity. The recipient holds the assets for the benefit of the *cestui que trust*.[144] The position is the same if the transfer is made to a volunteer, albeit the duty to account is different if the transferee takes without notice.[145] The same principle applies to fiduciaries other than private trustees who enjoy a power to dispose of their principal's property in their own name.[146]

Where the fiduciary's contract is within the letter of his mandate, but unauthorized because **1.68** it involves a breach of his duty of loyalty, the contract may be valid and binding at common law, but any disposition of assets made under it will be ineffective in equity.

The distinction between a voidable transfer, and the transfer of assets rendered ineffective **1.69** in equity, was underlined in *Independent Trustee Services Ltd v GP Noble Trustees Ltd*.[147] Lloyds LJ there explained that, in the former case, full legal and beneficial title passes, subject only to the transferor's equity to rescind, whereas in the case of a trustee's unauthorized disposition of trust assets (to a person other than a bona fide purchaser for value) the *cestui*

---

[142] *Rolled Steel Products (Holdings) Ltd v British Steel Corporation* [1986] 1 Ch 246 (CA) 303.

[143] *Foskett v McKeown* [2001] 1 AC 102, 108–109, 130. But beneficial title may be asserted against a trustee who reacquires the misapplied trust property from or via a bona fide purchaser for value without notice: *Gordon v Holland* (1913) 10 DLR 734 (PC—Canada) 743; *Re Stapleford Colliery Company* (1879) 14 ChD 432, 445.

[144] For a re-analysis, RC Nolan, 'Equitable Property' (2006) 122 LQR 232, 251, 259–60, 264–65. See also D Fox, 'Overreaching' in P Birks and A Pretto (eds), *Breach of Trust* (2002) chap 4.

[145] *Independent Trustee Services Ltd v GP Noble Trustees Ltd* [2013] Ch 91 (CA) 122–23.

[146] *Heinl v Jyske Bank (Gibraltar) Ltd* [1999] Lloyd's Rep Bank 511 (CA) 521.

[147] [2013] Ch 91 (CA).

24   I. INTRODUCTION

que trust 'have more than a "mere equity"; they still own their beneficial interests in the trust property unaffected by the disposition made without authority under the trust'.[148]

(3) Where the claimant is a party to the impugned transaction

The fair-dealing rule

1.70 The position just described is to be contrasted with the case where a trustee seeks to purchase or otherwise acquire an interest in the trust estate from his beneficiary. The beneficiary is said to be entitled to have the sale 'set aside' if the trustee cannot show that the transaction complied with the requirements of the fair-dealing rule.[149] It is generally thought that a contract and disposition of this kind is valid until rescinded rather than ineffective until ratified. That appears to have been confirmed in *Hill v Langley*,[150] where the Court of Appeal seemed to accept the trial judge's conclusion that he had a discretion whether or not to set the sale aside. Where a beneficial interest is purchased contrary to the fair-dealing rule, it therefore appears that title passes to the trustee, but defeasibly, subject to the beneficiaries' right to regain it by rescinding, and therefore subject to the ordinary bars to rescission.

1.71 The rule is more clearly established when a fiduciary who is not a trustee purchases or otherwise acquires assets from his principal under a contract vitiated by breach of fiduciary duty. Beneficial title in property passes, but may be regained if and when the principal rescinds.[151]

The self-dealing rule

1.72 Attempted transactions between a trustee and his trust, of which attempted purchases of trust assets are the most common example, are governed by the self-dealing rule.[152] No matter how fair the terms may be, self-dealing transactions are prohibited unless specifically authorized by the beneficiaries, by the court, by the terms of the trust, or by statute. This rule is designed to protect the beneficiaries against conflicts of interest.[153] The rule applies not only to conventional trusts, but also to company directors and indeed whenever a fiduciary holds assets in a custodial capacity.

---

[148] *Independent Trustee Services Ltd v GP Noble Trustees Ltd* [2013] Ch 91 (CA) 128.

[149] See the authorities reviewed in *Plowright v Lambert* (1885) 52 LT 646; *Tito v Waddell (No 2)* [1977] Ch 106, 241.

[150] (CA 29 January 1988) (rescission of purchase by trustee of beneficiary's interest under will). The court also seemed to assume that rescission could be barred if *restitutio in integrum* was impossible, and contemplated the transaction being set aside on the ordinary terms as to counter-restitution.

[151] *Daly v Sydney Stock Exchange Limited* (1985) 160 CLR 371, 387–90; approved by Millett J in *El Ajou v Dollar Land Holdings plc* [1993] 3 All ER 717, 735, albeit in the context of fraud rather than breach of fiduciary duty; *Greater Pacific Investments Pty Ltd v Australian National Industries Ltd* (1996) 39 NSWLR 143 (CA) 153; *Maguire v Makaronis* (1998) 188 CLR 449; *Johnson v EBS Pensioner Trustees Ltd* (ChD, 8 March 2001); [2002] Lloyd's Rep PN 309 (CA). There is Australian authority that the court has a discretion as to whether a proprietary interest will be granted where a fiduciary's contract with his principal is vitiated by breach of fiduciary duty: *Robins v Incentive Dynamics Pty Ltd* (2003) 175 FLR 286 (NSWCA) 301; also JD Heydon, MJ Leeming, and PG Turner, *Meagher, Gummow and Lehane's Equity Doctrines and Remedies* (5th edn, 2014) [5-250]; but cf [5-270]; see also Chap 16, paras [16.69]–[16.70].

[152] *Tito v Waddell (No 2)* [1977] 1 Ch 106, 224–25, 247–49.

[153] See M Conaglen, 'A Re-appraisal of the Fiduciary Self-dealing and Fair-dealing Rules' [2006] CLJ 366.

A trustee who circumvents the rule requiring that every contract has two parties and effects **1.73**
a valid contract and conveyance to himself or his nominee must still reckon with the limits
of his authority. Trustees and other custodial fiduciaries ordinarily lack authority to sell
trust property to themselves or related parties. The first part of this proposition was clearly
expressed by Lindley LJ in *Farrar v Farrar's Limited*: 'a power of sale does not authorise
the donee of the power to take the property subject to it at a price fixed by himself, even
although such price be the full value of the property.'[154] To this Millett LJ added in *Ingram
v IRC* that 'A trustee's power of sale does not authorize the trustee to sell the trust property
except to someone with whom he can deal at arm's length'.[155] These propositions constitute
the self-dealing rule.

A number of authorities indicate that an attempted purchase by a trustee is voidable at the **1.74**
option of any of the beneficiaries.[156] This might suggest that the beneficiaries' remedy is rescission. Bruce McPherson (an Australian judge, writing extra-judicially) points, however,
to a parallel line suggesting that such purchases are in fact void or ineffective in equity because the trustee cannot unilaterally extinguish the beneficial interests.[157] The idea that the
sale is voidable and liable to be set aside appears to have been used in some of the other cases
consistently with McPherson's view to mean nothing more than that the conveyance can be
set aside and the property recovered, or that the beneficiaries may elect whether to treat the
purported sale as void or else to ratify it and keep the proceeds.

In principle McPherson's view seems right. There can be no doubt that a simple transfer of **1.75**
property held in the name of the trust to the trustee personally without the consent of the
beneficiaries has no effect upon their beneficial title.[158] It is difficult to see that the position
is any different if at the same time the trustee deposits a sum of his own money to the trust
account; or dresses the transaction up as a formal sale; or purchases from himself at a public
auction. Even if a valid contract or conveyance can be effected, the purported sale in each of
these cases should be ineffective because the trustee's power of sale does not authorize a sale
to himself or his nominee.

Whatever doubts there may have been about this were put to rest by the Court of Appeal's **1.76**
decision in *JJ Harrison (Properties) Ltd v Harrison*.[159] That case involved a company director
who purchased a plot of land from the company without disclosing to the other directors
a qualification to the valuation and the existence of a planning application. Following the
sale the planning application was successful and the director soon resold the land for more

---

[154] (1888) 40 ChD 395 (CA) 401.

[155] [1997] 4 All ER 395 (CA) 425, on appeal [2000] 1 AC 293, 305, 310.

[156] *Campbell v Walker* (1800) 5 Ves Jun 678, 680; 31 ER 801; *Re Daly* (1907) 39 SCR 122; *Holder v Holder* [1968]
1 Ch 353 (CA) 398; *Re Sherman* [1954] Ch 653; *Ingram v IRC* [1997] 4 All ER 395 (CA) 424; [2000] 1 AC 293; see
also *Guinness plc v Saunders* [1990] 2 AC 663, 697–98. The issue was discussed in passing by the High Court of
Australia in *Clay v Clay* (2001) 202 CLR 410. The court said the transaction was voidable but does not appear to
have considered the question closed.

[157] BH McPherson, 'Self-Dealing Trustees' in AJ Oakley (ed), *Trends in Contemporary Trust Law* (1996) chap 6,
referring in particular to *Franks v Bolans* (1868) 3 Chap App 717, 718–19; *Denton v Donner* (1856) 23 Beav 285,
290; 53 ER 112; *Williams v Scott* [1900] AC 499 (PC). To this may be added *Morse v Royal* (1806) 12 Ves Jun 355,
372; 33 ER 134 and *Abacus Trust Co (Isle of Man) v Barr* [2003] Ch 409, 421, where Lightman J said that the self-
dealing rule is an exception to the general rule that 'a decision challenged on the ground of breach of fiduciary duty
is voidable and not void'.

[158] *Glennon v Federal Commissioner of Taxation* (1927) 127 CLR 503, 511–12.

[159] [2002] 1 BCLC 162 (CA).

26   I. INTRODUCTION

than ten times what he had paid. Rix LJ held that by operation of the self-dealing rule the director acquired the land subject to a constructive trust in the company's favour. He said that: 'a director, on appointment to that office, assumes the duties of a trustee in relation to the company's property. If, thereafter, he takes possession of that property, his possession "is coloured from the first by the trust and confidence by means of which he obtained it".[160] On this basis the remedy to recover the asset is simply an action to recover trust property.[161] This is quite different from rescission, which presupposes that the defendant has received undivided title subject only to the claimant's equity to recover title upon rescission.

Contracts procured by unauthorized agents

1.77   Where an agent sells or otherwise disposes of his principal's assets without actual or apparent authority and in breach of fiduciary duty owed to the principal, the other party to the contract does not obtain beneficial title if he is sufficiently aware of the breach of duty, or takes as a volunteer. As noted earlier, on the contractual plane, when this occurs the agreement will be ineffective until ratified.[162]

Application of the principle where directors misuse powers to alienate company property

1.78   The principle just noted is well established in the case of company directors who misuse their powers to alienate company assets to those aware that the powers have been misused, so that the director lacks both actual and apparent authority.[163] The disposition is denied effect in equity. The contractual counterparty is required to hold the assets received on trust for the company as from the moment of receipt.[164] The same principle applies if the recipient takes as a volunteer from the company without notice.[165] The transaction will be voidable only if the counterparty gives value and takes without notice of the director's breach of duty.[166] But if he takes with notice or is a volunteer, the property disposed of should be held on trust for the company as from the moment of receipt.[167]

---

[160] *JJ Harrison (Properties) Ltd v Harrison* [2002] 1 BCLC 162 (CA) [29].

[161] *JJ Harrison (Properties) Ltd v Harrison* [2002] 1 BCLC 162 (CA) [39].

[162] *Criterion Properties plc v Stratford UK Properties LLC* [2004] 1 WLR 1846 (HL); para [1.40].

[163] In such a case, s 40(1) of the Companies Act 2006 will have no application. See also s 41(2) of the Companies Act 2006 (transactions with directors or their associates voidable if authority for it depends upon the protection to outsiders conferred by s 40(1)).

[164] *Rolled Steel Products (Holdings) Ltd v British Steel Corporation* [1986] 1 Ch 246 (CA) 298, 303, 306–07 (moneys paid pursuant to a guarantee in improper exercise of directors' power); *Heinl v Jyske Bank (Gibraltar) Ltd* [1999] Lloyd's Rep Bank 511 (CA) 521, 533 (moneys paid under a loan pursuant to a fraud). It has been said that the transaction is in such a case 'void' rather than 'voidable': *GHML Trading Limited v Maroo* [2012] EWHC 61 (Ch) [171]. In Australia, *Grimaldi v Chameleon Mining NL* (2012) 200 FCR 296 (Full Ct) [254]; *Kalls Enterprises Pty Ltd (in liq) v Baloglow* (2007) 63 ACSR 557 (NSWCA) 586–88 (special leave to appeal refused [2008] HCA Trans 132); *Commonwealth v Davis Samuel Pty Ltd (No 7)* (2013) ACSR 258 (ACT Sup Ct) [1553]–[1565]; *Great Investments Ltd v Warner* (2016) 243 FCR 516 (Full Ct) [68], [69] ('strict liability' for dispositions of company property made without authority).

[165] *Clark v Cutland* [2004] 1 WLR 783 (CA) 792 (unauthorized payments made by company to pension trustee taking as a volunteer).

[166] *Richard Brady Franks Ltd v Price* (1937) 58 CLR 112 at 142. It is doubtful that this principle depends upon a distinction between abuses of a director's power to deal with company assets falling within, and outside, the director's authority, and insofar as the contrary is suggested in *Grimaldi v Chameleon Mining NL* (2012) 200 FCR 296 (Full Ct) [254], that part of the reasoning is unpersuasive.

[167] *Great Investments Ltd v Warner* (2016) 243 FCR 516 (Full Ct) [68]. For discussion in the context of a claim for specific performance, *ANZ Executors & Trustee Company Limited v Qintex Australia (receivers and managers appointed)* [1991] 2 Qd R 360 (CA) (covenant to procure subsidiary companies to execute a guarantee where group became insolvent). For the principal's rights against the agent who makes a secret profit, see now *FHR European Ventures LLP v Mankarious* [2015] AC 250 [8]–[9], [46]–[50].

Identity fraud

Just as in certain circumstances legal title to goods will not pass where a contract is rendered **1.79** void by the buyer's fraud as to his identity,[168] so a similar principle may sometimes apply in relation to equitable title. In *Collings v Lee*[169] the Court of Appeal held that beneficial title in the Collings' home had not passed to their buyer, one 'Styles', in circumstances where Styles was in fact an alias used by the fraudster Lee, whom Mr and Mrs Collings had retained as their agent to sell the property.

Would the result have been the same had the fraudster not been retained as the Collings' **1.80** agent, which had the effect that the sale and Lee's subsequent registration as owner was affected by breach of fiduciary duty and absence of authority? Nourse LJ, with whom the other members of the court agreed, emphasized that the critical reason why the transfer to 'Styles' was ineffective rather than merely voidable was that Mr and Mrs Collings had never intended to transfer ownership to him:

> The rationale of the principle, as it applies to a transfer of property, is that even where the transfer is obtained by fraudulent misrepresentation, the transferor nevertheless intends that the whole legal and beneficial ownership in the property shall pass to the transferee. But that was not this case. Mr and Mrs Collings did not intend to transfer the property to the first defendant and they did not intend to transfer it for no consideration. The first defendant acquired the property without their knowledge and consent and in breach of his fiduciary duty to them. The equitable interest remained vested in Mr and Mrs Collings.[170]

One view of this reasoning is that it implies that an immediate revesting of beneficial title **1.81** could have occurred absent any breach of fiduciary duty, and absent the fact that the sale involved an agent's unauthorized dealings. The key point was the absence of intention to transfer beneficial title. This alignment of voidable transfers with impaired intention, and wholly ineffective transfers with no intention, finds some support in the reasoning in *Twinsectra Limited v Yardley*[171] and, perhaps, also in the reasoning in *Nasrulla v Rashid*.[172] But the preferable analysis is that this alignment merely expresses the rationale for specific rules that regulate the behaviour of equitable title where property is transferred under a contract procured by fraud or other vitiating circumstance. It is these rules, and not judicial assessments of intention, that determine the location of beneficial title. The law has never sought to calibrate dispositive intention such that whether title passes turns on evidence of subjective intention, any more than it looks to subjective intention in determining whether a contract is formed.[173] Nor can the passing of beneficial title turn only on whether the contract is void or valid at common law. Unless the facts fall within one of the classes of case discussed in this part, or another recognized category of resulting or constructive trust, beneficial title to property should always follow legal title.

---

[168] *Cundy v Lindsay* (1878) 3 App Cas 459; *Ingram v Little* [1961] 1 QB 31 (CA); *Shogun Finance v Hudson* [2004] 1 AC 919.

[169] [2001] 2 All ER 332 (CA); noted D O'Sullivan, 'Distributing the Risk of Contract Fraud' (2001) 117 LQR 381.

[170] [2001] 2 All ER 332 (CA) 337.

[171] [1999] Lloyd's Rep Bank 438 (CA) 461 relied on by Nourse LJ in *Collings v Lee* [2001] 2 All ER 332 (CA) 337–38.

[172] [2020] Ch 37 (CA) [53], [58].

[173] *Norwich Union Fire Insurance Society v William H Price Ltd* [1934] AC 455 (PC—Aust) 463 (Lord Wright).

28   I. INTRODUCTION

1.82 *Collings v Lee* is therefore best regarded as an application of the established principles that regulate contracts procured by agents who lack both actual and apparent authority. It is orthodox that beneficial title does not pass where the contractual counterparty knows of the lack of authority. That must *a fortiori* be true where the contract has been procured by an agent to himself, and he is acting dishonestly, which was precisely the position as between the vendors and Lee.

Contracts that are the instrument of fraud

1.83 In *Halley v Law Society*[174] the Court of Appeal held that equitable title to sums paid to a solicitor escrow agent and then vested in the Law Society remained with the payer, the victim of a fraud, and did not pass to the intended payee, the fraudster, pursuant to the terms of the contract under which payment was made. There was no need for an election to rescind for the equitable interest to arise. Three strands of reasoning underpinned this conclusion. First, the sums were held on express trust by the escrow agent, and the court would not permit a trustee to execute a trust in favour of one whose claim to a beneficial interest was founded on his implication in a fraud.[175] Secondly, the payment having been made to an escrow agent, the payee's beneficial title depended on the court giving effect to the contract, and it would not do so because the contract was an instrument for fraud.[176] Thirdly, the relevant contract was not simply procured by fraud. The agreement was itself the instrument of a fraud and nothing else, and for that reason would be disregarded by the court.[177]

1.84 It is unclear whether the third of the court's reasons was free-standing, such that the result would have been the same even without the interposition of an escrow agent between payer and payee. In principle the third reason should not be free-standing. Whilst a distinction can be drawn between apparent contracts that are in fact void, and contracts valid until rescinded, no clear distinction exists between a contract procured by fraud, and one that is only an instrument of fraud.[178] Nor does the law recognize a concept of a 'sham contract' binding at common law but denied effect in equity by reason of the fraudulent design of one party to it.

1.85 Whilst it has since been said that *Halley v Law Society* is to be understood as if the contracts were void *ab initio*,[179] the decision has also been applied to an investment fraud by asking whether the arrangements could be characterized as 'a mere charade' or 'an instrument of fraud and nothing else' and 'no more than a vehicle for obtaining money by false pretences', and even if some form of consideration had been received.[180]

---

[174] [2003] WTLR 845, critically discussed HW Tang, 'Proprietary Relief Without Rescission' [2004] 63 CLJ 30. Also, *Re Crown Holdings (London) Limited (in liq)* [2015] EWHC 1876 (Ch), *Global Currency Exchange Network Limited v Osage 1 Limited* [2019] EWHC 1375 (Comm) (*Halley v Law Society* binding, notwithstanding doubt expressed in *Goff and Jones*).

[175] *Halley v Law Society* [2003] WTLR 845 [98]–[99] also [91], [96] (Mummery LJ), with whom Hale LJ agreed.

[176] *Halley v Law Society* [2003] WTLR 845 [47], [54] (Carnwath LJ), with whom Hale and Mummery LJJ agreed.

[177] *Halley v Law Society* [2003] WTLR 845 [45]–[47] (Carnwath LJ).

[178] In general, the effect of fraud on contracts and other consensual arrangements is to vitiate consent and to make the transaction voidable: *Prest v Petrodel Resources Ltd* [2013] 2 AC 415 [18] (Sup Ct).

[179] *Re Crown Holdings (London) Limited (in liq)* [2015] EWHC 1876 (Ch) [34](b) (traceable proceeds of valuable art deco furniture that had been stolen).

[180] *Global Currency Exchange Network Limited v Osage 1 Limited* [2019] 1 WLR 5865, 5879–80 [47] (alleged 'Ponzi scheme', but if 'real shares in a real company' obtained then *Halley* test not satisfied; investors nevertheless had a 'competing claim' consequent upon possible future rescission within CPR 86.1).

Similarly, in *Nolan v Minerva Trust Company Limited*[181] the Royal Court of Jersey applied **1.86** *Halley v Law Society* in deciding whether several investment frauds gave rise to an immediate constructive trust or only a contract voidable for fraud by asking whether the contract was 'the instrument of fraud, and nothing else',[182] which was equated with a transaction that was in truth 'no different from outright theft in the guise of a contract'.[183] The Royal Court held where the circumstances of the investment answered this description, a '*Halley* trust' was imposed, requiring immediate repayment from the time the funds were received.[184]

(4) Bribes

It has generally been thought that contracts procured by the bribery of one party's agent are **1.87** voidable at that party's instance rather than void.[185] This view fails to distinguish between two situations.[186] The first occurs where the agent did not actually conclude the contract on his principal's behalf, but instead advised the principal or the like. This was the situation in at least one and probably both of the two main cases usually cited in support of the general view that contracts procured by bribery are merely voidable,[187] and in that situation the general view seems to be correct.

It is more difficult to understand why the contract is voidable rather than void in the dif- **1.88** ferent situation where the bribed agent actually concludes the contract with the briber on behalf of his principal.[188] No agent has actual authority to secretly act against the interests of his principal,[189] and the counterparty is not entitled to rely on the agent's apparent authority where it is he himself who has bribed the agent.[190] Though it did not involve a bribe, *Heinl v Jyske Bank (Gibraltar) Ltd*[191] involved loan contracts arranged by a corrupt bank official. Nourse LJ explained the effect of the dealings in the following terms:

> Where an agent is known by the other party to a purported contract to have no authority to bind his principal, no contract comes into existence. The agent does not purport to

---

[181] [2014] 2 JLR 117; JRC 078A.

[182] *Nolan v Minerva Trust Company Limited* [2014] 2 JLR 117; JRC 078A [151]–[162], [274]–[275], [312]–[315], [333]–[334], [350]–[352], [401], [418] (claim failed), [379]–[380], [441] (claim succeeded).

[183] Applying *Barrett & Sinclair v McCormack* [1999] VUCA 11, where the Vanuatu Court of Appeal spoke of a transaction that was 'no different from outright theft in the guise of a contract'.

[184] *Nolan v Minerva Trust Company Limited* [2014] 2 JLR 117; JRC 078A [154], [161], [162], [170], [379] (the claim was for a third party's dishonest assistance in the fraudster's breach of a constructive trust). Cf *Nasrulla v Rashid* [2020] Ch 37 (CA) [53], [58] (outright theft contrasted with transaction procured by fraudulent misrepresentation).

[185] *Re a Debtor* [1927] 2 Ch 367 (CA); *Logicrose Ltd v Southend United Football Club Ltd* [1988] 1 WLR 1256, 1260; *Tajik Aluminium Plant v Ermatov (No 3)* [2006] EWHC 7 (Ch) [21]–[22]; P Finn, *Fiduciary Obligations* (1977) [515].

[186] A Berg, 'Bribery—Transaction Validity and other Civil Law Implications' [2001] LMCLQ 27, 39–41. See also H Beale (gen ed), *Chitty on Contracts* (33rd edn, 2018) [31-073], [31-074]; PG Watts and FMB Reynolds (eds), *Bowstead and Reynolds on Agency* (22nd edn, 2020) [8-218] (Art 96); and as to the company law aspects of the issue, RC Nolan, 'Directors' Self-Interested Dealings: Liabilities and Remedies' [1999] CfiLR 235, 239–40.

[187] *Panama and South Pacific Telegraph Company v India Rubber, Gutta Percha, and Telegraph Works Company* (1875) 10 Ch App 515; *Logicrose Ltd v Southend United Football Club Ltd* [1988] 1 WLR 1256. It also appears to have been the case in *Re a Debtor* [1927] 2 Ch 367 (CA). But cf *Bertram and Sons v Lloyd* (1904) 90 LT 357 (CA).

[188] Cf *Tajik Aluminium Plant v Ermatov (No 3)* [2006] EWHC 7 (Ch) [21]–[22]. See also Chap 16, para [16.55].

[189] PG Watts and FMB Reynolds (eds), *Bowstead and Reynolds on Agency* (22nd edn, 2020) Art 23.

[190] *Criterion Properties plc v Stratford UK Properties LLC* [2004] 1 WLR 1846 (HL) [31].

[191] [1999] Lloyd's Rep Bank 511 (CA).

30   I. INTRODUCTION

contract on his own behalf and the knowledge of the other party unclothes him of ostensible authority to contract on behalf of the principal. Whether or not such a transaction is accurately described as a void contract, it is plainly not voidable. If no contract comes into existence, there is nothing to avoid or rescind, nor can any property pass under it.[192]

1.89   It would seem to follow that a contract procured by a bribe and concluded by the corrupt agent purportedly on behalf of his principal should properly be treated as ineffective unless and until ratified rather than valid until set aside. If the agent has transferred any of his principal's assets to the counterparty in purported performance of the contract then these should be treated as being held on a constructive trust from the moment of receipt. Also, if the agent receives a secret commission, the money is held on constructive trust as from the moment of receipt, and the principal's claim to recover it is independent of any right to set aside the contract.[193]

(5) Apparent gifts made ineffective by resulting trust

1.90   In certain fairly well-defined situations, where a voluntary transfer of property is made *inter vivos*, there is a presumption that a gift is not intended, and if the presumption is not rebutted, a resulting trust is or continues to be imposed over the property in favour of the transferor.[194] The apparent gift is ineffective in equity. This is to be contrasted with the case where a gift of property is vitiated by mistake, undue influence, or other sufficient cause, and title passes subject to the donor's right to regain it upon rescission. There the gift is valid until rescinded. The rules applicable to the rescission of gifts are separately considered in Chapter 29.

(6) Other ineffective transactions

1.91   There are miscellaneous other cases where a trust is immediately imposed in respect of contractual and non-contractual payments of money. Some of the principal examples will be considered in turn.

The *Quistclose* trust and 'failure of basis'
1.92   When a trust is imposed upon the proceeds of a special purpose loan that cannot be fulfilled when the funds are received, in accordance with the principle recognized in *Barclays Bank Ltd v Quistclose Investments Ltd*,[195] it has been suggested that it is the initial failure of the basis of the transaction that explains why the law permits a proprietary claim for restitution.[196] However, after *Angove's Pty Ltd v Bailey*,[197] it is clear that in English law the

---

[192] *Heinl v Jyske Bank (Gibraltar) Ltd* [1999] Lloyd's Rep Bank 511 (CA) 521 and see 533. See also *Rolled Steel Products (Holdings) Ltd v British Steel Corporation* [1986] 1 Ch 246 (CA) 297–98, 303–04, 306–07; *Criterion Properties plc v Stratford UK Properties LLC* [2004] 1 WLR 1846 (HL).

[193] *FHR European Ventures LLP v Mankarious* [2015] AC 250.

[194] J Mowbray *et al* (eds), *Lewin on Trusts* (18th edn, 2008) [9-02]–[9-13]. Also R Chambers, *Resulting Trusts* (1997).

[195] *Barclays Bank Ltd v Quistclose Investments Ltd* [1970] AC 567; *Twinsectra Ltd v Yardley* [2002] AC 164.

[196] PBH Birks, *Unjust Enrichment* (2nd edn, 2005) 185–88. See also, A Burrows, *A Restatement of the English Law of Unjust Enrichment* (2012) 162–63.

[197] [2016] 1 WLR 3179 (Sup Ct).

circumstance that money has been paid for a consideration that will inevitably fail (as where the recipient is on the verge of ceasing to trade) will not support the imposition of a constructive trust, any more than a subsequent failure of the basis of the payment will do so.[198] The *Quistclose* trust is therefore best regarded as anomalous, and not one species of a wider *genus*.

Mistaken payments

In the case of a mistaken payment not made under a contract, there is some authority that a **1.93** trust may be imposed if the recipient realizes the mistake before the funds are dissipated,[199] and it has been held that a trust will arise if the recipient appreciates that the payer's mistake was the product of a fraud.[200]

Non-contractual payments procured by fraud

Where a payment is made other than pursuant to a valid contract, but was procured by a **1.94** fraud perpetrated by the payee (or by a third party of which the payee had notice) a constructive trust should be imposed from the moment of receipt. A bank's payment of money pursuant to a forged letter of credit or other payment instrument should be a familiar example.[201] In England and Wales there has, however, been some resistance to the proposition that a constructive trust is automatically imposed when money is obtained by fraud (unaccompanied by a breach of fiduciary duty), and even in the case of non-contractual payments it has been said that the paying party must elect to avoid the transaction before a proprietary interest can be asserted.[202] This is difficult to understand, for if the impugned payment was not made pursuant to a valid contractual obligation there is no agreement or obligation to set aside before a restitutionary right springs up, and it is not easy to see what there is to 'avoid'. The English approach appears to be founded upon a reluctance to recognize that equity will impose a constructive trust where a payment of money has been procured by fraud absent a breach of fiduciary duty, 'rescission' of the payment, or unless the facts give rise to some other recognized ground for the imposition of a trust.

Whilst some more recent decisions display a greater willingness to recognize the existence **1.95** of a constructive trust when money is obtained by fraud without requiring either a breach of fiduciary duty or an election to rescind,[203] the narrow view just described was reiterated in *National Crime Agency v Robb*.[204] It illustrates the difficulties that the narrow view can give rise to.

---

[198] *Angove's Pty Ltd v Bailey* [2016] 1 WLR 3179 (Sup Ct) at [30] and deciding that *Neste Oy v Lloyds Bank* [1983] 2 Lloyd's Rep 658 cannot be justified on the ground on which it was decided, and that *In re Japan Leasing* [1999] BPIR 911 was wrongly decided: at [31], [32].

[199] *Westdeutsche Landesbank Girozentrale v Islington LBC* [1996] AC 669, 715, considered in *Bank of America v Arnell* [1999] Lloyd's Rep Bank 399. In Australia, *Wambo Coal Pty Ltd v Ariff* (2007) 63 ACSR 429 [40] (Sup Ct NSW).

[200] *Bank of America v Arnell* [1999] Lloyd's Rep Bank 399; *Papamichael v National Westminster Bank plc* [2003] 1 Lloyd's Rep 341 [225].

[201] *Bank of Ireland v Pexxnet Limited* [2010] EWHC 1872 (Comm) [55]–[57].

[202] For example, *London Allied Holdings v Lee* [2007] EWHC 2061 (Ch) [266]–[276].

[203] Cf *Re Crown Holdings (London) Limited (in liq)* [2015] EWHC 1876 (Ch) [46]–[62]; *Angove's Pty Ltd v Bailey* [2016] 1 WLR 3179 (Sup Ct) [30]; *Nasrulla v Rashid* [2020] Ch 37 (CA) [58].

[204] [2015] Ch 520.

32   I. INTRODUCTION

1.96   In *National Crime Agency v Robb* it was held that the victims of a fraud that occurred only *after* investment contracts had been concluded and partly performed by instalment payments could rescind their contracts in order to claim a proprietary interest in the stolen funds.[205] That reasoning was evidently adopted because it was thought that with the money having been paid under a contract, no constructive trust could arise unless the contract was first rescinded.[206]

1.97   This reasoning is difficult to justify. The impairment of consent that makes a contract voidable also renders defeasible any title to money or property transferred under it;[207] rescission is said to be necessary before a proprietary interest may be asserted because that interest is inconsistent with the ownership rights established by the contract; and the contract must therefore be wiped away before a proprietary interest in money or property transferred may be asserted.[208] But this analysis has no application where a trust is asserted not because the contracting party's consent to pay money or to transfer property was impaired but as the law's response to the later misappropriation of money or property transferred under a contract. The misappropriation of the investor's money by the promoter Robb should have impressed those funds with a constructive trust as from the time of its receipt by Robb.[209] Rescission of the investment contracts was not possible because the investors' consent to contract and to pay the misappropriated money had not been impaired.[210] Rescission was also not necessary because the trust arising was not inconsistent with the continued existence of the contracts, albeit by choosing to enforce a constructive trust, the investors would thereby waive their right to enforce any contractual rights inconsistent with that trust.

1.98   The difficulty encountered in *National Crime Agency v Robb* does not arise under Australian law. Since the decision in *Black v S Freedman & Co*[211] it has been established that where money is stolen, or is otherwise obtained by a fraud that has not merely induced entry into a contract (in which case the contract must first be set aside before an equitable title may be asserted), the funds are impressed with a constructive trust as from the moment of receipt, and the defrauded party may trace their equitable interest into other hands or other

---

[205] [2015] Ch 520, 532–33 (purchasers of 'off the plan' residential development in Turkey).

[206] [2015] Ch 520, 530–31, esp at [44] ('[S]itting as I am at first instance I am bound to follow the approach of Atkin and Bankes LJJ in *Banque Belge pour l'Etranger v Hambrouck* [1921] 1 KB 321, 332 and 325, Rimer J in *Shalson v Russo*, and Millett J in *El Ajou v Dollar Land Holdings plc* [1993] 3 All ER 717, 734, that in the case of a voidable transaction a property interest only re-vests in the victim of fraud when the transaction is rescinded. Prior to that event, the victim's power to rescind constitutes a "mere equity" ').

[207] Para [1.27] above.

[208] Para [1.27] above.

[209] See *Angove's Pty Ltd v Bailey* [2016] 1 WLR 3179 (Sup Ct) 3193 [30] example (ii); *Nasrulla v Rashid* [2020] Ch 37 (CA) [53]–[58] (forged transfer of registered real property; legal title held on constructive trust). The corporate counterparty being the alter ego of Robb, a third party to the contracts, the trust should have been in favour of the defrauded investors.

[210] But cf the contrary view in K Handley, *Spencer Bower and Handley: Actionable Misrepresentation* (5th edn, 2014) [18.16] (post-contract fraud may possibly attract a right to judicial rescission in the exercise of equity's wider jurisdiction over fraud, citing *Panama and South Pacific Telegraph Company v India Rubber, Gutta Percha, and Telegraph Works Company* (1875) 10 Ch App 515).

[211] (1910) 12 CLR 105, 110: 'Where money is stolen, it is trust money in the hands of the thief'.

assets.[212] A constructive trust is likewise imposed over money obtained by selling stolen property.[213]

Property other than money taken by fraud

The principles just discussed should apply equally to those cases where a thief is able to acquire title to property taken. Subject to the operation of a particular statutory provision, the general rule should be that the thief is compelled to hold any title obtained in property taken on constructive trust for the victim. This was the approach of the Court of Appeal in *Nasrulla v Rashid*,[214] which held that whilst by operation of the Land Registration Act 1925 a forged transfer of real property conferred legal title in the fraudster, nevertheless the transferee was compelled to hold the title obtained on constructive trust for the victim.[215] In coming to that conclusion the Court of Appeal approved the analysis in *Snell's Equity*,[216] where the learned authors drew a distinction between the fraudulent taking of property wholly without a person's consent, triggering the imposition of a constructive trust of the thief's possessory title,[217] and a transaction induced by fraudulent misrepresentation, where the transferee obtains beneficial and legal title subject to an equity to rescind.[218]

1.99

---

[212] *Black v S Freedman & Co* (1910) 12 CLR 105, 110 (money stolen from employer passed on to wife); *Evans v European Bank Ltd* (2004) 61 NSWLR 75 (CA) [111], [113] (proceeds of credit card fraud); *Westpac Banking Corporation v Ollis* [2007] NSWSC 956 [18], [29]–[32] (exploiting bank error by writing 'an avalanche' of cheques; appeal dismissed: *Shields v Westpac Banking Corporation* [2008] NSWCA 268 [18]–[20]); *Wambo Coal Pty Ltd v Ariff* (2007) 63 ACSR 429 (Sup Ct NSW) [40] (paying away money knowing of payer's error); *Heperu Pty Ltd v Belle* (2009) 76 NSWLR 230 (CA) [92]–[93] (proceeds of misappropriated cheques); *MBF Australia Ltd v Malouf* [2008] NSWCA 214 [32] (cheque fraud); *Allianz Australia Insurance Limited v Rose Marie Lo-Guidice* [2012] NSWSC 145 [32], [33] (cheque fraud); *Lawrie v Hwang* [2012] QSC 422 [77], [164] (defrauding of mentally impaired man); *Sze Tu v Lowe* (2014) 89 NSWLR 317 (CA) 345–48 (stolen partnership money). As to tracing the proceeds of fraud, *Toksoz v Westpac Banking Corp* (2012) 289 ALR 557 (NSWCA) 579–80.

[213] *Kalls Enterprises Pty Ltd (in liq) v Baloglow* (2007) 63 ACSR 557 (NSWCA) [69].

[214] [2020] Ch 37 (CA).

[215] [2020] Ch 37 (CA) [53]–[58].

[216] J McGhee, *Snell's Equity* (33rd edn, 2015) at [26-012], [26-013].

[217] As to the holding on trust of a thief's possessory title, S Zogg, *Proprietary Consequences in Defective Transfers of Ownership* (2020) 425–28; R Chambers, 'Trusts and Theft' in E Bant and M Harding (eds), *Exploring Private Law* (2010).

[218] *Nasrulla v Rashid* [2020] Ch 37 (CA) [53], [58].

2

Rescission and Independent Claims

A. Introduction	2.01	(1) Distinction between profit-based	
B. Damages	2.03	remedies and rescission	2.16
C. Equitable Compensation	2.10	(2) Proprietary relief absent rescission	2.24
D. Disgorgement of Profits	2.14	(3) Personal accountability for profits	
		absent rescission	2.27

A. Introduction

2.01 The circumstances conferring a claim to rescind may also give rise to claims to damages or its equitable counterpart. Although these claims may arise out of the same circumstances, they are independent of rescission and certainly do not arise as a consequence of it. Rescission is only relevant to claims of this kind because, in most cases, it will affect their quantification.[1] There is a tendency to overlook these points, which can lead to confusion as to the entitlements that properly flow from rescission. There is a like tendency in relation to the distinction between claims to rescind and claims seeking to strip a fiduciary of unauthorized profits gained in the course of his engagement, though the relationship between these claims is more complex.

2.02 In what follows these and related issues are discussed in turn in connection with claims to damages, to equitable compensation, and to the disgorgement of profits.

B. Damages

2.03 A right to rescind is independent of, and cumulative with, any right the claimant may also have to damages in tort.[2] This is so even where both rights arise out of the same factual circumstances. In such a case, for example in a case of deceit, the claimant may claim rescission or damages or both.[3] A claimant may sue for damages even if he affirms the contract or if rescission is otherwise barred.[4]

---

[1] *London Allied Holdings Ltd v Lee* [2007] EWHC 2061 (Ch) [253]. In Australia, *Ivanof v Phillip M Levy Pty Ltd* [1971] VR 167; *Markovic v Coober Pedy Tours Pty Ltd South Australia* [1994] SASC 4401 [25]; *Cockburn v GIO Finance Ltd* (2001) 51 NSWLR 624 (CA) 634; *Scheur v Bell* [2004] VSC 71 [281]–[288].

[2] *Goldrei, Foucard & Son v Sinclair* [1918] 1 KB 180 (CA) 186–87. In Australia, *Sibley v Grosvenor* (1916) 21 CLR 469, 475; *O'Keefe v Taylor Estates Co Ltd* [1916] St R Qd 301 (Full Ct) 309–10. In Canada, *Yost v International Securities Co* (1918) 43 DLR 28 (Ont CA) and O'Halloran JA's dissenting judgment in *Jarvis v Maguire* (1961) 28 DLR (2d) 666 (BCCA) 672. By contrast the right to damages for breach of contract is extinguished upon rescission: see Chap 1, para [1.18]. Damages under the Misrepresentation Act 1967, s 2(2) are alternative to rescission: see Chap 28.

[3] *Newbigging v Adam* (1886) 34 ChD 682 (CA) 592.

[4] *Houldsworth v City of Glasgow Bank* (1880) 5 App Cas 317, 338; *Re Cape Breton Company* (1885) 29 ChD 795 (CA) 808. Affirmation may impact on causation and the measurement of loss in important ways, as to which see *Motortrak Limited v FCA Australia PTY Ltd* [2018] EWHC 1464 (Comm).

Observing that Chancery exercised a concurrent jurisdiction over frauds, Bowen LJ re- **2.04**
marked in *Newbigging v Adam* that Chancery could give a person defrauded 'complete indemnity' equivalent to what he could obtain in a common law court by coupling an action
for restitution with an action for damages in deceit.[5] An Australian judge has read this passage as indicating that in equity any loss occasioned by reason of the fraud would be made
good 'as part of the process of *restitutio in integrum*',[6] and this reading has been endorsed by
the High Court of Australia.[7]

Bowen LJ was of course correct to say that, prior to Judicature, Chancery had jurisdiction **2.05**
to give a claimant alleging fraud complete relief in the form of both restitution and damages for any further loss he may have suffered.[8] But the fact that both restitution and damages could be given in the same proceeding does not mean that they were not distinct, and
nothing in Bowen LJ's reasons indicates that he thought otherwise. This would involve a
confusion of the restitutionary function of rescission with the compensatory function of
damages, and would be inconsistent with high authority.[9]

Subject to the principle against double recovery, the measure of any damages to which **2.06**
the claimant may be entitled may repeat the restitution to which he would also be entitled by way of rescission. Thus in *Goldrei, Foucard & Son v Sinclair*[10] the claimants were
awarded £105 against the company they had contracted with as restitution, and upon
that judgment not being satisfied, £105 as damages against the agent who had fraudulently induced them to contract.[11] In that case the claimant had not suffered any extra-
neous loss. Had he done so, this could only have been made good by way of damages.
For example, expenses incurred preparing to perform a contract are not recoverable as
restitution but may be recoverable as damages,[12] as is the case with commission paid to
an estate agent.[13]

If the claimant does not have a cause of action sounding in damages, then the restitution to **2.07**
which he is entitled as a consequence of rescission may be the full extent of his relief, and
it may be inferior to the relief a claim in damages would offer. Thus in *Redgrave v Hurd*,[14]

---

[5] (1886) 34 ChD 682 (CA) 592.

[6] *McAllister v Richmond Brewing Company (NSW) Pty Ltd* (1942) 42 SR (NSW) 187.

[7] *Maguire v Makaronis* (1996) 188 CLR 449, 467–68, stating that the loss must have been 'directly occasioned'
by the falsity of the misrepresentation. See also *Munchies Management Pty Ltd v Belperio* (1988) 58 FCR 274 (Full
Ct); *Demagogue Pty Ltd v Ramensky* (1992) 110 ALR 608 (Full FCA); *Jonval Builders Pty Ltd v Commissioner for
Fair Trading* (2020) 104 NSWLR 1 (CA) [33]–[34].

[8] As to the jurisdiction of Chancery to award damages in cases of actual fraud, see *Peek v Gurney* (1873) LR 6
HL 377, 390.

[9] In particular *Goldrei, Foucard & Son v Sinclair* [1918] 1 KB 180 (CA); *Sibley v Grosvenor* (1916) 21 CLR 469;
Yost v International Securities Co (1918) 43 DLR 28 (Ont CA). See also *Restatement (Third) of Restitution* vol 2, 284
(2011).

[10] [1918] 1 KB 180 (CA).

[11] In *Ivanof v Phillip M Levy Pty Ltd* [1971] VR 167 the court held that, where the damage duplicates the amounts
recoverable as restitution in the way described in the text, the claimant may obtain judgment against a third party
such as a fraudulent agent even where it is not yet known whether the claimant will in fact recover that amount as
restitution.

[12] *Sibley v Grosvenor* (1916) 21 CLR 469.

[13] *Hayes v Ross (No 3)* [1919] NZLR 786, 791.

[14] (1881) 20 ChD 1 (CA).

36 I. INTRODUCTION

a case of innocent misrepresentation involving the sale of a solicitors' practice, the misled purchaser Hurd was awarded the return of his deposit by way of restitution. But because innocent misrepresentations do not sound in damages,[15] he was not compensated for having prepared to take up the practice by giving up his own practice and moving to Birmingham. *Aldrich v Norwich Union Life Ins Co Ltd*[16] provides a more recent example in a case involving non-disclosure in relation to an insurance contract.

2.08 Equally, the consequence of rescission may be that the claimant finds himself in a position that is financially better than if he had been paid damages. For example, if a sale of shares is induced by misrepresentation and the purchaser sues for damages when he learns the truth, if the shares have declined in value in the interval by the play of ordinary market forces, the purchaser will not recover the loss he suffered by the market decline.[17] His damages will be restricted to the difference between the contract price and the true open market value of the shares as at the date of purchase. The reason is that the subsequent market loss was not caused by the seller's default but rather by the combination of the market decline and the purchaser's decision not to sell.[18] Unless a bar has arisen a purchaser may, however, rescind the sale contract and recover the purchase money. The fact that the shares have declined in value does not prevent the purchaser from making *restitutio in integrum*.[19]

2.09 These differences are a consequence of it not being the function of rescission to compensate the claimant for whatever loss he may have suffered in connection with the contract.[20] It is said to be 'axiomatic' that rescission is concerned with restoring both parties to their original positions,[21] and then only in respect of obligations and advantages that have passed under the contract.[22] By contrast, damages are concerned with compensating the claimant alone for the loss he has suffered. While compensatory damages have sometimes been said to aim at the *restitutio in integrum* of the claimant, that means something quite different from *restitutio in integrum* upon rescission.

C. Equitable Compensation

2.10 Where a fiduciary has had contractual dealings with his principal, the principal may be entitled to have the contract set aside if the requirements of the fair-dealing rule have not been

---

[15] Nowadays with the exception of claims under s 2 of the Misrepresentation Act 1967.

[16] [2000] Lloyd's Rep IR 1 (CA) 7–8.

[17] *Waddell v Blockey* (1879) 4 QBD 678 (CA); *Cemp Properties (UK) Ltd v Dentsply Research Corporation* [1991] 2 EGLR 197 (CA). Where the misrepresentation is fraudulent there are exceptional circumstances in which the purchaser will be entitled to recover the loss he suffered in the market decline, such as where the misrepresentation also induced him to hold onto the shares or where by the nature of the transaction the purchaser was locked into holding them: *Smith New Court Securities Ltd v Citibank NA* [1997] AC 254.

[18] *South Australia Asset Management Corporation v York Montague* [1997] AC 191, 221.

[19] *Armstrong v Jackson* [1917] 2 KB 822; *William Sindall plc v Cambridgeshire CC* [1994] 1 WLR 1016 (CA) 1038; *Cheese v Thomas* [1994] 1 WLR 129 (CA) 135. In Australia, *JAD International Pty Ltd v International Trucks Australia Limited* (1994) 50 FCR 378 (Full Ct).

[20] *Aldrich v Norwich Union Life Ins Co Ltd* [2000] Lloyd's Rep IR 1 (CA) 7–8; *De Molestina v Ponton* [2002] 1 Lloyd's Rep 271, 287. In Australia, *Marks v GIO Australia Holdings Ltd* (1998) 196 CLR 494, 535; *Cockburn v GIO Finance (No 2)* (2001) 51 NSWLR 624 (CA); but cf *Vadasz v Pioneer Concrete (SA) Pty Ltd* (1995) 184 CLR 102, 115.

[21] *Cheese v Thomas* [1994] 1 WLR 129 (CA) 136.

[22] *Newbigging v Adam* (1886) 34 ChD 582 (CA) 595.

met. This is usually because the fiduciary has failed to disclose the full extent of his interest or some other fact material to the principal's decision. In these circumstances the principal may also have a claim to an equitable monetary remedy known as 'equitable compensation' in respect of any losses he has suffered, in the same way that if the ground for rescission were deceit, he might also have a remedy in damages.[23] In *Gwembe Valley Development Co v Koshy*[24] the Court of Appeal left open the question whether a claim for equitable compensation lies where the breach of fiduciary duty is less than deliberate and dishonest. Other cases suggest that the remedy may be available whenever there has been a violation of the fair-dealing rule.[25]

Save that the title to relief sounds in equity, equitable compensation is practically indistin- **2.11** guishable from damages,[26] and these terms are often used interchangeably. The English authorities treat equitable compensation as independent of and cumulative with rescission and its consequences in precisely the same way that damages are. Amongst other things, the fact some bar may prevent the claimant from rescinding his contract will not prevent him from instead suing for equitable compensation.[27] That is also the case in Canada,[28] but the position in Australia is less clear. *Tracy v Mandalay*,[29] a decision of the High Court of Australia, appears to preclude claims for equitable compensation where the contract in question has been affirmed, though this has been criticized.[30] Moreover, one Australian judge has held that even if the contract is rescinded, equitable compensation cannot be given as a cumulative remedy.[31] It is difficult to see any basis for either of these Australian rules.

It is important to appreciate that the term 'equitable compensation' is used in at least two **2.12** different senses.[32] To this point we have been concerned with the use of that term to identify an independent money remedy that aims to repair loss the claimant may have suffered by reason of the defendant's breach of an equitable duty. 'Equitable compensation', or more often simply 'compensation', is also sometimes used instead to refer to a sum that is awarded by way of restitution or counter-restitution upon rescission in equity.

Compensation of this latter variety is not calculated so as to repair a financial loss one of **2.13** the parties may have suffered, but according to the principles governing restitution and counter-restitution upon rescission. For instance, compensation may be calculated so as to provide a pecuniary substitute for an asset or some other benefit that the party in question

---

[23] See M Conaglan, 'Equitable Compensation for Breach of Fiduciary Dealing Rules' (2003) 119 LQR 246; M Conaglan, *Fiduciary Loyalty* (2010) 87–90.

[24] [2004] 1 BCLC 131 (CA) [143].

[25] *Swindle v Harrison* [1997] 4 All ER 705 (CA); *Longstaff v Birtles* [2002] 1 WLR 470 (CA).

[26] *Bristol and West Building Society v Mothew* [1998] Ch 1 (CA) 17 ('a distinction without a difference'); *Compagnia Seguros Imperio v Heath (REBX)* [2001] 1 WLR 112 (CA) 125. See the discussion in C Mitchell, 'Equitable Compensation for Breach of Fiduciary Duty' [2013] CLP 1.

[27] *Cavendish Bentinck v Fenn* (1887) 12 App Cas 652; *Re Leeds and Hanley Theatres of Varieties Ltd* [1902] 2 Ch 809 (CA); *Gwembe Valley Development Co v Koshy* [2004] 1 BCLC 131 (CA); *Hurstanger Ltd v Wilson* [2008] Bus LR 216 (CA). In the Cayman Islands, *AB jnr v MB* (unreported Grand Court, 13 August 2012) [444]–[508].

[28] *Proprietary Mines Ltd v MacKay* [1939] 3 DLR 215 (Ont CA), aff'd [1941] 1 DLR 240 (SCC).

[29] (1953) 88 CLR 215, 239.

[30] *Aequitas Ltd v AEFC* [2001] NSWSC 14 [428].

[31] *Aequitas Ltd v AEFC* [2001] NSWSC 14 [432].

[32] The Australian judge Austin J notes the distinction in *Aequitas Ltd v AEFC* [2001] NSWSC 14 [430]–[432]. A parallel distinction applies in other parts of equity, as to which see J McGhee and S Elliott (eds), *Snell's Equity* (34th edn, 2020) [20–028]ff.

38   I. INTRODUCTION

is unable to return *in specie*,[33] or it may be calculated to make good deterioration of a returnable asset.[34] Compensation is awarded in these cases as an element of the relief awarded upon rescission. It has been said that compensation of this variety is given 'in lieu of rescission',[35] but that needs to be elaborated as 'in lieu of the specific relief usually given upon rescission.'

D. Disgorgement of Profits

2.14   A fiduciary is ordinarily accountable for any unauthorized profits he gains in the course of his engagement. In the alternative to his right to enforce the fiduciary's personal accountability, the principal may have a proprietary remedy in respect of any asset in the fiduciary's hands that identifiably represents an unauthorized profit.[36] There is an area of potential overlap between these remedies and rescission in circumstances where the fiduciary gains his profit through a contract with his principal that does not meet the requirements of the fair-dealing rule.

2.15   The discussion under the first heading which follows is concerned with the independence of, and distinction between, the relief given upon rescission and the fiduciary's accountability for profits in cases caught by the fair-dealing rule. The discussion under the second and third headings which follow concerns the difficult question whether profit-based relief can be claimed without first rescinding the contract.

(1) Distinction between profit-based remedies and rescission

2.16   Bowen LJ remarked in *Re Cape Breton Company* that 'the right of the principal or *cestui que trust* to claim a profit made by an agent or trustee, seems to me to be wholly independent of the right to rescind the contract'.[37] He compared the relationship between the two to the relationship between the right to rescind and the right to claim damages in a case of deceit. Although the same factual circumstances may generate both rights, the rights may be exercised independently of one another, and if they are exercised there may be different consequences.

2.17   The rescinding party's entitlement is to be restored to his original position as regards the rights and obligations which have been created by the contract.[38] This means that he is entitled to restitution of whatever benefits the other party has received under the contract

---

[33]   Eg *McKenzie v McDonald* [1927] VLR 134; *Mahoney v Purnell* [1996] 3 All ER 61 (noted by PBH Birks, 'Unjust Factors and Wrongs: Pecuniary Rescission for Undue Influence' [1997] RLR 72); *Jennings v Cairns* [2003] EWHC 1115 (Ch). In Canada, *Kupchak v Dayson Holdings Co Ltd* (1965) 53 DLR (2d) 482 (BCCA). The word 'compensation' is used in the same way in s 65 of the Indian Contract Act 1872, as to which see *Govindram Seksaria v Radbone* (1947) 50 BOMLR 561 (PC—India) [8].

[34]   Eg *Erlanger v The New Sombrero Phosphate Company* (1878) 3 App Cas 1218, 1278.

[35]   *Bristol and West Building Society v Mothew* [1998] Ch 1 (CA) 17; *Compagnia Seguros Imperio v Heath (REBX)* [2001] 1 WLR 112 (CA) 125.

[36]   *FHR European Ventures LLP v Mankarious* [2015] AC 250.

[37]   (1885) 29 ChD 795 (CA) 808. Although Bowen LJ's judgment was a dissenting one, nothing in the majority judgments contradicts this remark.

[38]   *Newbigging v Adam* (1886) 34 ChD 582 (CA) 592–94. In Australia, *Brown v Smitt* (1924) 34 CLR 160, 166.

and also to be indemnified for any detriments he has suffered under the contract. By contrast, an account of profits is not a restitutionary remedy.[39] Its purpose is not to restore the claimant to his original position, but instead to deprive the fiduciary of whatever unauthorized profits, direct or indirect, he has gained within the course of his engagement.[40]

It is true that upon rescission each party must return not only the assets they received under **2.18** the contract or, in some cases, their traceable substitutes, but also any fruits such as dividends or rent receipts, and that it is sometimes necessary to take an account of these benefits.[41] This relief is, however, given on a different basis from an account of profits, and it is more circumscribed. It is given as an incident of the restitution of specific assets, and does not encompass consequential or indirect profits that the fiduciary may have been enabled to make by reason of the contract other than by exploiting an asset acquired under it.[42]

But although the rights and remedies are distinct, there is nonetheless a considerable **2.19** overlap between them. In those cases caught by the fair-dealing rule, it will always or almost always be the case that the no profits rule is also engaged to the extent the fiduciary has profited through the dealing.[43] This is because the profit the fiduciary made in the dealing will not have been sufficiently consented to by the principal and as such it will be unauthorized. Moreover, where the only profit the fiduciary has gained as a result of contractual dealings with his principal is the immediate profit arising from the advantageous terms of the bargain, the effect of rescission will be to strip him of that profit and transfer it to the principal. If the fiduciary has profited by reselling an asset he acquired from his principal or by reaping its fruits, that too will go to the principal. Though the relief in such cases is restitutionary, its financial effect is equivalent to an account of profits.

Notwithstanding this coincidental overlap, it is necessary to insist on the independence of **2.20** rescission and the accountability of a fiduciary for unauthorized profits for three reasons. First, it is possible in some cases to claim an account of profits even though rescission is barred, a topic considered later. Secondly, the measure of relief that an account of profits yields may, depending on the circumstances, be more extensive than the relief given as an incident of rescission. This will be so where the fiduciary has made profits that would not come within the rules governing restitution upon rescission. Thirdly, most of the grounds on which rescission may be had do not also generate a right to disgorgement of profits. Confusion of the relief given upon rescission with the remedy of account of profits might lead to a profits-based measure of relief being given under the rubric of rescission in a case where the ground for rescission does not warrant it.

The distinction between rescission and the accountability of a fiduciary for unauthorized **2.21** profits has not, however, always been observed. *O'Sullivan v Management Agency and*

---

[39] Eg *Murad v Al-Saraj* [2005] WTLR 1573 (CA) [108]. In Australia, *Harris v Digital Pulse Pty Ltd* (2003) 56 NSWLR 298 (CA) [414].

[40] *Boardman v Phipps* [1967] 2 AC 46; *Regal (Hastings) Ltd v Gulliver* [1967] 2 AC 134; and more recently *United Pan-Europe Ltd v Deutsche Bank AG* [2002] 2 BCLC 461 (CA) [47]; *Gwembe Valley Development Co Ltd v Koshy (No 3)* [2004] 1 BCLC 131 (CA) [137]–[138]; *Murad v Al-Saraj* [2005] WTLR 1573 (CA). In Australia, *Warman International Ltd v Dwyer* (1995) 182 CLR 544; *Maguire v Makaronis* (1996) 188 CLR 449.

[41] *Erlanger v The New Sombrero Phosphate Company* (1878) 3 App Cas 1218, 1278.

[42] *Caldicott v Richards* [2020] WTLR 823 [113]. Cf *McKenzie v McDonald* [1927] VLR 134, 146.

[43] The opposite proposition is not always true, for a contract caught by the fair-dealing rule may be set aside by the principal, if he wishes, even though it was not profitable for the fiduciary.

40   I. INTRODUCTION

Music Ltd[44] is a prominent example of a case in which they seem to have been conflated. That case involved a matrix of contracts regulating the arrangements between the claimant O'Sullivan, a singer and songwriter, and the defendants, who managed, produced, and promoted his work. The Court of Appeal rescinded the contracts and required, amongst other things, that the defendants account for the excessive profits they had made. This remedy was apparently viewed as an account of profits given as an element of *restitutio in integrum* upon rescission, and the Lord Justices referred indiscriminately to account of profits cases such as *Boardman v Phipps*[45] and rescission cases such as *Erlanger v The New Sombrero Phosphate Company*.[46] This confounds two distinct remedies.

2.22   In fact the references in *O'Sullivan*'s case to the accountability of a fiduciary for unauthorized profits appear to be a distraction because this principle was inessential to the result. While the Court of Appeal deprived the defendants of their excessive profits, it did not accede to the claimant's desire to have all of the profits. Instead, the defendants were allowed a reasonable sum for their skill and efforts including a fair profit element.[47] This allowance is best viewed as pecuniary counter-restitution for the services the defendants had provided. The net effect of the order was that O'Sullivan gained restitution of the rights in his music and of the fruits the defendants had gained by exploiting them, while the defendants received counter-restitution of the value of their services.

2.23   It is fair to say, however, that while the analysis offered by the Lord Justices in *O'Sullivan*'s case seems to have confused rescission with the accountability of a fiduciary for profits, there was no risk of error in the judgment itself. This is because if the sums awarded had gone beyond the legitimate scope of *restitutio in integrum* then the excess could be justified on the basis that the defendants were independently accountable for those sums as unauthorized profits.

(2) Proprietary relief absent rescission

2.24   An asset a fiduciary gains through contractual dealings with his principal in violation of the fair-dealing rule is not automatically held subject to a constructive trust even though it may be said to represent a profit in his hands.[48] Because such contracts are voidable rather than void, the fiduciary takes undivided title to whatever assets he gains under the contract.[49] It is only upon rescission that the principal acquires a beneficial title, though it appears that the title he then acquires is retrospective, at least to the extent necessary to allow the principal

---

[44] *O'Sullivan v Management Agency and Music Ltd* [1985] 1 QB 428 (CA). In New Zealand, *Estate Realties Ltd v Wignall* [1992] 2 NZLR 615.

[45] [1967] 2 AC 46.

[46] (1878) 3 App Cas 1218.

[47] Cf *Guinness v Saunders* [1990] 2 AC 663.

[48] Contrast the position of a trustee who attempts to buy from the trust estate in violation of the self-dealing rule, where the title of his beneficiaries will usually be unaffected, as to which see Chap 1, para [1.83].

[49] *Guinness Plc v Saunders* [1990] 2 AC 663, 698; *Lonrho Plc v Fayed (No 2)* [1992] 1 WLR 1, 11–12; *Halifax Building Society v Thomas* [1996] Ch 217 (CA) 228; *Re Ciro Citterio Menswear plc* [2002] 1 BCLC 672, 687–89. In Australia, *Daly v Sydney Stock Exchange Ltd* (1986) 160 CLR 371; *The Hancock Family Memorial Foundation Ltd v Porteous* (2000) 22 WAR 198 (Full Ct). There may be an exception for sums representing the amount by which a contract price has been inflated to cover the cost of paying a bribe to the claimant's agent: *Daraydan Holdings Ltd v Solland International Ltd* [2005] Ch 119, 137–40.

to trace through intermediate transactions in order to assert title in whatever exchange-product the fiduciary now holds.[50] To assert a constructive trust without first having the contract set aside involves, in Lord Goff's words, an attempt to 'short-circuit an unrescinded contract'.[51] It follows that once a bar arises precluding rescission, the principal loses all possibility of proprietary relief.

It stands to reason that the contractual regime should take priority in this way. If a principal **2.25** could at one and the same time maintain the contract and assert beneficial title in whatever assets he had transferred to his fiduciary, he would keep undivided title to whatever assets he received, as well as the benefit of any obligations the contract might impose on the fiduciary, while at the same time acquiring beneficial title in whatever assets he gave. This would plainly be unjust.

In *Grimaldi v Chameleon Mining NL (No 2)*,[52] the Federal Court of Australia questioned in **2.26** passing whether the rescission requirement should apply where a purchaser acquired company assets under an agreement which the purchaser knew to have been made by a director or officer in breach of his fiduciary duties to the company. The rescission requirement does not, in fact, apply in this scenario. The supposed purchase contract is ineffective for lack of authority, the purchaser is not a bona fide purchaser for value and, in consequence, the purchaser holds the asset subject to a constructive trust in favour of the company.[53] This is quite different from the purely bilateral scenario in which the rescission requirement applies.

(3) Personal accountability for profits absent rescission

The obstacles that prevent a principal from asserting beneficial title in whatever asset he has **2.27** given without first rescinding do not prevent the principal from instead claiming a pecuniary accounting and payment of the net profit the fiduciary gained through the contract without rescinding it. Three decisions of high authority confirm this possibility.[54]

There is, however, a longstanding rule that prevents a company from claiming an account of **2.28** the profits its promoter gained through a sale to the company while leaving that contract on foot.[55] Where this rule applies, if rescission has become barred then there is no possibility

---

[50] *Lonrho Plc v Fayed (No 2)* [1992] 1 WLR 1, 11–12; *El Ajou v Dollar Land Holdings* [1993] 3 All ER 717, 734; *Shalson v Russo* [2005] Ch 281 [122]–[127]. In Australia, *Daly v Sydney Stock Exchange Ltd* (1986) 160 CLR 371, 390 (Brennan J); *Greater Pacific Investments Pty Ltd v Australian National Industries Ltd* (1996) 39 NSWLR 153 (CA) 153–54; *Robins v Incentive Dynamics Pty Ltd* (2003) 175 FLR 286 (NSWCA) [82]. See further Chap 16, para [16.40].

[51] *Guinness Plc v Saunders* [1990] 2 AC 663, 698.

[52] (2012) 287 ALR 22 (FCA) [281].

[53] See Chap 1, para [1.78].

[54] *Gray v New Augarita Porcupine Mines Ltd* [1952] 3 DLR 1 (PC—Canada) 13; *Gwembe Valley Development Co Ltd v Koshy (No 3)* [2004] 1 BCLC 131 (CA) [137], [161]; *Akita Holdings Ltd v A-G of Turks and Caicos Islands* [2019] AC 250 (PC—TCI). Strictly speaking, the latter two involved contracts between the principal and a company controlled by the fiduciary rather than a contract to which the fiduciary himself was party. But in the *Akita Holdings* case, the Board treated the defendant company as standing in the same position as its controller, and reasoned that its liability arose by virtue of his fiduciary responsibility, so there is no meaningful distinction.

[55] *Erlanger v The New Sombrero Phosphate Company* (1878) 3 App Cas 1218, 1235 (Lord Cairns LC); *Re Cape Breton Company* (1885) 29 ChD 795 (CA), aff'd sub nom *Cavendish Bentinck v Fenn* (1887) 12 App Cas 652; *Ladywell Mining Company v Brookes* (1887) 35 ChD 400 (CA); *Jacobus Marler Estates Ltd v Marler* (1916) 114 LT 640n (HL). The last of these indicated that the rule might expand beyond the context of sales by promoters to their companies, but that has not been developed in later cases. In Australia, *Peninsular & Oriental Steam Navigation*

42   I. INTRODUCTION

of profits-based relief at all, personal or proprietary. The rule was established in a line of cases decided in the later part of the nineteenth century and the earlier part of the twentieth century.[56] While the rule has been approved in the House of Lords, as well as in the Privy Council on appeal from Canada and in the High Court of Australia, it has rarely been applied in the past century and it is difficult to reconcile with the permissive approach that is now generally applied.

The rule in *Re Cape Breton Company*

2.29 The seminal decision is that of the majority of the Court of Appeal in *Re Cape Breton Company*,[57] though Lord Cairns had expressed the same view a few years earlier in *Erlanger v The New Sombrero Phosphate Company*.[58] *Re Cape Breton Company* involved a purchase by the company in 1873 of three coal areas in Nova Scotia. The promoters, Fenn and his associates, had purchased the coal areas two years earlier for a price considerably less than the price at which they resold to the company. Fenn was one of the company's directors at the time of the resale, but he did not disclose his interest to the board. The company went into liquidation, following which the truth about the purchase came out. The company might have avoided the purchase, but instead in 1878 the contributories voted to adopt it and sell the coal areas.[59]

2.30 The purchase having been affirmed and the coal areas sold, rescission was out of the question. The case involved an attempt to hold Fenn liable under s 165 of the Companies Act 1865 in respect of the profit he had made, which turned on whether he was personally liable in equity. In deciding that the bar to rescission also precluded a pecuniary remedy for the disgorgement of profits, the Court of Appeal gave essentially three reasons.

2.31 The first, stressed by Cotton LJ, was that the alleged profit was incapable of sufficiently precise measurement.[60] That profit would be the difference between the contract price and the true market value of the coal areas at the date of the contract, but this true market value depended on what a willing purchaser might have paid, which was thought to be unascertainable. The second reason was, as Cotton LJ later put it, that 'the company keeping the mine could not make a new contract and say, we will keep it not at the price our trustee contracted to give for it, but at a different price'.[61] The third reason, which was emphasized by Fry LJ in a concurring judgment, was that the company had affirmed the contract.[62] The Court of Appeal's decision was upheld in the House of Lords.[63]

Co v Johnson (1938) 60 CLR 189; *Tracy v Mandalay Pty Ltd* (1953) 88 CLR 215; but cf *Aequitas Ltd v AEFC* [2001] NSWSC 14 [428]. In Canada, *Burland v Earle* [1902] AC 83 (PC); *Cook v Deeks* [1916] 1 AC 554 (PC); but cf *Proprietary Mines Ltd v MacKay* [1938] 3 DLR 631 (Ont CA), aff'd [1941] 1 DLR 240 (SCC). In New Zealand, *Cook v Evatt (No 2)* [1992] 1 NZLR 677.

[56] There is an interesting discussion of the earlier cases in M Lobban, '*Erlanger v The New Sombrero Phosphate Company* (1878)' in C Mitchell and P Mitchell (eds), *Landmark Cases in the Law of Restitution* (2006) chap 6.

[57] (1885) 29 ChD 795 (CA). The case came up on a preliminary point of law on assumed facts, but for simplicity this will be ignored in the following exposition.

[58] (1878) 3 App Cas 1218, 1235.

[59] These at any rate were the alleged facts, because the case came up to the Court of Appeal on a preliminary point of law.

[60] *Re Cape Breton Company* (1885) 29 ChD 795 (CA) 805.

[61] *Ladywell Mining Company v Brookes* (1887) 35 ChD 400 (CA) 408.

[62] *Re Cape Breton Company* (1885) 29 ChD 795 (CA).

[63] *Cavendish Bentinck v Fenn* (1887) 12 App Cas 652.

The decision might have been limited to cases in which the company chooses to affirm the contract.[64] Lindley LJ suggested that this was so one year later in *Lydney and Wigpool Iron Ore Company v Bird*,[65] speaking for a division of the Court of Appeal that included Cotton LJ. One year on again, however, giving the reasons of an identically constituted division of the Court of Appeal in *Ladywell Mining Company v Brookes*,[66] Cotton LJ said that the decision in *Re Cape Breton Company* did not turn on affirmation. The rule accordingly applies whatever the reason rescission is barred. In *Ladywell Mining Company* itself the company had never affirmed the purchase, but the landlord had recovered the mine in question and so *restitutio in integrum* was impossible. This was held to preclude an account of the promoters' profits. **2.32**

Bowen LJ's dissent

It is difficult to see that any of the reasons given in support of the rule in *Re Cape Breton Company* are good ones. While the rule has often been criticized over the years, it is difficult to improve on Bowen LJ's dissent in that very case. He could not see why Fenn, a director who had breached his fiduciary duty, should be allowed to retain a benefit he had received at the company's expense. Far from being excluded in cases where rescission has been barred, Bowen LJ considered that the right to recover secret profits is 'chiefly valuable' in those cases.[67] He pointed to the 'obvious analogy' with a right to claim damages for deceit, which persists even if the contract is affirmed or if rescission is otherwise barred. **2.33**

As to Cotton LJ's first reason, the supposed difficulty in measuring the profit, Bowen LJ observed that this is 'a difficulty which is dealt with every day in every branch of the High Court'.[68] There is, he said, 'no more impossibility... of arriving at a fair estimate of the real value of the property at the time of sale to the company, than in any other case where you have to determine the value of property by the evidence of experts'.[69] No modern court would disagree. As to Cotton LJ's second reason, his concern about writing a new contract for the parties, Bowen LJ replied that the company 'does not claim to be recouped part of the price as price, nor attempt in any way to vary the contract... Making a vendor return something which he ought not to have, is not altering the contract, it is insisting upon an incident which equity attaches to it'.[70] That incident is a liability to return any profit made. Nowadays we might put this point differently by saying that the claim to profits is founded on a breach of fiduciary duty rather than any variation of the contract. **2.34**

Bowen LJ said comparatively little about Fry LJ's contention that affirmation precluded profit-based relief beyond remarking that a person who affirms a contract does not release 'any right which is not inconsistent with the contract itself'.[71] Again that seems correct. There is nothing inconsistent about maintaining a contract in force while requiring the fiduciary to account for his profits. To this it may be added that in many cases the principal **2.35**

---

[64] This may be the case in Australia given the emphasis the High Court of Australia placed on affirmation in *Tracy v Mandalay Pty Ltd* (1953) 88 CLR 215.
[65] (1886) 33 ChD 85 (CA) 94.
[66] (1887) 35 ChD 400 (CA) 408.
[67] *Re Cape Breton Company* (1885) 29 ChD 795 (CA) 808.
[68] *Re Cape Breton Company* (1885) 29 ChD 795 (CA) 810.
[69] *Re Cape Breton Company* (1885) 29 ChD 795 (CA) 810.
[70] *Re Cape Breton Company* (1885) 29 ChD 795 (CA) 809.
[71] *Re Cape Breton Company* (1885) 29 ChD 795 (CA) 809.

44   I. INTRODUCTION

may have good reasons for wishing to affirm the contract, as in *Hitchens v Congreve*,[72] where Shadwell V-C observed that the company's business would be destroyed if it were required to return the mine in question as a condition of relief. Circumstances such as these do not justify a defaulting fiduciary in retaining profits he has gained at his principal's expense. And even if there were thought to be some justice in treating affirmation as decisive of the principal's rights, on the ground that at least it involves a free choice, it is much harder to justify the application of the rule where the right to rescind is lost because *restitutio in integrum* became impossible before the principal learnt of his rights.

Exceptions

2.36   In view of these criticisms, it is unsurprising that there are important exceptions which significantly limit the scope of the rule in *Re Cape Breton Company*.

Sale of principal's own property

2.37   First, the rule does not apply where the asset the fiduciary has sold to his principal was in fact the principal's property all along.[73] If the principal enjoyed undivided title then the contract would be void at law for the common mistake as to title.[74] If the principal instead enjoyed only beneficial title, then the contract has been said to be 'nugatory',[75] which presumably means void in equity on like grounds.[76] In these circumstances there is no contract to avoid, and the principal may recover the purchase price without returning the asset. It is accordingly important to know whether the fiduciary acquired the asset in question within the scope of his engagement, for if so the principal will have enjoyed beneficial title from that time forward subject to reimbursing the fiduciary for the original purchase price. It is fair to say that the principles governing this question have sometimes been manipulated in order to evade the rule in *Re Cape Breton Company*.[77]

Sales of regular trade supplies

2.38   Secondly, the rule in *Re Cape Breton Company* seems to have been ignored in a parallel line of authorities which all involve regular trade supplies by a fiduciary through his private business to another business which the fiduciary manages in his representative capacity.[78] In these circumstances the fiduciary is accountable for whatever profit he gains without any requirement that the supply contracts be set aside.

Sales of assets with a definite market value

2.39   Thirdly, there may be an exception to the rule where the asset in question is one that has a readily ascertainable market value, as in the case of quoted shares or many commodities. Where this is so, the first reason Cotton LJ gave in *Re Cape Breton Company* in support of

---

[72]   (1831) 4 Sim 420, 428; 58 ER 157, 160.

[73]   *Re Cape Breton Company* (1885) 29 ChD 795 (CA); *Gluckstein v Barnes* [1900] AC 240; *Burland v Earle* [1902] AC 83 (PC—Canada); *Jacobus Marler Estates Ltd v Marler* (1916) 114 LT 640n (HL); *Cook v Deeks* [1916] 1 AC 554 (PC—Canada); *Jubilee Cotton Mills v Lewis* [1924] AC 958.

[74]   *Bell v Lever Bros* [1932] AC 161, 218.

[75]   *Jacobus Marler Estates Ltd v Marler* (1916) 114 LT 640n (HL).

[76]   Cf *Cooper v Phibbs* (1867) LR 2 HL 149; *Earl of Beauchamp v Winn* (1873) LR 6 HL 223, 233.

[77]   Cf M Lobban, 'Erlanger v The New Sombrero Phosphate Company (1878)' in C Mitchell and P Mitchell (eds), *Landmark Cases in the Law of Restitution* (2006) chap 6, 157.

[78]   Eg *Bentley v Craven* (1853) 18 Beav 75, 52 ER 29; *Kuhlirz v Lambert Bros Ltd* (1913) 108 LT 565. See PD Finn, *Fiduciary Obligations* (1977) [528]–[529] and the other cases cited therein.

the rule will not apply, that reason being that the profit cannot be sufficiently ascertained. Cotton LJ himself left open for later decision those cases in which the asset in question has a 'definite market value',[79] and Lord Parker seems to have accepted that there is an exception in *Jacobus Marler Estates Ltd v Marler*,[80] though nothing turned on it in that case. It is surprising that there seem to be no subsequent cases that illustrate this exception or test its limits.[81] This may be because later cases accord little weight to Cotton LJ's first reason. It is Cotton LJ's second reason—his concern that the court should not make a new bargain for the parties—that has been emphasized.[82] That second reason, if it is a good one, applies equally where the asset in question has a definite market value.

---

[79] *Re Cape Breton Company* (1885) 29 ChD 795 (CA) 805.

[80] (1916) 114 LT 640n (HL).

[81] However, though the connection has not been explicitly drawn, some of the cases that illustrate the second exception identified—cases involving trade supplies—might be reconciled with *Re Cape Breton Company* on the basis that they involved goods with a definite market price.

[82] Eg *Burland v Earle* [1902] AC 83 (PC—Canada); *Cook v Deeks* [1916] 1 AC 554 (PC—Canada); *Tracy v Mandalay Pty Ltd* (1953) 88 CLR 215.

3

Historical Foundations

A.	**Introduction**	3.01	(3) The effect of fraud on contract		3.40
B.	**The Common Law**	3.04	(4) The effect of fraud on title		3.42
	(1) The effect of fraud on contract	3.05	(5) Rescission by election		3.53
	(2) The effect of fraud on title	3.06	D. **The Special Case of Insurance**		3.55
	(3) Rescission as a condition to restitution	3.16	(1) Special relationship between		
	(4) Termination *de futuro* and *ab initio*	3.30	common law and equity		3.56
	(5) Role of the forms of action	3.33	(2) Chancery courts' policy of limited		
C.	**Equity**	3.34	interference		3.59
	(1) Introduction	3.34	(3) Change from 'void' to 'voidable'		3.63
	(2) Orders effecting rescission	3.37			

A. Introduction

3.01   The courts of common law and Chancery developed separate and distinct doctrines of rescission, and at quite different points in time. The historical foundation of the two doctrines explains the great divide between the shape of rescission at common law and in equity—why the former is an automatic response to the innocent party's election, and the latter a remedy conferred by the court.

3.02   The two models were essentially a product of the different modes of enforcing rights at law and in equity before the Common Law Procedure Act 1852. This chapter first considers the common law model, and shows that the notion that a contract induced by fraud is voidable not void was largely a consequence of the decision that title passed under such a contract, which seems counter-intuitive to modern eyes.[1] The decision that title passed, but only defeasibly, at the option of the innocent party, was itself driven by a series of earlier choices about which forms of action lay in the context of a fraudulent sale. The discussion then traces the emergence of the separate rule that a contract must be 'rescinded' by the innocent party before personal claims for restitution are available.[2] That rule was also shaped more by practical concerns peculiar to the forms of action, than by a theory of contract law. These two groups of rules, the one concerned with title and the other with the right to personal claims to restitution, together produced the distinctive feature of rescission at law, that rescission and *restitutio in integrum* is fully effected by the election of the innocent party.

3.03   Whereas the shape of rescission at law was developed in the half-century or so before 1850, in the courts of Chancery a quite different form of relief had been administered since at

---

[1] The seminal case was *Load v Green* (1846) 15 M & W 216, 153 ER 828 (Parke B).
[2] The modern starting point is the decisions of Buller J in *Weston v Downes* (1778) 1 Doug 23, 99 ER 19 and *Towers v Barrett* (1786) 1 TR 133, 99 ER 1014.

least the time of Lord Nottingham, and doubtless before. Equitable rights were not articulated through the forms of action, and from at least the late seventeenth century the victim of fraud or imposition could bring a bill in equity seeking a decree setting aside his tainted transaction. The courts of Chancery did not proceed on a theory that rescission had been effected by the prior act of the party seeking relief. Their role was not to assess whether the claimant's election had given him an accrued form of action fit to be quantified by a jury, as it was at common law. The function of the court was instead to weigh all of the evidence placed before it, and to determine whether the transaction should be set aside, and if so on what terms. Court orders were essential for this purpose, and not least because absent those orders the transaction would usually be enforceable in a court of law. A decree in Chancery was, in a purely practical sense, essential if the contract was to be sterilized, and *restitutio in integrum* achieved. The distinctive feature of equitable rescission, that it is a remedy conferred by the court, in this way was entirely an effect of the mode of enforcing equitable rights in this context.

B. The Common Law

The principles of rescission applicable at common law were shaped by the rules regulating **3.04** the forms of action available when a contract had been procured by fraud. These rules were technical and practical, and help to explain both the structure and limitations of rescission at law.

(1) The effect of fraud on contract

During the eighteenth and until the middle of the nineteenth century contracts induced **3.05** by fraud tended to be described as 'void',[3] and the prevailing opinion in the cases and texts was that no title to chattels passed under such a bargain.[4] The distinction between apparent contracts that never existed, and those valid until rescinded, was not drawn. Contracts procured by fraud were consistently described as 'voidable', and valid until rescinded, only following Parke B's seminal decision in *Load v Green* in 1846.[5] At that time English contract

---

[3] J Powell, *Essay upon the Law of Contracts and Agreements* (1790) vi, 9–10, 140; S Comyn, *The Law of Contracts and Promises Upon Various Subjects* (2nd edn, 1824) 58, 168, 185, 186 ('contracts infected with fraud, are void both at law and in equity... every contract founded in fraud is void'); J Chitty, *A Practical Treatise on the Law of Contracts Not Under Seal* (T Chitty (ed)) (3rd edn, 1841) 407, 679 ('Fraud avoids a contract ab initio both at law and in equity'); cf 409, 415–16; C Addison, *A Treatise on the Law of Contracts and Rights and Liabilities Ex Contractu* (1847) 50; *Duffell v Wilson* (1808) 1 Camp 401, 402; 170 ER 999; *Hill v Gray* (1816) 1 Starke 435, 436; 171 ER 521, 521.

[4] Eg *Anon* (1704) 6 Mod 114, 87 ER 872 (Holt CJ); *Earl of Bristol v Wilsmore* (1823) B & C 514, 521; 107 ER 190, 192; *Ferguson v Carrington* (1829) 9 B & C 59, 59; 109 ER 22, 22 (Lord Tenterden). See also the jury directions in *Noble v Adams* (1816) 7 Taunt 59, 129 ER 24; the comments of Lord Denman in *Peer v Humphrey* (1835) 2 Ad & E 495, 498–99; 111 ER 191, 193; *Root v French* (1835) 13 Wendell 570, 571–72, 574 (SCNY). For texts, S Comyn *The Law of Contracts and Promises Upon Various Subjects* (2nd edn, 1824) 172, 174; J Chitty, *A Practical Treatise on the Law of Contacts Not Under Seal* (T Chitty (ed)) (3rd edn, 1841) 406; R Browne, *A Practical Treatise on Actions at Law* (1843) 427; J Chitty, *A Practical Treatise on the Law of Contracts Not Under Seal* (J Russell (ed)) (4th edn, 1850) 356.

[5] (1846) 15 M & W 216, 219; 153 ER 828, 829 'the transaction is not void except at the option of the seller ...'. Confirmation followed in *White v Garden* (1851) 10 CB 919, 138 ER 364 and *Clarke v Dickson* (1858) El Bl & El 148, 120 ER 463.

48   I. INTRODUCTION

law was coming to be organized by treatise writers around the principle of consent,[6] and this may explain the rapid acceptance of Parke B's analysis. The analysis was explicable on the basis that a consent sufficient to form a contract existed but, being defective, the misled party had a right to extinguish the bargain *ab initio*. Certainly this was the approach of the influential Pothier, who had been translated into English some 40 years earlier.[7] But evidence of a direct link between Parke B's reasoning and Pothier's *Treatise on Obligations* is so far missing.[8]

(2) *The effect of fraud on title*

3.06   *Load v Green*[9] established that title to goods obtained under a contract induced by fraud does pass, but defeasibly. Title passes subject to the transferor's right to regain it by electing to rescind, and before the fraudster disposes of the property in favour of an innocent purchaser. If that occurs the third party will gain an indefeasible title, the defrauded party is then unable to rescind, and must instead rely on a claim for damages in deceit.

3.07   This model was conditioned by a series of earlier choices about the forms of action available in the context of a fraudulent sale. Parke B's decision was apparently intended to reconcile and explain those earlier decisions, which it did through the device of defeasible title.[10]

3.08   The first of these choices was the rejection of assumpsit for goods sold and delivered as a count that was available against a fraudulent buyer. That form of action alleged that whereas the defendant was indebted to the claimant for certain goods sold and delivered to the defendant, at his special instance and request, the defendant in consideration thereof

---

[6] A Simpson, *A History of the Common Law of Contract: The Rise of The Action of Assumpsit* (1975) 265–69; D Ibbetson, *A Historical Introduction to the Law of Obligations* (1999) chap 12, esp 232–36; W Swain, 'The Classical Model of Contract: the Product of a Revolution in Legal Thought' (2010) 30 *Legal Studies* 513, 525–32; W Swain, *The Law of Contract 1670–1870* (2015) chaps 1 and 9. For the debate about the extent of the reworking of contract law around 'consent' at this time, see P Hamburger, 'The Development of Nineteenth-Century Consensus Theory of Contract' (1989) *Law and History Review* 241, 245–46; J Oldham, *The Mansfield Manuscripts and the Growth of English Law in the Eighteenth Century* (1992) vol 1, 213, 221–23. See also M Horwitz, 'The Historical Foundations of Modern Contract Law' (1974) 87 Harv LR 917, 936–52; P Atiyah, *The Rise and Fall of Freedom of Contract* (1979) 212–16, 405–408; A Simpson, 'The Horwitz Thesis and the History of Contract' (1979) 46 U of Chicago LR 533 (rejecting Horwitz's view); and J Baker, 'Review: The Rise and Fall of Freedom of Contract by PS Atiyah' (1980) 43 MLR 467, 468 (rejecting Atiyah's view).

[7] M Pothier, *A Treatise on the Law of Obligations or Contracts* (W Evans (tr)) (1806) 19: 'When a party has been induced to contract by the fraud of another, the contract is not absolutely and essentially void, because a consent, though obtained by surprise, is still a consent; but the contract is vicious, and the party surprised may institute a process for its rescission within ten years'. Cf error which 'annuls the agreement' at 12.

[8] For the role of Pothier in English contract law at this time, A Simpson, *A History of the Common Law of Contract: The Rise of The Action of Assumpsit* (1975) 256, 266–67; A Simpson, 'The Horwitz Thesis and the History of Contract' (1979) 46 U of Chicago LR 590; P Atiyah, *The Rise and Fall of Freedom of Contract* (1979) 406; J Baker, 'Review: The Rise and Fall of Freedom of Contract by PS Atiyah' (1980) 43 MLR 467, 469; D Ibbetson, *A Historical Introduction to the Law of Obligations* (1999) 215, 220; W Swain, 'The Classical Model of Contract: the Product of a Revolution in Legal Thought' (2010) 30 *Legal Studies* 513, 526–32; C Macmillan, *Mistakes in Contract Law* (2010) chap 5. Cf P Hamburger, 'The Development of Nineteenth-Century Consensus Theory of Contract' (1989) *Law and History Review* 241, 273 (Evan's translation an 'authoritative presentation of an already familiar and accepted civilian jurisprudence'); also H Colebrooke, *Treatise on Obligations and Contracts* (1818) 51, 53, 54, 220–23, 235–41. In India, W Swain, 'History and Drafting of the Indian Contracts Act 1872' (forthcoming, 2022) 8–11, 17 ('will theory' traced to Indian Contracts Act via Evans' translation of Pothier and Field's proposed Civil Code for New York).

[9] (1846) 15 M & W 216, 153 ER 828.

[10] Cf the different analysis in W Swadling, 'Rescission, Property, and the Common Law' (2005) 121 LQR 123.

3. HISTORICAL FOUNDATIONS   49

promised to pay the sum due, and had failed to do so.[11] The action led to an award of a sum of money assessed by the jury, either for the agreed price or value of the goods. It did not require the claimant to allege that he was or had been the owner of the goods, or had any right to possess them. Despite suggestions in the late eighteenth century that a defrauded vendor could reject the contract and bring assumpsit for goods sold and delivered (irrespective of whether a period of credit had expired),[12] a series of cases in the early nineteenth century held that he could not.[13]

These decisions determined that the proper remedy in such a case was a count in trover **3.09** or a plea of deceit, albeit the deceit form was said to have been little used.[14] Trover was the predecessor to the tort of conversion.[15] It required that at the time the defendant converted goods to his use, the claimant was in possession or had an immediate right to possess, and led to a verdict for damages assessed by the jury, but no right to recovery *in specie*.[16] It was not available where the claimant had irrevocably lost possession and a right to possess under a contract, even if the transferee was in breach.[17] But it was available when the sale had been procured by fraud, and in the early nineteenth century the courts began to associate bringing trover with the sale being 'rescinded' or 'treated as void'.[18]

The final feature of the landscape behind *Load v Green* was a separate group of cases **3.10** which held that trover did not lie against a bona fide purchaser from a fraudulent buyer,[19]

---

[11] JH Baker, 'The Use of Assumpsit for Restitutionary Money Claims 1600–1800' in E Schrage (ed), *Unjust Enrichment: The Comparative Legal History of the Law of Restitution* (1995) 31, 45.

[12] *De Symons v Minchwich* (1796) 1 Esp 430, 170 ER 409 (Eyre CJ).

[13] *Read v Hutchinson* (1813) 3 Camp 352, 353; 170 ER 1408, 1408 (defrauded vendor of seven pipes of red wine should have brought trover, not general *assumpsit*); *Ferguson v Carrington* (1829) 9 B & C 59, 59–60; 109 ER 22, 23 (defrauded vendor of goods should have brought trover); *Strutt v Smith* (1834) 1 CM & R 312, 313, 315; 149 ER 1099, 1100 (defrauded vendor of cotton yarns should have brought trover). The availability of trover to a defrauded vendor of goods was recognized in other cases, such as *Emanuel v Dane* (1812) 3 Camp 299, 300; 170 ER 1389, 1389; *Noble v Adams* (1816) 7 Taunt 59, 62; 129 ER 24, 25; *Earl of Bristol v Wilsmore and Page* (1823) 1 B & C 514, 521; 107 ER 190, 192.

[14] J Chitty, *A Practical Treatise on the Law of Contracts Not Under Seal* (J Russell (ed)) (4th edn, 1850) 364.

[15] See in particular s 49 of the Common Law Procedure Act 1852 (15 & 16 Vict c 76), also E Bullen and S Leake, *Precedents of Pleadings in Actions in the Superior Courts of Common Law with Notes* (1860) 173 fn (a). 'Trover' was an Anglo-Norman word connoting 'finding', and the claim was an action on the case for finding a thing lost. The loss and finding later became fictionalized.

[16] F Buller, *An Introduction to the Law Relative to Trials at Nisi Prius* (1772) 32; R Bridgman (ed), *An Introduction to the Law Relative to Trials at Nisi Prius* (7th edn, 1817) 32c; J Chitty, *Treatise on Pleading* (3rd edn, 1817) 149, 151; R Browne, *A Practical Treatise on Actions at Law* (1843) 425–26; E Bullen and S Leake, *Precedents of Pleadings in Actions in the Superior Courts of Common Law with Notes* (1860) 173. For further discussion in the rescission context, G Glenn, 'Rescission for Fraud in Sale or Purchase of Goods—Quasi Contractual Remedies as Related to Trover and Replevin' (1936) 22 Virginia LR 859, 880–82. Title vested in the fraudulent purchaser upon full satisfaction: *Brinsmead v Harrison* (1871) LR 6 HL 584; cf *Buckland v Johnson* (1854) 15 CB 145, 162; 139 ER 375, 382; R Browne, *A Practical Treatise on Actions at Law* (1843) 426.

[17] M Bacon, *A New Abridgment of the Law* (1736) 167; *Power v Wells* (1778) 2 Cowp 818, 819; 98 ER 1379, 1379 (exchange of horses); *Emanuel v Dane* (1812) 3 Camp 299, 300; 170 ER 1389, 1389 (exchange of watch for candlesticks); *Boyson v Thomas Cole* (1817) 6 M & S 14, 18, 21, 28; 105 ER 1148, 1149, 1150, 1153.

[18] *Read v Hutchinson* (1813) 3 Camp 352, 353; 170 ER 1408: 'If the contract is altogether rescinded, there is no sale. The defendant is not a purchaser of the goods, but a person who has tortiously got possession of them... the claimant should have brought trover, or an action in deceit' (Lord Ellenborough); *Emanuel v Dane* (1812) 3 Camp 299, 300; 170 ER 1389, 1389 (Lord Ellenborough); *Ferguson v Carrington* (1829) 9 B & C 59, 60; 109 ER 22: 'as long as the contract existed, the claimants were bound to sue on that contract. They might have treated that contract as void on the ground of fraud, and brought trover. By bringing this action they affirm the contract' (Parke J). See also *Strutt v Smith* (1834) 1 CM & R 312, 315; 149 ER 1099, 1100 (Parke B).

[19] *Sheppard v Shoolbred* (1841) Car & M 61, 63; 174 ER 409, 410 (vendor of woollen cloths on-sold by fraudulent purchaser unable to bring trover against sub-purchaser).

50 I. INTRODUCTION

who could himself bring trover if the defrauded vendor retook possession of the goods.[20]

3.11 There was no agreed explanation for why trover was available in these contexts, why it could be brought against a fraudulent buyer but not a subsequent bona fide purchaser, particularly given that contracts procured by fraud were said to be 'void'. The cases bordered on inconsistency, and different explanations for the rules were offered.[21] Nor was there any reasoned explanation for why trover was associated with rescission. If no title passed and the sale was 'void', that language seemed inappropriate.

3.12 The uncertainty as to how title behaved was fuelled by doubts about the effects of the widening of old legislation directed at the recovery of stolen goods. The legislation dated to 1529,[22] and was said to have the effect of revesting title in property taken upon conviction for felony, even if the property had been sold to an innocent purchaser in market overt.[23] In 1827 the legislation was widened to include felony or other misdemeanours involving unlawful taking or obtaining.[24] This widening led to doubts being cast on *Parker v Patrick*, which preceded *Load v Green* and seemed to give immunity to a bona fide purchaser from a fraudster.[25] Before *Load v Green* there were suggestions that *Parker v Patrick* was not good law after 1827 because of the change in legislation, and that was supported by the view that a contract procured by fraud was wholly void so that no title could pass to a third party.[26] Despite these doubts, in *Load v Green* Parke B followed *Parker v Patrick*, and explained the result in terms of a defeasible title.

3.13 Parke B's device of defeasible title explained why the vendor could bring trover against his fraudulent buyer:

---

[20] *Davis v Morrison* (1773) Lofft 185, 187; 98 ER 601, 602 (pawn of silver plate); *Parker v Patrick* (1793) 5 TR 175, 176; 101 ER 99, 99 (pawnbroker); *Wright v Lawes* (1799) 4 Esp 82, 83–84; 170 ER 649, 650 (sub-purchaser of four pipes of port).

[21] Some courts accepted that although no title passed under a contract induced by fraud, a general exception to the rule *nemo dat quod non habet* operated in favour of innocent sub-buyers: *Root v French* (1835) 13 Wendell 570 (SCNY) 572–74; perhaps also implicit in *Wright v Lawes* (1799) 4 Esp 82, 84; 170 ER 649, 650. Other courts suggested that an exception to the *nemo dat* rule applied if the vendor consented to the sub-sale: *Sheppard v Shoolbred* (1841) Car & M 61, 63; 174 ER 409, 410. There were also faint traces of an idea that title did in fact pass under a fraudulent contract (*Davis v Morrison* (1773) Lofft 185, 187; 98 ER 601, 602 (Lord Mansfield); *Parker v Patrick* (1793) 5 TR 175, 101 ER 99) or that it passed if the vendor affirmed the sale (see counsel's submissions and Talfourd J in *White v Garden* (1851) 10 CB 919, 923–24, 927; 138 ER 364, 366, 367).

[22] Restitution of Goods Stolen Act 1529 (21 Henry VIII c 11).

[23] Kelyng 48–49; 84 ER 1076; *Horwood v Smith* (1788) 2 TR 750, 755–56; 100 ER 404, 407–08 (stolen sheep); *Peer v Humphrey* (1835) 2 AD & E 495, 499; 111 ER 191, 193 (stolen oxen); *Scattergood v Sylvester* (1850) 15 QB 506, 117 ER 551 (cow and calf). The 1529 Act bolstered the early common law rights to recover property feloniously taken (J Kaye, 'Res Addiratae and Recovery of Stolen Goods' (1970) 86 LQR 379) by creating 'writs of restitution'. By the eighteenth century these writs were no longer used and trover was the preferred form of action: *Golightly v Reynolds* (1772) Lofft 88, 90; 98 ER 547, 548 (Lord Mansfield).

[24] Larceny (England) Act 1827 (7 & 8 Geo IV c 29), s 57.

[25] (1793) 5 TR 175, 101 ER 99. Lord Kenyon there held (following *Davis v Morrison* (1773) Lofft 158, 98 ER 99 (Lord Mansfield)) that the revesting legislation did not extend to the offence of obtaining goods by false pretences. A subsequent bona fide purchaser could therefore bring trover against a defrauded vendor, notwithstanding a conviction for obtaining by false pretences.

[26] *Peer v Humphrey* (1835) 2 AD & E 495, 499; 111 ER 191, 193; J Chitty, *A Practical Treatise on the Law of Contracts Not Under Seal* (T Chitty (ed)) (3rd edn, 1841) 415 fn (h). The authorities are reviewed in J Chitty, *A Practical Treatise on the Law of Contracts Not Under Seal* (J Russell (ed)) (4th edn, 1850) 363–64. For subsequent developments, see Larceny Act 1861 (24 & 25 Vict c 96), s 100; *Bentley v Vilmont* (1887) 12 App Cas 471 (PC); Powers of Criminal Courts (Sentencing) Act 2000, ss 148, 149. For a different account of this history, W Swadling, 'Rescission, Property, and the Common Law' (2005) 121 LQR 123.

As the goods were obtained by a fraudulent purchase, the claimants [sellers] had a right to disaffirm it, to revest the property in them, and recover their value in an action against the bankrupt [buyer].[27]

Defeasible title also reconciled that right with a sub-purchaser's entitlement to bring trover against the vendor. It gave the fraudster a title to sell, creating space for the further conclusion that a sub-sale could perfect that title as against the original seller.[28] The model also gave meaning to the insistence that bringing trover involved rescinding the sale, for it held that title revested only when the seller disaffirmed, which involved treating the contract as 'absolutely void'. This was, moreover, all consistent with the rule that trover did not lie for a mere breach of contract or warranty. **3.14**

It is difficult to escape the impression that Parke B intended to explain and clarify this area of the law, and that he did so through the device of defeasible title. The concept of a defeasible title was in this way conditioned by a series of earlier choices about which forms of action were available in this context. The rule that assumpsit for goods sold and delivered could not be used, but that trover could, was of decisive importance. This dictated that the parties' entitlements would be regulated through the incidence of rights to possess, and therefore ownership, foreclosing the possibility that rescission at law would involve purely personal claims to recover the value of property transferred. Further, it appears that Parke B's conclusion that a fraudulent sale was not absolutely void, but only voidable, followed from the conclusion that a defeasible title passed under it. This is counter-intuitive to modern eyes, but reflected both the primacy of the regime of the forms of action at the time, and also a dynamic in which principles of substantive law emerged as by-products of the availability of particular forms of action. **3.15**

(3) Rescission as a condition to restitution

Load v Green established that to regain title to goods sold, the defrauded seller must first elect to disaffirm the contract of sale, treating it as void. It was by that act that the defrauded seller obtained restitution by regaining legal title. The court's role was to enforce the proprietary rights so secured. **3.16**

A quite separate development established that a contract had to be first 'rescinded' before the common law would confer personal claims to restitution. This also proceeded on the basis that the court's role was to enforce the claimant's right to restitution, obtained when he elected to rescind. **3.17**

The rule emerged at the end of the eighteenth century as part of the working out of the relationship between general and special assumpsit, and is associated with the decisions of Buller J in *Weston v Downes*[29] and *Towers v Barrett*.[30] As in *Load v Green*, the rule was **3.18**

---

[27] *Load v Green* (1846) 15 M & W 216, 221; 153 ER 828, 830.

[28] This conclusion was foreshadowed in *Load v Green*, Parke B stating *obiter* that 'the transaction is not absolutely void, except at the option of the seller: he may elect to treat it as a contract, and he must do the contrary before the buyer has acted as if it were such, and resold the goods to a third party'. The rule was subsequently confirmed in *White v Garden* (1851) 10 CB 919, 138 ER 364.

[29] (1778) 1 Doug 23, 99 ER 19.

[30] (1786) 1 TR 133, 99 ER 1014.

52   I. INTRODUCTION

shaped by technical considerations relevant to the forms of action at that time. These background considerations will be discussed first, and Buller J's decisions after that.

The background to *Weston v Downes* and *Towers v Barrett*
Special and general assumpsit

3.19 Special assumpsit was the forebear of damages for breach of contract. It alleged non-performance of a promise ('assumpsit') supported by consideration. The assumpsit was 'special' because the promise and its non-performance were specifically described in the count itself.[31] The claim led to an award of damages assessed by the jury. The claimant bringing special assumpsit was required to prove at trial the particular facts alleged or the action would fail.[32] During the second half of the eighteenth century it was held that claims for breach of warranty (alleging that the defendant had falsely warranted the quality or character of articles sold)[33] could also be framed in a declaration for special assumpsit,[34] further widening its scope. Pleading breach of warranty in assumpsit conferred procedural advantages over the old form, the writ of deceit. Thereafter the old form remained relevant where the false statement was not a term of the contract as, for example, where it was a parole promise made in relation to a written contract.[35]

3.20 General assumpsit was different. It is the foundation for claims in what became known as 'quasi-contract', or in modern parlance, common law rights to restitution for unjust enrichment. The assumpsit was 'general' because the promise and its non-performance were recited in a very general way in the writ.[36] Few of the facts of the true complaint were alleged,

---

[31] E Lawes, *A Practical Treatise on Pleading in Assumpsit* (1810) 1–2; A Stephens, *The Law of Nisi Prius, Evidence in Civil Actions, and Arbitration Awards* (1842) vol 1, 232; D Ibbetson, *A Historical Introduction to the Law of Obligations* (1999) 148. The elements of the plea are discussed in J Saunders, *The Law of Pleading and Evidence in Civil Actions* (1828) vol 1, 111–36.

[32] R Bridgman (ed), *An Introduction to the Law Relative to Trials at Nisi Prius* (7th edn, 1817) 128a fn (b).

[33] As to the distinction between 'implied warranties', and 'express warranties' at this time, see the submissions in *Stuart v Wilkins* (1788) 1 Doug 18, 20; 99 ER 15, 16; M Lobban, 'Contractual Fraud in Law and Equity, c 1750–c 1850' (1997) 17 OJLS 441, 459–60; S Williston, 'What Constitutes an Express Warranty in the Law of Sales' (1908) 21 Harv LR 555, 555–56. On the early action for breach of warranty, J Ames, 'The History of Assumpsit' (1888) 2 Harv LR 1, 8; D Ibbetson, *A Historical Introduction to the Law of Obligations* (1999) 84–85; SFC Milsom, 'The Sale of Goods in the Fifteenth Century' (1961) 77 LQR 257, 278–82; A Simpson, *A History of the Common Law of Contract: the Rise of the Action of Assumpsit* (1975) 242–47; JH Baker, 'Bezoar-Stones, Gall-Stones, and Gem-Stones: A Chapter in the History of the Tort of Deceit' in A Burrows and A Rodger (eds), *Mapping the Law: Essays in Memory of Peter Birks* (2006) 547–559. For the action in the eighteenth century, see J Oldham, *The Mansfield Manuscripts and the Growth of English Law in the Eighteenth Century* (1992) vol 1, 232–40.

[34] See J Chitty, *Treatise on Pleading* (3rd edn, 1817) vol 1, 136, 140; vol 2, 136 fn (r); J Ames, 'The History of Assumpsit' (1888) 2 Harv LR 1, 8; S Williston, 'What Constitutes an Express Warranty in the Law of Sales' (1908) 21 Harv LR 555, 555–61; W Holdsworth, *A History of English Law* (A Goodhart *et al* (eds)) (7th edn, 1956) vol 8, 70; M Lobban, 'Contractual Fraud in Law and Equity, c 1750–c 1850' (1997) 17 OJLS 441, 450–60; JL Barton, 'Redhibition, Error, and Implied Warranty in English Law' (1994) 62 The Legal History Review 317, 310–20; D Ibbetson, *A Historical Introduction to the Law of Obligations* (1999) 223. Although *Stuart v Wilkins* (1788) 1 Doug 18; 99 ER 15 is usually regarded as the point of change, earlier cases have been found: M Lobban, 'Contractual Fraud in Law and Equity, c 1750–c 1850' (1997) 17 OJLS 441, 460 fn 116.

[35] Eg *Powell v Edmunds* (1810) 12 East 6, 11; 104 ER 3, 5; *Meyer v Everth* (1814) 4 Camp 22, 23; 171 ER 8, 8. The doctrine of the implied term inevitably ate away at this residual use of the old form of liability; see, for example, *Gardiner v Gray* (1815) 4 Camp 144, 171 ER 46. But breach of warranty was not wholly absorbed by special assumpsit. Its origin in the action on the case for deceit is reflected in the rule that a knowingly false statement of fact incorporated into a contract generates a cause of action in damages for the tort of deceit separate from the cause of action for breach of the contractual term (see esp S Williston, 'What Constitutes an Express Warranty in the Law of Sales' (1908) 21 Harv LR 555, 556, 559) and which, unlike the claim for damages for breach of the contractual term, survives rescission of the contract. See further Chap 2, para [2.03].

[36] E Lawes, *A Practical Treatise on Pleading in Assumpsit* (1810) 1–2; J Saunders, *The Law of Pleading and Evidence in Civil Actions* (1828) vol 1, 137–38; A Stephens, *The Law of Nisi Prius, Evidence in Civil Actions, and Arbitration Awards* (1842) vol 1, 232. The elements of pleas in general assumpsit are outlined in Saunders, 136–39.

3. HISTORICAL FOUNDATIONS 53

and many of those formally alleged did not have to be proved. In particular, the assumpsit or promise to pay did not require proof (and could not be traversed), and thereby became fictional or, as was sometimes said, 'implied' by the law. To succeed, the claimant was required to prove at trial those facts that were accepted as supporting the general words recited.[37] A claim for breach of warranty could not be framed in general assumpsit alone.[38]

The most important species of general assumpsit was *indebitatus* assumpsit. It alleged that **3.21** the defendant was indebted to the claimant and had failed to perform his promise to pay the debt.[39] Following pleading reforms in the early nineteenth century,[40] the claimant was also allowed to use this form of action to recover the reasonable value of services or goods, though the promise of a precise sum was averred but not proved, so that no 'debt' in fact existed. This saw the demise of the counts for *quantum meruit* (alleging failure to fulfil a promise to pay so much as the claimant deserved) and *quantum valebat* (alleging failure to pay the value of that given),[41] and paved the way for the 'common counts' in *indebitatus* assumpsit, which reflected the common fact patterns covered by the claim: that is, money had and received, goods sold and delivered, and work done.[42]

Relationship between special and general assumpsit
During the second half of the eighteenth century special and general assumpsit were regu- **3.22** larly pleaded together,[43] apparently on the basis that if the facts proved at trial did not match the special plea, they might support the general,[44] although other reasons were also given.[45]

---

[37] JH Baker, 'The Use of Assumpsit for Restitutionary Money Claims 1600–1800' in E Schrage (ed), *Unjust Enrichment. The Comparative Legal History of the Law of Restitution* (1995) 31, 33; S Comyn, *The Law of Contracts and Promises Upon Various Subjects* (2nd edn, 1824) 266 (in relation to money had and received); also F Buller, *An Introduction to the Law Relative to Trials at Nisi Prius* (1772) 129.

[38] Eg *Power v Wells* (1778) 2 Cowp 818, 819; 98 ER 1379, 1379 'the action for money had and received, with no other count, was an improper action to try the warranty'; see also the reporter's note.

[39] For development in the seventeenth century, JH Baker and S Milsom, *Sources of English Legal History: Private Law to 1750* (2nd edn, 2010)chap 18; JH Baker, 'The Use of Assumpsit for Restitutionary Money Claims 1600–1800' in E Schrage (ed), *Unjust Enrichment. The Comparative Legal History of the Law of Restitution* (1995).

[40] Uniformity of Process Act 1832, (2 & 3 Will IV, c 39); A Simpson, 'The Horwitz Thesis and the History of Contract' (1979) 46 U of Chicago LR 533, 587 fn 326; J Barton, 'Contract and *Quantum Meruit*: The Antecedents of *Cutter v Powell*' [1987] *Journal of Legal History* 48, 52.

[41] 'As... the claimant may now recover on the indebitatus count, though he do not prove that any given price was agreed upon, the quantum meruit and quantum valebat counts have fallen into total disuse': R Browne, *A Practical Treatise on Actions at Law* (1843) 486. See also J Saunders, *The Law of Pleading and Evidence in Civil Actions* (1828) vol 1, 137; E Bullen and S Leake, *Precedents of Pleadings in Actions in the Superior Courts of Common Law with Notes* (1860) 19 fn (a); J Barton, 'Contract and *Quantum Meruit*: The Antecedents of *Cutter v Powell*' [1987] *Journal of Legal History* 48, 52; JH Baker, 'The Use of Assumpsit for Restitutionary Money Claims 1600–1800' in E Schrage (ed), *Unjust Enrichment. The Comparative Legal History of the Law of Restitution* (1995) 34, fn 13; D Ibbetson, *A Historical Introduction to the Law of Obligations* (1999) 148, 149.

[42] F Buller, *An Introduction to the Law Relative to Trials at Nisi Prius* (1772) 128; R Browne, *A Practical Treatise on Actions at Law* (1843) 320; E Bullen and S Leake, *Precedents of Pleadings in Actions in the Superior Courts of Common Law with Notes* (1860) 19.

[43] This type of pleading is said to have been developed in the later years of the seventeenth century: J Barton (n 41) 52. For examples in the eighteenth century, see the pleadings extensively recited in J Wentworth, *A Complete System of Pleading* (1797, 1798), vols 2 and 3, and also J Oldham, *The Mansfield Manuscripts and the Growth of English Law of in the Eighteenth Century* (1992) vol 1, 228.

[44] A Simpson, *A History of the Common Law of Contract: The Rise of the Action of Assumpsit* (1975) 587: 'The available evidence indicates that a claimant used to set forth different counts in the same declaration... to have something to fall back on "lest he should fail in the proof" of his assumpsit'.

[45] E Lawes, *A Practical Treatise on Pleading in Assumpsit* (1810) 27: 'These special counts will not only have the effect of preventing the danger of not being permitted to give evidence on the general counts, but will also give a more distinct view of the true nature of the case to judge and jury, and more accurately direct the evidence ... It is also proper to add general counts in almost every case in assumpsit, lest the claimant should not be able to prove

54   I. INTRODUCTION

To side-step the objection that inconsistent facts were being alleged, the claimant would recite two entirely separate broken promises. The first was adapted to the requirements of special assumpsit, and the second to general assumpsit.[46]

3.23   The claimant's right to recover on the general count if he failed to prove the special count was the subject of some uncertainty. Lord Holt CJ seemed to permit this;[47] a view attributed to Lord Raymond held that the claimant had to elect at trial whether to proceed on special or general counts in assumpsit;[48] whereas Lord Mansfield appeared to reject that restriction.[49] Moreover, according to Professor Oldham,during most of Lord Mansfield's tenure, when the claimant did succeed in general assumpsit, there is no indication that this was premised upon a rescission of the contract under which the benefits had been conferred.[50] That changed decisivelyonly at the end of the eighteenth century[51] with the decisions of Buller J in *Weston v Downes*[52]and *Towers v Barrett*.[53]

his case, as stated in the special counts'. See also J Saunders, *The Law of Pleading and Evidence in Civil Actions* (1828) vol 1, 136–37.

[46] Eg Buller's pleading recorded in J Wentworth, *A Complete System of Pleading* (1797, 1798) vol 2, 126, read with the further details in vol 3, 55–56. See also *Hart v Longfield* (1703) 7 Mod 148, 149; 87 ER 1156, 1156; J Barton (n 41) 52; cf M Horwitz, 'The Historical Foundations of Modern Contract Law' (1974) 87 Harv LR 917, 934; A Simpson, *A History of the Common Law of Contract: The Rise of the Action of Assumpsit* (1975) 586–88; W Swain, '*Cutter v Powell* and the Pleading of Claims of Unjust Enrichment' [2003] RLR 46, 50–51.

[47] *Francam v Foster* (1693) Skinner 326, 90 ER 145, permitting a claimant who proved a contract different to that laid, so failing on the special count, to recover the value of work done in general assumpsit. Cf suggestions that *indebitatus* assumpsit did not lie to recover money paid under a bargain (*Anon* (1695) B & M 468; *Anon* (1697) B & M 469).

[48] *Weaver v Boroughs* (1726) 1 Str 648, 93 ER 757, as modified by the Lincoln's Inn MS Hill 12 (1) 6, reproduced J Barton, 'Contract and Quantum Meruit: the Antecedents of Cutter and Powell' [1987] *Journal of Legal History* 48, 52–53. As to how this case was received, Barton, 53–54, F Buller, *An Introduction to the Law Relative to Trials at Nisi Prius* (1772) 136.

[49] F Buller, *An Introduction to the Law Relative to Trials at Nisi Prius* (1772) 137, relying upon *Harris v Oke* in Winchester summer assizes 1759; *Payne v Bacomb* (1781) 2 Dougl 651, 99 ER 412; *Dutch v Warren* (1720) 1 Str 406, 93 ER 598.

[50] 'There is no indication that these actions were brought on a theory of rescission of the contract; usually the claim was described as the return performance that was alleged to have been promised': J Oldham, *The Mansfield Manuscripts and the Growth of English Law in the Eighteenth Century* (1992) vol 1, 230. See also P Atiyah, *The Rise and Fall of Freedom of Contract* (1979) 184.

[51] But cf *Dutch v Warren* (1720) 1 Str 406, 93 ER 598, as reported in *Moses v Macferlan* (1760) 2 Burr 1005, 1011; 97 ER 676, 680. See now also the manuscript report of *Dutch v Warren* in L Bonfield and LR Poos, 'Reports of Sir Peter King, Chief Justice of the Common Pleas 1714-22' (2013) 130 Selden Society 229–230 (and also at lx n 37 and cviii–cvix), which supports a conclusion that by as early as 1720, the Court of Common Pleas was aligning the right to bring money had and received for sums paid under a contract, with the making of an election to disaffirm the contract. The report records that on 18 August 1720 the plaintiff Dutch paid £262 10s to the defendant Warren in exchange for five shares in the Welch Copper Mines, to be transferred at the opening of the books on 22 August 1720. Warren refused to do this, telling Dutch that he 'might take his remedy'. At the subsequent trial of Dutch's claim for repayment of the £262 10s as money had and received, Warren argued that this claim would not lie, Dutch being confined to a claim for non-performance of the contract. After the jury had awarded damages of only £175 being the price of the stock as at 22 August 1720, on a motion by Chief Justice King, the Court of Common Pleas held that money had and received would indeed lie for the full amount paid over, explaining as follows (at 230):

> These actions have of late years been much extended beyond the rule of the ancient law, and the extending of them depends upon the notion of fraud. If a man takes my money to do a thing, and he refuses to do it, it is a fraud; and it is at the election of the party injured either to affirm the agreement bringing the action for the non-performance of it, or to disaffirm the agreement *ab initio* by reason of the fraud, and bring an action for the money paid by him, as so much money received to his use.

[52] (1778) 1 Doug 23, 99 ER 19.

[53] (1786) 1 TR 133, 99 ER 1014.

Weston v Downes and *Towers v Barrett*
The requirement for rescission

In *Weston v Downes* and *Towers v Barrett* Buller J said that money had and received was **3.24** only available where there was a special (express) contract if it was proved that the special contract had been rescinded.[54] Sir James Mansfield developed the principle in *Cooke v Munstone*,[55] holding that a claimant who failed to establish a plea of special assumpsit at trial could recover on a plea of general assumpsit only if the contract had been rescinded, or if that plea would have been available absent a special contract.[56]

In all three of these cases the court displayed a concern to prevent defendants being surprised at trial, by not knowing in advance the case to be answered.[57] A defendant to a plea of special assumpsit knew the case to be answered because the facts were specifically alleged in the count. A risk of surprise arose if at trial different facts were proved, of which the defendant had no notice, and the claimant sought to rely on those to establish a plea of general assumpsit, recited by general words.[58] The rescission requirement was apparently regarded as reducing the risk of surprise by aligning general assumpsit with rescinded contracts, and special assumpsit with the alternative scenario where the contract remained open, allowing the defendant to better know in advance the facts to be proved to establish each form of plea.[59] Buller J may also have been concerned to regulate more coherently the general relationship between the fictional promises implied by the law on which the claimant sued in general assumpsit, and the real promises actually given by the defendant, on which the claimant sued in special assumpsit.[60] **3.25**

---

[54] For discussion, W Swain, '*Cutter v Powell* and the Pleading of Claims of Unjust Enrichment' [2003] RLR 46, 51–53.

[55] (1805) 1 Bos & Pul 351, 127 ER 499; also eg *Rees v Lines* (1837) 8 Car & P 126, 129–30; 173 ER 427, 428.

[56] Sir James Mansfield did not spell out the meaning of this qualification. He probably intended to identify cases where it was proved at trial that there was no express contract, or a contract different from that alleged which had been wholly performed: see *Cooke v Munstone* (1805) 1 Bos & Pul 351, 355; 127 ER 499, 501. Indebitatus assumpsit had long been available when a special contract was fully performed on one side, and the rescission requirement was apparently never applied in that context, at least where the only outstanding performance was payment of a liquidated sum. The rule was apparently attributed to *Gordon v Martin* (1732) Fitz 302, 303; 94 ER 766, 767: see F Buller, *An Introduction to the Law Relative to Trials at Nisi Prius* (1772) 136; E Lawes, *A Practical Treatise on Pleading in Assumpsit* (1810) 4; see also R Browne, *A Practical Treatise on Actions at Law* (1843) 484; E Bullen and S Leake, *Precedents of Pleadings in Actions in the Superior Courts of Common Law with Notes* (1860) 20; E Williams, *Notes to Saunders' Reports by the Late Serjeant Williams* (1871) 366–67.

[57] Cf 'The ground of surprise... was never really sound': S Stoljar, 'The Doctrine of Failure of Consideration' (1959) 75 LQR 53, 75; also 57–58, 61. Also, F Dawson, 'Rescission and Damages' (1976) 39 MLR 214, 216 fn 17; S Lurie, 'Toward a Unified Theory of Breach: Tracing the History of the Rule that Rescission Ab Initio is not a Remedy For Breach of Contract' (2003) 19 JCL 250, 270–71.

[58] The risk of surprise created by the generalized form of the count for money had and received was well recognized, and was regarded as a brake on its availability: eg Sir John Strange notes to *Dutch v Warren* (1720) 1 Str 406, 93 ER 598; *Spurrier v Elderton* (1803) 4 Esp 1, 3; 170 ER 717, 718; S Comyn, *The Law of Contracts and Promises Upon Various Subjects* (2nd edn, 1824) 267. Lord Mansfield was particularly concerned to prevent the generalized nature of the plea of money had and received from causing surprise: eg *Lindon v Hooper* (1776) 1 Cowp 414, 418; 98 ER 1160, 1162–63; *Forrester v Hodgson* (1778) in J Oldham, *The Mansfield Manuscripts and the Growth of English Law in the Eighteenth Century* (1992) vol 1, 326–27, see also 186, 230; *Stevenson v Mortimer* (1778) 2 Cowp 805, 807; 98 ER 1372, 1373; *Longchamp v Kenny* (1779) 1 Doug 137, 138; 99 ER 91, 91.

[59] It subsequently became established that a claimant had to elect between general and special assumpsit, and that this election was to be made by electing to rescind or to affirm the contract: *Walstab v Spottiswoode* (1846) 15 M & W 501, 514; 153 ER 947, 953; *Goodman v Pocock* (1850) 15 QB 576, 580–83; 117 ER 577, 579–80.

[60] *Toussaint v Martinnant* (1787) 2 TR 100, 105; 100 ER 55, 57 (Buller J): 'Promises in law only exist where there is no express stipulation between the parties' (bonds taken as security). See also E Lawes, *A Practical Treatise on Pleading in Assumpsit* (1810) 15; *Cutter v Powell* (1795) 6 TR 320, 324; 101 ER 573, 576 (Lord Kenyon CJ): 'That where the parties have come to an express contract none can be implied has prevailed so long as to be reduced to an axiom in the law'. Also, D Ibbetson, *A Historical Introduction to the Law of Obligations* (1999) 279; M Dockray, '*Cutter v Powell*: A Trip Outside the Text' (2001) 117 LQR 664, 678–79, 681; W Swain, '*Cutter v Powell* and

56   I. INTRODUCTION

3.26   The cases that followed *Weston v Downes* generalized the rescission requirement beyond money had and received to all forms of general assumpsit, including for the value of services rendered and goods sold and delivered.[61]

Grounds for rescission

3.27   Subsequent cases also confirmed that rescission could occur by agreement,[62] or be founded on the defendant's unwillingness[63] or inability[64]to perform his side of the bargain.[65] Fraud was simply another ground for rescission.[66] There were only two material distinctions at this time between the right to rescind and bring general assumpsit in cases of fraud and in cases of mere non-performance. First, the defrauded purchaser of goods had the advantage that he could, by electing to disaffirm, unilaterally revest title, and thereby effect the failure of consideration necessary to bring money had and received. A purchaser who had simply bought non-conforming goods could not.[67] Secondly, a claimant alleging fraud was not permitted to bring general assumpsit to recover the value of goods sold or of services performed, but was required to sue in deceit or trover.[68] This restriction did not apply in

the Pleading of Claims of Unjust Enrichment' [2003] RLR 46, 51–53, 56; S Lurie, 'Toward a Unified Theory of Breach: Tracing the History of the Rule that Rescission Ab Initio is not a Remedy For Breach of Contract' (2003) 19 JCL 250, 270.

[61] See nn 62–64.

[62] Eg *Towers v Barrett* (1786) 1 TR 133, 99 ER 1014.

[63] Eg *Giles v Edwards* (1797) 7 TR 181, 182; 101 ER 920, 921 (vendor refused to cord wood); *Planche v Colburn* (1831) 8 Bing 14, 131 ER 305 (writing part of volume for series defendant discontinued); *Walstab v Spottiswood* (1846) 15 M & W 501, 153 ER 947 (money for shares defendant refused to issue); *Goodman v Pocock* (1850) 15 QB 576, 117 ER 577 (wrongful dismissal); *De Bernardy v Harding* (1853) 8 Ex 822, 824; 155 ER 1586, 1587; to similar effect Pollock CB in *Harrison v James* (1862) 7 H & N 804, 808; 158 ER 693, 695; *Bartholemew v Marwick* (1864) 15 CB (NS) 711, 143 ER 964. There had to be a 'total refusal to perform': *Ehrensperger v Anderson* (1848) 3 Ex 148, 158; 154 ER 793, 797.

[64] Eg *Grenville v Da Costa* (1797) Peake Add Cas 113, 114; 170 ER 213, 213 (deposit for estate payee unable to convey); *Hogan v Shee* (1797) 2 Esp 522, 170 ER 441 (£100 to secure position in East India company payee no power to give); also *Farrer v Nightingale* (1798) 2 Esp 639, 170 ER 481; *Bartlett v Tuchin* (1815) 6 Taunt 259, 128 ER 1034; *Roper v Coombes* (1827) 6 B & C 534, 108 ER 549.

[65] By the mid-nineteenth century it was said that the defendant's failure to perform had to be unjustified: *Fitt v Cassanet* (1842) 4 Man & G 898, 134 ER 369. *Abbelby v Meyers* (1867) LR 2 CP 651, 659. See further item three of the notes to *Dutch v Warren* (1720) 1 Str 406, 93 ER 598, 599; S Comyn, *The Law of Contracts and Promises Upon Various Subjects* (2nd edn, 1824) 304–33; T Chitty, A Denning, and C Harvey (eds), *A Selection of Leading Cases on the Various Branches of the Law* (13th edn, 1929) vol 1, 23, 45–46; E Williams, *Notes to Saunders' Reports* (1871) 367–69; S Williston, 'Repudiation of Contracts' (1901) 14 HLR 317, 317–31. Cf the critique in G Treitel, 'Some Problems of Breach of Contract' (1967) 30 MLR 139, 144–49; A Shea, 'Discharge for Performance of Contracts by Failure of Condition' (1979) 42 MLR 623; generally, B Crown, 'Restitution in Cases of Failure of Performance in Contracts and Misrepresentation' (DPhil thesis, 1979).

[66] *Gompertz v Denton* (1832) 1 C & M 207, 149 ER 376 (purchase of horse); *Campbell v Fleming* (1834) 1 AD&E 40, 42; 110 ER 1122, 1123 (purchase of shares); *Fitt v Cassanet* (1842) 4 Man & G 898, 134 ER 369 (purchase of palm oil scrapings); *Murray v Mann* (1848) 2 Ex 538, 154 ER 695 (purchase of horse); C Addison, *A Treatise on the Law of Contracts* (2nd edn, 1849) vol 1 150, 322; J Chitty, *A Practical Treatise on the Law of Contracts Not Under Seal* (J Russell (ed)) (4th edn, 1850) 549, 636. Cf until general acceptance of the rule that fraud made a contract voidable not void, money had and received was sometimes allowed where sums had been paid under a contract induced by fraud without any requirement for rescission, on the footing that the contract was void: eg *Hill v Gray* (1816) 1 Starke 435, 171 ER 521 (Lord Ellenborough).

[67] *Street v Blay* (1831) 2 B & AD 456, 109 ER 1212; applied *Murray v Mann* (1848) 2 Ex 538, 541–42; 154 ER 605, 606. For discussion of *Street v Blay*, S Williston, 'Rescission for Breach of Warranty' (1903) 16 Harv LR 46; (1904) 4 Columbia LR 195; F Burdick, 'Rescission for Breach of Warranty' (1904) 4 Columbia LR 1; S Stoljar, 'Conditions, Warranties and Descriptions of Quality in Sale of Goods—I' (1952) 15 MLR 425, 436–38 and S Stoljar, 'The Doctrine of Failure of Consideration' (1959) 75 LQR 53, 60. No return was needed if the plea was in special assumpsit: *Fielder v Starkin* (1788) 1 H BL 17, 126 ER 11.

[68] Goods sold: *Read v Hutchinson* (1813) 3 Camp 352, 353; 170 ER 1408, 1408; *Ferguson v Carrington* (1829) 9 B & C 59, 59–60; 109 ER 22, 23; *Strutt v Smith* (1834) 1 CM & R 312, 313, 315; 149 ER 1099, 1100. Services provided: *Selway v Fogg* (1839) 5 M & W 83, 151 ER 36.

cases of mere non-performance, where the general counts were available but trover and deceit were not.[69]

Need to elect to rescind

The line of cases beginning with *Weston v Downes* indicated that in order to effect the 're-   **3.28**
scission' required to bring general assumpsit, the claimant was required to manifest his
election to treat the contract as at an end, as by demanding the return of money paid,[70] or
tendering back goods purchased.[71] By failing to do so within a reasonable time, or acting
to affirm the contract, the claimant might lose the right to rescind, and thereby the right to
bring the restitutionary claim in general assumpsit.[72]

Conclusions

The modern rule that a contract must first be terminated before the common law will im-   **3.29**
pose a personal obligation to restore the value of benefits conferred emerged at the end of
the eighteenth century following the decisions of Buller J in *Weston v Downes*[73] and *Towers
v Barrett*.[74] The rule derived from a working out of the relationship between general and
special assumpsit. The reasons for its adoption are not particularly clear, but a principal
influence seems to have been to prevent surprise if both forms of action were relied on at
trial, as had been the practice. The rescission requirement attempted to remedy that difficulty, and this seems to have been at least as important as a concern to demarcate the incidence of rights based on fictional promises (general assumpsit) and real promises (special
assumpsit).

(4) *Termination* de futuro *and* ab initio

The rules just discussed fundamentally shaped the doctrine of rescission at common law.   **3.30**
All were worked out at a time when the common law did not draw the now familiar distinction between contracts terminated *de futuro* for breach or frustration and *ab initio* for initial
invalidating cause. This came much later. The first statements were in the late nineteenth
century,[75] but in England the distinction was only clearly stated and explained in the second
half of the twentieth century.[76]

---

[69] Goods sold: *Oxendale v Wetherell* (1829) 9 B & C 385, 109 ER 143; *Bartholemew v Marwick* (1864) 15 CB (NS)
711, 143 ER 964. Services provided: *Planche v Colburn* (1831) 8 Bing 14, 131 ER 305; *De Bernardy v Harding* (1853)
8 Ex 822, 824; 155 ER 1586, 1587.

[70] *Giles v Edwards* (1797) 7 TR 181, 182; 101 ER 920, 921 (demand repayment of 20 guineas).

[71] *Towers v Barrett* (1786) 1 TR 133, 136; 99 ER 1014, 1016 (buyer returned chaise purchased); *Grimaldi v White*
(1802) 4 Esp 95, 170 ER 654 (defendant dissatisfied with miniature painting purchased from claimant) 'if he means
to avail himself of that objection, he must return the picture; he must rescind the contract totally... he must either
abide by it, or rescind it *in toto* by returning the thing sold'.

[72] *Dr Compton's case* (referred to by Buller J in *Towers v Barrett* (1786) 1 TR 133, 136; 99 ER 1014, 1016);
Campbell v Fleming (1834) 1 AD & E 40, 42; 110 ER 1122, 1123.

[73] (1778) 1 Doug 23, 99 ER 19.

[74] (1786) 1 TR 133, 99 ER 1014.

[75] *Boston Deep Sea Fishing & Ice Co v Ansell* (1888) 39 ChD 339, 365 (Bowen LJ). But see also *Dutch v Warren*
(1720) 1 Str 406, 93 ER 598, as reported in *Moses v Macferlan* (1760) 2 Burr 1005, 1011; 97 ER 676, 680 and in the
manuscript note attributed to Sir Peter King, discussed n 51 above.

[76] *Heyman v Darwins Ltd* [1942] AC 356, 371–73, 398–99; *Johnson v Agnew* [1980] AC 367, 397; *Hurst v Bryk*
[2002] 2 AC 185, 193; M Albery, 'Mr Cyprian Williams' Great Heresy' (1975) 91 LQR 337. In Australia, *McDonald
v Dennys Lascelles Limited* (1933) 48 CLR 457, 476–77; *Mann v Paterson Constructions Pty Ltd* (2019) 267 CLR
560 [7]–[9], [30], [51], [69], [180], [190]; in New Zealand, *Hunt v Hyde* [1976] 2 NZLR 453, 457. See also, S Lurie,

58   I. INTRODUCTION

3.31   The late development of this distinction meant that the notion that there is no right to contractual damages when a contract is 'rescinded' for non-performance was able to survive well into the twentieth century,[77] alongside the now rejected notion that the consideration for a contractual payment can fail only if the contract is extinguished *ab initio*.[78]

3.32   Equally, although there is explanatory force in the notion that money is repayable and property revests following rescission for fraud because the contract is rescinded *ab initio*, this idea is divorced from the real reasons for the development of those rules. Both were more the product of now obsolete procedural rules about the availability of the forms of action, than they were motivated by theoretical considerations about the right to the return of benefits conferred under contracts of imperfect consent.

(5) Role of the forms of action

3.33   There was never a form of action for 'rescission'. The common law had no equivalent to the equitable bill to set aside a transaction, which will be discussed next. The common law of rescission was the by-product of a series of precise rules concerning the circumstances in which trover and general and special assumpsit would lie in relation to contracts procured by fraud. The central feature of the common law doctrine was that the defrauded party was himself empowered to rescind the contract by electing to disaffirm it. The court's role was confined to adjudicating whether a right to rescind had arisen and been exercised, and to give effect to that exercise by dismissing claims to enforce the contract, or by entering judgment in respect of rights to restitution that had arisen, following their quantification by the jury.

C. Equity

(1) Introduction

3.34   The equitable doctrine of rescission was quite different. Equitable rights were not articulated through the writs that gave rise to the forms of action in courts of law. Much of Chancery's jurisprudence was in fact generated by the inability of those forms of action to achieve justice, and by the constraints on investigation imposed by the rules of procedure and of evidence that accompanied them. A party wishing to rescind in equity brought a bill praying that the court set the transaction aside, and for consequential relief, on the ground that the transaction was improper or improperly procured in the manner recited in the bill.

'Toward a Unified Theory of Breach: Tracing the History of the Rule that Rescission Ab Initio is not a Remedy For Breach of Contract' (2003) 19 JCL 250, 261, 276–78.

[77]   *Horsler v Zorro* [1975] 1 Ch 302; M Albery, 'Mr Cyprian Williams' Great Heresy' (1975) 91 LQR 337; Chap 1, para [1.08].
[78]   *Fibrosa Spolka Akcyjna v Fairbairn Lawson Combe Barbour Limited* [1943] AC 32, 46–49, 52–53, 64, rejecting the approach in *Chandler v Webster* [1904] 1 KB 493 (CA) 499, 501. See also eg *Kettlewell v Refuge Assurance Company* [1908] 1 KB 545 (CA) 552 (Buckley LJ).

The facts surrounding entry into the transaction were put before the court in the bill and answer, by evidence from witnesses, and by means of bills for discovery.

The grounds for relief were typically described in the language of 'fraud', either 'actual' fraud **3.35** or *dolus malus*, or some lesser species of fraud, arising from the relation between the parties, or constructed because the bargain was contrary to the policy of the law.[79] The grounds for rescission both overlapped with and went well beyond the matters providing a defence at law to a claim to enforce a deed or parole agreement.

If the bill was successful, the court would itself effect rescission, and from at least the late **3.36** seventeenth century Chancery employed a well-recognized suite of orders to prevent the enforcement and undo the effects of contracts and gifts that offended equity's conscience, or which undermined the interests that it sought to protect.

(2) Orders effecting rescission

Chancery would prevent the enforcement of an executory transaction by orders for in- **3.37** junction and cancellation. The injunction might restrain an action at law,[80] or execution of a verdict obtained at law,[81] and it might be temporary pending investigation and trial in Chancery,[82] or permanent after that had occurred.[83] An order for cancellation provided for or permitted defacement of the relevant instrument,[84] in a manner that prevented or inhibited action on it at law. In early times cancellation probably prevented 'profert' of the deed, which was essential in proving it.[85] Before it was abolished by section 55 of the Common Law Procedure Act 1852, the requirement for profert was gradually relaxed at law, and at least by the early nineteenth century removal of the seal or other damage to a

---

[79] See in particular, *Chesterfield v Janssen* (1750) 1 Atk 301, 351–53; 26 ER 191, 224–25, where Lord Hardwicke LC described all of the grounds for rescission in the language of 'fraud'. See also the analysis of grounds for rescission in equity in J Newland, *A Treatise on Contracts within the Jurisdiction of Courts of Equity* (1806) chaps 20–22, 28–35, which followed Lord Hardwicke's classification. 'Actual fraud' was sometimes called 'moral fraud' in the nineteenth century: eg *Traill v Baring* (1864) 4 De G J & S 318, 328; 46 ER 942, 946; *Derry v Peek* (1889) 14 App Cas 337, 346–47, 356, 359–60, 362.

[80] *Pennell v Millar* (1857) 23 Beav 172, 182; 53 ER 68, 71 (loan secured on inheritance a catching bargain) 'Mr Dobson could not have enforced that covenant, by which Lord Huntingtower engaged to pay them, without being restrained by the injunction of this Court from doing so'.

[81] J Mitford, *A Treatise on the Pleadings in Suits in the Court of Chancery by English Bill* (2nd edn, 1787) 119; eg *Whittingham v Thornburg* (1690) 2 Vern 206, 23 ER 734; *Espey v Lake* (1852) 10 Hare 260, 68 ER 928.

[82] J Mitford, *A Treatise on the Pleadings in Suits in the Court of Chancery by English Bill* (2nd edn, 1787) 117; *Chesterfield v Janssen* (1750) 1 Atk 301, 302–03; 26 ER 191, 193; *Evans v Chesshire* (1803) Ves Sen Supp 300, 307, 313; 28 ER 532, 534, 536; *Fox v Wright* (1821) 6 Madd 111, 56 ER 1034. The injunction would usually be on the terms that the claimant paid the amount received under the impugned transaction: eg *Curling v Marquis Townsend* (1816) 19 Ves Jun 629, 633; 34 ER 649, 650–51.

[83] Eg *Blackwell v Redman* (1634) 1 Chan Rep 88, 22 ER 515; *Earl of Ardglasse v Muschamp* (1684) 1 Vern 237, 23 ER 438; *Turton v Benson* (1718) 1 P Wms 496, 496, 498; 24 ER 488, 489; *Davis v Duke of Marlborough* (1819) 2 Swans 108, 36 ER 555. Cf *Stent v Bailis* (1724) 2 P Wms 217, 24 ER 705 (frustration).

[84] Cancellation formerly involved court officers, and at one time the Chancellor himself, removing the seal from a deed, or cutting, tearing or 'damning' the instrument: R Preston (ed), *Sheppard's Touchstone of Common Assurances* (7th edn, 1820) 70. For reported examples, Tothill 26–28; 21 ER 113, 'Bonds'.

[85] J Gilbert, *The Law of Evidence* (1791) 112 (cf Chancery's less strict view: C Viner, *A General Abridgment of Law and Equity* (2nd edn, 1793) vol 12, 43–44). If a deed was sufficiently damaged this might also make it void or avoided in a way that supported a plea of *non est factum*: *Mathewson's case* (1597) 5 Co Rep 22b, 23a; 77 ER 84, 85; *Whelpdale's case* (1604) 5 Co Rep 119a, 77 ER 239; *Pigot's case* (1614) 11 Co Rep 26b, 27a; 77 ER 1177, 1178; Viner, 91 [17]; R Preston (ed), *Sheppard's Touchstone of Common Assurances* (7th edn, 1820) 53–54, 74.

60   I. INTRODUCTION

deed was of evidential relevance only.[86] From at least the late eighteenth century, the stated justification for this jurisdiction to grant injunctions and to cancel instruments was that the common law's procedures were inadequate to do justice.[87]

3.38   Executed and part-executed transactions were also unwound by Chancery upon proof of fraud or imposition. This was done using a set of orders that appear to have undergone little change between the late seventeenth and mid-nineteenth centuries. The orders were for restitution to the claimant by way of reconveyance of real property,[88] revesting of personal property[89] and the repayment of money,[90] and for counter-restitution and other adjustments by way of orders for conditional relief[91]and account,[92] and exceptionally by mandatory injunction.[93] These forms of order were largely unavailable at common law.

3.39   During this period there was no suggestion at all that the claimant obtained particular equitable entitlements at the time of any election to disaffirm, or that the court was giving effect to a rescission effected by the claimant. The equity of the party seeking rescission was to a decree that itself gave relief, in the form of court orders that either unwound or prevented the enforcement of the impugned transaction. The role of the party seeking relief was confined to confirming or ratifying the transaction, insofar as that was possible. One focus of the literature and the cases was therefore on whether or not the transaction was of a kind that was amenable to ratification.[94]

---

[86] *Perrott v Perrott* (1811) 14 East 423, 440; 104 ER 665, 671; *Alsager v Parker* (1842) 10 M & W 576, 581, 583–84; 152 ER 600, 603, 604; see also *Meiklejohn v Campbell* (1940) 56 TLR 663, 665; aff'd (1940) 56 TLR 704 (CA). Thereafter cancellation would be ordered to advertise the invalidity of the instrument, for the protection of the obligee and third parties. See also G Spence, *The Equitable Jurisdiction of the Court of Chancery* (1846) vol 1, 622–26.

[87] J Mitford, *A Treatise on the Pleadings in Suits in the Court of Chancery by English Bill* (2nd edn, 1787) 116, see also 103; *Evans v Chesshire* (1803) Ves Sen Supp 300, 307; 28 ER 532, 534; *Bright v Eynon* (1757) 1 Burr 390, 395–96; 97 ER 365, 367–68; also JN Pomeroy, *A Treatise on Equity Jurisprudence* (5th edn, 1941) vol 3, § 912.

[88] *Earl of Ardglasse v Muschamp* (1684) 1 Vern 237, 23 ER 438 (rent-charge obtained by fraud); *White v Small* (1682) 1 Chan Cas 103, 22 ER 867 (weak person imposed on to convey land); *Clarkson v Hanway* (1723) 2 P Wms 203, 24 ER 700 (weak person imposed on to convey land).

[89] *Newton v Hunt* (1833) 5 Sim 511, 58 ER 430 (sale of reversion in stock); *Nottidge v Prince* (1860) 2 Giff 446, 66 ER 103 (gift of shares).

[90] *Dyer v Tymewell* (1689) 2 Vern 123, 23 ER 688; *Booth v Warrington* (1714) 4 Brown 164, 2 ER 111. Cf repayment via an account: *Bridgeman v Green* (1755) 2 Ves Sen 627, 627, 629; 28 ER 399, 399, 401; aff'd (1755) Wilm 58, 97 ER 22 (HL).

[91] *Bill v Price* (1686) 1 Vern 467, 467; 23 ER 592, 592; *Lawley v Hooper* (1745) 3 Atk 278, 282; 26 ER 962, 964; *Chesterfield v Janssen* (1750) 1 Atk 301, 355; 26 ER 191, 226; *Benyon v Fitch* (1866) 35 Beav 570, 578; 55 ER 1018, 1021; *Peacock v Evans* (1809) 16 Ves Jun 513, 518; 33 ER 1079, 1081; *Croft v Graham* (1863) 2 De GJ & S 155, 161; 46 ER 334, 336.

[92] Formal order for account: eg *Englefeild v Englefeild* (1687) 1 Vern 446, 448; 23 ER 576, 577; *Charter v Trevelyan*, as reproduced in W Harrison and R Leach, *Seton on Decrees* (2nd edn, 1854) 302–03 (decisions reported (1835) 4 LJ Ch (NS) 209; (1839) 1 Beav 588, 48 ER 1069; (1844) 11 Cl & Fin 714, 8 ER 712; (1846) 9 Beav 140, 50 ER 297). Informal accounting or money adjustments: eg *Clarkson v Hanway* (1723) 2 P Wms 203, 204; 24 ER 700, 701; *Evans v Llewellin* (1787) 1 Cox 333, 341; 29 ER 1191, 1194; *Pickett v Loggon* (1807) 14 Ves Jun 215, 244; 33 ER 503, 515.

[93] *Donovan v Fricker* (1821) Jac 165, 166; 37 ER 813, 813 (rescission of sale of dwelling houses) defendants 'were at their own expense to reinstate as a private house, one of the houses which had been converted into a shop'; *Dunbar v Tredennick* (1813) 1 Ball & Beatty 304, 321–22 (sale of land in breach of fiduciary duty) 'let an injunction issue to put the claimant in possession of the lands'.

[94] H Ballow and J Fonblanque, *A Treatise of Equity* (1793) (first pub anon 1737 and attrib Henry Ballow) vol 1, 39, 131–33; *Chesterfield v Janssen* (1750) 1 Atk 301, 354; 26 ER 191, 226; J Newland, *A Treatise on Contracts within the Jurisdiction of Courts of Equity* (1806) 496–97; J Barton, 'The Enforcement of Hard Bargains' (1987) 103 LQR 118, 135.

(3) The effect of fraud on contract

Between the late seventeenth and mid-nineteenth centuries the cases paid very little atten- **3.40**
tion to the status of a transaction that could be but had not yet been set aside by the court. A
contract or gift sought to be rescinded was usually described in both the bill seeking relief
and in the court's decree as 'void', and as a transaction that 'ought to be set aside'.[95] However,
the terms 'void' and 'voidable' were used interchangeably, at least during the early nineteenth century,[96] and transactions that were ineffective at common law were regularly 'set
aside' in Chancery, in the same manner as those that were binding at law.[97]

The position changed significantly in a quite short period of time. During the 1850s and **3.41**
1860s courts of Chancery for the first time recognized that a contract induced by fraud was
not void, but only 'voidable',[98]which meant that it was valid until set aside.[99] 'Rescission' became identified with setting aside voidable contracts. This change followed and reflected the
rule that had recently emerged at common law, that a contract induced by fraud was valid
until rescinded, not void from the outset.[100] In 1862 it was held that the proper form of a decree for equitable rescission was not that the transaction was 'void', but that it be 'set aside',
changing the old form.[101]

---

[95] Prayers for relief: eg *Cooke v Clayworth* (1811) 18 Ves Jun 13, 34 ER 222 prayer that the written agreement
'be declared fraudulent and void, as against him; and may be decreed to be delivered up to be cancelled'; *Houghton
v Houghton* (1852) 15 Beav 278, 292; 15 ER 545, 551; *Jones v Ricketts* (1862) 31 Beav 130, 54 ER 1087. Orders for
rescission: eg *Addis v Campbell* (1841) 4 Beav 401, 416; 49 ER 394, 400 (sale of reversion rescinded) 'Decree, the in-
dentures... and the fine... and the recoveries, fraudulent and void against the Claimant'; *Gresley v Mousley* (1859) 4
De G & J 78, 100; 45 ER 31, 39. For statements to the effect that transactions procured by improper means are 'void',
Viscount Clermont v Tasburgh (1819) 1 Jac & W 112, 120; 37 ER 318, 321 (innocent misrepresentation); *Duranty's
case* (1858) 26 Beav 268, 274; 53 ER 901, 903 (misrepresentation); *Pennell v Millar* (1857) 23 Beav 172, 180–82; 53
ER 68, 71 (catching bargain). The language was the same at common law until *Load v Green* (1846) 15 M & W 216,
153 ER 828: para [3.05].
[96] Eg J Newland, *A Treatise on Contracts within the Jurisdiction of Courts of Equity* (1806) 496–97; *Addis v
Campbell* (1841) 4 Beav 401, 49 ER 394; contrast the submission in *Bromley v Holland* (1802) 7 Ves Jun 3, 5; 32
ER 2, 3.
[97] Contracts contrary to Annuity Acts: *Byne v Vivian* (1800) 5 Ves Jun 604, 31 ER 762; *Bromley v Holland* (1802)
7 Ves Jun 3, 32 ER 2; *Byne v Potter* (1800) 5 Ves Jun 609, 31 ER 765; *Hoffman v Cooke* (1801) 5 Ves Jun 623, 31 ER
772; *Holbrook v Sharpey* (1812) 19 Ves Jun 131, 34 ER 467; see generally S Campbell, 'Usury and Annuities of the
Eighteenth Century' (1928) 44 LQR 473. Usurious contracts: *Mason v Gardiner* (1793) 4 Bro CC 436, 29 ER 976;
Bosanquett v Dashwood (1734) Talb 38, 40; 25 ER 648, 649.
[98] *Vorley v Cooke* (1857) 1 Giff 230, 237–38; 65 ER 898, 901 (eds note); *Mixer's case* (1859) 4 De G & J 575, 586;
45 ER 223, 228; *Ormes v Beadle* (1860) 2 De G & J 333, 336; 45 ER 649, 651; *Oakes v Turquand* (1867) LR 2 HL
325, 345–46, 350; *Wright's case* (1871) 12 Eq Cas 331, 351; *Houldsworth v City of Glasgow Bank* (1880) 5 App Cas
317, 338.
[99] *Oakes v Turquand* (1867) LR 2 HL 325, 338 (in argument); *Reese River Silver Mining Co Ltd v Smith* (1869) LR
4 HL 64, 73; *Newbigging v Adam* (1886) 34 ChD 582, 592.
[100] *Mixer's case* (1859) 4 De G & J 575, 45 ER 223 was decided by Lord Campbell the year after as Lord Chief
Justice, he had decided *Clarke v Dickson* (1858) El Bl & El 148, 120 ER 463, which confirmed the new common law
rule that fraud renders a contract voidable not void. The decisions at common law in *The Deposit and General Life
Assurance Company Registered v Ayscough* (1856) 6 El & Bl 761, 762; 119 ER 1048, 1048; *White v Garden* (1851)
10 CB 919, 138 ER 364, and *Stevenson v Newnham* (1853) 13 CB 285, 138 ER 1208 were also cited in *Mixer's case*.
Clarke v Dickson (1858) El Bl & El 148, 120 ER 463 was later relied upon by Lord Chelmsford in *Oakes v Turquand*
(1867) LR 2 HL 325, 346 as authority that a contract induced by fraud is voidable not 'void'. In that case Mellish
QC also cited the leading common law cases of the time in submitting that 'voidable' meant valid till disaffirmed,
not void till affirmed (at 338), a submission adopted by Lord Hatherley in *Reese River Silver Mining Co Ltd v Smith*
(1869) LR 4 HL 64, 73.
[101] *Clark v Malpas* (1862) 4 De GF & J 401, 405; 45 ER 1238, 1240.

62   I. INTRODUCTION

(4) The effect of fraud on title

3.42   The principles governing the effect of fraud on title underwent a similar reorganization and clarification. By the middle of the nineteenth century it was well established that a claim to recover property upon rescission had a range of proprietary features. It passed to heirs at law,[102] successors in title under a settlement (whether made by the defrauded predecessor in title,[103] or an earlier predecessor of the defrauded party),[104] and executors,[105] and was enforceable against subsequent volunteers[106] and those taking with notice,[107] but not bona fide purchasers for value,[108] save where a chose in action was transferred.[109] It had also been held that an unexercised claim to recover property upon rescission could be devised by a subsequent will, permitting the devisee to recover legal title by a bill in equity.[110] Indeed, it was initially thought that a devisee could sue if the fraudulent conveyance occurred after the will was executed.[111] Later it was held that the conveyance would revoke the earlier will,[112] confining the right to sue to wills executed after the voidable conveyance.

---

[102] *Lyde or Joyner v Lyde or Joyner* (1616–1617) in J Ritchie, *Reports of Cases Decided by Francis Bacon in the High Court of Chancery (1617–1621)* (1932) 6; *Joy v Bannister (No 1)* (1617) in Ritchie, Reports of Cases Decided by Francis Bacon in the High Court of Chancery (1617–1621) (1932) 33; *Long v Long* (1620) in Ritchie, 218; *White v Small* (1682) 2 Cha Ca 103, 22 ER 867; *Coleby v Smith* (1683) 1 Vern 205, 23 ER 416; *Clark v Ward* (1700) Prec Cha 150, 24 ER 72; aff'd 4 Bro PC 70, 2 ER 48; *Clarkson v Hanway* (1723) 2 P Wms 203, 24 ER 700; *Hick v Mors* (1754) Amb 215, 27 ER 143; 3 Keny 117, 96 ER 1329; *Bates v Graves* (1793) 2 Ves Jun 288, 30 ER 637; 1 Ves Jun Supp 264, 34 ER 781; *Wood v Abrey* (1818) 3 Madd 417, 424; 56 ER 558, 561; *Charter v Trevelyan* (1844) 11 Cl & Fin 714, 8 ER 1273; *Clark v Malpas* (1862) 31 Beav 80, 54 ER 1067; aff'd 4 De GF & J 401, 45 ER 1238.

[103] *Earl of Ardglasse v Muschamp* (1684) 1 Vern 237, 23 ER 43 (claimant under settlement made by previous Earl living 'in riot and debauchery in London' rescinded rent-charge of estates procured by fraud); *Hawes v Wyatt* (1790) 2 Cox 263, 266; 30 ER 122, 124.

[104] *Englefeild v Englefeild* (1686–1687) 1 Vern 444, 23 ER 575 (son suing as remainder-man rescinded dispositions of estate by father for fraud); *Browne v Mitton* (1714) 4 Bro CC 167, 2 ER 114; *Addis v Campbell* (1841) 4 Beav 401, 49 ER 394.

[105] *Matthew v Hanbury* (1690) 2 Vern 188, 23 ER 723 (executor rescinded bonds in favour of testator's mistress for undue influence); *Chesterfield v Janssen* (1750) 1 Atk 301, 26 ER 191 (executors rescinding loan as catching bargain); *Nottidge v Prince* (1860) 2 Giff 246, 66 ER 103 (administrator rescinding gifts for undue influence); *Plowright v Lambert* (1885) 52 LT 646 (executor rescinding testator's sale of property for breach of fiduciary duty).

[106] *Joy v Bannister (No 2)* (1617) in J Ritchie, *Reports of Cases Decided by Francis Bacon in the High Court of Chancery (1617–1621)* (1932) 36 (husband of party guilty of duress 'charged with' that part of the estate received by him); *Wyatt v Wyatt* (1618–1620) in J Ritchie, Reports of Cases Decided by Francis Bacon in the High Court of Chancery (1617–1621) (1932) 126; *Gould v Okeden* (1731) 4 Brown 198, 2 ER 135 (rescission ordered against the successor in title of a fraudulent purchaser, taking by devolution on fraudster's death); *Small v Attwood* (1832) You 407, 535–38; 159 ER 1051, 1103–04 (donee wife of fraudster) (rev'd on another point *Attwood v Small* (1838) 6 Cl & Fin 232, 7 ER 684). See also Lord Commissioner Wilmot in *Bridgeman v Green* (1755) Wilm 58, 64–65; 97 ER 22, 25.

[107] *Dunbar v Tredennick* (1813) 1 Ball & Beatty 304, 318–19; *Addis v Campbell* (1841) 4 Beav 401, 49 ER 394.

[108] *Hawes v Wyatt* (1790) 2 Cox 263, 265; 30 ER 122, 123 (father purchased estate from son by undue influence) 'a purchaser from the father, for a valuable consideration, without notice, would certainly have holden it against the son himself'; rev'd on another point (1790) 3 Bro CC 156, 29 ER 463; *Bellamy v Sabine* (1857) 1 De G & J 566, 44 ER 842 (sale of land to attorney rescinded for breach of fiduciary duty, subsequent priority dispute assumed that both legal and equitable mortgagees took free from the equity to rescind; see also (1835) 2 Ph 425, 41 ER 1007; (1847) 2 Ph 446, 41 ER 1016); *Bowen v Evans* (1844) 1 J & Lat 178, 263–64 (plea of bona fide purchase of equitable interest defence to claim to rescind for fraud); aff'd (1848) 2 HLC 257, 9 ER 1090.

[109] *Turton v Benson* (1718) 1 P Wms 496, 24 ER 488; *Mangles v Dixon* (1852) 3 HLC 731, 10 ER 278.

[110] *Wilkinson v Brayfield* (1693) 2 Vern 307, 23 ER 799; 1 Eq Ca Abr 258, 21 ER 1031; *Blake v Johnson* (1700) Pre Cha 142, 24 ER 69; *Hawes v Wyatt* (1790) 2 Cox 263, 265–67; 30 ER 122, 123–24; *Drew v Merry* (1701) 1 Eq Ca Abr 176, 21 ER 969. See also C Viner, *A General Abridgment of Law and Equity* (2nd edn, 1793) vol 8, 63 [42] (release of testator's expectancy obtained by fraud; a devise of the residuary interest in the testator's goods and chattels passed the right to rescind the release to the devisee).

[111] *Hawes v Wyatt* (1790) 2 Cox 263, 265; 30 ER 122, 123; (1790) 3 Bro CC 156, 29 ER 463.

[112] *Cave v Holford* (1798) 3 Ves 650, 664; 30 ER 1203, 1210; *Harmood v Oglander* (1801) 6 Ves Jun 199, 215; 31 ER 1010, 1018; *Ex parte Earl of Illchester* (1803) 7 Ves Jun 348, 373; 32 ER 142, 151; *Simpson v Walker* (1831) 5 Sim 1, 58 ER 238; *Gresley v Mousley* (1859) 4 De G & J 78, 94; 45 ER 31, 37.

But before the middle of the nineteenth century there was no agreed description for the **3.43** proprietary interest conferred by an equity to rescind, save in the special cases of conveyances by fine vitiated by fraud[113] and fraudulent dispositions of testamentary property,[114] where it was established that equity imposed a trust from the time legal title passed. Even there, however, the trust arising was more fragile than an express trust, in that it could be defeated by acquiescence, or in some cases the statute of limitations, in a manner that claims against an express trustee could not.[115]

Outside those two categories the position was unclear. There were some suggestions that **3.44** equity always imposed a trust when a disposition of property was obtained by fraud or other undue means permitting rescission.[116] But the trust theory seems not to have been the dominant view. It was one among several descriptions of the interest that preceded a decree for rescission. It competed with, for example, the opinion that the rescinding party obtained an 'equity',[117] an interest akin to an equity of redemption,[118] and that a trust arose after a transaction was set aside,[119] and with decisions that focused on the court's decree as the source for restitution to the injured party.[120] In the literature, descriptions of the circumstances in which equity imposed a constructive trust regularly omitted the grounds for rescission, and discussions of rescission often made no mention of any constructive trust.[121]

---

[113] *Martin v Martin* in C Viner, *A General Abridgment of Law and Equity* (2nd edn, 1793) vol 13, 543 [12]; 2 Eq Ca 475, 22 ER 404; *Barnesly v Powel* (1749) 1 Ves Sen 284, 289; 27 ER 1034, 1037; *Bates v Graves* (1793) 1 Ves Jun Supp 264, 264; 34 ER 781, 781; *Pickett v Loggon* (1807) 14 Ves Jun 215, 234; 33 ER 503, 511; W Cruise, *An Essay on the Nature and Operation of Fines and Recoveries* (2nd edn, 1786) 314–15; H Ballow and J Fonblanque, *A Treatise of Equity* (1793) vol 1, 47–48 note (k); H Maddock, *A Treatise on the Principles and Practice of the High Court of Chancery* (1815) vol 1, 211–12; reporter's note in *Fermor's case* (1601) 3 Co Rep 77a, 79b; 76 ER 800, 809 fn (A1).

[114] *Thynn v Thynn* (1684) 1 Vern 296, 23 ER 47; C Viner, *A General Abridgment of Law and Equity* (2nd edn, 1793) vol 8, 166 [4] (executor wrongfully suppressing trust in favour of testator's wife); *Gosse v Tracy* (1715) 1 P Wms 288, 23 ER 1053 (draftsman fraudulently inserting devise to self); *Marriot v Marriot* (1726) Gilb 204, 25 ER 142 (asserting equity's 'notorious' power to declare that a legatee obtaining a legacy by fraud to be a trustee for the person entitled to it); *Barnesly v Powel* (1749) 1 Ves Sen 284, 27 ER 1034; see also G Palmer, 'History of Restitution in Anglo-American Law' (1989) 10 *Encyclopedia of Comparative Law* 3, 18–19.

[115] *Bonney v Ridgard* (1784) 1 Cox 145, 147, 149; 29 ER 1101, 1102, 1103 (acquiescence barred trust imposed by law); *Beckford v Wade* (1805) 17 Ves Jun 87, 97–100; 34 ER 34, 38–39 ('constructive trust' upon fraudulent sale of deceased estate outside trust exception in limitation statute); *Hovenden v Lord Annesley* (1806) 2 Sch & Lef 607, 633–35 (possession obtained by fraud is adverse and barred by lapse of time in manner that possession under an express trust is not); *Portlock v Gardner* (1842) 1 Hare 594, 607; 66 ER 1168, 1173 (agent of executor failing to pay over sums due to the estate a 'constructive trustee' and entitled to protection of limitation statute).

[116] *Lloyd and Jobson v Spillett* (1740) 2 Atk 148, 150; 26 ER 493, 494; *Bennett v Vade* (1742) 2 Atk 324, 327; 26 ER 597, 599; *Donovan v Fricker* (1821) Jacob 166, 167; 37 ER 813, 814; *Blake v Mowlatt* (1856) 21 Beav 603, 612; 52 ER 993, 996; *Gladstone v Hadwen* (1813) 1 M & S 517, 526–27; 105 ER 193, 197; J Hill, *A Practical Treatise on the Law Relating to Trustees* (1845) 117–18; G Spence, *The Equitable Jurisdiction of the Court of Chancery* (1846) vol 1, 453, vol 2, 511; cf vol 1, 622–27; A Underhill, *A Concise Manual on the Law Relating to Private Trusts and Trustees* (1878) 82; A Smith, *A Practical Exposition of the Principles of Equity* (1882) 99–100, 153–54.

[117] Right to rescind an 'equity' to 'have a vicious transaction rescinded and set aside' 'where it is necessary to replace the parties in status quo': J Adams, *The Doctrine of Equity* (1850) 166, 174. See also *Gregory v Gregory* (1815) G Coop 201, 204; 35 ER 530; aff'd (1821) Jac 631, 37 ER 989; *Roberts v Tunstall* (1844) 4 Hare 257, 67 ER 645.

[118] *Blake v Johnson* (1700) Pre Ch 142, 143; 24 ER 69, 69.

[119] *Bellamy v Sabine* (1835) 2 Ph 425, 441–42; 41 ER 1007, 1014.

[120] *Hick v Mors* (1754) Amb 215, 216; 27 ER 143, 143; *A-G v Vigor* (1803) 8 Ves Jun 256, 283; 32 ER 352, 363; *Huguenin v Baseley* (1807) 14 Ves Jun 273, 296; 33 ER 526, 535, 536.

[121] Lord Nottingham, 'Where Trusts Shall be Raised by Construction and Implication of Law, and Where Not' in D Yale (ed), *Lord Nottingham's 'Manual of Chancery Practice' and 'Prolegomena of Chancery and Equity'* (1965); H Ballow and J Fonblanque, *A Treatise of Equity* (1793) vol 2, chap 5 ('Of Uses raised by Operation of Law'), vol 1, chap 2 ('Want of Assent'); annotation at vol 1, 61 note (r), notes to vol 1, 111–15, 128–30; cf vol 1, 47–48 note (k) ('fines'); J Mitford, *A Treatise on the Pleadings in Suits in the Court of Chancery by English Bill* (2nd edn, 1787) 116–19; F Van Heythuysen, *The Equity Draftsman* (1816) 142–47, 202–15, (2nd edn, 1828) chap 2, 35–103; J Newland, *A Treatise on Contracts within the Jurisdiction of Courts of Equity* (1806); H Maddock, *A Treatise on the Principles and Practice of the High Court of Chancery* (1815) vol 1, 211–12; J Willis, *Pleadings in Equity* (1820) 118–85; H Seton, *Forms of Decrees in Equity* (1830) 217–23; W Harrison and R Leach (ed), *Seton on Decrees*, (2nd

64   I. INTRODUCTION

Stump v Gaby and *Phillips v Phillips*

3.45   After 1850 there were two key decisions that followed each other in quick succession. The first was *Stump v Gaby* in 1852.[122] It was followed in 1861 by Lord Westbury's seminal opinion in *Phillips v Phillips*.[123]

3.46   In *Stump v Gaby*, Lord St Leonards LC said that an entitlement to recover property on re-scission for 'fraud' (breach of fiduciary duty) could be devised, and described it as an 'equitable estate' in which the defrauded vendor 'remains the owner, subject to the repayment of the money which has been advanced' to buy it.[124] Lord St Leonards LC added that although he thought this point had already been decided, he was ready to make a new precedent:

> ... the whole legal fee-simple passed by the conveyance... whether the deed was or not such as could be maintained in a Court of Equity is another question, but there was no legal remedy, for the case is not put as one of such gross fraud as that the conveyance was, on the face of it, void at law.
>
> I do not deny that a deed may be so fraudulent as to be set aside at law; this however is not such a case; but I will assume that the conveyance might have been set aside in equity for fraud: what then is the interest of a party in an estate which he has conveyed to his attorney under such circumstances which would give a right in this Court to have the conveyance set aside? In the view of the Court he remains the owner, subject to the repayment of the money which has been advanced by the attorney, and the consequence is that he may devise the estate, not as a legal estate, but as an equitable estate... assuming the conveyance to have been voidable, the grantor had an equitable estate which he might have devised.[125]

3.47   But this analysis did not prevail. In *Phillips v Phillips*[126] Lord Westbury LC set out the three categories of case where he said the plea of bona fide purchase was most familiar, and appeared to reject the view of Lord St Leonards that this plea was generally available in favour of those asserting a purely equitable estate.[127] The third category of case in which the plea of bona fide purchase was 'familiar' and 'common' was as follows:

> Thirdly, where there are circumstances that give rise to an equity as distinguished from an equitable estate—as for example, an equity to set aside a deed for fraud, or to correct it for mistake—and the purchaser under the instrument maintains the plea of purchase for valuable consideration without notice, the Court will not interfere.[128]

---

edn, 1854) 299–306, (3rd edn, 1862) vol 1, 642–56. But cf J Story, *Commentaries on Equity Jurisprudence* (13th edn, 1886) vol 2, 5–8, 611.

[122]   (1852) 2 De M & G 623, 42 ER 1015.

[123]   (1861) 4 De G F & J 208, 45 ER 1164.

[124]   (1852) 2 De M & G 623, 630; 42 ER 1015, 1018.

[125]   *Stump v Gaby* (1852) 2 De M & G 623, 42 ER 1015. Lord St Leonards was correct that the point had already been decided. It had been decided in *Blake v Johnson* (1700) Pre Ch 142, 143; 24 ER 69, 69 a century and a half earlier. In *Blake v Johnson* the Lord Keeper and Master of the Rolls had held that the defrauded testator had an interest 'in the nature of an equity of redemption' that was able to be devised and assigned. An equity of redemption is an 'equitable estate', albeit not one where equity treats the transferor as one who 'remains the owner, subject to the repayment of the money which has been advanced', as was said in *Stump v Gaby*.

[126]   (1861) 4 De G F & J 208, 45 ER 1164.

[127]   E Sugden, *A Concise and Practical Treatise of the Law of Vendors and Purchasers of Estates* (14th edn, 1862) 791, 796–98; *Bowen v Evans* (1844) 1 Jo & Lat 178, 263–64. See also *Cave v Cave* (1880) 15 ChD 639, 646; *Latec Investments Limited v Hotel Terrigal Pty Limited* (1965) 113 CLR 265, 285.

[128]   *Phillips v Phillips* (1861) 4 De G F & J 208, 218; 45 ER 1164, 1167.

Phillips v Phillips[129] was a case about equitable priorities, not rescission. But in this passage **3.48** Lord Westbury appeared, in passing, to reject Lord St Leonards' conclusion that a right to recover land upon rescission conferred an equitable estate.

Whether that is what Lord Westbury intended to say is unclear. Writing 25 years after **3.49** *Phillips v Phillips*, in the first volume of the Harvard Law Review, Ames objected to what Lord Westbury seemed to be saying: 'The equity of a defrauded vendor is no less an equitable estate than the interest of *cestui que trust*… the fraudulent vendee is constantly called a constructive trustee'.[130] Ames went on to point out that Lord Westbury seemed to have said so himself elsewhere.[131]

But whatever may have been Lord Westbury's true intention, *Phillips v Phillips* came to **3.50** be understood as having decided that title to property passes at law and in equity under a voidable contract and that, pending rescission, the party entitled to rescind has only an 'equity'[132] or 'mere equity'[133] to recover it.

This squarely aligned equitable rescission with the rules developed at common law. As was **3.51** noticed earlier, these provided that legal title passes under a contract induced by fraud and may be recovered upon rescission,[134] and that until rescission the defrauded vendor enjoys no vested proprietary interest.[135]

Orders for reconveyance upon rescission

The year after *Phillips v Phillips* was decided a related uncertainty was resolved. It was held **3.52** in *Clark v Malpas*[136] that where the transaction involved a disposition of real property, a reconveyance should always be ordered as part of the decree for rescission. Although orders of this kind were known from at least the early seventeenth century,[137] and probably well before, a strand of cases in the eighteenth and nineteenth centuries had held that where

---

[129] *Phillips v Phillips* (1861) 4 De G F & J 208, 45 ER 1164.

[130] J Ames, 'Purchase for Value Without Notice' (1887) 1 Harv LR 1, 2; see also 4 fn 2, and J Ames, 'The History of Trover' (1897) 11 Harv LR 374, 386.

[131] *Eyre v Burmester* (1862) 10 HLC 90, 102–03; 11 ER 959; for further litigation, *Cory v Eyre* (1863) 1 De GJ & S 149, 46 ER 58; cf V Delany, [1957] Conv 195; also D O'Sullivan, 'The Rule in *Phillips v Phillips*' (2002) 118 LQR 296, 311–14, and for the contrary view, A Reilly, 'What were Lord Westbury's Intentions in *Phillips v Phillips*? Bona Fide Purchase of an Equitable Interest' (2021) 80 CLJ 156.

[132] *Tottenham v Green* (1863) 32 LJ Ch (NS) 201; *Ernest v Vivian* (1864) 33 LJ Ch (NS) 513; *Cave v Cave* (1880) 15 ChD 639, 649; *Bainbrigge v Browne* (1881) 18 ChD 188, 197; *Cloutte v Storey* [1910] 1 ChD 18, 24; *Fysh v Page* (1956) 96 CLR 233, 242; *Latec Investments Limited v Hotel Terrigal Pty Limited* (1965) 113 CLR 265, 277–78, 291 (cf 282, 284 where Taylor J expressed a preference for the term 'equitable interest'); *National Provincial Bank Ltd v Ainsworth* [1965] AC 1175, 1254; *Bristol and West Building Society v Mothew* [1998] 1 Ch 1 (CA) 22–23; *Greater Pacific Investments Pty Ltd v Australian National Industries Ltd* [1996] 39 NSWLR 143 (CA) 152–53; *Investors Compensation Scheme Ltd v West Bromwich Building Society* [1998] 1 WLR 896 (HL) 915, 916; *Barclays Bank v Boulter* [1999] 1 WLR 1919 (HL) 1925; *Twinsectra Limited v Yardley* [1999] Lloyd's Rep Bank 438 (CA) 461–62.

[133] *Latec Investments Limited v Hotel Terrigal Pty Limited* (1965) 113 CLR 265, 277, 290; *Tutt v Doyle* (1997) 42 NSWLR 10 (CA) 15 (claim for reconveyance for unilateral mistake).

[134] *Load v Green* (1846) 15 M & W 216, 221; 153 ER 828, 830; *Clough v London and North Western Railway Co* (1871) LR 7 Ex 26, 32.

[135] *Barclays Bank v Boulter* [1999] 1 WLR 1919 (HL) 1925.

[136] (1862) 4 De GF & J 401, 405; 45 ER 1238, 1240.

[137] *Waller v Waller* (1619) in J Ritchie, *Reports of Cases Decided by Francis Bacon in the High Court of Chancery (1617–1621)* (1932) 156; *Wyatt v Wyatt* (1618–1620) in J Ritchie, Reports of Cases Decided by Francis Bacon in the High Court of Chancery (1617–1621) (1932) 126; *Parke v Wannell* (1619) in J Ritchie, Reports of Cases Decided by Francis Bacon in the High Court of Chancery (1617–1621) (1932) 143, *Martin v Savage and Turner* (1672) 'all (was) set aside by decree, and a reconveyance ordered with an account of the mesne profits, because of the palpable fraud and *suppressio veri* and *suggestio falsi*' (fraudulent conveyance): D Yale (ed), *Lord Nottingham's 'Manual of Chancery Practice' and 'Prolegomena of Chancery and Equity'* (1965) 265–66.

66   I. INTRODUCTION

land was obtained under a transaction set aside by the court, an order cancelling the deeds of conveyance gave sufficient protection to the claimant's legal title.[138] This was notwithstanding that courts of Chancery recognized that cancellation did not of itself divest a title that had passed either by delivery or deed[139] (a rule adopted only later by the common law, which at one time seemed to discriminate between interests passing by delivery and by grant).[140] In 1862 the point was resolved, and it was held that a reconveyance should always be ordered.[141]

(5) Rescission by election

3.53   It was during this period of rapid development just after the middle of the nineteenth century that the suggestion was first made that rescission always occurs when a voidable transaction is disaffirmed, without any distinction being drawn between rescission at law and in equity. This suggestion was made by Lord Hatherley LC in *Reese River Silver Mining Co Ltd v Smith*,[142] a case that had been commenced in Chancery.[143]

3.54   This development apparently involved applying the model of rescission that had recently emerged at common law to rescission in equity, but without regard to the fact that it amounted to a fundamental break from the way that rescission had hitherto been effected in equity, or that the forms of action that had shaped the common law's approach were not relevant in a court of Chancery. Difficulties created by this unprincipled shift remain today. It has caused aspects of the law of rescission to become mired in uncertainty; in particular, as to the circumstances in which rescission can occur by electing to reject the transaction, and as to the consequences of disaffirming a contract that is voidable only in equity.[144]

---

[138] *Hawes v Wyatt* (1790) 3 Bro CC 156, 160; 29 ER 463, 465; *Bates v Graves* (1793) 2 Ves Jun 288, 295; 30 ER 637, 640; 1 Ves Jun Supp 263, 34 ER 781; *Houghton v Houghton* (1852) 15 Beav 278, 331; 51 ER 545, 562; *AG v Magdalen College Oxford* (1854) 18 Beav 223, 255; 52 ER 88, 100–01.

[139] *Leech v Leech* (1674) 2 Ch Rep 100, 21 ER 623; *Lady Hudson's case* (1704) 2 Eq Cas Abr 52, 22 ER 45, and in C Viner, *A General Abridgment of Law and Equity* (2nd edn, 1793) vol 12, 43; *Clavering v Clavering* (1704) Prec Chan 235, 24 ER 114; *Harrison v Owen* (1738) 1 Atk 520, 26 ER 328; *Re Way's Trust* (1864) 2 De G J & S 365, 46 ER 416; cf *Handcock v Berrey* (1888) 57 LJ (Ch) 793. Also JN Pomeroy, *Pomeroy's Equity Jurisprudence and Equitable Remedies* (2nd edn, 1919) vol 5, 3277–78.

[140] J Gilbert, *The Law of Evidence* (1791) 111–12. But other cases from this time held that even in cases where title passed by grant cancellation would not divest the interest: *Woodward v Aston* (1672) 1 Ven 296, 297; 86 ER 191 (grant of the office of clerk of the papers of the Kings Bench); *Nelthorpe v Dorrington* (1685) 2 Lev 113, 83 ER 475 (cancellation of assignment of goods of bankrupt). If it was ever accepted, a distinction between interests passing by delivery and by grant may have been produced by rules of evidence. If a person claiming a title derived solely from a deed had to prove that deed to establish title, title could be lost if the deed was defaced in a matter which prevented it being proved. But by the nineteenth century it was established that cancelling a deed would not affect property passing by delivery or by grant: *Bolton v Bishop of Carlisle* (1793) 2 Hl Bl 259, 263; 126 ER 540, 542 (cancellation of deed conveying interest in an advowson); *Perrott v Perrott* (1811) 14 East 423, 431; 104 ER 665, 668 (bond to pay money cancelled by obligee under mistaken belief that provision was made in will) (Lord Ellenborough, in argument). Also, *Moss v Mills and Boon* (1805) 6 East 144, 148; 102 ER 1242, 1243–44 (Lawrence J, in argument); *Doe d Lewis v Bingham* (1821) 4 B & Ald 672, 677; 106 ER 1082, 1084 (Holroyd J *obiter*); *Lord Ward v Lumley* (1860) 5 H & N 87, 656; 157 ER 1112, 1342; cf *Magennis v MacCollough* (c 1714–1727) Gilb Rep 235, 25 ER 163; *Doe d Archbishop of Berkley v Archbishop of York* (1805) 6 East 86, 102 ER 1219; *Doe d Courtail v Thomas* (1829) 9 B & C 288, 109 ER 107.

[141] *Clark v Malpas* (1862) 4 De GF & J 401, 405; 45 ER 1238, 1240.

[142] (1869) LR 4 HL 64. See Chap 11, paras [11.68]–[11.74].

[143] *Reese River Silver Mining Co Ltd v Smith* (1869) LR 4 HL 64, 73–74.

[144] See Chaps 10, 11, 12, and 15, paras [15.69]–[15.76].

D. The Special Case of Insurance

Insurance was in certain respects a special case. The proposing assured's obligation to make **3.55** full disclosure of facts relevant to the risk has been traced into the common law from the law merchant,[145] and numerous decisions at common law confirm the insurer's right to defend a claim for non-disclosure or misrepresentation on the part of the proposing assured.[146] But there are also decisions in Chancery where insurance policies were rescinded both for misrepresentation and non-disclosure.[147] The relationship between law and equity in this context is considered next.

(1) Special relationship between common law and equity

The courts of common law and equity both had jurisdiction over contracts of insur- **3.56** ance vitiated by non-disclosure and misrepresentation. Where the assured wished to enforce the policy, he would commence proceedings at common law, and could not do so in Chancery.[148] The insurer alleging misrepresentation or non-disclosure would raise that as a defence, and whether a good defence existed would be tried with the assured's claim on the policy. The insurer would often tender the premium money, or bring it into court, and the assured might bring a protective claim for repayment by adding a count for money had and received to his action on the policy.[149] At one point the practice was for the insurer defending on grounds of misrepresentation or non-disclosure to pay the premium into court,[150] but from early on that was not essential for the defence.[151] Premium income was repayable as money had and received,[152] either on the analysis that no risk attached under the policy,[153] or that the policy was made void.[154]

---

[145] P MacDonald Eggers, S Picken, and P Foss, *Good Faith and Insurance Contracts* (3rd edn, 2010) 81–85.

[146] The foundational case is *Carter v Boehm* (1766) 3 Burr 1909, 97 ER 1162; 1 Black W 593, 96 ER 342 (Lord Mansfield CJ).

[147] *Whittingham v Thornburgh* (1690) 2 Vern 206, 23 ER 734; 2 Eq Ca Abr 635, 22 ER 533; *De Costa v Scandret* (1723) 2 P Wms 169, 24 ER 686; *Duncan v Worrall* (1822) 10 Price 31, 42, 43; 147 ER 232, 236; *Barker v Walters* (1844) 8 Beav 92, 96; 50 ER 36, 38; *The Prince of Wales, &c Association Company v Palmer* (1858) 25 Beav 605, 53 ER 768; *Traill v Baring* (1864) 4 De G J & S 318, 46 ER 942; *The British Equitable Insurance Company v The Great Western Railway Company* (1869) 38 LJ Ch 132, 314 (NS); *Hoare v Bremridge* (1872) 8 Ch App 22; *London and Provincial Insurance Company v Seymour* (1873) LR 17 Eq 85.

[148] His bill would be dismissed as demurrable, the demand being one at law and the damage the subject of proof by a jury: *Dhegetoft v The London Assurance* (1728) Mos 84, 25 ER 285; *De Ghetoff v The London Assurance Company* (1720) 4 Brown's PC 525, 2 ER 295, discussed JA Park, *A System of Law of Marine Insurance* (F Hildyard (ed)) (8th edn, 1842) vol 2, 833–35.

[149] *Wilson v Duckett* (1762) 3 Burr 1361, 97 ER 874; *Middlewood v Blakes* (1797) 7 TR 162, 101 ER 911; *Penson v Lee* (1800) 2 Bos & Pul 330, 126 ER 1309; *Feise v Parkinson* (1812) 4 Taunt 640, 128 ER 482; *Anderson v Thornton* (1853) 8 Exch 425, 428; 155 ER 1415. See also G Spencer Bower, *The Law Relating to Actionable Non-Disclosure* (1915) [249].

[150] *Wilson v Duckett* (1762) 3 Burr 1361, 97 ER 874 (payment into court 'the usual course'); eg *Middlewood v Blakes* (1797) 7 TR 162, 101 ER 911.

[151] *Penson v Lee* (1800) 2 Bos & Pul 330, 126 ER 1309.

[152] The common law treated such claims with indulgence (*Penson v Lee* (1800) 2 Bos & Pul 330, 333; 126 ER 1309, 1311) and would in appropriate cases allow the assured to bring them in proceedings separate from those in which his action on the policy was tried, and held that by signing the policy the insurer was estopped from denying receipt of the premium: *Anderson v Thornton* (1853) 8 Exch 425, 428; 155 ER 1415 (Parke B).

[153] *Feise v Parkinson* (1812) 4 Taunt 640, 128 ER 482; *Anderson v Thornton* (1853) 8 Exch 425, 428; 155 ER 1415. This reasoning was consistent with the prevailing view that a policy vitiated by non-disclosure or misrepresentation was void.

[154] *Carter v Boehm* (1766) 3 Burr 1905, 1909; 97 ER 1162, 1164.

68   I. INTRODUCTION

3.57   On the other hand, if the insurer wished to obtain protection from a policy said to be vitiated by misrepresentation or non-disclosure, that would be done by a bill in equity seeking orders that the policy be delivered up to be cancelled, and that proceedings on it at law be restrained. If relief was granted it would usually include provisions for repayment of the premium.[155]

3.58   The special relationship between the equitable and common law jurisdictions in matters of insurance was explained by Lord Selborne LC in *Hoare v Bremridge*,[156] which was decided on the eve of the Judicature reforms:

> ... if there be a legal defence to a written instrument depending on facts not appearing upon the face of the instrument, the party charged on that instrument with some liability may come into a Court of Equity to get rid of it, notwithstanding the legal defence, because the evidence of those extrinsic facts upon which the defence depends might not be forthcoming at all times and under all circumstances. That would apply even perhaps to cases that were not strictly cases of fraud. But, independently of that, where a case of fraud is alleged, this court has an original and unquestionable jurisdiction. We proceed, therefore, upon the ground that this Court would have jurisdiction to deal with such a case as this at the hearing. But it is to be observed that it is only in an imperfect sense that a case of this kind is one of concurrent jurisdiction. Each party, to be an actor and to bring forward his own case, is not at liberty to choose this Court or the Court of Law as he pleases, but each, if he would be Claimant, must come the one into Equity and the other into a Court of Law. Each is *rectus in curiâ*. The assured cannot come into equity to sue on this policy; the office, the insurers, can come into equity only before they are sued, to have it delivered up and cancelled. Each, therefore, is suing, of necessity, in the proper Court, and in the only Court in which he can sue, to have that which he claims as his right. But what the one claims as his right in equity would constitute his defence at law; what the other claims as his right at law would constitute his defence in equity. That is the true state of the case.[157]

---

[155] Eg *Barker v Walters* (1844) 8 Beav 92, 96; 50 ER 36, 38. For Chancery proceedings after the Judicature reforms, see eg *London Assurance v Mansel* (1879) 11 ChD 363, 372. A direction was sometimes made that the premium be deducted from the costs that the assured would otherwise have to pay: eg *Whittingham v Thornburgh* (1690) 2 Vern 206, 23 ER 734; *De Costa v Scandret* (1723) 2 P Wms 169, 24 ER 686; *The British Equitable Insurance Company v The Great Western Railway Company* (1869) 38 LJ Ch 132. Chancery also exercised its ordinary jurisdiction to grant decrees for discovery and rectification: *De Ghetoff v The London Assurance Company* (1720) 4 Brown's PC 436, 2 ER 295; *Duncan v Worrall* (1822) 10 Price 31, 42; 147 ER 232, 236; JA Park, *A System of Law of Marine Insurance* (F Hildyard (ed)) (8th edn, 1842) vol 2, 835–36.

[156] (1872) 8 Ch App 22.

[157] *Hoare v Bembridge* (1872) 8 Ch App 22, 26–27. The term 'fraud' in this passage was probably intended to encompass both misrepresentation and knowing non-disclosure of material facts. Whether it also encompassed innocent non-disclosure sufficient to provide a defence at law is less clear. Lord Selborne LC proceeded on the basis that the case at hand was one of 'fraud' attracting equity's original jurisdiction, and the allegation was of knowing misrepresentation and non-disclosure. Innocent misrepresentation or non-disclosure by an assured had been characterized as 'fraud' or 'technical fraud' by LJ Turner in *Traill v Baring* (1864) 4 De G J & S 316, 328; 46 ER 941, 946. Non-disclosure of a change of circumstances prior to inception of the policy was described as 'fraud' in *The British Equitable Insurance Company v The Great Western Railway Company* (1869) 38 LJ Ch 132, 314 (NS). But Jessell MR indicated that knowing but not innocent non-disclosure was 'fraud' in *London Assurance v Mansel* (1879) 11 ChD 363, 368. In *Seaton v Heath* [1899] 1 QB 782 (CA) 792 Romer LJ observed that, in the case of insurance contracts, *uberrimae fides* was required both by the courts of law and by the courts of equity.

(2) Chancery courts' policy of limited interference

Hoare v Bembridge also illustrates the other distinctive feature of the treatment of contracts **3.59**
of insurance prior to the Judicature reforms. This was Chancery's policy of limited interference. The court affirmed the decision of Malins V-C dismissing a motion for an interlocutory injunction restraining the assured from continuing proceedings at law, the insurer
having earlier brought a bill seeking substantive relief in equity. It was said that although
there was a good equitable case stated by the bill, that was not a sufficient ground for an
injunction. Their Lordships indicated that an interlocutory injunction would rarely be
granted in cases involving insurance where there was a contested question. A trial before
a jury at common law was the proper forum for determining the issue, and there were no
grounds for thinking that Chancery would disturb a verdict at law.[158]

Chancery would therefore often send an insurer's claim for relief to the common law courts **3.60**
for trial,[159] or simply dismiss it.[160] The basis for declining jurisdiction was that the matters
alleged by the bill afforded a defence to a claim on the policy at common law, and there was
therefore no equity to warrant the interference of a court of Chancery.[161]

The policy of non-interference seems to have been rigorously applied during the late **3.61**
eighteenth and early nineteenth centuries. Lord Chief Baron Eyre's opinion was said to be
strongly against 'bills for discovery and injunction by Underwriters, in these cases, as filed
for the most part merely with a fraudulent intention to create delay',[162] and Lord Chief Baron
Richards said that 'I never remember one to have been acted on further than the dissolving
of the injunction'.[163] Richards LCB went on to express a strong opinion against 'the evil consequences' of a bill seeking cancellation of a policy of insurance, and only granted that relief
reluctantly, after the insurer had obtained a verdict at law.[164] His reluctance to entertain bills
for relief by insurers appears to have been based on the view that the matter was properly
dealt with at common law.[165]

Chancery judges seem to have been prepared to intervene more readily in favour of insurers **3.62**
in the second half of the nineteenth century. *Traill v Baring*[166] is a leading example. In *The
British Equitable Insurance Company v The Great Western Railway Company*,[167] a case of
non-disclosure in relation to life insurance, Malins V-C held that he was obliged to exercise
jurisdiction.[168] On appeal Giffard LJ said that 'If there is any one thing clearer than another,

---

[158] *Hoare v Bembridge* (1872) 8 Ch App 22, 26–29. There was no jury in Chancery proceedings.

[159] *Wilson v Duckett* (1762) 3 Burr 1361, 97 ER 874 (insurance of a ship procured by fraud). In *Carter v Boehm*
(1766) 3 Burr 1906, 1909; 97 ER 1162, 1163 Lord Mansfield said that 'Both sides had been long in Chancery', but
those proceedings appear never to have been reported.

[160] *Duncan v Worrall* (1822) 10 Price 31, 35; 147 ER 232, 234.

[161] *Duncan v Worrall* (1822) 10 Price 31, 42, 43, 44; 147 ER 232, 236, reporter's note; also *Brooking v Maudslay
Son & Field* (1888) 38 Ch 363, 644.

[162] *Duncan v Worrall* (1822) 10 Price 31, 42; 147 ER 232, 236.

[163] *Duncan v Worrall* (1822) 10 Price 31, 147 ER 232.

[164] *Duncan v Worrall* (1822) 10 Price 31, 45; 147 ER 232, 237.

[165] See also JA Park, *A System of Law of Marine Insurance* (F Hildyard (ed)) (8th edn, 1842) vol 2, 833–37.

[166] (1864) 4 De G J & S 316, 327, 331; 46 ER 941, 945, 947.

[167] (1869) 38 LJ Ch (NS) 132 (Malins V-C) (314 (on appeal). For argument on jurisdiction (1869) 38 LJ Ch
132, 134.

[168] *The British Equitable Insurance Company v The Great Western Railway Company* (1869) 38 LJ Ch (NS)
132, 136.

70   I. INTRODUCTION

it is that, in a case such as this, this Court has jurisdiction,' but with the qualification that 'In some cases, no doubt, of this character it will allow the question to go to a jury; but I must say, if ever a case was plain this case is plain, and there is no reason why it should go to a jury'.[169]

(3) Change from 'void' to 'voidable'

3.63   Until the second half of the nineteenth century policies of insurance procured by material misrepresentation and non-disclosure were generally described as 'void' or not binding, both by courts of law[170] and equity,[171] and in the literature.[172] The change to a description of the policy as 'voidable' probably occurred alongside the analogous reorganization of the status of contracts procured by fraud in the middle of the nineteenth century, discussed earlier. Before this change, there is no evidence that courts of law or equity regarded the policy as valid until set aside either by the election of the underwriter, or by order of the court.

---

[169] *The British Equitable Insurance Company v The Great Western Railway Company* (1869) 38 LJ Ch (NS) 132, 316. See also 136 (Malins V-C). Selwyn LJ added that 'The jurisdiction of the Court in cases of this description is fully established, and has been constantly exercised' (at 314).

[170] *Carter v Boehm* (1766) 3 Burr 1905, 1909; 97 ER 1162, 1164; (1746–1779) 1 Black W 593, 594; 96 ER 342, 343 ('the policy is void'); *Feise v Parkinson* (1812) 4 Taunt 640, 128 ER 482 ('the risk never attached'); *Anderson v Thornton* (1853) 8 Exch 425, 428; 155 ER 1415 ('The insurance never bound the defendant'). See also *Kettlewell v Refuge Assurance Company* [1908] 1 KB 545 (CA) 548, where Sir Gorrell Barnes said that when in *Duffell v Wilson* (1808) 2 Camp 401 Lord Ellenborough described a policy vitiated by the insurer's misrepresentation as 'void', he actually meant 'voidable' (cf Buckley LJ at 552).

[171] *Hoare v Bembridge* (1872) 8 Ch App 22, 22 (bill sought declaration that policy 'was void'); *London Assurance v Mansel* (1879) 11 ChD 363, 372 ('declare that the acceptance by the Plaintiffs of the Defendant's life was void and of no effect').

[172] JA Park, *A System of Law of Marine Insurance* (F Hildyard (ed)) (8th edn, 1842) vol 1, 403–04, 432–33 (insurance 'void from the beginning' and 'vacated and annulled by the least shadow of fraud or undue concealment'). See also G Spencer Bower, *The Law Relating to Actionable Non-Disclosure* (1915) 198.

Part II

GROUNDS

4

Misrepresentation

A.	Introduction	4.01	D. Representation must be Made by the	
B.	Types of Misrepresentation: Fraudulent, Negligent, Innocent	4.04	Representor to the Representee	4.74
			(1) Those by whom the representation may be made	4.74
	(1) Nature of fraudulent misrepresentation	4.05	(2) Those to whom the representation must be made	4.76
	(2) Importance of the distinction outside law of rescission	4.09	E. Representation must be False	4.81
	(3) Importance in relation to rescission	4.10	(1) Substantial correctness sufficient	4.83
			(2) Representation must be false at the time of reliance	4.88
	(4) Special vulnerability of contracts to rescission for fraud	4.13	(3) Continuing representations and changes of circumstances	4.90
C.	Representation	4.17	F. Representation must be Relied On	4.100
	(1) Representations of existing fact and of law	4.17	(1) Reliance and inducement: a question of causation	4.100
	(2) Representation may be a contractual term	4.20	(2) Ambiguous statements or conduct	4.103
	(3) Representation may be express or implied	4.26	(3) Causation: fraudulent misrepresentation	4.104
	(4) Passing on information generally not a representation	4.28	(4) Causation: non-fraudulent misrepresentation	4.105
	(5) Silence generally not a representation	4.29	(5) Presumption of reliance and onus of proof	4.110
	(6) Sources of implied representations	4.32	(6) Examples of non-reliance on a false representation	4.114
	(7) Determining what was represented (expressly and impliedly)	4.39	(7) Opportunity to discover truth does not disprove reliance	4.119
	(8) What are not representations	4.44	(8) Subsequent transactions	4.121
	(9) Materiality of the representation	4.62		

A. Introduction

A misrepresentation is a representation that is untrue. If certain conditions discussed in this **4.01** chapter are met, misrepresentation is a ground for rescission.[1] It may be contrasted with a mere mistake, not induced by a representation, which generally does not permit rescission. The way in which the representee's erroneous belief is brought about makes the critical difference as to whether a right to rescind arises.[2]

---

[1] In the case of contracts between consumers and traders misrepresentation may also be a misleading practice allowing the consumer to 'unwind' the contract under regulations (regs 27E and 27F) inserted into the Consumer Protection from Unfair Trading Regulations 2008 by the Consumer Protection (Amendment) Regulations 2014. Such statutory rights akin to rescission are beyond the scope of this chapter.

[2] For the special circumstances in which a contract may be rescinded for unilateral mistake, see Part A of Chap 6. As to the different rules relating to gifts, Chap 29.

74 II. GROUNDS

4.02   Each of the following elements must be present for a representee to be entitled to rescind a contract for misrepresentation: (i) a relevant 'representation' was made; (ii) it was made by, or with the knowledge of, the other party to the voidable contract; (iii) it was false; and (iv) it was relied upon by the representee. Typically the representee need only directly prove the first three elements. Although the fourth underpins rescission for misrepresentation, a rebuttable presumption of reliance arises where a *material* misrepresentation is made.[3] The onus then falls on the other party to disprove reliance by the representee.

4.03   It is not necessary to prove that the representor had a particular state of mind. He need not have acted fraudulently or negligently. Where rescission based on a misrepresentation is claimed it is only necessary to show that there was misrepresentation; then, however honestly it may have been made, however blameless the representor, the contract, having been obtained by misrepresentation, cannot stand.[4] Proving fraud in a rescission action does not *necessarily* place the claimant in a better position than if he had proved innocent misrepresentation.[5] But a number of special rules that may favour the rescinding party do apply to fraudulent misrepresentation. These are discussed later.[6]

B. Types of Misrepresentation: Fraudulent, Negligent, Innocent

4.04   Misrepresentations are conventionally classified into fraudulent and innocent according to the state of mind of the representor. 'If [behaviour by words or conduct] conveys a false impression, that is enough. If the false impression is created knowingly, it is a fraudulent misrepresentation. If it is created unwittingly, it is an innocent misrepresentation.'[7] A non-fraudulent misrepresentation can also be made negligently—that is, through a lack of care as to its truth or accuracy.

(1) Nature of fraudulent misrepresentation

4.05   The authoritative definition of fraud is contained in the speech of Lord Herschell in *Derry v Peek*: 'fraud is proved when it is shown that a false representation has been made (1) knowingly, or (2) without belief in its truth, or (3) recklessly, careless whether it be true or false.'[8] The touchstone is the defendant's state of mind vis-à-vis the falsity of the representation that he makes. A representor cannot commit fraud unless he intends or is willing that his representation should be understood in a sense which he knows to be false.[9] If he honestly believes the representation to be true in the sense in which he understands it when it is made, there is no fraud.[10] A false statement made through carelessness or even gross negligence,

---

[3] See para [4.110]ff.
[4] *Derry v Peek* (1889) 14 App Cas 337 (HL) 359; *Nash v Wooderson* (1884) 52 LT 49.
[5] *Goldrei, Foucard & Son v Sinclair and Russian Chamber of Commerce in London* [1918] 1 KB 180 (CA) 186.
[6] See paras [4.13]ff.
[7] *Curtis v The Chemical Cleaning & Dyeing Co Ltd* [1951] 1 KB 805 (CA) 808.
[8] (1889) 14 App Cas 337 (HL) 374.
[9] *Akerhielm v De Mare* [1959] AC 789 (PC—Eastern Africa) 805; *Gross v Lewis Hillman Ltd* [1970] Ch 445 (CA) 459; *Barton v County NatWest Ltd* [1999] All ER (D) 782 [32]; on appeal [2002] 4 All ER 494n (CA).
[10] *Sears v Minco Plc* [2016] EWHC 433 (Ch) [61].

but with an honest belief in its truth, is not fraudulent.[11] The test is subjective in the sense that the defendant must not have believed the representation to be true.[12]

The law treats a recklessly made false statement in the same way as a false statement made **4.06** knowingly.[13] Wilful ignorance of the falsehood of the statement—a shutting of one's eyes to the facts—is also fraudulent.[14] Although a negligently made false statement does not amount to fraud, the absence of reasonable grounds for making a false statement is not entirely irrelevant. It plays an evidentiary role in disproving honest belief. As Lord Herschell put it in *Derry v Peek*:

> I can conceive many cases where the fact that an alleged belief was destitute of all reasonable foundation would suffice of itself to convince the Court that it was not really entertained, and that the representation was a fraudulent one.[15]

The civil standard of proof applies to a finding of fraud, but as the allegation is a very serious **4.07** one, cogent evidence must be presented.[16] Before a finding of fraud can be made, it must be distinctly pleaded and also specifically put in cross-examination to the party or witness said to be responsible for the fraud.[17] It has been said that the finding itself must also be one that the court makes specifically.[18]

The tort of deceit requires that the fraudulent representation be made with the intention **4.08** that it should be acted on by the representee,[19] and the Court of Appeal has applied this requirement in a case concerning rescission for fraud.[20] That court has also held that where a fraudulent misrepresentation is made it gives rise to a rebuttable presumption of fact that the representor intends the representee to act in reliance on it.[21] But no motive for

---

[11] *Taylor v Ashton* (1843) 11 M & W 401, 152 ER 86; *Derry v Peek* (1889) 14 App Cas 337 (HL) 374–375; *Akerhielm v De Mare* [1959] AC 789 (PC—Eastern Africa); *Armitage v Nurse* [1998] Ch 241 (CA) 250; *Jaffray v Society of Lloyd's* [2002] EWCA 1101.

[12] But the defendant's own idiosyncratic views as to what is or is not dishonest will not provide a defence: *Ivey v Genting Casinos UK Ltd* [2018] AC 391 (Sup Ct).

[13] *Edgington v Fitzmaurice* (1885) 29 ChD 459 (CA) 481–82; see also *Derry v Peek* (1889) 14 App Cas 337 (HL) 350, 374; *AIC Ltd v ITS Testing Services (UK) Ltd (The Kriti Palm)* [2007] 1 All ER 667 (CA) 726; *Greenridge Luton One Ltd v Kempton Investments Ltd* [2016] EWHC 91 (Ch) [93].

[14] *Derry v Peek* (1889) 14 App Cas 337 (HL) 376.

[15] (1889) 14 App Cas 337 (HL) 375–76; *Akerhielm v De Mare* [1959] AC 789 (PC—Eastern Africa) 805.

[16] *Hornal v Neuberger Products Ltd* [1957] 1 QB 247 (CA); *Re H* [1996] AC 563; *Smith New Court Securities Limited v Scrimgeour Vickers (Asset Management) Ltd* [1997] AC 254, 274; *Barings plc v Coopers & Lybrand* [2002] 1 Lloyd's Rep PN 395, 407; *Re B* [2009] 1 AC 11 (HL); *Nadinic v Drinkwater* (2017) 94 NSWLR 518 (CA) [47].

[17] *Haringey LBC v Hines* [2010] EWCA Civ 1111; *Nadinic v Drinkwater* (2017) 94 NSWLR 518 (CA) [45]–[48], [102], [108]–[117] (finding of fraud not open given conduct of the trial); *Aquila Wsa Aviation Opportunities II Limited v Onur Air Tasimacilik AS* [2018] EWHC 519 (Comm).

[18] *Sgro v Australian Associated Motor Insurers Ltd* (2015) 91 NSWLR 325 (CA) [54]; *Nadinic v Drinkwater* (2017) 94 NSWLR 518 (CA) [49], [155].

[19] *Bradford Third Equitable Benefit Building Society v Borders* [1941] 2 All ER 205 (HL) 211.

[20] *Barton v County NatWest Ltd* [1999] All ER (D) 782 [43]; on appeal [2002] 4 All ER 494n (CA). The court treated the elements of the tort of deceit as the requirements for rescission for fraudulent misrepresentation without discussion. It is arguable that the requirements for rescission should differ. The elements of the tort of deceit shape the victim's entitlement to damages. But the right to damages is independent of and distinct from the right to rescind. See Chap 2, paras [2.03]ff. No authority appears to require an intention to induce for rescission for innocent misrepresentation. Such a requirement for innocent misrepresentation would be contrary to principle.

[21] *Goose v Wilson Sandford & Co* [2001] Lloyd's Rep PN 189 (CA) 201. But note that the authorities cited in the judgment in support of this proposition refer to a different presumption, ie that the representee was induced by the representation, not the presumption that the representor intended to induce.

76   II. GROUNDS

the making of the fraudulent representation needs to be shown by the representee.[22] It is not necessary to prove any intention to cheat, injure, or deceive.[23] It is no defence that the representor believed that he was justified in making the false representation or that in the circumstances no harm would result.[24] In Hong Kong, it has been held that mere silence is incapable of founding a claim for fraudulent misrepresentation, on the basis that mere silence cannot amount to a representation by words or conduct.[25]

(2) Importance of the distinction outside law of rescission

4.09   The distinction between fraudulent, negligent, and innocent misrepresentations is important outside the law of rescission. It determines the entitlement to recover compensation for misrepresentation. The representee has an action for the tort of deceit if the misrepresentation is fraudulent,[26] for the tort of negligence if the misrepresentation is negligent,[27] and under section 2(1) of the Misrepresentation Act 1967 if the misrepresentation is not fraudulent and the representor cannot prove that he made it honestly and on reasonable grounds. Even if the representor can prove the misrepresentation was truly innocent, he may still be required to pay damages in lieu of rescission under section 2(2) of that Act.[28] In jurisdictions that have not enacted legislation equivalent to sections 2(1) and 2(2) of the 1967 Act, and where the common law rules continue to apply, innocent misrepresentation confers no right to compensation, and the misled party must establish that it became a term of the contract, or rely on some other statutory provision, to obtain such relief.[29]

(3) Importance in relation to rescission

4.10   Before the Judicature reforms the distinction between fraudulent and non- fraudulent misrepresentation was vital because, save in the special case of insurance, the victim of a misrepresentation not amounting to fraud at common law had no right to rescind.[30] Courts of equity permitted rescission for misrepresentations that were not regarded as fraudulent at law, albeit the right was sometimes said to be based on 'equitable fraud', and until the late nineteenth century there was some uncertainty as to the effects of making a purely innocent

---

[22] *Smith v Chadwick* (1884) 9 App Cas 187 (HL) 201; *Edgington v Fitzmaurice* (1885) 29 ChD 459 (CA) 482. But motive may have some evidential value: *Goose v Wilson Sandford & Co* [2001] Lloyd's Rep PN 189 (CA) 201; *Barings plc v Coopers & Lybrand* [2002] 1 Lloyd's Rep PN 395, 407.

[23] *Foster v Charles* (1830) 7 Bing 105, 131 ER 40; *Derry v Peek* (1889) 14 App Cas 337 (HL) 374; *Eco3 Capital Limited v Ludsin Overseas Ltd* [2013] EWCA Civ 413; *Marme Inversiones 2007 SL v Natwest Markets Plc* [2019] EWHC 366 (Comm) [254].

[24] *Brown Jenkinson & Co Ltd v Percy Dalton (London) Ltd* [1957] 2 QB 621; *Jaffray v Society of Lloyd's* [2002] EWCA 1101 [66].

[25] *Xie Li Xin v Thompson* [2018] HKCFI 1096 [47](2) (fraudulent money-lending scheme).

[26] *Derry v Peek* (1889) 14 App Cas 337 (HL); *Doyle v Olby (Ironmongers) Ltd* [1969] 2 QB 158 (CA).

[27] *Hedley Byrne & Co Ltd v Heller & Partners Ltd* [1964] AC 465; *Esso Petroleum Co v Mardon* [1976] 1 QB 801 (CA); *Bristol and West Building Society v Mothew* [1998] Ch 1 (CA).

[28] *Atlantic Lines and Navigation Co Inc v Hallam Ltd (The Lucy)* [1983] 1 Lloyds Rep 188 (QB) 201–02.

[29] Eg in Australia, under ss 237–39 of the Australian Consumer Law (see also s 243 which replaced s 87 of the Trade Practices Act 1974).

[30] *Reynell v Sprye* (1852) 1 De GM & G 660, 708; 42 ER 710, 728; *Hopkins v Tanqueray* (1854) 15 CB 130, 139 ER 369; *Behn v Burness* (1863) 3 B & S 751, 753; 122 ER 281, 282; *Kennedy v The Panama, New Zealand, and Australian Royal Mail Co Ltd* (1867) LR 2 QB 580, 587.

pre-contractual representation. The modern rule that innocent misrepresentation provides a ground for rescission in equity was not clearly articulated until after the Judicature reforms.[31] The right to rescind for non-fraudulent misrepresentation continues to be equitable. Non-fraudulent misrepresentation is a ground for rescission at common law only in the special case of insurance.

In contrast, fraudulent misrepresentation is a ground for rescission both at law and in equity; there exists a so-called 'concurrent jurisdiction'.[32] Today the only meaningful category of fraud is fraud recognized by the common law, as defined in *Derry v Peek*.[33] With the refining of the grounds for equitable rescission the term 'equitable fraud' is now rarely used,[34] and does not describe any concrete ground for rescission. Nor does that label illuminate the reason why the law permits rescission in any given fact pattern, and should therefore be used with care.[35] **4.11**

In addition to its jurisdictional consequences, the distinction between fraudulent and non-fraudulent misrepresentation continues to be relevant as regards rescission because the law gives some special advantages to a victim of fraudulent misrepresentation. **4.12**

(4) Special vulnerability of contracts to rescission for fraud

Fraud unravels all.[36] Rescission is more readily available when a representation is fraudulent. The main ways in which this is so will now be summarized. First, fraudulent misrepresentations of opinion,[37] intention,[38] and law[39] have long been held to constitute grounds for rescission when an innocent misrepresentation to the same effect would not. That is probably because a false statement of opinion, intention, or law made without a belief in its truth is also a false representation of an existing fact, namely, that the representor holds the opinion, intention, or view as to the law that he expresses.[40] **4.13**

A representation is material if it would affect the judgement of a reasonable person in deciding to enter into the transaction, and the general rule is that a misrepresentation must be material to provide a ground for rescission.[41] However, that rule does not apply where the representation is made fraudulently.[42] Additionally, although it remains essential that the representee did in fact rely on the statement, a generous test of reliance is applied in fraud cases; it is enough that the representation was 'a' cause of the representee entering into the **4.14**

---

[31] *Redgrave v Hurd* (1881) 20 ChD 1 (CA) 12.
[32] *Peek v Gurney* (1871) LR 13 Eq 79 (CA); *Newbigging v Adam* (1886) 34 ChD 582 (CA) 592.
[33] (1889) 14 App Cas 337 (HL). But cf *Nadinic v Drinkwater* (2017) 94 NSWLR 518 (CA) [22].
[34] But cf *Nadinic v Drinkwater* (2017) 94 NSWLR 518 (CA) [22], [82], [102] (distinction relied upon).
[35] Cf Chap 29, para [29.16].
[36] *HIH Casualty & General Insurance v Chase Manhattan Bank* [2003] 2 Lloyd's Rep 61 (HL) [15], 'Once make out that there has been anything like deception, and no contract resting in any degree on that foundation can stand': *Reynell v Sprye* (1852) 1 De GM & G 660, 708; 42 ER 710, 728; *Takhar v Gracefield Developments Limited* [2020] AC 450 (Sup Ct) [43].
[37] See paras [4.48]–[4.49].
[38] *Edgington v Fitzmaurice* (1885) 29 ChD 459 (CA) 483.
[39] *West London Commercial Bank v Kitson* (1884) 13 QBD 360 (CA) 363.
[40] See paras [4.52] and [4.61].
[41] See para [4.62].
[42] See para [4.66].

78   II. GROUNDS

transaction.[43] A more stringent test of reliance probably applies when the representation is not fraudulent.[44]

4.15   Different mechanisms apply to rescission for fraudulent and non-fraudulent misrepresentation. Rescission is effected by election in the case of the former and by court order in the case of the latter.[45] The law also takes a more indulgent approach when a fraudster has absconded by dispensing with the normal rule that an election to rescind must be communicated. It is doubtful that this requirement is relaxed outside cases of fraud.[46]

4.16   Moreover, the statutory discretion conferred by section 2(2) of the Misrepresentation Act 1967, to bar rescission and award damages in lieu, is confined to non-fraudulent misrepresentation, and is not engaged in a case of fraud.[47] Other bars to rescission also operate differently when fraud is proved, in particular, the bar *restitutio integrum* impossible.[48]

C. Representation

(1) Representations of existing fact and of law

4.17   It is a long-standing rule that a misrepresentation must be a representation of a matter of existing fact.[49] It was, accordingly, long thought that an innocent misrepresentation of law does not give rise to a right to rescind.[50] Today, however, the position is probably different, for the following reasons.

4.18   In *Kleinwort Benson Ltd v Lincoln City Council*[51] the House of Lords abolished the bar to the recovery of money paid under a mistake of law, and thereby collapsed the distinction that formerly existed between mistake of fact and mistake of law as grounds for restitution. Following that watershed decision, the contention that this notoriously difficult distinction ought to continue to be drawn in the context of misrepresentation as a ground for rescission is difficult indeed. The cases indicate that the distinction is unlikely to survive. In *Pankhania v Hackney LBC*, Mr Rex Tedd, sitting as a Deputy High Court Judge, stated:

> I have concluded that the 'misrepresentation of law' rule has not survived the decision in the Kleinwort Benson case. Its historical origin is as an offshoot of the 'mistake of law' rule, created by analogy with it, and the two are logically interdependent ... The distinction between fact and law in the context of relief from misrepresentation has no more underlying

---

[43] See para [4.104].

[44] See paras [4.105]ff.

[45] Chap 10.

[46] Chap 11.

[47] Chap 28. See also Chap 27, which details bars to rescission for non-fraudulent misrepresentation that were developed by the courts.

[48] *Spence v Crawford* [1939] 3 All ER 271. See Chap 18.

[49] *Eaglesfield v The Marquis of Londonderry* (1876) 4 ChD 693 (CA) 709; *Smith v Chadwick* (1884) 9 App Cas 187 (CA); *British Airways Board v Taylor* [1976] 1 All ER 65 (HL) 68 Lord Wilberforce emphatically stressed that 'the distinction [between a statement of fact and a promise or statement of intention] is a real one and requires to be respected'.

[50] *Beattie v Lord Ebury* (1872) 7 Ch App 777, 801; on appeal LR 7 HL 102; *Eaglesfield v The Marquis of Londonderry* (1876) 4 ChD 693 (CA) 709. Cf fraudulent misrepresentations of law: *West London Commercial Bank v Kitson* (1884) 13 QBD 360 (CA) 363.

[51] [1999] 2 AC 349.

principle to it than it does in the context of relief from mistake … The rules of the common law should, so far as possible, be congruent with one another and based on coherent principle. The survival of the 'misrepresentation of law' rule following the demise of the 'mistake of law' rule would be no more than a quixotic anachronism.[52]

4.19 These were remarks made *obiter*, for the misrepresentation in question was held to be one of fact. But they were cited with apparent approval by the Court of Appeal in *Brennan v Bolt Burdon*,[53] which involved mistake rather than misrepresentation, and the indications are that it is only a matter of time before a court applies the reasoning in the *Kleinwort Benson* case to rescission for misrepresentation. The preferable view is that a non-fraudulent misrepresentation of law may, in an appropriate case, provide a ground for rescission.[54]

(2) Representation may be a contractual term

4.20 A representation was defined by Williams J in *Behn v Burness* as:

> … a statement, or assertion, made by one party to the other, before or at the time of the contract, of some matter or circumstance relating to it. Though it is sometimes contained in a written instrument, it is not an integral part of the contract; and consequently the contract is not broken though the representation proves untrue.[55]

4.21 A pre-contractual representation will become a term of the parties' agreement if that is what they intend, and as William J's formulation suggests, there was formerly some doubt as to whether rescission remained possible if this had occurred.[56] The doubt was resolved by section 1 of the Misrepresentation Act 1967, which provides that the fact that a misrepresentation has become a term of the contract does not bar rescission. Today a representation can be defined as a statement or assertion made before or at the time of the transaction, dealing with some matter or circumstance relating to it, whether it is a term of the transaction or not.

4.22 A contractual warranty does not always carry with it a representation as to the fact that is warranted.[57] A warranty is a promise that something is true, whereas a representation is a statement of fact.[58] Thus if a party 'warrants' something, it does not necessarily 'represent' it and, if no representation is made, the disappointed party will be confined to any contractual rights flowing from breach of the warranty, and unable to rescind *ab initio* for misrepresentation.[59] However, the terms of a

---

[52] [2002] EWHC 2441 [58].

[53] [2005] QB 303 (CA) 310, 317; *Mainstream Properties Limited v Young* [2005] All ER (D) 148 (CA) [84].

[54] *The Co-Operative Bank Plc v Hayes Freehold Ltd* [2017] EWHC 1820 (Ch) concerned an attempt to argue that there had been an implied misrepresentation that a party had the power to accept the surrender of a headlease. The argument failed on the facts.

[55] (1863) 3 B & S 751, 753; 98 ER 1361, 1362. As to the potential responsibility for misrepresentations made by a third party see Chap 9.

[56] *Pennsylvania Shipping Co v Compagnie Nationale de Navigation* [1936] 2 All ER 1167.

[57] *Sycamore Bidco Ltd v Breslin* [2012] EWHC 3443 (Ch); *Idemitsu Kosan Co Ltd v Sumitomo Corporation* [2016] 2 CLC 297.

[58] *Hunt v Optima (Cambridge) Ltd* [2015] 1 WLR 1346 (CA) [69].

[59] See R Zakrzewski, 'Representations and Warranties Distinguished' (2013) 28 BJIB & FL 341, particularly as to whether a knowingly false warranty may give rise to liability for fraudulent misrepresentation; *Idemitsu Kosan Co*

80   II. GROUNDS

contract may make it clear that certain statements constitute both a representation and a warranty.[60]

4.23 In jurisdictions that do not have an equivalent to section 1 of the 1967 Act the question of whether incorporation of a representation into a contract prevents rescission continues to be of practical importance. The preferable view is that a pre-contractual representation does not cease to be a representation because it is also made in the contract.[61] This point has been underlined in Australian courts,[62] but rejected in Canada.[63]

4.24 Moreover, if a representation was not made in oral negotiations but first appeared in the document signed by the parties, it is still a representation that potentially confers a right to rescind.[64] That principle too has been rejected by one Canadian appellate court, which held that a representation not made in the course of negotiations, but that first appeared as a term in a written contract, does not give rise to a right to rescind.[65] This is difficult to understand.[66] If the representee read the document before signing, the statement will be a pre-contractual representation made to him.[67] If he did not read it, then no right to rescind arises because there was no reliance on the representation, not because no representation was made.

4.25 A representation that is by the terms of an agreement deemed to be made at specified times does not give rise to a right to rescind if it becomes false after the date of the agreement. For example, in the common case of a borrower who makes a representation in a loan agreement that no event of default has occurred and that representation is deemed to be repeated at certain time intervals, the occurrence of an event of default does not give the lender a right to rescind the loan agreement. When repeated, the representation is not made before or at the time of the contract, and furthermore it cannot be said that the claimant relied on the false representation when entering into the transaction.[68]

Ltd v Sumitomo Corporation [2016] 2 CLC 297 [14] where it was stated that '[b]y contracting on terms by which he warrants something, the seller is not purporting to impart information; he is not making a statement to his buyer. He is making a promise, to which he will be held as a matter of contract in the sense that any breach of the warranty will be actionable as a breach of contract, subject to any other relevant terms of the contract and to general principles of the law of contract, for example as to remedies.' See also *SK Shipping Europe Plc v Capital Vlcc 3 Corp* [2021] 2 Lloyd's Rep 109.

[60] *SK Shipping Europe Plc v Capital Vlcc 3 Corp* [2021] 2 Lloyd's Rep 109 [119].

[61] *Compagnie Française des Chemins de Fer Paris-Orleans v Leeston Shipping Company Ltd* [1919] Lloyd's Rep 235, 238.

[62] *Alati v Kruger* (1955) 94 CLR 216, 220, 222; *Mihaljevic v Eiffel Tower Motors Pty Ltd and General Credits Ltd* (1973) VR 545, 566; *Kramer v McMahon* [1970] NSWLR 194, 204 (fraudulent misrepresentation) 'a statement in a contract may constitute a term of it and also act as a representation of fact (founding rescission) at one and the same time'. These cases make clear that when an actionable misrepresentation is also a term of the contract, the representee may either sue for breach of contract, or rescind *ab initio*.

[63] '[A] representation to induce a contract loses all force and effect as a representation inducing the contract once it is embodied in the contract as a term thereof': *Zien v Field* (1963) 41 DLR (2d) 394 (BCCA) 409 rev'd on another point [1963] SCR 632; see Chap 27, para [27.41].

[64] *Alati v Kruger* (1955) 94 CLR 216, 220, 222.

[65] *Abraham v Wingate Properties Limited* [1986] 1 WWR 568 (Man CA) [5].

[66] Williams J in *Behn v Burness* (1863) 3 B & S 751, 753; 98 ER 1361, 1362 refers to statements made 'at the time of the contract'.

[67] Language used in drafts circulated in the course of negotiations also ought to be capable of amounting to a representation, as was argued in *Bikam OOD v Adria Cable Sarl* [2012] EWHC 621 (Comm) [27]; *Idemitsu Kosan Co Ltd v Sumitomo Corporation* [2016] 2 CLC 297 [24].

[68] See also *Manifest Shipping Co Ltd v Uni-Polaris Insurance Co Ltd (The Star Sea)* [2003] 1 AC 469 (HL), where it was held that post-contract fraud does not permit an insurance contract to be rescinded *ab initio*.

(3) Representation may be express or implied

A representation may be made expressly, by written or oral communications,[69] or it may be implied from the representor's conduct. Writing for this purpose includes a plan or map[70] or a photograph.[71] A representation may be implied from very limited conduct. But the conduct must be clear.[72] A 'nod or a wink, or a shake of a head, or a smile' will, in some cases, be enough.[73] Whether a representation is made is a question of fact, and the conduct said to be a representation must be assessed in the context of all of the circumstances in which it occurred. **4.26**

Conduct that can give rise to a representation is therefore not limited to direct visual communication. It has been held to include much less direct means of communicating a fact, such as offering an item for sale in a particular market, concealing a flaw, or offering to enter into a particular type of transaction. Conduct that gives rise to an implied representation also includes the making of an express statement that, in the circumstances in which it is made, carries an implied representation. Each of these categories of implied representation is discussed later. However it should be noted that there is no rule of law that a particular statement carries a particular implied representation; all depends on the context.[74] **4.27**

(4) Passing on information generally not a representation

The mere passing on of information ought not to constitute a representation where the recipient is aware that the provider of the information is acting as a mere conduit;[75] however, the provider will be making a representation if he adopts the information as his own or, depending on the context, may be found to be representing impliedly that he is not aware that the information is inaccurate. A misrepresentation may also occur where the person passing on the information does not fairly set out the information; for example, where parts of a surveyor's report are passed on but qualifications are left out.[76] **4.28**

---

[69] In *Gestmin SGPS S.A. v Credit Suisse (UK) Limited* [2020] 1 CLC 428 [15]–[22] and [154]–[157], Leggatt J (as he then was) made a number of observations as to the evidential difficulties that arise in respect of oral misrepresentation claims based entirely on witnesses' recollections many years after the relevant events and concluded that the best approach was 'to place little if any reliance at all on witnesses' recollections of what was said in meetings and conversations, and to base factual findings on inferences drawn from the documentary evidence and known or probable facts'.

[70] *Re the Mount Morgan (West) Gold Mine Ltd* (1887) 56 LT 622; *Dabbs v Seaman* (1925) 36 CLR 538.

[71] *Newman v Pinto* (1887) 57 LT 31 (CA).

[72] *Property Alliance Group Ltd v Royal Bank of Scotland Plc* [2018] 1 WLR 3529 [129]; *Marme Inversiones 2007 SL v Natwest Markets Plc* [2019] EWHC 366 (Comm) [118]–[119].

[73] *Walters v Morgan* (1861) 3 De GF 7 J 718, 724; 45 ER 1056, 1059. In the criminal context, wearing a cap and gown in Oxford was held to amount to a representation that the wearer was a student: *R v Barnard* (1837) 7 C & P 784, 173 ER 342. Showing a purchaser around a property constituted a representation by conduct that an enclosed yard accessible from the property formed part of the property being sold: *Green Park Properties Ltd v Dorku Ltd* [2001] 1 HKLRD 139 (Hong Kong CA) 143.

[74] *Jaffray v Society of Lloyd's* [2002] EWCA 1101 [59].

[75] *Rehman v Santander UK Plc* [2018] EWHC 748 (QB) [37].

[76] *FoodCo UK LLP (t/a Muffin Break) v Henry Boot Developments Ltd* [2010] EWHC 358 (Ch) [218].

(5) Silence generally not a representation

4.29 The rules as to when a representation may be implied from silence cannot be understood in isolation. They are to a large extent a product of the principles regulating pre-contractual disclosure. Those principles are as follows: (i) there is no obligation to speak within the context of negotiations for an ordinary commercial contract;[77] (ii) ordinarily the failure to disclose a material fact which might influence the mind of a prudent contractor does not give a right to avoid the contract;[78] and (iii) mere silence is not a ground for rescission where there is no duty to make disclosure.[79]

4.30 These principles sit behind the general rule that mere silence is not a representation,[80] even when the other party is labouring under a self-deception,[81] and even if that is known to the first party.[82] However, it has been said that 'very little is sufficient to affect the application of that principle. If a word, a single word be dropped which tends to mislead the [counterparty], that principle will not be allowed to operate'.[83]

4.31 Furthermore, in the context of continuing representations that are later falsified, silence coupled with a prior representation may give rise to a misrepresentation.[84] Also, in some jurisdictions (but it appears not in England and Wales) a mistaken party is permitted to rescind for unilateral mistake. But this requires the non-mistaken party to have known of the mistake *and* to have engaged in sharp practice.[85] The right to rescind in such cases is consistent with the general rule described, for mere silence alone is not sufficient.

(6) Sources of implied representations

4.32 Whether a representation is implied depends on the context in which the relevant conduct takes place, and each case must therefore be assessed by reference to its particular facts. The following discussion outlines some of the fact patterns in which the courts have held that a contracting party made an implied representation.

---

[77] *Banque Keyser Ullmann SA v Skandia (UK) Insurance Co Ltd* [1990] 1 QB 665 (CA) 798; on appeal [1991] 2 AC 249; *ING Bank NV v Ros Roca SA* [2011] EWCA Civ 353 [92].

[78] *Bell v Lever Bros Ltd* [1932] AC 161, 227 (Lord Atkin).

[79] *Turner v Green* [1895] 2 Ch 205, 208 'Mere silence as regards a material fact which one party is not under an obligation to disclose to the other cannot be a ground for rescission'; *Carlish v Salt* [1906] 1 Ch 335, 338. As to the cases where a duty of disclosure is imposed, see Chap 5.

[80] *Fletcher v Krell* (1873) 42 LJ QB 55; *Davies v London and Provincial Marine Insurance Company* (1878) 8 ChD 469, 474; *Marcovitch v Liverpool Victoria Friendly Society* (1912) 28 TLR 188 (CA) 189; *Raiffeisen Zentralbank Osterreich AG v The Royal Bank of Scotland Plc* [2011] 1 Lloyd's Rep 123 [84]. In Hong Kong, it has been held that mere silence is incapable of founding a claim for fraudulent misrepresentation: *Xie Li Xin v Thompson* [2018] HKCFI 1096 [47](2).

[81] *Keates v Cadogan* (1851) 10 CB 591, 138 ER 234; *New Brunswick and Canada Railway and Land Co v Conybeare* (1862) 9 HLC 711, 11 ER 907; *Smith v Hughes* (1871) LR 6 QB 597, 607 where Blackburn J stated that 'there is no legal obligation on the vendor to inform the purchaser that he is under a mistake not induced by the misrepresentation of the vendor'.

[82] *Bell v Lever Bros Ltd* [1932] AC 161, 224, 227; *Banque Keyser Ullmann SA v Skandia (UK) Insurance Co Ltd* [1990] 1 QB 665 (CA) 798–99; *Westpac Banking Corp v Robinson* (1993) 30 NSWLR 668 (CA) 687–88.

[83] *Turner v Harvey* (1821) Jac 169, 178; 37 ER 814, 818 (Lord Eldon); *Barton v County NatWest Ltd* [1999] All ER (D) 782; on appeal [2002] 4 All ER 494n (CA).

[84] See paras [4.90]–[4.99].

[85] *Taylor v Johnson* (1983) 151 CLR 422. See Chap 7.

Implied from express statements, including partial disclosure

Representations may be implied from express oral or written statements. A purchaser of a **4.33** boat who states to the seller that the boat has a defective keel may make an implied representation that he has inspected the keel. This is a misrepresentation if no inspection was in fact made.[86] A reference to premises as 'offices' may carry a representation that there exist planning consents to use the premises in this manner.[87] A statement by a vendor's solicitor that the vendor is not aware of the property ever having been affected by dry rot would usually carry an implied representation that reasonable steps had been taken by the vendor to ascertain the existence of dry rot.[88]

As will be explained further, a statement of opinion may carry an implied representation **4.34** that the party making the statement has reasonable grounds for expressing that opinion.[89]

A statement or answer to a question may be literally true but involve a misrepresentation if **4.35** the representor omits qualifying or supplementary facts or information.[90] If a vendor's solicitors are asked whether land being sold is subject to restrictive covenants and they reply that they are not aware of any, the solicitors will usually be making an implied representation that inquiries have been made. If they have not been made the partial disclosure, though literally true, is a misrepresentation.[91] When an insured is asked whether he has ever made an insurance claim, and for further information if he has, and he states that he has and gives details of one claim, he is making an implied representation as to the absence of any additional claims. If there were such claims, the answer is literally true but constitutes a misrepresentation.[92] When a party negotiating for a sub-charter of a ship asks to see the head-charter because it wants the sub-charter to be on the same terms, and a copy is sent, but the telexes which qualify that document are innocently omitted, there is a misrepresentation as to the nature of the head-charter.[93] But an omission of this kind only gives rise to a right to rescind if it actually misleads. The rescinding party must show that the omission of relevant information makes what is stated misleading, and that he was misled by the representations made.[94]

James LJ summarized the principle in *Arkwright v Newbold*:

> Supposing you state a thing partially, you may make a false statement as much as if you misstated it altogether. Every word may be true but if you leave out something which qualifies

---

[86] *Goldsmith v Rodger* [1962] 2 Lloyd's Rep 249 (CA) 251.

[87] *Laurence v Lexcourt Holdings Ltd* [1978] 1 WLR 1128 (CA). A description of a development as consisting of 24 units was a misrepresentation where planning consent had only been granted for 12: *Thompson v Vincent* [2001] 3 NZLR 355.

[88] *Clinicare Ltd v Orchard* [2004] EWHC 1694.

[89] See paras [4.53]ff.

[90] *Curwen v Yan Yean Land Co Ltd* (1891) 17 VLR 745 (representor stated that he was buying shares in a company, but failed to state that he had other dealings with the company); *Galle Gowns Ltd v Licenses & General Insurance Co Ltd* (1933) 47 Lloyd's Rep 186 (representor stated that it had traded under a particular name, but failed to state that it had also traded under a different name); *Curtis v Chemical Cleaning and Dyeing Co Ltd* [1951] 1 KB 805 (representor stated that the waiver the customer was signing applied to one type of damage when it excluded all liability); *Spice Girls Ltd v Aprilia World Services BV* [2002] EWCA 15 [59] (representors stated that a pop group comprised five named individuals, but failed to state that one of them was about to leave).

[91] *Nottingham Patent Brick and Tile Co v Butler* (1866) 16 QBD 778 (CA); *William Sindall Plc v Cambridgeshire County Council* [1994] 1 WLR 1016 (CA) 1025.

[92] *Condogianis v Guardian Assurance Co Ltd* [1921] 2 AC 125 (PC—Australia).

[93] *Atlantic Lines and Navigation Co Inc v Hallam Ltd (The Lucy)* [1983] 1 Lloyds LR 188 (QB) 198.

[94] *McKeown v Boudard-Peveril Gear Co* (1896) 65 LJ Ch 735 (CA) 736.

84 II. GROUNDS

it, you may make a false statement. For instance, if pretending to set out the report of a surveyor, you set out two passages in his report, and leave out a third passage which qualifies
them, that is an actual misstatement.[95]

Implied from the nature of a transaction

4.36 An order for goods carries a representation that the purchaser intends to pay the price.[96]
For example, a purchase of goods on credit by a bankrupt who has no intention of paying
for them is a sale induced by fraud that entitles the seller to rescind the contract and retake his goods.[97] A bidder for goods at an auction 'must be taken to have made an implied
representation that he intended to pay for them'.[98] Similarly, in one case, ordering a meal
at a restaurant involved a representation that the customer had the funds to pay for it.[99]
Unauthorized use of a bank card and a credit card involves a false representation to the
seller that the buyer is entitled to use the card for the particular purchase.[100] In another
case, by accepting an order the person in control of a company represented by implication
that the business conducted by the company was trading properly and legitimately.[101] A
creditor may make an implied representation to a surety that there is nothing unusual in
the arrangements that the surety is guaranteeing.[102] In *Graiseley Properties Ltd v Barclays
Bank Plc*[103] the Court of Appeal refused to strike out an allegation that by proposing that
a particular benchmark (namely, LIBOR) ought to form the basis of a transaction in circumstances where the proposing bank had been involved in setting that benchmark, that
bank impliedly represented that this involvement was honest. In *Property Alliance Group
Ltd v Royal Bank of Scotland Plc*[104] the Court of Appeal held that a bank made implied representations in respect of proposed interest rate swaps to the effect that it was not itself
manipulating the benchmark reference rate and did not intend to manipulate it.

Implied from the market in which an item is offered

4.37 A representation that goods fit the description of the market at which they are offered may
be made by sending the goods to that market. The entry of an animal into a sale of bullocks

---

[95] (1887) 17 ChD 301 (CA) 318 (a case about damages for deceit, but the same principle applies to rescission).

[96] This is a representation that the purchaser holds a particular intention. See paras [4.60]ff regarding implied representations that an intention is honestly held.

[97] *Re Eastgate* [1905] 1 KB 465 (purchase of goods by rogue who did not intend to pay); *Contex Drouzhba Ltd v Wiseman* [2008] BCC 301 (CA): by signing a contract the director of a company impliedly represented that the company, which was insolvent at the time, had the capacity to pay for the goods subsequently ordered (a deceit case). The attempted sale of property by an undischarged bankrupt may also be fraudulent, for the property is not his to sell: *Re Hoffman ex p Worrell v Schilling* (1989) 85 ALR 145 (FC) 147; *Re Hoffman ex p Worrell v Schilling* (Full FCA, 14 August 1989). See also para [4.61].

[98] *Re Shackleton* (1875) 10 Ch App 446, 449.

[99] *Ray v Sempers* [1974] AC 370 (a criminal prosecution); *Graiseley Properties Ltd v Barclays Bank Plc* [2013] EWCA Civ 1372 [28].

[100] *R v Charles* [1977] AC 177; *R v Lambie* [1982] AC 449 (criminal prosecutions).

[101] *Lindsay v O'Loughnane* [2012] BCC 153 [103]. See also *Re Crown Holdings (London) Limited (In Liquidation)* [2015] EWHC 1876 (Ch), where by entering into contracts with customers, a company made implied representations as to its solvency.

[102] *Commercial Bank of Australia Ltd v Amadio* (1983) 151 CLR 447, 456. But the scope for implied represen-
tations of this nature is reduced where the parties conduct due diligence, enter into detailed agreements, and are represented by advisers: *Geest plc v Fyffes plc* [1999] 1 All ER 672, 685. See also Chap 5, paras [5.39]ff.

[103] *Graiseley Properties Ltd v Barclays Bank Plc* [2013] EWCA Civ 1372.

[104] [2018] 1 WLR 3529 (CA) [132]–[133]. Followed in this regard in *Marme Inversiones 2007 SL v Natwest Markets Plc* [2019] EWHC 366 (Comm) [142], [158], extending the implied representations so that they also included the representation that the bank did not intend to attempt to manipulate the benchmark rate.

and heifers is a representation that it is either a bullock or a heifer. If the animal is a herm-aphrodite, a misrepresentation is made.[105] Similarly, the offering for sale of a cow at a public market may involve a representation by conduct that the animal is not suffering from an in-fectious disease.[106] In another case, the offering for sale of a product in a shop that only sold new products involved a representation that the product was not second hand.[107]

Implied from concealment

It has been said that a misrepresentation 'may consist as much in the suppression of what **4.38** is true as in the assertion of what is false'.[108] The active concealment of a fact may give rise to an implied representation that the fact does not exist.[109] In one old case a representation as to the seaworthiness of a ship was made by concealing rotten timbers,[110] and in another a representation as to the condition of a gun was made by concealing a hole in its barrel.[111] The concealment of dry rot in a flat is a knowingly false representation that the flat does not suffer from dry rot.[112] Although mere silence does not constitute a representation, in con-cealment cases the representor is not *merely* silent. The representor's silence is coupled with a particular course of conduct (active concealment of a defect), albeit that conduct is not known to, and is kept secret from, the representee. It is this combination that gives rise to the making of a misrepresentation.

(7) Determining what was represented (expressly and impliedly)

To determine whether an express representation was made, and to what effect, the court **4.39** must consider what a reasonable person would have understood from the words in their context. To determine what, if any, implied representation was made, the court must con-sider what a reasonable person would have inferred was being represented implicitly by the representor's words and conduct, judged in their context.[113] It is helpful to ask whether, con-sidering the representor's clear words or clear conduct, a reasonable representee would nat-urally assume that what was the true state of facts did not exist and that, if it did, he would necessarily be informed of it.[114] Proof of necessity or obviousness will usually be important to show that an implied representation has been made, although neither is a necessary re-quirement.[115] As to the content of any implied representation, a court is unlikely to imply a representation that is vague, uncertain, ambiguous, imprecise, or otherwise elastic; and,

---

[105] *Gill v McDowell* [1903] 2 IR 463, 469.

[106] *Bodger v Nicholls* (1873) 28 LT 441, 445.

[107] *Gibson v National Cash Register Co* 1925 SC 500. For a case involving the sale of reproductions in an antique shop, *Edgar v Hector* 1912 SC 348.

[108] *Pulsford v Richards* (1853) 17 Beav 87, 96; 51 ER 965, 968.

[109] A deliberate concealment of a change of facts may well be fraudulent: *Reynell v Sprye* (1852) 1 De GM & G 660, 42 ER 710; *Incledon v Watson* (1862) 2 F & F 841, 175 ER 1312.

[110] *Baglehole v Walters* (1811) 3 Camp 154, 170 ER 1338; *Schneider v Heath* (1813) 3 Camp 506, 170 ER 1462.

[111] *Horsfall v Thomas* (1862) 1 H & C 90, 158 ER 813. However, in that case the misrepresentation did not induce the purchase as the purchaser did not examine the gun before the contract.

[112] *Gordon v Selico* [1986] EGLR 71 (CA).

[113] *IFE Fund SA v Goldman Sachs International* [2007] 1 Lloyd's Rep 264, 272; *Property Alliance Group Ltd v Royal Bank of Scotland Plc* [2018] 1 WLR 3529 (CA) [129]; *Marme Inversiones 2007 SL v Natwest Markets Plc* [2019] EWHC 366 (Comm) [115]; *Dhaliwal v Hussain* [2017] EWHC 2655 (Ch) [46].

[114] *Property Alliance Group Ltd v Royal Bank of Scotland Plc* [2018] 1 WLR 3529 (CA) [132]–[133].

[115] *Foster v Action Aviation Limited* [2013] EWHC 2439 (Comm) [93].

86   II. GROUNDS

more may be required in terms of express words or conduct, if a wide meaning or complex representation is to be implied.[116] Whether and what representation was impliedly made is to be considered in light of the express terms on which the parties dealt.[117] Any case of implied representation turns upon an assessment of all of the facts, and it is accordingly dangerous for allegations of implied representations to be dismissed summarily, in a factual vacuum.[118]

4.40   A statement is *prima facie* taken to bear 'the meaning in which it would be reasonably understood by the representee, that is to say, the natural and ordinary meaning which would be conveyed to a normal person'.[119] For example, when a shop is described as 'valuable business premises' the natural meaning is that it may be used for a variety of businesses, not only for dress-making.[120] The natural and ordinary meaning of words or conduct is determined objectively in the context of the circumstances in which the representation was made.[121] All the background knowledge which would reasonably have been available to the representee is also part of the context.[122] The principle was expressed by Mance LJ in *MCI WorldCom International Inc v Primus Telecommunications Inc* in the following terms:

> ... whether there is a representation and what its nature is must be judged objectively according to the impact that whatever is said may be expected to have on a reasonable representee in the position and with the known characteristics of the actual representee.[123]

In short, whether a particular representation has been made will depend on the nature and content of the statement, the context in which it was made, the characteristics of the maker, and of the person to whom it was made, and the relationship between them.[124]

4.41   If the representor intended to convey a particular meaning and the representee understood the words or actions in that subjective sense then that is the meaning of the representation.[125] But if the claimant construes statements or actions in a fanciful way, then he merely labours under a unilateral mistake and no misrepresentation can be attributed to the representor.

4.42   A document is to be read as a whole to determine whether it contains a particular representation.[126] The question is what idea would be conveyed to an ordinary man by a perusal of

---

[116] *Marme Inversiones 2007 SL v Natwest Markets Plc* [2019] EWHC 366 (Comm) [120]–[123].

[117] *Raiffeisen Zentralbank Osterreich AG v The Royal Bank of Scotland Plc* [2011] 1 Lloyd's Rep 123 [110].

[118] *Graiseley Properties Ltd v Barclays Bank Plc* [2013] EWCA Civ 1372 [25].

[119] *Spice Girls Ltd v Aprilia World Services BV* [2002] EWCA 15 [67]; *Krakowski v Eurolynx Properties Ltd* (1995) 183 CLR 563, 577.

[120] *Charles Hunt Ltd v Palmer* [1931] 2 Ch 287, 293; *Laurence v Lexcourt Holdings Ltd* [1978] 1 WLR 1128 (CA) (representation that premises were 'offices' was false as there was planning permission to use only one part as office space; rescission was granted).

[121] *Thomson v Weems* (1884) 9 App Cas 671, 685 (Lord Blackburn); *Occidental Worldwide Investment Corp v Skibs A/S Avanti (The Siboen and Sibotre)* [1976] 1 Lloyd's Rep 293, 318.

[122] The meaning of a representation is to be ascertained in much the same way as a statement forming part of a contract: *British Nuclear Group Sellafield Ltd v Gemeinschaftskernkraftwerk Grohnde GmbH* [2007] EWHC 2245 (Ch) [313].

[123] [2004] 2 All ER 833 (CA) 844.

[124] *Raiffeisen Zentralbank Osterreich AG v The Royal Bank of Scotland Plc* [2011] 1 Lloyd's Rep 123 [81]–[82]; *Mabanga v Ophir Energy Plc* [2012] EWHC 1589 (QB) [26]–[27].

[125] *Pigott v Stratton* (1859) 1 De GF & J 33, 50; 45 ER 271, 277; *EA Grimstead v McGarrigan* [1999] EWCA (Civ) 3029, 21; *Leni Gas and Oil Investments Ltd v Malta Oil Pty Ltd* [2014] EWHC 893 (Comm) [7].

[126] *Jaffray v Society of Lloyd's* [2002] EWCA 1101 [52]–[54] (a deceit case); *Global Flood Defence Systems Ltd v Johann Van Den Noort Beheer BV* [2016] EWHC 99 (IPEC).

the document, viewing each statement contained in it in the light of the other statements to be found there.[127] It may be necessary to read two or more documents together.[128] The overall approach is consistent with the general principles of contractual interpretation.[129]

It is no defence that the representor did not intend to convey the meaning that his words **4.43** or actions objectively conveyed. If a person uses such careless language that his statements read literally are untrue, although this literal sense is different from what he intended, he makes a misrepresentation.[130] The fact that the representor did not consider that he was making a representation is irrelevant.[131]

(8) What are not representations

The rule that a misrepresentation must be a representation of a matter of existing fact[132] re- **4.44** quires analysis of the following categories of case: (i) sales talk or mere puff; (ii) statements of opinion or belief; and (iii) statements as to the future (including promises and statements of intention). These generally do not involve any representation of existing fact. However, each case must be assessed on its own particular facts, and it will be seen that in some circumstances a statement of the kind just mentioned may constitute or carry a representation of fact. In particular, these distinctions are of little relevance where there is fraud. A fraudulent statement provides a ground for rescission whether it is a statement of law, opinion, or intention, for such statements involve a misstatement of the representor's state of mind, and thereby a misrepresentation of fact.[133]

Sales talk or mere puff

A statement that is so obviously laudatory of the merits of a product or service, and hence **4.45** to be dismissed as 'mere puff' or 'sales talk', is not a statement of fact.[134] Such statements also tend not to give rise to misrepresentations because they are too vague and incapable of verification.[135] They may also be characterized as opinions that the representee should recognize as not being based on particular facts. As the examples which follow demonstrate, whether a statement is to be characterized as mere puff depends on the circumstances of the particular case, especially on the context in which the statement was made.

Representations that land is 'fertile and improvable'[136] or uncommonly rich water **4.46** meadow,[137] or that a property is a 'prestigious retail development'[138] have been held to be

---

[127] *Aaron's Reefs v Twiss* [1896] AC 273, 279, see also 280–81; *Cargill v Bower* (1878) 10 ChD 502, 516.

[128] *Gross v Lewis Hillman Ltd* [1970] Ch 445 (CA) 458–59; *Oelkers v Ellis* [1914] 2 KB 139, 147–48.

[129] *Investors Compensation Scheme Ltd v West Bromwich Building Society* [1998] 1 WLR 896 (HL); said to be applicable to misrepresentations in *MCI WorldCom International Inc v Primus Telecommunications Inc* [2004] 2 All ER 833 (CA) 844.

[130] *Hallows v Fernie* (1868) 3 Ch App 467, 476.

[131] *Spice Girls Ltd v Aprilia World Services BV* [2002] EWCA 15 [57].

[132] *Eaglesfield v The Marquis of Londonderry* (1876) 4 ChD 693 (CA) 709; *Smith v Chadwick* (1884) 9 App Cas 187 (CA); *British Airways Board v Taylor* [1976] 1 All ER 65 (HL) 68; para [4.17].

[133] Para [4.13].

[134] *Robeson v Waugh* (1874) 2 R 63, 66.

[135] *Trower v Newcome* (1813) 3 Mer 704, 705; 36 ER 270–71 (a statement was 'so vague and indefinite that the court could not take notice of it judicially').

[136] *Dimmock v Hallett* (1866) 2 Ch App 21 (CA) 27.

[137] *Scott v Hanson* (1829) 1 Russ & M 128, 39 ER 49.

[138] *Chartered Trust v Davies* [1997] 2 EGLR 83, 86.

88   II. GROUNDS

mere sales talk and not representations of fact. A husband's statement to a surety wife about the prospects of his business has been characterized as mere puff.[139] Statements made in negotiations such as 'You can trust me' and 'There are no secrets between us' did not constitute statements of fact.[140] By way of contrast, statements that premises are let to 'a most desirable tenant',[141] that a business is a 'gold mine',[142] and that a car is 'absolutely mint'[143] have been found to be representations.

4.47 Even if a laudatory statement is held to be a representation, proof of reliance may be a stumbling block. It has been observed that a statement may be made so preposterous in its nature that nobody could believe that anyone was misled.[144] Mere puffs are not statements that the representee is entitled to take seriously.[145]

Statement of opinion or belief

4.48 As a general rule, a statement of opinion is not a representation of fact.[146] An opinion must be expressed as such, or it must be clear from the circumstances that the statement is merely one of opinion. Indicia of statements of opinion include qualifications such as 'I believe' or 'so I am told'.[147] The very fact that there is room for disagreement by experts suggests that what is expressed is an opinion rather than a statement of fact.[148] A contention or argument has been held to be similar to an opinion and not actionable as a misrepresentation.[149]

4.49 Statements that have been characterized as opinions include: a statement that there is no possibility that a rival railway line would be built;[150] a statement that land has capacity for farming 2,000 sheep;[151] an estimate of the value of household contents given by an applicant for insurance;[152] a statement as to the nature of an insurance policy made to a loss adjuster who had a copy of the policy schedule;[153] a statement as to the risk of default on a financial obligation;[154] an estimate of how much it would cost to complete a development;[155] statements as to the future availability of tax relief or potential commercial success;[156] a

---

[139] 'His statement, express or implied, that he would be able to trade his way out of his financial difficulties may have been an expression of over optimism but cannot be, and has not been, suggested to be a misrepresentation': *Royal Bank of Scotland v Etridge (No 2)* [2002] 2 AC 773, 858.

[140] *WPP Group plc v Reichmann* [2000] All ER (D) 1409 [52]–[53].

[141] *Smith v Land and House Property Corp* (1884) 28 ChD 7 (CA).

[142] *Senanayake v Cheng* [1966] AC 63 (PC—Singapore).

[143] *Fordy v Harwood* [1999] EWCA 1134 (replica vintage car was described in an advertisement as 'Absolutely mint. All the right bits and does it go' when in fact it had mechanical defects).

[144] *Bloomenthal v Ford* [1897] AC 156, 162.

[145] *MCI WorldCom International Inc v Primus Telecommunications Inc* [2004] 2 All ER 833 (CA) 844; *Shaftsbury House (Developments) Limited v Lee* [2010] EWHC 1484 (Ch) [35].

[146] *Hubbard v Glover* (1812) 3 Camp 313, 314–15; 170 ER 1394–95; *Anderson v Pacific Fire and Marine* (1872) LR 7 CP 65, 69.

[147] *Fordy v Harwood* [1999] EWCA 1134 (oral statements to the effect that car had 'all the right bits and that it had been constructed to an extremely high standard' were an ordinary use of language which amounted to statements of fact).

[148] *Irish National Insurance Company Ltd v Oman Insurance Company Ltd* [1983] 2 Lloyd's Rep 453, 462.

[149] *Kyle Bay Limited (t/a Astons Nightclub) v Underwriters Subscribing Under Policy Number 019057/08/01* [2007] 1 CLC 164; *Bikam OOD v Adria Cable Sarl* [2013] EWHC 1985 (Comm) [136]–[137].

[150] *New Brunswick and Canada Railway and Land Co v Conybeare* (1862) 9 HLC 711 (HL) 730; 11 ER 907, 915.

[151] *Bisset v Wilkinson* [1927] AC 177 (PC—NZ) 183–84.

[152] *Economides v Commercial Union Assurance plc* [1998] QB 587 (CA).

[153] *Kyle Bay Limited (t/a Astons Nightclub) v Underwriters Subscribing Under Policy Number 019057/08/01* [2007] 1 CLC 164.

[154] *Cassa di Risparmio della Repubblica di San Marino SpA v Barclays Bank Ltd* [2011] 1 CLC 701 [267].

[155] *Royal Bank of Scotland Plc v Chandra* [2011] EWCA Civ 192.

[156] *Brown v InnovatorOne Plc* [2012] EWHC 1321 (Comm) [903].

statement of the likely outcome of ongoing litigation;[157] and a statement of belief as to the continuing business of a company.[158] Many of these opinions took the form of statements as to the future, an important sub-category of opinions which is discussed in more detail later in this chapter.[159]

Where statements of opinion do involve representations of fact
Implied representation that opinion actually held

Lord Evershed MR stated in *Brown v Raphael* that 'a statement of opinion is always to this extent a statement of fact, that it is an assertion that the vendor does in fact hold the opinion which he states'.[160] If the representor does not hold the opinion then the expression of that opinion is a misrepresentation of fact.[161] What is being misrepresented in such a case is the state of the representor's mind, not the matter to which the opinion relates. This distinction is easy to lose sight of. For example, the seller of a business who states 'the business will make a net profit of £2 million in the next financial year' makes no representation of fact that the business will make those profits; the statement is one as to the future. If after it is sold the business earns only £1 million, there is no misrepresentation by reason of the shortfall. However, the seller's statement is likely to contain a representation as to his state of mind; that it is his opinion and belief that £2 million will be earned. If the seller does not truly hold this opinion at the time when the representation is made, and prior to entry into the contract if the representation is ongoing, then he misrepresents his state of mind. The representation is not false because the business earned only £1 million. It is false (and fraudulent) because the vendor did not have the belief represented when the statement was made.

4.50

Bowen LJ summed up the relevant principles in *Angus v Clifford*:

4.51

> [An affirmation of belief] is not the less false because the affirmation he makes is an affirmation about the state of his own mind. A man may tell a lie about the state of his own mind, just as much as he can tell a lie about the state of the weather, or the state of his own digestion. It makes, to be sure, the inquiry a difficult and complicated one, and probably an obscure one, as to what the state of his mind may have been, but once arrive at the inference of fact that the state of his mind was to his own knowledge not that which he describes it as being, then he has told a lie, just as if he made an intentional misstatement of something outside his own mind, and visible to the eyes of all men.[162]

A misrepresentation that an opinion is actually held will inevitably be fraudulent, because the party making it will be aware that he is not conveying what he truly believes.

4.52

---

[157] *Barnsley v Noble* [2014] EWHC 2657 (Ch) [202], upheld on appeal [2017] Ch 191 (CA).

[158] *Ardmair Bay Holdings Ltd v Craig* [2019] CSOH 58; [2020] SLT 549.

[159] See paras [4.57]ff.

[160] [1958] Ch 636 (CA) 641; also *Anderson v Pacific Fire and Marine Insurance Co* (1872) LR 7 CP 65, 69.

[161] *Bisset v Wilkinson* [1927] AC 177 (PC—NZ) 184; *Economides v Commercial Union Assurance Co plc* [1998] QB 587 (CA) 598, 608.

[162] [1891] 2 Ch 449 (CA) 470. See also *Edgington v Fizmaurice* (1885) 29 ChD 459 (CA) 483 where Bowen LJ famously stated that 'the state of a man's mind is as much a fact as the state of his digestion'.

II. GROUNDS

Implied representation that reasonable grounds for opinion exist

4.53   There is no general rule that when a person expresses a belief, a representation is made that he has grounds which reasonably support that belief.[163] But where there is a significant disparity in the relative knowledge or means of obtaining knowledge, the person who gives his opinion may also be impliedly making a representation that he has reasonable grounds for holding that opinion.[164] The principle was explained by Bowen LJ in *Smith v Land & House Property Corp*:

> In a case where the facts are equally well known to both parties, what one of them says to the other is frequently nothing but an expression of opinion. The statement of such opinion is in a sense a statement of fact, about the man's own mind, but only of an irrelevant fact, for it is of no consequence what the opinion is. But if the facts are not equally known to both sides, then a statement of opinion by the one who knows the facts best involves very often a statement of a material fact, for he impliedly states that he knows facts which justify his opinion.[165]

In that case, a representation had been made by the seller's agents that a hotel is 'let to Mr Frederick Fleck (a most desirable tenant)'. Mr Fleck was actually far from being that. He had been substantially in arrears in payments of rent and paid 'by driblets under pressure'. The ground for rescission was made out.

4.54   The crucial factor is the imbalance in the knowledge or the access to knowledge that exists between the parties. In *Brown v Raphael* Lord Evershed MR further elucidated Bowen LJ's formulation of the principle:

> Observe that he is not saying that one party must know all the facts; it suffices for the application of the principle if it appears that between the two parties one is better equipped with information or the means of information than the other.[166]

4.55   An expression of opinion or belief also does not carry an implication that it is based on reasonable grounds where wider practical and policy considerations militate against imposing an obligation to investigate the grounds for such an opinion or belief.[167] In *Sykes v*

---

[163] *Brown v Raphael* [1958] Ch 636 (CA) 642 (Lord Evershed MR); *Sykes v Taylor-Rose* [2004] EWCA 299; *Barnsley v Noble* [2014] EWHC 2657 (Ch) [211], upheld on appeal [2017] Ch 191 (CA).

[164] *Maredelanto Compania Naviera SA v Bergbau-Handel GmbH (The Mihalis Angelos)* [1971] 1 QB 164 (CA) 194, 197, 204–05 (contractual representation that a ship is 'expected ready to load' on a particular date involved an implied representation that the belief was honestly held and that there were reasonable grounds for it); *Hummingbird Motors Ltd v Hobbs* [1986] RTR 276, 281 (express warranty that to the best of the representor's knowledge and belief the odometer reading was correct imported an implied assertion that he knew no facts suggesting that it might be incorrect); *BG plc v Nelson Group Services (Maintenance) Ltd* [2002] EWCA 547 [35], [36] where Kennedy LJ stated 'Sometimes an expression of opinion may carry with it no implication other than that the opinion is genuinely held. But on other occasions, as in this case, the circumstances may be such as to give rise to the implied representation that the person knew of facts which justified his opinion'; *Avrora Fine Arts Investment Ltd v Christie, Manson & Woods Ltd* [2012] PNLR 35 [134] (opinion as to authenticity of painting). Cf *IFE Fund SA v Goldman Sachs International* [2007] 1 Lloyd's Rep 264, 272–73.

[165] (1884) 28 ChD 7 (CA) 15.

[166] [1958] Ch 636 (CA) 642. *Esso Petroleum Ltd v Mardon* [1976] QB 801 (CA), 818, 820 (Esso's statement as to likely capacity of a filling station was a misrepresentation actionable in damages as 'Esso professed to have—and did in fact have—special knowledge or skill in estimating the throughput of a filling station'); *Barings plc v Coopers & Lybrand* [2002] 1 Lloyd's Rep PN 395, 405–06 (sufficient knowledge imbalance existed between finance director of company and its auditors); *Creative Technology Ltd and another v Huawei International Pte Ltd* [2017] SGHC 201.

[167] *Economides v Commercial Union Assurance plc* [1998] QB 587 (CA) 599 (opinion as to value of goods kept in a flat by a family given for insurance purposes).

Taylor-Rose the vendors of a house answered the following question in the negative 'Is there any other information which you think the buyer may have a right to know?'[168] In fact, the vendors had discovered that it had been the scene of a gruesome murder. The court found that this was an honest answer. It did not carry a misrepresentation that the statement was based on objectively reasonable grounds.

In short, expressing an honest opinion does not give rise to a misrepresentation even if there **4.56** are no reasonable grounds for the opinion, if there is no disparity in the parties' relative knowledge or means of obtaining information about the subject matter of the opinion, or if the party who expresses the opinion could not be expected to possess sufficient knowledge as to its correctness, or where there are wider practical or policy considerations that count against the implication of a further representation that there exist reasonable grounds for the opinion stated. But it has been suggested that if a reasonable man, with the representor's knowledge of the relevant facts, could not honestly hold the opinion expressed, then the expression of such an opinion is to be treated as a misrepresentation of fact.[169]

Statement as to the future
Generally not a statement of fact
A statement as to a future state of affairs cannot be true nor false at the time it is made, since **4.57** the future cannot be predicted.[170] As Lewison J stated in *FoodCo UK LLP (t/a Muffin Break) v Henry Boot Developments Ltd*:

> Outside the realms of mythology and literature, no one can foretell the future. Even in those realms the prophecies of the Oracle of Delphi were always ambiguous, Cassandra was never believed, and the prophecies of the witches in Macbeth were downright obscure. The law has thus been wary of imposing liability for statements about the future.[171]

A statement as to the future is usually an opinion as to what will occur at a future time.[172] If made honestly, a statement as to what will happen in the future cannot be a misrepresentation,[173] unless it can be characterized as an opinion or belief which lacks reasonable grounds.[174] When the stated expectation does not eventuate, or the intention or promise is not carried out, the statement does not retrospectively become a misrepresentation.[175]

A statement of intention is a statement as to what the representor hopes or plans to do **4.58** or not do in the future. It is a representation of existing fact only insofar as it represents the speaker's state of mind, and is not actionable as a misrepresentation unless the person

---

[168] *Sykes v Taylor-Rose* [2004] EWCA 299. See also *Charles Lloyd Property Group Pty Ltd v Buchanan* [2013] VSC 148. Cf *Wang v Shao* [2018] BCSC 377 where a fraudulent misrepresentation was made as to the reasons for the sale of a house.

[169] *Economides v Commercial Union Assurance Co plc* [1998] QB 587 (CA) 598, 608. Cf *Sykes v Taylor-Rose* [2004] EWCA 299.

[170] *Bank Leumi le Israel BM v British National Insurance Co Ltd* [1988] 1 Lloyd's Rep 71.

[171] [2010] EWHC 358 (Ch) [193].

[172] *Barnsley v Noble* [2014] EWHC 2657 (Ch) [202], upheld on appeal [2017] Ch 191 (CA).

[173] *Beattie v Lord Ebury* (1872) 7 Ch App 777, 804; aff'd (1874) LR 7 HL 102 (HL). Contrast the position under ss 4 and 18 of the Australian Consumer Law which replaced ss 51A and 52 of the Australian Trade Practices Act 1974 (Cth).

[174] *Foster v Action Aviation Limited* [2013] EWHC 2439 (Comm) [97]. See [4.53]–[4.56].

[175] *Benham v United Guarantee and Life Assurance Co* (1853) 7 Exch 744, 155 ER 1149; *Hagen v ICI Chemicals & Polymers Ltd* (2002) IRLR 31 [131].

92   II. GROUNDS

making it does not honestly hold the intention he is expressing; or there is a representation that reasonable grounds exist for the intention expressed, when there are none;[176] or the representor knows that there is no ability to put into effect the intention which is represented.[177] A statement of a company's policy on a particular matter may be no more than a representation of its intention at the time of the statement, and when that policy and hence its intention changes, the earlier honestly made statement will not become a misrepresentation.[178] In contrast, a statement as to a third party's intentions is usually a statement of fact,[179] as is an agent's statement as to its principal's state of mind.[180]

4.59   A promise is a statement of what the representor undertakes to do or not do in the future. It is not a statement of fact.[181] A representation as to future conduct has no effect unless it constitutes a contractual promise.[182]

Implied representation that intention or promise honestly held or made

4.60   A statement of intention or a promise carries with it an implied representation as to the *present* state of mind of the representor.[183] As has been noted already, a representation as to a person's present state of mind is a representation of fact.[184] In *Edgington v Fitzmaurice*[185] a statement in a prospectus that the funds raised from the issue of shares would be used in the future to improve property and develop the company's business—a clear statement of intention—was held to be a false representation of fact. Similarly, a statement that an insurance syndicate would, as a matter of principle, not normally insure certain risks without a minimum level of deductible was a statement which gave rise to a representation of existing fact (namely, that the intention was presently held), and so was not only a mere statement of opinion, belief, or expectation.[186]

4.61   If the statement made asserts an intention that is not honestly held, or is a promise which is dishonestly made because the promisor falsely asserts that he intends to perform it, a fraudulent misrepresentation of fact is made.[187] So if a person who orders goods makes a knowingly false statement that he will pay for them, or will only resell them in a particular market, he makes a fraudulent misrepresentation of fact.[188] Similarly, accepting

---

[176]   *Wales v Wadham* [1977] 1 WLR 199, 211.

[177]   *C21 London Estates Ltd v Maurice Macneill Iona Ltd* [2017] EWHC 998 (Ch) [44]; *Inter Export LLC v Townley* [2018] EWCA Civ 2068 [34].

[178]   *Kleinwort Benson Ltd v Malaysia Mining Corp Berhad* [1989] 1 WLR 379—a letter which stated 'it is our policy to ensure that the business of [our subsidiary] is at all times in a position to meet its liabilities to you under the above arrangements' was found to have been a true representation of fact as to the representor's intention at the time it was made (as opposed to a promise as to its continuation).

[179]   *Viscount Clermount v Tasburgh* (1819) 1 Jac & W 112, 37 ER 318.

[180]   *Limit No 2 Ltd v Axa Versicherung AG* [2008] 2 CLC 673 (CA).

[181]   *Waterview Property Limited v Gardner* [2016] NZHC 2247 [61].

[182]   *Tudor Grange Holdings Ltd v Citibank* [1992] Ch 53, 67–68 (Browne-Wilkinson V-C).

[183]   As to implied representations see paras [4.32]ff; *BSkyB Limited, Sky Subscribers Services Limited v HP Enterprise Services UK Limited, Electronic Data systems LLC* [2010] EWHC 86 (TCC) [311]; *Waterview Property Limited v Gardner* [2016] NZHC 2247 [61].

[184]   Para [4.50].

[185]   (1885) 29 ChD 459 (CA) (claim for damages for deceit, not rescission).

[186]   *Limit No 2 Ltd v Axa Versicherung AG* [2008] 2 CLC 673 (CA) [17].

[187]   *Kettlewell v Refuge Assurance Co Ltd* [1908] 1 KB 545 (CA) (a statement that certain benefits would continue under an insurance contract without the need to pay a further premium); *British Airways Board v Taylor* [1976] 1 All ER 65 (HL) (a statement regarding a booking on a flight); also, para [4.36].

[188]   *Re Shackleton* (1875) 10 Ch App 446; *Ray v Sempers* [1974] AC 370 (fraudulent promises to pay; criminal prosecution); *Smith Kline & French Laboratories Ltd v Long* [1989] 1 WLR 1 (CA) (fraudulent misrepresentation as

prepayments for goods without intending to deliver them involves a fraudulent promise or representation of intention.[189]

(9) Materiality of the representation

Although the point is not free from doubt, it is suggested that with one exception,[190] a non- **4.62** fraudulent misrepresentation must be material if it is to confer a right to rescind,[191] and proof of materiality gives rise to a rebuttable presumption of reliance.[192]

Meaning of 'material'

A representation is material if it would influence the judgement of a reasonable person in **4.63** determining whether he will enter into the transaction. This definition, which is based on wording formerly in the Marine Insurance Act 1906,[193] is consistent with a number of judicial formulations of the concept.[194] The test is objective: it is concerned with the impact of the representation on a reasonable person, not with its impact on the particular claimant.[195] Taking a different point of view, a misrepresentation is immaterial if a reasonable person would consider it irrelevant in making his decision to enter into the transaction. A representation which also takes the form of a contractual warranty is always material.[196]

Effect of materiality: shifts onus of proving reliance

The materiality or otherwise of a representation determines who bears the onus of proving **4.64** or disproving that the representee relied on it.[197] If the statement was material, reliance is

---

to intention to resell medicine in Africa; deceit case); *Inter Export LLC v Townley* [2018] EWCA Civ 2068 (director misrepresented her company's ability to pay for cargo).

[189] *Re Gerald Cooper Chemicals Ltd* [1978] Ch 262 (issue was whether creditors defrauded; not a rescission case).
[190] Para [4.72]ff.
[191] *McDowall v Fraser* (1779) 1 Doug KB 260, 261; 99 ER 170 (Lord Mansfield); *Mathias v Yetts* (1882) 46 LT 497 (CA) 502 (Lord Jessel MR).
[192] Para [4.64].
[193] Marine Insurance Act 1906, ss 18(2) and 20(2) provided that 'material' circumstances and representations are those 'which would influence the judgment of a prudent insurer in fixing the premium, determining whether he will take the risk'. These provisions were omitted by s 21(2) of the Insurance Act 2015, with s 21(3) abolishing any rule of law to the effect of those provisions. However, by s 7(3) of the Insurance Act 2015, a circumstance is material if it would influence the judgement of a prudent insurer in determining whether to take the risk and, if so, on what terms. See also, Chap 5, paras [5.25], [5.28], [5.36], [5.37]; E Peel, *Treitel The Law of Contract* (15th edn, 2020) [9-023].
[194] A material misrepresentation 'is of such a nature as would induce a person to enter into the contract, or would tend to induce him to do so, or that it would be part of the inducement, to enter into the contract': *Smith v Chadwick* (1882) 20 ChD 27 (CA) 44 (Jessel MR) on appeal (1884) 9 App Cas 187 (HL) 196 (Lord Blackburn); *Mathias v Yetts* (1882) 46 LT 497 (CA) 502 (Lord Jessel MR). A material misrepresentation 'must be of such a nature as to be capable of inducing the representee to enter into the contract in question': *Lonrho plc v Fayed (No 2)* [1992] 1 WLR 1, 6 (Millett J). '[A] representation is material when its tendency, or its natural and probable result is to induce the representee to act on the faith of it in the kind of way in which he is proved to have in fact acted': *Downs v Chappell* [1996] 3 All ER 344 (CA) 351 (Hobhouse LJ). See also *Bate v Aviva Insurance UK Limited* [2014] EWCA Civ 334.
[195] *Downs v Chappell* [1996] 3 All ER 344 (CA) 351 (Hobhouse LJ).
[196] *Pawson v Watson* (1778) 2 Cowp 785, 788–90; 98 ER 1361, 1362–63; *Anderson v Fitzgerald* (1853) 4 HLC 484, 10 ER 551; *London Assurance v Mansel* (1879) 11 ChD 363; *Hambrough v Mutual Life Insurance Co of New York* (1895) 72 LT 140 (CA); *Paxman v Union Assurance Society* (1923) 39 TLR 424, 426.
[197] See paras [4.100]ff.

94   II. GROUNDS

rebuttably presumed.[198] The party against whom rescission is sought bears the onus of rebutting that presumption by proving that the representee did not in fact rely on the representation. Thus irrespective of whether it is a condition for obtaining relief, materiality assists the party seeking to rescind to prove reliance.

Materiality as a requirement for rescission

4.65   Materiality is not a necessary condition for relief in every case.[199] It need not be shown in cases of fraudulent misrepresentation. It is also not necessary in cases of non-fraudulent misrepresentation where the representor knew or ought to have known that the representee would rely on the immaterial representation. But it seems to be necessary in all other cases of non-fraudulent misrepresentation. These propositions will be considered in turn.

Fraudulent misrepresentation: materiality not required

4.66   A fraudulent misrepresentation confers a right to rescind even if the representation is not material.[200] A fraudulent misrepresentation gives rise to a particularly strong rebuttable presumption of inducement because there is a most powerful inference that the fraudulent party achieved his objective and that his fraud was actively in the mind of the recipient when the contract was made.[201] The position is not entirely clear, but it seems that it is not necessary to show the fraudulent misrepresentation is material for the presumption to arise.[202]

Non-fraudulent misrepresentation: materiality generally required

4.67   Materiality is generally necessary for rescission for innocent misrepresentation.[203]

4.68   As a matter of policy the better view is that a contract should not be capable of being set aside for a misrepresentation that was not material if (i) it was not fraudulent, and (ii) the representor could not have been expected to be aware that the representee would rely on it. In these circumstances the absence of materiality ought to be fatal to a rescission claim. An example of such a misrepresentation would be an innocently made false statement that what seems to be a fungible item was manufactured in a particular region in a case where the representee, unknown to the representor, collects items from that region and for that reason attaches special value to it.

4.69   Rescission for innocent misrepresentation allocates the risk that a statement of fact is false to one of two innocent parties. An objective of deterrence, which plays a role in relation to

---

[198] The 'presumption' is not a presumption of law but an inference of fact: *Zurich Insurance v Hayward* [2017] AC 142 (Sup Ct) [34]; *Van Eiprodukten v Rembrandt Enterprises* [2020] QB 551 (CA) [43].

[199] A Burrows, *A Restatement of the English Law of Contract* (2016) 192 takes the position that in general materiality is not a separate requirement.

[200] *Smith v Kay* (1859) 7 HLC 750 (HL), 11 ER 299; *Pan Atlantic Insurance Co Ltd v Pine Top Insurance Co Ltd* [1995] 1 AC 501, 533; *Barton v County NatWest Ltd* [1999] All ER (D) 782; on appeal [2002] 4 All ER 494n (CA). In Australia, *Nicholas v Thompson* [1924] VLR 554, 565, 575–77. Cf *Attwood v Small* (1838) 6 Cl & Fin 232, 502; 7 ER 684, 785; *Smith v Chadwick* (1884) 9 App Cas 187 (HL) (a deceit case).

[201] *Ross River Ltd v Waveley Commercial Ltd* [2008] 1 All ER 1004 [241]; *Bleasdale v Forster* [2011] EWHC 596 (Ch) [27]; *Zurich Insurance v Hayward* [2017] AC 142 (Sup Ct) [34]; *BV Nederlandse Industrie Van Eiprodukten v Rembrandt Enterprises* [2020] QB 551 (CA) [43]. The presumption was rebutted on evidence given in cross-examination in *Yukos Hydrocarbons Investments Ltd v Georgiades* [2020] EWHC 173 (Comm).

[202] *BV Nederlandse Industrie Van Eiprodukten v Rembrandt Enterprises* [2020] QB 551 (CA) [25], [43].

[203] *Smith v Chadwick* (1884) 9 App Cas 187 (HL) 190; *Lonrho plc v Fayed (No 2)* [1992] 1 WLR 1, 6 961, 966 (Millett J); *Pan Atlantic Insurance Co Ltd v Pine Top Insurance Co Ltd* [1995] 1 AC 501; E Peel, *Treitel The Law of Contract* (15th edn, 2020) [9-023].

fraud, does not seem to be relevant in the context of innocent misrepresentation. The argument for allowing rescission for *immaterial* non-fraudulent misrepresentation has been said to be the moral imperative that contracting parties should not benefit in any way from false statements they had made, or enforce contracts which are founded on such false statements.[204] This analysis suggests that materiality ought not to be required, but depends for its force upon an acceptance of a particular and contestable moral conclusion. A different reason for excluding materiality as a threshold requirement is that the test of materiality is inherently vague. The argument is that it is so difficult to draw a line between material and immaterial representations that it ought not to form a boundary of liability. Any adverse consequences of over-including misrepresentations could be mitigated by other means, such as the discretion to declare the contract subsisting and award damages in lieu conferred by section 2(2) of the Misrepresentation Act 1967.

An argument in favour of a requirement of materiality is that representors have reasonable **4.70** expectations that some statements are likely to be relied on, and so ought properly to be verified before they are made, and which statements are not of that kind. That distinction appears to underpin the rules relating to 'mere puffery', where an untrue statement characterized as mere sales talk will not provide a basis for rescission, notwithstanding the moral imperative to tell the truth.[205] That imperative also does not stand in the way of the rule that falsity must be substantial before a misstatement will confer a right to rescind.[206] The law does not categorically uphold the moral ideal that contracting parties must not mislead.

In favour of a requirement of materiality is that in practice it requires that a representee who **4.71** wishes to rely upon the truth of statements about apparently immaterial matters to convey that reliance by seeking and obtaining a contractual warranty about the matter, rather than placing reliance on remarks that may be made unadvisedly by a party unaware of their significance. A compelling argument can be made that in such a case the representee should seek a warranty if he or she is to be afforded the protection of the law. By insisting upon a warranty the representee will put the representor on notice that what a hypothetical reasonable person would not rely on is sought to be relied on by this particular party. Of course that would allow the representor to consider whether he will assume the risk of the fact not being true, and whether he ought to charge a higher price for the assumption of that risk.[207] On this analysis, which we would favour, if the representee attaches special value or importance to some stated matter or thing that a reasonable person in his position would not be expected to, and he transacts without providing any additional consideration in exchange for receiving that matter or thing or for an assurance that it exists, then it is just that he ought to be taken as accepting the risk that the matter or thing will not be received or will not exist.

Non-fraudulent misrepresentation: the special case where materiality not required
There is a special case where materiality ought not to be required in cases of non-fraudulent **4.72** misrepresentation. If the statement was not material—that is, if it would not influence the

---

[204] *Redgrave v Hurd* (1881) 20 ChD 1 (CA) 12–13 (Jessel MR). This argument does not, however, explain why the potentially far-reaching consequences of rescission should be visited upon the misrepresenting party.
[205] See para [4.45].
[206] See para [4.83].
[207] *EA Grimstead & Son Ltd v McGarrigan* [1999] EWCA (Civ) 3029, 34 (discussion of these policy factors in the context of exclusion clauses).

96 II. GROUNDS

judgement of a reasonable person—but the representor knew or ought to have known that the representee was likely to rely on the representation, then the claimant should be entitled to rescission.

4.73 This view is supported by scholars and has received some judicial support.[208] Policy considerations also support this view. A representor who knows that the representee will place reliance on what he states ought not to escape liability for his false statements merely because an ordinary person would not have relied on them. He has the opportunity to verify the statements or to charge a higher price for assuming the risk that they are false.

D. Representation must be Made by the Representor to the Representee

(1) Those by whom the representation may be made

4.74 To provide a ground for rescission the representation must have been made to the rescinding party by the counterparty to the transaction, by the counterparty's agent,[209] or by a third party with the knowledge of the counterparty.[210] A misrepresentation by an unconnected third party will not render a transaction voidable if the party against whom rescission is sought was unaware of it.[211]

4.75 It has been suggested that where a person requests the purported representor to verify propositions which the person had himself formulated, and the representor does so, that would amount to the giving of warranties, not the making of representations.[212] However, it is difficult to discern the rationale for this analysis.[213] Whether the adoption of such formulations constitutes a representation or a warranty must depend on the character and terms of the verification or confirmation. If the purported representor promises or warrants that the propositions are true, it will be a contractual warranty (unless that conclusion is inconsistent with other contractual terms). If the purported representor states, adopts, represents, or repeats the relevant propositions, they would amount to a statement of fact, and therefore a representation.

---

[208] HG Beale (ed), *Chitty on Contracts* (34th edn, 2021) quoted (in relation to a statement appearing in an earlier edition) with apparent approval in *Goff v Gauthier* (1991) 62 P & CR 388.

[209] *Awaroa Holdings Ltd v Commercial Securities and Finance Ltd* [1976] 1 NZLR 19, 30 (representation imputed to principal where the principal causes or authorizes the agent to make the representation); *Vald Nielsen Holding A/S and another v Baldorino and others* [2019] EWHC 1926 (Comm) [381]–[386] (email responses were found to have been agreed by the defendants); cf *Marme Inversiones 2007 SL v Natwest Markets Plc* [2019] EWHC 366 (Comm) [436]–[447] (when negotiating finance documentation, an arranger bank did not have apparent authority to make representations on behalf of the proposed syndicate banks, particularly on matters that the syndicate banks would not have knowledge of).

[210] *Erlson Precision Holdings Ltd v Hampson Industries plc* [2011] EWHC 1137 (Comm) [42]; *Georgallides v The Secretary of State for Business, Energy and Industrial Strategy* [2021] 1 BCLC 177 [167].

[211] See Chap 9. For the special rules relating to gifts, see Chap 29.

[212] *Parallel Media LLC v Chamberlain* [2014] EWHC 214 (QB) [48].

[213] It is also contrary to commercial practice whereby extensive schedules of 'warranties' are often prepared by purchaser's solicitors and the sellers are asked to both 'represent and warrant' that they are true. The propositions thereby constitute representations despite having been prepared by the purchaser's solicitors.

(2) Those to whom the representation must be made

The representation must have been made to the party who was misled, or his agent. This **4.76** encompasses representations made (i) directly to the representee; (ii) to a person whom the representor contemplated would receive the representation through a third person; or (iii) to a member of a class or the public generally who acted upon a representation addressed to that class or the public at large.[214] The representation can also be made to a machine acting on the misled party's behalf.[215]

The first fact pattern is self-explanatory. In the usual case there will have been a direct ex- **4.77** press statement by one contracting party to the other, or to his agent. However, *Cramaso LLP v Ogilvie-Grant*[216] provides an interesting extension of that notion. A misrepresentation was made to a person at the beginning of negotiations, and that person later became a member of a newly incorporated entity which entered into the agreement resulting from the negotiations. The Supreme Court held that in continuing and concluding the contractual negotiations with the corporate entity, through the natural person as its agent, without withdrawing the representation made earlier to the natural person, the representor had implicitly asserted the accuracy of that representation also to the corporate entity. The general principle is that 'where the representation is made to ... the agent prior to the commencement of his agency ... depending of course on the facts, the representor can equally be taken to be, by his conduct, implicitly repeating the representation previously made, and can therefore owe a duty in respect of the accuracy of the representation towards the agent's principal'.[217]

The second type of case arises where a representation is made by the representor to a third **4.78** party who communicates it to the claimant, in circumstances where the representor intended the statement to reach the claimant,[218] or knew that the claimant was relying on the misrepresentation when entering into the contract.[219] The latter context is consistent with the general rule discussed earlier in this chapter, that a misrepresentation made by a third party will vitiate a transaction if the defendant was aware that the claimant was relying on it. This principle could also provide an alternative basis for the decision in *Cramaso LLP v Ogilvie-Grant*.[220]

---

[214] *Swift v Winterbotham* (1873) LR 8 QB 244, 253 per Lord Cockburn CJ; on appeal sub nom *Swift v Jewsbury* (1874) LR 9 QB 301; *Richardson v Silvester* (1873) LR 9 QB 34, 36; *Commercial Banking Co of Sydney v RH Brown and Co* [1972] 2 Lloyd's Rep 360 (HCA); *Brown v InnovatorOne Plc* [2012] EWHC 1321 (Comm) [885]–[886]. These cases involved claims for damages rather than rescission, but the general principles for determining who is a representee ought to be the same in a rescission case. However, it has been suggested that in the case of tort they are less strictly applied as the representee also needs to establish a duty of care: HG Beale (ed), *Chitty on Contracts* (34th edn, 2021) [9-038].

[215] *Renault UK Ltd v FleetPro Technical Services Ltd* [2008] Bus LR D17 [122] (orders entered into a computer system).

[216] [2014] AC 1093; 2 WLR 317 (SC) [25], [30], [56].

[217] [2014] 2 WLR 317 (SC) [28].

[218] *McInerny v Lloyd's Bank Ltd* [1974] 1 Lloyd's Rep 246 (CA) 253 (Lord Denning MR) (a negligence case).

[219] This situation has arisen in a number of deceit cases: *Pilmore v Hood* (1838) 5 Bing NC 97, 132 ER 1042 (misrepresentation passed on by one prospective purchaser to another with the vendor's knowledge) distinguished in *Gross v Lewis Hillman Ltd* [1970] Ch 445 (CA) 461; *Clef Aquitaine SARL v Laporte Materials (Barrow) Ltd* [2001] QB 488 (CA) 502–03 (misrepresentation passed on by purchaser to his assignee).

[220] [2014] AC 1093; 2 WLR 317 (SC) but see [50]–[51].

98   II. GROUNDS

4.79   The third type of case (representations to a class of persons) is well illustrated by *Robinson v Wall*.[221] An interest in an estate was represented as being offered at auction without a reserve price. This was found to be a representation to the members of the public who chose to bid that there would be no minimum price. In fact there was a secret agreement between the vendors and a prospective purchaser whereby bids would be placed up to a certain pre-determined amount. The highest bidder discovered this after the property had been knocked down to him. He succeeded in defending an action for specific performance of the sale contract and recovered his deposit. In effect, the sale contract was voidable due to a misrepresentation made to the public at large, or perhaps to a class of which the complainant was a member.

4.80   In *Re National Patent Steam Fuel Co, ex p Worth*[222] a misled claimant fell outside of the class to whom a representation was made and consequently was denied relief. The claimant sought to avoid being placed on a list of contributories to a company on the basis that she had been misled into thinking that she was purchasing preference shares from a shareholder of the company when in fact the company had no power to issue such shares. It was held that a representation as to the power of the company to issue preference shares had only been made to those who took shares directly from the company. Consequently, the claimant who bought the shares from an existing shareholder was outside of that class and her contract with the company was not voidable.[223] A similar argument failed in *Taberna Europe CDO II Plc v Selskabet*.[224] The defendant bank issued subordinated loan notes. The claimant purchased such notes on the secondary market, rather than directly from the issuer. The defendant issuer had made a misrepresentation about its non-performing loans in an investor presentation originally directed to the attendees of investor roadshows who would purchase the new issue of securities. However, as the investor presentation had been put on the issuer's website, and the issuer had actively encouraged potential investors to view it there, the information it contained about non-performing loans was treated as having been directed to the claimant.

E.   Representation must be False

4.81   To be a misrepresentation, a representation must be false at the time of entry into the transaction. Falsity is assessed by comparing what was represented with the true facts. There is no misrepresentation if the statement is substantially true. But it is no defence to assert that the representation would be true if something were added to it.[225]

---

[221]   (1847) 2 Ph 372, 374–75; 41 ER 986, 988; *Richardson v Silvester* (1873) LR 9 QB 34 (false advertisement in newspaper gave rise to a cause of action in deceit).

[222]   (1859) 4 Drew 529, 62 ER 203; *Peek v Gurney* (1873) LR 6 HL 37 7 (fraudulent misrepresentation in a prospectus was not a representation made to a purchaser of shares in the market); *Collins v Associated Greyhound Racecourses Ltd* [1930] 1 Ch 1 (CA) (innocent misrepresentation in prospectus did not entitle undisclosed principal to rescind).

[223]   Cf *Possfund Ltd v Diamond* [1996] 1 WLR 1351, 1363 (negligence action by aftermarket purchaser of shares based on misrepresentations in prospectus not struck out because commercial practice in relation to prospectuses was found to have changed). For other examples of the special care that should be taken in considering the applicability of nineteenth century cases concerning voidable share allotments, see also Chap 23, Chap 24, and Chap 27.

[224]   [2017] QB 633 (CA).

[225]   Pollock CB observed that 'when a person is asked how old he is, and he states, in answer, a number of years less than his true age. It is trifling to say that that is a true answer which requires something to be added to it to make it true': *Cazenove v British Equitable Assurance Co* (1859) 6 CB NS 437, 144 ER 527.

Where answers are given to a questionnaire that is ambiguous, so that two meanings might reasonably be given to a particular question, it has been held that an answer correctly addressing either of those meanings would be true.[226] **4.82**

(1) Substantial correctness sufficient

No ground for rescission arises where the difference between what was represented and what was true would be considered not substantial or *de minimis* in the eyes of a reasonable person in the position of the representee.[227] If the representation is substantially correct, it is not a misrepresentation. In *With v O'Flanagan* Lord Wright MR stated that a representation, which does not constitute a term of the contract, is 'not like a warranty; it is not necessary [that] it should be strictly construed or strictly complied with; it is enough if it is substantially true; it is enough if it is substantially complied with.'[228] **4.83**

The common law test of substantial correctness, in the context of misrepresentation generally, has been held to be equivalent to that formerly set out in section 20(4) of the Marine Insurance Act 1906.[229] In *Avon Insurance v Swire* Rix J formulated the common law test as follows: **4.84**

> ...a representation may be true without being entirely correct, provided it is substantially correct and the difference between what is represented and what is actually correct would not have been likely to induce a reasonable person in the position of the claimants to enter into the contracts.[230]

Rix J eschewed the term 'material' in this context. This usefully avoids confusing the issue with the different and distinct question of materiality discussed earlier.[231] Materiality in that sense is concerned with the effect of the representation itself, not with calibrating the difference between what was true and what was false, in order to determine whether there has been a *mis*representation. Thus a statement by a seller that a car had travelled 101,865 miles **4.85**

---

[226] *Cheltenham Borough Council v Christine Susan Laird* [2009] EWHC 1253 (QB) [274].
[227] *McKeown v Boudard-Peveril Gear Co* (1896) 65 LJ Ch 735 (CA) 736–37 (trivial inaccuracies in prospectus did not make it false); *Seddon v North Eastern Salt Co Ltd* [1905] 1 Ch 326, 335 'representation was not untrue or substantially inaccurate'; *Allen v Universal Automobile Insurance Co Ltd* (1933) 45 Lloyd's LR 55, 58 (Lord Wright) (a representation that a car cost £285, when the truth was that it cost £271, just over 5 per cent less, was held to be substantial in the circumstances); *Toomey v Eagle Star Insurance Co Ltd (No 2)* [1995] 2 Lloyd's Rep 88 (whether a representation which was false only as regards 5 per cent of the subject matter was *de minimis* or material was a matter to be tried).
[228] [1936] Ch 575, 581. In *Pawson v Watson* (1778) 2 Cowp 785, 788–90; 98 ER 1361, 1362–63 (an insurance case) Lord Mansfield CJ drew a distinction between a misrepresentation in relation to which substantial falsity must be established and a warranty where a slight deviation constitutes a breach.
[229] Section 20(4) provided that 'A representation as to a matter of fact is true, if it be substantially correct, that is to say, if the difference between what is represented and what is actually correct would not be considered material by a prudent insurer'. Cf s 33(3) which requires a warranty to be 'exactly complied with'. Section 21(2) of the Insurance Act 2015 has now removed s 20 from the Marine Insurance Act 1906. However s 3(3)(c) of the Insurance Act 2015 provides that 'A fair presentation of the risk is one... in which every material representation as to a matter of fact is substantially correct' and s 7(5) goes on to state that 'A material representation is substantially correct if a prudent insurer would not consider the difference between what is represented and what is actually correct to be material'.
[230] [2000] 1 All ER 573 [17]; *Hagen v ICI Chemicals and Polymers Ltd* [2002] IRLR 31; *BSkyB Limited, Sky Subscribers Services Limited v HP Enterprise Services UK Limited, Electronic Data systems LLC* [2010] EWHC 86 (TCC) [313]; *Marme Inversiones 2007 SL v Natwest Markets Plc* [2019] EWHC 366 (Comm) [215].
[231] See paras [4.62]ff.

is material in the sense discussed earlier because it would influence a reasonable purchaser's decision to enter into the contract. If the car has actually travelled 102,307 miles the statement would be, strictly speaking, false. But applying the test of substantial correctness, a difference of less than 500 miles in the context of over 100,000 miles (less than 0.5%), would not have been likely to induce a reasonable person to enter, or to decline to enter, into the contract. Thus the test of falsity would not be satisfied. The representation is not a misrepresentation permitting rescission.

4.86 The requirement of a lack of 'substantial correctness' just discussed may appear to render the concept of 'materiality' redundant as a condition of liability. If the difference between what was represented and the true position would have been likely to induce a reasonable person to enter into the transaction, then the representation as a whole must have been likely to so induce a reasonable person, and thus must have been material. A representation that is not substantially correct will, therefore, always be material.

4.87 However, the two tests were treated as distinct in Sir Mackenzie Chalmers' Marine Insurance Act 1906, which codified a highly developed area of the common law relating to marine insurance, and which had been influential in shaping the principles of misrepresentation generally, and are still treated separately in the Insurance Act 2015.[232] Furthermore, as we have seen, the concept of materiality of the representation as a whole plays an important function in regulating the onus of proving reliance.[233] The requirement of a lack of substantial correctness and of materiality should be regarded as distinct and cumulative requirements in establishing a claim to rescind for innocent misrepresentation.

(2) Representation must be false at the time of reliance

4.88 The falsity of a representation is to be judged at the time when the representee altered his position in reliance on the representation, that is, the time of entry into the transaction.[234] Hence, if a representation is false when it was made but became true by the time of the contract, it provides no grounds for rescission.[235]

4.89 Similarly, if a representation is false when made but the representor informs the representee of the true facts before the transaction is entered into, then no ground for rescission will arise. In such circumstances it may be said that there was no longer any or any material representation, or it may be said that there was no inducement.[236]

---

[232] Section 20(2) of the Marine Insurance Act 1906 set out the test of materiality and s 20(4) set out the test of substantial correctness. Section 20 has now been omitted from the Act as part of the reforms brought in by the Insurance Act 2015. However, the test of materiality is now set out in s 7(3) of the Insurance Act 2015 and the test of substantial correctness in s 7(5).

[233] Paras [4.62]ff and paras [4.100]ff.

[234] *Briess v Woolley* [1954] AC 333, 353–54. This was a case concerning the tort of deceit rather than rescission but the same principle ought to apply.

[235] *Ship v Crosskill* (1870) LR 10 Eq 73, 86 (statement in a prospectus that more than half of a company's shares had been applied for was false when made but not when acted on by the claimant; not fraudulent misrepresentation); *Briess v Woolley* [1954] AC 333, 353–54 (deceit case).

[236] *Assicurazioni Generali v Arab Insurance Group* [2003] 1 All ER 140 (CA) [63].

(3) Continuing representations and changes of circumstances

In certain circumstances a representation will be treated as continuing.[237] When that occurs the representor is deemed to be repeating his representation at every successive moment during the interval between when it was made and when it was acted on, unless he withdraws or modifies it by timely notice to the representee in the meantime.[238] If a continuing representation is true when made but subsequently becomes false, then unless the representor informs the representee of the true facts before the contract is formed, a misrepresentation will have been made.[239] But a continuing representation may become spent after a certain period of time,[240] or cease to operate because it is forgotten,[241] or because there has been a material change of circumstances which makes the representation irrelevant.[242] Continuing representations of fact and intention will be discussed separately.

4.90

Whether a representation is continuing depends upon the importance of its subject matter to the transaction in question, the nature of the representation, and its context. If what is represented is peculiarly prone to change in the usual course of things, it is less likely that the representation is a continuing one at all, or one that can be expected to continue for a significant period of time.[243] A representation will not be construed as a continuing one where placing the risk of subsequent changes on the representor would impose an unreasonable burden on him, because it would require the representor to keep records of what was said, to keep track of relevant underlying facts and to monitor the situation to which the representation related; and that is particularly so where the representor would not receive a proportionate benefit for bearing such a burden.[244]

4.91

In *Cramaso LLP v Ogilvie-Grant*[245] the Supreme Court found that a change in the identity of the prospective contracting party had not affected the continuing nature of a representation.

4.92

---

[237] *With v O'Flanagan* [1936] Ch 575 (CA) 584 (Lord Wright MR); *Smith v Kay* (1859) 7 HLC 750, 769; 11 ER 299, 307; *Meluish v Milton* (1876) 3 ChD 27 (CA) 35 ('every day while they were living together [the bigamist wife] must be taken as continuously representing to [the husband] that she was his lawful wife'); *Ray v Sempers* [1974] AC 370 (criminal prosecution); *Jones v Dumbrell* [1981] VR 199, 203; *Cramaso LLP v Ogilvie-Grant* [2014] AC 1093; 2 WLR 317 (SC) [16]–[24], [57]; *Inter Export LLC v Townley* [2018] EWCA Civ 2068 [30]–[31].
[238] *Halsbury's Laws of England* (2003 reissue) vol 31 [754], cited with approval by Lord Tucker in *Briess v Woolley* [1954] AC 333, 354; *Lindsay v O'Loughnane* [2012] BCC 153 [90], [121] (a deceit case).
[239] *Traill v Baring* (1864) 4 De GJ & S 318, 326, 329; 46 ER 941, 945–46; *Davies v London and Provincial Marine Insurance Co* (1878) 8 ChD 469, 475; *With v O'Flanagan* [1936] Ch 575 (CA) 583; *Assicurazioni Generali v Arab Insurance Group* [2003] 1 All ER 140 (CA) [63]–[64]. A continuing misrepresentation made innocently may become fraudulent if the representor became aware of its falsity before the transaction was entered into: *Brownlie v Campbell* (1880) 5 App Cas 925 (HL) 950; *Abu Dhabi Investment Company v H Clarkson & Co Ltd* [2007] EWHC 1267. But it does not necessarily do so: *Davies v London Provincial Marine Insurance Co* (1878) 8 ChD 469; *Arkwright v Newbold* (1887) 17 ChD 301 (CA) 325, 329; *With v O'Flanagan* [1936] Ch 575 (CA) 584; *Thomas Witter Ltd v TBP Industries Ltd* [1996] 2 All ER 573, 587. A deliberate concealment of a change of facts is fraudulent: see para [4.38].
[240] *Occidental Worldwide Investment Corp v Skibs A/S Avanti (The Siboen and Sibotre)* [1976] 1 Lloyd's Rep 293, 324; *Limit No 2 Ltd v Axa Versicherung AG* [2008] 2 CLC 673 (CA) [26].
[241] *Briess v Woolley* [1954] AC 333, 344.
[242] *Cramaso LLP v Ogilvie-Grant* [2014] AC 1093; 2 WLR 317 (SC) [57].
[243] *Limit No 2 Ltd v Axa Versicherung AG* [2008] 2 CLC 673 (CA).
[244] *Bank of Tokyo-Mitsubishi UFJ Ltd v Baskan Gida Sanayi Ve Pazarlama AS* [2009] EWHC 1276 (Ch) [1015] (a gratuitous trade reference was not a continuing representation).
[245] [2014] AC 1093; 2 WLR 317 (SC) [25], [30]. See also para [4.77].

Representations of fact

4.93 A leading decision is *With v O'Flanagan*.[246] In January 1934, at the commencement of sale negotiations, the vendor of a medical practice stated that it had a turnover of £2,000 a year. The contract was signed on 1 May 1934. Between these two dates the vendor fell ill, patients stopped coming, and the practice became worthless. The vendor's failure to disclose the change of circumstances to the prospective purchaser was held to be a misrepresentation. Lord Wright MR held that rescission was possible as either the representor had not discharged his duty to inform the purchaser before the contract was made as to the falsehood of his earlier representation, or his original representation could be construed as a continuing one.[247] Romer LJ came to the same conclusion on the first basis only. He stated that the representor could not hold the purchaser to the bargain if owing to a change of circumstances before the contract was entered into, the representation would to the knowledge of the representor be untrue.[248] Clauson J agreed with both judgments. It is therefore not entirely clear whether the change in circumstances must actually be known to the representor before the earlier representation will be rendered a misrepresentation. The preferable view appears to be that such knowledge is unnecessary,[249] as the risk of subsequent changes in the facts ought to lie with the party making the representation. But the alternative is, we think, also arguable.[250]

Statements as to the future

Forecasts or projections

4.94 A forecast or projection may be characterized as an opinion or a statement as to the future, but in appropriate circumstances it may also be treated as carrying with it a continuing representation that circumstances on which it is based have not fundamentally changed. Where during the negotiations for the sale of a company, income forecasts had been rendered inaccurate by the loss of a major customer, the concealment of this change of circumstances was held to give rise to a fraudulent representation allowing the purchaser to rescind the sale and purchase agreement.[251]

Representations of intention

4.95 There is authority that suggests that a representation as to intention is not a continuing one; but this cannot be treated as a general rule. In *Wales v Wadham*[252] the representor's intention changed before the making of the contract, but there was held to be no duty to disclose that change of circumstances. A wife had represented in divorce proceedings that she had

---

[246] [1936] Ch 575. Applied in *Spice Girls Ltd v Aprilia World Service BV* [2002] EWCA 15 which in turn was applied in *Fitzroy Robinson Ltd v Mentmore Towers Ltd* [2009] BLR 505 (failure to inform client before contract was signed that a key team member had left) [160]. See also *Cleaver v Schyde Investments Ltd* [2011] 2 P & CR 21 (CA) [36].
[247] [1936] Ch 575, 583–84.
[248] [1936] Ch 575, 586.
[249] This is the position taken in Scots law, *Royal Bank of Scotland plc v James O'Donnell and Ian McDonald* [2014] CSIH 84; 2015 SC 258.
[250] In the context of insurance, a non-disclosure is not operative unless the person knew or ought to have known the information that was not disclosed. The same approach is taken in relation to 'family arrangements'—only material facts known to the family member must be disclosed. If this is the correct approach to the question, then knowledge is essential.
[251] *Erlson Precision Holdings Ltd v Hampson Industries plc* [2011] EWHC 1137 (Comm).
[252] [1977] 1 WLR 199.

no intention to remarry, but before a contract for her future financial provision was made, she became engaged to another man. Tudor Evans J stated that the wife had 'made an honest statement of her intention which was not a representation of fact, and I can find no basis for holding that she was under a duty in the law of contract to tell [the claimant] of her change of mind'.[253]

This analysis may be contrasted with the earlier decision of *Traill v Baring*,[254] which was not cited in the later cases. An insurance company was found to be under a duty to communicate a change of its intention to a reinsurance company. It had represented that it would not reinsure all of a risk that it had insured but then it did so after changing its mind on the matter. Rescission was granted.[255] **4.96**

As a matter of principle, an uncommunicated change of intention should be capable of amounting to a misrepresentation, at least in certain cases. A representation as to the state of a person's mind is a statement of existing fact,[256] and a representation regarding intention as at a particular date is a representation as to the representor's state of mind on that date. For as long as that representation of fact continues,[257] a change in the relevant intention would amount to a misrepresentation using the analysis in *With v O'Flanagan*.[258] In *Inter Export LLC v Townley*[259] a director's confirmation that a company had sufficient funds to pay for cargo was characterized as a continuing representation of present intention that the company would make the payment. **4.97**

As a further example, suppose A honestly tells B that A intends to build a housing estate within 12 months, and to do so next to shop premises that A owns. That is a representation as to A's state of mind, and true when made. The representation is made to induce B to enter into a ten-year lease of the shop from A. The common assumption is that B will sell to the residents of the future housing estate. After the representation of intention is made, but before the lease is signed, A changes his intention, and decides not to build the housing estate after all. He does not inform B, and A and B sign the lease. B ought to be able to rescind the lease for misrepresentation. B entered into the lease in reliance on the representation as to the state of A's mind, which B reasonably assumed to be continuing, and B could reasonably expect to be informed of changes to A's intentions in the circumstances.[260] **4.98**

---

[253] [1977] 1 WLR 199, 211. This decision was affirmed by the House of Lords in *Livesey v Jenkins* [1985] AC 424, 439, although that case overruled another of the reasons for that decision.
[254] (1864) 4 DeGJ & S 318, 46 ER 941.
[255] See also *Slough Estates plc v Welwyn and Hatfield DC* [1996] 2 PLR 50 (uncommunicated change of intention as to whether an agreement with a third party would be enforced amounted to deceit); *National Westminster Bank plc v Kotonou* [2006] All ER (D) 325 (guarantee rescinded because of a non-fraudulent failure to communicate a change in the bank's intentions).
[256] See para [4.51].
[257] In *Limit No 2 Ltd v Axa Versicherung AG* [2008] 2 CLC 673 (CA) [26] the Court of Appeal took the view that a misrepresentation of intention was a continuing one, but in that case the misrepresentation had ceased to be operative by the time the renewed contract was entered into some 19 months after the original misrepresentation had been made.
[258] See para [4.93].
[259] [2018] EWCA Civ 2068 [30]–[31], [33]–[35].
[260] It could be argued that B ought to have insisted on a covenant in the lease requiring A to build the housing estate. But such an argument ought not to allow A to take the benefit of a transaction that was procured by what would generally be considered to be sharp practice.

4.99 By way of contrast, *WPP Group plc v Reichmann* concerned an implied representation made by a landlord to a prospective tenant that the landlord intended to inform the tenant if other parties became interested in entering into a lease of the relevant premises. Ferris J noted the danger of giving binding effect to a non-contractual promise by stretching the concepts now being considered: of accepting that a statement as to future intention has no contractual effect, extracting from it an implied statement of fact as to the maker's state of mind, and then giving legal effect to the statement by treating it as a continuing one.[261] His Lordship avoided that outcome by finding that the particular representation of intention was *not* a continuing one, and thereby emphasizing that whether a change of intention gives rise to a misrepresentation, hinges on whether the particular representation of intention is construed as a continuing one.[262]

F. Representation must be Relied On

(1) Reliance and inducement: a question of causation[263]

4.100 For a misrepresentation to vitiate a claimant's consent to a transaction, there must be a causal link between the representation and the representee's conduct.[264] The representee must enter into the transaction in reliance on the misrepresentation; and the transaction must be induced by the misrepresentation.[265] Although a distinction has been drawn between reliance and inducement,[266] they are closely related concepts that are both concerned with causation. Reliance denotes the required causal link between the representee's conduct and the representation, viewed from the representee's perspective. Inducement signifies that same causal link, taking into account the representor's role in bringing about that reliance. It is not possible for there to be inducement without reliance.[267] There is no need to show intention to induce for rescission to be available as it is unnecessary for the representor even to be aware that he is making a representation.[268] Although a belief on the part of the representee that he believed the misrepresentation to be true can be very relevant for establishing reliance, it is not actually necessary to establish that the representee believed the misrepresentation.[269]

---

[261] [2000] All ER (D) 1409 (a deceit, not a rescission action). Cited with approval in the context of rescission in *Limit No 2 Ltd v Axa Versicherung AG* [2008] 2 CLC 673 (CA) [27].

[262] See para [4.91].

[263] This section of the first edition of this book was cited with approval by the Eastern Caribbean Supreme Court of Appeal in *East Pine Management Ltd v Tawney Assets Limited and others* [2014] BVIHCVAP 2012/0035 (ESCC CA, 24 March 2014) [23].

[264] *Marme Inversiones 2007 SL v Natwest Markets Plc* [2019] EWHC 366 (Comm) [281]; *Leeds City Council v Barclays Bank Plc* [2021] QB 1027 [144].

[265] *Pulsford v Richards* (1853) 17 Beav 87, 96; 51 ER 965, 968; *Attwood v Small* (1838) 6 Cl & Fin 232, 448; 7 ER 684, 765; *Mathias v Yetts* (1882) 46 LT 497 (CA) 502.

[266] *Downs v Chappell* [1997] 1 WLR 426 (CA) 433.

[267] This is derived from P Feltham, P Crampin, T Leech, and J Winfield, *Spencer Bower: Reliance-Based Estoppel* (5th edn, 2017) [5.4].

[268] *Spice Girls Ltd v Aprilia World Services BV* [2002] EWCA 15 [57]. Cf *Barton v County NatWest Ltd* [2002] 4 All ER 494n (CA) (necessary to show intention to induce to recover damages in deceit).

[269] *Zurich Insurance v Hayward* [2017] AC 142 (Sup Ct) [18], [23].

Where implied representations are pleaded, the claimant must prove that he understood that the representations alleged were in fact made; otherwise there can be no reliance.[270] Before or at the time of the transaction, the representee must have given some conscious thought to the fact that the implied representations were made.[271]

4.101

All of the circumstances must be considered in determining whether the claimant relied upon the misrepresentation in entering into the transaction.[272] Insistence that an express warranty to the same effect as the relevant representation be included in a contract is evidence of reliance.[273] The question of reliance is a question of fact.[274] It has been held that if it would have been unreasonable for the claimant to rely on the representation, this may show that the claimant did not in fact rely on the representation.[275] Reliance is rebuttably presumed as a matter of fact where a misrepresentation is proved to be material or, it seems, is fraudulent.[276]

4.102

(2) Ambiguous statements or conduct

Where the representor's statement or conduct was ambiguous—that is, capable of more than one meaning—the party seeking to rescind must satisfy the court of two things. First, that he was justified in understanding, and did understand it, in the sense alleged.[277] The principles according to which this is determined have already been discussed.[278] Secondly, he must prove that he actually relied on the statement or conduct in that particular sense.[279]

4.103

(3) Causation: fraudulent misrepresentation[280]

For rescission for fraud it is enough for the representee to prove that they were materially influenced by it in the sense that it was actively present to their mind when they decided to enter into the transaction, even if there were also other reasons for entering into it.[281] In

4.104

---

[270] *Brown v InnovatorOne Plc* [2012] EWHC 1321 (Comm) [904]. Cited in *Marme Inversiones 2007 SL v Natwest Markets Plc* [2019] EWHC 366 (Comm) [281].
[271] *Marme Inversiones 2007 SL v Natwest Markets Plc* [2019] EWHC 366 (Comm) [285]–[287].
[272] *Bloomenthal v Ford* [1897] AC 156, 162.
[273] *Thomas Witter Ltd v TBP Industries Ltd* [1996] 2 All ER 573, 595.
[274] *Zurich Insurance v Hayward* [2017] AC 142 (Sup Ct) [29], [68]; *Marme Inversiones 2007 SL v Natwest Markets Plc* [2019] EWHC 366 (Comm) [291].
[275] *Monde Petroleum SA v WesternZagros Limited* [2016] EWHC 1472 (Comm) [219] upheld on appeal [2018] 2 All ER (Comm) 867 (CA).
[276] See para [4.64]
[277] *Smith v Chadwick* (1884) 9 App Cas 187 (HL) 190 (a deceit case, but the same principle ought to apply to rescission); *EA Grimstead v McGarrigan* [1999] EWCA (Civ) 3029, 21.
[278] See para [4.39]ff.
[279] *Hallows v Fernie* (1868) 3 Ch App 467, 477 (ambiguity in a prospectus as to whether company owned steamships or was intending to acquire them; a rescission case); *Smith v Chadwick* (1884) 9 App Cas 187 (HL) (a deceit case); *Krakowski v Eurolynx Properties Ltd* (1995) 183 CLR 563, 577 'The sense in which a representation is understood by the representee is relevant to the question whether the representation induced the representee to act upon it.'
[280] This section of the first edition of this book was cited with approval by the Eastern Caribbean Supreme Court of Appeal in *East Pine Management Ltd v Tawney Assets Limited and others* [2014] BVIHCVAP 2012/0035 (ESCC CA, 24 March 2014) [23].
[281] *Van Eiprodukten v Rembrandt Enterprises* [2020] QB 551 (CA) [32]. A Burrows, *A Restatement of the English Law of Contract* (2016) 188, 191.

other words, the fraudulent misrepresentation need not have been the sole, dominant, or major cause that led the representee to enter into the transaction, but it must have been 'a' cause that influenced the decision to enter into the transaction.[282] In determining whether fraud induced the contract the courts are not prepared to speculate as to what would or would not have happened if the fraud had not been perpetrated.[283] It is said that in determining whether fraud induced a contract 'You cannot weigh the elements by ounces'.[284] It is generally irrelevant whether or not the injured party would have entered into the transaction in the absence of the fraud.[285] It is sufficient if the fraudulent misrepresentation is a matter but for which the representee 'might not' have reached the decision they did.[286] Rescission will be unavailable only if the representee's judgement was not influenced at all by the fraud.[287] In such a case the representor must prove that the representee would have entered into the contract had there been no representation, not that the representee might nonetheless have entered into it.[288] The burden is on the representor to rebut the presumption of inducement.[289]

(4) Causation: non-fraudulent misrepresentation

4.105 Different policy considerations apply where there is no dishonesty;[290] consequently a more stringent test of causation appears to be appropriate for non-fraudulent misrepresentations.[291] It is necessary to show that the non-fraudulent misrepresentation was a cause 'but for' which the transaction 'would not' have been entered into on the terms that were in fact agreed. That approach was implicit in authorities stating that the representee must have

---

[282] *Edgington v Fitzmaurice* (1885) 29 ChD 459 (CA) (a deceit rather than a rescission case) 481, 483; *Standard Chartered Bank v Pakistan National Shipping Corp (No 2)* [2003] 1 AC 959, 967; *BV Nederlandse Industrie Van Eiprodukten v Rembrandt Enterprises* [2020] QB 551 (CA) [32]. In Australia, *Gould v Vaggelas* (1985) 157 CLR 215, *Demetrios v Gikas Dry Cleaning Industries Pty Ltd* (1991) 22 NSWLR 561, 570. Cf *Cassa di Risparmio della Repubblica di San Marino SpA v Barclays Bank Ltd* [2011] 1 CLC 701 [233]. Cf N Venkatesan, 'Causation in Misrepresentation: Historical or Counterfactual? And "but for" What?' (2021) 137 LQR 201 where the special rule for fraud is doubted.
[283] *Reynell v Sprye* (1852) 1 De GM & G 660, 708–09; 42 ER 710, 728–29; *Smith v Kay* (1859) 7 HLC 750 (HL) 759; 11 ER 299, 303.
[284] *Arnison v Smith* (1875) 41 ChD 348 (CA) 369. In *Barton v Armstrong* [1976] AC 104 (PC—Australia) 118–19 it was noted in relation to fraud that 'in this field the court does not allow an examination into the relative importance of contributory causes'.
[285] *Occidental Worldwide Investment Corp v Skibs A/S Avanti (The Siboen and Sibotre)* [1976] 1 Lloyd's Rep 293, 324; *Downs v Chappell* [1997] 1 WLR 426 (CA) 433; *UCB Corporate Services Ltd v Williams* [2002] 3 FCR 448 (CA) [86], [89]; *Ross River Ltd v Waveley Commercial Ltd* [2008] 1 All ER 1004 [243]. Cf *Leni Gas and Oil Investments Ltd v Malta Oil Pty Ltd* [2014] EWHC 893 (Comm) [20].
[286] *BV Nederlandse Industrie Van Eiprodukten v Rembrandt Enterprises* [2020] QB 551 (CA) [49]; *Marme Inversiones 2007 SL v Natwest Markets Plc* [2019] EWHC 366 (Comm) [304].
[287] This was the conclusion in respect of a deceit claim in *Leni Gas and Oil Investments Ltd v Malta Oil Pty Ltd* [2014] EWHC 893 (Comm) [172]. Cf *Jurong Town Corp v Wishing Star Ltd* [2005] 3 SLR 283 (Singapore CA) where it was unsuccessfully argued that a public authority awarded a contract by reference *only* to price and had disregarded its other selection criteria that had been the subject of fraudulent misrepresentations by the counterparty. See also *Versloot Dredging BV v HDI Gerling Industrie Versicherung AG* [2017] AC 1 (Sup Ct).
[288] *BV Nederlandse Industrie Van Eiprodukten v Rembrandt Enterprises* [2020] QB 551 (CA).
[289] *Dadourian v Simms* [2009] 1 Lloyd's Rep 601 (CA); *Edwards v Ashik* [2014] EWHC 2454 (Ch); *Zurich Insurance v Hayward* [2017] AC 142 (Sup Ct); *Vald Nielsen Holding A/S and another v Baldorino and others* [2019] EWHC 1926 (Comm) [157]. In a recent case, that heavy burden was discharged and the presumption was rebutted: *Ahuja Investments Ltd v Victorygame Ltd* [2021] EWHC 2382 (Ch).
[290] Most importantly, deterrence does not play a predominant role.
[291] *Standard Chartered Bank v Pakistan National Shipping Corp (No 2)* [2003] 1 AC 959, 967 (Lord Hoffman).

altered his position by entering into the transaction on terms that are materially different from those he would have agreed to absent the misrepresentation.[292] Nonetheless some contrary authority existed suggesting that such a 'would not but for' test was not applicable.[293] However, it now seems settled that the test of causation in cases of non-fraudulent misrepresentation is that the transaction 'would not' have been entered into on the same terms 'but for' the misrepresentation.[294]

4.106 It has been held in a case involving fraudulent misrepresentation that inducement may consist in inducing a person to persevere in a decision already reached.[295] But where the representation is not fraudulent, it seems that the representee is required to establish more than that the representation encouraged or supported his prior decision.[296] The 'would not but for' test requires the party seeking to rescind to show that the representation caused him to change what he would otherwise have done.[297] In the case of a non-fraudulent misrepresentation, it is insufficient to show that the party 'might have' acted differently.[298] But a lower threshold is sufficient in cases of fraudulent misrepresentation.[299]

4.107 The inquiry should, it is suggested, always involve comparing the representee's actual position with the hypothetical position that would have obtained had the misrepresentation not been made. Rescission is only available for a non-fraudulent misrepresentation if the conclusion of that inquiry is that the transaction would not have been entered at all, or that it would have been concluded on materially different terms. If that is not established, there seems no sufficient justification for permitting the misled party to unwind the entire transaction.

4.108 In *Raiffeisen Zentralbank Osterreich AG v The Royal Bank of Scotland Plc* Christopher Clarke J considered whether the relevant question in applying the 'but for' test was what would the

---

[292] *The Larissa* [1983] 2 Lloyd's Rep 325, 332 (Hobhouse J) (a claim for damages rather than rescission); *Huyton SA v Distribuidora Internacional de Productos Agricolas SA de CV* [2003] 2 Lloyd's Rep 780 (CA) 852–53 (rescission claim).

[293] *Re Leeds Bank* (1887) 56 LJ Ch 321 (misrepresentations were 'of a most serious kind' but not expressly labelled fraudulent; fraud test applied); *UCB Corporate Services Ltd v Thomason* [2004] 2 All ER 774 (fraud test applied to innocent misrepresentation), aff'd [2005] 1 All ER 601 (CA).

[294] *Horry v Tate & Lyle Refineries Ltd* [1982] 2 Lloyd's Rep 416, 422 the misrepresentation 'has to be a factor without which the plaintiff would not have entered into the [transaction], and there may be other factors'; *Pan Atlantic Insurance Co Ltd v Pine Top Insurance Co Ltd* [1995] 1 AC 501; *Assicurazioni Generali v Arab Insurance Group* [2003] 1 All ER 140 (CA) [59] 'If the insurer would have entered into the contract on the same terms in any event, the representation or non-disclosure will not, however material, be an effective cause of the making of the contract and the insurer or reinsurer will not be entitled to avoid the contract.' *BV Nederlandse Industrie Van Eiprodukten v Rembrandt Enterprises* [2020] QB 551 (CA) [15]; *Marme Inversiones 2007 SL v Natwest Markets Plc* [2019] EWHC 366 (Comm) [304]. See A Burrows, *A Restatement of the English Law of Contract* (2016) 188, 191.

[295] *Barton v County NatWest Ltd* [1999] All ER (D) 782 [55], [60]; on appeal [2002] 4 All ER 494n (CA); *Kingspan Environmental Ltd v Borealis A/S* [2012] EWHC 1147 (Comm) [425], [498] (a claim under s 2(1) of the Misrepresentation Act 1967). See also the authorities cited at n 257 which decide that generally a fraudster cannot argue that the victim would have entered into the transaction in the absence of the fraud. Cf *Leni Gas and Oil Investments Ltd v Malta Oil Pty Ltd* [2014] EWHC 893 (Comm) [172].

[296] In *JEB Fasteners Ltd v Marks Bloom & Co* [1983] 1 All ER 583 (CA), a case concerning the tort of negligence, a useful distinction was drawn between 'reliance' in a narrow sense of 'inducement' or 'whole dependence' and a broader sense of 'encouragement or support'. As a matter of policy, the former ought to be required in relation to rescission for non-fraudulent misrepresentations, whilst the latter ought to suffice in relation to fraudulent misrepresentations. See also *Dadourian v Simms* [2009] 1 Lloyd's Rep 601 (CA) [99]; *Raiffeisen Zentralbank Osterreich AG v The Royal Bank of Scotland Plc* [2011] 1 Lloyd's Rep 123 [153], [159]–[162].

[297] *Raiffeisen Zentralbank Osterreich AG v The Royal Bank of Scotland Plc* [2011] 1 Lloyd's Rep 123 [171].

[298] *Raiffeisen Zentralbank Osterreich AG v The Royal Bank of Scotland Plc* [2011] 1 Lloyd's Rep 123 [195].

[299] *BV Nederlandse Industrie Van Eiprodukten v Rembrandt Enterprises* [2020] QB 551 (CA); *Marme Inversiones 2007 SL v Natwest Markets Plc* [2019] EWHC 366 (Comm) [304].

representee have done (a) if he had been told the truth, or (b) if no representation had been made to him at all?[300] His Lordship concluded that it was the latter inquiry that was relevant, because the representee must establish the causative impact of the representation on his decision.[301] The complaint is that he entered into the contract on the relevant terms as a result of what he was told.[302] If it is clear that the representee would not have entered into the contract unless the representation had been made, what would have happened if he knew the truth is irrelevant.[303] By way of contrast, in *Ross River Ltd v Waveley Commercial Ltd* Briggs J held in the context of a fraudulent misrepresentation, that in assessing inducement a comparison was to be carried out between the statement actually made and the truth, rather than between the statement made and silence; that is, where no statement was made.[304]

4.109 The difference between the analysis of Clarke J and that of Briggs J can be explained on the basis that in respect of fraudulent misrepresentation, a less stringent test of causation applies, and it is irrelevant that the representee may have entered into the transaction in the absence of the fraud. All that is needed is proof that the fraudulent representation had some effect on the representee's decision to enter into the transaction.[305] If that is the relevant question, in assessing the causative effect of the misstatement, a legitimate inquiry is what would have happened if the claimant had known the truth.

(5) Presumption of reliance and onus of proof

4.110 It was seen earlier[306] that a representation will be 'material' if it is capable of influencing the judgement of a reasonable person when considering whether or not to enter into the transaction. The inquiry is into the character of the statement judged objectively. Whether a representation 'induced' the contract is a separate question. That inquiry looks to the actual effect of the statement on the particular representee. A contract is induced by a representation if the representation was in fact relied upon by the particular representee.

---

[300] *Raiffeisen Zentralbank Osterreich AG v The Royal Bank of Scotland Plc* [2011] 1 Lloyd's Rep 123 [174].

[301] Cf *Atlantic Lines and Navigation Co Inc v Hallam Ltd (The Lucy)* [1983] 1 Lloyd's Rep 188 (QB) 200–01 where the court looked at whether the discrepancy between what was represented and the true state of facts would have had a material influence on the outcome of the bargain (rescission of sub-charter not possible because of absence of reliance on the misrepresentation).

[302] *Raiffeisen Zentralbank Osterreich AG v The Royal Bank of Scotland Plc* [2011] 1 Lloyd's Rep 123 [180].

[303] *Raiffeisen Zentralbank Osterreich AG v The Royal Bank of Scotland Plc* [2011] 1 Lloyd's Rep 123 [186]; *Marme Inversiones 2007 SL v Natwest Markets Plc* [2019] EWHC 366 (Comm) [297] where it was stated that 'where reliance has already been established without having to consider what would have happened had the claimant been told the truth, it is generally not relevant to ask what would have happened had the claimant been told the truth. ... [T]hat is an inquiry which is relevant if the position is that the claimant would have acted in the same way even had the truth been known since that is evidence which weighs against a conclusion that there was the requisite reliance.' See also *SK Shipping Europe Plc v Capital Vlcc 3 Corp* [2021] 2 Lloyd's Rep 109 [185]–[188].

[304] [2008] 1 All ER 1004 [243]. See also KR Handley, 'Causation in Misrepresentation' (2015) LQR 275, 278 where it is stated that 'The effect of a lie must be assessed by comparing it with the truth, and not with silence. The lie and its impact are historical facts. The effect of silence on the topic is a hypothetical and speculative question which the representee did not consider or have to consider at the time.' But contrast *Avonwick Holdings Ltd v Azitio Holdings Ltd* [2020] EWHC 1844 (Comm) [189] where Clarke J's approach in the *Raiffeisen* case was said to be applicable to fraudulent misrepresentation.

[305] See para [4.104].

[306] See paras [4.63]ff.

There is, however, an important connection between the conclusion that a representation is material, and analysis of its actual effect. That connection was explained by Lord Jessel MR in *Mathias v Yetts*: **4.111**

> ... if a man has a material misstatement made to him which may, from its nature, induce him to enter into the contract, it is an inference that he is induced to enter into the contract by it. You need not prove it affirmatively. The man who makes the material misstatement to induce the other to enter into the contract cannot be heard to say that he did not enter into it, to some extent, at all events, on the faith of that statement, unless he can prove one of two things: either in fact that the man did not rely upon it, and made inquiries and got information which showed that the misstatement was untrue, and still went on with the contract, that is one thing; or else that he said, expressly or impliedly, 'I do not care what your representations are; I shall not inquire about them. I shall enter into the contract taking the risk.'[307]

Accordingly, if the misrepresentation would influence the judgement of a reasonable person in determining whether to enter into the transaction, then the representee is presumed as a matter of fact (not law)[308] to have been induced to enter into the transaction; that is, to have entered the transaction in reliance on the misrepresentation. The representor then bears the onus of proving that the representee in fact did not rely on the representation.[309] **4.112**

But where the misrepresentation would not have induced a reasonable person to enter into the transaction (and so is not 'material'), in our view the representee should not be permitted to rescind even if he did in fact rely on the misrepresentation in entering into the transaction, unless the misrepresentation was fraudulent, or the representor knew or ought to have known that the particular representee was likely to act on the representation.[310] **4.113**

(6) Examples of non-reliance on a false representation

Knows that the representation is false

If at the time of the transaction the representee knows that the representation is false, in a typical case he cannot later claim to have acted in reliance on it.[311] It has been observed that: '[i]n a case depending upon alleged misrepresentation ... the defendant cannot adduce more conclusive evidence, or raise a more effectual bar to the plaintiff's case, than by showing that the plaintiff was from the beginning cognisant of all the matters complained of.'[312] It is also sufficient if the representee's duly authorized agent has this knowledge but **4.114**

---

[307] (1882) 46 LT 497 (CA) 502; *Gould v Vaggelas* (1984) 157 CLR 215, 236.
[308] Materiality only ever gives rise to a presumption of fact not law: *Smith v Land and House Property Corp* (1884) ChD 7 (CA) 16; *St Paul Fire and Marine Insurance Co (UK) Ltd v McConnell Dowell Constructors* [1995] 2 Lloyd's Rep 116 (CA). See also *Smith v Chadwick* (1884) 9 App Cas 187 (HL) 196; *Bate v Aviva Insurance UK Limited* [2014] EWCA Civ 334 [35].
[309] *Museprime Properties Ltd v Adhill Properties Ltd* [1990] 2 EGLR 196, 201–02; *Commission for New Towns v Cooper (GB) Ltd* [1995] Ch 259 (CA) 282; *Barton v County NatWest Ltd* [1999] All ER (D) 782 [57]–[58]; on appeal [2002] 4 All ER 494n (CA); *Dadourian v Simms* [2009] 1 Lloyd's Rep 601 (CA) [99]–[101].
[310] See paras [4.67]ff.
[311] *Jennings v Broughton* (1854) 5 De GM & G 126, 43 ER 818 (physical inspection of mine contradicted statements in advertisement); *Redgrave v Hurd* (1881) 20 ChD 1 (CA) 21 (Jessel MR); *Cooper v Tamms* [1988] 1 EGLR 257; *Peekay Intermark Ltd and Harish Pawani v Australia & New Zealand Banking Group Ltd* [2006] EWCA 386 [40].
[312] *Vigers v Pike* (1842) 8 Cl & F 562, 650; 8 ER 220, 253.

fails to pass it on.[313] The person resisting rescission bears the onus of showing that the representee or his agent actually knew that the representation was untrue.[314] Yet the principle that knowledge of the truth precludes reliance is not a categorical one. An exception is illustrated by *Zurich Insurance v Hayward*[315] where an insurance company was entitled to rescind the settlement of a fraudulent claim which it had settled not believing that it was genuine but in the belief that it was likely to succeed at trial. Lord Clarke observed that 'there may be circumstances in which a representee may know that the representation is false but nevertheless may be held to rely upon the misrepresentation as a matter of fact'.[316]

Not aware of misrepresentation

4.115 If the claimant is unaware of a representation that has been made, he cannot be relying on it.[317] As Lord Scott stated in *Royal Bank of Scotland v Etridge (No 2)*:

> ... a misrepresentation must, if it is to lead to an equitable or legal remedy, have led to a false impression about some material matter being held by the victim ... In the present case [the claimant] had no impression at all about the nature of the documents she was signing. No false impression had been planted on her by [the alleged misrepresentor].[318]

4.116 The position is the same if the representee forgets the representation before entering into the transaction.[319]

Not influenced by the misrepresentation

4.117 If the representee enters into the transaction solely for reasons that are entirely separate from the misrepresentation, then he does not rely on it.[320] A misrepresentation in a takeover

---

[313] *Bawden v London, Edinburgh & Glasgow Assurance Co* [1892] 2 QB 534 (CA) (a one-eyed man represented to insurance company's agent that he had no physical infirmity); *Strover v Harrington* [1988] Ch 390 (claimant's solicitors were informed that a prior representation was untrue but failed to communicate that fact to their client); contrast *Wells v Smith* [1914] 3 KB 722 (knowledge of agent who was a party to the fraud not imputed to the principal).

[314] *Peekay Intermark Ltd and Harish Pawani v Australia & New Zealand Banking Group Ltd* [2006] EWCA 386 [40].

[315] [2017] AC 142 (Sup Ct) [40]; 'Qualified belief or disbelief does not rule out inducement.'

[316] *Zurich Insurance v Hayward* [2017] AC 142 (Sup Ct) [44].

[317] *Re Northumberland and Durham District Banking Co, ex p Bigge* (1858) 28 LJ Ch 50 (purchaser of shares did not read false report about company); *Horsfall v Thomas* (1862) 1 H & C 90, 158 ER 813 (purchaser of gun did not inspect it and hence was unaware of a fraudulent attempt to conceal a defect); *Hunt v Optima (Cambridge) Ltd* [2015] 1 WLR 1346 (CA) (architects certificates confirming that flats were free from defects were issued after completion of purchases of the flats so the representations contained in the certificates could not have been relied on to enter into the relevant contracts); *Marme Inversiones 2007 SL v Natwest Markets Plc* [2019] EWHC 366 (Comm) [281], [287] (representee lacked awareness of implied representations); *Leeds City Council v Barclays Bank Plc* [2021] QB 1027.

[318] [2002] 2 AC 773, 855.

[319] *Briess v Woolley* [1954] AC 333, 344; *Wales v Wadham* [1977] 1 WLR 199 (CA).

[320] *Coaks v Boswell* (1886) 11 App Cas 232, 236 'if the vendor was not, in fact, misled, the contract could not be set aside'; *Seddon v North Eastern Salt Co Ltd* [1905] 1 Ch 326, 335 (representation as to losses incurred by business was not relied on by purchaser as 'he wanted the business, and that he intended to take the risk whatever it was'); *Royal Bank of Scotland v Etridge (No 2)* [2002] 2 AC 773, 855 'Judge Behrens found as a fact that if the nature and content of the documents had been explained to [the complainant], she would still have signed. So, if there had been any misrepresentation as to the nature and content of the documents, it had no relevant causative effect'; *Assicurazioni Generali v Arab Insurance Group* [2003] 1 All ER 140 (CA) [59]; *Involnert Management Inc v Aprilgrange Ltd* [2016] 1 All ER (Comm) 913; *Ahuja Investments Ltd v Victorygame Ltd* [2021] EWHC 2382 (Ch) (fraudulent misrepresentation not communicated to the complainant until just before exchange of contracts (by when he had already signed the contract); he had no interest in the subject matter of the misrepresentation). An argument that the representee relied on the belief that it was divine providence or intervention that had brought the investment opportunity to him, rather than the seller's representations, was rejected in *Re Krypton Nominees Pty Ltd* [2013] VSC 446.

target company's accounts was found not to have induced the share purchase contract as it did not have a 'real and substantial' role in inducing the claimant's entry into the contract. The claimant's reason for entering into the contract was to secure the services of the target company's directors.[321] Likewise a representee does not rely on a representation if he regards it as unimportant or is not aware of its significance.[322]

The representee is not induced by a representation if he relied on his own judgement or that of a third party.[323] In one case the purchasers of a company were found not to have relied on the financial information provided by the seller, but instead upon their own optimistic forecasts.[324] In an older case the earning capacity of a mine was misrepresented by the seller. The buyer commissioned an agent's report to verify the earning capacity, which stated that it was as large as had been represented. It was found that the buyer was not induced by the misrepresentation as he had relied upon the agent's report.[325] In *Peekay Intermark Ltd and Harish Pawani v Australia & New Zealand Banking Group Ltd*, the Court of Appeal held that a representee could not rescind for an innocent oral misrepresentation as to the nature of a transaction as the transaction was clearly explained in the terms and conditions of the contract, which he had signed without reading. It was held that the representee 'was induced to sign the documents and enter into the contract not by what [the representor] had told him, but by his own assumption that the investment product to which they related corresponded to the description he had previously been given'.[326] But the suggestion that the representee had not also relied on what he had been incorrectly told about the transaction is not easy to understand. It is also difficult to reconcile with *Redgrave v Hurd*, which is discussed in the next paragraph.

4.118

(7) Opportunity to discover truth does not disprove reliance

'No man can complain that another has too implicitly relied on the truth of what he has himself stated.'[327] If a representee has an opportunity to discover the falsity of a misrepresentation and does not take it, reliance is not negatived.[328] In *Redgrave v Hurd*[329] the buyer

4.119

---

[321] *JEB Fasteners v Marks, Bloom and Co* [1983] 1 All ER 583. See also *Sears v Minco Plc* [2016] EWHC 433 (Ch) [65].
[322] *Smith v Chadwick* (1884) 9 App Cas 187 (statement that a certain person was a director of a company could have influenced others to take shares but the claimant admitted that it had not influenced him); *The Attorney-General of New South Wales v Peters* (1924) 34 CLR 146, 152 (government considered the representations immaterial and entered the contract for political reasons).
[323] *Jennings v Broughton* (1854) 5 De GM & G 126, 43 ER 818. In *The Co-Operative Bank Plc v Hayes Freehold Ltd* [2017] EWHC 1820 (Ch) [122], [125], the claimant was found to have relied on its own lawyer's advice as to the counterparty's power to accept the surrender of a headlease rather than any implied misrepresentation that the counterparty had such power.
[324] *Welven Ltd v Soar Group Ltd* [2011] EWHC 3240 (Comm).
[325] *Attwood v Small* (1838) 6 Cl & F 232 (HL), 7 ER 684.
[326] [2006] EWCA 386 [52]. Followed in *Reinhard v Ondra LLP* [2015] EWHC 1869 (Ch); [2016] 2 BCLC 571 [116].
[327] *Reynell v Sprye* (1852) 1 De GM & G 660, 710; 42 ER 710, 729.
[328] *Directors of the Central Railway of Venezuela v Kisch* (1867) LR 2 HL 99, 120–21; *Redgrave v Hurd* (1881) 20 ChD 1 (CA) 13–14, 23; *Nocton v Ashburton* [1914] AC 932, 962; *Laurence v Lexcourt Holdings Ltd* [1977] 1 WLR 1128 (CA) 1137. In *Strover v Harrington* [1988] Ch 390, 410 Sir Nicholas Browne-Wilkinson stated 'The representee is under no duty of care to the representor to check on the accuracy of the representation. The representor is bound by his representations, however careless the representee may have been'.
[329] (1881) 20 ChD 1 (CA) 13 (Jessel MR).

was induced to purchase a share in a solicitor's practice by an innocent misrepresentation. He was given an opportunity to examine certain documents and so discover that the representation was false. He cursorily looked at them. Had he used reasonable diligence, he would have discovered the truth. Nonetheless he was entitled to rescind. Baggallay LJ stated:

> The mere fact that a party has the opportunity of investigating and ascertaining whether a representation is true or false is not sufficient to deprive him of his right to rely on a misrepresentation ... The person who has made the misrepresentation cannot be heard to say to the party to whom he has made that representation, 'You chose to believe me when you might have doubted me, and gone further'. The representation once made relieves the party from an investigation, even if the opportunity is afforded.[330]

4.120 Where a fraudulent misrepresentation is made, the representee is entitled to rescind no matter how negligent or careless he has been by not attempting to search out the true facts.[331] But in the case of non-fraudulent misrepresentations, three possible exceptions have been suggested to the general rule discussed. *First*, in *Redgrave v Hurd* itself Baggallay MR stated that the rule might not apply where the representee is aware of suspicious circumstances that put him upon inquiry that the representation is false.[332] However, this suggestion has not been further developed in subsequent authorities.[333] *Secondly*, there are some cases that have not applied the principle in *Redgrave v Hurd* where the representee actually investigates the non-fraudulent representation in a more than cursory way, but does not discover its falsehood through his own lack of due care.[334] This is consistent with principle if in such a case the purchaser actually relies on his own investigations and not on the misrepresentation or if due to the inquiries he is taken to know the true facts.[335] *Thirdly*, it has been argued by high academic authority that the rule does not apply to an innocent misrepresentation where it is reasonable to expect the representee to have made use of the opportunity to discover the truth.[336] But at least where the relief sought is rescission, this exception appears inconsistent with *Redgrave v Hurd*.[337]

---

[330] *Redgrave v Hurd* (1881) 20 ChD 1 (CA) 22–23.
[331] *Redgrave v Hurd* (1881) 20 ChD (CA) 13–14 (Jessel MR); *Alliance & Leicester Building Society v Edgestop Ltd* [1994] 2 All ER 38, 51; *Standard Chartered Bank v Pakistan National Shipping Corp (No 2)* [2003] 1 AC 959; *Flack v Pattinson* [2002] EWCA 1762; *Jurong Town Corp v Wishing Star Ltd* [2005] 3 SLR 283 (Singapore CA) [112]–[114].
[332] *Redgrave v Hurd* (1881) 20 ChD 1 (CA) 23.
[333] For the principles governing the bars of affirmation and delay where the representee becomes suspicious that a misrepresentation may have been made, Chaps 23 and 24.
[334] *Attwood v Small* (1838) 6 Cl & Fin 232 (HL), 7 ER 684 (no rescission where purchaser obtained own report as to the business which was acquired); *Clarke v Mackintosh* (1862) 4 Giff 134, 155–56; 66 ER 651, 659–60 (rescission of contract to purchase brewery denied where purchasers had opportunity to make own investigations as to the vague and inconsistent representations and partially did so); *Hartelid v Sawyer & McClockin Real Estate Ltd* [1977] 5 WWR 481 (rescission denied where garage size misrepresented in estate agent's specifications but buyer examined the property twice).
[335] In *Redgrave v Hurd* (1881) 20 ChD 1 (CA) 17 Jessel MR distinguished *Attwood v Small* as a case where the defendant knew the facts and placed no reliance on the representation.
[336] E Peel, *Treitel The Law of Contract* (15th edn, 2020) [9-033] relying on *Smith v Eric S Bush* [1990] 1 AC 831 (a negligence case).
[337] But note that the result in *Peekay Intermark Ltd and Harish Pawani v Australia & New Zealand Banking Group Ltd* [2006] EWCA 386 is potentially explicable on the basis of such a rule.

(8) Subsequent transactions

4.121 If a misrepresentation induces a transaction to which a second transaction is closely related it may be possible to rescind the second transaction.[338] An amendment or extension to a voidable contract will be voidable along with the original contract.[339] But a voidable subsequent transaction will not necessarily allow the original transaction to be rescinded with it.[340]

4.122 It seems that a voidable contract that has been brought to an end by agreement may be rescinded, even though the ground for rescission does not affect the agreement to cancel.[341] Rescission in this situation appears to entail erasing all remaining rights and obligations under the cancelled agreement, plus the agreement to cancel itself. The extinguishing of the later cancellation agreement is best regarded as an incidental effect of the rescission of the underlying agreement, although the precise basis for this is unclear.

4.123 A substitute contract may be voidable, where the original contract was vitiated by a misrepresentation. As Longmore LJ stated in *Yorkshire Bank Plc v Tinsley*:

> A substitute contract will often come into existence in a different factual context from an earlier contract and that factual context may show that the second contract is not a true substitute for the first. But if the factual situations are materially similar and, if it is a condition of the rescission or release of the original void or voidable bargain that the parties enter into a new bargain, that new bargain must be as open to attack as the old one.[342]

Principle dictates this conclusion where the representation relied on in respect of the first transaction is continuing and also relied on in entering into the second or substitute transaction.[343] Where a continuing representation has ceased to be operative, a subsequent or substitute contract will not be voidable.[344]

4.124 In *Graiseley Properties Ltd v Barclays Bank Plc*[345] the question arose whether the transfer of certain rights under a syndicated loan by means of a novation mechanism extinguished the equity to rescind arising from a misrepresentation which induced the original contract. The Court of Appeal suggested that in the relevant clauses of the syndicated loan agreement 'novation' might not be used in its strict legal sense of the old contract being discharged, or alternatively that any discharge and creation of a new contract may be partial so that the contract potentially remains voidable vis-à-vis the parties who did not acquire rights under it by novation.[346] Surprisingly, the simplest argument for preserving the equity to rescind in

---

[338] *Holliday v Lockwood* [1917] 2 Ch 47 (whether misrepresentation as to a shooting estate sold at an auction also vitiated the separate purchase of an adjoining farm at the same auction); *Ahuja Investments Limited v Victorygame Limited* [2020] EWHC 1153 (Ch).
[339] *Limit No 2 Ltd v Axa Versicherung AG* [2008] 2 CLC 673 (CA).
[340] *Ross River Ltd v Waveley Commercial Ltd* [2012] EWHC 81 (Ch) [254].
[341] *O'Kane v Jones* [2004] 1 Lloyd's Rep IR 174, 225–26. See also *Killick v Roberts* [1991] 1 WLR 1146 (CA). Cf *London Borough of Haringey v Hines* [2010] EWCA Civ 1111 [59].
[342] [2004] EWCA 816 [18]. See also *Samuel v Wadlow* [2007] EWCA 155 [49]–[63] (dealing with undue influence and substitute contracts).
[343] *Don Lodge Motel Limited v Invercargill Licensing Trust* [1970] NZLR 1105, 1113.
[344] *Limit No 2 Ltd v Axa Versicherung AG* [2008] 2 CLC 673 (CA).
[345] [2013] EWCA Civ 1372.
[346] *Graiseley Properties Ltd v Barclays Bank Plc* [2013] EWCA Civ 1372 [37]; *Bailey v Barclays Bank plc* [2014] EWHC 2882 (QB).

these circumstances appears not to have been dealt with before the court. It is well settled that the novation mechanism operates through an offer made by the borrower to the world at large to contract with any lender who signs a transfer certificate as transferee and fulfils any other stipulated conditions.[347] Yet if the borrower's consent to the original contract which contains this offer was vitiated by a misrepresentation, then equally each subsequent novation would also be tainted because each resulting contract is founded on flawed consent given in the original voidable contract. That is, the borrower's consent (granted upfront in the original contract) to each subsequent novation would be vitiated by the original misrepresentation, and any contract based upon such vitiated consent would be voidable along with the original contract. The situation could be different if the borrower actually executed each novation agreement, thereby consenting afresh to each substitute contract; however, the very purpose of a novation clause in a syndicated loan agreement is to render it unnecessary for the borrower to do that.

---

[347] Based on *Carlill v Carbolic Smokeball* [1893] 1 QB 256 (CA); *Argo Fund Ltd v Essar Steel Ltd* [2005] EWHC 600 [61].

5

Non-Disclosure

A. Introduction	5.01	(1) Fiduciary relationships	5.12
B. No General Duty of Disclosure	5.02	(2) Family arrangements	5.14
(1) Exceptional cases where non-disclosure permits rescission	5.04	(3) Relationships of trust and confidence	5.21
		E. Transactions where Disclosure is Required	5.24
C. Course of Dealings where Disclosure is Required	5.10	(1) Insurance	5.24
(1) Misrepresentation by silence	5.10	(2) Guarantees and suretyship	5.41
(2) Unilateral mistake	5.11	(3) Prospective partnerships	5.58
D. Relationships where Disclosure is Required	5.12	(4) Compromises	5.59
		(5) Sales of land	5.65

A. Introduction

This chapter considers the circumstances in which a contract may be rescinded because one of the parties failed to disclose material facts to the other before their agreement was concluded.[1] **5.01**

B. No General Duty of Disclosure

There is no general duty to make disclosure during the negotiations leading to the conclusion of a contract. If particular disclosures are wanted, the general rule is that they must be bargained for.[2] The Court of Appeal underlined the principle in the *Banque Keyser* case: **5.02**

> The general principle that there is no obligation to speak within the context of negotiations for an ordinary commercial contract... is one of the foundations of our law of contract, and must have been the basis of many decisions over the years. There are countless cases in which one party to a contract has in the course of negotiations failed to disclose a fact known to him which the other party would have regarded as highly material, if it had been

---

[1] In the case of contracts between consumers and traders a misleading omission may allow the consumer to 'unwind' the contract under regulations (regs 27E and 27F) inserted into the Consumer Protection from Unfair Trading Regulations 2008 by the Consumer Protection (Amendment) Regulations 2014. In some cases The Consumer Contracts (Information, Cancellation and Additional Payments) Regulations 2013 may also provide a right to cancel the contract. Such statutory rights akin to rescission are beyond the scope of this chapter.

[2] The existence of a market practice for parties to disclose particular matters to each other does not necessarily mean that a legal duty to disclose such matters arises: *National Westminster Bank Plc v Rabobank Nederland* [2007] EWHC 1056 (Comm) (no duty of disclosure arose between banks when restructuring a borrower's debts despite the fact that such disclosure was considered to be good commercial practice in the City of London).

revealed. However, ordinarily in the absence of misrepresentation, our law leaves that other party entirely without remedy.[3]

5.03 Ordinarily the failure to disclose a material fact which might influence the mind of a prudent contractor does not give a right to avoid the contract.[4] Silence is not a ground for rescission where there is no duty to make disclosure.[5] That the other contracting party may have been under a misapprehension that could be corrected by disclosure is of no consequence; the risk of mistake is allocated to the ignorant party. This is so even if the other party is aware of the first party's error.[6]

(1) Exceptional cases where non-disclosure permits rescission

5.04 In certain exceptional circumstances the law recognizes an exception to the general rule just discussed, and takes a different approach. In these circumstances, non-disclosure coupled with a relevant causal nexus makes the bargain voidable at the instance of the ignorant party. Non-disclosure where there is a duty to disclose has been said to be tantamount to an implied representation that there is nothing relevant to disclose.[7] The risk of mistake is shifted to the party with the superior knowledge. The cases are characterized not merely by asymmetric knowledge, but by an ingredient in the relationship between the parties that makes it unfair for one party to remain silent. The principal examples are usually thought to be as follows:[8]

- misrepresentation by silence;
- unilateral mistake;
- fiduciary relationships;
- family arrangements;
- insurance;
- surety contracts;
- prospective partnerships;
- compromises;
- sales of land.

5.05 The ingredient in the relationship between the parties that makes it unfair to remain silent is not the same for each type of case. There appear, however, to be three broad categories.

---

[3] *Banque Keyser Ullmann SA v Skandia (UK) Insurance Co Ltd* [1990] 1 QB 665 (CA) 798; also [1991] 2 AC 249.
[4] *Bell v Lever Bros Ltd* [1932] AC 161, 227 (Lord Atkin). But as regards the facts of *Bell v Lever Bros Ltd* some doubt has been expressed as to whether there is indeed no obligation to disclose one's own dishonesty or breach of statutory duty: *Graiseley Properties Ltd v Barclays Bank Plc* [2013] EWCA Civ 1372 [26].
[5] *Turner v Green* [1895] 2 Ch 205, 208; *Carlish v Salt* [1906] 1 Ch 335, 338.
[6] *Smith v Hughes* (1871) LR 6 QB 597, 607; *Bell v Lever Bros Ltd* [1932] AC 161, 224, 227; *Banque Keyser Ullmann SA v Skandia (UK) Insurance Co Ltd* [1990] 1 QB 665 (CA) 798–99; *Statoil ASA v Louis Dreyfus Energy Services LP* [2008] EWHC 2257 (Comm) [87]–[88]; *UTB LLC v Sheffield United Limited* [2019] EWHC 2322 (Ch). In Australia, *Westpac Banking Corp v Robinson* (1993) 30 NSWLR 668 (CA) 687–88; *Blackley Investments Pty Ltd v Burnie City Council (no 2)* [2011] TASFC 6 [16]–[20].
[7] *Conlon v Simms* [2008] 1 WLR 484 (CA) [130]. Cf HG Beale (ed), *Chitty on Contracts* (34th edn, 2021) [9-168] where it is argued that this proposition goes too far in that a breach of a duty to disclose should render the underlying contract voidable but should not sound in damages.
[8] Failure to comply with the special disclosure requirements that attend the issuing of securities often confers rights akin to rescission. But these rules are wholly creatures of statute and are therefore not considered here.

In the first category of case the ingredient is to be found in the course of the pre-contractual **5.06** dealings between the parties. That is so when non-disclosure amounts to misrepresentation by silence, or when it is coupled with unconscionable conduct permitting rescission for unilateral mistake. In these cases rescission is not permitted by reason of non-disclosure itself. Non-disclosure is, rather, the context in which other grounds for rescission operate, either misrepresentation or mistake.

In the second category of case it is the nature of the relationship between the parties over **5.07** and beyond their pre-contractual relationship that provides the ingredient making it unfair to remain silent. The principal member of this class is transactions between fiduciary and principal. Full disclosure of all of the relevant circumstances on the part of a fiduciary generally provides a defence to a claim to rescind for violation of the fair-dealing rule. Here, too, non-disclosure is a context in which some other ground for rescission operates, namely, breach of fiduciary duty. Family arrangements probably also fall into this category, but these are of much less practical importance, and overlap the third category.

In the third category of case the ingredient that makes it unfair for one party to remain silent **5.08** resides in the nature of the transaction itself. That is the position in contracts of insurance and guarantees.[9] In these cases the bargain is characterized by one of the contracting parties enjoying special access to relevant information, and a suspension of the normal principles of *caveat emptor* for essentially policy reasons. Contracts of compromise and sales of land are sometimes thought also to fall into this category. However, it will be seen that this is not so. Non-disclosure of material facts does not generally permit the rescission of compromises, and in the case of unregistered land confers purely contractual rights.

Non-disclosure itself is a ground for rescission only in the third of these three categories, **5.09** and in the case of family arrangements. In the other examples just discussed non-disclosure is better regarded as a context in which some other ground for rescission applies. For these reasons, although each member of the list set out earlier will be considered, misrepresentation by silence, unilateral mistake, and fiduciary relationships are each treated in detail elsewhere.[10]

C. Course of Dealings where Disclosure is Required

(1) Misrepresentation by silence

In exceptional circumstances silence itself amounts to a misrepresentation. The principal **5.10** example is a continuing representation that is subsequently falsified before the contract is concluded. A failure to notify the representee constitutes a misrepresentation, and rescission is permitted if the representee has relied on the falsified statement. In one of the leading cases a medical practitioner's representation about the vitality of his practice became a misrepresentation in circumstances where he stood by and said nothing after the practice died

---

[9] Cf in Australia and New Zealand, guarantees fall into the first category of case, because non-disclosure gives a right to rescind for misrepresentation. See paras [5.49], [5.50].
[10] See Chap 4, paras [4.29]–[4.31] (misrepresentation by silence); Chap 7, paras [7.12]ff (unilateral mistake); Chap 8, paras [8.03]-[8.17] (fiduciary relationships).

118　II. GROUNDS

away in the months preceding its sale.[11] Misrepresentation by silence is treated in detail in Chapter 4.[12]

(2) Unilateral mistake

5.11　In England it is likely that a contract may be rescinded in equity for unilateral mistake if an operative mistake has been made of which the other party was aware, and that party engaged in sharp practice or unconscionable conduct in connection with the mistake.[13] In Australia a contract may be rescinded for unilateral mistake if one contracting party knows that the other is labouring under a serious error, and takes advantage of that error in a manner that amounts to 'sharp practice'.[14] Singapore also permits rescission for unilateral mistake.[15] In all three jurisdictions knowledge and non-disclosure of the error is not alone sufficient to permit rescission.[16] There must be pre-contractual conduct that is so unconscionable that the court will not permit the bargain to stand. Rescission of a contract for unilateral mistake is considered in detail in Chapter 7. The more liberal rules that apply to the rescission of mistaken gifts are separately discussed in Chapter 29.

D. Relationships where Disclosure is Required

(1) Fiduciary relationships

5.12　A fiduciary is disabled from contracting with his principal unless certain conditions are satisfied. If they are not and the contract is *prima facie* voidable for failure to observe the so-called 'fair-dealing' rule, it can only be upheld if the fiduciary proves that he disclosed all matters material to the principal's decision and that the principal consented to the transaction. In this way disclosure coupled with consent provides a defence to a principal's claim to rescind.[17]

5.13　Fiduciary relationships therefore differ from the other types of case that are here discussed, in that non-disclosure is not part of the basis of the right to rescind, but rather disclosure is an ingredient that negatives it. In the other categories of case the onus of proving

---

[11] *With v O'Flanagan* [1936] Ch 575 (CA). In New Zealand, *Awaroa Holdings Ltd v Commercial Securities and Finance Ltd* [1976] 1 NZLR 19.
[12] See Chap 4, paras [4.29]–[4.31], [4.90]–[4.99]. As to whether silence can constitute 'misleading and deceptive conduct' for the purposes of a statutory prohibition on such conduct see *Charles Lloyd Property Group Pty Ltd v Buchanan* [2013] VSC 148.
[13] See Chap 7, paras [7.12]–[7.19].
[14] *Taylor v Johnson* (1983) 151 CLR 422.
[15] *Chwee Kin Keong v Digilandmall.com Pte Ltd* [2005] 1 SLR 502(R) (CA); affirmed *Olivine Capital Pte Ltd v Chia Chin Yan* [2014] 2 SLR 1371 (CA) [71]; *Quoine Pte Ltd v B2C2 Ltd* [2020] SGCA(I) 2; also, Chap 7, paras [7.22], [7.24]–[7.26].
[16] *Smith v Hughes* (1871) LR 6 QB 597, 607; *Bell v Lever Bros Ltd* [1932] AC 161, 224, 227; *Banque Keyser Ullmann SA v Skandia (UK) Insurance Co Ltd* [1990] 1 QB 665 (CA) 798–99; *Westpac Banking Corp v Robinson* (1993) 30 NSWLR 668 (CA) 687–88; *Blackley Investments Pty Ltd v Burnie City Council (No 2)* (2011) 21 Tas R 98 (Full Ct) [23]; *Chwee Kin Keong v Digilandmall.com Pte Ltd* [2005] 1 SLR 502(R) (CA); also, Chap 7, para [7.21] (where doubts about the position in Australia are noted at n 51).
[17] See Chap 8, paras [8.05]–[8.06].

non-disclosure is on the party seeking to rescind, whereas in the case of fiduciary relationships the fiduciary resisting rescission has the onus of proving full disclosure.

(2) Family arrangements

The old Chancery courts developed a rule that agreements between family members as to their respective claims to property, or which otherwise fell within the somewhat opaque category of 'family arrangements', could be set aside if one member of the family failed to disclose facts material to the other's rights, or, at one time, if the transaction was sufficiently tainted by mistake.[18] Mistakes arising from the compromise of doubtful rights between family members were, however, treated differently.[19] The rule was regarded as founded on the mutual trust and confidence that exists between the parties to a family arrangement.[20] **5.14**

The disclosure rule was developed and applied against a background of social and economic relationships that have now largely vanished. The rule was formulated in a context of 'family arrangements' that no longer exist. And although the disclosure rule seems to have been one facet of the special, paternal jurisdiction developed by the old courts of Chancery in favour of family arrangements,[21] this wider jurisdiction is itself now obsolete. For these reasons it might be thought that 'family arrangements' are today better understood as a fact pattern in which certain general principles of rescission tend to find expression, such as those concerned with unilateral mistake, undue influence, and breach of fiduciary duty. **5.15**

But this is not so. It is 'well established that there are a variety of agreements under the general head of family settlements where there is a duty to disclose',[22] and the principle has been affirmed in recent times.[23] In *Crowden v Aldridge*,[24] sixteen residuary beneficiaries who were the first cousins of the deceased signed a written direction to the executor requiring him to increase the distribution to one of the beneficiaries. Jonathan Sumption QC held that this was not a 'family arrangement' attracting a duty of disclosure, apparently because it consisted only in a binding unilateral direction and was not a contract or gift.[25] It might also have been material that the purpose of the arrangement was not to resolve a dispute. **5.16**

---

[18] Eg *Lansdown v Lansdown* (1730) 2 Jac & W 205, 37 ER 695; Sel Cas T King 364, 25 ER 441; *Griffith v Frapwel* (1732) 1 Ves Sen 401, 27 ER 1105; *Bingham v Bingham* (1748) 1 Ves Sen 126, 27 ER 934; Ves Sen Supp 79, 28 ER 462; *Cocking v Pratt* (1750) 1 Ves Sen 400, 27 ER 1105; 1 Ves Sen Supp 176, 28 ER 493; *Ramsden v Hylton* (1751) 2 Ves Sen 304, 28 ER 196; *Roberts v Roberts* [1905] 1 Ch 705 (CA). Also, E Hewitt and J Richardson, *White and Tudor's Leading Cases in Equity with Notes* (9th edn, 1928) vol 1, 192–93.
[19] *Stephens v Lord Viscount Bateman* (1778) 1 Bro CC 22, 28 ER 962; *Stone v Godfrey* (1853) 1 Sm & G 590, 65 ER 258; aff'd 5 De GM & G 76, 43 ER 798; E Hewitt and J Richardson, *White and Tudor's Leading Cases in Equity with Notes* (9th edn, 1928) vol 1, 188.
[20] J Story, *Commentaries on Equity Jurisprudence* (13th edn, 1886) vol 1 235.
[21] *Stapilton v Stapilton* (1739) 1 Atk 2, 26 ER 1; *Hoghton v Hoghton* (1852) 15 Beav 278, 300–06; 51 ER 545, 553–56; *Hoblyn v Hoblyn* (1889) 41 ChD 200, 204–06; *Cashin v Cashin* [1938] 1 All ER 536 (PC—Canada) 544.
[22] *Wales v Wadham* [1977] 1 WLR 199, 216.
[23] *Crowden v Aldridge* [1993] 1 WLR 433, 443; *Bank of Credit and Commerce International SA v Ali* [1999] 1 ICR 1068, 1077–78 (Lightman J); *Kuek Siang Wei v Kuek Siew Chew* [2015] 5 SLR 357 (CA) [63], [66]; *Yang Foo-Oi by Leung Ping Chiu, Roy, her next friend v Wai Wai Chen and Timford Resources Limited* (High Court of the HKSAR, 1739/2010, 29 November 2016, Chan J) [204]. In *Crowden v Aldridge* [1993] 1 WLR 433, 443 the court said that the cases are summarized in *Halsbury's Laws of England* (4th edn, reissue, 1984) vol 18 [315].
[24] [1993] 1 WLR 433.
[25] [1993] 1 WLR 433, 442.

5.17 Recent decisions of the Singapore Court of Appeal[26] and of the High Court of Hong Kong Special Administrative Region[27] discuss what will today count as a family arrangement attracting an obligation of disclosure. In *Kuek Siang Wei v Kuek Siew Chew*[28] the Singapore Court of Appeal concluded that a family arrangement is, broadly, an agreement between members of the same family which is intended to be generally and reasonably for the benefit of the family, and provided four examples of such arrangements.[29] That decision was followed in *Yang Foo-Oi v Wai Wai Chen*[30] where Justice Chan also cited with apparent approval the definition adopted in *Halsbury's Laws of England* (5th edn, Vol 91, §903), where it was said that:

> A family arrangement is an agreement between members of the same family, intended to be generally and reasonably for the benefit of the family either by compromising doubtful or disputed rights or by preserving the family property or the peace and security of the family by avoiding litigation or by saving its honour.

5.18 The two decisions were concerned with the valuation of assets to be distributed among family members, and explained that the obligation of disclosure is anchored partly in the circumstance that the parties to a family arrangement tend to not deal at arms-length and may repose trust and confidence in each other, and partly in policy considerations.[31] The obligation has been said to extend to such facts that are known to the family member as may reasonably affect another parties' determination as to whether they will enter into the agreement in question.[32]

Exception when the relationship is adversarial

5.19 The practical scope of the principle has been substantially narrowed in recent times, at least in England and Wales. It is now the case that whether disclosure must be made depends on how the family arrangement came to be effected; and there is no duty of disclosure when the negotiations involved neither side making full disclosure.[33] This prevents the principle applying when the relationship between the family members has broken down, and their dealings have become adversarial. Also, in Singapore, it has been held that the settlement of a dispute between a husband and wife contemplating divorce is 'antithetical to the underlying ethos of a family arrangement' for the reason that it contemplates an end to the family, rather than the preservation of family property, or the peace or security of the family, by avoiding litigation or saving its honour, which is the gist of 'family arrangements'.[34]

---

[26] *Kuek Siang Wei v Kuek Siew Chew* [2015] 5 SLR 357 (CA).
[27] *Yang Foo-Oi by Leung Ping Chiu, Roy, her next friend v Wai Wai Chen and Timford Resources Limited* (High Court of the HKSAR, 1739/2010, 29 November 2016, Chan J).
[28] [2015] 5 SLR 357 (CA).
[29] At [45]–[58], [66](a), (b).
[30] *Yang Foo-Oi by Leung Ping Chiu, Roy, her next friend v Wai Wai Chen and Timford Resources Limited* (High Court of the HKSAR, 1739/2010, 29 November 2016, Chan J).
[31] *Kuek Siang Wei v Kuek Siew Chew* [2015] 5 SLR 357 (CA) [63] (instrument set aside for non-disclosure of value of assets), applied *Yang Foo-Oi by Leung Ping Chiu, Roy, her next friend v Wai Wai Chen and Timford Resources Limited* (High Court of the HKSAR, 1739/2010, 29 November 2016, Chan J) [205]; also at [173]–[177], [180]–[183], [202]–[207], [230] (instruments distributing family fortune between children set aside for non-disclosure of *inter alia* value of assets).
[32] *Kuek Siang Wei v Kuek Siew Chew* [2015] 5 SLR 357 (CA) [62], [63], [65].
[33] *Wales v Wadham* [1977] 1 WLR 199, 218, approved on this point *Livesey v Jenkins* [1985] 1 AC 424, 439 (but overruling another of the reasons for decision in that case). It is unclear whether this represents the law in Singapore, following the reasons in *Kuek Siang Wei v Kuek Siew Chew* [2015] 5 SLR 357 (CA) [66](b)(i).
[34] *Tiong Swee Eng v Yeo Khee Siang* [2015] SGHC 116 [60] (and see also at [62]–[63]).

Separating spouses

In England and Wales there is an important exception to the principle just discussed in the case of financial arrangements entered into between separating spouses that are to be incorporated into a consent order. A duty of disclosure to the court arises in those cases, for the court is being asked to exercise its statutory power to make property adjustments or financial provision.[35] The duty extends to professional advisers.[36] Failure to comply renders the consent order voidable if it is substantially different from that which would have been made had proper disclosure taken place unless the non-disclosure is deliberate.[37] In the case of deliberate non-disclosure the consent order will be set aside if the party affected has a real prospect of doing better at a full hearing, unless the party at fault satisfies the court that when the order was made, the fraud would not have influenced a reasonable person to agree to the terms that were agreed, and nor, had it known the truth, would the court have made a significantly different order, whether or not the parties had agreed to it.[38] If the order is thereafter set aside (by a further court order) the recipient of assets transferred under it can retain those assets only by persuading the court to re-exercise a discretion in their favour on a renewed application for ancillary relief.[39]

5.20

(3) Relationships of trust and confidence

Where it is shown that one person reposes trust and confidence in another as to the management of their affairs, or in relation to the particular transaction sought to be impugned, and yet the relationship is not fiduciary in character, an obligation of candour and fairness is imposed upon the dominant party that requires him to disclose facts material to the decision to undertake the transaction.[40] In *Hewett v First Plus Financial Group plc*[41] the Court of Appeal held that in circumstances where a wife reposed trust and confidence in her husband, so as to give rise to an obligation of candour and fairness, the husband's failure to disclose an extra-marital affair rendered voidable her agreement to re-mortgage the family home. Whether that fact was material to be disclosed was to be determined on an objective test, and it did not matter whether the failure to make disclosure was deliberate or inadvertent, and nor was it relevant to inquire whether the transaction would have occurred even if disclosure had been made.[42]

5.21

---

[35] Matrimonial Causes Act 1973, ss 23–25; *Livesey v Jenkins* [1985] 1 AC 424; *Sharland v Sharland* [2016] AC 871 (fraud); *Gohil v Gohil (No 2)* [2016] AC 849 (fresh evidence). In Singapore, *BG v BF* [2007] 3 SLR(R) 233 (CA) [52], *Tiong Swee Eng v Yeo Khee Siang* [2015] SGHC 116 [62]–[63].
[36] *P v P (ancillary relief: consent order)* [2004] 1 Fam 1, 15–16.
[37] *Livesey v Jenkins* [1985] 1 AC 424, 445–46; see also *Pounds v Pounds* [1994] 1 WLR 1535 (CA) 1540; *S v S (ancillary relief: consent order)* [2003] 1 Fam 1, 6; *Norman v Norman (No 2) (Practice Note)* [2017] 1 WLR 2554 (CA) 2562–66 [46]–[60] (procedure); *CB v EB* [2020] EWFC 72 [54]–[57] (procedure). See also *Rick v Brandsema* [2009] 1 SCR 295 (SCC).
[38] *Sharland v Sharland* [2016] AC 871, applied *Goddard-Watts v Goddard-Watts* [2020] 4 WLR 51 (Fam) [61]–[64] (applying *Sharland* where the order is not a consent order).
[39] *Independent Trustee Services Ltd v GP Noble Trustees Ltd* [2013] Ch 91 (CA) [38], [42].
[40] *Hewett v First Plus Financial Group plc* [2010] 2 P & CR 22 (CA).
[41] [2010] 2 P & CR 22 (CA).
[42] *Hewett v First Plus Financial Group plc* [2010] 2 P & CR 22 (CA) [34]–[36]. The reasoning was applied in *Yang Foo-Oi by Leung Ping Chiu, Roy, her next friend v Wai Wai Chen and Timford Resources Limited* (High Court of the HKSAR, 1739/2010, 29 November 2016, Chan J) at [211]–[217] (setting aside agreements between mother and daughter as to the disposition of valuable family property).

5.22 In cases of this kind the ground for rescission is undue influence.[43] The non-disclosure is properly to be regarded as an ingredient in the abuse of confidence and trust at the heart of undue influence, and not as giving rise to an independent ground for rescission.

5.23 Whilst the decision in *Hewett v First Plus Financial Group* was concerned with a three-party case of the kind discussed in Chapter 9 of this work, the principles articulated apply equally in a two party case, where the impugned transfer is made instead to the party owing the duty of candour, rather than to a third party.[44] The principle is not confined to relationships between husband and wife, and should be engaged whenever there exists a relationship of trust and confidence sufficient to give rise to a presumption of undue influence.

E. Transactions where Disclosure is Required

(1) Insurance

5.24 The principles that apply at common law will be considered first, and then, more briefly, the rules established by the Consumer Insurance (Disclosure and Representations) Act 2012 and the Insurance Act 2015.

The common law

5.25 At common law contracts of insurance and treaties of reinsurance are contracts *uberrimae fide*, or of 'utmost good faith'.[45] Both parties are obliged prior to entry into the contract to disclose material facts, and non-disclosure gives the other a right to avoid it.[46]

5.26 The duty of disclosure is imposed by the general law, not the contract itself.[47] If a right to rescind arises, the court has no equitable jurisdiction to control its exercise.[48] On the other hand, there are authorities indicating that the insurer's obligation of good faith may itself impose some fetters on the exercise of the right to rescind, although the precise content of

---

[43] *Hewett v First Plus Financial Group plc* [2010] 2 P & CR 22 (CA) [24], [34], [37]. In Australia, the fact pattern might engage the doctrine of unconscionable conduct, if the mortgagor could be shown to be under a special disadvantage; cf *Permanent Mortgages Pty Ltd v Vandenbergh* (2010) 41 WAR 353, 397–403, (son's deliberate concealment from aged mother of purpose of obtaining mortgage over her home).

[44] For discussion of the distinction between two and three party cases in this context see D O'Sullivan, 'Developing *O'Brien*' (2002) 118 LQR 337.

[45] *Manifest Shipping Co Ltd v Uni-Polaris Insurance Co Ltd (The Star Sea)* [2003] 1 AC 469, 492 (Lord Hobhouse); *Pan Atlantic Insurance Co Ltd v Pine Top Insurance Co Ltd* [1995] 1 AC 501 (Lord Mustill); H Bennett, 'Mapping the doctrine of utmost good faith in insurance contract law' [1999] LMCLQ 165.

[46] The rule was codified in the Marine Insurance Act 1906, s 17, but applied to all forms of insurance. Section 17 of the Marine Insurance Act 1906 was altered by s 14(3) of the Insurance Act 2015 Act (and had previously been altered by s 2(5) of the Consumer Insurance (Disclosure and Representation) Act 2012, which was itself removed by the Insurance Act 2015).

[47] *Strive Shipping Corporation v Hellenic Mutual War Risks Association (The Grecia Express)* [2002] 2 Lloyd's Rep 88, 129; *Banque Keyser Ullmann SA v Skandia (UK) Insurance Co Ltd* [1990] 1 QB 665 (CA) 779–80; *Manifest Shipping Co Ltd v Uni-Polaris Insurance Co Ltd (The Star Sea)* [2003] 1 AC 469, 493.

[48] *Brotherton v Aseguradora Colseguros SA* [2003] 2 All ER (Comm) 298 (CA); *Drake Insurance plc v Provident Insurance plc* [2004] QB 601 (CA) (pet to appeal to HL refused [2004] 1 WLR 1394).

this limitation (if it exists) is yet to be worked out.[49] Breach of the duty to disclose confers no right to damages.[50]

The reason for the rule is the special nature of the insurance bargain. The insurer purchases a risk the extent of which depends upon matters peculiarly within the knowledge of the assured. Without disclosure of facts material to the risk the insurer cannot properly assess its likelihood or extent, and so whether he wishes to take it on, or at what price.[51] **5.27**

Disclosures to be made by proposing assured

The reason for the rule shapes the extent of the duty. A fact is material to be disclosed if it would influence the judgement of a prudent insurer in fixing the premium, or in determining whether he will take the risk.[52] The test is not whether the matter would have had a decisive effect on the prudent insurer's decision, but whether it would have had an effect on the mind of the prudent insurer in estimating the risk.[53] The matter need not increase the risk; it must simply affect the prudent underwriter's assessment of it.[54] It has been said that whether a fact is material rests upon the court's own appraisal of the relevance of the disputed fact to the subject matter of the insurance.[55] **5.28**

Material facts must be disclosed if they are known to the assured.[56] Wilful ignorance is equated with actual knowledge for this purpose,[57] as is knowledge of an agent imputed to the assured.[58] An assured is deemed to know every circumstance which in the ordinary **5.29**

---

[49] *Drake Insurance plc v Provident Insurance plc* [2004] QB 601 (CA). The argument that the obligation of good faith should limit an insurer's right of rescission is made in M Clarke, 'Rescission: a bridge too far for insurance good faith' [2012] LMCLQ 611. Contrast *Banks v Insurance Company of the West Indies (Cayman) Ltd* [2016] (2) CILR 442 (CA) [75], [93], [94], [96] (insurer's right to avoid for non-disclosure not conditional upon insurer acting in good faith). In Australia, exercise of an insurer's right to rescind might also be subject to equitable control, if it is shown that exercise of the right was, in the circumstances, 'unconscientious': *Greencapital Aust Pty Ltd v Pasminco Cockle Creek Smelter Pty Ltd (subject to Deed of Company Arrangement) (no 3)* [2018] NSWSC 1956 [74]–[76] (termination for failure to achieve conditions; reversed on other grounds [2019] NSWCA 53). Cf the statutory power to control exercise of the right to avoid certain policies in Australia and New Zealand: Insurance Contracts Act 1984 (Aust) ss 9, 31; Insurance Law Reform Act 1977 (NZ) ss 4–7.

[50] *Banque Keyser Ullmann SA v Skandia (UK) Insurance Co Ltd* [1990] 1 QB 665 (CA); aff'd [1991] 2 AC 249, 280; *Manifest Shipping Co Ltd v Uni-Polaris Insurance Co Ltd (The Star Sea)* [2003] 1 AC 469, 493.

[51] *Carter v Boehm* (1766) 3 Burr 1905, 97 ER 1162; 1 Black W 593, 96 ER 342; *Versloot Dredging BV v HDI Gerling Industrie Vericherung AG (DC Merwestone)* [2017] AC 1 [54], [114].

[52] Marine Insurance Act 1906, s 18(2), which codified the common law. That test has been held to apply to all forms of insurance, not only marine insurance: *Locker and Woolf Ltd v Western Australian Insurance Co Ltd* [1936] 1 KB 408 (CA) 415. Prior to 12 August 2016, s 18(6) of the Marine Insurance Act 1906 provided that s 18 of that Act did not apply to a contract of marine insurance that was a consumer insurance contract within the meaning of the Consumer Insurance (Disclosure and Representations) Act 2012. From 12 August 2016, s 18(6) was removed, along with the balance of s18, by s 21(2) of the Insurance Act 2015.

[53] *Pan Atlantic Insurance Co Ltd v Pine Top Insurance Co Ltd* [1995] 1 AC 501; *St Paul Fire and Marine Insurance Co Ltd v McConnell Dowell Constructors Ltd* [1995] 2 Lloyd's Rep 116 (CA) 124. The terms 'estimating', 'assessing', 'weighing', and 'appreciating' the risk are used in these two cases, apparently interchangeably.

[54] *St Paul Fire and Marine Insurance Co Ltd v McConnell Dowell Constructors Ltd* [1995] 2 Lloyd's Rep 116 (CA) 126.

[55] *Brit UW Ltd v F & B Trenchless Solutions Ltd* [2016] Lloyd's Rep IR 69 [102]; *Banks v Insurance Company of the West Indies (Cayman) Ltd* [2016](2) CILR 442 (CA) [53]; *Niramax Group Limited v Zurich Insurance plc* [2020] EWHC 535 (Comm) [133](iii) (and explaining the relevance of expert opinion evidence in the court's assessment).

[56] 'The duty is a duty to disclose, and you cannot disclose what you do not know. The obligation to disclose, therefore, necessarily depends on the knowledge you possess': *Joel v Law Union and Crown Insurance Co* [1908] 2 KB 863 (CA) 884.

[57] *Blackburn Low & Co v Vigors* (1887) 12 App Cas 531, 543; *Economides v Commercial Union Assurance Co Ltd* [1998] QB 587 (CA) 601–02, 607.

[58] The circumstances in which an agent's knowledge will be imputed to the assured are summarized in *Simner v New India Assurance Co Ltd* [1995] 1 Lloyd's Rep IR 240.

course of business ought to be known to him.[59] However, in non-marine cases where the assured does not effect the insurance in the course of business, the duty is confined to matters actually known to the assured.[60]

5.30 There are several exceptions to the assured's duty of disclosure at common law. They were formerly listed in section 18(3) of the Marine Insurance Act 1906 and applied to all types of insurance.[61] Disclosure need not be made of circumstances that diminish the risk, that are known or presumed to be known to the insurer, have been waived by him,[62] or that are superfluous by reason of a warranty in the policy.

Disclosures to be made by insurer

5.31 For his part the insurer's duty of disclosure extends at least to all facts known to him which are material either to the nature of the risk sought to be covered or the recoverability of a claim under the policy which a prudent insured would take into account in deciding whether or not to place the risk for which he seeks cover with that insurer.[63] Facts that would not provide a defence to a claim under the policy need not be disclosed.[64]

Non-disclosure after entry into the contract

5.32 The obligation of good faith continues after entry into a contract of insurance until litigation commences, whereupon it is superseded by the rules governing the conduct of the litigation.[65] However, it is only pre-contractual non-disclosures that confer a right to terminate *ab initio*.[66] The obligation to make disclosure after entry into the contract is more limited and confers a right to damages and possibly to terminate *de futuro*, but not *ab initio*. The principles were explained by Lord Hobhouse in *The Star Sea*:

> The right to avoid referred to in section 17 is different. It applies retrospectively. It enables the aggrieved party to rescind the contract ab initio. Thus he totally nullifies the contract. Everything done under the contract is liable to be undone. If any adjustment of the parties' financial positions is to take place, it is done under the law of restitution not under the law of contract. This is appropriate where the cause, the want of good faith, has preceded and been material to the making of the contract. But, where the want of good faith first occurs later, it becomes anomalous and disproportionate that it should be so categorised and entitle the aggrieved party to such an outcome...

---

[59] *Proudfoot v Montefiore* (1867) LR 2 QB 511; Marine Insurance Act 1906, s 18(1).
[60] *Economides v Commercial Union Assurance Co Ltd* [1998] QB 587 (CA) 601.
[61] Section 18(3) has now been replaced by the statutory regime established by the Consumer Insurance (Disclosure and Representations) Act 2012 and the Insurance Act 2015.
[62] This includes (a) waiver by reason of the questions asked in the proposal, and (b) waiver by failure to inquire after a fair presentation of the risk is made that discloses facts which would raise in the mind of a reasonable insurer at least the suspicion that there were other circumstances which would or might vitiate the presentation: *WISE (Underwriting Agency) Ltd v Grupo Nacional Provincal SA* [2004] 2 Lloyd's Rep 483 (CA); see also *Container Transport International Inc v Oceanus Mutual Underwriting Association (Bermuda) Ltd* [1984] 1 Lloyd's Rep 476; *Marc Rich & Co AG v Portman* [1997] 1 Lloyd's Rep 225 (CA) 233–34. In Australia, Insurance Contracts Act 1984 (Cth) ss 9, 21(2).
[63] *Banque Keyser Ullmann SA v Skandia (UK) Insurance Co Ltd* [1991] 2 AC 249, 268.
[64] *Banque Keyser Ullmann SA v Skandia (UK) Insurance Co Ltd* [1991] 2 AC 249, 268.
[65] *Manifest Shipping Co Ltd v Uni-Polaris Insurance Co Ltd (The Star Sea)* [2003] 1 AC 469, 505.
[66] A contract of marine insurance is deemed to be concluded when the proposal of the assured is accepted by the insurer, whether the policy is issued then or not: Marine Insurance Act 1906, s 21; and see *Cory v Patton* (1872) LR 7 QB 304; *Manifest Shipping Co Ltd v Uni-Polaris Insurance Co Ltd (The Star Sea)* [2003] 1 AC 469, 496.

A coherent scheme can be achieved by distinguishing a lack of good faith which is material to the making of the contract itself (or some variation of it) and a lack of good faith during the performance of the contract which may prejudice the other party or cause him loss or destroy the continuing contractual relationship. The former derives from requirements of the law which pre-exist the contract and are not created by it although they only become material because a contract has been entered into. The remedy is the right to elect to avoid the contract. The latter can derive from expressor implied terms of the contract; it would be a contractual obligation arising from the contract and the remedies are the contractual remedies provided by the law of contract.[67]

Inducement

5.33 To provide a ground for rescission, the non-disclosure must not only be material; it must also have induced the bargain.[68] The test of inducement is the same as the general law of contract.[69] The non-disclosure must therefore have been an inducement to contract, but need not have been the sole or principal cause.[70] The insurer or reinsurer must show that the non-disclosure (or misrepresentation) was an effective cause of its entry into the contract on the terms of the policy or treaty concluded. It must therefore show at least that, but for the relevant non-disclosure (or misrepresentation), it would not have entered the contract on those terms.[71] Whilst 'materiality' looks to the hypothetical prudent underwriter, 'inducement' looks at the effects of the non-disclosure on the actual underwriter.[72] It is therefore said that 'materiality' imports an objective inquiry, whereas the test of 'inducement' is subjective.[73]

Onus of proof

5.34 The onus of proving materiality rests on the party alleging the right to rescind. It may be that, by analogy with the rules for misrepresentation, once materiality is proved there is a rebuttable presumption of inducement. The point has not been authoritatively determined in the context of non-disclosure by a proposing assured. It does seem that if there is *prima facie* evidence of concealment, the assured is required to call evidence that he did in fact make proper disclosure.[74]

---

[67] *Manifest Shipping Co Ltd v Uni-Polaris Insurance Co Ltd (The Star Sea)* [2003] 1 AC 469, 494–95, also, *Versloot Dredging BV v HDI Gerling Industrie Vericherung AG (DC Merwestone)* [2017] AC 1, 10, 31.
[68] *Pan Atlantic Insurance Co Ltd v Pine Top Insurance Co Ltd* [1995] 1 AC 501, *Versloot Dredging BV v HDI Gerling Industrie Vericherung AG (DC Merwestone)* [2017] AC 1, 20–21. The bargain means the precise contract that was written, including its terms: *Synergy Health (UK) Ltd v CGU Insurance plc* [2011] Lloyd's Rep IR 500 [185].
[69] *St Paul Fire and Marine Insurance Co Ltd v McConnell Dowell Constructors Ltd* [1995] 2 Lloyd's Rep 116 (CA) 124.
[70] See Chap 4, para [4.104], but see also paras [4.105]–[4.109].
[71] *Assicurazioni Generali SpA v Arab Insurance Group* [2003] 1 All ER 140 (CA) [62]; *Niramax Group Limited v Zurich Insurance plc* [2020] EWHC 535 (Comm) [133](iv).
[72] *St Paul Fire and Marine Insurance Co Ltd v McConnell Dowell Constructors Ltd* [1995] 2 Lloyd's Rep 116 (CA) 125 col 1. As to the distinction between materiality and inducement in the context of misrepresentation, see Chap 4, para [4.110]. For the proposition that a court should exercise caution in assessing whether inducement has been established, *Niramax Group Limited v Zurich Insurance plc* [2020] EWHC 535 (Comm) [134], [164]–[166] (caution because rescission a draconian remedy and due to risk of hindsight bias).
[73] *Versloot Dredging BV v HDI Gerling Industrie Vericherung AG (DC Merwestone)* [2017] AC 1, 22.
[74] *Glicksman v Lancashire and General Insurance Co* [1925] 2 KB 593 (CA) 605, 610–12; aff'd but without discussion of the onus of proof [1927] AC 139.

Consumer insurance contracts—the Consumer Insurance (Disclosure and Representations) Act 2012

5.35 The Consumer Insurance (Disclosure and Representations) Act 2012 makes significant changes to the framework of rules described, in cases where insurance is obtained by consumers under contracts or variations agreed after the Act came into force on 6 April 2013.[75] The legislation applies to insurance contracts between an individual assured who enters the contract wholly or mainly for purposes unrelated to their trade, business, or profession, and an insurer who enters the contract by way of its business of insurance.[76] The proposing assured's obligation of disclosure is abolished, and replaced with a statutory duty to take reasonable care to not make a misrepresentation to the insurer.[77] The insurer's general law right of rescission in cases of misrepresentation and non-disclosure is replaced with a statutory regime in which rescission is available in a limited class of cases, and where the consequences of a qualifying misrepresentation are otherwise calibrated to its effects on the insurer.[78] The legislation also creates special rules for life insurance, agents, and insurance contracts obtained for the benefit of third parties,[79] and contains provisions adapted to preventing circumvention of the legislation by agreement.[80]

Non-consumer insurance contracts—the Insurance Act 2015

5.36 The Insurance Act 2015 came into force on 12 August 2016 and applies to contracts entered or variations agreed after that time.[81] Pursuant to the Act, for 'non-consumer insurance contracts',[82] the common law duty of disclosure is abolished[83] and replaced by the duty of fair presentation by which the proposing assured must disclose material circumstances that the insured knows or ought to know, or must give the insurer sufficient information to put a prudent insurer on notice that it needs to make enquiries for the purpose of revealing those circumstances.[84]

5.37 A circumstance is material if it would influence the judgement of a prudent insurer in determining whether to take the risk and, if so, on what terms.[85] The Act also identifies matters that need not be disclosed,[86] when a matter will be known and what matters ought to be

---

[75] Section 12(4).
[76] Section 1.
[77] Sections 2 and 11. Whether a consumer has exercised reasonable care is to be determined in accordance with the requirements set out in s 3 of the Act.
[78] Sections 4 and 5 and Sched 1.
[79] Sections 7, 8, 9, and 12 and Scheds 1 and 2.
[80] Sections 6 and 10.
[81] The Act received Royal Assent on 12 February 2015 and came into force 18 months later, and applies to contracts entered and variations agreed from that time: ss 22 and 23.
[82] 'Non-consumer insurance contracts' are contracts of insurance that are not 'consumer insurance contracts' within the meaning of the Consumer Insurance (Disclosure and Representations) Act 2012: ss 1, 2(1). For the scope and operation of the Consumer Insurance (Disclosure and Representations) Act 2012, see para [5.35].
[83] By s 14, any rule of law permitting a party to a contract of insurance to avoid the contract on the ground that utmost good faith has not been observed by other party is abolished, and the common law rule that a contract of insurance is one of utmost good faith is modified to the extent required by the Act.
[84] Section 3(1),(4). Material representations of fact must also be substantially correct and material representations as to expectations or belief must be made in good faith: s 3(3)(c). Disclosure must be made in a way that would be reasonably clear and accessible to a prudent insurer: s 3(3)(b).
[85] Section 7(3).
[86] Section 3(5): absent enquiry, circumstances that diminish the risk, that the insurer knows or ought to know or is presumed to know, or is something as to which the insurer waives information.

known by insurer and insured,[87] and when a representation will be regarded as substantially correct.[88]

5.38 The Insurance Act 2015 also abolishes the common law right to rescind a contract of insurance for non-disclosure (and misrepresentation).[89] It provides that if the insurer or reinsurer can show that a non-disclosure (or misrepresentation) amounting to a breach of the duty of fair presentation would have caused the risk to be declined or insurance to be offered only on different terms, the insurer or reinsurer obtains the remedies set out in Schedule 1 to the Act.[90] The Schedule 1 remedies are calibrated to the significance of the non-disclosure (or misrepresentation) and the culpability of the proposing assured.

5.39 The insurer or reinsurer may rescind for non-disclosure by a proposing assured only if it establishes that (a) the breach was deliberate or reckless or (b) it was not but the insurer or reinsurer would not have provided cover on any terms had proper disclosure (or no misrepresentation) been made.[91] In addition, if the breach of the duty of fair presentation was neither deliberate nor reckless, premium income must be returned when the contract is avoided; but it need not be if the insurer or reinsurer establishes that the breach was deliberate or reckless.[92]

Other Commonwealth jurisdictions

5.40 In each of Australia, New Zealand, and Canada legislation has also substantially reformed the English common law in favour of the proposing assured. Australian legislation obliges insurers providing certain classes of insurance to notify the proposing assured of their duty of disclosure, failing which compliance with the duty to disclose is regarded as having been waived.[93] Moreover, for some types of insurance the policy may be avoided only where the non-disclosure is fraudulent, and even then the court has power to disregard the avoidance in certain circumstances.[94] Canadian law has similarly been overtaken by legislation enacted by each of the different Provinces,[95] and in New Zealand the English common law as to disclosure has also been altered by legislation in favour of the proposing assured,[96] although it has been argued that New Zealand law requires further statutory reform.[97]

---

[87] Sections 4, 5, 6.
[88] A material representation is substantially correct if a prudent insurer would not consider the difference between what is represented and the true position to be material: s 7(5).
[89] Section 14(1), also ss 3, 8 and Sched 1.
[90] Section 8(1),(2), Sch 1.
[91] Section 8(1),(5),(6) and Sched 1, paras 2–5.
[92] Schedule 1, paras 2(b), 3, 4, 8(b), 9(2). The Insurance Act 2015 also reforms the common law as to warranties (ss 9, 10) and other breaches of the insurance policy (s 11) in a manner favourable to the insured. An insurer may continue to refuse to pay any fraudulent claim (ss 12, 13) but must pay a claim within a reasonable time (s 13A). Sections 15 to 17 limit the right to contract out of the Act.
[93] Insurance Contracts Act 1984 (Cth) ss 9, 21A, 22; Insurance Contract Regulations 2017 Reg 7, 8. The insurer itself must also provide a key fact sheet in the case of certain insurance contracts: ss 33A–D; Insurance Contract Regulations 2017 Reg 11–13.
[94] Insurance Contracts Act 1984 (Cth) ss 9, 28–33.
[95] C Brown and A Mercer, *Introduction to Canadian Insurance Law* (4th edn, 2018); *Canadian Indemnity Co v Johns-Manville Co* [1990] 2 SCR 549.
[96] Insurance Law Reform Act 1977 (NZ), ss 4–7.
[97] H Wham, '"If They Wanted to Know, Why Didn't They Ask?" A Review of the Insured's Duty of Disclosure' (2014) 20 Auckland Univ LR 73, 100. The New Zealand Government has announced a review of insurance contract law, and the terms of reference for the review released in March 2018 included a review of disclosure obligations and remedies for non-disclosure. An exposure draft Bill was released for consultation between 24 February 2022 and 4 May 2022.

(2) Guarantees and suretyship

No general duty to disclose

5.41 Contracts of guarantee and insurance are similar in that both involve the transfer and the purchase of a contingent risk. However, the relationship between the parties is materially different and for this reason ordinary guarantees are not regarded as bargains *uberrimae fide*.[98] The key difference is said to be that:

> The risk undertaken is generally known to the surety, and the circumstances generally point to the view that as between the creditor and surety it was contemplated and intended that the surety should take upon himself to ascertain exactly what risk he was taking upon himself.[99]

5.42 Although wider statements can be found in some older authorities,[100] the rule today is that a creditor owes no general duty to disclose material facts to an intended surety.[101]

Duty to disclose unusual features

5.43 A creditor does however owe a limited duty to make disclosure to an intended surety. The duty is peculiar to guarantees and other suretyship contracts and does not apply to contracts generally. Breach of the duty makes the guarantee voidable at the option of the surety.[102] The Court of Appeal has suggested *obiter* that non-disclosure to a proposing surety takes effect as a misrepresentation on which the surety has relied,[103] and Mr Justice Teare has since expressed that opinion in strong terms, deciding as follows:

> If the correct jurisprudential analysis of the limited duty of disclosure is not implied representation it is difficult to know what it is. It is certainly not a duty to disclose matters which are material for a guarantor to know and a more limited duty of disclosure is not known to the law of contract. Both the cases and the textbooks indicate that implied representation is the correct analysis. That is also the analysis suggested by an analysis of the guarantor's

---

[98] *North Shore Ventures Ltd v Anstead Holdings Inc* [2012] Ch 31 (CA) [14], [29] (Sir Andrew Morritt C, with whose reasons Smith and Tomlinson LJJ agreed); *Deutsche Bank AG v Unitech Global Ltd (No 2)* [2013] 2 Lloyd's Rep 629 [47].

[99] *Seaton v Heath* [1899] 1 QB 782 (CA) 792–93, cited with approval on this point *Royal Bank of Scotland plc v Etridge (No 2)* [2002] 2 AC 773, 848. To similar effect, *Lee v Jones* (1864) 17 CB (NS) 482, 503; 141 ER 194 (Blackburn J). In Australia, *Commercial Bank of Australia Ltd v Amadio* (1983) 151 CLR 447, 454–57 (Gibbs CJ). The restriction on the duty of disclosure in the case of a loan guarantee is said to be justified by commercial necessity: *North Shore Ventures Ltd v Anstead Holdings Inc* [2012] Ch 31 (CA) [30] (referring to the speech of Lord Campbell in *Hamilton v Watson* (1845) 12 Cl & F 109, 8 ER 1339 (HL Sc)).

[100] *Pidcock v Bishop* (1825) 3 B & C 605, 610; 107 ER 857; *Owen v Homan* (1851) 3 Mac & G 378, 396–97; 42 ER 307 (Lord Truro LC) (but cf on appeal (1853) 4 HLC 997, 10 ER 752).

[101] *Hamilton v Watson* (1845) 12 Cl & F 109, 119; 8 ER 1339 (HL Sc); *The North British Insurance Co v Lloyd* (1854) 10 Ex 523, 533–35; 156 ER 545; *Lee v Jones* (1864) 17 CB (NS) 482, 503; 141 ER 194; *Seaton v Heath* [1899] 1 QB 782 (CA) 792; *North Shore Ventures Ltd v Anstead Holdings Inc* [2012] Ch 31 (CA) [14], [29], [31]. For the special rules that apply where a wife guarantees her husband's debts, see Chap 9, Part C.

[102] *Royal Bank of Scotland plc v Etridge (No 2)* [2002] 2 AC 773 [350] (Lord Scott, with whose reasons Lord Nicholls agreed). *Deutsche Bank AG v Unitech Global Ltd (No 2)* [2013] 2 Lloyd's Rep 629 [56]. Cf in Canada, *Toronto Dominion Bank v Rooke* (1983) 3 DLR (4th) 715 (BCCA): effect of non-disclosure is 'to entirely release the guarantors from their obligation... the guarantee was therefore voided...'.

[103] *North Shore Ventures Ltd v Anstead Holdings Inc* [2012] Ch 31 (CA) [29], [33] (Sir Andrew Morritt C, with whose reasons Smith and Tomlinson LJJ agreed). The position was expressed more tentatively in *Credit Lyonnais Bank Nederland v Export Credit Guarantee Department* [1996] 1 Lloyd's Rep 200, 216: 'It may be that, in general, there is an implied representation that unusual matters, material to the guarantee, do not exist'. See also W Courtney, J O'Donovan, and J Phillips, *The Modern Contract of Guarantee* (4th English edn, 2020) [4-403].

position. In the absence of disclosure he would assume that there are no unusual features of the contractual relationship between the creditor and the debtor. Thus a failure to disclose amounts to an implied representation that there are no unusual features. I am therefore satisfied that implied representation is the correct analysis. That being so the remedy is rescission.[104]

If this is the correct analysis, English law now aligns with the position adopted in Australia and New Zealand. The courts there have held that the right to rescind following a relevant non-disclosure to a proposing surety is founded upon the non-disclosure giving rise to a misrepresentation.[105]

5.44 The precise ambit of the duty of disclosure has been said to be unclear,[106] and formulations with different emphases may be found.[107] In *Royal Bank of Scotland plc v Etridge (No 2)*[108] Lord Nicholls said that it encompassed any unusual feature of the contract between the creditor and the debtor which makes it materially different in a potentially disadvantageous respect from what the guarantor might naturally expect. Lord Scott said that the obligation should extend to unusual features of the contractual relationship between the creditor and the principal debtor, or between the creditor and other creditors of the principal debtor, that would or might affect the rights of the surety.[109]

5.45 Lord Scott's formula was adopted in *North Shore Ventures Ltd v Anstead Holdings Inc*.[110] The Court of Appeal there held that a creditor owed no duty to disclose facts or matters which were not unusual features of the contractual relationship between the creditor and the debtor, or between the creditor and other creditors of the debtor.[111] The creditor's duty of disclosure was held to be as stated by Lord Campbell in *Hamilton v Watson*.[112] The obligation is to disclose to the surety any contract or other dealing between creditor and debtor so as to change the position of the debtor from what the surety might naturally expect, but not other matters relating to the debtor which might be material for the surety to know.[113]

5.46 The unusual feature must be something not known to the intended surety.[114] It is not enough that the creditor reasonably believes that the surety knows of the unusual circumstance;

---

[104] *Deutsche Bank AG v Unitech Global Ltd (No 2)* [2013] 2 Lloyd's Rep 629 [56].
[105] Discussed at paras [5.49]–[5.51].
[106] *Royal Bank of Scotland plc v Etridge (No 2)* [2002] 2 AC 773, 812.
[107] *Hamilton v Watson* (1845) 12 Cl & F 109, 119; 8 ER 1339; *Lee v Jones* (1864) 17 CB (NS) 482, 503–04; 141 ER 194; *London General Omnibus Co Ltd v Holloway* [1912] 2 KB 72 (CA) 78. In Australia, *Union Bank of Australia Ltd v Puddy* [1949] VLR 242, 247 (Fullagar J); *Goodwin v National Bank of Australasia Ltd* (1968) 117 CLR 173, 175; *Commercial Bank of Australia Ltd v Amadio* (1983) 151 CLR 447, 454–57; *Westpac Banking Corp v Robinson* (1993) 30 NSWLR 668 (CA). In New Zealand, *Scales Trading Ltd v Far Eastern Shipping Co Public Ltd* [1999] 3 NZLR 26 (CA).
[108] [2002] 2 AC 773, 812. The language is that used in *Levett v Barclays Bank plc* [1995] 1 WLR 1260, 1275 (Michael Burton QC).
[109] *Royal Bank of Scotland plc v Etridge (No 2)* [2002] 2 AC 773, 848. Both Lord Nicholls and Lord Scott referred with approval to the discussion in J O'Donovan and J Phillips, *The Modern Contract of Guarantee* (3rd edn, 1996) 122–31. See now W Courtney, J O'Donovan, and J Phillips, *The Modern Contract of Guarantee* (4th English edn, 2020) [4-05]–[4-21].
[110] [2012] Ch 31 (CA).
[111] *North Shore Ventures Ltd v Anstead Holdings Inc* [2012] Ch 31 (CA) [31] (Sir Andrew Morritt C, with whose reasons Smith and Tomlinson LJJ agreed).
[112] (1845) 12 Cl & F 109, 8 ER 1339.
[113] *North Shore Ventures Ltd v Anstead Holdings Inc* [2012] Ch 31 (CA) [14], [27]–[31], [57], [63]; applied, *Deutsche Bank AG v Unitech Global Ltd (No 2)* [2013] 2 Lloyd's Rep 629 [45]–[52].
[114] *Levett v Barclays Bank plc* [1995] 1 WLR 1260, 1273; *North Shore Ventures Ltd v Anstead Holdings Inc* [2012] Ch 31 (CA).

what matters is whether the surety is in fact aware of the relevant fact or matter.[115] If the surety is aware of the unusual circumstance there can be no misrepresentation on which the surety relied, and therefore no right to rescind can arise.[116] Importantly, the unusual feature must relate to the transaction between creditor and debtor or transactions between the creditor and other creditors of the debtor;[117] unusual features of transactions between the debtor and third parties need not be disclosed.[118]

5.47 Matters relating only to the debtor's credit generally need not be disclosed even if they indicate a parlous financial situation.[119] Moreover, in the case of ordinary cash guarantees, unusual features of the transaction between debtor and creditor do not extend to suspicions that the debtor is guilty of fraud in relation to the transaction.[120] It has also been held that no disclosure needed to be made where the creditor knew that the debtor had committed forgery and embezzlement,[121] or that the customer's bankrupt husband was able to draw on her account and orders had been given not to pay some cheques.[122] Similarly disclosure was not required of the circumstance that principals of the debtor company were being investigated for alleged embezzlement in Switzerland and their bank accounts there had been frozen, and that there was a risk that part of the loan funds would be frozen if paid into a Swiss bank account.[123] There could likewise be no obligation to disclose unlawful manipulations of the LIBOR exchange rate by one party to a credit agreement, for that conduct was not a feature of the contractual arrangement between the creditor and debtor.[124] The limited duty of disclosure to guarantors did not extend to a duty to inform the guarantor as to the potential consequences of the debtor later entering into a related interest rate–hedging transaction.[125] The duty to disclose unusual facts is not a continuing duty.[126] However, arguably the duty revives in relation to amendments to the guarantee and possibly in respect of requests for the guarantor to consent to variations to the contract between the creditor and the debtor which would otherwise have discharged the guarantee.[127]

---

[115] *North Shore Ventures Ltd v Anstead Holdings Inc* [2012] Ch 31 (CA) [46], [48].
[116] *North Shore Ventures Ltd v Anstead Holdings Inc* [2012] Ch 31 (CA) [33].
[117] *Royal Bank of Scotland plc v Etridge (No 2)* [2002] 2 AC 773, 848.
[118] *Credit Lyonnais Bank Nederland v Export Credit Guarantee Department* [1996] 1 Lloyd's Rep 200, 226–27, aff'd on other grounds [2000] 1 AC 486.
[119] *Wythes v Labouchere* (1859) 3 De G & 593, 609; 44 ER 1397. In Australia, *Commercial Bank of Australia Ltd v Amadio* (1983) 151 CLR 447, 454–57; *Westpac Banking Corp v Robinson* (1993) 30 NSWLR 668 (CA) 697; *Radin v Commonwealth Bank of Australia* [1998] FCA 1361.
[120] *National Provincial Bank of England Ltd v Glanusk* [1913] 3 KB 335; followed on this point *Credit Lyonnais Bank Nederland v Export Credit Guarantee Department* [1996] 1 Lloyd's Rep 200, 227; cf *Far Eastern Shipping Co Public Ltd v Scales Trading Ltd* [2001] Lloyd's Rep Bank 29 (PC—NZ). See also *North Shore Ventures Ltd v Anstead Holdings Inc* [2012] Ch 31 (CA) [29].
[121] *Fitzgerald v Jacomb* (1873) 4 AJR 189 (FC Sup Ct Vict).
[122] *Cooper v National Provincial Bank Ltd* [1946] KB 1. For a list of matters that need not be disclosed, W Courtney J O'Donovan, and J Phillips *The Modern Contract of Guarantee* (4th English edn, 2020) [4-20].
[123] *North Shore Ventures Ltd v Anstead Holdings Inc* [2012] Ch 31 (CA) [37], [46], [53]. For a list of matters that need not be disclosed, W Courtney, J O'Donovan, and J Phillips, *The Modern Contract of Guarantee* (4th English edn, 2020) [4-020].
[124] *Deutsche Bank AG v Unitech Global Ltd (No 2)* [2013] 2 Lloyd's Rep 629 [51]–[52]. Similarly there could be no obligation to disclose the alleged unsuitability of the terms of the credit agreement, of which the creditor was alleged to have been aware: [2013] 2 Lloyd's Rep 629 [49]–[50]. Cf *Deutsche Bank AG v Unitech Global Ltd* [2013] EWCA Civ 1372 (an appeal in a related case).
[125] *Barclays Bank Plc v Borkhatria* [2018] EWHC 1326 (Comm).
[126] *Barclays Bank Plc v Borkhatria* [2018] EWHC 1326 (Comm) [32]–[33].
[127] *Barclays Bank Plc v Borkhatria* [2018] EWHC 1326 (Comm) [34]–[35].

It is possible for a creditor to contract out of the duty of disclosure by making it clear to the surety that no disclosure would be made and that the creditor leaves it to the surety to ascertain for itself all material facts relating to the transaction,[128] presumably in circumstances where it is possible for the surety to do this; that is, where the information regarding the unusual feature is not solely in possession of the creditor. **5.48**

The duty in other Commonwealth jurisdictions
Australia
Australian law requires a creditor to disclose to the intended surety circumstances that are not naturally to be expected in the transaction between the creditor and debtor.[129] The circumstances must be such that non-disclosure amounts to a representation that no such circumstances exist, and it is the misrepresentation from silence arising from non-disclosure that founds the right to rescind.[130] **5.49**

The New South Wales Court of Appeal has said that 'mere non-disclosure in breach of the special rule will not itself be sufficient to avoid the guarantee, rather, general equitable principles governing rescission will apply'.[131] These 'general equitable principles governing rescission' to which the court referred appear to be the established bars to rescission; certainly that is the proposition to be derived from *MacKenzie v Royal Bank of Canada*,[132] which the court referred to as authority in connection with its formulae.[133] **5.50**

New Zealand
New Zealand law also views the right to rescind as deriving from the creditor's non-disclosure giving rise to a misrepresentation, with the result that the regime established by the Contract and Commercial Law Act 2017 (NZ) probably governs the right to rescind guarantees affected by non-disclosure. The Court of Appeal initially formulated the principle thus: 'A creditor's failure to disclose to a guarantor a material fact known to him will vitiate the guarantee if the non-disclosure amounts to a misrepresentation. That will be so if the fact is inconsistent with the presumed basis of the contract of guarantee.'[134] But it was later said in the *Scales Trading* litigation that 'There is little if any difference between the "unusual", the "different from natural expectation", and the "presumed basis of the contract"'.[135] The Court **5.51**

---

[128] *Trade Indemnity Co Ltd v Workington Harbour and Dock Board (No 1)* [1937] AC 1 (HL) 17–18.
[129] *Goodwin v National Bank of Australasia Ltd* (1968) 117 CLR 173, 175 (existence of guarantee given by debtor to creditor not required to be disclosed). The obligation probably does not extend to the creditworthiness of other co-sureties: *Behan v Obelon Pty Ltd* (1985) 167 CLR 326.
[130] *Goodwin v National Bank of Australasia Ltd* (1968) 117 CLR 173, 175; *Commercial Bank of Australia Ltd v Amadio* (1983) 151 CLR 447, 455; *Westpac Banking Corp v Robinson* (1993) 30 NSWLR 668 (CA) 688–90 (and disapproving the view expressed in *Behan v Obelon Pty Ltd* [1984] 2 NSWLR 637, 639); *Zachariadis v Allforks Australia Pty Ltd* (2009) 26 VR 47 (CA) [73]. See also *Credit Lyonnais Bank Nederland v Export Credit Guarantee Department* [1996] 1 Lloyd's Rep 200, 216 'It may be that, in general, there is an implied representation that unusual matters, material to the guarantee, do not exist'.
[131] *Westpac Banking Corp v Robinson* (1993) 30 NSWLR 668 (CA) 690. W Courtney, J O'Donovan, and J Phillips *The Modern Contract of Guarantee* (4th English edn, 2020) [4-32] is to similar effect.
[132] [1934] 1 AC 468 (PC—Canada) 475–76.
[133] *Westpac Banking Corp v Robinson* (1993) 30 NSWLR 668 (CA) 690. The obligation to make disclosure has common law origins, and it is likely that the surety also obtains a common law right to rescind: Chap 10, para [10.23].
[134] *Westpac Securities Ltd v Dickie* [1991] 1 NZLR 657 (CA) 662–63.
[135] *Scales Trading Ltd v Far Eastern Shipping Co Public Ltd* [1999] 3 NZLR 26 (CA). Also, *Shivas v Bank of New Zealand* [1990] 2 NZLR 327 (HC); *Chapman v Westpac New Zealand Limited* [2018] NZHC 1986 [31]–[39], [53]; P Watts, 'Rescission of Guarantees for Misrepresentation and Actionable Non-Disclosure' (2002) 61 CLJ 301.

of Appeal went on to say that non-disclosure involves an implied representation there is nothing unusual in the contract to be guaranteed, and that the Contractual Remedies Act 1979 (NZ) probably governs the right to rescind in such cases.[136]

Canada

5.52 In Canadian law the creditor's duty is to disclose material facts,[137] and this means facts connected to the dealings between debtor and creditor which are the subject of the guarantee, which would be likely to affect the mind of a reasonable guarantor, and which the guarantor would expect not to exist.[138] For example, in *Toronto Dominion Bank v Rooke*[139] the British Columbia Court of Appeal held that a guarantee of a company's debts was unenforceable in circumstances where, when obtaining the guarantor's consent to an increase in borrowing, the creditor bank neglected to disclose that the company's directors had established a competing business. This was said to be something that the guarantors would expect not to exist, and made the guarantee unenforceable. It is doubtful that disclosure of this circumstance would have been required under English law, at least if the point arose before the guarantee was first given.[140]

Duty to disclose varies with the circumstances

5.53 The extent of disclosure required may vary as between different types of guarantee.[141] A more stringent requirement existed in the case of so-called 'fidelity bonds' guaranteeing the honesty of an employee. Although now largely obsolete, they featured in reported cases in the nineteenth and early twentieth century.[142] The employer giving the bond had to disclose to the surety any acts of dishonesty by the employee that he has notice of and, if there was dishonesty, a failure to disclose it is an implied misrepresentation.[143] However, the distinction between fidelity and other guarantees has been doubted in more recent authority.[144]

5.54 Canadian law draws a distinction between 'accommodation sureties', who enter into a guarantee in the expectation of little or no remuneration and for the purpose of accommodating others or assisting them in the accomplishment of their plans, and 'compensation sureties'

---

[136] *Scales Trading Ltd v Far Eastern Shipping Co Public Ltd* [1999] 3 NZLR 26 (CA). The Privy Council did not express a view on the point in the subsequent appeal, and overturned the Court of Appeal's decision on other grounds: *Far Eastern Shipping Co Public Ltd v Scales Trading Ltd* [2001] Lloyd's Rep Bank 29 (PC—NZ). The Contractual Remedies Act 1979 (NZ) has since been replaced by the provisions in Subpart 3 of Part 2 of the Contract and Commercial Law Act 2017 (NZ).

[137] 'To what extent is there an obligation upon a creditor to disclose before a guarantee is given? It is clear on the authorities that the duty is to disclose to a surety a material fact': *Bank of Montreal v Collum* (2004) 29 BCLR (4th) 18 (BCCA).

[138] *Toronto Dominion Bank v Rooke* (1983) 3 DLR (4th) 715 (BCCA) (Esson JA); *Bank of Montreal v Collum* (2004) 29 BCLR (4th) 18 (BCCA) [35], [40].

[139] (1983) 3 DLR (4th) 715 (BCCA).

[140] *National Provincial Bank of England Ltd v Glanusk* [1913] 3 KB 335, 339 (no need to disclose suspicion that debtor, agent of the surety, was defrauding the surety by making improper payments out of overdrawn, guaranteed account).

[141] *Levett v Barclays Bank plc* [1995] 1 WLR 1260, 1273. That case was cited with apparent approval by the Court of Appeal in *Lloyds TSB Bank plc v Shorney*, The Times, 25 October 2001.

[142] *Railton v Mathews* (1844) 10 Cl & Fin 934, 943; 8 ER 993 (HL Sc); *London General Omnibus Co Ltd v Holloway* [1912] 2 KB 72 (CA).

[143] *London General Omnibus Co Ltd v Holloway* [1912] 2 KB 72 (CA).

[144] *North Shore Ventures Ltd v Anstead Holdings Inc* [2011] 1 All ER (Comm) 81 [119] and [2012] Ch 31 (CA) [30].

who act for profit. The former are afforded greater protection than the latter.[145] There are some suggestions that this distinction extends to the surety's entitlement to insist upon disclosure, and that it shapes the facts that are material to be disclosed in a given case.[146]

Materiality and inducement
Materiality

The English authorities do not suggest that the circumstances not disclosed must be in some **5.55** sense 'material' before there is a right to set aside the guarantee. It is sufficient if they are relevantly unusual, and have the requisite connection with the transaction between debtor and creditor. That also seems to be the approach in Australia. In Canada, on the other hand, as has just been observed, the gist of the duty is to disclose material facts, which are facts that would be likely to affect the mind of a reasonable surety, and that the surety would expect not to exist.[147]

Inducement or reliance

The non-disclosure must have induced the giving of the guarantee. This conclusion may **5.56** be drawn as a creditor's failure to disclose unusual features in the transaction involves an implied representation that none exist, and the right to rescind flows from the implied misrepresentation by silence.[148] Since non-disclosure takes effect in that way,[149] inducement is a condition of rescission, just as it is for misrepresentation generally. Thus if the guarantor knew of the unusual matter not disclosed then the failure of the creditor to disclose that matter could not have constituted a misrepresentation on which the surety relied, and the non-disclosure would not permit rescission.[150]

There is a rebuttable presumption that a representee has relied upon 'material' represen- **5.57** tations.[151] An argument can be made that there should be a similar presumption where a guarantee is entered after a creditor has failed to disclose unusual features in his transaction with the debtor.

(3) Prospective partnerships

A duty of disclosure arises between prospective partners who are in negotiations to enter **5.58** into a partnership:

> [T]principle of caveat emptor does not apply to the making of a partnership agreement, and that in negotiating such an agreement a party owes a duty to the other negotiating

---

[145] *Citadel General Assurance Co v Johns-Manville Canada Inc* [1983] 1 SCR 513; *Manulife Bank of Canada v Conlin* [1996] 3 SCR 415, 428.
[146] *Bank of Montreal v Collum* (2004) 29 BCLR (4th) 18 (BCCA) [37]–[45].
[147] *Toronto Dominion Bank v Rooke* (1983) 3 DLR (4th) 715 (BCCA) (Esson JA); *Bank of Montreal v Collum* (2004) 29 BCLR (4th) 18 (BCCA) [35], [40]. Petition for leave to appeal dismissed [2004] SCCA No 412.
[148] *North Shore Ventures Ltd v Anstead Holdings Inc* [2012] Ch 31 (CA) [29].
[149] See also *Conlon v Simms* [2008] 1 WLR 484 (CA) [130].
[150] *North Shore Ventures Ltd v Anstead Holdings Inc* [2012] Ch 31 (CA) [33].
[151] *Mathias v Yetts* (1882) 46 LT 497 (CA) 502; *Baker v LSREF III Wight Ltd* [2016] 2 WLUK 408; [2016] BPIR 509 (duty may also exist in respect of prospective joint venturers); Chap 4, paras [4.110]–[4.113].

parties to disclose all material facts of which he has knowledge and of which the other negotiating parties may not be aware.[152]

In the absence of fraud, breach of this duty will generally permit rescission only and will not confer a claim for damages.[153]

(4) Compromises

5.59 There are certain old cases that may suggest that there is a general duty of disclosure before a compromise is entered. Many of these cases are discussed in *The Law Relating to Compromises*, where it is said that compromises are contracts *uberrimae fide*, and non-disclosure of material facts not known to the other renders the agreement voidable.[154] But all of the authorities cited appear to be concerned with fact patterns peculiar to their time, involving compromises of uncertain claims to family assets by members of the family.[155] They are best understood as founded on the special requirement for disclosure in 'family arrangements', considered separately earlier, and not as establishing principles that govern compromises generally. It is suggested that the true principle is that stated by Lightman J in *BCCI v Ali*,[156] and is that there is no general duty of disclosure when agreeing a compromise, unless it involves a 'family arrangement'. The same opinion is expressed in *White and Tudor's Leading Cases*.[157] Compromises are not contracts *uberrimae fide*.[158] The House of Lords' reasoning in *BCCI v Ali* seems, indeed, to have regarded both of these propositions as self-evident.[159] In *Silver Queen Maritime Ltd v Persia Petroleum Services plc* Lindblom J concluded that:

---

[152] *Conlon v Simms* [2008] 1 WLR 484 (CA) [127]–[128].
[153] *Conlon v Simms* [2008] 1 WLR 484 (CA) [129].
[154] WD Edwards, *The Law Relating to Compromises of Litigation, Disputes and Differences with a Chapter on Family Arrangements and Similar Transactions* (1925) 141–47, discussing principally *Pusey v Desbouvrie* (1734) 3 P Wms 315, 24 ER 1081; *Gibbons v Caunt* (1799) 4 Ves 840, 849; 31 ER 435; *Gordon v Gordon* (1816–21) 3 Swans 400, 477; 36 ER 910; *Grove v Perkins* (1834) 6 Sin 576, 583; 58 ER 510; *Sturge v Sturge* (1849) 12 Beav 229, 50 ER 1049; *Brooke v Lord Mostyn* (1864) 2 De GJ & Sm 373, 416; 46 ER 419. Edwards also said that the indications to the contrary in *Turner v Green* [1895] 2 Ch 205 were against the current of authority.
[155] *Pusey v Desbouvrie* (1734) 3 P Wms 315, 24 ER 1081 (inconclusive comments *obiter* as to possibility of setting aside daughter's election to take one part of father's estate instead of another, where ignorant of rights); *Gibbons v Caunt* (1799) 4 Ves 840, 849; 31 ER 435 (Lord Eldon LC stating requirement for full understanding of rights in order to validly compromise claims under will); *Gordon v Gordon* (1816–21) 3 Swans 400, 477; 36 ER 910 (compromise of claims between two brothers in respect of family estate rescinded after 19 years; proved that younger brother had knowingly failed to disclose parent's secret marriage ceremony, contrary to his claim of elder brother's illegitimacy); *Grove v Perkins* (1834) 6 Sin 576, 583; 58 ER 510 (conveyance of husband's interest in deceased estate to wife set aside for lack of disclosure as to its extent and value); *Sturge v Sturge* (1849) 12 Beav 229, 244–45; 50 ER 1049 (rescission of conveyance of interest in estate by one brother to others in ignorance of extent of his right to it and without full disclosure by other brothers, who alleged a compromise of family differences); *Brooke v Lord Mostyn* (1864) 2 De GJ & Sm 373, 416; 46 ER 419 (statement *obiter* that compromise between persons of full age may be set aside if knowledge on one side withheld, but in the context of non-disclosure of documents to a court sanctioning infant's compromise); rev on other grounds (1866) LR 4 HL 304.
[156] *Bank of Credit and Commerce International SA v Ali* [1999] 1 ICR 1068, 1077–78.
[157] E Hewitt and J Richardson, *White and Tudor's Leading Cases in Equity with Notes* (9th edn, 1928) vol 1, 192.
[158] *Wales v Wadham* [1977] 1 WLR 199, 215–16; *Livesey v Jenkins* [1985] 1 AC 424, 439.
[159] *Bank of Credit and Commerce International SA v Ali* [2002] 1 AC 251 See further, D Foskett, *Foskett on Compromise* (9th edn, 2020) [4-38]–[4-39]. Cf settlements where one party suppresses a fact or document that would totally destroy his claim, or which is made in circumstances where one party knows his claim to be baseless: D Foskett, *Foskett on Compromise* (9th edn, 2020) at [4-40].

the idea that the negotiation of agreements to settle hostile litigation generally gives rise to a duty of disclosure is misconceived. The existence of such a duty would not be consistent with the general position that parties negotiating for a contract do not owe duties of disclosure to each other. An agreement to settle litigation is not, or at least normally is not, a contract *uberrimae fidei*.[160]

It is suggested that this passage accurately states the law. A similar principle has been recognized in Singapore.[161]

Releases unsupported by consideration

In *BCCI v Ali*[162] Lightman J also said that there was a distinction between a release of rights that was supported by consideration, and one that was not. In the former case there was no general duty of disclosure, but there was in the latter.[163] A similar distinction seems to have been drawn by Tudor Evans J in *Wales v Wadham*.[164] **5.60**

There is a basis in principle for this distinction. A release wholly unsupported by consideration is akin to a gift, and gifts are more easily rescinded than are simple contracts; in particular, a serious unilateral mistake as to the effects of a deed of gift will permit it to be set aside, but the same mistake will not affect the enforceability of a reciprocal contract.[165] If a similar distinction was to be recognized in the case of releases, the beneficiary of a deed of release would naturally be obliged to make full disclosure of material facts if the release was to be upheld, for, absent disclosure, it would be vulnerable to rescission for unilateral mistake. **5.61**

However, although this distinction was not specifically discussed in the appeals in *BCCI v Ali*, the reasoning of both the Court of Appeal and House of Lords appears to be against it.[166] In particular, Lord Nicholls and Lord Hoffmann considered the right to equitable relief when the beneficiary of a release fails to disclose that the other may have a claim, without suggesting that it made any difference whether valuable consideration was given.[167] Accordingly, although there is both authority and principle in favour of a general duty of disclosure when a release is given without consideration, the weight of authority is against that view. **5.62**

General releases

A general release is a release of all rights that the releasing party may have against the beneficiaries of the release.[168] In *BCCI v Ali* Lord Hoffmann commented on general releases in the following terms: **5.63**

---

[160] [2010] EWHC 2867 (QB) [130].
[161] *Tiong Swee Eng v Yeo Khee Siang* [2015] SGHC 116 [59] (no obligation of disclosure in settlement agreements, including disputes between husband and wife, citing with approval J Cartwright, *Misrepresentation and Non-Disclosure* (3rd edn, 2012) [16-02] and chap 17).
[162] *Bank of Credit and Commerce International SA v Ali* [1999] 1 ICR 1068, 1077–78.
[163] *Bank of Credit and Commerce International SA v Ali* [1999] 1 ICR 1068.
[164] [1977] 1 WLR 199, 215–16.
[165] See Chap 29, para [29.19].
[166] *Bank of Credit and Commerce International SA v Ali* [2000] 1 ICR 1410 (CA) 1421, 1458; [2002] 1 AC 251, 267, 279.
[167] *Bank of Credit and Commerce International SA v Ali* [2002] 1 AC 251, 267, 279.
[168] As to the construction of general releases, *Bank of Credit and Commerce International SA v Ali* [2002] 1 AC 251; *Satyam Computer Services Ltd v Unpaid Systems Ltd* [2008] 1 All ER (Comm) 737 [74]–[80], [2008] EWCA Civ 487 [79]–[84]; *Marsden v Barclays Bank plc* [2016] 2 Lloyd's Rep 420 (QB) [44]–[49].

... a transaction in which one party agrees in general terms to release another from any claims upon him has special features. It is not difficult to imply an obligation upon the beneficiary of such a release to disclose the existence of claims of which he actually knows and which he also realises may not be known to the other party... a person cannot be allowed to rely upon a release in general terms if he knew that the other party had a claim and knew that the other party was not aware that he had a claim. I do not propose any wider principle...[169]

5.64 It is doubtful that non-disclosure of the kind described confers a right to rescind the whole release. The equity of the releasing party appears to extend only to obtaining a defence to the claim of which he was ignorant.[170] The precise content of that defence remains somewhat opaque.[171]

(5) Sales of land

5.65 At common law a vendor of unregistered land makes an implied promise to show a good title. Failure to do so is a breach of contract unless the purchaser is aware at the date of contract of the defect in title, or it is so obvious as to be 'patent'. The correct view seems to be that it is this contractual relationship that produces the principle that a vendor of unregistered land is bound to disclose latent defects in his title. Failure to comply with the so-called obligation to disclose confers no right in the purchaser to rescind *ab initio*. Instead, it gives rise to purely contractual rights and obligations. These are a right in the purchaser to complete and recover damages for breach of the implied term, or to terminate and recover the deposit, unless the defect is such that the bargain can be substantially performed, in which case the vendor may have specific performance with compensation.[172]

5.66 Non-disclosure gives a right to set aside a contract for the sale of unregistered land *ab initio* only if it is coupled with positive statements or concealment that amount to pre-contractual misrepresentation,[173] or, in Australia, Canada, and New Zealand, if the non-disclosure accompanies a sufficiently serious mistake as to the property being sold.[174] In both cases it is not the non-disclosure itself that permits rescission. Non-disclosure is, instead, the context in which a claim to rescind for misrepresentation or mistake arises.

---

[169] *Bank of Credit and Commerce International SA v Ali* [2002] 1 AC 251, 279. See also at 267 per Lord Nicholls. Lord Bingham preferred to express no view on this point: at 264. See also *Yukos Hydrocarbons Investments Ltd v Georgiades* [2020] EWHC 173 (Comm) where it was held that a principle of sharp practice may apply to vitiate a general release.

[170] See the reasoning in *Bank of Credit and Commerce International SA v Ali* [2000] 1 ICR 1410 (CA) 1421, 1458, which appears to have been endorsed by Lord Hoffmann in *Bank of Credit and Commerce International SA v Ali* [2002] 1 AC 251, 279. In Australia, *Grant v John Grant & Sons Pty Ltd* (1954) 91 CLR 112, 130.

[171] For analysis of the older authorities, *Grant v John Grant & Sons Pty Ltd* (1954) 91 CLR 112.

[172] JT Farrand and A Clarke (eds), *Emmet's Notes on Perusing Titles and on Practical Conveyancing* (19th edn, 1986) chap 4, part 3, 'Non-Disclosure'; also G Battersby, *Williams Contracts for Sale of Land and Title to Land* (4th edn, 1975) 94–101, 746, 752.

[173] In the older cases the courts regarded rescission in equity for concealment of a defect in title, and damages for breach of covenant as to title, as cumulative remedies; eg *Mostyn v The West Mostyn Coal and Iron Co* [1875] 1 CPD 145. This is no longer the law. Rescission *ab initio* erases the contract, and with it claims to damages for breach: see Chap 1, para [1.18].

[174] See Chap 7, paras [7.31]–[7.33]. In Hong Kong it has been decided that any such duty of disclosure does not extend to tenancies: *Fortune Global Development Ltd v Shung Cheong Food Trading Ltd* [2002] 2 HKLRD 447 [83]–[84].

6

Duress and Undue Influence

A. Introduction	6.01	C. Undue Influence	6.75
B. Duress	6.05	(1) Introduction	6.75
(1) Introduction	6.05	(2) Two ways of proving undue influence	6.76
(2) First requirement: illegitimate pressure	6.09	(3) Actual undue influence: undue influence proved directly	6.80
(3) Second requirement: coercion in the sense of no practical choice or alternative	6.46	(4) Presumed undue influence: undue influence proved with the assistance of a presumption	6.94
(4) Third requirement: causation	6.61	(5) Severable transactions	6.120

A. Introduction

A contract or as the case may be, gift, is able to be rescinded if the consent of one of the parties is impaired by pressure or influence exerted by the other, or by a third party with the counterparty's knowledge.[1] The doctrines engaged in such a case are duress and undue influence. This chapter describes the circumstances in which duress and undue influence provide a ground for rescinding a contract.[2] These grounds overlap because illegitimate pressure is capable of giving rise to both duress and undue influence.[3] But although they are linked in this way, duress and undue influence are separate grounds for rescinding.[4] Duress is the narrow doctrine developed by the common law courts, and undue influence the wider one created by the courts of Chancery.

6.01

The two doctrines differ in scope. Duress is concerned with threats and demands, whereas neither is necessary to establish undue influence. Undue influence covers more subtle

6.02

---

[1] For third party situations, see Chap 9. For the special rules for gifts, where knowledge is not required, see Chap 29.

[2] In the case of contracts between consumers and traders similar events may also constitute aggressive practices allowing the consumer to 'unwind' the contract under regulations (regs 27E and 27F) inserted into the Consumer Protection from Unfair Trading Regulations 2008 by the Consumer Protection (Amendment) Regulations 2014. Such statutory rights akin to rescission are beyond the scope of this chapter. See The Law Commission and the Scottish Law Commission, *Report on Consumer Redress for Misleading and Aggressive Practices* (Scot Law Com No 226, Law Com No 332) and the Department for Business, Innovation and Skills, *Reform of Consumer Law—Government Response to Consultations on Misleading and Aggressive Practices and the European Consumer Rights Directive* (August 2013).

[3] *Barton v Armstrong* [1976] AC 104 (PC—Australia) 118; *Royal Bank of Scotland v Etridge (No 2)* [2002] 2 AC 773, 795.

[4] Birks and Chin argue that duress and actual undue influence ought to be treated as one doctrine based on illegitimate pressure, and presumed undue influence as a separate doctrine that is founded on weakness brought about by a relationship of excessive dependence: PBH Birks and NY Chin, 'On the Nature of Undue Influence' in J Beatson and D Friedmann (eds), *Good Faith and Fault in Contract Law* (1995)chap 3 at 63–64, 67. However, such a rationalization has not found favour with the courts.

II. GROUNDS

influences than duress.[5] Whereas duress requires proof of pressure, undue influence does not.[6] Furthermore, only duress requires an absence of choice. The existence of a practical alternative course of action does not bar a finding of undue influence.

6.03 Remarks *obiter* have been made to the effect that both duress[7] and undue influence[8] are wrongs. Precisely what is intended by this label is unclear. On one view, if indeed they were wrongs, then the law would be imposing duties not to coerce or unduly influence others into transactions, and injunctions and perhaps compensation should be available to prevent or redress such wrongs, even in situations where rescission is barred. But the better view is that these doctrines only confer a right to have the transaction set aside, give no right to compensation or injunctive relief absent rescission, and do not entail breach of a legal duty.[9] That certainly appears to be the case in relation to presumed undue influence, where the courts have stressed that no wrongdoing is required in order to rescind, and that the law's intervention is founded on broader notions of public policy.[10] A finding of duress or undue influence need not mean that the defendant contravened any legal obligation, but only that the transaction is morally or socially unacceptable and ought not stand.[11] Nonetheless, compensation is also available alongside rescission in the not uncommon situation where the acts that constituted duress or undue influence also involved a tort or breach of contract.[12]

6.04 This chapter first examines duress in Part B, and then undue influence in Part C.

B. Duress

(1) Introduction

6.05 Duress comprises illegitimate pressure, arising from a threat coupled with a demand, exerted on the party seeking to avoid a transaction. For the victim to be capable of being

---

[5] See J Cartwright, *Unequal Bargaining: A Study of Vitiating Factors in the Formation of Contracts* (1991) 174; N Enonchong, *Duress, Undue Influence and Unconscionable Dealing* (3rd edn, 2018) [1-1003].

[6] *BCCI v Aboody* [1990] 1 QB 923 (CA) 967–69; *Dunbar Bank plc v Nadeem* [1998] 3 All ER 876 (CA) 883 (Millett LJ).

[7] *Universe Tankships Inc of Monrovia v International Transport Workers Federation (The Universe Sentinel)* [1983] 1 AC 366, 400: Lord Scarman stated that duress is actionable as a tort if it causes damage or loss.

[8] Undue influence was repeatedly said to be based on wrongdoing in *Royal Bank of Scotland v Etridge (No 2)* [2002] 2 AC 773. See also *YS GM Marfin II LLC v Lakhani* [2020] EWHC 2629 (Comm).

[9] PBH Birks, 'Undue Influence as Wrongful Exploitation' [2004] 120 LQR 34. Birks and Chin argue that both duress and undue influence are claimant-sided grounds in that they are concerned with impaired consent; they are to be contrasted with unconscionable bargains where the court intervenes because of the morally culpable behaviour of the dominant party: PBH Birks and NY Chin, 'On the Nature of Undue Influence' in J Beatson and D Friedmann (eds), *Good Faith and Fault in Contract Law* (1995) chap 3 at 58. Cf D Capper, 'Undue Influence and Unconscionability: a Rationalisation' (1998) 114 LQR 479. See *Al Nehayan v Kent* [2018] EWHC 333; (Comm); [2018] 1 CLC 216 [224].

[10] *Allcard v Skinner* (1887) 36 ChD 145 (CA), 171, 187, 191; *Cheese v Thomas* [1994] 1 WLR 129 (CA); *Hammond v Osborn* [2002] EWCA 885 [30]–[32]; *Jennings v Cairns* [2003] EWCA 1935 [33]–[35]; *Niersmans v Pesticcio* [2004] EWCA 372 [20]; *Goodchild v Bradbury* [2006] EWCA 1868 [25]–[27]; *Hackett v Crown Prosecution Service* [2011] EWHC 1170 (Admin) [64].

[11] *CTN Cash and Carry Ltd v Gallaher Ltd* [1994] 4 All ER 714 (CA) 719 (Lord Scarman). For example, there may be no wrongful (and hence unlawful) conduct on the part of an elderly person's helper whose gift is liable to be rescinded on the basis of undue influence: see para [6.96]. Similarly, a transaction vitiated by innocent misrepresentation is liable to be set aside even though it involved no unlawful conduct.

[12] Lord Scarman was probably alluding to this in *The Universe Sentinel*: see n 7. See also Chap 2 and *Al Nehayan v Kent* [2018] EWHC 333 (Comm); [2018] 1 CLC 216 [225].

coerced in law the circumstances must be such that the victim has no practical alternative course other than acting as is demanded. Furthermore, the illegitimate pressure must actually cause the victim to enter into the transaction. As with the other grounds for rescission, the courts focus on the process by which the contract is made, not on its terms. The gravamen is a lack of procedural fairness, not substantive unfairness whereby the terms of the contact are more favourable to one party than to the other.[13]

Types of duress

Duress is conventionally divided into three categories. The criterion of the classification is the target of the threat that generates the pressure: (i) duress to the person involves threats of physical harm or constraint; (ii) duress of property involves threats to seize, retain, or damage property; and (iii) economic duress overlaps with duress of property and involves threats to harm economic interests. The underlying principles are similar, for 'all that matters to the plaintiff is that, metaphorically speaking, a club has been used. It does not matter to the plaintiff what the club is made of—whether it is a physical club or an economic club or an otherwise illegal club'.[14]

6.06

Requirements for rescission for duress

All categories of duress amounting to a ground for rescission require proof of three elements:[15] (i) there must be illegitimate pressure arising from a threat coupled with a demand; (ii) the effect of the pressure must be coercion in the sense of an absence of practical choice; and (iii) the pressure must be a sufficient cause of the victim's entry into the transaction.

6.07

Authorities concerning the recovery of non-contractual payments

Some of the authorities commonly cited in relation to each of these elements involved claims for the recovery of non-contractual payments rather than for the rescission of contracts. These cases provide some guidance as to the general principles that govern the rescission of contracts for duress. They are based on similar policy motivations but involve one material difference. In a contract case there is an additional interest in upholding bargains that weighs heavily against rescission. Contract cases require a balance to be struck between the *security of bargains* on the one hand, and the potential injustice of upholding contracts procured through illegitimate pressure on the other. Mere payment cases only need to strike a balance between the *security of receipts*, and the injustice of upholding payments made because of illegitimate pressure. That is why a unilateral causative mistake allows the payer to recover a mistaken payment, but not to rescind a contract based on such a mistake.[16] It

6.08

---

[13] *Hart v O'Connor* [1985] AC 1000 (PC—NZ) 1017. See further J Beatson, *The Use and Abuse of Unjust Enrichment* (1991) 109–10.
[14] *Rookes v Barnard* [1964] AC 1129, 1209 (Lord Devlin) (comments made in the context of the tort of intimidation but equally applicable to rescission).
[15] These elements are derived from Dyson J's judgments in *DSND Subsea Ltd v Petroleum Geoservices ASA* [2000] BLR 530, 545 and *Carillion Construction Limited v Felix (UK) Limited* [2001] BLR 1. Applied in *Adam Opel GmbH and another v Mitras Automotive (UK) Ltd* [2007] EWHC 3205 (QB) [25]; *Amsalem v Raivid* [2008] EWHC 3028 (TCC) [78]; *Kolmar Group AG v Traxpo Enterprises Pvt Ltd* [2011] 1 All ER (Comm) 46 [92]; *LCP Holding Limited v Hombergh Holdings BV* [2012] EWHC 3643 (QB) [34]; *Deutsche Bank AG v Sebastian Holdings Inc* [2013] EWHC 3463 (Comm) [1125]; *Holyoake v Candy* [2017] EWHC 3397 (Ch) [398]; *Pakistan International Airline Corp v Times Travel (UK) Ltd* [2021] 3 WLR 727 (Sup Ct) [1], [78]–[79].
[16] See also Chap 29, especially paras [29.18] and [29.19].

follows that more may need to be shown to rescind a contract for duress, than to recover a non-contractual payment on the basis of duress.

(2) First requirement: illegitimate pressure

Pressure: threat and demand

6.09 The complainant must show that he was subjected to pressure. This pressure arises from a demand to enter into the transaction backed by a threat to harm the complainant's physical well-being, goods, or economic interests.

Demand

6.10 A demand that the claimant enter into the impugned transaction may be made explicitly or implicitly. The form of words is not determinative of whether a demand has or has not been made. That depends upon the context. A statement made in the form of a request or offer could actually be an implicit demand. An extreme example would be a request for a discount made while a weapon was brandished at the seller. The presence of a threat can turn what is otherwise an offer or a request into a demand.

Threat

General principles

6.11 A threat is a declaration of an intention to inflict harm, and is to be distinguished from a warning and from an offer. In the case of a warning, the person issuing it does not have control over whether the harm will be inflicted. In the case of a true offer, the person making it does not intend to inflict any harm if it is rejected. These distinctions are explored further in the next two sub-sections because they circumscribe the availability of rescission for duress, particularly in the context of the renegotiation of existing contracts.[17]

6.12 The threat will usually be made by the counterparty to the transaction or his agent. But a threat from another source is sufficient, provided that the party taking advantage is aware at the time of the transaction that it had been made.[18] The threat may be aimed at a party to the transaction or a related person or, arguably, even a stranger.[19] To constitute sufficient pressure, the threatened harm must be serious.[20] But, as will be seen, the causative effect of the pressure on the complainant is determined according to the state of mind and circumstances of the person threatened.[21] It is not necessary to show bad faith to prove that a threat had been made. A threat is still a threat even if made in good faith.[22]

---

[17] See paras [6.32]ff.
[18] *Kesarmal v Valliappa Chettiar* [1954] 1 WLR 380 (PC—Malaya) (complainant forced to transfer land to another in occupied Malaya by Japanese officers). The rule is different for gifts: knowledge is not necessary. See also Chap 9, especially para [9.05].
[19] *Kaufman v Gerson* [1904] 1 KB 591 (threats of criminal prosecution made against complainant's husband); *Royal Boskalis Westminster NV v Mountain* [1999] QB 674 (threats made against complainant's employees); *Gulf Azov Shipping Co Ltd v Idisi* [2001] Lloyd's Rep 727.
[20] In *Universe Tankships Inc of Monrovia v International Transport Workers Federation (The Universe Sentinel)* [1983] 1 AC 366, 383 the financial consequences would have been 'catastrophic'; in *B & S Contracts and Design Ltd v Victor Green Publications Ltd* [1984] ICR 419, 426 the consequences would have been grave reputational damage and very heavy claims.
[21] See para [6.62].
[22] In *Ware & De Freville Ltd v Motor Trade Association* [1921] 3 KB 40 (CA) 82 Atkin LJ stated that a threat 'does not necessarily involve any feeling of hostility or ill-will'; see also *Mason v The State of New South Wales* (1959) 102

A threat may be made directly,[23] or it may be made indirectly.[24] An indirect, or 'veiled', **6.13** threat was made in *B & S Contracts and Design Ltd v Victor Green Publications Ltd*.[25] A company was obliged to erect exhibition stands pursuant to a contract with the complainant. The company's disgruntled workers threatened to strike, which would have prevented the company from performing its contract with the complainant. The company indicated to the complainant that if the complainant made an additional payment, which would be passed on to the workers, then they would not strike and the work would proceed. This indication was held to be a veiled threat.

Distinguished from a warning
Warnings must be distinguished from threats.[26] Not every indication that a party will **6.14** commit a breach of contract if the other party does not agree to modify the terms of the contract is a threat. For example, a builder's request for additional payment or time for performance coupled with a statement that default will otherwise occur because of bankruptcy or a lack of subcontractors, does not necessarily involve a threat.[27]

Both a threat and a warning suggest that harm may come to the recipient of the communi- **6.15** cation. The distinction between them lies in the condition to that harm occurring. In the case of a threat, the infliction of the harm is conditional on the acts or omissions of the person making the threat. In the case of a warning, the harm is not so conditioned. The risk of the harm is outside that person's control. So, if A says to B 'If you walk across my land, my dog will bite you!', this will be a threat if the dog is under A's control. However, if A utters the same words to B in circumstances where A has no control over his dog, the communication is simply a warning.

The form and content of a communication does not determine whether it is a threat or a **6.16** warning. It is the context, and in particular the capacity to control the infliction of harm, that determines whether or not the communication is a threat. The core feature of a threat,

---

CLR 108, 141 (Windeyer J) and *Adam Opel GmbH and another v Mitras Automotive (UK) Ltd* [2007] EWHC 3205 (QB) [34]. But bad faith is a factor taken into consideration in determining whether pressure is illegitimate: *DSND Subsea Ltd v Petroleum Geoservices ASA* [2000] BLR 530, *Carillion Construction Limited v Felix (UK) Limited* [2001] BLR 1. See para [6.33] and also n 77.

[23] *Barton v Armstrong* [1976] AC 104 (PC—Australia) (threats to kill); *North Ocean Shipping Co Ltd v Hyundai Construction Co Ltd (The Atlantic Baron)* [1979] QB 705 (threat not to deliver a ship under ship-building contract).
[24] It had been suggested by some commentators that *Borrelli v Ting* [2010] UKPC 21, where a contract was set aside for economic duress brought about by opposition to a proposed scheme of arrangement, showed that threatened conduct was not required. However, an alternative interpretation of the case is that the relevant agreement was entered into due to the indirect or veiled threat to block the relevant scheme that if that agreement was not signed.
[25] [1984] ICR 419, 426, 428.
[26] *Equiticorp Finance Ltd v Bank of New Zealand* (1992) 29 NSWLR 260, 298–99. Compare the distinction sometimes drawn between threats and warnings in the field of economic tort: *Conway v Wade* [1909] AC 506, 510; *Hodges v Webb* [1920] 2 Ch 70, 87–89; *Rookes v Barnard* [1964] AC 1129, 1166. See J Beatson, *The Use and Abuse of Unjust Enrichment* (1991) 118–20; S Smith, 'Contracting Under Pressure: A Theory of Duress' [1997] CLJ 343, 346–50. Cf PBH Birks, 'The Travails of Duress' [1990] LMCLQ 342, 346.
[27] In *William v Roffey Bros & Nicholls (Contractors) Limited* [1991] QB 1 an agreement to pay more for the performance of work which was already contracted for was upheld (though in this case there was no threat or warning by the party seeking amendment); R Halson, 'Opportunism, Economic Duress and Contractual Modifications' (1991) 107 LQR 649; HG Beale (ed), *Chitty on Contracts* (34th edn, 2021) [10-050]; PBH Birks, *An Introduction to the Law of Restitution* (rev edn, 1989) 183.

II. GROUNDS

as opposed to a warning, is defendant-focused: it looks at whether the infliction of harm was or was not within the defendant's control.

Distinguished from an offer

6.17 Bigwood argues that a distinction ought to be made between threats and offers, rather than between threats and warnings.[28] An offer, unlike a threat, does not reduce the recipient's available choices for action; it increases them. He argues that an offer is a proposal to make the claimant better off if he accepts the proposal (or at least no worse off if he rejects it) whereas a threat is a proposal to make the claimant worse off if he rejects the proposal. For example, a proposal by a private physician to treat an illness for £100 is an offer because it is a proposal to make the patient better off and will not make him worse off if he rejects it; a proposal by a public physician to treat an illness for £100 (when he is already required to do so at no charge) is a threat because it is a proposal to make the patient worse off (by withholding free treatment if he rejects it). This distinction is an attractive one, but has not yet been recognized in the cases.

6.18 The core feature of a threat, as opposed to an offer, is claimant-focused: it looks at whether or not the proposal is to make the claimant worse off if he rejects it. In short, a threat requires the potential infliction of harm. But recognition of this does not make the distinction between threats and warnings redundant. As was shown in the previous section, the infliction of harm must be within the defendant's control.

Types of threat

6.19 The threat may be against a person's physical well-being, property, or economic interests. These three types of threat are considered in turn.

6.20 **Threats against a person: duress to the person**   Duress to the person may involve actual or threatened violence or actual or threatened unlawful constraint.[29] The *locus classicus* in this area is the Privy Council decision in *Barton v Armstrong*.[30] Armstrong, the former chairman of a company, threatened Barton, the managing director of the company, with death on a number of occasions. Barton subsequently entered into a contract with Armstrong to purchase Armstrong's shares in the company. Overturning the decision below, the Privy Council held that the threats of physical violence rendered the deed void so far is it concerned Barton.[31] The case has generally been regarded as one involving rescission of a voidable contract.[32] The expression 'void as against Barton' appears to have been shorthand for the proposition that it was rescindable by him.

---

[28] R Bigwood, *Exploitative Contracts* (2003) 295–301. See also R Bigwood, 'Coercion in Contract: The Theoretical Constructs of Duress' *Uni of Toronto LJ* 201, 212.

[29] *Cumming v Ince* (1847) 11 QB 117, 116 ER 418 (complainant confined by her daughters in a lunatic asylum until she entered into a transaction); *Scott v Sebright* (1886) 12 PD 21 (complainant coerced into contract of marriage through fear and terror); *Williams v Bayley* (1886) LR 1 HL 200 (threat to bring criminal prosecution rendered contract voidable in equity although it would have been valid at law; this case may also be viewed as one of actual undue influence, see 216 cf 212); *Royal Boskalis Westminster NV v Mountain* [1999] QB 674 (threat by foreign government to use complainant's employees as 'human shields'); *Antonio v Antonio* [2010] EWHC 1199 (QB) (shareholders' agreements entered into by the victim of an abusive relationship set aside); *Holyoake v Candy* [2017] EWHC 3397 (Ch) [397]; *Al Nehayan v Kent* [2018] EWHC 333 (Comm); [2018] 1 CLC 216 [214].

[30] [1976] AC 104 (PC—Australia).

[31] [1976] AC 104, 120.

[32] Cf D Lanham, 'Duress and Void Contracts' (1966) 29 MLR 615 who argued that duress renders a contract void, not merely voidable. A contract procured by duress to the person was held to be voidable by the Hong Kong

Threats against property: duress of property Formerly, on the authority of *Skeate v* **6.21**
Beale,[33] the courts refused to recognize unlawful threats to detain another person's goods
as a ground for rescinding an executory contract to pay money. But money actually paid
for the release of wrongfully detained goods or to avoid their seizure could be recovered
as money had and received.[34] This apparent inconsistency appears to have been expunged
from the law.[35]

The modern position is best represented by the remarks made *obiter* by Kerr J in *The Siboen* **6.22**
and The Sibotre:

> ... if I should be compelled to sign a lease or some other contract for a nominal but legally
> sufficient consideration under an imminent threat of having my house burnt down or a
> valuable picture slashed, though without any threat of physical violence to anyone, I do not
> think that the law would uphold the agreement...[36]

In *The Alev*[37] Hobhouse J applied cases on economic duress to a situation involving duress **6.23**
of goods and concluded that the principle that agreements are voidable if entered into under
duress of goods or economic duress is now well established.

It is safe to conclude that, though not expressly overruled, *Skeate v Beale* no longer repre- **6.24**
sents the law. Subject to the point already made about the law's concern with upholding
bargains,[38] authorities in which money paid otherwise than under a contract has been recovered for duress of goods, or property generally, provide some guidance in determining
when a contract may be rescinded for duress of property. Cases of this nature have included
threats to seize, retain, or sell silver plate,[39] a ship,[40] documents of insurance,[41] an animal,[42]
deeds of title,[43] and land.[44] The complainant need not be the owner of the relevant goods,

---

Court of Appeal in *Mir v Mir* [2013] HKCA 144 (deed rescinded despite a 10 day delay between assault and execution of deed).

[33] (1840) 11 Ad & El 983, 113 ER 688 (tenant not entitled to rescind promise to make a larger payment of rent than was actually owed which had been exacted by the landlord under the threat of the levying of distress, ie the sale of the tenant's goods).
[34] *Astley v Reynolds* (1731) 2 Str 915, 93 ER 938 (claimant entitled to recover interest he paid over legal rate to pawnbroker to obtain the return of his silver plate); *Maskell v Horner* [1915] 3 KB 106 (market stall holder entitled to recover toll money obtained from him, without any legal right, under the threat of seizure and sale of his goods); *Tamvaco v Simpson* (1866) LR 1 CP 363; *Government of Spain v North of England SS Co Ltd* (1938) 61 Lloyd's LR 44.
[35] The different interests identified in para [6.08] help to explain why the different rules arose.
[36] *Occidental Worldwide Investment Corp v Skibs A/S Avanti (The Siboen and The Sibotre)* [1976] 1 Lloyd's Rep 293, 335–36; supported by *North Ocean Shipping Co Ltd v Hyundai Construction Co Ltd (The Atlantic Baron)* [1979] QB 705, 715; app'd in *Pao On v Lau Yiu Long* [1980] AC 614 (PC—Hong Kong) 636.
[37] *Vantage Navigation Corporation v Suhail & Saud Bahwan Building Materials (The Alev)* [1989] 1 Lloyd's Rep 138, 145. See also *Lloyds Bank Ltd v Bundy* [1975] QB 326 (CA) 337 (Lord Denning MR); *Woolwich Equitable Building Society v IRC (No 2)* [1993] AC 70, 164 (Lord Goff); *Royal Boskalis Westminster NV v Mountain* [1999] QB 674 (threat by foreign government to retain dredging fleet). There is a significant overlap between duress to goods and economic duress: see A Burrows, *The Law of Restitution* (3rd edn, 2011) 266.
[38] See para [6.08].
[39] *Astley v Reynolds* (1731) 2 Str 915, 93 ER 938.
[40] *Somes v British Empire Shipping Co* (1860) 8 HLC 338, 11 ER 459.
[41] *Shaw v Woodcock* (1827) 7 B & C 73, 108 ER 652.
[42] *Green v Duckett* (1883) 11 QBD 275.
[43] *Wakefield v Newbon* [1844] 6 QB 276, 115 ER 107.
[44] *Close v Phipps* (1844) 7 Man & G 586, 590; 135 ER 236, 238 (threat of sale of estate); *Kanhaya Lal v National Bank of India* (1913) 29 TLR 314 (PC—India) (threat of sale of mill).

and it should be sufficient if he has a proprietary interest such as possession of the goods that are threatened or seized.[45]

6.25 **Threats against economic interests: economic duress** Economic duress occurs where a party is forced to enter into a transaction through threats to economic interests. The threats must give rise to illegitimate economic pressure; mere commercial pressure does not count.[46] The possibility of rescinding on the basis of threats to economic interests was first recognized by Kerr J in *The Siboen and the Sibotre*.[47] Within less than a decade, the ground was firmly established by the House of Lords in *The Universe Sentinel*.[48]

6.26 Examples of threats against economic interests that have been considered by the courts have included a threat to declare insolvency if a charterparty was not modified to reduce the rate of hire;[49] a threat to withhold the delivery of a ship under a ship-building contract unless a higher price was agreed;[50] a threat to break a share purchase agreement unless the complainants gave a guarantee against losses which the purchasers might suffer if the shares fell in value;[51] a threat by a union not to lift a strike that prevented the claimants' ship from leaving port unless the claimants made certain payments, including a payment to its welfare fund;[52] a threat by a supplier of components to cease supply which would halt production unless a payment was made;[53] a threat to breach a supply contract unless a smaller quantity was accepted at a higher price;[54] and a threat by an airline to reduce the supply of airline tickets to a travel agent if the agent did not agree to waive its claims for unpaid commission.[55] Not all of these were found to give rise to illegitimate pressure.

Pressure must be illegitimate

6.27 A transaction can be rescinded on the basis of duress only where the complainant has been subjected to illegitimate pressure.[56] Even strong pressure to enter into a transaction will not suffice unless it crosses the threshold of illegitimacy. As Lord Wilberforce and Lord Simon stated in *Barton v Armstrong*:

---

[45] *Fell v Whittaker* (1871–72) LR 7 QB 120.
[46] See para [6.38].
[47] *Occidental Worldwide Investment Corp v Skibs A/S Avanti (The Siboen and the Sibotre)* [1976] 1 Lloyd's Rep 293; noted J Beatson (1976) 92 LQR 496; approved in *Pao On v Lau Yiu Long* [1980] AC 614 (PC—Hong Kong).
[48] *Universe Tankships Inc of Monrovia v International Transport Workers Federation (The Universe Sentinel)* [1983] AC 366.
[49] *Occidental Worldwide Investment Corp v Skibs A/S Avanti (The Siboen and the Sibotre)* [1976] 1 Lloyd's Rep 293 (where the pressure was found to be mere commercial pressure).
[50] *North Ocean Shipping Co Ltd v Hyundai Construction Co Ltd (The Atlantic Baron)* [1979] QB 705 (economic duress found but rescission barred due to affirmation).
[51] *Pao On v Lau Yiu Long* [1980] AC 614 (PC—Hong Kong).
[52] *Universe Tankships Inc of Monrovia v International Transport Workers Federation (The Universe Sentinel)* [1983] AC 366.
[53] *Adam Opel GmbH and another v Mitras Automotive (UK) Ltd* [2007] EWHC 3205 (QB).
[54] *Kolmar Group AG v Traxpo Enterprises Pvt Ltd* [2011] 1 All ER (Comm) 46.
[55] *Pakistan International Airline Corp v Times Travel (UK) Ltd* [2021] 3 WLR 727 (Sup Ct).
[56] *Barton v Armstrong* [1976] AC 104 (PC—Australia) 121 (duress to the person); *Universe Tankships Inc of Monrovia v International Transport Workers Federation (The Universe Sentinel)* [1983] 1 AC 366, 384 (economic duress). Contrast the position in Canada where it has been suggested that, at least in the case of economic duress forcing a variation of a contract, illegitimate pressure is not a requirement: *Greater Fredericton Airport Inc v NAV Canada* [2008] NBCA 28; (2008) 280 DLR (4th) 405 [46]. However, this unorthodox position has not been taken in all cases: cf *Taber v Paris Boutique & Bridal Inc* [2010] ONCA 157.

... in life, including the life of commerce and finance, many acts are done under pressure, sometimes overwhelming pressure, so that one can say that the actor had no choice but to act. Absence of choice in this sense does not negate consent in law: for this the pressure must be one of a kind which the law does not regard as legitimate.[57]

In *The Universe Sentinel*[58] Lord Scarman provided a framework for assessing illegitimacy by reference to the two factors that combine to give rise to illegitimate pressure, namely, the threat and the demand. In determining whether pressure was illegitimate, it is necessary to consider: (i) the nature of the threat, in particular whether it was unlawful or lawful; and (ii) the nature of the demand that the threat was made to support. Generally a threat of unlawful conduct will be regarded as giving rise to illegitimate pressure, and conversely, a threat of lawful conduct will be regarded as not crossing that boundary. But both principles are subject to exceptions that depend upon the nature of the demand.[59]

6.28

The question of legitimacy is not simply an inquiry into the presence or absence of good faith on the part of the defendant.[60] In *Lloyds Bank Ltd v Bundy*[61] Lord Denning MR stated that a contract may be avoided for duress even where the stronger party makes his claim in good faith honestly believing that he is entitled to make the demand. Consistently with this, it is not necessary for the stronger party to be aware that the complainant is acting under duress.[62] But although good faith does not *necessarily* render pressure legitimate, some authorities had suggested that good faith and bad faith were sometimes relevant factors to be taken into account in determining illegitimacy.[63] However, in *Pakistan International Airline Corp v Times Travel (UK) Ltd*,[64] the Supreme Court refused to treat the presence of bad faith as a touchstone of illegitimacy in the case of lawful act duress, in contrast to the position that had been taken by Lord Burrows in his minority judgement and also the Court of Appeal in that case.[65]

6.29

Threats of unlawful acts
Generally speaking, the threat of any form of unlawful action will be regarded as illegitimate.[66] An unlawful act is an act that constitutes a breach of a legal duty, whether imposed

6.30

---

[57] [1976] AC 104 (PC—Australia) 121 (dissenting on the application of the principles to the facts).
[58] *Universe Tankships Inc of Monrovia v International Transport Workers Federation (The Universe Sentinel)* [1983] AC 366, 401; *R v Attorney-General for England and Wales* [2003] UKPC 22 (PC—NZ) [16].
[59] *Pakistan International Airline Corp v Times Travel (UK) Ltd* [2021] 3 WLR 727 (Sup Ct) [1] 'the court in focusing on the nature and justification of the demand ... has regard to, among other things, the behaviour of the threatening party including the nature of the pressure which it applies, and the circumstances of the threatened party.'
[60] *Pakistan International Airline Corp v Times Travel (UK) Ltd* [2021] 3 WLR 727 (Sup Ct) [1], [95]. Contrast the position taken by the Court of Appeal in the same case ([2020] Ch 98 (CA)) and followed in *Adare Finance DAC v Yellowstone Capital Management SA* [2020] EWHC 2760 (Comm); [2021] 2 BCLC 140 [84]–[85].
[61] [1975] QB 326 (CA) 337; In *Huyton SA v Peter Cremer Gmbh & Co* [1999] 1 Lloyd's Rep 620, 637 Mance J expressed the view that it is 'difficult to accept that illegitimate pressure applied by a party who believes bona fide in his case can never give grounds for relief against an apparent compromise'.
[62] *North Ocean Shipping v Hyundai Construction (The Atlantic Baron)* [1979] QB 705 (the defendant shipyard was ignorant of the lucrative time charter the complainant was negotiating).
[63] *Huyton v Cremer* [1999] 1 Lloyd's Rep 620, 637; *DSND Subsea Ltd v Petroleum Geoservices ASA* [2000] BLR 530 [13]. See also para [6.33] and, as to the meaning of bad faith, n 80. Cf *Occidental Worldwide Investment Corp v Skibs A/S Avanti (The Siboen and the Sibotre)* [1976] 1 Lloyd's Rep 293, 335.
[64] [2021] 3 WLR 727 (Sup Ct).
[65] [2020] Ch 98 (CA); followed in *Adare Finance DAC v Yellowstone Capital Management SA* [2020] EWHC 2760 (Comm); [2021] 2 BCLC 140 [84]–[85].
[66] *R v Attorney-General for England and Wales* [2003] UKPC 22 [16].

by the common law or statute.[67] It includes a crime, a tort, or a breach of contract. It can also include a breach of international law.[68]

6.31 **Threat to commit a crime or a tort** A threat to commit a crime invariably gives rise to illegitimate pressure.[69] This is also true of a threat to commit a tort, which may include trespass, conversion,[70] interference with contractual relations,[71] defamation,[72] intimidation,[73] malicious prosecution, or abuse of the process of the court.[74] If a crime or a tort is threatened, it is not necessary to inquire further into the nature of the demand. The pressure is illegitimate.

6.32 **Threat to commit a breach of contract** A threatened breach of contract generally constitutes illegitimate pressure. For example, a threat by a sole supplier to breach a contract to supply components vital for the manufacture of cars gave rise to illegitimate pressure,[75] as did a threat to breach a sale contract by proposing to actually provide a smaller quantity than ordered at a higher price on a 'take it or leave it basis'.[76] But authorities and commentators have suggested that a threatened breach need not always give rise to illegitimate pressure.[77] The view has been expressed that a threat to break a contract unless money is paid by the other party can, but by no means always will, constitute duress.[78]

6.33 Some commentators had argued that demands for amendments that were made in good faith ought not to constitute illegitimate pressure if the demands were fair or reasonable in the sense that they would redress an imbalance in the original agreement.[79] However, an attempt to apply such a rule would place the courts in a very difficult position. It would be necessary to adjudicate the substantive fairness of an agreement and also the substantive fairness of the amendment. It is doubtful whether such a rule is acceptable as a matter of principle or policy. Yet it is clear that the law must provide some room for the binding renegotiation of existing contracts, even though it may be clear that unlawful infringements of rights will follow if the negotiations break down.[80]

6.34 It may also be that a 'threat' to break a contract that does not give rise to illegitimate pressure is not actually a threat in the eyes of the law. As was noted earlier, warnings of inevitable

---

[67] *Alf Vaughan v Royscot Trust plc* [1999] 1 All ER 856.
[68] *Ukraine v Law Debenture Trust Corp Plc* [2019] QB 1121 (CA).
[69] *Barton v Armstrong* [1976] AC 104 (PC—Australia).
[70] *Vantage Navigation Corp v Bahwan Building Materials (The Alev)* [1989] 1 Lloyd's Rep 138.
[71] *Universe Tankships Inc of Monrovia v International Transport Workers Federation (The Universe Sentinel)* [1983] AC 366; *Dimskal Shipping Co SA v International Transport Workers Federation (The Evia Luck)* [1992] 2 AC 152.
[72] *Norreys v Zeffert* [1939] 2 All ER 187, 189–90.
[73] *D&C Builders Ltd v Rees* [1966] 2 QB 617 (CA).
[74] *Metall und Rohstoff v Donaldson Lufkin & Jenrette Inc* [1990] 1 QB 391 (CA) 469–70.
[75] *Adam Opel GmbH and another v Mitras Automotive (UK) Ltd* [2007] EWHC 3205 (QB).
[76] *Kolmar Group AG v Traxpo Enterprises Pvt Ltd* [2011] 1 All ER (Comm) 46.
[77] *North Ocean Shipping Co Ltd v Hyundai Construction Co Ltd (The Atlantic Baron)* [1979] QB 705. See also A Burrows, *The Law of Restitution* (3rd edn, 2011) 273; N Enonchong, *Duress, Undue Influence and Unconscionable Dealing* (3rd edn, 2018) [3-003]–[3-004]. Cf S Smith, 'Contracting Under Pressure: A Theory of Duress' [1997] CLJ 343, 347–48; G Virgo, *The Principles of the Law of Restitution* (2nd edn, 2006) 208, 218; R Bigwood, *Exploitative Contracts* (2003) 340–44.
[78] *B & S Contracts and Design Ltd v Victor Green Publications Ltd* [1984] ICR 419, 428.
[79] A Burrows, *The Law of Restitution* (3rd edn, 2011) 275.
[80] Where no breach of contract is threatened—but rather a lawful exercise of legal rights if the amendment is not agreed to—the resulting pressure will generally be legitimate: *Pakistan International Airline Corp v Times Travel (UK) Ltd* [2021] 3 WLR 727 (Sup Ct).

consequences that will flow if a contract is not renegotiated, and offers which will not make the claimant worse off if rejected, do not amount to threats.[81] It may be that conduct of this kind is properly characterized as a warning that unless a party obtains more time or funds or other advantage, it will be impossible to fulfil his contractual obligations, or as an offer to resolve the commercial predicament.[82] If A says to B that unless B allows A more time, A will be unable to make payments under a contract, that may be a warning as to an inevitable future state of affairs, rather than a threat to breach the contract.

Consequently it may be that any *threat* to breach a contract, by definition being within the defendant's control and not amounting to an offer, is to be treated as giving rise to illegitimate pressure. When a defendant refuses to make a contractual payment even though he has the funds to do so he makes a threat and exerts illegitimate pressure, but when he cannot make the payment due to a lack of funds he does neither. As this example suggests, however, the classification that is offered is likely to produce difficult questions as to what was and was not within the defendant's control at the time the alleged threat was made. **6.35**

If the contrary view is taken that some threats to breach a contract do not give rise to illegitimate pressure, demands made in bad faith backed by such threats should always be taken to give rise to illegitimate pressure.[83] Demands made in bad faith would include demands that were aimed at exploiting the complainant by securing an advantage that is unrelated to the original contract or at imposing unfair or unreasonable terms.[84] **6.36**

Threats of lawful acts
A threat of a lawful act made by one commercial party to another in nearly all cases will not amount to illegitimate pressure. This is informed by a judicial concern to maintain certainty and finality in commercial dealings, and not to create liability on the basis of what is otherwise lawful conduct.[85] However, the possibility of lawful act duress has been recognized in the House of Lords, the Privy Council, and the Supreme Court.[86] Where the threatened act is lawful, it is necessary to consider the nature of the demand that the threat is coupled with. If the demand is unlawful or unconscionable,[87] the threat may give rise to illegitimate pressure. **6.37**

Legitimate pressure based on lawful acts Commercial pressure is legitimate.[88] It accompanies many contracts, and exists wherever one party is in a stronger bargaining position **6.38**

---

[81] See paras [6.14]–[6.18].
[82] *William v Roffey Bros & Nicholls (Contractors) Limited* [1991] QB 1 (subcontractor obtaining additional payments from contractor in such circumstances).
[83] *D&C Builders Ltd v Rees* [1966] 2 QB 617 (CA) 626 '[The defendants] really behaved very badly. They knew of the plaintiffs' financial difficulties and used their awkward situation to intimidate them.'
[84] Moore-Bick J's formulation of the test of bad faith in *Niru Battery v Milestone Trading Ltd* [2002] EWHC 1425 [135] may be useful in this respect, albeit the context there was different: '[bad faith] is capable of embracing a failure to act in a commercially acceptable way and sharp practice of a kind that falls short of outright dishonesty as well as dishonesty itself'; approved on appeal [2003] EWCA 1446 [164].
[85] *CTN Cash and Carry Ltd v Gallaher Ltd* [1994] 4 All ER 714 (CA) 718–19.
[86] *Universe Tankships Inc of Monrovia v International Transport Workers Federation (The Universe Sentinel)* [1983] 1 AC 366, 400 (Lord Scarman) (*obiter*); *R v Attorney-General for England and Wales* [2003] UKPC 22 (PC—NZ) [16] '[T]he fact that the threat is lawful does not necessarily make the pressure legitimate.' (*obiter*); *Borrelli v Ting* [2010] UKPC 21; *Pakistan International Airline Corp v Times Travel (UK) Ltd* [2021] 3 WLR 727 (Sup Ct).
[87] *Pakistan International Airline Corp v Times Travel (UK) Ltd* [2021] 3 WLR 727 (Sup Ct) [3], [17], [20].
[88] *Lloyds Bank Ltd v Bundy* [1975] QB 326 (CA) 336 (Lord Denning MR) 'No bargain will be upset which is the result of the ordinary interplay of [market] forces'; *Atlas Express Ltd v Kafco (Importers and Distributors) Ltd* [1989] QB 833, 839.

148   II. GROUNDS

than the other party.[89] Illegitimate pressure must be distinguished from the rough and tumble of the pressure of normal commercial bargaining[90] and the hurly burly of commercial life.[91] Threats to not contract,[92] to take business elsewhere, to withdraw a discretionary discount, to terminate lawfully an existing contract, or to exercise other contractual rights[93] are part of ordinary commercial negotiations.[94]

6.39 Threats to enforce legal rights through civil proceedings, if not involving an abuse of legal process, also do not amount to illegitimate pressure. Lord Goff stated in *Woolwich Equitable Building Society v IRC*[95] that 'where money has been paid under pressure of actual or threatened legal proceedings for its recovery, the payor cannot say that for that reason the money has been paid under compulsion and is therefore recoverable by him'. His Lordship's remarks were directed at the recovery of money, but the same principle prevents the rescission of bargains which are struck following threatened legal proceedings. It is not economic duress for a creditor to threaten to bring proceedings against his debtor, even if this is likely to be disastrous for the debtor, and even if the creditor spells out why it will be so.[96]

6.40 Similarly, threats to retake possession of leased goods in accordance with a contractual right to repossession have been held to be legitimate. This was despite the fact that relief from forfeiture may have been available and that the defendants had demanded a substantial premium for not retaking the goods.[97] Threats to withdraw a customer's credit terms and to require upfront payment for future shipments made to back a demand for a payment which was actually not due were found not to amount to duress. The suppliers were at liberty not to enter into future contracts with the claimants and to cease granting credit.[98] A lawful threat to do acts that the complainant perceived as a public humiliation was also found not to be illegitimate, even though it may have involved 'overwhelming pressure'.[99] A threat by

---

[89] *Universe Tankships Inc of Monrovia v International Transport Workers Federation (The Universe Sentinel)* [1983] AC 366, 384 (Lord Diplock).
[90] *DSND Subsea Ltd v Petroleum Geoservices ASA* [2000] BLR 530.
[91] *LCP Holding Limited v Hombergh Holdings BV* [2012] EWHC 3643 (QB) [42].
[92] *Smith v Charlick (William) Ltd* (1924) 34 CLR 38, 56, 64–65 (threat not to supply in future not duress); *Hardie and Lane Ltd v Chilton* [1928] 2 KB 306; *Leyland Daf Ltd v Automotive Products plc* [1994] 1 BCLR 244 (CA) 249–50 'In general, in the absence of a contractual or statutory obligation, one person is not compelled to trade with another. He cannot be forced to supply goods to someone else if he does not wish to do so'; see also 257; *Dold v Murphy* [2020] NZLR 313 (threat by a minority shareholder not to sell unless offered a higher price); the leading case of *Pakistan International Airline Corp v Times Travel (UK) Ltd* [2021] 3 WLR 727 (Sup Ct) involved a legitimate threat not to contract.
[93] '[A]ny right given by contract may be exercised… no matter how wicked, cruel or mean the motive may be which determines the enforcement of the right': *Allen v Flood* [1898] AC 1, 46. Cf what may be an increasing inclination of the courts to imply terms requiring good faith: *Abu Dhabi National Tanker Co v Product Star Shipping Ltd (The Product Star) (No 2)* [1993] 1 Lloyd's Rep 397 (CA); *Paragon Finance plc v Staunton* [2002] 2 All ER 248 (CA); *Burger King v King Franchises* [2013] EWHC 1761 (Comm) [24].
[94] *Flying Music Co Ltd v Theater Entertainment SA* [2017] EWHC 3192 (QB) (threat to exercise contractual rights unless a guarantee was provided was not illegitimate). See also *Barclays Bank Plc v Borkhatria* [2018] EWHC 1326 (Comm) and *Adare Finance DAC v Yellowstone Capital Management SA* [2020] EWHC 2760 (Comm); [2021] 2 BCLC 140.
[95] [1993] AC 70, 165.
[96] *Holyoake v Candy* [2017] EWHC 3397 (Ch) [236], [401].
[97] *Alf Vaughan v Royscot Trust plc* [1999] 1 All ER 856, 863; *Westpac v Cockerill* (1998) 152 ALR 267 (FCA) (threat to enforce security by appointing receiver not duress).
[98] *CTN Cash and Carry Ltd v Gallaher Ltd* [1994] 4 All ER 714 (CA) 718 (a claim for the recovery of money rather than rescission). Similarly in *National Merchant Buying Society Limited v Bellamy* [2012] EWHC 2563 (Ch) [30]–[31] threats to withdraw credit were legitimate and justified because changes in circumstances had made it less secure to continue to extend it.
[99] *R v Attorney-General for England and Wales* [2003] UKPC 22 (PC—NZ) [15] and [20].

an airline to reduce lawfully the supply of airline tickets to a travel agent whose business was reliant on selling such tickets was not illegitimate.[100]

Illegitimate pressure based on lawful acts The Privy Council held in *R v Attorney-General for England and Wales*[101] that a threat of a lawful act may give rise to a ground for rescission if the demand is unlawful or is not justified or reasonable. In that case a demand that a member of an elite military unit sign a confidentiality undertaking was found not to be unlawful nor unreasonable or unjustified in the circumstances. 6.41

In *CTN Cash and Carry Ltd v Gallaher Ltd*,[102] a demand was made by a supplier to a customer for a payment that was not actually due. It was backed by a threat of lawful action that would be harmful to the customer. The demand was found not to give rise to duress as the supplier genuinely considered that the money was due to it. Steyn LJ concluded: 6.42

> Outside the field of protected relationships, and in a purely commercial context, it might be a relatively rare case in which 'lawful act duress' can be established. And it might be particularly difficult to establish duress if the defendant bona fide considered that his demand was valid. In this complex and changing branch of the law I deliberately refrain from saying 'never'.[103]

In *Borrelli v Ting*[104] the Privy Council held that a settlement agreement was voidable due to illegitimate pressure based on a threat of lawful acts, namely, opposition to a proposed scheme of arrangement. The defendant agreed to withdraw his opposition to the scheme if liquidators agreed not to pursue claims against him. As his opposition to the scheme had not been in good faith, but for the improper motive of escaping claims arising from the insolvency,[105] and he had used forgery and false evidence as part of that opposition (although that was past unlawful conduct and not a threat of future unlawful conduct), his conduct was found to be unconscionable and the transaction liable to rescission on the ground of duress.[106] In *Progress Bulk Carriers Ltd v Tube City IMS LLC* the High Court also recognized that duress could arise by lawful means; however, on the facts it flowed from a prior repudiation of a contract between the parties which, together with conduct since that breach, placed the complainant in a position where it had no alternative but to submit to the demands.[107] Cooke J stated that 'the more serious the impropriety and the greater the 6.43

---

[100] *Pakistan International Airline Corp v Times Travel (UK) Ltd* [2021] 3 WLR 727 (Sup Ct).
[101] [2003] UKPC 22 [18] and [20]; *Daniel v Drew* [2005] EWCA 507 [40]; *Universe Tankships Inc of Monrovia v International Transport Workers Federation (The Universe Sentinel)* [1983] 1 AC 366, where Lord Scarman stated at 401: 'Duress can, of course, exist even if the threat is one of lawful action: whether it does so depends upon the nature of the demand.'
[102] [1994] 4 All ER 714 (CA) (an action for the recovery of money paid rather than rescission).
[103] [1994] 4 All ER 714, 719. The court approved the statement of Professor Birks that the law ought not be such that 'those who devise outrageous but technically lawful means of compulsion must always escape restitution': PBH Birks, *An Introduction to the Law of Restitution* (rev edn, 1989) 177. See also J Steyn, 'The Role of Good Faith and Fair Dealing in Contract Law: A Hair-Shirt Philosophy?' [1991] Denning LJ 131, 140–41.
[104] [2010] UKPC 21.
[105] *Borrelli v Ting* [2010] UKPC 21 [28].
[106] *Borrelli v Ting* [2010] UKPC 21 [32].
[107] [2012] EWHC 273 (Comm) [30], [39]–[40]. Lawful act duress was also accepted as possible in *Burger King v King Franchises* [2013] EWHC 1761 (Comm) [24] but not found on the facts. See also *Ryan v Tiuta International Ltd* [2014] 11 WLUK 703; [2015] BPIR 123 (a party who had committed breaches of contract took advantage of the innocent party's commercial position to illegitimately pressurise that party into accepting terms of a settlement by threatening to withhold consent to an intercreditor arrangement that was necessary for the innocent party to raise more funding).

moral obloquy which attaches to the conduct, the more likely the pressure is to be seen as illegitimate.'[108]

6.44 In *Al Nehayan v Kent*, Leggatt LJ proposed that a demand coupled with a threat to commit a lawful act would be regarded as illegitimate if (a) the defendant has no reasonable grounds for making the demand and (b) the threat would not be considered by reasonable and honest people to be a proper means of reinforcing the demand.[109] However, in *Times Travel (UK) Ltd v Pakistan International Airlines Corp*,[110] the Supreme Court considered this to be an insufficiently precise standard for determining when legal rights could not be exercised. Instead the Supreme Court narrowed the doctrine of lawful act economic duress significantly. Lord Hodge (with whom Lord Reed, Lord Lloyd-Jones, and Lord Kitchin agreed) held that there were only two circumstances, underpinned by a high standard of unconscionability, in which lawful act duress would lead to rescission. The first was where the defendant used knowledge of criminal activity on the part of the claimant (or a member of the claimant's family) to obtain a benefit by a threat to report the activity or commence a prosecution.[111] This may be seen as an example of blackmail, which often involves a threat of a lawful act, but is itself unlawful.[112] Because a blackmailer's demand is itself unlawful, blackmail always gives rise to illegitimate pressure.[113] The second was where the defendant, having exposed himself to a civil claim by the claimant, 'deliberately manoeuvres the claimant into a position of vulnerability by means which the law regards as illegitimate and thereby forces the claimant to waive his claim'.[114] The majority held that neither set of circumstances pertained in the present case. It was not prepared to accept that a demand by a stronger party even if made in bad faith would, without more, give rise to lawful act duress.[115]

6.45 On the other hand, Lord Burrows held that lawful act economic duress could be made out in a wider range of circumstances, namely where 'the demand is made in bad faith in the particular sense that the threatening party does not genuinely believe that it is owed what it is claiming to be owed or does not genuinely believe that it has a defence to the claim being waived by the threatened party'.[116] Thus, had such bad faith been made out, Lord Burrows would have granted rescission for lawful act economic duress in the present case.[117]

---

[108] *Progress Bulk Carriers Ltd v Tube City IMS LLC* [2012] EWHC 273 (Comm) [43].
[109] [2018] EWHC 333 (Comm); [2018] 1 CLC 216 [188]. See also *Times Travel (UK) Ltd v Pakistan International Airlines Corp* [2017] EWHC 1367 (Ch) [253] and [259]–[263] (overturned on appeal).
[110] [2021] UKSC 40; [2021] 3 WLR 727.
[111] Such cases being *Williams v Bayley* (1866) LR 1 HL 200; *Kaufman v Gerson* [1904] 1 KB 591; *Mutual Finance Ltd v John Wetton & Sons Ltd* [1937] 2 KB 389; J Beatson, *The Use and Abuse of Unjust Enrichment* (1991) 129–34. Transactions brought about by such threats have also been rescinded on the basis of undue influence: see para [6.84];
[112] *Universe Tankships Inc of Monrovia v International Transport Workers Federation (The Universe Sentinel)* [1983] 1 AC 366, 401; *Al Nehayan v Kent* [2018] EWHC 333 (Comm); [2018] 1 CLC 216 [230].
[113] Lord Atkin stated in *Thorne v Motor Trade Association* [1937] AC 797, 806 that: 'The ordinary blackmailer normally threatens to do what he has a perfect right to do—namely, communicate some compromising conduct to a person whose knowledge is likely to affect the person threatened ... What he has to justify is not the threat, but the demand of money.' Lord Wright noted at 822 that 'a legal liberty (that is something that a man may do with legal justification) may form the basis of blackmail'.
[114] Ibid [4]. Such cases being *Borrelli v Ting* [2010] Bus LR 1718 and *The Cenk K* [2012] 2 All ER (Comm) 855.
[115] Ibid [50]–[52].
[116] Ibid [102].
[117] Ibid [132].

(3) Second requirement: coercion in the sense of no practical choice or alternative

Development of the coercion requirement

Duress connotes coercion, compulsion, or constraint. The earlier authorities on economic duress stressed that the complainant's will must have been overborne by the pressure.[118] If this requirement was satisfied, the complainant was regarded as having acted without free will, and as not actually having consented to the transaction. This was always a fiction, for a person intends to do something even when he is coerced into doing it.

6.46

The House of Lords departed from this formulation of the coercion requirement in *Universe Tankships Inc of Monrovia v International Transport Workers Federation (The Universe Sentinel)*.[119] Lord Scarman held that '[t]he classic case of duress is, however, not the lack of will to submit but the victim's intentional submission arising from the realization that there is no other practical choice open to him'.[120] Consequently the rhetoric of the 'overborne will' has been abandoned.[121]

6.47

Test of coercion: absence of practical or real choice

The effect of the illegitimate pressure must be such that the complainant has no practical choice—or 'no reasonable or practical alternative'[122]—but to submit to the demand and enter into the transaction.[123] The test is whether the victim of the illegitimate pressure nevertheless had a real choice and could, if he had wished, equally well have resisted the pressure and, for example, pursued alternative legal redress.[124] The absence of real choice establishes that the illegitimate pressure was capable of being coercive as a matter of law.[125]

6.48

If the claimant had courses of action reasonably open to him other than submission to the demand, then the claimant is precluded from asserting that he was coerced into the transaction. In *Huyton SA v Peter Cremer GmbH & Co*, Mance J held that it was 'self-evident that relief may not be appropriate if an innocent party decides, as a matter of choice, not to

6.49

---

[118] *Occidental Worldwide Investment Corp v Skibs A/S Avanti (The Siboen and the Sibotre)* [1976] 1 Lloyd's Rep 293, 336; *North Ocean Shipping Co Ltd v Hyundai Construction Co Ltd (The Atlantic Baron)* [1979] QB 705, 717, 719; *Pao On v Lau Yiu Long* [1980] AC 614 (PC—Hong Kong) 635–36; *Hennessy v Craigmyle & Co Ltd* [1986] ICR 461 (CA) 468; *Vantage Navigation Corp v Bahwan Building Materials (The Alev)* [1989] 1 Lloyd's Rep 138, 145 (Hobhouse J). The 'overborne will' theory was trenchantly criticized by Atiyah: PS Atiyah, 'Economic Duress and the "Overborne Will"' (1982) 98 LQR 197, 200. Cf D Tiplady 'Concepts of Duress' (1983) 99 LQR 188; PS Atiyah, 'Duress and the Overborne Will Again' (1983) 99 LQR 353.

[119] [1983] AC 366.

[120] [1983] AC 366, 400.

[121] *Universe Tankships Inc of Monrovia v International Transport Workers Federation (The Universe Sentinel)* [1983] 1 AC 366, 384 (Lord Diplock), 400 (Lord Scarman); *Crescendo Management Pty Ltd v Westpac Banking Corporation* (1988) 19 NSWLR 40 (CA) 45–46 (McHugh JA); *Enimont Overseas AG v Rojugotanker Zadar (The Olib)* [1991] 2 Lloyd's Rep 108; *Dimskal Shipping Co SA v International Transport Workers Federation (The Evia Luck)* [1992] 2 AC 152; *Al Nehayan v Kent* [2018] EWHC 333 (Comm); [2018] 1 CLC 216 [189]. See also *Lynch v DPP of Northern Ireland* [1975] AC 653, 670, 675, 680, 690–91, 695, 703, 709 (this case was concerned with duress in the context of criminal law but the same analysis is applicable to the civil law concept).

[122] *Borrelli v Ting* [2010] UKPC 21 [31], [35].

[123] *Universe Tankships Inc of Monrovia v International Transport Workers Federation (The Universe Sentinel)* [1983] 1 AC 366, 400 (Lord Scarman); *Enimont Overseas AG v Rojugotanker Zadar (The Olib)* [1991] 2 Lloyd's Rep 108, 114 (threats by carriers to sell cargo and not allow its inspection unless they were paid outstanding freight and other costs did not amount to duress).

[124] *Huyton SA v Peter Cremer GmbH & Co* [1999] 1 Lloyd's Rep 620, 636.

[125] Though it does not prove that the claimant was actually coerced by the illegitimate pressure. See para [6.60].

II. GROUNDS

pursue an alternative remedy which any and possibly some other reasonable persons in his circumstances would have pursued'.[126]

Factors taken into account in determining practical alternatives

6.50 The factors which are taken into account in determining the 'practicality' of alternative courses of action include, in the context of economic duress,[127] the time pressures to which the complainant was subject, the availability of alternative parties to contract with, the risks to the complainant's business and relationships with third parties if supply were disrupted, and the availability and sufficiency of the complainant's legal remedies against the party issuing the threats.[128]

6.51 The principles are well illustrated in *Atlas Express Ltd v Kafco (Importers and Distributors) Ltd*.[129] Kafco was a small company which imported baskets and re-sold them domestically. It obtained a valuable contract to supply Woolworths, a large supermarket chain. Kafco retained a national firm of carriers to deliver their goods to Woolworths. Some time after the contract had been signed the carriers realized that they had underestimated their costs and demanded a higher price. They threatened to cease deliveries unless that price was paid. Kafco had insufficient time to find and engage a different carrier to ensure that its goods would continue to reach Woolworths before Christmas. While protesting, it agreed to the amendment of the price. Subsequently it refused to pay the higher price and argued that the new contract had been vitiated by duress.

6.52 The court found that the pressure applied had been illegitimate and Kafco had no practical alternative but to agree to the terms. Dangers to established business relationships, lack of time, and lack of alternative suppliers were factors that were treated as material to establishing the absence of a practical alternative.

6.53 The fact that the complainant would itself be forced to breach contracts with other counterparties, or to incur significant costs under them, if it did not give in to the demand, has also been a key factor showing absence of a practical alternative in a number of cases.[130]

Monopoly supplier and practical alternatives

6.54 A practical alternative may exist though the party applying pressure is a monopoly supplier.[131] So in *CTN Cash and Carry Ltd v Gallaher Ltd*,[132] economic duress was not proved

---

[126] [1999] 1 Lloyd's Rep 620, 638. The inquiry appears to be an objective one based on what the reasonable man would have seen as his alternatives, rather than a subjective one based on what the complainant actually believed to have been his alternatives. This approach has attracted criticism: P Chandler, 'Economic Duress: Clarity or Confusion?' [1989] LMCLQ 270, 275–57; C Mitchell *et al*, *Goff & Jones: The Law of Unjust Enrichment* (9th edn, 2016) [10–75].

[127] Lord Scarman also suggests in *Universe Tankships Inc of Monrovia v International Transport Workers Federation (The Universe Sentinel)* [1983] 1 AC 366, 400 that the absence of choice can also be proved by protest or the absence of independent advice. However, the preferable view is that these factors go more towards establishing the element next discussed, ie causation.

[128] The New Zealand Court of Appeal has also examined in this context the characteristics of the victim, the relationship between the parties, and the availability of professional advice to the victim: *McIntyre v Nemesis DBK Ltd* [2009] NZCA 329 [67].

[129] [1989] QB 833. See also *Adam Opel GmbH and another v Mitras Automotive (UK) Ltd* [2007] EWHC 3205 (QB) a case of economic duress involving a refusal by a sole supplier to continue to provide components for cars.

[130] *Adam Opel GmbH and another v Mitras Automotive (UK) Ltd* [2007] EWHC 3205 (QB); *Kolmar Group AG v Traxpo Enterprises Pvt Ltd* [2011] 1 All ER (Comm) 46.

[131] *Smith v Charlick (William) Ltd* (1924) 34 CLR 38; *Eric Gnapp Ltd v Petroleum Board* [1949] 1 All ER 980 (CA) 986; PBH Birks, *An Introduction to the Law of Restitution* (rev edn, 1989) 178.

[132] [1994] 4 All ER 714 (CA) (an action for the recovery of money paid rather than rescission).

even though the sole distributors of a very popular brand of cigarettes threatened not to supply the product in the future if the claimants did not make the payment which was demanded but was not actually due. The court held that 'the fact that the defendants were in a monopoly position cannot therefore by itself convert what is not otherwise duress into duress'.[133] This is consistent with the principle that mere inequality of bargaining power does not provide a ground for rescission.[134]

Failure to sue and practical alternatives
In *Pao On v Lau Yiu Long*[135] the complainants had an alternative course open to them after threats to breach a share purchase agreement had been made together with a demand for a guarantee. They could have sued for specific performance of the agreement that the other party had threatened to breach instead of entering into the guarantee which they later sought to rescind for economic duress. A failure to utilize an avenue for legal redress, such as an action for an order for specific performance, an award of damages, or an order for the return of goods, may militate against a finding of duress.[136]

6.55

But it will not do so in all circumstances. Of central importance is whether legal redress would provide a *practical* alternative. In some cases it will not. The delay inherent in obtaining a judicial remedy may mean that pursuing a legal action is not practical. In the case of duress of goods, the complainant may have 'such an immediate want of his goods that an action ... would not do his business'.[137] In *Adam Opel GmbH v Mitras Automotive (UK) Ltd*[138] an application for an injunction to prevent a breach of a supply contract was held not to be a practical alternative because of the actual and perceived uncertainties of litigation and ambiguity in the relevant documentation. Similarly, the availability of a cause of action for wrongful interference with non-fungible goods may be inadequate as an order for their redelivery is only available at the court's discretion.[139]

6.56

Urgency
Waiting and seeing whether threats will be carried out may not be a practical alternative. In *The Alev*[140] a carrier detained cargo in breach of contract and demanded that the owners of the cargo enter into an agreement providing for additional payments before it would be released. Hobhouse J held that the owners could not just ignore the threats and wait to see

6.57

---

[133] *CTN Cash and Carry Ltd v Gallaher Ltd* [1994] 4 All ER 714 (CA) 717 (Steyn LJ).
[134] *Hart v O'Connor* [1985] AC 1000 (PC—NZ).
[135] [1980] AC 614 (PC—Hong Kong).
[136] *Morley (t/a Morley Estates) v Royal Bank of Scotland Plc* [2021] EWCA Civ 338 [54] (complainant was not coerced as he had explored a number of alternatives, including threatening an emergency application to court for an injunction).
[137] *Astley v Reynolds* (1795) 2 Str 915, 916; 93 ER 939; *Kanahaya Lal v National Bank of India* (1913) 29 TLR 314; *Maskell v Horner* [1915] 3 KB 106 (CA) 122; *North Ocean Shipping Co Ltd v Hyundai Construction Co Ltd (The Atlantic Baron)* [1979] QB 705, 719. In *Vantage Navigation Corp v Bahwan Building Materials (The Alev)* [1989] 1 Lloyd's Rep 138, 146–47 Hobhouse J characterized the case as 'a clear example of the situation where the legal remedies are inadequate to meet the victim's legitimate commercial needs or to negative the compulsion operating upon him'.
[138] [2007] EWHC 3205 (QB) [32]–[32]. The court also noted the absurdity of the notion that the more blatantly unjustified and illegal the action threatened (and hence the clearer the complainant's right to sue), the more readily the defendant would be able to escape liability in duress if suing were treated as a practical alternative.
[139] Torts (Interference with Goods) Act 1977, s 3(2)(a) and (3)(b).
[140] *Vantage Navigation Corp v Bahwan Building Materials (The Alev)* [1989] 1 Lloyd's Rep 138, 146.

what would happen because being deprived of the goods seriously disrupted their business. His Lordship also noted that there was a risk that the deliberate contract breaker might convert the goods or otherwise seriously affect the owners' ability to recover them. Accordingly, waiting and seeing was not regarded as a realistic or reasonable alternative course.

Distinguishing lack of practical choice from causation

6.58 There has been some doubt whether the lack of an alternative course must be separately proved as a condition of rescinding, or whether it is merely an evidentiary issue that goes toward establishing causation, that is, that it assists in showing that the complainant was actually coerced.[141] The authorities tended, however, to treat the requirement as a separate element,[142] and this view is to be preferred as a matter of principle. The Supreme Court has now put this beyond doubt.[143]

6.59 Coercion is the gist of duress, and connotes an absence of choice. It ought to have an objective element, both to provide certainty, and to ensure that rescission is not too readily available. If the complainant had a practical option not to enter into the transaction, that should be the end of the inquiry, and he should be precluded from saying that he was nonetheless coerced into it.

6.60 Conversely, the lack of a practical alternative need not carry with it the conclusion that coercion has in fact occurred. A person may enter into a transaction for reasons unrelated to the illegitimate pressure that had been exerted; for example, because it is thought to be an excellent business opportunity[144] or a way out of their difficult situation.[145] In other words, just because a person has no practical choice but to enter into a transaction, it does not necessarily follow that a particular factor—namely illegitimate pressure stemming from a threat and a demand—is a cause of the complainant's entry into the transaction. Coercion need not equate with causation.

---

[141] *Pao On v Lau Yiu Long* [1980] AC 614 (PC—Hong Kong) 635 (alternative course treated as a relevant factor for establishing coercion of the will).

[142] *Hennessy v Craigmyle & Co Ltd* [1986] ICR 461 (CA) 468; *Carillion Construction Limited v Felix (UK) Limited* [2001] BLR 1 (Dyson J), applied in the cases noted at n 15; and *Adare Finance DAC v Yellowstone Capital Management SA* [2020] EWHC 2760 (Comm); [2021] 2 BCLC 140 [80]. Cf *Huyton SA v Peter Cremer GmbH & Co* [1999] 1 Lloyd's Rep 620; *Kolmar Group AG v Traxpo Enterprises Pvt Ltd* [2011] 1 All ER (Comm) 46 [92]. This approach finds support in the literature: J Beatson, *The Use and Abuse of Unjust Enrichment* (1991) 122–26; HG Beale (ed), *Chitty on Contracts* (34th edn, 2021) [10-044], [10-046]; J Beatson, A Burrows, and J Cartwright, *Anson's Law of Contract* (31st edn, 2020) 377. However, some commentators have taken a contrary view: E Peel, *Treitel The Law of Contract* (15th edn, 2020) [10-009]; N Enonchong, *Duress, Undue Influence and Unconscionable Dealing* (3rd edn, 2018) [4-022]–[4-023]. Burrows took a hybrid position with the absence of a reasonable alternative only being required in relation to situations involving threats to break a contract: A Burrows, *The Law of Restitution* (3rd edn, 2011) 270; A Burrows, *A Restatement of the English Law of Unjust Enrichment* (2012) 10; A Burrows, *A Restatement of the English Law of Contract* (2016) 195, 198.

[143] *Pakistan International Airline Corp v Times Travel (UK) Ltd* [2021] 3 WLR 727 (Sup Ct).

[144] Cf *Barton v Armstrong* [1976] AC 104 (PC—Australia).

[145] *Morley (t/a Morley Estates) v Royal Bank of Scotland Plc* [2021] EWCA Civ 338 [55]–[56], where it was held that '[i]n the end the agreement concluded was the agreement which [the complainant] wanted and had originally proposed'.

(4) Third requirement: causation

6.61 The final requirement is that the illegitimate pressure must be a sufficient cause of the transaction. If the complainant has shown that he was subjected to illegitimate pressure which left him with no practical alternative but to submit, he must still prove causation before duress will be made out. The test of causation in relation to duress to the person is well established. It is sufficient if the illegitimate pressure was 'a' cause of the complainant's entry into the transaction. The test in relation to duress of goods and economic duress is not yet authoritatively settled. It will be suggested that it ought to be the same for all types of duress.

Causation is subjective

6.62 Whereas the absence of a practical alternative is determined objectively, that is, by reference to what a reasonable person would have done, causation involves a subjective test. The effect of the illegitimate pressure is judged according to the state of mind and circumstances of the actual person threatened. Butt J stated in *Scott v Sebright*:

> It has sometimes been said that in order to avoid a contract entered into through fear, the fear must be such as would impel a person of ordinary courage and resolution to yield to it. I do not think that is an accurate statement of the law. Whenever from natural weakness of intellect or from fear—whether reasonably entertained or not—either party is actually in a state of mental incompetence to resist pressure improperly brought to bear, there is no more consent than in the case of a person of stronger intellect and more robust courage yielding to a more serious danger.[146]

Causation: duress to the person

6.63 In the case of duress to the person, the threat must be one of the reasons why the complainant entered into the transaction, but it does not have to be the sole or main reason. That was established in *Barton v Armstrong*.[147] Armstrong's threats were one of the reasons why Barton entered into the share purchase agreement. Another was Barton's opinion that the transaction was a good business arrangement. Nonetheless, a majority of the Privy Council held that the agreement was vitiated by duress. Lord Cross observed that, when fraudulent misrepresentation is pleaded as a ground for rescission, there is no need to prove that the false statement was the only reason for entry into the transaction 'for in this field the court does not allow an examination into the relative importance of contributory causes' and concluded:

> Their Lordships think that the same rule should apply in cases of duress and that if Armstrong's threats were 'a' reason for Barton's executing the deed he is entitled to relief even though he might well have entered into the contract if Armstrong had uttered no threats to influence him to do so.[148]

---

[146] (1866) 12 PD 21, 24.
[147] [1976] AC 104 (PC—Australia); *Al Nehayan v Kent* [2018] EWHC 333 (Comm); [2018] 1 CLC 216 [190].
[148] *Barton v Armstrong* [1976] AC 104, 118–19.

6.64 The Board went on to decide, also by analogy with the rules applicable to fraud, that in the case of duress to the person it was for the party seeking to resist rescission to show that the threats contributed nothing to the other party's decision to enter into the transaction.[149]

Causation: duress of property and economic duress

6.65 Some commentators have suggested that whereas duress to the person will not be tolerated in any circumstances and hence the courts have adopted a very generous test of causation, the same policy does not apply to duress of property and economic duress, and so a stricter test of causation ought to apply in that context.[150] And in *Huyton SA v Peter Cremer GmbH*, Mance J stated that the 'relaxed view of causation in the special context of duress to the person cannot prevail in the less serious context of economic duress'.[151] It has been suggested that the illegitimate pressure must have been a predominant cause of the transaction or alternatively that a 'but for' test applies. The principal authorities will be discussed next.

6.66 The view that the duress must be a 'predominant cause' for entry into the transaction has been associated with Lord Goff's statement in *The Evia Luck*[152] that 'economic pressure may be sufficient to amount to duress ... provided at least that the economic pressure may be characterized as illegitimate and constituted a significant cause inducing the plaintiff to enter into the relevant contract'. But this sentence does not appear to have been intended to reformulate the causation test; it was presented as a mere summary of existing authorities.[153] It appears that 'significant' in this context means no more than 'material', which would not be a departure from the test espoused by the Privy Council in relation to duress to the person.

6.67 The 'but for' test provides that in the absence of illegitimate pressure the agreement would not have been made at all or at least not on the same terms. It finds support in the reasons of Mance J, as he then was, in *Huyton SA v Peter Cremer GmbH*.[154] However, no authority is cited for the application of such a test in this context, and it involves a departure from the test applied in relation to duress to the person, fraud, and also undue influence.[155] Moreover, Mance J appeared to treat the absence of a practical alternative as no more than a factor to be taken into account in determining causation. Yet, as was noted earlier, the better view is that it is a separate element.[156] The formulation of the appropriate test of causation

---

[149] *Barton v Armstrong* [1976] AC 104, 120. See also *Antonio v Antonio* [2010] EWHC 1199 (QB).

[150] J Cartwright, *Unequal Bargaining: A Study of Vitiating Factors in the Formation of Contracts* (1991) 168; S Smith, 'Contracting Under Pressure: A Theory of Duress' [1997] CLJ 343, 354–56; A Burrows, *The Law of Restitution* (3rd edn, 2002) 270; A Burrows, *A Restatement of the English Law of Unjust Enrichment* (2012) 10; A Burrows, *A Restatement of the English Law of Contract* (2016) 199; HG Beale (ed), *Chitty on Contracts* (34th edn, 2021) [10-034], [10-040]. Cf PBH Birks, *An Introduction to the Law of Restitution* (rev edn, 1989) 179–84; N Enonchong, *Duress, Undue Influence and Unconscionable Dealing* (3rd edn, 2018) [4-010]–[4-011].

[151] [1999] 1 Lloyd's Rep 620, 636.

[152] *Dimskal Shipping Co SA v International Transport Workers Federation (The Evia Luck)* [1992] 2 AC 152, 165. This language was used in *DSND Subsea Ltd v Petroleum Geoservices ASA* [2000] BLR 530; *Carillion Construction Limited v Felix (UK) Limited* [2001] BLR 1; *Cantor Index Ltd v Shortall* [2002] All ER(D) 161.

[153] Lord Goff referred with approval to *Barton v Armstrong* [1976] AC 104 (PC—Australia), *Pao On v Lau Yiu Long* [1980] AC 614 (PC—Hong Kong) and *Cresendo Management Pty Ltd v Westpac Banking Corporation* (1988) 19 NSWLR 40 (CA) where the fraud test of causation was applied in relation to duress.

[154] [1999] 1 Lloyd's Rep 620, 636. Applied in *Kolmar Group AG v Traxpo Enterprises Pvt Ltd* [2011] 1 All ER (Comm) 46 [92]. See also *Al Nehayan v Kent* [2018] EWHC 333 (Comm); [2018] 1 CLC 216 [190].

[155] As to duress to the person see para [6.63], as to fraud see Chap 4, para [4.104], as to undue influence see para [6.89]. It would, however, mirror the test of causation for non-fraudulent misrepresentation: see Chap 4, para [4.105].

[156] See paras [6.58]ff.

must depend on whether the lack of the complainant's practical alternatives is treated as a separate element to be proved, or as a mere factor going to causation.

6.68 In particular, if, as has been suggested here, the former approach is correct, and a complainant must separately prove that he had no practical alternative but to submit to the demand, the less stringent test of causation seems clearly to be appropriate. That is because the two requirements of illegitimate pressure and lack of practical alternative are in practice both more difficult to satisfy in the case of duress of property or economic duress than they are in the case of duress to the person. That being the case, there is no need for a further restriction on relief in such cases in the guise of a stricter causation requirement. Rescission ought, therefore, to be available if the illegitimate pressure was 'a' factor that caused the complainant to enter into the transaction. The same test ought to apply to all types of duress.[157]

Factors relevant to causation

6.69 Causation is a question of fact to be decided on the evidence in each particular case. The authorities do, however, offer some guidance as to the factors that are relevant. One factor is the length of time that passed between when the threat was made and the transaction was entered into. A lapse of some months may suggest that the illegitimate pressure was no longer operating on the defendant's mind.[158]

6.70 It is relevant whether the complainant protested at the time of the transaction or shortly thereafter, and also whether the complainant regarded the transaction as binding on him or still open.[159] If the complainant did protest this goes towards showing that he entered into the transaction due to the illegitimate pressure rather than for another reason, such as because he thought it was a good business deal.

6.71 While the presence of protest helps to establish duress, its absence is by no means conclusive. As Lord Scarman stated in *The Universe Sentinel*:

> The victim's silence will not assist the bully, if the lack of any practicable choice but to submit is proved. The present case is an excellent illustration. There was no protest at the time, but only a determination to do whatever was needed as rapidly as possible to release the ship. Yet nobody challenges the judge's finding that the owner acted under compulsion.[160]

6.72 Another factor taken into account is whether the complainant had taken independent advice before entering into the transaction.[161] But again the presence of independent advice is

---

[157] This is the approach adopted by the Court of Appeal of New South Wales in *Cresendo Management Pty Ltd v Westpac Banking Corporation* (1988) 19 NSWLR 40 (CA) 46 (McHugh JA).
[158] *Shivas v Bank of New Zealand* [1990] 2 NZLR 327, 350.
[159] *Occidental Worldwide Investment Corp v Skibs A/S Avanti (The Siboen and the Sibotre)* [1976] 1 Lloyd's Rep 293, 336; *Maskell v Horner* [1915] 3 KB 106 (CA) (protests made over a number of years and became a joke); *Atlas Express Ltd v Kafco (Importers and Distributors) Ltd* [1989] QB 833. Also *DSND Subsea Ltd v Petroleum Geoservices ASA* [2000] BLR 530; *Burger King v King Franchises* [2013] EWHC 1761 (Comm) [26]. In *Morley (t/a Morley Estates) v Royal Bank of Scotland Plc* [2021] EWCA Civ 338 [55], the fact that the complainant did not take steps to rescind the agreement until five years had passed was significant in negating any finding of coercion.
[160] *Universe Tankships Inc of Monrovia v International Transport Workers Federation (The Universe Sentinel)* [1983] AC 366, 400.
[161] *Pao On v Lau Yiu Long* [1980] AC 614 (PC—Hong Kong) 635–36; *Hennessy v Craigmyle & Co Ltd* [1986] ICR 461 (CA) 470; *Dawson v Bell* [2016] EWCA Civ 96; [2016] 2 BCLC 59. See also the Canadian case of *Burin Peninsula Community Business Development Corporation v Grandy* [2010] NLCA 69 (where the absence of legal advice was an important factor in establishing duress).

not conclusive.[162] In *The Universe Sentinel*[163] the shipowners took legal advice before they made the payment. This did not stand in the way of a finding of duress.

6.73 Yet another factor that has been taken into consideration is whether, after the illegitimate pressure was removed, the complainant took steps to avoid the transaction.[164] A delay in acting to rescind may therefore have a dual function: it may evidence a defence of affirmation, or it may go to undermine the claim that the contract was ever sufficiently vitiated.

Voluntary conduct

6.74 There is said to be no actionable duress if the party seeking rescission acted voluntarily.[165] But what labels such as 'voluntariness', 'submission to an honest claim', or an attempt 'to close a transaction' mean is not certain. If they are references to the absence of an overborne will, they are premised on a now defunct theory of duress.[166] The preferable approach is that suggested by Burrows: they ought to be treated as conclusions that the elements of duress have not been satisfied.[167]

C. Undue Influence

(1) Introduction

6.75 People are routinely influenced by events and experiences of everyday life that do not disable them from freely exercising their will. An 'undue influence' exists only when the influence exerted is so great that it compromises the freedom of a person to act independently.[168] Also, as the term suggests, 'undue influence' involves the improper exercise of influence over another. In the eye of the law, it means that influence has been misused.[169] The doctrine is equitable, and the ways in which influence may be misused have a correspondingly unlimited scope: they 'include cases of coercion, domination, victimisation and all the

---

[162] In *Williams v Bayley* (1886) LR 1 HL 200 (HL) 202, 211–12, 215, 219 a transaction which a father entered in order to prevent his son being prosecuted for forgery was set aside despite the fact that the father's solicitor had been present when discussions took place, because when 'the bankers began to exert pressure on the father, the solicitor left, remonstrating with all parties against the impropriety of what they were about to do'.

[163] *Universe Tankships Inc of Monrovia v International Transport Workers Federation (The Universe Sentinel)* [1983] AC 366, 400.

[164] *North Ocean Shipping Co Ltd v Hyundai Construction Co Ltd (The Atlantic Baron)* [1979] QB 705; *Pao On v Lau Yiu Long* [1980] AC 614 (PC—Hong Kong) 635–36; *DSND Subsea Ltd v Petroleum Geoservices ASA* [2000] BLR 530.

[165] *Pao On v Lau Yiu Long* [1980] AC 614 (PC—Hong Kong); *Maskell v Horner* [1915] 3 KB 106 (CA) 118 (an action for the recovery of money paid rather than the rescission of an executory contract).

[166] See paras [6.46]ff.

[167] A Burrows, *The Law of Restitution* (3rd edn, 2011) 255–56.

[168] *Hart v Burbidge* [2013] EWHC 1628 (Ch) [49]. In *Esquire (Electronics) Ltd v The Hong Kong And Shanghai Banking Corporation Ltd* [2007] 3 HKLRD 439 [123] it was said that it is difficult to see how a corporation could be subject to undue influence, but it was mooted that such a situation could arise if, for example, its banker was a trusted adviser. There is Australian authority that a corporation may be able to obtain relief for undue influence: *Commonwealth Bank of Australia v Ridout Nominees Pty Ltd* [2000] WASC 37 [59]; *Lawrie v Hwang* [2012] QSC 422 [155] (equitable compensation). The Australian position appears to be preferable. Cf *Wallis Trading Inc v Air Tanzania Co Ltd* [2020] EWHC 339 (Comm) [117].

[169] *Royal Bank of Scotland v Etridge (No 2)* [2002] 2 AC 773, 800 (Lord Nicholls); *YS GM Marfin II LLC v Lakhani* [2020] EWHC 2629 (Comm) [83]–[96] but this probably does not require that that the influencing party must subjectively know that he is acting wrongly.

6. DURESS AND UNDUE INFLUENCE

insidious techniques of persuasion'.[170] A contract or gift is voidable when procured by conduct of this kind.

(2) Two ways of proving undue influence

Undue influence may be established in one of two ways: (i) by proving directly that undue influence was exercised; or (ii) by proving that a presumption of undue influence arose from (a) a relationship of influence, and (b) the nature of the transaction, with that presumption not being rebutted by the other party. In the leading case of *Royal Bank of Scotland v Etridge (No 2)* ('*Etridge*') Lord Nicholls explained the distinction in the following terms: **6.76**

> Equity identified broadly two forms of unacceptable conduct. The first comprises overt acts of improper pressure or coercion such as unlawful threats ... The second form arises out of a relationship between two persons where one has acquired over another a measure of influence, or ascendency, of which the ascendant person then takes unfair advantage.[171]

The first form is conventionally called 'actual undue influence', and the second 'presumed undue influence'. In both cases the fact of undue influence must be proved by the party asserting it. But in the first case it is to be proved by evidence that undue influence was in fact exercised. In the second the complainant benefits from a rebuttable evidential presumption that undue influence was in fact exercised. The term 'presumption' describes a shift in the evidential onus on a question of fact.[172] **6.77**

Two prerequisites must be satisfied before there is such a shift in the onus of proof, that is, before a presumption of undue influence arises. One is that the complainant reposed trust and confidence in the other party, or that the other party acquired ascendancy over the complainant. This relationship of trust and confidence or acquired ascendancy may be proved by evidence or, alternatively, irrebuttably presumed as a matter of law following proof that the relationship was one of a recognized class.[173] The other prerequisite for a presumption of undue influence to arise is that the transaction must not be readily explicable by the relationship between the parties.[174] The type and weight of the resultant presumption varies from case to case depending on the nature of the particular relationship and of the impugned transaction. The type and weight of evidence needed to rebut it also varies accordingly.[175] **6.78**

---

[170] *Royal Bank of Scotland v Etridge (No 2)* [2002] 2 AC 773, 816 (Lord Clyde); *R v Attorney-General* [2003] UKPC 22 [21] 'Undue influence has concentrated in particular upon the unfair exploitation by one party of a relationship which gives him ascendancy or influence over the other.' Cf n 208.
[171] *Royal Bank of Scotland v Etridge (No 2)* [2002] 2 AC 773, 795.
[172] *Royal Bank of Scotland v Etridge (No 2)* [2002] 2 AC 773, 797 (Lord Nicholls), 840 (Lord Scott). Presumed undue influence was formerly divided into 'class 2A' and 'class 2B' undue influence: *BCCI v Aboody* [1990] 1 QB 923 (CA) 953; *Barclays Bank v O'Brien* [1994] 1 AC 180, 189–90 (Lord Browne-Wilkinson). However in *Etridge* the utility of this classification, particularly category 2B, was seriously doubted: 816 (Lord Clyde), 822 (Lord Hobhouse), 843 (Lord Scott).
[173] *Royal Bank of Scotland v Etridge (No 2)* [2002] 2 AC 773, 773, 797, 820, 841. But the transaction must still 'call for explanation' in order to raise a presumption of undue influence even if it is between parties to such a relationship, such as solicitor and client, where influence is automatically presumed: at 820, 841.
[174] *Royal Bank of Scotland v Etridge (No 2)* [2002] 2 AC 773, 796, 798 (Lord Nicholls), also 853 (Lord Scott).
[175] *Royal Bank of Scotland v Etridge (No 2)* [2002] 2 AC 773, 773, 797, 840.

6.79 Each form of undue influence will be considered in turn. It must, however, be kept steadily in mind that the second form is in substance merely a subset of the first. It is undue influence proved with the assistance of an inference that the law permits to be drawn from particular facts. The two species are not mutually exclusive, nor are they alternatives.[176]

(3) Actual undue influence: undue influence proved directly
First requirement: exercise of undue influence

6.80 To establish this ground the complainant must prove more than just that he was influenced by the other party to enter into the transaction. The law accepts that in everyday life people constantly attempt to influence and persuade others to enter into transactions.[177] The complainant must prove that he was *unduly* influenced to enter into the particular transaction. The other party's conduct must prevent the complainant from bringing a free will and properly informed mind to bear on the proposed transaction.[178] There must be domination on the one side and an undermining of the independence of mind on the other.[179] The complainant must prove affirmatively that the other party exerted undue influence on him to enter into the particular transaction that is impugned.[180]

6.81 The question is not whether the complainant understood the transaction, but how the intention to enter into it was produced. Parties are free to enter into transactions which they do not understand; the doctrine protects against victimization, not folly.[181]

6.82 Lord Nicholls in *Etridge* underlined that there is no fixed definition to be applied in assessing whether influence has been brought to bear in an 'undue' manner:

> The means used is regarded as an exercise of improper or 'undue' influence, and hence unacceptable, whenever the consent thus procured ought not fairly to be treated as the expression of a person's free will. It is impossible to be more precise or definitive. The circumstances in which one person acquires influence over another, and the manner in which influence may be exercised, vary too widely to permit of any more specific criterion.[182]

Thus each case turns on its own facts, and in determining whether influence was undue, decisions will tend to be reached more by impression, or by analogy with decided cases, than by the application of precise rules.

6.83 In *Etridge*[183] Lord Nicholls and Lord Hobhouse referred to actual undue influence as an equitable wrong committed by the dominant party against the

---

[176] *Royal Bank of Scotland v Etridge (No 2)* [2002] 2 AC 773, 854, 872 (Lord Scott); *Annulment Funding Co Ltd v Cowey* [2010] EWCA Civ 711 [50], [54].
[177] *Royal Bank of Scotland v Etridge (No 2)* [2002] 2 AC 773, 794 (Lord Nicholls).
[178] *CIBC Mortgages plc v Pitt* [1994] 1 AC 200, 209 (Lord Browne-Wilkinson).
[179] *Smith v Kay* (1859) 7 HLC 750, 11 ER 299; *Bank of Montreal v Stuart* [1911] AC 120 (PC—Canada).
[180] *Barclays Bank plc v O'Brien* [1994] 1 AC 180, 189 (Lord Browne-Wilkinson).
[181] *Hugenin v Baseley* (1807) 14 Ves 273, 300; *Davies v AIB Group (UK) Plc* [2012] EWHC (Ch) 2178 [8]; *YS GM Marfin II LLC v Lakhani* [2020] EWHC 2629 (Comm).
[182] [2002] 2 AC 773, 795, also 816 (Lord Clyde).
[183] [2002] 2 AC 773, 820, 822 (Lord Hobhouse) and 796, 801, 802 (Lord Nicholls). Lord Hobhouse also asserted that the wrong of undue influence is 'typically some express conduct overbearing the other party's will'. As was noted at paras [6.46]–[6.48] the overborne will theory in the context of duress was trenchantly criticized and has been abandoned. It does not seem to have a useful function to play in explaining undue influence and ought not to reappear in this context.

other.[184] It is not clear exactly what was intended by the use of this label. Certainly it was not intended to suggest that undue influence is to be characterized as a breach of duty giving rise to rights to compensation, and it may be that an essentially moral judgement is denoted.[185] As outlined at the beginning of this chapter, however, it is unnecessary to characterize undue influence as a wrong for rescission to be available, and it is suggested that such a characterization is difficult to sustain if actual undue influence and presumed undue influence are indeed the same doctrine merely proved in different ways, as was stressed in *Etridge*.[186]

Examples of actual undue influence
Actual undue influence has been found where there were threats to prosecute someone connected with the complainant,[187] or to bring a civil claim against the complainant personally.[188] The principle has been applied to set aside transactions procured by threats to prosecute a husband,[189] a brother[190] and a son.[191] Some commentators have argued that in this area the doctrine of actual undue influence is subsumed by common law duress.[192] This would not seem to be correct, particularly because duress requires a threat coupled with a demand, which need not be present for undue influence to be exercised. Likewise, duress requires that the influenced party has no practical alternative but to submit, and undue influence may exist notwithstanding the existence of a practical alternative. For example, blackmail always involves threats and unjustified demands which give rise to illegitimate pressure. If the victim has no practical alternative but to submit to blackmail then the doctrine of duress is engaged and actual undue influence may be superfluous. However, in some circumstances the victim's practical alternative, or perhaps even the best alternative in the eyes of a reasonable bystander, might be to inform the police rather than to submit, and if that is so duress would not be made out. Yet in such cases the transaction could still be voidable for actual undue influence.

6.84

Actual undue influence has been found to have been exercised by an older man over an inexperienced young man,[193] by a member of a religious group who 'took possession, so to speak of the whole life of the deceased',[194] by a carer over an elderly person,[195] an employee

6.85

---

[184] Similarly in *Davies v AIB Group (UK) Plc* [2012] EWHC (Ch) 2178, it was said that the complainant must prove a legal or equitable wrong to establish undue influence without the benefit of any presumption: [10] and [113].
[185] Thus in *Evans v Lloyd* [2013] EWHC 1725 (Ch) [38] it was pointed out that undue influence has 'a connotation of impropriety'.
[186] See paras [6.03] and [6.96]. In particular it would be a major departure from the reasoning in the seminal case of *Allcard v Skinner* (1887) 36 ChD 145 (CA).
[187] *Mutual Finance Ltd v John Wetton & Sons Ltd* [1937] 2 KB 389, 396.
[188] *Daniel v Drew* [2005] EWCA 507 [40] (vulnerable and elderly lady).
[189] *Kaufman v Gerson* [1904] 1 KB 591.
[190] *Mutual Finance Ltd v John Wetton & Sons Ltd* [1937] 2 KB 389.
[191] *Williams v Bayley* (1866) LR 1 HL 200 (HL) 209–10 (this case may also be viewed as one of illegitimate pressure, that is, duress, see 212 cf 216); 'If you are aware that a crime has been committed, you shall not convert that crime into a source of profit or benefit to yourself', per Lord Westbury at 220.
[192] HG Beale (ed), *Chitty on Contracts* (34th edn, 2021) [10-089]; A Burrows, *The Law of Restitution* (3rd edn, 2011) 255.
[193] *Smith v Kay* (1859) 7 HLC 750, 11 ER 299.
[194] *Morley v Loughman* [1893] 1 Ch 736, 756. Also *Norton v Relly* (1764) 2 Eden 286, 28 ER 908; *Nottidge v Prince* (1860) 2 Giff 246, 66 ER 103; *Lyon v Home* (1868) LR 6 Eq 655.
[195] *Langton v Langton* [1995] 2 FLR 890 (elderly person who lived with carers feared that if he did not enter into the transaction, the carers would no longer look after him); *Killick v Pountney* [2000] WTLR 41; *Desir v Alcide* [2015] UKPC 24 [55].

over an employer,[196] and by a person with whom another was abnormally infatuated.[197] And, not infrequently in recent cases, by a husband over a wife.[198] Actual undue influence may be exercised by a husband over his wife where he does not allow her to make an independent and informed decision as to the transaction, as by abusing the confidence he has through misinformation or by making a choice for them both.[199] Undue influence has also been found to arise from a husband's concealment of an affair prior to his wife's assent to a transaction.[200] It has also been found to result from pressure resulting from anxiety and unwitting misrepresentations, due to an absence of understanding of the transaction, made by one co-habiting partner to another.[201]

6.86 It has been suggested that actual undue influence could comprise acts of overt persuasion, emotional blackmail, bullying, or threats; but not a promise sincerely given.[202] Mild emotional blackmail blurted out in the course of a domestic argument and a desire to prevent manifest unhappiness were insufficient to show that independent judgement was being overborne.[203] The provision of a desirable internship to the brother of an employee of the claimant who was responsible for entering into trades with an investment bank did not amount to undue influence.[204] In theory it is said to be possible for actual undue influence to operate as a ground for rescission without proof of any particular act in relation to the transaction in question.[205]

Proving actual undue influence

6.87 Whether a transaction has been brought about by undue influence is a question of fact. The party seeking rescission must prove that the transaction was brought about by the exercise of undue influence.[206] The evidence required to discharge the burden of proof depends on the nature of the alleged undue influence, the personality of the parties, their relationship, the extent to which the transaction cannot readily be accounted for by the ordinary motives of ordinary persons in such relationships, and all the circumstances of the case.[207] There is said to be 'a vast penumbra of facts which bear upon the question whether actual undue influence was exerted. The vulnerability of one party must feature in that analysis. So does the

---

[196] *Bridgeman v Green* (1755) Wilm 58, 97 ER 22 (HL) (footman servant and master); *Re Craig* [1971] Ch 95 (secretary-companion and her elderly employer).
[197] *Sutton v Mishcon de Reya* [2003] EWHC 3166 [25] (transfer of all the complainant's wealth as part of a sexual master-slave role play 'must have been the result of his own (self willed it may be said) mental and emotional subjection to the will of the claimant, and the latter's actual domination of [the complainant]'). Cf *Louth v Diprose* (1992) 175 CLR 621 (transfer of house by man infatuated with woman rescinded on the grounds of unconscionability).
[198] *Bank of Montreal v Stuart* [1911] AC 120 (PC—Canada) 136–37 (wife 'had no will of her own... she was ready to sign and do anything [her husband] told her to do'); *BCCI v Aboody* [1990] QB 923 (CA) 926 (wife was a 'mere channel through which the will of [the husband] operated'); *CIBC Mortgages plc v Pitt* [1994] 1 AC 200; *Bank of Scotland v Bennett* [1997] 1 FLR 801 (wife was told by husband that their marriage was dependent upon her assent to the transaction).
[199] *Royal Bank of Scotland v Etridge (No 2)* [2002] 2 AC 773, 800 (Lord Nicholls).
[200] *Hewett v First Plus Financial Group plc* [2010] EWCA Civ 312 [24]ff.
[201] *Annulment Funding Co Ltd v Cowey* [2010] EWCA Civ 711.
[202] *Thompson v Foy* [2009] EWHC 1076 (Ch) [112].
[203] *Darjan Estate Co plc v Hurley* [2012] 1 WLR 1782 [38]–[40]. See also a consideration of similar facts in *Barclays Bank plc v O'Brien* [1993] QB 109 (CA) 141.
[204] *Libyan Investment Authority v Goldman Sachs International* [2016] EWHC 2530 (Ch) [194], [427].
[205] *Morley v Elmaleh* [2009] EWHC 1196 (Ch) [607].
[206] *BCCI v Aboody* [1990] QB 923 (CA) 967.
[207] *Royal Bank of Scotland v Etridge (No 2)* [2002] 2 AC 773, 796 (Lord Nicholls).

forcefulness of the personality of the other'.²⁰⁸ Actual undue influence may arise from the exploitation of a vulnerable person,²⁰⁹ in which case there will be an overlap with the doctrine of unconscionable bargains.²¹⁰ It has been pointed out that it is unlikely that a court would ever find that undue influence in the one case consisted both of coercion and abuse of trust and confidence, as people do not usually trust those who coerce them.²¹¹ Evidence of reluctance to sign may assist in showing that the complainant's state of mind was 'I do not want to sign this document but I am being *forced* to do so'.²¹² On the other hand, the fact that independent advice was given may have an emancipating effect.²¹³

Whether an ordinary person would have been influenced in the same circumstances is irrelevant. The question is whether the particular party seeking rescission was subjected to actual undue influence.²¹⁴ Thus there is no equivalent to the requirement of materiality that must be satisfied in cases of non-fraudulent misrepresentation. This is because undue influence is treated in a similar way to fraud at common law, a similarity also apparent in relation to the requirement of causation. **6.88**

Second requirement: causation
The undue influence must have had some effect in inducing or bringing about the transaction. However, it appears to be irrelevant that the complainant would still have entered into the transaction in the absence of the undue influence. In *UCB Corporate Services Ltd v Williams* Jonathan Parker LJ stated: **6.89**

> As Lord Browne-Wilkinson said in *CIBC v Pitt* (at p 209B): 'Actual undue influence is a species of fraud.' That being so, I cannot see any reason in principle why (for example) a husband who has fraudulently procured the consent of his wife to participate in a transaction should be able, in effect, to escape the consequences of his wrongdoing by establishing that had he not acted fraudulently, and had his wife had the opportunity to make a free and informed choice, she would have acted in the same way.²¹⁵

Thus it is sufficient if the undue influence was simply 'a' reason why the complainant entered the transaction. The causal element will be missing only in the unusual case where the influence exerted had no effect at all on the decision to enter the transaction. **6.90**

Causation is judged by looking at the situation at the time the transaction was entered into. A transaction will not become retrospectively tainted by undue influence merely because the counterparty fails to perform his side of the bargain.²¹⁶ **6.91**

---

²⁰⁸ *Daniel v Drew* [2005] EWCA 507 [32].
²⁰⁹ *Liddle v Cree* [2011] EWHC 3294 (Ch) [9].
²¹⁰ See Chap 7, para [7.62]ff.
²¹¹ *Thompson v Foy* [2009] EWHC 1076 (Ch) [101].
²¹² *Howard v Howard-Lawson* [2012] EWHC 3258 (Ch) [89] (emphasis retained).
²¹³ *Re Brindley (Deceased)* [2018] EWHC 157 (Ch) [113]–[122].
²¹⁴ *Re Brocklehurst's Estate* [1978] Ch 14 (CA) 40 (strong-willed autocrat made generous gift to a friend in a lower socio-economic group); *Daniel v Drew* [2005] EWCA 507 [41] (threats of civil action made by nephew against vulnerable old aunt to procure her resignation as trustee of a family trust).
²¹⁵ [2002] 3 FCR 448 (CA) [86], [91]; applied in *UCB Group Ltd v Hedworth* [2003] EWCA 1717 [77]. The Court of Appeal expressly declined to follow *BCCI v Aboody* [1990] 1 QB 923 (CA) 971 where the opposite view had been expressed.
²¹⁶ *Thompson v Foy* [2009] EWHC 1076 (Ch) [101].

6.92 As in the case of other grounds for rescission, a substitute contract will be voidable where the original contract was vitiated by undue influence if the substitute contract cannot fairly be regarded as an exercise of the complainant's free will.[217]

Matters not required to be shown

6.93 There is no need to show a prior relationship of trust and confidence or a history of influence. Actual undue influence does not depend on a pre-existing relationship between the parties, though it usually derives from such a relationship.[218] Although they are indicia of actual undue influence, neither coercion, nor pressure, nor deliberate concealment is necessary to establish actual undue influence.[219] Nor is it necessary to show that the defendant acted with malign intent[220] or that he knew that he was exerting undue influence.[221] It is not essential that the transaction should be disadvantageous to the complainant, either financially or in any other way.[222] Nor it is necessary to prove that the party against whom rescission is sought derived a direct personal benefit from the transaction.[223]

(4) Presumed undue influence: undue influence proved with the assistance of a presumption

Nature of presumed undue influence

6.94 No specific overt acts of persuasion are necessary for rescission to be available on the basis of presumed undue influence. The parties' relationship may be such that, without more, one of them is disposed to agree to a course of action proposed by the other. If the complainant places trust in the dominant party to look after his affairs and interests, and the latter betrays this trust by preferring his own interests, the dominant party's influence arising from the parties' relationship has been abused.[224]

6.95 For the presumption of undue influence to arise, the complainant must prove a relationship of influence and also show that the transaction calls for an explanation. Only then does the onus of disproving undue influence shift to the defendant. In *Etridge* Lord Nicholls explained that:

> On proof of these matters the stage is set for the court to infer that, in the absence of a satisfactory explanation, the transaction can only have been procured by undue influence. In other words, proof of these two facts is prima facie evidence that the defendant abused the influence he acquired in the parties' relationship. He preferred his own interests. He did

---

[217] *Yorkshire Bank Plc v Tinsley* [2004] EWCA 816; *Samuel v Wadlow* [2007] EWCA 155. See also Chap 4, para [4.121]. Cf *Davies v AIB Group (UK) Plc* [2012] EWHC (Ch) 2178 [119].
[218] *Royal Bank of Scotland v Etridge (No 2)* [2002] 2 AC 773, 820 (Lord Hobhouse).
[219] *Dunbar Bank plc v Nadeem* [1998] 3 All ER 876 (CA) 883 (Millett LJ).
[220] *Bank of Credit International v Aboody* [1990] 1 QB 923 (CA) 969–70.
[221] *Papouis v Gibson-West* [2004] EWHC 396.
[222] *Royal Bank of Scotland v Etridge (No 2)* [2002] 2 AC 773, 796 (Lord Nicholls), also 841 (Lord Scott); and see *CIBC Mortgages plc v Pitt* [1994] 1 AC 200, 209 (Lord Browne-Wilkinson). Cf also *Thompson v Foy* [2009] EWHC 1076 (Ch) [99].
[223] *Ellis v Barker* (1871) 7 Ch App 104; *Allcard v Skinner* (1887) 36 ChD 145 (CA); *Bullock v Lloyds Bank Ltd* [1955] Ch 317; *Naidoo v Naidu*, The Times, 1 November 2000.
[224] *Royal Bank of Scotland v Etridge (No 2)* [2002] 2 AC 773, 795 (Lord Nicholls).

not behave fairly to the other. So the evidential burden then shifts to him. It is for him to produce evidence to counter the inference which otherwise should be drawn.[225]

The presumption is a forensic tool to assist the complainant in establishing his case, and as Cotton LJ observed in the leading case of *Allcard v Skinner*:[226] **6.96**

> ... the court interferes, not on the ground that any wrongful act has in fact been committed by the donee, but on the ground of public policy, and to prevent the relations which existed between the parties and the influence arising there from being abused.

This explanation has been endorsed on a number of occasions by the Court of Appeal.[227] Yet it does not sit comfortably with the observations made in the House of Lords that undue influence is founded on wrongdoing.[228]

First requirement: relationship of influence
Relationship may be proved or presumed

A relationship of influence may be proved or presumed.[229] Relationships of influence proved directly will be considered first.[230] The classes of relationship where influence is irrebuttably presumed will be identified in the next section.[231] Relationships of influence are infinitely various and cannot be listed exhaustively. The key indicium of such a relationship is that one party has reposed sufficient trust and confidence in the other.[232] But as Lord Nicholls noted in *Etridge* even this is not comprehensive: **6.97**

> The principle is not confined to cases of abuse of trust and confidence. It also includes, for instance, cases where a vulnerable person has been exploited. Indeed, there is no single touchstone for determining whether the principle is applicable. Several expressions have been used in an endeavour to encapsulate the essence: trust and confidence, reliance, dependence or vulnerability on the one hand and ascendancy, domination or control on the other. None of these descriptions is perfect. None is all embracing. Each has its proper place.[233]

All the surrounding circumstances are taken into account in determining whether a sufficient relationship of influence existed.[234] Factors which have been particularly relevant have included the strength of the reliance by the complainant on the other party,[235] the history **6.98**

---

[225] [2002] 2 AC 773, 796, also 821 (Lord Hobhouse); *Papouis v Gibson-West* [2004] EWHC 396 [5].
[226] (1887) 36 ChD 145 (CA) 171, 187 (Lindley LJ), 191 (Bowen LJ). Birks argued that such cases are not cases of pressure in the nature of bullying or domination but rather cases where the claimant 'could not *vis-à-vis* this defendant be expected to keep his guard up and his judgment clear': PBH Birks, *An Introduction to the Law of Restitution* (rev edn, 1989) 205. As regards the former, the vitiating factor is defendant-sided; as regards the latter, it is complainant-sided: see n 9.
[227] *Cheese v Thomas* [1994] 1 WLR 129 (CA); *Hammond v Osborn* [2002] EWCA 885 [30]–[32]; *Jennings v Cairns* [2003] EWCA 1935 [33]–[35]; *Niersmans v Pesticcio* [2004] EWCA 372 [20]; *Goodchild v Bradbury* [2006] EWCA 1868 [25]–[27].
[228] See para [6.83].
[229] *National Commercial Bank (Jamaica) Ltd v Hew* [2003] UKPC 51 [31].
[230] Formerly known as Class 2B cases: *Barclays Bank plc v O'Brien* [1994] 1 AC 180, 189.
[231] Formerly known as Class 2A cases: *Barclays Bank plc v O'Brien* [1994] 1 AC 180, 189.
[232] *Re Brocklehurst's Estate* [1978] Ch 14, 41.
[233] [2002] 2 AC 773, 795–96; *Evans v Lloyd* [2013] EWHC 1725 (Ch) [39]–[40]. In *Malik (Deceased) v Shiekh* [2018] 4 WLR 86 it was stressed that the principle is not limited to cases where trust and confidence was reposed, but extends to cases where there was evidence of dependence or vulnerability.
[234] *Lloyd's Bank Ltd v Bundy* [1975] QB 326 (CA) 341–42.
[235] *Goldsworthy v Brickell* [1987] 1 Ch 378 (CA) 401.

and duration of the relationship,[236] and, it seems, the nature of the transaction entered into.[237] However, a relationship of influence ought not to be inferred only from the fact that a transaction was improvident.[238] And this factor must be distinguished from the separate requirement that the transaction 'calls for an explanation' which also looks to its content.[239]

6.99 No particular acts of persuasion have to be shown—it is necessary to show a *relationship of trust and confidence*. The trust and confidence must be generally reposed in relation to some general aspect of the complainant's affairs, such as management of finances, the other party's role as adviser, or the entrustment of the other party to look after the complainant. Evidence of particular dealings between the parties will often assist in establishing the existence of a relevant relationship.[240] A relationship of trust and confidence is to be distinguished from a mere friendship based on equality and mutual interests.[241] The relationship of trust and confidence must pre-date the impugned transaction. If a claimant enters into a transaction that calls for explanation, and in the course of that transaction reposes trust and confidence in the defendant, the evidential presumption will not arise.[242]

Examples of relationships of influence arising without a presumption of influence

6.100 A sufficient relationship of influence has been proved to have arisen in a wide variety of relationships. These include husband and wife,[243] parties to a long-standing sexual and emotional relationship,[244] siblings,[245] banker and customer,[246] farm manager and elderly farmer,[247] adviser and young man,[248] son and retired

---

[236] *Lloyds Bank Ltd v Bundy* [1975] QB 326 (CA) (many years); *Goldsworthy v Brickell* [1987] 1 Ch 378 (CA) (only few months of reliance before first agreement was signed).

[237] *Huguenin v Baseley* (1807) 14 Ves Jun 273, 296; 33 ER 526; *Zamet v Hyman* [1961] 1 WLR 1142 (CA) 1149 ('extravagantly one-sided', 'astonishing' document); *Alec Lobb (Garages) Ltd v Total Oil Great Britain Ltd* [1983] 1 WLR 87, 94–95; on appeal [1985] 1 WLR 173 (CA) 181–83; *Credit Lyonnais Bank Nederland NV v Burch* [1997] 1 All ER 144 (CA) 154–55 ('where the transaction is so extravagantly improvident that it is virtually inexplicable on any other basis, the inference will be readily drawn'). This is an instance of the substantive fairness of the transaction being taken into account when a judgment of its procedural fairness is being made.

[238] *Tufton v Sperni* [1952] 2 TLR 516 (CA) 530; Lord Romilly's view in *Hoghton v Hoghton* (1852) 15 Beav 278, 298; 51 ER 545, 553 that a donee of a large gift must always prove that it was made freely and with sufficient understanding was rejected in *Barclays Bank plc v O'Brien* [1994] 1 AC 180, 193–94.

[239] See paras [6.105]ff.

[240] *Morley v Elmaleh* [2009] EWHC 1196 (Ch) [598]–[599].

[241] *Morley v Elmaleh* [2009] EWHC 1196 (Ch) [614].

[242] *Perwaz v Perwaz* [2018] UKUT 325 (TCC).

[243] *Re Lloyd's Bank Ltd; Bomze and Lederman v Bomze* [1931] 1 Ch 289, 302 'it is not difficult for the wife to establish her title to relief'. In *Barclays Bank plc v O'Brien* [1994] 1 AC 180, 190–91, 196 Lord Browne-Wilkinson stated that 'the sexual and emotional ties between the parties provide a ready weapon for undue influence: a wife's true wishes can easily be overborne because of her fear of destroying or damaging the wider relationship between her and her husband if she opposes his wishes'. In *Bank of China (Hong Kong) Ltd v Wong Kam Ho Trust* [2014] 1 HKLRD 41 [34] it was held that trust and confidence is not unusual between husband and wife; 'It is as much in Hong Kong as in the United Kingdom "a part of every healthy marriage"'. Cf *Royal Bank of Scotland v Etridge (No 2)* [2002] 2 AC 773, 800 where Lord Nicholls noted that 'statements or conduct by a husband which do not pass beyond the bounds of what may be expected of a reasonable husband in the circumstances should not, without more, be castigated as undue influence'. For undue influence of a wife over an ill husband, *Simpson v Simpson* [1989] Fam Law 20.

[244] *Massey v Midland Bank plc* [1995] 1 All ER 929 (CA).

[245] *Northern Rock Building Society v Archer* [1999] Lloyd's Rep 32.

[246] *Lloyds Bank Ltd v Bundy* [1975] QB 326 (CA) 347; *National Commercial Bank (Jamaica) Ltd v Hew* [2003] UKPC 51. Cf *National Westminster Bank plc v Morgan* [1985] 1 AC 686, 708–09; *Cornish v Midland Bank plc* [1985] 3 All ER 513 (CA); *Alec Lobb (Garages) Ltd v Total Oil GB Ltd* [1985] 1 WLR 173 (CA); *National Westminster Bank plc v Waite* [2006] EWHC 1287 [45].

[247] *Goldsworthy v Brickell* [1987] Ch 378 (CA).

[248] *Tate v Williamson* (1866) LR 2 Ch App 55.

parent,[249] son-in-law and elderly father-in-law,[250] nephew and elderly aunt[251] or uncle,[252] great-nephew and great-uncle,[253] carer and elderly or disabled person,[254] executor and young woman,[255] employer and junior employee,[256] employer's insurers and employee,[257] manager and musician,[258] member of association's committee and fellow member of the committee,[259] a solicitor and former client,[260] and an older man and a quasi step-daughter who was described as a successful career woman.[261] But these are merely examples and, as Lord Scarman observed in *National Westminster Bank plc v Morgan*,[262] '[t]he relationships which may develop a dominating influence of one over another are infinitely various. There is no substitute in this branch of the law for a "meticulous examination of the facts"'. In a recent case the fact that a power of attorney was granted by a partially disabled mother to her son was a key factor that showed such a relationship of influence.[263] But the significance of a grant of a power of attorney will, of course, vary from case to case.[264]

No relationship of influence was found where a valuable gift was made by a 'strong-willed, autocratic and generous man, whom [the recipient] liked, respected and looked up to as a social superior',[265] or by a 'a tough, strong-willed, highly intelligent individual' who easily dismissed others as incompetent and was prepared to falsify documents if it served her interests.[266] Addiction to drugs, family loyalties, business partnerships, and impecuniosity do not generally give rise to a relationship of influence.[267] No relationship of dependence was found in a case where a man had lived with a farming family from the age of 14 to 79, and worked on the family's farm, for the court accepted that whilst his life was very simple, the man was independently minded and had made his own decision to give property to his adopted family.[268] No protected relationship of trust and confidence arose between a

6.101

---

[249] *Avon Finance Co Ltd v Bridger* [1985] 2 All ER 281 (CA); *Coldunell Ltd v Gallon* [1986] QB 1184 (CA); *Greene King plc v Stanley* [2001] EWCA 1966; *Abbey National Bank plc v Stringer* [2006] EWCA 338; *Thompson v Foy* [2009] EWHC 1076 (Ch) [103] (no sufficient trust and confidence in relationship between mother and daughter); *Re Brindley (Deceased)* [2018] EWHC 157 (Ch); *Re Chin (Deceased)* [2019] EWHC 523 (Ch).
[250] *Mahoney v Purnell* [1996] 3 All ER 61.
[251] *Inche Noriah v Shaik Allie Bin Omar* [1929] AC 127 (PC—Straits Settlements).
[252] *Goodchild v Bradley* [2006] EWCA 1868.
[253] *Cheese v Thomas* [1994] 1 WLR 129 (CA).
[254] *Re Craig* [1971] Ch 95; *Langton v Langton* [1995] 2 FLR 890; *Murphy v Rayner* [2011] EWHC 1 (Ch) [323].
[255] *Grosvenor v Sherratt* (1860) 28 Beav 659, 54 ER 520.
[256] *Credit Lyonnais Bank Nederland NV v Burch* [1997] 1 All ER 144 (CA) 154–55 (Millett LJ); *Trustees of Beardsley Theobalds Retirement Benefit Scheme v Yardley* [2011] EWHC 1380 (QB).
[257] *Horry v Tate & Lyle Refineries Ltd* [1982] 2 Lloyd's Rep 416.
[258] *O'Sullivan v Management Agency and Music Ltd* [1985] QB 428 (CA).
[259] *Tufton v Sperni* [1952] 2 TLR 516 (CA) 523 'If a number of persons join together for the purpose of furthering some charitable or altruistic objective, it would seem not unreasonable to conclude that in regard to all matters related to that objective, each "necessarily reposes confidence" in the others and each possesses accordingly that "influence which naturally grows out of confidence"'; *Roche v Sherrington* [1982] 1 WLR 599.
[260] *Demerara Bauxite Co Ltd v Hubbard* [1923] AC 673 (PC—British Guiana).
[261] *Jolly v Watson* (unreported, High Court of Justice of the Isle of Man, 1 March 2012) [339].
[262] [1985] AC 686, 709.
[263] *Hackett v Crown Prosecution Service* [2011] EWHC 1170 (Admin) [54].
[264] *Morley v Elmaleh* [2009] EWHC 1196 (Ch) [610] no inference of a relationship of trust and confidence was drawn from the grant of a power of attorney, or that fact that the complainant had previously signed a will leaving her property to the other party to the challenged gift.
[265] *Re Brocklehurst's Estate* [1978] Ch 14 (CA) 36.
[266] *Morley v Elmaleh* [2009] EWHC 1196 (Ch) [612].
[267] *Irvani v Irvani* [2000] 1 Lloyd's Rep 412 (CA) 425; *Hughes v Hughes* [2005] EWHC 469 [109], [116] (no relationship of influence found between mother and son as to the former's financial affairs).
[268] *Evans v Lloyd* [2013] EWHC 1725 (Ch).

sovereign wealth fund and an investment bank, which had not become a trusted adviser to the fund as had been alleged, but there remained a banker–customer relationship.[269]

Relationships where influence is irrebuttably presumed

6.102 Some relationships always, as a matter of law, give rise to an irrebuttable presumption of influence. Lord Nicholls explained these classes of relationship in *Etridge*:

> The law has adopted a sternly protective attitude towards certain types of relationship in which one party acquires influence over another who is vulnerable and dependent and where, moreover, substantial gifts by the influenced or vulnerable are not normally to be expected... In these cases the law presumes, irrebuttably, that one party had influence over the other. The complainant need not prove he actually reposed trust and confidence in the other party. It is sufficient for him to prove the existence of the type of relationship.[270]

6.103 The following relationships have been recognized as giving rise to the irrebuttable presumption of a relationship of sufficient influence: parent and child[271] (including step-parent and step-child),[272] guardian and ward,[273] doctor and patient,[274] solicitor and client,[275] religious or spiritual adviser and disciple,[276] trustee and beneficiary,[277] and possibly fiancés.[278] It has been observed that in such recognized relationships of undue influence 'it would seem that you only have to look at the relative status of the parties in order to presume that the requisite degree of trust and confidence is there'.[279] The following relationships have been

---

[269] *Libyan Investment Authority v Goldman Sachs International* [2016] EWHC 2530 (Ch).
[270] [2002] 2 AC 773, 797, also 842 (Lord Scott).
[271] *Wright v Vanderplank* (1856) 8 De GM & G 133, 44 ER 340; *Lancashire Loans Ltd v Black* [1934] 1 KB 380 (CA) (presumption arose even though child had married). But after the child attains sufficient maturity, the relationship moves out of this class where influence is irrebuttably presumed and a relationship of influence must be proved on the facts: *Bainbridge v Browne* (1881) 18 ChD 188, 196; *Re Pauling's Settlement Trusts* [1964] Ch 303 (CA) 337; similarly no presumption arises where rescission is sought against the child: *Coles v Reynolds* [2020] EWHC 2151 (Ch) [115].
[272] *Kempson v Ashbee* (1874) 10 Ch App 15 (stepfather and stepdaughter); *Powell v Powell* [1900] 1 Ch 243, 246 (stepmother and stepdaughter).
[273] *Archer v Hudson* (1844) 7 Beav 551, 50 ER 126; *Taylor v Johnston* (1882) 19 ChD 603, 608; *Wright v Carter* [1903] 1 Ch 27 (CA) 49.
[274] *Billage v Southee* (1852) 9 Hare 534, 68 ER 623; *Mitchell v Homfray* (1881) 8 QBD 587; *Radcliffe v Price* (1902) 18 TLR 446; *Goldsworthy v Brickell* [1987] Ch 378 (CA) 404.
[275] *Wright v Carter* [1903] 1 Ch 27 (CA) 57; *Goldsworthy v Brickell* [1987] Ch 378 (CA) 404; *Liles v Terry* [1895] 2 QB 679 (property gifted by client to solicitor's wife); *Wintle v Nye* [1959] 1 WLR 284 (HL) (will drawn up by beneficiary solicitor). For the relationship of solicitor and former client see n 241. The presumption of undue influence as between solicitor and client was rebutted in respect of part of a transaction in *Pathania v Adedeji* [2010] EWHC 3085 (QB).
[276] *Allcard v Skinner* (1887) 36 ChD 145 (property given by nun to her mother superior over the course of the nun's eight years as a member of the order); *Huguenin v Baseley* (1807) 14 Ves Jun 273, 33 ER 528; *Lyon v Home* (1868) LR 6 Eq 655; *Morley v Loughnan* [1893] 1 Ch 736; *Roche v Sherrington* [1982] 2 All ER 426; *Curtis v Curtis* [2011] EWCA Civ 1602.
[277] *Ellis v Barker* (1871) 7 Ch App 104; *Thomson v Eastwood* (1877) 2 App Cas 215; *Beningfield v Baxter* (1886) 12 App Cas 167 (PC—Natal); *Wright v Carter* [1903] 1 Ch 27 (CA).
[278] *Lovesy v Smith Re Lloyds Bank Ltd* [1931] 1 Ch 289, 302; *Leeder v Stevens* [2005] EWCA 50. Cf *Zamet v Hyman* [1961] 1 WLR 1442 (CA). The High Court of Australia rejected the argument that a presumption arose between fiancés in *Thorne v Kennedy* (2017) 263 CLR 85.
[279] *Goldsworthy v Brickell* [1987] Ch 378 (CA) 401. In *R v Attorney-General for England and Wales* [2003] UKPC 22 [41]–[43] Lord Scott (dissenting) appeared to treat the relationship between a senior officer and soldier as within this list. The majority was prepared to assume a relationship of influence but concluded in effect that the transaction did not call for an explanation: [24].

held not to give rise to the irrebuttable presumption: husband and wife,[280] principal and agent,[281] banker and customer,[282] nephew and aunt,[283] and siblings.[284]

6.104 In a case falling within the category described in this section, two distinct presumptions are at play: (i) the law irrebuttably presumes that one party possessed influence over the other,[285] and, provided that the transaction calls for an explanation, (ii) an evidential presumption arises that the influence has been abused.[286]

Second requirement: transaction calls for an explanation
6.105 In order for the burden of proof to shift from the complainant to the other party, the complainant must show not only that the other party possessed influence over him but also that the transaction was one that is not readily explicable by the relationship between the parties.[287] As Lord Nicholls explained in *Etridge*:

> ... something more is needed before the law reverses the burden of proof, *something which calls for an explanation*. When that something more is present, the greater the disadvantage to the vulnerable person, the more cogent must be the explanation before the presumption will be regarded as rebutted.[288]

6.106 This requirement must be satisfied whether the influence is proved by evidence or presumed because the relationship falls within one of the established classes just discussed. This limitation is necessary for, as Lord Nicholls observed, it would be absurd for the law to presume that every gift by a child to a parent, or every transaction between a client and his solicitor or a patient and his doctor, was procured by undue influence unless the contrary was affirmatively proved. A presumption of this scope would be too far-reaching.[289]

6.107 The touchstone is that the transaction must not be explicable by reference to the ordinary motives on which people act.[290] As Lindley LJ stated in *Allcard v Skinner* 'if the gift is so large as not to be reasonably accounted for on the ground of friendship, relationship, charity, or other ordinary motives on which ordinary men act, the burden is upon the donee to support the gift'.[291] The test is an objective one.[292] Transactions which may satisfy the

---

[280] *Bank of Montreal v Stuart* [1911] AC 120 (PC—Canada) 137; *Yerkey v Jones* (1939) 63 CLR 649, 675; *Barclays Bank plc v O'Brien* [1994] 1 AC 180. See D O'Sullivan (2002) 118 LQR 337. Cf *Royal Bank of Scotland v Etridge (No 2)* [2002] 2 AC 773, 842 where Lord Scott stated 'I would assume that in every case in which a wife and husband are living together that there is reciprocal trust and confidence between them'. His Lordship added at 866 that 'the trust and confidence of a wife in her husband... is accentuated in a Hassidic marriage'.
[281] *Re Coombe* [1911] 1 Ch 723 (CA) 728.
[282] *National Westminster Bank plc v Morgan* [1985] AC 686, 707.
[283] *Randall v Randall* [2004] EWHC 2258 [45].
[284] *Pesticcio v Huet* (2003) [2003] EWHC 2293 (Ch).
[285] *Royal Bank of Scotland v Etridge (No 2)* [2002] 2 AC 773 [18] (Lord Nicholls).
[286] In *Niersmans v Pesticcio* [2004] EWCA 372 [3] the two presumptions were erroneously collapsed into one.
[287] *Royal Bank of Scotland v Etridge (No 2)* [2002] 2 AC 773, 798 (Lord Nicholls).
[288] *Royal Bank of Scotland v Etridge (No 2)* [2002] 2 AC 773, 799 (emphasis added).
[289] *Royal Bank of Scotland v Etridge (No 2)* [2002] 2 AC 773, 798. See, eg, *Fielder v Smith* [2005] All ER(D) 264 (guarantee of company's liability for disbursements given by client to solicitor upheld as it did not call for an explanation).
[290] *Royal Bank of Scotland v Etridge (No 2)* [2002] 2 AC 773, 798, 800 (Lord Nicholls), also 841 (Lord Scott).
[291] (1887) 36 ChD 145 (CA) 185; *National Westminster Bank plc v Morgan* [1985] AC 686, 703-07. In *Smith v Cooper* [2010] EWCA Civ 722 Lloyd LJ stated at [60] that the phrase 'a transaction which calls for explanation' was used in the *Etridge* case as shorthand for the formula in *Allcard v Skinner* extracted earlier. This approach was applied in *Hackett v Crown Prosecution Service* [2011] EWHC 1170 (Admin) [52].
[292] *Vale v Armstrong* [2004] EWHC 1160 [44].

170 II. GROUNDS

requirement of calling for an explanation include a large gift,[293] sale by the complainant at an undervalue,[294] or a purchase by the complainant at an excessive price.[295]

6.108 The disadvantage that the complainant suffers, or may potentially suffer,[296] as a result of the transaction is important, but it is not conclusive. Something more than mere disadvantage to the complainant is required. A gift is often disadvantageous but is not necessarily something that calls for explanation in the context of the parties' relationship.[297] Similarly, a guarantee by a wife of her husband's business debts may be disadvantageous to her but not call for an explanation because the business is potentially of great benefit to the family.[298] The nature of the parties' relationship is a crucial factor.[299]

6.109 The previous formulation of this requirement, that there be a 'manifest disadvantage',[300] has been abandoned.[301] But earlier decisions on what constituted manifest disadvantage may provide guidance as to what satisfies the present test. In *BCCI v Aboody*[302] it was stated that whether there was manifest disadvantage in a surety case must depend on two factors, namely (i) the seriousness of the risk of enforcement to the surety, in practical terms, and (ii) the benefits gained by the surety in accepting the risk. The balance between risk and reward was also determinative in a case involving a joint purchase of a house by an elderly person and a carer. It involved a manifest disadvantage because the former 'used all his money, and it was not an insignificant amount, in buying a right which was seriously insecure and which tied him to this particular house'.[303]

6.110 In determining whether a transaction calls for an explanation, the court takes into account the particular transaction and the particular relationship between the parties.[304] As regards the nature of the transaction, the court considers the balance between, on the one hand, the value transferred or risks assumed by the complainant relative to his overall wealth and,

---

[293] *Watson v Huber* [2005] All ER(D) 156 (gifts of 48% of gross estate of grandmother of four grand-daughters to her step-sister required an explanation).
[294] *Mahoney v Purnell* [1996] 3 All ER 61; *Leeder v Stevens* [2005] EWCA 50 (transfer of 50% interest in a house in exchange for payment of £5,000 mortgage).
[295] *Tufton v Sperni* [1952] 2 TLR 516 (CA) 526.
[296] *Hammond v Osborn* [2002] EWCA 885 (donor gave away nearly all of his liquid assets thereby incurring a future tax liability which he would not be able to meet); *Goodchild v Bradley* [2006] EWCA 1868 (donor gave away land adjacent to his house without appreciating its development potential which would depreciate the value of his house by £45,000).
[297] *Royal Bank of Scotland v Etridge (No 2)* [2002] 2 AC 773, 841 (Lord Scott) 'Some transactions will obviously be innocuous and innocent. A moderate gift as a Christmas or birthday present will be obviously innocuous and innocent.' Transfer of property between mother and daughter to allow the latter to raise finance by way of mortgage was readily explicable on ordinary motives on which people act (*Thompson v Foy* [2009] EWHC 1076 (Ch)), as was an attempt at family tax planning (*Hurst v Green* [2020] EWHC 344 (Ch) [62]). The importance of context was emphasized in *Evans v Lloyd* [2013] EWHC 1725 (Ch) [43], [62]–[64], where a gift of practically all of a man's property to employers he had been living with for 56 years and treated as family did not call for an explanation. Estate-planning measures could provide an explanation for a gift: *Tociapski v Tociapski* [2013] EWHC 1770 (Ch) [17] (an action to set aside a will).
[298] *Royal Bank of Scotland v Etridge (No 2)* [2002] 2 AC 773, 799–800 (Lord Nicholls).
[299] *Gorjat v Gorjat* [2010] EWHC 1537 (Ch) (transfer of money from sole account to an account held jointly with second wife did not call for an explanation).
[300] *National Westminster Bank plc v Morgan* [1985] AC 686, 703 (Lord Scarman), clarified in *CBI Mortgages plc v Pitt* [1994] 1 AC 200, 208–09.
[301] *Royal Bank of Scotland v Etridge (No 2)* [2002] 2 AC 773, 799 (Lord Nicholls). For a comparison of the two formulations, EC Mujih, 'From manifest disadvantage to transactions that call for explanation: have the difficulties been eliminated ten years after Royal Bank of Scotland Plc v Etridge (No.2)?' (2012) 27 JIBLR 295.
[302] [1990] QB 923 (CA) 965.
[303] *Cheese v Thomas* [1994] 1 WLR 129 (CA) 134; *Vale v Armstrong* [2004] EWHC 1160 [50].
[304] *Niersmans v Pesticcio* [2004] EWCA 372 [20].

on the other, the financial and non-financial benefits that the complainant received or expected to receive in return.[305] These factors are weighed in light of the particular relationship that pertained as between the parties[306] and any other circumstances relevant to that relationship.[307] Thus the consideration that is exchanged is judged in the context of the circumstances of the transaction.[308]

6.111 It has been held that the transaction must be of such a nature that a person in the position of the complainant, acting in the way that such a person might ordinarily be expected to act, would not have entered into the transaction unless he was subjected to undue influence,[309] but the authorities are in conflict on this point. In *Chater v Mortgage Agency Services Number Two Ltd* the Court of Appeal stated:

> Insofar as the passage cited from Lord Scarman's speech in *Morgan* suggests a higher test, we prefer the reformulated test given by Lord Nicholls [in *Etridge* at [14]]. We detect a possible distinction between a transaction explicable *only* on the basis that undue influence had been exercised to procure it (Lord Scarman [in *Morgan*]) and one which called for an explanation, which if not given would enable the court to infer that it could only have been procured by undue influence (Lord Nicholls [in *Etridge*]).[310]

This is the preferable view after *Etridge*. A transaction which calls for an explanation is sufficient to raise the rebuttable presumption. There ought to be no further need for the claimant to show that the transaction is only explicable on the basis that undue influence had been exerted.

Third requirement: counterparty's failure to rebut presumption of undue influence
6.112 When a presumption of undue influence arises, the onus shifts from the party who is alleging undue influence to the party who is denying it. The weight of that presumption varies from case to case, depending upon the particular nature of the relationship, and on the nature of the particular impugned transaction. The type and weight of evidence needed to rebut the presumption therefore also varies, depending upon the weight of the presumption itself.[311]

---

[305] *Hammond v Osborn* [2002] EWCA 885 (transaction called for explanation where elderly donor gave away 91% of his liquid assets, incurring a large tax liability, to his neighbour who had provided him with general care). Ward LJ stated at [58] that it was 'an act of generosity wholly out of proportion to the kindness shown to him. Looking at the matter objectively, it was an irrational decision, not a good one'; *Brown v Stephenson* [2013] EWHC 2531 (Ch) [128] (transfer of half share in property into a partnership in exchange for building services could be accounted for on grounds on which ordinary men or women act); *Malik (Deceased) v Shiekh* [2018] 4 WLR 86; *Paull v Paull* [2018] EWHC 2520 (Ch); *YS GM Marfin II LLC v Lakhani* [2020] EWHC 2629 (Comm) [78]–[79] (granting of guarantees did not call for an explanation where the guarantors owned the ultimate holding company of the companies whose debts they guaranteed).
[306] *National Commercial Bank (Jamaica) Ltd v Hew* [2003] UKPC 51 [34].
[307] *Coles v Reynolds* [2020] EWHC 2151 (Ch) [117].
[308] *Bridgeman v Green* (1757) Wilm 58, 62; 97 ER 22, 24 (HL) (transaction whereby a master gave a large part of his substantial wealth to his servant 'must alarm and raise jealousies and suspicions in every man's mind who hears of it'); *Vale v Armstrong* [2004] EWHC 1160 (transfer of home to great-nephew at 50% undervalue and an undocumented promise of a lifetime licence to occupy called for an explanation). Cf *Hughes v Hughes* [2005] EWHC 469 (transfer of home by mother to son at undervalue did not call for explanation).
[309] *National Westminster Bank Plc v Morgan* [1985] AC 686, 704 (Lord Scarman) and *Turkey v Awadh* [2005] EWCA 382 [39].
[310] [2003] EWCA 490 (CA) [30].
[311] *Royal Bank of Scotland plc v Etridge (No 2)* [2002] 2 AC 773, 840 (Lord Scott).

172   II. GROUNDS

6.113 Once the onus has shifted, it is for the dominant party to show that the influence did not actually operate in the particular case.[312] Unless the defendant introduces evidence to counteract the inference of undue influence that the complainant's evidence justifies, the complainant will succeed.[313] Evidence of a prior assertion by the complainant that he was not put under any pressure by the dominant party does not suffice.[314]

6.114 To rebut the presumption the dominant party must prove that the transaction was the result of the free exercise of independent will.[315] He must prove that the party claiming rescission had, before entering into the transaction, been placed in such a position as would enable him to form an entirely free and unfettered judgement, independent altogether of any sort of control.[316] In short, it is necessary to establish that the complainant entered into the transaction only after full, free, and informed thought about it.[317] In order to prove this, it must be shown *inter alia* that he understood the nature and effect of the transaction. The nature and the effect of the transaction are distinct concepts. Understanding the effect of a transaction includes understanding the value of what is given or exchanged and its impact on the remainder of one's assets.[318]

6.115 The fact that the complainant understood the nature and effect of the transaction may be established, for example, by showing that he obtained and acted upon legal advice.[319] But understanding, let alone advice, does not automatically disprove undue influence.[320] It has been observed that 'it is not sufficient to show that the complainant understood what he was doing and intended to do it. The problem is not lack of understanding but lack of independence'.[321] Lord Nicholls stated in *Etridge*:

> Proof that the complainant received advice from a third party before entering into the impugned transaction is one of the matters a court takes into account when weighing all the evidence. The weight, or importance, to be attached to such advice depends on all the circumstances. In the normal course, advice from a solicitor or other outside adviser can be expected to bring home to a complainant a proper understanding of what he or she is about to do. But a person may understand fully the implications of a proposed transaction, for instance, a substantial gift, and yet still be acting under the undue influence of another. Proof

---

[312] *Allcard v Skinner* (1887) 36 ChD 145 (CA) 181 (Lindley LJ).
[313] *Royal Bank of Scotland v Etridge (No 2)* [2002] 2 AC 773, 843 (Lord Scott).
[314] *Goodchild v Bradley* [2006] EWCA 1868.
[315] *Inche Noriah v Shaik Allie Bin Omar* [1929] AC 127 (PC—Straits Settlements) 135. Lord Hailsham LC further stated that the court must be satisfied 'that the donor was acting independently of any influence from the donee and with the full appreciation of what he was doing'; also, *Allcard v Skinner* (1887) 36 ChD 145 (CA) 171 (Cotton LJ). What is important is independence of will, not independence in a financial sense: *Evans v Lloyd* [2013] EWHC 1725 (Ch) [58].
[316] *Archer v Hudson* (1844) 7 Beav 551, 560; 49 ER 1180, 1183.
[317] *Zamet v Hyman* [1961] 1 WLR 1442 (CA) 1446 (Lord Evershed MR); *Re Craig* [1971] Ch 95, 105; *Goldsworthy v Brickell* [1987] 1 Ch 378 (CA) 408–09; *Hammond v Osborn* [2002] EWCA 885 [25].
[318] *Randall v Randall* [2004] EWHC 2258 [37].
[319] *Re Brindley (Deceased)* [2018] EWHC 157 (Ch).
[320] *Huguenin v Baseley* (1807) 14 Ves Jun 273, 300; 33 ER 526, 536 (Lord Eldon LC); *Allcard v Skinner* (1887) 36 ChD 145 (CA) 185 (Lindley LJ); *Leeder v Stevens* [2005] EWCA 50 [19]; *Thorne v Kennedy* (2017) 263 CLR 85.
[321] J McGhee (ed), *Snell's Equity* (32nd edn, 2010) 270 quoted with approval in *Hammond v Osborn* [2002] EWCA 885 [39]; *Smith v Cooper* [2010] EWCA Civ 722 [61]. Cf *Garcia v National Australia Bank Ltd* (1998) 194 CLR 395, 409. See D O'Sullivan (2002) 118 LQR 337, 339.

of outside advice does not, of itself, necessarily show that the subsequent completion of the transaction was free from the exercise of undue influence.[322]

6.116 The fact that independent advice was received does not automatically lead to the conclusion that the presumption is rebutted. Independent advice will not rebut the presumption, first, if the dominant party knew, or ought to have known, that the person giving the advice had not discharged his duties or not satisfied himself that the complainant understood it. Secondly, such advice will not suffice if the dominant party possessed material information which was not available to the adviser. Thirdly, the presumption will not be rebutted on this basis if the transaction was one which no competent adviser could properly advise the complainant to enter.[323]

6.117 For it to be given significant weight, legal advice must have been independent, that is, given by a lawyer who was not acting for the dominant party.[324] It is not sufficient that the lawyer acted for the parties jointly but did not know one client better than the other:[325]

> [I]ndependent advice is advice to and for the benefit of the one party alone given by an adviser whose duty it is to consider the position of that party and to advise her … so that she can give thought, free from any influence of or dependence on the other party, as to whether she really does want to enter into the transaction, bearing in mind its full implications from her point of view.[326]

It must have been given by a person who was fully acquainted with the facts.[327] It will not suffice if it was based on an incorrect understanding of the facts.[328] The advice must be imparted 'with a knowledge of all relevant circumstances and must be such as a competent and honest adviser would give if acting solely in the interests of the donor'.[329] Especially careful advice will usually be required where the party is suffering from a mental impairment or learning difficulty.[330] And generally, the lawyer must have ensured that the party understood and intended to enter and carry out the transaction.[331] But it is not generally the adviser's role to approve or veto the transaction.[332] Fletcher Moulton LJ stated in *Re Coomber*:

---

[322] *Royal Bank of Scotland v Etridge (No 2)* [2002] 2 AC 773, 798, also 840 (Lord Scott); *Niersmans v Pesticcio* [2004] EWCA 372 [23]; *Murphy v Rayner* [2011] EWHC 1 (Ch) [328].
[323] *Credit Lyonnais Bank Nederland NV v Burch* [1997] 1 All ER 144 (CA) 155–56 (Millett LJ).
[324] *Powell v Powell* [1900] 1 Ch 243. The lawyer does not have to be a qualified solicitor; he can be a legal executive: *Royal Bank of Scotland v Etridge (No 2)* [2002] 2 AC 773, 868 (Lord Scott).
[325] *Smith v Cooper* [2010] EWCA Civ 722 [56]; *Moursi v Doherty* [2019] EWHC 830 (Ch). Cf *Evans v Lloyd* [2013] EWHC 1725 (Ch) [72]–[73] where advice would have been sufficient even though the lawyer was instructed and paid for by the recipient of the property.
[326] *Smith v Cooper* [2010] EWCA Civ 722 [56].
[327] *Tate v Williamson* (1866) LR 2 Ch App 55, 65; *Wright v Carter* [1903] 1 Ch 27 (CA); *HSBC Bank Plc v Brown* [2015] EWHC 359 (Ch).
[328] *Paull v Paull* [2018] EWHC 2520 (Ch); *Moursi v Doherty* [2019] EWHC 830 (Ch).
[329] *Inche Noriah v Shaik Allie Bin Omar* [1929] AC 127 (PC—Straits Settlements) (the advice was inadequate because the lawyer was not aware that the complainant was giving away substantially the whole of her property); *Niersmans v Pesticcio* [2004] EWCA 372 [23] Mummery LJ stated that the solicitor's advice 'was not such as a competent adviser would give, if acting solely in the interests of [the complainant]'; *Vale v Armstrong* [2004] EWHC 1160 [55].
[330] *Hackett v Crown Prosecution Service* [2011] EWHC 1170 (Admin) [74].
[331] *Re Brindley (Deceased)* [2018] EWHC 157 (Ch).
[332] In *Powell v Powell* [1900] 1 Ch 243, 247 it was suggested that the lawyer must go further and 'satisfy himself that the gift is one which it is right and proper for the donor to make under all the circumstances' or veto the transaction and refuse to act further if the client persists. See also *Credit Lyonnais Bank Nederland NV v Burch* [1997] 1 All ER 144 (CA) 156 (Millett LJ). This was disapp'd by Lord Nicholls in *Royal Bank of Scotland v Etridge (No 2)*

All that is necessary is that some independent person, free from any taint of the relationship, or of the consideration of interest which would affect the act, should put clearly before the person what are the nature and the consequences of the act. It is for adult persons of competent mind to decide whether they will do an act, and I do not think that independent and competent advice means independent and competent approval. It simply means that the advice shall be removed entirely from the suspected atmosphere; and that from the clear language of an independent mind, they should know precisely what they are doing.[333]

A solicitor's advice may be insufficient if the solicitor is chosen by the dominant party, who is present in the room when the transaction is initially discussed, even if that person waits outside while advice is being given to the claimant alone; in such a scenario the claimant has no space to think.[334]

6.118 Independent advice as to the nature of the transaction given by a non-lawyer may therefore be enough.[335] But even strong views expressed against the transaction or advice given by a family member may prove to be no substitute for independent advice from a professional.[336] What must be shown is that the nature and effect of the transaction had been fully explained to the complainant by an independent and competent person so completely as to satisfy the court that the complainant acted independently of any influence from the other party and with a full appreciation of what he was doing.[337]

6.119 Independent advice is not a mandatory requirement for rebutting a presumption of undue influence. Independence of mind may be shown even in cases where no advice was received from a third party, or where it was received but disregarded.[338] Where the presumption of undue influence is not a heavy one, an explanation of the transaction by the dominant party himself might even suffice to rebut the presumption.[339] The presumption was also rebutted in the absence of independent advice where the decision to make a generous gift was not a spur of the moment decision but something the giver had considered for some time, had discussed with his doctor, and had sent letters of thanks for the care and support provided by the recipients of the gift.[340]

(5) Severable transactions

6.120 Where a part of a transaction or part of a series of transactions was not affected by undue influence, it may be possible to set aside the severable affected part but not the part that is

[2002] 2 AC 773, 807, but his Lordship added 'there may, of course, be exceptional circumstances where it is glaringly obvious that the [complainant] is being grievously wronged. In such a case the solicitor should decline to act further'.

[333] *Re Coomber* [1911] 1 Ch 723, 730 app'd in *Royal Bank of Scotland v Etridge (No 2)* [2002] 2 AC 773, 807.
[334] *Sollis v Leyshon* [2018] EWHC 2853 (Ch) [77].
[335] *Inche Noriah v Shaik Allie Bin Omar* [1929] AC 127 (PC—Straits Settlements) 135 (Lord Hailsham): '[T]heir Lordships are not prepared to accept the view that independent legal advice is the only way in which the presumption can be rebutted.'
[336] *Smith v Cooper* [2010] EWCA Civ 722 [69].
[337] *Inche Noriah v Shaik Allie Bin Omar* [1929] AC 127, 135.
[338] *Re Brocklehurst's Estate* [1978] Ch 141 (CA).
[339] *Hammond v Osborn* [2002] EWCA 885 [28].
[340] *Bateman v Overy* [2014] EWHC 432 (Ch) [126]–[131].

unaffected by undue influence, provided that is not necessary to rewrite the wording of what remains and the removal of the affected part does not alter the character of the remaining transaction or the balance of rights and obligations that comprise the remaining transaction.[341]

---

[341] *Barclays Bank plc v Caplan* [1998] 1 FLR 532; *Pathania v Adedeji* [2010] EWHC 3085 (QB). Cf *Annulment Funding Co Ltd v Cowey* [2010] EWCA Civ 711 [75]–[79].

7

Mistake, Impaired Capacity, and Unconscionable Bargains

A. Introduction	7.01	(1) First requirement: serious disadvantage relative to the counterparty	7.75
B. Mistake	7.02		
(1) Common mistake	7.07		
(2) Unilateral mistake	7.12	(2) Second requirement: weakness exploited in morally culpable manner	7.80
(3) Special doctrines of rescission for mistake	7.27	(3) Third requirement: transaction overreaching and oppressive	7.89
C. Impaired Capacity: Mental Infirmity and Intoxication	7.41	(4) Possible defence: counterparty shows that transaction was fair, just, and reasonable	7.93
(1) Mental infirmity	7.45	(5) Role of independent advice	7.97
(2) Drunkenness or intoxication	7.65	(6) Other Commonwealth jurisdictions	7.103
D. Unconscionable Bargains: Exploitation	7.69		

A. Introduction

7.01 Each of the three grounds considered in this Chapter involves a situation where the complainant could not bargain to protect his interests adequately because of an impairment. The complainant may have been incapable of obtaining a fair bargain due to a misapprehension of the true facts or due to a lack of understanding caused by mental infirmity or intoxication, or because he was labouring under a serious disadvantage such as poverty and ignorance. In each of these situations, the counterparty's knowledge of the impairment is relevant, but it is not always sufficient to lead to rescission. In the case of unilateral mistake and so-called 'unconscionable bargains', some morally reprehensible, exploitative, or otherwise unconscionable conduct must also be shown. Knowledge goes towards establishing the moral unacceptability of the counterparty's conduct. It is only in the case of mental infirmity and intoxication that mere knowledge of the complainant's impairment suffices for rescission. That is because the vitiation of consent in such cases is more profound,[1] and perhaps also because contracting with knowledge of such a condition is itself morally culpable.

B. Mistake

7.02 All misrepresentations involve a mistake. But there the mistake is of a particular kind; it is induced by a representation. Misrepresentation is considered in Chapter 4. This part

---

[1] See *Barclays Bank plc v Schwartz*, The Times, 2 August 1995 (CA).

concerns situations where the mistake is self-induced or spontaneous. The point of substantive distinction is that the other party has not been responsible for the error. When such a mistake is shared by both parties it is conventionally called a 'common mistake', or sometimes and less accurately a 'mutual mistake'. Where only one party is mistaken the misapprehension is usually called a 'unilateral mistake'. Consent to a contract may be impaired to the same degree in a case of misrepresentation, common mistake, and unilateral mistake, but the scope for rescission varies.

Misrepresentation is always a ground for rescission. Common mistake is no longer a ground for rescission at all, at least in England and Wales. As is explained in Part B(1) of this Chapter, if it operates at all, common mistake renders a contract void, not voidable. Unilateral mistake alone appears not to be sufficient for rescinding a contract in England and Wales. In Australia it provides a ground only when accompanied by knowledge and conduct on the part of the non-mistaken party that sufficiently affects conscience. **7.03**

The law draws a sharp distinction between mistakes induced by misrepresentation and those that are not. The courts intervene more readily when one party has been responsible for the other's misunderstanding, for several reasons. One is that a person is not to be allowed to benefit from his own false statements.[2] A second is that the law has an interest in protecting the integrity of the bargaining process, and that interest is engaged in cases of misrepresentation, but not unilateral or common mistake.[3] **7.04**

The second reason may also explain why unilateral mistake operates quite differently in cases of gifts. A donor's serious unilateral mistake as to the effect of a deed of gift will make it voidable, but the same mistake will not permit a contract to be rescinded. Gifts are more easily rescinded for unilateral mistake than contracts because the law's interest in protecting the integrity of the bargaining process, and in upholding bargains themselves, is not engaged in cases of gifts even if effected by deed.[4] Similarly a payment made other than under a contract and not intended as a gift may be recovered if induced by a causative unilateral mistake.[5] The payee need not establish the additional facts needed to rescind a contract so as to recover sums paid thereunder. **7.05**

There are also certain types of contract that are particularly vulnerable to rescission for mistake. In these cases rescission will be permitted for a mere unilateral mistake, absent factors affecting the other party's conscience. The law regarding these special cases is not without difficulty. But the list appears to include conveyances of unregistered land[6] and the special cases where non-disclosure is said to provide a ground for rescission.[7] **7.06**

---

[2] *Redgrave v Hurd* (1881) 20 ChD 1, 12–13.
[3] This thesis is developed in J Cartwright, *Unequal Bargaining: A Study of Vitiating Factors in the Formation of Contracts* (1991).
[4] See *Pitt v Holt* [2013] 2 AC 108 [114]; *Van der Merwe v Goldman* [2016] 4 WLR 71. Chap 29, paras [29.22]–[29.33].
[5] *Barclays Bank Ltd v WJ Simms Son & Cooke (Southern) Ltd* [1980] 1 QB 677.
[6] Paras [7.28]ff.
[7] See Chap 5.

(1) Common mistake

Not a ground for rescission in England and Wales

7.07 A common mistake is a mistake shared by both parties. It was formerly thought to be a ground for rescinding contracts in equity in England and Wales.[8] But in *Great Peace Shipping Ltd v Tsavliris Salvage (International) Ltd*[9] the Court of Appeal held that there was no such doctrine; if common mistake operates at all, it takes effect at common law, and renders the contract void.[10]

7.08 In *The Great Peace*[11] the Court of Appeal held that the test to be applied to determine whether a common mistake rendered a contract void is based on the test applied in determining whether a contract is discharged through frustration. The court stated that:

> ... the following elements must be present if common mistake is to avoid a contract: (i) there must be a common assumption as to the existence of a state of affairs; (ii) there must be no warranty by either party that that state of affairs exists; (iii) the non-existence of the state of affairs must not be attributable to the fault of either party; (iv) the non-existence of the state of affairs must render performance of the contract impossible; (v) the state of affairs may be the existence, or a vital attribute, of the consideration to be provided or the circumstances which must subsist if performance of the contractual adventure is to be possible.[12]

7.09 Common mistakes that will render a contract void include mistakes as to the existence,[13] identity, or fundamental character of the subject matter of the contract.[14] A mistake that renders a contract void may be one of fact or law.[15] If the contract is void, there is of course nothing to rescind. Claims for the restitution of benefits conferred under the apparent agreement are regulated by their own principles.[16]

Other Commonwealth jurisdictions[17]

7.10 In Australia there had been considerable resistance to the notion that common mistake permits rescission in equity,[18] and *The Great Peace* has been followed in

---

[8] *Solle v Butcher* [1950] 1 KB 671 (CA) treated as correct or binding in *Grist v Bailey* [1967] Ch 532, 538–39; *Magee v Pennine Insurance Co Ltd* [1969] 2 QB 507 (CA) 514–15; *Amalgamated Investment & Property Co Ltd v John Walker & Sons Ltd* [1977] 1 WLR 164 (CA) 176; *Laurence v Lexcourt Holdings Ltd* [1978] 1 WLR 1128; *Associated Japanese Bank (International) Ltd v Credit du Nord SA* [1989] 1 WLR 255, 266; *William Sindall plc v Cambridgeshire County Council* [1994] 1 WLR 1016 (CA) 1034–35, 1039–140, 1042; *Nutt v Reed* (1999) 96(42) LSG 44 (CA).

[9] [2003] QB 679 (CA).

[10] '[T]here is no jurisdiction to grant rescission of a contract on the ground of common mistake where that contract is valid and enforceable on the ordinary principles of contract law': [2003] QB 679 (CA) 725. Accepted by way of *obiter* in *Pitt v Holt* [2013] 2 AC 108 (SC) [115]. For a historical survey of the development of the law in this area see C MacMillan, *Mistakes in Contract Law* (2010).

[11] *Great Peace Shipping Ltd v Tsavliris Salvage (International) Ltd (The Great Peace)* [2003] QB 679 (CA).

[12] *Great Peace Shipping Ltd v Tsavliris Salvage (International) Ltd* [2003] QB 679 (CA) 703.

[13] Enshrined in Sale of Goods Act 1893, s 6, which states 'Where there is a contract for the sale of specific goods, and the goods without the knowledge of the seller have perished at the time when the contract is made, the contract is void'; see also *Associated Japanese Bank (International) Ltd v Crédit du Nord SA* [1989] 1 WLR 255, 269. In Australia, *McRae v Commonwealth Disposals Commission* (1951) 84 CLR 377 (existence of tanker to be salvaged).

[14] *Krell v Henry* [1903] 2 KB 740.

[15] *Brenan v Bolt Burdon* [2005] QB 303 (CA).

[16] See further Chap 1, paras [1.49]ff.

[17] For a comparative survey, D Capper, 'Common Mistake in Contract Law' (2009) Sing Jo of Legal Studies 457 (and arguing in favour of a more flexible and discretionary response to common mistake).

[18] *Baird v BCE Holdings Pty Ltd* (1996) 40 NSWLR 374; see also JD Heydon, MJ Leeming, and PG Turner, *Meagher, Gummow and Lehane's Equity Doctrines and Remedies* (5th edn, 2015) [14-065].

Queensland.[19] The law has also been said to be unclear and there is now some doubt whether there exists any equitable jurisdiction to set aside a contract for common mistake.[20] New Zealand has its own distinctive rules in relation to common mistake, deriving from the Contractual Mistakes Act 1977 (NZ) and now enacted in Subpart 2 of Part 2 of the Contract and Commercial Law Act 2017 (NZ).[21]

7.11 In Singapore, common mistake continues to provide a basis for rescission in equity.[22] Some parts of Canada also recognize a right to rescind for common mistake,[23] and Canada also has its own distinct doctrine of 'error in *substantialibus*', discussed later in this chapter.[24]

(2) Unilateral mistake

7.12 At common law a mere unilateral mistake is not sufficient to vitiate a contract.[25] Where the mistake is as to the terms of the contract and is known to the other party it will prevent the contract from coming into existence in the first place.[26] In such a case there is no agreement between the parties; no meeting of the minds. But if the mistake concerns a fact relating to a quality of the subject matter of the contract, but that fact does not form a term of the contract, then the contract will be binding even if the other party knew of this mistake.[27] In England and Wales, there is authority that after the decision in *The Great Peace* there is no equitable jurisdiction to set a contract aside on the basis of unilateral mistake,[28] although the matter has not been settled at appellate level.[29] The position is different in other parts of the Commonwealth. England and Wales will be considered first, and the approach in other parts of the Commonwealth will be considered after that.

England and Wales

7.13 A mere unilateral mistake is an insufficient ground for rescission. In *BP Oil International Ltd v Target Shipping Ltd* Andrew Smith J observed that 'The law does not consider that it

---

[19] *Australia Estates Pty Ltd v Cairns City Council* [2005] QCA 328; *Menegazzo v Pricewaterhousecoopers (A Firm)* [2016] QSC 94. But the application of the decision in the *Cairns City Council* case, to a transfer of land, is doubtful: see para [7.28].

[20] *Schwartz Family Co Pty Ltd v Capitol Carpets Pty Ltd* [2019] NSWSC 238 [91], but cf at [106]–[110]. Contrast the position taken in Victoria: *Rees v Rees* [2016] VSC 452.

[21] For the origins and operation of this legislation, W Swain, 'A Reputation for Boldness: Statutory Reform of Contract Law in New Zealand' in T Arvind and J Steele (eds), *Contract Law and the Legislature* (2020) 113–18.

[22] *Chwee Kin Keong v Digilandmall.com Pte Ltd* [2005] 1 SLR(R) 502; *Olivine Capital Pte Ltd v Chia Chin Yan* [2014] 2 SLR 1371 (CA) [63], [69].

[23] *re Kelowna Mountain Development Services Ltd* [2014] BCSC 1791 [70]–[73] (rescission for common mistake permitted in Alberta and Ontario but the position in British Columbia less clear following the decision in *Great Peace*).

[24] Para [7.34] below.

[25] *Smith v Hughes* (1871) LR 6 QB 597 (CA) 603, 607; *Food Corporation of India v Antclizo Shipping Corporation (The Antclizo)* [1987] 2 Lloyd's Rep 130 (CA) 146.

[26] *Statoil ASA v Louis Dreyfus Energy Services LP (The 'Harriette N')* [2009] 1 All ER (Comm) 1035 [87], [96]; *Merrill Lynch International v Amorim Partners Ltd* [2014] EWHC 74 (QB) [55].

[27] *Statoil ASA v Louis Dreyfus Energy Services LP (The 'Harriette N')* [2009] 1 All ER (Comm) 1035 [88].

[28] *Statoil ASA v Louis Dreyfus Energy Services LP (The 'Harriette N')* [2009] 1 All ER (Comm) 1035 [105]; *UTB LLC v Sheffield United Limited* [2019] EWHC 2322 (Ch) [280].

[29] Cf the statements *obiter* in *Riverlate Properties Ltd v Paul* [1975] 1 Ch 133 (CA) 145 and in *Commission for the New Towns v Cooper (Great Britain) Ltd* [1995] Ch 259 (CA) 280.

is necessarily unconscionable or otherwise improper for one commercial party to benefit from another commercial party's misunderstanding of the meaning or implications of a contract, and he is under no general duty to draw attention to mistakes or misunderstandings that he knows or suspects that the other has or might have made.'[30]

7.14 A number of English authorities had suggested that in appropriate circumstances a court could order rescission of a contract on the grounds of a unilateral mistake of one of the parties coupled with additional circumstances. In particular in *Huyton v Distribuidora Internacional de Productos Agricolas SA de CV*[31] Andrew Smith J held that the court had an equitable jurisdiction to set aside a contract on the grounds of unilateral mistake. That decision and earlier authorities appeared to decide that for rescission to be possible, the misled party needed to prove that:[32] (i) an operative mistake had been made;[33] (ii) the non-mistaken party knew of the mistake;[34] and (iii) the non-mistaken party engaged in sharp practice or other unconscionable conduct in connection with the mistake.[35]

7.15 However, in *Statoil ASA v Louis Dreyfus Energy Services LP (The 'Harriette N')* Aikens J emphatically rejected the existence of an equitable jurisdiction to order rescission on the grounds of a unilateral mistake. His Lordship held that there was no equitable jurisdiction to grant rescission of a contract where a party made a unilateral mistake as to a fact or state of affairs which was the basis on which the terms of the contract were agreed, but that assumption did not become a term of the contract. His Lordship held that the Court of Appeal's decision in *Great Peace* strongly suggests that this was now English law.[36]

7.16 On the other hand, in *Commission for the New Towns v Cooper (Great Britain) Ltd*, a decision of the Court of Appeal not cited in *The 'Harriette N'*, Stuart-Smith LJ posited a scenario whereby:

---

[30] [2012] 2 Lloyd's Rep 245 [203] (reversed on a point of construction [2013] 1 Lloyd's Rep 561). The observation was made in the context of rectification but is of general application.

[31] [2003] 2 Lloyd's Rep 780, 838 (unilateral mistake not considered on appeal, [2003] 2 Lloyd's Rep 780 (CA) 854).

[32] These elements were referred to by the Supreme Court of Jamaica in *Continental Petroleum Products Ltd v Scotia DBG Investments Ltd* [2016] JMSC Civ 219 [39].

[33] An operative mistake (i) does not concern a matter the risk of which has been allocated by the contract: *Associated Japanese Bank (International) Ltd v Credit du Nord SA* [1989] 1 WLR 255, 268 (a case of common mistake) applied in the context of unilateral mistake in *Kalsep Ltd v X-Flow BV, The Times*, 3 May 2001; *Huyton v Distribuidora Internacional de Productos Agricolas SA de CV* [2003] 2 Lloyd's Rep 780, 838 (unilateral mistake not considered on appeal, [2003] 2 Lloyd's Rep 780 (CA) 854); (ii) concerns a matter of real importance: *Huyton v Distribuidora Internacional de Productos Agricolas SA de CV* [2003] 2 Lloyd's Rep 780, 838; and (iii) goes to the subject matter of the contract as opposed to its commercial consequences: *Clarion Ltd v National Provident Institution* [2000] 1 WLR 1888, 1905–06.

[34] *Riverlate Properties Ltd v Paul* [1975] 1 Ch 133 (CA) 145; *OT Africa Line Ltd v Vickers plc* [1996] 1 Lloyd's Rep 700, 704. In both of these decisions the claim for rescission appeared to fail because of a lack of knowledge of the unilateral mistake, not because of an absence of equitable jurisdiction.

[35] *Riverlate Properties Ltd v Paul* [1975] 1 Ch 133 (CA) 145 (suggesting something approaching sharp practice may have led to a different conclusion regarding rescission); *Commission for the New Towns v Cooper (Great Britain) Ltd* [1995] Ch 259 (CA) 280; *OT Africa Line Ltd v Vickers plc* [1996] 1 Lloyd's Rep 700, 704 ('rescission would be available where it is simply inequitable for one party to seek to hold the other to a bargain objectively made'); *Huyton v Distribuidora Internacional de Productos Agricolas SA de CV* [2003] 2 Lloyd's Rep 780, 838; *Thames Trains Ltd v Adams* [2006] EWHC 3291 [56] (failure to inform counterparty of more favourable offer that had been sent to it but not yet received was not sharp practice).

[36] [2009] 1 All ER (Comm) 1035 [105] followed in *UTB LLC v Sheffield United Limited* [2019] EWHC 2322 (Ch) [280]. The suggestion that a unilateral mistake would vitiate a contract where the counterparty contributed to or was partially responsible for the mistake (where the mistake was unknown to the other party) was also doubted in *Deutsche Bank (Suisse) SA v Khan* [2013] EWHC 482 (Comm) [265]–[268].

... A intends B to be mistaken as to the construction of the agreement, so conducts himself that he diverts B's attention from discovering the mistake by making false and misleading statements, and B in fact makes the very mistake that A intends, then notwithstanding that A does not actually know, but merely suspects, that B is mistaken, and it cannot be shown that the mistake was induced by any misrepresentation ...[37]

His Lordship concluded that 'A's conduct is unconscionable and he cannot insist on performance in accordance to the strict letter of the contract; that is sufficient for rescission.'[38] Whether this analysis remains applicable after the decision in *The Great Peace* is unclear.

Moreover, different considerations arguably apply where there has been a mistake not as to the terms or meaning of the contract,[39] but about its subject matter, and the non-mistaken party knows of the mistake and also engages in sharp practice. In such a case the contract will not be void at common law[40] or susceptible to rectification.[41] Rescission on the grounds of unconscionability would also not be possible.[42]

7.17

There would appear to be a lacuna in the law if a court lacked power to order rescission in such a situation.[43] The issue might rarely arise in practice because the non-mistaken party's conduct in hurrying negotiations or trying to divert attention from the mistake may often involve an implied misrepresentation by conduct permitting rescission,[44] but that seems an insufficient reason for allowing what would otherwise appear to be a lacuna in the law.

7.18

Compared to rectification

Where there is a unilateral mistake as to the terms of a written contract and the error is known to the other party, the mistaken party may seek rectification of the instrument recording the contract.[45] Sharp practice need not be established to rectify an agreement for unilateral mistake.[46] Knowledge of a mistake coupled with a failure to draw it to the mistaken party's attention are enough if the mistake is 'calculated to benefit' the non-mistaken party (or is detrimental to the mistaken party).[47] In contrast, all of the cases indicate that rescission for unilateral mistake would require proof of 'sharp practice' or 'unconscionability'.

7.19

---

[37] [1995] Ch 259 (CA) 280.
[38] [1995] Ch 259 (CA) 280.
[39] Where other doctrines tend to come into play, such as the common law principle preventing a contract arising where parties are not truly *ad idem* and the equitable principles permitting rectification for unilateral mistake in appropriate cases.
[40] See para [7.07].
[41] *Fredrick E Rose (London) Ltd v William H Pim Junior & Co Ltd* [1953] 1 QB 450 (CA) 461.
[42] See Part D of this chapter.
[43] Cf H Beale, *Mistake and Non-Disclosure of Facts* (2012) 81–82, 89, 98 who proposes that a party should be able to avoid a contract where there was simply a unilateral mistake of which the other party knew, or perhaps even ought to have known, but 'contrary to good faith and fair dealing, caused the contract to be concluded by leaving the mistaken party in error'. On the other hand A Burrows *A Restatement of the English Law of Contract* (OUP 2016) 176, 183 takes the position that there is no scope for rescission for a unilateral mistake.
[44] Particularly given the special rules about misrepresentation by concealment discussed in Chap 4, para [4.38].
[45] *Roberts (A) & Co Ltd v Leicestershire County Council* [1961] Ch 555; *Agip SpA v Navigazione Alta Italia SpA (The Nai Genova and The Nai Superba)* [1984] 1 Lloyd's Rep 353 (CA) 359; *Traditional Structures Ltd v HW Construction Ltd* [2010] EWHC 1530 (TCC); [2010] CILL 2899 [25]–[33]; *Liberty Mercian Ltd v Cuddy Civil Engineering Ltd* [2013] EWHC 2688 (TCC); [2014] BLR 179 [139]–[146]. See also *The Leopardstown Club Ltd v Templeville Developments Ltd* [2010] IEHC 152 [7.78]–[7.110] (survey of English and Irish authorities).
[46] *Thomas Bates and Son Ltd v Wyndham's (Lingerie) Ltd* [1981] 1 WLR 505 (CA) 515, 520, 522; *George Wimpey UK Ltd v VI Components Ltd* [2005] EWCA 7.
[47] *Thomas Bates and Son Ltd v Wyndham's (Lingerie) Ltd* [1981] 1 WLR 505 (CA) 515–16; *George Wimpey UK Ltd v VI Components Ltd* [2005] EWCA 7; *Littman v Aspen Oil (Broking) Ltd* [2005] EWCA 1579.

The difference seems justified, for rescission entails quite different consequences; in particular, the whole agreement must be set aside (at least in England), whereas following rectification the parties are bound by an agreement different from that recorded in writing. In *Commission for New Towns v Cooper (GB) Ltd*[48] Stuart-Smith LJ explained that the principles were different 'for the simple reason that in rescission the court simply undoes the bargain, provided the parties can be restored to their original position; in rectification for unilateral mistake the original bargain is undone and a different one imposed'.

Other Commonwealth jurisdictions

7.20 The circumstances in which a unilateral mistake will permit rescission in Australia have been more fully developed, and were spelt out by the High Court of Australia in *Taylor v Johnson*:

> ... a party who has entered into a written contract under a serious mistake about its contents in relation to a fundamental term will be entitled in equity to an order rescinding the contract if the other party is aware that circumstances exist which indicate that the first party is entering the contract under some serious mistake or misapprehension about either the content or subject matter of that term and deliberately sets out to ensure that the first party does not become aware of the existence of his mistake or misapprehension.[49]

7.21 The courts have emphasized that before rescission will be granted, it is necessary to demonstrate unconscionable conduct on the part of the non-mistaken party.[50] Knowledge of the unilateral mistake whilst merely staying silent about it is probably insufficient.[51]

7.22 The Court of Appeal of Singapore has taken a similar approach. A unilateral mistake coupled with actual or constructive knowledge of the mistake and 'sharp practice' or 'unconscionable conduct' will permit rescission.[52]

7.23 In New Zealand the law is set out in the Contract and Commercial Law Act 2017 (NZ).[53]

---

[48] [1995] Ch 259 (CA) 278.

[49] (1983) 151 CLR 422, 432 (Mason ACJ, Murphy and Deane JJ). See also *Deputy Commissioner of Taxation (NSW) v Chamberlain* (1990) 93 ALR 729 (contract where a party moved with alacrity to take advantage of an offeror's clerical or arithmetical error set aside).

[50] *Gallinar Holdings Pty Ltd v Riedel* [2014] NSWSC 476 [34]–[35] ('The question is whether the plaintiff purchaser played such a part in the vendor's labouring and continuing to labour under the mistake that it is unconscientious for it to seek to hold the vendor to the contract.')

[51] *Blackley Investments Pty Ltd v Burnie City Council (No 2)* (2011) 21 Tas R 98 [23]; Chap 5, para [5.11]. But cf *Toma v Olcorn* [2019] VSCA 116 [28]–[31], [63], [68] (buyer stayed silent and 'opportunistically' took advantage of vendor's mistake about the operation of a rent adjustment clause; principles expressed in the context of rectification—*Leibler v Air New Zealand Ltd [No 2]* [1999] 1 VR 1 [68] (CA)—were applied to permit rescission). Also, *Schwartz Family Co Pty Ltd v Capitol Carpets Pty Ltd* [2019] NSWSC 238 [82] (a suggestion that rescission for unilateral mistake is permitted where the non-mistaken party merely remains silent is not supported by the authority cited, *Westpork Pty Ltd v Bio-Organics Pty Ltd* [2018] WASC 291 [116]).

[52] *Chwee Kin Keong v Digilandmall.com Pte Ltd* [2005] 1 SLR 502(R) (CA) (the defendant mistakenly offered commercial printers on its website for $66 when their ordinary retail price was $3,854; the plaintiffs ordered 1606 units over the internet; rescission of the contracts was upheld on appeal); affirmed, *Olivine Capital Pte Ltd v Chia Chin Yan* [2014] 2 SLR 1371 (CA) [71]; see also the analysis in *Quoine Pte Ltd v B2C2 Ltd* [2020] SGCA(I) 2 [169]–[178] (Lord Mance IJ, dissenting as to the result).

[53] Sections 24(1)(a)(i) (other party must know of mistake), 24(1)(b) (materiality of mistake), 24(1)(c) (contractual allocation of risk), 24(1)(3) (parties must be arms-length), 25 (not mere error of interpretation), 27 (self-induced mistakes), 28 (relief available), 31 (third parties protected), and 32 (proper law of contract not New Zealand); *King v Williamson* (1994) 2 NZ ConvC 95; *Tri-star Customs and Forwarding Ltd v Denning* [1999] 1 NZLR 33 (CA) (constructive notice is not sufficient for relief under the former Contractual Mistakes Act 1977); *Janus Nominees Ltd v Fairhall* [2009] 3 NZLR 757.

Machine-generated contracts

7.24 In *Quoine Pte Ltd v B2C2 Ltd*[54] the Singapore Court of Appeal considered the operation of the doctrine of unilateral mistake in circumstances where sale transactions effected automatically by a machine were later reversed by the defendant platform provider. The defendant did this after it learned that errors had occurred in its automated platform for trading cryptocurrencies, and which had caused parcels of 'ethereum' to be sold at 250 times their market value. The trades having been brought about by what the Court of Appeal described as a 'deterministic algorithmic program', the parties did not know until the next morning that the contracts had been concluded. It was held that the relevant inquiry was whether the person who had written the program for the plaintiff seller of the ethereum understood when the program was written that a trade of the kind that occurred, almost a year later, must have been the result of a mistake. Because the programmer did not so understand, and emphasizing that no-one was in fact aware of a mistake until after the contracts had been concluded, the Court of Appeal held that rescission for unilateral mistake was unavailable. Neither knowledge of a mistake, or unconscionable conduct, was established on the facts.[55] The contracts were therefore enforceable according to their terms.

7.25 Dissenting, Lord Mance IJ held that the trades were voidable in equity for mistake.[56] His Lordship considered that it was wrong to focus upon the state of mind of the programmer at the time the algorithms were written, rather than what such a person would have known if he had in fact been aware of the trades when they occurred.[57] If a reasonable trader on the exchange would have realized that a fundamental mistake had occurred, relief in equity should be available.[58] Constructive notice and unconscionability were not required in the case of machine-generated contracts in the same way as is necessary for a contract concluded between human beings: it was enough if a person foreseeing or being involved in the transaction would have realized that it had been affected by a fundamental mistake, as both parties in fact did once they learned of the aberrant trades.[59]

7.26 It is suggested that the dissenting opinion of Lord Mance IJ is to be preferred, including because it meets what his Lordship described as the clear justice of the case and the natural expectations of reasonable traders.[60]

---

[54] [2020] SGCA(I) 2, discussed eg K Low and E Mik, 'Lost in Transmission: Unilateral Mistakes in Automated Contracts' (2020) 136 LQR 563, J Fu, 'Algorithmic Contracts: Who is to Blame?' (2020) 12 Sing LR 1, V Ooi and K Soh, 'Rethinking Mistake in the Age of Algorithms: *Quoine Pty Ltd v B2C2 Ltd*' (2020) 31 Kings LJ 36. At first instance, *B2C2 Ltd v Quoine Pte Ltd* [2019] 4 SLR 17 (Sing Int Comm Ct).
[55] *Quoine Pte Ltd v B2C2 Ltd* [2020] SGCA(I) 2 [78], [89]–[92], [96], [108]–[111], [112]–[128] (Menon CJ, Leong JA, Prakash JA, and French IJ; Mance IJ dissenting) (as to how the matter was analysed given that the claim was against the platform provider, who had reversed the trades, see [55], [78], [160]).
[56] *Quoine Pte Ltd v B2C2 Ltd* [2020] SGCA(I) 2 [207] (also, [162]–[178], [179]–[181]).
[57] *Quoine Pte Ltd v B2C2 Ltd* [2020] SGCA(I) 2 [193]–[195].
[58] *Quoine Pte Ltd v B2C2 Ltd* [2020] SGCA(I) 2 [200].
[59] *Quoine Pte Ltd v B2C2 Ltd* [2020] SGCA(I) 2 [204]. Lord Mance IJ said that insofar as unconscionability may be relevant, it was unconscionable for a trader to retain the benefit of a transaction which he would and did recognize was due to some major error as soon as he came to learn of it: at [205]–[206].
[60] *Quoine Pte Ltd v B2C2 Ltd* [2020] SGCA(I) 2 [196], [203]. For criticism of the reasoning of the majority, K Low and E Mik, 'Lost in Transmission: Unilateral Mistakes in Automated Contracts' (2020) 136 LQR 563, 566–69.

(3) Special doctrines of rescission for mistake

7.27 This section considers transactions that are said to be particularly vulnerable to rescission for mistake. It focuses on the rules relating to completed conveyances of land, and touches at the end on compromises, family arrangements, and gifts.

Completed conveyances of land
Early English authorities

7.28 Two well-known eighteenth-century cases,[61] and a group of cases in the late nineteenth and early twentieth century,[62] indicate that a completed disposition of an estate or interest in unregistered land may be rescinded in equity if the intention of the parties was impaired by a sufficiently fundamental common mistake about the title to be conveyed. The principle probably emerged as a practical response to the difficulties in ascertaining title to unregistered land at that time. It ameliorated the harshness of the rule that a completed conveyance of land could not be rescinded for non-fraudulent misrepresentation.[63]

England and Wales today

7.29 The decision in *The Great Peace*[64] implies that the old English authorities just discussed are no longer good law. The Court of Appeal there held that common mistake does not provide a ground for rescission in equity. Although it did not specifically consider the possibility of a special rule for dispositions of land, the court expressly disapproved *Solle v Butcher*,[65] and that case concerned a lease of real property rescinded for mistake.

7.30 *The Great Peace* has probably also abrogated the court's former power to put the recipient of a mistaken conveyance of land to an election either to correct the mistake or to permit rescission.[66]

Australia

7.31 The High Court of Australia has followed the early English authorities to hold that, apart from the special case where the vendor has no title at all to the land purported to be sold:

> ... it is clearly established that equity will not undo a sale of land after conveyance unless there has been fraud or there is such a discrepancy between what has been sold and what

---

[61] *Lansdown v Lansdown* (1730) 2 Jac & W 205, 37 ER 695; Sel Cas T King 364, 25 ER 441; *Bingham v Bingham* (1748) 1 Ves Sen 126, 27 ER 934; Ves Sen Supp 79, 28 ER 462.

[62] *Brownlie v Campbell* (1880) 5 App Cas 925, 937 ('error in *substantialibus*'); *Re Tyrell* (1900) 82 LT 675 ('error in the substance of what was purchased'); *Debenham v Sawbridge* [1905] 2 Ch 98, 109 (assumed that non-total failure of consideration might be sufficient); *Angel v Jay* [1911] 1 KB 666, 673–74 ('failure of consideration'). See also the cases discussed by Dixon CJ in *Svanosio v McNamara* (1956) 96 CLR 186.

[63] *Legge v Croker* (1811) 1 Ball & Beaty 506, 514–15; *Edwards v M'Leay* (1818) 2 Swan 287, 289; 36 ER 625, 626; *Wilde v Gibson* (1848) 1 HLC 605, 633; 9 ER 897, 909; *Brownlie v Campbell* (1880) 5 App Cas 925, 938; *Angel v Jay* [1911] 1 KB 666, 671–73; *Elder v Auerbach* [1949] 2 All ER 692 (CA) 699; *Hill v Harris* [1965] 1 QB 601; *Laurence v Lexcourt Holdings* [1978] 1 WLR 1128 (CA) 1134; Chap 24, Part B.

[64] *Great Peace Shipping Ltd v Tsavliris Salvage (International) Ltd (The Great Peace)* [2003] QB 679 (CA).

[65] [1950] 1 KB 671 (CA).

[66] *Garrard v Frankel* (1862) 30 Beav 445, 458–59; 54 ER 961, 966–67; *Harris v Pepperell* (1867) LR 5 Eq 1, 4–5; *Bloomer v Spittle* (1872) LR 13 Eq 427, 431; *Paget v Marshall* (1884) 28 ChD 255; *Solle v Butcher* [1950] 1 KB 671 (CA) 696; *Riverlate Properties Limited v Paul* [1975] Ch 133 (CA) 141–45 (confirming that mere unilateral mistake is insufficient); *Topham v Topham Group Ltd* [2003] 1 BCLC 123 [23]. Cf *May v Platt* [1900] 1 Ch 616, 632 where Farwell J said that these decisions ought to be regarded as founded on fraud. In Canada, *Devald v Zigeuner* (1958) 16 DLR (2d) 285.

has been conveyed that there is a total failure of consideration, or what amounts practically to a total failure of consideration.[67]

The principle should apply equally to registered and unregistered land.[68] Despite this, the Queensland Court of Appeal has held that *The Great Peace* governs mistaken conveyances of land.[69] But the court misunderstood *Svanosio v McNamara*,[70] and its reasoning is to this extent unpersuasive. Unless and until the Australian High Court changes the law established in *Svanosio v McNamara, The Great Peace* does not provide reliable guidance as to the right to rescind conveyances of land affected by mistake in Australia. There is an equitable jurisdiction to rescind for mistake if the error involves a total failure of consideration or what amounts practically to that.[71]

New Zealand

In *Watson v Cullen*[72] a completed sale of land was rescinded because of a mistake about its dimensions, the plaintiff and defendant being at cross purposes as to the shape of the block to be conveyed. A more restrictive approach was adopted by Speight J in *Montgomery and Rennie v Continental Bags (NZ) Limited*.[73] His Honour cited *Svanosio v McNamara*[74] with approval, and held that a completed conveyance of land may be rescinded only if there is fraud or a total failure of consideration, or its equivalent. Speight J's reasons indicate that the right to rescind for total failure of consideration applies equally to registered and unregistered land. The scope for relief from mistake was later expanded in New Zealand by the Contractual Mistakes Act 1977 and is now set out in the Contract and Commercial Law Act 2017 (NZ).[75]

The Canadian doctrine of error in substantialibus

Canada has developed its own special rules. The Supreme Court of Canada has fashioned a doctrine of 'error in *substantialibus*' which provides that any transaction, whether involving land or not, may be rescinded if there is a sufficient discrepancy between the thing promised and that delivered.[76]

The language of 'error in *substantialibus*' derives from Lord Selborne's speech in *Brownlie v Campbell*,[77] a Scots case in which his Lordship quoted with approval a passage from Bell's

---

[67] *Svanosio v McNamara* (1956) 96 CLR 186, 198–99, 209; rule re-stated *Pukallus v Cameron* (1982) 180 CLR 447, 449. See also *Pamamull v Albrizzi (Sales) Pty Ltd (No 2)* [2011] VSCA 260 [133].
[68] *Montgomery and Rennie v Continental Bags (NZ) Limited* [1974] NZLR 884, 889.
[69] *Australia Estates Pty Ltd v Cairns City Council* [2005] QCA 328 [56]–[58].
[70] (1956) 96 CLR 186.
[71] Cf rectification of conveyances for common and unilateral mistake: *Lukacs v Wood* (1978) 19 SASR 520, 529–30 (rectification of conveyancing error unknown to both parties that involved an 'error in *substantialibus*', applying *Svanosio v McNamara* (1956) 96 CLR 186); *Tutt v Doyle* (1997) 42 NSWLR 10 (CA) (rectification of conveyance for unilateral mistake, applying *Taylor v Johnson* (1983) 151 CLR 422).
[72] (1886) 5 NZLR 17.
[73] [1974] NZLR 884, 889.
[74] (1956) 96 CLR 186.
[75] Sections 24 to 32; *Conlon v Ozolins* [1984] 1 NZLR 489 (CA) 498.
[76] *Cole v Pope* (1898) 29 SCR 291; *Redican v Nesbit* [1924] SCR 135; *Shortt v MacLennan* [1959] SCR 3; *Di Cenzo Construction Co Ltd v Glassico* (1978) 90 DLR 127, 140 (Ont CA); *Betker v Williams* (1991) 86 DLR (4th) 395 (BCCA); *Romank v Achtem* [2009] BCSC 1757 [18]–[23].
[77] (1880) 5 App Cas 925, 937.

Principles where that term was used.[78] The reception of this Scots doctrine into Canadian law has been criticized by scholars,[79] but is firmly established and regularly applied.[80]

7.36 There is some uncertainty as to how substantial the discrepancy must be. It has been said that the courts employ a flexible concept of error as to 'substantial matters' and will permit rescission whenever justice seems to require it.[81] Certainly there need not be a total failure of consideration. A mistake as to the quality of the thing is enough in some cases.[82] It is sufficient if what is received is so different from that which was bargained for that the contracting party can be said to have received 'something totally different'.[83]

7.37 The doctrine applies to errors arising from mistake and misrepresentation, and to contracts involving real property or other kinds of assets. But it is of special importance to completed conveyances of land in Canada, where completion continues to bar rescission for non-fraudulent misrepresentation.[84] It also has some significance in ameliorating the harshness of the rule in *Seddon*'s case. That rule, which has gained some purchase in Canada, provides that completion bars rescission for non-fraudulent misrepresentation if the contract involves a transfer of personal as opposed to real property.[85] The existence of these bars to rescission provides much of the explanation and justification for the continued vitality of the error in *substantialibus* doctrine in Canada. The bars have been abolished in England,[86] and for this reason at least, the excision of common mistake from the grounds for rescission in England[87] should not be thought a good reason for rolling back the Canadian doctrine of 'error in *substantialibus*'.

Compromises and family arrangements

7.38 Old cases can be found that may indicate that contracts of compromise are especially vulnerable to rescission for mistake in equity.[88] But the modern approach is against this, and assimilates contracts of compromise to general principle.[89] If it

---

[78] GJ Bell, *Principles of the Law of Scotland* (8th edn, 1885) s 893; GHL Fridman, 'Error in Substantialibus: A Canadian Comedy of Errors' (1978) 56 Can Bar Rev 603, 604–606; see also *Stewart v Kennedy (No 2)* (1890) 15 App Cas 108 (re-stating Scots law); FH Lawson, 'Error in Substantia' (1936) 52 LQR 79, 103–105 (comparing civilian and English law). This kind of language also appears in *Kennedy v The Panama, New Zealand and Australian Royal Mail Company Limited* (1867) LR 2 QB 589, where Blackburn J likewise drew upon Roman jurisprudence.

[79] GHL Fridman, 'Error in Substantialibus: A Canadian Comedy of Errors' (1978) 56 Can Bar Rev 603.

[80] For example, *Intrawest Corp v No 2002 Taurus Ventures Ltd* (2006) 54 BCLR (4th) 173; *Chase v Spence* [2006] AJ 733 (Alberta QB) [33]; *Houle v Knelsen Sand and Gravel Ltd* [2015] ABQB 659 [68]–[73].

[81] SM Waddams, *The Law of Contracts* (6th edn, 2010) [424]; *Barclays Bank v Metcalfe & Mansfield* [2011] ONSC 5008 [160].

[82] GHL Fridman, *The Law of Contract in Canada* (6th edn, 2011) 766. See also *Skogan v Worthman* [2010] MBQB 194 [22]; *Olfman v RBC Life Insurance Company* [2013] MBQB 142 [35] where it was said that the error must change the essence of the subject matter of the contract, whether or not there is a failure of consideration. Cf *Bloor Street West Ltd v Moksha Yoga Studio* [2013] ONSC 6501 [27] where it was suggested that the error must undermine the entire value of the consideration.

[83] *Houle v Knelsen Sand and Gravel Ltd* [2015] ABQB 659 [72] (sale of license to extract gravel where fivefold overestimation of the quantity of gravel available).

[84] *Cole v Pope* (1898) 29 SCR 3; *Redican v Nesbitt* (1923) SCR 135; *Shortt v MacLennan* (1959) SCR 3; *Kingu v Walmar Ventures Ltd* (1986) 10 BCLR (2d) 15 (BCCA) 20–21 (McLachlin JA); *Intrawest Corp v No. 2002 Taurus Ventures Ltd* (2006) 54 BCLR (4th) 173 [66]. The bar has been abolished by legislation in New Brunswick: Law Reform Act 2011, s 6(1) (New Brunswick). See further Chap 27, paras [27.14]–[27.15].

[85] See Chap 27, para [27.32].

[86] Misrepresentation Act 1967.

[87] *Great Peace Shipping Ltd v Tsavliris Salvage (International) Ltd (The Great Peace)* [2003] QB 679 (CA).

[88] Eg *Gibbons v Caunt* (1799) 4 Ves 840, 849; 31 ER 435 (Lord Eldon).

[89] *Brennan v Bolt Burdon (a firm)* [2005] QB 303 (CA); *Elston v King and Roscoe* [2020] EWHC 55 (Ch).

operates at all, common mistake makes a compromise void by negativing or nullifying consent.[90]

There are also old cases suggesting that settlements between family members are peculiarly vulnerable to rescission for mistake.[91] But it is doubtful that any special rules continue to exist today. Allegations of mistake in the compromise of a family dispute are likely to be determined by the application of the general principles just discussed. The exception is where the mistake follows a relevant non-disclosure by one of the family members, in which case the family arrangement is voidable by reason of that non-disclosure. This principle is separately discussed in Chapter 5.[92]

7.39

Gifts
Gifts are more easily rescinded for mistake than are reciprocal contracts. The relevant principles are separately discussed in Chapter 29.

7.40

C. Impaired Capacity: Mental Infirmity and Intoxication

Rescission for mental infirmity and intoxication is governed by specific rules that are distinct from the general principles applicable to unconscionable bargains that are discussed in Part D.[93]

7.41

Rescission for impaired capacity is more readily available than rescission as an unconscionable bargain. The party seeking rescission on the basis of impaired capacity does not have to show exploitation or other morally culpable conduct, nor does he have to demonstrate undervalue. Once impaired capacity is proved, the contract is voidable if the other party was aware of the impairment. The counterparty is given no opportunity of proving that the transaction ought to be upheld as being fair, just, and reasonable.

7.42

The law therefore gives greater protection to those suffering from impaired capacity than to those labouring under other types of disability. This is best explained by the tendency for the vitiation of consent to be more profound in such cases as the affected party may be unaware that his autonomy is impaired. This was emphasized by Millett LJ in *Barclays Bank plc v Schwartz*.[94] His Lordship observed that while illiteracy, inability to comprehend English,

7.43

---

[90] *Brennan v Bolt Burdon (a firm)* [2005] QB 303 (CA). As to principles of construction applied in determining whether there has been any mistake in the first place, *Bank of Credit and Commerce International SA v Ali (No 1)* [2002] 1 AC 251; *Brennan v Bolt Burdon (a firm)* [2005] QB 303 (CA). For the possibility of rescission for unilateral mistake where the party to whom a general release was given knew that the other party had or might have a claim, and knew also that the other party was ignorant of this: *Bank of Credit and Commerce International SA v Ali (No 1)* [2002] 1 AC 251, 267. In Australia, *Grant v John Grant & Sons Pty Ltd* (1954) 91 CLR 112.
[91] *Lansdown v Lansdown* (1730) 2 Jac & W 205, 37 ER 695; Sel Cas T King 364, 25 ER 441; *Griffith v Frapwel* (1732) 1 Ves Sen 401, 27 ER 1105; *Bingham v Bingham* (1748) 1 Ves Sen 126, 27 ER 934; Ves Sen Supp 79, 28 ER 462; *Cocking v Pratt* (1750) 1 Ves Sen 400, 27 ER 1105; 1 Ves Sen Supp 176, 28 ER 493; *Ramsden v Hylton* (1751) 2 Ves Sen 304, 28 ER 196; *Roberts v Roberts* [1905] 1 Ch 705 (CA); E Hewitt and J Richardson, *White and Tudor's Leading Cases in Equity with Notes* (9th edn, 1928) vol 1, 192–93.
[92] Paras [5.14]–[5.18].
[93] *Hart v O'Connor* [1985] AC 1000 (PC—NZ) (mental infirmity); *Barclays Bank plc v Schwartz, The Times*, 2 August 1995 (CA).
[94] *The Times*, 2 August 1995 (CA).

mental incapacity, and drunkenness each affect a person's understanding of a transaction, yet:

> Mental incapacity and drunkenness might not only deprive the sufferer of understanding of the transaction, but also deprive him of the awareness that he did not understand it. An illiterate knew that he could not read. A man who was unfamiliar with English was aware of that fact. If he signed a document which he did not understand he had only himself to blame.[95]

7.44 The rule applied to incapacity is also to be contrasted with that applied to unilateral mistake. There it is not enough that the other party was aware of the mistaken party's error: in those jurisdictions where rescission is possible,[96] sharp practice or other unconscionable conduct must be shown. In such cases the mistaken party is necessarily unaware that he lacks a full understanding, yet the law still requires more than mere knowledge by the counterparty. But all contracting entails the risk of mistake, and there is no good reason why that risk should be borne by the other party absent culpable conduct on his part. It should therefore not be surprising that the law adopts a more protective stance to mental infirmity and drunkenness than it does to a mere unilateral mistake.

(1) Mental infirmity

7.45 A complete lack of mental capacity will render a transaction void.[97] Mental infirmity falling short of total incapacity will in certain circumstances render a transaction voidable.[98] The person seeking rescission must show that (i) when he entered into the transaction he was so affected by mental infirmity that he did not know what he was doing, and (ii) the counterparty to the transaction knew of this infirmity.[99]

7.46 In contradistinction to contracts, gifts are probably void if made with impaired mental capacity, irrespective of the donee's knowledge.[100]

Development of the requirements

7.47 Until the mid-nineteenth century, a maxim prevailed whereby a person was said to be unable to 'stultify' himself by pleading his own incapacity in defence to an action on a contract.[101]

---

[95] *The Times*, 2 August 1995 (CA).
[96] Paras [7.20]ff.
[97] *Daily Telegraph Newspaper Co v McLaughlin* [1904] AC 776 (PC—Australia). A person who lacks mental capacity is liable for necessaries supplied to that person: Sale of Goods Act 1979, s 3; Mental Capacity Act 2005, s 7. This may be because a plea of *non est factum* may be available: *Sutton v Sutton* [2009] EWHC 2576 (Ch) [51]; *Ford by his Tutor Beatrice Ann Watkinson v Perpetual Trustees Victoria Ltd* [2009] NSWCA 186.
[98] *Masterman-Lister v Brutton & Co (Nos 1 and 2)* [2002] 1 WLR 1511 (CA) 1533–34. Fridman draws a distinction between a lack of cognition (knowledge of what one is doing) which absolutely negates capacity and a lack of intelligence (appreciation of the consequences of one's actions) which is variable in effect: GHL Fridman, 'Mental Incompetency' (1963) 79 LQR 502, 523.
[99] The onus of proving mental incapacity lies with the person asserting it: *Collins by her next friend Poletti v May* [2000] WASC 29 [54].
[100] *Re Beaney Dec'd* [1978] 1 WLR 771 (gift); *The Special Trustees for Great Ormond Street Hospital for Children v Rushin* [2003] All ER (D) 598 (contract and gift distinguished); *Williams v Williams* [2003] EWHC 742 (gift); cf *Sutton v Sutton* [2009] EWHC 2576 (Ch) [46] (concluding that it is unclear whether a gift affected by impaired capacity is void or voidable); also Chap 29, para [29.21].
[101] WGH Cook, 'Mental Deficiency and the English Law of Contract' (1921) 21 Col LR 424, 429.

7. MISTAKE, IMPAIRED CAPACITY, AND UNCONSCIONABLE BARGAINS

This common law rule was finally abandoned in *Molton v Camroux*.[102] But it was held that unsoundness of mind *per se* was insufficient to vitiate a contract. In that seminal case the contract was not rescinded because the defendants had not been aware of the claimant's lunacy at the time of the transaction, and had not taken advantage of the claimant. In the early cases 'taking advantage' of an infirmity appeared to be treated as an alternative ground for rescission which could operate in the absence of knowledge.[103] Even if it was an alternative ground, the jurisdiction appears to have been superseded.[104]

7.48 *Imperial Loan Co v Stone*,[105] the other watershed decision in this area, made it clear that both executed and executory contracts could be rescinded on the basis of known mental infirmity. In that case the defendant signed a promissory note. His defence to the claim to enforce the note pleaded that, at the time at which he signed it, he was so insane as to be incapable of knowing what he was doing and that the claimant knew of this insanity. The jury found that the defendant suffered from insanity at the relevant time but could not agree as to whether the claimant had knowledge of that fact. The trial judge found for the defendant. On appeal, a new trial was ordered by the Court of Appeal.[106] Lord Esher laid down the following principle:

> When a person enters into a contract, and afterwards alleges that he was so insane at the time that he did not know what he was doing, and proves the allegation, the contract is as binding on him in every respect, whether it is executory or executed, as if he had been sane when he made it, unless he can prove further that the person with whom he contracted knew him to be so insane as not to be capable of understanding what he was about.[107]

7.49 Similarly, Lopes LJ stated:

> In order to avoid a fair contract on the ground of insanity, the mental capacity of the one must be known to the other of the contracting parties. A defendant who seeks to avoid a contract on the ground of insanity, must plead and prove, not merely his incapacity, but also the plaintiff's knowledge of that fact, and unless he proves these two things he cannot succeed.[108]

7.50 In *Hart v O'Connor*[109] the question arose as to whether a contract with a mentally infirm person could be set aside on the basis that its terms were 'unfair' where the counterparty had not been aware of the incapacity at the time of the contract. The court reviewed the authorities and concluded that a contract entered into by a person of unsound mind who is ostensibly sane, such that the other party is unaware of his mental infirmity, could not

---

[102] (1848) 2 Exch 487, 154 ER 584; aff'd (1849) 4 Exch 17, 154 ER 1107.
[103] *Molton v Camroux* (1848) 2 Exch 487, 154 ER 584; aff'd (1849) 4 Exch 17, 154 ER 1107. See also *Campbell v Hooper* (1855) 3 Sm & Giff 153, 159; 65 ER 603, 606 '[T]he money was honestly paid, *and no advantage taken* by the plaintiff, nor any knowledge by him of the lunacy' (emphasis added).
[104] *Ayres v Hazelgrove* (QB, 9 February 1984); *Irvani v Irvani* [2000] 1 Lloyd's Rep 412 (CA) 425 where it was stated that 'It is now firmly decided that a contract cannot be set aside on grounds of lack of capacity unless the handicap is known to the other party', referring to *Hart v O'Connor* [1985] AC 1000 (PC—NZ). Cf *Blomley v Ryan* (1956) 99 CLR 362, 405 where Fullager J listed 'infirmity of body or mind' as an example of a special disadvantage which engages the doctrine of unconscionability.
[105] [1892] 1 QB 599 (CA). Applied in *Wiltshire v Cain* (1958–60) 2 Barb LR 149.
[106] See also *Baldywn v Smith* [1900] 1 Ch 588.
[107] *Imperial Loan Co v Stone* [1892] 1 QB 599 (CA) 601.
[108] *Imperial Loan Co v Stone* [1892] 1 QB 599 (CA) 601, 603.
[109] [1985] AC 1000 (PC—NZ).

be set aside 'by reason of "unfairness"' unless such unfairness amounts to equitable fraud which would have enabled the complaining party to avoid the contract even if he had been sane'.[110] Consequently, such a contract stands unless it can be rescinded as an unconscionable bargain.

Requisite mental infirmity

7.51 The person asserting a right to rescind on this basis must have been unable to appreciate the general nature and effect of the transaction he had entered into. The question left to the jury in *Imperial Loan Co v Stone*[111] was whether, when the person claiming insanity entered into the transaction, he was so insane as not to be capable of understanding what he did.

7.52 The level of understanding that is required is relative to the nature and complexity of the transaction viewed in its context.[112] As Hallett J stated in *Manches v Trimborn*:

> ... the degree of mental capacity which must be possessed varies with every case, as it seems to me, according to the nature of the transaction in question ... [T]he degree of mental incapacity which the defence would have to establish to [the jury's] satisfaction was such a degree of incapacity as would interfere with the capacity of the defendant to understand substantially the nature and effect of the transaction into which she was entering.[113]

7.53 In that case the defendant, who suffered from senile degeneration, sought to avoid liability arising from a cheque that she had signed. The court held that it was sufficient if she could show that she was incapable of understanding the wider transaction of which the cheque was a part. It was not necessary for her to prove that she did not understand that she was signing a cheque.[114]

7.54 The effect of the transaction includes its relative value as compared to the aggregate value of the complainant's assets.[115] A higher level of mental capacity is required for the transfer of a home than would be required for the transfer of bric-a-brac.[116] It is also relevant whether the transaction is an outright gift or whether the party retains some dominion over the assets.[117]

---

[110] *Hart v O'Connor* [1985] AC 1000 (PC—NZ) 1027.
[111] *Imperial Loan Co v Stone* [1892] 1 QB 599 (CA).
[112] *Dunhill v Burgin* [2014] 1 WLR 933 (Sup Ct) [13] (capacity is to be judged in relation to the decision or activity in question and not globally).
[113] (1946) 115 LJKB 305, 307; *Gibbons v Wright* (1954) 91 CLR 423, 438 applied in relation to a gift by Martin Nourse QC in *Re Beaney (Dec'd)* [1978] 1 WLR 770; *Re K* [1988] Ch 310 and *Re W* [2001] Ch 609 (CA) (claims to set aside enduring powers of attorney); *Williams v Williams* [2003] EWHC 742 (gift case); *Masterman-Lister v Brutton & Co* [2002] EWCA Civ 1889 [58]; *Re Smith (Deceased)* [2015] 4 All ER 329.
[114] See also *Public Trustee (WA) v Brumar Nominees Pty Ltd* [2012] WASC 161 [14] where it was stated that 'Ordinarily, understanding the nature of the transaction means understanding its broad operation or the "general purport" of the instrument, but in some cases it may mean the effect of a wider transaction which the instrument is a means of carrying out'.
[115] In *Gorjat v Gorjat* [2010] EWHC 1537 (Ch) [134] it was argued that this principle could have the result that someone with £2 million of assets who gave away £1 million to one child and shortly thereafter gave away the remaining £1 million to their other child would need less capacity to make the first gift than the second. This shows that the principle must be applied in context rather than in isolation.
[116] *Re Beaney (Dec'd)* [1978] 1 WLR 771, 774 (a case involving a gift); followed in *Re Sutton (Dec'd)* [2009] EWHC 2576 (Ch) [11], [26].
[117] *Gorjat v Gorjat* [2010] EWHC 1537 (Ch) [138].

7. MISTAKE, IMPAIRED CAPACITY, AND UNCONSCIONABLE BARGAINS

Mental infirmity is not established merely because a party was under a delusion, even if the delusion was connected with the subject matter of the transaction. *Jenkins v Morris*[118] concerned a lease of a farm granted while the lessor was suffering delusions, including a delusion that the farm was impregnated with sulphur. The validity of the lease was challenged on the basis that the delusions showed that he lacked mental capacity. It was held that the delusions were not conclusive. The question was whether 'the delusions to which he was subject had not so far affected the general faculties of his mind as to render him incompetent to deal with the property which was the subject of the lease'.[119]

7.55

Generally evidence of previous episodes of mental disorder is not sufficient to prove a lack of capacity at a different time.[120] The transaction itself can provide evidence of mental infirmity, and it has been said that 'the circumstances attending the contract, though not conclusive, are, perhaps, of the greatest importance on the one side or the other'.[121]

7.56

In Re Smith (Deceased)[122] it was held that these common law principles continue to apply to inter vivos gifts despite the coming into force of the Mental Capacity Act 2005. The Act is concerned with the jurisdiction of the Court of Protection to deal with welfare issues of living persons who have mental incapacity, and lays down its own principles for determining mental incapacity. The common law principles also ought to continue to apply to contracts.

7.57

Those under the protection of the court
Authority under earlier legislation suggests that an order as to the management of a person's affairs or the appointment of a receiver made by a Court of Protection[123] has the effect that any transactions entered into by that person (the patient) are void; the order appears to deprive the patient of his or her legal capacity to contract, as such capacity would be inconsistent with the court's powers.[124] But some doubt as to the status of the patient's contracts is introduced by a modern court's power to make orders for 'the carrying out of any contract entered into by the patient'.[125] If this power applies to contracts entered into after the management order was made, which it might not, they could be potentially binding on the other party, that is, they are valid if ratified by the court, or perhaps the receiver.

7.58

The Mental Capacity Act 2005 probably further alters any rule that contracts entered into by patients of the Court of Protection are void in cases where deputies have been appointed to manage the patient's affairs. The Act provides that a deputy ceases to have power to make decisions on behalf of the patient in relation to particular matters if he knows or reasonably believes that the patient has capacity in relation to those matters.[126] The general common

7.59

---

[118] (1880) 14 ChD 674 (CA).
[119] *Jenkins v Morris* (1880) 14 ChD 674 (CA) 685.
[120] *Hall v Warren* (1804) 9 Ves Jun 605, 32 ER 738; *McAdam v Walker* (1813) 1 Dow 148, 3 ER 654.
[121] *Hassard v Smith* (1872) IR 6 Eq 429, 434.
[122] [2015] 4 All ER 329.
[123] Mental Health Act 1983, ss 95, 96, 99; Mental Capacity Act 2005, ss 16–19.
[124] *Re Walker* [1905] 1 Ch 160 (CA) and *Re Marshall* [1920] 1 Ch 284 (deeds made by persons subject to orders in lunacy held to be void); *Re Beaney (Dec'd)* [1978] 1 WLR 770, 772; GHL Fridman, 'Mental Incompetency' (1963) 79 LQR 502. Cf *Hall v Warren* (1804) 9 Ves Jun 605, 32 ER 738; *Hassard v Smith* (1872) IR 6 Eq 429. The fact that a person was a patient of the Court of Protection did not conclusively determine whether he had capacity some years before the order was made but it was treated as 'of some evidential assistance': *Pesticcio v Huet* (2003) 73 BMLR 57; on appeal *Niersmans v Pesticcio* [2004] EWCA 372 (point not considered on appeal).
[125] Mental Health Act 1983, s 96(1)(h); Mental Capacity Act 2005, s 18(1)(f).
[126] Mental Capacity Act 2005, s 20(1).

law principles discussed in this section will therefore cover situations where deputies have been appointed to manage a patient's property, the deputy knows or reasonably believes that the patient has capacity in relation to a particular matter concerning his property, and the patient enters a transaction in relation to that matter.[127]

7.60 In Australia, there is authority that the appointment of a financial administrator to the affairs of an impaired adult has the effect that the adult is stripped of capacity to enter into contracts, or undertake other juristic acts, that are thenceforth to be undertaken by the administrator.[128]

Knowledge of mental infirmity

7.61 For mental infirmity that does not render a contract void to affect its enforceability at all, the other party to the contract must know of it.[129] The knowledge required was spelt out in *Hassard v Smith*:

> The knowledge of the lunacy or incapacity ... must be understood to mean not merely actual knowledge, but that which must be presumed, from circumstances known to the other contracting party, sufficient to lead any reasonable person to conclude that, at the time the contract was made, the person with whom he was dealing was of unsound mind.[130]

7.62 Thus the requisite knowledge includes actual knowledge, including the wilful shutting of one's eyes to the true facts,[131] and type (iv) constructive knowledge on the *Baden* scale: knowledge of circumstances which would indicate the facts to an honest and reasonable man.[132] *Obiter dicta* appears to suggest that it might even extend to such notice as would have put a prudent person on inquiry as to the fact of the mental infirmity,[133] that is, type (v) constructive knowledge on that scale.

7.63 In *York Glass Co v Jubb* the claim failed as the counterparty 'did not know and had no reason to know that [the complainant] was out of his mind at the time'. To obtain rescission the defendant had to prove 'that the other party knew either that he was of unsound mind, or such facts about him that he (the other party) must be taken to have been aware that he was of unsound mind'. Recently in *Dunhill v Burgin*[134] the Supreme Court confirmed by way of obiter dictum that constructive knowledge will suffice. Baroness Hale stated that a contract made by a person who lacks capacity is valid unless the other party to the contract knew or

---

[127] See also, P Bartlett, *Blackstone's Guide to the Mental Capacity Act 2005* (2nd edn, 2008) [3.110]–[3.111].
[128] *Bergmann v Daw* [2010] QCA 143 (entry into contract of sale); *McIvey v St Vincent's Hospital (Melbourne) Ltd* [2005] VSCA 233 (filing notice of appeal).
[129] *Molton v Camroux* (1849) 4 Exch 17, 19; 154 ER 1107, 1108; *Imperial Loan Co v Stone* [1892] 1 QB 599 (CA) 601, 602, 603; *York Glass Co v Jubb* (1925) 42 TLR 1 (CA); *Hart v O'Connor* [1985] AC 1000 (PC—NZ); *Fineland Investments Ltd v Pritchard* [2011] EWHC 113 (Ch) [82].
[130] (1872) IR 6 Eq 429. However, precisely what type of knowledge will suffice has not been free from doubt. Contrast *The Public Trustee (WA) v Brumar Nominees Pty Ltd* [2012] WASC 161 [91]–[96] (actual knowledge required); and *Collins by her next friend Poletti v May* [2000] WASC 29 [68] (constructive knowledge will suffice).
[131] *Grant v Imperial Trust Co* [1935] 3 DLR 660 (SCC).
[132] *Baden v Société Générale pour Favoriser le Developpement du Commerce et de l'Industrie en France SA* [1993] 1 WLR 509, 575–76, where Peter Gibson J noted that knowledge can comprise: (i) actual knowledge; (ii) wilfully shutting one's eyes to the obvious; (iii) wilfully and recklessly failing to make such inquiries as an honest and reasonable man would make; (iv) knowledge of circumstances which would indicate the facts to an honest and reasonable man; and (v) knowledge of circumstances which would put an honest and reasonable man on inquiry.
[133] *Greenslade v Dare* (1855) 20 Beav 284, 288, 290; 52 ER 612, 614, 615.
[134] [2014] 1 WLR 933 (Sup Ct).

ought to have known that she lacked that capacity.[135] This proposition, although not uncontroversial,[136] has been applied in a number of subsequent High Court cases.[137]

The amount of time that the defendant had spent with the complainant prior to the transaction is a relevant factor in judging his knowledge of the mental infirmity.[138] It has been held that evidence that a person had a general reputation of insanity in the neighbourhood in which he resided did not prove that the counterparty knew of that person's impaired capacity.[139]

7.64

(2) Drunkenness or intoxication

Drunkenness has the same effect on a contract as unsoundness of mind.[140] In extreme cases, it seems that it may render the contract void at law.[141] For this to occur, the defendant must be 'wholly incapable of any reflective or deliberate act, so that, in fact, he was utterly unconscious of the nature of the acts he did'.[142] But in less extreme cases, drunkenness may render a contract voidable.[143] Although historically the cases have focused on drunkenness, the same principles ought to apply to all forms intoxication, whether induced by alcohol or narcotics.[144] As with mental infirmity, intoxication alone is not a ground for rescission.[145] The other party to the contract must also know of it at the time the agreement is concluded.[146] A drunken person who lacks capacity is liable for necessaries supplied to that person.[147]

7.65

Requisite intoxication
It is trite to say that there are degrees of intoxication. A contract is not rendered voidable simply because one party enjoyed wine with lunch before signing it. To have this effect, the intoxication must be very serious. The party must be in such a state 'as not to know what he is doing'.[148] The authorities on mental infirmity imply that the degree of intoxication must

7.66

---

[135] *Dunhill v Burgin* [2014] 1 WLR 933 (Sup Ct) [1] and [25].
[136] A Burrows, *A Restatement of the English Law of Contract* (2016) 219; HG Beale (ed), *Chitty on Contracts* (34th edn, 2021) [11-078]–[11-088].
[137] Followed in *Josife v Summertrot Holdings Ltd* [2014] EWHC 996 (Ch) [19]–[20]; *Mackay v Wesley* [2020] EWHC 1215 (Ch) [125].
[138] *Ayres v Hazelgrove* (QB, 9 Feb 1984) 'a strange old lady, eccentric in the extreme and one whom, within a very short time, let alone in forty minutes, would have made it manifestly plain by her conduct that she was suffering from a mental incapacity'.
[139] *Greenslade v Dare* (1855) 20 Beav 284, 290; 52 ER 612.
[140] *Moulton v Camroux* (1849) 4 Exch 17, 19; 154 ER 1107, 1108.
[141] *Pitt v Smith* (1811) 3 Camp 33, 170 ER 1296 (claimant plied with drink by counterparty); *Fenton v Holloway* (1815) 1 Stark 126, 171 ER 422; *Shaw v Thackray* (1853) 1 Sm & G 537, 539; 65 ER 235, 236.
[142] *Hawkins v Bone* (1865) 4 F & F 311, 314; 176 ER 578, 580 (Pollock CB). Fridman's distinction between lack of cognition (knowledge of what one is doing) which would render a contract void and a lack of intelligence (appreciation of the consequences of one's actions) which would render it voidable may prove a useful distinction in this respect: GHL Fridman, 'Mental Incompetency' (1963) 79 LQR 502, 523. For a historical overview, W Swain, 'Without the Power to Drink or Contract' (2020) 24 The Edin LR 26–48.
[143] *Cooke v Clayworth* (1811) 18 Ves 12, 34 ER 222; *Say v Barwick* (1812) 1 Ves & B 195, 35 ER 76; *Matthews v Baxter* (1873) LR 8 Exch 132.
[144] *Irvani v Irvani* [2000] 1 Lloyd's Rep 412 (CA) 425 (defence of incapacity based on drug addiction unsuccessful on the facts).
[145] *Cory v Cory* (1747) 1 Ves Sen 19, 27 ER 864; *Cooke v Clayworth* (1811) 18 Ves 12, 15–16; 34 ER 222, 223.
[146] *Moulton v Camroux* (1849) 4 Exch 17, 19; 154 ER 1107, 1108.
[147] Sale of Goods Act 1979, s 3.
[148] *Gore v Gibson* (1845) 13 M & W 623, 626–27; 153 ER 260, 261–62. References in this decision to the contract being void were read as references to it being voidable in *Matthews v Baxter* (1873) LR 8 Exch 132; *Moulton v Camroux* (1849) 4 Exch 17, 19; 154 ER 1107, 1108.

be at a level that interferes with the person's capacity to understand substantially the nature and effect of the transaction into which he is entering.[149] That the complainant's intoxication was self-induced is not material.[150]

Knowledge of intoxication

7.67 Knowledge of the claimant's intoxicated state is required for rescission to be available.[151] The rules for determining knowledge in the context of mental infirmity ought to apply in this context, for the principles that underlie the vitiating effect of the two forms of incapacity are the same.[152] Exceedingly irrational behaviour, in an environment where alcohol is provided, may indicate to those who are present that a person's capacity is impaired by alcohol.[153]

7.68 It is well settled that encouragement or the provision of alcohol or drugs by the counterparty, or other attempts to get the claimant intoxicated in order to induce him to enter into a contract, will permit rescission if the claimant does succumb.[154] According to older authorities intoxication could also provide a ground for rescission where the counterparty had 'taken advantage' of the other's incapacity.[155] But any jurisdiction to rescind in the absence of knowledge of the intoxication has probably been superseded, as in the case of mental infirmity.[156]

D. Unconscionable Bargains: Exploitation[157]

7.69 This ground for rescission[158] is often associated with the language of 'constructive fraud', or sometimes 'equitable fraud'. This is 'fraud presumed or inferred from the circumstances

---

[149] *Manches v Trimborn* (1946) 115 LJKB 305, 307. See paras [7.51]ff. See also *Resorts World at Sentosa Pte Ltd v Lee Fook Kheun* [2018] SGHC 173.

[150] 'The fact that the defendant's condition was the result of his own self-indulgence could make no difference': *Blomley v Ryan* (1956) 99 CLR 362, 429.

[151] *Moulton v Camroux* (1849) 4 Exch 17, 19; 154 ER 1107, 1108; *Gore v Gibson* (1845) 13 M & W 623, 626; 153 ER 260, 261 where Parke B equated the entry into a contract with a person who is totally drunk where this was to known to the counterparty with actual fraud.

[152] See paras [7.61]ff. Accordingly constructive knowledge of the intoxication ought to suffice, in line with *Dunhill v Burgin* [2014] 1 WLR 933 (Sup Ct).

[153] *Hawkins v Bone* (1865) 4 F & F 311, 315; 176 ER 578, 580 (bid blurted out at an auction where wine had been provided).

[154] *Johnson v Medlicott* (1734) 2 Eq Cas Abr 186n, 22 ER 160; *Cooke v Clayworth* (1811) 18 Ves 12, 17; 34 ER 222, 223 (claimant not drawn to drink as 'the drinking was not introduced on account of his coming there, nor after he came there: but a company engaged in drinking, he joined them'); *Say v Barwick* (1812) 1 Ves & B 195, 35 ER 76 (minor induced into a 'habit of intoxication'); *Blomley v Ryan* (1956) 99 CLR 362, 405 where Fullagar J stated that 'where the court is satisfied that a contract disadvantageous to the party affected has been obtained by "drawing him to drink", or there has been real unfairness in taking advantage of his condition, the contract will be set aside'.

[155] *Cory v Cory* (1747) 1 Ves Sen 19, 27 ER 864; *Cooke v Clayworth* (1811) 18 Ves 12, 15–16; 34 ER 222, 223.

[156] See paras [7.47]ff. Cf *Blomley v Ryan* (1956) 99 CLR 362, 405, where 'drunkenness' is listed as an example of a special disadvantage which engages the doctrine of unconscionability.

[157] This para uses the term 'exploitation' in its title as a marker for the core facts enlivening the doctrine. It adopts the terminology used by Andrew Burrows in *The Law of Restitution* (3rd edn, 2011) 244 which in turn appears to be based on *Alec Lobb (Garages) Ltd v Total Oil Great Britain Ltd* [1983] 1 WLR 87, 94–95. The more common labels are 'unconscionable conduct' or 'unconscionable bargains'. As to the terminology for this ground, see also *Commercial Bank of Australia Limited v Amadio* (1983) 151 CLR 447, 461 (Mason J).

[158] In the case of contracts between consumers and traders similar circumstances may also constitute aggressive practices allowing the consumer to 'unwind' the contract under regulations (regs 27E and 27F) inserted into the Consumer Protection from Unfair Trading Regulations 2008 by the Consumer Protection (Amendment) Regulations 2014. Such statutory rights akin to rescission are beyond the scope of this chapter. Refer to The Law Commission and the Scottish Law Commission, *Report on Consumer Redress for Misleading and Aggressive*

or conditions of the parties contracting—weakness on one side, usury on the other, or extortion, or advantage taken of that weakness'.[159] Lord Selborne LC explained in *Earl of Aylesford v Morris* that:

> Fraud does not here mean deceit or circumvention; it means an unconscientious use of the power arising out of these circumstances and conditions; and when the relative position of the parties is such as *prima facie* to raise this presumption, the transaction cannot stand unless the person claiming the benefit of it is able to repel the presumption by contrary evidence, proving it to have been in point of fact, fair, just and reasonable.[160]

For England and Wales, the core requirements of this ground for rescission were enumerated by Peter Millett QC in *Alec Lobb (Garages) Ltd v Total Oil Great Britain Ltd*: **7.70**

> ... if the cases are examined, it will be seen that three elements have almost invariably to have been present before the court has interfered. First, one party has been at a serious disadvantage to the other, whether through poverty, or ignorance, or lack of advice, or otherwise, so that circumstances existed of which unfair advantage could be taken ... secondly, this weakness of the one party has been exploited by the other in some morally culpable manner ... and thirdly, the resulting transaction has been not merely hard or improvident, but overreaching and oppressive. Where there has been a sale at an undervalue, the undervalue has almost always been substantial, so that it calls for an explanation, and is in itself indicative of the presence of some fraud, undue influence, or other such feature. In short, there must, in my judgment, be some impropriety, both in the conduct of the stronger party and in the terms of the transaction itself (though the former may often be inferred from the latter in the absence of an innocent explanation) which in the traditional phase 'shocks the conscience of the court', and makes it against equity and good conscience of the stronger party to retain the benefit of a transaction he has unfairly obtained.[161]

The requirements identified by Lord Millett are therefore that (i) the rescinding party was at a serious disadvantage relative to the counterparty; (ii) the weakness was exploited in a morally culpable manner; and (iii) the resulting transaction was overreaching and oppressive. This part will focus on these three requirements and a possible defence if the counterparty can nonetheless demonstrate that the transaction was fair, just, and reasonable. It will then conclude with a discussion of the important role that the absence of independent advice plays in relation to the above matters. **7.71**

Practices (Scot Law Com No 226, Law Com No 332) and the Department for Business, Innovation and Skills, *Reform of Consumer Law—Government Response to Consultations on Misleading and Aggressive Practices and the European Consumer Rights Directive* (August 2013).

[159] *Earl of Chesterfield v Janssen* (1751) 2 Ves Sen 125, 157; 28 ER 82, 101.
[160] (1873) 8 Ch App 484 (CA) 490–91; see also *Hart v O'Connor* [1985] AC 1000 (PC—NZ) 1024.
[161] *Alec Lobb (Garages) Ltd v Total Oil Great Britain Ltd* [1983] 1 WLR 87, 94–95 (on appeal [1985] 1 WLR 173 (CA) 181–83); *Credit Lyonnais Bank Nederland NV v Burch* [1997] 1 All ER 144 (CA) 152–53 (Millett LJ); *Strydom v Vendside Limited* [2009] EWHC 2130 (QB) [35]–[36]; *Pakistan International Airline Corp v Times Travel (UK) Ltd* [2021] 3 WLR 727 (Sup Ct) [24]. In Hong Kong the three requirements are the same: *Lo Wo v Cheung Chan Ka* [2001] HKCA 302. In Australia the requirements are more liberal in that there is no need to prove that the transaction was overreaching and oppressive: *Commercial Bank of Australia v Amadio* (1983) 151 CLR 447; *Turner v Windever* [2003] NSWSC 1147 [105]; *Holz v Davis* [2010] QSC 452 [44]. Nonetheless in most cases where relief has been granted against unconscionable dealing in Australia there has been no, or inadequate, consideration: *Permanent Mortgages Pty Ltd v Vandenbergh* (2010) 41 WAR 353 [244].

7.72 At the outset it is to be underlined, however, that the doctrine of unconscionable bargains is interpreted and applied restrictively in English courts. Although the authorities are treated here in some detail, the doctrine is not highly developed or regularly employed. On the contrary, it is rarely used, and is sometimes regarded as anomalous. The lack of development of the doctrine is in part because English appellate courts have not embraced 'unconscionability' as an organizing principle for equitable doctrines in the same way that has occurred in some other Commonwealth jurisdictions.

7.73 The Privy Council has confirmed that undue influence and unconscionable bargains are distinct doctrines. Unconscionable bargains involve the exploitation of a vulnerability but do not depend on a relationship of actual or presumed confidence. However the two are based on a common foundation: equity's concern to protect the vulnerable from economic harm.[162]

7.74 In *Langton v Langton*[163] the court concluded that the equitable jurisdiction relating to unconscionable bargains does not apply to gifts, as they are not 'bargains'. This decision is not without difficulty, and was not followed in *Evans v Lloyd*.[164] It is considered in the context of the rescission of gifts.[165] Going forward it may be more appropriate to refer to this ground of rescission as one dealing with 'unconscionable transactions' rather than 'bargains'.

(1) First requirement: serious disadvantage relative to the counterparty

7.75 The first requirement is that the complainant must have been at a serious disadvantage relative to the counterparty.[166] Sources of sufficiently serious disadvantage have included poverty and ignorance,[167] financial strife or 'distressed circumstances',[168] old age,[169] youth

---

[162] *Lawrence v Poorah* [2008] UKPC 21 [20]. In Australia the difference has been said to be that unconscionable conduct focuses more on the unconscientious conduct of the defendant in dealing with the party under the special disadvantage, whereas undue influence looks more to the quality of the independence of the consent or assent of the disponor: *Bridgewater v Leahy* (1998) 194 CLR 457 [75]; *Permanent Mortgages Pty Ltd v Vandenbergh* (2010) 41 WAR 353 (SC-WA) [215].

[163] [1995] 2 FLR 890, 908–09, approved in *Randall v Randall* [2004] EWHC 2258 (Ch) [94]; cf *Hamburg v Goldstein* [2002] EWCA 122.

[164] [2013] EWHC 1725 (Ch) [52].

[165] See Chap 29, para [29.16].

[166] In *Blomley v Ryan* (1956) 99 CLR 362, 405 Fullager J listed examples of such special disadvantage as 'poverty and need of any kind, sickness, age, sex, infirmity of body or mind, drunkenness, illiteracy, or lack of assistance or education where assistance or explanation is necessary'. He said: 'The common characteristic seems to be that they have the effect of placing one party at a serious disadvantage vis-à-vis the other.' The requirement was not made out in *Nosworthy v Instinctif Partners Ltd* [2019] 2 WLUK 469 by a departing employee who sought to challenge the effectiveness of 'bad leaver' provisions as unconscionable.

[167] *Evans v Llewellin* (1787) 1 Cox 334, 29 ER 1191; *Fry v Lane* (1888) 40 ChD 312; cf *Norwich Union Life Insurance Society v Qureshi* [1999] Lloyd's Rep 263 (a person who was a Name at Lloyd's was not poor).

[168] *Wood v Abrey* (1818) 3 Madd 417, 423; 56 ER 558, 560; *Earl of Aylesford v Morris* (1873) 8 Ch App 484; *Watkin v Watson-Smith, The Times*, 3 July 1986 (a desire for a quick sale). '[N]ecessitous men are not, truly speaking, free men, but, to answer a present exigency, will submit to any terms that the crafty may impose on them': *Vernon v Bethell* (1762) 2 Eden 110, 113; 28 ER 838, 839. Cf *Heritage Travel and Tourism Ltd v Windhorst* [2021] EWHC 2380 (Comm) [47] (financial problems were insufficient given the complainant's considerable commercial experience and sophisticated financial expertise).

[169] *Longmate v Ledger* (1860) 2 Giff 157, 66 ER 67 (a man advanced in years with a known weak and eccentric disposition sold property for a price greatly below its value); *Watkin v Watson-Smith, The Times*, 3 July 1986 (frail 80-year-old signed contract to sell a house for one tenth of its value); *Boustany v Pigott* (1995) 69 P & CR 298 (PC—Antigua and Barbuda) (elderly landlady 'quite slow' in her affairs entered into 10-year lease with no rent review clause).

and inexperience,[170] lack of education,[171] and illness.[172] These sources are often present in combination when the doctrine is made out, and are usually coupled with an absence of independent advice.[173] The effect of the serious disadvantage must be such as to give the stronger party dominion over the weaker[174] or, considering the effect from the perspective of the other party, that the weaker party is unable to judge for himself.[175] The Australian High Court held that a pathological compulsion to gamble did not constitute a special disadvantage vis-à-vis a casino operator.[176]

The earliest cases often concerned 'expectant heirs'. They were young men who expected to inherit wealth from family members in the future, and who used that expectancy to finance a profligate lifestyle. They were usually inexperienced and heavily indebted, and borrowed money secured by their future inheritance on very disadvantageous terms.[177] There were many such cases in the late seventeenth and eighteenth centuries, and the rules developed were heavily influenced by policy considerations.[178] Economic and social change saw this jurisdiction eventually die out, but it evolved to protect other persons whom the courts saw as particularly vulnerable.[179] In the landmark case of *Fry v*

7.76

---

[170] *Earl of Aylesford v Morris* (1873) 8 Ch App 484; *Multiservice Bookbinding v Marden* [1979] Ch 84, 110 (Browne-Wilkinson J): 'The classic example of an unconscionable bargain is where advantage has been taken of a young, inexperienced or ignorant person to introduce a term which no sensible well-advised person or party would have accepted.'

[171] *Clark v Malpas* (1862) 4 De GF & J 401, 405; 45 ER 1238, 1240 (a man 'who could read only with difficulty, who could write only his name' who was in a humble station of life and suffering illness sold property at undervalue); *Baker v Monk* (1864) 4 De GJ & S 388 (CA), 46 ER 968 (old woman in humble life, of slender education, sold property for small annuity); *Singla v Bashir* [2002] EWHC 883 [7] (complainant was illiterate and had a poor command of English). Cf *Barclays Bank v Schwartz*, *The Times*, 2 August 1995 (CA) where a businessman's argument that his illiteracy and unfamiliarity with the English language amounted to a special disability was rejected.

[172] *Clark v Malpas* (1862) 4 DeG F & J 401, 405; 45 ER 1238, 1240 (vendor died 36 hours after executing documents). Cf *Irvani v Irvani* [2000] 1 Lloyd's Rep 412 (CA) where a businessman's argument that his addiction to heroin amounted to a special disability was rejected. The Court of Appeal in Singapore accepted the argument that acute grief could amount to an infirmity that was sufficient to engage a narrow doctrine of unconscionability: *BOM v BOK* [2018] SCA 83.

[173] *Chagos Islanders v Attorney-General* [2003] EWHC 2222 [580] complainants had reasonable prospects of showing that they were 'illiterate, ignorant or ill educated and very poor and in real need of money' (issue not considered on appeal [2004] EWCA 997). See paras [7.97]ff as to the role of independent advice.

[174] *Earl of Aylesford v Morris* (1873) 8 Ch App 484, 491; *James v Kerr* (1880) 40 ChD 449, 460 which suggests that the weaker party needs to be 'practically at the mercy' of the other; *Adare Finance DAC v Yellowstone Capital Management SA* [2020] EWHC 2760 (Comm) [69] where it was held that the weaker party must be under 'a disadvantage which renders it vulnerable to unconscientious conduct by the other party. In other words, the weaker party is in the power of the stronger party. It is unlikely that this requirement will be established where there is no substantial inequality of bargaining power'.

[175] *Blomley v Ryan* (1956) 99 CLR 362, 392; *Commercial Bank of Australia v Amadio* (1983) 151 CLR 447, 467. This principle is based on *Clark v Malpas* (1862) 4 DF & J 401, 404; 45 ER 1238, 1240 where the weaker party was 'unable of himself to judge' and *Wiltshire v Marshall* (1866) 14 LT 396, 397 where the issue was 'whether the person did exercise any degree of judgment in making the contract'.

[176] *Kakavas v Crown Melbourne Ltd* (2013) 250 CLR 392; 298 ALR 35 (HCA).

[177] For later examples, *Earl of Aylesford v Morris* (1873) 8 Ch App 484 (a 'foolish and extravagant' expectant heir borrowed money at over 60% interest to pay off large debts); *O'Rorke v Bolingbroke* (1877) 2 App Cas 814. See also J Newland, *A Treatise on Contracts within the Jurisdiction of Courts of Equity* (1806).

[178] *Earl of Aylesford v Morris* (1873) 8 Ch App 484 (Lord Selborne LC) 492: 'Great Judges have said that there is a principle of public policy in restraining this [ie 'catching bargains with expectant heirs']; that this system of undermining and blasting, as it were, in the bud the fortunes of families, is a public as well as a private mischief'. Special protection for sellers of reversionary interests was abolished by the Sales of Reversions Act 1867, consolidated in s 174 of the Law of Property Act 1925. The general principles of equity continue to apply. See further, JP Dawson, 'Economic Duress—An Essay in Perspective' (1947) 45 Michigan LR 253, 267–68.

[179] This process is ongoing. In *Multiservice Bookbinding v Marden* [1979] Ch 84, 110 Browne-Wilkinson J stated 'I do not think the categories of unconscionable bargains are limited: the court can and should intervene where the bargain has been procured by unfair means'. In *Credit Lyonnais Bank Nederland v Burch* [1997] 1 All ER 144 (CA)

Lane[180] Kay J reviewed the authorities and held that:

> The circumstances of poverty and ignorance of the vendor, and absence of independent advice, throw upon the purchaser, when the transaction is impeached, the onus of proving in Lord Selbourne's words [in *Earl of Aylesford v Morris*], that the purchase was 'fair, just and reasonable'.[181]

7.77 The concept of poverty and ignorance is ambulatory in that it is measured against contemporary levels of wealth and education. In *Cresswell v Potter*[182] a Post Office telephonist who had previously worked as a van driver was found to have been poor and ignorant. Megarry J stated:

> I think that the plaintiff may fairly be described as falling within whatever is the modern equivalent of 'poor and ignorant.' Eighty years ago, when *Fry v Lane* was decided, social conditions were very different from those which exist today. I do not, however, think that the principle has changed, even though the euphemisms of the 20th century may require the word 'poor' to be replaced by 'a member of the lower income group' or the like, and the word 'ignorant' by 'less highly educated.' The plaintiff has been a van driver for a tobacconist, and is a Post Office telephonist. The evidence of her means is slender. The defendant told me that the plaintiff probably had a little saved, but not much; and there was evidence that her earnings were about the same as the defendant's, and that these were those of a carpenter. The plaintiff also has a legal aid certificate.
>
> In those circumstances, I think that the plaintiff may properly be described as 'poor' in the sense used in *Fry v Lane*, where it was applied to a laundryman who, in 1888, was earning £1 a week. In this context, as in others, I do not think that 'poverty' is confined to destitution. Further, although no doubt it requires considerable alertness and skill to be a good telephonist, I think that a telephonist can properly be described as 'ignorant' in the context of property transactions in general and the execution of conveyancing documents in particular.[183]

7.78 In that case, the victim's 'ignorance' was assessed in relation to the type of transaction in question, rather than as to matters generally.[184] This decision was followed in *Backhouse v Backhouse*[185] where the weaker party was 'certainly not wealthy' but was 'an intelligent woman'. The requirement was also satisfied in *Boustany v Pigott*[186] where the weaker party was a wealthy elderly landlady who had become 'quite slow' and had handed the management of her affairs to her cousin. The requirement that the claimant is 'poor and ignorant' was also met where the donor of property had left school at 14, was an agricultural worker employed by the donee, and was dependent on the donee for board and accommodation.[187]

---

151 Nourse LJ stated that this ground for rescission was 'in good heart and capable of adaptation to different transactions entered into in changing circumstances'.

[180] (1888) 40 ChD 312, 322.
[181] *Fry v Lane* (1888) 40 ChD 312, 322.
[182] [1978] 1 WLR 255n.
[183] *Cresswell v Potter* [1978] 1 WLR 255n, 257–58.
[184] *Cresswell v Potter* [1978] 1 WLR 255n, 260. See also *Chagos Islanders v Attorney-General* [2003] EWHC 2222 [559] (issue not considered on appeal [2004] EWCA 997).
[185] [1978] 1 WLR 243.
[186] (1995) 69 P & CR 298 (PC—Antigua and Barbuda).
[187] *Evans v Lloyd* [2013] EWHC 1725 (Ch) [75]–[76].

7. MISTAKE, IMPAIRED CAPACITY, AND UNCONSCIONABLE BARGAINS

In short, to establish this requirement, the claimant must prove that his circumstances were such that that he laboured under a serious disadvantage vis-à-vis the other party.[188] But although this is supported by the tide of authority, one decision of the Court of Appeal appears to suggest that a special disadvantage is not a necessary condition for relief. In *Credit Lyonnais Bank Nederland NV v Burch*[189] the court suggested *obiter* that a transaction was an unconscionable bargain without considering whether any special disadvantage was present. On the facts there appeared to be no disadvantage analogous to the disadvantages that had been present in prior cases.[190] The terms of the transaction were, however, unusual and startling. A junior employee granted a mortgage over her home to secure her employer's business debts. She had no financial interest in the business and was unaware of the level of its indebtedness. It has been suggested that gross undervalue gives rise to a rebuttable inference that one party was at a special disadvantage relative to the other.[191] But this takes the doctrine too far and is difficult to reconcile with *Hart v O'Connor*.[192] The *Burch* decision ought to be confined to its special facts, and not regarded as authority that no special disadvantage must be present before the doctrine is engaged.

7.79

(2) Second requirement: weakness exploited in morally culpable manner
The general principle

The second requirement is that the weakness of the complainant must have been exploited by the counterparty in some morally culpable manner. This requirement is concerned with the stronger party's conduct before or at the time of the transaction,[193] in particular in light of his or her knowledge of the other party's special disadvantage.[194] This requirement has been recognized for some time. In the early case of *Wood v Abrey*, Leach V-C concluded that 'a Court of Equity will inquire whether the parties really did meet on equal terms; and if it

7.80

---

[188] In a number of cases companies have claimed to have been at a serious disadvantage vis-à-vis their counterparty: *Alec Lobb (Garages) Ltd v Total Oil (Great Britain) Limited* [1985] 1 WLR 173 (CA); *Burmah Oil Co v Governor of the Bank of England, The Times*, 4 July 1981. Although the doctrine does not yet appear to have been applied in favour of a legal person, such an outcome is possible if all three requirements were satisfied. See also *Pakistan International Airline Corp v Times Travel (UK) Ltd* [2021] 3 WLR 727 (Sup Ct) [77].
[189] [1997] 1 All ER 144 (CA).
[190] As observed in R Hooley and J O'Sullivan, 'Undue Influence and Unconscionable Bargains' [1997] LMCLQ 17, 23.
[191] N Enonchong, *Duress, Undue Influence and Unconscionable Dealing* (3rd edn, 2018) [18-007].
[192] [1985] AC 1000 (PC—NZ). See also *White and Carter (Councils) Ltd v McGregor* [1962] AC 413, 445; *Multiservice Bookbinding v Marden* [1979] chap 84, 112 (Browne-Wilkinson J).
[193] *Liddle v Cree* [2011] EWHC 394 (Ch) [83]–[92]. In *Gustav & Co Ltd v Macfield Ltd* [2008] NZSC 47 [5], [21] the New Zealand Supreme Court held that unconscionability should be assessed at the date a contract was entered into, not at the date it became unconditional. The court sought to avoid overlap with the doctrine of frustration which would occur if supervening unconscionability became a ground for rescission.
[194] *Adare Finance DAC v Yellowstone Capital Management SA* [2020] EWHC 2760 (Comm) [69] where it was held that the stronger party should have been aware, or had the means of becoming aware, of the weaker party's disadvantage or weakness and had acted cynically to take advantage of or exploit that weakness; *Minder Music Ltd v Sharples* [2015] EWHC 1454 (IPEC) at [34]–[35] was a case where the doctrine was not engaged as it was not shown that there was sufficient knowledge of the weakness. A Burrows, *A Restatement of the English Law of Contract* (2016) 211 states that the better view is that knowledge of the weakness and substantive unfairness is required. In New Zealand, it has been held that constructive knowledge of the weakness is sufficient. A contract may be voidable if the party against whom rescission is sought 'ought to have known of [the weakness]; when a reasonable man would have adverted to the possibility of its existence': *Nichols v Jessup* [1986] 1 NZLR 226 (CA) 235 (Somers J). See N Bamforth, 'Unconscionability as a Vitiating Factor' [1995] LMCLQ 538, 549–50 for a discussion of the subjective and the objective approaches to constructive fraud in English law.

be found that the vendor was in distressed circumstances, *and that advantage was taken of that distress*, it will avoid the contract'.[195] The conduct to be shown has been characterized as 'victimisation, which can consist of either of the active extortion of a benefit or the passive acceptance of a benefit in unconscionable circumstances'.[196]

7.81 In *Boustany v Pigott* Lord Templeman further explained the character of the conduct that must be present in the following terms:

(1) It is not sufficient to attract the jurisdiction of equity to prove that a bargain is hard, unreasonable or foolish; it must be proved to be unconscionable, in the sense that 'one of the parties to it has imposed the objectionable terms in a morally reprehensible manner, that is to say, in a way which affects his conscience': *Multiservice Bookbinding v Marden* [1979] Ch 84, 110.

(2) 'Unconscionable' relates not merely to the terms of the bargain but to the behaviour of the stronger party, which must be characterized by some moral culpability or impropriety: *Lobb (Alec) (Garages) Limited v Total Oil (Great Britain) Limited* [1983] 1 WLR 87, 94.

(3) Unequal bargaining power or objectively unreasonable terms provide no basis for equitable interference in the absence of unconscientious or extortionate abuse of power where exceptionally, and as a matter of common fairness, 'it was not right the strong should be allowed to push the weak to the wall': *Lobb (Alec) (Garages) Limited v Total Oil (Great Britain) Limited* [1985] 1 WLR 173, 183.

(4) A contract cannot be set aside in equity as 'an unconscionable bargain' against a party innocent of actual or constructive fraud. Even if the terms of the contract are 'unfair' in the sense that they are more favourable to one party than the other ('contractual imbalance'), equity will not provide relief unless the beneficiary is guilty of unconscionable conduct: *Hart v O'Connor* [1985] AC 1000 applied in *Nichols v Jessup* [1986] NZLR 226.

(5) 'In situations of this kind it is necessary for the plaintiff who seeks relief to establish unconscionable conduct, namely that unconscientious advantage has been taken of his disabling condition or circumstances': per Mason J in *Commercial Bank of Australia Ltd v Amadio* (1983) 46 ALR 402, 413 [also (1983) 151 CLR 447].[197]

7.82 In summary, the behaviour of the stronger party must be morally culpable in that he or she has exploited or taken advantage of the weaker party's disadvantage.[198] In the case before the court in *Pigott*, this requirement was met. The lessees had approached the elderly landlady when her cousin whom they knew managed her affairs was away, persuaded her to grant the lease on very disadvantageous terms and took her to a lawyer's office to have the document drafted and signed.

---

[195] (1818) 3 Madd 417, 423; 56 ER 558, 560 (emphasis added).
[196] *Hart v O'Connor* [1985] AC 1000 (PC—NZ) 1024. See also *Alec Lobb (Garages) Ltd v Total Oil (Great Britain) Limited* [1985] 1 WLR 173 (CA), 182.
[197] *Boustany v Piggott* (1995) 69 P & CR 298 (PC—Antigua and Barbuda) 303.
[198] *Jones v Morgan* [2001] EWCA 995 [35]; *Singla v Bashir* [2002] EWHC 883 [28]; *Kakavas v Crown Melbourne Ltd* (2013) 250 CLR 392; 298 ALR 35 (HCA) [20].

In *Kakavas v Crown Melbourne Ltd*[199] the High Court of Australia held that equitable intervention does not relieve a plaintiff from the consequences of improvident transactions conducted in the ordinary and undistinguished course of a lawful business. The Court held that a plaintiff who voluntarily engages in risky business has never been able to call upon equitable principles to be redeemed from the coming home of risks inherent in the business. The plaintiff must be able to point to conduct on the part of the defendant, beyond the ordinary conduct of the business, which makes it just to require the defendant to restore the plaintiff to his or her previous position. In that case a person said to be addicted to gambling failed to establish that the casino operator had engaged in unconscionable conduct. **7.83**

Applications of the general principle
In *Alec Lobb (Garages) Ltd v Total Oil Great Britain Ltd*,[200] Peter Millett QC cited *Clark v Malpas*[201] as an example of a case where this requirement was satisfied, namely, 'where a poor illiterate man was induced to enter into a transaction of an unusual nature, without proper independent advice,[202] and in great haste'.[203] Some of the reasons that the requirement was found to be lacking in the *Alec Lobb* case were that the stronger party 'did not press [the weaker] for a quick decision; there was no undue haste' and that '[t]hey had no reason to believe … that they were acquiring the site at an undervalue'.[204] Similarly in *Harrison v Guest*[205] the requirement was not made out as the vendor first made the offer of sale, and the purchaser advised him to take time to consider it. The offer was not 'snapped up' by the stronger party. **7.84**

It is clear that English law now requires morally culpable conduct on the defendant's part, and that, contrary to Lord Denning's suggestion in *Lloyds Bank Ltd v Bundy*,[206] mere inequality of bargaining power is not sufficient.[207] This was stressed by the Privy Council in *Hart v O'Connor* where this exploitation requirement was found not to have been satisfied: **7.85**

> [The stronger party] acted with complete innocence throughout. He was unaware of the vendor's unsoundness of mind. The vendor was ostensibly advised by his own solicitor. The [stronger party] had no means of knowing or cause to suspect that the vendor was not in receipt of and acting in accordance with the most full and careful advice. The terms of the bargain were the terms proposed by the vendor's solicitor, not terms imposed by the [stronger party] or his solicitor. There was no equitable fraud, no victimisation, no taking

---

[199] (2013) 250 CLR 392; 298 ALR 35 (HCA) [20]. See also [117] and [161] (proof of a 'predatory state of mind' is required). Followed in *PT Ltd v Spuds Surf Chatswood Pty Ltd* [2013] NSWCA 446 [93]–[106] and *Donnelly v Australia and New Zealand Banking Group Ltd* [2014] NSWCA 145.
[200] [1983] 1 WLR 87, 94; on appeal [1985] 1 WLR 173 (CA).
[201] (1862) 4 De GF & J 401, 45 ER 1238. The weaker party was also dying.
[202] In *Portman Building Society v Dusangh* [2000] 2 All ER 221 (CA) 235 Ward LJ suggests that 'It may be that the absence of legal advice is not so much an essential freestanding requirement, but rather a powerful factor confirming the suspicion of nefarious dealing which the presence of advice would serve to dispel.' Thus absence of advice is not an element but a factor to be considered in determining whether morally culpable conduct occurred.
[203] Haste was an important factor in *Evans v Llewellin* (1787) 1 Cox 333, 340; 29 ER 1191, 1194 where a sale was set aside because 'the party was taken by surprise; he had not sufficient time to act with caution, and therefore though there was no actual fraud, it is something like fraud, for an undue advantage was taken of his situation'.
[204] *Alec Lobb (Garages) Ltd v Total Oil Great Britain Ltd* [1983] 1 WLR 87, 95.
[205] (1860) 8 HLC 481, 492; 11 ER 517.
[206] [1975] QB 326, 339; *Arrale v Costain Engineering Ltd* [1976] 2 Lloyd's Rep 98; *Levison v Patent Steam Carpet Cleaning Co Ltd* [1978] QB 69, 78–79.
[207] *Pakistan International Airline Corp v Times Travel (UK) Ltd* [2021] 3 WLR 727 (Sup Ct) [26].

7.86 Morally culpable conduct was also lacking in *Portman Building Society v Dusangh*.[209] An elderly illiterate man, with poor proficiency in English and on a low income, took out a £33,750 mortgage over his home in order to raise funds for his son's business venture. The father, son, and the building society were advised by the same solicitor. The son's business failed and the mortgagee building society sought to enforce the charge. The Court of Appeal found that the father was not entitled to rescission. There was no exploitation of the father by the son. Ward LJ stated: 'True it may be that the son gained all the advantage and the father took all the risk, but this cannot be stigmatized as impropriety. There was no exploitation of father by son such as would prick the conscience and tell the son that in all honour it was morally wrong and reprehensible.'[210] Similarly, there was no exploitation as between the building society and the father. Simon Brown LJ stated:

> I simply cannot accept that building societies are required to police transactions of this nature to ensure that parents (even poor and ignorant ones) are wise in seeking to assist their children ... [The father's] situation was not exploited by the building society. The building society did not act in a morally reprehensible manner.[211]

Similarly there was no moral culpability in a family's acceptance of a gift of practically all the property of a former employee who had lived with them for 56 years at the time of the gift.[212]

7.87 This requirement, which requires the claimant to establish some victimization or exploitation, may be contrasted with a literal interpretation of *Fry v Lane*,[213] which only requires the claimant to show (i) poverty and ignorance, (ii) sale at an undervalue, and (iii) lack of independent advice, before the onus is placed on the defendant to show that the transaction was fair, just, and reasonable.[214] On this formulation, the party seeking rescission is not required to prove any morally culpable conduct. But the modern approach is exemplified by *Boustany v Pigott* and the authorities discussed therein, and requires that exploitation be established before the bargain can become voidable. *Fry v Lane* is not to be read literally today.[215]

7.88 Impropriety may sometimes be inferred from unfairness of contractual terms, or gross undervalue, in the absence of an adequate explanation.[216] Where inferences of morally

---

[208] [1985] AC 1000 (PC—NZ) 1028. Doubts that inequality of bargaining power can itself be a ground for rescission were also expressed in *National Westminster Bank plc v Morgan* [1985] AC 686, 708 (Lord Scarman); *CTN Cash and Carry Ltd v Gallaher Ltd* [1994] 4 All ER 714 (CA) 717 (Steyn LJ).
[209] [2000] 2 All ER 221 (CA).
[210] *Portman Building Society v Dusangh* [2000] 2 All ER 221 (CA) 232.
[211] *Portman Building Society v Dusangh* [2000] 2 All ER 221 (CA) 229.
[212] *Evans v Lloyd* [2013] EWHC 1725 (Ch) [75]–[76].
[213] (1888) 40 ChD 312. This interpretation was followed in *Cresswell v Potter* [1978] 1 WLR 255n; *Backhouse v Backhouse* [1978] 1 WLR 243; *Watkin v Watson-Smith*, The Times, 3 July 1986; *Langton v Langton* [1995] 2 FLR 890.
[214] See also *Baker v Monk* (1864) 4 De GJ & S 388, 394; 46 ER 968 where an improvident transaction was set aside although the court did not wish to enter into the question of whether the stronger party's conduct was improper, and was content to believe that there was 'no actual moral fraud' on the part of the stronger party.
[215] For the view that treating *Fry v Lane* as articulating an independent ground for relief is both superfluous and perilous, N Bamforth, 'Unconscionability as a Vitiating Factor' [1995] LMCLQ 538, 547–48.
[216] *Credit Lyonnais Bank Nederland NV v Burch* [1997] 1 All ER 144 (CA) 153; *Hart v O'Connor* [1985] AC 1000 (PC—NZ) 1017–18; *Morley v Loughnan* [1893] 1 Ch 736, 754. See also *Blomley v Ryan* (1956) 99 CLR 362 (HCA)

culpable conduct are drawn from undervalue, the approaches in *Fry v Lane* and in *Boustany v Pigott* are not actually as far apart as may at first glance appear. Nonetheless, they still represent an important difference in emphasis, and could certainly lead to different results on the same facts.

(3) Third requirement: transaction overreaching and oppressive

The third requirement is that the resulting transaction has been not merely hard or improvident, but overreaching and oppressive.[217] This looks to the overall effect of the transaction.[218] It has been said that the transaction must be such that it 'shocks the conscience of the court'; it must call for an explanation.[219] The focus is on the inequality between the value of what the weaker party has transferred and what he has received in return.[220] The undervalue must be substantial or considerable.[221] The question is whether the contract was oppressive, not whether it was unreasonable.[222]

7.89

The fact that the transaction is on standard terms, for example a standard form guarantee and mortgage, will not absolve the stronger party if the terms operate oppressively in the particular circumstances. In *Burch*'s case it was said: 'It could not have helped the bank to say that it used its standard form. A mortgagee who uses such a form without regard to its impact on the individual case acts at his peril.'[223]

7.90

Care must be taken in assessing this requirement. It was not made out in *Portman Building Society v Dusangh*[224] where an elderly immigrant father mortgaged his home in order to

7.91

---

485. Cf *Kalsep Ltd v X-Flow BV*, *The Times*, 3 May 2001 where Pumfrey J refused to set aside 'an exceptionally improvident agreement, ignorantly and foolishly entered into'.

[217] *Fineland Investments Ltd v Pritchard* [2011] EWHC 113 (Ch) [81].
[218] For the view that *dicta* in Australian case law that this requirement is not required (*Blomley v Ryan* (1956) 99 CLR 362, 405) would not be followed in England and that there, unlike in the United States, the overall transaction must be overreaching and oppressive rather than just a particular aspect of it, see HG Beale (ed), *Chitty on Contracts* (34th edn, 2021) [10-165]. See also N Enonchong, *Duress, Undue Influence and Unconscionable Dealing* (3rd edn, 2018) [18-003].
[219] *Alec Lobb (Garages) Ltd v Total Oil Great Britain Ltd* [1983] 1 WLR 87, 94–95 (Peter Millett QC); *Credit Lyonnais Bank Nederland NV v Burch* [1997] 1 All ER 144 (CA) 152–53 (Millett LJ).
[220] *Adare Finance DAC v Yellowstone Capital Management SA* [2020] EWHC 2760 (Comm) [69], [74].
[221] *Clark v Malpas* (1862) 4 DeG F & J 401, 45 ER 1238 (ill man sold property for annuity and £100 on his death to whoever he would appoint; consideration may have been as low as one-quarter of true value); *Fry v Lane* (1888) 40 ChD 312, 318, 322–23 (an estate which was worth £425 at the time had been sold for £170); *Cresswell v Potter* [1978] 1 WLR 255n (wife transferred her interest in the matrimonial home for an indemnity against mortgage liability; there was substantial equity in the house); *Backhouse v Backhouse* [1978] 1 WLR 243 (wife transferred interest in the matrimonial home to estranged husband for a release of her liability on the mortgage); *Boustany v Piggott* (1995) 69 P & CR 298 (PC—Antigua and Barbuda) (prior lease was at $833 per month and included a covenant to repair; the new lease did not include the covenant and the rent was set at $1000 per month for a 10-year term with a 10-year option; the new lease was set aside); *Credit Lyonnais Bank Nederland NV v Burch* [1997] 1 All ER 144 (CA) (employee guaranteed employer's overdraft but had no stake in employer's business); *Lo Wo v Cheung Chan Ka* [2001] HKCA 302 (price offered to three illiterate elderly sisters was found to be ridiculous in view of the price which had been paid to the co-owner of the same flat).
[222] *Strydom v Vendside Limited* [2009] EWHC 2130 (QB) [39]. Cf *Adare Finance DAC v Yellowstone Capital Management SA* [2020] EWHC 2760 (Comm) [69] where it was held that it must be unfair and unreasonable.
[223] *Credit Lyonnais Bank Nederland NV v Burch* [1997] 1 All ER 144 (CA) 151.
[224] [2000] 2 All ER 221 (CA). Other recent cases where this requirement was not made out include *Mitchell v James* [2001] All ER 116 (sale of part of garage business); *Jones v Morgan* [2001] EWCA 995 (land transferred in expectation of future loans); *Singla v Bashir* [2002] EWHC 883 (sale of flat for reduced price, a right to occupy it for three years and a modest additional payment).

raise funds for his son's business venture. Simon Brown LJ concluded that '[t]he transaction, although improvident, was not "overreaching and oppressive." In short, the conscience of the court is not shocked'.[225]

7.92 An agreement is not oppressive merely because aspects of it turn out to a party's disadvantage;[226] the matter must be determined on the facts as they are at the time the contract is entered into.[227] Also, it is clear that inadequate consideration is of itself insufficient to vitiate a transaction,[228] for it 'is trite that equity will not rewrite an improvident contract where there is no disability on either side'.[229]

(4) Possible defence: counterparty shows that transaction was fair, just, and reasonable

7.93 According to the older authorities, the party against whom rescission is sought may sustain the transaction by showing that the transaction was 'fair, just and reasonable'.[230] This may be done by proving that the weaker party knew of the undervalue of the consideration that he was receiving and intended the transaction to be partly a gift[231] or, as discussed in Part 5, that his consent was not vitiated because he acted with the benefit of independent advice.

7.94 In assessing what is fair, just, and reasonable in relation to a transaction where the stronger party lends money to the weaker, the court has regard to the nature and degree of the risk run by the lender and any other relevant criterion, including whether there was any real bargaining between the parties.[232] It has also been regarded as relevant that the stronger party was unaware that he was obtaining the property at undervalue, that the weaker party relied on the advice of a parent, and that the weaker party could not have afforded independent professional advice even if it had been insisted on.[233] The claimant's delay in seeking rescission is another factor that also appears to have been treated as relevant to this inquiry.[234]

7.95 There does not appear to be a modern reported case in which the claimant has succeeded in proving the other three requirements set out earlier, so as to establish a *prima facie* claim to rescind, but has been denied relief because the defendant has been able to show that the transaction was fair, just, and reasonable. It is difficult to contemplate a situation where a party has been shown to have exploited the weakness of another in a morally culpable manner to acquire property at a substantial undervalue, and yet the court concludes that nonetheless the transaction was fair, just, and reasonable.

---

[225] *Portman Building Society v Dusangh* [2000] 2 All ER 221 (CA), 229.
[226] *Irvani v Irvani* [2000] 1 Lloyd's Rep 412 (CA) 425.
[227] *Strydom v Vendside Limited* [2009] EWHC 2130 (QB) [39].
[228] *Wood v Abrey* (1818) 3 Madd 417, 423; 56 ER 558, 560; *Longmate v Ledger* (1860) 2 Giff 157, 163; 66 ER 67, 69; *O'Rorke v Bolingbroke* (1877) 2 App Cas 814, 834 ('Standing alone, mere undervalue is worth little').
[229] *White and Carter (Councils) Ltd v McGregor* [1962] AC 413, 445; *Multiservice Bookbinding v Marden* [1979] Ch 84, 112 (Browne-Wilkinson J).
[230] *Earl of Aylesford v Morris* (1873) 8 Ch App 484 (CA) 490–91; *Cresswell v Potter* [1978] 1 WLR 255n, 260.
[231] *Whalley v Whalley* (1821) 3 Bligh 1, 4 ER 506.
[232] *Earl of Aylesford v Morris* (1873) 8 Ch App 484 (CA) 496.
[233] *O'Rorke v Bolingbroke* (1877) 2 App Cas 814, 835, 837.
[234] *Cresswell v Potter* [1978] 1 WLR 255n, 260.

7.96 This defence only appears to have a real role to play if the requirements for setting aside a transaction are the more limited ones established in *Fry v Lane*.[235] It then functions as a safety-valve. But, as explained earlier, the law has moved on and now also requires the weaker party to prove unconscionable exploitation or victimization.[236] It is suggested that for the stronger party to prove that the transaction was 'fair, just, and reasonable' will rarely if ever be possible once a *prima facie* case is made out that the transaction is an unconscionable bargain. If this defence continues to exist, it is probably confined to cases where the inference of advantage taking or exploitation is drawn only from undervalue.[237] In a case of this kind, the requirement affords the stronger party an appropriate opportunity to show that the transaction ought to be upheld.

(5) Role of independent advice

7.97 Absence of independent advice, coupled with a special disadvantage and undervalue, has been held to have the consequence that the transaction calls for an explanation by the stronger party.[238] Yet it is not a requirement for relief: 'Such advice is neither always necessary nor always sufficient. It is not a panacea. The result does not depend mechanically on the presence or absence of legal advice.'[239] But absence of independent advice, although not a strict requirement, continues to be an important factor in the modern authorities. The advice expected depends on the nature of the transaction. Megarry J noted in *Cresswell v Potter* that:

> ... [t]he absence of the aid of a solicitor is ... of especial significance if a conveyancing matter is involved. The more usual it is to have a solicitor, the more striking will be his absence, and the more closely will the courts scrutinise what was done.[240]

7.98 Absence of independent advice is a factor that cuts across a number of the points discussed earlier. If the supposedly weaker party had the benefit of suitable independent advice, his disadvantage relative to the other party may be mitigated or removed.[241] The presence of independent advice may also make it more difficult for the claimant to establish that the defendant exploited his weakness in a morally culpable manner.[242] Finally, the fact that the weaker party was independently advised may also assist the defendant in convincing the court that the transaction ought to stand as one that was fair, just, and reasonable.[243]

---

[235] (1888) 40 ChD 312: (1) poverty and ignorance; (2) sale at an undervalue; and (3) lack of independent advice.
[236] See paras [7.80]ff.
[237] See paras [7.88]ff.
[238] *Fry v Lane* (1888) 40 ChD 312, 321–24; *Earl of Aylesford v Morris* (1873) 8 Ch App 484, 491–92, 495.
[239] *Credit Lyonnais Bank Nederland NV v Burch* [1997] 1 All ER 144 (CA) 156 (Millett LJ).
[240] [1978] 1 WLR 255n, 258.
[241] In *Jones v Morgan* [2001] EWCA 995 it was held at [40] that 'it is for a solicitor to advise the naïve, the trusting or the unbusinesslike in their dealings with the more astute. In such a case the client relies on the solicitor to protect his interests; and, if the solicitor is competent and fulfils his role, the imbalance which would otherwise exist by reason of the client's naïveté, trust and lack of business experience is redressed. The parties meet on equal terms, at least in that respect'.
[242] See paras [7.80]ff; *Alec Lobb (Garages) Ltd v Total Oil Great Britain Ltd* [1983] 1 WLR 87, 95; on appeal [1885] 1 WLR 173 (CA).
[243] See paras [7.93]ff.

7.99 What constitutes independent advice is considered in some detail in Chapter 6 in the context of undue influence.[244] Similar principles ought to apply in this context.[245] Where one lawyer acts for both parties, the weaker party is unlikely to be considered to have received independent advice. One lawyer acted for both vendor and purchaser in a number of cases where a transaction was set aside as an unconscionable bargain.[246] Similarly, where it was unclear which party a lawyer had acted for, a lease was set aside although the lawyer who had drafted it 'forcibly pointed out … [its] disadvantages' to the weaker party.[247] The experience of the lawyer who has advised the weaker party and the quality of the advice given have also been material in some of the authorities.[248]

7.100 The mere opportunity to obtain independent advice is generally not sufficient. Megarry J observed in *Cresswell v Potter*:

> … what matters, I think, is not whether [the weaker party] could have obtained proper advice but whether in fact she had it; and she did not. Nobody, of course, can be compelled to obtain independent advice; but I do not think that someone who seeks to uphold what is, to him, an advantageous conveyancing transaction can do so merely by saying that the other party could have obtained independent advice, unless something has been done to bring to the notice of that other party the true nature of the transaction and the need for advice.[249]

Megarry J concluded that if the weaker party was provided with information as to the true nature of the transaction and a recommendation that she ought to consider getting independent advice, and that party proceeded 'in the teeth of that information' to enter into the transaction, that situation may be treated as one where independent advice had been provided.[250]

7.101 However, whether urging the weaker party to seek advice would assist the stronger party depends on the particular circumstances of the case. By way of contrast, in *Credit Lyonnais Bank Nederland NV v Burch*[251] the court held that the bank's admonitions to seek independent advice did not suffice. Nourse LJ stated that the mortgagor needed at least to have actually received such advice.

7.102 Even actual independent advice may be insufficient to save a transaction. Some transactions are so tainted or improvident that they may not be upheld, even if independent advice was received.[252]

---

[244] See Chap 6, paras [6.115]–[6.118].
[245] In *Credit Lyonnais Bank Nederland NV v Burch* [1997] 1 All ER 144 (CA) 156 Millett LJ stated that in unconscionable bargain and undue influence cases 'the role of the independent advisor, while not identical, is not dissimilar'.
[246] *Longmate v Ledger* (1860) 2 Giff 157, 66 ER 67; *Clark v Malpas* (1862) 4 De GF & J 401, 45 ER 1238; *Baker v Monk* (1864) 4 De GJ & S 388 (CA), 46 ER 968; *Fry v Lane* (1888) 40 ChD 312.
[247] *Boustany v Pigott* (1995) 69 P & CR 298 (PC—Antigua and Barbuda) 304.
[248] *Fry v Lane* (1888) 40 ChD 312, 323 (inexperienced solicitor who acted for both parties did not properly protect the vendors); *Multiservice Bookbinding v Marden* [1979] Ch 84, 111 ('the borrowers were represented by independent solicitors of repute').
[249] *Cresswell v Potter* [1978] 1 WLR 255, 259; *Chagos Islanders v Attorney-General* [2003] EWHC 2222 [560] (issue not considered on appeal [2004] EWCA 997).
[250] [1978] 1 WLR 255, 260; *K v K* [1976] 2 NZLR 31, 38; cf *Moffat v Moffat* [1984] 1 NZLR 600 (CA).
[251] [1997] 1 All ER 144 (CA) 152.
[252] *Alec Lobb (Garages) Ltd v Total Oil Great Britain Ltd* [1985] 1 WLR 173 (CA) 182; *Boustany v Pigott* (1995) 69 P & CR 298 (PC—Antigua and Barbuda). Also, *Credit Lyonnais Bank Nederland NV v Burch* [1997] 1 All ER 144 (CA) 153 (Millett LJ): 'The cases show that it is not sufficient that [the weaker party] should have received independent advice unless she has acted on that advice.'

(6) Other Commonwealth jurisdictions

Appellate courts in Australia,[253] New Zealand,[254] and Canada[255] have each developed a more generalized doctrine of unconscionable conduct as a ground for rescission. As was noted at the beginning of the discussion, English law has taken a more conservative path, and has so far tended to restrict rather than expand the scope of this ground for rescission.[256]

7.103

---

[253] *Blomley v Ryan* (1956) 99 CLR 362, 405, 415; *Commercial Bank of Australia v Amadio* (1983) 151 CLR 447, 474; *Louth v Diprose* (1992) 175 CLR 621; *Kakavas v Crown Melbourne Ltd* (2013) 250 CLR 392; 298 ALR 35 (HCA). See also ss 20–22 of the Australian Consumer Law which replaced ss 51AA, AB, and AC of the Trade Practices Act 1974. Section 20 prohibits corporations engaging in 'conduct that is unconscionable within the meaning of the unwritten law, from time to time'. Sections 21 and 22 prohibit unconscionable conduct in supplying goods and services in consumer and business transactions respectively, and identify factors that the courts may take into account in assessing whether conduct is unconscionable.

[254] *Nichols v Jessup* [1986] 1 NZLR 226 (CA).

[255] *Morrison v Coast Finance Ltd* (1965) 55 DLR (2d) 710 (BCCA) 713; *Harry v Kreutziger* (1978) 95 DLR (3d) 231 (BCCA) (question is whether the transaction, seen as a whole, is sufficiently divergent from community standards of commercial morality); *Simpson v Moffat Communications Ltd* [1983] BCJ No 2089 (BCCA); *Gindis v Brisbourne* (2000) 72 BCLR (3d) 19 (BCCA); *Braut v Stec* (2005) 51 BCLR (4th) 15 (BCCA).

[256] See also para [7.72]. For a comparative analysis see D Capper, 'The unconscionable bargain in the common law world' (2010) LQR 403.

8
Conflict of Interest

A. Introduction	8.01	(2) Disclosure and advice	8.42
B. Transactions with Fiduciaries	8.03	(3) Substantive fairness	8.45
(1) Nature and basis of the fair-dealing rule	8.05	(4) Implication of counterparty	8.46
		D. Bribery	8.49
(2) Scope of the fair-dealing rule	8.11	(1) Rescission at law and in equity	8.51
(3) Compliance with the fair-dealing rule	8.17	(2) Elements of bribery	8.52
C. Double Employment	8.34	(3) Implication of counterparty	8.61
(1) Consent to adverse duty or interest	8.38	E. Causation Irrelevant	8.72

A. Introduction

8.01 This chapter is concerned to identify the circumstances in which transactions may be set aside because a fiduciary has allowed an adverse interest or duty to cloud the single-minded loyalty he owes his principal. These may be transactions between a fiduciary and his principal (Part B), or transactions that are in some way mediated by a fiduciary (Part C).

8.02 This chapter is not concerned with attempts by trustees to purchase from or sell to their trust and other transactions regulated by the self-dealing rule. Those transactions are void rather than voidable and so there is no question of rescission.[1]

B. Transactions with Fiduciaries

8.03 Transactions between a fiduciary and his principal are regulated by the fair-dealing rule. These transactions are 'not voidable ex debito justitæ, but can be set aside by the beneficiary unless the trustee can show that he has taken no advantage of his position and has made full disclosure to the beneficiary, and that the transaction was fair'.[2] The onus falling on a fiduciary seeking to uphold a transaction with his principal is not a light one. The fiduciary 'must show to demonstration, for that must not be left in doubt, that no industry he was bound to exert would have got a better bargain' for his principal.[3]

8.04 These cases have sometimes been treated under the rubric of abuse of confidence, but that term is potentially misleading.[4] Transactions may be avoided under the fair-dealing rule even though the fiduciary has behaved with scrupulous honesty, and even though the

---

[1] See Chap 1, paras [1.72]–[1.76].
[2] *Tito v Waddell (No 2)* [1977] Ch 106, 241. In Australia, *Clay v Clay* (2001) 202 CLR 410 [50]–[51].
[3] *Gibson v Jeyes* (1801) 6 Ves 266, 271; 31 ER 1044, 1047.
[4] *Bank of Credit and Commerce International SA v Aboody* [1990] 1 QB 923 (CA) 962.

failure to disclose a material fact was inadvertent.[5] It is also not necessary to the operation of the rule that the fiduciary sought or obtained any unfair personal advantage in the dealing.[6] If proper disclosure has not been made, a transaction may be set aside even though the price was fair and the terms were such as might have been agreed between parties dealing at arm's length.[7]

(1) Nature and basis of the fair-dealing rule

Basis of the rule

Where a fiduciary deals with his principal in circumstances involving a conflict between his personal interest and his duty towards his principal, there is a particular danger that he will be tempted to favour his own interests by disregarding his duty to a greater or lesser extent. The fiduciary's bias may not be conscious, and it may not manifest itself in a manner that is easily susceptible of proof. It is because of the danger of abuse and the difficulty of proof that the burden of upholding such transactions is thrown onto the fiduciary.[8] Transactions are avoided under the fair-dealing rule not because there has necessarily been any misconduct in the particular case, but because of a concern to protect principals as a class from exploitation by fiduciaries as a class.[9] **8.05**

The burden that falls on a fiduciary seeking to uphold a transaction with his principal requires him to prove that he has carried out whatever duties he may have owed the principal in relation to that transaction.[10] In most cases what is required is that the fiduciary make full disclosure and, where his role is advisory, that he give such advice as he would if the principal were dealing with a third party. The concern in such cases is that the fiduciary should not deal from a position of informational advantage.[11] **8.06**

Relationship with presumed undue influence

The origins of the fair-dealing rule are intertwined with the origins of the doctrine of presumed undue influence, and the distinctions drawn between the two in the modern cases were not always observed in earlier times.[12] In practice they frequently overlap, most commonly in cases involving solicitors, who typically stand in a fiduciary relationship with their clients and who are also presumed to enjoy influence over them. In cases of overlap there may be two independent grounds for rescission. **8.07**

But while these doctrines may sometimes yield the same result, the basis on which a transaction may be avoided for unfair dealing is 'quite independent of the existence of undue **8.08**

---

[5] *Ex p James* (1803) 8 Ves 337, 345; 32 ER 385, 388; *Pisani v A-G for Gibraltar* (1874) LR 5 PC 516 (Gibraltar) 538; *Bristol and West Building Society v Mothew* [1998] Ch 1 (CA) 18.
[6] *Ex p Lacey* (1802) 6 Ves 626, 627; 31 ER 1228, 1229; *Ex p James* (1803) 8 Ves 337, 348; 32 ER 385, 389.
[7] *Aberdeen Railway Co v Blaikie* (1854) 1 Mac 461, 472; *McPherson v Watt* (1877) 3 App Cas 254 (HL Sc) 264.
[8] *Aberdeen Railway Co v Blaikie* (1854) 1 Mac 461, 472; *Bray v Ford* [1896] AC 44, 51.
[9] *CIBC Mortgages plc v Pitt* [1994] 1 AC 200, 209.
[10] *McMaster v Byrne* [1952] 1 All ER 1362 (PC—Canada) 1368.
[11] See M Conaglan, 'A Re-appraisal of the Fiduciary Self-dealing and Fair-dealing Rules' [2006] CLJ 366.
[12] Eg *Edwards v Meyrick* (1842) 2 Hare 60, 67 ER 25; *Rhodes v Bates* (1865) LR 1 Ch App 252; *Tate v Williamson* (1866) LR 2 Ch App 55.

influence'.[13] The fair-dealing rule is largely concerned to ensure that in dealing with their principals, fiduciaries do not enjoy informational advantages by reason of their position. By contrast, the doctrine of undue influence is concerned to ensure that the personal influence or ascendancy of one person over another is not abused.[14] Not all fiduciaries enjoy personal influence over their principals.[15] There is no presumption of undue influence, for instance, between principal and agent.[16] Equally, many of the relationships that would support a presumption of undue influence are not fiduciary in nature. Moreover, the fair-dealing rule requires that to uphold the transaction the fiduciary prove that the terms were not disadvantageous to the principal,[17] or else that a gift was intended.[18] With presumed undue influence it is the rescinding claimant who must prove that the transaction 'is not readily explicable by the relationship of the parties', which is usually done by reference to its disadvantageous terms.[19]

Contractual disability

8.09 While it is possible to take a contrary view,[20] the fair-dealing rule is best viewed as a contractual disability inherent in the relationship between the parties.[21] A fiduciary is disabled from conclusively contracting with his principal in relation to matters falling within the scope of his engagement except where the requirements of the rule are satisfied. As Megarry J put it in *Tito v Waddell*, 'the fair-dealing rule is essentially a rule of equity that certain persons (including trustees) are subject to certain consequences if they carry through certain transactions without, where appropriate, complying with certain requirements'.[22]

8.10 The failure of a fiduciary to make full disclosure or to give appropriate advice may also amount to a breach of fiduciary duty, and the principal may be entitled to compensatory relief on this basis.[23] But the bare attempt by a fiduciary to transact with his principal does not necessarily amount to a breach of duty,[24] and the fact that the requirements of the fair-dealing rule are not satisfied does not necessarily mean that the fiduciary has breached a fiduciary duty in a technical sense sufficient to support a claim for compensatory relief.[25] Quite simply, the entitlement to avoid the contract does not depend on any breach of an

---

[13] *Bank of Credit and Commerce International SA v Aboody* [1990] 1 QB 923 (CA) 963. In *CIBC Mortgages plc v Pitt* [1994] 1 AC 200, 209 Lord Browne-Wilkinson suggested that the apparent distinctions between the two doctrines might need to be reconsidered, but that possibility has since been rejected in *Royal Bank of Scotland plc v Etridge (No 2)* [2002] 2 AC 773 [24]. See further M Conaglan, *Fiduciary Loyalty* (2010) 236–41.
[14] [2002] 2 AC 773 [6], [8].
[15] Eg *Pisani v A-G for Gibraltar* (1874) LR 5 PC 516 (Gibraltar) 537; *Allison v Clayhills* (1907) 97 LT 709, 714; *Moody v Cox* [1917] 2 Ch 71 (CA) 79–80.
[16] *Re Coomber* [1911] 1 Ch 723 (CA).
[17] *Thomson v Eastwood* (1877) 2 App Cas 215 (HL Ir) 236.
[18] *Coles v Trecothick* (1804) 9 Ves 234, 248; 32 ER 592, 598; *Hatch v Hatch* (1804) 9 Ves 292, 297; 32 ER 615, 617.
[19] *Royal Bank of Scotland plc v Etridge (No 2)* [2002] 2 AC 773 [21].
[20] M Conaglan, 'Equitable Compensation for Breach of Fiduciary Dealing Rules' (2003) 119 LQR 246.
[21] *Tito v Waddell (No 2)* [1977] Ch 106, 248; *Movitex Ltd v Bulfield* [1988] BCLC 104; *JJ Harrison (Properties) Ltd v Harrison* [2002] 1 BCLC 162 (CA) [33] but cf *Gwembe Valley Development Co Ltd* [2004] 1 BCLC 131 (CA) [107]–[108]. This is how the rule has traditionally been understood: eg J Hill, *The Law Relating to Trustees* (1845) 554–61.
[22] *Tito v Waddell (No 2)* [1977] Ch 106, 249; *JJ Harrison (Properties) Ltd v Harrison* [2002] 1 BCLC 162 (CA) [33].
[23] *Swindle v Harrison* [1997] 4 All ER 705 (CA); *Longstaff v Birtles* [2002] 1 WLR 470 (CA).
[24] *Tito v Waddell (No 2)* [1977] Ch 106, 248–49.
[25] *Gwembe Valley Development Co Ltd v Koshy (No 3)* [2004] 1 BCLC 131 (CA) [143]. See also P Finn, *Fiduciary Obligations* (1977) [471]: 'The term "duty" in the [no conflicts rule] is used in no technical sense. It does not mean, for example, that the existence of a fiduciary relationship depends upon it being shown that the undertaking given embodies duties of a legally enforceable character.'

equitable duty on the part of the fiduciary. Given their common provenance, it is not surprising that the fair-dealing rule should in this way resemble the doctrine in accordance with which contracts are avoided for undue influence.[26]

(2) Scope of the fair-dealing rule
Relationships to which the rule applies
While most of the reported cases involve dealings between trustees and their beneficiaries and solicitors and their clients, the fair-dealing rule applies to transactions involving fiduciaries of all sorts. At the highest level of generality, a fiduciary has been said to be 'someone who has undertaken to act for or on behalf of another in a particular matter in circumstances which give rise to a relation of trust and confidence. The distinguishing obligation of a fiduciary is the obligation of loyalty'.[27] As a consequence, a fiduciary must not allow an unauthorized and conflicting duty or interest to cloud his dedication to his principal.[28]

8.11

Transactions falling outside of the scope of the relationship
The fair-dealing rule does not apply to transactions falling outside of the scope of the fiduciary relationship in question.[29] In *Allison v Clayhills*[30] Parker J gave the example of a solicitor engaged to conduct a slander action who meets his client on the hunting field and bargains and buys from him a horse, each relying on his own knowledge of horseflesh. The judge said that 'this transaction will stand on the same footing as a transaction between strangers, because the matter is entirely outside the confidential relationship between the parties, and the solicitor owes his client no duty whatever in the particular matter'.[31]

8.12

The critical question is whether the transaction entails a conflict between the fiduciary's duty to his principal and his personal interest, and so it is always necessary to determine whether the fiduciary owes his principal any duty in relation to the transaction in question.[32] The cases largely fall into two categories.[33] The first includes those where the fiduciary has in the course of his engagement acquired knowledge that is material to the transaction, usually knowledge about the asset he is purchasing from his principal.[34] Here the fiduciary's duty is to disclose what he knows.[35] The second includes cases where the principal is entitled to be advised by the fiduciary in relation to the transaction.[36] It is not necessary to the application

8.13

---

[26] *Agnew v Länsförsäkringsbolagens AB* [2001] 1 AC 223, 264–65; *Pesticcio v Huet* [2004] EWCA Civ 372 [20].
[27] *Bristol and West Buildings Society v Mothew* [1998] Ch 1 (CA) 18.
[28] *Aberdeen Railway Co v Blaikie* (1854) 1 Mac 461, 471–72; *Parker v McKenna* (1874) LR 10 Ch App 96, 118; *Bray v Ford* [1896] AC 44, 51.
[29] *Montesquieu v Sandys* (1811) 18 Ves 302, 313; 34 ER 331, 336; *Cane v Allen* (1814) 2 Dow 289, 297; 3 ER 869, 872; *Jones v Thomas* (1837) 2 Y & C Ex 498, 519–20; 160 ER 493, 502; *Edwards v Meyrick* (1842) 2 Hare 60, 68–70; 67 ER 25, 28–29; *Knights v Majoribanks* (1849) 2 Mac & G 10, 12–13; 42 ER 4, 5–6; *Holman v Loynes* (1854) 4 De G M & G 270, 281; 43 ER 510, 515; *McPherson v Watt* (1877) 3 App Cas 254 (HL Sc) 270.
[30] (1907) 97 LT 709, 712.
[31] (1907) 97 LT 709, 712.
[32] (1907) 97 LT 709, 711–12; *Demerara Bauxite Company, Limited v Hubbard* [1923] AC 673 (PC—British Guiana) 675–76.
[33] It may be that the fiduciary enjoys or is presumed to enjoy a personal influence or ascendancy over the client, in which case the doctrine of undue influence may also be engaged.
[34] Eg *Cane v Allen* (1814) 2 Dow 289, 294; 3 ER 869, 871; *McPherson v Watt* (1877) 3 App Cas 254 (HL Sc) 271.
[35] *Allison v Clayhills* (1907) 97 LT 709, 712; *McMaster v Byrne* [1952] 1 All ER 1362 (PC—Canada) 1368.
[36] Eg *Montesquieu v Sandys* (1811) 18 Ves 302, 313; 34 ER 331, 336; *Holman v Loynes* (1854) 4 De G M & G 270, 43 ER 510; *McPherson v Watt* (1877) 3 App Cas 254 (HL Sc) 271–72.

of the rule that the fiduciary has been specifically instructed in relation to the transaction or that he is entitled to charge for his services.[37]

Termination of relationship

8.14 Some of the early cases tended to suggest that a fiduciary might only transact with his principal if the relationship is first dissolved by common consent,[38] but that idea was soon repudiated.[39] A fiduciary may transact with his principal during the subsistence of their formal relationship provided the principal is put at arm's length for the purposes of the transaction.

8.15 Conversely, the fair-dealing rule may continue to apply to transactions concluded after the formal relationship between the parties has been terminated.[40] It has been said to be impossible precisely to define the circumstances in which this will occur.[41] Most commonly, however, it is where the fiduciary continues to enjoy the benefit of knowledge gained in the course of his engagement.[42] It may also be that the relationship between the parties has been such that the principal is entitled to expect that the fiduciary will advise him in relation to the transaction, for example in the case of a regular client.[43]

Types of transactions to which the rule applies

8.16 Most of the cases to which the fair-dealing rule has been applied have involved contracts of sale. In *Johnson v EBS Pensioner Trustees Ltd*,[44] which involved a contract of guarantee, the defendant solicitors argued that the rule only applies to contracts of sale. But while this argument found favour with Patten J,[45] the Court of Appeal held there to be no such restriction.[46] The rule would seem to apply whatever the nature of the transaction.

(3) Compliance with the fair-dealing rule

8.17 A transaction between fiduciary and principal will only stand if the fiduciary affirmatively proves that it was a fair one,[47] or, as Lord St Leonards LC put it in *Lewis v Hillman*, 'open and fair, and free from all objection'.[48] This commonly requires the fiduciary to prove four things: (i) that the principal consented to the fiduciary having an adverse interest; (ii) that the fiduciary disclosed all facts material to his principal's decision; (iii) that the transaction

---

[37] *McPherson v Watt* (1877) 3 App Cas 254 (HL Sc) 262; *Allison v Clayhills* (1907) 97 LT 709, 711; *McMaster v Byrne* [1952] 1 All ER 1362 (PC—Canada).
[38] *Gibson v Jeyes* (1801) 6 Ves 266, 277; 31 ER 1044, 1049; *Re Lacey* (1802) 6 Ves 625, 626; 31 ER 1228, 1228; *Ex p James* (1803) 8 Ves 337, 348; 32 ER 385, 389.
[39] *Coles v Trecothick* (1804) 9 Ves 234, 246; 32 ER 592, 597; *Morse v Royal* (1806) 12 Ves 355, 372–73; 33 ER 134, 140–41; *Cane v Allen* (1814) 2 Dow 289, 294; 3 ER 869, 871.
[40] *Demerara Bauxite Company, Limited v Hubbard* [1923] AC 673 (PC—British Guiana) 675–76; *McMaster v Byrne* [1952] 1 All ER 1362 (PC—Canada) 1367–68.
[41] *McMaster v Byrne* [1952] 1 All ER 1362 (PC—Canada) 1368.
[42] *Re Bole's & British Land Co's Contract* (1902) 71 LJ Ch 130; *Allison v Clayhills* (1907) 97 LT 709, 712.
[43] *McMaster v Byrne* [1952] 1 All ER 1362 (PC—Canada) 1367–68; *Longstaff v Birtles* [2002] 1 WLR 470 (CA). See the discussion of these cases in M Conaglan, *Fiduciary Loyalty* (2010) 190–95.
[44] [2002] Lloyd's Rep PN 309 (CA).
[45] (ChD 8 March 2001) [42].
[46] [2002] Lloyd's Rep PN 309 (CA) [48], [50], [67].
[47] *CIBC Mortgages plc v Pitt* [1994] 1 AC 200, 209.
[48] *Lewis v Hillman* (1852) 3 HLC 606, 629; 10 ER 239, 249.

was substantively fair or that a gift was intended; and (iv) where the fiduciary's role involves giving advice, that the principal received disinterested advice. These will be discussed in turn.

Consent to adverse interest

The first requirement is that the fiduciary prove that the principal consented to the fiduciary having an adverse interest in the transaction. Often it will be obvious to the principal that he is dealing with his fiduciary and his consent will be implicit in his willingness to deal.[49] But there have been several cases where the principal did not appreciate that he was dealing with his fiduciary instead of a third party, or where he did not appreciate the extent of his fiduciary's interest.[50] Where it is not obvious, full disclosure of the nature and extent of the interest is necessary; it is not enough that the fiduciary merely discloses that he has an interest or makes statements apt to put the principal on enquiry.[51] Provided rescission has not become barred, a contract concluded without fully informed consent to the adverse interest may be avoided without further question.

8.18

The informed consent requirement is most often considered in relation to transactions involving companies and their directors.[52] A transaction between a company and one of its directors, or one in which a director is materially interested, is liable to be set aside in equity at the instance of the company unless the director discloses the nature and extent of his interest and the company approves the transaction.[53] Equity requires that the director disclose his interest to the shareholders in general meeting and that they approve it,[54] disclosure to the board alone being deemed inadequate because the whole board would not be in a position to exercise independent and unbiased judgement in the matter.[55]

8.19

With important exceptions where shareholder approval remains mandatory,[56] this equitable rule is abrogated by section 180(1) of the Companies Act 2006 where the conflict is authorized by the board and also where the director sufficiently discloses his interest.[57] Disclosure must be made in advance either at a meeting of the board or by written notice

8.20

---

[49] *Kregor v Hollins* (1913) 109 LT 225 (CA) 230 (a bribery case); *Bristol and West Building Society v Mothew* [1998] Ch 1 (CA) 19; *Pedashenko v Blacktown City Council* (1996) 39 NSWLR 189, 203.

[50] *Randall v Errington* (1805) 10 Ves 423, 426; 32 ER 909, 910; *Lewis v Hillman* (1852) 3 HLC 607, 630; 10 ER 239, 249; *McPherson v Watt* (1877) 3 App Cas 254 (HL Sc); *Fullwood v Hurley* [1928] 1 KB 498 (CA); *Swindle v Harrison* [1997] 4 All ER 705 (CA); *Johnson v EBS Pensioner Trustees Ltd* [2002] Lloyd's Rep PN 309 (CA); *Hurstanger Ltd v Wilson* [2008] Bus LR 216 (CA) [44]. In Australia, *Maguire v Makaronis* (1997) 188 CLR 449.

[51] *Hurstanger Ltd v Wilson* [2008] Bus LR 216 (CA) [34]–[35].

[52] See generally RC Nolan, 'Directors' Self-interested Dealings: Liabilities and Remedies' [1999] CfiLR 235.

[53] *Transvaal Lands Co v New Belgium (Transvaal) Land and Development Co* [1914] 2 Ch 488 (CA); *Hely-Hutchinson v Brayhead Ltd* [1968] 1 QB 549 (CA) 585, 589, 594; *Guinness plc v Saunders* [1988] BCLC 607 (CA) 612–13.

[54] *Aberdeen Railway Co v Blaikie* (1854) 1 Mac 461, 471–72; *North-West Transportation Co Ltd v Beatty* (1887) 12 App Cas 589 (PC—Canada) 593–94.

[55] *Benson v Heathorn* (1842) 1 Y&CCC 326, 342–43; 62 ER 909, 916–17; *Imperial Mercantile Credit Association v Coleman* (1871) LR 6 Ch App 556, 567–68; *Gray v New Augarita Porcupine Mines Ltd* [1952] 3 DLR 1 (PC—Canada) 13.

[56] Companies Act 2006, ss 188 to 210 (eg long-term service contracts, substantial property transactions, loans to directors). The consequences of not obtaining shareholder approval in such cases are themselves regulated by the 2006 Act.

[57] Section 180 brought into the primary legislation, with some revisions, the approach previously contained in regs 85–86 of Table A under the Companies Act 1985. The abrogation is subject to contrary provision in a company's constitution but this is uncommon if not unknown.

to all the other directors.[58] The 2006 Act clarifies that a director need not disclose interests of which the other directors are aware or of which they ought reasonably to be aware.[59] The contract must be presented for consideration and approval and not as a fait accompli.[60] The nature and extent of the interest must be disclosed in terms sufficient to allow the board to make an informed decision;[61] it is not enough for a director to simply state that he has an interest.[62] It is no longer the case that disclosure must be made at a board meeting.[63] While the Companies Act 2006 regulates the disclosure that must be made to preclude rescission, where the legislative requirements are not met it is the general law that supplies the right to rescind.[64]

Complete disclosure

8.21 The second requirement is that the fiduciary prove that he dealt with his principal openly by making complete disclosure. This requirement is strictly upheld. If proper disclosure is not made, the transaction may be set aside even though it was substantively fair,[65] even though the failure to disclose was inadvertent,[66] and even though full disclosure would not have made a difference to the principal's decision.[67]

8.22 The disclosure requirement has been said to extend to 'everything that is material, or may be material, to the judgement of his client', disclosure of which must of course be made 'before the transaction is completed'.[68] What is required will differ from case to case, but commonly includes any fact bearing on the contract price or the other terms,[69] and any fact bearing on the character of the asset in question in the case of a sale. The extent of the disclosure that is required can depend on the sophistication and intelligence of the principal.[70]

8.23 The test for materiality in this context is an objective one in that the fiduciary must disclose all facts that would be material to the decision of a reasonable man whether to enter a transaction of the kind in question.[71] Materiality is not to be determined subjectively by

---

[58] Companies Act 2006, ss 177(2), 184 (notice in writing) and 185 (general notice). Disclosure to a committee of the board is not sufficient: *Guinness plc v Saunders* [1988] BCLC 607 (CA); *Gwembe Valley Development Co Ltd v Koshy (No 3)* [2004] 1 BCLC 131 (CA) [51], [59]; both decided under the Companies Act 1985.

[59] Companies Act 2006, s 177(6)(b). As to the position under earlier legislation, see *Woolworths Ltd v Kelly* (1991) 4 ACSR 431 (NSWCA) and *Lee Panavision Ltd v Lee Lighting Ltd* [1992] BCLC 22 (CA) 33. A director will also comply with s 177 if he does not disclose an interest of which he is not aware unless he ought reasonably to be aware of it, and he will also comply with s 177 if the interest is one which cannot reasonably be regarded as likely to give rise to a conflict of interest.

[60] *Re Nuneaton Borough AFC Ltd (No 2)* [1991] BCC 44, 59–60.

[61] *Fairford Water Ski Club Ltd v Cohoon* [2021] BCC 498 (CA) [45]. Cf *Demite Ltd v Protec Health Ltd* [1998] BCC 638, 649; *Clydebank Football Club Ltd v Steedman* 2002 SLT 109, 116–17.

[62] *Gray v New Augarita Mines Ltd* [1952] 3 DLR 1 (PC—Canada) 14.

[63] Companies Act 2006, s 177(2)(a); *Fairford Water Ski Club Ltd v Cohoon* [2021] BCC 498 (CA) [31].

[64] *Hely-Hutchinson v Brayhead Ltd* [1968] 1 QB 549 (CA) 589, 594; *Guinness plc v Saunders* [1990] 2 AC 663, 697; *Fairford Water Ski Club Ltd v Cohoon* [2021] BCC 498 (CA) [28].

[65] *Ex p Lacey* (1802) 6 Ves 626, 31 ER 1228; *McPherson v Watt* (1877) 3 App Cas 254 (HL Sc) 264.

[66] *Bristol and West Building Society v Mothew* [1998] Ch 1 (CA) 18.

[67] See para [8.72].

[68] *Moody v Cox* [1917] 2 Ch 71 (CA) 80.

[69] Eg *Dougan v MacPherson* [1902] AC 197 (HL Sc) (a valuation); *Moody v Cox* [1917] 2 Ch 71 (CA) (a valuation); *Demerara Bauxite Company, Limited v Hubbard* [1923] AC 673 (PC—British Guiana) (a rival offer); *JJ Harrison (Properties) Ltd v Harrison* [2002] 1 BCLC 162 (CA) (a valuation); *Gwembe Valley Development Co Ltd v Koshy (No 3)* [2004] 1 BCLC 131 (CA) (source and scale of profit). In Australia, *Blackham v Haythorpe* (1917) 23 CLR 156 (probability that Crown would purchase at a higher price); *Pedashenko v Blacktown City Council* (1996) 39 NSWLR 189 (planning changes).

[70] *Farah Constructions Pty Ltd v Say-Dee Pty Ltd* (2007) 230 CLR 89 [107].

[71] *McMaster v Byrne* [1952] 1 All ER 1362 (PC—Canada) 1367.

reference to the probable reaction of the individual in question.[72] That the fiduciary knew that his principal was determined to sell and would not be deflected from that course does not render an otherwise material fact immaterial.[73]

The fiduciary need not disclose facts that are already known to the principal,[74] nor that the principal can be expected to deduce for himself,[75] nor facts the fiduciary does not himself know.[76] *BLB Corporation v Jacobsen*, a decision of the High Court of Australia, indicates that for this purpose a fiduciary will be taken to know facts of which he has been wilfully blind but not those his ignorance of which stemmed from mere imprudence.[77] This reflects the concern of the rule, which is that the fiduciary should not enjoy an informational advantage in dealing with his principal.

8.24

There are suggestions in some of the older cases that the disclosure requirement does not extend beyond material facts the fiduciary has learned in the course of his engagement.[78] That is plainly not the law; 'it does not matter in the least how or under what circumstances the information was acquired'.[79] In *Spector v Ageda*,[80] which involved a solicitor who knew from prior dealings but did not disclose that the debt which her client sought to repay might in fact be invalid, Megarry J explained that a 'solicitor must put at his client's disposal not only his skill but also his knowledge'.

8.25

Substantive fairness

In addition to proving that he has made complete disclosure, to sustain a transaction with his principal the fiduciary must also prove that the price and other terms were substantively fair.[81] That is, he must show that the contract was as advantageous to the principal as it could have been if he had been dealing with a third party at arm's length.[82] This requirement has puzzled at least one commentator,[83] but Conaglan has suggested that substantive fairness is best understood as fulfilling an evidentiary function, for it tends to indicate informed consent.[84] As one judge put it, to 'demonstrate to conviction' that a fiduciary has done his

8.26

---

[72] [1952] 1 All ER 1362 (PC—Canada); *Johnson v EBS Pensioner Trustees Ltd* [2002] Lloyd's Rep PN 309 (CA) [72], [83].
[73] See further para [8.72].
[74] *Johnson v Bones* [1970] 1 NSWR 28; *Hanson v Lorenz & Jones (a firm)* [1987] FTLR 23 (CA) (although that case involved advice rather than disclosure).
[75] *Farah Constructions Pty Ltd v Say-Dee Pty Ltd* (2007) 230 CLR 89 [108].
[76] *Clark Boyce v Mouat* [1994] 1 AC 428 (PC—NZ) 437.
[77] (1974) 48 ALJR 372. See also *Bristol and West Building Society v Mothew* [1998] Ch 1 (CA). If the fiduciary owed his principal a duty of care to investigate the matter in question then the principal may have a cause of action for compensatory relief.
[78] Eg *Coles v Trecothick* (1804) 9 Ves 234, 246–47; 32 ER 592, 597 ('information acquired by him in the character of trustee').
[79] *Dougan v MacPherson* [1902] AC 197 (HL Sc) 204.
[80] [1973] 1 Ch 30, 48.
[81] *Gibson v Jeyes* (1801) 6 Ves 266, 271; 31 ER 1044, 1047; *Cole v Trecothick* (1804) 9 Ves 234, 246–47; 32 ER 592, 597; *Marquis of Clarincade v Henning* (1861) 30 Beav 174, 185; 54 ER 855, 859; *Pisani v A-G for Gibraltar* (1874) LR 5 PC 516 (Gibraltar) 537; *Thomson v Eastwood* (1877) 2 App Cas 215 (HL Ir) 236; *Wright v Carter* [1903] 1 Ch 27 (CA) 60, 61; *Demerara Bauxite Company, Limited v Hubbard* [1923] AC 673 (PC—British Guiana) 681–82; *Bank of Credit and Commerce International SA v Aboody* [1990] 1 QB 923 (CA) 963; *CIBC Mortgages plc v Pitt* [1994] 1 AC 200, 209; *Bristol and West Building Society v Mothew* [1998] Ch 1 (CA) 18; *Johnson v EBS Pensioner Trustees Ltd* [2002] Lloyd's Rep PN 309 (CA) [68].
[82] *Gibson v Jeyes* (1801) 6 Ves 266, 271; 31 ER 1044, 1047; *Savery v King* (1856) 5 HLC 627, 656; 10 ER 1046, 1058; *Pisani v A-G for Gibraltar* (1874) LR 5 PC 516 (Gibraltar) 536–37; *Demerara Bauxite Co Ltd v Hubbard* [1923] AC 673, 682.
[83] JC Shepherd, *The Law of Fiduciaries* (1981) 169.
[84] M Conaglan, *Fiduciary Loyalty* (2010) 129–38.

duty 'will usually be beyond possibility in a case where anything to his client's detriment has occurred'.[85]

8.27 Consistently with Conaglan's suggestion, the substantive fairness requirement is subject to an exception or qualification in that there is nothing to stop a principal who wishes to do so from making a gift to his fiduciary or from contracting with him on terms favourable to the fiduciary.[86] A gift or a favourable contract will only be upheld, however, where the fiduciary proves that this is indeed what the principal intended and also that the principal appreciated the true value of the asset in question.[87]

8.28 Provided the requirements of the fair-dealing rule are met, the fact the fiduciary later makes a profit out of the contract will not entitle the principal to avoid it, for example where the fiduciary later resells what he had bought at a time when values are higher.[88] In such cases the fiduciary may be required to prove, however, that the likelihood of the increase in values was not known to him at the time of the transaction.[89]

Disinterested advice

8.29 Additional considerations come into play in relation to solicitors and other fiduciaries whose role involves advising the principal. Here there is a danger not only that the principal will not be apprised of all of the facts he is entitled to know, but also that he will not be given the disinterested advice he is entitled to receive. To sustain the transaction, the fiduciary must therefore prove that the principal received such advice.[90]

Independent advice

8.30 There is no difficulty on this front if the principal takes independent advice in relation to the transaction, and so it is prudent for the fiduciary to advise that he do so.[91] In terms of whether independent advice is required, there is a range of possibilities. In some circumstances the fiduciary must insist that his principal is independently advised;[92] in others he must advise his principal to take independent advice but he may act if his principal declines to do so;[93] and finally there are circumstances where the transaction may be upheld provided only that the fiduciary himself gives proper advice to the extent advice is needed.[94]

8.31 No definite test has been laid down for deciding between these possibilities. In general the more acute the conflict of interest, the more complicated the transaction, and the less sophisticated the principal, the greater the likelihood that independent advice will be

---

[85] *Spector v Ageda* [1973] 1 Ch 30, 47.
[86] *Coles v Trecothick* (1804) 9 Ves 234, 248; 32 ER 592, 598; *Hatch v Hatch* (1804) 9 Ves 292, 297; 32 ER 615, 617; *Selsey v Rhoades* (1824) 2 Sim & St 41, 49–50; 57 ER 260, 263–64; *Hunter v Atkins* (1834) 3 My & K 113, 134–36; 40 ER 43, 51–52.
[87] *Coles v Trecothick* (1804) 9 Ves 234, 248; 32 ER 592, 598; *Hatch v Hatch* (1804) 9 Ves 292, 297; 32 ER 615, 617.
[88] *Edwards v Meyrick* (1842) 2 Hare 60, 67 ER 25; *Demerara Bauxite Co Ltd v Hubbard* [1923] AC 673, 681.
[89] *Andrews v Mowbray* (1807) Wils Ex 71, 109; 159 ER 835, 851.
[90] *Allison v Clayhills* (1907) 97 LT 709.
[91] Independent advice may also assist in rebutting an inference of undue influence.
[92] Eg *Commonwealth Bank of Australia v Smith* (1991) 102 ALR 453, 477–78; *Witten-Hannah v Davis* [1995] 2 NZLR 141 (CA); *Longstaff v Birtles* [2002] 1 WLR 470 (CA).
[93] Eg *Willis v Barron* [1902] AC 271, 284; *Haira v Burbery Mortgage Finance & Savings Ltd* [1995] 3 NZLR 396 (CA).
[94] Eg *Readdy v Pendergast* (1886) 55 LT 767; *Wright v Carter* [1903] 1 Ch 27 (CA) 54–55 (Vaughan Williams LJ), but cf 60 (Stirling LJ); *Allison v Clayhills* (1907) 97 LT 709; *Demerara Bauxite Co Ltd v Hubbard* [1923] AC 673, 681; *McMaster v Byrne* [1952] 1 All ER 1362 (PC—Canada) 1369.

required. In *Wright v Carter*[95] Vaughan Williams LJ indicated that the fact a transaction is manifestly fair tends to make independent advice unnecessary.

What advice needs to be given

Where the principal does not take independent advice, to sustain the transaction the fiduciary must prove that he gave his principal all of the advice he would have given if instead he was advising in relation to a transaction with a third party.[96]   **8.32**

What that advice is depends upon the scope of the fiduciary's engagement and the duties it entails in the particular circumstances.[97] A solicitor will usually be obliged to advise on the nature and legal effect of the transaction,[98] although obviously there is no need to do so if the client already understands what he is getting into.[99] In many circumstances a solicitor's duty will go beyond this, and he may, for example, be required to advise on other modes of sale that might be more advantageous.[100] In other cases the scope of the engagement will circumscribe the adviser's duty. Thus in *Hanson v Lorenz & Jones*, where a client had entered into a business venture with his solicitors, the Court of Appeal held that their duty as solicitors did not extend to advising on the financial prudence or imprudence of the transaction.[101]   **8.33**

C. Double Employment

Depending on the scope and nature of his engagement, by undertaking to act for parties with opposing interests a fiduciary may assume potentially conflicting duties. Provided there is 'a reasonable apprehension of a potential conflict, not a mere theoretical possibility',[102] the fiduciary will be in breach of the double employment rule unless he obtains the informed consent of both to the dual role.[103] This may be so even though the potentially conflicting engagements relate to separate transactions;[104] but the mere fact a fiduciary acts for multiple parties is unobjectionable if they do not have potentially opposing interests.[105]   **8.34**

---

[95] *Wright v Carter* [1903] 1 Ch 27 (CA) 54–55.
[96] *Gibson v Jeyes* (1801) 6 Ves 266, 271, 278; 31 ER 1044, 1046–47, 1050; *Cane v Allen* (1814) 2 Dow 289, 299; 3 ER 869, 872–73; *Demerara Bauxite Co Ltd v Hubbard* [1923] AC 673, 681.
[97] *Pisani v A-G for Gibraltar* (1874) LR 5 PC 516 (Gibraltar) 536–40; *Hanson v Lorenz & Jones (a firm)* [1987] FTLR 23 (CA); *Clark Boyce v Mouat* [1994] 1 AC 428 (PC—NZ) 436–37; *Beach Petroleum NL v Kennedy* (1999) 48 NSWLR 1 (CA) [188].
[98] *Allison v Clayhills* (1907) 97 LT 709.
[99] *Hanson v Lorenz & Jones (a firm)* [1987] FTLR 23 (CA).
[100] *Pisani v A-G for Gibraltar* (1874) LR 5 PC 516 (Gibraltar) 536.
[101] *Hanson v Lorenz & Jones (a firm)* [1987] FTLR 23 (CA). See also *Clark Boyce v Mouat* [1994] 1 AC 428 (PC—NZ) 436–37; *Citicorp Australia Ltd v O'Brien* (1996) 40 NSWLR 398.
[102] *Marks & Spencer plc v Freshfields Bruckhaus Deringer* [2004] 1 WLR 2331 [9], [15] aff'd [2004] EWCA Civ 741; *Ratiu v Conway* [2006] 1 All ER 571 (CA) [59]; *Paton v Rosesilver Group Corp* [2017] EWCA Civ 158 [33]. See also *Boardman v Phipps* [1967] 2 AC 46, 124; *Queensland Mines Ltd v Hudson* (1978) 52 ALJR 399 (PC—Aus) 400.
[103] *Bristol and West Building Society v Mothew* [1998] Ch 1 (CA) 18.
[104] *Marks & Spencer plc v Freshfields Bruckhaus Deringer* [2004] 1 WLR 2331 [16], aff'd [2004] EWCA Civ 741 [11]; *Ratiu v Conway* [2006] 1 All ER 571 (CA) [96].
[105] *Farrington v Rowe McBride & Partners* [1985] 1 NZLR 83 (CA) 92. As to the circumstances in which a lawyer may act for clients with opposing commercial interests, see *Strother v 3464920 Canada Inc* [2007] 2 SCR 177 [54]–[55].

8.35 There is a similar potential for a conflict where a fiduciary acts for his principal in a transaction with a counterparty with whom the fiduciary is personally connected in some way, though the fiduciary is not actually instructed by him. This may be because the fiduciary has a material financial interest in the counterparty or because they are related by blood or marriage, to give the two most common examples. Here there is no potential conflict of duty and duty, but the governing principles are the same.[106]

8.36 In extreme cases it may be altogether impossible for a fiduciary to act fairly for opposing parties.[107] More commonly a fiduciary may properly act for opposing parties provided the requirements of the fair-dealing rule are met, including the requirement that both principals consent to dual representation.[108] A principal who does not receive fair treatment may be entitled to avoid the transaction.[109]

8.37 It is not necessary to repeat the requirements of the fair-dealing rule here. There are, however, certain aspects of those requirements that can operate in special ways in double employment cases.

(1) Consent to adverse duty or interest

8.38 It is essential that the principal give his fully informed consent to his fiduciary's adverse duty or interest.[110] Where the fiduciary himself deals with his principal, the fiduciary's adverse interest will usually be self-evident, in which case consent to that interest will be implicit in the principal's willingness to deal. Informed consent is more often an issue in double employment cases.

8.39 There is no precise formula for determining what the principal must be told in any particular case.[111] In general he must be told that there is a potential conflict between the parties, what the nature of that potential conflict is, and what its ramifications are. In this regard, the fiduciary must typically explain what would happen in the event of an actual conflict arising, for example that the fiduciary may be disabled from disclosing to each party the full knowledge which he possesses as to the transaction, or that he may be disabled from giving advice to one party which conflicts with the interests of the other.[112] The principal must be told what his rights are and that he is in part surrendering them,[113] if that is indeed what he is doing.

---

[106] *Moody v Cox* [1917] 2 Ch 71 (CA) 81–82, 84–85; *Beach Petroleum NL v Kennedy* (1999) 48 NSWLR 1 (CA) [202].
[107] *Farrington v Rowe McBride & Partners* [1985] 1 NZLR 83 (CA) 90; *Tuiara v Frost & Sutcliffe (a firm)* [2003] 2 NZLR 833 [81].
[108] *Clark Boyce v Mouat* [1994] 1 AC 428 (PC—NZ) 435; *Bristol and West Building Society v Mothew* [1998] Ch 1 (CA) 18; *Johnson v EBS Pensioner Trustees Ltd* [2002] Lloyd's Rep PN 309 (CA).
[109] *Moody v Cox* [1917] 2 Ch 71 (CA); *North & South Trust Co v Berkeley* [1971] 1 WLR 470, 485.
[110] *Fullwood v Hurley* [1928] 1 KB 498 (CA); *Clark Boyce v Mouat* [1994] 1 AC 428 (PC—NZ) 435; *Hurstanger Ltd v Wilson* [2008] Bus LR 216 (CA) [35]; *Rosetti Marketing Ltd v Diamond Sofa Co Ltd* [2013] Bus LR 543 (CA) [22].
[111] *Life Association of Scotland v Siddal* (1861) 3 De G F & J 58, 73; 45 ER 800, 806; *Maguire v Makaronis* (1997) 188 CLR 449, 466.
[112] *Clark Boyce v Mouat* [1994] 1 AC 428 (PC—NZ) 435.
[113] *Boulting v ACTAT* [1963] 2 QB 606 (CA) 636.

The fiduciary must ensure that the principal fully understands and appreciates these things, and so the extent of the explanation that is required may depend on the sophistication of the principal.[114] Depending on the circumstances, the fiduciary may have to bring the significance of the conflict home by recommending that his principal take independent advice,[115] or even in some cases by insisting on it.[116]

8.40

It is not enough that the principal is informed of the dual engagement and the potential conflict; he must also consent to it. In some cases consent will be implicit in the fiduciary's instructions, as where a mortgage lender instructs the purchaser's solicitors to also put their security in place.[117] Here the lender chooses the solicitor precisely because he is already acting for the purchaser, and so the conflict is of his own making.

8.41

(2) Disclosure and advice

The fact that a fiduciary has obtained his client's informed consent to the dual engagement is not the end of the matter. In addition, the fiduciary must not allow his dual engagement to inhibit the service that he provides to each principal. He must act in good faith in the interests of each and must not act with the intention of furthering the interests of one principal to the prejudice of the other. The fiduciary must serve each as faithfully as if he were his only principal.[118]

8.42

Amongst other things, a doubly employed fiduciary must give each principal the same disclosure and the same advice that he would have given had he been acting with an undivided loyalty.[119] This is so even where a potential conflict matures into an actual one, so that the fiduciary comes under irreconcilable duties.[120] For example, the existence of a duty of confidentiality owed to one principal does not affect a fiduciary's duty to make full disclosure to another.[121] The only qualification to this occurs where the fiduciary and client agree that the fiduciary's obligations are to be limited in some way. Any limitation of this sort must usually be clearly explained.[122]

8.43

In exceptional cases a limitation on the fiduciary's duties may be implied in the dealings between the parties. For example, in *Kelly v Cooper*[123] the Privy Council decided that an estate agent was not bound to disclose to one vendor client information concerning an offer

8.44

---

[114] *Taylor v Schofield Peterson* [1999] 3 NZLR 434 (CA) 440; *Strother v 3464920 Canada Inc* [2007] 2 SCR 177 [55].
[115] Eg *Willis v Barron* [1902] AC 271, 284; *Haira v Burbery Mortgage Finance & Savings Ltd* [1995] 3 NZLR 396 (CA) 407.
[116] Eg *Commonwealth Bank of Australia v Smith* (1991) 102 ALR 453 (FCA) 477–78; *Tuiara v Frost & Sutcliffe (a firm)* [2003] 2 NZLR 833.
[117] *Bristol and West Building Society v Mothew* [1998] Ch 1 (CA) 18–19; *Paton v Rosesilver Group Corp* [2017] EWCA Civ 158 [34]. See also *Kelly v Cooper* [1993] AC 205 (PC—Bermuda) 215; *Tuiara v Frost & Sutcliffe (a firm)* [2003] 2 NZLR 833 [49].
[118] *Bristol and West Building Society v Mothew* [1998] Ch 1 (CA) 19.
[119] *Moody v Cox* [1917] 2 Ch 71 (CA) 83; *Hilton v Barker Booth and Eastwood (a firm)* [2005] 1 WLR 567 (HL).
[120] *Moody v Cox* [1917] 2 Ch 71 (CA); *Hilton v Barker Booth and Eastwood (a firm)* [2005] 1 WLR 567 (HL).
[121] *Mortgage Express Ltd v Bowerman & Partners (a firm)* [1996] 2 All ER 836 (CA) 845–46; *Hilton v Barker Booth and Eastwood (a firm)* [2005] 1 All ER 651 (HL).
[122] *Clark Boyce v Mouat* [1994] 1 AC 428 (PC—NZ) 435.
[123] [1993] AC 205 (PC—Bermuda) 215. See also *Bolkiah v KPMG* [1999] 2 AC 222, 235 and *CH Offshore Limited v Internaves Consorcio Naviero SA* [2021] 1 Lloyd's Rep 465 [74].

received by another client who was a rival vendor, notwithstanding the lack of any express agreement to this effect.[124] The House of Lords has more recently made clear in *Hilton v Barker Booth and Eastwood*[125] that a limitation of this sort will only be implied if one of the conventional tests for the implication of terms is satisfied.[126] The fact that the performance of a duty owed to one principal would otherwise involve the breach of a duty owed to another principal is not itself a reason for implying a term excluding either duty.[127]

(3) Substantive fairness

8.45 There is some indication that the substantive fairness requirement that applies to dealings between a fiduciary and his principal applies equally in cases where the fiduciary instead mediates a transaction between two principals,[128] but this is not emphasized in the cases. Where the principals decide the price between themselves on the basis of considerations to which the fiduciary is not privy, it is difficult to see why this requirement should apply. Substantive unfairness may nonetheless prompt questions about whether the fiduciary gave the disclosure and advice that he ought to have.

(4) Implication of counterparty

8.46 Though it is the fiduciary who fails his principal, nonetheless the transaction with the counterparty may be set aside if he is sufficiently implicated. Deciding whether the counterparty is implicated does not usually pose much difficulty in cases where the fiduciary was instructed to act for both parties. The counterparty will be implicated if he knew that the fiduciary failed his other principal, and for this purpose the fiduciary's knowledge will be imputed to the counterparty on conventional agency principles.[129]

8.47 More difficult are cases where the fiduciary was not actually acting for the counterparty, so that the fiduciary's knowledge cannot be imputed to him. These are cases where the fiduciary was instead financially interested in the counterparty or personally related to him or the like. In cases of this type it is open to question whether actual knowledge on the part of the counterparty of the fiduciary's failure is necessary, or whether some form of constructive knowledge will suffice to implicate him.

8.48 This question does not seem to have been considered in any real detail in any reported case. *Cowan de Groot Properties Ltd v Eagle Trust plc*[130] involved a transaction between two

---

[124] Cf *Mortgage Express Ltd v Bowerman & Partners (a firm)* [1996] 2 All ER 836 (CA) 845, where a conflict of duty was instead avoided by an implied waiver of confidentiality.
[125] [2005] 1 WLR 567 (HL). Noted J Getzler, 'Inconsistent Fiduciary Duties and Implied Consent' (2006) 122 LQR 1.
[126] See also *Rosetti Marketing Ltd v Diamond Sofa Co Ltd* [2013] Bus LR 543 (CA) [27], where Lord Neuberger MR said it was highly questionable whether the reasoning in *Kelly v Cooper* should be extended to other types of agency, at least in the absence of clear evidence to support the extension.
[127] In Canada, *Strother v 3464920 Canada Inc* [2007] 2 SCR 177 [51].
[128] *Bristol and West Building Society v Mothew* [1998] Ch 1 (CA) 18.
[129] *Turner v Trelawney* (1841) 12 Sim 49, 59 ER 1049; *North & South Trust Co v Berkeley* [1971] 1 WLR 470, 485; *O'Sullivan v Management Agency and Music Ltd* [1985] QB 428 (CA) 464. For the view that only actual knowledge will suffice, see M Conaglan, *Fiduciary Loyalty* (2010) 161, fn 81.
[130] [1991] BCLC 1045.

companies mediated by a director of one who also had an undisclosed financial interest in the other. Knox J assumed that constructive knowledge of the director's failure to disclose his interest would suffice.[131] On the facts of that case, however, Knox J did not consider that the counterparty's knowledge of the director in question's character and habits combined with the fact he was known not to trouble himself with what he viewed as legal technicalities was sufficient to put the counterparty on inquiry. It is at least arguable, however, that Knox J was wrong to assume that anything short of actual knowledge or wilful blindness might suffice,[132] for constructive knowledge is not sufficient in allied areas such as deceit and undue influence.[133]

D. Bribery

Bribery is said to be 'an evil practice which threatens the foundations of any civilised society'.[134] A principal who discovers that his agent has been suborned has the benefit of an array of legal and equitable remedies against both the agent and the briber.[135] Amongst other options, if the briber has procured a contract with the principal, the principal may be entitled to avoid it.[136]

8.49

While bribery is contrary to English public policy and contracts to bribe are unenforceable, contracts which have been procured by bribes are not unenforceable on grounds of public policy.[137] It is at least arguable, however, that if the contract in question was in fact concluded by the suborned agent on his principal's behalf, then it is void rather than voidable on the basis that the agent lacked authority to conclude a contract in fraud of his principal. This argument is discussed elsewhere.[138] For present purposes it is assumed, consistently with what is perhaps the more widely shared view, that such contracts are merely voidable. On any view a contract which is not concluded by a corrupt agent, but in relation to which he instead advises or plays some similar role, is voidable rather than void.

8.50

(1) Rescission at law and in equity

Contracts procured by bribery may be avoided either at law or in equity.[139] The ground for rescission at law is fraud.[140] It is not fraudulent misrepresentation, for of necessity there is

8.51

---

[131] [1991] BCLC 1045, 1116–17.
[132] But cf P Finn, *Fiduciary Obligations* (1977) [446], whose view is that even actual knowledge may not suffice.
[133] See Chap 9, para [9.05].
[134] *A-G for Hong Kong v Reid* [1994] 1 AC 324 (PC—NZ) 330.
[135] For a useful summary see *Daraydan Holdings Ltd v Solland International Ltd* [2005] Ch 119 [51]–[56].
[136] *Panama and South Pacific Telegraph Co v India Rubber, Gutta Percha, and Telegraph Works Co* (1875) LR 10 Ch App 515; *Logicrose Ltd v Southend United Football Club Ltd* [1988] 1 WLR 1256. A bribe will not justify the rescission of a contract if it was not paid or intimated before the date of formation but was instead given in the course of performance of the contract, though such a bribe may found a claim for damages for breach of contract and may justify the termination of the contract: *Armagas Ltd v Mundogas SA (The Ocean Frost)* [1985] 1 Lloyd's Rep 1, 21–22; *Ross River Limited v Cambridge City Football Club Limited* [2008] 1 All ER 1004 [220]–[225]; *Tigris International NV v China Southern Airlines Co Ltd* [2014] EWCA Civ 1649 at [143]. But compare *National Crime Agency v Robb* [2015] 3 WLR 23 at [50]–[51], which appears to be incorrect, a view shared by PG Turner [2016] CLJ 206.
[137] *Honeywell International Middle East Limited v Meydan Group LLC* [2014] EWHC 1344 (TCC) [184]–[185].
[138] See Chap 1, paras [1.78]–[1.80].
[139] *Wood v Commercial First Business Ltd* [2022] Ch 123 (CA) [98]–[99].
[140] *Mahesan v Malaysia Government Officers' Co-operative Housing Society Ltd* [1979] AC 374 (PC—Malaysia) 383; *Petrotrade Inc v Smith* [2000] 1 Lloyd's Rep 486, 490.

no representation.[141] Bribery is also viewed in equity as a fraud on the principal.[142] More specifically, contracts procured by bribery may be avoided in equity because, without the knowledge and consent of his principal, the agent has put himself in a position where his duty and his interest may conflict.[143] As with rescission for deceit, the elements of the ground appear to be the same at law and in equity, and it seems that the same body of special presumptions assist the defrauded principal whether he rescinds at law or in equity.

(2) Elements of bribery

For the purposes of the civil law a bribe means the payment of a secret commission, which only means (i) that the person making the payment makes it to the agent of the other person with whom he is dealing; (ii) that he makes it to that person knowing that that person is acting as the agent of the other person with whom he is dealing; and (iii) that he fails to disclose to the other person with whom he is dealing that he has made that payment to the person whom he knows to be the other person's agent.[144]

8.52 This definition has been generally accepted,[145] but it requires elaboration in a number of respects.

Character of the agent

8.53 It has sometimes been said that there must be a fiduciary relationship between the claimant and the payee of the bribe,[146] but it has also been said that in bribery cases this concept is 'used in a very loose, or at all events a very comprehensive sense'.[147] In *Alexander v Webber*,[148] for example, a chauffeur was treated as a fiduciary where his employer relied on his advice in deciding whether to purchase an automobile. In *Wood v Commercial First Business Limited*, however, the Court of Appeal has now held that the right question is simply whether the agent owed a duty to provide information, advice, or recommendation on an impartial or disinterested basis.[149] In some cases that duty may be correctly described as fiduciary but this is inessential. Where there is a fiduciary relationship, that may affect the analysis and character of the available remedies,[150] but rescission is available in all cases.

---

[141] [1979] AC 374 (PC—Malaysia) 383 ('the claim based on bribery is not a species of deceit but a special form of fraud where there is no representation made to the principal of the agent let alone reliance').

[142] *Panama and South Pacific Telegraph Co v India Rubber, Gutta Percha, and Telegraph Works Co* (1875) LR 10 Ch App 515, 526; *Boston Deep Sea Fishing and Ice Company v Ansell* (1888) 39 ChD 339 (CA) 368.

[143] *Barry v The Stoney Point Canning Co* (1917) 55 SCR 51, 73; *Logicrose Ltd v Southend United Football Club Ltd* [1988] 1 WLR 1256, 1260; *Anangel Atlas Compania Naviera SA v Ishikawajima-Harima Heavy Industries Ltd* [1990] 1 Lloyd's Rep 167, 171; *Hurstanger Ltd v Wilson* [2008] Bus LR 216 (CA) [34].

[144] *Industries and General Mortgage Co Ltd v Lewis* [1949] 2 All ER 573, 575. See also *Hovenden & Sons v Millhof* (1900) 83 LT 41 (CA) 43.

[145] Eg *Taylor v Walker* [1958] 1 Ll L R 490, 511; *Armagas Ltd v Mundogas SA (The Ocean Frost)* [1985] 1 Lloyd's Rep 1, 18; *Anangel Atlas Compania Naviera SA v Ishikawajima-Harima Heavy Industries Ltd* [1990] 1 Lloyd's Rep 167, 171; *Petrotrade Inc v Smith* [2000] 1 Lloyd's Rep 486, 489–90; *Novoship (UK) Limited v Mikhaylyuk* [2012] EWHC 3586 (Comm) [104]; *Wood v Commercial First Business Limited* [2022] Ch 123 (CA).

[146] Eg *Prince Eze v Conway* [2019] EWCA Civ 88 [39]–[43].

[147] *Reading v The King* [1949] 2 KB 232 (CA) 236. See also *Reading v The King* [1951] AC 507, 516.

[148] [1922] 1 KB 642.

[149] *Wood v Commercial First Business Limited* [2022] Ch 123 (CA) [48], [92], [102].

[150] *Wood v Commercial First Business Limited* [2022] Ch 123 (CA) [49].

Necessity of conflict of interest

8.54 One key to determining whether or not a payment constitutes a bribe is whether it puts the agent into a position where his duty and his interest may realistically conflict.[151] It is accordingly necessary that at the time the payment is made there is an open question whether the principal will deal with the payor or on what terms,[152] and that the agent is in a position to influence the principal in some way. A gratuity given after the matter has been concluded will not constitute a bribe provided there was no earlier indication that it would be given.[153]

8.55 But while it is necessary that the payment bring about a conflict of interest, there is no need to prove that the agent has actually been influenced to act against his principal's interests or that the principal was in fact disadvantaged in any way.[154] The 'court will presume in favour of the principal, and as against the briber and the agent bribed, that the agent was influenced by the bribe; and this presumption is irrebuttable'.[155]

Secrecy

8.56 Another essential characteristic of a bribe is that it is kept secret from the agent's principal. It has even been said that 'the real evil is not the payment of money, but the secrecy attending it'.[156]

8.57 If the fact or even the possibility of payment is disclosed then the payment is not secret and so there is no bribe.[157] There may nonetheless be a breach of the agent's fiduciary duty if the full circumstances of the payment are not disclosed or if the principal does not give his informed consent to the arrangement,[158] though a failure to object may be sufficient evidence of assent.[159] The distinction is an important one because absent secrecy the claimant will not gain the advantage of the special presumptions applicable in a case of bribery, and also apparently because absent secrecy the court has a discretion whether to grant rescission.[160]

8.58 The fact that it is common practice in a particular industry for one party to make payments of a particular type to the agent of their counterparty does not negate the inference of

---

[151] *Anangel Atlas Compania Naviera SA v Ishikawajima-Harima Heavy Industries Ltd* [1990] 1 Lloyd's Rep 167, 171. See also *Eden v Ridsdale's Railway Lamp & Lighting Co* (1889) 23 QBD 368, 373; *Barry v The Stoney Point Canning Co* (1917) 55 SCR 51, 73; *Alexander v Webber* [1922] 1 KB 642, 644; *Taylor v Walker* [1958] 1 Ll L R 490, 509; *Logicrose Ltd v Southend United Football Club Ltd* [1988] 1 WLR 1256, 1260; *Petrotrade Inc v Smith* [2000] 1 Lloyd's Rep 486, 490; *Imageview Management Ltd v Jack* [2009] Bus LR 1034 (CA) [38] ('realistic possibility of a conflict of interest').
[152] *Eden v Ridsdale's Railway Lamp & Lighting Co* (1889) 23 QBD 368 (CA) 372.
[153] *The Parkdale* [1897] P 53 (DC).
[154] *Harrington v The Victoria Graving Dock Company* (1878) 3 QBD 549; *Shipway v Broadwood* [1899] 1 QB 369 (CA); *Re a Debtor* [1927] 2 Ch 367 (CA).
[155] *Hovenden & Sons v Millhof* (1900) 83 LT 41 (CA) 43.
[156] *Shipway v Broadwood* [1899] 1 QB 369 (CA) 373. See also *Panama and South Pacific Telegraph Co v India Rubber, Gutta Percha, and Telegraph Works Co* (1875) LR 10 Ch App 515, 526; *Taylor v Walker* [1958] 1 Ll L R 490, 513.
[157] *Hurstanger Ltd v Wilson* [2008] Bus LR 216 (CA) [40]; *McWilliam v Norton Finance (UK) Limited* [2015] 2 BCLC 730 (CA). See also *Azevedo v IMCOPA –Importacao, Exportaacao e Industria de Oleos Ltda* [2014] 1 BCLC 72 (CA) [63]. The law on half-secret commissions is fully reviewed and discussed in *Wood v Commercial First Business Limited* [2020] CTLC 1.
[158] *Hurstanger Ltd v Wilson* [2008] Bus LR 216 (CA) [40]; *Bulfield v Fournier* (1894) 11 TLR 62; cf *Medsted Associates Limited v Canaccord Genuity Wealth (International) Limited* [2019] 1 WLR 4481 (CA). As to the agency issues that arise in determining to whom a disclosure to a company may be made, see *Ross River Limited v Cambridge City Football Club Limited* [2008] 1 All ER 1004 [209]–[217].
[159] *Kregor v Hollins* (1913) 109 LT 225 (CA) 230.
[160] *Hurstanger Ltd v Wilson* [2008] Bus LR 216 (CA) [48]; *Ross River Limited v Cambridge City Football Club Limited* [2008] 1 All ER 1004 [203].

bribery if the payment compromises the position of the agent. The courts have on a number of occasions held common industry practices to amount to bribery.[161] However proof of a market practice coupled with proof that the principal was aware of that practice may in an appropriate case negate secrecy and therefore avoid a finding of bribery.[162]

Benefits that may constitute bribes

8.59 A bribe need not take the form of a payment of money, although that is most common. It has been said that any transfer or promise of money or money's worth other than for full consideration may constitute a bribe.[163] But even this definition does not go nearly far enough. Probably any benefit that is realistically capable of influencing an agent may constitute a bribe.[164] For example, in *Panama and South Pacific Telegraph Co*[165] the granting of a subcontract to carry out work laying an underwater telegraph cable was held to be a bribe notwithstanding that the subcontract was not said to be on unusually favourable terms. That case also indicates that a tacit understanding that the agent will receive a benefit will in appropriate circumstances suffice.

8.60 A bribe may be a gift or it may consist in remuneration for the agent's services to the payer.[166] Payments or other benefits to third parties whom the agent wishes to benefit may constitute a bribe provided the agent is thereby put in a real position of conflict.[167] The payment or benefit need not be linked to a particular transaction provided the agent is tainted by the bribery at the time of the transaction in question.[168] Consequently, bribery in relation to one transaction will taint subsequent transactions provided the potential conflict of interest remains a real possibility. A benefit that is trivial and honestly conferred will not be treated as a bribe,[169] there being no realistic possibility of influence.

(3) Implication of counterparty

8.61 There is usually no difficulty implicating the counterparty in cases involving the corruption of an agent. Having given the bribe, the counterparty will usually be aware of the circumstances founding the principal's title to avoid the contract. There is no need to prove that the counterparty acted dishonestly or with the intention of corrupting the agent. Bribes are

---

[161] *Bulfield v Fournier* (1894) 11 TLR 62; *Alexander v Webber* [1922] 1 KB 642, 644; *Taylor v Walker* [1958] 1 Ll L R 490, 514.
[162] *Secretary of State for Justice v Topland Group plc* [2011] EWHC 983 (QB) [65]–[80].
[163] *Armagas Ltd v Mundogas SA (The Ocean Frost)* [1985] 1 Lloyd's Rep 1, 19; *Prince Eze v Conway* [2019] EWCA Civ 88 [36].
[164] *Petrotrade Inc v Smith* [2000] 1 Lloyd's Rep 486, 489. See further discussion and references in P Finn, *Fiduciary Obligations* (1977) [501]–[504], and see *Kings Security Systems Ltd v King* [2021] EWHC 325 (Ch) [150]–[152].
[165] *Panama and South Pacific Telegraph Co v India Rubber, Gutta Percha, and Telegraph Works Co* (1875) LR 10 Ch App 515.
[166] Eg *Eden v Ridsdale's Railway Lamp & Lighting Co* (1889) 23 QBD 368 (CA) (gift); *Rhodes v Macalister* (1923) 29 Com Cas 19 (CA) 27 (remuneration).
[167] *Novoship (UK) Limited v Mikhaylyuk* [2012] EWHC 3586 (Comm) [107].
[168] *Daraydan Holdings Ltd v Solland International Ltd* [2005] Ch 119 [53]; *Fiona Trust v Privalov* [2010] EWHC 3199 (Comm) [73]; *Novoship (UK) Limited v Mikhaylyuk* [2012] EWHC 3586 (Comm) [109].
[169] *Kregor v Hollins* (1913) 109 LT 225 (CA) 230.

irrebuttably presumed to be given with an intention to induce the agent to act favourably to the paying counterparty and unfavourably to the principal.[170]

It might happen, however, that the counterparty is not aware of all of the circumstances that would otherwise constitute his payment as a bribe. It is of the essence of a bribe that it is made for the personal benefit of the agent. The counterparty will not be implicated if he believed that his payment was made for the benefit of the principal rather than the agent,[171] for example not realizing that the bank account to which he paid was that of the agent rather than the principal. The test is one of actual knowledge; wilful blindness will suffice but constructive knowledge will not.[172]

8.62

The same reasoning does not apply to the question whether the agent's benefit has been or will be disclosed to the principal. It is no answer to an allegation of bribery that the counterparty believed the agent to be an honest man who would himself disclose it.[173] Nor, apparently, is it even an answer that the agent told the counterparty that the benefit had already been disclosed and that there was no reason to doubt this.[174] To be safe, the counterparty must disclose the benefit himself.

8.63

Two special situations need to be considered. The first is where the bribe is paid not by the counterparty himself but by his agent. The second is where the bribe is instead paid by a third party.

8.64

Bribe paid by agent

Of course the fact the bribe is given by the counterparty's agent rather than by the counterparty personally will not make a difference provided the agent acted within his authority. More difficult is the situation that occurred in *The Ocean Frost*.[175] There the counterparty neither knew of the bribe paid by his agent nor authorized it. The Court of Appeal nonetheless unanimously considered that the contract might have been rescinded on the basis the bribing agent was acting in the course of his employment,[176] though in light of other findings this conclusion was not necessary to the decision.

8.65

In reaching this conclusion, the Lord Justices referred to a Canadian case which treated the point as being governed by the doctrine of vicarious liability rather than the doctrine of authority.[177] Goff LJ evidently preferred this approach because it avoided the anomalous result an authority analysis might yield, namely that the counterparty's title under the contract

8.66

---

[170] *Hovenden & Sons v Millhof* (1900) 83 LT 41 (CA) 43; *Industries and General Mortgage Co Ltd v Lewis* [1949] 2 All ER 573, 576; *Taylor v Walker* [1958] 1 Ll L R 490, 512; *Armagas Ltd v Mundogas SA (The Ocean Frost)* [1985] 1 Lloyd's Rep 1, 19.
[171] *Logicrose Ltd v Southend United Football Club Ltd* [1988] 1 WLR 1256, 1261.
[172] *Logicrose Ltd v Southend United Football Club Ltd* [1988] 1 WLR 1256, 1261.
[173] *Grant v Gold Exploration and Development Syndicate Ltd* [1900] 1 QB 233 (CA) 249–50; *Armagas Ltd v Mundogas SA (The Ocean Frost)* [1985] 1 Lloyd's Rep 1, 20; *Logicrose Ltd v Southend United Football Club Ltd* [1988] 1 WLR 1256, 1262; *Ross River Limited v Cambridge City Football Club Limited* [2008] 1 All ER 1004 [251]; *Wood v Commercial First Business Limited* [2020] CTLC 1 [140].
[174] *Taylor v Walker* [1958] 1 Ll L R 490, 513.
[175] *Armagas Ltd v Mundogas SA (The Ocean Frost)* [1986] AC 717 (CA). The bribery point did not arise on further appeal to the House of Lords. See also *Petrotrade Inc v Smith* [2000] 1 Lloyd's Rep 486, 490 (not a rescission case).
[176] [1986] AC 717 (CA) 744–45, 755, 769.
[177] *Barry v The Stoney Point Cannery Co* (1917) 55 SCR 51, 80.

could not be attacked notwithstanding that he is vicariously liable to pay damages for the fraud of his agent.[178] The consequence, however, is that the counterparty's contract may be set aside notwithstanding that in giving the bribe his agent has acted for his own personal benefit and contrary to express instructions.[179] It is open to question whether vicarious liability is the correct doctrine where the remedy sought does not duplicate a remedy that might have been had against the agent, and where that remedy is not damages in tort.

Bribe paid by third party

8.67 Where the bribe is instead paid by a third party, the availability of rescission will depend on whether the counterparty's conscience is sufficiently affected by the payment.[180] In *The Ocean Frost*, Goff LJ suggested that it might be inequitable for an entirely innocent counterparty to enforce a contract discovered to have been procured by a stranger's bribery.[181] That would be anomalous. It is well established that to avoid a contract induced by the deceit of a third party, it is necessary to prove that the counterparty actually knew of the deceit.[182] It is difficult to see any ground for distinction between fraud by way of deceit and fraud by way of bribery. Consistently with this, attempts to rescind contracts where the counterparty's conscience is unaffected by the bribery have all failed,[183] and Goff LJ's suggestion is now a dead letter.[184]

8.68 In line with the established position in relation to deceit, it might be thought that a counterparty's conscience would only be sufficiently affected where it actually knew of the bribery. However, the courts have recognized an exception to that general rule in this particular context. In *Logicrose Limited v Southend United Football Club Limited*,[185] Millett J said in passing that if a party to a transaction made a payment for the personal benefit of another party's agent, and did not disclose it to the principal, he could not later defend the transaction by claiming that he believed the agent was an honest person who would disclose it. The Court of Appeal then took this further in *UBS AG v Kommunale Wasserwerke Leipzig GmbH*,[186] formulating the general principle to be derived from *Logicrose* and earlier cases as follows:

> Where a party to an intended transaction deals with the other party's agent secretly and behind his back, and dishonestly assists that agent to abuse his fiduciary duties to the other party so as to bring that transaction about, then the first party's conscience may be affected not merely by the particular form of abuse by the agent of which it actually knew, but also by any other abuse which the agent chose to employ to bring about the transaction with the first party.

---

[178] *Armagas Ltd v Mundogas SA (The Ocean Frost)* [1986] AC 717 (CA) 745.
[179] *Lloyd v Grace, Smith & Co* [1912] AC 716, which was cited in *Barry v The Stoney Point Cannery Co* (1917) 55 SCR 51, 80.
[180] *UBS AG v Kommunale Wasserwerke Leipzig GmbH* [2017] 2 Lloyd's Rep 621 (CA) [106].
[181] *Armagas Ltd v Mundogas SA (The Ocean Frost)* [1986] AC 717 (CA) 745.
[182] See Chap 9, para [9.05].
[183] *Armagas Ltd v Mundogas SA (The Ocean Frost)* [1985] 1 Lloyd's Rep 1, 20; *Chancery Client Partners Ltd v MRC 957 Ltd* [2016] Lloyd's Rep FC 578 [23].
[184] *UBS AG v Kommunale Wasserwerke Leipzig GmbH* [2017] 2 Lloyd's Rep 621 (CA) [106]; *Donegal International Limited v Zambia* [2007] 1 Lloyd's Rep 397 [496].
[185] [1988] 1 WLR 1256 at 1262.
[186] [2017] 2 Lloyd's Rep 621 (CA) [113].

8.69 In that case UBS had made a secret arrangement with Wasserwerke Leipzig's agents under which the agents would deliver derivatives business from their clients. UBS therefore knew that the agents had disabled themselves from giving disinterested advice, and so put themselves in a conflicted position, and this was alone a sufficient ground for setting aside the derivatives contracts between UBS and Wasserwerke Leipzig.[187] What UBS did not know was that the agents had a corrupt relationship with one of Wasserwerke Leipzig's two managing directors and that as part of the transaction they paid him a bribe. Notwithstanding UBS's ignorance, the Court of Appeal considered that bribery gave an independent basis for rescission. UBS's conscience was sufficiently affected by the bribe because of its secret arrangement with the agents, and in particular the fact that through that arrangement UBS dishonestly assisted the agents to abuse their fiduciary duties.[188]

8.70 It is difficult to understand the significance of the alternative, bribery-based ground for rescission where UBS's secret arrangement with the agents was essential to that ground but that secret arrangement was alone sufficient to support rescission. Kelshiker is right to observe that 'the two lines of reasoning collapse into one analysis',[189] but worse still it is one analysis with a fifth wheel, being the bribery. The Court of Appeal therefore made *UBS AG v Kommunale Wasserwerke Leipzig GmbH* more complicated than it needed to be. UBS knew that Wasserwerke Leipzig' agents had disabled themselves from giving disinterested advice. That knowledge was sufficient to warrant rescission of the contract consistently with a long-established and clear legal rule that applies across the law of rescission.[190] The elaboration of Millett J's limited exception to this rule was superfluous.

8.71 The Court of Appeal also confused matters by applying the test for dishonest assistance.[191] That is a different cause of action with different consequences and elements which have been tailored accordingly. The relief is compensatory and to obtain it the claimant must prove assistance and dishonesty. To obtain the different and often less extreme remedy of rescission on the basis of third-party wrongdoing, it is not necessary to prove either that the counterparty assisted that wrongdoing or that he acted dishonestly. Instead, on conventional principles, what must be shown is actual knowledge of the factual circumstances that are treated by the court as impairing the other party's consent; no more and no less. The Court offered no reason for departing from those principles.

E. Causation Irrelevant

8.72 Causation is not a relevant concept in determining whether a contract between fiduciary and principal should be set aside.[192] That full disclosure or disinterested advice would not in the circumstances have made a difference to the principal's decision will not save the

---

[187] *UBS AG v Kommunale Wasserwerke Leipzig GmbH* [2017] 2 Lloyd's Rep 621 (CA) [156].
[188] *UBS AG v Kommunale Wasserwerke Leipzig GmbH* [2017] 2 Lloyd's Rep 621 (CA) [119].
[189] P Kelshiker, 'Rescission and Attribution of Knowledge in Multi-party Cases of Dishonest Assistance' (2018) 134 LQR 363.
[190] See Chap 9, para [9.05].
[191] This aspect of the Court of Appeal's decision is defended by R Lee, 'Relief for Bribes in Equity' (2019) 13 J of Eq 122.
[192] *Maguire v Makaronis* (1997) 188 CLR 449, 467.

transaction.[193] Lord Thankerton famously expressed the principle in this way in *Brickenden v London Loan and Savings Co*:

> When a party, holding a fiduciary relationship, commits a breach of duty by non-disclosure of material facts, which his constituent is entitled to know in connection with the transaction he cannot be heard to maintain that disclosure would not have altered the decision to proceed with the transaction because the constituent's action would be solely determined by some other factor, such as the valuation of another party of the property proposed to be mortgaged. Once the Court has determined that the non-disclosed facts were material, speculation as to what course the constituent, on disclosure, would have taken is not relevant.[194]

8.73 The same holds where the fiduciary was not a party to the transaction but instead mediated it: 'causation is not a requirement of the equitable right to rescind, where the decision-making of the party seeking rescission has been undermined by a conflict of interest on the part of its fiduciary adviser which the counterparty resisting rescission either assisted, or of which it knew.'[195]

---

[193] *McMaster v Byrne* [1952] 1 All ER 1362 (PC—Canada); *Swindle v Harrison* [1997] 4 All ER 705 (CA); *Gwembe Valley Development Co Ltd v Koshy (No 3)* [2004] 1 BCLC 131 (CA) [144]–[146] (going on to observe at [147] that causation does matter if the principal seeks to establish loss for the purpose of claiming equitable compensation). Lord Wilberforce's remarks in *NZ Netherlands Society 'Oranje' Inc v Kuys* [1973] 1 WLR 1126 (PC—NZ) 1131–32 can be read as contradicting this, but they can equally be read as meaning that the facts he had in mind were not objectively material.
[194] *Brickenden v London Loan and Savings Co* [1934] 3 DLR 465 (PC—Canada) 469.
[195] *UBS AG v Kommunale Wasserwerke Leipzig GmbH* [2017] 2 Lloyd's Rep 621 (CA) [155]. See also *Logicrose Limited v Southend United Football Club Limited* [1988] 1 WLR 1256 at 1260.

9
Third Party Wrongdoing

A. Introduction	9.01	C. Surety Contracts	9.07
B. Contracts	9.03	(1) Constructive notice	9.08
(1) The basic rule precluding rescission	9.03	(2) Circumstances in which special measures must be taken	9.14
(2) Agency	9.04		
(3) Knowledge of misconduct	9.05	(3) Special measures that immunize the security	9.18
(4) Relationship with unilateral mistake	9.06		
		D. Gratuitous Dispositions	9.21

A. Introduction

9.01 This chapter concerns the situation where A contends that his transaction with B is voidable because his consent was vitiated by some factor for which a third party, C, was responsible. The question to be addressed is how far B must be implicated in order for A to rescind. Provided A can implicate B, A's right to rescind will be subject to the same bars and governed by the same principles that apply in an ordinary two party situation.[1]

9.02 An important example of this scenario occurs where A, a wife, seeks to rescind a security she gave to B, a bank, in support of finance the bank extended to a business operated by C, the husband. The special rules that have been developed to govern cases of this general type are discussed in Part C of this chapter.

B. Contracts

(1) The basic rule precluding rescission

9.03 The simple fact that the third party, C, has wrongfully caused A to contract with B will not entitle A to avoid that contract.[2] If A has a claim it is against C, usually for damages or equitable compensation.

---

[1] *TSB Bank Plc v Camfield* [1995] 1 WLR 430 (CA) 437.
[2] *Sturge v Starr* (1833) 2 My & K 195, 196; 39 ER 918, 919; *Pulsford v Richards* (1853) 17 Beav 87, 95; 51 ER 965, 968; *Re The Liverpool Borough Bank (Duranty's case)* (1858) 26 Beav 268, 270–71; 53 ER 901, 902; *Re The United Kingdom Ship Owning Company, Limited (Felgate's case)* (1865) 2 De G J & S 456, 465; 46 ER 451, 455; *Bainbrigge v Browne* (1881) 18 Ch 188, 197; *Talbot v Von Boris* [1911] 1 KB 854 (CA); *Armagas Ltd v Mundogas SA (The Ocean Frost)* [1985] 1 Lloyd's Rep 1, 18–20; *Royal Bank of Scotland plc v Etridge (No 2)* [2002] 2 AC 773 [40], [144]; *Chancery Client Partners Ltd v MRC 957 Ltd* [2016] Lloyd's Rep FC 578.

(2) Agency

9.04 Of course if C was B's agent or sub-agent then the case will be treated as if B had himself committed the wrongful act,[3] and C's knowledge will be imputed to B,[4] provided that C made the representation within the scope of his actual or apparent authority.[5] It makes no difference that the agent may have been acting in his own interests.[6] B will also be responsible if he adopts C's unauthorized misrepresentation before the contract is made,[7] or if before that time the agent is given the authority necessary to make the representation in question.[8]

(3) Knowledge of misconduct

9.05 A will also be entitled to avoid the contract if B knew before the contract was concluded of C's misrepresentation or other wrongful inducement.[9] Nothing more is required and nothing less will suffice. This applies to all of the grounds for rescission, even innocent misrepresentation,[10] except that the Court of Appeal has recognized a qualification in a limited class of cases involving the abuse of fiduciary relations.[11] Knowledge in this context means actual knowledge of the factual circumstances that are treated by the court as impairing A's consent, such as a material misrepresentation or a relationship sufficient to raise a presumption of undue influence.[12] Constructive knowledge is not enough, and nor is suspicion,[13] but as in related areas of the law actual knowledge encompasses wilfully shutting one's eyes

---

[3] *Mullens v Miller* (1892) 22 ChD 194, 198; *Lynde v Anglo-Italian Hemp Spinning Co* [1896] 1 Ch 178, 182–83; *Wauton v Coppard* [1899] 1 ChD 92; *Goldrei, Foucard & Son v Sinclair* [1918] 1 KB 180 (CA); *Anglo-Scottish Sugar Beet Corporation, Limited v Spalding Urban District Council* [1937] 2 KB 607; *Armagas Ltd v Mundogas SA (The Ocean Frost)* [1985] 1 Lloyd's Rep 1, 18–20; *Krakowski v Eurolynx Properties Ltd* (1995) 183 CLR 563, 582–84, applied in *Spice Girls Ltd v Aprilia World Services BV* [2002] EWCA 15 [57].
[4] *Archer v Hudson* (1844) 7 Beav 551, 560–61; 49 ER 1180, 1183–84; aff'd (1846) 15 LJ Ch 211, 213.
[5] *Gordon v Selico Co Ltd* [1986] 1 EGLR 71 (CA) 75; *First Energy (UK) Ltd v Hungarian International Bank Ltd* [1993] 2 Lloyd's Rep 194 (CA) 204; *MCI Worldcom International Inc v Primus Telecommunications plc* [2004] 2 All ER (Comm) 833 [25]; *Gaydamak v Leviev* [2012] EWHC 1740 (Ch). As to the test for determining whether a fraud is committed within the scope of an agent's authority, see *Dubai Aluminium v Salaam* [2003] 2 AC 366 [23], [122], [129]. Cf *Armagas Ltd v Mundogas SA (The Ocean Frost)* [1986] AC 717 (CA) 744–45, 755, 769, a case of bribery where the Court of Appeal held *obiter* that it would be sufficient that the agent was acting within the course of his employment, as to which see Chap 8, paras [8.65]–[8.66].
[6] *Bank of Credit and Commerce International SA v Aboody* [1990] 1 QB 923 (CA) 972.
[7] *Bradford Third Equitable Benefit Buildings Society v Borders* [1941] 2 All ER 205 (HL) 211.
[8] *Briess v Woolley* [1954] AC 333, 353–54.
[9] *Stone v Compton* (1838) 5 Bing NC 142, 156–57; 132 ER 1059, 1065; *Spencer v Handley* (1842) 4 Man & G 414, 418; 134 ER 169, 171; *Cobbett v Brock* (1855) 20 Beav 524, 528, 531; 52 ER 706, 707, 708; *Kempson v Ashbee* (1874) 10 Ch App 15, 21; *Bainbrigge v Browne* (1881) 18 Ch 188, 197; *Lynde v Anglo-Italian Hemp Spinning Co* [1896] 1 Ch 178, 183; *Talbot v Von Boris* [1911] 1 KB 854 (CA); *Kesarmel v NKV Valliappa Chettiar* [1954] 1 WLR 380 (PC—Malaya); *O'Sullivan v Management Agency and Music Ltd* [1985] QB 428 (CA); *Barclays Bank plc v O'Brien* [1994] 1 AC 180, 197; *Credit Lyonnais Bank Nederland NV v Burch* [1997] 1 All ER 144 (CA) 152; *Royal Bank of Scotland plc v Etridge (No 2)* [2002] 2 AC 773 [40], [144]; *UBS AG v Kommunale Wasserwerke Leipzig GmbH* [2017] 2 Lloyd's Rep 621 (CA) [108], [110].
[10] *Lynde v Anglo-Italian Hemp Spinning Co* [1896] 1 Ch 178, 183. See also *Re Metropolitan Coal Consumer's Association (Karberg's case)* [1892] 3 Ch 1 (CA) 13.
[11] *UBS AG v Kommunale Wasserwerke Leipzig GmbH* [2017] 2 Lloyd's Rep 621 (CA) [113]. See Chap 8, para [8.69].
[12] *Bainbrigge v Browne* (1881) 18 Ch 188, 197.
[13] *UBS AG v Kommunale Wasserwerke Leipzig GmbH* [2017] 2 Lloyd's Rep 621 (CA) [120], [347].

to the obvious and wilfully and recklessly failing to make enquiries that an honest and reasonable man would.[14] The onus of proving knowledge lies on the rescinding party.[15]

(4) Relationship with unilateral mistake

Cartwright has pointed out that the entitlement to rescind on account of a counterparty's knowledge of a third party's misrepresentation sits uneasily with the established approach to mistake and duties of disclosure in the formation of a contract.[16] In particular, since *Smith v Hughes*[17] it has been understood that a vendor is under no obligation to inform the purchaser that he is in some way mistaken, provided the vendor himself is not responsible for the mistake. It is difficult to explain why the fact the vendor knows that the purchaser's mistake has been induced by a third party's misrepresentation should make a difference, though it clearly does on the authorities. 9.06

C. Surety Contracts

In *Barclays Bank plc v O'Brien*[18] the House of Lords fashioned special rules to govern a particular situation that has become increasingly prevalent. The central example of this situation occurs where a wife guarantees her husband's business debts, often exposing her interest in the matrimonial home. There is a particular danger that in persuading his wife to stand surety, the husband will take advantage of the influence that he may enjoy over her, or else that he may misrepresent the state of his business or the extent of the guarantee.[19] 9.07

(1) Constructive notice

On conventional principles the creditor would not be affected by the husband's misconduct, and the wife would not be entitled to avoid the guarantee, unless the creditor or its agent actually knew of the circumstances in which her consent was procured. The courts have, however, long been especially concerned about the vulnerability of sureties such as wives and elderly relations. Before *O'Brien* this concern had been partially met by treating the husband as the agent of the creditor for the purpose of imputing his misconduct to the bank, but only where the bank entrusted him with the task of obtaining the wife's signature.[20] 9.08

---

[14] *Owen v Holman* (1853) 4 HLC 997, 1034–35; 10 ER 752, 767; *Logicrose Ltd v Southend United Football Club Ltd* [1988] 1 WLR 1256, 1261; *Royal Bank of Scotland plc v Etridge (No 2)* [2002] 2 AC 773 [144], where Lord Scott referred in this connection to *Commission for New Towns v Cooper (Great Britain) Ltd* [1995] Ch 259 (CA) 281; *Economides v Commercial Assurance Co plc* [1998] QB 587 (CA) 601–02, 607; *Donegal International Ltd v Zambia* [2007] 1 Lloyd's Rep 397 [464].
[15] *Talbot v Von Boris* [1911] 1 KB 854 (CA).
[16] J Cartwright, *Misrepresentation, Mistake and Non-disclosure* (5th edn, 2019) [4.81].
[17] (1867) LR 6 QB 597, 607.
[18] [1994] 1 AC 180.
[19] The applicability of the special rules in cases of misrepresentation, including innocent misrepresentation, was confirmed in *Annulment Funding Company Limited v Cowey* [2010] BPIR 1304 (CA) [64] and *Royal Bank of Scotland plc v Chandra* [2011] Bus LR D149 (CA).
[20] Eg *Avon Finance Co Ltd v Bridger* [1985] 2 All ER 281 (CA); *Kings North Trust Ltd v Bell* [1986] 1 WLR 119 (CA); *Coldunell Ltd v Gallon* [1986] QB 1184 (CA).

9.09 In *O'Brien*[21] the House of Lords held this approach to be artificial and unsatisfactory. While there may be cases in which the husband acts as the creditor's agent, Lord Browne-Wilkinson said that these would be very rare.[22] The mere fact that the creditor left the husband to procure his wife's signature is not enough to constitute him as their agent without distorting that concept.

9.10 Instead the House of Lords held that the security would be vulnerable to avoidance at the instance of the wife if the bank had either actual or, what was novel, constructive notice of the facts giving rise to her equity.[23] In broad terms, where the circumstances known to the creditor disclose a risk that the wife's consent may have been improperly procured, the creditor will be fixed with constructive notice of any impropriety there may have been unless it takes certain specified steps designed to minimize that risk. Where the creditor is fixed with constructive notice, the wife will be entitled to avoid the security on proof that it was in fact procured by undue influence or misrepresentation.

9.11 While Lord Browne-Wilkinson spoke of the concept of constructive notice as if it would be familiar, it soon became clear that the concept is a new one, not to be equated with the conventional principles of constructive notice applicable in conveyancing transactions. Those conventional principles regulate the situation where a purchaser acquires from his vendor real property which is subject to the undisclosed interest of a third party. In this situation the purchaser is fixed with constructive notice of the third party's interest, and takes subject to it, if that interest would have been uncovered by reasonable inquiries.[24]

9.12 By contrast the wife in the situation regulated by the doctrine of constructive notice recognized in *O'Brien* deals directly with the creditor. The creditor does not acquire her interest through her husband, and in the usual case where the wife offers as security a charge over her share in the matrimonial home, there is no defect in her title. Moreover, the measures a creditor must take in order to avoid constructive notice do not consist in making inquiries.

9.13 The novelty of this doctrine was recognized by the House of Lords eight years later in *Royal Bank of Scotland plc v Etridge (No 2)*,[25] a decision which has been largely successful in settling a number of difficult issues that had emerged in the wake of *O'Brien*. In particular, in that case their Lordships reformulated and clarified the scope of the *O'Brien* principle as well as the special measures that a creditor must take to immunize its security where the principle applies.

(2) Circumstances in which special measures must be taken

9.14 It is now clear that the *O'Brien* principle applies to surety transactions where the relationship between the surety and the debtor is non-commercial and the transaction is not on its

---

[21] [1994] 1 AC 180, 195. The House of Lords also rejected the theory that a wife standing surety for her husband's debts enjoys the 'special equity' against the creditor recognized by the High Court of Australia in *Yerkey v Jones* (1939) 63 CLR 649, 675. That theory has since been reconfirmed by the High Court of Australia in *Garcia v National Australia Bank Limited* (1998) 194 CLR 395.
[22] [1994] 1 AC 180, 195.
[23] [1994] 1 AC 180, 195.
[24] Law of Property Act 1925, s 199.
[25] [2002] AC 773 [39]–[41], [145]–[147].

face financially advantageous to the surety.[26] If the creditor knows that this is so, the burden of proof of which lies with the surety,[27] it will only avoid being fixed with constructive notice of any impropriety by taking special measures. The two key circumstances will be discussed in turn, followed by a discussion of the special measures a creditor must take to immunize his security.

Non-commercial relationship

9.15 While the central example of a case to which the principle applies is the relationship between husband and wife, its scope is much wider than this. It encompasses all other familial relationships, such as the relation between parents and children and between more extended family members. Cohabitation is not necessary.[28] The principle goes further still, and has been applied in a case where a junior employee provided security for her employer's overdraft.[29] In *Etridge* Lord Nicholls considered the scope of the principle and concluded that the only sensible limitation was that it should apply in all cases where the relationship between the surety and the debtor is non-commercial but not where their relationship is commercial in nature.[30]

Transaction not on its face financially advantageous to surety

9.16 A transaction by which one party stands surety for the debts of another, without more, will be treated by the courts as one that on its face is not to the financial advantage of the surety.[31] By contrast, a transaction by which funds are advanced to a husband and wife jointly is on its face financially advantageous to the wife, though the principle will apply if the creditor is aware that the loan is being made for the husband's purposes as distinct from joint purposes.[32] In this regard the creditor cannot shut its eyes to what it knows, but it need not enquire as to the purposes of a joint advance.[33]

9.17 More difficult are cases in which the advance is made to a company in which the surety is involved. In *Etridge* the House of Lords held that the *O'Brien* principle would apply notwithstanding that the surety might be a shareholder or a director or officer, because these factors 'are not a reliable guide to the identity of the persons who actually have the conduct of the company's business'.[34] There may be cases in which the creditor reliably knows that the surety actively participates in the actual conduct of the business, but it would rarely be prudent to assume on this basis that the *O'Brien* principle does not apply.

---

[26] *Royal Bank of Scotland plc v Etridge (No 2)* [2002] AC 773 [41], [43]–[49], [87]. In Hong Kong, *Li San Ying v Bank of China (HK) Limited* (2004) 7 HKCFAR 579 (Lord Scott NPJ).
[27] *Barclays Bank plc v Boulter* [1999] 1 WLR 1919 (HL) 1925.
[28] *Royal Bank of Scotland plc v Etridge (No 2)* [2002] AC 773 [47]; *Massey v Midland Bank plc* [1995] 1 All ER 929 (CA) 933.
[29] *Credit Lyonnais Bank Nederland NV v Burch* [1997] 1 All ER 144 (CA).
[30] *Royal Bank of Scotland plc v Etridge (No 2)* [2002] AC 773 [87]–[89].
[31] *Royal Bank of Scotland plc v Etridge (No 2)* [2002] AC 773 [43].
[32] *Royal Bank of Scotland plc v Etridge (No 2)* [2002] AC 773 [48]; *CIBC Mortgages plc v Pitt* [1994] 1 AC 200.
[33] *Mortgage Agency Services Number Two Ltd v Chater* [2003] EWCA Civ 490 [63]–[67].
[34] *Royal Bank of Scotland plc v Etridge (No 2)* [2002] AC 773 [49]. Eg, *Mahon v FBN Bank (UK) Limited* [2012] 2 BCLC 83, where the wife was the sole shareholder and company secretary. As to joint advances to husband and wife partnerships, see *O'Neill v Ulster Bank Ltd* [2016] BPIR 126 (NICA).

(3) Special measures that immunize the security

9.18 In *O'Brien*, Lord Browne-Wilkinson said that for the future a creditor could avoid being fixed with constructive notice if it insists that the wife attend a private meeting with a representative of the creditor at which she is told of the extent of her liability as surety, warned of the risk, and urged to take independent advice.[35] In practice lending institutions have been understandably reluctant to assume responsibility for advising intending sureties in this manner. They have instead insisted that the intending surety take independent advice from a solicitor.

9.19 Much of the focus in *Etridge* was on this practice in light of complaints that such advice could be perfunctory and inapt to protect vulnerable sureties. Notwithstanding these complaints, the House of Lords confirmed that a creditor's security will usually be immunized from challenge if it insists that the surety obtain independent legal advice, provided certain safeguards are complied with.[36] The burden of proving compliance rests with the creditor.[37] The creditor proceeds at its own risk, however, if the creditor knows that the solicitor has not duly advised the surety or knows facts from which it ought to realize that the surety has not received appropriate advice.[38] Absent special circumstances such as these, the creditor is entitled to assume that the solicitor has done his job properly and deficiencies in his advice are a matter between the surety and the solicitor.[39]

9.20 So far as the safeguards are concerned, Lord Nicholls identified four in respect of future transactions.[40] First, the creditor should check directly with the surety the name of the solicitor she wishes to act for her, and not proceed until it has received an appropriate response directly from the surety. Secondly, the creditor should send the solicitor such financial information as it possesses relevant to the advice he is to give.[41] Thirdly, if exceptionally the creditor believes or suspects that the surety's consent has been improperly procured, then it should insist that the surety is advised by a solicitor independent of the debtor,[42] and inform the solicitor of the facts on which this belief or suspicion is based. Fourthly, the creditor should obtain from the solicitor a written confirmation that he has given appropriate independent advice.[43] The creditor is not required to advise the surety about the wisdom of

---

[35] *Barclays Bank plc v O'Brien* [1994] 1 AC 180, 196. Though if the creditor knows facts indicating that impropriety is not only possible but probable, then it must insist on independent advice: 197.
[36] *Royal Bank of Scotland plc v Etridge (No 2)* [2002] AC 773 [56], [171].
[37] *Barclays Bank plc v Boulter* [1999] 1 WLR 1919 (HL) 1925.
[38] *Royal Bank of Scotland plc v Etridge (No 2)* [2002] AC 773 [57]. See the discussion of the solicitor's role and the advice that should be given in *Padden v Bevan Ashford* [2012] 1 WLR 1759 (CA).
[39] *Royal Bank of Scotland plc v Etridge (No 2)* [2002] AC 773 [78], [175]. In ordinary cases the solicitor will not be taken to act as the creditor's agent when advising the surety even if the solicitor is also acting for the creditor in the transaction: [77], [178].
[40] *Royal Bank of Scotland plc v Etridge (No 2)* [2002] AC 773 [79]. In respect of past transactions, Lord Nicholls indicated at [80] that the creditor would usually be protected if a solicitor who was acting for the surety in the transaction had given the creditor confirmation to the effect that he had brought home to the surety the risk she was running by standing as surety.
[41] *Royal Bank of Scotland plc v Etridge (No 2)* [2002] AC 773 [189].
[42] *Royal Bank of Scotland plc v Etridge (No 2)* [2002] AC 773 [174]. Except in this special case, the creditor may safely accept a confirmation of independent advice given by a solicitor who also acts for both the husband and the creditor itself.
[43] See *Kapoor v National Westminster Bank plc* [2010] EWHC 2986 (Ch). In Hong Kong, *Wing Hang Bank Limited v Kwok Lai Sim* [2009] 4 HKC 71 (CA).

entering the transaction or to give its opinion of the financial state or business prospects of the debtor.[44]

D. Gratuitous Dispositions

Gifts and other gratuitous dispositions procured by the misconduct of a third party may be set aside without proof of knowledge or even constructive knowledge on the part of the donee. This is illustrated by cases involving third party misrepresentation,[45] undue influence,[46] and breach of fiduciary duty.[47] This aligns with the proposition that a gratuitous disposition made by reason of a sufficient unilateral mistake may be set aside even though the donee did not know of the mistake,[48] though the same mistake would not make a contract voidable.[49]

9.21

---

[44] *Royal Bank of Scotland plc v Etridge (No 2)* [2002] AC 773 [172].
[45] *Scholefield v Templer* (1859) 4 De G & J 429, 433–34; 45 ER 166, 168; *Hunter BNZ Finance Ltd v CG Maloney* (1988) 18 NSWLR 420, 433–34 (cheque).
[46] *Bridgeman v Green* (1755) Wilm 58, 62; 97 ER 22, 25; *Huguenin v Baseley* (1807) 14 Ves 273, 288–90; 33 ER 526, 532–33; *Bullock v Lloyds Bank Ltd* [1955] Ch 317. See P Ridge, 'Third Party Volunteers and Undue Influence' (2014) 130 LQR 112.
[47] *Barron v Willis* [1900] 2 Ch 121 (CA) 133.
[48] *Pitt v Holt* [2013] 2 AC 108.
[49] *Riverlate Properties Ltd v Paul* [1975] 1 Ch 133 (CA) 140–45. See Chap 29, para [29.19].

Part III

RESCISSION BY ELECTION AND BY COURT ORDER

10

Common Law, Equity, and Fusion

A. Introduction	10.01	C. Overview of the Distinctions between Rescission at Law and in Equity	10.20
B. Persistence of the Distinction between Rescission at Law and in Equity	10.03	(1) Introduction	10.20
		(2) Grounds for rescission	10.23
(1) Absence of fusion	10.03	(3) Bars to rescission	10.30
(2) The principle that rules of equity prevail	10.10	(4) Differences between rescinding at law and in equity	10.34
(3) Reform	10.15	(5) Interaction between the common law and equitable doctrines	10.39

A. Introduction

Chapter 3 outlined the differences between the common law and equitable doctrines of rescission as they had developed before the Judicature reforms. Those differences were not the subject of much attention in the literature at the time, and the Judicature reforms further obscured the relationship between them. Neither the separate origins of rescission at law and in equity, nor the different mechanisms each employed to effect rescission, are well understood. This has hampered the development of clear rules regulating the relationship between the two doctrines, and their relationship remains uncertain today. A key question is how far, if at all, there has been a fusion or synthesis of the principles of common law and equity in this area. **10.01**

The conclusion reached here is that there has not been any fusion and that there remain two distinct kinds of rescission.[1] That one has common law and the other equitable origins is, however, of limited importance in itself. Of practical significance is that each confers separate rights, and permits rescission to occur in quite different ways. The origin of those rights is of less importance than their delineation. Accordingly, after first addressing the question of fusion, this chapter goes on to summarize the key differences between rescission at law and in equity, and the relationship that now seems to obtain between them. **10.02**

---

[1] Also, JD Heydon, MJ Leeming, and PG Turner, *Meagher, Gummow and Lehane's Equity Doctrines and Remedies* (5th edn, 2015) [25–125] 'the Judicature legislation has the capacity to obscure what are two quite distinct remedies'. S Zogg, *Proprietary Consequences in Defective Transfers of Ownership* (2020) 139–40, 157–58, 163–64 and *ff* argues that there has been no fusion in relation to the grounds for and proprietary consequences of rescission, but that there is fusion for contractual rights and the bar *restitutio in integrum* impossible. A Burrows, *A Restatement of the English Law of Contract* (2nd edn, 2020) §34(3) concludes that the only significant remaining distinction between rescission at law and in equity is that laches applies to equitable rescission only, and that in principle differences between the two 'should be minimised'.

B. Persistence of the Distinction between Rescission at Law and in Equity

(1) Absence of fusion

10.03 The Uniformity of Process Act 1832 and Common Law Procedure Act 1852 significantly reformed the system of common law pleadings. In weakening the formal strictures of the forms of action, this legislation assisted in the development of the principles of rescission at common law. But it in no way abolished them. Likewise the Judicature Acts of 1873 and 1875 did not abolish the doctrine of equitable rescission or combine the separate rules for rescission developed at law and in equity.[2] Unless subsequent case law has combined them, the separate doctrines of rescission developed at law and in equity must each continue to operate.

10.04 The evidence of fusion is not strong. On the contrary, many of the principal authorities proceed on the basis that both the equitable and common law doctrines continue to operate side by side. This was assumed by Lord Wright in *Spence v Crawford*,[3] and Lord Blackburn's speech in *Erlanger v The New Sombrero Phosphate Company*[4] explained the different machinery available to courts of law and equity to effect a restoration of the status quo upon rescission without inquiring whether the Judicature Acts made any, or if so, what difference.[5] Appellate courts have since continued to refer to the differences explained by Lord Blackburn, whilst underlining that the effect of the Judicature Acts is that rescission may be ordered pursuant to equitable principles even if restoration of the status quo is not possible at common law.[6] This assumes the parallel working of the two different regimes. That was also the analysis of the High Court of Australia in *Alati v Kruger*,[7] where it was regarded as uncontroversial that both common law and equitable principles continue to operate.[8] The Court of Appeal has since said that *Alati v Kruger* explains the distinction between rescission at law and in equity.[9]

10.05 Moreover, several of the leading decisions are explicable only on the basis that common law principles were involved, and others on the basis that the court was giving equitable relief. Mr Caldwell's rescission of the contract for the sale of his motor car in *Car and Universal Finance Co Ltd v Caldwell*[10] involved the exercise of a common law right. It was the common

---

[2] For the background and effects of the Judicature Acts, see J McGhee and S Elliott (eds), *Snell's Equity* (34th edn, 2020) [1-015]–[1-033]; JD Heydon, MJ Leeming, and PG Turner, *Meagher, Gummow and Lehane's Equity Doctrines and Remedies* (5th edn, 2015) [2-005]–[2-125]. For the problems with Chancery procedure prior to the Judicature reforms, see M Lobban, 'Preparing for Fusion: Reforming the Nineteenth-Century Court of Chancery, Part I' (2004) 22 *Law and History Review* 389; M Lobban, 'Preparing for Fusion: Reforming the Nineteenth-Century Court of Chancery, Part II' (2004) 22 *Law and History Review* 565; also J Getzler, 'Chancery Reform and Law Reform' (2004) 22 *Law and History Review* 601.
[3] [1939] 3 All ER 271 (HL Sc) 290.
[4] (1878) 3 App Cas 1218, 1278.
[5] The relevant events in that case occurred before the Judicature Acts.
[6] But cf *Halpern v Halpern (No 2)* [2008] QB 195 (CA) [69].
[7] (1955) 94 CLR 216, 223–24.
[8] For a recent restatement of the law in Australia, *Nadinic v Drinkwater* (2017) 94 NSWLR 518 (CA) [28]–[30]; also, *Jonval Builders Pty Ltd v Comr for Fair Trading* (2020) 383 ALR 334 (NSWCA) [28]–[34], *Harvard Nominees Pty Ltd v Tiller* [2020] FCAFC 229 [96] (rescission at law effected by election and in equity by court order and subject to discretion of the court).
[9] *O'Sullivan v Management Agency and Music Limited* [1985] QB 428 (CA) 457. See also *Halpern v Halpern (No 2)* [2007] QB 88; [2008] QB 195 (CA).
[10] [1965] 1 QB 525 (CA).

law that gave him the power, by his own act, to extinguish the contract *ab initio*, and to regain legal title to the car he had sold, once the fraud came to light.

This stands in sharp contrast with *Johnson v EBS Pensioner Trustees Ltd*,[11] where the Court of Appeal rejected the submission that a solicitor's client had an equivalent right unilaterally to rescind a charge and guarantee for breach of fiduciary duty. It was stressed that when a principal wishes to rescind a contract for breach of fiduciary duty, the court is asked to exercise a discretion to grant equitable relief, and at first instance Patten J underlined that the discretion is to intervene in the enforcement of legal rights.[12] **10.06**

In *Goldsworthy v Bricknell*[13] the Court of Appeal likewise characterized the right to rescind for undue influence as 'an equitable right', and therefore liable to be defeated by equitable defences. Characterizing particular rights to rescind as 'equitable' presupposes that the agreement is valid at common law. If it was void or had been avoided at law, then logically no equity to rescind could arise. **10.07**

Nor is there any evidence that the various grounds for rescission developed in equity, but unknown at common law, now also confer a right to extinguish a contract by electing to reject it, in the manner permitted by the common law. Decisions such as *Johnson v EBS Pensioner Trustees Ltd* and *Goldsworthy v Bricknell* suggest that the contrary is true. **10.08**

Statements can certainly be found to the effect that former distinctions between the equitable and common law doctrines of rescission no longer apply.[14] But these have tended to be made by judges in passing, and without elaboration or the benefit of argument. They should be treated with care. The weight of authority supports the conclusion that the principles of rescission at common law and in equity remain distinct and separate doctrines, operating side by side, albeit in a manner that is sometimes overlooked.[15] Recent authorities considering claims to rescind for bribery have underlined the differences between the doctrines at law and in equity, including for the purpose of explaining why the remedy is a matter of right rather than judicial discretion.[16] **10.09**

---

[11] [2002] Lloyd's Rep PN 309 (CA); Chap 11, paras [11.90]–[11.92].
[12] [2002] Lloyd's Rep PN 309 (CA) [32], [56]–[57], [78]–[79]; (ChD, 8 March 2001) [46] (Patten J), followed *Hurstanger Ltd v Wilson* [2008] Bus LR 216 (CA) [48]–[51].
[13] [1987] Ch 378 (CA) 409–10.
[14] *Society of Lloyd's v Lyons* [1997] CLC 1398 (CA) (Saville LJ); *Drake Insurance plc v Provident Insurance plc* [2003] Lloyd's Rep IR 781, 788 (Moore-Bick J).
[15] See also S Worthington, 'The Proprietary Consequences of Rescission' [2002] 10 RLR 28, 32; A Lodder, *Enrichment in the Law of Unjust Enrichment* (2012) 118 (describing rescission at law as a self-help remedy, and equitable rescission as requiring a court order). That rescission at law and in equity attract quite different principles continues to be accepted in Australia: Chap 11, paras [11.97]–[11.101].
[16] *Conway v Prince Eze* [2018] EWHC 29 (Ch) [148], [154], [156] ('the discretionary remedy of rescission in equity does not abolish the position at common law ... [r]escission at common law is a legal, not an equitable remedy') (appeal dismissed [2019] EWCA Civ 88); *Wood v Commercial First Business Limited* [2021] EWCA Civ 471 [98]–[101] (doctrines of rescission at law and in equity are distinct, and the remedy at common law is a matter of right and not judicial discretion). See also *Ceviz v Frawley* [2021] EWHC 8 (Ch) [120] (absent fraud rescission at common law by self-help is not available, and the right to rescind is equitable, at discretion of the court); *IGE USA Investments Limited v The Commissioner for Her Majesty's Revenue and Customs* [2021] Ch 423 (CA) (rescission at law for fraud is not subject to any limitation period whereas equitable rescission for fraud is subject to a 6-year time-bar where facts would support a claim for damages in deceit).

(2) The principle that rules of equity prevail

10.10 A principle of the Judicature reforms is that in cases of conflict or variance between the rules of equity and the common law with respect to the same subject matter, the rules of equity shall prevail.[17] Does that principle have any application to the law of rescission?

10.11 There are two locations, in particular, where that principle might be thought to be relevant. The first is the notion that rescission at law is effected by the act of the injured party, whereas in equity it is brought about by court order. The second is the discrepancy between the rules applied by the common law and equity in determining whether *restitutio in integrum* is possible. But neither of these differences involves the application of different common law and equitable 'rules' within the meaning of the priority principle. The differences are, rather, consequences of the different mechanisms employed by the common law and equity to effect rescission.[18] They are the product of substantive rights, and the principle that equitable rules prevail in cases of conflict is not engaged.[19] There is no more 'conflict' than exists between legal and equitable titles.[20]

10.12 In *Halpern v Halpern (No 2)*[21] the Commercial Court regarded the distinction between rescission at law and in equity as uncontroversial, and this appears to have been accepted in the Court of Appeal.[22] But in considering the argument that there is no obligation to make counter-restitution following rescission for duress at common law, Carnwath LJ commented *obiter* that the submission faced an uphill battle in circumstances where it was accepted that counter-restitution is required when rescinding for undue influence in equity, and that since the Judicature reforms the rules of equity prevail.[23] This must be correct. If the common law does not require counter-restitution following rescission for duress, it must be provided in accordance with equitable principles, for the facts constituting duress at law will equally permit rescission in equity, and in equity counter-restitution is mandatory.

10.13 But even this narrow point is not properly to be regarded as an instance where there is a conflict between the rules of common law and equity, and where equitable rules must therefore prevail. That is because the common law almost certainly does require counter-restitution upon rescission for duress, and there is therefore no conflict between the common law and equitable rules in this respect. Conversely, if counter-restitution is not possible at law by reason of the common law's limited mechanisms for compelling it, rescission in equity will be ordered if *restitutio in integrum* remains possible by reference to its more flexible doctrine. But, as suggested above, here too there is no conflict between the rules of common law and equity calling for application of the statutory priority rule. Equity's response presupposes the relative poverty of the rights conferred by the common law. There is no conflict

---

[17] Judicature Act 1873, s 25(11), reproduced Senior Courts Act 1981, s 49.
[18] As to the difference between rescission as a self-help and judicial remedy, see Chap 11. For the difference between common law and equity as to the possibility of *restitutio in integrum*, see Chap 18.
[19] The same conclusion is reached in JD Heydon, MJ Leeming, and PG Turner, *Meagher, Gummow and Lehane's Equity Doctrine and Remedies* (5th edn, 2015) [25-120] (approving this passage in the first edition).
[20] FW Maitland, *Equity and the Forms of Action* (1929) 16–18.
[21] [2007] 1 QB 88.
[22] *Halpern v Halpern (No 2)* [2008] QB 195 (CA).
[23] *Halpern v Halpern (No 2)* [2008] QB 195 (CA) [63]–[69].

between them, any more than there is a conflict between the right to damages for breach of contract, and the right to seek its specific performance.

10.14 The only point where the statutory priority rule might possibly find expression is in the notion that a court order setting aside a contract in accordance with equitable principles extinguishes it at common law, which was not the case before the Judicature reforms.[24] The law of rescission is otherwise untouched by the principle that in cases of conflict or variance between the rules of equity and the common law with respect to the same subject matter, the rules of equity prevail.

(3) Reform

10.15 A system that does not distinguish between rescission at law and in equity would no doubt be simpler, but then so would a system of property law devoid of the distinction between legal and equitable titles, or a law of contract untrammelled by equitable constraints. Simple rules are not necessarily just, and nor are they necessarily useful. In determining whether reform should be attempted by trying to fuse the common law and equitable principles of rescission the question is not whether there is a simpler alternative, but whether the existence of separate doctrines works injustice, or is otherwise indefensible.[25] It has not so far been suggested that the existing system is unjust, and it does indeed seem defensible for the following reasons.[26]

10.16 The key question of substance when contemplating a fused set of rules is whether the right to rescind by election, as opposed to court order, should be abolished, expanded, or remain as it currently is, confined to instances where rescission is available according to common law principles.[27] If the right is to be expanded it is necessary to know both exactly how the law should rescind part-executed transactions in such cases, and why contracting parties should be entitled to self-help rescission. As to the first question, it is in fact very difficult to formulate a system that achieves automatic *restitutio in integrum* once a part-executed transaction is disaffirmed, outside the simple cases where rescission at law is possible.[28] As to the second question, there do not appear to be compelling reasons for extending self-help rescission beyond its current field of operation, within the boundaries of rescission at law.

---

[24] See Chap 12, para [12.07]. For the old law, Chap 3, para [3.37].
[25] As to the wider debate about the fusion of common law and equitable principles, 'Part I: The Fusion Debate' in S Degeling and J Edelman, *Equity in Commercial Law* (2005); A Burrows, 'We Do This at Common Law But That in Equity' (2002) 22 OJLS 1; J Getzler, 'Patterns of Fusion' in P Birks (ed), *Classification of Obligations* (1997); see also, K Barker, 'Equitable Title and Common Law Conversion: The Limits of the Fusionist Ideal' [1998] 6 RLR 150.
[26] Also, JD Heydon, MJ Leeming, and PG Turner, *Meagher, Gummow and Lehane's Equity Doctrine and Remedies* (5th edn, 2015) [25-125] (approving these passages in the first edition).
[27] See Chap 11, paras [11.53]–[11.56]. Rescission is not, in substance, effected by an election when a contract is not voidable according to orthodox common law principles, even in cases of fraud. See Chap 11, paras [11.60], [11.108]–[11.110], Chap 12, paras [12.11]–[12.21], Chap 15, paras [15.69]–[15.76].
[28] For some of the difficulties with the concept that rescission follows the making of an election where the contract is not voidable at law, see Chap 11, paras [11.108]–[11.110], Chap 12, paras [12.11]–[12.21], Chap 15, paras [15.69]–[15.76]. See also Chap 18, para [18.30]. For the view that an election to disaffirm confers a vested obligation to make counter-restitution and is effective to bring about rescission in equity by unilateral act, S Zogg, *Proprietary Consequences in Defective Transfers of Ownership* (2020) 147, 158.

10.17 That is, in particular, because rescission often has quite radical consequences for the parties affected by it. Permitting rescission by election gives the innocent party extensive rights, and the power to cause significant prejudice to the other contracting party in a manner that is, necessarily, unmediated by judicial control. It should be proscribed accordingly. Whilst there seems no good reason for abolishing the self-help form of rescission altogether,[29] restricting the right to cases where rescission is possible at law appears to be a proportionate and justified limitation. In practice rescission at law is available in comparatively narrow classes of case, involving plainly wrongful conduct,[30] profoundly impaired consent,[31] or policy considerations anchored in commercial necessity.[32] A power to rescind by election seems justified in each of these instances. It is much more difficult to see that it is justified whenever a transaction is voidable only in equity, not least because extreme forms of the equitable grounds for rescinding tend to overlap with the grounds for rescission at common law.[33] It has been recently argued that the underlying nature and purpose of the remedy of equitable rescission speaks in favour of it continuing to be regarded as a form of relief administered by the court, and subject to judicial control.[34]

10.18 The most commercially significant context for rescission at law is the insurance market. Contracts of insurance and reinsurance that are affected by non-disclosure or misrepresentation are always voidable at common law,[35] and the insurance market has been predicated on precisely that model of rescission. Risks are written and priced on the assumption that the underwriter enjoys an unconditional right to avoid the policy upon discovering a material non-disclosure or misrepresentation, and on the assumption that there is no need for a court order or for a judicial discretion to be exercised in his favour.[36] When the extent of the common law right to rescind contracts of insurance and reinsurance has been found wanting, the rules have been reformed by Parliament in respects that go far beyond what could be accommodated by the natural evolution of the common law.[37] The other principal context for rescission at law is executory contracts procured by fraud or duress, and completed sales of goods procured by fraud. In each of those contexts it seems to be appropriate that the injured party has a power to restore the status quo by simply electing to reject the transaction, free from the constraint of judicial control.[38]

---

[29] For the contrary argument, see J O'Sullivan, 'Rescission as a Self Help Remedy: A Critical Analysis' [2000] 59 CLJ 509.

[30] Fraud (including bribery) or duress: Chaps 4 and 6.

[31] Contracting with knowledge that the other party is suffering from mental infirmity or intoxication: Chap 7.

[32] Insurance (albeit the principles are now altered by statute) and, if voidable at law, guarantees: Chap 5.

[33] Dishonest breaches of fiduciary tend to involve fraud, and actual undue influence coupled with threats will usually amount to duress.

[34] A Reilly, 'Is the "Mere Equity" to Rescind a Legal Power? Unpacking Hohfeld's Concept of "Volitional Control"' (2019) 39 OJLS 779, 805–06 (and drawing upon the analysis of N McBride, 'Rescission' in G Virgo and S Worthington (eds), *Commercial Remedies: Resolving Controversies* (CUP 2017) 155).

[35] See para [10.41].

[36] See also *Brotherton v Aseguradora Colseguros SA* [2003] 2 All ER (Comm) 298 (CA); *Drake Insurance plc v Provident Insurance plc* [2004] QB 601 (CA); para [10.29].

[37] Consumer Insurance (Disclosure and Representations) Act 2012 and Insurance Act 2015, which tip the balance strongly toward the insured, whilst conferring greater remedial flexibility if insurance is affected by misrepresentation and non-disclosure (discussed Chap 5, paras [5.35]–[5.39]). In Australia, Parliament has given the courts power to control the right to rescind certain kinds of insurance policies: Insurance Contracts Act 1984 (Cth), ss 9, 28–33 (and see also Chap 5, para [5.40]).

[38] See *Conway v Prince Eze* [2018] EWHC 29 (Ch) [148] ('uncompromising stance' common law adopts against secret commissions reflected in lack of discretionary control on victim's right to rescind at common law, approving G Howells (2010) LQR 617, 636); appeal dismissed [2019] EWCA Civ 88). See also Chap 12, paras [12.17]–[12.19].

10.19 In the vast majority of cases rescission is a remedy administered by the court acting on equitable principles and in a manner sensitive to the particular circumstances of the case. That is as it should be. The more powerful species of self-help rescission is in practice restricted to discrete classes of case in which its availability is appropriate. Properly understood, the law is not in need of reform. Whilst the promise of simplicity may at first make fusion attractive, upon closer examination the dualism that exists seems to be both useful and just. The preferable way forward is for incremental development of the doctrines of rescission at law and in equity with a clear eye to the differences between them, always sensitive to the strong policy considerations that underpin how the law should respond to impaired transactional autonomy.[39]

C. Overview of the Distinctions between Rescission at Law and in Equity

(1) Introduction

10.20 The structure of rescission at common law was in substance a by-product of the availability of different forms of action and emerged relatively late in the day, during the first half of the nineteenth century, alongside a reorganization of the law of contract generally. Equitable rescission is much older and was shaped by different forces. It originated in the Court of Chancery's jurisdiction to grant relief against transactions tainted by conduct offensive to conscience or which undermined the interests that those courts sought to protect.[40]

10.21 The Judicature reforms effectively halted the development of the principles governing rescission at law in England. Thereafter it has usually been sufficient for a litigant to turn to equity's more developed and flexible principles and there has been little pressure to further elaborate or clarify the common law rules.[41]

10.22 The doctrine of rescission at law remains a much narrower doctrine than its equitable counterpart.[42] It mainly operates in three contexts: executory contracts induced by fraud or duress; executed contracts for the sale of goods or payments of money induced by fraud; and contracts of insurance and reinsurance affected by misrepresentation or non-disclosure by the proposing assured.[43] Equitable rescission, by contrast, is available on these and other grounds, and applies to all types of transaction.

---

[39] See also A Reilly, 'Is the "Mere Equity" to Rescind a Legal Power? Unpacking Hohfeld's Concept of "Volitional Control"' (2019) 39 OJLS 779, 805–06.

[40] See Chap 3.

[41] The position was quite different in the United States of America. There the distinction continued to be of practical importance because claims based upon rescission at law were generally tried by a jury, whilst claims to rescind in equity were not. This appears to have underpinned the elaboration of the rules regulating rescission at law that has occurred in the United States. See further Chap 14, paras [14.63]–[14.65].

[42] Also, JD Heydon, MJ Leeming, and PG Turner, *Meagher, Gummow and Lehane's Equity Doctrines and Remedies* (5th edn, 2015) [25-125] listing five essential differences between rescission at law and in equity.

[43] The common law rules will, however, only apply to risks written before the Insurance Act 2015 applies, and for consumer insurance contracts, before operation of the Consumer Insurance (Disclosure and Representations) Act 2012, as to which see Chap 5, para [5.35]–[5.39].

(2) Grounds for rescission

Grounds for rescission at law

10.23 Contracts may be rescinded at common law if induced by fraud,[44] bribery,[45] or duress,[46] and contracts of insurance for material non-disclosure and non-fraudulent misrepresentation.[47] There is also a specialized common law right to rescind contracts for mental infirmity,[48] and probably also for intoxication.[49] The limited obligation of disclosure owed by a creditor to an intended surety has principally common law origins.[50] An Australian court has described the surety's right to rescind for non-disclosure as equitable,[51] but the common law origin of the obligation to make disclosure implies that the right to rescind arises at common law.

10.24 Although there are older[52] and equivocal[53] suggestions that certain kinds of mistake permit rescission at common law, in England, since the decision in *Bell v Lever Bros Ltd*,[54] if mistake operates at all at common law, it makes a contract void, not voidable.[55] This is also the law in Australia.[56] Contracts cannot be rescinded at common law for mistake. It is sometimes said that a contract may be rescinded at common law if there is a total failure of consideration,[57]

---

[44] *Load v Green* (1846) 15 M & W 216, 153 ER 828; *Clarke v Dickson* (1858) El Bl & El 148, 120 ER 463; *Clough v London and North Western Railway Co* (1871) LR 7 Ex 26; *Car and Universal Finance Co Ltd v Caldwell* [1965] 1 QB 525 (CA); *HIH Casualty v Chase Manhattan* [2003] 1 All ER 349 (HL) [98] (Lord Hobhouse). In Australia, *Coastal Estates Pty Ltd v Melevende* [1965] VR 433 (Full Ct); *Hunter BNZ Finance Ltd v CG Maloney Pty Ltd* (1988) 18 NSWLR 420; *Nadinic v Drinkwater* (2017) 94 NSWLR 518 (CA) [23].

[45] Contracts procured by bribes are not enforceable, and may be 'vacated', at common law (*Harrington v The Victoria Graving Dock Company* (1878) 3 QBD 549; *Shipway v Broadwood* [1899] 1 QB 369 (CA) 372), and it is now clear that they may be rescinded at law: *Mahesan v Malaysia Government Officers' Co-operative Housing Society Ltd* [1979] AC 374 (PC—Malaysia) 383; *Hurstanger Ltd v Wilson* [2007] 1 WLR 2351 (CA) [47]; *Conway v Prince Eze* [2018] EWHC 29 (Ch) [148]–[156] (appeal dismissed [2019] EWCA Civ 88); *SK Shipping Europe plc v Capital VLCC 3 Corp* [2021] 2 Lloyd's Rep 109 [240] (appeal dismissed [2022] EWCA Civ 231); *Wood v Commercial First Business Limited* [2021] EWCA Civ 471 [98]–[101].

[46] *Whelpdale's case* (1604) 5 Co Rep 119a 77 ER 239; *Enimont Overseas AG v RO Jugotanker Zadar (The Olib)* [1991] 2 Lloyd's Rep 108, 118; *Dimskal Shipping Co SA v International Transport Workers Federation (The Evia Luck)* [1992] 2 AC 152, 165; *Halpern v Halpern (No 2)* [2007] 1 QB 88; also [2008] QB 195 (CA).

[47] *Carter v Boehm* (1766) 3 Burr 1909, 97 ER 1162; 1 Black W 593, 96 ER 342; *Manifest Shipping Co Ltd v Uni-Polaris Insurance Co Ltd (The Star Sea)* [2003] 1 AC 469 (and which are now to be read in the light of the Insurance Act 2015). See also *SK Shipping Europe plc v Capital VLCC 3 Corp* [2021] 2 Lloyd's Rep 109 [240] (noting the limited grounds for rescinding a contract at common law).

[48] *Molton v Camroux* (1848) 2 Exch 487, 154 ER 584; aff'd (1849) 4 Exch 17, 154 ER 1107; *Imperial Loan Co v Stone* [1892] 1 QB 599 (CA); *Gibbons v Wright* (1954) 91 CLR 423; *Hart v O'Connor* [1985] AC 1000 (PC—NZ).

[49] *Moulton v Camroux* (1849) 4 Exch 17, 19; 154 ER 584 (Patteson J); *Matthews v Baxter* (1873) LR 8 Exch 132, reading 'void' in *Gore v Gibson* (1845) 13 M & W 623, 626, 627; 153 ER 260 as 'voidable'.

[50] *Pidcock v Bishop* (1825) 3 B & C 605, 610; 107 ER 857; *Hamilton v Watson* (1845) 12 Cl & F 109, 119; 8 ER 1339 (HL Sc); *The North British Insurance Co v Lloyd* (1854) 10 Ex 523, 533–35; 156 ER 545; *Lee v Jones* (1864) 17 CB (NS) 482, 503; 141 ER 194; *Seaton v Heath* [1899] 1 QB 782 (CA) 792.

[51] *Westpac Banking Corp v Robinson* (1993) 30 NSWLR 668 (CA) 690.

[52] *Cox v Prentice* (1815) 3 M & S 344, 350; 105 ER 641, 643 (Bayley J); *Kennedy v The Panama, New Zealand, and Australian Royal Mail Company Limited* (1867) LR 2 QB 580, 587–88 (Blackburn J).

[53] *Re Goldcorp Exchange Ltd* [1995] 1 AC 74 (PC—NZ) 103 (apparently referring to rescission at law); *Eldan Services Ltd v Chandag Motors Ltd* [1990] 3 All ER 459, 462 (statements *obiter* in interlocutory application might imply that rescission to found money had and received may occur in cases of mistake); *Abram Steamship Company Limited v Westville Shipping Company Limited* [1923] AC 773, 781 (Scots case where English authorities also referred to).

[54] [1932] AC 161.

[55] *Great Peace Shipping Ltd v Tsavliris Salvage (International) Ltd (The Great Peace)* [2003] QB 679 (CA) [28]–[29], [50], [73]–[76], [118], [153]; see also *Shogun Finance Ltd v Hudson* [2004] 1 AC 919 [123]–[125].

[56] *McRae v Commonwealth Disposal Commission* (1951) 84 CLR 377.

[57] H Beale (ed), *Chitty on Contracts* (34th edn, 2021) vol 1, [7-112]; K Mason, JW Carter, and GJ Tolhurst, *Mason & Carter's Restitution Law in Australia* (3rd edn, 2016) [1320], [1325].

but this is inaccurate. Failure of consideration is a condition to the recovery of money paid under a contract that is sought to be rescinded, not a ground for rescission itself.[58]

Grounds for rescission in equity

Equity permits rescission for fraud, and duress, mental impairment, and intoxication that would permit rescission at common law. It also recognizes a right to rescind a contract on several other grounds that do not apply at common law. These are as follows: 10.25

- non-fraudulent misrepresentation;
- actual and presumed undue influence;
- non-compliance with the fiduciary fair-dealing rules;
- certain unilateral mistakes;
- unconscionable conduct.

A donor is also permitted to rescind a gift in equity for a serious unilateral mistake.[59] Common mistake was formerly thought to be a ground for rescinding a contract in equity in England and Wales.[60] In *The Great Peace*,[61] however, the Court of Appeal held that there is no such doctrine. If common mistake operates at all, it takes effect at common law, and renders the contract void.[62] 10.26

Source of right to rescind contracts of insurance

Modern authorities disagree as to whether the right to rescind contracts of insurance for actionable non-disclosure has common law or equitable origins.[63] Two cases proceed on the basis that this is a common law right,[64] while two others state that it has equitable origins.[65] It has been said that the controversy over the source of the power to avoid for non-disclosure remains unresolved.[66] 10.27

---

[58] In a case where there has been a total failure of consideration the party seeking to recover money paid will need to identify a right to terminate the contract *de futuro*, either for breach or anticipatory breach of an express term or implied term, or because the agreement has been repudiated, and then exercise his right to terminate on that basis. Questions of failure of consideration arise in determining the separate question of whether, after termination, money paid under the contract is recoverable on the ground that there has been, or the paying party can effect, a total failure of consideration.

[59] *Ogilvie v Littleboy* (1897) 13 TLR 399 (CA) 400; aff'd *Ogilvie v Allen* (1899) 15 TLR 294 (HL); *Pitt v Holt* [2013] 2 AC 108; Chap 29.

[60] *Solle v Butcher* [1950] 1 KB 671 (CA) (Lord Denning MR), treated as correct or binding in *Grist v Bailey* [1967] Ch 532, 538–39; *Amalgamated Investment & Property Co Ltd v John Walker & Sons Ltd* [1977] 1 WLR 164 (CA) 176; *Associated Japanese Bank (International) Ltd v Credit du Nord SA* [1989] 1 WLR 255, 266; *William Sindall plc v Cambridgeshire County Council* [1994] 1 WLR 1016 (CA) 1034–35, 1039–40, 1042, and applied in *Nutt v Reed* (1999) 96(42) LSG 44 (CA).

[61] *Great Peace Shipping Ltd v Tsavliris Salvage (International) Ltd (The Great Peace)* [2003] QB 679 (CA).

[62] *Great Peace Shipping Ltd v Tsavliris Salvage (International) Ltd (The Great Peace)* [2003] QB 679 (CA).

[63] The right, formerly codified for marine insurance in s 18(1) of the Marine Insurance Act 1906, is now proscribed by statute in the case of 'consumer insurance contracts' in the manner set out in ss 2 and 11 and Sched 1 of the Consumer Insurance (Disclosure and Representations) Act 2012, and for 'non-consumer insurance contracts' in the manner set out in ss 3 to 8 and Sched 1 of the Insurance Act 2015. See further Chap 5, paras [5.35]–[5.39].

[64] *Pan Atlantic Insurance Co Ltd v Pine Top Insurance Co Ltd* [1993] 1 Lloyd's Rep 496 (CA) 503 (Steyn LJ); *Svenska Handelsbanken v Sun Alliance and London Insurance plc* [1996] 1 Lloyd's Rep 519, 552 (Rix J).

[65] *Banque Keyser Ullmann SA v Skandia (UK) Insurance Co Ltd* [1990] 1 QB 665 (CA) 779 (Slade LJ) (whose analysis was approved in passing by Lord Templeton in *Banque Financière de la Cité SA v Westgate Insurance Co Ltd* [1991] 2 AC 249, 280); *Strive Shipping Corporation v Hellenic Mutual War Risks Association (The Grecia Express)* [2002] Lloyd's Rep IR 669, 716.

[66] *Pan Atlantic Insurance Co Ltd v Pine Top Insurance Co Ltd* [1995] 1 AC 501, 544 (Lord Mustill), after ref to *Banque Keyser Ullmann SA v Skandia (UK) Insurance Co Ltd* [1990] 1 QB 665 (CA) 779 (Slade LJ).

10.28 Chapter 3 explained that the true position appears to be that for some time before the Judicature reforms contracts of insurance could be rescinded for non-disclosure and misrepresentation both at common law and in equity. When not conferred by statute, an insurer's entitlement to rescind for misrepresentation and non-disclosure is therefore best regarded as a right arising concurrently at common law and in equity.

10.29 Whether rescission for non-disclosure is a common law or equitable right has featured in cases considering the extent of judicial control of an insurer's right to rescind.[67] English courts have disavowed a discretionary power to control the exercise of an insurer's right to rescind, and have been similarly slow to find limits on that right in the insurer's obligation of utmost good faith.[68] This is true to the relationship between law and equity before the Judicature reforms. Instead of asserting a jurisdiction to control an underwriter's right to defend at law for non-disclosure or misrepresentation, Chancery confined its role to providing procedural assistance to common law actions by way of bills for discovery, and protecting an insurer by decrees for injunction and cancellation where appropriate.[69]

(3) Bars to rescission

10.30 Both the common law and equity recognize four general bars to rescission: *restitutio in integrum* impossible, intervention of third party rights, affirmation, and delay. These bars are considered in Chapters 18, 20, 23, and 24 respectively.

10.31 There are however bars to rescission that are peculiar to the common law and to equity. These are noted briefly at [10.32] and [10.33] below.

Bars to rescission peculiar to the common law

10.32 There are three supervening events that will bar the rescission of a contract at common law if they occur before there is an effective election to disaffirm it, but which will not prevent rescission in equity. Each is rooted in an inability to make restitution or counter-restitution, and may be regarded as founded on the impossibility of *restitutio in integrum* at common law. The bars are as follows:

- An interest in unregistered or registered land has been transferred by the party wishing to rescind. The contract cannot be rescinded because title to the land cannot be regained at common law.[70]
- The rescinding party receives an intangible benefit under the contract, being a benefit other than money or property, such as the use of property, or a service. This bar

---

[67] *Strive Shipping Corporation v Hellenic Mutual War Risks Association (The Grecia Express)* [2002] Lloyd's Rep IR 669 [271]; *Drake Insurance plc v Provident Insurance plc* [2003] Lloyd's Rep IR 781 [31]; *Brotherton v Aseguradora Colseguros SA* [2003] 2 All ER (Comm) 298 (CA) [34]; cf *Drake Insurance plc v Provident Insurance plc* [2004] 1 Lloyd's Rep 268 (CA) [93] (Rix LJ).

[68] *Brotherton v Aseguradora Colseguros SA* [2003] 2 All ER (Comm) 298; *Drake Insurance plc v Provident Insurance plc* [2004] 1 Lloyd's Rep 268 (CA). Also, P MacDonald Eggers and S Picken, *Good Faith and Insurance Contracts* (4th edn, 2017) [16.90]–[16.95]; M Clarke, 'Rescission: A Bridge too Far for Insurance Good Faith' [2012] LMCLQ 611.

[69] See Chap 3, paras [3.59]–[3.62].

[70] See Chap 14, paras [14.23]–[14.28]. As to cases where land is received by the party seeking to rescind, see Chap 14, paras [14.60], [14.74].

exists because the common law does not permit the rescinding party to give counter-restitution of benefits of this kind.[71]
- Possibly, wholly or partly performed contracts under which the rescinding party has provided services. If this bar exists, it is because the common law refuses to permit restitution when services are provided under a contract induced by fraud.[72]

Bars to rescission in equity

Equity is not restricted by the three bars to rescission peculiar to the common law (for which, see [10.32]). On the other hand, equity developed its own rules barring rescission for non-fraudulent misrepresentation in certain cases. All of these bars have been abolished in England,[73] but remain important in other Commonwealth jurisdictions.[74] English courts may also have recently recognized a new bar to equitable rescission, engaged when the effects of rescission would be disproportionate to the blameworthiness of the conduct that permits it.[75] **10.33**

(4) Differences between rescinding at law and in equity

There are four main differences between rescission at law and in equity. Each is treated in more detail in Chapters 11 to 15. The following is a summary of what is found there. **10.34**

Extinction of contract

In the first place, when rescission occurs at common law, any contract between the parties is extinguished *ab initio* from the moment the rescinding party elects to disaffirm it. In equity, the contract is set aside only when the court so orders. **10.35**

Recovery of money

Secondly, the party rescinding at common law is entitled to recover sums paid as a debt imposed by law; in the language of the forms of action, as money had and received to the payer's use. This right arises at the moment the transaction is disaffirmed. Interest formerly ran from that date, but probably not anymore.[76] In equity, on the other hand, the rescinding party has an equitable entitlement to be repaid an equivalent sum, and interest runs from the date on which the money was first received. Also, an equitable proprietary claim in respect of money paid arises following rescission for fraud, and perhaps other grounds. No common law proprietary claim to money has so far been recognized when rescission occurs at common law. **10.36**

---

[71] See Chap 14, para [14.86], Chap 18, paras [18.21]–[18.25].
[72] See Chap 14, paras [14.41]–[14.44]. It is also unclear whether the common law permits the party wishing to rescind to regain title to chattels sold, where the ground for rescission does not involve fraud. See Chap 14, paras [14.07]–[14.09].
[73] Misrepresentation Act 1967.
[74] See Chap 27.
[75] See Chap 28, para [28.36].
[76] *Sempra Metals Limited v Inland Revenue Cmrs* [2008] AC 561.

Recovery of property

10.37 Thirdly, the party rescinding at common law automatically regains legal title to property transferred when he elects to rescind. When rescission occurs in equity, legal title is obtained only pursuant to the court's order, although in cases of fraud an equitable title may arise when the transaction is disaffirmed. This difference affects the kinds of claims available to the rescinding party to vindicate his proprietary interest, as well as the vulnerability of his rights to competing claims by third parties.

Counter-restitution

10.38 Fourthly, the rescinding party's obligation to make counter-restitution is different when rescission occurs at law and in equity. Upon disaffirming a contract voidable at law, legal title to property received automatically revests in the transferor; the rescinding party comes to owe a debt imposed by law in respect of money received; and in certain circumstances, he must tender back that which was received as a condition of rescinding. In equity, the obligation to return benefits received does not generally arise upon an election to disaffirm, and is imposed as a condition of the court granting the relief sought. There is also no requirement to offer counter-restitution.

(5) Interaction between the common law and equitable doctrines

10.39 There are three classes of case to consider:

- the transaction is voidable at law when the innocent party elects to disaffirm it;
- the transaction was initially voidable at law but a bar that prevents it being rescinded at law supervenes before the innocent party elects to disaffirm;
- the ground for rescission is recognized only in equity.

These categories are considered in turn.

First class: voidable at law at the time of an election to rescind

10.40 When a transaction is voidable at common law and remains so at the date of an effective election to disaffirm it, that election will, if coupled where necessary with a tender of benefits received, automatically effect rescission at law. Once this happens there is no scope for rescission to occur in equity. The contract is gone, and both parties have vested common law rights to restitution. Equity can have no work to do in effecting rescission. Its role is confined to protecting or enforcing the common law rights that have arisen, as by way of injunction, or supplementing those rights where that is necessary to do justice, as where an equitable proprietary interest arises in the proceeds of money repayable upon rescission at law.[77]

10.41 The most important member of this class is contracts of insurance vitiated by non-disclosure or misrepresentation by a proposing assured. These are always initially voidable at common law. Moreover, in practice, the right to rescind is later lost only because of affirmation, and that will bar rescission equally at law and in equity. For this reason, the rescission of

---

[77] See Chap 16, para [16.07].

a contract of insurance or a treaty of reinsurance invariably occurs pursuant to exclusively common law principles. The other members of this class are wholly executory contracts vitiated by causes that permit rescission at law. These causes are fraud, duress, incapacity and intoxication, and possibly non-disclosure by creditor to surety. Completed contracts are also within this class if there has been a payment of money or transfer of title to goods, as long as matters have not so changed that *restitutio in integrum* has become impossible.

In these fact patterns, there is no established equitable jurisdiction to control the exercise of the common law rights, and events that occur between the date of the election to rescind and the commencing of proceedings are incapable of undoing the effects of the rescission that has occurred. Equity is confined to enforcing and protecting the common law rights secured by the rescission, and does not seek to control them. **10.42**

Second class: voidable at law but a supervening event bars rescission at law before there is an election to rescind

The position is different where the transaction was once voidable at law but, before the party entitled to rescind elects to disaffirm it, events occur that bar rescission at common law. Here the power to rescind that existed at common law is lost by the supervening event. **10.43**

In some instances the supervening event barring rescission at common law will also bar rescission in equity, as where the rescinding party has earlier elected to affirm the transaction. In other instances, however, the event barring rescission at common law will not also prevent rescission in equity. The most important member of this class is contracts involving property that are procured by fraud; in particular, where the innocent party has conveyed an interest in real property, or where the transferee has used or otherwise dealt with other property in a way that makes *restitutio in integrum* impossible at law, but not in equity. **10.44**

If it matters, the right to rescind in equity that arises where a parallel right of rescission at law has been lost by some supervening event ought not to be regarded as founded on a jurisdiction to assist the common law or to enforce common law rights. The rescinding party enjoys a wholly separate equitable entitlement to rescind. There is no evidence that prior to the Judicature reforms, in a case of this kind, a court of Chancery would decree rescission on the footing that it was assisting the exercise of common law rights. The indications are that in those cases where rescission at law would be unavailable because of some supervening bar, Chancery would exercise its own separate and original jurisdiction to grant rescission.[78] There is no reason why the position should be any different today. **10.45**

The effects of an election to disaffirm in this situation are uncertain. The conclusion in Chapter 12 is that it will not cause the contract to become extinguished. That only occurs pursuant to a court order for rescission. Disaffirming will, however, crystallize an equitable interest in assets transferred or their traceable substitute in cases of fraud.[79] Save that it **10.46**

---

[78] If this is correct, it should be unsurprising. A principled body of rules for setting aside transactions for fraud and duress existed in Chancery long before the common law developed an equivalent coherent jurisprudence, which only really happened in the first half of the nineteenth century. By the time the common law rules had become settled, in the middle of the nineteenth century, there was only a short pause before the Judicature reforms removed entirely the possibility of courts of Chancery assisting the courts of law in the manner contemplated. See further JN Pomeroy, *A Treatise on Equity Jurisprudence* (5th edn, 1941) vol 3, § 912. Cf *Alati v Kruger* (1955) 94 CLR 216, 223–24.

[79] See Chap 16, paras [16.25]–[16.40].

might in some circumstances prevent or postpone certain of the bars to rescission, the act of disaffirming has no other effect in cases of this kind.

Third class: ground for rescission recognized in equity only

10.47 A third and different category of case arises when rescission is sought on grounds that permit rescission in equity but not at common law; that is, for non-fraudulent misrepresentation, undue influence, breach of fiduciary duty, unilateral mistake, and unconscionable conduct. In all of these cases there never was a right to rescind at law. An election to disaffirm does not extinguish any contract between the parties. That occurs only when a court order for rescission is made.[80] Nor, it seems, does an election to disaffirm the transaction confer a vested equitable interest in any assets transferred. Instead, a proprietary interest is obtained only when a court order for rescission is granted, after which the law will regard beneficial title as having been vested in the rescinding party as from the start, at least for the purposes of bringing a tracing claim.[81]

---

[80] See Chap 12.
[81] See Chap 16, paras [16.41]–[16.43].

11
Electing to Rescind

A. Introduction	11.01	
B. How an Election to Rescind is Made	11.03	
(1) Communicating an unequivocal intention to disaffirm	11.03	
(2) Conduct must be unequivocal	11.15	
(3) Disaffirming by pleading	11.19	
(4) The need for communication	11.30	
(5) Rescission as a defence	11.41	
(6) Need for a tender or return of benefits at the time of electing	11.48	
(7) Special requirements when defending a call on shares	11.50	
C. Transactions Voidable at Law	11.53	
(1) Election effects rescission	11.53	
(2) Election to rescind irrevocable	11.57	
D. Transactions Voidable only in Equity	11.59	
(1) Summary	11.59	
(2) Historical context	11.62	
(3) The 'rescission by election' line of authority	11.67	
(4) The 'rescission by court order' line of authority	11.85	
(5) Other common law jurisdictions	11.97	
(6) Conclusions	11.107	
(7) Whether election to rescind is irrevocable	11.113	

A. Introduction

11.01 A voidable transaction is valid until rescinded. The party entitled to rescind is not obliged to do so; he has a choice to either affirm the transaction or to set it aside. When the transaction is affirmed the right to rescind is lost by waiver. The principles governing affirmation are considered in Chapter 23. This chapter considers the making of the converse choice, where the innocent party elects to rescind rather than to affirm.

11.02 The chapter is concerned with two distinct questions. The first is how an election to rescind is made. That is considered in Part B. The second question concerns the legal consequences that flow from making an election to rescind. This is relatively straightforward if the transaction is voidable at law. As set out in Part C, if the transaction is voidable at law when the election to rescind is made, the act of disaffirming itself effects rescission. But when a contract or gift is voidable in equity and not at common law the consequences of electing to disaffirm are less clear. Part D reviews the main authorities. The conclusion is that an election to disaffirm never causes rescission in such cases, but that proprietary rights to restitution are conferred when a transaction is rejected for fraud.

B. How an Election to Rescind is Made

(1) Communicating an unequivocal intention to disaffirm

11.03 The general rule is that an election to rescind is made by communicating to the other party to the transaction, in an unequivocal way, an intention to disaffirm it.[1] It is sufficient for the rescinding party to make clear that he wishes to reject or call off the transaction,[2] or 'not to be bound by it'[3] or otherwise to 'rescind' it.[4]

Communication by words or conduct

11.04 The election may be communicated by 'express words or acts'.[5] No particular form is necessary,[6] and the question of whether the innocent party has disaffirmed is to be determined in the circumstances of each case.[7] The election may be by letter, as where solicitors state that their clients 'claim a rescission of their contract with you',[8] and whether all of the stated grounds for rescission are later established or not.[9] Alternatively, the election may be by conduct that involves unequivocally asserting rights incompatible with a subsisting contract, such as demanding repayment of the price,[10] or demanding damages in respect of rights compromised under a voidable release.[11] Merely claiming damages for fraud would seem to be equivocal conduct for the right to damages, for the tort of deceit is wholly independent of any right that may exist to also set aside the contract by reason of that fraud.[12]

Retaking possession

11.05 Retaking possession of goods sold unambiguously asserts rights incompatible with a subsisting contract. That occurred in *Re Eastgate*,[13] where furniture and other chattels were sold to a fraudster who took them without intending to pay. The vendor retook possession of the items after the rogue absconded, and this was held to be an effective rescission. The

---

[1] The principles are codified in New Zealand in the Contract and Commercial Law Act 2017, s 41. Affirmation is regulated by s 38.
[2] *Clough v London and North Western Railway Co* (1871) LR 7 Ex 26, 34, 35.
[3] *United Shoe Machinery Company of Canada v Brunet* [1909] AC 330 (PC—Canada) 339.
[4] *Potter v Dwyer* [2011] EWCA Civ 1417 [56].
[5] *Clough v London and North Western Railway Co* (1871) LR 7 Ex 26, 32.
[6] *Chapman v Greater Midland Insurance Pty Ltd* [1981] 1 NSWLR 479, 483.
[7] *Boynton v Monarch Life Insurance Co of New Zealand Ltd* [1973] 1 NZLR 606, 614, app'd *Chapman v Greater Midland Insurance Pty Ltd* [1981] 1 NSWLR 479, 485 (insurance).
[8] *The Westville Shipping Company Limited v Abram Steamship Company Limited* 1922 SC 571, 575; *Abram Steamship Company Limited v Westville Shipping Company Limited* [1923] AC 773, 781–82; *Tenji v Henneberry & Associates Pty Ltd* (2000) 98 FCR 324 (Full Ct) [113]–[114].
[9] *Peyman v Lanjani* [1985] Ch 457 (CA) 503 (termination for defect in title, but principles expressed as applying to rescission *ab initio*).
[10] *Shuman v Coober Pedy Tours Pty Ltd* (1994) 175 LSJS 159 (demand for repayment of price paid for fossilized dinosaur bone): 'The letter does not use the words "avoid" "rescind" or "disaffirm", but I think the intention to do so is made clear by the claim for restitution'.
[11] *Cockerill v Westpac Banking Corporation* (1996) 142 ALR 227 (FCA) 288.
[12] Compare *Simmer v Copithorne* [2018] ABQB 525 [16]–[18], [20] (re-listing for sale residential and commercial property in Alberta earlier bought under a contract procured by fraud, and commencing proceedings to recover damages for fraud, did not involve an unequivocal election to rescind the purchase *ab initio*, in the circumstances of the case).
[13] [1905] 1 KB 465.

possibility of rescinding by retaking possession has been suggested both before and since *Re Eastgate*, and appears to be accepted.[14]

However, unless the contract is voidable at common law, retaking possession will, although constituting an election to rescind, also constitute a wrongful conversion. This is because it is only when the contract is voidable at law that the injured party is able to regain legal title to property transferred by simply electing to disaffirm. A mere equitable title confers no right to immediate possession, and does not permit chattels to be retaken.[15]

11.06

Mere non-performance

At the other end of the spectrum, mere non-performance of which the other party is aware may, in exceptional cases, evince an unequivocal intention to disaffirm. The principles that apply to acceptance of a repudiatory breach should apply to voidable contracts by analogy.[16] In an Australian case it was held that an employee's contract to purchase shares in his employer's drilling business was rescinded when, after having indicated that he was considering his position, the employee left the business and took up alternative employment.[17]

11.07

Keeping the election open

When the party entitled to rescind becomes aware of the facts that permit him to do so, he is not required to make a choice then and there, but may keep his options open, at least until lapse of time itself bars rescission, or other events occur that have that effect. The leading statement of the principle is that in *Clough*'s case:

11.08

> ... the question is, has the person on whom the fraud was practised, having notice of the fraud, elected not to avoid the contract? or has he elected to avoid it? or has he made no election? We think that so long as he has made no election he retains the right to determine it either way.[18]

Underwriters are entitled to a reasonable time to investigate information coming to light before they are required to decide whether to avoid the policy or not.[19] Other victims of misrepresentation and non-disclosure have a similar entitlement.[20]

11.09

---

[14] *Moyce v Newington* (1878) 4 QBD 32, 35 (*obiter*). Counsel for both parties in *Car and Universal Finance Co Ltd v Caldwell* [1965] 1 QB 525 (CA) accepted that rescission could be effected by retaking possession of goods, but Davies LJ noted (at p 558) that apart from *Re Eastgate*, no very clear authority had been cited for this conclusion. In Australia, *MacFarlane v Heritage Corp (Australia) Pty Ltd* [2003] QSC 353 [80], aff'd [2004] QCA 183.

[15] As to recaption, see also Chap 14, paras [14.18]–[14.20].

[16] *Vitol SA v Norelf Ltd (The Santa Clara)* [1996] AC 800.

[17] *Re Hoffman ex p Worrell v Schilling* (Full FCA, 14 August 1989) [22] (rescission for fraud).

[18] *Clough v London and North Western Railway Co* (1871) LR 7 Ex 26, 35 followed on this point *Gordon v Street* [1899] 2 QB 641 (CA) 649. In Australia, *Tropical Traders Ltd v Goonan* (1964) 111 CLR 41, 55 ('rescission' for late payment); *Sargent v ASL Developments* (1974) 131 CLR 634, 656 ('rescission' pursuant to terms of contract); *Champtaloup v Thomas* [1976] 2 NSWLR 264 (CA) 268 ('rescission' pursuant to terms of contract); *Cockerill v Westpac Banking Corporation* (1996) 142 ALR 227 (FCA) 280–82; *Galafassi v Kelly* [2014] NSWCA 190 [88] (repudiation).

[19] *McCormick v National Motor and Accident Insurance* (1934) 49 Lloyd's Rep 362 (CA) 365–66 (Scrutton LJ); *Insurance Corporation of the Channel Islands Ltd v McHugh and Royal Hotel Limited* [1997] Lloyd's Rep IR 94, 132 (Mance J); *Callaghan and Hedges t/a Stage 3 Discotheque v Syndicate 1049* [2000] Lloyd's Rep IR 125, 133.

[20] *Erlanger v The New Sombrero Phosphate Company* (1878) 3 App Cas 1218, 1251–53, 1258–59; *Lagunas Nitrate Company v Lagunas Syndicate* [1899] 2 Ch 392 (CA) 454; *Senanayake v Cheng* [1966] AC 63 (PC—Singapore) 79; *Fiona Trust & Holding Corporation v Privalov* [2007] 1 All ER (Comm) 81 [36].

III. RESCISSION BY ELECTION AND BY COURT ORDER

May be justified by facts not known at the time

11.10 It has been said *obiter* that a party electing to rescind may justify his action by reference to the true facts at the time the contract was entered into, and is not restricted to those matters advanced by or known to him when the election is made; and that the law regarding rescission *ab initio* in this respect is the same as that applicable to termination for breach.[21]

Knowledge of the rescinding party

11.11 Questions as to knowledge of the facts and of the right to rescind do not ordinarily arise when there is an election to disaffirm.[22] The issue tends to be whether and, if so, when a sufficiently unequivocal intention to rescind was communicated.

Overlapping claims to rescind *ab initio* and to terminate for breach

11.12 There is support for the view that rescission may be granted by the court in favour of a party who has sought to terminate for breach, but is not in fact entitled to do so.[23]

11.13 In the converse situation, it has been held by an Australian court that a party purporting to rescind *ab initio* for misrepresentation may rely upon that conduct as an election to terminate for breach of contract.[24]

11.14 It is difficult to find examples of a court being called upon to decide whether the victim of a misrepresentation later incorporated into a contract has by rejecting the agreement elected to rescind it *ab initio* or instead to terminate the agreement for breach of condition. The difference may, of course, be significant, not least because by rescinding *ab initio* the innocent party will lose his right to damages for breach of contract. In principle merely rejecting the agreement ought not to involve an election to rescind, for such conduct is ordinarily equivocal, being equally consistent with the innocent party having decided to terminate for breach. In Singapore, there is authority that in such a case the innocent party must choose whether to treat the contract as terminated for breach of condition, or instead to treat it as rescinded *ab initio*,[25] and that both claims may be pursued as alternatives unless the right to pursue one of the two has been lost by waiver.[26] In Canada, re-listing for sale a property earlier purchased under a contract procured by fraud and seeking damages for fraud was found to be consistent with terminating the agreement for breach rather than rescinding it *ab initio* for fraud.[27] In the result, the victims' right to recover damages for

---

[21] *Drake Insurance plc v Provident Insurance plc* [2004] 1 Lloyd's Rep 268 (CA) [69] (Rix LJ); *Occidental Worldwide Investment Corp v Skibs A/S Avanti (The Siboen and Sibotre)* [1976] 1 Lloyd's Rep 293, 337–38. The principle was affirmed in *Li Cho Kwan v Oliveiro Lana* (unreported, High Court of Hong Kong Special Administrative Region, 23 March 2016) [104] (misrepresentation in sale of shares).

[22] *Insurance Corporation of the Channel Islands Ltd v The Royal Hotel Limited* [1998] Lloyd's Rep IR 151, 162 'The claim to avoid demonstrates of itself at one and the same time awareness of the choice and its making'; also R Handley, 'Exploring Election' (2006) 122 LQR 82, 83.

[23] *The Siboen and Sibotre* [1976] 1 Lloyd's Rep 293, 337. In Australia, *Commonwealth Homes and Investment Co Ltd v MacKellar* (1939) 63 CLR 351, 378, 380, 381 (Dixon J); *Landers v Schmidt* [1983] 1 Qd R 188 (Full Ct) (statutory right to rescind). See also *O'Kane v Jones* [2005] 1 Lloyd's Rep IR 174, 226.:

[24] *Highfield Property Investments Pty Ltd v Commercial and Residential Developments (SA) Pty Ltd* [2012] SASC 165 [301].

[25] *RBC Properties Pte Ltd v Defu Furniture Pte Ltd* [2014] SGCA 62 [137] (innocent party required to choose whether to rescind for misrepresentation or to terminate for repudiatory breach of contract).

[26] *Creative Technologies Ltd v Huawei International Pte Ltd* [2017] SGHC 201 [252], [253] (rescission for misrepresentation and damages for breach could be advanced as alternatives, the right to seek rescission not having been lost following express reservation of rights).

[27] *Simmer v Copithorne* [2018] ABQB 525.

breach of contract, which would have been extinguished by a rescission *ab initio*, continued to subsist.[28]

(2) Conduct must be unequivocal

The conduct of the rescinding party must unequivocally demonstrate an intention to disaffirm the transaction. **11.15**

Subsequent acts of rescinding party

Where the rescinding party's conduct is equivocal, it appears that his subsequent actions may be taken into account in determining whether there has been an election to rescind. This is the preferable interpretation of *Drake Insurance plc v Provident Insurance plc*.[29] Following a motor vehicle accident on 2 July, by letter dated 2 August the insurer of the vehicle wrote to the insured and purported to avoid the policy for non-disclosure. Two vehicles were in fact insured under the policy, and thereafter the insurer continued to receive premium payments for both vehicles. The insurer also conducted itself in a manner consistent with the policy remaining on foot in respect of the second vehicle, which had not been involved in the accident. The Court of Appeal held that it was not possible to rescind the policy as to one vehicle only, and that the whole of the relevant period of time had to be looked at to determine whether there had been an effective election to rescind. It was found that in all the circumstances, no valid election had been made. **11.16**

An election to disaffirm an insurance policy for non-disclosure is irrevocable because the act of disaffirming puts an end to the contract.[30] There is no indication that the Court of Appeal intended to cast doubt on that principle. *Drake Insurance* is best regarded as a case where the election to disaffirm was, looked at in isolation, equivocal. An unequivocal election required the insurer to rescind the whole of the policy in respect of both vehicles, and it was unclear whether the letter of 2 August purported to do so. In those circumstances it was appropriate to look at the underwriter's subsequent conduct to determine whether there had been an unequivocal election to rescind. Any other interpretation of the case cannot be reconciled with the fundamental rule that a communicated election to disaffirm a contract voidable at law is irrevocable.[31] **11.17**

Attempting to rescind part only

An attempt to elect to rescind part and to affirm another part of a contract is ineffective as an election to rescind, unless the part sought to be rescinded can be treated as an independent contract.[32] **11.18**

---

[28] *Simmer v Copithorne* [2018] ABQB 525 [16]–[18], [20], [47], [48].
[29] [2004] 1 Lloyd's Rep 268 (CA) [100]–[104]. Contrast *Northcote Housing Association v Dixon* (ChD, 30 November 2001) 7 (lease procured by fraudulent misrepresentation; acceptance of rent after letter electing to rescind; held that there had been a valid election to rescind).
[30] See further paras [11.57]–[11.58]. The position has since been modified by legislation, as to which see Chap 5, paras [5.35]–[5.39].
[31] That principle had been applied by Moore-Bick J at first instance: *Drake Insurance plc v Provident Insurance plc* [2003] 1 All ER (Comm) 759, 769.
[32] *United Shoe Machinery Company of Canada v Brunet* [1909] AC 330 (PC—Canada) 340; *Potter v Dyer* [2011] EWCA Civ 1417 [58]; and see *Restatement (First) of Restitution* 276–77 (1937), and Chap 19.

In the context of misrepresentation, the Court of Appeal has explained that:[33]

> The representee's right of election is a right to decide whether to rescind the transaction and so be put in the position as if it had never taken place, or to be bound by the transaction notwithstanding that it was induced by misrepresentation and could, if the representee so wished, be set aside. There is no scope, therefore, for ... a middle course under which the representee elects neither to rescind the transaction nor to affirm its full force and effect, but affirms the transaction only to the extent of the misrepresentation that was made. That would be to treat the misrepresentation as a promise pursuant to a contract, even though no contract has been made or broken.

(3) Disaffirming by pleading

General rule

11.19 An election to rescind may be made in an originating process or pleading. The leading decision is *Clough v London and North Western Railway Co*,[34] where the Court of Exchequer rejected the submission that an election to rescind had to be made before proceedings commenced, and held that it could be made in an appropriately worded plea:

> Neither can we see the principle or discover the authority for saying that it is necessary that there should be a declaration of his intention to rescind prior to the plea. It seems to us clear, on principle, that a statement in a plea by the party from whom the property passed, that he claims back the property on the ground that he was induced to part with it by fraud, is as unequivocal a determination of his election to avoid the transaction as could well be made ... And no authority was cited on the argument, nor are we aware of any, for saying that this unequivocal expression of his determination of his election must be preceded by some act in pais.[35]

11.20 The principle has been repeatedly applied. In the Australian case of *Nicholas v Thompson*,[36] after citing *Clough*'s case, the Full Court of the Supreme Court of Victoria held that:

> ... the issue and service of the writ in the present case, claiming rescission on the ground that the plaintiffs were induced to enter into the contract by the fraud of the defendant, was a definite election on their part to avoid the contract, and it was unnecessary to prove any prior election to disaffirm.[37]

11.21 In *Hunter BNZ Finance Ltd v CG Maloney Pty Ltd*[38] the Supreme Court of New South Wales held that a finance company had rescinded a fraudulent transaction involving the delivery of certain cheques by bringing proceedings for their conversion against the collecting bank. Adam J underlined in *Coastal Estates Pty Ltd v Melevende*[39] that if it is to operate as an

---

[33] *Potter v Dyer* [2011] EWCA Civ 1417 [58] (in explaining why evidence of affirmation was fatal to a proposed plea of fraudulent misrepresentation).
[34] (1871) LR 7 Ex 26.
[35] *Clough v London and North Western Railway Co* (1871) LR 7 Ex 26, 35–36.
[36] [1924] VLR 554 (Full Ct).
[37] *Nicholas v Thompson* [1924] VLR 554 (Full Ct) 582.
[38] (1988) 18 NSWLR 420, 437A. See also *Westpac v Markovic* (1985) 82 FLR 7, 10.
[39] [1965] VR 433 (Full Ct) 439–40, 450.

election to rescind 'the writ or summons ... must by its terms evince an unequivocal intention to treat the contract as at an end'.[40]

If a claim form or pleading does not demonstrate an unequivocal intention to avoid the contract, as where a claimant vendor seeks to recover both the property transferred and the price payable, it will not be effective as an election to rescind,[41] unless the court construes the pleading as involving claims in the alternative.[42]

11.22

Different kinds of pleadings

The principle has also been applied in the case of a defence,[43] defence and counter-claim,[44] and reply.[45] Indeed, it has been said that a defence of fraud implies an election to rescind the contract, for otherwise the plea would be defective.[46] An insurer's pleaded defence of non-disclosure, relied upon as one ground for resisting liability, coupled with oral submissions that the policy was avoided, has been held sufficiently to evince an election to rescind a policy of insurance.[47]

11.23

Amendment to pleading

An election to rescind may be made by amended pleadings served before or during the trial, as where the facts giving rise to the right only become fully apparent at that time.[48]

11.24

Applies equally to equitable rescission

The principle applies equally when rescission is sought in equity: 'There is no principle that the equitable remedy of rescission is unavailable unless sought by notice given before action brought'.[49] In *Shalson v Russo*,[50] Rimer J held that a defrauded lender had impliedly elected to rescind his loan by bringing a proprietary claim to its traceable proceeds, that being consistent only with rescission.[51] The same approach was taken in *London Allied Holdings Limited v Lee*, another fraud case.[52]

11.25

---

[40] *Coastal Estates Pty Ltd v Melevende* [1965] VR 433 (Full Ct) 449, also 439–40, 450. See also *Alati v Kruger* (1955) 94 CLR 216, 222; *Ivanof v Phillip M Levy Pty Ltd* [1971] VR 167, 169; *Chapman v Greater Midland Insurance Pty Ltd* [1981] 1 NSWLR 479, 485; *MacFarlane v Heritage Corp (Australia) Pty Ltd* [2003] QSC 353 [80], aff'd [2004] QCA 183.

[41] *LHK Nominees Pty Ltd v Kenworthy* [2001] WASC 205 [51]–[55]; *Commonwealth v Davis Samuel Pty Ltd (No 7)* (2013) ACSR 258 (ACT Sup Ct) [1566]–[1570].

[42] *London Allied Holdings Limited v Lee* [2007] EWHC 2061 (Ch) [279].

[43] *Chapman v Greater Midwest Insurance Pty Ltd* [1981] 1 NSWLR 479, 489.

[44] *Kupchak v Dayson Holdings Ltd* (1965) 53 WWR 65 (BCCA) 77.

[45] *Cockerill v Westpac Banking Corporation* (1996) 142 ALR 227 (FCA) 288.

[46] *Dawes v Harness* (1875) LR 10 CP 166, 167–168; *M'Millan v Sampson* (1884) 10 VLR 74, 77.

[47] *Chapman v Greater Midwest Insurance Pty Ltd* [1981] 1 NSWLR 479, 489.

[48] *Steedman v Frigidaire Corporation* [1933] 1 DLR 161 (PC—Canada) (amendment made at trial following discovery of bribe); *Black King Shipping Corporation and Wayang (Panama) SA v Mark Ranald Massie (The Litsion Pride)* [1985] 1 Lloyd's Rep 513, 517 (underwriters' 'precautionary avoidance during the trial by the points of rejoinder would be valid'); *West Sussex Properties Ltd v Chichester District Council* [2000] EWCA Civ 205 (common mistake); *Khoury v Government Insurance Office* (1984) 165 CLR 622 (insurer amending defence to plead non-disclosure after hearing rumours). See also *Clough v London and North Western Railway Co* (1871) LR 7 Ex 26 (fraud emerging during trial).

[49] *West Sussex Properties Ltd v Chichester District Council* [2000] EWCA Civ 205 [12].

[50] [2005] Ch 281.

[51] *Shalson v Russo* [2005] Ch 281 [120], [127].

[52] [2007] EWHC 2061 (Ch) [279] (fraudulent obtaining of £1m 'deposit', and where the payment was construed as voidable, so requiring an election to rescind). In Australia, *MBF Australia Ltd v Malouf* [2008] NSWCA 214 [64] (commencement of proceedings in Equity Division of the Supreme Court an act of rescission if no earlier election); *Commonwealth v Davis Samuel Pty Ltd (No 7)* (2013) ACSR 258 (ACT Sup Ct) [1566]–[1570] (prayer for

11.26 A different result was reached in the Australian case of *Hancock Family Memorial Foundation Ltd v Porteous*.[53] The court rejected the submission that, by bringing proceedings which included claims for a constructive trust, the claimants had elected to rescind loans said to have been made in breach of fiduciary duty. The court stated that the relief claimed was consistent with maintaining the contracts of loan on foot.[54] This is difficult to understand, particularly because the court went on to decide that the failure to seek and obtain orders for rescission of the loans was fatal to the claim for a constructive trust.[55]

Form of plea

11.27 Where the party entitled to rescind asserts that the contract was and remains voidable at common law or may be avoided in equity by election, and does not allege any prior disaffirmation, the appropriate plea would seem to be an averral that the injured party 'now' or 'hereby' elects to rescind. If it is claimed that the contract is voidable in equity but the power to rescind is vested exclusively in the court, it ought to be sufficient for the rescinding party to ask the court to order that the contract be rescinded. A prayer for relief in those terms should itself constitute a sufficient election to rescind.[56]

Rescission as a plea in the alternative

11.28 An effective election to rescind may be made in an originating process or pleading that contains alternative claims founded on the premise that the contract remains in force and has not been and cannot be rescinded. The existence of the alternative claims does not make the election equivocal.[57]

Disaffirming by oral submission in court

11.29 In principle there is no reason why a contract may not be effectively disaffirmed by oral statements in court, as where the facts conferring the right to rescind only emerge during trial. This analysis has been endorsed in Australia.[58]

(4) The need for communication

11.30 The general rule is that to be effective, an election to disaffirm a voidable contract must be communicated to the other party to it. There is, however, an exception to the rule,

---

declaration that funds transfers were 'void and illegal' coupled with relief seeking restitution sufficient for an election to rescind).

[53] (2000) WAR 198 (Full Ct) 215.
[54] *Hancock Family Memorial Foundation Ltd v Porteous* (2000) WAR 198 (Full Ct) 215.
[55] In *Daly v Sydney Stock Exchange Ltd* (1985) 160 CLR 371, 390 the failure to rescind a loan procured by breach of fiduciary duty was also said to be fatal to the assertion of a constructive trust. But there the injured party, Mrs Daly, did not commence proceedings against the fiduciary stockbrokers who had received the moneys. Proceedings were instead commenced against a third party, the Sydney Stock Exchange, which had a statutory obligation to indemnify for trust losses.
[56] See also Chap 12, paras [12.04]–[12.06] and *Horsler v Zorro* [1975] Ch 302, 310.
[57] *Coastal Estates Pty Ltd v Melevende* [1965] VR 433 (Full Ct) 440, 450; *London Allied Holdings Limited v Lee* [2007] EWHC 2061 (Ch) [279] (alternative claim to enforce contract); see also *Johnson v Agnew* [1980] AC 367, 398; *Clough v The London and North Western Railway Company* [1871] LR 8 Ex 26, 38.
[58] *Chapman v Greater Midwest Insurance Pty Ltd* [1981] 1 NSWLR 479, 489.

established by *Car and Universal Finance Co Ltd v Caldwell*,[59] the outer limits of which remain unclear.

Prior to *Caldwell*'s case

11.31 The rule requiring communication was formerly applied even where goods were obtained under a contract procured by fraud and the fraudster could not be found. That is demonstrated by *Moyce v Newington*.[60] The defendant sold sheep to a fraudster in exchange for a worthless cheque. After he discovered the fraud and found that the buyer had taken the sheep away, the defendant contacted the police. The fraudster then sold the sheep to the claimant. Finding his sheep on the claimant's premises, the defendant retook them. He was held to have committed a conversion. The outcome turned on the effect of a statute giving rights of restitution for goods acquired by false pretences.[61] However, delivering the reasons of the Queen's Bench Division, Cockburn CJ said as follows:

> The question which in some cases might be a very material one, as well as of some nicety, viz what, on the part of the defrauded seller, short of retaking possession of the thing sold, will amount to an avoidance of the contract, does not arise in the present instance. The defendant not knowing what had become of his sheep, or where to find Wale, his buyer, had done and could do nothing, beyond giving notice to the police, up to the time when the sheep were bought by the plaintiff.
>
> We must take it, therefore, as incontestable, that but for the subsequent conviction of Wale for having taken these sheep by false pretences, no question could be raised as to the title of the plaintiff.[62]

11.32 It was therefore held that if the rescinding party does not actually contact the fraudster at all, but merely evinces an election to disaffirm by contacting the police, this is insufficient to rescind and regain title.[63]

11.33 On the other hand, the court in *Re Eastgate*[64] did not ask whether, in retaking possession of his furniture and other goods sold, the vendor communicated an intention to rescind to his fraudulent buyer. He had issued a summons for the price, the fraudster promptly absconded, and five days later the vendor, with the landlord's permission, broke into the purchaser's former residence and retook possession. The summons treated the contract of sale as valid. On the reported facts no election to rescind had been communicated to the dishonest purchaser.

11.34 Despite the decision in *Re Eastgate*, before *Caldwell*'s case[65] the accepted view was that communication was essential to an election to rescind.[66] *Caldwell*'s case established that this

---

[59] [1965] 1 QB 525 (CA).
[60] (1878) 4 QBD 32, 35–36.
[61] Although the court's interpretation of s 100 of the Larceny Act 1861 (24 & 25 Vict c 96) (repealed Theft Act 1968, s 32(3) Pt 1, Sched 3; see now s 148 of the Powers of Criminal Courts (Sentencing) Act 2000) was overruled in *Bentley v Vilmont* (1887) LR 12 HL 471, the House of Lords cast no doubt on the communication point discussed here.
[62] *Moyce v Newington* (1878) 4 QBD 32, 35–36.
[63] This was also the approach in *Maclead v Kerr* 1965 SC 253, 257.
[64] [1905] 1 KB 465.
[65] *Car and Universal Finance Co Ltd v Caldwell* [1965] 1 QB 525 (CA).
[66] This was recognized by Upjohn LJ in *Car and Universal Finance Co Ltd v Caldwell* [1965] 1 QB 525 (CA) 554 (citing *Kerr on Fraud and Mistake* (7th edn, 1952) 530, D Finneman and A James (eds) *Benjamin on Sale* (8th edn, 1950) 441, and *Pollock on Contracts* (13th edn, 1950) 467).

Caldwell's case

11.35 The only issue in *Caldwell's* case was whether Mr Caldwell had rescinded the sale of his motor vehicle for fraud by notifying the police and the Automobile Association three days before it had been sold to a bona fide purchaser for value without notice.[67] Both the trial judge (who was Lord Denning MR), and a unanimous Court of Appeal, decided that although in general an election to rescind must be communicated to the other party to the transaction, in the exceptional circumstances of the case, Caldwell's actions in contacting the police and the Automobile Association the day after the fraud were effective to rescind and revest title in the car in him.

11.36 *Caldwell's* case indicates that communication can be dispensed with if three conditions are met. First, communication must not be practicable; secondly, the conduct of the other party must prevent them from insisting on communication; and, thirdly, upon discovering the facts conferring a right to rescind, the party rescinding must promptly do everything reasonable to demonstrate a public unequivocal intention to disaffirm. The decision confirms that communication need only be made to the other party to the transaction, so that interested third parties can be left out of account.[68]

Scope of the rule

11.37 Later decisions have not much amplified the exception recognized in *Caldwell's* case. In *Newtons of Wembley Ltd v Williams*[69] the doctrine was applied in similar circumstances, and the Court of Appeal noted that the vendor 'took all available steps they could to recover the car and disaffirm the sale'.[70] It has been suggested that the exception only applies where the fraudster cannot be reached.[71]

11.38 The decision was criticized at the time,[72] and one influential commentator doubted that it could be supported by the reasons given by the Court of Appeal.[73] The Law Reform Commission has recommended that it be reversed by legislation.[74] Despite this, the decision

---

[67] *Car and Universal Finance Co Ltd v Caldwell* [1965] 1 QB 525 (CA) 528–30. The contest was between the defrauded vendor, Mr Caldwell, and the purchaser at the end of a chain of sales, Car and Universal Finance Co Ltd. It had inter-pleaded in Mr Caldwell's claim against an earlier sub-buyer, Motobella, which had purchased with notice from the fraudster. Car and Universal Finance had sold the car and paid the proceeds into court pursuant to a court order. The issue was who was entitled to those proceeds: [1963] 2 All ER 547, 548.

[68] Unless the third party relies on the Factors Act 1889, s 2, where notice to the third party may prevent the Act applying: s 2(2). See further, *Gray v Smith* [2013] EWHC 4136 (Comm) [109]–[117], [132]–[138].

[69] [1965] 1 QB 560 (CA).

[70] *Newtons of Wembley Ltd v Williams* [1965] 1 QB 560 (CA) 571; cf 'where one party to a contract had done all he could to evince to the other party his intention to rescind it': *Tenax Steamship Co Ltd v The Brimness (owners)* [1975] 1 QB 929 (CA) 945.

[71] *Empresa Cubana de Fletes v Lagonisi Shipping Co Ltd* [1971] 1 QB 488 (CA) 505 (citing *Caldwell's* case when discussing exercise of a contractual right to terminate).

[72] W Cornish, 'Rescission Without Notice' (1964) 27 MLR 472, 478; but cf F Odgers, 'Note to *Car and Universal Finance v Caldwell* [1963] 2 All ER 547' [1963] CLJ 180, 181–82; G Fridman, 'Rescission of a Voidable Contract' (1963) 113 *The Law Journal* 459, 460–61. *Moyce v Newington* (1878) 4 QBD 32, 35–36 appears not to have been brought to the attention of the trial judge or the Court of Appeal.

[73] 'What *Car and Universal Finance v Caldwell* must be taken to decide is that in the particular case the fraudulent representor had impliedly agreed to be affected by constructive communication': A Turner (ed), *Turner and Spencer Bower: The Law of Actionable Misrepresentation* (3rd edn, 1974) 261. This analysis was, however, not carried through to later editions of the work.

[74] 12th Report (1966) [16].

remains good law in England and Wales. It was affirmed by a reconstituted Court of Appeal soon after it was handed down,[75] has been referred to with approval in later cases,[76] and has been applied at least once.[77] Moreover, the rule in *Caldwell*'s case has been codified in New Zealand by section 41(1)(b) of the Contract and Commercial Law Act 2017,[78] and legislation in other jurisdictions has also adopted it.[79]

It has been said that the decision can only be justified, if at all, by the strong need to protect victims of fraud, and that it should not be applied in cases of negligent or innocent misrepresentation.[80] The decision has also been read down, and treated as authority for the proposition that rescission need not be communicated to a fraudulent buyer of goods who has made it impossible or impracticable for the defrauded seller to communicate with him, but not for any wider proposition.[81] **11.39**

Dispensing with communication protects the previous owner at the expense of a later buyer, strengthening the sanctity of ownership by sacrificing the security of transactions. This shift in the balance created by *Caldwell*'s case was cancelled out by treating the fraudster as a buyer in possession with the consent of the seller, so that anyone buying from him gained an indefeasible title conferred by statute.[82] The statutory provisions will, however, not invariably apply, and the third party is protected only insofar as he can bring himself within their scope.[83] **11.40**

(5) Rescission as a defence

The fact that a contract is induced by fraud is not of itself a defence to actions at law to enforce it. Fraud gives a right to rescind, and it is the rescission that provides a defence.[84] **11.41**

---

[75] *Newtons of Wembley Ltd v Williams* [1965] 1 QB 560 (CA).
[76] *Empresa Cubana de Fletes v Lagonisi Shipping Co Ltd* [1971] 1 QB 488 (CA) 505 (discussing exercise of a contractual right to terminate; the decision was rev'd on another point in *The Laconia* [1977] AC 850); *Tenax Steamship Co Ltd v The Brimness (Owners)* [1975] 1 QB 929 (CA) 945 (although the case concerned the timing of a notice of termination for breach rather than rescission for fraud); *National Employers' Mutual General Insurance Association Ltd v Jones* [1990] 1 AC 24 (CA) 33 (May LJ) (reciting the decision in *Newtons of Wembley Ltd v Williams* [1965] 1 QB 560 without disapproval).
[77] *Chartered Trust plc v Conloy* (Romford County Court, 22 May 1998) (rescission of sale of car for fraud by notifying police). The principle in *Caldwell*'s case was also recognized (but not applied) by McInerney J in *Ivanof v Phillip M Levy Pty Ltd* [1971] VR 167.
[78] 'The cancellation of a contract by a party does not take effect—(a) before the time at which the cancellation is made known to the other party; or (b) before the time at which the party cancelling the contract shows, by some clear means that is reasonable in the circumstances, an intention to cancel the contract, if—(i) it is not reasonably practicable for the cancelling party to communicate with the other party; or (ii) the other party cannot reasonably expect to receive notice of the cancellation because of that other party's conduct in relation to the contract': Contract and Commercial Law Act 2017 (NZ), s 41(1) (formerly Contractual Remedies Act 1979 (NZ), s 8). The Act applies to all forms of misrepresentation, and not merely fraud.
[79] Australian Consumer Law and Fair Trading Act 2012 (Vict), s 26(1)(b).
[80] E Peel, *Treitel: The Law of Contract* (15th edn, 2020) [9-105].
[81] *Spriggs v Wessington Court Schools Ltd* [2005] 1 Lloyd's Rep IR 474, 483.
[82] *Newtons of Wembley Ltd v Williams* [1965] 1 QB 560 (CA), applying ss 2 and 9 of the Factors Act 1889 (agent in possession with consent of seller; see also Sale of Goods Act 1979, s 25). The two decisions are discussed in W Cornish, 'Rescission Without Notice' (1964) 27 MLR 472 and J Thornley, 'Sales by Persons with Voidable Titles and Buyers in Possession' [1965] CLJ 24.
[83] See also *National Employers' Mutual General Insurance Association Ltd v Jones* [1990] 1 AC 24 (statutory provisions do not apply where agent takes from a thief or purchases from a thief); *Gray v Smith* [2013] EWHC 4136 (Comm) [109]–[117], [132]–[138].
[84] *Dawes v Harness* (1875) LR 10 CP 166, 167–68; *United Shoe Machinery Company of Canada v Brunet* [1909] AC 330 (PC—Canada) 338; *Coastal Estates Pty Ltd v Melevende* [1965] VR 433 (Full Ct) 441; see also *Gordon v*

Likewise misrepresentation or non-disclosure by a proposing assured does not itself provide a defence on the policy. The insurer must elect to rescind.[85] This principle should apply to all grounds for rescission.[86]

11.42 The difference between rescission at law and in equity is that in the former case, disaffirming the contract generates defences to claims upon it by extinguishing the agreement *ab initio*, whereas in the latter, the defence exists because of the injured party's entitlement to have the contract set aside by the court. Accordingly, if that right is lost after the contract is disaffirmed, so is the defence.[87]

11.43 The position is otherwise where the contract is sought to be enforced in equity, by way of an order for specific performance. Circumstances such as fraud, or undue influence, that would permit rescission of the contract may cause specific performance to be refused on discretionary grounds, even though the passage of time or changes in circumstances have caused the right to rescind to be lost.[88]

Supposed limitations on electing when rescission used as a defence

11.44 It ought to make no difference to the steps required to rescind whether rescission is alleged as a cause of action or as a defence. Despite this, there are suggestions to the contrary in both the literature and the cases. It is said that a prior disaffirmation is needed, and also that no benefit must be received. Neither of these suggested limitations is well founded. Each will be considered in turn.

Limitation that disaffirmance prior to proceeding is necessary

11.45 It has been said that one distinction between the use of misrepresentation as a cause of action and as a defence is that in the former rescission may be effected by a claim or counterclaim, and it is unnecessary to allege or prove disaffirmance, whereas in the latter the rescinding party must plead and prove the misrepresentation, and that the contract 'having become voidable on that ground, it was in fact avoided by him within a reasonable time after discovery of the truth'.[89] But this principle is contrary to both *Clough's* case[90] and *Dawes v Harness*.[91] Further, there is no good authority that the onus of proof as to affirmation

---

Street [1899] 2 QB 641 (CA) 644, 650–51. A defence of set-off founded upon damages for deceit is in principle also available, and in that event no rescission need be proved: *O'Keefe v Taylor Estates Co Ltd* [1916] St Rep Qd 301 (Full Ct) 309 (agreement for agistment).

[85] *Graham v Western Australian Insurance Company Ltd* (1931) 40 Lloyd's Rep 64, 66–67 (no defence because insurer had never sought to avoid the policy—premium income exceeded the loss); *West v National Motor and Accident Union Ltd* [1955] 1 Lloyd's Rep 207 (CA) 210 (no defence because insurer accepted that it had not elected to avoid). The result is different if by the terms of the policy the non-disclosure or misrepresentation provides a defence. There the insurer can defend without rescinding. Pre-contractual misrepresentation is to be further distinguished from a case where a claim itself is misrepresented, so as to forfeit rights to indemnity: *Black King Shipping Corporation and Wayang (Panama) SA v Mark Ranald Massie (The Litsion Pride)* [1985] 1 Lloyd's Rep 513, 514–15; *Manifest Shipping Co Ltd v Uni-Polaris Insurance Co Ltd (The Star Sea)* [2003] 1 AC 469, 494; *Axa General Insurance v Gottlieb* [2005] 1 Lloyd's Rep IR 369, 375–76.

[86] See *Webster v Havyn Pty Ltd* [2004] NSWSC 227 [32]–[43] (vendor able to give contractual notice to complete notwithstanding his misrepresentations, when purchaser had not elected to rescind).

[87] See Chap 12, para [12.10].

[88] *AH McDonald and Company Pty Ltd v Wells* (1931) 45 CLR 506, 513; *Capcon Holdings plc v Edwards* [2007] EWHC 2662 (Ch) [65].

[89] *Halsbury's Laws of England* (5th edn, 2013 reissue) vol 76, [786].

[90] *Clough v London and North Western Railway Co* (1871) LR 7 Ex 26.

[91] (1875) LR 10 CP 166, 167–68.

switches to the rescinding party when rescission is relied upon as a defence. The onus remains with the party against whom rescission is sought.[92]

11.46 It has also been said that a requirement for prior disaffirmance only applies when a defence is being raised to executed contracts, and not to wholly executory agreements.[93] Yet whether the contract is executory or part performed should make no difference. The approach suggested is contrary to *Clough*'s case, where the sale contract had been partly performed. This supposed limitation was considered and correctly rejected in *Chapman v Greater Midwest Insurance Pty Ltd*.[94] Rescission for the purpose of defending a contractual claim need not be preceded by a prior disaffirmance, but may be effected by an appropriate plea.

Limitation that no benefit must have been received

11.47 It is also sometimes said that the rescinding party must allege and prove *inter alia* that he or she has taken no benefit under the contract when a defence of rescission is relied upon. This notion has old roots. It was mentioned as far back as Sir John Strange's notes to *Dutch v Warren*.[95] At that early point, the supposed limit was probably a product of restrictions on the count for money had and received. But if it ever existed, the limitation was removed long ago by the common law,[96] and was never recognized in equity.

(6) Need for a tender or return of benefits at the time of electing

11.48 When a contract may be set aside in equity there is no need for the party wishing to rescind to tender or return benefits received, for the court is able to ensure counter-restitution by orders for conditional relief.[97]

11.49 But if what is wanted is to rescind the contract at common law the position is more uncertain. Although the matter is not free from doubt, it seems that no return or tender is required in respect of money or chattels, but that steps must be taken if shares have been acquired. If some other kind of property has been purchased by the party wishing to rescind, there is an argument that rescission at law is in principle possible if he is able to, and does, return title to that property when the contract is disaffirmed.[98]

---

[92] *WISE (Underwriting) Agency Ltd v Grupo Nacional Provincal SA* [2004] 2 Lloyd's Rep 483 (CA) 509; Chap 23, para [23.111].
[93] *Meldon v Lawless* (1869) 18 WR 261 (CP Ir) 262; *Academy of Health and Fitness Pty Ltd v Power* [1973] VR 254, 259–60.
[94] [1981] 1 NSWLR 479, 487–88. See also P Winfield (ed), *Pollock's Principles of Contract* (13th edn, 1950) 468; D McDonnell and J Monroe (eds), *Kerr on the Law of Fraud and Mistake* (7th edn, 1952) 531, 650; K Handley (ed), *Spencer Bower and Handley Actionable Misrepresentation* (5th edn, 2014) [18.06].
[95] (1720) 1 Str 406, 406; 93 ER 598, 599. The point does not, however, appear to have featured in the reasons delivered in *Dutch v Warren* itself: see Chap 3, n 51 at [3.23]. See also, *Academy of Health and Fitness Pty Ltd v Power* [1973] VR 254, 262.
[96] *Street v Blay* (1831) 2 B & AD 456, 109 ER 1212.
[97] *Jervis v Berridge* (1873) 8 Ch App 351, 357. In Australia, *Commercial Bank of Australia Limited v Amadio* (1983) 151 CLR 447, 468; *Tenji v Henneberry & Associates Pty Ltd* (2000) 98 FCR 324 (Full Ct) [115].
[98] See Chap 14, paras [14.52]–[14.62].

(7) Special requirements when defending a call on shares

11.50 *First National Reinsurance Company v Greenfield*[99] establishes that shareholders induced to subscribe for shares by a company's misrepresentation remain liable for calls until the moment their name is removed from the register of members. A defence to a call exists if the shareholder's name is removed by the company or by a court, or the member has a right to have that happen. Once the right to rectify is lost, the defence is also lost. That was what happened to Mr Greenfield. He had notified the company that he was rescinding his allotment for misrepresentation, refused to pay calls, and demanded that the company refund the sums he had paid, and remove his name from the register of members. The company refused and made a call. Several months later it successfully brought proceedings to enforce the call. Mr Greenfield's defence that he had a right to rescind the allotment and to have the register rectified was rejected. The Court of Appeal held that Mr Greenfield's seven or eight-month delay in taking steps to have his name removed from the register meant that he had lost that right. He therefore had no defence to the claim to enforce the call.

11.51 A short period of delay is sufficient to bar the right to rescind. Lush J underlined that for a defence to exist, if the company did not rectify the register, the shareholder must have disaffirmed and then either commenced rectification proceedings or given an undertaking to do so.[100] Both Lush J and McCardie J emphasized that this was necessary to protect the integrity of the register, which represented to creditors the extent of the company's creditworthiness.[101]

11.52 Partly paid shares are rarely issued today; equity finance is typically raised by placing fully paid shares. The rules developed in *Greenfield*'s case are accordingly of much less practical importance than they once were.[102]

C. Transactions Voidable at Law

(1) Election effects rescission

11.53 Rescission at common law is effected by the rescinding party's election to disaffirm the voidable transaction, in the sense that all the constituent elements that make up rescission follow from that election. After the election, and if necessary a tender of benefits received, the transaction is completely rescinded, and the judicial process need be invoked only for the purpose of declaring or enforcing the rights secured.

11.54 Although strictly a statement of Scots law, the following passage from the speech of Lord Atkinson in *Abram Steamship Company Limited v Westville Shipping Company Limited*

---

[99] [1920] 2 KB 260 (CA).
[100] *First National Reinsurance Company v Greenfield* [1920] 2 KB 260 (CA) 271, 280. McCardie J appeared to agree: 277–79.
[101] *First National Reinsurance Company v Greenfield* [1920] 2 KB 260 (CA) 272, 276.
[102] See also Chap 24, paras [24.88]–[24.90] (discussing when delay bars the right to rescind allotments of shares); *Haas Timber & Trading Co Pty Ltd v Wade* (1954) 94 CLR 593, 604 (the changed significance of members' registers since the nineteenth century removes the reason for the old rule requiring special promptness in electing to rescind; allotment of fully paid shares).

summarizes the doctrine of rescission at common law, and underlines the automatic nature of the consequences that flow from the rescinding party's election to disaffirm:

> When one party to a contract expresses by word or act in an unequivocal manner that by reason of fraud ... inducing him to enter into the contract he has resolved to rescind it, and refuses to be bound by it, the expression of his election, if justified by the facts, terminates the contract, puts the parties in statu quo ante and restores things, as between them, to the position in which they stood before the contract was entered into ... if the other party to the contract questions the right of the first to rescind, thus obliging the latter to bring an action at law to enforce the right he has secured for himself by his election, and the latter gets a verdict, it is an entire mistake to suppose that it is this verdict which by itself terminates the contract and restores the antecedent status. The verdict is merely the judicial determination of the fact that the expression by the plaintiff of his election to rescind was justified, was effective, and put an end to the contract. Questions as to whether the judgment relates back to a date earlier than its own are really irrelevant.[103]

More recently, in *Halpern v Halpern (No 2)* Nigel Teare QC (as his Lordship then was) observed that it was not disputed before him that at common law 'The act which brings the contract to an end is the act of the party who avoids or rescinds the contract'.[104] In *IGE USA Investments Limited v The Commissioner for Her Majesty's Revenue and Customs* the Court of Appeal likewise stated that 'It remains common ground in this court that rescission of a contract at common law for fraudulent misrepresentation is a self-help remedy which does not require the intervention of the court'.[105] Similarly, in Australia, the Full Court of the Federal Court recently reaffirmed that 'it should be recalled that at common law, rescission occurs by election'.[106]

11.55

This feature of rescission at law was also underlined in the Australian case of *Coastal Estates Pty Ltd v Melevende*.[107] An executory sale of land had been induced by fraudulent misrepresentations, and the County Court in Melbourne duly entered a judgment requiring the vendor to refund the sums it had received. The County Court had at the time a statutory jurisdiction that did not extend to equitable relief. On the vendor's appeal, the Supreme Court of Victoria rejected the argument that the County Court had no jurisdiction to give the relief that had been awarded. It held that the buyer had exercised a common law right, and did not seek equitable relief: 'The plaintiff came to the court not to have the contract rescinded by the court, but to obtain relief on the basis that he had already himself rescinded it, and that in circumstances where there were no adjustments to be made which required recourse being had to the processes of equity.'[108] The purchaser's claim to repayment was a common law action for money had and received, founded on a failure of consideration.[109]

11.56

---

[103] *Abram Steamship Company Limited v Westville Shipping Company Limited* [1923] AC 773, 781. See further paras [11.75]–[11.76].
[104] [2007] 1 QB 88, 94–95.
[105] [2021] Ch 423 (CA) 435 [20]. See also, S Zogg, *Proprietary Consequences in Defective Transfers of Ownership* (2020) 144–45 (that rescission at common law is a self-help remedy is plainly established by the case law and widely accepted by commentators).
[106] *Harvard Nominees Pty Ltd v Tiller* [2020] FCAFC 229 [96] 'it should be recalled that at common law, rescission occurs by election; in equity rescission occurs by court order and, like all equitable remedies, is subject to equitable defences and the discretion of the court', to be exercised in order to achieve 'practical justice'.
[107] [1965] VR 433. See also *Alati v Kruger* (1955) 94 CLR 216, 223–24; *McFarlane v Heritage Corp* [2003] QSC 353 [80].
[108] *Coastal Estates Pty Ltd v Melevende* [1965] VR 433, 434.
[109] *Coastal Estates Pty Ltd v Melevende* [1965] VR 433.

(2) Election to rescind irrevocable

11.57 An election to rescind a contract voidable at common law is necessarily irrevocable. The election, and where necessary tender back of benefits received, puts an end to the contract, revests legal title to property transferred, and creates a debt in respect of sums paid. Vested rights of action accrue to enforce the restructured rights and obligations.[110] These consequences are by their nature permanent.

11.58 The irrevocability of the decision to rescind a contract voidable at law does not follow from the application of a doctrine of election. The choice is irrevocable because of the nature of the legal consequences flowing from it. This may be contrasted with the making of a decision to affirm. There it is a doctrine of waiver by election that prevents the injured party from afterwards seeking to exercise a right to rescind. The right to rescind is lost because it is waived.[111]

D. Transactions Voidable only in Equity

(1) Summary

11.59 The law on this topic is enormously confused, and in need of reappraisal. Two quite separate groups of cases have grown up that cannot be reconciled. One says that the innocent party can rescind by electing, the other that they must obtain a court order to rescind.[112] The conclusion reached here is that when a transaction is voidable in equity, it is only in cases of fraud that an election to rescind is effective. This conclusion is best supported by the authorities, and is explicable as a matter of principle as an instance of equity assisting or following the common law. It has the advantage of explaining the group of cases which establish that equitable title to money or property may be obtained when a voidable transaction is disaffirmed for fraud,[113] and is consistent with the absence of good authority that this may also occur when a transaction is set aside for other reasons.[114]

11.60 However, even when a transaction is procured by fraud, if it is not voidable at common law, there is only a weak sense in which an election to disaffirm it causes rescission. The act of disaffirming does not extinguish the contract.[115] It simply triggers an equitable interest in assets transferred, burdened by any obligation to make counter-restitution. The contract

---

[110] Chap 14.
[111] *Sargent v ASL Developments Ltd* (1974) 131 CLR 634, 640–41.
[112] See also JD Heydon, MJ Leeming, and PG Turner, *Meagher, Gummow & Lehane's Equity: Doctrines and Remedies* (5th edn, 2015) [25-105] (election line of authority commencing with *Reese River Silver Mining Co Ltd v Smith* (1869) LR 4 HL 64 (HL) 'does not withstand scrutiny'). For the view that a court order is not required to effect rescission, even in equity, S Zogg, *Proprietary Consequences in Defective Transfers of Ownership* (2020) 146–48 ff and A Burrows, *A Restatement of the English Law of Contract* (2nd edn 2020) §34(4) 179–80.
[113] *Alati v Kruger* (1955) 94 CLR 216, 224; *Lonhro plc v Fayed (No 2)* [1992] 1 WLR 1, 11–12; *Shalson v Russo* [2005] Ch 281, 320–22.
[114] Chap 16, paras [16.30]–[16.32].
[115] For the contrary view, S Zogg, *Proprietary Consequences in Defective Transfers of Ownership* (2020) 146, 157 (who also concludes that there has been a fusion of law and equity 'on the contractual level' but not 'on the proprietary level').

itself is only erased, and legal title is only recovered, by and pursuant to the terms of a court order.[116]

Engagement with this issue is impossible without reference to the historical context in which it arises. That is undertaken next, and is followed by a review of the principal modern authorities. **11.61**

(2) Historical context

Before about 1870 rescission in equity was always regarded as occurring pursuant to the terms of a court decree. There was no suggestion that the party seeking to set aside a transaction in a Court of Chancery did so by electing to disaffirm it, or that the role of the court was to enforce a rescission previously effected. The equity of the innocent party was to a decree that itself gave relief, in the form of orders declaring the transaction to be void, that unwound what had been done, and that prevented the further enforcement of the transaction. These were orders for injunction, cancellation, reconveyance, account, and conditional relief. Rescission occurred pursuant to those orders.[117] **11.62**

Had the point been focused upon, it would have been obvious that there was a significant structural difference between this approach and the doctrine of rescission developed by the common law courts. That was based on a theory of rescission as a 'self-help' remedy, where the court enforced the rights secured by a prior election to rescind. In contrast, Courts of Chancery regarded rescission as a form of relief conferred by the court. It was the court itself that effected the rescission through its orders. However, for reasons that are unclear, the distinction escaped attention in both the authorities and the literature of the time. **11.63**

But this was not so in the United States. There, the association of self-help rescission with the common law, and court-ordered rescission with equity, became well recognized.[118] *Gould v Cayuga County National Bank*[119] came to be a leading statement of the distinction. The New York Court of Appeals pithily observed that rescission at law was 'an action ... as upon a rescission' whilst rescission in equity 'proceeds for a rescission', and Earl J stressed that: **11.64**

> ... the difference between an action to rescind a contract and one brought, not to rescind it, but based upon the theory that it has already been rescinded, is as broad as a gulf. They depend on different principles and require different judgments.[120]

---

[116] See further Chap 12, paras [12.11]–[12.21], Chap 15, paras [15.69]–[15.72], Chap 16, para [16.20].
[117] See further Chap 3, paras [3.37]–[3.39].
[118] The distinction was focused upon in the United States because the jurisdictional origin of the right governed whether the matter would be tried by a jury. If the claim arose at law, it could be tried by a jury, and if it was equitable, it would not. The enduring importance of the jury in civil trials in the United States ensured that the issue retained a vitality and relevance that it did not in England.
[119] 86 NY 75, 83–84 (1881) (compromise induced by fraud).
[120] *Gould v Cayuga County National Bank* 86 NY 75, 83–84 (1881). For the view that this decision no longer provided reliable guidance for American law, D Dobbs and C Roberts, *Law of Remedies* (3rd edn, 2018) 477 n 532. But see also at 423 explaining that rescission at law occurs by unilateral act, whereas rescission in equity happens when the court declares it.

11.65 Holmes J made the same point somewhat later,[121] and it has been repeated in other courts in the United States.[122] The distinction was formerly enshrined in the Californian Civil Code,[123] and remains alive in several of the States today.[124]

11.66 Notwithstanding the significant technical obstacles to the adoption of an election-based approach to equitable rescission in England, from about 1870 there began to develop a line of authority which held that rescission always occurred when the innocent party elected to disaffirm.[125] These authorities betray a lack of awareness of the distinction between the structure of rescission at law and in equity. At the same time, a different line of authority continued to treat equitable rescission as a remedy conferred by the court, the availability and terms of which were in the court's discretion, in accordance with Chancery's established approach. The two lines of authority do not separate into instances of rescission at law and in equity. They cannot be reconciled, and present no coherent picture. Each of the two groups of cases will be considered in turn.[126]

(3) The 'rescission by election' line of authority
Three foundational cases

11.67 The election line of authority is anchored in three cases. These are Lord Hatherley LC's speech in *Reese River Silver Mining Co Ltd v Smith*,[127] the speech of Lord Atkinson in *Abram Steamship Company Limited v Westville Shipping Company Limited*,[128] and the judgment of Megarry J in *Horsler v Zorro*.[129] It will be seen that, properly understood, none provide a reliable basis for the view that rescission always occurs when the voidable transaction is disaffirmed, irrespective of whether the right has legal or equitable origins. The three cases will be taken in turn.

Reese River Silver Mining v Smith

11.68 Lord Hatherley LC's speech in *Reese River Silver Mining Co Ltd v Smith*[130] is the foundation for the 'election' line of authority. It appears to suggest that the right to rescind is always

---

[121] *Thomas v Beals* 154 Mass 51, 27 NE 1004 (1891).
[122] See the cases listed in W Allen, 'Annotation: Action involving Rescission or Right to Rescind Contract and to Recover amount Paid thereunder as one at Law or in Equity' (1935) 95 American Law Rep Annotated 1000, 1000–101, 1003–10.
[123] The separate provision for rescission by election and by court decree in the California Civil Code sects 1688–1691 (rescission by election), and sects 3406–3408 (rescission by court decree), enacted in 1872, was held to follow the distinction between rescinding at law and in equity: *Philpott v Superior Court* 36 P2d 635, 641 (1934); *McCall v Superior Court* 36 P2d 643, 646–47 (1934); discussed W Allen, 'Annotation: Action involving Rescission or Right to Rescind Contract and to Recover amount Paid thereunder as one at Law or in Equity' (1935) 95 American Law Rep Annotated 1000, 1008. In 1961 sects 3406–3408 were abolished, and changes made to ss 1688–1691.
[124] D Dobbs and C Roberts, *Law of Remedies* (3rd edn, 2018) 423 and also 473 § 4.7: 'Under this "at law" procedure for restitution, the court does not effect the rescission upon which restitution is based; the plaintiff effects the rescission, and the court gives a judgment for the restitution that is needed.' As to the requirement for a tender of counter-restitution when rescinding at common law in the United States, see Chap 14, paras [14.63]–[14.65].
[125] Chap 3, paras [3.53]–[3.54].
[126] See also the discussion of this issue in J O'Sullivan, 'Rescission as a Self Help Remedy: A Critical Analysis' [2000] 59 CLJ 509; and also M Bryan, 'Rescission, Restitution and Contractual Ordering: the Role of Plaintiff Election' in AJ Robertson (ed), *The Law of Obligations: Connections and Boundaries* (2004) 59.
[127] (1869) LR 4 HL 64.
[128] [1923] AC 773, 781, 785.
[129] [1975] 1 Ch 302, 310.
[130] (1869) LR 4 HL 64.

vested in the aggrieved party not the court, and is exercised by electing to disaffirm. The speech has been very influential, but the context in which it was made is usually overlooked.[131] The context significantly qualified what Lord Hatherley said.

11.69 After stating that because the prospectus Mr Smith relied on contained fraudulent misrepresentations, the allotment to him of 100 shares in the Reese River Silver Mining Co Ltd was 'voidable' not 'void',[132] Lord Hatherley said as follows:

> It appeared to your Lordships [in *Oakes v Turquand* [1867] LR 2 HL 325], and with all humility I would say it appears to me, perfectly correct to say that the agreement subsists until rescinded; that is to say, in this sense—until rescinded by the declaration of him whom you sought to bind by it, that he no longer accepts the agreement, but entirely rejects and repudiates it. It is not meant, I apprehend, by that expression, 'until rescinded', used by any of your Lordships at the time when that case was argued before the House, to say that the rescission must be an act of some Court of competent authority, and that, until the rescission by that Court of competent authority takes place takes place, the agreement is subsisting in its full rigour.[133]

11.70 Mr Smith had commenced proceedings in Chancery, and on one view these statements are a general comment about the working of rescission, whether at law or in equity. But this interpretation does not withstand scrutiny. The case was not concerned with the rescission of a contract under the general law. It was concerned with a shareholder's statutory right to escape particular liabilities, imposed by a mixture of statute and contract. The only issue before the court was whether Mr Smith's name was to be removed from the list of contributories, thus permitting him to escape pro-rata liability for the company's debts in the liquidation. Although Mr Smith brought a bill in equity, the court was exercising a statutory power. Mr Smith's right to have his name removed was conferred by the relevant companies legislation.[134] Although the proceedings were instituted in Chancery, they could equally have been brought in a common law court.[135]

11.71 The House of Lords held that when Mr Smith notified the company that he rejected the allotment of 100 shares for fraud, he ceased to be a member and the company came under a statutory obligation to amend the register of members to show this.[136] When the directors failed to amend the register, the legislation empowered the court to do so, and also to amend the list of contributories to which Mr Smith's name was improperly added.[137]

---

[131] See also the discussion of *Reese*'s case in *IGE USA Investments Limited v The Commissioner for Her Majesty's Revenue and Customs* [2021] Ch 423 (CA) 455 [96]–[97] (decision does not provide unequivocal support for the proposition that equitable rescission for fraud is a self-help remedy), J O'Sullivan 'Rescission as a Self Help Remedy: A Critical Analysis' [2000] 59 CLJ 509, 533–36 and JD Heydon, MJ Leeming, and PG Turner, *Meagher, Gummow & Lehane's Equity: Doctrines and Remedies* (5th edn, 2015) [25-105].
[132] (1869) LR 4 HL 64, 71, 72.
[133] *Reese River Silver Mining Co Ltd v Smith* (1869) LR 4 HL 64, 73 and see also 74–75.
[134] Companies Act 1862, ss 25, 35, 98; *Reese River Silver Mining Co Ltd v Smith* (1869) LR 4 HL 64, 75–76, 77, 80–81.
[135] The statute permitted the application to be brought before a court of equity or common law: Companies Act 1862, s 35. Mr Smith's desire to restrain the company from suing to enforce a call made Chancery the appropriate forum for his claim: (1869) LR 4 HL 64, 67, 81.
[136] Companies Act 1862, s 25; *Reese River Silver Mining Co Ltd v Smith* (1869) LR 4 HL 64, 75–76, 77, 80–81.
[137] Companies Act 1862, ss 35, 98; *Reese River Silver Mining Co Ltd v Smith* (1869) LR 4 HL 64, 75–76, 80–81.

11.72 In coming to this conclusion, the other members of the House of Lords did not adopt Lord Hatherley's analysis. Lord Hatherley had held that upon Mr Smith's rejection of the shares his contract with the company 'was at an end' and 'avoided'.[138] Lord Westbury, on the other hand, held that Mr Smith's right was to pursue a bill in equity to cancel his relations with the company though winding up had commenced.[139] To similar effect, Lord Colonsay concluded that Smith was 'entitled to be regarded as if that [rescission of his contract] had been done by the Court at the time he demanded it'.[140]

11.73 The House of Lords focused upon the question of timing in this way because it had recently been decided in *Oakes v Turquand*[141] that a shareholder induced to take shares by the company's fraud lost his right to escape liability as a contributory once winding up commenced.[142] The issue of substance was whether an exception to this rule existed when the shareholder elected to disaffirm the allotment before winding up had commenced, even though his name remained on the list of members. Rescission would protect the shareholder at the expense of the company's creditors, and other shareholder contributories, whose share of the company's liabilities would be increased accordingly.

11.74 Notwithstanding that the case was concerned with statutory rights under the Companies Act 1862, not with the rescission of contracts at law or in equity, and that both Lord Westbury and Lord Colonsay concluded that Mr Smith's contract of allotment had not been rescinded when he disaffirmed it, Lord Hatherley's general statement became the foundation for subsequent cases holding that rescission always occurs by an election to disaffirm.

Abram Steamship v Westville Shipping

11.75 The next significant statement was the speech of Lord Atkinson in *Abram Steamship Company Limited v Westville Shipping Company Limited*.[143] That was on appeal from the Court of Session in Scotland[144] and involved a dispute governed by Scots law.[145] The ground for rescission pleaded[146] and accepted by Lord Atkinson[147] was 'essential error'. That is a ground for rescinding ('reducing' in Scots law) a contract in Scotland,[148] but not in English law.

11.76 Lord Atkinson cites English cases involving rescission at law and in equity without distinction, and in particular, relies on the opinion of Lord Hatherley in the *Reese River Silver Mining* case.[149] However, in circumstances where the matter was on appeal from Scotland and was governed by Scots law, and the claim was for reduction for 'essential error', Lord Atkinson cannot have been purporting to state English law. Insofar as his description of

---

[138] *Reese River Silver Mining Co Ltd v Smith* (1869) LR 4 HL 64, 74, 75.
[139] *Reese River Silver Mining Co Ltd v Smith* (1869) LR 4 HL 64, 77–78.
[140] *Reese River Silver Mining Co Ltd v Smith* (1869) LR 4 HL 64, 79.
[141] (1867) LR 2 HL 325.
[142] For this bar to rescission, see Chap 25, Part C.
[143] [1923] AC 773, 781, 785. See para [11.54].
[144] *The Westville Shipping Company Limited v Abram Steamship Company Limited* 1922 SC 571.
[145] The reports proceed on this basis, although the proper law of the contract (which was concluded by correspondence between parties in Wales and Scotland) was not discussed by the Court of Session or House of Lords.
[146] *The Westville Shipping Company Limited v Abram Steamship Company Limited* 1922 SC 571, 575.
[147] *Abram Steamship Company Limited v Westville Shipping Company Limited* [1923] AC 773, 781, 784, 787.
[148] W McBryde, *The Law of Contract in Scotland* (3rd edn, 2007) [15–104] but cf [15–12]; W Gloag, *The Law of Contract: A Treatise on the Principles of Contract in the Law of Scotland* (2nd edn, 1985) 440–41, 456.
[149] *Abram Steamship Company Limited v Westville Shipping Company Limited* [1923] AC 773, 782–83.

rescission reflects English law at all, it well describes rescission at common law, but not rescission in equity.[150] It is not reliable authority for how and when rescission occurs in equity.

Horsler v Zorro
Nevertheless, in *Horsler v Zorro*, Megarry J drew no distinction between rescission at law and in equity, and relied upon Lord Hatherley's speech in the *Reese River Silver Mining* case and Lord Atkinson's speech in the *Abram Steamship* case in concluding that:

11.77

> ... the process of rescission is essentially the act of the party rescinding, and not of the court. Of course, if matters are disputed, the dispute may have to be determined by the court, and until the decision it may not be known whether there is a proper and effectual rescission: but that does not mean that there is no rescission until the court speaks.[151]

Megarry J was, however, not concerned with rescission *ab initio* at all. Titus Zorro had repudiated a contract for the sale of his house in London to Mr and Mrs Horsler, who sought to 'rescind' the contract and recover damages. Adopting what was later described as 'Mr Cyprian Williams' great heresy',[152] Megarry J held that the Horslers had a right to 'rescind' the contract and be restored to their former position 'as if the contract had never been made', but no right to damages, thereby confusing the entitlement to extinguish a contract *ab initio* as a response to a vice in its formation, and to terminate it *de futuro* by reason of a subsequent breach.[153] He therefore relied on *Lee v Soames*,[154] where a repudiated contract for the sale of land was said to have been 'rescinded on November 8, 1887, the date of a letter whereby one of the parties purported to rescind the contract'.[155] But the innocent party's right to terminate for repudiation by communicating his election to disaffirm is uncontroversial, and governed exclusively by common law principles. *Lee v Soames* provides no support for the view that equitable rescission occurs upon an election to disaffirm.

11.78

Like the *Reese River Silver Mining* and *Abram Steamship* cases, *Horsler v Zorro* is not good authority that rescission *ab initio* always follows an election to disaffirm, and still less that rescission pursuant to equitable principles does so. However, all of the decisions after 1975 that propound the election model of rescission outside cases governed by the common law, are based entirely on the authority of these three cases. For the reasons outlined, none provides a stable foundation for that view.

11.79

Recent decisions
Several more recent decisions have added to the election line of authority. The most important of these are *The Lucy*,[156] *TSB Bank plc v Camfield*,[157] *Allied Irish Bank plc v Byrne*,[158] *Society of Lloyd's v Lyons*,[159] *Drake Insurance plc v Provident Insurance plc*,[160] and *Brotherton*

11.80

---

[150] Also, Lord Atkinson was best known as a common law lawyer.
[151] *Horsler v Zorro* [1975] 1 Ch 302, 310.
[152] M Albery, 'Mr Cyprian Williams' Great Heresy' (1975) 91 LQR 336; see further Chap 1, para [1.08].
[153] *Horsler v Zorro* [1975] 1 Ch 302, 309, 314, 316. The mistake was corrected in *Johnson v Agnew* [1980] AC 367.
[154] (1888) 36 WR 884.
[155] *Horsler v Zorro* [1975] 1 Ch 302, 310.
[156] *Atlantic Lines and Navigation Co Inc v Hallam Ltd (The Lucy)* [1983] 1 Lloyd's Rep 188, 202.
[157] [1995] 1 WLR 430 (CA) 438–39.
[158] [1995] 2 FLR 325.
[159] [1997] CLC 1398 (CA).
[160] [2003] Lloyd's Rep IR 78 [31]–[32].

III. RESCISSION BY ELECTION AND BY COURT ORDER

v Aseguradora Colseguros SA.[161] The first four of these cases are either equivocal or otherwise unpersuasive,[162] but the more recent two decisions are emphatic in their endorsement of the election model.

11.81 The decision of Moore-Bick J in *Drake Insurance plc v Provident Insurance plc*[163] is authority for the proposition that rescission on any ground, and whether founded on principles having their origin in the common law or equity, is always effected by an election to disaffirm. At issue was an insurer's right to rescind a policy of motor vehicle insurance for non-disclosure by the proposing assured. Moore-Bick J cited the speech of Lord Atkinson in the *Abram Steamship* case and the decision of Megarry J in *Horsler v Zorro* to conclude as follows:

> Whatever the true origin of the insurer's right to avoid for non-disclosure, it is in the nature of a right to rescind the contract and its exercise is subject to the same principles as apply to the exercise of the right to rescind generally. Although equity recognised a right of rescission in a wider range of circumstances than did the common law, modern authorities do not suggest that a distinction is to be drawn between the principles that apply to the exercise of that right in different cases. Whenever a right to rescind arises it is exercisable at the election of the injured party. Moreover, it does not require the intervention of the court but is effective immediately upon the communication by the injured party of his decision to rescind the contract ... in my view the same principles apply to the avoidance of a contract of insurance for non-disclosure ... The insurer does not need to invoke the assistance of the court, nor does the court have jurisdiction to declare that his right to avoid has been lost retrospectively by subsequent events ...[164]

11.82 The decision of Moore-Bick J was overturned on appeal on other grounds,[165] and the Court of Appeal did not directly consider the correctness of the reasoning quoted.[166] But his statement of general principle was fully endorsed by the Court of Appeal in *Brotherton v Aseguradora Colseguros SA*.[167] That case considered a reinsurer's right to rescind its treaty of reinsurance for non-disclosure by the proposing reinsured. After approving the statement of law by Moore-Bick J quoted earlier, and also citing the *Abram Steamship* case and *Horsler v Zorro*, Mance LJ held that:

---

[161] [2003] 2 All ER (Comm) 298 (CA) [27], [44]–[48].
[162] *Atlantic Lines and Navigation Co Inc v Hallam Ltd (The Lucy)* [1983] 1 Lloyd's Rep 188, 202 only underlines that s 2(2) of the Misrepresentation Act 1967 assumes that a representee can claim rescission occurred when an election was made, and does not positively assert that. The passages in *TSB Bank plc v Camfield* [1995] 1 WLR 430 (CA) 438–39 (Roche LJ) were a minority view, and proceed from the erroneous premise that in a case of non-fraudulent misrepresentation the court is not being asked to grant equitable relief or equitable relief to which terms may be attached. *Allied Irish Bank plc v Byrne* [1995] 2 FLR 325, 353–54 is inconsistent with the later Court of Appeal decision in *Johnson v EBS Pensioner Trustees Ltd* [2002] Lloyd's Rep PN 309 (CA). *Society of Lloyd's v Lyons* [1997] CLC 1398 (CA) quotes with approval from H Beale (ed), *Chitty on Contracts* (27th edn, 2004) [6–067], but the passage cited is founded on cases that do not support the court's broad proposition that in cases of misrepresentation, the act of rescission avoids the contract retroactively *ab initio* (ie *Car and Universal Finance Co Ltd v Caldwell* [1961] 1 QB 525, *Abram Steamship Company Limited v Westville Shipping Company Limited* [1923] AC 773, *Horsler v Zorro* [1975] Ch 302, 310).
[163] [2003] Lloyd's Rep IR 78 [31]–[32].
[164] *Drake Insurance plc v Provident Insurance plc* [2003] Lloyd's Rep IR 78.
[165] *Drake Insurance plc v Provident Insurance plc* [2004] 1 Lloyd's Rep 268 (CA).
[166] But see [2004] 1 Lloyd's Rep 268 (CA) [69], [138].
[167] [2003] 2 All ER (Comm) 298 (CA).

It is clear that rescission in the general law of contract is by act of the innocent party operating independently of the court ... I see no basis for saying that avoidance of an insurance contract for non-disclosure or misrepresentation is any different ...[168]

11.83 Buxton LJ also expressly approved the reasoning of Moore-Bick J, and also cited *Abram Steamship* and *Horsler v Zorro* in deciding that:

... rescission is an act of the party, effective as soon as made, and regarded by the courts as so effective provided that the appropriate circumstances for rescission existed at that time ... There is no authority for the appellant's argument that the court retains some power of equitable intervention to control the exercise of that right to rescind ... The appellant however sought to avoid this general jurisprudence of the law of rescission by urging that insurance was a special case ... This argument does not circumvent the difficulties arising from the nature of rescission that have already been set out.[169]

11.84 These statements are very clear. Notwithstanding the limitations of the three cases on which this view is based, looked at in isolation, the reasoning in *Brotherton* establishes that, in English law, rescission is always an automatic response to an effective election to disaffirm, and the court's role is confined to recognizing and giving effect to the rights thereby secured. That conclusion is, however, inconsistent with the second line of cases considered next. Its authority is also undermined by the circumstance that the reasoning in both *Brotherton* and *Drake Insurance* was unnecessary to the conclusion reached. It was unnecessary because an insurer's right to avoid for non-disclosure is a common law right, and before the Judicature reforms equity exercised a concurrent jurisdiction characterized by a policy of very limited interference.[170] It should therefore be uncontroversial that an underwriter's right to avoid for non-disclosure can be fully exercised by a communicated election to disaffirm, and free from judicial control. Insurance is no different in this respect from all other common law rights to rescind.

(4) The 'rescission by court order' line of authority

11.85 Another line of authority continues to approach rescission in equity as something that occurs when the court orders it, reflecting the traditional approach of courts of Chancery.[171] In these cases the court does not purport to give effect to a prior election to disaffirm, and pays no attention to when or how the contract was disaffirmed, save for the purpose of adjudicating defences of affirmation, acquiescence, or laches. The court simply examines the facts in the light of the plea seeking relief, and refuses or grants rescission on appropriate terms.

11.86 Several well-known cases illustrate this approach.[172] They do so in different ways. In some cases the court indicated that whether rescission would be ordered, and the terms that

---

[168] *Brotherton v Aseguradora Colseguros SA* [2003] 2 All ER (Comm) 298 (CA) [27].
[169] *Brotherton v Aseguradora Colseguros SA* [2003] 2 All ER (Comm) 298 (CA) [45]–[48].
[170] See Chap 3, paras [3.56]–[3.62], Chap 10, paras [10.27]–[10.29].
[171] Chap 3, paras [3.39], [3.53]–[3.54].
[172] *Cooper v Phibbs* (1867) LR 2 HL 149 (mistake); *Allcard v Skinner* (1887) 36 ChD 145 (CA) (undue influence); *Spence v Crawford* [1939] 3 All ER 271 (HL Sc) (a Scots case involving fraud and said by the House of Lords to be governed by the same principles as English law); *Solle v Butcher* [1950] 2 KB 671 (CA) (mistake); *O'Sullivan v*

would be imposed, were both matters within the discretion of the court. This characterizes rescission as relief conferred by the court, not a right vested in the innocent party. If the right was vested in the party and exercisable by election the court could not have a discretion as to whether rescission will occur, or as to its terms.[173]

11.87 A leading statement of this approach is the speech of Lord Wright in *Spence v Crawford*.[174] When discussing rescission for fraud Lord Wright said that 'The remedy is equitable. Its application is discretionary, and, where the remedy is applied, must be moulded in accordance with the exigencies of the particular case'.[175] Likewise in *Cheese v Thomas*,[176] in considering rescission for undue influence, Sir Donald Nicholls V-C observed that 'a court in the exercise of this jurisdiction is a court of conscience ... As with the jurisdiction to grant relief, so with the precise form of the relief to be granted, equity as a court of conscience will look at all the circumstances and do what fairness requires'. Similar statements are to be found in relation to rescission for mistake.[177]

11.88 In other cases in this group the court indicates that the nature of the right is to have the transaction set aside by the court, and in assessing defences of delay, it is the delay in coming to seek that relief, and not a delay in electing to disaffirm, which is relevant. So, in *Goldsworthy v Bricknell*, Nourse LJ (with whom Parker LJ and Sir John Megaw agreed) analysed the elderly claimant's right to rescind a tenancy agreement for undue influence in the following terms:

> Goulding J was in my opinion correct in holding that the tenancy agreement was in the first instance liable to be set aside at the suit of the plaintiff. I now turn to consider whether he was also correct in holding that the plaintiff had afterwards affirmed it and thereby lost his right to do so ...
>
> I think it desirable to consider in general terms both the nature of the plaintiff's right and the defences which could have defeated it.
>
> The characteristics of the right which are material for present purposes were these. First, it was an equitable right and as such liable to be defeated by equitable defences. Secondly, although it was a right to set aside a contractual transaction, it arose outside of and not under the contract. Thirdly, it was in substance no different from other equitable rights to

---

Management Agency and Music Ltd [1985] 1 QB 428 (CA) (undue influence); *Goldsworthy v Brickell* [1987] Ch 378 (CA) (undue influence); *Gibbon v Mitchell* [1990] 3 All ER 338 (mistaken gift); *Cheese v Thomas* [1994] 1 WLR 129 (CA) (undue influence); *Barclays Bank plc v O'Brien* [1994] 1 AC 180 (undue influence/misrepresentation); and, more recently, *Johnson v EBS Pensioner Trustees Ltd* [2002] Lloyd's Rep PN 309 (CA) (breach of fiduciary duty) and *Hurstanger Ltd v Wilson* [2008] Bus LR 216 (CA) (breach of fiduciary duty).

[173] For the view that the existence of judicial discretion is consistent with rescission in equity being effected by act of the party, S Zogg, *Proprietary Consequences in Defective Transfers of Ownership* (2020) 147. The analysis offered does not, however, appear to explain how a court could properly consider events following an election to rescind, in assessing whether rescission will be ordered or on what terms.
[174] [1939] 3 All ER 271 (HL Sc).
[175] *Spence v Crawford* [1939] 3 All ER 271 (HL Sc) 288.
[176] [1994] 1 WLR 129 (CA) 137.
[177] *Seiff v Fox* [2005] 1 WLR 3811, 3821 (Lloyd LJ, sitting as Vice Chancellor of the County Palatine of Lancaster): 'In equity, rectification or rescission may be available in cases of mistake, but these are discretionary remedies, granted only on equitable principles, which enable the court to ensure that relief is not granted in circumstances in which it would lead to injustice. Moreover the courts have developed principles which limit the availability of the remedy.'

set aside completed transactions, for example a beneficiary's right to set aside a purchase by his trustee of the trust property.

The equitable defences which would usually be regarded as being available to defeat such a right are laches, acquiescence and confirmation.[178]

11.89 This statement reflects equity's approach to rescission before the Judicature reforms. The right is to have the transaction set aside at the suit of the claimant, not by simply informing the other party that the contract is rejected. Rather than generating new rights and obligations, an election to disaffirm might at most preserve the existing equity to the court's assistance, by preventing or postponing the operation of defences of laches, acquiescence, or confirmation.

11.90 The reasons of Lindley LJ in *Allcard v Skinner* provide another example of this pattern of analysis, this time in the context of a gift:

> Gifts liable to be set aside by the Court on the ground of undue influence have always been treated as voidable and not void ... Moreover, such gifts are voidable on equitable grounds only. A gift intended when made to be absolute and irrevocable, but liable to be set aside by a Court of Justice ... is very different from a loan which the borrower knows he is under an obligation to repay ... if the donor desires to have his gift declared invalid and set aside, he ought, in my opinion, to seek relief within a reasonable time after the removal of the influence under which the gift was made. If he does not the inference is strong, and if the lapse of time is long the inference becomes inevitable and conclusive, that the donor is content not to call the gift in question, or, in other words, that he elects not to avoid it, or, what is the same thing in effect, that he ratifies and confirms it. This view is ... conformable to the well-settled rules relating to other voidable transactions ...[179]

11.91 Lindley LJ therefore says that the transaction is set aside by the court, and that the right to do so may be lost by failing to seek relief. He does not say that the transaction is set aside by an act of the party imposed upon, and may be lost by a failure to disaffirm.[180]

11.92 Further, in cases involving transfers of real property vitiated by a significant mistake not providing a ground for rectification, there is a long line of authority to the effect that the party benefiting from the mistake can be put to an election by the court, either to correct the mistake or accept rescission.[181] This doctrine is inconsistent with the rescinding party having a right to rescind by disaffirming. Cases involving 'partial' rescission are equally inconsistent with rescission by election, because the extent to which rescission occurs is entirely at the court's discretion.[182]

---

[178] *Goldsworthy v Bricknell* [1987] Ch 378 (CA) 409–10.
[179] *Allcard v Skinner* (1887) 36 ChD 145 (CA) 186–87. Cf Cotton LJ at 173, 175—stock gifted was 'held in trust' and relief not akin to rescinding a voidable contract.
[180] See also *Allcard v Skinner* (1887) 36 ChD 145 (CA) 171: 'In such a case the Court sets aside the voluntary gift.'
[181] *Garrard v Frankel* (1862) 30 Beav 445, 458–59; 54 ER 961, 966–67; *Harris v Pepperell* (1867) LR 5 Eq 1, 4–5; *Bloomer v Spittle* (1872) LR 13 Eq 427, 431; *Paget v Marshall* (1884) 28 ChD 255; *Solle v Butcher* [1950] 1 KB 671 (CA) 696; *Riverlate Properties Limited v Paul* [1975] Ch 133 (CA) 141–45 (confirming that mere unilateral mistake is insufficient); *Topham v Topham Group Ltd* [2003] 1 BCLC 123 [23]. This jurisdiction may now have been abolished in England: *Great Peace Shipping Ltd v Tsavliris Salvage (International) Ltd (The Great Peace)* [2003] QB 679 (CA). In other parts of the Commonwealth, *Devald v Zigeuner* (1958) 16 DLR (2d) 285; *Luckas v Wood* (1978) 19 SASR 520; *Tutt v Doyle* (1997) 42 NSWLR 10 (CA).
[182] See Chap 19, where it is concluded that partial rescission is available in Australia, but not in England.

11.93 More recently, in *Johnson v EBS Pensioner Trustees Ltd*[183] the Court of Appeal reiterated the old rule that equitable rescission is a form of discretionary relief. Both Patten J at first instance and the Court of Appeal would have refused to order the rescission of a charge and guarantee assuming it to have been voidable by reason of the solicitor creditor's breach of fiduciary duty to his client. Relying on the reasons of Roch LJ in *TSB Bank plc v Camfield*,[184] counsel for the solicitor's client submitted that the court had no discretion to refuse rescission. Rescission was said to be a right vested in the client and not the court, which had been fully exercised by his prior election to reject the contract.[185] This submission was rejected. Patten J said:

> ... whatever may be the position in relation to a claim to rescind based on misrepresentation it needs to be stressed that the right to rescission on grounds of undue influence or abuse of confidence or on grounds of breach of fiduciary duty does depend upon the exercise of a discretion by the court to intervene in the enforcement of legal rights.[186]

11.94 The Court of Appeal unanimously agreed. They also rejected the submission that the right to rescind was vested in the solicitor's client, and that it had been exercised, so as to leave the court no discretion to refuse to rescind.[187] Dyson LJ said that:

> ... when exercising the equitable jurisdiction [to rescind], the court considers what fairness requires not only when addressing the question of the precise form of relief, but also when considering whether the remedy should be granted at all.[188]

11.95 This reasoning has since been affirmed by the Court of Appeal in *Hurstanger Ltd v Wilson*,[189] and in *UBS AG (London Branch) v Kommunale Wasserwreke Leipzig Gmbh*, where the Court of Appeal explained that a discretion to refuse rescission on equitable grounds exists if the remedy would be unfair or disproportionate, or if a more suitable form of relief is available,[190] or if the claimant does not come to equity with clean hands.[191] These decisions are authority that, whatever may be the position in cases of misrepresentation (which the court in *Johnson v EBS Pensioner Trustees Ltd* put to one side), rescission for undue influence and breach of fiduciary duty is an equitable remedy conferred by the court, which the court has a discretion to grant or withhold. Indeed, even in the case of misrepresentation, the Court of Appeal has stated that it is not controversial that the right of the representee is to elect to rescind rather than to affirm the contract, and that in such a case it is the court that effects rescission by its order, which in some cases it will refuse to do.[192]

---

[183] (ChD, 8 March 2001) [46] (at first instance); [2002] Lloyd's Rep PN 309 (CA) [32], [56]–[57], [78]–[79]; followed *Hurstanger Ltd v Wilson* [2008] Bus LR 216 (CA) [48]–[51]. See also *Runciman v Walter Runciman* [1992] BCLC 1084; *PT Royal Bali Leisure v Hutchinson & Co Trust Co Ltd* [2004] EWHC 1014 (Ch) [123].
[184] [1995] 1 WLR 430 (CA) 438; para [11.77].
[185] *Johnson v EBS Pensioner Trustees Ltd* (ChD, 8 March 2001) [46] (at first instance); [2002] Lloyd's Rep PN 309 (CA) [32], [56], [76].
[186] *Johnson v EBS Pensioner Trustees Ltd* (ChD, 8 March 2001) [46].
[187] *Johnson v EBS Pensioner Trustees Ltd* [2002] Lloyd's Rep PN 309 (CA) [32], [56]–[57], [78]–[79]. See also to similar effect, *Seiff v Fox* [2005] 1 WLR 3811 [79].
[188] *Johnson v EBS Pensioner Trustees Ltd* [2002] Lloyd's Rep PN 309 (CA) [79].
[189] [2007] 1 WLR 2351 (CA) [48]–[51] (breach of fiduciary duty).
[190] [2017] EWCA Civ 1567 [157]; also at [162]–[168] (declining to refuse rescission of complex derivate transaction affected by bribery and breach of fiduciary duty; cf also [370]–[371]). For the proposition that bribery also permits rescission at common law, whereupon the same discretion to refuse relief is not engaged, *Conway v Prince Eze* [2018] EWHC 29 (Ch) [156] (appeal dismissed [2019] EWCA Civ 88).
[191] [2017] EWCA Civ 1567 [170]–[171], [370]–[371].
[192] *Islington London Borough Council v Uckac* [2006] 1 WLR 1303 (CA) [26].

The uncertainty in the authorities was recently discussed in *SK Shipping Europe plc v Capital VLCC 3 Corp*[193] where Foxton J concluded that the better view is that equitable rescission is effected by order of the court, rather than the court confirming the efficacy of a prior rescission by one of the parties.[194] However, the Court of Appeal subsequently observed that it was 'highly controversial' whether rescission for misrepresentation is not a self-help remedy but depends upon a court order for rescission,[195] and the uncertainty as to the position where equitable rescission is sought for fraud was further underlined by Henderson LJ in *IGE USA Investments Limited v The Commissioner for Her Majesty's Revenue and Customs*.[196]

11.96

(5) Other common law jurisdictions

Australia

The leading decision in Australia is *Alati v Kruger*.[197] The High Court of Australia there described equity's response to a contract that, whilst procured by fraud, cannot be rescinded at common law. The judgment provides a reasoned explanation for when and why rescission in equity occurs upon an election to disaffirm, and was adopted by Dunn LJ in *O'Sullivan v Management Agency and Music Ltd*,[198] who said that it explained the distinction between rescission at law and in equity. The case concerned the sale of a fruit shop that had been induced by fraudulent misstatements about its turnover, and the High Court said as follows:

11.97

> If the case had to be decided according to the principles of the common law, it might have been argued that at the date when the respondent issued his writ he was not entitled to rescind the purchase, because he was not then in a position to return to the appellant *in specie* that which he had received under the contract ... But it is necessary here to apply the doctrines of equity, and equity has always regarded as valid the disaffirmance of a contract induced by fraud even though precise *restitutio in integrum* is not possible ...
>
> It is not that equity asserts a power by its decree to avoid a contract which the defrauded party himself has no right to disaffirm, and to revest property the title to which the party cannot affect. Rescission for misrepresentation is always the act of the party himself: *Reese River Silver Mining Co v Smith* (1869) LR 4 HL 64 at 73. The function of a court in which proceedings for rescission are taken is to adjudicate upon the validity of the purported disaffirmance as an act avoiding the transaction *ab initio*, and, if it is valid, to give effect to it and make appropriate consequential orders ... Of course a rescission which the common law courts would not accept as valid cannot of its own force revest the legal title to property which had passed, but if a court of equity would treat it as effectual the equitable title to such property revests upon the rescission.[199]

In the context in which it was made, the statement that 'rescission for misrepresentation is always the act of the party himself' appears to refer to fraudulent misrepresentation. The

11.98

---

[193] [2021] 2 Lloyd's Rep 109 [240] – [242].
[194] Ibid [241].
[195] *SK Shipping Europe plc v Capital VLCC 3 Corp ('C Challenger')* [2022] EWCA Civ 231 [89] (per Males LJ, Phillips LJ and Carr LJ agreeing).
[196] [2021] EWCA Civ 534 [91] (authorities in such a state of disarray that only the Supreme Court can reconcile them, Asplin and Birss LJJ agreeing: at [100]–[101]).
[197] (1955) 94 CLR 216.
[198] [1985] QB 428 (CA) 457.
[199] *Alati v Kruger* (1955) 94 CLR 216, 223–24.

III. RESCISSION BY ELECTION AND BY COURT ORDER

statement follows a discussion of rescission for fraud at law and in equity, and the case cited as authority (*Reese's* case) was itself concerned with fraud.

11.99 There is no evidence that the old courts of Chancery had ever in fact adopted the practice described in this passage, of recognizing that equitable title to property revested following the disaffirmance of a contract for fraud.[200] But there is no reason why a court exercising dual common law and equitable jurisdiction could not adopt that strategy if it so chose, and in endorsing this approach *Alati v Kruger* developed new principles. The principle is that in cases of fraudulent misrepresentation equity assists the common law by recognizing that an election to disaffirm that does not cause rescission at law, will be effective to rescind in equity, at least to the extent of revesting beneficial title in property transferred. This reasoning implies that when the ground for rescission is recognized only in equity, the situation may be different. That point is underlined by the authors of *Equity Doctrines and Remedies*:

> When dealing with contracts voidable at law, equity confirms the rescission by the aggrieved party whose act is operative. The position is quite different when equity deals with a contract or disposition which is not voidable at law, as Nolan and Cloherty have observed. The decision in such cases cannot be expressed as merely confirming a rescission already made at law by election of the party concerned no longer to be bound.[201]

11.100 The authors conclude that '[t]he plaintiff in the auxiliary and exclusive jurisdictions will be seeking not a declaration that he or she has already validly rescinded, but a decree of the court taking effect from its date'.[202] However, authorities involving fraud have come to be cited as applicable in cases involving innocent misrepresentation, but that this overlooks the fact that equity and law have a concurrent jurisdiction to rescind for fraud, but only equity rescinds for innocent misrepresentation.[203]

11.101 The pattern described is displayed in the older Australian authorities, where the courts had said that rescission is effected by election of the innocent party in cases involving both fraudulent[204] and non-fraudulent misrepresentation,[205] as well as undue

---

[200] The lack of evidence is not surprising, for the common law model of rescission did not emerge until the middle of the 19th century, only a few decades before the Judicature reforms: see Chap 3, Part B. This left comparatively little time for equity to develop a concurrent jurisdiction of the kind described in *Alati v Kruger*. Nor was it obvious what practical scenario might have led a court of Chancery to formulate relief of the kind suggested, of holding that rescission in equity was triggered by an election to disaffirm, or even what equity existed to support such relief.

[201] JD Heydon, MJ Leeming, and PG Turner, *Meagher Gummow and Lehane Equity Doctrines and Remedies* (5th edn, 2015) [25-095] (citing R Nolan and A Cloherty, 'Taxing Times for Re Hastings-Bass' (2010) 126 LQR 513, 515–16).

[202] JD Heydon, MJ Leeming, and PG Turner, *Meagher Gummow and Lehane Equity Doctrines and Remedies* (5th edn, 2015) [25-100] (and at [24-085] of the fourth edition), adopted, eg, in *Permanent Mortgages Pty Ltd v Vandenbergh* (2010) 41 WAR 353, 426 (secured loan affected by unconscionable conduct), *Sheahan v Thompson (No 2)* [2015] NSWSC 871 [151]–[152] (letter of rescission not effective because deed voidable only on equitable grounds), and *Thomas v Arthur Hughes Pty Ltd* [2015] NSWSC 1027 [72] (dispositions of company property by directors in breach of fiduciary duty).

[203] RP Meagher, JD Heydon, and MJ Leeming, *Equity Doctrines and Remedies* (4th edn, 2002) [24-075]. Cf JD Heydon, MJ Leeming, and PG Turner, *Meagher, Gummow and Lehane's Equity Doctrines and Remedies* (5th edn, 2015) [25-095] where this observation is omitted, and the confusion affecting the English authorities is underlined: at [25-105].

[204] *Alati v Kruger* (1955) 94 CLR 216, 223–24; *Kramer v McMahon* [1970] 1 NSWLR 194, 206, 207; *Krakowski v Eurolynx Properties Ltd* (1995) 183 CLR 563.

[205] *Simons v Zartom Investments Pty Ltd* [1975] 2 NSWLR 30, 34; *Academy of Health and Fitness Pty Ltd v Power* [1973] VR 254, 259; *JAD International Pty Ltd v International Trucks Australia Limited* (1994) 50 FCR 378 (Full Ct) 380, 386, 394; *Shuman v Coober Pedy Tours Pty Ltd* (1994) 175 LSJS 159 [17], [25], [26]–[30] (innocent

influence.[206] There are also suggestions to this effect in cases involving breach of fiduciary duty,[207] although the reasoning in other cases appears to contradict that approach.[208] More recent Australian authorities have, however, tended to reassert the idea that rescission in equity is a remedy conferred by order of the court, whereas at common law it is brought about by the act of the party entitled to rescind.[209]

New Zealand

11.102 In New Zealand rescission for misrepresentation is governed by the statutory scheme established by the Contract and Commercial Law Act 2017, which abolishes the distinction between termination *de futuro* and *ab initio* and confers on the court a wide discretion as to what relief should be given.[210] In cases not caught by the Act the Court of Appeal of New Zealand has expressed the view that rescission is always effected by the election of the innocent party, even though the ground for rescission may be exclusively equitable:

> ... rescission is the act of the party seeking to set the contract aside; until there is an election to that end, the contract remains on foot. It follows that rescission is effective from the date it is communicated to the other side and not from the date of any judgment in subsequent litigation which may in some cases be brought to obtain the assistance of the Court: Cheshire and Fifoot's Law of Contract (9th ed, 1976) p 265. Where a party lacks capacity and cannot therefore make a decision to rescind, the Court takes on itself the decision to set the contract aside.[211]

11.103 This view is evidently founded on the opinion expressed in the literature to which the court referred. However, for the reasons set out earlier, that opinion should be treated with care.

Canada

11.104 The point considered here seems not to have been much discussed by Canadian appellate courts. Whilst there are instances of Canadian courts citing English authority to the effect that rescission is the act of the innocent party,[212] Professor Fridman concludes that rescission at law occurs when there is an election to reject a transaction that is voidable at law,

---

misrepresentation and common mistake); *Cockerill v Westpac Banking Corporation* (1996) 142 ALR 227 (FCA) 288 (misrepresentation and economic duress); *Scheur v Bell* [2004] VSC 71 [250], [261].

[206] *Cockburn v GIO Finance Ltd* (2001) 51 NSWLR 624 (CA) 634, 638 (mortgagee with notice mortgagor's consent vitiated by father's undue influence).
[207] *Daly v Sydney Stock Exchange Ltd* (1985) 160 CLR 371, 388–89; *Greater Pacific Investments Pty Ltd v Australian National Industries Ltd* (1996) 39 NSWLR 143 (CA) 153; *Hancock Family Memorial Foundation Ltd v Porteous* (2000) WAR 198 (Full Ct) 217; *Southern Cross Mine Management Pty Ltd v Ensham Resources Pty Ltd* [2005] QSC 233 [676].
[208] *Maguire v Makaronis* (1998) 188 CLR 449.
[209] For example, *Sheahan v Thompson (No 2)* [2015] NSWSC 871 [151]–[152]; *Thomas v Arthur Hughes Pty Ltd* [2015] NSWSC 1027 [72]; *Perpetual Trustees Victoria Ltd v Burns* [2015] WASC 234 [264]; *Nadinic v Drinkwater* (2017) 94 NSWLR 94 (CA) [28]–[30]; *Harvard Nominees Pty Ltd v Tiller* [2020] FCAFC 229 [96]. Also, JD Heydon, MJ Leeming, and PG Turner, *Meagher, Gummow and Lehane's Equity Doctrines and Remedies* (5th edn, 2015) [25-095], [25-105], [25-110], [25-125].
[210] Contract and Commercial Law Act 2017 (NZ), ss 37, 42–49.
[211] *O'Connor v Hart* [1983] NZLR 280 (CA) 295 (unconscionable bargain); the point was not considered on appeal to the Privy Council: [1985] 1 NZLR 159 (PC—NZ).
[212] Eg *Bevan v Anderson and Peace River Sand & Gravel Co* (1957) 12 DLR (2d) 69 (Alta SC) 76–77 (innocent misrepresentation), citing English textbooks and Lord Atkins' speech in *Abram Steamship Company Limited v Westville Shipping Company Limited* [1923] AC 773, 781.

and that rescission in equity is a remedy conferred by the court.[213] If this analysis correctly reflects Canadian law, it remains true to the historical position.[214]

Hong Kong

11.105 The Hong Kong Court of Appeal has held that rescission is not effected by an election to rescind if that act does not by itself effect a *restitutio in integrum*, notwithstanding the statements of principle in *Abram Steamship* and subsequent cases.[215]

Jersey

11.106 In Jersey it is established that the equity to set aside a voluntary disposition for mistake gives the claimant a right to orders setting the disposition aside, as well as an entitlement to set it aside by his or her own act.[216] In a leading case the donor elected to set the gift aside after obtaining a declaration of her right to do so by executing an instrument styled a 'deed of avoidance', in circumstances where it mattered for fiscal reasons that the transaction was set aside by the donor rather than by the court.[217]

(6) Conclusions

Cases present no clear picture

11.107 The 'rescission by election' and 'rescission by court order' lines of authority conflict and cannot be reconciled.[218] On the one hand there are cases saying that rescission is always effected by the act of the innocent party.[219] On the other hand, there is authority that rescission for undue influence,[220] breach of fiduciary duty,[221] and mistake[222] is a remedy conferred by the court and effected by its orders. There are also cases stating that rescission for misrepresentation is effected by an election to rescind.[223] But these are inconsistent with Lord's Wright's speech in *Spence v Crawford*,[224] which said that rescission for fraud is a discretionary, equitable remedy.

---

[213] G Fridman, *The Law of Contracts* (5th edn, 2006) 810–13.
[214] See Chap 3.
[215] *Amuse Hong Kong Ltd v Chan Tin Kim* [1994] HKCA 369 [21]–[23].
[216] *In re S Trust* [2011] JLR 375 [51], [52]–[57], esp [55]: 'The action which avoids the gift is thus in equity the action of the donor and not the Court, although the Court may of course be asked to declare that the donor has that right and even, at the request of the donor, that the gift has been set aside'.
[217] *In re S Trust* [2011] JLR 375 [1], [52], [53].
[218] In *Halpern v Halpern (No 2)* [2007] 1 QB 88, 94–95 Sir Nigel Teare (then Nigel Teare QC) observed that it was not disputed that at common law it is the act of the party that rescinds the contract, but declined to offer a view on the debate before him as to whether this was also true of equitable rescission. The point was not considered on appeal: [2008] QB 195 (CA).
[219] *Reese River Silver Mining Co Ltd v Smith* (1869) LR 4 HL 64, 73; *Abram Steamship Company Limited v Westville Shipping Company Limited* [1923] AC 773, 781, 785; *Horsler v Zorro* [1975] 1 Ch 302, 310; *Drake Insurance plc v Provident Insurance plc* [2003] Lloyd's Rep IR 78 [31], [32]; *Brotherton v Aseguradora Colseguros SA* [2003] 2 All ER (Comm) 298 (CA) [27], [44]–[48].
[220] *Johnson v EBS Pensioner Trustees* [2002] Lloyd's Rep PN 309 (CA); *Allcard v Skinner* (1887) 36 ChD 145 (CA) 186–87; *O'Sullivan v Management Agency and Music Ltd* [1985] 1 QB 428 (CA); *Goldsworthy v Brickell* [1987] Ch 378 (CA); *Cheese v Thomas* [1994] 1 WLR 129 (CA); cf *Allied Irish Bank plc v Byrne* [1995] 2 FLR 325, 353–54.
[221] *Johnson v EBS Pensioner Trustees* [2002] Lloyd's Rep PN 309 (CA); *Hurstanger Ltd v Wilson* [2008] Bus LR 216 (CA) [48]–[51]. In Australia, *Maguire v Makaronis* (1998) 188 CLR 449.
[222] *Cooper v Phibbs* (1867) LR 2 HL 149; *Gibbon v Mitchell* [1990] 1 WLR 1304.
[223] *TSB Bank plc v Camfield* [1995] 1 WLR 430 (CA); *Society of Lloyd's v Lyons* [1997] CLC 1398 (CA).
[224] [1939] 3 All ER 271 (HL Sc) 288.

Difficulties with the 'election' line of authority

There are substantial difficulties with the election line of authority. In the first place, the election model is contrary to the long-established approach of the Court of Chancery, which regarded rescission as a remedy conferred by the court and effected by its orders.[225] Secondly, for the reasons explained earlier, the election model has no solid foundation in authority. It is based on three cases that, properly understood, do not support its application when the transaction is voidable only in equity.[226]

11.108

Perhaps even more importantly, the cases do not really explain what occurs after an election to rescind a contract that is voidable in equity, and their practice is against the notion that rescission has been effected by an earlier election. This notion would preclude the possibility of the right to rescind being lost by reason of subsequent events. But the practice of the courts is to look at all of the circumstances up to the date of judgment in assessing whether the right survives. They also take account of all of the events up to that time in determining the terms on which rescission will be granted. That is not easy to reconcile with rescission having occurred when the transaction was disaffirmed.[227]

11.109

There is one other principled difficulty in the way of a blanket application of the election model. Where benefits have been received by the party who wishes to rescind, if the transaction is set aside in equity, the obligation to restore these benefits is typically imposed by an order for conditional relief. The transaction is set aside and restitution ordered on condition that the rescinding party makes specified counter-restitution, and if the condition is not satisfied the equity to relief is lost. The agreement then remains enforceable according to its terms. This technique of ensuring that the innocent party makes full restitution is not compatible with the transaction having been set aside at an earlier point in time. That is because unless and until the rescinding party in fact provides the counter-restitution that is required, the agreement is not rescinded.[228]

11.110

Conclusions

The law in this area is confused and in need of reappraisal. The view that rescission always occurs when the innocent party elects to rescind has no firm foundation in authority or principle. Despite this, judicial statements at the highest level can be found to support it. The Court of Appeal has stated that the authorities are in such a state of disarray that only the Supreme Court can reconcile them.[229]

11.111

Perhaps the best reconciliation of the authorities is that, where a transaction is not voidable at law, it is only in cases of fraud that an election to disaffirm leads to rescission in any sense.[230] This conclusion fits most of the rival authorities, and is explicable as a matter of

11.112

---

[225] See Chap 3.
[226] *Reese River Silver Mining Co Ltd v Smith* (1869) LR 4 HL 64; *Abram Steamship Company Limited v Westville Shipping Company Limited* [1923] AC 773; *Horsler v Zorro* [1975] 1 Ch 302; paras [11.67]–[11.79].
[227] These points are underlined in J O'Sullivan, 'Rescission as a Self Help Remedy: A Critical Analysis' [2000] 59 CLJ 509. See also Chap 12, paras [12.11]–[12.21]. For the limits of the court's discretion, Chap 13, paras [13.07]–[13.25].
[228] Chap 15, paras [15.50]–[15.52], [15.73]–[15.74].
[229] *IGE USA Investments Limited v The Commissioner for Her Majesty's Revenue and Customs* [2021] Ch 423 (CA) 454 [91].
[230] See also JD Heydon, MJ Leeming, and PG Turner, *Meagher, Gummow and Lehane's Equity Doctrine and Remedies* (5th edn, 2015) [25-110] (discussing this passage in the first edition and reaffirming the view that where a transaction is voidable in equity, it is only in cases of fraud that an election to rescind is effective).

principle as an instance of equity assisting or following the common law. It maintains a symmetry with the group of cases establishing that equitable title to money or property may be obtained when a voidable transaction is disaffirmed for fraud.[231] Even in a case of fraud, however, if the transaction is not voidable at common law, the preferable view is that there is only a weak sense in which the election to disaffirm causes rescission. It does not extinguish the contract and does not affect legal title. The contract is only erased, and legal title is only recovered, pursuant to the terms of a court order for rescission.[232] Instead, the election takes effect by conferring a proprietary right to restitution, burdened by any obligation to make counter-restitution.[233]

(7) Whether election to rescind is irrevocable

11.113 An election to disaffirm a contract voidable at law is necessarily irrevocable because the effect of the election is to put an end to the contract and to restore the *status quo ante*. But numerous statements can be found to the effect that an election to rescind is always irrevocable, not merely when it causes the contract to be set aside at law,[234] and there is only slender authority to the contrary.[235] In principle, however, an election to rescind a transaction voidable only in equity should be revocable. The electing party should be able to change his mind and thereafter sue upon the contract unless the right to do so is lost by estoppel, or rescission has in fact occurred pursuant to the terms of a court order, or the election has generated vested equitable rights in favour of the innocent party,[236] as in a case of fraud.[237]

11.114 This approach accords with principle. The equity to rescind may be lost by events that occur after there has been an election to disaffirm; for example, where matters so change that *restitutio in integrum* becomes impossible, or the transaction is set aside on terms that the rescinding party is unable or refuses to satisfy, or (at least in Australia) the rescinding party acts unconscientiously so as to disentitle himself to relief.[238] It cannot be right that the election to rescind remains irrevocable, even though the right to rescind has been lost. Nor is the other party to the transaction prejudiced by the injured party being permitted to change his mind, for the right to do so is subject to estoppel.

11.115 The approach suggested here accords with the American *Restatement of Restitution* and *Restatement of Contract*, where it is said that an election to rescind is not irrevocable unless

---

[231] *Alati v Kruger* (1955) 94 CLR 216, 224; *Lonhro plc v Fayed (No 2)* [1992] 1 WLR 1, 11–12; *Shalson v Russo* [2005] Ch 281, 320–22. Also, Chap 16, Part C.
[232] See Chap 12, paras [12.11]–[12.21], Chap 15, paras [15.69]–[15.72], Chap 16, para [16.20].
[233] See Chap 15, para [15.70], Chap 16, paras [16.21]–[16.22].
[234] *Clough v London and North Western Railway Co* (1871) LR 7 Ex 26, 34, 36; *Coastal Estates Pty Ltd v Melevende* [1965] VR 433 (Full Ct) 443, 451; *Peyman v Lanjani* [1985] Ch 457 (CA) 494, 500 (which comments appear directed equally to rescission *ab initio*); *Baird v BCE Holdings Pty Ltd* (1996) 40 NSWLR 374, 378; *Drake Insurance plc v Provident Insurance plc* [2003] 1 All ER (Comm) 759 [35]–[37].
[235] *Radferry Pty Ltd v Starborne Holdings Pty Ltd* (Full FCA, 18 December 1998) (purchaser resiled from election to rescind, affirmed and sought relief on basis contract on foot).
[236] *Scheur v Bell* [2004] VSC 71 [245], [248], [250], [261] (rescission occurred when an election to rescind made; held that affirmatory conduct must occur before that election).
[237] See Chap 16, paras [16.25]–[16.29].
[238] *Alati v Kruger* (1955) 94 CLR 216, 225; *Krakowski v Eurolynx Properties Ltd* (1995) 183 CLR 563. Also, *Kang v Eau* [2010] EWHC 1837 (QB) [32] (affirmation of contract after notice of rescission caused any right to rescind to be lost).

the rescinding party has also recovered what he gave, obtained a final judgment for rescission, or become estopped from enforcing the contract.[239]

The notion that an election to rescind is irrevocable is connected with the idea that it involves an election between rights.[240] But that is also difficult to accept. When a party holding two inconsistent rights loses one by electing to enforce the other, the right is lost by waiver. It is difficult to accept that the right to sue upon a contract voidable in equity is waived by an election to disaffirm it, for the right to rescind may itself thereafter be lost, leaving the innocent party with neither of the two original rights. That is not the function of the doctrine of election between rights. It is of the essence of that doctrine that loss of one of the two inconsistent rights confers the benefit of enjoying the other.[241] That feature of the doctrine prevents it operating to deny the electing party both of his inconsistent rights, as opposed to compelling a choice between them. Electing to disaffirm a contract voidable in equity does not confer the benefit of enjoying the right to rescind, for it continues to be subject to the same bars that operated before an election was made.

11.116

However, despite these principled objections, the cases support the view that an election to disaffirm a voidable contract always engages the doctrine of election between rights, and is wholly irrevocable.

11.117

---

[239] *Restatement (First) of Restitution* § 68(2) (1937) and Reporter's Note at 282; *Restatement (Second) of Contract* vol 3, § 382 (1981) and Reporter's Note at 242–43. The point does not appear to have been taken up in the *Restatement (Third) of Restitution* § 54 (2011).
[240] Authorities at n 235; also *Oliver Ashworth (Holdings) Ltd v Ballard (Kent) Ltd* [2000] Ch 12 (CA) 28.
[241] *Sargent v ASL Developments Ltd* (1974) 131 CLR 634, 640–41.

12

Extinction of the Contract

A. Introduction	12.01	(1) Contract set aside by court order	12.07
B. Rescission at Common Law	12.04	(2) Contract set aside by election?	12.11
C. Rescission in Equity	12.07	(3) Discretion to grant rescission	12.22

A. Introduction

12.01 A core feature of rescission is that it extinguishes *ab initio* any contract between the parties. Exactly what that entails is considered in Chapter 1. This chapter addresses the separate question of *when* a contract comes to be set aside *ab initio*.

12.02 The position at common law is straightforward. When a contract is voidable at common law, it is automatically extinguished at the moment the innocent party elects to disaffirm it. But when a contract is not voidable at law, the position is more complicated and comparatively unsettled. The conclusion here is that in cases of this kind, where the transaction is not voidable at law when it is disaffirmed, an election to disaffirm does not bring the contract to an end. That instead requires a court order for rescission.

12.03 The common law will be considered first, and then the position where a transaction is voidable only in equity.

B. Rescission at Common Law

12.04 The common law empowers the party entitled to rescind to extinguish his contract *ab initio* by simply communicating his choice to reject it.[1] The rescission is automatic, and nothing can thereafter revive the contract. In these respects the right to rescind at law resembles a contracting party's entitlement to terminate for repudiation or breach of condition, which is also exercisable as of right by communicating an intention to cancel the agreement.

12.05 The effect of extinguishing a contract *ab initio* is that 'the contract is treated in law as never having come into existence',[2] albeit the law does recognize that there once was a

---

[1] *Halpern v Halpern (No 2)* [2007] 1 QB 88, 94–95; *Abram Steamship Company Limited v Westville Shipping Company Limited* [1923] AC 773, 781. In Australia, *Alati v Kruger* (1955) 94 CLR 216, 223–24; *Coastal Estates Pty Ltd v Melevende* [1965] VR 433 (Full Ct) 434. In Canada, G Fridman, *The Law of Contracts* (5th edn, 2006) 810–13. In the USA, *Gould v Cayuga County National Bank* 86 NY 75, 83–84 (1881); *Thomas v Beals* 154 Nass 51, 27 NE 1004 (1891) (Holmes J); *Philpott v Superior Court* 36 P2D 635, 641 (1934).

[2] *Johnson v Agnew* [1980] AC 367, 393.

contract.³ With certain narrow exceptions considered elsewhere, all rights and obligations existing by virtue of a contract at the moment of termination are dissolved.⁴ The extinction of a contract *ab initio* is to be contrasted with the effects of terminating it *de futuro* for breach or frustration.⁵

The fact that an agreement may have been procured by fraud is not itself a defence to an action at law to enforce it. Fraud gives a right to rescind, and it is the rescission that provides a defence.⁶ It has therefore been said that a pleaded defence of fraud implies an allegation that the defendant has disaffirmed the contract, for otherwise the plea would be defective.⁷ The principle applies equally to contracts of insurance vitiated by actionable non-disclosure or misrepresentation by a proposing assured. An insurer must elect to disaffirm the policy in order to obtain a defence to a claim upon it.⁸

12.06

C. Rescission in Equity

(1) Contract set aside by court order

General rule

A court's order that a contract be set aside extinguishes it *ab initio* at common law and in equity.⁹ This has been so since the Judicature Acts. Before then, the position was quite different. A decree by a court of Chancery directing that a contract be set aside did not extinguish it at common law. Rather, the decree prevented the contract being enforced in a court of law, and would be supported where necessary by orders for injunction and cancellation.¹⁰ The rule today, that the court's order extinguishes the contract both at law and in equity,

12.07

---

³ *Mackender v Feldia AG* [1967] 2 QB 590 (CA) 603 (Diplock LJ); *FAI General Insurance Company Ltd v Ocean Marine Mutual Protection and Indemnity Association Ltd* (1997) 41 NSWLR 559, 563, app'd *Brit Syndicates Limited v Grant Thornton* [2006] EWHC 341 (Comm) [24].

⁴ See Chap 1, paras [1.14]–[1.17].

⁵ *Johnson v Agnew* [1980] AC 367, 393; *Hurst v Bryk* [2002] 1 AC 185, 193–94; *Manifest Shipping Co Ltd v Uni-Polaris Insurance Co Ltd (The Star Sea)* [2003] 1 AC 469 [51]. In Australia, *McDonald v Dennys Lascelles Limited* (1933) 48 CLR 457, 476–77. In Canada, *Guarantee Company of North America v Gordon Capital Corporation* [1999] 3 SCR 423, 439–41. See also, M Albery, 'Mr Cyprian Williams' Great Heresy' (1975) 91 LQR 337; Chap 1, Part B.

⁶ *Dawes v Harness* (1875) LR 10 CP 166, 167–68; see also *Gordon v Street* [1899] 2 QB 641 (CA) 644, 650–51. In Canada, *United Shoe Machinery Company of Canada v Brunet* [1909] AC 330 (PC—Canada) 338. In Australia, *O'Keefe v Taylor Estates Co Ltd* [1916] St Rep Qd 301 (Full Ct) 309; *Coastal Estates Pty Ltd v Melevende* [1965] VR 433 (Full Ct) 441. The position is otherwise when the claim made is for specific performance. Fraud may provide a defence though the innocent party's right to rescind has been lost by subsequent events, in the exercise of the court's discretion to grant or refuse equitable relief: *AH McDonald and Company Pty Ltd v Wells* (1931) 45 CLR 506, 513; *Capcon Holdings plc v Edwards* [2007] EWHC 2662 (Ch) [65]. See also Chap 11, paras [11.41]–[11.42].

⁷ *Dawes v Harness* (1875) LR 10 CP 166, 167–68; *M'Millan v Sampson* (1884) 10 VLR 74, 77.

⁸ *Graham v Western Australian Insurance Company Ltd* (1931) 40 Lloyd's Rep 64, 66–67 (no defence because insurer had never sought to avoid the policy, premium income exceeded insured loss). Some policies provide that there is no liability in the event of misrepresentation or non-disclosure. An election is not normally required for the underwriter to take advantage of such a clause.

⁹ 'A contract obtained by fraud, being voidable and not void, remains until it is set aside, and when it is set aside it is treated both at law and in equity as non-existing': *Newbigging v Adam* (1886) 34 ChD 582 (CA) 592 (Bowen LJ), aff'd (1888) 13 App Cas 305; *Lagunas Nitrate Company v Lagunas Syndicate* [1899] 2 Ch 392 (CA) 444. In Australia, *Academy of Health and Fitness v Power* [1973] VR 254, 258; *Maguire v Makaronis* (1996) 188 CLR 449, 474–75. Megarry J said that when making an order for rescission, the court should direct that 'the contract ought to be rescinded': *Horsler v Zorro* [1975] 1 Ch 301, 302. The more complete form is an order that the contract ought to be and is now rescinded. For the earlier forms of order, see Chap 3, para [3.37].

¹⁰ Chap 3, para [3.37].

might be regarded as an example of equitable principles prevailing over those formerly recognized at law.[11] But a simpler analysis is that it is a consequence of the order having been made by a court exercising a dual common law and equitable jurisdiction.

Delivery up and cancellation

12.08 Orders for the delivery up and cancellation of instruments now have a purely evidential function, and serve to protect the rescinding party and the public by, in the case of delivery up, removing the instrument from the defendant's possession, and in the case of cancellation, advertising its invalidity.[12]

Injunction

12.09 The practice of issuing injunctions to restrain action at law became redundant with the Judicature reforms.[13] However, where payment under the rescinded contract is to be made by a negotiable instrument such as a bill of exchange, the taking of steps to enforce or indorse the instrument might still be prohibited by an injunction.

Defence to contractual claims

12.10 Prior to a judgment for rescission, the party entitled to that relief has a defence to claims at law and in equity to enforce the contract, or founded upon its existence. The defence is an entitlement to have the contract rescinded by the court. Where a defence of this kind is to be pleaded, it is therefore in principle necessary also to plead a counter-claim seeking orders for rescission, although in practice this is sometimes overlooked.

(2) Contract set aside by election?

12.11 Can a contract that is not voidable according to the principles of the common law be set aside by an election to disaffirm it? For the reasons that follow, it is suggested that it cannot be. When a contract is not voidable at law at the time it is disaffirmed, it remains in existence unless and until set aside pursuant to an order of the court.

When rescission in equity is said to follow an election

12.12 It is unclear when the injured party is said to be able to rescind by disaffirming, even though the transaction is not voidable at law. The conclusion in Chapter 11 is that this is confined to cases of fraud where the contract cannot be rescinded at law because of the limits of the restitutionary rights afforded by the common law; as, for example, where land has been conveyed, or services received. Authority can, however, be found to support a much wider view than this, and which suggests that rescission occurs upon election whatever the ground relied upon.[14]

---

[11] Judicature Act 1873, s 25(11), now Superior Courts Act 1981, s 49(1); also *Halpern v Halpern (No 2)* [2008] QB 195 (CA) [69].
[12] See further Chap 29, para [29.86]. For the previous function of orders for cancellation, see Chap 3, para [3.37].
[13] For the position before the Judicature reforms, see Chap 3, para [3.37].
[14] See Chap 11, paras, [11.59], [11.67]–[11.84].

The cases provide no real guidance as to what happens to a contract when it is disaffirmed **12.13**
in circumstances where rescission at law is not possible, either because mutual restitution is
not possible at law, or because the ground for rescission is purely equitable. The question is
therefore to be approached as a matter of principle. This is attempted next.

Election does not cause extinction of the contract
There are several difficulties with the view that an election erases the contract when it is not **12.14**
voidable at law, and these exist irrespective of whether the ground for rescission is legal or
equitable. If the contract is not voidable at law, it can only be set aside in accordance with
equitable principles. Conventional equitable principles enjoin the court to look at all of the
events up to the date of judgment in deciding whether rescission should be granted, and if
so on what terms.[15] If after having rejected the contract the injured party so conducts himself that the equity to rescind is lost, a theory that the contract had been extinguished by the
election would also require that it is subsequently revived. This is highly artificial. It is also
unsatisfactory for the parties' contractual rights to be left so uncertain, gone at one moment,
and back the next.[16]

Moreover, it is fundamental that a contract cannot be extinguished *ab initio* upon rescission **12.15**
without both parties at that point obtaining vested rights to recover benefits passing under
it. But equity has never supposed that fixed rules exist by which precise entitlements to restitution and counter-restitution can be determined *a priori*, and has always insisted on a
discretionary moulding of the relief to fit the circumstances of the case, as they exist at the
date of judgment.[17] It is precisely the limits of predetermined rules for mutual restoration,
automatically engaged upon an election to rescind, that helps to curtail the availability of rescission at law.[18] A rule that election causes the contract to be extinguished *ab initio* cannot
easily be reconciled to this approach to *restitutio in integrum*.

For these reasons, it would seem that when a contract is not voidable at common law, but rescission is nevertheless said to occur when the injured party elects to disaffirm it, that election does not cause the contract to be extinguished. Its effects are more limited. The election **12.16**
may postpone the operation of bars to rescission and, in cases of fraud, will crystallize the
innocent party's personal claim to assets transferred into a vested equitable interest in those
assets, or their exchange product.

---

[15] See also J O'Sullivan 'Rescission as a Self-Help Remedy: A Critical Analysis' [2000] 59 CLJ 509, 541; cf *Drake Insurance plc v Provident Insurance plc* [2003] Lloyd's Rep IR 78 [31]–[32]; approved *Brotherton v Aseguradora Colseguros SA* [2003] 2 All ER (Comm) 298 (CA) [27], [44]–[48]; JD Heydon, MJ Leeming, and PG Turner, *Meagher, Gummow and Lehane's Equity Doctrines and Remedies* (5th edn, 2014) [25-090], [25-100]. See also Chap 11, para [11.109].

[16] See also *Atlantic Lines and Navigation Co Inc v Hallam Ltd (The Lucy)* [1983] 1 Lloyd's Rep 188, 202, noting the 'formidable difficulties' in the notion that s 2(2) of the Misrepresentation Act 1967 allowed a court to declare subsisting a contract that had been rescinded by a prior disaffirmation. Contrast Misrepresentation Act 1972 (SA), s 7(5): 'Where a contract has been rescinded but is subsequently declared to be subsisting under subsection (3), the respective rights and liabilities of the contracting parties will be determined in all respects as if the contract had never been rescinded.' Cf rescission at law, where subsequent events cannot revive the contract: Chap 11, paras [11.57]–[11.58].

[17] See also Chap 11, para [11.109], Chap 13, paras [13.07]–[13.11].

[18] Chap 18, paras [18.23], [18.24]; also Chap 14, paras [14.21]–[14.28], [14.46]–[14.48].

Executory contracts

12.17 In the case of a purely executory contract complete *restitutio in integrum* is achieved simply by extinguishing the contract *ab initio*. The second of the two considerations just discussed therefore does not apply.[19] Is it therefore possible to set aside an executory contract by electing to reject it, even though the contract is not voidable at law? An affirmative answer has the significant attraction of permitting the injured party to restore the *status quo ante* without incurring the time and expense of litigation. That view is, however, incompatible with the notion, recently reaffirmed by the Court of Appeal, that the court retains a discretion whether an executory contract should be set aside for breach of fiduciary duty,[20] or other equitable ground.[21] The innocent party cannot enjoy a vested right to extinguish the contract by electing to disaffirm it if the court also has a discretion to grant or withhold rescission. This is so irrespective of whether the court is seen as enjoying a generalized discretion, or, as is preferable, a discretion as to the application of recognized bars to rescission.

12.18 The issue does not arise where the ground for rescission is fraud or duress or other cause recognized by the common law. Nor does it arise if an election to rescind is accepted by the other party, and rescission occurs by agreement. That is because in the case of executory contracts there is an exact overlap in the bars to rescission that arise at law and in equity.[22] If the bargain is voidable at all, it will be voidable at law, and may be set aside by disaffirmance.

12.19 It may at first appear to be unsatisfactory that the availability of the valuable right to extinguish an executory contract by electing to reject it depends on the accident of whether the ground for rescinding is recognized at law or only in equity. But this objection is not as compelling as it first appears. Concerns that the quality of the defendant's conduct may not justify the consequences flowing from rescission led to the imposition of specific bars to rescission for non-fraudulent misrepresentation, which were abolished only in exchange for a general statutory discretion to refuse rescission in such cases.[23] Precisely the same concern applies to the other grounds for rescission in equity, particularly breach of fiduciary duty and presumed undue influence. The potential consequences of rescinding on equitable grounds may well be quite disproportionate to the blameworthiness of the conduct complained of, particularly where the consent of the complainant was not in truth impaired in any significant way. If that is so, judicial control over the exercise of the right to rescind in equity seems essential, and even at the cost of depriving the injured party of the freedom to undo his bargain by unilateral act.

Extinction of the contract 'in equity'?

12.20 Should a contract that cannot be rescinded at law, either because the ground for rescission is recognized only in equity, or because *restitutio in integrum* is not possible at law, be treated as avoided in equity as from the moment of election? Whilst this is superficially plausible, upon analysis it seems an unnecessary refinement. It is unnecessary because there is no practical difference between the contractual rights and obligations that arise when a contract is valid until set aside by a court order, and when it is said to be avoided in equity

---

[19] See para [12.15].
[20] *Hurstanger Ltd v Wilson* [2007] 1 WLR 2351 (CA) [48]–[51].
[21] *Johnson v EBS Pensioner Trustees Ltd* (ChD, 8 March 2001) [46]; [2002] Lloyd's Rep PN 309 (CA) [79].
[22] The bars diverge only when the transaction is partly executed. See Chap 10, para [10.32].
[23] Misrepresentation Act 1967, s 2; see Chaps 27 and 28.

following an election to disaffirm. In both cases it is the entitlement of the rescinding party to a judgment extinguishing the contract *ab initio* that provides a defence to claims for debts, damages, or to enforce other contractual rights. Similarly, equity will refuse the wrongdoer specific performance or other relief in aid of his contractual rights so long as the other party has the benefit of an equity to rescind, irrespective of whether the contract is regarded as having been set aside in equity when it was disaffirmed.

Conclusions
For these reasons the position would appear to be that if a contract is not voidable at law when the innocent party acts to reject it, his disaffirmation does not cause the contract to be extinguished. That is the case whether the ground for rescission is legal but *restitutio in integrum* is not possible at law, or the ground relied upon sounds only in equity. In both of these cases the contract between the parties is set aside only after a court order is obtained, and in accordance with its terms. The notion of a contract being set aside in equity following an election to disaffirm it is an unnecessary refinement that the law should not embrace.

12.21

(3) Discretion to grant rescission

Where rescission does not take effect automatically upon the election of the innocent party, rescission requires an order of the court. In making this order the court exercises a discretion, but it is a discretion guided by settled principles.[24]

12.22

Those principles have been articulated over the years in the definition of the circumstances in which rescission will be barred on one ground or another. If rescission has become barred then the court will exercise its discretion to refuse rescission. By contrast, it is well established that if *restitutio in integrum* is possible, and if rescission is not otherwise barred, then the innocent party is entitled to have the contract rescinded as a matter of right.[25] Thus the court only exercises a discretion in the weak sense that it has a jurisdiction to refuse to rescind the contract, and will exercise it according to criteria established through the definition of the bars.

12.23

It is nonetheless true that in deciding whether certain of the bars apply and in working out the financial consequences of rescission the courts are often called upon to make fine judgments, and that these judgments occasionally turn on the balance of prejudice between the parties. Those judgments are, however, again guided by settled principles.

12.24

---

[24] Recent authorities to this effect include *Johnson v EBS Pensioner Trustees Limited* [2002] Lloyd's Rep PN 309 (CA); *Wilson v Hurstanger Ltd* [2007] 1 WLR 2351 (CA); and *UBS AG v Kommunale Wasserwerke Leipzig GmbH* [2017] 2 Lloyd's Rep 621 (CA). The first case is best understood as involving an unconventional application of the *restitutio in integrum* bar and in the second the discretion was used similarly to the statutory 'bar' that may be applied where rescission for innocent misrepresentation would have disproportionate effects: see Chap 18, paras [18.113], [18.114] and Chap 28, Part E.

[25] *Lagunas Nitrate Company v Lagunas Syndicate* [1899] 2 Ch 392 (CA) 456 (Rigby LJ). Though he was dissenting in that case, Rigby LJ's remarks have been specifically approved both in the House of Lords and in the High Court of Australia: see *Spence v Crawford* [1939] 3 All ER 271 (HL Sc) 280 and *Brown v Smitt* (1924) 34 CLR 160, 165. See also *West Sussex Properties Ltd v Chichester DC* [2000] EWCA Civ 205 [34]. In Australia see also *Kirwan v Cresvale Far East Ltd* (2002) 44 ACSR 21 (NSWCA) [140]–[142] and *Nadinic v Drinkwater* (2017) 94 NSWLR 518 (CA) [140]–[141].

Part IV

RESTITUTIO IN INTEGRUM

13

General Principles of *Restitutio in Integrum*

A. Objective	13.01	(4) Fiscal consequences	13.32
B. Judicial Discretion	13.07	(5) Contribution under the Marine Insurance Act 1906	13.33
C. Heretical Approaches	13.14	(6) Interest and income	13.34
D. Retrospective Effects	13.26	E. Other Cases	13.35
(1) Introduction	13.26	(1) Replacement contracts	13.35
(2) Contractual rights	13.27	(2) Contract terminated by agreement	13.36
(3) Property rights	13.29		

A. Objective

The basic objective of the relief given upon rescission is to restore the parties to their original positions or, where rescission occurs in equity, as near to those positions as may be.[1] **13.01**

Restoring the parties to their original positions does not involve restoring them to those positions in all respects, but only 'as regards the rights and obligations which have been created by the contract'.[2] The parties are released from the obligations created by the contract, have returned to them any advantages transferred under the contract, and are indemnified for any detriments incurred pursuant to the contract. This is what is meant by *restitutio in integrum* when that term is used in connection with rescission, and this is also what is meant when it is said that the parties should be returned to the *status quo ante*. **13.02**

The object of an award of damages is also sometimes said to be *restitutio in integrum*.[3] The use of overlapping terminology obscures a fundamental difference of principle. The relief given upon rescission is bilateral, restitutionary, and often specific in nature, whereas damages are unilateral, compensatory, and always pecuniary. **13.03**

The distinction between the relief given upon rescission and damages requires emphasis because it is not always understood. The availability of rescission and consequential orders is not conditional on identification of a loss.[4] The object of the relief given upon rescission is **13.04**

---

[1] *Hanson v Keating* (1844) 4 Hare 1, 67 ER 537; *Clarke v Dickson* (1858) El Bl & El 148, 154–55; 120 ER 463, 466; *The Western Bank of Scotland v Addie* (1867) LR 1 Sc App 145, 165; *Erlanger v The New Sombrero Phosphate Company* (1878) 3 App Cas 1218, 1278; *Newbigging v Adam* (1886) 34 ChD 582 (CA) 588; *Hulton v Hulton* [1917] 1 KB 813 (CA) 825; *Cheese v Thomas* [1994] 1 WLR 129 (CA) 137; *Independent Trustee Services Ltd v GP Noble Trustees Ltd* [2013] Ch 91 (CA) [115]. In Australia, *Mayfair Trading Co Pty Ltd v Dreyer* (1958) 101 CLR 428. The object is certainly not to punish the defendant, even in a case of fraud: *Spence v Crawford* [1939] 3 All ER 280 (HL Sc) 289.
[2] *Newbigging v Adam* (1886) 34 ChD 582 (CA) 592–94; *Smith v Cooper* [2010] 2 FLR 1521 (CA) [201]. In Australia, *Brown v Smitt* (1924) 34 CLR 160, 166. In Singapore, *RBC Properties Pte Ltd v Defo Furniture Pte Ltd* [2015] 1 SLR 997 (CA) [126].
[3] Eg *Hungerfords v Walker* (1989) 171 CLR 125, 143.
[4] *Jonval Builders Pty Ltd v Commissioner for Fair Trading* (2020) 104 NSWLR 1 (CA) [43].

not to restore the claimant to his pre-contractual position in the sense of making good whatever financial loss he may have suffered by reason of the misrepresentation or other event that entitles him to rescind.[5] It is only the immediate consequences of the contract itself that must be reversed. If following rescission the claimant will still be suffering losses, for example as a result of expenses he has incurred in connection with the contract but not under it, or by reason of a foregone opportunity, those losses are only recoverable as damages. If the claimant does not have a claim for damages, then those losses will be irrecoverable.

13.05 Just as rescission can leave uncompensated losses, so it can also leave windfalls. The rescinding claimant in *Banwaitt v Dewji* had been fraudulently induced to pay the defendant US$750,000 under an investment agreement.[6] The claimant paid about £318,000 out of his sterling account, converting to US dollars en route to the defendant's account. Since that time the US dollar had appreciated so that restitution of US$750,000 would greatly enrich the claimant compared with his sterling position before the transaction. This windfall did not concern the Court of Appeal, which required the defendant to repay the dollar amount he received.

13.06 To put the point another way, damages are designed to adjust the claimant's financial position to achieve an equivalence with the position he would have occupied had the wrong not been committed or had the obligation been performed. In working out the consequences of rescission the court makes no similar adjustment. Rescission may produce a windfall for one of the parties in financial terms or it may leave one of them in a worse position financially than if the contract had never been made. The exercise is simply one of unravelling the transaction.

B. Judicial Discretion

13.07 Where a claimant is able to rescind at law, the consequences of his election to do so take effect automatically. The role of the court in such a case is to pronounce upon the efficacy of that election and give effect to its consequences by awarding judgment on claims and cross-claims for restitution of benefits that have previously passed under the contract. There is no scope for the exercise of judicial discretion in deciding what those consequences should be. Discretion would be inconsistent with the automatic effect of rescission.

13.08 By contrast, where a claimant is unable to rescind at law, rescission may nonetheless be possible in equity.[7] In a simple case exact *restitutio in integrum* may be possible, but frequently the passage of time and changing circumstances make matters more complex. Where this is so, the court may often facilitate rescission by making discretionary adjustments of various types, moulded in accordance with the exigencies of the particular case so as to achieve the practically just result of substantial *restitutio in integrum*.[8] 'Substantial *restitutio*

---

[5] *Aldrich v Norwich Union Life Ins Co Ltd* [2000] Lloyd's Rep IR 1 (CA) 7–8; *De Molestina v Ponton* [2002] 1 Lloyd's Rep 271, 287. In Australia, *Cockburn v GIO Finance Limited* (No 2) (2001) 51 NSWLR 624 (CA).
[6] [2014] EWCA Civ 67 [86].
[7] *Alati v Kruger* (1955) 94 CLR 216, 223–24; *O'Sullivan v Management Agency and Music Ltd* [1985] QB 428 (CA) 457.
[8] *Erlanger v The New Sombrero Phosphate Company* (1878) 3 App Cas 1218, 1278–79; *Spence v Crawford* [1939] 3 All ER 271 (HL Sc) 288. In Australia, *Alati v Kruger* (1955) 94 CLR 216, 223–24.

in integrum' means that the parties should be placed in positions sufficiently equivalent to their original positions that no injustice is suffered.[9] That is what is meant by practical justice in this connection.

Relief in equity is discretionary but it is given on settled restitutionary principles and not by reference to the judge's personal conception of what would be fair as between the parties.[10] In exercising its discretion to achieve a practically just result, the court should keep the basic objective of restoring both parties to their original positions firmly in mind.[11] Colman J explained the principle in *De Molestina v Ponton* in the following terms: 13.09

> The scope of the equitable discretion in a rescission claim is confined to adjustments to achieve substantial restitution to accommodate events that have occurred after the contract has come into force and does not extend to the general reconstruction of the bargain to achieve an objectively overall fair result.[12]

The discretion the court enjoys is confined to working out the detail of how the parties are to be restored as nearly as may be to their original positions. It is not a discretion whether or to what extent the parties should be restored to those positions. If by the use of its powers the court can achieve practical justice by restoring the parties substantially to their original positions, then the parties are entitled to this as a matter of right.[13] Thus in *Kirwan v Cresvale Far East Ltd*,[14] the New South Wales Court of Appeal held, differing from the trial judge, that the notion of practical justice does not permit a refusal of restitution if restitution is practicable. The discretion the court enjoys in working out the consequences of rescission may be compared to its freedom in fixing the quantum of compensatory damages. 13.10

The same principle applies to the court's related power to impose terms on a rescinding claimant as a condition of his relief. As an application of the maxim 'he who seeks equity must do equity', a court will only order restitution in favour of a rescinding claimant on condition that the claimant restores the defendant to his original position. The discretionary power of the court to put a claimant on terms is a limited one, to be exercised according to established principles. In *TSB Bank plc v Camfield*,[15] Nourse LJ referred with evident approval to a submission that such terms are only appropriate where they are necessary to bring about *restitutio in integrum*. The power cannot be used effectively to reshape the parties' bargain along lines the court may consider to be fair. In the foundational case *Hanson v Keating*, Wigram V-C said that the terms on which a claimant may be put 'must be determined *aliunde* by strict rules of law, and not by any arbitrary determinations of the Court'.[16] 13.11

---

[9] *Northern Bank Finance Corporation Limited v Charlton* [1979] IR 129 (SC) 213: '… rescission will only be granted where a true restitution of the original position can be attained, or can be attained to such an extent that no injustice will be suffered.'
[10] *De Molestina v Ponton* [2002] 1 Lloyd's Rep 271, 287.
[11] *Cheese v Thomas* [1994] 1 WLR 129 (CA) 137.
[12] [2002] 1 Lloyd's Rep 271, 287–88.
[13] *Lagunas Nitrate Company v Lagunas Syndicate* [1899] 2 Ch 392 (CA) 456 (Rigby LJ). Though he was dissenting in that case, Rigby LJ's remarks have been specifically approved both in the House of Lords and in the High Court of Australia: see *Spence v Crawford* [1939] 3 All ER 271 (HL Sc) 280 and *Brown v Smitt* (1924) 34 CLR 160, 165. See also *West Sussex Properties Ltd v Chichester DC* [2000] EWCA Civ 205 [34].
[14] (2002) 44 ACSR 21 (NSWCA) [140]–[142].
[15] [1995] 1 WLR 430 (CA) 434. See also *Dunbar Bank plc v Nadeem* [1998] 3 All ER 876 (CA) 883; *Savery v King* (1856) 5 HLC 627, 666–67; 10 ER 1046, 1062–63.
[16] *Hanson v Keating* (1844) 4 Hare 1, 5; 67 ER 537, 538. See also *United States of America v Macrae* (1867) LR 3 HL 89.

IV. RESTITUTIO IN INTEGRUM

13.12 A difficult line must sometimes be drawn between those cases in which the circumstances have so changed that it is no longer possible to restore the defendant to his original position, so that rescission is barred, and those cases in which the court can achieve satisfactory practical justice by making adjustments between the parties. To an extent this depends on the court's willingness to undermine the defendant's reliance on the security of the contract in question. As a conscious wrongdoer, a fraudster will not usually be entitled to rely on the security of the contract he procured.[17] This lies behind Lord Thankerton's comment in *Spence v Crawford* that a fraudulent purchaser 'is not entitled in bar of restitution to found on dealings with the subject matter purchased, which he has been enabled by his fraud to carry out'.[18] A conscious wrongdoer has no title to complain that he has changed his position on the faith of the contract and would be prejudiced if it were set aside.

13.13 Lord Wright similarly commented in the same case that '[t]he court will be less ready to pull a transaction to pieces where the defendant is innocent, whereas in a case of fraud the court will exercise its jurisdiction to the full'.[19] Neither Lord Thankerton nor Lord Wright were, however, calling into question even a fraudster's right to complete restitution of whatever advantages he may have conferred upon the claimant. Immediately after the passage extracted earlier, Lord Wright continued as follows:

> Restoration, however, is essential to the idea of restitution. To take the simplest case, if a plaintiff who has been defrauded seeks to have the contract annulled and his money or property restored to him, it would be inequitable if he did not also restore what he had got under the contract from the defendant. Though the defendant has been fraudulent, he must not be robbed, nor must the plaintiff be unjustly enriched, as he would be if he both got back what he had parted with and kept what he had received in return.[20]

C. Heretical Approaches

13.14 The propositions formulated earlier are consistent with all of the main English authorities and reflect the attitude of the English courts in recent times, as exemplified in *TSB Bank plc v Camfield*[21] and in *De Molestina v Ponton*.[22] It would be impossible to contend, however, that the courts have always adhered to this restitutionary model of rescission. There are a number of cases, particularly in Australia, in which the courts have departed from it, assuming a more generous discretion to do justice according to their understanding of the merits of the case.

13.15 These cases largely proceed from an unconventional interpretation of Lord Blackburn's injunction in *Erlanger v The New Sombrero Phosphate Company*[23] that the court should

---

[17] Cf *Coleman v Myers* [1977] 2 NZLR 225 (CA).
[18] *Spence v Crawford* [1939] 3 All ER 271 (HL Sc) 281.
[19] *Spence v Crawford* [1939] 3 All ER 271 (HL Sc) 288. See also *Lagunas Nitrate Company v Lagunas Syndicate* [1899] 2 Ch 392 (CA) 434.
[20] *Spence v Crawford* [1939] 3 All ER 271 (HL Sc) 288–89. See also *Wood v Commercial First Business Limited (Dissolved)* [2021] EWHC 1403 (Ch) [40].
[21] [1995] 1 WLR 430 (CA).
[22] [2002] 1 Lloyd's Rep 271.
[23] (1878) 3 App Cas 1218, 1278.

exercise its discretion to achieve practical justice. Whereas this has conventionally been understood as an injunction to restore both parties to their original positions as nearly as may be, given changes in circumstance, there are cases in which practical justice has been viewed as an objective in itself, and one that takes priority over restoring the parties to their original positions. That is to say, a number of judgments appear to hold that practical justice should be achieved *even at the expense* of restoring the parties to their original positions. This represents a fundamentally different conception of rescission, if not of legal philosophy.

13.16 Fox LJ's remarks in *O'Sullivan*'s case may provide an English example of this.[24] He said that, '[the] question is not whether the parties can be restored to their original positions; it is what does the justice of the case require?'[25] More recently Carnwath LJ has tentatively suggested that 'perhaps … for the purposes of "practice justice", the primary objective may not always need to be to restore both parties to their previous positions'.[26] A like idea was expressed by the Full Court of the Federal Court of Australia in *JAD International Pty Ltd v International Trucks Australia Limited*.[27] There the court said that:

> … there is a large measure of discretion available to the Court in deciding what it will order by way of restitution … Although a perfect restitution to the *status quo ante* may in fact be practically achievable in a given case, the Court may be justified, even where the misrepresentation was innocently made, in ordering rescission on terms that give the claimant rather less than that … [The claimant's] entitlement is to be restored only to the extent that will achieve what is practically just as between both parties.[28]

13.17 It is difficult to be sure what lay behind these various remarks. The idea expressed in these passages appears, however, to be that upon rescission the court's overriding object is to achieve practical justice, and that this qualifies or takes priority over the court's concern to restore the parties to their original positions.[29]

13.18 This idea is inconsistent with the way in which the principles governing the relief given upon rescission have conventionally been understood, the central tenet of which is that the restoration of the parties to their original positions is the criterion of practical justice. From this conventional viewpoint the idea that practical justice should be done at the expense of restoring the parties to their original positions is difficult to understand. It is not clear what alternative criterion of justice is being proposed. The proposal may simply be that justice should be done according to the judge's personal conception of what seems fair in all of the circumstances.[30]

---

[24] *O'Sullivan v Management Agency and Music Ltd* [1985] QB 428 (CA).
[25] *O'Sullivan v Management Agency and Music Ltd* [1985] QB 428 (CA) 466–67. See also 458, 471, and *GHLM Trading Limited v Manoo* [2012] EWHC 61 (Ch) [172].
[26] *Halpern v Halpern* [2008] QB 195 (CA) [74].
[27] (1994) 50 FCR 378 (Full Ct).
[28] *JAD International Pty Ltd v International Trucks Australia Limited* (1994) 50 FCR 378 (Full Ct) 387.
[29] But note that this heresy has been repudiated in New South Wales: *Kirwan v Cresvale Far East Ltd* (2002) 44 ACSR 21 (NSWCA) [140]–[142]: 'The notion of doing what is practically just is concerned with practicality. It does not deny that there must be restitution.'
[30] This paragraph was endorsed by Leeming JA in *Nadinic v Drinkwater* (2017) 94 NSWLR 518 (CA) [140]. It is perhaps unsurprising that some other Australian courts should adopt the unstructured approach described in the text given the long shadow the Competition and Consumer Act 2010 (formerly the Trade Practices Act 1974) casts over commercial litigation in that country. Section 243 of Sched 2 of that legislation accords Australian courts very wide remedial powers when rescinding contracts concluded in contravention of the 2010 Act. Though the exercise of these powers is to be guided by the principles developed in equity, it is not constrained by them and the power created by the provision extends even to reforming the transaction. See *Kizbeau Pty Ltd v WG & B Pty Ltd* (1995)

13.19 A more sophisticated version of the same idea finds expression in the High Court of Australia's decision in *Vadasz v Pioneer Concrete (SA) Pty Ltd*.[31] Vadasz had given Pioneer Concrete a guarantee in support of his company's trade debts. As a result of Pioneer Concrete's misrepresentation Vadasz had believed himself to be guaranteeing only subsequent indebtedness, whereas in fact the guarantee encompassed the company's past indebtedness as well. Upon the company's failure to pay, Pioneer Concrete sued Vadasz on his guarantee, and by his defence Vadasz sought to rescind.

13.20 In the joint judgment the High Court highlighted Lord Blackburn's injunction that the court should craft its relief so as to achieve practical justice.[32] The court then articulated a principle in accordance with which practical justice might be done. That principle it expressed as follows: 'The concern of equity, in moulding relief between the parties is to prevent, nullify, or provide compensation for, wrongful injury.'[33] This the court took to be 'the ordinary function of civil remedies, including equitable remedies'.[34]

13.21 On this basis, according to the joint judgment, one asks what the rescinding party would have done if the misrepresentation had not been made. 'If it appears that the [rescinding] party would not have entered the contract at all if the true position were known, the contract may be set aside in its entirety.'[35] By contrast, if absent the misrepresentation the rescinding party would have been prepared to contract on different terms, then the court should craft its relief so as to give the other party the benefit of those different terms. In *Vadasz's* case that meant requiring that Vadasz should discharge the company's subsequent indebtedness, but not its past indebtedness, as a condition of rescinding the guarantee. The court considered that this would be a practically just result both for Vadasz and for Pioneer Concrete.

13.22 Thus the joint judgment provided a criterion by which a court might apply the injunction to craft relief so as to achieve practical justice. This criterion may be expressed through two propositions. First, the rescinding party is to be placed in the position he would have occupied if the misrepresentation or other vitiating factor had not occurred. Secondly, the other party is to be placed in no worse a position than is necessary in order to satisfy the first proposition. Those two propositions appear to represent the ratio of *Vadasz's* case.

13.23 The High Court's approach compares favourably with those cases in which courts have simply posited an apparently unprincipled discretion to achieve practical justice. Nonetheless, the High Court's approach is objectionable in that it blurs the line between damages and rescission.[36]

---

184 CLR 281, 298; *Marks v GIO Australia Holdings Ltd* (1998) 196 CLR 494; *Tenji v Henneberry & Associates Pty Ltd* (2006) 98 FCR 324 (Full Ct) (each considering the predecessor provision in s 87 of the Trade Practices Act 1974); and see E Bant and JM Paterson, 'Exploring the Boundaries of Compensation for Misleading Conduct: The Role of Restitution under the Australian Consumer Law' (2019) 41 Sydney LR 155.

[31] (1995) 184 CLR 102. See also *Bridgewater v Leahy* (1998) 194 CLR 457.
[32] *Vadasz v Pioneer Concrete (SA) Pty Ltd* (1995) 184 CLR 102, 112–14.
[33] *Vadasz v Pioneer Concrete (SA) Pty Ltd* (1995) 184 CLR 102, 115. Cf *Amadio Pty Ltd v Henderson* (1998) 81 FCR 149 (Full Ct) 197.
[34] *Vadasz v Pioneer Concrete (SA) Pty Ltd* (1995) 184 CLR 102, 115.
[35] *Vadasz v Pioneer Concrete (SA) Pty Ltd* (1995) 184 CLR 102.
[36] See further Chap 19, para [19.36].

13.24 It ought to be immediately apparent that the first of the two propositions set out earlier—that the rescinding party should be placed in the position he would have occupied if the misrepresentation had not occurred—describes the objective of an award of compensatory damages. It is a unilateral objective, focusing on the position of the injured party only. In order to achieve this objective the court must proceed by asking a counter-factual question pursuant to a causal inquiry linking the injury to the misrepresentation or other wrongful act.

13.25 While the High Court described this objective as being 'the ordinary function of civil remedies', in fact compensation for injury or loss is only the function of compensatory damages and its equitable counterpart. Other remedies have other functions and objectives. Specific performance, for example, functions to secure the performance of contractual obligations. The function of the relief given upon rescission, as it is conventionally understood, is the restitutionary one of restoring both parties to their original positions.[37]

D. Retrospective Effects

(1) Introduction

13.26 The theory of rescission is that the parties are restored to their former positions by the unwinding of the transaction between them. This is so both at law and in equity and is one of the doctrine's unifying features. A literal unwinding is not possible. However, following rescission the law treats the parties *as if* the transaction had in fact never taken place in certain respects. These retrospective effects of rescission are now summarized.

(2) Contractual rights

13.27 When a contract is rescinded the law regards it as having been extinguished *ab initio*, such that 'the contract is treated in law as never having come into existence'.[38] Accrued contractual rights are extinguished, including any rights to payment of liquidated sums or damages for breach.[39]

13.28 If a variation to a contract is rescinded the original contract is automatically revived.[40] The parties' rights and obligations are thereafter governed by the original bargain. Similarly, the

---

[37] *Newbigging v Adam* (1886) 34 ChD 582 (CA) 589, 592–93.
[38] *Johnson v Agnew* [1980] AC 367, 393; see also *Manifest Shipping Co Ltd v Uni-Polaris Insurance Co Ltd (The Star Sea)* [2003] 1 AC 469, 494–95. But cf the comments in *FAI General Insurance Company Ltd v Ocean Marine Mutual Protection and Indemnity Association Ltd* (1997) 41 NSWLR 559, 563, followed *Brit Syndicates Limited v Grant Thornton* [2006] EWHC 341 (Comm) [24]; see Chap 1, para [1.16]. Similarly, where a consent order is set aside, 'it is to be treated, as far as possible, as if it had never happened, or at any rate never had any legal effect': *Independent Trustee Services Ltd v GP Noble Trustees Ltd* [2013] Ch 91 (CA) [113].
[39] There are exceptions for arbitration clauses, and possibly for jurisdiction clauses and contractual rights of investigation conferred by a policy of insurance: see Chap 1, para [1.16].
[40] *North Ocean Shipping Co Ltd v Hyundai Construction Co Ltd (Atlantic Baron)* [1979] QB 705; *Occidental Worldwide Investment Corp v Skibs A/S Avanti (The Siboen and Sibotre)* [1976] 1 Lloyd's Rep 293, 337, 339. In Canada, *Baytex Energy Ltd v Canada* 2015 ABQB 278 [62].

rescission of a compromise revives the rights and obligations that it had put an end to.[41] It has been held that, by analogy, an agreement to make an interim payment under a voidable policy of insurance will fall away automatically upon rescission of the policy.[42]

(3) Property rights

13.29 The retrospective consequences of rescission extend beyond the contract itself. The rule in England is that when a transaction is set aside in equity, equitable title to assets that have been transferred to the defendant revests retrospectively for the purposes of bringing a tracing claim, at least in cases of fraud,[43] misrepresentation[44] and breach of fiduciary duty.[45] Similarly, rescission of a purchase contract will deprive the purchaser of a defence of bona fide purchase for value should the asset prove to have been misdirected from a trust, although that defence would have been available before the contract was rescinded.[46]

13.30 An Australian judge has held that where a fraudster has obtained possession of chattels under a voidable agreement, rescission at common law does not generate retrospective liability for conversion.[47] This is consistent with the English principle that the retrospective revesting of equitable title following rescission in equity does not create retrospective liability for breach of trust.[48]

13.31 In the unusual case of *Killick v Roberts*[49] the Court of Appeal held that a lease procured by fraud remained voidable despite having been replaced by a statutory tenancy. Rescinding the lease also had the effect of rescinding the statutory tenancy, thereby extinguishing the tenant's right to possess and permitting the landlord to regain the premises.[50] This accords with the principle that a contract terminated by agreement may be effectively rescinded, considered in paragraph [13.36] in Part E of this chapter.

---

[41] *Magee v Pennine Insurance* [1969] 2 QB 507 (CA); *Baghbadrani v Commercial Union Assurance Co plc* [2000] 1 Lloyd's Rep 94, 119–20; *Insurance Corporation of the Channel Islands Ltd v The Royal Hotel Ltd* [1998] Lloyd's Rep IR 151, 173–74; *Samuel v Wadlow* [2007] EWCA Civ 155 [65]; *Crystal Palace FC (2000) Limited v Dowie* [2007] IRLR 682 [209].

[42] *Insurance Corporation of the Channel Islands Ltd v The Royal Hotel Ltd* [1998] Lloyd's Rep IR 151, 173–74, referring to *Magee v Pennine Insurance* [1969] 2 QB 507 (CA).

[43] *Lonrho plc v Fayed (No 2)* [1992] 1 WLR 1, 11–12; *El Ajou v Dollar Land Holdings plc* [1993] 3 All ER 717, 735; *Shalson v Russo* [2005] Ch 281, 320–22; see also *Halifax Building Society v Thomas* [1996] Ch 217 (CA) 226.

[44] *Bristol and West Building Society v Mothew* [1998] Ch 1 (CA); *Twinsectra Limited v Yardley* [1999] Lloyd's Rep Bank 438 (CA) 461–62.

[45] *Daly v Sydney Stock Exchange* (1985) 160 CLR 371, 387–90; *Greater Pacific Investments Pty Ltd v Australian National Industries Ltd* (1996) 39 NSWLR 143 (CA) 153, which would probably be followed in England on this point.

[46] *Independent Trustee Services Ltd v GP Noble Trustees Ltd* [2013] Ch 91 (CA). Noted B Häcker, 'The Effect of Rescission on Bona Fide Purchase' (2012) 128 LQR 493.

[47] *Perpetual Trustees Australia Ltd v Heperu Pty Ltd* (2009) 76 NSWLR 195 (CA) 212–14 (cheque fraud).

[48] *Lonrho plc v Fayed (No 2)* [1992] 1 WLR 1, 11–12; *Bristol and West Building Society v Mothew* [1998] Ch 1 (CA); *Independent Trustee Services Ltd v GP Noble Trustees Ltd* [2013] Ch 91 (CA) [67]. See also *Gany Holdings (PTC) SA v Khan* [2018] UKPC 21 (BVI) [60]–[61] (order to account imposed no obligation to compensate in respect of dispositions by appointee prior to instrument of appointment being set aside).

[49] [1991] 1 WLR 1146 (CA).

[50] [1991] 1 WLR 1146 (CA). Contrast *London Borough of Haringey v Hines* [2010] EWCA Civ 1111 [59] (not deciding whether trial judge erred in deciding that landlord incapable of rescinding a long lease granted under 'right to buy' provisions of part V of the Housing Act 1985, by reason of *Rushton v Worcester City Council* [2002] HLR 9 (CA)).

(4) Fiscal consequences

13.32 Unless a taxing statute says otherwise, the right of the state to charge tax on a transaction is subject to the effect of that transaction as defined by the general law, so that the tax effects of a transaction will be annulled retrospectively if the transaction is avoided.[51] For example, income received between the date of transfer and the date of a revesting in the original owner by virtue of rescission is treated as belonging to that original owner.[52] It has been said that while Parliament is competent to legislate for a different result, that would require express words or at least necessary implication in the relevant legislation.[53] In a well-known line of cases, culminating with *Pitt v Holt*, the only object of the remedy was to avoid a fiscal liability,[54] and there are also decisions in Canada and in Australia in which fiscal consequences have been reversed.[55]

(5) Contribution under the Marine Insurance Act 1906

13.33 Where a relevant risk is double insured, section 80 of the Marine Insurance Act 1906 entitles the paying insurer A to contribution from the other insurer B even if B's policy has been cancelled since the date of the loss. However, if the second insurer is able to rescind his policy then B is not required to contribute, it being 'as if B had never been on risk at all'.[56]

(6) Interest and income

13.34 Interest is payable in respect of money received under a voidable transaction as from the date of receipt rather than the date that an election to rescind was made.[57] Likewise the fruits of assets are to be repaid as from the date of their receipt, not from the time the agreement was disaffirmed.[58]

---

[51] *IRC v Spence* (1941) 24 TC 312; *AC v DC* [2012] EWHC 2032 (Fam) [31]–[41]; *Bainbridge v Bainbridge* [2016] WTLR 943 [37]–[39].
[52] *Wright v National Westminster Bank plc* [2014] EWHC 3158 (Ch) [25].
[53] *Bainbridge v Bainbridge* [2016] WTLR 943 [39]. By contrast, s 150 of the Inheritance Tax Act 1984 confirms that the ordinary position applies in that context, as to which see *AC v DC* [2012] EWHC 2032 (Fam) [34]–[35].
[54] *Gibbon v Mitchell* [1990] 1 WLR 1304; *Sieff v Fox* [2005] 1 WLR 3811; *Pitt v Holt* [2013] 2 AC 108.
[55] In Canada, *Re Kelowna Mountain Development Services Ltd* [2014] BCSC 1791 [106]–[109]. In Australia, *Baird v BCE Holdings Pty Ltd* (1996) 40 NSWLR 374, 388; *United Enterprises v Freyer* [2005] 1 Qd R 337. See also *Akron Securities Ltd v Iliffe* (1997) 41 NSWLR 353 (CA) 370 (party receiving tax benefits not required to account to the other for those benefits upon rescission of tax shelter transaction); *Koutsonicolis v Principe (No 2)* (1987) 48 SASR 328, 335 (liability for tax upon rescission).
[56] *Legal and General Assurance Society Ltd v Drake Insurance Co Ltd* [1992] QB 887 (CA) 893; *O'Kane v Jones* [2004] 1 Lloyd's Rep 389 [213].
[57] *Adam v Newbigging* (1886) 34 ChD 582 (CA) 585, aff'd (1888) 13 App Cas 308. See further Chap 17, paras [17.18], [17.21].
[58] See Chap 17, paras [17.03]–[17.06].

E. Other Cases

(1) Replacement contracts

13.35 Where the effects of undue influence or some other ground for rescission render the contract voidable, and is continuing when a replacement agreement is concluded, that replacement may be set aside just as the original contract could be. But there is no rule that a contract concluded in replacement of another is voidable merely because the first agreement had been.[59] In one case it was common ground that the rescission of a contract of sale procured by misrepresentation revived an earlier contract that it had replaced, and also undid the termination of that earlier agreement, for it had been brought to an end by operation of the now rescinded agreement.[60]

(2) Contract terminated by agreement

13.36 On the other hand, it seems that a voidable contract that has been brought to an end by agreement may be rescinded, even though the ground for rescission does not affect the agreement to cancel. Rescission in this situation appears to entail erasure of all remaining rights and obligations under the cancelled agreement, plus the agreement to cancel itself. The extinguishing of the later cancellation agreement is best regarded as an incidental effect of the rescission of the underlying agreement, although the precise basis for this is unclear.[61]

---

[59] *Samuel v Wadlow* [2007] EWCA 155 [56]–[57], reinterpreting suggestions to that effect in *Yorkshire Bank plc v Tinsley* [2004] 1 WLR 2380 (CA).

[60] *BV Nederlandse Industrie Van Eiprodukten v Rembrandt Enterprises Inc* [2019] 1 All ER (Comm) 543 [136] (appeal dismissed [2019] 1 Lloyd's Rep 491 (CA)).

[61] *O'Kane v Jones* [2005] 1 Lloyd's Rep IR 174, 225–26. Rescission would appear to be unavailable where the agreement to cancel the contract constitutes an election to not rescind it *ab initio*.

14

Mutual Restitution: Rescission at Law

A. Introduction	14.01	(1) Nature of the obligation to make counter-restitution	14.45
B. Restitution of Benefits Transferred	14.02	(2) The need for a return or tender of benefits received	14.52
(1) Nature of the right to restitution	14.02	(3) Security for counter-restitution	14.66
(2) Restitution of property transferred	14.03	(4) Counter-restitution of property received	14.69
(3) Substitutive restitution of property transferred	14.29	(5) Counter-restitution for money received	14.76
(4) Restitution for money paid	14.36	(6) Counter-restitution for services received	14.86
(5) Restitution for services provided	14.41		
C. Counter-restitution of Benefits Received	14.45		

A. Introduction

14.01 This chapter outlines the rights to mutual restitution that arise when rescission occurs at common law. It first considers the restitution of benefits conferred by the rescinding party, and then the obligation of that party to provide counter-restitution. Property, money, and services are treated separately.

B. Restitution of Benefits Transferred

(1) Nature of the right to restitution

14.02 Upon rescission the common law gives exclusively proprietary rights to restitution in respect of property transferred, and exclusively personal rights in respect of money paid.[1] These rights arise automatically upon the innocent party disaffirming the transaction. Where property has been disposed of, claims to substitutes may be brought. In principle, a claim to recover the value of services provided should also be available, but the limited authority on the point is against this possibility. The following discussion considers property first, then money, and concludes with services.

---

[1] For the possibility of a proprietary claim to money upon rescission at law, see Chap 16, paras [16.05]–[16.09].

(2) Restitution of property transferred

Chattels
Fraud

14.03 When a contract is voidable for fraud, and a legal title to chattels has been transferred in accordance with its terms, that title is automatically revested in the innocent transferor when he elects to disaffirm.[2]

14.04 This rule was formulated by Baron Parke in *Load v Green*.[3] It emerged as a way of reconciling earlier cases concerned with the availability of trover in the context of fraudulent sales. These had held that trover, not assumpsit for goods sold and delivered, was the proper count against a fraudulent purchaser in possession, but that trover would not lie against a bona fide purchaser from the fraudster, who could himself bring trover if the defrauded vendor retook possession. The device of a defeasible title that could be regained before an innocent sub-sale, but not thereafter, neatly explained this otherwise contradictory body of decisions. Though today explicable in terms of the theory that the contract subsists until rescinded, whereupon it is set aside as from the beginning, the device of defeasible title was in fact shaped by the requirements of the forms of action.[4]

14.05 The authorities all concern sales procured by fraud. However, the rule must apply to all contracts under which a legal title to goods is transferred, and therefore equally applies to a pledge, hire, bailment, or any other agreement conferring a right to possess. In cases of this kind, where less than full ownership is transferred, and the fraudster's title is created by the transaction itself, rescission revests title by extinguishing it.

14.06 The cases draw no distinction between situations where title to chattels passes by force of a contractual provision, and those where it passes by an act of delivery, or some other event collateral to the contract, such as indorsement of a bill of lading. It is sufficient if the agreement between the parties was induced by fraud. There is no need to show any further nexus between the fraud and the delivery or other collateral event.

Duress

14.07 It has long been established that duress makes a contract voidable at common law, and provides a defence to claims to enforce the contract.[5] Duress also permits rescission at law so as to recover sums paid.[6] There is, however, so far no clear English authority that duress also provides a ground for undoing a completed transaction, so as to recover legal title to

---

[2] *Load v Green* (1846) 15 M & W 216, 221; 153 ER 828, 830; *Clough v London and North Western Railway Co* (1871) LR 7 Ex 26, 32; *Car and Universal Finance Co Ltd v Caldwell* [1965] 1 QB 525 (CA); *Hunter BNZ Finance Ltd v CG Maloney Pty Ltd* (1988) 18 NSWLR 420, 432–33. The principle has also been affirmed in cases where a third party gains a paramount interest in the property before rescission, thereby preventing title revesting: *White v Garden* (1851) 10 CB 919, 138 ER 364; *Stevenson v Newnham* (1853) 13 CB 285, 138 ER 1208; *Kingsford v Merry* (1856) 11 Ex 577, 156 ER 960 rev on other grounds (1856) 1 H & N 503, 156 ER 1299 and subsequently aff'd *Pease v Gloahec* (1866) LR 1 PC 219, 230; *Truman (Limited) v Attenborough* (1910) 26 TLR 601; *Whitehorn Bros v Davison* [1911] 1 KB 463 (CA).
[3] (1846) 15 M & W 216, 153 ER 828.
[4] See Chap 3, para [3.15].
[5] *Whelpdale's case* (1604) 5 Co Rep 119a, 77 ER 239.
[6] *Enimont Overseas AG v RO Jugotanker Zadar (The Olib)* [1991] 2 Lloyd's Rep 108, 118 (rescission to claim money had and received); *Dimskal Shipping Co SA v International Transport Workers Federation (The Evia Luck)* [1992] 2 AC 152, 165 (money had and received implied in the reference to failure of consideration).

property transferred under it, in the same way that fraud does.[7] In fact, there appear to be no reported examples of common law claims in England to regain goods sold, bailed, or otherwise disposed of under a contract procured by duress. At the same time, however, there are no decisions rejecting that possibility, and a New Zealand court has held that duress permits rescission so as to regain legal title.[8] Nor have the English cases considered when legal title will pass if a contract is induced by duress. At a certain point duress should make an apparent agreement void, and negative the intention necessary to pass legal title.[9]

Where title does pass, the rescinding party will be able to rescind the contract in equity and thereby recover property transferred, and that will usually provide adequate relief. However, in some cases it may matter whether rescission at law is also available. This will be so where the injured party wishes to exercise a right of recaption, for which a legal title is necessary,[10] or if there is a bona fide purchase of the legal title after the party imposed upon disaffirms.[11] **14.08**

There seems no good reason why the victim of duress actionable at common law should not be permitted to regain legal title to goods sold by electing to rescind. There should be symmetry between the effects of fraud and duress in this respect.[12] **14.09**

Non-contractual transfers of chattels
Absent a simple contract, legal title to chattels may pass by deed, or by delivery coupled with an intention to transfer title.[13] **14.10**

In Australia it has been held that where A transfers legal title in goods to B by reason of C's fraudulent misrepresentations, and there is no contract between A and B, B obtains a voidable title that A is able to regain by disaffirming the transfer. That was decided in *Hunter BNZ Finance Ltd v CG Maloney Pty Ltd*.[14] The Supreme Court of New South Wales held that the claimant finance company was able to revest legal title in cheques it had delivered to the defendant supplier of goods following fraudulent misrepresentations by the supplier's customer.[15] This permitted the claimant to bring a claim in conversion against the recipients of the cheques, which were worth the sums payable on their face. Giles J did not analyse the case as one where the finance company had rescinded its financing agreement with the fraudster, but as a case where A transferred title to goods to B by reason of C's fraud, and that title was voidable at the instance of A.[16] This reasoning has been subsequently **14.11**

---

[7] The authority that might favour this view is *Universe Tankships Inc of Monrovia v International Transport Workers Federation* [1983] AC 366, 385, although it is unclear whether Lord Diplock contemplated common law rather than equitable rights to recover property obtained by duress, and contractual rather than non-contractual transfers.
[8] *Irons v Wang* [2004] DCR 830 (DC, NZ).
[9] *Fairbanks v Snow* 13 NE 596, 598 (1887) duress 'to the height of such bodily compulsion as turns the ostensible party into a mere machine' (Holmes J).
[10] *MCC Proceeds Inc v Lehman Bros International (Europe)* [1998] 4 All ER 675 (CA); for recaption, see para [14.18].
[11] For that will defeat an equitable interest in the property but cannot take away a legal title regained by the rescinding party: Chap 21, paras [21.55]–[21.70].
[12] Cf *Halpern v Halpern (No 2)* [2007] 1 QB 88, 91–92; on appeal [2008] QB 195 (CA).
[13] *Cochrane v Moore* (1890) 25 QB 57 (CA), discussed F Pollock, 'Gifts of Chattels Without Delivery' (1890) 24 LQR 446, 446–51; see also W Holdsworth, *A History of English Law* (A Goodhart et al (eds)) (7th edn, 1956) vol 7, 503–509.
[14] (1988) 18 NSWLR 420. Cf *Citibank NA v Brown Shipley & Co Ltd* [1991] 2 All ER 690.
[15] *Hunter BNZ Finance Ltd v CG Maloney Pty Ltd* (1988) 18 NSWLR 420, 433–34, 437.
[16] *Hunter BNZ Finance Ltd v CG Maloney Pty Ltd* (1988) 18 NSWLR 420, 432–34.

308   IV. RESTITUTIO IN INTEGRUM

approved, and appears to represent the law in Australia.[17] There are no equivalent decisions in England and Wales, and it is unclear whether the same approach would be taken there.

14.12 The result might be different if it was B rather than C who was the author of the fraud practised on A. Where goods were delivered under an agreement rendered void by reason of a fraudulently induced mistake as to identity, it has been held that no legal title passed to the fraudster, notwithstanding that the seller delivered the goods to the fraudster with that apparent intention.[18] The circumstances evidently prevented there being a sufficient intention to transfer title, though that point was not discussed in the cases.[19] Similarly, where a cheque fraud was such that no contract ever arose it has been held that title to cheques delivered by the victim did not pass.[20] These decisions imply that where fraud induces a gift or other non-contractual transfer of goods intended to be effected by delivery, or the delivery of goods under a void contract, legal title may not pass because the fraud negates the dispositive intention required to do so.[21]

Other tangible legal personal property

14.13 As just noted, title in cheques is capable of being revested in the original owner upon the disaffirmance of the relevant transaction for fraud.[22] The same principle should apply to other forms of legal personal property capable of being possessed, such as bills of lading, bills of exchange, promissory notes, or certificates to bearer shares.

Remedies once legal title is regained
Conversion

14.14 Although formerly trover,[23] and later detinue,[24] were available upon rescission at law, with the abolition of these torts in England the rescinding party's claim is for conversion in accordance with the Torts (Interference with Goods) Act 1977.[25] It is therefore for damages or specific restitution plus damages.[26]

---

[17] *Orix Australia Corporation Ltd v M Wright Hotel Refrigeration Pty Ltd* (2000) 15 FLR 267, 272–73; *Sanwa Australia Finance Ltd v Finchill Pty Ltd* [2001] NSWCA 466. Cf the notion of a retrospective conversion after title is regained has since been disapproved: *Perpetual Trustees Australia Ltd v Heperu Pty Ltd* (2009) 76 NSWLR 195 (CA) 212–14: para [14.15].

[18] *Cundy v Lindsay* (1878) 3 App Cas 459, 466, 469, 471 (handkerchiefs delivered); *Ingram v Little* [1961] 1 QB 31 (CA) (car delivered); see also *Shogun Finance Ltd v Hudson* [2004] 1 AC 919; *Citibank NA v Brown Shipley & Co Ltd* [1991] 2 All ER 690, 700.

[19] See also *Shogun Finance Ltd v Hudson* [2004] 1 AC 919 [6]–[11].

[20] *Citibank Ltd v Papandony* [2002] NSWCA 375 [64]–[65]; *MBF Australia Ltd v Malouf* [2008] NSWCA 214 [65]–[72] (but cf at [32]); *Perpetual Trustees Australia Ltd v Heperu Pty Ltd* (2009) 76 NSWLR 195 (CA) [71].

[21] See also Chap 29, para [29.09].

[22] *Hunter BNZ Finance Ltd v CG Maloney Pty Ltd* (1988) 18 NSWLR 420; *Orix Australia Corporation Ltd v M Wright Hotel Refrigeration Pty Ltd* (2000) 15 FLR 267; *Sanwa Australia Finance Ltd v Finchill Pty Ltd* [2001] NSWCA 466; *MBF Australia Ltd v Malouf* [2008] NSWCA 214 [64].

[23] *Emanuel v Dane* (1812) 3 Camp 299, 300; 170 ER 1389, 1389; *Noble v Adams* (1816) 7 Taunt 59, 62; 129 ER 24, 25; *Earl of Bristol v Wilsmore and Page* (1823) 1 B & C 514, 521; 107 ER 190, 192; see further Chap 3.

[24] *Truman (Limited) v Attenborough* (1910) 26 TLR 601 (detinue implicit); *Whitehorn Bros v Davison* [1911] 1 KB 463 (CA) 463 fn (1); *Newtons of Wembley Ltd v Williams* [1965] 1 QB 560 (CA) 561. The claim was only for the item *in specie* at the discretion of the court: Common Law Procedure Act 1854 (17 & 18 Vict c 125), s 78 (changing the common law rule that the discretion lay with the defendant: E Bullen and S Leake, *Precedents of Pleadings in Personal Actions in The Superior Courts of Common Law* (3rd edn, 1868) 313). Trover was the preferred form before the reforms brought by the Common Law Procedure Act 1854. Also, S Green and J Randall, *The Tort of Conversion* (2009) 31–33.

[25] Conversion is also available in those jurisdictions where no equivalent legislation is enacted: eg *MacFarlane v Heritage Corp (Aust) Pty Ltd* [2003] QSC 353 [84] (sale of yacht induced by fraud). Detinue is also available in those jurisdictions where it has not been abolished.

[26] Torts (Interference with Goods Act) 1979, s 3; see generally, S Green and J Randall, *The Tort of Conversion* (2009) chap 7. If the party against whom rescission is sought is convicted of stealing, the rescinding party might

No retrospective liability for conversion

No liability can arise until the recipient converts the goods to his or her own use. Whilst there is Australian authority that the act of conversion may occur before the point in time when title is revested, so that retrospective liability for conversion is possible,[27] this analysis has since been disapproved, and does not represent the law in Australia.[28] A liability in conversion can arise only if the relevant conduct occurs after title is revested by the injured party's election. 14.15

Similarly, the English approach to equitable rescission mandates that the retrospective revesting of equitable title does not carry retrospective liability for breach of trust.[29] 14.16

Legal title required

Equitable ownership is not sufficient to support a claim for conversion.[30] Accordingly, in those cases where the rescinding party obtains an equitable title by electing to disaffirm, no right to sue for conversion arises. 14.17

Recaption

Recaption is the exercise of a self-help right to recover possession.[31] Instead of suing in conversion the rescinding vendor may exercise that right, retaking possession of what has become his property. This happened in *Re Eastgate*,[32] where the vendor obtained the landlord's consent to enter the fraudulent purchaser's rented rooms, and retook the furniture and other goods that he had sold to the fraudster. 14.18

Recaption carries risks. If unbeknown to the vendor a paramount right to possess has already passed to a third party, the vendor becomes liable for conversion upon retaking the goods.[33] Recaption may also make the rescinding party liable to the other contracting party for acts done while effecting the recapture, and it is unclear to what extent English law 14.19

---

obtain one of the orders for restitution set out in s 148 of the Powers of Criminal Courts (Sentencing) Act 2000. These include orders for the return of the property taken or its substitute.

[27] *Hunter BNZ Finance Ltd v CG Maloney Pty Ltd* (1988) 18 NSWLR 420, approved *Orix Australia Corporation Ltd v M Wright Hotel Refrigeration Pty Ltd* (2000) 15 FLR 267, 272–73 and *Sanwa Australia Finance Ltd v Finchill Pty Ltd* [2001] NSWCA 466 [29].
[28] *Perpetual Trustees Australia Ltd v Heperu Pty Ltd* (2009) 76 NSWLR 195 (CA) 212–14 (cheque fraud).
[29] *Lonrho plc v Fayed (No 2)* [1992] 1 WLR 1, 11–12; *Bristol and West Building Society v Mothew* [1998] 1 Ch 1 (CA) 22–23.
[30] *MCC Proceeds Inc v Lehman Bros International Europe* [1998] 4 All ER 675 (CA); noted K Barker, 'Equitable Title and Common Law Conversion: The Limits of the Fusionist Ideal' [1998] 6 RLR 150.
[31] For discussion, *Toyota Finance Australia Ltd v Dennis* (2002) 58 NSWLR 101 (CA), noted (2003) 77 ALJ 223; F Pollock and R Wright, *An Essay on Possession in the Common Law* (1888) 78–80; CA Branston, 'Forcible Recaption of Chattels' (1912) 28 LQR 262; W Holdsworth, *A History of English Law* (A Goodhart et al (eds)) (7th edn, 1956) vol 3, 279–80; F Lawson and H Teff, *Remedies of English Law* (2nd edn, 1980) 28; AM Dugdale et al (eds), *Clerk and Lindsell on Torts* (23rd edn, 2020) [29-14] and [29-15]; J Goudkamp and D Nolan, *Winfield & Jolowicz on Tort* (20th edn, 2020) [18-42]–[18-47].
[32] [1905] 1 KB 465.
[33] This occurred in *White v Garden* (1851) 10 CB 919, 138 ER 919 (quantity of iron retaken by defrauded vendor after it was sold to a bona fide purchaser for value, who successfully brought trover for it). Cf *MacFarlane v Heritage Corp (Aust) Pty Ltd* [2003] QSC 353 [80] (defrauded vendor's attempt to recapture his yacht, sold for 'trade dollars', thwarted by water police).

excuses a recapturing party for what would otherwise be wrongful conduct.[34] It has been said that less latitude is given where the initial taking is not wrongful,[35] and an Australian court has held that force may not be used where the taking was not wrongful from its inception.[36] That is the position where a voidable title passes, in that the transferee has a right to possess unless and until the transaction is avoided. On the other hand, the taking is 'wrongful' in the sense that it was procured by fraud or other conduct permitting rescission, and another Australian judge has said that 'I should not regard a physical resumption of property [sold] as improper, where it was a reasonable course of action adopted on legal advice'.[37]

14.20 In principle, the fact that the rescinding party commits a wrong in retaking possession of the goods should not cut down his right to retain that possession.[38]

Property not recoverable on rescission at law
Intangible legal property

14.21 Rescission at law cannot revest title in intangible legal property, such as the chose in action represented by a credit balance in a bank account, because the common law knows no mechanism by which that revesting may occur. For transactions involving choses in action and other property that cannot be possessed, a proprietary interest may only be obtained by rescinding in equity.

14.22 The principle is well illustrated in relation to shares. Save in the case of bearer shares, legal title to shares is generally conferred by entry of the shareholder's name in the company's register of members, in that it is generally only registered shareholders who enjoy the full complement of statutory and contractual rights that comprise a share,[39] and registration is treated as conferring legal title to shares in equity.[40] Where registration does confer ownership, an election to disaffirm a transfer of shares induced by fraud or duress is incapable of revesting legal title in the transferor. That can only happen when the register of members is amended. For this reason a contract or gift under which shares have been transferred may, save in the exceptional case of bearer shares, only be set aside in equity.[41] When decreeing

---

[34] n 31. In some jurisdictions statute authorizes the use of reasonable force to recover chattels; see eg *Toyota Finance Australia Ltd v Dennis* (2002) 58 NSWLR 101 (CA) [68].

[35] F Lawson and H Teff, *Remedies of English Law* (2nd edn, 1980) 28; AM Dugdale et al (eds), *Clerk and Lindsell on Torts* (23rd edn, 2020) [29-14]; J Goudkamp and D Nolan, *Winfield & Jolowicz on Tort* (20th edn, 2020) [18-46].

[36] *Toyota Finance Australia Ltd v Dennis* (2002) 58 NSWLR 101 (CA), but cf the dissenting opinion of Handley JA.

[37] *Waters Motors Pty Ltd v Cratchley* (1964) 80 WN (NSW) 1165, 1176 (Else Mitchell J) (although the case concerned equitable rescission).

[38] F Pollock and R Wright, *An Essay on Possession in the Common Law* (1888) 78–80.

[39] *Borland's Trustee v Steel Bros and Co* [1901] 1 Ch 279, 288; *Soden v British and Commonwealth Holdings plc* [1995] 1 BCLC 686, 696; [1998] AC 298 (CA) 309; P Davies, S Worthington, and C Hare (eds), *Gower: Principles of Modern Company Law* (11th edn, 2020) [26-005]; G Barton, 'The Legal Nature of a Share' in N Palmer and E McKendrick (eds), *Interests in Goods* (2nd edn, 1998) 111; Companies Act 2006, s 112(2).

[40] Equitable title to shares is conferred by a right to be registered as a member on allotment (*National Westminster Bank plc v IRC* [1995] 1 AC 111, 126) or transfer (*Milroy v Lord* (1862) 4 De GF & J 264, 45 ER 1185; *Re Rose, Midland Bank Executor and Trustee Co v Rose* [1949] Ch 78; *Re Rose, Rose v IRC* [1952] Ch 499 (CA) 510–11). Registration also confers legal title for the purpose of equitable priority disputes (*Ireland v Hart* [1902] 1 Ch 552), and registration as the holder without intent to take beneficial ownership confers a bare legal title (*Hardoon v Belilios* [1901] AC 118).

[41] *Civil Service Co-operative Society v Blyth* (1914) 17 CLR 601, 613; *Sons of Gwalia Limited v Margaretic* (2007) 231 CLR 160 [55] (discussing rescission by a recipient rather than a transferor of shares); *Nadinic v Drinkwater* (2017) 94 NSWLR 518 (CA) [28]–[31].

rescission the court will make appropriate orders for revesting title, typically by directing the transferee to execute a re-transfer.[42]

Unregistered land
At common law an executory contract for the sale or purchase of an interest in land may be rescinded for fraud, and a deposit or like sum paid is recoverable as money had and received.[43] If the conveyance has been completed and a legal estate passed the claimant may recover damages in deceit.[44]

14.23

Although there is some text book authority to the contrary,[45] it seems fairly clear that at common law there can be no rescission of a contract pursuant to which an interest in unregistered land has passed, because the common law does not allow the conveying party to recover legal title by electing to disaffirm, or by other unilateral act. The defrauded transferor may only obtain rescission in equity.[46] This rule is founded on the way in which *Feret v Hill*[47] has been interpreted, and that decision and its later reception will be briefly considered.

14.24

Feret had obtained a lease and possession of a house from Hill by fraudulently misrepresenting that it would be used to carry on the business of perfumer, when in fact he intended to operate a brothel. Upon discovering that his house had been converted into a brothel Hill forcibly evicted Feret, who successfully brought ejectment to recover possession. By allowing Feret to bring ejectment the court recognized that at the time of his eviction he was lawfully in possession with an exclusive right to possess. As has been observed since, the foundation of Feret's cause of action was his possession of the premises, not the agreement under which he had been put into possession.[48]

14.25

There were two separate themes in the court's reasons, which were further complicated by suggestions that Hill's defence was in the nature of a plea of *non est factum*.[49] First, some members of the court emphasized that the misrepresentation was merely 'collateral' to the contract or its purpose,[50] implying that the result might have been different if it was not.[51] Secondly, it was said that after the estate vested in Feret upon completion of the lease and

14.26

---

[42] See Chap 15, para [15.11].
[43] *Flight v Booth* (1834) 1 Bing (NC) 370, 376; 131 ER 1160, 1162; *Coastal Estates Pty Ltd v Melevende* [1965] VR 433 (Full Ct).
[44] *Dobell v Stevens* (1825) 3 B & C 623, 107 ER 864; also *Ekins v Tresham* (1675) 1 Lev 102, 83 ER 318; *Lysney v Selby* (1705) 2 Ld Raym 1118, 92 ER 240; *Small v Attwood* (1832) You 406, 460–61; 159 ER 1051, 1073.
[45] T Williams and J Lightwood, *A Treatise on the Law of Vendor and Purchaser of Real Estate and Chattels Real* (4th edn, 1936) vol 2, 671, 794; D McDonnell and J Monroe (eds), *Kerr on the Law of Fraud and Mistake* (7th edn, 1952) 530–31.
[46] For literature supporting that view, JD Heydon, MJ Leeming, and PG Turner, *Meagher, Gummow and Lehane's Equity Doctrines and Remedies* (5th edn, 2014) [25-050] ; E Sugden, *A Concise and Practical Treatise of the Law of Vendors and Purchasers of Estates* (14th edn, 1862) 243–44, 246, 248, 253 (implying that title may only be recovered in equity).
[47] (1854) 15 CB 207, 223–27; 139 ER 400, 406–08. Cf *Lovell v Hicks* (1836) 2 Y & C Ex 46, 48; 160 ER 306, 308 per Wigram (later Wigram V-C) and Heathfield of counsel: 'when an estate has been conveyed away under circumstances of fraud, you cannot recover it at law, but must come to equity.'
[48] *Gollan v Nugent* (1988) 166 CLR 18, 29.
[49] *Feret v Hill* (1854) 15 CB 207, 213, 219; 139 ER 400, 403, 405.
[50] (1854) 15 CB 207, 223–24, 227; 139 ER 400, 407–408.
[51] This is particularly given that the same court had recently held, in *Evans v Edmonds* (1853) 13 CB 777, 138 ER 1407, that the gross fraud perpetrated there made the deed 'voidable' insofar as the obligee did not have to perform it.

his entry into possession, it could not by operation of law be revested, at least by reason of a misrepresentation about the use to which the premises would be put.[52] This was supported by policy considerations.[53]

14.27 The second ground for the decision was not universally accepted at the time,[54] and on one reading of *Feret v Hill* a rescinding party might be able to regain title to land if the fraud went beyond a misstatement as to the intended use of the premises. Despite this, with one exception,[55] subsequent cases interpreted *Feret v Hill* as resting upon a rule that once an estate has passed it cannot be regained at common law by disaffirming the transaction for fraud, irrespective of the kind of fraud practised.[56] *Feret v Hill* has therefore become accepted as authority that a completed contract for conveying an interest in unregistered land cannot be rescinded at law, because the common law does not empower the defrauded party to revest title. He must instead seek relief in equity.

Registered land

14.28 By analogy with the rule developed in relation to unregistered land, completed contracts that create or dispose of interests in registered land cannot be rescinded at law, for neither the legislation nor the common law confers a right in the transferor to unilaterally regain title. Title is instead to be regained by a claim founded on equitable principles, which if successful will end in orders for rectification of the register, or that the registered owner execute and deliver a registrable re-transfer.[57]

(3) Substitutive restitution of property transferred

Proceeds

Disposal to purchaser with notice

14.29 Where the fraudster disposes of property to a purchaser with notice, the rescinding party may either recover damages in conversion, or instead bring money had and received in respect of the proceeds. It has been said that this involves waiver of the tort of conversion,[58]

---

[52] *Feret v Hill* (1854) 15 CB 207, 209; 139 ER 400, 401 (Williams J); 15 CB 207, 223–24; 139 ER 400, 407 (Jervis CJ); 15 CB 207, 225–26; 139 ER 400, 407–08 (Maule J).

[53] Maule J referred to the 'inconvenient and mischievous consequences if we were to hold that a title once vested might afterwards be impeached, on the ground that one of the contracting parties had been induced by a fraudulent misrepresentation of the other as to the uses to which he meant to apply the premises':15 CB 207, 225–26; 139 ER 400, 407–08. This echoes the reasoning of Chancery judges in denying the possibility of rescinding a completed disposition of land for non-fraudulent misrepresentation: see *Clare v Lamb* (1875) LR 10 CP 334, 338–39. See further Chap 27.

[54] See the reporter's critique of *Feret v Hill* in *Cavaleiro v Puget* (1865) 4 F & F 537, 542; 176 ER 680, 683 note (a): 'that "an estate had passed", surely was untenable; for if the agreement was voidable by reason of fraud, then an estate did not pass, as the lessor had an option to, and elected to avoid it *ab initio*; and if the agreement was avoided an estate could not be deemed to have passed under it.'

[55] *Gordon v Chief Commissioner of Metropolitan Police* [1910] 2 KB 1080 (CA) 1089, which emphasized both the first and second grounds for the decision.

[56] *Canham v Barry* (1855) 15 CB 597, 611–12; 139 ER 558, 564–65; *R v Saddlers' Company* (1863) 10 HLC 303, 422; 11 ER 217, 228; *Taylor v Chester* (1869) LR 4 QB 309, 311–12. See also *Alexander v Rayson* [1936] 1 KB 169 (CA) 184 and *Alati v Kruger* (1955) 94 CLR 216, 224–25 where the view was expressed that title to a lease may be recovered in equity for misrepresentation.

[57] See further Chap 15, paras [15.08]–[15.09].

[58] *Hunter BNZ Finance Ltd v Maloney* (1988) 18 NSWLR 420, 433, also 441 (cheque). As to 'waiver of tort' generally, *United Australia v Barclays Bank Ltd* [1941] AC 1.

but that analysis is redundant. The sums are held to the use of the defrauded vendor because they represent the proceeds of the sale of what has become, upon rescission, his property.[59]

Presumably, once the rescinding party obtains satisfaction, title in the property will revest in the third party, rather than the initial transferee.   **14.30**

Disposal to innocent purchaser
Although it has been argued that a defrauded vendor may rescind and bring money had and received for the proceeds of a subsequent re-sale, even though the sale has been to a bona fide purchaser,[60] there is no clear authority in favour of this view. It is generally assumed that once a paramount interest has passed to a third party, rescission is barred.[61]   **14.31**

But cases concerned with voidable preferences have not taken this approach. The assignee in bankruptcy has been permitted to set aside a voidable sale and claim the proceeds of goods re-sold to a bona fide purchaser, for reasons that would seem equally to apply to rescission at common law.[62] In *Marks v Feldman*[63] Kelly CB said that the reason was that the bankrupt never received a good title to the chattels or their proceeds; rather, he obtained a defeasible title, and 'when the goods have been converted into money the assignee becomes entitled to maintain an action for money had and received ... the transaction remaining in effect the same, the remedy only differing'.[64] There does not seem to be any reason why the analysis should be any different if the transaction is voidable at common law, rather than under the bankruptcy legislation there considered.   **14.32**

Exchange product
Subject to the objections noticed earlier in relation to claims to the proceeds of sale, in principle legal title to exchange substitutes should be able to be asserted upon rescission at law, if the fact pattern admits of such a claim.[65] The circumstances that must be present will, however, rarely occur in practice. It must have been possible to obtain back legal title in the asset that was originally transferred. The contract or gift must, therefore, have been one involving chattels or other tangible legal personal property.[66] A 'clean' substitution must then have taken place, in that the substitute was acquired only using the original asset. Legal title in   **14.33**

---

[59] *Buckland v Johnson* (1854) 15 CB 145, 139 ER 375 (the reasoning in which is unaffected by the subsequent overruling of the case in *Brinsmead v Harrison* (1871) LR 6 CP 584).

[60] G Glenn, 'Rescission for Fraud in Sale or Purchase of Goods—Quasi Contractual Remedies as Related to Trover and Replevin' (1936) 22 Virginia LR 859, 878–79.

[61] *White v Garden* (1851) 10 CB 919, 138 ER 364; *Stevenson v Newnham* (1853) 13 CB 285, 138 ER 1208. Cf *Hill v Perrott* (1810) 3 Taunt 274, 128 ER 109.

[62] *Marks v Feldman* (1870) LR 5 QB 275 (Ex), overturning the decision of the Court of Queen's Bench, which had held that money had and received was unavailable because when the goods were sold they were the goods of the bankrupt, and the money received for their sale was therefore also his: (1869) LR 4 QB 481, 484–86.

[63] (1870) LR 5 QB 275 (Ex). As to the position under the earlier legislation, *Young v Billister* (1860) 8 HLC 682, 693; 11 ER 596, 601 (Blackburn J).

[64] (1870) LR 5 QB 275, 281 (Ex).

[65] *Gladstone v Hadwen* (1813) 1 M & S 517, 526–27; 105 ER 193, 197 (creditor entitled to retain possession of two recovered bank notes, the exchange product of bills of exchange obtained by the debtor's fraud). Lord Ellenborough decided that case before the concept of a title voidable at law had been developed in *Load v Green* (1846) 15 M & W 216, 153 ER 828. However, the reasoning employed turned on the creditor's right to recover legal title in equity, and it is implicit that the result would have been the same if he could have recovered title at law. See also *Small v Attwood* (1832) You 407, 535–38; 159 ER 1051, 1103–04 (rev'd on other grounds *Attwood v Small* (1838) 6 Cl & Fin 232, 7 ER 684).

[66] See paras [14.03], [14.13], [14.21], [14.23], [14.28].

that substitute must also be capable of being vested in the rescinding party by operation of law. The substitute must therefore itself be tangible legal personal property. Because of these difficulties, a claim to exchange substitutes will rarely be capable of arising upon rescission at law. The case would have to be one where chattels are bartered for other chattels, a cheque is delivered and its proceeds are received in cash that remains separately identified, or, perhaps, identified cash is paid over and then used to buy identified chattels.[67]

Personal claims to the value of chattels

14.34 Rejecting earlier suggestions to the contrary,[68] a series of cases in the early nineteenth century held that a defrauded vendor could not bring a personal claim for the value of goods sold (assumpsit for goods sold and delivered) against his dishonest buyer, but must seek either damages in deceit, or assert a proprietary interest in order to bring trover.[69]

14.35 Notwithstanding that they were difficult to reconcile with cases holding that this form of action was available when a contract of sale was repudiated,[70] or against a fraudster's accomplice receiving the goods sold,[71] these decisions were accepted as correct at the time[72] and have not since been questioned by English courts. Although they have been criticized by scholars,[73] and some American courts have come to a different conclusion,[74] the cases seem to have established a general rule that a defrauded vendor cannot rescind and maintain a personal claim for the value of property transferred. A proprietary interest must be asserted. If it cannot be asserted, either because the goods have ceased to exist or become subject to a third party's paramount claim, rescission is said to be unavailable.[75] The claimant must then, if he has a right to do so, sue for damages in tort or for breach of contract. If the issue was to arise today, it is unclear whether a modern court would follow the approach charted by the early authorities.[76]

---

[67] If legal title can be asserted to cash upon rescission at law, which is doubtful: Chap 16, paras [16.05]–[16.09].
[68] *De Symons v Minchwich* (1796) 1 Esp 430, 170 ER 409.
[69] *Read v Hutchinson* (1813) 3 Camp 352, 170 ER 1408; *Ferguson v Carrington* (1829) 9 B & C 59, 109 ER 22; *Strutt v Smith* (1834) 1 CM & R 312, 149 ER 1099. The overruling of *De Symons*' case was noted in *Bradbury v Anderton* (1834) 1 CM & R 486, 489; 149 ER 1171, 1173. These cases were probably precipitated by the greater separation between the count for goods sold and delivered and trover effected in *Bennett v Francis* (1801) 2 Bos & Pul 550, 126 ER 1433.
[70] *Oxendale v Wetherell* (1829) 9 B & C 385, 109 ER 143; *Bartholemew v Marwick* (1864) 15 CB (NS) 711, 143 ER 964.
[71] *Hill v Perrott* (1810) 3 Taunt 274, 128 ER 109.
[72] See eg J Chitty, *A Practical Treatise on the Law of Contracts Not Under Seal* (J Russell (ed)) (4th edn, 1850) 358; E Bullen and S Leake, *Precedents of Pleadings* (3rd edn, 1868) 39.
[73] C Mitchell et al, *Goff and Jones: The Law of Unjust Enrichment* (9th edn, 2016) [36-10] (supporting the view of Peter Birks that the rescinding party ought to be entitled to receive the money value of benefits transferred, whether comprising money, specific assets, or services); D Friedmann, 'Valid, Voidable, Qualified and Non-Existing Obligations: An Alternative Perspective on the Law of Restitution' in A Burrows (ed), *Essays on the Law of Restitution* (1991) 247, 267, fn 78; G Palmer, *The Law of Restitution* (1978) vol 1, [3.16]; A Lodder, *Enrichment in the Law of Unjust Enrichment* (2012) 128–29.
[74] See the cases cited in G Palmer, *The Law of Restitution* (1978) vol 1, 329, fn 18; J Dawson and G Palmer, *Cases on Restitution* (2nd edn, 1969) 316–31; also *Philpott v Superior Court* 36 P2d 635, 641 (1934).
[75] But cf if rescission to assert a personal or proprietary claim to substitutes is possible: paras [14.29]–[14.33].
[76] For the view that a court today need not follow the older cases, C Mitchell et al, *Goff and Jones: The Law of Unjust Enrichment* (9th edn, 2016) [36-10]. An innovation of the kind suggested would require a court to explain the juridical basis for requiring a person to pay for the value of property in their hands that they own and to which they have a paramount right to possess. The common law has never recognised such a right. It has instead always anchored the obligation to pay for the value of chattels to a wrongful interference in the possession or right of possession of another person, and as a remedy to vindicate rights of ownership.

(4) Restitution for money paid

Money had and received

14.36 Upon electing to disaffirm a contract voidable at law, and where necessary also tendering back benefits received, the party rescinding obtains a right to be repaid sums that he has paid under the contract.[77] The right is to be repaid an equivalent sum. In the language of the forms of action, the money received by the payee is held for the use of the payer on the ground that it has been paid for a consideration that has failed. As such, it is recoverable as money had and received,[78] which is a debt imposed by operation of law. The principle has been applied in cases involving rescission for fraud,[79] duress,[80] and non-disclosure and misrepresentation by an insurer.[81]

Failure of consideration

14.37 The right to repayment arises because the consideration for it has wholly failed. The consideration fails on rescission because the contract is terminated and any benefits received under it are returned. Where an interest in goods has passed, the title acquired is revested and given up.[82] Sums received are held to the use of the other party to the transaction, so that the rescinding party becomes indebted in respect of them.[83] If the rescinding party has obtained the benefit of contractual rights under the voidable contract, such as a right of indemnity under an insurance policy, or the chance of profit under a bargain, rescission extinguishes those rights *ab initio*.[84] It is therefore the rescinding party himself who brings about the failure of consideration, and he does so by electing to disaffirm the voidable transaction.

Rights accrue unconditionally

14.38 In seeking judgment for the amount due the rescinding party asks the court to enforce rights that accrued unconditionally when the contract was disaffirmed. He does not ask the court to rescind the contract.[85]

---

[77] As to interest, see Chap 17, paras [17.21]–[17.22].
[78] Equitable rescission does not confer a claim for money had and received, and there is no need to show a failure of consideration to recover sums paid: *Senanayake v Cheng* [1966] AC 63 (PC—Singapore) 76–77; *With v O'Flanagan* [1936] 1 Ch 575 (CA) 585–86; *Re Australian Slate Quarries Ltd* (1930) 31 St Rep NSW 1, 4; *Wilson v Brisbane City Council* [1931] St R Qd 360, 379; *Mihaljevic v Eiffel Tower Motors Pty Ltd and General Credits Ltd* [1973] VR 545, 565; Chap 15, paras [15.33]–[15.36].
[79] *Street v Blay* (1831) 2 B & AD 456, 462; 109 ER 1212, 1214; *Murray v Mann* (1848) 2 Ex 538, 540–42; 154 ER 605, 606; *Clarke v Dickson* (1858) El Bl & El 148, 120 ER 463 (count did not lie because rescission barred); *Murray v Larsen* [1953] 2 Lloyd's Rep 453, 464; *Coastal Estates Pty Ltd v Melevende* [1965] VR 433 (Full Ct) 434, 439, 454–55.
[80] *Enimont Overseas AG v RO Jugotanker Zadar (The Olib)* [1991] 2 Lloyd's Rep 108, 118; *Dimskal Shipping Co SA v International Transport Workers Federation (The Evia Luck)* [1992] 2 AC 152, 165.
[81] *Kettlewell v Refuge Assurance Company* [1908] 1 KB 545 (CA) 550, 551; aff'd [1909] AC 243 (where the false representation was made after inception of the policy to induce the assured to continue to keep it on foot, and she sued to recover only the premiums paid after the representations had been made); *Drake Insurance plc v Provident Insurance plc* [2004] 1 Lloyd's Rep 268 (CA) 287 (Rix LJ) (avoidance and recovery of premium only remedy of assured rescinding for non-disclosure).
[82] *Street v Blay* (1831) 2 B & AD 456, 109 ER 1212; *Murray v Mann* (1848) 2 Ex 538, 154 ER 605.
[83] *Clough v London and North Western Railway Co* (1871) LR 7 Ex 26, 37.
[84] *Kettlewell v Refuge Assurance Company* [1908] 1 KB 545 (CA); aff'd [1909] AC 243 (rejecting an argument to the contrary); *Coastal Estates Pty Ltd v Melevende* [1965] VR 433 (Full Ct) 441.
[85] *Coastal Estates Pty Ltd v Melevende* [1965] VR 433 (Full Ct) 434, 447–48; *McCall v Superior Court* 36 P 2d 643, 647 (1934); also W Allen, 'Annotation: Action Involving Rescission or Right to Rescind Contract and to Recover Amount Paid thereunder as one at Law or in Equity' (1935) 95 American Law Rep Annotated 1000, 1004.

Non-contractual payments

14.39 Unlike the position when goods are transferred,[86] fraud and duress are unlikely to prevent legal title to money from passing when a payment is made other than under a contract.[87] The payer has a claim for money had and received that will arise from the time the sum was paid. There is no need for the payer to elect to disaffirm the payment to obtain a right of restitution. The claim is in substance one for recovery of a mistaken payment and principles of rescission have no role to play.[88]

Proprietary claims

14.40 The possibility of bringing a proprietary claim in respect of money following rescission at law is separately discussed in Chapter 16.

(5) Restitution for services provided

14.41 Executed contracts for services should in principle be capable of being rescinded at common law. By disaffirming the contract the party providing the service ought to extinguish the contract *ab initio* and obtain a right to be paid the value of the services provided as a debt imposed by law; that is, a claim in the nature of the common count for work done.[89]

14.42 But the very limited authority on the point is against this possibility. The principal authority is the old case of *Selway v Fogg*.[90] Selway had agreed with Fogg to remove a pile of rubbish for £15. It was established at trial that the contract had been induced by fraudulent misrepresentations about the depth of rubbish to be removed, and that the value of the work was in fact about £20. Selway carried away all of the rubbish, was paid £15, and then sued in general assumpsit for work and labour to recover the difference between what was paid and the value of his work. Selway was non-suited; that is, his claim was dismissed on the ground that the form of action did not lie. The Court of Exchequer upheld the non-suit on two grounds. First, by going on with the contract after discovering the truth, he had affirmed the agreement and lost the right to rescind.[91] Secondly, even if Selway had rejected the contract for fraud upon discovering the truth, his remedy lay in damages for deceit not general assumpsit. In coming to this conclusion the court drew upon contemporary decisions barring assumpsit for goods sold and delivered when chattels were purchased by fraud.[92]

14.43 The striking feature of *Selway v Fogg* is its apparent inconsistency with cases that had confirmed the availability of general assumpsit to recover the value of services provided under

---

[86] See paras [14.07], [14.12].
[87] *Sinclair v Brougham* [1924] AC 398, 418; *Barclays Bank Ltd v Simms* [1980] 1 QB 677, 689; *Westdeutsche Landesbank Girozentrale v Islington LBC* [1996] AC 669, 689. See also *Norwich Union Fire Insurance Society Ltd v WM H Price Ltd* [1934] AC 455 (PC—Aust); *Porter v Latec Finance (Qld) Pty Ltd* (1964) 111 CLR 177.
[88] See further Chap 29, para [29.35].
[89] Prior to the 1832 reforms, the form of action was for a *quantum meruit*: R Browne, *A Practical Treatise on Actions at Law* (1843) 486; Chap 3, para [3.21].
[90] (1839) 5 M & W 83, 151 ER 36.
[91] Cf *Grant Campbell & Co v Devon Lumber Co Ltd* (1914) 7 OWN 209 (Ont SC, App Div).
[92] *Selway v Fogg* (1839) 5 M & W 83, 86; 151 ER 36, 37 (Parke B), citing *Read v Hutchinson* (1813) 3 Camp 351, 170 ER 352 and *Ferguson v Carrington* (1829) 9 B & C 59, 109 ER 22, in which he had given judgment as Parke J. *Selway v Fogg* exemplified a wider trend toward restricting the availability of the common counts in the contractual context at the time.

a repudiated contract. This occurred, for example, in *Planche v Colburn*,[93] *De Bernardy v Harding*,[94] and *Prickett v Badger*.[95] The point of practical distinction was that the claimants there had no right to sue in deceit, which was available to the victim of fraud. *Selway v Fogg* can be further contrasted with decisions in the old Admiralty Court where salvage agreements were rescinded for the salvor's duress, and an award made for the reasonable value of the salvage performed.[96]

Although *Selway v Fogg* seems to be authority that English law recognizes no claim to recover the value of services provided under a contract induced by fraud, in principle a claim of this kind should be allowed.[97] There is no good reason for permitting the recovery of the value of services provided under a repudiated contract, but not under a contract induced by fraud or duress. The rule has the potential to cause injustice. Where the market value of services provided exceeds the loss that can be compensated by damages in deceit or breach of contract the wronged contractor is denied that excess without good reason. The availability of equitable rescission means that the point will usually not matter; but it might in the exceptional case where it makes a difference whether the rescinding party can extinguish the contract simply by disaffirming it, as where events after the election would have barred equitable rescission. Executed contracts for services should be capable of being rescinded at common law.

14.44

C. Counter-restitution of Benefits Received

(1) Nature of the obligation to make counter-restitution

The party rescinding at law must make counter-restitution for whatever benefits he may have received under the transaction. The principle is that 'no man can at once treat the contract as avoided by him, so as to resume the property which he parted with under it, and at the same time keep the money or other advantages which he has obtained under it'.[98] That the other party may be guilty of fraud or duress is no reason to deny him restitution.[99]

14.45

Unlike equity, the common law does not grant conditional relief, setting aside contracts and ordering restitution on condition that the rescinding party provide specified counter-restitution. The court is restricted to either enforcing a common law obligation to provide

14.46

---

[93] (1831) 8 Bing 14, 131 ER 305.
[94] (1853) 8 Exch 822, 155 ER 1586.
[95] (1856) 1 CB (NS) 296, 140 ER 123.
[96] *The Medina* [1876] 1 P 272 aff'd [1876] 2 P 5; *The Port Caldedonia and The Anna* [1903] P 184.
[97] *S-244 Holdings Ltd v Seymour Building Systems Ltd* (1994) 93 BCLR (2d) 34 (BCCA), where a building contract was rescinded for innocent misrepresentation and the rescinding contractor was entitled to recover for the work he had done by way of 'quantum meruit'. (Strictly speaking the award should have been for an equitable allowance or account, because innocent misrepresentation provides a ground for rescinding in equity but not at law, but nothing turns on that.) Cf New Zealand, where there is no right to a quantum meruit claim where the Contract and Commercial Law Act 2017 (NZ) applies: *Brown & Doherty Ltd v Whangarei County Council* [1990] 2 NZLR 63 (but cf also Contract and Commercial Law Act 2017 (NZ), s 45(d)).
[98] *Clough v London and North Western Railway Co* (1871) LR 7 Ex 26, 37, codified in the Indian Contracts Act 1872, s 64 ('party rescinding a voidable contract shall, if he have received any benefit thereunder from another party to such contract, restore such benefit, so far as may be, to the person from whom it was received').
[99] *Halpern v Halpern (No 2)* [2007] QB 88, 93.

counter-restitution that accrued when the contract was brought to an end, or recognizing that it has in fact been provided by the actions of the rescinding party. If there is no obligation to be enforced, and no return in fact, there is a logical and practical difficulty in recognizing that rescission has occurred.[100]

14.47 These limits on counter-restitution at common law have come to be regarded as limits on the right to rescind. The explanation given in *Hogan v Healy* is that:

> If, therefore, the right to rescind existed, notwithstanding benefits received by the defrauded party and incapable of being returned, the law would not alone afford him a remedy co-extensive with the injury sustained, but in addition would confer upon him a benefit, to the extent of the advantages which he had retained under the contract.[101]

14.48 So, if the benefits received cannot be returned, the common law does not stir, for fear of conferring a remedy that does not do justice. To this is added the principled objection that retention of bargained-for benefits is inconsistent with the extinction of the contract *ab initio*:

> So long as part of the consideration is retained, the party is not permitted to allege that his retention is unlawful; and rightful retention involves the continued existence of the contract under which alone the consideration can be rightfully held.[102]

Two categories of case

14.49 The benefits that can be returned upon rescission at common law are therefore of two kinds. First, there are those in respect of which an obligation to make counter-restitution is imposed by the common law itself. Into this category falls money and chattels. In the second class are benefits where, although there is no right enforceable against the rescinding party, if sufficient steps are taken to return the benefits, rescission can occur. In this category are shares, and possibly other legal property.

14.50 The practical importance of the distinction between the two categories is that in the former, there is a right to rescind even if no positive steps are taken to return the benefit received, whereas in the latter, a failure to take any positive steps will prevent rescission from occurring.

Lack of clarity in the law

14.51 Before the Judicature reforms the distinction between and scope of these two categories was not clearly spelled out. The structure of rescission at law emerged relatively late in the day, and in England its development was effectively halted by the Judicature reforms. Thereafter, it was usually sufficient for a litigant to turn to equity's more developed and flexible principles, and there was no pressure to further elaborate the common law principles. The result is a somewhat muddled and misunderstood body of rules, and in which the authorities do not speak with one voice. The next section attempts to describe the position today as to when a party wishing to rescind is obliged to tender back benefits received in order to effectively set aside a transaction at common law.

---

[100] See also A Lodder, *Enrichment in the Law of Unjust Enrichment* (2012) 124.
[101] (1877) IR 11 CL 119 (Ex Ch) 122. See also *Clough v London and North Western Railway Co* (1871) LR 7 Ex 26, 37.
[102] *Hogan v Healy* (1877) IR 11 CL 119 (Ex Ch) 121–22.

(2) The need for a return or tender of benefits received

Although the point is not free from doubt, English law appears to provide that a tender is not generally required when rescinding at common law. This is not because conditional relief is available; it is not.[103] Rather, no tender is required because when the transaction is disaffirmed the guilty party obtains a vested right to restitution, and the rescinding party becomes subject to a corresponding obligation to make counter-restitution, and a tender serves no purpose. It is required only when shares are acquired, and perhaps in certain other cases considered later in this chapter.

14.52

Chattels

There is probably no need to either return or tender back chattels received in order to effectively rescind at common law. The authorities are, however, not all one way.

14.53

The early cases, decided before *Street v Blay*,[104] seemed to regard a return of goods purchased as necessary before a count in money had and received would lie, and irrespective of the ground for 'rescission'.[105] *Street v Blay*[106] decided that in cases of fraud the defrauded buyer was empowered to revest title in the vendor, apparently by rejecting the contract.[107]

14.54

By the time of *Lawton v Elmore*[108] in 1858 it was established that there was no need to aver a return of goods purchased to allege a defence of fraud, and the court seemed to accept that rescission could occur without a return of goods purchased. It was noted, however, that cases where fraud was relied on as a defence to calls upon shares rest on different principles. If there was doubt on this point, it should have been removed by the decision in *Grimoldby v Wells*[109] 20 years later, which held that the buyer of non-conforming goods need not offer to return them in order to terminate the contract. If this is the case for breach of contract, it should *a fortiori* be so where a purchase is procured by fraud.

14.55

Money

From quite early on the common law seems not to have required the insurer to pay insurance premiums into court, or to tender them back, as a condition of defending an action on the policy for misrepresentation or non-disclosure.[110] The sums were recoverable from the insurer as money had and received whether or not they had been tendered back.

14.56

Although the decision is in some respects equivocal, *Clough v London and North Western Railway*[111] appears to indicate that a tender of sums received is also not necessary when

14.57

---

[103] Cf *Jervis v Berridge* (1873) 8 Ch App 351, 357.
[104] (1831) 2 B & AD 456, 109 ER 1212.
[105] *Fielder v Starkin* (1788) 1 H BL 17, 126 ER 11 (horse purchased died after claimant attempted its return) Heath J: 'If this had been an action for money had and received to the claimant's use, an immediate return of the mare would have been necessary; but as it is brought on the express warranty, there was no necessity for a return to make the defendant liable'; *Grimaldi v White* (1802) 4 Esp 95, 170 ER 654 (defendant dissatisfied with miniature painting purchased from claimant): 'if he means to avail himself of that objection, he must return the picture; he must rescind the contract totally ... he must either abide by it, or rescind it *in toto* by returning the thing sold.' For the lack of differentiation between rescission for pre-contractual fraud and subsequent breach at this time, see Chap 3, para [3.27].
[106] (1831) 2 B & AD 456, 109 ER 1212.
[107] *Murray v Mann* (1848) 2 Ex 538, 154 ER 605. See also Chap 3, paras [3.27], [3,28].
[108] (1858) 27 LR Exch (NS) 141.
[109] (1875) LR 10 CP 391; see now Sale of Goods Act 1979, s 36.
[110] *Penson v Lee* (1800) 2 Bos & Pul 330, 126 ER 1309.
[111] (1871) LR 7 Ex 26, 32–33, 36–37. The judgment was written by Blackburn J, but delivered by Mellor J: *Scarfe v Jardine* (1882) 7 App Cas 345.

rescinding a sale of goods for fraud at law. The court noted, however, that if the paying party indicated a willingness to receive back the sums paid, a refusal to do so would be grounds for inferring an affirmation. In *Hogan v Healy*[112] the Exchequer Chamber in Ireland said *obiter* that if the rescinding party did tender back money received, but the other refused to accept it, that would not prevent rescission, but expressed no opinion on whether a tender was necessary in the first place.

14.58 On balance the authorities indicate that the innocent party is not required to tender back money received in order to rescind at common law. This makes sense as a matter of principle. The innocent party is obliged to repay sums received because the consequences of electing to rescind are such as to render it money received for a consideration that has failed: the contract has been extinguished *ab initio*, and the rescinding party has obtained vested rights to recover benefits conferred. Sums received are therefore automatically repayable by the rescinding party, and the wrongdoer has an independently enforceable right to payment. In those circumstances there seems to be no good reason for requiring the rescinding payee to tender the money back.

Exception for shares

14.59 The position is different for shares. By disaffirming an allotment or transfer of shares, a shareholder is unable to revest legal title. The register of members must be amended.[113] The limited authority on the point indicates that to rescind at law so as to obtain a right to claim back the price paid, a defrauded allottee or transferee is probably required to tender back the shares received.[114] The point is unlikely to matter in practice because a purchaser of shares who is able to rescind at law will also be able to rescind in equity, and that can be done without tendering the shares back.

Other assets

14.60 English law has not considered whether rescission at law is possible by tendering back other forms of property, or the value of non-money benefits; for example, by tendering an executed instrument for the re-transfer of land, or a cheque for services rendered. If the tender permits the guilty party to receive back what he gave, there would seem to be no principled objection to it, or to the law recognizing that rescission at law has occurred.

Contrary authority

14.61 Statements in English,[115] Irish,[116] and Australian[117] cases can be found which seem to say that a party rescinding at law must always plead and prove that he has in fact restored, or

---

[112] (1877) IR 11 CP 119 (Ex Ch) 123–24.

[113] Save in the unusual case where bearer shares are purchased, where possession confers title.

[114] *Clarke v Dickson* (1858) El Bl & El 148, 120 ER 463; *Kennedy v The Panama, New Zealand, and Australian Royal Mail Company Limited* (1867) LR 2 QB 580. For the steps that a shareholder must take to defend a call on shares, see Chap 11, paras [11.50]–[11.52].

[115] *The Deposit and General Life Assurance Company Registered v Ayscough* (1856) 6 El & Bl 761, 762; 119 ER 1048, 1048.

[116] *Meldon v Lawless* (1870) 18 WR 261 (CP Ir) 262 (claim for rent under a lease defended on the ground of fraud; plea bad on demurrer because *inter alia* it failed to say that defendant placed lessor as far as possible in the position he stood before the contract); to similar effect *Anderson v Costello* (1871) 19 WR 628 (CP Ir).

[117] *The Picturesque Atlas Publishing Co Ltd v Phillipson* (1890) 16 VLR 675 (Full Ct) 679 (vendor's fraud in inducing contract for sale of 42 books no defence to action for goods sold and delivered, because defendant purchaser had made no attempt to return seven books delivered).

taken steps to restore, benefits received. But for the reasons explained below, these should not be regarded as good authority for that proposition.

The English decision is a comment made *obiter* by Crompton J in *The Deposit and General Life Assurance Company Registered v Ayscough* to the effect that a defence of fraud to an action on a contract might always require a plea that benefits received have been returned.[118] But that is directly contrary to the later decision of Pollock CB in *Lawton v Elmore*,[119] and is also difficult to reconcile with the principle established in *Grimoldby v Wells*[120] that the buyer of non-conforming goods need not offer to return them in order to terminate the contract. The Irish cases are best regarded as instances where *restitutio in integrum* was impossible at law, and are also not consistent with *Lawton v Elmore*.[121] They should not be regarded as authority for a general rule that a tender is required. The Australian decision in *The Picturesque Atlas Publishing Co Ltd v Phillipson*[122] is best understood as an instance of affirmation: where a failure to tender back seven parts of a colonial atlas purchased and delivered was, in the particular circumstances, inconsistent with an election to rescind the sale.

14.62

Contrast with the United States of America

The law in the United States developed differently. Actions based on rescission at law were generally tried by a jury, whereas a claim for equitable rescission was tried by a judge alone.[123] This difference, and the enduring importance of the civil jury trial in America, has seen the distinction between the two forms of rescission receive greater attention, and to elaboration of the principles for rescission at law.

14.63

The principal elaboration has been the development of a rule that proceedings to enforce rights arising on rescission at common law can only be brought if the party seeking to rescind has sufficiently restored or tendered the consideration received.[124] This is said to be a central distinction between rescission at law and in equity. In equity rescission is effected by the court, the court can ensure counter-restitution to the defendant, and no prior tender

14.64

---

[118] (1856) 6 El & Bl 761, 762; 119 ER 1048, 1048: 'When the record shews that the contract has been executed so far that the defendant has received a benefit, I have doubted whether, in an action on the contract, the plea of fraud must not shew that he has restored what he received.' The case at hand was said to be governed by a different, statutory regime. But the statement was quoted without disapproval by Lord Halsbury LC in *Aaron's Reefs Limited v Twiss* [1896] AC 273, 278. See also *Clough v London and North Western Railway Co* (1871) LR 7 Ex 26, 32–33, 36–37.
[119] (1858) 27 LR Exch (NS) 141.
[120] (1875) LR 10 CP 391; see now Sale of Goods Act 1979, s 36.
[121] (1858) 27 LR Exch (NS) 141.
[122] (1890) 16 VLR 675 (Full Ct) 679.
[123] JN Pomeroy, *A Treatise on Equity Jurisprudence* (5th edn, 1941) vol 1, § 358a; D Dobbs, 'Pressing Problems for the Plaintiff's Lawyer in Rescission: Election of Remedies and Restoration of Consideration' (1972) 26 Ark L Rev 322, 323, fn 6.
[124] *Thayer v Turner* 49 Mass 550 (1844); *Gould v Cayuga County National Bank* 86 NY 75 (1881); *ETC Corp v Title Guarantee & Trust Co* 271 NY 124, 2 NE 2d 284, 3 NE 2d 471, 105 ALR 999 (1936); Anon, 'Equity—Rescission—Lack of Offer to Return Benefits' (1926) 36 Yale LJ 879; W Cook, 'Necessity of Restitution in Suits for Rescission Based on Fraud' (1929) 29 Columbia LR 791, 792–95, 798; J Phillips, 'Contracts: Rescission: Notice Required: Cal Civ Code para 1691' (1931) 19 Cal LR 424, 427; LS Tellier, 'Annotation' (1936) 105 American Law Rep Annotated 1003, 1004; H Kohford, 'Rescission at Law and In Equity' (1948) 36 Cal LR 606, 607–608, 610, 613; D Dobbs, 'Pressing Problems for the Plaintiff's Lawyer in Rescission: Election of Remedies and Restoration of Consideration' (1972) 26 Ark L Rev 322, 341–52; D Dobbs and C Roberts, *Law of Remedies* (3rd edn, 2018) § 4.7;

is therefore required.[125] For rescission at law, however, it is said that 'return of the property which he obtained is part of the act of rescission',[126] and that 'the tender itself effectuates the rescission'.[127]

14.65 Several explanations for the tender rule have been given. It has been said that one seeking to recover shall not put the other party to an action to regain what he gave, and that tender might result in mutual restoration and the avoidance of a lawsuit.[128] In some cases, however, it seems to have been supposed that restoration or tender was necessary because the defendant would otherwise have no claim to recover what was given.[129] This fits the explanation for excluding the requirement in cases of equitable rescission. Although the tender rule has been criticized,[130] it has also been codified in various States.[131] More recently, however, the rule has been undermined by statutory and judicial moves to abolish it generally, or in particular contexts.[132] Presumably that abolition has accompanied either a rule that the innocent party comes under a vested obligation to make counter-restitution, or an acceptance that the rescission is effected by the court rather than by the act of the innocent party. The *Third Restatement of Restitution* states that restitution or a tender of restitution by the claimant is *not* a prerequisite to rescission, if the restitution due to him can be reduced by, or made subject to, his obligation to make counter-restitution.[133]

Restatement (First) of Restitution § 65(d) (1937) (but cf the approach adopted in the *Third Restatement*, discussed at para [14.65]); *Restatement (Second) of Contracts* vol 3, § 384 (1981).

[125] *Brown v Norman* 65 Miss 369, 4 So 293 (1888). See also *Gould v Cayuga County National Bank* 86 NY 75, 83–84 (1881); *Vail v Reynolds* 118 NY 297, 302, 23 NE 301, 303 (1890); *McGowan v Blake* 134 App Div 165, 118 NY Supp 905 (1909); *ETC Corp v Title Guarantee & Trust Co* (n 123); Anon, 'Equity—Rescission—Lack of offer to Return Benefits' (1926) 36 Yale LJ 879; W Cook, 'Necessity of Restitution in Suits for Rescission Based on Fraud' (1929) 29 Columbia LR 791, 795; J Phillips, 'Contracts: Rescission: Notice Required: Cal Civ Code para 1691' (1931) 19 Cal LR 424 427; W Allen, 'Annotation: Action Involving Rescission or Right to Rescind Contract and to Recover Amount Paid thereunder as one at Law or in Equity' (1935) 95 American Law Rep Annotated 1000,1001; LS Tellier, 'Annotation' (1936) 105 American Law Rep Annotated 1003, 1004; H Kohford, 'Rescission at Law and In Equity' (1948) 36 Cal LR 606, 607, 610, 613; *Restatement (First) of Restitution* § 260 (1937); D Dobbs and C Roberts, *Law of Remedies* (3rd edn, 2018) § 4.7.
[126] *Gould v Cayuga County National Bank* 86 NY 75, 82 (1881).
[127] *Brown v Techdata Corp Inc* 238 Ga 622, 626, 234 SE2d 787, 791 (1977); also D Dobbs, *Law of Remedies* (2nd edn, 1993) vol 1, 673 where return or tender is construed as part of rescission at law.
[128] See *Thayer v Turner* 49 Mass 550, 552 (1844); *Gould v Cayuga County National Bank* 86 NY 75, 79–80 (1881); W Cook, 'Necessity of Restitution in Suits for Rescission Based on Fraud' (1929) 29 Columbia LR 791, 792.
[129] *Brown v Norman* 65 Miss 369, 377–78, 4 So 293, 294–95 (1888); D Dobbs, 'Pressing Problems for the Plaintiff's Lawyer in Rescission: Election of Remedies and Restoration of Consideration' (1972) 26 Ark L Rev 322, 342; D Dobbs and C Roberts, *Law of Remedies* (3rd edn, 2018) 473–74.
[130] See eg *Nab v Hills* 92 Idaho 877, 884; 452 P2d 981, 988 (1969); W Cook, 'Necessity of Restitution in Suits for Rescission Based on Fraud' (1929) 29 Columbia LR 791, 798 (tender as 'useless ceremony'); D Dobbs, 'Pressing Problems for the Plaintiff's Lawyer in Rescission: Election of Remedies and Restoration of Consideration' (1972) 26 Ark L Rev 322, 346–49; D Dobbs and C Roberts, *Law of Remedies* (3rd edn, 2018) 473–74, 476–77, § 4.7 and refs therein.
[131] Eg formerly Californian Civil Code s 1691; W Cook, 'Necessity of Restitution in Suits for Rescission Based on Fraud' (1929) 29 Columbia LR 791.
[132] D Dobbs and C Roberts, *Law of Remedies* (3rd edn, 2018) 473–74, 476–77, § 4.7.
[133] *Restatement (Third) of Restitution* § 54(5) (2011). The reporters state that the rule adopted 'explicitly eliminates previous requirements that the claimant tender restitution to the other party as a precondition of rescission. No distinction is recognised between rescission "at law" and "in equity"' (vol 2, cmt j at 285). However, the reporters also state that the effect of the distinction between rescission at law and in equity on the right to jury trial was outside the scope of the work. The *Restatement* concludes that the tender rule gave an American court exercising common law jurisdiction 'nearly as much discretion to allow rescission or withhold it as the chancellors enjoyed in equity', and that in substance it was applied as a rule regulating the propriety of rescission in the particular case before the court: *Restatement (Third) of Restitution* vol 2, 268 (2011).

(3) Security for counter-restitution

14.66 Counter-restitution in equity is effected through conditional relief, and one effect of that approach is to secure the obligation to provide counter-restitution. It is secured on the relief that the court gives to the rescinding party, in that the relief cannot be obtained save at the price of effecting counter-restitution.[134] At common law a similar security is afforded when counter-restitution is effected by a revesting of legal title in chattels purchased, which follows a purchaser's election to rescind, or if the benefits received are in fact returned.

14.67 But the position is different if when the contract is set aside by an election to disaffirm, the guilty party obtains only a personal right to recover back what he gave, such as a claim to receive back the price he paid, or payment for services or other non-money benefit that he has conferred. Where that occurs the guilty party is compelled to give up the contract, and what he received under it, in exchange for an unsecured claim against the rescinding party. Where the rescinding party is or becomes insolvent, the guilty party is compelled to return benefits obtained under the transaction for division among unsecured creditors, of which he becomes one. This cannot occur when counter-restitution is effected by orders for conditional relief, or where it is given *in specie*.

14.68 This consideration militates in favour of retaining the common law's strict approach to counter-restitution, and shutting the door to rescission when benefits other than money or chattels are received, unless the benefit has in fact been returned, or the innocent party is allowed to rescind by tendering it back.

(4) Counter-restitution of property received

Chattels
Right to revest title by disaffirming

14.69 In the seminal case of *Street v Blay*[135] it was decided that the defrauded buyer of goods was empowered to revest title, and thereby to effect a failure of consideration sufficient to found an action for the price as money had and received. The revesting of title in the goods apparently occurred when the buyer elected to reject the purchase, for Lord Tenderden CJ referred to the buyer's right to 'by his own act ... revest title in the seller'.[136] The principle was applied in *Murray v Mann*,[137] where a livery-stable keeper made fraudulent misstatements when selling a horse. The court confirmed that title in the horse revested in the vendor, and the obligation to repay the price arose, 'when the contract was avoided',[138] which was 'the moment the purchaser chose to declare it void'.[139] The date this occurred was not spelled out, but seems to have been when the misled buyer returned the horse.

---

[134] Chap 15, paras [15.50]–[15.51], [15.56].
[135] (1831) 2 B & AD 456, 109 ER 1212. See also Chap 3, paras [3.27]–[3.28].
[136] *Street v Blay* (1831) 2 B & AD 456, 462; 109 ER 1212, 1214.
[137] (1848) 2 Ex 538, 154 ER 605.
[138] *Murray v Mann* (1848) 2 Ex 538, 540; 154 ER 605, 606 (Platt B).
[139] *Murray v Mann* (1848) 2 Ex 538, 541; 154 ER 605, 606 (Parke B).

14.70 In *Murray v Larsen*,[140] on the other hand, the purchaser of a houseboat rescinded the sale for fraudulent misrepresentation as to the vessel's seaworthiness. Pearson J held that title in the vessel revested in the vendor as a consequence of rescission, but the assumption seems to have been that this occurred when the court gave judgment.[141] However, the earlier authorities discussed indicate that title should have revested when the plaintiff buyer told the seller that he wished to repudiate the contract. The rule ought also to apply irrespective of the kind of interest that has been acquired under the contract. It should not matter whether the agreement is a hire, pledge, bailment, attornment, or other species of transaction involving title to chattels.

Position of rescinding transferee in possession

14.71 If after electing to rescind the buyer retains possession of goods purchased, what is the extent of his obligations in relation to those goods? The point appears not to have been considered in the reported cases. The rescinding buyer becomes an involuntary bailee, and it is suggested that his rights and duties are analogous to those of a buyer who rejects non-conforming goods. He therefore cannot deal with the goods without the express or implied authority of the owner, and has a limited obligation to care for them.[142]

Property not revested by an election to rescind
Shares

14.72 Save in the special case of bearer shares, an election to disaffirm a purchase of shares induced by fraud or duress is incapable of revesting legal title, for that can occur only when the register is amended. However, it appears that this does not prevent a shareholder obtaining a right to recover the price at common law if he takes appropriate steps to return the shares, at least where the contract was induced by fraud.[143]

14.73 This appears to be the premise of *Clarke v Dickson*[144] and *Kennedy v The Panama, New Zealand, and Australian Royal Mail Company Limited*.[145] Although the claimant was unsuccessful in both cases, the court in each proceeded on the basis that, if a share allotment is tainted by fraud, the shareholder has a right to recover the price paid as money had and received once he communicates his rejection of the transaction, and is in a position to return the shares issued, and perhaps offers them back. The implication is that the result is the same if shares are purchased from another shareholder, not from the company itself. Precisely what the shareholder is required to do to return the shares is not spelled out in either case. The point is now of limited practical importance, because a share allotment or purchase procured by fraud may also be rescinded in equity without any plea or offer of counter-restitution.

---

[140] [1953] 2 Lloyd's Rep 453, 464.
[141] *Murray v Larsen* [1953] 2 Lloyd's Rep 453, 464.
[142] M Bridge (ed), *Benjamin's Sale of Goods* (11th edn, 2020) [12-1067]; also, K Handley, *Spencer Bower and Handley: Actionable Misrepresentation* (5th edn, 2014) [16.21]. See also cases involving rescission in equity: *Maturin v Tredinnick* (1864) 10 LT 331, 332; *Imperial Ottoman Bank v Trustees, Executors and Securities Investment Corp* [1895] WN 23, 13 R 287; *Alati v Kruger* (1955) 94 CLR 216; *Kramer v McMahon* [1970] 1 NSWLR 194.
[143] Cf in Australia it has been said that a subscriber for shares cannot rescind at law by his own act, but must turn to equitable principles: *Civil Service Co-operative Society v Blyth* (1914) 17 CLR 601, 613, as explained in *Sons of Gwalia Limited v Margaretic* (2007) 231 CLR 160 [55], [58].
[144] (1858) El Bl & El 148, 120 ER 463.
[145] (1867) LR 2 QB 580.

Other forms of property

Right to revest title by unilateral act   The English authorities have not considered whether a party induced to contract by fraud or duress is able to rescind the agreement at common law if property other than chattels or shares have been received. In principle rescission at common law should be possible whenever the injured party himself is able to revest legal title in the transferor, and takes the necessary steps to do so. This possibility appears to exist for many forms of property, for legal title may generally be conveyed though the transferee is ignorant of the transfer,[146] and an executed deed is capable of conveying legal title to most forms of property; the principal exceptions being those instances where registration is necessary to perfect title,[147] or to create it.[148]

14.74

Practical considerations   In most cases, executing instruments to re-transfer title to a party guilty of fraud or duress in the manner contemplated earlier will not be the preferred course of action. The value of being able to rescind at common law in most cases will not be worth the price of giving up title to property received. Rescission in equity will usually be more attractive, for in equity the injured party is able to postpone returning property received until he has the benefit of a court order in his favour.[149] Doing what is necessary to return legal title probably only makes sense if the relevant property has no value, or the innocent party has a particular interest in being able to rescind immediately at law, as where he wishes to urgently regain legal title to personal property transferred, or to extinguish onerous contractual obligations.

14.75

(5) Counter-restitution for money received

Money had and received

Where money is received by the party rescinding at law, by electing to disaffirm the contract he becomes indebted in respect of those sums. The sums are held for the use of the party against whom rescission is sought, and are recoverable by him as money had and received on the ground that they have been paid for a consideration that has failed.[150]

14.76

Failure of consideration

The consideration for the payment will fail when a sale of goods is rescinded because title to the goods is returned to the rescinding vendor.[151] If sums have been paid by the rescinding party, they are also recoverable as money had and received,[152] and where the rescinding party has conferred the benefit of contractual rights under the voidable contract, such as a right of indemnity under an insurance policy, or the chance of profit under a bargain, rescission extinguishes those rights *ab initio*.[153]

14.77

---

[146] *Butler and Baker's case* (1591) 3 Co Rep 25, 26 b–27 a; 76 ER 684, 689; *Standing v Bowring* (1885) 31 ChD 282 (CA).
[147] As in the case of shares.
[148] As in the case of registered land.
[149] See Chap 15, paras [15.51], [15.56], but cf [15.54].
[150] The rescinding party's obligation to pay interest on money repayable is discussed in Chap 17.
[151] See paras [14.03], [14.09].
[152] See para [14.36].
[153] *Kettlewell v Refuge Assurance Company* [1908] 1 KB 545 (CA); aff'd [1909] AC 243.

IV. RESTITUTIO IN INTEGRUM

Obligation arises when election to rescind

14.78 In each of the cases just considered the contract is extinguished and the consideration fails at the moment the contract is disaffirmed, and it is therefore at that point that the law imposes a debt in respect of sums received by the rescinding party.

Insurance premiums at common law

14.79 These principles find regular expression when an insurer rescinds a policy of insurance for non-disclosure or misrepresentation by a proposing assured at common law. Policies of insurance and treaties of reinsurance are voidable for non-disclosure or misrepresentation at common law,[154] and the rule is that the rescinding insurer must return all premium income received under the policy.[155] Premium income is therefore recoverable as money had and received to the use of the assured when the policy is set aside at common law.[156] The money is received for the use of the assured because it has been paid for a consideration that, following rescission of the policy, has failed.

Fraud exception for marine insurance at common law

14.80 The common law recognized an exception for marine insurance where the assured was guilty of fraud; there the premium was not recoverable.[157] It is unclear how far, if at all, the fraud exception applied to other classes of insurance, or was recognized in equity. An early Chancery decision permitted the recovery of premiums where marine insurance had been obtained by fraud,[158] but this was before the fraud exception became established at common law,[159] and there are some suggestions that Chancery subsequently followed the common law's approach.[160]

14.81 In England the common law exception became codified in section 84(3)(a) of the Marine Insurance Act 1906. It stated that where the policy is avoided by the insurer as from the commencement of the risk, the premium is returnable 'provided that there has been no fraud or illegality on the part of the assured'.[161] Whether premium income is repayable upon the rescission of a non-marine policy for fraud appears not to have been decided.

---

[154] See Chap 10, paras [10.28], [10.40]–[10.42]. The right to rescind is significantly modified by the Insurance Act 2015 in respect of policies concluded after 12 August 2016: see Chap 5, paras [5.35]–[5.39].
[155] *Graham v Western Australian Insurance Company Ltd* (1931) 40 Lloyd's Rep 64, 66–67; *Cornhill Insurance Company Ltd v L & B Assenheim* (1937) 58 Lloyd's Rep 27, 31.
[156] Eg *Penson v Lee* (1800) 2 Bos & Pul 330, 333; 126 ER 1309, 1311; *Anderson v Thornton* (1853) 8 Exch 425, 155 ER 1415. *Kettlewell v Refuge Assurance Company* [1908] 1 KB 545 (CA) 550, 551; aff'd [1909] AC 243 (where the assured not the insurer rescinded, and the action was confined to premium paid after the representations had been made).
[157] *Feise v Parkinson* (1812) 4 Taunt 640, 128 ER 482; *Anderson v Thornton* (1853) 8 Exch 425, 428; 155 ER 1415; *Rivaz v Geruss Bros & Co* (1880) 6 QBD 222, 229–30.
[158] *De Costa v Scandret* (1723) 2 P Wms 169, 24 ER 686, where the reporter's note contrasts the position at common law, but by reference to later common law cases.
[159] In 1762 the position remained open at common law: *Wilson v Duckett* (1762) 3 Burr 1361, 1362; 97 ER 874, 875. The fraud exception was apparently only settled in 1795 in *Chapman v Fraser* BR Trin 33 Geo 3: reporter's note (a) to *Penson v Lee* (1800) 2 Bos & Pul 330, 332; 126 ER 1309, 1310; see the discussion in JA Park, *A System of Law of Marine Insurance* (F Hildyard, ed) (8th edn, 1842) vol 1, 452–57.
[160] See *Duncan v Worrall* (1822) 10 Price 31, 147 ER 232 where a policy of marine insurance induced by misrepresentation, alleged to be fraudulent, was cancelled without any mention of the return of premium. It is unclear whether the premium had been returned in the parallel proceedings at law.
[161] By para 17 of Sched 1 to the Consumer Insurance (Disclosure and Representations) Act 2012, s 84 of the Marine Insurance Act 1906 is to be read subject to the provisions of that schedule in relation to contracts of marine insurance which are consumer insurance contracts and para 12 of Sched 1 of the Insurance Act 2015 is to like effect for non-consumer insurance contracts. See further Chap 5, para [5.35]–[5.39].

Statutory modification of the common law for insurance premiums

14.82 Today, if the policy is a 'consumer insurance contract'[162] that has been avoided by the insurer,[163] the obligation to return premium income is spelled out in paragraphs 2 and 5 of Schedule 1 of the Consumer Insurance (Disclosure and Representations) Act 2012.

14.83 If a consumer insurance contract is rescinded for fraud, the insurer 'need not return any of the premiums paid, except to the extent (if any) that it would be unfair to the consumer to retain them'.[164] It is difficult to see when it would ever be 'unfair' to the dishonest insured for the insurer to retain premium income. Unfairness sufficient to compel restitution might, perhaps, arise if the premium income is substantial, and not returning all or part of it is thought to be unfair when measured against the conduct of the insured.[165]

14.84 For 'non-consumer insurance contracts'[166] if breach of the duty of fair presentation[167] gives the insurer a right to avoid the contract and the insurer does so,[168] the insurer may refuse all claims but must return the premiums paid if the breach was neither deliberate nor reckless; but if it is, the insurer need not return the premium paid.[169]

Sums received for goods sold

14.85 Outside the insurance context, the fact patterns coming before the courts tend to be sales in which the injured party is an unpaid vendor. Where some money is received, however, it will automatically become repayable following an election to rescind. Thus in *Clough v London and North Western Railway*[170] the court noted that £68 received by the London Pianoforte Company from one Adams, as part-payment for nine pianofortes that he had induced them to sell by fraud, was 'money which, in consequence of the rescission of the contract, they held for the use of Adams', once an election to rescind had been made.[171]

---

[162] That is 'a contract of insurance between—(a) an individual who enters into the contract wholly or mainly for purposes unrelated to the individual's trade, business or profession, and (b) a person who carries on the business of insurance and who becomes a party to the contract by way of that business (whether or not in accordance with permission for the purposes of the Financial Services and Markets Act 2000)': Consumer Insurance (Disclosure and Representations) Act 2012, s 1.

[163] The right of rescission is proscribed in the manner set out in ss 2–5 and Sched 1 of the Consumer Insurance (Disclosure and Representations) Act 2012.

[164] Para 2 of Sched 1 of the Consumer Insurance (Disclosure and Representations) Act 2012, which applies equally to marine and non-marine insurance.

[165] The provision applies also where the misrepresentation is 'reckless', and it may be that the proviso for 'unfairness' is confined to conduct that is 'reckless' rather than intentional.

[166] A 'non-consumer insurance contract' is a contract of insurance that is not a consumer insurance contract, and that term has the same meaning as in the Consumer Insurance (Disclosure and Representations) Act 2012: Insurance Act 2015, s 1.

[167] Insurance Act 2015, s 3.

[168] Rescission for non-disclosure is available under the Insurance Act 2015 if the insurer can establish that either (a) the breach was deliberate or reckless (s 8(1), (5), (6) and para 2 of Sched 1), or (b) it was not, but the insurer would *not* have provided cover on any terms had disclosure been made (paras 3, 4, 5 of Sched 1).

[169] Schedule 1, para 2(b), 3, 4, 8(b), 9(2).

[170] (1871) LR 7 Ex 26.

[171] *Clough v London and North Western Railway* (1871) LR 7 Ex 26, 37. There are however passages in the judgment that may suggest a different analysis: see esp 32–33, 36–37. In practice a court is likely to hesitate before permitting a fraudster to sue to recover the price paid, if the rescinding vendor has obtained no rights of value.

(6) Counter-restitution for services received

14.86 Although the point has not been specifically considered in the cases, the receipt of bargained-for services by the party wishing to rescind is likely to bar to rescission at common law. That is because the common law confers no cause of action for restitution in favour of the party providing the services, and the rescinding party is unable to restore their benefit by his own act, save perhaps by tendering payment for them. The same restriction does not apply in equity. Partly or wholly performed contracts for the purchase of services may therefore be set aside in equity, but the right to rescind at common law is doubtful.

15

Mutual Restitution: Rescission in Equity

A. Introduction	15.01	(1) Nature of the obligation to make counter-restitution	15.45
B. Restitution of Benefits Transferred	15.03	(2) Counter-restitution of property received	15.63
(1) Nature of the right to restitution	15.03	
(2) Restitution of property transferred	15.04	(3) Counter-restitution for money received	15.65
(3) Substitutive restitution of property transferred	15.14	(4) Counter-restitution for services received	15.67
(4) Restitution for money paid	15.33	D. Equitable Rescission by Election	15.69
(5) Restitution for services provided	15.39	(1) Restitution	15.69
C. Counter-restitution of Benefits Received	15.44	(2) Counter-restitution	15.73

A. Introduction

This chapter outlines how mutual restitution occurs when a transaction is set aside in equity. It first considers the restitution of benefits conferred by the party who rescinds, and then the obligation of that party to make counter-restitution for benefits that he has received under the transaction. Property, money, and services are each considered separately. Questions of interest, rent, dividends, and other benefits that represent the time value of assets, as well as compensation for deterioration, indemnity, and the like, are all deferred to Chapter 17, which reviews the financial adjustments that are incidental to rescission. **15.01**

There is a key difficulty in describing the workings of equitable rescission. That difficulty is to determine the proper treatment of the authorities that indicate rescission always occurs upon the injured parties' election to repudiate the transaction, without discrimination between the common law and equity. The main problem is that these authorities provide almost no guidance at all as to exactly how rescission, and in particular mutual restitution, is to occur in such a case, if not effected pursuant to the principles recognized by the common law. This problem is compounded by the fact that the cases contradict each other as to when rescission occurs upon election in this way.[1] Because of these uncertainties, the principles that appear to govern mutual restitution when rescission in equity is said to follow an election to disaffirm are considered separately, at the end of the chapter. **15.02**

---

[1] See Chap 11, Part D.

B. Restitution of Benefits Transferred

(1) Nature of the right to restitution

15.03 The equity to rescind carries a right to the restitution of benefits conferred under the transaction. The rescinding party is generally given an exclusively proprietary claim in respect of property transferred, and an exclusively personal one to reclaim money, but both of these general rules are subject to certain exceptions considered later. In all cases where the party wishing to rescind has received benefits for which counter-restitution must be made, or is otherwise required to take steps to effect *restitutio in integrum,* his right to restitution is conditional upon that occurring. The assertion of proprietary claims upon equitable rescission is treated in more detail in Chapter 16.

(2) Restitution of property transferred

15.04 When giving judgment for rescission the court will make orders directed at re-vesting title to property transferred if it remains both *in specie* in the hands of the other party to the transaction and free of paramount interests in favour of third parties. The form of order varies depending on what is necessary for title to be revested.

15.05 Title may have originally passed by operation of a contract or deed of gift, or by a collateral event, such as execution of an instrument of transfer, delivery (as in the case of chattels), or registration (as in the case of registered land and shares). It is sufficient if the agreement itself was vitiated by misrepresentation, undue influence, or some other ground for rescission. There is no need to show any further nexus between the conduct permitting rescission and the delivery or other collateral event by which title passed. The facts that render the contract voidable also render the transfer of property defeasible, and that is so whether title passed by force of the contract itself or some collateral event of the kind just discussed. As Rigby LJ said in *Lagunas Nitrate Company v Lagunas Syndicate*:

> The completion of the contract by assignment would not in any way affect this right [to rescind], since any deeds executed for the purposes of completion would be tainted by the same weakness as the original agreement.[2]

15.06 Where property is created by the voidable transaction, as in the case of a share allotment,[3] or the grant of a lease or charge, rescission will at once revest and extinguish the relevant interest.

Unregistered land

15.07 Where an estate in unregistered land is conveyed, the court will order the transferee to execute a reconveyance.[4] Title is revested by and pursuant to that instrument, not the order itself. An order for reconveyance is appropriate following the rescission of a transfer of a fee simple or leasehold estate, or where an estate is conveyed by way of legal mortgage. The

---

[2] [1899] 2 Ch 392 (CA) 452 (purchase of a mine).
[3] *Plimer v Duke Group Limited (in liq)* (2001) 207 CLR 165 [20].
[4] *Clark v Malpas* (1862) 4 De GF & J 401, 45 ER 1238.

court probably has power to order execution of an instrument of transfer by a Registrar or other court official, as where the transferor refuses to do so or cannot be found.[5]

Registered land
Rectification of register
Legal title to registered land is sometimes returned by an order rectifying the register, or directing that this be done in the manner permitted by the relevant legislation.[6] In England, it had formerly been held that the power was to be found in section 82(1)(a) or (b) of the Land Registration Act 1925.[7] Under the Land Registration Act 2002 the power to alter the register is conferred by section 65 and paragraph 2 of Schedule 4. Paragraph 2(b) (bringing the register up to date) permits alteration of the register consequent upon an order for rescission.[8] The power to rectify to correct a mistake (para 2(a)(a) of Sched 4) might be engaged if the transaction was rescinded before the date of registration of the transfer, charge, or other disposition sought to be recovered or extinguished upon rescission, but it will not be if rescission occurs only after the date of registration.[9]

15.08

Execution of registrable transfer
Australian courts have held that whether or not the relevant legislation confers a power to amend the register, the court may order the transferee to execute and deliver a registrable transfer in favour of the transferor,[10] and that course has been adopted in cases of mistake[11] and undue influence.[12] This mirrors the approach to unregistered land, and orders of this kind should also be available in England and Wales.

15.09

Obtaining possession of land
The purchaser of land in possession may be ordered to deliver up possession, either at the time of reconveyance[13] or forthwith.[14] There is authority that this may be ordered even

15.10

---

[5] Cf *Spence v Crawford* [1939] 3 All ER 271 (HL Sc) 285 (shares).
[6] *Norwich Peterborough Building Society v Steed* [1993] Ch 116 (CA) 132–33 *(obiter)*. In Australia, *Maguire v Makaronis* (1996) 188 CLR 449, 459, 478, 500.
[7] *Norwich Peterborough Building Society v Steed* [1993] Ch 116 (CA) 132–33. See also *Re Leighton's Conveyance* [1936] 1 All ER 667.
[8] *NRAM Ltd v Evans* [2018] 1 WLR 639 (CA) 653 [59], [60] (approving the analysis in *Ruoff & Roper, Registered Conveyancing* loose-leaf ed, 46.009) (leave to appeal refused [2018] 1 WLR 1563 (Sup Ct)). Because the equity to recover property upon rescission seems to be a 'right ... excepted from the effect of registration' within the meaning of para 2(c) of Sched 4, that provision should also confer power to alter the register consequent upon an order for rescission. See also s 108(2) and (4) of the 2002 Act (orders for rectifying or setting aside a document), S Cooper and E Lees, 'Interests, Powers and Mere Equities in Modern Land Law' (2017) 37 OJLS 435, 439–41; E Cook and P O'Connor, 'Purchaser Liability to Third Parties in the English Land Registration System: A Comparative Perspective' (2004) 120 LQR 640, 641–42.
[9] *NRAM Ltd v Evans* [2018] 1 WLR 639 (CA) 651–53 [53]–[59]; see also *Antoine v Barclays Bank plc* [2019] 1 WLR 1958 (CA) 1974–75 [44]–[49] (leave to appeal refused [2019] 1 WLR 5630 (Sup Ct)). See also Sched 4, para 1, 3 and Sched 8, para 1(1)(a) (indemnity for mistake).
[10] *Breskvar v Wall* (1971) 126 CLR 376, 387, 408–09, 413. See also *Frazer v Walker* [1967] AC 569 (PC—NZ) 585; *Boyd v Mayor of Wellington* [1924] NZLR 1174, 1223; *Barry v Heider* (1914) 19 CLR 197, 213–14.
[11] *Luckas v Wood* (1978) 19 SASR 520, 531; *Tutt v Doyle* (1997) 42 NSWLR 10 (CA) 19, 20–21. In the case of a voidable mortgage, a duly executed discharge of mortgage has been ordered: *McNally v GIO Finance Ltd* (14 September 1994); *Cockburn v GIO Finance Ltd* (2001) 51 NSWLR 624 (CA) 627, 634.
[12] *Freeman v Brown* [2001] NSWSC 1028 [87].
[13] Eg *Trasler v Purser* (1848, VC) reproduced in W Harrison and R Leach, *Seton on Decrees* (2nd edn, 1854) 302: 'and let the defendant ... also deliver up possession of the premises comprised in the said deeds to the plaintiff ... And let the defendant reconvey the premises ...'.
[14] *Dunbar v Tredennick* (1813) 1 Ball & Beatty 304, 321–22 (sale of land in breach of fiduciary duty) 'let an injunction issue to put the plaintiff in possession of the lands'.

before the rescinding party has repaid the price received.[15] But that would appear to be appropriate only where acceptable undertakings have been given to secure repayment, for the general rule is that the other party has no independently enforceable right to counter-restitution, which is provided by the rescinding party as the price for his relief.[16] Orders for possession are also made when a lease is rescinded against a lessee in possession.[17]

Shares

15.11 The owner of shares is usually ordered to reassign them by executing an appropriate instrument of transfer,[18] and in one case a court official was authorized to do so.[19] Legal title revests in accordance with that assignment, not the court's order,[20] although equitable title will probably pass once a decree for rescission is made.[21] There is no suggestion in the cases that it matters whether the rescinding party could acquire equivalent shares in the marketplace. An order for reassignment will be made even if the shares are wholly fungible and publicly traded.[22]

Chattels

15.12 Title to chattels will also be revested by an appropriate order. An order that possession be delivered back to or to the order of the rescinding party may be sufficient.[23] Where title has passed by delivery of a bill of lading, or the right to collect goods requires presentation of an original bill of lading or other document of title, the rescinding party should be entitled to orders for delivery or, where appropriate, indorsement of the relevant instrument. There are few reported cases involving equitable rescission and chattels; they are mostly decided at common law.[24] However, by analogy with the decisions concerning voidable share transfers, the right to restitution should not require that the chattels are in any way unique.

---

[15] *Trevelyan v Charter* (1846) 9 Beav 140, 142; 50 ER 297, 297.
[16] See para [15.62].
[17] *Killick v Roberts* [1991] 1 WLR 1146 (CA); *Northcote Housing Association v Dixon* (ChD, 30 November 2001) 8; *Classic International Pty Ltd v Lagos* (2004) 60 NSWLR 241, 250.
[18] *Newton v Hunt* (1833) 5 Sim 511, 58 ER 430 (sale of reversionary interest in stock); *Blake v Mowlatt* (1856) 21 Beav 603, 52 ER 993 (sale of shares); *Transvaal Lands Company v New Belgium (Transvaal) Land and Development Company* [1914] 2 Ch 488 (CA) 505 (rescission of allotment for breach of fiduciary duty).
[19] *Spence v Crawford* [1939] 3 All ER 271 (HL Sc) 285 (rescission of sale of shares for fraud).
[20] *Gutnick v Indian Farmers Fertiliser Cooperative Limited* (2016) VR 732 (CA) [22] 'It is not until the order of the court or tribunal is executed by alteration of the register that legal title is restored'.
[21] *Indian Farmers Fertiliser Cooperative Limited v Gutnick* [2015] VSC 724 [76], accepted as correct in *Gutnick v Indian Farmers Fertiliser Cooperative Limited* (2016) 49 VR 732 (CA) [15] (counter-restitution of shares).
[22] Cf the extra-judicial opinion expressed by Lord Millett, that specific relief will not be ordered upon rescission where the property is not unique: P Millett, 'Restitution and Constructive Trusts' (1998) 114 LQR 399, 416; P Millett, 'The Law of Restitution: Taking Stock' (1999) 14 *Amicus Curiae* 4, 8; also P Millett, 'Proprietary Restitution' in S Degeling and J Edelman (eds), *Equity in Commercial Law* (2005) 309, 320 fn 31, endorsing the approach in W Swadling, 'Rescission, Property, and the Common Law' (2005) 121 LQR 123. This opinion is not supported by the cases. The experience in the USA is also against it. As between the First and Second *Restatement of Contracts*, the right to specific restitution was enlarged, and the 'inadequacy of legal rights' test abandoned: *Restatement (Second) of Contracts* vol 3, § 372 and Reporter's Note at 208 (1981). The position in the *Second Restatement* is that the party entitled to restitution by reason of his avoidance of the contract is generally entitled to either claim money value, or the thing *in specie*: Cmt a at 205.
[23] *Alati v Kruger* (1955) 94 CLR 216, 229 (purchase of fruit shop procured by fraud) as to counter-restitution rather than restitution: rescinding purchaser to 'deliver or tender to the defendant...the chattels mentioned in the schedule to the contract...as are in his possession or control' upon being repaid by defendant.
[24] Cf cases of innocent misrepresentation, eg *Goldsmith v Roger* [1968] 2 Lloyd's Rep 249 (fishing vessel); Chap 27, para [27.53].

Other property

Intellectual property rights transferred under a rescinded contract will be ordered to be returned by way of reassignment, redelivery, or other appropriate order.[25] Orders to retransfer property are also made when a voidable gift is rescinded.[26]

15.13

(3) Substitutive restitution of property transferred

It often happens that assets passing under a contract sought to be rescinded have been sold on, consumed or destroyed, or for some other reason it is no longer possible to restore them to their original owner. Chapter 18 considers the question whether a rescinding claimant who is unable to give specific counter-restitution can instead insist that the other contracting party accept a substitute, usually a sum of money. The related question considered under this head is what happens when the problem is the other way around, where it is the defendant rather than the claimant who no longer has the specific asset received.[27] The issue is whether the claimant can insist that the defendant make substitutive restitution in some form.

15.14

Possible substitutes include a replacement asset purchased in the market; the proceeds of the wrongdoer's resale; or any traceable exchange product remaining in his hands; and a pecuniary sum representing the value of the asset. These will be considered in turn.

15.15

Replacement asset

Where the asset in question is a fungible it would in theory be possible to insist that the defendant purchase a substitute in the market and return that.[28] This has never been tested in England, but it was considered and rejected by the Supreme Court of Michigan in *Gray v Trick*.[29]

15.16

Proceeds

In equity it has long been possible, where the defendant has resold some or even all of the assets he acquired under the transaction being set aside, for the rescinding claimant to recover the proceeds of that resale. There are many cases to this effect involving land,[30] but there are also cases involving shares,[31] and no distinction seems to have been drawn. The claim is

15.17

---

[25] *O'Sullivan v Management Agency and Music Ltd* [1985] 1 QB 428 (CA) 432, 459, 469, 473 (copyright).
[26] Eg *Nottidge v Prince* (1860) 2 Giff 246, 271; 66 ER 103, 113 (rescission of gift of securities for undue influence); *Allcard v Skinner* (1887) 36 ChD 145 (CA) (gifts induced by undue influence; right to rescind barred by delay).
[27] It may also be that the defendant has the asset but the court considers that it would be unjust to require that he return it *in specie*, as in the Canadian case *Kupchak v Dayson Holdings Co Ltd* (1965) 53 DLR (2d) 482 (BCCA) 486.
[28] Cf *Smith New Court Securities Ltd v Citibank NA* [1997] AC 254, 262.
[29] 243 Mich 388, 220 NW 741 (SC 1928); noted (1928–29) 42 Harv LR 438.
[30] *Fox v Mackreth* (1788) 2 Bro CC 44, 29 ER 224, aff'd (1791) 4 Bro PC 258, 2 ER 175; *Whichcote v Lawrence* (1798) 3 Ves 740, 30 ER 1248; *Randall v Errington* (1805) 10 Ves 423, 32 ER 909; *Trevelyan v Charter* (1835) 4 LJ (NS) 209, aff'd (1844) 11 Cl & Fin 714, 8 ER 1273; *Edwards v Brown* (1845) 2 Coll 100, 63 ER 654; *Gresley v Mousley* (1859) 4 De G & J 78, 45 ER 31. In Australia, *Blackham v Haythorpe* (1917) 23 CLR 156; *Pedashenko v Blacktown City Council* (1996) 39 NSWLR 189; *Hartigan v International Society for Krishna Consciousness Ltd* [2002] NSWSC 810 [98].
[31] *New Sombrero Phosphate Company v Erlanger* (1877) 5 ChD 73 (CA) 125; *Lagunas Nitrate Company v Lagunas Syndicate* [1899] 2 Ch 392 (CA) 434; *Estate Properties Ltd v Wignall* [1992] 2 NZLR 615, 631 (constructive trust over proceeds).

personal rather than proprietary, so it matters not what has since become of the proceeds. The sums are typically quantified by an accounting upon rescission.

15.18 Many of the cases involve fiduciary defendants, and an order requiring an accounting of the proceeds of sale subject to counter-restitution by the claimant of what he received has the effect that the defendant is made to account for his profits. But while the relief has the coincidental effect of depriving the faithless fiduciary of the advantage he has made, it is properly to be understood as one of the ordinary incidents of rescission in equity, rather than relief founded upon any principle peculiarly applicable to those occupying a fiduciary office. This is clear from the fact that the same relief may be had against non-fiduciary defendants, as in a case of fraud or undue influence.[32]

Exchange product

15.19 Where rescission occurs in equity, the claimant gains a retrospective beneficial title sufficient to entitle him to trace through intermediate transactions. If as a result of that process he can identify assets in the defendant's hands that represent the assets the defendant acquired under the voidable transaction, the claimant will be entitled to assert a proprietary claim and recover them on this basis.[33] This is further discussed in Chapter 16.

Value of asset

15.20 The more difficult question is whether the claimant can instead insist that the defendant make restitution by paying a sum representing the value of the asset that he gave. This possibility will be especially important to the rescinding party where he does not have a cause of action for damages and the asset he gave has been lost by the defendant in a manner that yielded neither proceeds nor a traceable residue. The term 'pecuniary rescission' is sometimes used in this connection.

Authorities

15.21 Surprisingly, this question does not seem to have arisen in equity until modern times, perhaps because in most cases there will be proceeds or an exchange product that the rescinding party can claim. In *Boyd & Forrest v The Glasgow Railway Company* Lord Atkinson said, in the course of discussing whether counter-restitution could be made in money, that 'Courts of Equity, when they set aside contracts, direct, as ancillary to the main relief but never in substitution for it, that money is to be paid by one litigant to the other'.[34] That was a Scottish case, and it is fair to say that Lord Atkinson's views have been largely ignored in England.[35]

---

[32] *Edwards v Brown* (1845) 2 Coll 100, 63 ER 654 (catching bargain); *Lagunas Nitrate Company v Lagunas Syndicate* [1899] 2 Ch 392 (CA) 434 (example of fraudulent representation). In Australia, *Hartigan v International Society for Krishna Consciousness Ltd* [2002] NSWSC 810 [98] (undue influence).

[33] *Small v Attwood* (1832) You 407, 535–38; 159 ER 1051, 1103–04; *Lonrho plc v Fayed (No 2)* [1992] 1 WLR 1, 11–12; *El Ajou v Dollar Land Holdings plc* [1993] 3 All ER 717, 735; *Halifax Building Society v Thomas* [1996] Ch 217 (CA) 226; *Bristol and West Building Society v Mothew* [1998] 1 Ch 1 (CA) 22–23; *Twinsectra Limited v Yardley* [1999] Lloyd's Rep Bank 438 (CA) 461–62; *Pesticcio v Huet* (2003) 73 BMLR 57 [134]; *Shalson v Russo* [2005] Ch 281, 320–22. In Australia: *Daly v Sydney Stock Exchange* (1985) 160 CLR 371, 387–90. In NZ, *Estate Properties Ltd v Wignall* [1992] 2 NZLR 615, 631. In the USA, *American Sugar Refining Co v Fancher* (1895) NE 206 (SCNY) 208–09.

[34] (1915) SC 20 (HL) 30.

[35] Eg *O'Sullivan v Management Agency and Music Limited* [1985] 1 QB 428 (CA), where *Boyd & Forrest* was cited but evidently not followed.

15.22 It is true, however, that at the time Lord Atkinson wrote there appears to have been no case in which a court of equity had awarded the rescinding party a sum of money representing the value of the asset he had given as opposed to the proceeds of its resale. Since that time, however, there has been one English case and several elsewhere in the Commonwealth in which the courts appear to have allowed a claimant a substitutive sum where the asset in question was no longer available.[36] The English case is *Mahoney v Purnell*.[37]

15.23 That case involved the sale of a hotel business by a father-in-law to his son-in-law. Their relationship was one of trust and confidence, and May J held that the son-in-law had abused his fiduciary position. The difficulty was that the hotel had since been sold and the proceeds lost, and the company had gone into liquidation. In these circumstances May J considered that practical justice required a balancing of the value the father-in-law surrendered with the value he received and an award of the difference. This remedy May J described as 'akin to damages',[38] but he also said that it was an 'adjunct to setting aside the agreement'.[39] He seems to have had in mind a restitutionary remedy and this has been said to be an example of 'pecuniary rescission'.[40]

15.24 While *Mahoney v Purnell* is without precursor in England, the Australian case *McKenzie v McDonald*[41] is very similar. It involved a contract for the exchange of properties between a principal and agent. By the time the action was commenced the agent had sold the farm he had acquired to a third party, but Dixon J considered that substantial restitution could be achieved by an order requiring that the agent pay the difference in value of the two properties as at the date of sale.[42] Canadian cases to the same effect have involved fraudulent misrepresentation rather than the abuse of trust and confidence.[43]

Measure

15.25 Such authorities as there are conflict as to the measure of the pecuniary sum the defendant must pay in circumstances where the asset in question has changed in value since the date of the original sale. A number of cases take the measure to be the value of the asset at the date of the sale, including *Mahoney v Purnell*.[44] In that case the business in question had since become insolvent so that measurement by reference to present values would have rendered the remedy valueless. By contrast, in the Canadian case *McCarthy v Kenny*[45] the defendant

---

[36] In some Canadian cases the courts have awarded damages for the value of the asset even though the ground for the action would not ordinarily support a right to damages relief: *Treadwell v Martin* (1976) 67 DLR (3d) 493 (NBSC—App Div) 504–05 (undue influence); *Dusik v Newton* (1985) 62 BCLR 1 (BCCA) (unconscionable bargain). See also *Fleischhaker v Fort Garry Agencies Ltd* (1957) 11 DLR (2d) 599 (Man CA), where the defendant was given an option whether to accept rescission or pay damages.
[37] [1996] 3 All ER 61.
[38] *Mahoney v Purnell* [1996] 3 All ER 61, 88.
[39] *Mahoney v Purnell* [1996] 3 All ER 61, 89.
[40] PBH Birks, 'Unjust Factors and Wrongs: Pecuniary Rescission for Undue Influence' [1997] RLR 72.
[41] [1927] VLR 134.
[42] *McKenzie v McDonald* [1927] VLR 134, 146–47. Note that Dixon J considered that owing to the special terms of the resale, the resale price could not be taken as the measure of the defendant's liability. This contrasts with the usual approach in equity, which is to allow the rescinding party to claim the proceeds whatever they may be.
[43] *McCarthy v Kenny* [1939] 3 DLR 556 (Ont SC) (shares); *Kupchak v Dayson Holdings Co Ltd* (1965) 53 DLR (2d) 482 (BCCA) (land). See also *Bank of Montreal v Murphy* (1985) 6 BCLR (2d) 169 (BCCA) (*obiter*).
[44] [1996] 3 All ER 61. In Australia, *McKenzie v McDonald* [1927] VLR 134; *Hartigan v International Society for Krishna Consciousness Inc* [2002] NSWSC 810 [104]. In Canada, *Kupchak v Dayson Holdings Co Ltd* (1965) 53 DLR (2d) 482 (BCCA).
[45] [1939] 3 DLR 556 (Ont SC). In Australia, *Koutsonicolis v Principe (No 2)* (1987) 48 SASR 328.

fraudster was required to account at present values for such of the shares in question as he had sold on, the shares having appreciated since the date of the original sale.

15.26 It seems doubtful that these cases are to be reconciled on the basis that the court will adopt the valuation date most favourable to the claimant. The theory of rescission would seem to favour present values, because if the defendant were able to return the asset *in specie* that is the value the claimant would receive.[46]

Discussion

15.27 A fair consensus amongst English scholars favours allowing claims to pecuniary restitution upon rescission.[47] This was the view of Professor Birks, who considered that the traditional position rested upon a 'squeamishness' about valuing non-money benefits that is out of line with the usual willingness of the courts to estimate asset values. It appears that pecuniary restitution is given in the United States.[48]

15.28 This viewpoint has some attractions, but if the law is to develop in this direction convincing answers will need to be found to a number of questions. The problem of measure has already been discussed. A further question is whether 'pecuniary rescission' is a financial remedy given in lieu of setting aside the contract (as May J may have had in mind in *Mahoney v Purnell*), or whether restitution can be required in money upon the setting aside of the contract.

15.29 Moreover, if rescinding parties are to be entitled to claim the monetary value of what they have transferred, it would be necessary to explain how that entitlement relates to their entitlement to claim what proceeds there may be in cases where the defendant has sold the asset on. Would the true criterion be the value of the asset, with the proceeds of a resale simply being taken as a rebuttable measure of that value, as Dixon J seems to have considered to be the case in *McKenzie v McDonald*? Or would the rescinding party instead be entitled to claim the greater of the proceeds or the true value, on the theory that he should not be prejudiced if the defendant has sold on less than market terms? Another approach would be that a claim to the value is only available where the asset was lost in a manner that did not yield proceeds. Presumably it would not be open to the rescinding party to claim substitutive restitution where the defendant still holds the actual asset, but if the measure is taken to be values ruling at the date of sale, even that might be open to question in an appropriate case.

15.30 One major concern would be to develop a mechanism to ensure that the defendant is not unjustifiably prejudiced in being required to make substitutive restitution by a payment of the asset's monetary value. If he parted with the asset in question in return for proceeds then the defendant cannot complain if he is required to give these up. But here we are concerned

---

[46] See C Mitchell, 'Equitable Compensation for Breach of Fiduciary Duty' [2013] CLP 1, 10–14. See also E Bant, 'Reconsidering the Role of Election in Rescission' (2012) 32 OJLS 467, arguing that these cases can be reconciled according to the date when the claimant elects to rescind.

[47] Eg PBH Birks, *Unjust Enrichment* (2nd edn, 2005) 226–28; A Burrows, *The Law of Restitution* (3rd edn, 2010) 249–50; A Lodder, *Enrichment in the Law of Unjust Enrichment* (2012) 128–31.

[48] *Restatement (Second) of Contracts* vol 3, 205 (1981): 'A party who has a right to restitution ... because he has avoided the contract, generally has a choice of either claiming a sum of money in restitution or seeking specific restitution if the benefit is something that can be returned to him'. See also HC Black, *A Treatise on the Rescission of Contracts and Cancellation of Written Instruments* (1916) vol 2, 1453.

with those cases in which, for one reason or another, there are no proceeds, or the claimant says that they do not represent the value of the property transferred.

Where the defendant is a conscious wrongdoer it is difficult to see that pecuniary restitution would be unjustly prejudicial,[49] provided a satisfactory value can be placed upon the asset. The difficulty arises where the defendant's misconduct was not reprehensible, as in a case of innocent misrepresentation or presumed undue influence. The same considerations that would give rise to a defence of change of position, were the claim one for money had and received, equally argue against requiring that the defendant pay a sum of money where the asset itself was lost in circumstances leaving no residue of wealth. The concern is about innocent defendants being left worse off than if the contract had never been made in the first place. It may be observed that it is in precisely those cases where the defendant's conduct is not reprehensible that pecuniary rescission is most important, for in those cases the claimant is unlikely to have an alternative claim for compensatory damages. **15.31**

Pecuniary rescission also involves a re-modelling of the principles of property law as they are currently understood. The theoretical basis for this innovation would require careful thought. **15.32**

(4) Restitution for money paid

Where money has been paid, the rescinding party is entitled to orders for the repayment of an equivalent sum with interest, minus any deductions allowed in favour of the other party on an accounting upon rescission.[50] The payer usually has a purely personal right to payment,[51] but may assert a proprietary claim in cases of fraud, and probably breach of fiduciary duty.[52] **15.33**

The payment will often have been the price for whatever was purchased under the voidable contract, such as a share in a partnership,[53] a professional practice,[54] a business,[55] shares[56] or land,[57] or for the hire of a vessel.[58] But the money might equally have been paid under a loan[59] or as a gift,[60] or under a bill of exchange.[61] **15.34**

---

[49] Cf *Lipkin Gorman (a firm) v Karnaple Limited* [1991] 2 AC 548, 588.
[50] As to the payment of interest, see Chap 17.
[51] *Re Goldcorp Exchange* [1995] 1 AC 74 (PC—NZ) 102.
[52] Chap 16, paras [16.49]–[16.58].
[53] *Rawlins v Wickham* (1858) 1 Giff 355, 65 ER 954; (1858) 3 De G & J 304, 42 ER 1285 (partnership for country banking business; net payments repayable); *Newbigging v Adam* (Bacon VC, 5 May 1886); aff'd (1886) 34 ChD 582 (CA); order varied (1888) 13 App Cas 308 (HL) (partnership for manufacturing textiles; net payments repayable).
[54] *Redgrave v Hurd* (1881) 20 ChD 1 (CA) (solicitor's practice; deposit repayable); *With v O'Flanagan* [1936] 1 Ch 575 (CA) 585–86 (medical practice).
[55] *Kramer v McMahon* [1970] 1 NSWLR 194 (bakery; price minus deductions repayable).
[56] *Capel and Co v Sim's Ships Composition Company* (1888) 58 LT (NS) 807, 810; *Karberg's case* [1892] 3 ChD 1 (CA); *Kent v Freehold Land and Brickmaking Company* (1867) LR 4 Eq Ca 588, 601 (rev'd on other grounds [1868] 3 Ch App 493); *Re Australian Slate Quarries* (1930) 31 St Rep NSW 1, 4.
[57] *Edwards v M'Leay* (1815) Coop 311, 35 ER 568; aff'd (1818) 2 Swans 287, 36 ER 625; *Berry v Armistead* (1836) 2 Keen 221, 48 ER 613; *Wilson v Brisbane City Council* [1931] St R Qd 360, 379.
[58] *Compagnie Chemin de fer Paris-Orleans v Leeston Shipping Company (Limited)* [1919] 1 Lloyd's Rep 235, 239.
[59] *Daly v Sydney Stock Exchange Ltd* (1985) 160 CLR 371.
[60] *Booth v Warrington* (1714) 4 Brown 164, 2 ER 111 (gift of 1000 guineas induced by fraud ordered to be repaid); *Bridgeman v Green* (1755) 2 Ves Sen 627, 627, 629; 28 ER 399, 399, 401; aff'd (1755) Wilm 58, 97 ER 22 (HL) (repayment by bill for account); *Re Glubb* [1900] 1 ChD 354 (CA) 361–62.
[61] *Dyer v Tymewell* (1689) 2 Vern 123, 23 ER 688 (bill of exchange extorted from drawer, the payee ordered to repay the £50 received with interest).

15.35 At the turn of the eighteenth century the common law courts developed a rule that money paid under a contract is, in general, not repayable until the contract has first been brought to an end.[62] Today, that rule applies whether rescission is regarded as occurring at law or in equity. There is now a general rule to the effect that:

> ... where money is paid under a legally effective transaction, neither misrepresentation nor mistake vitiates consent or gives rise by itself to an obligation to make restitution. The recipient obtains a defensible right to the money, which is divested if the payer rescinds or otherwise withdraws from the transaction. If the payer exercises his right of rescission in time ... the obligation to make restitution may follow.[63]

15.36 The right to repayment upon equitable rescission is imposed by principles of equity, not the common law. It is not a claim for money had and received, and there is no need to allege or demonstrate any failure of consideration.[64]

Repayment and account

15.37 Where payments have been made or received on both sides, and the sum due upon rescission is unclear, the amount payable may be quantified through an accounting.[65] Allowances are made at the court's direction.[66] The account is *sui generis* and unlike the obligation of a trustee to render an account, or a fiduciary's obligation to account for profits.[67] It seems not to have been based on a theory that the recipient was accountable as a constructive trustee.[68] Since early times accounts were ordered without any real concern for their basis, as a procedural device allowing Chancery judges to unwind bargains that had been set aside, and that continues to be their function today.

Lien to secure right to repayment

15.38 Where the purchase of a property is rescinded, the rescinding vendor's right to the repayment of the price paid is sometimes protected by a lien over the property to be returned by

---

[62] Chap 3, paras [3.16]–[3.29].
[63] *Portman Building Society v Hamlyn Taylor Neck (a firm)* [1998] 4 All ER 202 (CA) 208.
[64] *Senanayake v Cheng* [1966] AC 63 (PC—Singapore) 76–77; *With v O'Flanagan* [1936] 1 ChD 575 (CA) 585–86; *Re Australian Slate Quarries* (1930) 31 St Rep NSW 1, 4; *Wilson v Brisbane City Council* [1931] St R Qd 36, 379; *Mihaljevic v Eiffel Tower Motors Pty Ltd and General Credits Ltd* [1973] VR 545, 565. Contrast the right to repayment arising at common law: Chap 14, para [14.36].
[65] Eg *Bridgeman v Green* (1755) 2 Ves Sen 627, 627, 629; 28 ER 399, 399, 401; aff'd (1755) Wilm 58, 97 ER 22 (HL).
[66] *Englefeild v Englefeild* (1687) 1 Vern 446, 448; 23 ER 576, 577 (also (1686) 1 Vern 444, 23 ER 575) (conveyance rescinded for fraud; court to direct how far defendant charged with rents and profits actually received); *Matthew v Hanbury* (1690) 2 Vern 188, 23 ER 723 (bond rescinded for undue influence; defendant to account 'for what should appear justly due'); *Mitford v Featherstonaugh* (1752) 2 Ves Sen 446, 28 ER 284 (terms of an account more or less favourable to defendant depending upon whether conduct unconscionable); *Claughton v Price* (1997) 30 HLR 396 (CA) 408 (rescission of sale of property from patient to psychiatrist for undue influence; trial judge had a discretion to ignore 'strict accounting practice' in awarding relief).
[67] The nearest parallel was probably accounts directed in cases of usurious loans (*Bosanquett v Dashwood* (1734) Talbot 38, 25 ER 648) and void annuities (*Byne v Vivian* (1800) 5 Ves Jun 604, 31 ER 762; *Bromley v Holland* (1800) 5 Ves Jun 610, 31 ER 766; rev'd (1802) 7 Ves Jun 3, 32 ER 2; *Holbrook v Sharpey* (1812) 19 Ves Jun 131, 34 ER 467).
[68] *Mildmay v Duckett* (1678) case 822 in D Yale (ed), *Lord Nottingham's 'Manual of Chancery Practice' and 'Prolegomena of Chancery and Equity'* (1965) 633, 636 (orders for an account said to be equally appropriate where a constructive trust was declared over deeds procured by fraud, and if the alternative course was taken of setting them aside); also *Lucas v Adams* (1724) 9 Mod 118, 120; 88 ER 352, 353 (account upon rescission of release of promissory note obtained by undue influence—no property on which trust could attach). Cf *Donovan v Fricker* (1821) Jacob 166, 168; 137 ER 813, 814.

way of counter-restitution. The lien may be specified by the court,[69] or arise by means of orders providing that the property is to be returned by the innocent party only when the price is repaid.[70] Counter-restitution is therefore effected by conditional relief, but on terms that protect the rescinding party from the risk of the other's insolvency.[71]

(5) Restitution for services provided

15.39 Although there does not appear to be any authority directly establishing the point, a contract under which services have been provided by the rescinding party is in principle capable of being set aside in equity.[72] Upon rescission the party providing the services will become entitled to an account for the expenses incurred in providing the services,[73] or perhaps their value including a profit element,[74] with an allowance for any sums received.

15.40 This may be contrasted with Scots law, which does not permit a partly completed contract for services to be reduced (rescinded). That was established in *Boyd and Forrest v Glasgow Railway*,[75] and although it has in the past been said that this decision represents English law, it is better regarded as establishing only that Scotland adopts the restrictive approach of the English common law, which has also denied the right to rescind when services are provided by the party wishing to rescind.[76]

15.41 There is little discussion in the cases as to the amount payable in respect of services provided by the rescinding party. Cases decided in connection with restitutionary claims of other types indicate that there is likely to be no single answer.[77]

15.42 That is in part because services may be of many different types, ranging from those that produce a saleable end-product, such as the building of a boat, to 'pure' services that leave no valuable residue, such as the performance of a concert. Particularly in the case of services designed to produce an end-product, there is obviously an important difference between cases in which the services are partially performed and wholly performed, for partial performance may be of no benefit at all.

---

[69] *Imperial Ottoman Bank v Trustees, Executors and Securities Investment Corp* [1895] WN 23, 13 R 287 (voidable purchase of debentures; lien in favour rescinding purchaser); *Lagunas Nitrate Company v Lagunas Syndicate* [1899] 2 Ch 392 (CA) 461 (*obiter*, rescission being refused). See also *Bellamy v Sabine* (1857) 1 De G & J 566, 574; 44 ER 842, 846 (counsel's submissions); *Trevelyan v Charter* (1846) 9 Beav 140, 142; 50 ER 297. Cf *Cooper v Phibbs* (1867) LR 2 HL 149 where a lien in respect of expenses in improving the estate arose independently of rescission, by reason of the fact that the respondent incurred the expenditure when a trustee. See also *Norway v Rowe* (1812) 19 Ves Jun 144, 159; 34 ER 472 (Lord Eldon).

[70] *Erlanger v The New Sombrero Phosphate Company* (1878) LR 3 App Cas 1218, 1266; *New Sombrero Phosphate Company v Erlanger* (1876) 5 ChD 73, 126 (purchase of island); *Armstrong v Jackson* [1917] 2 KB 822, 831 (purchase of shares); *Alati v Kruger* (1955) 94 CLR 216, 229 (purchase of fruit shop).

[71] See also *Restatement (Second) of Contracts* vol 3, § 380(3) (1981): 'If the other party rejects an offer by the party seeking avoidance to return what he has received, the party seeking avoidance if entitled to restitution can, after the lapse of a reasonable time, enforce a lien on what he has received by selling it and crediting the proceeds toward his claim in restitution'; also vol 3, note (b), 234.

[72] Certainly rescission is possible where the party rescinding has received services: *O'Sullivan v Management Agency and Music Ltd* [1985] QB 428 (CA).

[73] *Ormes v Beadle* (1860) 2 Giff 166, 176; 66 ER 70, 75; rev'd on another point (1860) 2 De G F & J 333, 45 ER 649.

[74] *O'Sullivan v Management Agency and Music Ltd* [1985] QB 428 (CA) (counter-restitution).

[75] 1915 SC 20 (HL).

[76] As to the common law rule, see Chap 14, paras [14.41]–[14.44].

[77] C Mitchell et al, *Goff and Jones: The Law of Unjust Enrichment* (9th edn, 2016) [5-36]–[5-49].

15.43 Two points may be ventured. First, the contractually agreed price does not govern. Having said that, unless the misrepresentation or other vitiating factor obviously distorted the true value of the work, the agreed price may be evidence of its market value.[78] Secondly, where it is the claimant who wishes to be paid for services he has provided to a blameless defendant, it seems appropriate to award only the actual benefit the defendant has received, even if it exceeds the expenses incurred. But that may not be the appropriate measure where the defendant is guilty of some wrongdoing. In that case it may well be that the rescinding party should be permitted to recover the greater of expenses or value, and possibly with a profit element.

C. Counter-restitution of Benefits Received

15.44 The general rule is that the party seeking to rescind is entitled to set aside his transaction and to recover back benefits conferred only if he returns all benefits received under the transaction. There must be mutual restitution. The restoration of benefits received by the party rescinding is here called 'counter-restitution'.[79]

(1) Nature of the obligation to make counter-restitution

15.45 When rescission occurs in equity, counter-restitution is effected in two ways; it occurs by orders for conditional relief, and as part of an accounting upon rescission. Each technique will be considered in turn.

Counter-restitution by conditional relief
Nature of conditional relief

15.46 Conditional relief, also called relief on terms, is a general equitable doctrine not confined to the law of rescission. The court awards particular equitable relief, but only on certain conditions or terms. These must be satisfied in order to obtain the relief awarded. When employed in the context of rescission, the relief typically comprises orders for the transaction to be set aside and appropriate restitution provided, and the condition is that the party seeking that relief makes counter-restitution, and does whatever else is required to effect *restitutio in integrum*.[80]

---

[78] Cf *Way v Latilla* [1937] 3 All ER 759 (HL) 764 and C Mitchell et al, *Goff and Jones: The Law of Unjust Enrichment* (9th edn, 2016) [5-045], and see also [5-042] (costs of performance plus modest profit as approximation of value of benefit).

[79] *Independent Trustee Services Ltd v GP Noble Trustees Ltd* [2013] Ch 91 (CA) [54].

[80] *Hulton v Hulton* [1917] 1 KB 813 (CA) 825; *Cheese v Thomas* [1994] 1 WLR 129 (CA) 136; *Midland Bank plc v Greene* [1995] 1 FLR 365, 378; *Investors Compensation Scheme Ltd v West Bromwich Building Society* [1998] 1 WLR 896 (HL) 916; *Caldicott v Richards* [2020] EWHC 767 (Ch) [120]. In Australia, *Brown v Smitt* (1924) 34 CLR 160, 172 (Isaacs and Rich JJ); *Greater Pacific Investments Pty Ltd v Australian National Industries* (1996) 39 NSWLR 143 (CA) 151; *Maguire v Makaronis* (1996) 188 CLR 449, 477–78; *Bridgewater v Leahy* (1998) 194 CLR 457, 473, 494. In Canada, *Lindsay Petroleum v Hurd* (1874) 5 App Cas 221 (PC—Canada) 245–46. In the USA, *Walker v Galt* 171 F2d 613, 615 (1948).

'He who seeks equity must do equity'

15.47 Since early times the courts have recognized that conditions are imposed pursuant to the maxim 'he who seeks equity must do equity'.[81] The connection was made explicit by Lord Cottenham LC in *Sturgis v Champneys*, who also emphasized that the conditions need not reflect obligations that would be independently enforceable in a court of equity:

> Hence arises the extensive and beneficial rule of this Court, that he who asks for equity must do equity, that is, this Court refuses its aid to give to the Plaintiff ... without imposing upon him conditions which the Court considers he ought to comply with, although the subject of the condition should be one which this Court would not otherwise enforce.[82]

15.48 In *Hanson v Keating*, Sir James Wigram VC observed that:

> ... the well-established rule of this Court that the Plaintiff who would have equity must do equity ... cannot *per se* decide what terms the Court should impose upon the Plaintiff as the price for the decree it gives him. It decides in the abstract that the Court giving the Plaintiff the relief to which he is entitled will do so only upon the terms of him submitting to give the Defendant such corresponding rights (if any) he also may be entitled to in respect of the subject matter of the suit.[83]

15.49 The Vice Chancellor went on to identify rescission as one familiar context for conditional relief, where it functions to permit the court 'to remit both parties to their original positions'.[84]

Effects of conditional relief

15.50 Conditional relief renders the party seeking rescission ineligible for equitable relief if he does not satisfy the conditions imposed. The order is self-executing and the claim to rescind is automatically dismissed if the conditions are not satisfied.[85] Formerly the decree would impose terms and state that in default the bill was to be dismissed, either expressly[86] or by implication, as by an order for relief 'on' or 'upon' certain terms.[87] The more complete form

---

[81] R Francis, *Maxims of Equity* (1727) 3–4; H Ballow and J Fonblanque, *A Treatise of Equity* (1793) (first pub anon 1737 and attrib Henry Ballow) 130; 1 Eq Cas Abr 88, 21 ER 899; Reporter's Notes to *Rich v Sydenham* (1671) 1 Chan Ca 202, 22 ER 762. For the connections between conditional relief and rescission, see also H Maddock, *A Treatise on the Principles and Practice of the High Court of Chancery* (1815) vol 1, 184; E Daniell, *A Treatise on the Practice of the High Court of Chancery* (1837) vol 1, 497–98; J Hill, *A Practical Treatise on the Law Relating to Trustees* (1845) 122; G Spence, *The Equitable Jurisdiction of the Court of Chancery* (1846) vol 1, 626; J Adams, *The Doctrine of Equity* (1850) 191; J Story, *Commentaries on Equity Jurisprudence, First English Edition* (W Grigsby (ed)) (1884) [693], [694], [696]; W Harrison and R Leach, *Seton on Decrees* (2nd edn, 1854) 299.

[82] *Sturgis v Champneys* (1839) 5 My & Cr 97, 102; 41 ER 308, 310 (assignee in bankruptcy's obligation to make provision for bankrupt's wife when enforcing rights in equity).

[83] *Hanson v Keating* (1844) 4 Hare 1, 4–5; 67 ER 537, 538; followed *Gibson v Goldsmid* (1854) 5 DeG M & G 757, 765–66; 43 ER 1064, 1067–68; *USA v McRae* (1867) LR 3 HL 79, 89; cf *Colvin v Hartwell* (1837) 5 Cl & Fin 484, 522; 7 ER 488, 504: 'the true meaning of that maxim [is] ... that a man, who comes to seek the aid of a Court of Equity to inforce a claim, must be prepared to submit in that suit to any directions which the known principles of a Court of Equity may make it proper to give' (Earl of Devon), followed *Langman v Handover* (1929) 43 CLR 334, 351.

[84] *Hanson v Keating* (1844) 4 Hare 1, 6; 67 ER 537, 539, discussed *Mayfair Trading Co Pty Ltd v Dreyer* (1958) 101 CLR 428, 452 (Dixon CJ). For examples of the codification of conditional relief upon equitable rescission, Indian Contracts Act 1872, s 19A; Contracts Act 1950 (Malaysia), s 20; Specific Relief Act 1950 (Malaysia), s 37.

[85] Cf *Gamatronic (UK) Limited v Hamilton* [2016] EWHC 2225 (QB) [224], discussed para [15.54].

[86] Eg *Lawley v Hooper* (1745) 3 Atk 278, 282; 26 ER 962, 964 (undue influence); *Benyon v Fitch* (1866) 35 Beav 570, 578; 55 ER 1018, 1021 (catching bargain).

[87] Eg *Bill v Price* (1686) 1 Vern 467, 467; 23 ER 592, 592; *Chesterfield v Janssen* (1750) 1 Atk 301, 355; 26 ER 191, 226; *Peacock v Evans* (1809) 16 Ves Jun 513, 518; 33 ER 1079, 1081 (heir 'addicted to drinking, extravagant, improvident, and necessitous').

that made the sanction of dismissal explicit was preferred by the time of the Judicature reforms,[88] but both forms are used today.[89]

15.51 At the heart of this device are the twin propositions that the claimant gains no right to relief until the terms imposed by the court are met,[90] and that he has a choice whether or not to comply with those conditions.[91] There are two corollaries to this. First, the entitlement to counter-restitution articulated in the terms imposed is effectively secured by whatever relief is granted to the rescinding party, for the right to that relief is postponed until the terms are satisfied.[92] Secondly, the party against whom rescission is sought has no independent claim to have the terms satisfied.[93] Whether or not this will occur is wholly at the option of the rescinding party.[94] The defendant has no entitlement to counter-restitution independent of rescission, and the right to rescind is vested exclusively in the other party.

Failure to satisfy conditions

15.52 If the terms of relief are rejected or cannot be satisfied, rescission is denied and the voidable transaction remains *prima facie* enforceable according to its terms. Before the Judicature reforms dismissal of the bill to rescind would often leave the transaction enforceable at

---

[88] *Croft v Graham* (1863) 2 De GJ & S 155, 161; 46 ER 334, 336; *Earl of Aylesford v Morris* (1873) 8 Ch App 484, 485, 498. See also *Lindsay Petroleum v Hurd* (1874) 5 App Cas 221 (PC—Canada) 245.

[89] *Hulton v Hulton* [1917] 1 KB 813 (CA) 821 gist of defendant's plea is 'that the plaintiff ought to be put upon terms'; *Midland Bank plc v Greene* [1995] 1 FLR 365, 378 (undue influence) ordering rescission on terms, in default of which 'the action will be dismissed' (following *Lodge v National Union Investment Company Limited* [1907] 1 Ch 300, 312, an illegal loan case).

[90] For 'it is by submitting to this condition that the party makes out an equitable title to the relief of the court': *Mayfair Trading Co Pty Ltd v Dreyer* (1958) 101 CLR 428, 451–52 (Dixon CJ). Also, *Dunbar Bank plc v Nadeem* [1998] 3 All ER 876 (CA) 884: 'I reject Mr Price's submission that, had the cross appeal not succeeded, Mrs Nadeem would have had an unqualified unconditional right to rescission. She never had any such right. Her right to rescission was conditional on her making counter restitution' (Millett LJ). Also, *Lindsay Petroleum Co v Hurd* (1874) LR 5 PC 221 (PC—Canada) 245.

[91] Eg *Duke of Sutherland v Heathcote* [1891] 1 ChD 475 (CA) 468 (unsuccessful claim to *inter alia* rescind a lease of coal for common mistake): 'the only possible right which the Plaintiff could have would be to have the lease set aside on equitable terms, one of which would be giving up possession of the property leased. The Plaintiff was not prepared to do this, and it is plain, therefore, that he is not entitled to have that lease...set aside'. Cf the analogous principle employed in relation to conditional claims for specific performance: *South Western Mineral Water Company Ltd v Ashmore* [1967] 1 WLR 1110. See also *Australand Corporation (Qld) P/L v Johnson* [2007] QCA 302 [124]–[127] (Keane JA).

[92] Chancery formerly made use of this feature of conditional relief by decreeing relief in a manner said to turn the vitiated transaction into a 'mortgage' or 'security' constructed by law. Though regularly used for catching bargains with heirs and reversioners (eg *Edwards v Burt* (1852) 2 De GM & G 55, 64; 42 ER 791, 795), this device was also applied in cases of undue influence (*Billage v Southee* (1852) 9 Hare 534, 541; 68 ER 623, 626), duress (*Hawes v Wyatt* (1790) 3 Bro CC 155, 157, 160; 29 ER 463, 464, 465), fraud (*Wharton v May* (1799) 5 Ves Jun 27, 69; 31 ER 454, 475), breach of fiduciary duty (*Plowright v Lambert* (1885) 52 LT 646, in A Ingpen, F Bloxam, and H Garrett (eds), *Seton on Decrees* (7th edn, 1912) vol 3, 2254–55) and unconscionable conduct (*Neville v Snelling* (1880) 15 ChD 679, 705). The courts recognized that they were constructing a mortgage in these cases (*Hick v Mors* (1754) 3 Keny 117, 127, 129; 96 ER 1329, 1333), treating the defendant as if a mortgagee (*Bellamy v Sabine* (1835) 2 Ph 425, 428, 442; 41 ER 1007, 1009, 1014) and the claimant as bringing a bill to redeem (*Benyon v Fitch* (1866) 35 Beav 570, 578; 55 ER 1018, 1021). Cf Chancery's practice of giving relief against penalties by transforming the transaction into a security, a power that has been said to underpin the equity of redemption: *G and C Kreglinger v New Patagonia Meat and Cold Storage Company Limited* [1914] AC 25, 35. This practice, and the equity of redemption itself, also relied upon the technique of conditional relief.

[93] That party therefore need not plead any cause of action to obtain the counter-restitution to which he is entitled as the price of the contract being rescinded: *Peak Hotels and Resorts Limited v Tarek Investments Ltd* [2015] EWHC 1997 (Ch) [114] (and also at [125]–[135], [138], in determining that the court had no power to order an interim payment in respect of sums payable as counter-restitution; but see *Deutsche Bank AG v Unitech Global Limited* [2016] 1 WLR 3598 (CA) [83] where such an order was made; see further para [15.55]).

[94] *Peak Hotels and Resorts Limited v Tarek Investments Ltd* [2015] EWHC 1997 (Ch) [135] (doubting that the court has power to make a compulsory order for counter-restitution).

common law. Rather than disturbing this pattern, the fused administration of law and equity allows its more efficient operation, for the court can where appropriate specify that in default of complying with the conditions imposed, judgment should be entered in favour of the party seeking to enforce the agreement, rather than simply allowing him to bring proceedings in a different court.[95]

Orders of this kind may be appropriate when rescission is the only defence to a claim brought to enforce an agreement. That was the position in *Maguire v Makaronis*.[96] Solicitors advanced funds to their clients on the security of a charge over certain real property. Following defaults in repayment the solicitors brought possession proceedings, and their client borrowers counter-claimed for a declaration that the mortgage was void. The mortgage was held to be voidable for breach of fiduciary duty. Overturning the decision of the Victorian Court of Appeal, the High Court of Australia held that the loan and security could only be set aside on terms that the outstanding principal was repaid with commercial interest. An order for conditional relief was made in those terms. The court specified that in default of the borrowers making the repayment imposed as a term of relief, judgment was to be entered for possession in favour of the solicitors.[97]

15.53

In *Gamatronic (UK) Limited v Hamilton*[98] the claimant's unwillingness to return shares received under the transaction sought to be rescinded, articulated at the outset of trial, led the court to conclude that rescission should be refused or the claim to rescind treated as withdrawn.

15.54

The Court of Appeal has held that an interim payment may be ordered in respect of sums that would be repayable as counter-restitution in respect of a loan sought to be set aside by the borrower.[99] The circumstance that the right to counter-restitution might be enforced by an order for conditional relief, and that the borrower was not required to offer counter-restitution, did not stand in the way of the conclusion that an interim payment should be ordered in circumstances where at least that sum would be payable whether rescission was granted or not. The answer may well be different, however, where the party seeking an interim payment has no claim other than by counter-restitution provided to him as an incident of rescission.

15.55

Lien

Conditional relief effectively secures the guilty party's entitlement to restitution on the relief awarded to the innocent party, for relief is granted only if the prescribed counter-restitution is first made.[100] Where a vendor rescinds his sale, the purchaser

15.56

---

[95] As was the case before the Judicature reforms; eg *Waller v Dalt* (1676) Dickens 7, 11; 21 ER 169, 170.
[96] (1998) 188 CLR 449, applied *Permanent Mortgages Pty Ltd v Vandenbergh* (2010) 41 WAR 353, 427–8 (rescinding party to 'do equity' by returning benefit received under mortgage, comprising a portion only of the sums advanced).
[97] *Maguire v Makaronis* (1998) 188 CLR 449, 477–78 (and cf *Carter v Palmer* (1837) 11 Bli NS 397, 419–20; 6 ER 378, 386). See also *Midland Bank plc v Greene* [1995] 1 FLR 365, 378, 379.
[98] [2016] EWHC 2225 (QB) [224].
[99] *Deutsche Bank AG v Unitech Global Limited* [2016] 1 WLR 3598 (CA) [83], [86]; and cf *Peak Hotels and Resorts Limited v Tarek Investments Ltd* [2015] EWHC 1997 (Ch) [138] (decided before *Deutsche Bank*).
[100] See para [15.51]. Cf *Perpetual Trustees Victoria Ltd v Burns* [2015] WASC 234 [273]–[277], [281] (secured loan procured by unconscionable conduct; counter-restitution made by order for repayment of principal plus simple interest, with the debt due to be unsecured; conditional relief refused on the basis that the obtaining of

has a purchaser's lien to secure repayment to him of the part of the price that he has paid.[101]

Counter-restitution by accounting

15.57 When both parties to the transaction are obliged to make payments of money as an incident of rescission, counter-restitution is typically not effected by conditional relief, but by deducting the sums due from the party rescinding from the amounts payable by the other party. The process of accounting permits the court to both identify and quantify the benefits to be returned on both sides. So for example in *Sibley v Grosvenor*, where the claimants had bought a grazing property on the faith of fraudulent misrepresentations, the court made provision for restitution and counter-restitution through the following order for an account:

> ... 3. Account of purchase money and interest thereon at 5 per cent per annum from times of payment. 4. Account of all sums expended by plaintiffs in substantial repairs and lasting improvements on the land together with interest thereon on 5 per cent from the time of disbursement. 5. Inquiry as to the proper rent to be paid by the plaintiffs during the period of their occupation of the land. The amount so found for occupation rent to be set off against the amounts found in taking the accounts no 3 and 4. 6. Balance to be paid by defendant Loughnan to plaintiffs. 7. Reserve further consideration as to defendant Grosvenor's liability in respect of such balance in event of non-recovery from defendant Loughnan.[102]

15.58 Counter-restitution may be effected through an accounting when property is sold rather than purchased by the rescinding party, the defendant purchaser being ordered to return the property and pay the fruits of its use to be determined on an accounting, but minus the price paid.[103]

Right limited to insisting on proper allowances

15.59 The right of the defendant entitled to counter-restitution is limited to insisting that proper allowances are made in the accounting. He has no entitlement independent of rescission to receive the sums deducted in his favour in taking the account, and the right to rescind is exclusively that of the other party. The deduction does not derive from any independently enforceable right to payment, and confers no right of set-off or counterclaim. This is underlined in cases when the account leaves a balance due from the rescinding party. In such cases relief may properly be made conditional upon the rescinding party paying the

---

security was part of the plaintiff's imposition and exploitation); also, *Jams 2 Pty Ltd v Stubbings (No 4)* [2019] VSC 482.

[101] *Hughes v Macpherson & UBC Home Loans Limited* [1999] EWCA Civ 1006 (sale of house set aside for undue influence) citing *Whitbread v Watt* [1901] 1 Ch 911 (Farwell J), and applying conveyancing principles developed in the context of termination for breach of condition. Cf *Imperial Ottoman Bank v Trustees, Executors and Securities Investment Corp* [1895] WN 23; 13 R 287 (voidable purchase of debentures; lien in favour rescinding purchaser).
[102] (1916) 21 CLR 269, 476. To similar effect, *Lagunas Nitrate Company v Lagunas Syndicate* [1899] 2 Ch 392 (CA) 461 (Rigby LJ) (where rescission was denied); *Kramer v McMahon* [1970] 1 NSWLR 194, 210–11; *Midland Bank plc v Greene* [1995] 1 FLR 365, 378–79.
[103] Eg *Clarkson v Hanway* (1723) 2 P Wms 203, 206; 24 ER 700, 701; *Evans v Llewellin* (1787) 1 Cox 333, 341; 29 ER 1191, 1194 defendant to 'account for rents and profits ... out of which he was to retain 200 guineas paid to the plaintiffs'; *Pickett v Loggon* (1807) 14 Ves Jun 215, 244; 33 ER 503, 515 'an account of the rents of profits from the time of filing the Bill: the £1046 [price], and interest from the same time, to be deducted'. For off-setting upon rescission, see further Chap 17, paras [17.30]–[17.31].

balance so determined,[104] which assumes that the innocent party has a choice whether to pay that sum as a condition of relief, or to decline to do so.[105] The defendant's right is limited to insisting on proper allowances.

No need to offer counter-restitution

Although there were once certain classes of case in which a bill to set aside a transaction was demurrable if it did not contain an offer to repay sums received,[106] in *Jervis v Berridge*[107] Lord Selborne LC held that no such offer was generally required. Equity could always ensure rescission occurred on proper terms by making orders for conditional relief, and there was no need for an express offer for that power to be exercised.[108] The old rule has survived to an uncertain extent in cases where equitable relief is sought in the context of unlawful transactions.[109] There is also some authority that the position is different if rescission is raised as a defence,[110] but there is no principled reason for that, and the notion is inconsistent with recent authority.[111]   **15.60**

Although an offer of counter-restitution is not necessary to rescind in equity, it may be in the interests of the rescinding party to do so in order to meet arguments that *restitutio in integrum* is impossible, or that the transaction has been affirmed.[112]   **15.61**

No independently enforceable right to counter-restitution

It is apparent from the survey undertaken above that the obligation to make counter-restitution upon equitable rescission is fundamentally different from the equivalent obligation that arises upon rescission at common law. At common law rescission confers a vested right to counter-restitution in favour of the party against whom rescission is sought. The obligation accrues unconditionally. In equity, on the other hand, the party against whom   **15.62**

---

[104] Eg *Lawley v Hooper* (1745) 3 Atk 278, 282; 26 ER 962, 964; *Neesom v Clarkson* (1842) 2 Hare 163, 176; 67 ER 68 as reported in W Harrison and R Leach, *Seton on Decrees* (2nd edn, 1854) 299–300.

[105] Cf *Hollis v Bulpett* (1865) 13 WR 492, 12 LT 293; A Ingpen, F Bloxam, and H Garrett (eds), *Seton on Decrees* (7th edn, 1912) vol 2, 1312 (defendant unable to claim for the balance of an accounting in his favour when no offer to pay by claimant and no independent right to payment).

[106] *Mason v Gardiner* (1793) 4 Bro CC 436, 438; 29 ER 976, 977 (usurious secured loan); *Whitmore v Francis* (1820) 8 Price 616, 619; 146 ER 1314, 1315 (usurious loan); see also *Godbolt v Watts* (1795) 2 Anst 543, 544; 145 ER 961, 962 (indemnity obtained by fraud); *Aguilar v Aguilar* (1820) 5 Madd 414, 56 ER 953 and notes thereto, suggesting a general rule that a rescinding party must expressly offer to do equity; cf *Barker v Walters* (1844) 8 Beav 92, 96; 50 ER 36, 38.

[107] (1873) 8 Ch App 351, 357.

[108] *Jervis v Berridge* (1873) 8 Ch App 351. In Australia, *The Commercial Bank of Australia Limited v Amadio* (1983) 151 CLR 447, 468 'it matters not that the respondents have not offered to do equity' (rescission of mortgage and guarantee unconscionably procured); *Tenji v Henneberry & Associates Pty Ltd* (2000) 98 FCR 324 (Full Ct) [115] (lack of offer to account for rent received no bar to equitable rescission). In the USA, *Brown v Norman* 65 Miss 369, 4 So 293 (1888); *Parker v Baltimore Paint and Chemical Corp* 39 FDR 567 (Colo 1966); *Restatement (Third) of Restitution* vol 2, § 54(5), Cmt. j 285, Reporter's Notes 294 (2011).

[109] The court in *Jervis v Berridge* (1873) 8 Ch App 351, 358 put to one side cases involving penalties, forfeiture, usurious and other unlawful transactions, and mortgages. The need for an offer to restore was later confirmed in *Lodge v National Union Investment Co* [1907] 1 Ch 300 and *Langman v Handover* (1929) 43 CLR 334, which concerned money-lending legislation. But the scope of these decisions was undermined by *Kasumu v Baba-Egbe* [1956] AC 539 (PC-West Africa) and *Mayfair Trading Co Pty Ltd v Dreyer* (1958) 101 CLR 428, and by the subsequent abolition of money-lending statutes in most jurisdictions.

[110] *Steedman v Frigidaire Corporation* [1933] 1 DLR 161 (PC—Canada).

[111] *Deutsche Bank AG v Unitech Global Limited* [2016] 1 WLR 3598 (CA) [86] (borrower defending claim upon loan for misrepresentation).

[112] See eg *Kramer v McMahon* [1970] 1 NSWLR 194, 209; *Preda v Australian Imaging & Ultrasound Distributors Pty Ltd* [2007] NSWSC 155 [61]–[63] (undertakings to court offered by rescinding party to make necessary counter-restitution).

rescission is sought has no independently enforceable right. When it is imposed by an award of conditional relief, the obligation to make counter-restitution depends entirely upon whether the rescinding party is content to do equity by accepting the terms imposed by the court. Whether counter-restitution will be provided (and whether rescission will occur) is entirely at the option of the injured party. Equally, if counter-restitution occurs through the making of allowances in an accounting, the extent of the defendant's right is to have all proper allowances included in the account. He has no independent entitlement to be paid those sums.

(2) Counter-restitution of property received

15.63 Property must be returned if it remains *in specie* in the hands of the rescinding party and free of paramount interests in favour of third parties.[113] The court will direct that land be re-conveyed,[114] shares acquired in the market[115] and upon allotment[116] to be re-transferred, and the redelivery of chattels purchased,[117] such as stock-in-trade remaining in a business.[118] Contractual rights against third parties may also be returned.[119] The order will be tailored to the type of title acquired, and coupled where appropriate with orders for possession.[120] Where a gift is rejected by the donee, the court will make orders to revest title in the donor in a process analogous to counter-restitution upon rescission.[121]

15.64 It is often said that the party wishing to rescind must return any property received, and if he cannot do so, rescission will not be permitted. The basis and true scope of this rule is discussed in Chapter 18.

(3) Counter-restitution for money received

15.65 Sums received by the rescinding party under the voidable transaction must be repaid upon rescission.[122] If the amounts so payable are less than the sums recoverable by way of

---

[113] In principle, rescission may itself permit assertion of a third party interest in assets to be restored by way of counter-restitution, as in the exceptional case where so long as it stands, the voidable transaction creates a bar to the assertion of that interest, or where the revesting of the asset affects the enforceability of the third party's interest: *Independent Trustee Services Ltd v GP Noble Trustees Ltd* [2013] Ch 91 (CA) [56]–[57].

[114] *Lindsay Petroleum v Hurd* (1874) 5 App Cas 221 (PC—Canada); *Edwards v M'Leay* (1815) Coop 311, 35 ER 568; aff'd (1818) Swans 287, 36 ER 625 (fraud). Cf *Hart v Swaine* (1877) 7 Ch 42, 47 (declaration that deed inoperative indorsed on the deed and delivered up to plaintiff; no order for reconveyance).

[115] *Transvaal Lands Company v New Belgium (Transvaal) Land and Development Company* [1914] 2 ChD 488 (CA) 505 (breach of fiduciary duty). Cf *Oeklers v Ellis* [1914] 2 KB 139, 152 (shares extinguished by winding up, purchaser to pay dividend received on winding up). It has been held in Australia that an order in favour of the purchaser of shares for rescission and repayment of the price will revest equitable title in the shares received, if unaccompanied by a consequential order for returning legal title to the shares: *Indian Farmers Fertiliser Cooperative Limited v Gutnick* [2015] VSC 724 [76], accepted on appeal as being an 'unimpeachable' statement of principle: *Gutnick v Indian Farmers Fertiliser Cooperative Limited* (2016) 49 VR 732 (CA) [15].

[116] *Capel and Co v Sim's Ships Composition Company* (1888) 58 LT (NS) 807; *Karberg's case* [1892] 3 ChD 1 (CA).

[117] *JAD International Pty Ltd v International Trucks Australia Limited* (1994) 50 FCR 378 (Full Ct) (truck).

[118] *Alati v Kruger* (1955) 94 CLR 216, 229; *Kramer v McMahon* [1970] 1 NSWLR 194, 210.

[119] *Abram Steamship Company Limited v Westville Shipping Company Limited* [1923] AC 773 (Scots law; benefit of shipbuilding contract). Cf *Ballantyne v Raphael* (1889) 15 VLR 538, 558.

[120] *Erlanger v The New Sombrero Phosphate Company* (1878) LR 3 App Cas 1218, 1266; *New Sombrero Phosphate Company v Erlanger* (1876) 5 ChD 73, 126 (possession of island in West Indies purchased by rescinding party).

[121] *Re Paradise Motor Co Ltd* [1968] 1 WLR 1125 (CA) 1143; Chap 29, para [29.13].

[122] The payment of interest on sums to be repaid as counter-restitution is considered in Chap 17.

restitution, the lesser sum is deducted from the greater in an accounting upon rescission.[123] In that event, counter-restitution is effected by making the appropriate allowance. If, on the other hand, the balance favours the party against whom rescission is sought, the contract will be set aside and orders for restitution made on condition that the rescinding party pays the balance owing.[124] The obligation to repay is, in effect, secured by the relief awarded.

Before the Judicature reforms, when an insurer obtained a decree in Chancery setting aside a policy of insurance it was normally a condition of relief that premium income be repaid.[125] Today, however, the right to repayment of premium income following rescission is governed by statute.[126]   **15.66**

(4) Counter-restitution for services received

When the rescinding party receives the benefit of services under a voidable transaction, upon rescission he will usually be required to make counter-restitution by paying for them,[127] often by way of an allowance in an accounting.[128] The court has a discretion as to whether expenses only are recoverable, or the reasonable value of what was received, including a profit element.[129]   **15.67**

The cases provide limited guidance as to valuation. Fault should play some role.[130] Where the party providing the services is blameless or comparatively so, the court will be concerned to protect him. It may then be appropriate to quantify counter-restitution as the greater of the market value of the services actually performed, or the cost of performing them, and also to allow a profit element, though this will be modest compared with the profits that might have been obtained in the market, under a freely negotiated bargain.[131] But in cases of conscious wrongdoing, the attitude of the court should be different, and counter-restitution should be measured by the lesser of value and expenses, and the allowance of a profit element reduced as the court thinks fit in all the circumstances.   **15.68**

---

[123] Eg *Clarkson v Hanway* (1723) 2 P Wms 203, 206; 24 ER 700, 701; *Evans v Llewellin* (1787) 1 Cox 333, 341; 29 ER 1191, 1194; *Pickett v Loggon* (1807) 14 Ves Jun 215, 244; 33 ER 503, 515.
[124] Eg *Lawley v Hooper* (1745) 3 Atk 278, 282; 26 ER 962, 964; *Neesom v Clarkson* (1842) 2 Hare 163, 176; 67 ER 68 as reported in W Harrison and R Leach, *Seton on Decrees* (2nd edn, 1854) 299–300; para [15.57].
[125] Eg *Barker v Walters* (1844) 8 Beav 92, 96; 50 ER 36, 38. The court would sometimes direct that the amount be deducted from the costs that the assured would otherwise have to pay: *Whittingham v Thornburgh* (1690) 2 Vern 206, 23 ER 734; *De Costa v Scandret* (1723) 2 P Wms 169, 24 ER 686, and *The British Equitable Insurance Company v The Great Western Railway Company* (1869) 38 LJ Ch 132.
[126] Consumer Insurance (Disclosure and Representations) Act 2012 and the Insurance Act 2015, discussed Chap 14, para [14.82]–[14.84] and Chap 5, para [5.35]–[5.39]. For the common law as to premium income, Chap 14, para [14.79]–[14.81].
[127] *Atlantic Lines and Navigation Co Inc v Hallam Ltd (The Lucy)* [1983] 1 Lloyd's LR 188, 202 (*obiter* in a case of innocent misrepresentation); *O'Sullivan v Management Agency and Music Ltd* [1985] QB 428 (CA) (undue influence by managers of musician).
[128] *Rees v De Bernardy* [1896] 2 Ch 437, 450 (rescission of unconscionable bargain also void for champerty) 'plaintiffs having offered before me to allow to the defendant such reasonable sum as the Court may think just for his services rendered and expenses incurred in reference to the intestate's property, I direct an inquiry to ascertain what sum ought to be so allowed to the defendant'.
[129] *O'Sullivan v Management Agency and Music Ltd* [1985] QB 428 (CA); see also *Guinness plc v Saunders* [1990] 2 AC 663.
[130] Cf as to services provided by the rescinding party: para [15.43].
[131] *O'Sullivan v Management Agency and Music Ltd* [1985] QB 428 (CA).

D. Equitable Rescission by Election

(1) Restitution

Proprietary claims

15.69 When money or property has been transferred under a contract obtained by fraud, the party defrauded may, by electing to disaffirm the contract, vest in himself an equitable interest in the asset or its traceably identified proceeds.[132] No equivalent right has yet been recognized for other grounds of rescission.[133]

15.70 If the rescinding party has also received benefits for which counter-restitution must be given, the obligation to return those benefits must in principle burden the equitable interest that arises. The innocent party is able to assert ownership in equity, but only upon condition that appropriate counter-restitution is provided.[134] His equitable interest is in this respect akin to an equity of redemption.[135]

Personal claims

15.71 Although there is no authority on the point, in principle if equitable rescission occurs when the transaction is disaffirmed, the guilty party must automatically become obliged to account for the value of benefits conferred in respect of which no proprietary interest may be asserted, such as the value of services provided, or the time value of assets transferred.

Claims are contingent

15.72 These claims to restitution are weak, for they must in principle remain contingent on the persistence of the innocent party's right to court orders effecting rescission. The claims described earlier will therefore be lost if events occur that extinguish the equity to orders for rescission, as, for example, where disaffirmation is followed by unexcused delay or other conduct that would lead to unjustified prejudice were rescission to be granted.[136]

(2) Counter-restitution

15.73 The cases are largely silent as to the content of the obligation to make counter-restitution when a transaction is said to be capable of being set aside in equity by an election to disaffirm it. In principle, an obligation to make counter-restitution must accrue when the election is made, but only conditionally, subject to the court eventually ordering rescission. If this is the correct analysis, when the innocent party communicates his decision to reject the transaction, the wrongdoer gains no independently enforceable right to counter-restitution.

---

[132] *Lonrho plc v Fayed (No 2)* [1992] 1 WLR 1, 11–12; *Shalson v Russo* [2005] Ch 281, 320–22; *Independent Trustee Services Ltd v GP Noble Trustees Ltd* [2013] Ch 91 (CA) [52]–[55]. In Australia, *Alati v Kruger* (1955) 94 CLR 216, 224.
[133] Chap 16, paras [16.25]–[16.40].
[134] Paras [15.50], [15.51], Chap 16, para [16.62].
[135] Chap 16, para [16.62].
[136] See Chaps 18, 24.

15.74 The alternative view is that the election generates an unconditional obligation to provide counter-restitution that is independently enforceable by the party against whom rescission is sought.[137] But although this mirrors the common law model of rescission, it cannot be reconciled with equity's established pattern, which is to require counter-restitution through grants of conditional relief.[138] Unconditional rights to counter-restitution also cannot logically be reconciled with the possibility, which must remain, of the right to rescind being lost by reason of events subsequent to the making of the election to rescind.[139] They also appear to be contrary to authority. In *Hughes v Macpherson*[140] the Court of Appeal said that when a vendor sets aside a sale, the purchaser has a purchaser's lien to secure repayment to him of the portion of the price that he has paid.[141] That makes the right to restitution conditional upon the rescinding party providing counter-restitution.[142]

15.75 In Australia there is authority that in cases of fraud, by electing to rescind the defrauded party may automatically revest equitable title in property received. The leading decision is *Alati v Kruger*,[143] where Kruger bought Alati's fruit shop in Brisbane, and in so doing took an assignment of Alati's lease of the premises. The sale was held to be voidable for Alati's fraudulent misrepresentation as to the shop's turnover, and to have been rescinded in equity when Kruger elected to disaffirm it. The High Court of Australia indicated that but for the covenant requiring the landlord's consent to reassignment, equitable title in the lease would have revested in equity when Kruger elected to rescind.[144] Similarly, in *Kramer v McMahon*,[145] McMahon fraudulently exaggerated the turnover of his rural bakery to induce Kramer to buy it. After signing the agreement, paying the deposit to a stakeholder, and going into business for a trial period, Kramer discovered the misrepresentation. Before completion, he wrote to McMahon and rejected the deal. Helsham J held that because of the fraud no equitable title may ever have passed, but even if it did, it would revest when the plaintiff elected to rescind because of the fraud.[146]

---

[137] This form of order forecloses the possibility that the bargain will become enforceable according to its terms if the party seeking rescission cannot provide the required counter-restitution, which is the effect of conditional relief.
[138] See paras [15.46]–[15.56]. See also Chap 11, para [11.110]. Cf in Australia s 243 of Sched 2 of the Competition and Consumer Act 2010 permits orders for rescission and restitution that are not conditional on the claimant satisfying orders for counter-restitution: *MacFarlane v Heritage Corp (Aust) Pty Ltd* [2004] QCA 183 (fraudulent purchase of a yacht for 'trade dollars', considering the predecessor provision in s 87 of the Trade Practices Act 1974).
[139] Also Chap 11, para [11.109].
[140] *Hughes v Macpherson & UBC Home Loans Limited* [1999] EWCA Civ 1006.
[141] The court invoked conveyancing principles concerned with termination for breach of condition, citing *Whitbread v Watt* [1901] 1 Ch 911 (Farwell J).
[142] But cf the unusual orders made by Evans-Lombe J in *Investors Compensation Scheme Ltd v West Bromwich Building Society* [1999] 1 Lloyd's Rep PN 496, 546 which are probably confined to their facts (sums due under voidable mortgage reduced to amounts due as counter-restitution upon rescission; but mortgagor had never had unfettered access to funds).
[143] (1955) 94 CLR 216.
[144] *Alati v Kruger* (1955) 94 CLR 216, 224.
[145] [1970] 1 NSWLR 194.
[146] *Kramer v McMahon* [1970] 1 NSWLR 194, 209, see also 206. In *Gutnick v Indian Farmers Fertiliser Cooperative Limited* (2016) 49 VR 732 (CA) [15], [22]–[27], [29] it was held that equitable title to shares purchased under a contract procured by fraud revested when the order for rescission was made. However, whether an equitable title had instead passed before that time, when the contract was disaffirmed, was not argued, the question being whether the absence of a consequential order for reconveyance permitted double recovery (which it did not: at [30]).

15.76 It is unclear whether these decisions would be followed in England.[147] Moreover, although on its face this analysis mirrors the common law rule that title to chattels automatically revests when the buyer elects to disaffirm for fraud,[148] it was recognized in *Alati v Kruger* that the equity to rescind could be lost by events occurring between the date of election and judgment.[149] If that were to happen it must follow that equitable title revests back in the injured party, and the bargain remains enforceable. This is quite unlike the position at common law. An election to disaffirm a purchase that is voidable at law has consequences that are by their nature final and permanent, and which cannot be undone.

---

[147] For discussion in the context of the setting aside of a consent order, *Independent Trustee Services Ltd v GP Noble Trustees Ltd* [2013] Ch 91 (CA) [43], [44], [115], [125] (no automatic revesting of title upon consent order being set aside; title passes when effect is given to any consequential orders for restoring the status quo). Cf *Gutnick v Indian Farmers Fertiliser Cooperative Limited* (2016) 49 VR 732 (CA) [15], [22]–[27], [29] (equitable title revests when order for rescission is made even absent a consequential order for counter-restitution).

[148] See Chap 14, para [14.69].

[149] 'There remains, however, the question whether the respondent lost his right to such a decree by his conduct in discontinuing the business and leaving the premises before judgment was given in the action. The remedy is discretionary (*Story on Equity*, (3rd English edn, 1920) 293, 294, 295), and if the respondent had acted unconscientiously during the pendency of the action, as by causing the loss of a valuable leasehold and goodwill by discontinuing the business and abandoning the premises without giving the appellant a reasonable opportunity to take them back, no doubt the court might refuse relief': *Alati v Kruger* (1955) 94 CLR 216.

16
Proprietary Claims

A. Introduction	16.01	(1) Title passes pending rescission	16.12
B. Proprietary Claims upon Rescission at Law	16.02	(2) Recovering title	16.19
(1) Property	16.02	(3) When does disaffirmation confer an equitable interest?	16.25
(2) Money	16.05	(4) Retrospective equitable title	16.41
(3) Tracing into substitutes	16.10	(5) Proprietary claims in respect of money paid	16.45
C. Proprietary Claims upon Equitable Rescission	16.12	(6) Nature of the proprietary interest arising upon equitable rescission	16.59

A. Introduction

One of the attractions of rescission as a remedy is the possibility of asserting proprietary claims to money or property transferred, or their traceable substitute. There is, however, some uncertainty as to when a proprietary claim may be brought, and as to the nature of the interest that is conferred. This chapter considers the availability, and nature, of proprietary claims upon rescission at law and in equity.[1] The theoretical basis for the right to recover title upon rescission is considered in Chapter 1, and is not discussed again here.[2]

16.01

B. Proprietary Claims upon Rescission at Law

(1) Property

When a contract is voidable for fraud, and a legal title to chattels has been transferred in accordance with its terms, that title is automatically revested in the transferor when he elects to disaffirm.[3] There is no equivalent authority when chattels have been sold under a contract

16.02

---

[1] For a valuable comparative study, B Häcker, *Consequences of Impaired Consent Transfers* (2013), chaps V, VIII. See also the careful analysis in S Zogg, *Proprietary Consequences in Defective Transfers of Ownership* (2020) chaps 4, 5.

[2] Chap 1, paras [1.25]–[1.28], arguing that the impairment of consent that permits rescission of the contract also renders imperfect the transfer of title to property, and that rescission involves the realization of that defect in title. Title is not revested because the contract itself is extinguished *ab initio*.

[3] *Load v Green* (1846) 15 M & W 216, 221; 153 ER 828, 830; *Clough v London and North Western Railway Co* (1871) LR 7 Ex 26, 32; *Car and Universal Finance Co Ltd v Caldwell* [1965] 1 QB 525 (CA); *Hunter BNZ Finance Ltd v CG Maloney Pty Ltd* (1988) 18 NSWLR 420, 432–33. The principle has also been affirmed in cases where a third party gains a paramount interest in the property before rescission, thereby preventing title revesting: *White v Garden* (1851) 10 CB 919, 138 ER 364; *Stevenson v Newnham* (1853) 13 CB 285, 138 ER 1208; *Kingsford v Merry* (1856) 11 Ex 577, 156 ER 960 rev'd on other grounds (1856) 1 H & N 503, 156 ER 1299 and subsequently aff'd *Pease v Gloahec* (1866) LR 1 PC 219, 230; *Truman (Limited) v Attenborough* (1910) 26 TLR 601; *Whitehorn Bros v Davison* [1911] 1 KB 463 (CA).

voidable for duress. However, assuming that the duress is not so extreme that it prevents title passing,[4] the rule should probably be same.[5]

16.03 Contracts of insurance may be rescinded at law for material non-disclosure and non-fraudulent misrepresentation,[6] and there is also a specialized common law right to rescind contracts for mental infirmity,[7] and probably also for intoxication.[8] It is more doubtful that these other grounds for rescission at law permit the recovery of legal title, but the point seems not to have been decided either way.

16.04 Title to real property and to intangible property cannot be recovered upon rescission at law, and in cases of this kind resort must be had to equity.[9]

(2) Money

16.05 David Fox has argued that in principle one who pays money under a contract induced by fraud may, by rescinding, recover legal title in its traceably identified proceeds.[10] But the cases have not so far recognized such a right. The claim to be repaid sums paid under a contract induced by fraud has always been a personal claim for money had and received. To the extent that they deal with the point at all, the cases seem to reject the proprietary analysis.[11]

16.06 There seems, however, to be no reason in principle why legal title may not be recovered in bank notes and coins paid under a contract procured by fraud, in the same way that title may be regained to other tangible personal property, as long as the cash remains separately identified in the hands of the payee.

16.07 The point will not matter in most cases, because where a contract induced by fraud is rescinded at common law the rescinding party should obtain an equitable proprietary interest in the traceable proceeds of sums paid.[12] Equity's response in a case where rescission occurs at law might be said to spring from the failure of the common law to provide complete

---

[4] *Fairbanks v Snow* 13 NE 596, 598 (1887) duress 'to the height of such bodily compulsion as turns the ostensible party into a mere machine' (Holmes J).
[5] *Irons v Wang* [2004] DCR 830 (DC, NZ); *Halpern v Halpern (No 2)* [2007] 1 QB 88, 91–92.
[6] *Carter v Boehm* (1766) 3 Burr 1909, 97 ER 1162; 1 Black W 593, 96 ER 342; *Manifest Shipping Co Ltd v UniPolaris Insurance Co Ltd (The Star Sea)* [2003] 1 AC 469. For statutory modification of the right, Chap 5, paras [5.35]–[5.39].
[7] *Molton v Camroux* (1848) 2 Exch 487, 154 ER 584; aff'd (1849) 4 Exch 17, 154 ER 1107; *Imperial Loan Co v Stone* [1892] 1 QB 599 (CA); *Gibbons v Wright* (1954) 91 CLR 423, 153 ER 260; *Hart v O'Connor* [1985] AC 1000 (PC—NZ).
[8] *Moulton v Camroux* (1849) 4 Exch 17, 19; 154 ER 584; *Matthews v Baxter* (1873) LR 8 Exch 132, reading 'void' in *Gore v Gibson* (1845) 13 M & W 623, 626, 627; 153 ER 260 as 'voidable'. Guarantees might also be voidable at law if the creditor fails to disclose unusual features of the transaction.
[9] See Chap 14, paras [14.21]–[14.28].
[10] D Fox, 'The Transfer of Legal Title to Money' [1996] 4 RLR 60, 63–64, 67–70; D Fox, *Property Rights in Money* (2008) [5.147].
[11] *Re Goldcorp Exchange Ltd* [1995] 1 AC 74 (PC—NZ) 102–03; *Eldan Services Ltd v Chandag Motors Ltd* [1990] 3 All ER 459, 462.
[12] *El Ajou v Dollar Land Holdings plc* [1993] 3 All ER 717, 734; *Bank Tejarat v Hong Kong and Shanghai Bank* [1995] 1 Lloyd's Rep 239, 248; *Halifax Building Society v Thomas* [1996] Ch 217 (CA) 226; *Shalson v Russo* [2005] Ch 281, 320–22; *Global Currency Exchange Network Limited v Osage 1 Limited* [2019] 1 WLR 5865, 5880 [52], 5886 [74], 5888 [84]. In Australia, *Westpac Banking Corp v Markovic* (1985) 82 FLR 7. In Jersey, *Nolan v Minerva Trust Company Limited* [2014] 2 JLR 117; JRC 078A. For authority that even fraud after entry into the contract permits rescission to assert a proprietary interest in money paid, *National Crime Agency v Robb* [2015] Ch 520 (discussed Chap 1, paras [1.95]–[1.97]).

redress, and to involve equity assisting the common law.[13] But the simpler analysis is that the fraud itself automatically generates an equitable proprietary interest once the transaction is disaffirmed, which is equity's response to the facts whether or not the transaction is also rescinded at common law.

Non-contractual payments[14]

The reasoning of Atkin LJ in *Bank Belge Pour L'Etranger v Hambrouck* may suggest that although legal title will pass where a non-contractual payment is procured by fraud, by disaffirming the payment, the payer can obtain a legal proprietary interest in it: **16.08**

> I will assume therefore that this is a case not of a void but of a voidable transaction by which Hambrouck obtained a title to the money until the plaintiffs elected to avoid his title, which they did when they made their claim in this action. The title would then revest in the plaintiffs subject to any title acquired in the meantime by any transferee for value without notice of the fraud.[15]

Whether Atkin LJ contemplated a revesting of legal or of equitable title remains unclear.[16] Although he held that a personal claim for money had and received was available as against the recipient of the funds paid, identified using equity's tracing rules, he appeared to leave open whether a common law proprietary claim would also have been available, had the funds been traced into cash or goods over which a possessory claim could have been maintained.[17] In practice, however, the point is unlikely to matter, because in most cases a common law proprietary claim will not be capable of arising. The case would have to be one where cash was paid and remained separately identified in the hands of the payee, or only the cash paid was used to buy identified goods.[18] **16.09**

(3) Tracing into substitutes

The orthodox view is that rescission is barred once the property sold has been acquired by a subsequent bona fide purchaser for value. This bar is, however, only defensible insofar as it protects the rights of the innocent third party, and rescission should be permitted if it can occur on terms that do not interfere with those rights. Accordingly, where property has **16.10**

---

[13] *American Sugar Refining Co v Fancher* 145 NY 552, 40 NE 206 (NYCA) 209 col 1 (1895); see also *Alati v Kruger* (1955) 94 CLR 216, 224, where the High Court of Australia contemplated equitable intervention on the ground that the rules of rescission at law were inadequate.

[14] See also Chap 1, paras [1.94]–[1.98].

[15] *Bank Belge Pour L'Etranger v Hambrouck* [1921] 1 KB 321 (CA) 332. See also Bankes LJ at 325: 'I will assume that Hambrouck obtained a voidable title to the proceeds of the cheques'. Scrutton LJ appeared to proceed on the basis that no title passed: at 329. See also *Re Duncan* [1899] 1 Ch 387, 391–92, where Romer J appears to have contemplated *obiter* the recovery of title to money at law by rescinding for fraud.

[16] The reasoning of Atkin LJ has subsequently been relied upon as authority that an equitable proprietary interest arises in the proceeds of sums paid under a contract rescinded for fraud: *Shalson v Russo* [2005] Ch 281, 320–24. See also *National Crime Agency v Robb* [2015] Ch 520, 530–31.

[17] *Bank Belge Pour L'Etranger v Hambrouck* [1921] 1 KB 321 (CA) 333–35. See also D Fox, 'The Transfer of Legal Title to Money' [1996] 4 RLR 60, 67–69.

[18] There is no suggestion in the cases that upon rescission the common law vests legal title in money in the rescinding party, in the same way that statute vests legal title to credit balances in a trustee in bankruptcy, in the manner discussed in *Trustee of the Property of FC Jones & Sons (a firm) v Jones* [1997] Ch 159 (CA).

IV. RESTITUTIO IN INTEGRUM

been on-sold, that onward sale should not itself bar rescission, if it can occur without disturbing the third party's title.

16.11 Rescission at common law is probably capable of conferring a right to assert legal title to traceable substitutes for the thing initially transferred.[19] In practice the case would have to be one involving a subsequent barter of identified chattels, or, if proprietary claims may be brought in respect of cash, a cash payment applied in purchasing identified chattels, or perhaps the identifiable cash proceeds of a cheque.[20]

C. Proprietary Claims upon Equitable Rescission

(1) Title passes pending rescission

16.12 Although the point was formerly the subject of some uncertainty, it is now settled that title to property passes at law and in equity under a voidable contract, and that a claim to recover title upon equitable rescission is properly described as an 'equity'[21] or 'mere equity'.[22] This is said to not be an interest in that property, or a chose in action,[23] but a personal right to recover title when rescission occurs.[24] The principle is that 'before rescission, the owner has no proprietary interest in the original property; all he has is the "mere equity" of his right to set aside the voidable contract'.[25]

---

[19] *Gladstone v Hadwen* (1813) 1 M & S 517, 526–27; 105 ER 193, 197; also, *Small v Attwood* (1832) You 407, 535–38; 159 ER 1051, 1103–04. See Chap 14, para [14.33].

[20] Assuming both that legal title could be claimed in the cash, and that equity's tracing rules may be relied upon.

[21] *Tottenham v Green* (1863) 32 LJ Ch (NS) 201; *Ernest v Vivian* (1864) 33 LJ Ch (NS) 513; *Cave v Cave* (1880) 15 ChD 639, 649; *Bainbrigge v Browne* (1881) 18 ChD 188, 197; *Cloutte v Storey* [1910] 1 ChD 18, 24; *National Provincial Bank Ltd v Ainsworth* [1965] AC 1175, 1254; *Bristol and West Building Society v Mothew* [1998] 1 Ch 1 (CA) 22–23; *Investors Compensation Scheme Ltd v West Bromwich Building Society* [1998] 1 WLR 896 (HL) 915, 916; *Barclays Bank v Boulter* [1999] 1 WLR 1919 (HL) 1925; *Twinsectra Limited v Yardley* [1999] Lloyd's Rep Bank 438 (CA) 461–62. Australia, *Fysh v Page* (1956) 96 CLR 233, 242; *Latec Investments Limited v Hotel Terrigal Pty Limited* (1965) 113 CLR 265, 277–78, 291 (cf 282, 284 where Taylor J expressed a preference for the term 'equitable interest'); *Greater Pacific Investments Pty Ltd v Australian National Industries Ltd* [1996] 39 NSWLR 143 (CA) 152–53.

[22] *Latec Investments Limited v Hotel Terrigal Pty Limited* (1965) 113 CLR 265, 277, 290; *Tutt v Doyle* (1997) 42 NSWLR 10 (CA) 15 (claim for reconveyance for unilateral mistake); *National Crime Agency v Robb* [2015] Ch 520, 531 [43], [44] (fraud); *Global Currency Exchange Network Limited v Osage 1 Limited* [2019] 1 WLR 5865, 5886 [74] (fraud); *Vale SA v Steinmetz* [2020] EWHC Comm 3051 [9](ii).

[23] '[A] chose in action is property, something capable of being turned into money ... a claim to rescission is a right of action but can in no way be described as a chose in action or part of a chose in action': *Investors Compensation Scheme Ltd v West Bromwich Building Society* [1998] 1 WLR 896 (HL) 915, 916. Cf *National Crime Agency v Robb* [2015] Ch 520, 539 [80] right or power to rescind for fraud 'was a property right (albeit not a legal or equitable interest)'.

[24] 'The equity to rescind is a personal right against the fraudster. It is established law that a party with an equity to rescind a contract does not have any proprietary interest in the property transferred under that contract': *In the matter of Crown Holdings (London) Limited (in liq)* [2015] EWHC 1876 (Ch) [38].

[25] *Twinsectra Limited v Yardley* [1999] Lloyd's Rep Bank 438 (CA) 461–62. See also *Lonrho plc v Fayed (No 2)* [1992] 1 WLR 1, 11–12; *El Ajou v Dollar Land Holdings plc* [1993] 3 All ER 717, 735; *Collings v Lee* [2001] 2 All ER 332 (CA) 335–36; *Barclays Bank plc v Boulter* [1999] 1 WLR 1919 (HL) 1925; *Shalson v Russo* [2005] Ch 281, 316, 320–21; *Independent Trustee Services Ltd v GP Noble Trustees Ltd* [2013] Ch 91 (CA) 128; *National Crime Agency v Robb* [2015] Ch 520, 531; *Global Currency Exchange Network Limited v Osage 1 Limited* [2019] 1 WLR 5865, 5886 [74]. Paragraph [16-12] of the second edition was cited with apparent approval in *In the matter of Crown Holdings (London) Limited (in liq)* [2015] EWHC 1876 (Ch) [39].

16.13 The same or a similar principle has been recognized in Australia,[26] New Zealand,[27] Canada,[28] Hong Kong,[29] and Jersey.[30]

16.14 United States literature contains a few suggestions that equity immediately and automatically imposes a constructive trust when property is transferred under a voidable transaction.[31] The term 'voidable', on this view, focuses on legal not equitable ownership.[32] Scholars have argued that English law is, or should be, the same in this respect.[33] These arguments have, however, not been accepted by the courts in England.[34]

16.15 Nor is there any convincing authority in favour of the immediate and automatic constructive trust approach in Australia or New Zealand, where the cases are rather to the contrary. In *Nolan v Minerva Trust Company Limited* the Royal Court of Jersey rejected a submission that a trust arose immediately where a contract was procured by fraudulent misrepresentation and held that Jersey law was the same as English law on this point.[35] It has also been said that Canadian law does not permit the imposition of a constructive trust while a valid, albeit voidable, contract remains on foot, because while it remains the contract is a 'juristic reason' for the enrichment that precludes proprietary restitution in this form.[36]

---

[26] *Alati v Kruger* (1955) 94 CLR 216, 224; *Fysh v Page* (1956) 96 CLR 233, 242; *Daly v Sydney Stock Exchange* (1985) 160 CLR 371, 387–89; *Cockburn v GIO Finance Ltd* (2001) 51 NSWLR 624 (CA) 634.
[27] *Estate Properties Ltd v Wignall* [1992] 2 NZLR 615, 631.
[28] *First Island Financial Services Ltd v Novastar Developments (Kelowna, Orchard Gardens) Ltd* (unreported, BCCA, 5 December 2000) (Southin JA, with whom the other members of the BCCA agreed).
[29] *Crown Master International Trading Co Ltd v China Solar Energy Holdings Ltd* [2015] 4 HKC 505 [58] (shares).
[30] *Nolan v Minerva Trust Company Limited* [2014] 2 JLR 117; JRC 078A [151] (investment fraud; claim for third party's alleged dishonest assistance in the fraudster's breach of a constructive trust).
[31] J Ames, 'Purchase for Value Without Notice' (1887) 1 Harv LR 1, 2: 'The equity of a defrauded vendor is no less an equitable estate than the interest of *cestui que trust* ... the fraudulent vendee is constantly called a constructive trustee', also, J Ames, 'The History of Trover' (1897) 11 Harv LR 374, 386; *Restatement (First) of Restitution* § 166 (1937): 'Where the owner of property transfers it, being induced by fraud, duress or undue influence of the transferee, the transferee holds the property upon a constructive trust for the transferor'. See also Reporter's Notes at 674–79. Cf the more general statement in *Restatement (Third) of Restitution* § 55(1) and cmts e and f (2011). It is difficult to find reliable guidance in contemporary American texts and cases, as to the proprietary consequences that follow when property is transferred under a contract procured by fraud or other ground permitting rescission, and it may be that the doctrine described by Ames and in the first *Restatement of Restitution* is no longer the law in the United States.
[32] PBH Birks, *Unjust Enrichment* (2nd edn, 2005) 184.
[33] G Elias, *Explaining Constructive Trusts* (1990) 66–67; R Chambers, *Resulting Trusts* (1997) chap 7. As to the fiduciary context, RC Nolan, 'Dispositions Involving Fiduciaries: The Equity to Rescind and the Resulting Trust' in P Birks and F Rose (eds), *Restitution and Equity* (2000) 146.
[34] See also S Worthington, 'The Proprietary Consequences of Rescission' [2002] 10 RLR 28.
[35] [2014] 2 JLR 117; JRC 078A [151]: '...it is not the law of Jersey that a constructive trust arises immediately if a contract has been procured by a fraudulent misrepresentation. On the contrary, the law of Jersey is, we conclude, the same as English law so that (save in the case of a Halley trust) a constructive trust will not arise out of a contract which has been procured by a fraudulent misrepresentation unless and until the contract has been rescinded.' For discussion of the 'Halley trust', Chap 1, paras [1.83]–[1.86].
[36] *Canadian Imperial Bank of Commerce v Melnitzer* (1993) 1 ETR (2d) 1, 35–36; aff'd (1997) 50 CBR (3d) 79 (Ont CA); *Royal Bank of Canada v Harowitz* (1994) 17 OR (3d) 671. Absence of juristic reason is one of the elements of a claim for a constructive trust in Canadian law. The reasoning in the cases cited implies that the proprietary interest conferred upon rescission is a remedial constructive trust, awarded at the court's discretion to reverse unjust enrichment, and in accordance with the principles governing the award of a constructive trust that have been developed by the Supreme Court of Canada. See also *American Reserve Energy Corp v McDorman* (2002) 117 ACWS (3d) 82 (Nfld and Labrador, CA); *Cherrington v Mayhew's Perma-Plants Ltd* (1990) 71 DLR (4th) 371 (BCCA) 377–78.

The 'equity' to rescind

16.16 The entitlement to a judgment directing that a voidable contract or gift be set aside is an 'equity' to rescind, in the sense that it is an entitlement to the equitable relief conferred by that judgment. Used in this sense, the term 'equity' connotes simply a claim to rescind.

16.17 But the term 'equity' is also used in a different sense, to describe the right to obtain a proprietary interest in specific assets upon rescission. Used in this sense, the term 'equity' is employed interchangeably with 'mere equity'.[37] That is a personal right of a particular kind. It is a right to obtain a proprietary interest in the future, and is therefore best described as a kind of 'power'.[38]

16.18 There is an ongoing debate in the literature as to what kind of 'power' the equity to rescind truly comprises.[39]

(2) Recovering title

16.19 If the equity to recover property on rescission is a power enabling the obtaining of a proprietary interest in the future, at what future point does that interest arise? There is, in this respect, a distinction between legal and equitable title, and as to equitable title, between cases where the innocent party obtains an equitable interest by electing to disaffirm the transaction, and when he does not. Legal and equitable title will be taken in turn.

---

[37] The 'mere equity' label that has been criticized as not capturing the proprietary indicia of a claim to rescind: *Latec Investments Limited v Hotel Terrigal Pty Limited* (1965) 113 CLR 265, 281, 284–85. There has also been criticism of any attempt to fit the equity to rescind into a 'rigid hierarchy' of equitable interests JD Heydon, MJ Leeming, and PG Turner, *Meagher, Gummow and Lehane's Equity Doctrines and Remedies* (5th edn, 2014) [4-180] (distinguishing personal and proprietary equities to rescind); cf M Neave and M Wienberg, 'The Nature and Function of Equities' (1978) 6 Uni of Tas LR 24. For further discussion of 'mere equities' see W Wade, 'Equitable Interests and "Mere Equities"' [1955] CLJ 158; R Megarry, 'Mere Equities, The Bona Fide Purchaser and the Deserted Wife' (1955) 71 LQR 480, 490–92; A Everton, '"Equitable Interests" and "Equities"—In Search of a Pattern' [1976] Conv 209; M Neave and M Wienberg, 'The Nature and Function of Equities' (1979) 6 Uni of Tas LR 115; V Annetta, 'Priority Rights in Insolvency—The Doctrinal Basis for Equity's Intervention' (1992) 20 Aust Bus LR 311, 316–17; D Skapinker, 'Equitable Interests, Mere Equities, "Personal" Equities and "Personal Equities"—Distinctions With a Difference' (1994) 68 ALJ 593; R Chambers, *Resulting Trusts* (1997) chap 7; D O'Sullivan, 'The Rule in *Phillips v Phillips*' (2002) 118 LQR 296; B Häcker, 'Proprietary Restitution after Impaired Consent Transfers: A Generalised Power Model' [2009] CLJ 324; M Balen, 'What is the Status of a Restitutionary Power to Revest Title in Insolvency' (2011) 22 KLJ 85; M Balen, 'Exploring Proprietary Restitution: The Relationship between Rescission and Insolvency' (2011) 22 KLJ 228; S Cooper & E Lees, 'Interests, Powers and Mere Equities in Modern Land Law' (2017) 37 OJLS 435; A Reilly, 'Is the "Mere Equity" to Rescind a Legal Power? Unpacking Hohfeld's Concept of "Volitional Control"' (2019) 39 OJLS 779; A Reilly, 'What were Lord Westbury's Intentions in *Phillips v Phillips*? Bona Fide Purchase of an Equitable Interest' (2021) 80 CLJ 156; J Wells, "What is a mere equity?: an investigation of the nature and function of so-called 'mere equities'" (unpublished PhD thesis, January 2019).

[38] PBH Birks, *Unjust Enrichment* (2nd edn, 2005) 299–300; KR Handley, *Estoppel by Conduct and Election* (2nd edn, 2016) 255; *National Crime Agency v Robb* [2015] Ch 520, 531 [44] ('the victim's power to rescind constitutes a "mere equity"'). Cf D Fox, *Property Rights in Money* (2008) [6.36]–[6.37] (preferring the term 'title' to 'power').

[39] B Häcker, 'Proprietary Restitution after Impaired Consent Transfers: A Generalised Power Model' [2009] CLJ 324; B Häcker, *Consequences of Impaired Consent Transfers* (2013) 129–30, developed 131–59, 163, 324 (power *in rem*); M Balen, 'What is the Status of a Restitutionary Power to Revest Title in Insolvency' (2011) 22 KLJ 85, 86–87; A Reilly, 'Is the "Mere Equity" to Rescind a Legal Power? Unpacking Hohfeld's Concept of "Volitional Control"' (2019) 39 OJLS 779, 804–05 (rejecting the analysis of Professor Häcker and arguing that an equity to rescind is not a vested power but merely a 'procedural power' in the nature of a 'transformative remedy', as described by R Zakrzewski, *Remedies Reclassified* (2015) 59, 151); S Zogg, *Proprietary Consequences in Defective Transfers of Ownership* (2020) 139, 178–80 (party entitled to rescind holds two distinct powers, one *in personam* to avoid the contract and a second *in rem* to revest ownership).

Legal title

16.20 Equitable rescission leads to recovery of legal title only pursuant to, and in accordance with, the terms of a court order for rescission.[40] This is to be contrasted with rescission at common law, where legal title is revested immediately once the transaction is disaffirmed.[41]

Equitable title

16.21 In most cases there is no point in time at which assets transferred under a transaction voidable in equity are capable of being impressed with a constructive trust, or other equitable proprietary interest. Before the order is made the party seeking to have the transaction set aside has a personal claim to recover the assets by means of a court order in his favour, and enjoys no equitable interest in the property.[42] Once an order for rescission is made, the right to the asset is to be ascertained in accordance with its terms, and the equity to rescind merges in the order. In this scenario, there is no point in time at which the rescinding party obtains an equitable interest in assets transferred. The position is perhaps different if the judgment for rescission contains no consequential order by which title is to be transferred to the rescinding party. If judgment in that form is entered, there is Australian authority that the order for rescission imposes, or recognizes, a constructive trust over property received by the party against whom rescission is granted.[43]

16.22 But it is different in those cases where the innocent party has a power to obtain an equitable title by electing to disaffirm. In this fact pattern an equitable title arises on and from the moment that the transaction is disaffirmed. A power to assert equitable title in this way is valuable, because it allows the rescinding party to obtain priority over subsequent equitable interests, which will defeat a mere equity to rescind,[44] and gives more secure rights in an insolvency.[45]

16.23 A power to revest equitable title by electing to disaffirm should, in principle, also confer more extensive rights against third parties who thereafter receive or deal with money or property that has been transferred under the contract. If the trust that follows an election to rescind supports a claim for knowing receipt or dishonest assistance,[46] those claims provide potentially valuable remedies against third parties who receive the subject matter of the contract or its traceable product with notice of the circumstances permitting rescission, or who dishonestly assist the contracting party to breach the trust that has arisen by dealing with that money or property adversely to the rescinding party. By contrast, those claims are not available against a third party who receives or deals with money or property that is the

---

[40] See Chap 15, paras [15.04]–[15.13].
[41] See Chap 14, paras [14.03]–[14.13].
[42] See para [16.12]. See also A Burrows, *A Restatement of the English Law of Unjust Enrichment* (2012) 162, arguing that rescission does not give rise to any 'interim trust' of property received by the counterparty, and instead has the effect of 'revesting rights' to property in the rescinding party.
[43] *Indian Farmers Fertiliser Cooperative Limited v Gutnick* [2015] VSC 724 [76] (decree of rescission in favour of purchaser of shares included no consequential order for legal title to the shares to be transferred to the fraudulent vendor; held that equitable title to shares revested by order for rescission; accepted on appeal as being 'unimpeachable' as a statement of principle: *Gutnick v Indian Farmers Fertiliser Cooperative Limited* (2016) 49 VR 732 (CA) [15]). Also, *Thomas v Arthur Hughes Pty Ltd* [2015] NSWSC 1027 [73] (declarations of constructive trust made in respect of securities and cash transferred by directors in breach of fiduciary duty).
[44] See Chap 21, para [21.69].
[45] See Chap 25, paras [25.05], [25.18].
[46] Paras [16.65]–[16.66] below.

subject of an unexercised claim to rescind, for the trust retrospectively arising following rescission is said to not create retrospective liability in those dealing with the subject matter of the contract.[47]

16.24 For the reasons that follow it appears that English law empowers the rescinding party to assert an equitable interest when he disaffirms whenever the contract has been induced by fraud. There is so far no good authority that the same right exists when rescission is available on other grounds. But this is a developing area of law, and it may be that the distinction between fraud and other grounds for rescinding will turn out to be more apparent than real. The principal authorities are considered next.

(3) When does disaffirmation confer an equitable interest?
Fraud

16.25 Disaffirming a voidable transaction confers an equitable interest in assets transferred if the transaction was procured by fraud. The key authorities are *Lonrho plc v Fayed (No 2)*[48] and *Shalson v Russo*,[49] behind both of which is the Australian case of *Alati v Kruger*.[50] In that case the High Court of Australia held as follows:

> Equity has always regarded as valid the disaffirmance of a contract induced by fraud even though precise *restitutio in integrum* is not possible, if ... it can do what is practically just between the parties, and by so doing restore them substantially to the *status quo* ... Rescission for misrepresentation is always the act of the party himself: *Reese River Silver Mining Co v Smith* (1869) LR 4 HL 64 at 73. The function of a court in which proceedings for rescission are taken is to adjudicate upon the validity of the purported disaffirmance as an act avoiding the transaction *ab initio*, and, if it is valid, to give effect to it and make appropriate consequential orders ... Of course a rescission which the common law courts would not accept as valid cannot of its own force revest the legal title to property which had passed, but if a court of equity would treat it as effectual the equitable title to such property revests upon the rescission.[51]

---

[47] *Lonrho plc v Fayed (No 2)* [1992] 1 WLR 1, 11, 12; *Bristol and West Building Society v Mothew* [1998] 1 Ch 1 (CA) 22–23; cf *Bank Tejarat v Hong Kong and Shanghai Bank* [1995] 1 Lloyd's Rep 239, 248.
[48] [1992] 1 WLR 1, 11–12.
[49] [2005] Ch 281, 320–22, discussed D Fox, *Property Rights in Money* (2008) [6.31].
[50] (1955) 94 CLR 216, 224. The reasoning in *Alati v Kruger* almost certainly shaped the analysis of Brennan J in *Daly v Sydney Stock Exchange Ltd* (1986) 160 CLR 371, 387–90, which was in turn endorsed by Millett J in *Lonrho plc v Fayed (No 2)* [1992] 1 WLR 1. But cf Australian authority, and also academic argument, in favour of the view that even in cases of fraud, beneficial title vests in the rescinding party only after an order for rescission is made: *Latec Investments Limited v Hotel Terrigal Pty Limited* (1965) 113 CLR 265, 290–91, cited with approval *Daly v Sydney Stock Exchange Ltd* (1985) 160 CLR 371, 389. See also *Latec Investments* at 278; *Svanasio v McNamara* (1956) 96 CLR 186, 197–98; *Breskvar v Wall* (1971) 126 CLR 376, 387; A Everton, '"Equitable Interests" and "Equities"—In Search of a Pattern' [1976] Conv 209, 214–15 (adopting the submissions of counsel in *Gresley v Mousley* (1859) 4 De G & J 78, 45 ER 31). See also *Gutnick v Indian Farmers Fertiliser Cooperative Limited* (2016) 49 VR 732 (CA) [15], [23], [25], [29] (equitable title to shares acquired by fraud revested by order declaring agreement rescinded).
[51] *Alati v Kruger* (1955) 94 CLR 216, 223–24. This passage was approved by the Court of Appeal in *O'Sullivan v Management Agency and Music Ltd* [1985] QB 428 (CA) 457 and more recently in *Independent Trustee Services Ltd v GP Noble Trustees Ltd* [2013] Ch 91 (CA) 117.

16.26 It seems from the context that the reference to equitable title revesting 'upon the rescission' refers to a rescission that follows an election to disaffirm, and that the High Court contemplated a rescinding party obtaining an equitable title to property transferred after he elected to rescind.[52]

16.27 In *Lonrho plc v Fayed (No 2)*[53] Millett J considered a submission that the vendor of shares could bring claims for breach of fiduciary duty against the buyer because the sale was voidable for fraud. In explaining why this submission was misconceived, Millett J said as follows:

> A contract obtained by fraudulent misrepresentation is voidable, not void, even in equity. The representee may elect to avoid it, but until he does so the representor is not a constructive trustee of the property transferred pursuant to the contract...: see *Daly v Sydney Stock Exchange Ltd* (1986) 160 CLR 371, 387–390, per Brennan J. It may well be that if the representee elects to avoid the contract and set aside a transfer of property made pursuant to it the beneficial interest in the property will be treated as having remained vested in him throughout, at least to the extent necessary to support a tracing claim. But the representee's election cannot retrospectively subject the representor to fiduciary obligations of the kind alleged ... Even after the representee has elected to avoid the contract and reclaim the property, the obligations of the representor would in my judgment be analogous to those of a vendor of property contracted to be sold, and would not extend beyond the property actually obtained by the contract and liable to be returned.[54]

Millett J seems here to indicate that an equitable title arises at the time the defrauded party elects to disaffirm the sale, and not when an order for rescission is made.

16.28 In *Shalson v Russo*[55] Rimer J held that advances procured by a sophisticated fraud became the legal and beneficial property of the payee company, and rejected the submission that the company automatically held the funds subject to a constructive trust. After reviewing the authorities, Rimer J went on to say as follows:

> There was no evidence satisfying me that Mr Mimran had unequivocally affirmed the loan contracts since discovering the frauds, and I accept that his issue of the Part 20 claims (the proprietary claims which are consistent only with an implied rescission) did evince a sufficient intention to rescind them.
>
> The question then arises as to the consequence of such rescission. I heard virtually no argument on this... However, I did understand Mr Smith's secondary position to be that, if it was necessary for him to rely on rescission, then rescission there had indeed been and its effect was to revest in Mr Mimran the title to the money he had been induced to advance to Westland, carrying with it a right to trace onwards.
>
> Rescission is an act of the parties which, when validly effected, entitles the party rescinding to be put in the position he would have been in if no contract had been entered into in the first place. It involves a giving and taking back on both sides... There is, however,

---

[52] The High Court's statements were made in the context of the purchase of a business procured by the vendor's fraud, and the reference to a revesting of equitable title referred to a divesting of title to property obtained by the defrauded party, not recovering title in property transferred by him. The reasoning must, however, apply *a fortiori* to such a case.
[53] [1992] 1 WLR 1.
[54] *Lonrho plc v Fayed (No 2)* [1992] 1 WLR 1, 11–12.
[55] [2005] Ch 281, 316, 320–21.

also a line of authorities supporting the proposition that, upon rescission of a contract for fraudulent misrepresentation, the beneficial title which passed to the representor under the contract revests in the representee. The representee then enjoys a sufficient proprietary title to trace, follow and recover what, by virtue of such revesting, can be regarded as having always been in equity his own property...

I hold, therefore, that upon the implied rescission of the loan contracts effected by bringing his Part 20 claim, Mr Mimran had revested in him the property in the money he advanced to Westland entitling him at least to trace it into assets into which it was subsequently applied.[56]

16.29 The claim to trace the proceeds of the loan into a large yacht failed on the facts, primarily because they had been paid into an overdrawn account.[57] Rimer J's reasons do make clear, however, that if an unbroken tracing chain could have been established, the defrauded lender would have had obtained a proprietary interest in the yacht from the moment that the loan was disaffirmed.[58] The Court of Appeal has subsequently approved this analysis. In *Independent Trustee Services Ltd v GP Noble Trustees Ltd* Patten LJ said that:

Rescission avoids the contract ab initio. In relation to assets transferred to the representor, the better view (encapsulated in the authorities reviewed by Rimer J in *Shalson v Russo*) is that title revests in the representee retrospectively once the election to rescind the contract is made.[59]

Grounds for rescission other than fraud

16.30 Outside cases of fraud there is no clear authority that an election to disaffirm will vest an equitable proprietary interest in money or property transferred. The cases are ambiguous. They betray an uncertainty as to whether a court order for rescission is needed before a proprietary interest can arise.

Principal authorities

16.31 The starting point is the reasoning of Brennan J in *Daly v Sydney Stock Exchange Ltd*,[60] which Millett J adopted in *Lonrho plc v Fayed (No 2)*.[61] Patrick Partners, a firm of stockbrokers on the brink of collapse, had obtained an investment loan from Dr Daly in breach of fiduciary duty. The firm later became insolvent. Dr Daly had assigned the deposits to his wife, who was entitled to compensation out of a stock exchange fidelity fund if the firm was a 'trustee' of the money he had invested within the meaning of the legislation regulating the fund. The firm was held not to be a trustee. In the course of his reasons, Brennan J (with whom Wilson J agreed) said as follows:

---

[56] *Shalson v Russo* [2005] Ch 281, 321, 324.
[57] *Shalson v Russo* [2005] Ch 281, 328–29.
[58] Although the point was not discussed in the judgment, it is apparent that the absence of any traceable proceeds would not have prevented the loan from being rescinded and Mr Mimran obtaining a personal claim to repayment as an incident of rescission.
[59] [2013] Ch 91 (CA) [53]. His Lordship's observations at [52] imply that the passage quoted was concerned with rescission for fraudulent misrepresentation.
[60] (1985) 160 CLR 371, 387–90.
[61] [1992] 1 WLR 1.

Irrespective of the fairness of its terms, equity regards a contract made between a fiduciary and the person to whom he stands in a fiduciary relationship as voidable if the fiduciary has breached his fiduciary duty in respect of the contract. If property is transferred to the fiduciary pursuant to the contract, the transfer may be set aside in consequence of avoiding the contract... The contract and the transfer are voidable, but not void. If the transfer is set aside, the fiduciary transferee (and, no doubt, a volunteer or a purchaser with notice of the circumstances) holds the property transferred on a constructive trust for the transferor which a court of equity will enforce subject to any accounts or inquiries that may be necessary to do equity to the transferee. The transferor may elect to avoid the contract and to assert his title to the land or other property transferred assuming it still exists in specie or, being money, can be traced.

The principles governing the setting aside of contracts of purchase or sale are applicable to contracts of loan...

It may be said that a party who elects to avoid a contract and set aside a transfer of property made pursuant to the contract had an equitable interest in the property from the beginning... and his equitable interest arose before, and does not depend upon the court's decree... If a decree setting aside the conveyance is made, the plaintiff's equitable title is treated 'as having been, from the first, a trustee for the grantor, who, therefore, has an equitable estate, not a mere right of suit'...

But where property has been sold and conveyed, the purchaser's beneficial title must be ascertained by reference to the sale so long as it stands; the vendor cannot insist on an equitable interest in the property if he does not choose to enforce his equity to avoid the sale... Similarly, until the lender elects to avoid the contract of loan, he cannot assert an equitable title to the money lent. He cannot at once leave the contract on foot and deny the borrowers the title to the money which the contract confers... the borrower cannot be made a trustee of the money without his consent so long as the contract stands...

In equity, Patrick Partners' title to the money lent was imperfect from the beginning by reason of their failure to discharge their duty as a fiduciary... and, had the contract of loan been avoided, Mrs Daly's rights as against Patrick Partners might have been determined as though the firm had from the beginning held the money lent on a constructive trust for Dr and then Mrs Daly... a beneficial title that is imperfect and liable to be divested by relation back in the event of avoidance of the contract of loan.[62]

16.32 Two points may be noted. First, Brennan J states that following rescission, a beneficial title might be deemed to have existed from the time the relevant transfer of property or money is made, so that it is 'imperfect and liable to be divested by relation back'. Secondly, it is unclear whether that title is said to come into being when the transaction is disaffirmed, or when an order for rescission is made. Support for both views can be found in the reasoning.[63]

---

[62] (1985) 160 CLR 371, 387–89.
[63] The phrase 'The transferor may elect to avoid the contract and to assert his title to the land or other property transferred assuming it still exists in specie or, being money, can be traced' suggests that the title might arise when an election is made. But the observation that 'If a decree setting aside the conveyance is made, the plaintiff's equitable title is treated "as having been, from the first, a trustee for the grantor, who, therefore, has an equitable estate, not a mere right of suit"' implies that no title arises until an order for rescission is made: (1985) 160 CLR 371, 387–89.

16.33 In *El Ajou v Dollar Land Holdings plc*, when discussing the effects of purchasing rather than selling shares under a contract voidable for fraud, Millett J said as follows:

> ... if the other victims of fraud can trace their money in equity it must be because, having been induced to purchase the shares by false and fraudulent misrepresentations, they are entitled to rescind the transaction and revest equitable title to the purchase money in themselves, at least to the extent necessary to support an equitable tracing claim: see *Daly v Sydney Stock Exchange Ltd* (1986) 160 CLR 371 at 387–390 per Brennan J. There is thus no distinction between their case and the plaintiffs. They can rescind the purchases for fraud ... But if this is correct, as I think it is, then the trust which is operating in these cases is not some new model remedial constructive trust, but an old-fashioned institutional resulting trust. This may be of relevance in relation to the degree of knowledge required on the part of a subsequent recipient to make him liable.[64]

16.34 This passage is neutral as to when the beneficial interest arises, but makes clear that it arises retrospectively for the purpose of maintaining a tracing claim. In *Bristol and West Building Society v Mothew*, a case of negligent misrepresentation, Millett LJ said as follows:

> The right to rescind for misrepresentation is an equity. Until it is exercised the beneficial interest in any property transferred in reliance on the representation remains vested in the transferee. In *El Ajou v Dollar Land Holdings plc* [1993] 3 All ER 717 at 734 I suggested that on rescission the equitable title might revest in the representee retrospectively at least to the extent necessary to support an equitable tracing claim. I was concerned to circumvent the supposed rule that there must be a fiduciary relationship or retained beneficial interest before resort may be had to the equitable tracing rules.[65]

16.35 Millett LJ here suggests that title to property revests retrospectively upon rescission for misrepresentation, but does not specify whether, to exercise the equity to rescind, the misrepresentee may simply elect to disaffirm, or must also obtain a court order. The analysis proposed by Millett LJ was endorsed by a unanimous Court of Appeal in *Twinsectra Limited v Yardley*:

> ... the distinction of importance here is that between non-consensual transfers and transfers pursuant to contracts which are voidable for misrepresentation. In the latter case, the transferor may elect whether to avoid or affirm the transaction and, until he elects to avoid it, there is no constructive (resulting) trust; in the former case, the constructive trust arises on the moment of transfer. The result, so far as third parties are concerned, is that, before rescission, the owner has no proprietary interest in the original property; all he has is the 'mere equity' of his right to set aside the voidable contract. That equity binds volunteers and those taking with notice of the equity, but not purchasers for value without notice ... the general position seems to me that summarised in Underhill and Hayton (15th ed at p 372(f)). It is there stated that equity imposes a constructive trust on property where a transferor's legal and equitable title in his property has passed to the transferee according to basic principles of property law but in circumstances (eg involving fraud and misrepresentation) where the transferor has an equitable right (ie mere equity) to recover the

---

[64] *El Ajou v Dollar Land Holdings plc* [1993] 3 All ER 717, 734. This passage was not doubted on appeal: [1994] 2 All ER 685 (CA).
[65] [1998] 1 Ch 1 (CA) 22–23.

property by having the transfer set aside, and the court declares that from the outset the transferee has held the property to the transferor's order, though nowadays it seems better to regard a restitutionary resulting trust as arising.[66]

16.36 This reasoning also indicates that title to property revests retrospectively, 'from the outset', upon rescission for misrepresentation. However, the Court of Appeal does not make clear when beneficial title revests. The second quoted sentence implies that this occurs when the transferor 'elects to avoid' the transaction; the last sentence indicates that it revests when the party misled obtains relief from the court.[67]

Confusion

16.37 This uncertainty as to when equitable title revests tends to create confusion. The potential problems are illustrated by the Australian case of *Handcock Family Memorial Foundation Ltd v Porteous*,[68] which concerned, among other things, the availability of proprietary claims over assets said to be the traceable proceeds of loans obtained in breach of fiduciary duty. The court first cited the analysis of the New South Wales Court of Appeal in *Greater Pacific Investments Pty Ltd v Australian National Industries Ltd*, where the lack of certainty as to when equitable title revests was made explicit:

> In general, where there is a contract for the sale of property by A to B made in breach of fiduciary duty owed to A by B ... pursuant to which legal title to the property has been transferred from A to B, the transaction is in equity voidable at the instance of A, who may (if necessary) obtain an order for rescission setting it aside. Unless and until A effectively avoids the transaction and (if necessary) obtains an order for rescission, B's property rights as a result of the transaction remain unaffected. However if A does effectively avoid the transaction and (if necessary) obtain an order for rescission, the parties will be treated in equity as if the transaction had never been effected; in other words equity will treat B as if he had held the property in trust for A, that is, as a constructive trustee, ab initio. A constructive trust arises in such circumstances as a consequence of the effective avoidance or rescission of the transaction. Where, for whatever reason, the transaction has not been and cannot be effectively avoided and rescission is unavailable, it remains effective and no constructive trust can arise: see generally *Daly v Sydney Stock Exchange* (1986) 160 CLR 371 at 386–390, per Brennan J.[69]

16.38 After referring to this passage, the court in *Porteous* held that an order for rescission was required 'where a party to the proceedings disputes the effectiveness of the rescission alleged, or where third parties' interests are involved', and because that was the present case, 'before any constructive trust could be declared, it was essential for the appellants to seek and obtain orders for the rescission of the contracts of loan'.[70] But this is confused. As a matter of

---

[66] [1999] Lloyd's Rep Bank 438 (CA) 461–62. This aspect of the decision was not reviewed by the House of Lords on appeal: [2002] 2 AC 164.
[67] The decision in *Independent Trustee Services Ltd v GP Noble Trustees Ltd* [2013] Ch 91 (CA) [53] emphasized the first of these two alternatives. Patten LJ there said that the better view 'is that title revests in the representee retrospectively once the election to rescind the contract is made' before going on to quote *Twinsectra* at [53] (extracted earlier at para [16.35]); see also [55], [58].
[68] (2000) WAR 198 (Full Ct).
[69] *Greater Pacific Investments Pty Ltd v Australian National Industries Ltd* (1996) 39 NSWLR 143 (CA) 153.
[70] *Handcock Family Memorial Foundation Ltd v Porteous* (2000) WAR 198 (Full Ct) 217. See also *LHK Nominees Pty Ltd v Kenworthy* [2001] WASC 205.

IV. RESTITUTIO IN INTEGRUM

principle the entitlement to obtain a beneficial interest without a court order cannot depend on either the attitude of the counter-party to the transaction, or whether third party rights are involved. For any given ground of rescission the right must be exercisable by an election to disaffirm, or only arise upon a court order, and its priority as against adverse third party claims determined in accordance with the established priority rules.

Resolving the uncertainty

16.39   The law in this area is uncertain and in need of reappraisal.[71] There is, however, no obviously attractive solution. The right to obtain a vested equitable interest by electing to rescind confers real advantages whilst exposing third parties to more extensive liability.[72] A rule that confines this right to cases of fraud may be supported on the ground that the victims of fraud are particularly deserving of protection. On the other hand, it is well arguable that the victims of other conduct that permits rescission are equally deserving of such protection; for example, those contracting by reason of duress or actual undue influence.

16.40   It is suggested that there is no clear answer as a matter of principle or policy, and that in those circumstances the law should adopt the simplest solution consistent with the whole of the authorities, and which least prejudices innocent third parties. The law should therefore provide that where a transaction is voidable in equity but not at law, the act of electing to rescind confers a proprietary interest only where fraud is involved. In all other cases, a court order must be obtained before a vested proprietary interest can arise. A different view has, however, been expressed by Birke Häcker and other scholars, who argue that the law should always permit a rescinding claimant to obtain a proprietary interest in money or property transferred as from the moment the transaction is disaffirmed, irrespective of the ground for rescission.[73] Other scholars have endorsed a third model, in which the law recognizes a personal right in the rescinding party to recover property when a decree for rescission is made, without a trust arising at an earlier point in time.[74]

(4) Retrospective equitable title

16.41   The cases emphasize that once rescission occurs, equitable title is to be regarded as having been vested in the rescinding party from the outset, when ownership was first transferred.[75]

---

[71] It has been described as being 'not an easy area of law' that 'remains in a state of flux': *The Bell Group Ltd (in liq) v Westpac Banking Corporation* (2008) 70 ACSR 1 [4801] and see [4797] (identifying different points in time at which 'the equity recognized by the imposition of a constructive trust' might arise when a transaction is set aside for breach of fiduciary duty). The uncertainty is discussed in A Burrows, *A Restatement of the English Law of Unjust Enrichment* (2012) 161–62.

[72] See paras [16.22], [16.23].

[73] B Häcker, 'Proprietary Restitution after Impaired Consent Transfers: A Generalised Power Model' (2009) CLJ 324, 325, 359–60. Also, M Balen, 'Exploring Proprietary Restitution: The Relationship between Rescission and Insolvency' (2011) 22 KLJ 228, 236–37 and E Bant, 'Reconsidering the Role of Election in Rescission' (2012) 32 OJLS 467.

[74] A Burrows, *A Restatement of the English Law of Unjust Enrichment* (2012) 161–62; also, J O'Sullivan, 'Rescission as a Self Help Remedy: A Critical Analysis' [2000] 59 CLJ 509. See also A Lodder, *Enrichment in the Law of Unjust Enrichment and Restitution* (2012) 133–34; N Skead, 'Undue Influence and the Remedial Constructive Trust' (2008) 2 *Journal of Equity* 143, 153–54; Chap 11, Part D, esp [11.108]–[11.109]. The American approach, of recognizing that a trust arises as from the time that title passes under a voidable transaction, has not been adopted by English law: see paras [16.12]–[16.15].

[75] See paras [16.27]–[16.37], also *Caldicott v Richards* [2020] EWHC 767 (Ch) [109].

This has been said to follow the rescission of a contract for fraud,[76] non-fraudulent misrepresentation,[77] breach of fiduciary duty,[78] and even mistake,[79] and the rule appears to be a general one.[80] Voidable gifts probably follow the same pattern.[81]

Retrospective title confers a right to trace
Beneficial title is deemed to revest retrospectively for the purpose of allowing the rescinding   16.42
party to bring a tracing claim.[82] In *Bristol and West Building Society v Mothew*[83] Millett LJ made clear that the concept of retrospective beneficial title is intended to reconcile the right to trace upon rescission with the requirement that there be a retained beneficial interest. The law ought, however, to recognize that an unexercised equity to recover property on rescission may itself be traced.[84] Introducing a fictional retrospective title seems unnecessary.[85] An unexercised claim to recover property on rescission has so many proprietary features that it should be capable of being traced.[86] In particular, it is enforceable against any subsequent transferee of the property who gives no value or takes with notice,[87] descends upon death by operation of law,[88] and may be devised,[89] and also passes by conveyance[90] and assignment.[91] The inchoate interest that exists should be capable of being traced for so

---

[76] *Lonrho plc v Fayed (No 2)* [1992] 1 WLR 1, 11–12; *El Ajou v Dollar Land Holdings plc* [1993] 3 All ER 717, 735; *Shalson v Russo* [2005] Ch 281, 320–22; see also *Halifax Building Society v Thomas* [1996] Ch 217 (CA) 226.

[77] *Bristol and West Building Society v Mothew* [1998] 1 Ch 1 (CA) 22–23; *Twinsectra Limited v Yardley* [1999] Lloyd's Rep Bank 438 (CA) 461–62.

[78] *Daly v Sydney Stock Exchange* (1985) 160 CLR 371, 387–90, apparently endorsed on this point in England in the *Lonrho* and *El Ajou* cases. See also *Greater Pacific Investments Pty Ltd v Australian National Industries Ltd* (1996) 39 NSWLR 143 (CA) 153.

[79] *Bainbridge v Bainbridge* [2016] WTLR 898 (Ch) [30]–[32] (retrospective revesting of title permitting a tracing claim also available in the case of a trust deed rescinded for unilateral mistake).

[80] It appears to have been so treated in *Independent Trustee Services Ltd v GP Noble Trustees Ltd* [2013] Ch 91 (CA) [53].

[81] *Pesticcio v Huet* (2003) 73 BMLR 57 [134].

[82] See paras [16.25]–[16.33].

[83] [1998] 1 Ch 1 (CA) 22–23.

[84] Cf *Estate Properties Ltd v Wignall* [1992] 2 NZLR 615, 631 where a personal claim to traceable substitutes was permitted upon rescission without reference to a retrospective title. See also RC Nolan, 'Dispositions Involving Fiduciaries: The Equity to Rescind and the Resulting Trust' in P Birks and F Rose (eds), *Restitution and Equity* (2000) 131; D Fox, *Property Rights in Money* (2008) [6.58]. For an extended defence of the proposition that an unexercised power to recover property upon rescission is capable of being traced, B Häcker, *Consequences of Impaired Consent Transfers* (2013) 289–94, 320; also, S Zogg, *Proprietary Consequences in Defective Transfers of Ownership* (2020) 184–86. Contrast S Worthington, 'The Proprietary Consequences of Rescission' [2002] 10 RLR 28, 59–60.

[85] It has been also said to create a risk of confusion, and to complicate analysis: D Fox, *Property Rights in Money* (2008) [6.58].

[86] Cf *American Sugar Refining Co v Fancher* NE 206, 208–09 (1895), where a tracing claim was permitted by reference to *Small v Attwood* (1832) You 407, 535–38; 159 ER 1051, 1103–04 without invoking the notion of a retrospective equitable title, albeit in a jurisdiction that has not adopted the English notion that full beneficial title passes under a contract procured by fraud. Also, B Häcker, *Consequences of Impaired Consent Transfers* (2013) 289–90.

[87] *Twinsectra Limited v Yardley* [1999] Lloyd's Rep Bank 438 (CA) 461–62; *Daly v Sydney Stock Exchange* (1985) 160 CLR 371, 388; volunteers: *Gould v Okeden* (1731) 4 Brown 198, 2 ER 135; *Small v Attwood* (1832) You 407, 535–38; 159 ER 1051, 1103–04 (rev'd on other grounds *Attwood v Small* (1838) 6 Cl & Fin 232, 7 ER 684); *Charter v Trevelyan* (1842, 1844) 11 Cl & Fin 714, 8 ER 1273; *Vane v Vane* (1873) 8 Ch App 383, 397; notice: *Dunbar v Tredennick* (1813) 1 Ball & Beatty 304, 318–19; *Addis v Campbell* (1841) 4 Beav 401, 49 ER 394.

[88] *Charter v Trevelyan* (1842, 1844) 11 Cl & Fin 714, 8 ER 1273; *Clark v Malpas* (1862) 31 Beav 80, 54 ER 1067; aff'd 4 De GF & J 401, 45 ER 1238.

[89] *Stump v Gaby* (1852) 2 De M & G 623, 42 ER 1015; *Gresley v Mousley* (1859) 4 De G & J 78, 45 ER 31; *Allcard v Skinner* (1887) LR 36 ChD 145 (CA) 187; see also *Re Sherman dec'd* [1954] 1 Ch 653.

[90] Conveyance of estate following voidable sale or other disposition of it: *Earl of Ardglase v Muschamp* (1684) 1 Vern 237, 23 ER 43; *Dickinson v Burrell* (1866) 1 Eq Cas 337, 342–43; *Melbourne Banking Corporation Ltd v Brougham* (1882) 8 App Cas 307, 311; *Fitzroy v Cave* [1905] 2 KB 364 (CA) 371; *Investors Compensation Scheme Ltd v West Bromwich Building Society* [1998] 1 WLR 896 (HL) 916.

[91] *Daly v Sydney Stock Exchange* (1985) 160 CLR 371 (assignment of benefit of voidable loan).

long as the equity to rescind persists, and should cease to be traceable only once the right to rescind is lost.

16.43 In *National Crime Agency v Robb* it was held that the rule in *Re Hallett's Estate* was to be applied when tracing funds paid under a transaction later rescinded.[92]

Retrospective title creates no retrospective liability

16.44 In *Lonrho plc v Fayed (No 2)*[93] Millett J emphasized that the beneficial title arising on the rescission of a contract for fraud cannot retrospectively impose fiduciary obligations, and in *Bristol and West Building Society v Mothew*, in the context of misrepresentation, he said that:

> Whether or not there is retrospective vesting for tracing purposes it is clear that on rescission the equitable title does not revest retrospectively *so as to cause an application of trust money which was properly authorised when made to afterwards be treated as a breach of trust*.[94]

Whilst formerly the Australian approach to rescission at common law provided that once legal title is regained all intermediate possessors become retrospectively liable for conversion,[95] this has since been disapproved.[96] It is only possession after title is revested that can generate a liability in conversion.[97]

(5) Proprietary claims in respect of money paid
Claim is generally to traceable substitute

16.45 Although the cases speak of equitable title to money 'revesting' upon rescission,[98] there is no real sense in which equitable title to money revests, as occurs when property is transferred. Rather, title vests in the rescinding party for the first time. Claims to money paid upon rescission are invariably claims to traceable substitutes because of the way in which contractual payments are made. The usual method is by the transfer of funds between bank accounts pursuant to a cheque, credit card or electronic funds transfer, or in the commercial sphere, by letter of credit or other documentary credit. But unlike the situation where property is transferred or cash paid over, in this situation no interest in any *res* is transferred.[99]

---

[92] [2015] Ch 520, 534 [58]. In the circumstances of that case the rule was applied also to payments on behalf of persons who had not elected to rescind: at [75], [76].
[93] [1992] 1 WLR 1, 11, 12.
[94] [1998] 1 Ch 1 (CA) 22-23 (emphasis in original), approved *Independent Trustee Services Ltd v GP Noble Trustees Ltd* [2013] Ch 91 (CA) [67], and see also at [76], [81]; also, *Nasrulla v Rashid* [2020] Ch 37 [53]. Also, D Fox, *Property Rights in Money* (2008) [6.63]. This view is consistent with *Bank Tejarat v Hong Kong and Shanghai Bank* [1995] 1 Lloyd's Rep 239, 248. The trust there relied upon to found a claim for knowing assistance, in respect of the period *before* the fraud was discovered, was based upon an equitable title that it was conceded—perhaps wrongly—arose by reason of the fact that the claimant's payment was made by operative mistake. Tuckey J's reference to the claimant being able to revest equitable title upon rescission for the customer's fraud (at 248) was confined to the separate question of tracing.
[95] *Hunter BNZ Finance Ltd v CG Maloney Pty Ltd* (1988) 18 NSWLR 420, 439; app'd *Orix Australia Corporation Ltd v M Wright Hotel Refrigeration Pty Ltd* (2000) 15 FLR 267, 272-73.
[96] *Perpetual Trustees Australia Ltd v Heperu Pty Ltd* (2009) 76 NSWLR 195 (CA) 212-14 (cheque fraud).
[97] *Perpetual Trustees Australia Ltd v Heperu Pty Ltd* (2009) 76 NSWLR 195 (CA).
[98] *El Ajou v Dollar Land Holdings plc* [1993] 3 All ER 717, 734; *Bank Tejarat v Hong Kong and Shanghai Bank* [1995] 1 Lloyd's Rep 239, 248; *Shalson v Russo* [2005] Ch 281, 324.
[99] *R v Preddy* [1996] AC 815, 834-35, 841.

There is simply a correspondence between a debit to the payer's account and a credit to the payee's. The only property in respect of which a proprietary interest can arise is the chose in action represented by the new or increased credit balance in the payee's bank account.[100] That is a new asset in which the rescinding payer necessarily had no proprietary interest before rescission. There can be no revesting of equitable title in such an asset. The claim is to title in a new asset.[101]

The result is the same when cash is paid into a bank account pursuant to a voidable transaction. Again, any proprietary claim arising is in respect of a new asset. If cash is paid and mixed with other cash, there too a new asset arises. This is the mixture of cash held by the payee. 16.46

A true revesting of equitable title to money only occurs when payment is made in cash, and the specific notes and coins paid over are identifiable in the payee's hands. In this case, upon rescission, the payee might be compelled to hold the very notes and coins received on trust for the payer. Save in this rare situation, a proprietary claim in respect of money paid under a rescinded transaction is always a claim to a new and substitute asset.[102] 16.47

Nature of the interest
The authorities provide limited guidance as to whether the interest in money arising upon rescission consists of beneficial ownership, a charge, or an equitable lien. In principle a pro-rata beneficial ownership should be obtained, for the interest asserted by the rescinding party appears to be in the nature of a constructive trust.[103] There is Australian authority that the extent of the proprietary interest is at the discretion of the court,[104] but this is unsatisfactory and does not represent English law.[105] Special rules apply where a partner rescinds the partnership agreement for fraud or misrepresentation; by statute, a lien is given in respect of certain sums contributed to the partnership.[106] 16.48

When rescission confers a proprietary claim to money
The grounds for rescission that confer a proprietary claim in respect of money are surprisingly unclear. It might be thought that in principle there is no reason to distinguish between the different grounds for rescission, and that there should be one rule for all. But to date the authorities only clearly recognize the right in cases of fraud, and for the reasons explained later in this chapter, it is suggested that the right should be expanded with care. 16.49

The discussion that follows excludes Canadian law, because there the right to assert a proprietary claim to money upon rescission appears to depend not on the ground for rescinding, 16.50

---

[100] There is no traceable asset if the payment is made into an overdrawn account not thereby placed in credit: eg *Shalson v Russo* [2005] Ch 281, 328.
[101] Also, *Vale SA v Steinmetz* [2020] EWHC Comm 3051 [9](iv); S Zogg, *Proprietary Consequences in Defective Transfers of Ownership* (2020) 511.
[102] See also, D Fox, *Property Rights in Money* (2008) [6.44].
[103] See paras [16.60]–[16.61].
[104] *Robins v Incentive Dynamics Pty Ltd* (2003) 175 FLR 286 (NSWCA) 301.
[105] *Vale v Steinmetz* [2020] EWHC Comm 3051 [22]–[23]; *Angove's Pty Ltd v Bailey* [2016] 1 WLR 3179 (Sup Ct) 3191 [27]; paras [16.65]–[16.68] below.
[106] Partnership Act 1890, s 41 (rescinding partner is entitled to a lien on or right of retention of surplus partnership assets after satisfying partnership liabilities, for any sum paid to purchase a share in the partnership and any capital contributed, together with certain rights of subrogation and indemnity). In conferring a right of lien, the 1890 Act followed *Mycock v Beatson* (1879) 13 ChD 384.

Fraud

16.51 A series of English cases indicate that a proprietary claim is available when a payment transaction is set aside for fraud.[108] There is also Australian authority to that effect.[109]

Breach of fiduciary duty

16.52 **Australia and New Zealand** In Australia and New Zealand a proprietary claim to money is conferred upon rescission for breach of fiduciary duty. The leading Australian authority is the judgment of Brennan J in *Daly v Sydney Stock Exchange*.[110] In the New Zealand case of *Estate Properties Ltd v Wignall*[111] Tipping J set aside a purchase of shares for breach of fiduciary duty and declared that the fiduciary purchaser held the proceeds of their sale on constructive trust for his vendor principal, and his reasons indicate that the result would have been the same had money rather than shares been transferred.[112]

16.53 **England and Wales** The English authorities are less clear. Brennan J's analysis in *Daly v Sydney Stock Exchange*[113] has been cited with approval in relation to rescission for fraud, but without specifically endorsing its application in a case of breach of fiduciary duty.[114] In *Guinness plc v Saunders* Lord Goff rejected the submission that a constructive trust could be imposed in respect of sums paid under a contract voidable for breach of fiduciary duty, saying:

> ... the money was on this approach paid not under a void, but under a voidable, contract. Under such a contract, the property and the money would have vested in Mr Ward (who, I repeat, was ex hypothesi acting in good faith); and Guinness cannot short-circuit an unrescinded contract simply by alleging a constructive trust.[115]

16.54 Lord Goff did not also say that upon the rescission of the contract posited, Guinness could in fact have asserted a constructive trust, and it is not obvious whether that was implicit. It

---

[107] *Canadian Imperial Bank of Commerce v Melnitzer* (1993) 1 ETR (2d) 1, 35–36; aff'd (1997) 50 CBR (3d) 79 (Ont CA).
[108] *El Ajou v Dollar Land Holdings plc* [1993] 3 All ER 717, 734; *Bank Tejarat v Hong Kong and Shanghai Bank* [1995] 1 Lloyd's Rep 239, 248; *Halifax Building Society v Thomas* [1996] Ch 217 (CA) 226 (discussed in PBH Birks, 'The Proceeds of Mortgage Fraud' (1996) 10 TLI 2, 3); *Shalson v Russo* [2005] Ch 281, 320–22; *Independent Trustee Services Ltd v GP Noble Trustees Ltd* [2013] Ch 91 (CA) 116–17; *National Crime Agency v Robb* [2015] Ch 520, 531–32; *Global Currency Exchange Network Limited v Osage 1 Limited* [2019] 1 WLR 5865, 5876–77, 5880; *Vale SA v Steinmetz* [2020] EWHC Comm 3051 [9](ii); and see D Fox, *Property Rights in Money* (2008) [6.38].
[109] *Westpac Banking Corp v Markovic* (1985) 82 FLR 7. Although in *Olympic Airways v Alysandratos* [1999] VSC 244 the court rejected a submission that sums paid under a contract rescinded for fraud were held on constructive trust, that decision is contrary to the trend of Australian authority, set out in the decisions referred to in Chap 1, para [1.93].
[110] (1985) 160 CLR 371, 388–90. See also *Handcock Family Memorial Foundation Ltd v Porteous* (2000) 22 WAR 198 (Full Ct) 214, 220; *Robins v Incentive Dynamics Pty Ltd* (2003) 175 FLR 286 (NSWCA) 301.
[111] [1992] 2 NZLR 615.
[112] *Estate Properties Ltd v Wignall* [1992] 2 NZLR 615, 631.
[113] (1985) 160 CLR 371, 388–90.
[114] *El Ajou v Dollar Land Holdings plc* [1993] 3 All ER 717, 734 (Millett J).
[115] *Guinness plc v Saunders* [1990] 2 AC 663, 698.

is suggested that, as a matter of principle, a proprietary interest should be available in such cases.

Bribes
The position is different if all or part of the price paid under a contract is in the nature of a bribe or secret commission. Where that is the case equity imposes a constructive trust from the time the sums are received, and the principal is not required to rescind in order to assert a proprietary interest in the traceable proceeds of the payment.[116]

16.55

Other grounds for rescission
Authority can be found against[117] and in support of[118] the availability of a proprietary claim to money following rescission for causes that do not involve any fraud or breach of fiduciary duty. But the weight of authority is against a blanket rule in favour of proprietary claims. In particular, in the vast majority of reported cases the rescinding party's right was to repayment of an equivalent sum, and there was no suggestion that a proprietary claim also existed. So, in the common case of a completed sale rescinded by the purchaser, the seller must repay the price received plus interest, and no mention is made of any proprietary claim. This is the consistent pattern in the reported cases. Examples include purchases of a professional practice,[119] business,[120] shares[121] and land,[122] and into a partnership,[123] and the same approach is displayed in relation to the rescission of payment transactions that do not involve a purchase.[124] The inference is that the claim to repayment was thought to be wholly personal.

16.56

More recently, in *Global Currency Exchange Network Limited v Osage 1 Limited* Andrew Henshaw QC, sitting as a Judge of the High Court, cited with apparent approval a passage from *Lewin on Trusts* in which the learned authors stated that '[i]t is the element of fraud which causes equity to impose a constructive trust in such circumstances, and so there is no trust when a contract is rescinded for a non-fraudulent misrepresentation'.[125]

16.57

---

[116] *Daraydan Holdings Ltd v Solland International Ltd* [2005] Ch 119, 137–40 (proprietary claims permitted in respect of bribes built into the price of completed contracts not sought to be rescinded).
[117] *Re Goldcorp Exchange* [1995] 1 AC 74 (PC—NZ) 102. See also *Westdeutsche Landesbank Girozentrale v Islington London Borough Council* [1996] AC 669.
[118] *West Sussex Properties Ltd v Chichester District Council* [2000] EWCA Civ 205 [34]–[35]. See also *Bristol and West Building Society v Mothew* [1998] 1 Ch 1 (CA) 22–23 (Millett LJ); *Bainbridge v Bainbridge* [2016] WTLR 898 (Ch) [32] (authorities concerning fraud extended to trust deed set aside for unilateral mistake).
[119] *Redgrave v Hurd* (1881) 20 ChD 1 (CA) (solicitor's practice; deposit repayable).
[120] *Kramer v McMahon* [1970] 1 NSWLR 194 (bakery; price minus deductions repayable).
[121] *Kent v Freehold Land and Brickmaking Company* (1867) LR 4 Eq Ca 588, 601; *Capel and Co v Sim's Ships Composition Company* (1888) 58 LT (NS) 807, 810 col 2; *Karberg's case* [1892] 3 ChD 1 (CA); *Re Australian Slate Quarries* (1930) 31 St Rep NSW 1, 4.
[122] *Edwards v M'Leay* (1815) Coop 311, 35 ER 568; aff'd (1818) 2 Swans 287, 36 ER 625; *Berry v Armistead* (1836) 2 Keen 221, 48 ER 613; *Wilson v Brisbane City Council* [1931] St R Qd 360, 379.
[123] *Rawlins v Wickham* (1858) 1 Giff 355, 65 ER 954; (1858) 3 De G & J 304, 42 ER 1285 (country banking partnership; net payments repayable); *Newbigging v Adam* (Bacon VC, 5 May 1886); aff'd (1886) 34 ChD 582 (CA); varied (1888) 13 App Cas 308 (partnership for manufacturing textiles; net payments repayable).
[124] *Dyer v Tymewell* (1689) 2 Vern 123, 23 ER 688 (bill of exchange extorted from drawer, the payee ordered to repay the £50 received with interest); *Compagnie Chemin de Fer Paris-Orleans v Leeston Shipping Company (Limited)* [1919] 1 Lloyd's Rep 235, 239 (hire of vessel); rescinded gifts of money: *Booth v Warrington* (1714) 4 Brown 164, 2 ER 111; *Bridgeman v Green* (1755) 2 Ves Sen 627, 627, 629; 28 ER 399, 399, 401; aff'd (1755) Wilm 58, 97 ER 22 (HL); *Re Glubb* [1900] 1 ChD 354 (CA) 361–62.
[125] [2019] 1 WLR 5865, 5876 [40], citing *Lewin on Trusts* 19th edn [7.030] (although the allegation in that case was one of fraud).

16.58 The restrictive view is to be preferred as a matter of policy. It is usually when the payee becomes insolvent or bankrupt that it matters whether a proprietary claim is available. But that the payee is guilty of conduct permitting rescission is not a sufficient reason for preferring the claims of the rescinding payer over unpaid trade and other unsecured creditors; the risk of insolvency should be allocated equally between these various parties.[126] Cases involving fraud, breach of fiduciary duty and bribery are to be regarded as exceptional, and justified by policy considerations that do not apply to the other grounds for rescission.

(6) Nature of the proprietary interest arising upon equitable rescission

Prospective and retrospective interests

16.59 It has been seen that, somewhat confusingly, the law recognizes two different kinds of proprietary interest upon equitable rescission. The first arises prospectively in response to an election to rescind for fraud.[127] The second arises retrospectively once a contract or gift transferring property is set aside by court order, irrespective of the ground for rescission.[128] Whilst the interest arising when an election is made is a real interest, the retrospective interest is entirely fictional, not least because before the order was made the transferor enjoyed a purely personal claim, and afterwards his claim to the relevant assets merges in the court's order.[129] There is therefore no point at which the transferor could in fact have held the relevant assets on trust.[130]

Description of interest

16.60 There is no agreed label for the proprietary interest that arises upon equitable rescission; and the nomenclature has bloomed. The interest has been variously described as an 'equitable interest',[131] an 'equitable estate'[132] and a 'beneficial interest',[133] and also as 'equitable title',[134] a 'constructive trust',[135] and 'not some new model remedial constructive trust, but an old-fashioned institutional resulting trust'.[136] The interest has also been called a 'remedial constructive trust',[137] 'a constructive (resulting) trust',[138] 'restitutionary resulting trust',[139]

---

[126] R Goode, 'Ownership and Obligation in Commercial Transactions' (1987) 103 LQR 433, 438–41, 444, 460 (and cf also *Angove's Pty Ltd v Bailey* [2016] 1 WLR 3179 (Sup Ct) 3191, citing Goode's analysis with approval). However, this argument would favour confining the rescinding vendor to a personal claim, but in fact he has a proprietary one.

[127] See paras [16.26]–[16.30].

[128] See para [16.41].

[129] See para [16.21].

[130] But cf the recognition in Australia that an order for rescission unaccompanied by an order for restitution will give rise to a constructive trust of assets transferred under the contract: para [16.21] above.

[131] *Latec Investments Limited v Hotel Terrigal Pty Limited* (1965) 113 CLR 265, 277–78, 291.

[132] *Latec Investments Limited v Hotel Terrigal Pty Limited* (1965) 113 CLR 265, 291.

[133] *Lonrho plc v Fayed (No 2)* [1992] 1 WLR 1, 12.

[134] *Alati v Kruger* (1955) 94 CLR 216, 224; *Twinsectra Limited v Yardley* [1999] Lloyd's Rep Bank 438 (CA) 461–62.

[135] *Daly v Sydney Stock Exchange Ltd* (1985) 160 CLR 371, 387–90; *Greater Pacific Investments Pty Ltd v Australian National Industries Ltd* (1996) 39 NSWLR 143 (CA) 153; *Estate Properties Ltd v Wignall* [1992] 2 NZLR 615, 631.

[136] *El Ajou v Dollar Land Holdings plc* [1993] 3 All ER 717, 734.

[137] *Robins v Incentive Dynamics Pty Ltd* (2003) 175 FLR 286 (NSWCA) 301.

[138] *Twinsectra Limited v Yardley* [1999] Lloyd's Rep Bank 438 (CA) 461–62. Similarly, *Halley v Law Society* [2003] WTLR 845 [99] 'A resulting trust might then affect, or a constructive trust might then be imposed on, the property transferred under the contract'.

[139] *Twinsectra Limited v Yardley* [1999] Lloyd's Rep Bank 438 (CA) 461–62.

and as analogous to the purchaser's rights against a vendor of property contracted to be sold.[140]

16.61 The label 'constructive trust' seems most appropriate where the rescinding party has received nothing under the transaction, for upon rescission full beneficial title revests pursuant to a trust imposed by the law irrespective of the presumed intention of the parties.[141] The trust is in that sense constructed (or the circumstances are 'construed'), and falls outside the established categories of resulting trust. Whilst there is support in the literature for describing the interest as a resulting trust,[142] in *National Crime Agency v Robb* the term 'constructive trust' was said to be preferable.[143] In that case, and in a later decision, the proprietary interest arising upon rescission was also described as a 'rescission trust'.[144]

16.62 The position is more complicated if the rescinding party is required to provide counter-restitution or otherwise do equity upon rescission. In these cases the entitlement to set the transaction aside and to recover benefits transferred depends upon satisfying terms imposed by the court, and if those terms are not satisfied, rescission and restitution will not occur.[145] A right to recover an asset that is conditional in this way is more akin to an equity of redemption than a trust.[146] An equity of redemption is a vested equitable estate consisting of a claim to recover property upon terms articulated through conditional relief,[147] and has the same structure as an order for rescission on terms.[148] But the equity of redemption is increasingly unfamiliar today, and the proprietary interest arising upon equitable rescission is probably best described as a constructive trust, or a rescission trust, even when counter-restitution must be provided.[149]

Fiduciary and other personal obligations
Fiduciary duties

16.63 Whether the interest arising is to be regarded as a constructive trust, or a constructed equity of redemption, in either case it appears that the party holding the asset is subject to limited

---

[140] *Lonrho plc v Fayed (No 2)* [1992] 1 WLR 1, 11–12.
[141] *Angove's Pty Ltd v Bailey* [2016] 1 WLR 3179 (Sup Ct) 3193 A-B [30]; cf *Williams v Central Bank of Nigeria* [2014] AC 1189, 1197–99 [9]–[11].
[142] D Fox, *Property Rights in Money* (2008) [6.40]–[6.42]; A Lodder, *Enrichment in the Law of Unjust Enrichment and Restitution* (2012) 133. Cf B Häcker, *Consequences of Impaired Consent Transfers* (2009) 128 (trust can equally be described as 'resulting' or 'constructive'). Against the 'resulting trust' label, A Burrows, *A Restatement of the English Law of Unjust Enrichment* (2012) 160–61. Cf also the discussion of the basis for the resulting trust in W Swadling, 'Explaining Resulting Trusts' (2008) 124 LQR 72, and in *Anderson v Mcpherson [No 2]* [2012] WASC 19 [88]–[116].
[143] [2015] Ch 520, 532 [49], approving G Virgo, *The Principles of Equity and Trusts* (2012) 300.
[144] *National Crime Agency v Robb* [2015] Ch 520, 530 [40]; *Vale SA v Steinmetz* [2020] EWHC Comm 3051 [9](i); S Zogg, *Proprietary Consequences in Defective Transfers of Ownership* (2020) 437.
[145] *Lindsay Petroleum Co v Hurd* (1874) LR 5 PC 221 (PC—Canada) 245; *Mayfair Trading Co Pty Ltd v Dreyer* (1958) 101 CLR 428, 451–52 (Dixon CJ); *Dunbar Bank plc v Nadeem* [1998] 3 All ER 876 (CA) 884; *Maguire v Makaronis* (1998) 188 CLR 449, 477–78.
[146] *Blake v Johnson* (1700) Pre Ch 142, 24 ER 69. For discussion of the contrasting obligations to make counter-restitution in cases of rescission and trust, RC Nolan, 'Dispositions Involving Fiduciaries: The Equity to Rescind and the Resulting Trust' in P Birks and F Rose (eds), *Restitution and Equity* (2000) 133, 141.
[147] The equity is a right to an order that the mortgagee reconvey the mortgaged estate, on condition that the redeeming mortgagor pays the sums due in equity, as determined on an accounting, with the bill to redeem being dismissed upon default in payment: A Ingpen, F Bloxam, and H Garrett (eds), *Seton on Decrees* (7th edn, 1912) vol 3, chap 47, esp 1885, 1887.
[148] For possible historical links between the equity to redeem and to rescind, see Chap 15, para [15.51], n 88.
[149] Cf *National Crime Agency v Robb* [2015] Ch 520, 530 [40]; *Vale SA v Steinmetz* [2020] EWHC Comm 3051 [9](i).

fiduciary obligations. In *Lonrho plc v Fayed (No 2)*[150] Millett J said that they were analogous to the obligations of a vendor of property contracted to be sold. After rejecting the notion that the recipient of property subject to an equity to rescind could become retrospectively subject to the fiduciary obligations of an express trustee, Millett J went on to describe the position after an election to rescind in the following terms:

> Even after the representee has elected to avoid the contract and reclaim the property, the obligations of the representor would in my judgment be analogous to those of a vendor of property contracted to be sold, and would not extend beyond the property actually obtained by the contract and liable to be returned.[151]

16.64 David Fox has argued that a party holding money or property following an effective election to rescind owes fiduciary duties in relation to those assets only if for some other reason he was a fiduciary in relation to them, because the status of trustee was imposed on him by operation of law.[152] If, however, following the imposition of the trust the party holding the assets sells or otherwise disposes of them, his personal liability to account will be similar to that of an express trustee. Insofar as the liability to account for the value of the property or its proceeds is to be characterized as fiduciary, a trustee of assets following an effective election to rescind is properly regarded as being subject to fiduciary duties in relation to those assets.

Knowing receipt and dishonest assistance

16.65 Surprisingly, there is so far no authority as to whether a third party who receives property transferred under a voidable transaction may be liable as a knowing recipient. There is likewise limited guidance as to whether a third party can be liable for dishonestly assisting in a breach of trust for assisting in the abstraction of assets under a voidable transaction[153]

16.66 It has been said that neither form of liability can be imposed retrospectively.[154] If available, claims of this kind can therefore only be maintained if the injured party is empowered to regain equitable title by electing to rescind,[155] and in respect of receipt or assistance that occurs after that election has been made.[156]

16.67 Whether the law should permit claims for knowing receipt or dishonest assistance in such a case is not straightforward. A third party who receives goods sold under a contract voidable at common law that the vendor has disaffirmed is strictly liable for the items received, and

---

[150] [1992] 1 WLR 1.
[151] *Lonrho plc v Fayed (No 2)* [1992] 1 WLR 1, 11–12.
[152] D Fox, *Property Rights in Money* (2008) [6.62].
[153] But see *Bank Tejarat v Hong Kong and Shanghai Bank* [1995] 1 Lloyd's Rep 239, 248; *Estate Properties Ltd v Wignall* [1992] 2 NZLR 615, 633. The reasoning in *Nolan v Minerva Trust Company Limited* [2014] 2 JLR 117; JRC 078A [151] suggests that if a constructive trust were to arise after an election to rescind, a claim for dishonest assistance would be capable of arising against a third party who acted after that time.
[154] *Lonrho plc v Fayed (No 2)* [1992] 1 WLR 1, 11, 12; *Bristol and West Building Society v Mothew* [1998] 1 Ch 1 (CA) 22–23; cf *Bank Tejarat v Hong Kong and Shanghai Bank* [1995] 1 Lloyd's Rep 239, 248.
[155] The circumstances in which equitable title to money or property transferred under a voidable contract may be obtained by disaffirming the transaction are discussed in Part C(3) above.
[156] See also RC Nolan, 'Dispositions Involving Fiduciaries: The Equity to Rescind and the Resulting Trust' in P Birks and F Rose (eds), *Restitution and Equity* (2000) 131, 136, 142.

notice is relevant only if statutory defences are relied upon.[157] Symmetry with this approach would suggest that the claims should be available.

16.68 But the question is really one of policy, not of logic. If it is only the victims of fraud who may gain equitable title by electing to disaffirm the transaction it is difficult to see why claims for knowing receipt and dishonest assistance should not be available. Having received property with notice that it had been obtained under a transaction tainted by fraud, or dishonestly assisted in disposing of the property, the third party can hardly complain if they are required to account for the value of the property. But if this indeed the law, the timing of the injured party's rejection of the transaction becomes critical to the allocation of liability. The third party is liable if the receipt or assistance occurs after the transaction is disaffirmed, but not if it took place before that time. It is not obvious why this should be so. Perhaps the justification is that it is an inevitable consequence of the rule that a contract induced by fraud is voidable and not void, and it is in that way an incident of the balance that the law has struck between the competing interests engaged in cases of impaired transactional autonomy. Resolution of the question should await determination by a court confronted with a fact pattern in which the answer matters.[158]

Discretion to grant a proprietary interest?
16.69 In principle both the entitlement to a proprietary interest upon rescission and the extent of that interest should be governed by fixed and pre-determined rules. The proprietary interests arising upon rescission should not be subject to judicial discretion. In Australia, however, Mason P has said that when a loan is procured by breach of fiduciary duty, the proprietary interest in its proceeds arising upon rescission is a 'remedial constructive trust', the availability and scope of which is discretionary:

> In general, the court will need to be satisfied that a remedial constructive trust (or charge if that suffices) is necessary to protect the legitimate rights of the plaintiff and does not do injustice to the rights of third parties, such as creditors ... A full proprietary remedy is not always necessary or appropriate and it is not automatic. Sometimes the interests of innocent third parties such as creditors will mean that the plaintiff will be confined to a personal remedy or the narrower remedial constructive charge. But a remedial constructive trust will generally be appropriate where profit can be traced into identifiable property in the hands of the defaulting beneficiary or the agent of the defaulting beneficiary.[159]

16.70 Although subsequently approved by other intermediate appellate courts in Australia,[160] and consistent with Canadian law,[161] this view will not be followed in England, for there

---
[157] Whether the third party had notice or was acting bona fides is relevant if s 25 of the Sale of Goods Act 1979 or ss 2 and 9 of the Factors Act 1889 are relied upon: see Chap 11, para [11.40], Chap 14, para [14.14].
[158] The question will tend to matter if the third party retains no traceable proceeds over which a constructive trust may be asserted and no claim is available against the third party for deceit, unlawful means conspiracy, or other tort. See also the reasoning in *Nolan v Minerva Trust Company Limited* [2014] 2 JLR 117; JRC 078A, where the availability of a claim for dishonest assistance came to depend upon whether sums paid over pursuant to investment contracts procured by fraud were immediately impressed with a 'Halley trust' or only a mere equity to rescind: see Chap 1, paras [1.85]–[1.86].
[159] *Robins v Incentive Dynamics Pty Ltd* (2003) 175 FLR 286 (NSWCA) 301, see also at 298.
[160] *Mernda Developments Pty Ltd (in liq) v Alamanda Property Investments No 2 Pty Ltd* (2011) 86 ACSR 277 (Vict CA) [47]–[49], [56] (secured loan by company voidable for director's breach of duty); *Grimaldi v Chameleon Mining NL* (2012) 200 FCR 296 [277], [281] (payments made in breach of director's duties).
[161] *Canadian Imperial Bank of Commerce v Melnitzer* (1993) 44 ACWS (3d) 1303; aff'd (1997) 75 ACWS (3d) 584 (Ont CA).

the remedial constructive trust remains an alien concept.[162] In *Vale SA v Steinmetz* it was rightly held that the proprietary consequences of rescission follow automatically and are not a matter for judicial discretion.[163] The approach of Mason P is also objectionable on the ground that absent a legislative mandate it should form no part of the judicial function to adjust property rights on a discretionary basis. Rights of property should arise and be lost only in accordance with pre-determined rules. Moreover, specific bars to rescission already protect the interests of innocent third parties to which Mason P refers. His Honour's suggestion that the rights of unsecured creditors should affect whether a proprietary interest is awarded is also unpersuasive. Save in the special case of a shareholder's claim to rescind against a company in liquidation, the law of rescission has never given any protection to the rights of unsecured creditors.[164] A preference for protecting their interests should militate in favour of a refusal to permit proprietary interests upon rescission at all, or outside narrow categories of case, and does not justify a discretion to decide whether property rights exist or not.[165]

---

[162] *Westdeutsche Landesbank Girozentrale v Islington London Borough Council* [1996] AC 669, 714, 716; *Shalson v Russo* [2005] Ch 281, 320; also, *Angove's Pty Ltd v Bailey* [2016] 1 WLR 3179 (Sup Ct) 3191 [27] 'English law is generally averse to the discretionary adjustment of property rights, and has not recognized the remedial constructive trust favoured in some jurisdictions'.

[163] [2020] EWHC Comm 3051 [22]–[23].

[164] See Chaps 20, 25. But cf now *In the matter of Crown Holdings (London) Limited (in liq)* [2015] EWHC 1876 (Ch) where it was held that a claim to recover assets following rescission cannot be asserted against a company in liquidation, discussed Chap 25, paras [25.05]–[25.06].

[165] See also *Daraydan Holdings Ltd v Solland International Ltd* [2005] Ch 119, 138, 140; R Goode, 'Ownership and Obligation in Commercial Transactions' (1987) 103 LQR 433, 438–41, 444, 460; *Angove's Pty Ltd v Bailey* [2016] 1 WLR 3179 (Sup Ct) 3190 [25], 3191 [27], 3192–93 [30].

17

Financial Adjustments

A. Introduction	17.01	(4) Indemnity	17.23
B. Restitution and Counter-restitution	17.02	(5) Offsetting equivalent benefits	17.30
(1) Benefits derived from land and chattels	17.03	C. Compensation	17.32
		(1) Improvements and repairs	17.35
(2) Joint acquisitions	17.14	(2) Deterioration and depreciation	17.55
(3) Interest	17.15	(3) Irrelevant detriments	17.61

A. Introduction

17.01 This chapter is concerned with the financial allowances and adjustments that are sometimes made as an incident of the restoration of the parties to their original positions upon rescission. Most of the types of allowance and adjustment discussed in this chapter are available only upon rescission in equity. The onus of proof will usually fall on the claiming party.[1]

B. Restitution and Counter-restitution

17.02 The following sections address a number of issues that may arise relating to the restitution and counter-restitution that must be made upon rescission.

(1) Benefits derived from land and chattels

17.03 Upon rescission, in addition to returning the assets they received under the contract, each party is usually required to account for the benefits they have gained from ownership of those assets. Restitution of these benefits is incidental to the restitution of the assets themselves. It must be distinguished from the accountability of a fiduciary for unauthorized profits gained in the course of his engagement, which rests upon a different principle.[2]

17.04 The simplest cases are those where the benefit has consisted in money derived from an asset. In these cases the order will be one for an accounting of the income or net profits the owner of the asset in question has received. Orders have accordingly been made in respect of rents

---

[1] *Salt v Stratstone Specialist Ltd* [2016] RTR 17 (CA) [30].
[2] See Chap 2, para [2.18].

and profits derived from land,[3] dividends paid in respect of shares,[4] the net profits made by working a mine,[5] and the net profits of a business.[6]

17.05 Equally, where a party has enjoyed the actual use or occupation of an asset he gained under a contract, upon rescission the court may direct that he pay a reasonable user or occupation rent. Such awards have often been made in respect of the occupation of land,[7] but the same principle applies where the use of chattels is concerned.[8] For example, where the purchaser of a motor vehicle rescinds after using the vehicle for a period of time, the court will typically require that he give an allowance for the use he has had.[9] User or occupation rent is charged not only from the date rescission is notified, but throughout the period of possession.[10]

17.06 An account of income or profits, and an account of user or occupation rent, are two different ways of allowing for the benefit a party has had from the ownership of a particular asset. The two are mutually incompatible in that it would be double counting to charge a purchaser of land who let it to tenants both with the rents he has received and with an occupation rent for the same period.

Measure of use value

17.07 There is not much discussion in the cases of the measure of the user or occupation rent that may be charged upon rescission.[11] It will usually be the prevailing market price of hiring or

---

[3] Eg *York Buildings Co v Mackenzie* (1795) 8 Bro PC 42, 3 ER 432; *Trevelyan v White* (1839) 1 Beav 588, 48 ER 1069; *Gibson v D'Este* (1843) 2 Y & CCC 542, 63 ER 243; *Salter v Bradshaw* (1858) 26 Beav 161, 165–66; 53 ER 858, 860; *Haygarth v Wearing* (1871) LR 12 Eq 320. In Australia, *Wilson v Brisbane City Council* (1931) St R Qld 360.

[4] Eg *Gillette v Peppercorn* (1840) 3 Beav 78, 49 ER 31; *Allcard v Skinner* (1887) 36 ChD 145 (CA); *Armstrong v Jackson* [1917] 2 KB 822; *Spence v Crawford* [1939] 3 All ER 271 (HL Sc) 284. In Canada, *McCarthy v Kenny* [1939] 3 DLR 556 (Ont SC). In Hong Kong, *Acute Result Holdings Limited v Lioncap Global Management Limited* [2019] HKCFI 1580 [14]. Cf *Caldicott v Richards* [2020] EWHC 767 (Ch) [120], in the special circumstances of which the defendant was permitted to retain the dividends.

[5] *Small v Attwood* (1832) You 407, 159 ER 1051, rev'd on other grounds (1838) 6 Cl & Fin 232, 7 ER 684; *Lagunas Nitrate Company v Lagunas Syndicates* [1899] 2 Ch 392 (CA) 461. Where the working of the mine has the dual effect of generating a profit and depleting the asset, the award of profits may equally be justified as a convenient measure of compensation for deterioration.

[6] *Carter v Golland* [1937] 4 DLR 513 (Ont CA); *Kramer v McMahon* (1969) 89 WN (Pt 1) (NSW) 584; *Forum Development Pte Ltd v Global Accent Trading Pte Ltd* [1995] 1 SLR 474 (CA) 481.

[7] Eg *York Buildings Co v Mackenzie* (1795) 8 Bro PC 42, 48 ER 1069; *Donovan v Fricker* (1821) Jac 165, 37 ER 813; *Gibson v D'Este* (1843) 2 Y & CCC 542, 63 ER 243; *Cooper v Phibbs* (1867) LR 2 HL 149; *Goldsworthy v Bricknell* [1987] Ch 378 (CA); *Cheese v Thomas* [1994] 1 WLR 129 (CA); *Claughton v Price* (1997) 30 HLR 396 (CA). In both of the latter cases the occupation rent was offset against the interest otherwise payable on the purchase money. In Australia, *Sibley v Grosvenor* (1916) 21 CLR 469; *Brown v Smitt* (1924) 34 CLR 160; *Alati v Kruger* (1955) 94 CLR 216.

[8] *Atlantic Lines and Navigation Co Inc v Hallam Ltd (The Lucy)* [1983] 1 Lloyd's Rep 188, 202.

[9] *Salt v Stratstone Specialist* Ltd [2016] RTR 17 (CA). In Canada, *F & B Transport Ltd v White Truck Sales Manitoba Ltd* (1964) 47 DLR (2d) 419 (Man QB), aff'd (1965) 49 DLR (2d) 670 (Man CA). It is often sensible in such cases for the court to offset the value of the purchaser's use of the vehicle against the value of the vendor's use of the purchase money and so to award neither a user nor interest: eg *Addison v Ottawa Auto and Taxi Co* (1913) 16 DLR 318 (Ont SC (App Div)).

[10] *Hayes v Ross (No 3)* [1919] NZLR 786. See to like effect in relation to the final rejection of goods by a consumer: ss 24(8)–(10) and 58(5)–(6) of the Consumer Rights Act 2015.

[11] There has, however, been considerable discussion of parallel issues in cases involving tortious interference with property rights. See in particular *Swordheath Properties Ltd v Tabet* [1979] 1 WLR 285 (CA); *Ministry of Defence v Ashman* [1993] 2 EGLR 102 (CA); *Ministry of Defence v Thompson* [1993] 2 EGLR 107 (CA); *Lunn Poly Limited v Liverpool & Lancashire Properties Limited* [2007] L & TR 6 (CA). See also *Attorney-General v Blake* [2001] 1 AC 268; *Experience Hendrix LLC v PPX Enterprises Inc* [2003] 1 All ER (Comm) 830; and *Morris-Garner v One Step (Support) Ltd* [2019] AC 649. Notable decisions in cognate jurisdictions include *Inverugie Investments Ltd v Hackett* [1995] 1 WLR 713 (PC—Bermuda); *Roberts v Rodney District Council* [2001] 2 NZLR 402; *Finesky Holdings Pty Ltd v Minister of Transport for Western Australia* [2002] WASCA 206; *Pell Frischmann Engineering Limited v Bow Valley Iran Limited* [2011] 1 WLR 2370 (PC—Jersey).

leasing the asset in question, which is its objective use-value.[12] Consistently with cases in cognate areas of the law of restitution, this objective market value is the price which a reasonable person in the position of the paying party would have had to pay for the use taking into account conditions which increased or decreased the objective value of the use to any reasonable person in that position.[13] It may sometimes be appropriate to ascertain this value by reference to the result of a hypothetical negotiation between a reasonable willing buyer and a reasonable willing seller.[14]

There are circumstances in which this objective value does not fairly reflect the value of the use of the asset to the paying party so that he should be charged with a lesser value. The South Australian case *Koutsonicolis v Principe*[15] is an example. The vendor of a house had fraudulently concealed defects in the foundations that resulted in very bad cracking one year after the purchasers took possession. The purchasers rescinded but, lacking the means to purchase another property, were effectively locked into living in the house against their wishes during the protracted litigation. Because the benefit of living in the house was an unwanted one, White J charged the purchasers with an occupation rent much below the house's market rental value. This ruling may reflect the principle of subjective devaluation.[16] The purchasers did not subjectively place the same value on occupying the house that the market generally may have.

By contrast, where it is a wrongdoer who has used or occupied an asset, he would presumably be charged with its objective use-value. Having wrongfully extracted the asset from his seller, he can hardly now say that the asset has not been worth its market price to him. Where the wrong in question is technical rather than reprehensible, as with innocent misrepresentation, it is easier to imagine cases in which the actual benefit would be taken to be less than the asset's objective use-value.

Measure where asset not actually used
A further question concerns the sum if any that is payable where a person has owned an asset he received under a contract, but he has not actually used or occupied it and he has not deployed it economically. An example might be a purchaser of land who neither occupies it nor lets it to a tenant, but instead allows the land to sit empty and unused during his period of ownership.[17] In these cases the owner receives no actual benefit from the asset, although it might be said that he has the unrealized but objective benefit of the asset's market hire value during his period of ownership.

This issue was, in earlier times at least, framed in this branch of the law by asking whether the owner is accountable on the footing of wilful default. Accountability on the footing of wilful default is accountability not only for the actual receipts in the form of rent or other

---

[12] No user will be payable where the asset was in fact useless, as, for example, the defective heating equipment in *Kellogg Brown & Root Inc v Aerotech Herman Nelson Inc* (2004) 238 DLR (4th) 594 (Man CA) [66].
[13] *Benedetti v Sawiris* [2014] AC 938.
[14] See *Pell Frischmann Engineering Limited v Bow Valley Iran Limited* [2011] 1 WLR 2370 (PC—Jersey) for a general discussion of this approach in a non-rescission context.
[15] (1987) 48 SASR 328, 331.
[16] *Ministry of Defence v Ashman* [1993] 2 EGLR 102 (CA); *Benedetti v Sawiris* [2014] AC 938. But cf Lord Reed JSC's approach to subjective devaluation in the latter case, which is conceptually stronger than that of the majority.
[17] Similar issues arise where the asset has been deployed economically but not to best effect, for example where land has been let at an undervalue.

income derived from an asset, but also for the receipts that would have been gained if ordinary care had been taken to maximize the asset's economic return.[18] Thus to hold a party accountable on the footing of wilful default is to hold that party accountable for the objective use-value of the asset in question rather than simply the actual benefit he has had.

17.12 One line of cases holds that where a contract is rescinded a party returning an asset is only obliged to account on the footing of wilful default where he extracted the asset from his counter-party by fraud or equivalent misconduct.[19] Accordingly, where it is the vendor who rescinds, he will be entitled to be paid the objective use-value of the asset where his purchaser has been guilty of fraud or equivalent misconduct. A purchaser who is only guilty of innocent misrepresentation may only, on this view, be charged with the value of the actual benefit he has had from the asset. It also follows from this view that where the rescinding party is the purchaser, he will only be accountable to the vendor for the actual benefit he has had from the asset.

17.13 In the well-known case of *Gibson v D'Este*,[20] however, a defrauded purchaser of land was upon rescission directed to account on the footing of wilful default. Similarly, although not framed in the same terms, in *Cheese v Thomas* the Court of Appeal required the rescinding party to account for an occupation rent in respect of a period of time when he was not using the house on the basis that it continued to be available to him.[21] This is consistent with the approach of the majority of the House of Lords in *Sempra Metals Limited v IRC*.[22] That case concerned restitution of the use value of money paid by mistake and the central issue that divided the House was whether the interest should be calculated by reference to the actual benefit the government had gained by investing the money or paying down its debts or, instead, by reference to an objective market value represented by the government's cost of borrowing. Lord Hope and Lord Nicholls held, with Lord Walker's support, that the government had been enriched by the opportunity to use the money to reduce its debts irrespective of what the government may actually have done in consequence of the receipts. The approach in *Gibson v D'Este* and *Cheese v Thomas* therefore appears to be correct.[23]

---

[18] The terms 'wilful' and 'wilful default' are used in a special sense in connection with accounts in equity. See *Armitage v Nurse* [1998] Ch 241 (CA) 252; *Leeds City Brewery v Platts* [1925] Ch 532, 533; J McGhee and S Elliott (eds), *Snell's Equity* (34th edn, 2020) [20-024].

[19] *Howell v Howell* (1837) 2 My & Cr 478, 40 ER 722; *Adam v Sworder* (1863) 2 De G J & S 44, 46 ER 291; *Tate v Williamson* (1866) LR 2 Ch 55 (see the order in A Ingpen, F Blochman, and G Garrett (eds), *Seton on Judgments and Orders* (7th edn, 1912) 2253). See also the Australian case *Coastal Estates Pty Ltd v Melevendes* [1965] VR 433 (Full Ct), where Sholl J said at 440–41 that a court of equity would not debit a rescinding purchaser of land with any sum in respect of the technical right of possession he had enjoyed in the land now being returned, the purchaser having visited the land only in order to inspect it. It seems likely, however, that the vacant land in that case had no rental value.

[20] (1843) 2 Y & CCC 542, 63 ER 243. See TC Williams, *The Law of Vendor and Purchaser of Lands* (4th edn, 1936) 820. See also in Canada *Lambert v MacKenzie* [1949] OWN 758 (CA).

[21] [1994] 1 WLR 129 (CA) 138F-G.

[22] [2008] 1 AC 561. See the discussion of this point in *Sempra Metals* in *Littlewoods Retail Limited v HMRC* [2014] STC 1761 [350]–[373]. Other cases decided outside the rescission context but that support that same conclusion include *Dimond v Lovell* [2002] 1 AC 384, 397 and *Lewisham LBC v Masterson* (2000) 80 P & CR 117 (CA) 122–23.

[23] See AVM Lodder, *Enrichment in the Law of Unjust Enrichment and Restitution* (2012) 76, 96, 98.

(2) Joint acquisitions

In the case of a simple sale, mutual restitution involves the purchaser returning the asset and the seller returning the purchase money. It is not relevant that the asset may have appreciated or depreciated as a result of market fluctuations.[24] This approach is not appropriate where the rescinded transaction, properly analysed, consists in a joint acquisition and the defendant is not guilty of conscious wrongdoing. In a case of this type mutual restitution requires that the asset be divided proportionately to the parties' contributions so that market gains or losses are shared proportionately.[25] Where the contributions of the parties are not specified by the contract, as for example in the informal context of a personal relationship, the contributions that are relevant for this purpose are those that relate directly to the acquisition and improvement of the joint asset.[26]

17.14

(3) Interest

The analysis of interest differs significantly depending whether the right to rescind is enforceable in equity or at law.

17.15

Rescission in equity

Upon rescission the court will generally direct that sums paid under the contract or by way of gift be returned with interest.[27] Likewise, a party returning an asset is liable to pay interest on any income derived from it for which he is accountable;[28] and he is entitled to interest on any outlays for which he is entitled to be reimbursed.[29] In *Coleman v Myers*[30] the New Zealand Court of Appeal refused to award, instead of interest, the actual profits a recipient had made through use of the money he had been paid.

17.16

Interest is thus awarded as an incident of full restitution.[31] The principle was said in *Karberg's* case to be 'that where a contract was rescinded, interest on money actually paid under it ought to be allowed, not by way of damages, but on the ground that the parties were to be restored as far as possible to their original position.'[32]

17.17

---

[24] See the cases cited in n 111.
[25] *Cheese v Thomas* [1994] 1 WLR 129 (CA). See M Chen-Wishart, 'Loss Sharing, Undue Influence and Manifest Disadvantage' (1994) 110 LQR 174.
[26] *Smith v Cooper* [2010] 2 FLR 1521 (CA).
[27] *National Commercial Bank (Jamaica) Limited v Hew* [2003] UKPC 51 [43] (Jamaica). In Australia, *Maguire v Makronis* (1996) 188 CLR 449, 475–77.
[28] There appears to be an exception where assets are returned by a trustee upon the sale being set aside by his beneficiary: *Silkstone and Haigh Moor Coal Company v Edey* [1900] 1 Ch 167. That decision was not, however, made with enthusiasm and it is anomalous. The same case also supports the obvious proposition that where profits have been retained within a business now being returned, there is no need to account for the profits separately.
[29] *Gibson v D'Este* (1843) 2 Y & CCC 542, 581; 63 ER 243, 259–60.
[30] [1977] 2 NZLR 225 (CA) 337.
[31] *Erlanger v The New Sombrero Phosphate Company* (1876) 5 ChD 73 (CA) 125 aff'd (1878) 3 App Cas 1218; *Newbigging v Adam* (1886) 34 ChD 582 (CA) 585 aff'd (1888) 13 App Cas 308; *Investors Compensation Scheme Ltd v West Bromwich Building Society* [1998] 1 WLR 896 (HL) 916. In Australia, *Alati v Kruger* (1955) 94 CLR 216; *Maguire v Makronis* (1996) 188 CLR 449, 475–77.
[32] *Re Metropolitan Coal Consumers' Association (Karberg's case)* [1892] 3 Ch 1 (CA) 17; *Wood v Commercial First Business Limited (Dissolved)* [2021] EWHC 1403 (Ch) [14].

17.18 Equitable interest generally runs from the date on which the money was originally paid, income was received, or expenses incurred, down until the date of judgment.[33] Equitable interest is always discretionary, however, and so in exceptional circumstances the court may select a different starting date.[34] Exceptional circumstances may exist where the claimant has been guilty of egregious and unwarranted delay in bringing his claim;[35] and where the defendant did not know and could not reasonably be expected to have known that the claimant was likely to rescind, and so was in no position to tender payment or make provision for payment.[36] But the overriding consideration will usually be that the recipient of money has enjoyed the benefit of it from the date of receipt.[37]

17.19 Where interest is given in equity the court enjoys a jurisdiction to order that it be compounded. That jurisdiction has traditionally been exercised only in discrete and limited categories of case, being cases where the money was obtained and retained by fraud, and cases where the money was used by a fiduciary commercially for their own benefit.[38] *O'Sullivan*'s case is a well-known example of the latter.[39] The decision of the House of Lords in *Sempra Metals*[40] was not based on the equitable jurisdiction, but the majority's warmth towards compound interest indicated that these limitations would quickly be reappraised.[41] But that warmth was not in evidence in *Prudential Assurance*,[42] in which the Supreme Court overruled *Sempra Metals*, and the early modernization of the law in this area now seems less likely. Most recently, in *Wood v Commercial First Business Limited (Dissolved)* the court applied the old approach.[43]

17.20 There is some indication that the Australian courts take a broader approach. The Full Court of the Federal Court of Australia held in *JAD International Pty Ltd v International Trucks Australia Ltd*[44] that the court may award compound interest whenever the evidence shows that, in being out of his money, the party entitled has incurred a loss that is measured by compound interest. That was a case of innocent misrepresentation, but the same principle ought to apply in all cases where there is equitable jurisdiction.

---

[33] *York Buildings Co v Mackenzie* (1795) 8 Bro PC 42, 3 ER 432; *Newbigging v Adam* (1886) 34 ChD 582 (CA) 585 aff'd (1888) 13 App Cas 308; *Re Metropolitan Coal Consumers' Association (Karberg's case)* [1892] 3 Ch 1 (CA) 17; *Wood v Commercial First Business Limited (Dissolved)* [2021] EWHC 1403 (Ch) [16]–[17]. In Australia, *Alati v Kruger* (1955) 94 CLR 216, 220.
[34] See *BP Exploration Co (Libya) Ltd v Hunt (No 2)* [1979] 1 WLR 783, 846 and *Westdeutsche Landesbank Girozentrale v Islington LBC* [1994] 4 All ER 890 (CA) 963, 970.
[35] *Corbett v Barking, Havering and Brentwood Health Authority* [1991] 2 QB 408 (CA). In Australia, *Hartigan v International Society for Krishna Consciousness Ltd* [2002] NSWSC 810 [104].
[36] *West Sussex Properties Ltd v Chichester DC* [2000] EWCA Civ 205 [37]; *Allied London Investments Ltd v Hambro Life Assurance plc* [1985] 1 EGLR 45.
[37] *Westdeutsche Landesbank Girozentrale v Islington LBC* [1994] 4 All ER 890 (CA) 971.
[38] *Johnson v The King* [1904] AC 817 (PC—Sierra Leone) 822; *President of India v La Pintada Compania Navigacion SA* [1985] AC 104, 116; *Westdeutsche Landesbank Girozentrale v Islington LBC* [1996] AC 669; *Black v Davies* [2005] EWCA Civ 531 [81]–[88].
[39] *O'Sullivan v Management Agency and Music Ltd* [1985] QB 428 (CA) 461-62, 474. The point had been conceded. Interest on other sums paid under the same contract was not compounded because the money had been used by the fiduciary for purposes that also benefited the claimant.
[40] *Sempra Metals Limited v Inland Revenue Commissioners* [2008] 1 AC 561.
[41] See, in this regard, Lord Mance's remarks at [239].
[42] *Prudential Assurance Co Ltd v HMRC* [2019] AC 929.
[43] [2021] EWHC 1403 (Ch) [21].
[44] (1994) 50 FCR 378 (Full Ct) 392. Other Australian cases in which compound interest was given include *Maguire v Makaronis* (1996) 188 CLR 449, 475–77 and *Krakowski v Trenorth Ltd* (Vict SC, 7 May 1996).

Rescission at law

17.21 Sums paid under a contract later rescinded at law are recoverable by an action for money had and received. Interest is not available as part of the restitution given in that action.[45] This longstanding rule was overturned by the House of Lords in *Sempra Metals*,[46] but the rule was then reinstated by the Supreme Court in *Prudential Assurance*.[47] Lord Macnaghten once posited an exception where the money was obtained and retained by fraud,[48] but there is no room for this in the Supreme Court's reasoning. Interest is therefore only available by grace of legislation. The courts have construed section 35A of the Senior Courts Act 1981 to bring such claims within its purview, notwithstanding that a claim for restitution is not strictly one in debt.[49]

17.22 Restricting claimants to statutory interest has three unfortunate consequences. First, compound interest is not available under the statute and so it is not available whatever the justice of the case, where practical merits would usually favour compound interest.[50] Secondly, statutory interest runs only from the date on which the cause of action arose, and in a case of rescission at law that is the date on which the claimant elects to rescind.[51] Third, if the defendant repays before the claim is brought, there is no jurisdiction to award interest. The decision in *Prudential Assurance* is, in this context at least, a retrograde step.[52]

(4) Indemnity

17.23 As Bowen LJ observed in *Adam v Newbigging*,[53] upon rescission there must be a giving back and taking back not only of advantages that have passed under the contract, but also of obligations. He explained that 'complete rescission would not be effective unless the misrepresenting party not only hands back the benefits which he has himself received—but also re-assumes the burden which under the contract the injured person has taken upon himself'.[54] The burden the injured party assumed in consideration of the contract is thus treated as a benefit to the misrepresenting party within the rule requiring restitution upon rescission.[55] That it is a benefit to the misrepresenting party is evident from the fact that he contracted for it. Cotton LJ stressed in the same case that the award of an indemnity is not tantamount to an award of damages for the misrepresentation, but that 'it is working out the proper result of setting aside a contract'.[56]

---

[45] See the line of cases running from *Walker v Constable* (1798) 1 B & P 306, 126 ER 919 to *Frühling v Schroeder* (1835) 2 Bing NC 77, 132 ER 31.
[46] *Sempra Metals Limited v Inland Revenue Commissioners* [2008] 1 AC 561.
[47] *Prudential Assurance Co Ltd v HMRC* [2019] AC 929.
[48] *Johnson v The King* [1904] AC 817 (PC—Sierra Leone) 822.
[49] *BP Exploration (Libya) Ltd v Hunt (No 2)* [1979] 1 WLR 783, 836–37 aff'd [1983] 2 AC 352; *Woolwich Equitable Building Society v Inland Revenue Commissioners* [1993] AC 70.
[50] Since 31 January 1997 compound interest has, however, been available if the case is decided by way of arbitration: Arbitration Act 1996, s 49.
[51] Cf *Star v O'Brien* (1996) 22 ACSR 434 (NSWCA) 443.
[52] See also the criticisms made in A Burrows, 'In Defence of Unjust Enrichment' [2019] CLJ 521, 538–41 and C Mitchell, 'End of the Road for the Overpaid Tax Litigation?' [2019] Supreme Court Year Book 1, 16–17.
[53] (1886) 34 ChD 582 (CA) 595.
[54] (1886) 34 ChD 582 (CA) 594.
[55] See the analysis of this case in A Burrows, *The Law of Restitution* (3rd edn, 2011) 246–47 and in E Bant, 'Rescission, Restitution and Compensation' in S Degeling and J Varuhas, *Equitable Compensation and Disgorgement of Profit* (2017) chap 13.
[56] *Newbigging v Adam* (1886) 34 ChD 582 (CA) 589.

17.24 The court may order an indemnity where, under the terms of the contract, one of the parties has conferred a benefit on a third party or incurred a liability towards one. For example, in two of the principal English authorities men induced to join partnerships by misrepresentations as to the state of the business or the extent of its debts were indemnified against such of the partnership liabilities as they had discharged or might in future be required to discharge.[57] In a more recent case from Singapore the rescinding tenant was entitled to be indemnified for sums he had expended renovating the premises as he had been required to do under the lease.[58]

17.25 It is usually thought that the indemnity only extends to those obligations or outlays that a claimant has been required by the contract to incur. That is the natural reading of Bowen LJ's remarks in *Adam v Newbigging*, and that was also the view taken by Farwell J in *Whittington v Seale-Hayne*.[59] The claimant had leased a poultry farm on the strength of an innocent misrepresentation as to its sanitary condition when in fact the water supply was poisoned. While entitled to be indemnified in respect of certain rates and repairs which he had been bound by the lease to pay or carry out, the claimant did not recover for the losses he incurred running the operation, including the loss of poultry and medical costs resulting from the poisoning of his manager.[60] Those operating losses could only be recovered as damages, for which the claimant did not have a cause of action.

17.26 It is arguable, however, that an indemnity should also be given in respect of outlays incurred as a necessary consequence of the contract, and for which the defendant vendor would otherwise have been responsible, even though the contract between the two did not require that these payments should be made. This would encompass, for example, rates and taxes paid in respect of land being returned upon rescission of a sale.[61] Had the contract never been made, the obligation to pay the rates would inevitably have fallen on the vendor's shoulders, and so upon rescission of the sale the payment can be treated as a discharge of the vendor's liability and so an incontrovertible benefit to him. On any view, however, the indemnity is restitutionary and not in the nature of compensatory damages.

17.27 Those cases all concern the rescinding claimant's entitlement to be indemnified for expenses and liabilities he has incurred. The question there concerns the scope of the claimant's right to restitution. While there appear to be no cases in which an indemnity has been ordered in favour of a defendant, in principle the same relief ought to be available where he has incurred expenses or liabilities in consideration of the rights he gained under the contract.[62]

17.28 Where one of the parties is entitled to be indemnified in respect of sums he has paid to third parties in the past, the amount is awarded as an item of the restitution his counter-party must pay. By contrast, orders for an indemnity in respect of undischarged or contingent future

---

[57] *Newbigging v Adam* (1886) 34 ChD 582 (CA) (the indemnity point was not contested on further appeal: (1888) 13 App Cas 308); *Rawlins v Wickham* (1858) 3 De G & J 304, 44 ER 1285.
[58] *Forum Development Pte Ltd v Global Accent Trading Pte Ltd* [1995] 1 SLR 474 (CA) 482. Cf *RBC Properties Pte Ltd v Defo Furniture Pte Ltd* [2015] 1 SLR 997 (CA) where the fitting out work was not required by the lease.
[59] (1900) 82 LT 49.
[60] In Australia, *Blackley Investments Pty Ltd v Burnie City Council (No 2)* (2011) 21 Tas R 98 (Full Ct) [38].
[61] See *Restatement (Third) of Restitution* vol 2, 282 (2011). But see *Koutsonicolis v Principe (No 2)* (1987) 48 SASR 328, 335. *Pedashenko v Blacktown City Council* (1996) 39 NSWLR 189 is difficult to explain because the council returning property to the rescinding party had presumably not been required to pay the rates to itself.
[62] *Spence v Crawford* [1939] 3 All ER 271 (HL) 289–90.

liabilities characteristically take the form of a declaration. Thus the order in *Newbigging v Adam* declared that the defendants were jointly and severally bound to indemnify the claimant against 'all outstanding debts, claims, demands, and liabilities which the Plaintiff had become or might become subject to, or be liable to pay for or on account or in respect of the dealings and transactions of the partnership'.[63]

17.29 Declaratory relief is disadvantageous to the beneficiary of the indemnity because he remains primarily liable to the third party, and therefore subject to the risk that the counter-party will not be able to pay on the indemnity. Where it is the defendant who is to be indemnified, it may sometimes be possible to avoid this disadvantage by an order that, instead of declaring the defendant's right of indemnity, directs that the claimant should secure the release of the obligation in question as a condition of his relief.[64] Under an order of this type the claimant is free to choose how to secure the release of the obligation, for example by paying off the business's debts or by procuring a novation of the guarantee.

(5) Offsetting equivalent benefits

17.30 Even where exact restitution and counter-restitution is possible, the court enjoys a discretion to spare the parties a wasteful exchange of equivalent benefits by directing that they be offset against each other and so ignored. Thus where contracts for the sale of land or chattels are set aside, the courts have often directed that the interest the vendor would otherwise have to pay on the purchase money he has received should be offset against the user or occupation rent the purchaser would otherwise have to pay.[65] In other cases sums payable by way of counter-restitution have been allowed out of costs.[66] These cases illustrate the scope of the discretion to achieve practical justice by treating the question of restitution and counter-restitution in the round.

17.31 Scrutton LJ's reasons in *Hulton v Hulton*[67] indicate that the court may offset equivalent benefits even where *restitutio in integrum* would otherwise be impossible and even though the benefits are incapable of financial expression. The wife in that case sought to set aside a deed of separation on the ground of fraud. She had received under the deed £2,500 for her maintenance, but the Court of Appeal held that this sum did not need to be returned. According to Scrutton LJ, the sum was instead offset against equivalent benefits the husband had received during the five-year life of the deed in the form of 'freedom from molestation, freedom from proceedings by the wife for restitution of conjugal rights, and other

---

[63] *Newbigging v Adam* (1886) 34 ChD 582 (CA) 584–85. See also *Rawlins v Wickam* (1858) 1 Giff 355, 65 ER 954, aff'd (1858) 3 De G & J 304, 44 ER 1285, where the claimant had requested an order that the defendant execute an indemnity but was granted a declaration instead.
[64] Eg *Waters Motors Pty Ltd v Cratchley* [1964] 80 WN (NSW) 1165.
[65] Land cases include *Cheese v Thomas* [1994] 1 WLR 129 (CA); *Langton v Langton* [1995] 2 FLR 890; and *Claughton v Price* (1997) 30 HLR 396 (CA). In Australia, *Freeman v Brown* [2001] NSWSC 1028. As to chattels, see the Canadian automobile cases: *Addison v Ottawa Auto and Taxi Co* (1913) 16 DLR 318 (Ont SC (App Div)); *McKinnon v Brockinton* (1921) 60 DLR 303 (Man CA); and *Wiebe v Butchart's Motors Ltd* [1949] 4 DLR 838 (BCCA).
[66] Eg *Da Costa v Scandret* (1723) 2 P Wms 170, 24 ER 686; *Hulton v Hulton* [1917] 1 KB 813 (CA) 820.
[67] *Hulton v Hulton* [1917] 1 KB 813 (CA).

very considerable advantages'.[68] *Hulton v Hulton* is rightly regarded as a striking illustration of the scope of the court's discretion to achieve substantial *restitutio in integrum*.

C. Compensation

17.32 Any alteration to assets which have passed under a contract will bar rescission altogether at law. In equity rescission may be barred altogether where the alteration has been of such a magnitude as to change the nature of the asset in question.[69]

17.33 Where the nature of the asset has not been changed, however, equity is more flexible. In such cases the court will make financial adjustments to compensate for intervening improvements or deterioration to the assets, thereby making substantial *restitutio in integrum* possible.[70] In fixing the amount of the compensatory allowance the court exercises an element of discretion, but the decision whether to compensate is not itself properly speaking discretionary. As Rigby LJ put it in *Lagunas Nitrate Company v Lagunas Syndicate*, '[i]f substantially compensation can be made, rescission with compensation is ex debito justitiæ'.[71]

17.34 The term 'compensation' is used in this connection in a sense that is different from the sense in which that term is used in connection with damages. In connection with damages compensation consists in a money equivalent to the injury or loss that a person has suffered. The compensation is calculated so as to repair the injury or loss. Compensation as part of the relief given upon rescission is different. It consists in a money equivalent for the improvement or the deterioration, and so is calculated on a substitutive basis.[72] Compensation in this sense is given by way of perfecting the restitution and counter-restitution that must be made upon rescission.

(1) Improvements and repairs

17.35 Compensation is sometimes given in respect of improvements and repairs carried out by a party in possession of an asset he has received under a contract now being rescinded. Most of the cases involve improvements and repairs to land and buildings, as, for example, the erection of a manor house in the early case *York Buildings Co v Mackenzie*.[73] But the same principles apply in respect of chattels.[74] Naturally, compensation will not be given for the cost of repairs necessitated by the possessor's own mistreatment of the asset, but it will be given if the deterioration resulted from ordinary use.

---

[68] *Hulton v Hulton* [1917] 1 KB 813 (CA) 826.
[69] See further Chap 18, para [18.85].
[70] *Erlanger v The New Sombrero Phosphate Company* (1878) 3 App Cas 1218, 1278; *Lagunas Nitrate Company v Lagunas Syndicate* [1899] 2 Ch 392 (CA) 456.
[71] *Lagunas Nitrate Company v Lagunas Syndicate* [1899] 2 Ch 392 (CA) 456. In Australia, *Brown v Smitt* (1924) 34 CLR 160, 165.
[72] As to the difference between reparative compensation and substitutive compensation, see J McGhee and S Elliott (eds), *Snell's Equity* (34th edn, 2020) [20-28], *Agricultural Land Management Limited v Jackson (No 2)* (2014) 48 WAR 1 [333]–[375] and *Sim Poh Ping v Winsta Holdings Pte Ltd* [2020] 1 SLR 1199 [125].
[73] (1795) 8 Bro PC 42, 3 ER 432.
[74] Eg the repair of a truck in the Canadian case *F & B Transport Ltd v White Truck Sales Manitoba Ltd* (1964) 47 DLR (2d) 419 (Man QB), aff'd (1965) 49 DLR (2d) 670 (Man CA).

17.36 Compensation as such is only appropriate where the party in possession has carried out repairs or improvements at his own instance. Where the contract actually required that they be undertaken, the sum expended may instead be recovered by way of indemnity under the principle in *Newbigging v Adam* discussed earlier.[75]

17.37 Different considerations apply depending whether the claim to rescind is made by a vendor seeking to recover an asset or by a purchaser seeking to return one.

Vendor's claims

17.38 A rescinding vendor seeking to recover an asset must usually compensate the purchaser for improvements and repairs that he has made to it.

17.39 Compensation will not, however, generally be required where the purchaser carried out improvements or repairs at a time when he knew, or perhaps had reasonable notice, of the defect in his title,[76] with the likely exception of emergency repairs. Certainly, compensation will only exceptionally be given in respect of work carried out after the purchaser learns of the vendor's election to rescind.[77]

17.40 While there are comparatively few cases, on the same principle fraudsters are often refused compensation for improvements,[78] and this probably extends to other conscious wrongdoers. They can always protect their position before incurring the outlay by disclosing their wrongdoing and inviting the vendor to affirm the contract. Even a fraudster is not to be robbed, however, and so it seems likely that compensation will be given where his outlay will unequivocally benefit the vendor. This might be the case with repairs necessary to preserve the asset, improvements that it is clear the vendor desires, or valuable improvements to a marketable commercial asset.[79] This is subject to the proviso that the improvement or repair is carried out honestly and not, as it is put in the old cases, for the purpose of 'improving the vendor out of his estate' where he is unable to pay for it.[80]

17.41 While a conscious wrongdoer may not be entitled to be compensated for his outlays, there are many cases where the defendant's conduct has fallen short of this in which compensation has been given. Thus, compensation has often been given where contracts have been set aside for undue influence or against fiduciaries who have purchased from their principals.[81] These are species of equitable fraud, but allowances are given provided the vice in the transaction was not conscious or intentional.

17.42 It is often said that the repairs or improvements for which compensation will be given must be substantial, permanent, or lasting in nature.[82] Lord Truro spoke in *Mill v Hill* of

---

[75] (1886) 34 ChD 582 (CA). Eg *Forum Development Pte Ltd v Global Accent Trading Pte Ltd* [1995] 1 SLR 474 (CA) 482.
[76] *Kenney v Browne* (1796) 3 Ridg PC 462, 518. In Australia, *Brown v Smitt* (1924) 34 CLR 160, 165.
[77] *Edwards v M'Leay* (1818) 2 Swans 287, 36 ER 625.
[78] *Kenney v Browne* (1796) 3 Ridg PC 462, 518. And see *Restatement (First) of Restitution* § 158, cmt d (1937).
[79] Cf *Restatement (First) of Restitution* § 158 cmt c and d (1937).
[80] *Kenney v Browne* (1796) 3 Ridg PC 462, 518; *Ex p Hughes* (1802) 6 Ves 617, 31 ER 1223; *Stepney v Biddulph* (1865) 13 WR 576.
[81] Eg *York Buildings Co v Mackenzie* (1795) 8 Bro PC 42, 3 ER 432; *Ex p Bennett* (1805) 10 Ves 381, 32 ER 893; *Mill v Hill* (1852) 3 HLC 828, 10 ER 330; *O'Sullivan v Management Agency and Music Ltd* [1985] QB 428 (CA) 466.
[82] Eg *Ex p Bennett* (1805) 10 Ves 381, 32 ER 893 ('substantial and lasting'); *Trevelyn v White* (1839) 1 Beav 588, 48 ER 1069 ('substantial repairs and lasting improvements'); *Mill v Hill* (1852) 3 HLC 828, 10 ER 330 ('permanent improvement'). In Australia, *Sibley v Grosvenor* (1916) 21 CLR 469 ('substantial repairs and lasting improvements')

'permanent improvement in the pecuniary value of the estate', and said that no compensation would be given for improvements which are matters of personal taste or convenience,[83] though tasteful improvements favoured by the market would presumably warrant compensation. In *Ex p Bennett* Eldon LC gave compensation not only for substantial and lasting improvements and repairs, but also for minor or impermanent alterations 'such as have a tendency to bring the estate to a better sale'.[84] That was a case in which the land was to be sold at auction for the benefit of an insolvent estate, and so there was a prospect of realizing the value of impermanent alterations. In *Lambert v MacKenzie*[85] the Ontario Court of Appeal refused to compensate for the cost of digging and drilling holes, attempting to determine whether there was gravel in the land, where the result was to demonstrate that there was none.

17.43 In many of the older cases compensation was measured by the sum actually laid out on the improvement or repair,[86] on the basis, of course, that it is one tending to enhance the market value of the asset. This is a convenient approach because the amount expended will often be no greater than the actual increase in the asset's market value while also being more easily susceptible to proof.

17.44 Nevertheless, the amount expended will not always be reflected in an equivalent improvement in the asset's market value, and there are also early cases in which compensation was measured by the actual improved value of the asset.[87] More recently, in *Holder v Holder*,[88] Cross J noted that the older authorities conflicted and preferred those measuring compensation by the actual increase in the market value of the asset. He gave these reasons:

> It would be inequitable that the beneficiaries should get the benefit of any expenditure made in good faith by [the purchaser] which he would not have made if he had not thought that he owned the land and which has enhanced its value and will be reflected in the purchase price. On the other hand, there is no reason in equity why the [purchaser] should be given credit for expenditure which did not increase the value of the land or the value of which is exhausted before the resale or reconveyance which may not take place until many years after the original conveyance to him.[89]

17.45 That case involved improvements made to a farm by a trustee who had purchased the land from his trust. Similarly, in *JAD International Pty Ltd v International Trucks Australia Ltd*[90]

and *Brown v Smitt* (1924) 34 CLR 160 ('permanent lasting and substantial'). In Canada, *Lambert v MacKenzie* [1949] OWN 758 (CA) 759 ('permanent and substantial').

[83] *Mill v Hill* (1852) 3 HLC 828, 869; 10 ER 330, 346.
[84] *Ex p Bennett* (1805) 10 Ves 381, 400; 32 ER 893, 900. In Australia, *Brown v Smitt* (1924) 34 CLR 160. In Canada, *Lambert v MacKenzie* [1949] OWN 758 (CA) 759.
[85] [1949] OWN 758 (CA) 759.
[86] *Ex p Hughes* (1802) 6 Ves 617, 31 ER 1223; *Ex p Bennett* (1805) 10 Ves 381, 32 ER 893; *Edwards v M'Leay* (1818) 2 Swans 287, 36 ER 625; *Small v Attwood* (1832) Young 407, 159 ER 1051; *Gibson v D'Este* (1843) 2 Y & CCC 542, 63 ER 243; *Cooper v Phibbs* (1867) LR 2 HL 149; *Lagunas Nitrate Company v Lagunas Syndicate* [1899] 2 Ch 392 (CA). In Australia, *Sibley v Grosvenor* (1916) 21 CLR 469. A deduction may be appropriate where the improver has enjoyed the improvement for a period of time, as in *Jonval Builders Pty Ltd v Commissioner for Fair Trading* (2020) 104 NSWLR 1 (CA) [62].
[87] Eg *Robinson v Ridley* (1821) 6 Madd 2, 56 ER 988.
[88] [1968] Ch 353.
[89] *Holder v Holder* [1968] Ch 353, 373–74.
[90] (1994) 50 FCR 378 (Full Ct). The court cited as support the High Court of Australia's decision in *Brown v Smitt* (1924) 34 CLR 160. The order in that case is, however, unclear. The High Court directed inquiries both of the

the Full Court of the Federal Court of Australia held that compensation should only be given for the increase in the sale value of the asset attributable to the purchaser's efforts. In that case the court refused an allowance in respect of work on a truck's gearbox where there was no satisfactory basis for thinking it had improved the truck's value in the market.

Two principles appear to be in play. The first is that the rescinding vendor should not, in recovering the asset in question, be enriched at the expense of the purchaser, as he would be if he took the benefit of a valuable improvement or repair without paying compensation. That principle argues for a measure according to the actual increase in value realizable by the rescinding vendor. The second principle is that the purchaser should not be prejudiced where he has honestly changed his position on the faith of the voidable contract by expending sums improving and repairing the asset in question. This second principle may help to explain the authorities measuring compensation by the actual amount of the outlay. 17.46

While it would go beyond the decided authorities, on the basis of these two principles the correct measure should depend on whether the purchaser is entitled to have his position protected, as he would be, for example, in a case of mistake, innocent misrepresentation, or presumed undue influence.[91] Where the purchaser is entitled to protection, compensation should be in the amount of his actual outlay, so that he is left no worse off than if the contract had never been made. This should extend to outlays that have not produced an alteration favoured by the market. But where the purchaser's conduct is such that he does not merit protection, the sole purpose of compensation should be to ensure that the vendor is not unjustly enriched. In these cases the compensation should be measured by the actual increase in the market value of the asset, provided that is less than the cost of the work. 17.47

Purchaser's claims

Different considerations apply where it is the rescinding purchaser who has improved or repaired an asset he is now returning to the vendor. The question in cases of this variety is whether the rescinding purchaser is entitled to force the vendor to pay for the alteration. 17.48

Eldon LC's decision in *Edwards v M'Leay*[92] is authority that a rescinding purchaser is entitled to compensation for sums expended in making necessary repairs. The repairs being necessary, it stands to reason that the purchaser should be compensated, because he has spared the vendor the expense. Of course, no allowance will be given where the repair was necessitated by the purchaser's own fault. 17.49

Improvements and non-necessary repairs are more problematic, because the vendor may not have wanted them. In *Cheese v Thomas*, Nicholls V-C remarked that a rescinding purchaser 'will not necessarily be entitled to a further payment from the defendant; it may not be just to require the defendant to pay for improvements he does not want'.[93] While the Vice-Chancellor seems to have implied that there may be circumstances in which a rescinding 17.50

amount expended on improvements and repairs, and of the extent to which the value of the land had thereby been improved. Possibly the intention was that the purchaser should be compensated for the lesser of the two amounts.

---

[91] Cf *Restatement (First) of Restitution* § 158 cmt d (1937).
[92] (1818) 2 Swans 287, 36 ER 625. Similarly *Hart v Swaine* (1877) 7 ChD 42. In Australia, *Brown v Smitt* (1924) 34 CLR 160, 165.
[93] *Cheese v Thomas* [1994] 1 WLR 129 (CA) 137.

purchaser would be compensated for improvements, there appears to be no English authority in which such an order has been made.

17.51 The issues were discussed in some detail by the High Court of Australia in *Brown v Smitt*.[94] The claimant in that case had purchased grazing land on the faith of fraudulent statements. On rescinding the sale, he sought compensation for improvements he had made by way of clearing the land and providing for a permanent water supply. The High Court was divided three–two as to the claimant's entitlement to compensation. The majority considered that the claimant should be compensated, tersely highlighting the supposed injustice in the vendor receiving at no cost a valuable benefit upon rescission where he had procured the sale by fraud. It is not clear whether the majority intended that its decision should cover cases falling short of intentional misconduct.

17.52 The minority judges, Isaacs and Rich JJ, would have refused to compensate the claimant 'as part of the process of rescission'.[95] While their view has not prevailed in Australia, it accords better with the principles underpinning rescission. Referring to *Newbigging v Adam*,[96] they pointed out that rescission involves the 'undoing of all that was done directly or indirectly by force of the contract'.[97] The minority judges took this proposition as the foundation of their analysis, which was as follows:

> True, the vendor gets those improvements without paying for them. But he is not asking for them, and he is not bound to purchase them. Annulling one contract does not justify creating another; and, without another contract, what justification exists for compelling the vendor defendant to pay the value of the improvements? They are not the direct outcome of the contract, nor do they come into existence by force of the contract ... The allowance of permanent improvements to a plaintiff who throws back to the vendor the property the latter transferred to him is *ex facie* not restitution unless it is the result of some obligation created by the contract.[98]

17.53 Isaacs and Rich JJ distinguished the position of a rescinding purchaser from that of a rescinding vendor, where compensation for improvements is uncontroversial. As to the latter, they said that:

> The allowance of permanent improvements to a defendant rests on a totally different footing. There the governing principle is that 'he who seeks equity must do equity' ... In such a case it is a condition of obtaining rescission and of thereby being restored to the *status quo ante*.[99]

17.54 In the view of Isaacs and Rich JJ, the cost of improvements made by a rescinding purchaser is properly recoverable only as damages in tort, if it is recoverable at all.

---

[94] (1924) 34 CLR 160. See also *Jonval Builders Pty Ltd v Commissioner for Fair Trading* (2020) 104 NSWLR (CA) 1, where the plaintiff purchasers made the improvements by reason of the wrongdoing and the improvements would benefit the defendant vendors. In Canada, see *Lambert v MacKenzie* [1949] OWN 758 (CA), where the rescinding purchaser's claim for compensation failed on the facts, but was not said to be bad in principle.
[95] *Brown v Smitt* (1924) 34 CLR 160, 169.
[96] (1886) 34 ChD 582 (CA).
[97] *Brown v Smitt* (1924) 34 CLR 160, 169.
[98] *Brown v Smitt* (1924) 34 CLR 160, 170–72.
[99] *Brown v Smitt* (1924) 34 CLR 160, 172.

(2) Deterioration and depreciation

17.55 Circumstances often arise in which the deterioration of an asset in the hands of a rescinding purchaser is not so extreme as to make *restitutio in integrum* impossible. Deterioration of this sort can instead be made good by a compensating monetary adjustment, although there are circumstances in which deterioration does not call for any adjustment.

17.56 A rescinding purchaser is only required, as a condition of rescission, to compensate the vendor for deterioration that resulted from the purchaser's fault.[100] Ordinary wear or tear is for this reason not compensable.[101] More importantly, the purchaser will not be required to pay compensation where the asset has depreciated owing to the play of market forces.[102] Furthermore, the purchaser will not be responsible for deterioration that is the product of some inherent vice in the asset.[103] This was decided by the House of Lords in *Adam v Newbigging*.[104] Their Lordships there held that the claimant was entitled to rescind an agreement of partnership notwithstanding that the business had failed in the interim with large liabilities, because the failure was due to the aggravation of the partnership's pre-existing insolvency rather than any fault of the claimant.

17.57 In *Adam v Newbigging*[105] the misrepresentation entitling the claimant to rescind had related to the firm's solvency and profitability, but it is not essential that the cause of the deterioration was the subject matter of the misrepresentation or non-disclosure founding the claim to rescind. What is essential is that the rescinding party is not himself responsible for the deterioration. Provided this is so, the deterioration will not bar rescission and it will not require any adjustment. This is clear from the cases holding that depreciation owing to the accidental play of market forces is not compensable.[106]

17.58 Once a purchaser has notified his election to rescind and given the vendor a reasonable opportunity to take the asset in question back, he is no longer responsible for maintaining it. Should the vendor contest the rescission, the purchaser will not be responsible if the asset deteriorates during the course of their dispute.[107]

17.59 The discussion thus far has been concerned with the circumstances in which a rescinding purchaser must pay compensation for deterioration to assets he is returning. There are

---

[100] *Lagunas Nitrate Company v Lagunas Syndicate* [1899] 2 Ch 392 (CA) 456–57; *Spence v Crawford* [1939] 3 All ER 271 (HL Sc) 279–80. In Australia, *Balfour v Hollandia Raventhorpe NL* (1978) 18 SASR 240 (in Banco) 258; *Akron Securities Ltd v Iliffe* (1997) 143 ALR 457 (NSWCA). The precise standard of fault has not been discussed in the cases, though in *Kramer v McMahon* (1969) WN (Pt 1) (NSW) 584, 595 Helsham J asked whether the business in question had deteriorated from 'want of reasonable care by the plaintiffs'.
[101] *Kramer v McMahon* (1969) WN (Pt 1) (NSW) 584, 594–95.
[102] *Blake v Mowatt* (1856) 21 Beav 603, 613; 52 ER 993, 997; *The Western Bank of Scotland v Addie* (1867) LR 1 Sc App 145, 166; *Armstrong v Jackson* [1917] 2 KB 822, 829; *Cheese v Thomas* [1994] 1 WLR 129 (CA) 135; *Smith New Court Securities Ltd v Scrimgeour Vickets (Asset Management) Ltd* [1994] 1 WLR 1271 (CA) 1280. In Australia, *Balfour v Hollandia Raventhorpe NL* (1978) 18 SASR 240 (in Banco) 258; *JAD International Pty Ltd v International Trucks Australia Ltd* (1994) 50 FCR 378 (Full Ct).
[103] *Adam v Newbigging* (1888) 13 App Cas 308; *Lagunas Nitrate Company v Lagunas Syndicate* [1899] 2 Ch 392 (CA) 456–57; *Spence v Crawford* [1939] 3 All ER 271 (HL Sc) 279; *Senanayake v Cheng* [1965] AC 63 (PC—Singapore). In Canada, *Gearhart v Kraatz* (1918) 40 DLR 26 (Sask SC (App Div)).
[104] (1888) 13 App Cas 308.
[105] (1888) 13 App Cas 308.
[106] See n 98.
[107] *Maturin v Tredinnick* (1864) 10 LT(NS) 331. In Australia, *Alati v Kruger* (1955) 94 CLR 216, 225–26, 228. In Canada, *O'Flaherty v McKinlay* [1953] 2 DLR 514 (Nfld SC—Full Ct).

390   IV. RESTITUTIO IN INTEGRUM

understandably fewer cases in which a vendor has sought to recover an asset which has deteriorated in the hands of a purchaser, but compensation for deterioration has been awarded in cases of this sort as well.[108] Where the purchaser was not at fault, as, for example, in a case of mistake, one would expect the courts to be slow to make such awards.

17.60   The rescission cases do not address the question whether the measure of compensation is the loss of market value attributable to the deterioration or the cost of reinstating the asset. This is a question requiring a fine judgment as to the circumstances of the particular case and the comparative fault of the parties. Where the loss of market value is greater than the cost of reinstatement, the cost of reinstatement would seem to be the correct measure. More difficult problems arise where the asset can only be reinstated at a cost greater than the anticipated recovery in the asset's market value. The fair solution to problems of this variety probably depends on whether it is possible to reinstate the asset, whether it would be reasonable to do so, and whether the beneficiary of the adjustment actually intends to reinstate.[109]

(3) Irrelevant detriments

17.61   No adjustment will be made for detriments suffered as a consequence of or in connection with the contract but not pursuant to it. For example, in *Redgrave v Hurd*,[110] a case of innocent misrepresentation involving the sale of a solicitors' practice, the misled purchaser was not compensated for the expenses he had incurred in preparing to take up the practice and moving to Birmingham. While he had incurred these expenses as a consequence of the transaction now being avoided, the contract did not oblige him to incur them and so they were not properly compensable.

17.62   The most common detriment of this type is transaction expenses, such as the cost of instructing a solicitor or the commission paid to a stockbroker or an estate agent. Unless the party incurring these expenses was obliged to do so by the contract,[111] the expenses will not call for compensation as an element of *restitutio in integrum*.[112] The same is true of expenses incurred preparing to perform a contract.[113] Similarly, compensation will not be ordered as an element of the relief given upon rescission for the loss the claimant may have suffered by foregoing other opportunities in favour of the opportunity the contract had seemed to present.[114]

---

[108] *Ex p Bennett* (1805) 10 Ves 381, 400; 32 ER 893, 900. In New Zealand, *Hayes v Ross (No 3)* [1919] NZLR 786, 789.
[109] The tort and contract cases addressing like problems are usefully collected in A Tetterborn, *The Law of Damages* (2nd edn, 2010) chap 12 and [19.87]ff.
[110] (1881) 20 ChD 1 (CA). *Blackley Investments Limited v Burnie City Council (No 2)* (2011) 21 Tas R 98 (Full Ct) is an Australian example.
[111] Eg where the defendant vendor was bound by a contract for the sale of land to prove title, he may recover the cost of investigating title as an indemnity under the principle in *Whittington v Seale-Hayne* [1900] WN 31: *Carlish v Salt* [1906] 1 Ch 335.
[112] *McAllister v Richmond Brewing Company (NSW) Pty Ltd* (1942) 42 SR (NSW) 187; *Hayes v Ross (No 3)* [1919] NZLR 786; *Forum Development Pte Ltd v Global Accent Trading Pte Ltd* [1995] 1 SLR 474 (CA) 482.
[113] *Sibley v Grosvenor* (1916) 21 CLR 469.
[114] *Newbigging v Adam* (1886) 34 ChD 582 (CA) 589.

17.63 This principle is also illustrated by a line of nineteenth-century cases involving mortgages of reversionary interests by expectant heirs. In these cases the creditor sought to protect his interest in the reversion by obtaining an insurance policy on the life of the heir. The question was whether upon rescission of the mortgage the creditor was entitled to an allowance for the cost of the premiums he had paid to keep up the policy. While allowances were given in early cases,[115] Romilly MR decided in *Pennell v Millar*[116] that no allowance should be given. As he is reported to have later put it in *Bromley v Smith*, '[t]here was nothing to compel them to insure; it was done for their own security'.[117]

17.64 Where, however, the rescinding claimant also has a cause of action sounding in damages, he may be able to obtain compensation in this way for wasted transaction expenses and other detriments he has suffered as a consequence of the transaction. In principle these expenses are compensated by way of damages rather than restitution, but in fraud cases this is a distinction without a difference, since a court of equity has always had jurisdiction to award both in a single proceeding. It is only where there is no claim for damages that it becomes important to identify those detriments that can only be compensated in that way.[118] As a consequence, while there are several fraud cases in which items of this type were taken into account when working out the consequences of rescission,[119] the orders in these cases are best understood as blending elements of restitution and damages.

17.65 The Canadian case *Lewis v Howson*[120] appears to go beyond this. Upon rescission of a sale of a farm for misrepresentation, the Saskatchewan Court of Appeal awarded the claimant sums in respect of wages lost during the time he spent at the farm, various expenses he had incurred including the cost of moving to the farm and later moving back, and the cost of hiring help at the farm. These sums were not given by way of damages, and in any event fraud does not appear to have been alleged. If that is so, then the decision is inconsistent with principle.[121]

17.66 A party against whom rescission is sought will not have a claim to damages and so he will generally have to suffer detriments of the type identified earlier. The only exception occurs in those cases where the defendant is blameless and the detriment is sufficiently serious that the court is prepared to bar rescission altogether on the ground that there has been a material change of circumstances[122] or because rescission would have a disproportionate effect.[123]

---

[115] *Hoffman v Cooke* (1800/01) 5 Ves 622, 31 ER 772; *Edwards v Burt* (1852) 2 De G M & G 55, 42 ER 791 (consent order).
[116] (1857) 23 Beav 172, 53 ER 68.
[117] *Bromley v Smith* (1859) 26 Beav 644, 53 ER 1047. See also *Fry v Lane* (1888) 40 ChD 312.
[118] *McAllister v Richmond Brewing Company (NSW) Pty Ltd* (1942) 42 SR(NSW) 187. For example in cases of mistake, innocent misrepresentation, undue influence, and non-disclosure by an applicant for insurance.
[119] Eg *Edwards v M'Leay* (1818) 2 Swans 287, 36 ER 625 and *Gibson v D'Este* (1843) 2 Y & CCC 542, 63 ER 242.
[120] [1928] 2 WWR 197 (Sask CA). That decision was upheld in the Supreme Court of Canada but it is unclear whether this issue was raised on appeal: [1929] SCR 174.
[121] See *Bell v Robutka* (1966) 55 DLR (2d) 436 (Alta CA) 443.
[122] See Chap 18, paras [18.105]ff.
[123] See Chap 28.

18

Restitutio in Integrum Impossible

A.	Basic Principles	18.01	(1) Counter-restitution impossible	18.48
	(1) Purpose of the bar	18.03	(2) Substitutive counter-restitution	18.52
	(2) The role of fault	18.09	(3) The future of substitutive counter-	
	(3) The role of delay	18.12	restitution	18.62
B.	The Bar at Law and in Equity	18.17	E. Counter-restitution: Miscellaneous	
	(1) The bar at law	18.18	Issues	18.77
	(2) The bar in equity	18.27	(1) Possession, occupation, and use of	
	(3) Persistence of the distinction	18.30	asset	18.77
C.	Where Counter-restitution Not		(2) Asset changed	18.85
	Required	18.33	(3) Asset depreciated owing to market	
	(1) Benefits obtained other than		decline	18.93
	under the contract	18.34	(4) Services	18.99
	(2) Defendant's fault	18.36	(5) Other intangible benefits	18.102
	(3) Asset lost following tender	18.37	(6) Money	18.103
	(4) Costless benefits	18.39	F. Prejudicial Change of Circumstances	18.106
	(5) Insurance fraud	18.40	(1) Unjustified prejudice	18.107
	(6) Benefits the defendant was		(2) Money committed to joint	
	bound to confer	18.43	purposes	18.118
	(7) Worthless assets and services	18.46	(3) Reversible change of circumstances	18.119
	(8) Set-off	18.47	G. Miscellaneous Issues	18.121
D.	Counter-restitution and		(1) Date of assessment	18.121
	Unavailable Assets	18.48	(2) Onus of proof	18.124

A. Basic Principles

18.01 An election to rescind will usually be ineffective, and a claim seeking rescission will usually fail, where *restitutio in integrum* is impossible.[1] The requirement is that 'the party seeking [rescission] is able to put those against whom it is asked in the same situation in which they stood when the contract was entered into'.[2] This bar applies whatever the ground for rescission and whether that ground sounds at law or in equity,[3] though the bar operates less

---

[1] *Erlanger v The New Sombrero Phosphate Company* (1878) 3 App Cas 1218, 1278 is the most widely cited authority. See M Lobban, '*Erlanger v The New Sombrero Phosphate Company* (1878)' in C Mitchell and P Mitchell (eds), *Landmark Cases in the Law of Restitution* (2006) chap 6. In Australia, *Urquhart v Macpherson* (1878) 3 App Cas 831 (PC—Australia); *AH McDonald and Company Pty Ltd v Wells* (1931) 45 CLR 506; *Alati v Kruger* (1955) 94 CLR 216. In Canada, *Dominion Royalty Corporation v Goffatt* [1935] SCR 565; *Proprietary Mines Ltd v MacKay* [1939] 3 DLR 215 (Ont CA), aff'd [1941] 1 DLR 240 (SCC).

[2] *The Western Bank of Scotland v Addie* (1867) LR 1 Sc App 145, 164–65; and see *Spence v Crawford* [1939] 3 All ER 271 (HL Sc) 279.

[3] Eg *O'Sullivan v Management Agency and Music Limited* [1985] 1 QB 428 (CA) 458 (undue influence/breach of fiduciary duty); *Logicrose Ltd v Southend United Football Club Ltd* [1988] 1 WLR 1256, 1263 (bribery); *Halpern v Halpern (Nos 1 and 2)* [2008] QB 195 (CA) [72] (duress). In Australia, *Nadinic v Drinkwater* (2017) 94 NSWLR 518 (CA) [27].

restrictively in equity. The Court of Appeal has emphasized that rescission should be the normal remedy for misrepresentation, unless *restitutio in integrum* is truly impossible.[4]

The term *restitutio in integrum* was borrowed from Scots law as late as 1878.[5] It has been said to be 'somewhat vague' and to require careful handling.[6] Some judges and commentators have attempted to anglicize and modernize the nomenclature by speaking instead of counter-restitution being impossible.[7] While the modernizing impulse cannot be criticized, this suggestion risks obscuring the fact that a claimant's inability to make counter-restitution is only one of the reasons why *restitutio in integrum* may be impossible. As discussed below, the bar also applies where the circumstances have irreversibly changed since the contract was made such that the defendant would be unjustifiably prejudiced if the contract were now set aside.

18.02

(1) Purpose of the bar

Protection of defendant

The purpose of the *restitutio in integrum* bar is to protect the defendant from being put, upon rescission, in an unjustifiably worse position than he occupied before the contract was made.[8] It is true that the bar is frequently described in terms of the possibility of restoring both parties to their pre-contractual positions.[9] The authorities are clear, however, that the bar is only concerned with the position of the defendant. The claimant is entitled to take what he can get even though it is less than what he gave, and so the fact he cannot be fully restored to his original position will not preclude rescission.[10]

18.03

This was decided by the House of Lords in *Spence v Crawford*.[11] Spence sought the return of shares he had sold to Crawford. The company's capital had been increased since the time of sale such that the shares now comprised only a minority interest. This did not bar rescission because, according to Lord Thankerton, it was for Spence to say 'whether he is content to take the number of shares sold by him, though they no longer amount to one-half of the issued capital'.[12] Lord Thankerton noted in this regard 'that the condition of relief is the restoration of the defender to his pre-contract position, and that no stress is placed on whether

18.04

---

[4] *Salt v Stratstone Specialist Limited* [2016] RTR 17 (CA) [24], [31].
[5] *Erlanger v The New Sombrero Phosphate Company* (1878) 3 App Cas 1218, 1278, drawing upon *The Western Bank of Scotland v Addie* (1867) LR 1 Sc App 145.
[6] *Armstrong v Jackson* [1917] 2 KB 822, 828.
[7] *Dunbar Bank plc v Nadeem* [1998] 3 All ER 876 (CA) 883; *Johnson v EBS Pensioner Trustees Ltd* [2002] Lloyd's Rep PN 309 (CA) [58]; *Halpern v Halpern (No 2)* [2007] QB 88 [4]; G Virgo, *The Principles of the Law of Restitution* (3rd edn, 2015) 25; A Burrows, *A Restatement of the English Law of Contract* (2016) [34(5)(c)].
[8] See, to similar effect, *Restatement (Third) of Restitution* vol 2, 279 (2011).
[9] Eg *Clarke v Dickson* (1858) El Bl & El 148, 120 ER 463; *The Sheffield Nickel and Silver Plating Company Limited v Unwin* (1877) 2 QBD 214 (CA) 224; and *Erlanger v The New Sombrero Phosphate Company* (1878) 3 App Cas 1218, 1278.
[10] This accords with the rule applicable in a purchaser's claim for specific performance, for he is also entitled to take what he can get: *Mortlock v Buller* (1804) 10 Ves Jun 292, 315–16; 32 ER 857, 866; *Thames Guarantee Ltd v Campbell* [1985] QB 210 (CA) 235.
[11] [1939] 3 All ER 271 (HL Sc). See also *Clough v The London and North Western Railway Company* (1871) LR 7 Ex 26, 35; and *Armstrong v Jackson* [1917] 2 KB 822, 828–29. In Australia, *Urquhart v Macpherson* (1878) 3 App Cas 831 (PC—Australia) 838.
[12] *Spence v Crawford* [1939] 3 All ER 271 (HL Sc) 282. See also 279 (referring to *The Western Bank of Scotland v Addie* (1867) LR 1 Sc App 145, 164–65) and 289.

the pursuer is so restored'.[13] *Spence v Crawford* was a Scottish case, but Lord Thankerton said that this doctrine is the same in England.[14]

Bar not only concerned to prevent unjust enrichment of the claimant

18.05 Following a scholarly lead, Carnwath LJ has suggested that the *restitutio in integrum* bar is concerned in part at least to prevent the unjust enrichment of the claimant at the defendant's expense, for it prevents him from retaining what he has received whilst recovering what he has given.[15] That the unjust enrichment principle has a role to play in explaining the counter-restitution requirement has been recognized in the highest courts.[16]

18.06 Prevention of the claimant's unjust enrichment cannot, however, fully explain the bar. The focus of the cases is on the position of the defendant rather than on the enrichment the claimant has received. It is the fact the defendant would not be sufficiently restored to his original position that engages the bar. *Restitutio in integrum* may be impossible even though the claimant offers to return all of the benefits he has received if the circumstances have changed such that rescission would unjustifiably prejudice the defendant.[17]

Relationship with the defence of change of position

18.07 The *restitutio in integrum* bar bears some resemblance to the defence of change of position that has developed in other areas of the law of restitution.[18] The relationship between the two has excited considerable scholarly discussion.[19] It would be difficult to argue that the *restitutio in integrum* bar is simply the change of position defence under a different rubric, at least as that defence is conventionally understood.[20] However the two share the same purpose. Both are concerned to prevent the defendant from being left in an unjustifiably worse position than he would have occupied if the contract or transfer had never been made. The *restitutio in integrum* bar protects the defendant in the context of a decision whether to extinguish a bilateral agreement whereas the change of position defence protects the

---

[13] *Spence v Crawford* [1939] 3 All ER 271 (HL Sc) 279. See also *Bouygues Offshore v Utisol Transport Contractors Ltd* [1996] 2 Lloyd's Rep 153 (SC South Africa) 159.

[14] *Spence v Crawford* [1939] 3 All ER 271 (HL Sc) 280.

[15] *Halpern v Halpern (Nos 1 and 2)* [2008] QB 195 (CA) [74], citing GH Treitel, *The Law of Contract* (11th edn, 2003) 380. See also NY Nahan, 'Rescission: A Case for Rejecting the Classical Model' (1997) 27 UWALR 66; M Chen-Wishart, 'Unjust Factors and the Restitutionary Response' (2000) 20 OJLS 557, 566; A Burrows, *The Law of Restitution* (3rd edn, 2011) 249; and PBH Birks, *Unjust Enrichment* (2nd edn, 2005) 225–27.

[16] *Spence v Crawford* [1939] 3 All ER 271 (HL Sc) 288–89; *National Commercial Bank (Jamaica) Limited v Hew* [2003] UKPC 51 [43] (Jamaica).

[17] See further Part E of this chapter.

[18] *Lipkin Gorman (a firm) v Karnaple Ltd* [1991] 2 AC 548, 580.

[19] M Chen-Wishart, 'Loss Sharing, Undue Influence and Manifest Disadvantage' (1994) 110 LQR 174; M Chen-Wishart, 'Unjust Factors and the Restitutionary Response' (2000) 20 OJLS 557; P Hellwege, 'Unwinding Mutual Contracts: *Restitutio in Integrum* v. the Defence of Change of Position' in D Johnston and R Zimmermann (eds), *Unjustified Enrichment: Key Issues in Comparative Perspective* (2002) chap 9; S Worthington, 'The Proprietary Consequences of Rescission' [2002] RLR 28, 55–59; D Friedmann, 'Reversible Transfers—The Two Categories' [2003] RLR 1; B Häcker, 'Proprietary Restitution after Impaired Consent Transfers: a Generalised Power Model' [2009] CLJ 324, 347–49; E Bant, *The Change of Position Defence* (2009) chap 4; A Burrows, *The Law of Restitution* (3rd edn, 2011) 570; C Mitchell et al, *Goff and Jones The Law of Unjust Enrichment* (9th edn, 2016) [31-15]; A Lodder, *Enrichment in the Law of Unjust Enrichment and Restitution* (2012) 122–25.

[20] The *restitutio in integrum* bar does not, and cannot, operate *pro tanto* in the way the change of position defence does. Moreover, if the defendant's counter-performance is viewed as the relevant change of position, the bar requires counter-restitution even if the defendant was a wrongdoer, but there would be no defence of change of position in these circumstances. Cf *Spence v Crawford* [1939] 3 All ER 271 (HL Sc) 288 with *Lipkin Gorman (a firm) v Karnaple Ltd* [1991] 2 AC 548, 580.

defendant in the context of a decision whether to reverse a unilateral transfer. These different contexts explain the differences between the operation of the bar and the defence.

18.08 It is also necessary to ask whether the change of position defence, as such, can cut back the restitution and counter-restitution that must be made upon rescission. As explained earlier,[21] the *restitutio in integrum* bar is only concerned with ensuring that the defendant is not unjustifiably prejudiced and so a claimant may, if he wishes, rescind even though he will not receive full restitution. There is therefore no reason in principle why, following rescission, the restitution the defendant must make should not be cut back by a defence of change of position, provided he is in good faith and not a wrongdoer. Allowing the defendant a change of position defence, where appropriate, is preferable to barring rescission altogether. This step has not been taken in any English case but it has been taken in Australia.[22] It would, however, be contrary to principle and inconsistent with the *restitutio in integrum* bar to apply change of position in the other direction, as cutting back the counter-restitution the claimant must give as a condition of rescinding.[23]

(2) The role of fault

18.09 Fault plays an important role in the functioning of the bar that is not always openly recognized. *Restitutio in integrum* does not require that upon rescission the defendant should be placed in a position no worse than the position he occupied before the contract was made, but instead that he should not be placed in an unjustifiably worse position. Prejudicial changes of circumstance for which the claimant is responsible, or which are the result of accidental misfortune, will usually bar rescission.[24] However, those changes for which the defendant is responsible do not bar rescission,[25] and nor do changes owing to inherent defects in the contractual subject matter.[26]

18.10 Related to this, the *restitutio in integrum* bar has a more limited application where the defendant has been guilty of fraud or other conscious misconduct.[27] This is essentially for two reasons. The first is that a conscious wrongdoer is in practice more likely to be responsible for changes to the contractual subject matter that would otherwise make *restitutio in integrum* impossible. The second is that a defendant is not generally entitled to rely on

---

[21] See para [18.03].
[22] *Bathurst Regional Council v Local Government Financial Service Pty Ltd (No 5)* [2012] FCA 1200 [3322]; *Moore v The National Mutual Life Association of Australasia Limited* [2011] NSWSC 416 [99]. The latter decision is difficult to understand in that the ground for rescission was fraudulent misrepresentation: see [105].
[23] The counter-restitution the claimant must give may, however, be cut back where the defendant caused the inability to make complete counter-restitution. See part C below.
[24] *Houldsworth v City of Glasgow Bank* (1880) 5 App Cas 317, 338 (Lord Blackburn). In fact it is difficult to find authorities involving accidents and so the application of the bar in such cases is open to question. Depreciation in the value of an asset owing to the play of market forces might be said to be accidental, and yet it will not always bar rescission: *Armstrong v Jackson* [1917] 2 KB 822.
[25] *Clarke v Dickson* (1858) El Bl & El 148, 155; 120 ER 463, 466; *Lagunas Nitrate Co v Lagunas Syndicate* [1899] 2 Ch 392 (CA) 456–57 (Rigby LJ), approved in *Spence v Crawford* [1939] 3 All ER 271 (HL Sc) 279–80.
[26] *Adam v Newbigging* (1888) 13 App Cas 308. In Canada, *Gearhart v Kraatz* (1918) 40 DLR 26 (Sask SC (App Div)) 29–30.
[27] *Lagunas Nitrate Co v Lagunas Syndicate* [1899] 2 Ch 392 (CA) 434; *Spence v Crawford* [1939] 3 All ER 271 (HL Sc) 279–81, 288–89; *O'Sullivan v Management Agency and Music Ltd* [1985] QB 428 (CA) 458. In Canada, *Redican v Nesbitt* [1924] SCR 135 and *Kellogg Brown & Root Inc v Aerotech Herman Nelson Inc* (2004) 238 DLR (4th) 594 (Man CA) [57]–[63].

changes he has made to his position in reliance on the security of a contract he knows to have been procured by his own wrongdoing.[28]

18.11 This must not be taken too far. Subject to these points, the requirement of *restitutio in integrum* applies equally where the defendant has been guilty of conscious wrongdoing.[29] As Lord Wright put it in *Spence v Crawford*, '[t]he defendant has been fraudulent, he must not be robbed'.[30] Each case must be considered on its particular facts in order to determine whether the changes that have occurred are changes for which the defendant should be held responsible by reason of his misconduct.

(3) The role of delay

18.12 In the course of his landmark discussion of the *restitutio in integrum* bar in *Erlanger v The New Sombrero Phosphate Company*,[31] Lord Blackburn made these remarks:

> ... a Court of Equity requires those who come to it to ask its active interposition to give them relief, should use due diligence, after there has been such notice or knowledge as to make it inequitable to lie by. And any change which occurs in the position of the parties or the state of the property after such notice or knowledge should tell much more against the party *in môra*, than a similar change before he was *in môra* should do.

18.13 Lord Blackburn then referred to the classic exposition of the doctrine of laches in *Lindsay Petroleum Company v Hurd*,[32] and said that the question 'whether the balance of justice or injustice is in favour of granting the remedy or withholding it' depends 'on the degree of diligence which might reasonably be required, and the degree of change which has occurred'.[33] On this view the claimant's culpable delay is a factor tending to make *restitutio in integrum* impossible because during the period of such delay the claimant is more likely to be held responsible for the risk that the circumstances may change in a way that would prejudice the defendant were the contract to be rescinded. That is also how the relationship between delay and the *restitutio in integrum* bar is treated in the other principal English authorities.[34]

18.14 Lord Blackburn's achievement in *Erlanger*'s case was to synthesize into a unified doctrine disparate strands of authority, tracing their provenance to both sides of the jurisdictional divide, all based upon the same fundamental principle. So far as the relationship with delay is concerned, Lord Blackburn drew on the cases in equity where the claimant's prejudicial laches had been held to bar rescission. Those cases had never before been explained in terms of the impossibility of making *restitutio in integrum*, and indeed it is very difficult to find any earlier case in equity in which this precise notion had been articulated, save in the

---

[28] *Spence v Crawford* [1939] 3 All ER 271 (HL Sc) 281.
[29] Eg *Sheffield Nickle and Silver Plating Co v Unwin* (1877) 2 QBD 214 (CA) 223–24 and the decision of the Supreme Court of Eire in *Northern Bank Finance v Charlton* [1979] IR 149. In Australia, *Greater Pacific Investments Pty Ltd v Australian National Industries* (1996) 39 NSWLR 143 (CA) 152. In New Zealand, *Kenny v Fenton* [1971] NZLR 1 (CA) 18.
[30] *Spence v Crawford* [1939] 3 All ER 271 (HL Sc) 288.
[31] *Erlanger v The New Sombrero Phosphate Company* (1878) 3 App Cas 1218, 1279.
[32] (1874) LR 5 PC 239.
[33] *Erlanger v The New Sombrero Phosphate Company* (1878) 3 App Cas 1218, 1279.
[34] Eg *Lagunas Nitrate Company v Lagunas Syndicate* [1899] 2 Ch 392 (CA) 433–34; *Armstrong v Jackson* [1917] 2 KB 822, 828–29; *Holder v Holder* [1968] Ch 353 (CA) 394.

special case of marriage contracts[35] and the odd later case applying the reasoning in *Clarke v Dickson*.[36] But as Lord Blackburn perceived, at bottom that is what the defence of prejudicial laches was concerned with. On the common law side of the divide, the same idea had been expressed only a few years earlier in a passage in *Clough v The London and North Western Railway Company*[37] that Lord Blackburn also treated as an application of the *restitutio in integrum* bar.

The organizing principle is that the defendant should not as a result of rescission be placed in an unjustifiably worse position than the position he would have occupied had the contract never been made. Where the claimant delays in electing to rescind, it will necessarily be difficult to justify any substantial prejudice the defendant might upon rescission suffer by reason of a change of circumstances occurring during the period of that delay. This is particularly so where the change in circumstances was foreseeable,[38] as for example in the case of a perishable asset or an asset liable to fluctuate in value.[39] Certainly rescission would be barred where the claimant was hoping to speculate at the defendant's risk. As Lord Blackburn put it, '[if] no steps to repudiate a lottery ticket were taken till after the ticket came up blank, so that the purchaser, if it came up a prize, might have kept it, it would surely be inequitable to set aside the contract then.'[40]

18.15

The relationship between delay and the *restitutio in integrum* bar is viewed differently by some judges in Australia. In *JAD International*,[41] the Full Court of the Federal Court of Australia held that a decline in the market value of the asset the claimant must return, occurring during a period of culpable delay, is not relevant to the question whether *restitutio in integrum* remains possible. Rather, that prejudicial change of circumstances is instead to be considered by the court in deciding whether to refuse relief on the ground of delay. The Federal Court took this to be the effect of *Fysh v Page*,[42] a decision of the High Court of Australia. On this view laches or delay operates independently of the *restitutio in integrum* bar.

18.16

B. The Bar at Law and in Equity

The scope of the *restitutio in integrum* bar depends on the capacity of the claimant and the law to undo what changes there may have been that affect the defendant's position. Although the underlying rationale of the bar is the same, it operates differently at law than it does in

18.17

---

[35] *North v Ansell* (1731) 2 P Wms 618, 24 ER 885; notes at 2 Eq Ca Abr 391, 22 ER 335; H Maddock, *A Treatise on the Principles and Practice of the High Court of Chancery* (1815) vol 1, 215. Suggestions that a general rule existed in J Adams, *The Doctrine of Equity* (1850) and J Hill, *A Practical Treatise on the Law Relating to Trustees* (1845) rely upon *Anglesey v Annesley* (1741) 1 Bro 289, 299; 1 ER 573, 580 and *King v Hamlet* (1834) 2 My & K 456, 39 ER 1018, both of which are explicable on other grounds.
[36] (1858) El Bl & El 148, 120 ER 463; see *Mixer's case* (1859) 4 De G & J 575, 45 ER 223.
[37] (1871) 7 LR Ex 26, 35: 'if in consequence of his delay even the position of the wrong-doer is affected, it will preclude him from exercising his right to rescind.'
[38] *Nelson v Rye* [1996] 1 WLR 1378, 1392: 'the plaintiff's knowledge that the delay will cause [substantial] prejudice is a factor to be taken into account.'
[39] *Lagunas Nitrate Company v Lagunas Syndicate* [1899] 2 Ch 392 (CA) 433–34.
[40] *Erlanger v The New Sombrero Phosphate Company* (1878) 3 App Cas 1218, 1281.
[41] *JAD International Pty Ltd v International Trucks Australia Ltd* (1994) 50 FCR 378 (Full Ct) 388. See also *Baburin v Baburin (No 2)* [1991] 2 Qd R 240 (Full Ct).
[42] (1956) 96 CLR 233, 242–43.

equity because rescission at law is a right of self-help that, upon being exercised, takes immediate and automatic effect. In practice the bar circumscribes the availability of rescission much more closely at law than it does in equity. The two need to be considered separately.

(1) The bar at law

18.18 As has been explained in Chapter 10, there is no common law action for rescission. The mechanism of rescission at common law is that the claimant announces the avoidance of the contract and then brings an action to recover what he has transferred under it, supposing that the common law recognizes an action apt to recover the type of asset in question. That action may only succeed, however, if the court concludes that the claimant has effectively rescinded the contract, and that can only be done if the defendant is completely restored to his original position.[43]

18.19 There is no difficulty with *restitutio in integrum* where the defendant's obligations remain wholly executory. But even where those obligations have been performed, *restitutio in integrum* may be achieved in three different ways depending on the nature of the benefit the claimant has received.[44]

18.20 First, the claimant may return or tender whatever it is he has received under the contract. Secondly, title to the asset the claimant has received may automatically revest in the defendant. This does not occur in the case of land, but it does occur where a sale of goods is rescinded for fraud and probably duress. It appears that tender is not a condition of rescission where title revests automatically.

18.21 Thirdly, where the defendant has paid money to the claimant, he may automatically acquire a claim to recover it as money had and received. For example, the rescission of an insurance contract by an insurer for misrepresentation or non-disclosure on the part of the assured may be effective at common law even though the insurer does not tender the premium money because the assured automatically acquires a claim to recover it. The defendant's acquisition of this claim satisfies the requirement of *restitutio in integrum*.

18.22 *Restitutio in integrum* sufficient to support an election to rescind at law will be possible where the consideration the claimant has received is such that by one of these three methods the defendant can be completely restored to his original position. The requirement is a strict one, however, and if any aspect of the consideration provided by the defendant is not restored in one of these three ways then the attempt to rescind will be ineffective. Since the claimant may nonetheless be able to rescind in equity, and since he is usually entitled to recoup his loss by an action in damages, the unavailability of rescission at law is not a denial of justice.

18.23 The strictness of the doctrine at common law is illustrated by the seminal cases of *Hunt v Silk* and *Blackburn v Smith*.[45] Both of these were decided on the proposition that where the

---

[43] The leading cases are *Hunt v Silk* (1804) 5 East 449, 102 ER 1142; *Blackburn v Smith* (1848) 2 Ex 783, 154 ER 707; and *Clarke v Dickson* (1858) El Bl & El 148, 120 ER 463.
[44] See generally Chap 14, where the authorities supporting the following propositions are identified.
[45] *Hunt v Silk* (1804) 5 East 449, 102 ER 1142; *Blackburn v Smith* (1848) 2 Ex 783, 154 ER 707. These were both in fact cases of termination for breach, but the distinction between that and rescission *ab initio* was not drawn at that

claimant has enjoyed the possession of land under a contract, however briefly, it is impossible for him to restore the defendant to his original position. As Parke B put it in *Blackburn v Smith*: 'How can [the purchaser] rescind when he has had possession of the land? There can be no rescission of the contract, unless the parties can be placed in the status quo.'[46] A surrender of present possession would not restore to the defendant the benefit the claimant enjoyed during the period of his possession.

In *Erlanger v The New Sombrero Phosphate Company*,[47] Lord Blackburn attributed the strict approach of the common law courts to the comparative poverty of their adjudicative machinery, particularly when it came to making financial adjustments. This may be part of the explanation, but it is difficult to understand why the jury was not thought capable in many cases. After all, one of the reasons damages were rarely given in equity was precisely that the jury was deemed uniquely fit to quantify them.[48] Moreover, if the issue were simply one of adjudicative machinery, the administrative fusion of the common law and equity courts wrought by the Judicature reforms should have provoked a reappraisal, for all of the machinery formerly available only in Chancery is now available when purely legal rights are in issue.

18.24

The reason for the common law's strict approach instead springs from the fact that rescission at common law takes effect automatically upon notice. While the parties may need to resort to the court in order to have their claims for the recovery of benefits enforced, there is no scope for a discretionary adjustment of benefits between them. In these circumstances rescission can only occur if at the moment it is announced the defendant is completely restored to his original position, either because he has received back everything he gave or because he has acquired a claim to recover it. If the defendant were not completely restored to his original position, then he would be unfairly prejudiced to that extent and there would be no mechanism for reversing that prejudice.

18.25

It seems to follow that in principle executed contracts may only be rescinded at law either where the asset the claimant has received can be specifically returned to the defendant or where the benefit is of such a nature that the common law affords the defendant a claim to recover it. In practice rescission is rarely available at law except where the defendant's obligations remain executory; where the defendant has only paid money, as in the case of a contract for insurance; and where the defendant has transferred chattels to the claimant that have not been used and that remain in the same condition.

18.26

(2) The bar in equity

The *restitutio in integrum* bar has a more limited scope in equity than it does at common law, at least where the claimant has not been guilty of laches. The requirement is not that

18.27

---

time as it is nowadays, and these cases have always been treated as authority in relation to rescission for fraud. See eg *Clark v Dickson* (1858) El Bl & El 148, 120 ER 463.

[46] (1848) 2 Ex 783, 790; 154 ER 707, 710.
[47] (1878) 3 App Cas 1218, 1278. See also *Winterbottom v Ingham* (1845) 7 QB 611, 115 ER 620.
[48] J Story, *Commentaries on Equity Jurisprudence* (13th edn, 1886) vol 2, para 794a.

the defendant be restored to the very same position he was in before the contract was made. Rather, the concern of equity is to achieve a practically just result.[49] This means that *restitutio in integrum* will be possible in equity provided the defendant can be put in as good a position as before, what is known as substantial *restitution in integrum*.[50] Rescission occurs in equity by order of the court, and the claimant's obligation to make *restitutio in integrum* is imposed upon him as a condition of the relief he seeks. At that stage the court may make discretionary adjustments of various types to ensure that the defendant is not unfairly prejudiced by the rescission of the contract.[51]

18.28 The scope of the bar is accordingly coextensive with the scope of the court's ability and willingness to ensure that the defendant is put in as good a position as before by way of discretionary adjustments. That topic is addressed in detail in the course of this chapter. It may be observed at this point that there are two fundamental questions, the answers to which largely determine the scope of the bar.

18.29 The first question is in what circumstances a claimant who is unable to make specific counter-restitution of what he has received may instead restore the defendant to his original position by paying an equivalent sum of money. The second question is in what circumstances *restitutio in integrum* will be barred by other changes of circumstances that have occurred, apart from changes to the asset or its availability, the effect of which would be to prejudice the defendant were the contract now set aside. Both of these questions are controversial.

(3) Persistence of the distinction

18.30 The restrictiveness of the *restitutio in integrum* bar as it is applied by the common law is often viewed as archaic and treated with a degree of scorn. It has been suggested that the differences between the bar as it is applied by the common law and in equity should not be allowed to persist, and it has also been suggested that the strictures of the common law bar have in practice been relaxed so that equity's more flexible approach now prevails generally.[52]

18.31 These views are misplaced and tend to stem from a misunderstanding of the reasons why the bar operates as it does at common law. The cardinal distinguishing feature of rescission at law is that it involves the exercise of a right of self-help. Rescission occurs upon the claimant's election, and all of the consequences follow immediately and automatically. There is no opportunity or room for a discretionary judicial adjustment between the parties. Rescission can only occur in this way if the defendant can be immediately and automatically

---

[49] *Erlanger v The New Sombrero Phosphate Company* (1878) 3 App Cas 1218, 1278. See also eg *O'Sullivan v Management Agency and Music Ltd* [1985] 1 QB 428 (CA) 458, 466; *Cheese v Thomas* [1994] 1 WLR 129 (CA) 136; *Midland Bank plc v Greene* [1995] 1 FCR 374. In Australia, *Alati v Kruger* (1955) 94 CLR 216, 223–24; *Taheri v Vitek* [2014] NSWCA 209 [96]. See further Chap 13, paras [13-08]–[13.10].
[50] *Compagnie Française des Chemins de Fer Paris-Orleans v Leeston Shipping Company Ltd* [1919] 1 Lloyd's Rep 235, 238.
[51] *Earl Beauchamp v Winn* (1873) LR 6 HL 223, 232.
[52] Eg *Halpern v Halpern (Nos 1 and 2)* [2008] QB 195 (CA) [69]; PBH Birks, *Unjust Enrichment* (2nd edn, 2005) 227; HG Beale (ed), *Chitty on Contracts* (33rd edn, 2019) [7-125]; C Mitchell et al, *Goff and Jones: The Law of Unjust Enrichment* (9th edn, 2016) [31-02]–[31-03].

restored to his original position, otherwise he would be unfairly prejudiced and left without a satisfactory remedy. That this is possible only in certain limited circumstances explains the restrictiveness of the bar at law. The bar will necessarily remain restrictive for so long as it remains possible to rescind on a self-help basis.[53]

There is nonetheless a degree of truth in the view that the more flexible approach of equity now prevails. In cases of fraud and duress,[54] equity exercises a concurrent jurisdiction with the common law. If a contract remains wholly executory, or if the common law *restitutio in integrum* bar can be satisfied, then the claimant may rescind at law on a self-help basis. But if this is not possible then the claimant may apply to the court, which, acting in its equity jurisdiction, will often be able to make whatever discretionary adjustments are necessary.[55] For this reason it may fairly be said that equity's more flexible approach does prevail except where for some particular reason the claimant requires the benefits of self-help rescission.

18.32

C. Where Counter-restitution Not Required

Restitutio in integrum is impossible where the claimant cannot make sufficient counter-restitution of whatever he has received under the contract. The general rule is that the claimant must return all of the assets and other benefits he has received, and this is so irrespective of the wrongfulness of the defendant's conduct.[56] There are, however, certain assets and other benefits that a claimant will not be required to return as a condition of the relief he seeks.[57]

18.33

(1) Benefits obtained other than under the contract

Counter-restitution need only be made in respect of assets and other benefits that the claimant received under the contract. This was the reason Millett J gave in *Logicrose Ltd v Southend United Football Club Ltd*[58] for refusing to order the rescinding party to account for a £70,000 bribe the counterparty had paid his agent as an inducement to procure the contract. This was notwithstanding that the agent had since paid the bribe over to the rescinding party. Millett J said that 'a principal who elects to rescind a contract is bound to return the benefits he has received under the contract, but no more; he is not bound to treat money paid to his agent otherwise than under the contract as if it were paid under it'.[59]

18.34

Likewise, there is no obligation to account for benefits the claimant has received as a result of the contract but not under it. For example, the Australian case *Akron Securities Ltd v*

18.35

---

[53] Cf J O'Sullivan's view that self-help rescission should be abolished: 'Rescission as a Self-Help Remedy: A Critical Analysis' [2000] CLJ 509.
[54] In the case of duress, see *Halpern v Halpern (Nos 1 and 2)* [2008] QB 195 (CA).
[55] *Alati v Kruger* (1955) 94 CLR 216, 223–24; *O'Sullivan v Management Agency and Music Ltd* [1985] QB 428 (CA) 457.
[56] *Spence v Crawford* [1939] 3 All ER 271 (HL Sc) 288; *Gamatronic (UK) Ltd v Hamilton* [2017] BCC 670 is a recent authority that confirms the vitality of the rule. In Australia, *Greater Pacific Investments Pty Ltd v Australian National Industries* (1996) 39 NSWLR 143 (CA) 152.
[57] See also *Restatement (First) of Restitution* § 65 (1937).
[58] [1988] 1 WLR 1256. See also *Marr v Tumulty*, 256 NY 15, 175 NE 356 (CA 1931) (Cardozo J).
[59] [1988] 1 WLR 1256, 1264.

Illife[60] involved contracts comprising a tax shelter scheme that were subsequently set aside at the instance of the purchaser of the scheme. Mason P said that *restitutio in integrum* did not require that the rescinding purchaser should account for the value of the tax benefit he had received as a result of the scheme while it was on foot.[61]

(2) Defendant's fault

18.36 Counter-restitution is not required, and *restitutio in integrum* will not be impossible, where the claimant's inability to return a particular asset or other benefit is the result of the defendant's wrongdoing.[62] *Hine v McCallum*,[63] a Canadian case, provides a good illustration. Rescission was granted in that case even though the rescinding purchaser of a farm was no longer able to return the land or chattels, these having been seized by creditors in realization of securities held against them. The creditors, however, were those of the vendor not the rescinding purchaser, and the vendor had concealed the encumbrances at the time of the sale.

(3) Asset lost following tender

18.37 Once a purchaser has notified his election to rescind and given the vendor a reasonable opportunity to take the asset in question back, he is no longer responsible for maintaining it. Should the vendor contest the rescission, the purchaser will not be responsible if the asset is lost during the course of their dispute.[64] This was decided in *Maturin v Tredinnick*,[65] in which the shares in question were forfeit during the course of the dispute owing to a failure to pay calls.

18.38 The same principle was applied by the High Court of Australia in *Alati v Kruger*.[66] That case involved a failing fruit business, the principal asset of which was its lease. Following the close of argument at trial, but before the judge delivered his judgment, the rescinding purchaser closed down the business and the landlord re-entered the premises. The High Court held that the purchaser had acted fairly and that he 'was under no duty to go on indefinitely, working for nothing and incurring losses'.[67] The court indicated, however, that it would have refused rescission had the purchaser brought about the loss of the leasehold and

---

[60] (1997) 41 NSWLR 353 (CA).
[61] *Akron Securities Ltd v Illife* (1997) 41 NSWLR 353 (CA) 370. That decision appears to have been overlooked by the same court in *HP Mercantile Pty Ltd v Dierickx* [2013] NSWCA 479 [134], where a tax advantage was viewed as a returnable benefit. See also *Amadio Pty Ltd v Henderson* (1998) 81 FCR 149 (Full Ct) 200 (illegality).
[62] *Rees v De Bernardy* [1896] 2 Ch 437, 446. In Hong Kong, *Crown Master International Trading Co Ltd v China Solar Energy Holdings Ltd* [2015] 4 HKC 505 [56].
[63] [1925] 2 DLR 403 (Man KB) 410.
[64] *Maturin v Tredinnick* (1864) 10 LT(NS) 331. In Australia, *Alati v Kruger* (1955) 94 CLR 216, 225–26, 228. In Canada, *O'Flaherty v McKinlay* [1953] 2 DLR 514 (Nfld SC—Full Ct); *Stewart v Complex 329 Ltd* (1990) 109 NBR (2d) 117.
[65] (1864) 10 LT(NS) 331.
[66] (1955) 94 CLR 216, 225–26, 228. See also *Kramer v McMahon* (1969) 89 WN (Pt 1) (NSW) 584, where immediately upon notice of rescission mortgagees took possession. Cf *Butler v Croft* (1973) 27 P & CR 1. In Canada, *O'Flaherty v McKinlay* [1953] 2 DLR 514 (Nfld SC— Full Ct).
[67] *Alati v Kruger* (1955) 94 CLR 216, 226.

the goodwill by discontinuing the business and abandoning the premises without giving the vendor a reasonable opportunity to take them back.[68]

(4) Costless benefits

A rescinding claimant need not return benefits the conferral of which did not put the defendant to any expense, for upon rescission the defendant is not prejudiced. This is illustrated by *Spence v Crawford*.[69] Upon the share sale in that case the fraudulent purchaser assumed the innocent vendor's liability to the bank for the business's debts. Rescission was not barred because, as events transpired, the company prospered and so the bank never claimed on the guarantee.

18.39

(5) Insurance fraud

The Marine Insurance Act 1906 provides that an insurer who avoids a marine insurance policy in circumstances of fraud on the part of the assured need not return any premium that has been paid.[70] It was for a long time not clear whether the rule applicable to marine insurance also applied to other forms of insurance. The framers of the Marine Insurance Act 1906 adopted the practice of the common law courts in insurance cases.[71] Those were cases in which the assured made a claim on the policy which the insurer defended by rescinding. But if instead the insurer sought pre-emptively to have the policy delivered up and cancelled, its claim was in Chancery. The practice in Chancery appears to have been that the premium would have to be paid back or allowed out of the costs as a condition of the insurer's relief.[72]

18.40

This uncertainty has now been resolved by further legislation. The Insurance Act 2015 provides that where there has been a deliberate or reckless breach of the duty of fair presentation in relation to a non-consumer insurance contract entitling the insurer to rescind, the premium need not be returned.[73] The Consumer Insurance (Disclosure and Representations) Act 2012 makes the same provision for misrepresentations in relation to consumer insurance contracts except that there is a power to require repayment of the premium where retention would be unfair to the consumer.[74]

18.41

These are anomalous exceptions to the general principle that even a fraudster is *prima facie* entitled to counter-restitution.[75] The premium is capable of return, and once the policy is set

18.42

---

[68] Cf *Campbell v Back Office Investments Pty Ltd* (2008) 66 ACSR 359 (NSWCA); on appeal (2009) 238 CLR 304 [107]–[109], where the parties shared responsibility for the loss of the business.
[69] [1939] 3 All ER 271 (HL Sc).
[70] Marine Insurance Act 1906, ss 84(1) and 84(3)(a).
[71] Eg *Chapman v Fraser* (1793) in JA Park, *A System of law of Marine Insurance* (F Hilyard (ed)) (8th edn, 1842) 456; *Rivaz v Gerussi* (1880) 6 QBD 222 (CA) 230.
[72] Eg *Whittingham v Thornburgh* (1690) 2 Vern 206, 23 ER 734; *Da Costa v Scandret* (1723) 2 P Wms 170, 24 ER 686; *Barker v Walters* (1844) 8 Beav 92, 96; 50 ER 36, 38. In Canada, *Brophy v North American Life Assurance Co* (1902) 32 SCR 261, 270, 276.
[73] Sched 1, s 8(2).
[74] Sched 1, s 4(3).
[75] *Spence v Crawford* [1939] 3 All ER 271 (HL Sc) 288.

aside the insurer has no title to retain it. Allowing the insurer to retain the premium could only be justified as a punitive measure, but English civil courts do not punish fraudsters.[76]

(6) Benefits the defendant was bound to confer

18.43 Counter-restitution is not required of benefits which the defendant was in any event legally bound to confer without charge. For example, *Hulton v Hulton*[77] involved a separation deed procured by the fraud of the husband. Upon rescission, his claim to have repaid the annual sums of £500 he had paid under the deed was refused on the ground, amongst others, that absent the deed the husband would have been bound to pay at least that amount as maintenance.[78] The same principle applies if, for example, a government or company official charges for a service he ought to provide for free.[79] The claimant is entitled to recover the charge without making any allowance for the value of the service.

18.44 The *Rembrandt Enterprises* case involved an original contract for the supply of egg products which had been replaced by a contract on the same terms except for a higher price.[80] The intermediate resale of the eggs did not prevent the purchaser from rescinding the variation contract because rescission reinstated the original contract with the consequence that the seller had been bound to supply the same egg product. The net result was that the seller had to repay the excess price charged under the rescinded variation contract.

18.45 *Allason v Campbell*,[81] an unreported decision of the Court of Appeal, indicates that the principle may extend further to benefits the defendant would inevitably have conferred on the claimant even though there was no legal obligation to do so. That case involved the rescission of an agreement compromising a libel action. The defendant had already performed the agreement by printing an apology, but the Court of Appeal held that this did not bar rescission because a printed apology would have fallen short of the minimum settlement terms in any event.

(7) Worthless assets and services

18.46 In equity at least, there is no obligation to return assets that were worthless from the beginning, as with the broken heaters in issue in *Kellogg Brown & Root Inc v Aerotech Herman Nelson Inc*.[82] The same principle was applied by the Court of Appeal in *Phosphate Sewage*

---

[76] *Spence v Crawford* [1939] 3 All ER 280 (HL) 289; *Broome v Cassell* [1972] AC 1027, 1076, 1030–31. The position taken in the text agrees with P MacDonald Eggers et al, *Good Faith and Insurance Contracts* (4th edn, 2018) [16.64] and [16.122] but disagrees with J Bird et al, *MacGillivray on Insurance Law* (14th edn, 2018) [8-30], the editors of which favour the view that the premium should be irrecoverable on the basis that contracts of insurance require utmost good faith so that fraud is especially unforgivable.
[77] [1917] 1 KB 813 (CA).
[78] *Hulton v Hulton* [1917] 1 KB 813 (CA) 821.
[79] *Guinness plc v Saunders* [1990] 2 AC 663.
[80] *BV Nederlandse Industrie Van Eiprodukten v Rembrandt Enterprises Inc* [2019] 1 All ER (Comm) 543, this point unaffected by the appeal [2019] 3 WLR 1113 (CA).
[81] (CA) 26 February 1998.
[82] (2004) 238 DLR (4th) 594 (Man CA) [66]. *KSH Farm Limited v KSH Plant Limited* [2021] EWHC 1986 (Ch) [650] is another example.

Company v Hartmont.[83] That case involved a sale of foreign mining concessions which were either void or voidable by the foreign government at the time they were sold to the claimant, which had since been avoided, and which were in any event incapable of being worked economically. Similarly, in *Halpern v Halpern*[84] Carnwath LJ said that counter-restitution would not be required in respect of the retiling of a roof if it transpired that the work was unnecessary and that the workman had caused the homeowner to agree to the work by means of fraud or duress.

(8) Set-off

A claimant may be entitled to set off a sum he would otherwise have to return against a separate obligation that his counterparty owes him.[85]

D. Counter-restitution and Unavailable Assets

(1) Counter-restitution impossible

The basic rule

Perhaps the central example of a case in which *restitutio in integrum* will sometimes be impossible occurs where the claimant has received an asset which he is no longer able to return. This may be because he has sold the asset or given it away.[86] He may have encumbered it in a way that prevents him from now returning it.[87] It may also be that the asset no longer exists, having been extinguished or consumed or otherwise destroyed.[88] Subject to the possibility of substitutive counter-restitution, the unavailability of the asset in question operates as a bar both at law and in equity.

Some assets available and some not

Where the claimant has received several assets under the same contract, rescission will be barred unless he can return all of them. There is an exception where the contract can be severed into a series of discrete sales.[89] For example, contracts for the sale of identical shares may be severable so that if the purchaser resells some shares before he learns of his right to rescind, he will still be entitled to rescind in respect of the shares that remain in his hands.[90]

---

[83] (1875) 5 ChD 394 (CA) 454–55.
[84] [2008] QB 195 (CA).
[85] *Keatley v Churchman* (1922) 65 DLR 357 (Alta SC (App Div)) 361.
[86] *The Sheffield Nickel and Silver Plating Company Limited v Unwin* (1877) 2 QBD 214, 224 (patent alienated); *Re Cape Breton Company* (1885) 29 ChD 795 (CA) 803 (coal areas sold); *Re Leeds Hanley Theatre of Varieties Ltd* [1902] 2 Ch 809 (CA). In Canada, *Dominion Royalty Corp v Goffatt* [1935] 1 DLR 780 (Ont CA), aff'd [1935] 4 DLR 736 (SCC) (alienation of leasehold); *Proprietary Mines Ltd v MacKay* [1939] 3 DLR 215 (Ont CA), aff'd [1941] 1 DLR 240 (SCC) (alienation of claim against bankrupt estate).
[87] *Dimsdale v Dimsdale* (1856) 3 Drew 556, 577; 61 ER 1015, 1024; *Re Worssam* (1882) 46 LT 584, 591–92; *Dunbar Bank plc v Nadeem* [1998] 3 All ER 876 (CA) 887. In Singapore, *Liberty Sky Investments Ltd v Goh Seng Heng* [2019] SGHC 39 (beneficial interest in shares).
[88] *Clark v Dickson* (1858) El Bl & El 148, 155; 120 ER 463, 466; *Ladywell Mining Co v Brookes* (1887) 35 ChD 400 (CA) 414 (lease extinguished). In Australia, *AH Macdonald and Company Pty Ltd v Wells* (1931) 45 CLR 506, 512–13 (patents extinguished).
[89] See further Chap 19, para [19.06].
[90] *Maturin v Tredennick* (1864) 10 LT 331; *Re The Mount Morgan (West) Gold Mine Limited* (1887) 56 LT 622.

Asset recovered

18.50 What if the claimant has sold the asset but he recovers it before attempting to rescind? The earliest cases to consider this situation gave conflicting answers. *Street v Blay*,[92] a common law case, decided that the intermediate sale would bar rescission, while *Gillette v Peppercorn*,[93] a case in Chancery, decided that it would not.[94] Thirty years later, in the Chancery case *Re Bank of Hindustan*,[95] Wickens V-C held that the effect of an intermediate sale is to bar rescission, apparently because the right to rescind is then lost and cannot be revived. *Gillette v Peppercorn* was not mentioned even though both cases involved share sales. It may be possible to square the two cases on the basis that *Gillette v Peppercorn* involved a breach of fiduciary duty whereas *Re Bank of Hindustan* involved only an innocent misrepresentation.

18.51 The view taken in *Re Bank of Hindustan*[96] was later adopted in two Scottish cases also involving innocent misrepresentations, both of which are decisions of the House of Lords.[97] In one of these, *Abram Steamship Company*, their Lordships founded their decision on an exception that Wickens V-C had also recognized. The exception is that the right to rescind can be revived if the claimant reacquires the asset through the avoidance of the resale contract. The theory appears to be that the avoidance of that contract takes effect *ab initio* so that the parties are restored to their original positions including any rights to rescind they may have enjoyed.

(2) Substitutive counter-restitution

18.52 While rescission is usually barred where the asset in question cannot be returned, it is sometimes possible to make sufficient *restitutio in integrum* by instead offering the defendant some form of substitute.[98] Possible substitutes are first, in the case of fungibles, an identical asset purchased in the market; secondly, where the asset has been resold, the proceeds of that resale; and thirdly, a sum of money representing the value of the asset. The

---

[91] See also the cases concerning sales of multiple lots of land: *Thorpe v Fasey* [1949] 1 Ch 649, 665 and in Canada *Fleming v Mair* (1921) 58 DLR 318 (Sask CA).
[92] (1831) 2 B & Ad 456, 109 ER 1212.
[93] (1840) 3 Beav 78, 85; 49 ER 31, 33.
[94] See also *Dimsdale v Dimsdale* (1856) 3 Drew 556, 577; 61 ER 1015, 1024, where Kindersley V-C indicated what where an asset has been mortgaged, the claimant may nonetheless rescind upon first repaying the mortgage. The claimant in *Boulter v Stocks* (1913) 47 SCR 440, 442 was similarly able to rescind a contract by which he had bought a farm which he had then leased out upon obtaining the cancellation of the lease.
[95] (1873) LR 16 Eq 417, 431–32.
[96] (1873) LR 16 Eq 417.
[97] *Edinburgh United Breweries Ltd v Molleson* [1894] AC 90 (HL Sc); *Abram Steamship Company, Limited v Westville Shipping Company, Limited* [1923] AC 773 (HL Sc).
[98] The related question whether a claimant can claim against a defendant restitution of a substitute where the defendant no longer has the actual asset he received is considered in Chap 14, paras [14.29]ff (law) and Chap 15, paras [15.14]ff (equity).

term 'pecuniary rescission' is sometimes used to describe the situation where restitution or counter-restitution is given by way of a pecuniary substitute.

Views differ and authority may be found supporting a range of possibilities. On one view rescission is essentially a specific remedy. Representative is Nourse LJ's *obiter dictum* in *Smith New Court Securities Ltd v Scrimgeour Vickers (Asset Management) Ltd*[99] that a contract cannot be rescinded where the claimant can no longer return the very asset he received, in that case quoted shares that had been sold on. On further appeal, Lord Browne-Wilkinson indicated a different view, doubting Nourse LJ's *obiter dictum* and saying that in the case of quoted shares a claimant can make substantial *restitutio in integrum* by returning identical shares purchased in the market.[100] It has even been suggested by Lord Millett that, by analogy with the specific performance of contracts, the consequences of rescission should only be worked out specifically where a pecuniary equivalent would be inadequate.[101]

No substitutive counter-restitution at law

Rescission has always been treated by common lawyers as being specific in nature, in the sense that if its consequences cannot be worked out specifically, then they cannot be worked out at all. Accordingly, at common law *restitutio in integrum* is impossible except where the claimant can return the very same asset in materially the same condition.[102] The difficulty is that the common law does not recognize an action that would allow the defendant to recover from the claimant the value of the asset. Certainly if the asset has been sold or otherwise alienated, that is an absolute bar to rescission even if the asset has been reacquired.[103] Substitutive counter-restitution is unknown at common law.[104]

Substitutive counter-restitution in equity

Equity has always been more willing than the common law to make pecuniary adjustments where circumstances have changed such that the claimant is no longer in a position to make exact *restitutio in integrum*. Equity will allow compensation for any collateral benefits the claimant may have received, and also for any deterioration in the asset.[105] Provided substantial *restitutio in integrum* is possible, that is all that practical justice requires.

This flexibility has not usually, however, extended to allowing substitutive counter-restitution. Thus Lord Atkinson remarked in *Boyd & Forrest v The Glasgow Railway Company* that it is not 'competent to a person, bound to restore what he has got under a contract which he asks to have set aside, to put a money value on the thing to be restored by him and pay over or allow credit for that sum instead of returning the thing itself'.[106] He took this to be true as much in equity as at law, for the financial allowances given in equity in working out

18.53

18.54

18.55

18.56

---

[99] [1994] 1 WLR 1271 (CA) 1280.
[100] *Smith New Court Securities Ltd v Citibank NA* [1997] AC 254, 262. See the discussion of this suggestion in Part D(3) of this chapter.
[101] PJ Millett, 'Restitution and Constructive Trusts' (1998) 114 LQR 399, 416.
[102] *Clarke v Dickson* (1858) El Bl & El 148, 120 ER 463. In Australia, *Alati v Kruger* (1955) 94 CLR 216, 223.
[103] *Street v Blay* (1831) 2 B & Ad 456, 109 ER 1212; *Hogan v Healy* (1877) IR 11 CL 119 (Ex Ch) 121; *The Sheffield Nickel and Silver Plating Company Limited v Unwin* (1877) 2 QBD 214, 224.
[104] Cf PBH Birks, *Unjust Enrichment* (2nd edn, 2005) 226.
[105] *Erlanger v The New Sombrero Phosphate Company* (1878) 3 App Cas 1218, 1278.
[106] 1915 SC (HL) 20, 28–29.

408 IV. RESTITUTIO IN INTEGRUM

the rescission of a contract are, Lord Atkinson said, 'ancillary to the main relief but never in substitution for it'.[107]

18.57 There is, however, a somewhat eclectic collection of cases spanning three centuries in which claimants who have resold assets have been allowed to rescind upon accounting to the defendant for the proceeds of the resale or else the value of the asset. These are almost all cases in which the contracting parties expected that the claimant would resell, and in which he did so before learning of the facts entitling him to rescind.

18.58 A Canadian case involving a sale of 60 dozen cigarette lighters from a wholesaler to a retailer provides a good example.[108] The retailer had resold 13 dozen lighters, but Urquhart J said that full *restitutio in integrum* is not necessary where the articles are bought 'with the intention that they be immediately put into trade and resold'.[109] Instead it was sufficient that the retailer return the unsold lighters and account for the price of the others. Similarly, the claimant in *Savary v King*,[110] a decision of the House of Lords, had resold an insurance policy, but he was allowed to rescind upon accounting for the proceeds of that resale. The Lord Chancellor observed that the defendant solicitor had specifically suggested that the policy be resold.

18.59 Although it was not expressed, the same idea explains the earliest cases of the type. These involved sales of trading goods to expectant heirs at inflated prices and with long repayment periods.[111] The sales were in fact disguised loans at above-market interest rates. The idea was that the heir would immediately resell the goods at their true value, enjoy the proceeds of that resale, and repay the original purchase price when he gained his expectancy. These contracts could be rescinded upon payment of a pecuniary substitute for the goods. In one of these cases, *Barker v Vansommer*,[112] Thurlow LC specifically considered whether the rescinding heir should account for the proceeds of the resale or instead the price that would have been realized had the goods been resold to best advantage, the goods having instead been resold as a single lot. Thurlow LC decided that on the facts of that case the measure should be the amount actually realized because both parties had anticipated that the goods would be resold in the way that they were.

18.60 The same pattern may be found in cases involving the rescission of business sale agreements. In the famous Australian case *Alati v Kruger*,[113] the sale of a fruit business was set aside on terms that the purchaser account for the value of the inventory he had acquired as part of the business and subsequently resold, as both parties necessarily expected that he would. *Carter v Golland*,[114] a case from Ontario, furnishes another example. Giving the judgment of the Court of Appeal, Middleton JA reasoned that by contrast with a sale of a determinate asset, in the sale of a business 'both parties contract with regard to a circulating

---

[107] 1915 SC (HL) 20, 30.
[108] *Trans-Canada Trading Co Limited v M Loeb Limited* [1947] 2 DLR 849 (Ont HC).
[109] *Trans-Canada Trading Co Limited v M Loeb Limited* [1947] 2 DLR 849, 858.
[110] (1856) 5 HLC 627, 667; 10 ER 1046, 1063.
[111] *Bill v Price* (1686) 1 Vern 467, 23 ER 592; *Barker v Vansommer* (1782) 1 Bro CC 149, 28 ER 1046; *Smith v Kay* (1859) 7 HLC 750, 774; 11 ER 299, 309.
[112] (1782) 1 Bro CC 149, 151–52; 28 ER 1046, 1047.
[113] (1955) 94 CLR 216, 225.
[114] [1937] 4 DLR 513 (Ont CA). See also *Wandinger v Lake* (1977) 78 DLR (3d) 305 (Ont HC). In New Zealand, *Fulton v Reay* [1926] NZLR 195; *Root v Badley* [1960] NZLR 756, 763.

stock, to things coming and going in the daily transaction of the business rather than to the specific list of chattels'.[115]

Middleton JA's remark seems to go to the heart of these cases. It is difficult to see why the availability of substitutive counter-restitution should depend upon whether the parties expected a resale. The key to these cases instead seems to be that the assets in question were not regarded by the parties as having any special importance or value. The cases all involved trading commodities or financial instruments, valuable only for their economic potential. That is also true of *Nicholl*'s case,[116] where Chelmsford LC remarked that had the claimant acted timeously, he might have rescinded the contract by which he took shares in the defendant company, accounting for the proceeds of his resale. That case seems to have been forgotten, however, for nowadays a resale of shares is generally thought to bar rescission.[117] **18.61**

(3) The future of substitutive counter-restitution

It should be possible to make counter-restitution by paying a sum of money much more frequently than is generally thought to be possible. The conventional view, of which Lord Atkinson's *obiter dictum* in *Boyd & Forrest*[118] is representative, sits poorly with the authorities. The earlier cases reviewed in the last section indicate that there has never been a general bar to pecuniary counter-restitution in equity. The conventional view appears to have migrated comparatively recently from the common law. **18.62**

Fungibles
While most of the cases reviewed in the last section can be explained on the basis that the parties both expected a resale, it is also possible to detect a wider principle that counter-restitution can be given in money whenever the asset in question is a fungible. This wider principle was adopted in the first *Restatement of Restitution*.[119] There does not seem to be any good reason why pecuniary counter-restitution should not be possible in cases involving fungibles, which are in their nature interchangeable. **18.63**

As has been noted, in *Smith New Court Securities*[120] Lord Browne-Wilkinson suggested that where the rescinding party has resold quoted shares, the requirement of substantial *restitutio in integrum* may be satisfied by the return of substitute shares purchased in the market.[121] The logic of this would seem to extend to fungibles of all types.[122] **18.64**

This suggestion is open to two criticisms. The first is that it is difficult to see what is achieved by the return of a substitute asset as opposed to an equivalent sum of money. The second is that where the rescinding party has sold the asset into a falling market, if he were allowed to **18.65**

---

[115] *Carter v Golland* [1937] 4 DLR 513 (Ont CA) 517.
[116] *Re Royal British Bank (Nicholl's case)* (1859) 3 De G & J 387, 431; 44 ER 1317, 1335.
[117] *Smith New Court Securities Ltd v Citibank NA* [1994] 1 WLR 1271 (CA) 1280. In Australia, *Cadence Asset Management Pty Ltd v Concept Sports Limited* [2005] 147 FCR 435 (Full Ct) [3].
[118] *Boyd & Forrest v The Glasgow Railway Company* 1915 SC (HL) 20, 30.
[119] *Restatement (First) of Restitution* § 66 (1937).
[120] *Smith New Court Securities Ltd v Citibank NA* [1997] AC 254, 262.
[121] This is apparently allowed in the United States: *Watson v Massachusetts Mutual Life Insurance Co*, 140 F2d 673 (DC Cir 1943), cert denied 322 US 746 (1944).
[122] Cf *Restatement (First) of Restitution* § 65(4) (1937).

return a substitute purchased at a lower price then he would gain a windfall profit at the expense of the wrongdoer.[123] On these facts Cardozo J required the rescinding party in *Marr v Tumulty*[124] instead to account for the proceeds of his resale.

Non-fungibles

18.66 The more contentious question is whether pecuniary counter-restitution should also be possible where the asset in question has individual characteristics. The position taken in the first *Restatement of Restitution* is that specific counter-restitution is required in such cases, even where the asset is a chattel with a definite market value.[125] Somewhat confusingly, the first *Restatement of Restitution* at the same time allows pecuniary counter-restitution in respect of services, provided there is no serious difficulty in estimating their value.

18.67 In England, pecuniary counter-restitution can plainly be made in respect of services, save probably in the case of self-help rescission at law. That was decided by the Court of Appeal in *O'Sullivan v Management Agency and Music Ltd*,[126] and there are a number of other cases to the same effect.[127] If pecuniary counter-restitution can be given in respect of services, there can be no general objection to pecuniary counter-restitution of unavailable assets, even though the assets may have individual characteristics. Services are not inherently any less difficult to value.

18.68 This argument has been advanced by a number of scholars including Professor Birks and Lord Burrows.[128] They contend that the conventional view rests upon a 'squeamishness' about valuing non-money benefits that is out of line with the usual willingness of the courts to estimate asset values. Lord Burrows goes so far as to say that, because it can be effected in money, counter-restitution is always possible, and that the only significance of the bar is to ensure that counter-restitution is made in some form.[129]

18.69 Though its outer limits have not been tested, this basic argument has been accepted at first instance in New Zealand and also in passing by Steyn LJ in *SIB v Pantell SA*.[130] Neither of those cases involved rescission in the usual sense: the New Zealand case involved a claim to recover money paid to a knowing recipient in return for shares; and *SIB v Pantell SA* involved a claim to rescind under the Financial Services Act 1986. Nonetheless, both situations are closely analogous to conventional rescission.

18.70 The argument also finds support in a small number of cases in which the court has directed that the wrongdoer should make restitution in money where the asset he has received is now unavailable, though pecuniary restitution as opposed to counter-restitution raises

---

[123] R Halson, 'Rescission for Misrepresentation' [1997] RLR 89.
[124] 256 NY 15, 175 NE 356 (CA 1931).
[125] *Restatement (First) of Restitution* § 66(3) (1937).
[126] [1985] 1 QB 428 (CA). See the analysis of this case in Chap 2, paras [2.21]–[2.23].
[127] See Part E(4) of this chapter.
[128] PBH Birks, *Unjust Enrichment* (2nd edn, 2005) 226–28; A Burrows, *The Law of Restitution* (3rd edn, 2011) 250; A Burrows, *A Restatement of the English Law of Contract* (2016) [34(5)(c)]. See also S Zogg, *Proprietary Consequences in Defective Transfers of Ownership* (2020) 152–53.
[129] A Burrows, *The Law of Restitution* (3rd edn, 2011) 541–42.
[130] *Equiticorp Industries Group Ltd v The Crown (No 47)* [1998] 2 NZLR 481, 646–51; *SIB v Pantell SA* [1992] 3 WLR 896 (CA) 912–13. See also *Jolly v Watson* (unreported, High Court of Justice of the Isle of Man, 1 March 2012), Ord 2010/77, where compensation was given in lieu of rescission for undue influence where the Deemster considered that it would be unfair to require the claimant to surrender the purchased property that was now her home.

some distinct issues.[131] From an English standpoint *Mahoney v Purnell*[132] is the most important of these. That case involved a sale of shares in a private company by a father-in-law to his son-in-law, which was set aside on the ground of presumed undue influence. The company had since gone into liquidation, but May J considered that the contract could still be avoided, requiring the son-in-law to pay equitable compensation for the value of the shares. Though May J said that this award was 'akin to damages', he also said that the award was given 'as an adjunct to setting aside the agreement'.[133] The award is best understood as pecuniary restitution.[134] Parallel cases in Australia and in Canada have involved pecuniary restitution of land.[135]

18.71 In principle there is much to recommend the idea that pecuniary counter-restitution should be possible even where the unavailable asset has individual characteristics. Equity only requires substantial *restitutio in integrum*, and this essentially means that the wrongdoer should not be placed in a position that is unjustifiably worse than the position he occupied before the contract was made. On this basis the criterion should be whether the wrongdoer would be unjustifiably prejudiced by receiving back money instead of the actual asset. The fact that an asset has individual characteristics does not necessarily mean that pecuniary counter-restitution would be unjustifiably prejudicial.

18.72 So far as sales are concerned, it seems that the only circumstance in which pecuniary counter-restitution should be impossible occurs where the asset's value cannot be reliably estimated.[136] Lord Burrows is right to point out that it is always possible to estimate an asset's value, but some estimates are in their nature more reliable than others. Where the value of an asset could only be estimated at the price of considerable speculation, whether because of the nature of the asset or because of the poverty of the evidence adduced by the rescinding party, pecuniary counter-restitution may be unjust.[137] The courts would presumably be more willing to speculate against a conscious wrongdoer than against a comparatively blameless defendant.

18.73 It is tempting to say that pecuniary counter-restitution should also be impossible where the asset has unique characteristics, as, for example, do plots of land. This would align with the availability of specific performance of contracts for the sale of land and unique goods, damages not being an adequate substitute. But while it is possible to imagine cases in which the wrongdoer has a justifiable interest in recovering the very asset he has parted with, in general the analogy with the doctrine of the inadequacy of damages is not a good one. Where counter-restitution is in question, the vendor has, by selling the asset, demonstrated his desire to part with it notwithstanding any unique qualities it may have. In some cases uniqueness may nevertheless be a factor tending to make the asset incapable of sufficiently reliable valuation.

---

[131] See Chap 15, paras [15.20]–[15.32].
[132] [1996] 3 All ER 61.
[133] [1996] 3 All ER 61, 88–89.
[134] PBH Birks, 'Unjust Factors and Wrongs: Pecuniary Rescission for Undue Influence' [1997] RLR 72.
[135] *McKenzie v McDonald* [1927] VLR 134; *Kupchak v Dayson Holdings Co Ltd* (1965) 53 DLR (2d) 482 (BCCA).
[136] Outside cases involving simple sales or exchanges, however, there are many situations in which the financial adjustments required to achieve substantial *restitutio in integrum* by a pecuniary substitute would be infeasible. *Land Enviro Corp Pty Ltd v HTT Huntley Heritage Pty Ltd* [2012] NSWSC 382 [910]–[914] is an example.
[137] *AH McDonald and Company Pty Ltd v Wells* (1931) 45 CLR 506, 513.

Measure

18.74 What few authorities there are provide little guidance as to the measure of pecuniary counter-restitution where that is possible. It is necessary to distinguish between cases where the rescinding party has resold the asset and cases where the asset has become unavailable in some other way.

18.75 Where the asset has been resold, the usual measure should be the proceeds of the resale. That was the measure given in most of the cases discussed in Part D(2) of this chapter. Provided the resale was at arm's length, the proceeds are likely to give a fair indication of the asset's true market value. To award less than the proceeds, for example where the asset has since declined further in value, would allow the rescinding party to gain a windfall profit at the wrongdoer's expense.[138] By contrast, where the asset might with reasonable diligence have fetched a higher price, it may be appropriate to require that the rescinding party pay instead that higher amount.[139] It is possible to imagine cases where the rescinding party should be given an allowance for his skill and effort in successfully marketing a substantial asset.

18.76 Where the asset has become unavailable other than by way of a resale, it will be necessary to value the asset on some other basis. A difficult question may arise if the market value of the asset has changed since the date of the original sale. If specific counter-restitution were still possible, the wrongdoer would receive back an asset now worth more or less than it was. This suggests that present values should rule, as the pecuniary sum is given in substitution for specific restitution. However in *Fulton v Reay*,[140] a New Zealand case, the judge considered this question and awarded instead the market value of certain sheep at the date the claimant first took possession of them, and a like order was made by another New Zealand judge more recently in respect of shares.[141]

E. Counter-restitution: Miscellaneous Issues

(1) Possession, occupation, and use of asset

Rescission generally possible

18.77 In general the simple fact a purchaser has possessed, occupied, or used an asset will not prevent him from rescinding the sale.[142] Upon rescission the purchaser may return the asset

---

[138] Cf *Marr v Tumulty*, 256 NY 15, 175 NE 356 (CA 1931).
[139] Cf *Barker v Vansommer* (1782) 1 Bro CC 149, 151–52; 28 ER 1046, 1047.
[140] [1926] NZLR 195. The decision is criticized in KR Handley, *Spencer Bower and Handley Actionable Misrepresentation* (5th edn, 2014) [16.18], the author of which prefers present values.
[141] *Equiticorp Industries Group Ltd v The Crown (No 47)* [1998] 2 NZLR 481, 652–54. See also *Jolly v Watson* (unreported, High Court of Justice of the Isle of Man, 1 March 2012), Ord 2010/77 [373], where compensation was given in lieu of rescission for undue influence by reference to values at the date of the transaction.
[142] *Compagnie Française des Chemins de Fer Paris-Orleans v Leeston Shipping Company Ltd* [1919] 1 Lloyd's Rep 235; *Salt v Stratstone Specialist Ltd* [2016] RTR 17 (CA). In Australia, *Brown v Smitt* (1924) 34 CLR 160; *Alati v Kruger* (1955) 94 CLR 216. In Canada, *Lindsay Petroleum Company v Hurd* (1874) LR 5 PC 221, 240; *Addison v Ottawa Auto and Taxi Co* (1913) 16 DLR 318 (Ont SC (App Div)); *Kellogg Brown & Root Inc v Aerotech Herman Nelson Inc* (2004) 238 DLR (4th) 594 (Man CA) [57]–[63]. In New Zealand, *Root v Badley* [1960] NZLR 756. But cf *Emhill Pty Ltd v Bonsoc Pty Ltd (No 2)* [2007] VSCA 108 [38], where the Court of Appeal of Victoria appears to have assumed that counter-restitution cannot be made of the benefit of a tenancy.

and account to the defendant for the benefit he has enjoyed if any. The deterioration of the asset in his hands is a different matter and is treated further below.

Steedman v Frigidaire Corp,[143] a decision given on appeal to the Privy Council from Canada, is difficult to understand. The case concerned a purchase of refrigeration equipment procured by a bribe given by the vendor to the purchaser's agent. Before learning of the bribe, the purchaser installed the equipment in market stalls, which he then let to tenants. Giving the advice of the Board, Lord Macmillan said that *restitutio in integrum* had not been shown to be possible. He observed that on the contrary, the purchaser appeared to have 'exercised or authorised acts of ownership or use in relation to at least a large part of the equipment installed, by letting it out to be operated by his tenants'.[144] In principle, however, matters such as these may require an allowance but they do not preclude rescission provided the purchaser can return the units. *Steedman v Frigidaire Corp* seems to have been quietly forgotten in Canada.[145]   **18.78**

More restrictive common law rules
The general proposition set out earlier[146] reflects the rule developed in equity. Very different rules apply if for one reason or another the claimant wishes to rescind at law. Rescission may only occur at law if at the moment rescission is announced the defendant is completely restored to his former position. Where the defendant's obligations are not wholly executory, this will only be possible if the benefit the claimant has received is either of such a nature that he can return or tender it *in specie*, or if it is such that the law will recognize an action by the defendant to recover it.   **18.79**

Land
Different rules have developed at law in relation to land and chattels. So far as land is concerned, a completed conveyance or lease of land cannot usually be rescinded, the reason being that the common law has no mechanism to unwind the conveyance and so restore the vendor to his original rights.[147] There may be an exception to this where the purchaser has not been in possession of the land and he is able to tender the title documents and so effect *restitutio in integrum* in that way.   **18.80**

Rescission is also usually impossible where the conveyance or lease has not been completed but the purchaser or lessee has been let into possession of the land, however brief the period of possession may have been. This was first established in *Hunt v Silk*,[148] which involved a lease and where the period of possession was only a few days. The rule was consolidated in relation to sale transactions in *Blackburn v Smith*.[149]   **18.81**

The reason rescission is precluded is that the benefit of intermediate possession, being unspecified in value, is incapable of return or tender, and the common law has no action by which the vendor might recover that benefit.[150] It follows that if rescission were allowed   **18.82**

---

[143] [1933] 1 DLR 161 (PC—Canada).
[144] [1933] 1 DLR 161 (PC—Canada) 165.
[145] *Kellogg Brown & Root Inc v Aerotech Herman Nelson Inc* (2004) 238 DLR (4th) 594 (Man CA) [57]–[63].
[146] See para [18.77].
[147] See Chap 14, paras [14.24]–[14.28].
[148] (1804) 5 East 449, 102 ER 1142.
[149] (1848) 2 Ex 783, 154 ER 707.
[150] *Winterbottom v Ingham* (1845) 7 QB 611, 115 ER 620; *Markey v Coote* (1876) Ir 10 CL 149.

upon the purchaser surrendering present possession, he would be unjustly enriched to the extent of the benefit he had enjoyed by his intermediate possession.

18.83 An Australian case suggests that this rule may be displaced, notwithstanding that the purchaser has received a 'theoretical or technical' right to possession pending completion, if he did not have 'any actual possession or enjoyment of the land'.[151] The land in that case comprised bare development plots, which appear to have had no rental value, and the purchaser's only act in relation to them was to inspect. In these circumstances the Full Court of the Supreme Court of Victoria held that the contract could be rescinded for fraud at law.

Chattels

18.84 The common law has a different rule where chattels are concerned, at least in cases of fraud and probably in cases of duress as well. Here the fact the purchaser has taken possession of the chattel does not preclude rescission provided he can return it unused and in the same condition.[152] For this reason rescission is possible at law in respect of an executed sale of goods transactions. There is no financial adjustment in respect of the purchaser's mere possession of the chattel, which is apparently treated as being of no intrinsic benefit to him. There are few cases, but presumably any significant use of the article will make *restitutio in integrum* impossible at law on the grounds that the benefit of that use would be incapable of restoration. So, for example, rescission would be impossible where a person sought to return jewellery after wearing it or a car after driving it.

(2) Asset changed

18.85 McCardie J said in *Armstrong v Jackson* that '[i]f mere deterioration of the subject-matter negatived the right to rescind, the doctrine of rescission would become a vain thing'.[153] In equity mere deterioration usually warrants only a compensating allowance,[154] and then only if the deterioration was the fault of the rescinding purchaser. A change in the asset may, however, make *restitutio in integrum* impossible in two circumstances.[155]

Delay

18.86 Rescission may be barred if an asset the claimant must return deteriorates after he sufficiently learns of the facts entitling him to rescind but before he exercises his rights. This is illustrated by a line of nineteenth-century cases concerning purchases of mines, one of the central questions in each being whether the purchase could be rescinded notwithstanding that the purchaser had worked the mine and in some cases largely exhausted it. In *Vigers v Pike*[156] and in *Lagunas Nitrate Company v Lagunas Syndicate*[157] rescission was

---

[151] *Coastal Estates Pty Ltd v Melevende* [1965] VR 433 (Full Ct) 440.
[152] *Street v Blay* (1831) 2 B & Ad 456, 109 ER 1212; *Murrary v Mann* (1848) 2 Ex 538, 154 ER 605; *Udell v Atherton* (1861) 7 H & N 172, 158 ER 437.
[153] *Armstrong v Jackson* [1917] 2 KB 822, 829.
[154] Cf *Whittle v Filaria Pty Ltd* [2004] ACTSC 45 [219], in which *restitutio in integrum* was said to be impossible where hotel units depreciated owing to neglect and unwise commercial decisions on the part of the rescinding purchaser.
[155] This is subject to the possibility of substitutive counter-restitution discussed in Part D of this chapter.
[156] (1842) 8 Cl & Fin 562, 650; 8 ER 220, 253.
[157] [1899] 2 Ch 392 (CA) 433–34.

barred mainly because the claimants had continued working the mines with a view to profit after they had learned of the misrepresentations. By contrast, in *Attwood v Small*[158] and in *Erlanger v The New Sombrero Phosphate Company*[159] the claimants were not held to have been guilty of laches and rescission was granted upon an accounting of the profits they had gained by working the mines.

Asset has changed its nature

Where an asset in the hands of the rescinding purchaser has, by reason of events for which the vendor is not responsible, been altered to such an extent as to have changed its nature, *restitutio in integrum* will usually be impossible.[160] In *Clarke v Dickson*,[161] Crompton J gave the example of a butcher who had bought live cattle seeking to return the slaughtered carcasses. That case itself involved a share sale, and rescission was barred on the ground amongst others that the shares had changed their nature, the company having been converted into a joint-stock corporation.[162] Similarly, in an Australian case involving the sale of a boarding house, *restitutio in integrum* was held to be impossible because the building had since been condemned.[163]

18.87

The distinction between a change in the nature of an asset and lesser changes that do not bar rescission is illustrated by cases concerning automobile purchases. Provided the purchaser's use of the vehicle, and so its deterioration, has been ordinary, rescission is usually possible subject to an allowance.[164] The fact that an automobile sold as new has been registered for the first time does not preclude rescission.[165] By contrast, the British Columbia Court of Appeal held *restitutio in integrum* to be impossible in *Brook v Wheaton Pacific Pontiac Buick GMC Ltd*,[166] where the automobile had been driven a long distance and had been involved in an accident resulting in major repairs.

18.88

Where an interest in a business has been sold it may be incapable of return if the basic nature of the business has changed in the interim. Thus *restitutio in integrum* was said to be impossible in *Northern Bank Finance v Charlton*,[167] a decision of the Supreme Court of Eire, where the company in question had changed from one operating licensed premises to substantially a property holding company. There are several English cases to the same effect, including cases where the changes in the company's business were not so fundamental.[168]

18.89

---

[158] (1838) 6 Cl & Fin 232, 7 ER 684.
[159] (1878) 3 App Cas 1218.
[160] *Clarke v Dickson* (1858) El Bl & El 148, 120 ER 463; *The Western Bank of Scotland v Addie* (1867) LR 1 Sc App 145. In Canada, *Gearhart v Kraatz* (1918) 40 DLR 26 (Sask SC (App Div)) 29–30; *O'Flaherty v McKinlay* (1951) 30 MPR 172 (Nfld CA) 188–89.
[161] (1858) El Bl & El 148, 153; 120 ER 463, 465.
[162] (1858) El Bl & El 148, 154. See also *The Western Bank of Scotland v Addie* (1867) LR 1 Sc App 145.
[163] *Sargent v Campbell* [1972] Argus LR 708, 711.
[164] Eg the Canadian cases *Addison v Ottawa Auto and Taxi Co* (1913) 16 DLR 318 (Ont SC (App Div)); *Wiebe v Butchart's Motors Ltd* [1949] 4 DLR 838 (BCCA); and *F & B Transport Ltd v White Truck Sales Manitoba Ltd* (1964) 47 DLR (2d) 419 (Man QB), aff'd (1965) 49 DLR (2d) 670 (Man CA).
[165] *Salt v Stratstone Specialist Ltd* [2016] RTR 17 (CA).
[166] (2000) 76 BCLR (3d) 246 (CA). Cf *Mckinnon v Brockington* (1921) 60 DLR 303 (Man CA). See also *Waterloo Motors Ltd v Flood* [1931] 1 DLR 762 (NBCA).
[167] [1979] IR 149 (SC) 210.
[168] *Thomas Witter Ltd v TBP Industries Ltd* [1996] 2 All ER 573, 587; *Capcon Holdings plc v Edwards* [2007] EWHC 2662 (Ch); *Rayden v Edwardo Ltd* [2008] EWHC 2689 (Comm). See also *The Sheffield Nickel and Silver Plating Company, Limited v Unwin* (1877) 2 QBD 214 (CA) 223–34.

The fact a business has failed may preclude rescission,[169] but not where the failure was due to an inherent vice that existed at the time of the sale, and especially not where the misrepresentation related to that vice.[170]

18.90 Repairs and other alterations tending to enhance the market value of the asset the claimant must return will not preclude rescission,[171] although the rescinding party may not be entitled to recoup the cost of the work.[172]

More restrictive rule at law

18.91 The discussion to this point has been concerned only with rescission in equity. In equity mere deterioration does not bar rescission because it can be compensated by an allowance. By contrast, if a purchaser were permitted to rescind at common law and return an asset which had deteriorated, the vendor would have no action to recover compensation. It would seem to follow that any non-trivial alteration that is not the result of an inherent vice in the asset should bar rescission. While there is very little authority, *Udell v Atherton*[173] appears to support this. In that case rescission was said to be unavailable where the purchaser of a log had cut it, and so discovered that the log was partially rotten contrary to a fraudulent representation made by the vendor's agent.

18.92 Looked at from another perspective, the rule at common law in a case of fraud or duress may be the same as the rule that applies where a purchaser rejects goods for non-conformity, and in principle it should not be more restrictive. The latter rule is, however, surprisingly underdeveloped. The editor of *Benjamin's Sale of Goods*[174] suggests that damage or deterioration owing to misuse or accidental causes should preclude rejection but that damage or deterioration caused by fair wear and tear, reasonable testing, fitting, and the like should not.

(3) Asset depreciated owing to market decline

18.93 Absent culpable delay, the fact the asset the rescinding claimant received has declined in value as a result of the ordinary play of market forces will not prevent him from making sufficient *restitutio in integrum* by simply returning it.[175] For example, the shares at issue in *Armstrong v Jackson*[176] had been worth £3 5 shillings each when sold in 1910 and were

---

[169] Eg *Campbell v Back Office Investments Pty Ltd* (2008) 66 ACSR 359 (NSWCA); on appeal (2009) 238 CLR 304 [107]–[109], where the failure was the result of the breakdown in the relationship between the two shareholders and their agreement to sell.
[170] *Adam v Newbigging* (1888) 13 App Cas 308; *Senanayake v Cheng* [1965] AC 63 (PC—Singapore).
[171] Eg *Mckinnon v Brockington* (1921) 60 DLR 303 (Man CA); *Guest v Beecroft* (1957) 22 WWR 481 (BCSC) 486.
[172] See Chap 17, paras [17.35]ff.
[173] (1861) 7 H & N 172, 158 ER 437. In Australia, *Jonval Buildings Pty Ltd v Commissioner of Fair Trading* (2020) 104 NSWLR 1 (CA).
[174] M Bridge (ed), *Benjamin's Sale of Goods* (11th edn, 2021) [12-1061].
[175] *Gillette v Peppercorn* (1840) 3 Beav 78, 85; 49 ER 31, 33; *Blake v Mowatt* (1856) 21 Beav 603, 52 ER 993; *The Western Bank of Scotland v Addie* (1867) LR 1 Sc App 145, 166; *Armstrong v Jackson* [1917] KB 822, 828–29; *Cheese v Thomas* [1994] 1 WLR 129 (CA) 135; *William Sindall Plc v Cambridge CC* [1994] 1 WLR 1016 (CA); *Salt v Stratstone Specialist Ltd* [2016] RTR 17 (CA) (where Longmore LJ suggested that the depreciation of an automobile might warrant a compensatory adjustment). In Australia, *Fysh v Page* (1956) 96 CLR 233, 242; *Balfour v Hollandia Ravensthorpe NL* (1978) 18 SASR 240; *JAD International Pty Ltd v International Trucks Australia Ltd* (1994) 50 FCR 378 (Full Ct); *Akron Securities v Illife* (1997) 41 NSWLR 353 (CA); *Amadio Pty Ltd v Henderson* (1998) 81 FCR 149 (Full Ct) 198 (illegality). In Hong Kong, *Crown Master International Trading Co Ltd v China Solar Energy Holdings Ltd* [2015] 4 HKC 505 (adopting this passage).
[176] [1917] KB 822.

worth only 5 shillings when the claimant purchaser exercised his right to rescind in 1917, and yet that was not a bar. Nicholls V-C remarked in *Cheese v Thomas* that '[a] defendant cannot be heard to protest that such an outcome is unfair when he is receiving back the very thing he persuaded the plaintiff, by undue influence or misrepresentation, to buy from him'.[177]

It is necessary to be clear about the limits of this proposition. First, it does not apply where the depreciation is caused by the conduct of the parties rather than market fluctuations, as in an Australian case where the value of shares in a private company declined in consequence of the breakdown of the relationship between the shareholders and their agreement to sell the business.[178] Secondly, the proposition does not apply where, as in *Cheese v Thomas* itself, the transaction was a joint venture between the parties by which the risk of a market decline was to be shared.[179] **18.94**

Thirdly, once a claimant sufficiently learns of his right to rescind, the position changes and any substantial depreciation in the value of the asset he must return occurring before he determines his election will usually render *restitutio in integrum* impossible.[180] This is particularly so where it is foreseeable that the asset might decline in value, as in the case of speculative assets.[181] In cases of this type a claimant must act quickly once he learns of his rights or risk losing them. Certainly a claimant cannot knowingly speculate at the defendant's risk, hoping to keep the asset if it performs well and return it if not.[182] **18.95**

The editors of *McGregor on Damages* argue that the rule excluding any consideration of market depreciation except where there has been delay does not apply in cases of innocent misrepresentation.[183] This is difficult to sustain on current authorities. While it is true that most of the authorities in which the rule has been applied involved frauds or the like, the Court of Appeal proceeded on the basis that the rule applies in cases involving blameless misconduct in two of the most important recent cases in the area, *Cheese v Thomas*[184] and *William Sindall*.[185] In Australia, the Federal Court has specifically applied the rule in a case of innocent misrepresentation,[186] and, as far as one can tell, the rule is also applied in those cases in the United States.[187] The editors refer to *Lagunas Nitrate Company v Lagunas Syndicate*[188] as an innocent misrepresentation case in which the rule was not applied, but that is difficult to see. In explaining that *restitutio in integrum* was impossible, Lindley LJ's emphasis was on the claimant's board's delay in asserting its rights once it was in a position **18.96**

---

[177] *Cheese v Thomas* [1994] 1 WLR 129 (CA) 135.
[178] *Campbell v Back Office Investments Pty Ltd* (2008) 66 ACSR 359 (NSWCA); on appeal (2009) 238 CLR 304 [107]–[109]. In Hong Kong, *Crown Master International Trading Co Ltd v China Solar Energy Holdings Ltd* [2015] 4 HKC 505 [56].
[179] See Chap 17, para [17.14].
[180] *Armstrong v Jackson* [1917] KB 822. In Australia, *Fysh v Page* (1956) 96 CLR 233. See the explanation of this case in *JAD International Pty Ltd v International Trucks Australia Ltd* (1994) 50 FCR 378 (Full Ct), which is not consistent with the approach of English courts for reasons given in Part A(3) of this chapter.
[181] *Lagunas Nitrate Company v Lagunas Syndicate* [1899] 2 Ch 392 (CA) 433–34.
[182] *Erlanger v The New Sombrero Phosphate Company* (1878) 3 App Cas 1218, 1281.
[183] J Edelman et al, *McGregor on Damages* (21st edn, 2020) [49-083].
[184] [1994] 1 WLR 129 (CA) 135 (presumed undue influence).
[185] *William Sindall Plc v Cambridge CC* [1994] 1 WLR 1016 (CA) (innocent misrepresentation).
[186] *JAD International Pty Ltd v International Trucks Australia Ltd* (1994) 50 FCR 378 (Full Ct).
[187] *Seneca Wire & Mfg Co v AB Leach & Co*, 247 NY 1, 159 NE 700 (CA 1928); *Restatement (First) of Restitution* § 13 ill 16 (1937).
[188] [1899] 2 Ch 392 (CA).

to do so, the fact that instead it continued working out the mine with a view to profit, and the fact that a phosphate mine was at that time a highly speculative asset.[189]

18.97 The suggestion made by the editors of *McGregor on Damages* is nonetheless an attractive one.[190] The rule allowing a claimant to make sufficient counter-restitution by returning an asset that may have depreciated considerably in value can be hard on a defendant whose misconduct was blameless. This is particularly so where absent the sale to the claimant, the defendant would instead have sold to someone else while the asset's market value was holding up; and where the claimant equally might have sold but chose not to.

18.98 The rationale offered in *Armstrong v Jackson*,[191] that 'the shares are the same shares', depends upon a problematic and metaphysical distinction between an asset's intrinsic qualities and other characteristics such as its market value. It is not obvious that that distinction has any justificatory force. The focus of justification should instead be on the question which of the parties should bear the loss occasioned by the market decline. It is easy to see that a conscious wrongdoer should bear this loss. The law has a weaker interest in protecting him from the harm suffered by adverse market movements, and in any event he might have foreseen that the market would decline by the time the claimant learned that he had been cheated. But where the defendant was blameless and equally ignorant of the true position, a substantial market decline should arguably be treated as a pure accident, and so bar rescission.

(4) Services

18.99 In their nature, services performed under a contract cannot be specifically returned upon rescission. If rescission is viewed as essentially a specific remedy, then the fact the claimant has had the benefit of the defendant's services should preclude *restitutio in integrum*.[192] That is not, however, the attitude that has been taken by the courts in modern times. The fact the defendant has performed services will not usually prevent *restitutio in integrum* because a financial allowance can be given.

18.100 Executed contracts of salvage have since the nineteenth century been rescinded in Admiralty for fraud or duress upon payment by the rescinding owner of a reasonable sum for the salvor's services.[193] The question does not seem to have arisen outside of that context until the 1980s.[194] In *Atlantic Lines & Navigation Co Inc v Hallam Ltd*,[195] a case involving a partly performed charter-party, Mustill J considered the main authorities and concluded

---

[189] *Lagunas Nitrate Company v Lagunas Syndicate* [1899] 2 Ch 392 (CA) 433–34.
[190] The application of the rule in cases of innocent misrepresentation has been criticized in the United States: GE Palmer, *The Law of Restitution* (1978) vol 1, s 3.8; D Dobbs, *The Law of Remedies* (2nd edn, 1993) vol 2, s 9.3(2) (but the criticism does not appear in the shorter D Dobbs and C Roberts, *The Law of Remedies* (3rd edn 2018)). Cf *Restatement (First) of Restitution* § 13 reporter's note h (1937).
[191] [1917] KB 822, 828.
[192] Cf *Boyd & Forrest v The Glasgow Railway Company* 1915 SC (HL) 20.
[193] *The Medina* (1875) 1 PD 272 aff'd (1876) 2 PD 5; *The Port Caledonia and the Anna* [1903] P 184.
[194] But see *Rees v De Barnardy* [1896] 2 ChD 437, 450, where the claimant offered to pay for the services and no point was taken about this. In Canada, *S-244 Holdings Ltd v Seymour Building Systems Ltd* [1994] 8 WWR 185 (BCCA).
[195] [1983] 1 Lloyd's Rep 188, 202.

that the fact the claimant had received the benefit of services did not bar rescission. The point was not essential to his disposition of that case, but rescission was soon afterwards ordered and an allowance for services given by the Court of Appeal in *O'Sullivan*'s case,[196] which concerned executed contracts for the management of a musician. In *Guinness plc v Saunders*[197] Lord Goff said he had no doubt that it would have been possible to set aside the service contract between Guinness and its director Ward with an allowance for the services he had performed in securing the success of Guinness's takeover bid.[198]

There appears to be no authority specifically concerning the question whether a contract may be rescinded on a self-help basis where the defendant has performed services.[199] It is doubtful that this would be possible given that it is not usually possible to make counter-restitution of benefits of unspecified value at common law.[200] But in the case of monetary receipts the common law bar can be satisfied on the basis the defendant acquires a claim to recover the sum, and it is arguable by analogy that a contract for services can be rescinded on the basis the defendant automatically acquires a claim for the value of the services. **18.101**

(5) Other intangible benefits

Restitutio in integrum will be impossible if the innocent party has received intangible benefits in their nature incapable of return or quantification. *Hogan v Healy*,[201] an Irish case, provides a clear illustration of this. *Restitutio in integrum* was impossible in that case because in consideration for the promissory notes the obligor now sought to avoid, the fraudster had married the obligor's daughter. Palles CJ observed that marriage is 'of such a nature that to return it is impossible'.[202] More recently, in *Society of Lloyds v Leighs*,[203] the Court of Appeal held that one of the reasons the Lloyds Names in that case could not rescind their contracts of membership was that they had enjoyed the benefit of being able to transact insurance business in the Lloyds market and this benefit is incapable of return. An Australian case suggests that the opportunity to profit under a distributorship agreement is similar.[204] The destruction of documents under the terms of the agreement may provide another example, though that would depend on the identity and nature of the documents.[205] But where the intangible benefit in question is capable of quantification, rescission should be possible as it was in *O'Sullivan*'s case.[206] **18.102**

---

[196] *O'Sullivan v Management Agency and Music Ltd* [1985] QB 428 (CA).
[197] [1990] 2 AC 693, 698.
[198] See *415703 BC Ltd v JEL Investments Ltd* 2010 BCSC 202, adopting the analysis in this paragraph.
[199] Though in *Halpern v Halpern (Nos 1 and 2)* [2008] QB 195 (CA) [73] Carnwath LJ gave an example which contemplates that a contract for services may be rescinded on grounds of duress.
[200] Eg *Hunt v Silk* (1804) 5 East 449, 102 ER 1142.
[201] (1877) 11 IR 119 (Ex Ch). In Australia, *AH McDonald and Company Pty Ltd v Wells* (1931) 45 CLR 506, 513 (opportunity to exploit patents).
[202] (1877) 11 IR 119 (Ex Ch) 124.
[203] [1997] 6 Re LR 289 (CA). See also *Society of Lloyds v Khan* [1998] 3 FCR 93.
[204] *Chint Australasia Pty Ltd v Cosmoluce Pty Ltd* [2008] NSWSC 635 [132].
[205] *Halpern v Halpern (Nos 1 and 2)* [2008] QB 195 (CA) [75]. Cf *Hulton v Hulton* [1917] 1 KB 813 (CA), where *restitutio in integrum* was not impossible because the documents had been destroyed at the instance of the party now resisting rescission.
[206] *O'Sullivan v Management Agency and Music Ltd* [1985] QB 428 (CA).

(6) Money

18.103 There is generally no difficulty in making counter-restitution where the claimant has received money providing he is in a position to repay an equal sum together with interest. Where rescission is sought in equity, repayment will be made a condition of the claimant's relief. Where instead the claimant by his own act rescinds a contract capable of being avoided at common law, if he does not repay or tender then the defendant will automatically acquire a claim for the amount as money paid under a failed consideration.[207]

18.104 Where the innocent party has become insolvent, it is not usually enough to offer instead to allow the wrongdoer a claim in the insolvency. *Restitutio in integrum* was held to be impossible for this reason by the New South Wales Court of Appeal in *Greater Pacific Investments Pty Ltd v Australian National Industries*,[208] in circumstances where such claims were likely to realize only 50 cents on the dollar. The insolvency in that case was not the result of the wrongdoing in question, as Mclellan J noted, and the result presumably might have been different if it were. That is because of the familiar principle that *restitutio in integrum* will not be impossible where the defendant's wrongdoing is the cause of the claimant's inability to make complete counter-restitution.

18.105 Browne-Wilkinson J's unreported decision in *Alman v Associated Newspapers Ltd*[209] involved a question of some practical importance to cases involving large sums. The claimants sought to recover a company they had sold to the defendants, but were not in a position to repay the £1.5 million odd the defendants had since put into the company. They led evidence, however, indicating that they would have a reasonable chance of raising the money given two to three months, and asked that the order should be conditional upon payment being made within that timeframe. Browne-Wilkinson J considered that this would leave the business in a position of unacceptable uncertainty during the conditional period and held that *restitutio in integrum* was impossible. He allowed, however, that such an order might be appropriate in a case where there was not a commercial business to be run.

F. Prejudicial Change of Circumstances

18.106 In *Erlanger v The New Sombrero Phosphate Company*, Lord Blackburn spoke of *restitutio in integrum* being impossible not only by reason of a change in 'the state of the property' but also by reason of a change 'in the position of the parties'.[210] Consistently with this, rescission may be barred not only where counter-restitution is impossible, but also where other circumstances have irreversibly changed such that the defendant would be unjustifiably prejudiced if the contract were rescinded.[211] The operation of this principle is limited because, as discussed later, a wrongdoer is not usually entitled to complain that he would be prejudiced by reason of steps he has taken in reliance on the security of the contract.[212]

---

[207] See Chap 14, paras [14.56]–[14.58].
[208] (1996) 39 NSWLR 143 (CA) 151–52.
[209] (ChD) 20 June 1980.
[210] *Erlanger v The New Sombrero Phosphate Company* (1878) 3 App Cas 1218, 1279. See also 1278.
[211] Cf *Restatement (Third) of Restitution* § 54(6) (2011): 'a change of circumstances unfairly prejudicial to the defendant, justifies denial of the remedy'.
[212] Cf *Lipkin Gorman (a firm) v Karnaple Ltd* [1991] 2 AC 548, 580.

(1) Unjustified prejudice

18.107 Changes of circumstances only bar rescission if the defendant would be *unjustifiably* prejudiced upon rescission. There is no single test whether any particular prejudice would be justifiable or not. The question is one of degree and each case must be considered on its particular facts.[213] Two factors that are frequently of particular significance are the wrongfulness of the defendant's conduct and the extent of any delay on the part of the innocent party in asserting his rights.

Conscious wrongdoing

18.108 In general it is much easier to justify the defendant being prejudiced upon rescission where he has been guilty of fraud or some other form of conscious wrongdoing. Thus Lord Thankerton said in *Spence v Crawford* that 'broadly' a fraudulent purchaser 'is not entitled in bar of restitution to found on dealings with the subject matter purchased, which he has been enabled by his fraud to carry out'.[214]

18.109 Spence and the fraudster Crawford had each held 50% of the company's shares. Following the sale of Spence's shares to Crawford, the company's capital was increased and one Richardson acquired a modest shareholding. Richardson had originally been Crawford's accomplice, but they subsequently fell out and Richardson moved into Spence's camp. The consequence was that upon rescission and the return to Spence of his shares, in alliance with Richardson he would enjoy control of the company, something Spence had not enjoyed before the original sale. Whilst the change of circumstance was such that rescission would establish a fundamentally new balance of power within the company, Lord Thankerton considered that this could be ignored because the change was a consequence of Crawford's 'dealings with the fruits of his fraud'.[215]

18.110 Lord Thankerton did not express his views in universal terms, and it seems that in an appropriate case *restitutio in integrum* may be impossible by reason of a change in circumstances even where the wrongdoer has been guilty of fraud. *Spence v Crawford* may be contrasted in this regard with *Coleman v Myers*,[216] a decision of the New Zealand Court of Appeal.

18.111 That case also involved a sale of shares in a company which the vendor now sought to rescind for fraud and also for breach of fiduciary duty. The vendor's shares had been sold as a part of a wider takeover of the company, following which the purchaser had declared a very substantial dividend in order to finance the purchase. The difficulty was that by the time the vendor moved to rescind, the compulsory acquisition provision in the applicable companies legislation could no longer be operated as it might have been at the time of the sale. Moreover, if the sale were rescinded, the innocent vendor would take the benefit of the enormous dividend that had since been declared, which would not have been declared had

---

[213] *Erlanger v The New Sombrero Phosphate Company* (1878) 3 App Cas 1218, 1279.
[214] *Spence v Crawford* [1939] 3 All ER 271 (HL Sc) 281. See also *UBS AG v Kommunale Wasserwerke Leipzig GmbH* [2017] 2 Lloyd's Rep 621 (CA) [221], where the court disregarded losses a fraudster would suffer under hedging contracts it had entered in reliance on the contracts which were now being rescinded.
[215] *Spence v Crawford* [1939] 3 All ER 271 (HL Sc).
[216] [1977] 2 NZLR 225 (CA). See also in Canada *Kupchak v Dayson Holdings Co Ltd* (1965) 53 DLR (2d) 482 (BCCA), although there the effect of the fraudster's reliance expenditure was only to bar specific relief and a pecuniary award was given.

IV. RESTITUTIO IN INTEGRUM

the sale never occurred. The majority considered that these changes of circumstances were sufficient to bar rescission notwithstanding the fraud.[217]

Comparatively blameless misconduct

18.112 The considerations that preclude a fraudster from standing on changes he has made to his position on the faith of the contract do not apply where the defendant is comparatively free from blame, as in a case of innocent misrepresentation. Though he did not need to express a concluded view, Lord Thankerton said that the result in *Spence v Crawford* might well have been different if the case had instead involved only an innocent misrepresentation. He explained that:

> If the purchaser of the shares thereby gained ample control of the company, both parties being aware that that was the purpose of their acquisition, and thereafter disposed of so many of the shares as still left him in control if the contract stood, but would not do so if the contract were rescinded, it may be that, if the contract were reducible for fraudulent misrepresentation, there would be no bar to restitution, and that, if the misrepresentation were without fraud, it might be held to provide such a bar.[218]

18.113 Accordingly, *restitutio in integrum* was held by the Court of Appeal to be impossible in *Holder v Holder*[219] because the purchaser of a farm had incurred liabilities that he would not be able to recoup. The sale had been in technical breach of the fiduciary dealing rules, and the purchaser had not been guilty of any reprehensible conduct. The liabilities in question comprised his costs of financing the purchase and his costs of making improvements to the farm beyond the compensable value of the improvements.[220]

18.114 Similarly, *Alman v Associated Newspaper Group Ltd*[221] involved an attempt by a vendor to rescind the sale of his business for innocent misrepresentation. One of the reasons why Browne-Wilkinson J held *restitutio in integrum* to be impossible was that the purchaser had introduced considerable know-how and inventive skills into the company, the value of which was incapable of quantification. It is difficult to think that this would have been a material factor tending against rescission if the representation had been fraudulent.

18.115 A different approach has been taken where, on the faith of a guarantee, a lender advances money to the borrower. It is generally assumed that outlays of this type will not defeat a claim to rescind the guarantee even on grounds that do not impute any real blame to the lender, such as innocent misrepresentation. It does not matter that the sums may be irrecoverable from the defaulting borrower. The authority for this is *MacKenzie v Royal Bank of Canada*, an appeal to the Privy Council from Canada, in which Lord Atkin said that '[t]he mere fact that the party making the representation has treated the contract as binding and has acted on it does not preclude relief'.[222] No reasons were given for this.

---

[217] *Coleman v Myers* [1977] 2 NZLR 225 (CA) 361, 379, but cf Woodhouse J at 327.
[218] *Spence v Crawford* [1939] 3 All ER 271 (HL Sc) 281–82.
[219] [1968] Ch 353 (CA) 395, 400, 406.
[220] [1968] Ch 353 (CA) 380–81.
[221] (ChD) 20 June 1980.
[222] [1934] AC 468 (PC—Canada) 476.

MacKenzie's case illustrates Palmer's caution against unthinkingly applying in cases of innocent misrepresentation principles developed to deal with the consequences of fraud.[223] More recently, in *Johnson v EBS Pensioner Trustees Ltd*[224] the Court of Appeal reached the opposite conclusion in a case involving a technical and unintentional breach of fiduciary duty, though *MacKenzie*'s case does not appear to have been cited. It may be that *MacKenzie*'s case is to be explained as depending upon a special rule designed to protect vulnerable sureties, something Mr Johnson was not.[225]

18.116

Delay
Prejudicial changes of circumstance that occur once the innocent party has sufficiently learned the facts entitling him to rescind will usually bar rescission, even in a case of fraud.[226] This is because it is difficult to justify prejudice to the defendant which would have been avoided if the innocent party had acted promptly. The extent to which the innocent party might have anticipated the prejudicial change of circumstances will often be a material factor in the court's decision.[227] These cases are discussed elsewhere.[228]

18.117

(2) Money committed to joint purposes

Rescission may be barred, or the restitution to which the innocent party is entitled may be circumscribed, if the defendant has *bona fide* committed money to joint purposes. Although rescission was ultimately not available in *Allcard v Skinner*,[229] the Court of Appeal made clear that the novice nun could only in any event have recovered so much of the funds gifted to the Lady Superior as had not been devoted to charitable purposes with which the nun was at the time associated and anxious to promote. Cotton LJ said that there would have been no bar if the funds had been applied by the Lady Superior for her own selfish purposes, or if they had been obtained by fraud.[230]

18.118

(3) Reversible change of circumstances

The only changes of circumstances that will bar rescission are those that are irreversible. Where the defendant can avoid any detriment by simply rearranging his affairs then there is

18.119

---

[223] GE Palmer, *The Law of Restitution* (1978) vol 1, s 3.8. Burrows suggests that *MacKenzie*'s case may need to be reconsidered: A Burrows, *The Law of Restitution* (3rd edn, 2011) 252. See also P Watts, 'Rescission of Guarantees for Misrepresentation and Actionable Non-disclosure' [2002] CLJ 301.
[224] [2002] Lloyd's Rep PN 309 (CA). Cf *Vadasz v Pioneer Concrete (SA) Pty Ltd* (1995) 184 CLR 102.
[225] However, in *UBS AG v Kommunale Wasserwerke Leipzig GmbH* [2017] 2 Lloyd's Rep 621 [225] the Court of Appeal treated the principle in *MacKenzie*'s case as applicable to contracts of a very different type, albeit that was a fraud case.
[226] *Clough v The London and North Western Railway Company* (1871) 7 LR Ex 26, 35; *Armstrong v Jackson* [1917] 2 KB 822, 828–29.
[227] *Nelson v Rye* [1996] 1 WLR 1378, 1392.
[228] Part A(3) of this chapter and Chap 24. See also *Cheese v Thomas* [1994] 1 WLR 129 (CA). Cf M Chen-Wishart, 'Loss Sharing, Undue Influence and Manifest Disadvantage' (1994) 110 LQR 174.
[229] (1887) 36 ChD 145 (CA) 170–71. See also *Cheese v Thomas* [1994] 1 WLR 129 (CA). Cf M Chen-Wishart, 'Loss Sharing, Undue Influence and Manifest Disadvantage' (1994) 110 LQR 174.
[230] *Allcard v Skinner* (1887) 36 ChD 145 (CA) 170–71.

no bar. In other cases it may be possible to craft relief such that the innocent party is able to rescind upon assuming the detriment or making it good.

18.120 For example, the fraudulent purchaser in *Spence v Crawford*[231] had posted certain stocks with the company's bank as security for its overdraft, which the bank had later realized at a time when values were low. Lord Thankerton said that *restitutio in integrum* was satisfied by the innocent party's offer to give credit sufficient to compensate the purchaser for the current value of the stocks.[232] In another case a settlement agreement was rescinded notwithstanding that employment claims of the wrongdoer were now time barred on the basis of the claimant's undertakings to enable such claims to be addressed.[233] In an Australian case the High Court indicated that a guarantor might have been entitled to rescind had he offered to pay the creditor, a trade supplier, an amount equivalent to the value of the goods it had supplied on the faith of the guarantee.[234]

G. Miscellaneous Issues

(1) Date of assessment

18.121 The date as at which the question whether rescission is possible falls to be considered appears to depend on whether the rescission in question is to be effected by court order or by the act of the rescinding party.[235] *Lagunas Nitrate Company v Lagunas Syndicate*,[236] for example, was a case of innocent misrepresentation, and so rescission was only available by court order. Accordingly, in deciding whether *restitutio in integrum* remained possible the Lords Justice took into account the continued working and depletion of a mine during the pendency of the suit.[237]

18.122 By contrast, *Alati v Kruger*[238] was a fraud case in which the claimant sought to return a fruit business he had bought from the defendant, and the High Court of Australia explained that rescission had been effected by the act of the claimant in issuing his writ. Consistently with this, the High Court reasoned that the question whether *restitutio in integrum* was possible fell to be determined in the circumstances as they existed at the commencement of the action, being the date at which the claimant elected to rescind.[239]

18.123 The High Court's reasoning in *Alati v Kruger* was subject to an important qualification.[240] The court said it had a discretion to refuse relief, notwithstanding that *restitutio in integrum*

---

[231] [1939] 3 All ER 271 (HL Sc).
[232] *Spence v Crawford* [1939] 3 All ER 271 (HL Sc) 283.
[233] *Kings Security Systems Ltd v King* [2021] EWHC 325 (Ch) [190].
[234] *Vadasz v Pioneer Concrete (SA) Pty Ltd* (1995) 184 CLR 102, 112. See also *Waters Motors Pty Ltd v Cratchley* [1964] 80 WN (NSW) 1165, where the vendor of a business succeeded in rescinding by offering to indemnify the purchaser for his liability under a personal guarantee given to the company's bank.
[235] JD Heydon, MJ Leeming, and PG Turner, *Meagher, Gummow and Lehane Equity Doctrine and Remedies* (5th edn, 2015) [25-090], [25-125].
[236] [1899] 2 Ch 392 (CA).
[237] [1899] 2 Ch 392 (CA) 433, 458–59, 463–64. Cf *Abram Steamship Company Limited v Westville Shipping Company Limited* [1924] AC 773.
[238] (1955) 94 CLR 216, 224.
[239] (1955) 94 CLR 216, 222–23. See also *Kramer v McMahon* (1969) 89 WN (NSW) (Pt 1) 584.
[240] See the critique of this aspect of the High Court's decision in J O'Sullivan, 'Rescission as a Self-Help Remedy: A Critical Analysis' [2000] CLJ 509, 539–41.

may have been possible at the date of election, if the claimant had during the pendency of the action 'acted unconscientiously ... as by causing the loss of a valuable leasehold and goodwill by discontinuing the business and abandoning the premises without giving [the defendant] a reasonable opportunity to take them back'.[241] In fact the defendant had refused to take the business back when offered and so relief was granted. Nonetheless, the practical effect of this qualification is that the possibility of *restitutio in integrum* will be assessed as at the date of judgment where the claimant has since election unjustifiably put it out of his power to restore the defendant to his previous position. This qualification presumably does not apply where rescission takes effect by self-help at law rather than in equity, so that there is no discretion to refuse relief.

(2) Onus of proof

Lord Blackburn said in *Erlanger v The New Sombrero Phosphate Company*[242] that once the rescinding party had established that at one time he had title to rescind, the onus fell on the party resisting rescission to prove that *restitutio in integrum* was no longer possible. The same view had been expressed in the Court of Appeal 20 years earlier in *Rawlins v Wickham*.[243] This view is consistent with the *restitutio in integrum* bar operating as a defence to a claim to rescind. However, the basic rule is subject to an important exception in that a rescinding purchaser must prove that he is able to return what he received in substantially the same condition, for the sensible reason that he is in the best position to know whether this is possible.[244]

18.124

---

[241] *Alati v Kruger* (1955) 94 CLR 216, 225.
[242] (1878) 3 App Cas 1218 at 1283, see also 1286.
[243] *Rawlins v Wickham* (1858) 3 De G & J 304, 321; 44 ER 1285, 1292. See also *Oelkers v Ellis* [1914] 2 KB 139, 152. In Canada, *Redican v Nesbitt* [1924] 1 DLR 536 (SCC) 549; *Zien v Field* (1963) 41 DLR (2d) 394 (BCCA) 420–22, rev'd on other grounds (1963) 42 DLR (2d) 708 (SCC).
[244] *Thomas Witter Ltd v TBP Industries Ltd* [1996] 2 All ER 573, 587. In Canada, *Steedman v Frigidaire Corp* [1933] 1 DLR 161 (PC—Canada) 165. In Australia, *N & M Gangemi Nominees Pty Ltd v Hypax Pty Ltd* [1997] FCA 1167. In Singapore, *Liberty Sky Investments Limited v Goh Seng Heng* [2019] SGHC 39.

19
Partial Rescission

A. Introduction	19.01	(2) Former exception in cases of mistaken dispositions of real property	19.22
B. Partial Rescission	19.02		
(1) Rationale	19.03	F. Rescission on Terms Elsewhere in the Commonwealth	19.26
(2) Rule applies to bargains	19.05		
(3) Unilateral dispositions	19.08	(1) Australia: *Vadasz v Pioneer Concrete*	19.26
C. Adjustment of Insurance Contracts	19.09	(2) New Zealand	19.31
D. Rescission Against Third Party Wrongdoers	19.10	(3) Canada	19.32
		(4) Hong Kong	19.33
E. Rescission on Terms	19.17	G. Comment	19.34
(1) *TSB Bank Plc v Camfield*	19.18		

A. Introduction

19.01 Partial rescission properly so called involves setting aside one part of a contract while leaving other obligations in force. The expression is often, however, used imperfectly to refer to the process whereby the court sets the contract aside in its entirety, but as a condition of relief places the claimant on terms the effect of which is to reform the bargain in some way. These two processes need to be treated separately. Also discussed in this chapter is the statutory adjustment of insurance contracts and the situation where A wishes to 'virtually' rescind his contract with B as against the wrongdoer C.

B. Partial Rescission

19.02 It is a long-standing rule both of the common law and of equity that a contractual bargain cannot be rescinded in part unless that part is properly severable.[1] 'If it cannot be rescinded *in toto*, it cannot be rescinded at all'.[2]

---

[1] *Myddleton v Lord Kenyon* (1794) 2 Ves 391, 408; 30 ER 689, 697; *Rawlins v Wickham* (1858) 3 De G & J 304, 321–22; 44 ER 1285, 1292. In Australia, *Urquhart v MacPherson* (1878) 3 App Cas 831 (PC—Australia); *Emhill Pty Ltd v Bonsoc Pty Ltd (No 2)* [2007] VSCA 108 [38]. In Canada, *United Shoe Machinery Company of Canada v Brunet* [1909] AC 330 (PC—Canada) 340; *Kingu v Walmar Ventures Ltd* (1986) 10 BCLR (2d) 15 (CA) 20; *Mirage Consulting Ltd v Astra Credit Union Ltd* [2017] MBQB 63. In Ireland, *Hogan v Healy* (1877) 11 IR 119 (Ex Ch) 121; *Northern Bank Finance v Charlton* [1979] IR 149 (SC) 209. But in New Zealand, while the common law position was recognised in *Paki v Attorney-General of New Zealand* [2015] 1 NZLR 67 (NZSC) [278], s 9 of the Contractual Remedies Act 1979 arguably permits a form of partial rescission, as to which see P Watts, 'Partial Rescission: Disentangling the Seedlings, but not Transplanting them' in E Bant and M Harding (eds), *Exploring Private Law* (2013) chap 19.

[2] *The Sheffield Nickel and Silver Plating Company Limited v Unwin* (1877) 2 QBD 214 (CA) 223.

(1) Rationale

The rule against partial rescission has two bases. The most general and fundamental is that the court should not involve itself in the rewriting of bargains along lines it may consider to be fair.[3] Where the court cannot say which part of the consideration the claimant received related to which of his obligations—in other words, where the contract is not severable—the court cannot properly erase only some of the obligations. A *fortiori* a claimant cannot avoid his obligations while insisting that the defendant's obligations should remain on foot or, what is in effect the same thing, while refusing to make *restitutio in integrum*.[4] The rule against partial rescission and the rule requiring *restitutio in integrum* are for this reason closely related.

19.03

The second basis is technical and only applies where rescission takes effect automatically on the claimant's election, as it does at common law. Since rescission takes place automatically upon the claimant's election, there is no scope for the exercise of judicial discretion in working out the consequences of that election, and so rescission must necessarily in these cases be all or nothing. Roch LJ made this point in *TSB Bank Plc v Camfield*,[5] although on the facts of that case it seems inapplicable. The ground for rescission was innocent misrepresentation, so that rescission could only occur by the order of the court.

19.04

(2) Rule applies to bargains

The rule against partial rescission applies to bargains rather than individual contracts. Rescission will accordingly be refused where the contract in question is part of a wider transaction, the components of which are commercially interdependent in the sense that they were contracted each in consideration or contemplation of the others and were intended to be performed together.[6] For example, in *Maguire v Makaronis*[7] the High Court of Australia reversed the decision of the court below, which had been to rescind a mortgage while leaving the underlying contractual covenants intact. The effect of that had been to leave the borrower in possession of the loan money while depriving the lender of his security. The High Court considered this to involve an impermissible reformation of a single bargain comprised of two instruments.

19.05

---

[3] *Myddleton v Lord Kenyon* (1794) 2 Ves 391, 408; 30 ER 689, 697.
[4] *The Sheffield Nickel and Silver Plating Company Limited v Unwin* (1877) 2 QBD 214 (CA) 223. In Australia, *AH MacDonald & Co Pty Ltd v Wells* (1931) 45 CLR 507, 512; *Emhill Pty Ltd v Bonsoc Pty Ltd (No 2)* [2007] VSCA 108 [38]. In Ireland, *Hogan v Healy* (1877) 11 IR 119 (Ex Ch) 121.
[5] [1995] 1 WLR 430 (CA) 438–39.
[6] *Holliday v Lockwood* [1917] 2 Ch 47; *De Molestina v Ponton* [2002] 1 Lloyd's Rep 271; *Murad v Al-Saraj* [2004] EWHC 1235 (Ch) [294]–[298]; *NGM Sustainable Developments Ltd v Wallis* [2015] EWHC 2089 (Ch); *UBS AG v Kommunale Wasserwerke Leipzig GmbH* [2017] 2 Lloyd's Rep 621 [316]; *Deutsche Bank AG v Unitech Global Ltd* [2017] EWHC 1381 (Comm) [43] (citing but distinguishing this paragraph); *Marme Inversiones 2007 SL v Natwest Markets plc* [2019] EWHC 366 (Comm) [336]–[338] (citing this paragraph). In Australia, *AH MacDonald & Co Pty Ltd v Wells* (1931) 45 CLR 507; *HP Mercantile Pty Ltd v Dierickx* (2013) 306 ALR 53 (NSWCA) [133]. In Canada, *Kingu v Walmar Ventures Ltd* (1986) 10 BCLR (2d) 15 (CA) 20; *415703 BC Ltd v JEL Investments Ltd* [2010] BCSC 202; *Mirage Consulting Ltd v Astra Credit Union Ltd* [2017] MBQB 63 (the last two citing this paragraph).
[7] (1997) 188 CLR 449, 474–75. See also *National Commercial Bank (Jamaica) Limited v Hew* [2003] UKPC 51 (Jamaica) [43].

19.06 By contrast, where a contract or wider transaction is severable according to conventional principles, there is usually no difficulty with rescinding one severable part and leaving the remainder on foot.[8] In effect the court must find that the obligations in respect of which rescission is claimed form a self-contained bargain.[9] There may be cases, however, in which a defendant would suffer unjustified prejudice if one agreement were set aside in circumstances where a second independent agreement remained on foot, such that substantial *restitutio in intregrum* is not possible.[10]

19.07 *Deutsche Bank AG v Unitech Global Limited* questioned how these principles apply to the relationships between a creditor, a primary debtor, and a surety.[11] In support of a summary judgment application, the creditor argued that the surety could not rescind its commitment where the loan itself could not be rescinded, because these were the interdependent parts of a single bargain. In a case where the creditor's misconduct was not deliberate,[12] this argument would have some merit, for rescission would effectively reform the tripartite bargain in circumstances where the creditor would not have advanced the credit without the benefit of the guarantee.[13] That would, however, be inconsistent with a line of authorities in which guarantees have been rescinded separately from the primary debt,[14] for which reason Cooke J dismissed the application.

(3) Unilateral dispositions

19.08 Because it is concerned with bargains, the rule against partial rescission does not apply to gifts and other unilateral dispositions. Thus in *Barron v Willis*[15] the House of Lords upheld a declaration that certain deeds were not binding on the plaintiff so far as they deprived her of a power of appointment she had enjoyed under an earlier deed. Without having had independent advice, the plaintiff had been induced to execute these aspects of the deeds by her family solicitor in circumstances where their practical effect was to ensure that the solicitor's son would receive a gift. Where gifts are concerned there is no question of rebalancing a bargain or depriving the defendant of a benefit for which he has paid. Another way of looking at it is that a purely gratuitous element of a wider transaction can always or almost always be severed.[16]

---

[8] *Barclays Bank Plc v Caplan* [1998] 1 FLR 532, 546–47; *Drake Insurance plc v Provident Insurance plc* [2004] 1 Lloyd's Rep 268 (CA) [103]; *Raiffeisen Bank International AG v Asia Coal Energy Ventures Ltd* [2020] EWHC 2602 (Comm) [245]. In Australia, *Urquhart v Macpherson* (1878) 3 App Cas 831 (PC—Australia); *Vitek v Taheri* (2014) 87 NSWLR 403 (CA) [99]. In New Zealand, *Don Lodge Motel Limited v Invercargill Licensing Trust* [1970] NZLR 1105.

[9] Eg the cases involving sales of identical shares: *Maturin v Tredennick* (1864) 10 LT 331; *Re The Mount Morgan (West) Gold Mine Limited* (1887) 56 LT 622. Cf *Dominion Paper Box Co v Crown Tailoring Co* (1918) 43 DLR 557 (Ont SC) 560, which seems doubtful. Contrast the cases involving sales of multiple lots of land: *Thorpe v Fasey* [1949] 1 Ch 649, 665 and in Canada *Fleming v Mair* (1921) 58 DLR 318 (Sask CA).

[10] See the argument advanced in *Taheri v Vitek* (2014) 87 NSWLR 403 (CA) [98], unsuccessfully on the facts of that case.

[11] [2017] EWHC 1381 (Comm).

[12] Compare *Moody v Condor Insurance Ltd* [2006] 1 WLR 1847, where the fraud was that of the principal debtor.

[13] See Chap 18 [18.105]ff and Chap 19 [19.45].

[14] Most prominently *Mackenzie v Royal Bank of Canada* [1934] AC 468 (PC—Canada).

[15] [1902] AC 271. See also *Kennedy v Kennedy* [2015] WTLR 837, *Bainbridge v Bainbridge* [2016] WTLR 943 [21]–[23], and *MacKay v Wesley* [2020] WTLR 1359.

[16] *Wright v Carter* [1903] 1 Ch 27 (CA). See also *Niersman v Pesticco* [2004] EWCA Civ 372; *Kennedy v Kennedy* [2015] WTLR 837 [46].

C. Adjustment of Insurance Contracts

Legislation provides for a form of partial rescission of insurance contracts where the proposing insured's misrepresentation or breach of his duty of fair presentation was neither deliberate nor reckless.[17] If the insurer would not have entered the contract on any terms then it may avoid the contract and refuse all claims. However, if the insurer would have entered the contract but on different terms, then the outcome depends on whether those hypothetical different terms relate to the amount of the premium. If not, then the insurer may require that the contract be treated as if it had been entered into on those different terms. If instead the only difference is that the premium would have been higher, then any claim will be proportionately reduced.

19.09

D. Rescission Against Third Party Wrongdoers

Where a third party C improperly causes A to contract with B, A may have a right against C irrespective of whether the contract can be rescinded. It has sometimes been suggested that A is entitled in these circumstances to rescind, or 'virtually' rescind, the contract with B as against C. This may be seen as a form of partial rescission because the effect would be to rescind the contract so far as A is concerned but not so far as B or C is concerned. An argument along these lines succeeded in an older Australian case, but failed more recently in the Supreme Court of Eire and in Hong Kong.[18]

19.10

The Australian case is *Curwen v Yan Lean Land Company Limited*,[19] a decision of the Full Court of the Supreme Court of Victoria from the late nineteenth century. The defendant in question was the promoter of a company formed to buy land, and the claimant was one of the shareholders in that company, having bought his shares on the faith of a misrepresentation made by the defendant. The claimant sought to rescind the share purchase not against the company, which had sold him the shares, but against the promoter. At first instance the judge acceded to this. He ordered that the defendant should repay the purchase money and indemnify the claimant against future calls, in return for which he would be entitled to take a transfer of the claimant's shares if he wished them.

19.11

On appeal the defendant protested that there was no evidence of loss sufficient to support an award of damages, and that the purchase contract could not be rescinded against him because he was not party to it and had not received the purchase price. The Full Court nonetheless upheld the trial judge's order. Mr Justice A'Beckett described the relief as 'virtual' rescission and said that it was not a form of damages.[20] Rather, the relief was 'intended to place the plaintiff and defendant as nearly as practicable in the position in which they would have stood if the plaintiff had not acted upon the misrepresentation made to him by the defendant'.[21] The fact the defendant was not party to the contract was not seen as an

19.12

---

[17] Consumer Insurance (Disclosure and Representations Act) 2012 schedule 1 (consumer business); Insurance Act 2015 schedule 1 (non-consumer business).
[18] See also *Sibley v Grosvenor* (1916) 21 CLR 469 (Isaacs J) and *Jarvis v Maguire* (1961) 28 DLR (2d) 667 (BCCA) (Davey JA), both dissenting judgments.
[19] (1891) 17 VLR 745 (Full Ct).
[20] *Curwen v Yan Lean Land Company Limited* (1891) 17 VLR 745 (Full Ct) 748, 753.
[21] *Curwen v Yan Lean Land Company Limited* (1891) 17 VLR 745 (Full Ct) 753.

IV. RESTITUTIO IN INTEGRUM

objection, for the company was merely a device through which the defendant had got hold of the claimant's money.[22]

19.13 The Irish case is *Northern Bank Finance Corp Ltd v Charlton*.[23] That case arose out of a takeover bid in relation to which the claimant bank advised and acted as the defendant promoters' agent. The facts are complex but in essence the result of the bid was that the defendants acquired certain shareholdings, personally and through their holding company, which subsequently became worthless. During the course of the takeover bid the advising bank had made a series of fraudulent misrepresentations concerning the contribution made by one of the other promoters, and these misrepresentations had induced the defendants to continue with the bid. Amongst other relief the defendants sought against the bank, they claimed to rescind the share purchase agreements. That is, they wanted the bank to take the shares and refund the purchase money the defendants had paid to the third party vendors.

19.14 This relief was granted at trial, but the order was reversed by a narrow majority on appeal. Mr Justice Henchy expressed the main reason, echoed by the other two majority judges, as follows:

> [The order made at trial] so far from restoring the *status quo ante* results in a situation which never before existed. In this case the return of the purchase money might be said to restore the purchasers' former position, but the compulsory subrogation whereby the misrepresentor would be required to step into the purchaser's shoes and take over ownership of the property bought, which the misrepresentor never owned, would have the effect of thrusting on the misrepresentor a wholly new factual and legal situation which would be incompatible with the mutuality and fairness inherent in the concept of restoring the *status quo ante*.[24]

19.15 Mr Justice Henchy went on to refer to Bowen LJ's remark in *Newbigging v Adam* that upon rescission there must be 'a giving back and a taking back on both sides',[25] and said that the 'compulsory acquisition by the bank of those shares could not be said to be a "taking back" since the bank had never owned those shares'.[26] Accordingly he said that the mutuality that rescission requires was lacking, and Griffin J described the relief given by the trial judge as an impermissible form of partial rescission.[27]

19.16 The decision on this point in *Northern Bank Finance* almost certainly represents English law as well.[28] The relief sought against the bank was not rescission and it could not be justified on any other basis. The purchasers' right, if any, was in damages. The key to *Curwen* seems to have been the willingness of the majority to treat the promoter as the true party of interest under the share sale agreement. That decision must be regarded as doubtful. In *Magic Score* a judge in Hong Kong considered these cases and preferred the approach in *Northern Bank Finance*.[29]

---

[22] *Curwen v Yan Lean Land Company Limited* (1891) 17 VLR 745 (Full Ct) 754–55.
[23] [1979] IR 149 (SC).
[24] [1979] IR 149 (SC) 197.
[25] *Newbigging v Adam* (1886) 34 ChD 582 (CA) 595.
[26] *Northern Bank Finance Corp Ltd v Charlton* [1979] IR 149 (SC) 198.
[27] *Northern Bank Finance Corp Ltd v Charlton* [1979] IR 149 (SC) 197 and 209.
[28] HG Beale (ed), *Chitty on Contracts* (33rd edn, 2019) [7-121].
[29] *Magic Score Ltd v The Hong Kong and Shanghai Banking Corporation Limited* [2006] HKCU 1029 [80]–[86].

E. Rescission on Terms

19.17 As has been explained, the mechanism of rescission in equity is that the court orders that the contract be rescinded in its entirety on condition that the claimant comply with certain terms. While the court exercises a discretion in crafting these terms, this discretion is to be exercised in accordance with settled principle.[30] The relevant principle has traditionally been that the terms should be crafted so as to ensure that the claimant makes substantial *restitutio in integrum*.[31] The power to put a party on terms is not to be used to reform the transaction.

(1) TSB Bank Plc v Camfield

19.18 Following a conflict of opinions in the High Court,[32] the principle that a rescinding claimant may only be put on such terms as are necessary to ensure *restitutio in integrum* was challenged in the Court of Appeal in *TSB Bank Plc v Camfield*.[33]

19.19 In that case a bank sought to enforce a legal charge granted by a wife to secure loan facilities for her husband's business to an unlimited extent. The husband had innocently misrepresented the extent of the charge, and the bank had not taken sufficient steps to see that the wife was properly advised. The trial judge rescinded the security on terms that the wife pay the amount she had thought she was securing. Orders of this character are sometimes described as partial rescission because the practical effect is to rescind the contract save to the extent the claimant would have committed himself absent the circumstances now entitling him to rescind.

19.20 The Court of Appeal overturned the trial judgment. Lord Justice Nourse, with whom the other Lords Justice agreed, accepted the submission that the court's power to put a party claiming rescission on terms is limited to terms necessary to ensure *restitutio in integrum*.[34] That doctrine had no application because the wife had not received anything that she might now be required to return. In the words of Ferris J, with whom Nourse LJ agreed, rescission 'is an all or nothing process'.[35] The court does not have the power to put a claimant on terms where the effect is to reform the transaction.[36]

19.21 As a result, the traditional approach to the terms on which a rescinding party may be put must now be regarded as being in English law beyond challenge below the Supreme Court.[37]

---

[30] *Hanson v Keating* (1844) 4 Hare 1, 5; 67 ER 537, 538.
[31] Eg *Savery v King* (1856) 5 HLC 627, 666–67; 10 ER 1046, 1062–63.
[32] *Allied Irish Banks Plc v Byrne* [1995] 2 FLR 325 and *Bank Melli Iran v Samadi-Rad*, (ChD, 9 February 1994).
[33] [1995] 1 WLR 430 (CA).
[34] [1995] 1 WLR 430 (CA) 432, 437. See also *Dunbar Bank plc v Nadeem* [1998] 3 All ER 876 (CA) 883.
[35] *TSB Bank Plc v Camfield* [1995] 1 WLR 430 (CA) 436.
[36] Similarly, there can be no 'partial affirmation', which is to say an affirmation by which the representee elects neither to rescind the transaction nor to affirm its full force and effect but instead to affirm it only as having a particular represented effect: *Potter v Dyer* [2011] EWCA Civ 1417 [58].
[37] The decision in *TSB Bank Plc v Camfield* has been treated as binding in *Castle Phillips Finance v Piddington* [1995] 1 FLR 783 (CA) and in *De Molestina v Ponton* [2002] 1 Lloyd's Rep 271 [67], where Colman J said that 'the present state of English law is not in any doubt at all ... whatever the position in Australia may be'.

(2) Former exception in cases of mistaken dispositions of real property

19.22 An exception to the traditional approach has been recognized in a parallel line of authority involving the rescission in equity of dispositions of real property affected by mistake. Lord Justice Denning's judgment in *Solle v Butcher*[38] is the *fons et origo* of this exception.

19.23 That case involved a lease of a flat which both parties mistakenly believed to be free from rent control, as a result of which the rent was fixed at a level above that at which the property had previously been let. Had the landlord then appreciated that the flat was subject to rent control, he would have been able to increase the permitted rent by serving a notice, but that was not done. When the truth emerged, the tenant sued to recover the excess rent he had paid. In response the landlord sought to rescind the lease for mistake, in connection with which he claimed restitution of a sum representing the value of the tenant's occupation.

19.24 Lord Justice Denning considered that the lease was voidable in equity for common mistake, but thought that the tenant should be given the choice whether to surrender possession or to stay on with a new lease at the rent that would be permitted were a notice given. Referring to an old line of cases beginning with *Garrard v Frankel*,[39] Denning LJ therefore set the lease aside on terms that the landlord give undertakings the effect of which would afford the tenant this choice.[40] The power to put a claimant on terms was thus used not to ensure that the defendant was restored to his original position, but instead to reform the transaction in line with what would have been done if no mistake had been made.

19.25 Though rescission has been given on comparable terms a couple of times since *Solle v Butcher* was decided,[41] it has never been suggested that this form of relief has any application beyond mistake in equity, and moreover the principle appears to be confined to dispositions of real property. Even within that sphere, two developments indicate that this aspect of *Solle v Butcher* no longer represents the law. First, in *Riverlate Properties Ltd v Paul*[42] the Court of Appeal expressed considerable doubt about the *Garrard v Frankel* line of cases on which Denning LJ had relied. Secondly, and more importantly, in *The Great Peace*[43] the Court of Appeal reconsidered and overruled *Solle v Butcher* insofar as the court had in that case recognized an equitable jurisdiction to rescind contracts concluded on the basis of a common mistake. Though the Court of Appeal was concerned in *The Great Peace* with the ground for relief rather than its nature, the effect of the court's conclusion is that contracts concluded on the basis of a common mistake can no longer be set aside on terms.[44]

---

[38] [1950] 1 KB 671 (CA). Bucknill LJ agreed with the terms of the order.
[39] (1862) 30 Beav 445, 54 ER 961. The other cases in this line are *Harris v Pepperell* (1867) LR 5 Eq 1; *Bloomer v Spittle* (1872) LR 13 Eq 427; and *Paget v Marshall* (1884) 28 ChD 255.
[40] *Solle v Butcher* [1950] 1 KB 671 (CA) 697.
[41] *Grist v Bailey* [1967] Ch 532, 543 and *Topham v Charles Topham Group Ltd* [2003] 1 BCLC 123 [23], in both of which the point was conceded.
[42] [1975] Ch 133, 141–45. Cf *Topham v Charles Topham Group Ltd* [2003] 1 BCLC 123 [23].
[43] *Great Peace Shipping Ltd v Tsavliris Salvage (International) Ltd (The Great Peace)* [2003] QB 679 (CA).
[44] *Great Peace Shipping Ltd v Tsavliris Salvage (International) Ltd (The Great Peace)* [2003] QB 679 (CA) [161].

F. Rescission on Terms Elsewhere in the Commonwealth

(1) *Australia:* Vadasz v Pioneer Concrete

Soon after the decision in *TSB Bank Plc v Camfield*, the High Court of Australia repudiated the Court of Appeal's reasoning in the very similar case of *Vadasz v Pioneer Concrete (SA) Pty Ltd*.[45] Vadasz had given Pioneer Concrete a guarantee in support of his company Vadipile's trade debts. As a result of Pioneer Concrete's misrepresentation, Vadasz had believed himself to be guaranteeing only subsequent indebtedness, whereas in fact the guarantee encompassed the company's past indebtedness as well. Upon the company's failure to pay, Pioneer Concrete sued Vadasz on his guarantee, and by his defence Vadasz claimed to rescind. The High Court upheld the trial judge's decision rescinding the guarantee on condition that Vadasz pay to Pioneer Concrete not the full amount, but the amount of the subsequent indebtedness that he would have agreed to pay had he not been misled.[46]

19.26

In the joint judgment the High Court reasoned that in framing the terms on which a claimant is to be put, the court should be concerned to achieve a practically just result. The court took the measure of practical justice to be the 'wrongful injury' the rescinding party has suffered as a result of the misrepresentation, the concern of the court in moulding relief being 'to prevent, nullify, or provide compensation for' that injury.[47] The High Court distinguished its earlier decision in *Commercial Bank of Australia Ltd v Amadio*,[48] where a mortgage was set aside in its entirety, on the ground that the Amadios would not have entered the transaction at all had they appreciated their son's true financial position. In reaching its conclusion, the High Court was plainly influenced by the fact that while the advances were made to Vadasz's company, his purpose in giving the guarantee was to procure the advances and he stood to benefit personally from the operations of the company.[49]

19.27

The principle adopted by the High Court in *Vadasz* is subject to two important limitations. First, as the distinction the High Court drew between that case and *Amadio* illustrates, the principle only applies where absent the circumstances entitling the claimant to rescind, he would still have entered the contract though on different and perhaps more limited terms.[50] If he would not have contracted at all then the contract must be rescinded in its entirety.

19.28

Secondly, relief of the sort given in *Vadasz* is only available where rescission is claimed on certain grounds. *Vadasz* was a case of misrepresentation. There had been a question whether the misrepresentation was made fraudulently or innocently, but that was left open in the High Court because the court held that the appeal would succeed either way.[51] The principle established in that case has since also been applied by lower courts in cases of

19.29

---

[45] (1995) 184 CLR 102.
[46] In a case involving a debt and mortgage procured unconscionably, the New South Wales Court of Appeal has cited *Vadasz* in support of the proposition that the plaintiff's entitlement was not to be relieved of the debt and to avoid the mortgage but instead to have the mortgage treated as valid and the debt that it secured appropriately reduced: *Donnelly v Australia and New Zealand Banking Group Ltd* [2014] NSWCA 145 [72].
[47] *Vadasz v Pioneer Concrete (SA) Pty Ltd* (1995) 184 CLR 102, 115.
[48] (1983) 151 CLR 447, 481.
[49] *Vadasz v Pioneer Concrete (SA) Pty Ltd* (1995) 184 CLR 102, 112, 113.
[50] *Dowdle v Pay Now For Business Pty Ltd* [2012] QSC 272 [119].
[51] *Vadasz v Pioneer Concrete (SA) Pty Ltd* (1995) 184 CLR 102, 110.

economic duress and of unconscionability.[52] In *Maguire v Makaronis*,[53] however, the High Court held that the same principle does not apply where an instrument is rescinded on grounds that a fiduciary has failed to give his beneficiary sufficient disclosure of his interest in a dealing between them. This was said to be on the basis that the equity raised by the breach of duty in such cases is to have the whole transaction rescinded.

19.30 It is difficult to understand the scope of the exception to the principle in *Vadasz* introduced by *Maguire v Makaronis*. The reason given in that case why the principle did not apply is not a reason at all but a statement of a conclusion. It begs the question, why is the equity in a case involving fiduciary misconduct one to have the whole transaction rescinded? The answer to that question cannot depend upon the degree of wrongfulness of the misconduct in question, for in *Vadasz* itself the High Court was prepared to apply the principle even if the misrepresentation in that case were properly treated as fraudulent. It is for these reasons impossible to anticipate whether the Australian courts will apply the *Vadasz* principle in, for example, a case of undue influence.

(2) New Zealand

19.31 The conflict between the decisions in *TSB Bank Plc v Camfield* and *Vadasz* was considered by the New Zealand Court of Appeal in *Scales Trading Company Ltd v Far Eastern Shipping Company Public Ltd*.[54] That case involved a claim to rescind a guarantee for non-disclosure of aspects of the underlying trading relationship contrary to Russian exchange control legislation. The New Zealand Court of Appeal favoured the High Court of Australia's approach, and held that the rescinding party could do so on condition that it paid the amount it would have agreed to had full disclosure been made. Mr Justice McGechan said that this approach accorded with the thrust of modern New Zealand legislation in the field of contracts, and that it was 'in the spirit of equity' because it avoided 'the rigidity of all or nothing solutions'.[55] The question did not need to be decided on further appeal to the Privy Council.[56]

(3) Canada

19.32 The issue has not been considered in Canada.[57]

---

[52] *Cockrill v Westpac Banking Corporation* (1996) 142 ALR 227 (FCA) (economic duress); *NZI Capital Corp Ltd v Poignand* (1997) ATPR 41–586 (FCA), *Micarone v Perpetual Trustees* [1999] SASC 265 (Full Ct), *Dowdle v Pay Now For Business Pty Ltd* [2012] QSC 272, *Perpetual Trustees Victoria Ltd v Burns* [2015] WASC 234, *Jams 2 Pty Ltd v Stubbings (No 4)* (2019) 59 VR 1 (unconscionability). See also *Bridgewater v Leahy* (1998) 194 CLR 457, a subsequent decision of the High Court of Australia which is difficult to reconcile with any recognized or comprehensible principle.
[53] (1996) 188 CLR 449, 472.
[54] [1999] 3 NZLR 26 (CA).
[55] [1999] 3 NZLR 26 (CA) 44–45. See also *Sayers v Burton* (2009) 11 NZCPR 39 [118]–[120].
[56] *Scales Trading Ltd v Far Eastern Shipping Co Public Ltd* [2001] 1 NZLR 513 (PC—NZ).
[57] But see *Bank of Montreal v Murphy* (1985) 6 BCLR (2d) 169 (BCCA).

(4) Hong Kong

Following some uncertainty,[58] in 2009 the Court of Appeal in Hong Kong followed *TSB v Camfield*.[59]   **19.33**

G. Comment

TSB Bank Plc v Camfield and *Vadasz* excited considerable scholarly comment.[60] It is generally appreciated that *Vadasz* represents a departure from the traditional orthodoxy represented by *TSB Bank Plc v Camfield*. Opinions differ, however, whether *Vadasz* introduces a welcome measure of flexibility into this branch of Australian law or whether justice was achieved in that case through a distortion of elementary principles.   **19.34**

Lord Justice Nourse recognized in *TSB Bank Plc v Camfield* the 'morality, or perhaps the justice in an abstract sense'[61] of the solution that came to be adopted in the *Vadasz*'s case, and it is easy to see why. The law in England concerning the rescission of guarantees is hard on creditors. The creditor makes an advance to the borrower on the faith of the guarantee. The guarantor and the borrower are frequently closely related. In most cases the one is either the spouse or the owner of the other. Although the advance is made to the borrower, the guarantor often expects to benefit from it indirectly. If without any real fault on the creditor's part it transpires that he has made an innocent misrepresentation, or that the creditor has constructive notice of a misrepresentation made by the borrower, then the guarantor will escape his obligation and the creditor will be left to prove for what he can get in the borrower's insolvency.   **19.35**

In point of principle, however, the solution adopted in *Vadasz* is difficult for an English lawyer to understand.[62] The High Court of Australia seems to have treated rescission as a compensatory remedy,[63] with the consequence that the rescinding claimant should be put on terms designed to ensure that he does not end up in a position better than the position he would have occupied had the misconduct in question not occurred. That confuses the function of rescission with that of damages. The relief given upon rescission is designed not to compensate but to restore the parties to their original positions so far as the advantages   **19.36**

---

[58] *Citic Ka Wah Bank Ltd v Lau Kam Luen* [2008] 2 HKLRD 167 [33]–[37] and the earlier authorities cited.
[59] *Wing Hang Bank Limited v Kwok Lai Sim* [2009] 4 HKC 71 (CA) [64]–[67].
[60] L Proksch, 'Rescission on Terms' [1996] RLR 71; JW Carter and G Tolhurst, 'Rescission, Equitable Adjustment and Restitution' (1996) 10 JCL 167; D O'Sullivan, 'Partial Rescission for Misrepresentation in Australia' (1997) 113 LQR 16; M Chen-Wishart, 'Unjust Factors and the Restitutionary Response' (2000) 20 OJLS 557; A Robertson, 'Partial Rescission, Causation and Benefit' (2001) 17 JCL 163; P Watts, 'Rescission of Guarantees for Misrepresentation and Actionable Non-disclosure' [2002] CLJ 301; DJ Meikle, 'Partial Rescission—Removing the Restitution from a Contractual Doctrine' (2003) 19 JCL 40; J Poole and A Keyser, 'Justifying Partial Rescission in English Law' (2005) 121 LQR 273; P Watts, 'Partial Rescission: Disentangling the Seedlings, but not Transplanting them' in E Bant and M Harding (eds), *Exploring Private Law* (2013) chap 19.
[61] *TSB Bank plc v Camfield* [1995] 1 WLR 430 (CA) 437.
[62] The case has received a mixed reception in Australia. See the criticisms in KR Handley, *Spencer Bower & Handley on Actionable Misrepresentation* (5th edn, 2014) [16.07] and see JD Heydon, *Heydon on Contract* (2019) [31-310]–[31-330].
[63] Cf s 237 of the Australian Competition and Consumer Act 2010, which conditions rescission under that legislation on proof of loss, though once this condition is satisfied the resulting remedy itself is not compensatory. See *Tenji v Henneberry & Associates Pty Ltd* (2000) 98 FCR 324 (Full Ct) [12].

IV. RESTITUTIO IN INTEGRUM

and detriments passing under the contract are concerned.[64] If the claimant has not received anything, there is nothing for him to give back.

19.37 The High Court's approach is also objectionable on another ground.[65] In many cases a claimant may rescind even though it may be proved that he would have entered the same contract in any event.[66] The approach adopted by the High Court in *Vadasz*'s case subverts this proposition. As noted earlier, the High Court explained that in crafting the relief given upon rescission, the court must ask what would have happened had the misrepresentation not been made. Where the claimant would not have entered the contract at all, total rescission would be appropriate; and where he would have entered the contract on modified terms then relief would be given reflecting those modified terms. But what happens in a case where, but for the vitiating factor, the claimant would nonetheless have contracted on the very same terms? On the approach taken in *Vadasz*'s case, the answer would seem to be that the contract should be enforced according to its full terms. That contradicts the proposition that, so far as many grounds are concerned, a claimant is entitled to rescind in these circumstances.

19.38 This contradiction came home to the High Court of Australia in *Maguire v Makaronis*,[67] which came up on appeal only one year after *Vadasz*. The Makaronises sought to rescind a mortgage they had granted to their solicitors as security for a loan. The solicitors had not drawn the Makaronises' attention to the fact that the solicitors were to be the mortgagees, and so on the face of it the Makaronises were entitled to rescind. The trial judge had, however, found that even if the identity of the mortgagees had been revealed, the Makaronises would nonetheless have signed the mortgage because they needed funds urgently and because the loan was on market terms. The principle adopted in *Vadasz* would suggest that in these circumstances the contract should be enforced according to its full terms. It is perhaps not surprising that the High Court avoided facing this contradiction by holding that the *Vadasz* principle does not apply in cases involving fiduciary misconduct.[68]

19.39 A number of scholars have proposed an alternative analysis of the decision in *Vadasz* which avoids these complications and reconciles the decision with the traditional rule that a claimant should only be put on terms directed towards ensuring *restitutio in integrum*.[69] The suggestion is that the sum Vadasz was required to pay as a condition of relief should be regarded as representing counter-restitution of the benefit Vadasz gained through Pioneer Concrete's advances. This analysis finds support in one of the dominant threads of the High Court's reasoning. The joint judgment states that 'the justification for not setting aside the transaction in its entirety or in doing so subject to conditions' is 'to prevent one party obtaining an unwarranted benefit at the expense of the other'.[70]

---

[64] *Newbigging v Adam* (1886) 34 ChD 582 (CA) 589, 592–93.
[65] See A Robertson, 'Partial Rescission, Causation and Benefit' (2001) 17 JCL 163, 168–73.
[66] This is true for fraud (Chap 4), duress (Chap 6), abuse of trust and confidence (Chap 8), and undue influence (Chap 6), but not for innocent misrepresentation.
[67] (1996) 188 CLR 449.
[68] (1996) 188 CLR 449, 472. The High Court also expressed reservations about the trial judge's view of the facts.
[69] L Proksch, 'Rescission on Terms' [1996] RLR 71; JW Carter and G Tolhurst, 'Rescission, Equitable Adjustment and Restitution' (1996) 10 JCL 167; M Chen-Wishart, 'Unjust Factors and the Restitutionary Response' (2000) 20 OJLS 557; P Watts, 'Partial Rescission: Disentangling the Seedlings, but not Transplanting them' in E Bant and M Harding, *Exploring Private Law* (2013) chap 19. Cf A Robertson, 'Partial Rescission, Causation and Benefit' (2001) 17 JCL 163.
[70] *Vadasz v Pioneer Concrete (SA) Pty Ltd* (1995) 184 CLR 102, 114.

19. PARTIAL RESCISSION 437

While in some ways attractive, this view is inconsistent with high authority. In *MacKenzie v* **19.40**
Royal Bank of Canada, Lord Atkin advised that the plaintiff guarantor had not 'received anything under the contract which she is unable to restore'.[71] Similarly, in *National Commercial Bank (Jamaica) Ltd v Hew*, Lord Millett explained that, 'A surety incurs a liability but obtains no benefit ... there is nothing for him to disgorge by way of counter-restitution.'[72] This proposition underpinned Nourse LJ's reasons in *TSB Bank Plc v Camfield*[73] as well as the disposition of one of the cases in *RBS plc v Etridge (No 2)*.[74] The approach described in the previous paragraph would therefore require the courts to take a more expansive view of the benefit received by a guarantor than they have until now. That benefit may be viewed in at least three ways.

First, there is the objective economic benefit that the guarantor may gain indirectly as a **19.41**
result of the advances that the creditor makes, for example by participating in the fruits of the borrower's business. Whether a guarantor gains an indirect benefit of this type is contingent on the facts of each particular case and any such benefit will rarely be coextensive with the amount the guarantor intended to secure. For this reason, the approach in *Vadasz* itself cannot be justified by reference to the objective indirect benefits that a guarantor may have received, if any. Certainly there was no finding on this point in *Vadasz*. Moreover, the principle in *Newbigging v Adam*[75] does not require counter-restitution of benefits that the rescinding party acquires indirectly as a consequence of the contract as opposed to directly under the contract.

Secondly, the principle in *Newbigging v Adam* does require indemnification for detriments **19.42**
either party has incurred under the terms of the contract, and this extends to indemnifying for payments made to third parties. A lender's advances to a borrower could be brought into account on this basis if the guarantee specifically required the lender to make those advances, though that is not always the case. The consequence of this approach would, however, be that the guarantor would be required to indemnify the creditor to the full extent of his advances.

Thirdly, drawing on scholarly developments in the theory of unjust enrichment, Chen- **19.43**
Wishart directs attention instead to the subjective value that the guarantor places on the creditor making the advances.[76] She argues that the guarantor is subjectively benefited to the extent he freely intended to guarantee those advances, so that this is the measure of the counter-restitution he must make. Chen-Wishart compares the situation to one where a purchaser has been induced to pay too much, and argues that here the price he would freely have paid is the measure of the benefit he received. Chen-Wishart also compares the situation to one in which by one party's outlay the other party has been saved an expense he would otherwise have had to incur to achieve his desired end.

---

[71] [1934] AC 468 (PC—Canada) 476.
[72] [2003] UKPC 51 [42].
[73] [1995] 1 WLR 430 (CA) 434.
[74] [2002] AC 773 (Mrs Moore's case). See also *Deutsche Bank AG v Unitech Global Limited* [2017] EWHC 1381 (Comm).
[75] (1886) 34 ChD 582 (CA).
[76] M Chen-Wishart, 'Unjust Factors and the Restitutionary Response' (2000) 20 OJLS 557, 572–76.

19.44 Chen-Wishart's analysis of the guarantor's benefit has the advantage over the other two analyses that it actually explains the decision in *Vadasz* and the distinction the High Court of Australia drew with its earlier decision in *Amadio*. Where, as in *Amadio*, the guarantor would not freely have signed at all, on Chen-Wishart's approach they cannot be said to have placed any subjective value on the lender's advances, and rescission should be granted without any term as to payment. Chen-Wishart suggests that *MacKenzie* can be explained on the same basis.

19.45 But notwithstanding its attractions, Chen-Wishart's approach is not without difficulty. Assuming that it is legitimate to take account of the guarantor's subjective valuation of the creditor's performance in the novel way Chen-Wishart proposes, it is nonetheless the case that a guarantor chooses not to put his own money into the venture but only accepts a risk of having to do so. At the time a guarantee is given the guarantor usually considers the business to be capable of meeting its obligations and so likely discounts the possibility of a call on the guarantee. It is at least arguable that the subjective value the guarantor places on the creditor's advances must be discounted accordingly, and so will only very exceptionally be coextensive with the amount they intend to secure.

19.46 Another solution to the problem posed by these guarantee cases would be to reconsider whether *restitutio in integrum* is possible where, honestly and on the faith of a guarantee, a lender advances credit to a borrower. Changes of position of this type have generally been taken to be irrelevant since the decision in *McKenzie v Royal Bank of Canada*, which also involved a guarantee.[77] Lord Atkin said that *restitutio in integrum* was not impossible because the 'mere fact that the party making the representation has treated the contract as binding and has acted on it does not preclude relief'.[78] But Lord Atkin did not explain why this was so. It is difficult to understand how a lender who is not a conscious wrongdoer is sufficiently restored to his original position where on the faith of the guarantee he has irrecoverably advanced funds to a third party.[79] More recently, in *Johnson v EBS Pensioner Trustees Ltd*, the Court of Appeal reached the opposite conclusion, holding that a guarantee could not be rescinded in part because the guarantor had not reimbursed the lender for the amounts it had advanced to the borrower.[80]

---

[77] [1934] AC 468 (PC—Canada).
[78] [1934] AC 468 (PC—Canada) 476.
[79] See further Chap 18, [18.115]–[18.116].
[80] [2002] Lloyd's Rep PN 309 (CA) [58] (Mummery LJ) and [82] (Dyson LJ).

Part V
THIRD PARTIES

20
Intervention of Third Party Rights

A. Introduction	20.01	C. Protection of Other Third Party Rights	20.28
B. Protection of Third Party Property Rights	20.06	(1) Multilateral contracts	20.31
(1) The bar at law	20.09	(2) Contracts relating to the subject matter of the voidable transaction	20.33
(2) The bar in equity	20.23	(3) The winding-up bar	20.36

A. Introduction

20.01 Rescission is barred 'where innocent parties have, in reliance on the fraudulent contract, acquired rights which would be defeated' if the contract were set aside.[1] This reflects in part at least a jurisdictional limit,[2] for 'as a general rule it is clear that a judgment or order will not be made if it would affect the rights of third parties who are not before the court'.[3] Rescission will not be barred, however, if relief can be crafted in a way that does not impinge on the rights of innocent third parties.[4]

20.02 The intervention of third party rights is routinely identified as one of the four main bars to rescission, and yet there are very few cases in which the bar has been successfully invoked. In relation to the central case—that of third party property rights—it has been suggested that the bar should be abolished.[5]

20.03 The intervention of third parties rights bar is sometimes run together with or treated as an aspect of the *restitutio in integrum* impossible bar,[6] but the two are fundamentally distinct. The former serves to protect the rights of third parties, while the latter serves to protect the justifiable interests of the party against whom rescission is sought.[7]

---

[1] *Tennent v The City of Glasgow Bank and Liquidators* (1879) 4 App Cas 615 (HL Sc) 620-21. In Australia, *Hunter BNZ Finance Ltd v CG Maloney Pty Ltd* (1988) 18 NSWLR 420, 433-34. In Canada, *Redican v Nesbitt* [1924] 1 DLR 536 (SCC) 549. In New Zealand, *Fenton v Kenny* [1969] NZLR 552, 556.

[2] *Northern Bank Finance Corp Ltd v Charlton* [1979] IR 149 (SC) 197.

[3] *Senanayake v Cheng* [1966] AC 63 (PC—Singapore) 80; *Crociani v Crociani* (Royal Court of Jersey 11 September 2017) para 724 ('we do not think we have jurisdiction to set aside an agreement governed by foreign law involving a third party which is not before us').

[4] Eg *Bainbridge v Bainbridge* [2016] WTLR 943 [20]; *Waters Motors Pty Ltd v Cratchley* (1964) 80 NSW WN 1165, 1177.

[5] B Häcker, 'Rescission and Third Party Rights' [2006] RLR 1 and further developed in B Häcker, *Consequences of Impaired Consent Transfers* (2013) chap 7.

[6] *Senanayake v Cheng* [1966] AC 63 (PC) 79; *Thomas Witter Ltd v TBP Industries Ltd* [1996] 2 All ER 573, 588; *Huyton SA v Distribuidora Internacional de Productos Agricolas SA de CV* [2003] 2 Lloyd's Rep 780 (CA) 845-46.

[7] See further Chap 18, paras [18.03]-[18.04].

20.04 The third party rights bar is a defence to a claim to rescind. If the defendant wishes to raise that defence then he carries the burden of pleading and proof.[8]

20.05 The central case of third party property rights will be treated first in Part B. That will be followed in Part C by a discussion of other applications of the bar.

B. Protection of Third Party Property Rights

20.06 The central case occurs where A sells an asset to B, who induces the sale by fraud or the like. Before A discovers the fraud and moves to avoid the sale, B resells the asset to C, who knows nothing of B's fraud. In these circumstances C acquires an indefeasible title both at law and in equity.[9]

20.07 It is generally accepted by text writers that the intervention of C's rights in the asset will also bar rescission of the original sale.[10] The bar to rescission seems to be viewed as necessary to the protection of C's title. But the bar has never applied in equity, so that its practical effect is on any view much more limited than the standard texts suggest. Even at common law, the status of the bar is open to question.

20.08 Where the third party acquires his rights from the innocent claimant who now wishes to rescind, rather than from the wrongdoer, the third party rights bar is not engaged.[11] If the claimant has parted with an asset he acquired from the wrongdoer, or has given a third party a security interest over it, the difficulty he may face will instead be one of making sufficient counter-restitution.[12]

(1) The bar at law

20.09 While text writers generally accept that the intervention of third party property rights will bar rescission of the contract between A and B,[13] so far as the common law is concerned this proposition is not well established in point of authority and difficult to justify in point of principle.[14]

---

[8] *Redican v Nesbitt* [1924] 1 DLR 536 (SCC) 549. Cf *Thomas Witter Ltd v TBP Industries Ltd* [1996] 2 All ER 573, 588, though that case involved a confusion between the third party rights bar and the *restitutio in integrum* impossible bar.

[9] *White v Garden* (1851) 10 CB 919, 138 ER 364; *Cundy v Lindsay* (1878) 3 App Cas 459, 463–64 (law); *Hawes v Wyatt* (1790) 2 Cox 263, 30 ER 122 (equity). In Hong Kong, *Crown Master International Trading Co Ltd v China Solar Energy Holdings Ltd* [2015] 4 HKC 505 [59] (shares, citing this paragraph).

[10] Cf s 195(2)(c) of the Companies Act 2006, relating to avoidance of substantial property transactions, and see in this regard *The Funding Corporation Block Discounting Limited v Lexi Holdings plc* [2011] EWHC 3101 (Ch).

[11] Cf *Stewart v Complex 329 Ltd* (1990) 109 NBR (2d) 117; *Thomas Witter Ltd v TBP Industries Ltd* [1996] 2 All ER 573, 588.

[12] *Dunbar Bank plc v Nadeem* [1998] 3 All ER 876 (CA) 887. In Ireland, *Hogan v Healy* (1877) 11 IR 119 (Ex Ch) 121. In Singapore, *Liberty Sky Investments Limited v Goh Seng Heng* [2019] SGHC 39 is properly a case about the *restitutio in integrum* impossible bar.

[13] Eg A Burrows, *A Restatement of the English Law of Contract* (2016) [34(5)(b)].

[14] A view shared by S Zogg, *Proprietary Consequences in Defective Transfers of Ownership* (2020) 191–201.

The authorities

20.10 The third party rights bar is associated with a small collection of cases decided by the common law courts in the middle of the nineteenth century involving sales of goods procured by the purchaser's fraud. Chief amongst these is *White v Garden*,[15] a decision of the Court of Common Pleas.

20.11 *White v Garden* decided that in a contest between A and C for title to the asset, in that case 50 tons of iron, the bona fide third party purchaser C would prevail provided the resale occurred before A's election to rescind.[16] Although that proposition decided the issue in the case, *White v Garden* has also been taken to stand as authority for a second proposition. This second proposition is that where a third party in the position of C acquires indefeasible title from B, A is henceforth barred from rescinding his contract with B. The protection accorded to C therefore has a contractual as well as a proprietary dimension, and the incidental effect of the former is to protect B. This is the origin of what has come to be known as the third party rights bar.

20.12 It is doubtful that the judges who decided *White v Garden* intended this second proposition. The case involved a contest between litigants in the position of A and C. There was no question whether the fraudster in the position of B would be similarly protected, and Cresswell J expressly remarked that the fraudster 'could not have enforced the contract'.[17] The question whether C's title should prevail had been argued by one of the parties as being the question whether A was entitled to rescind the contract by which he parted with the asset,[18] but that is not how any of the judges who decided the case expressed themselves.

20.13 Nevertheless, *White v Garden* has been routinely cited as the chief authority for the application of the supposed bar in cases of this nature.[19] *Clough v The London and North Western Railway Company*,[20] a decision of the Court of Exchequer, is also commonly cited. There the court remarked that a defrauded claimant will be precluded from exercising his right to rescind if 'an innocent third party has acquired an interest in the property'.[21] There was, however, no third party involvement in the transaction with which that case was concerned.

20.14 A different analysis underpins a line of cases involving pledges rather than resales. A pledge confers a right to possess chattels by way of security for the pledgee's debt. The pledgor retains title burdened by that security. In *Kingsford v Merry*,[22] Pollock CB proceeded on the basis that the intervention of the pledgee's interest did not bar rescission.

---

[15] (1851) 10 CB 919, 138 ER 364.
[16] See also *Stevenson v Newnham* (1853) 13 CB 285, 138 ER 1208; *Babcock v Lawson* (1880) 5 QBD 284 (CA), and s 23 of the Sale of Goods Act 1979.
[17] *White v Garden* (1851) 10 CB 919, 926; 138 ER 364, 367.
[18] *White v Garden* (1851) 10 CB 919, 920; 138 ER 364, 365.
[19] Part of the explanation for this reception may lie in a collection of earlier cases holding that following rescission a personal claim cannot be maintained for the value of the goods transferred. See *Read v Hutchinson* (1813) 3 Camp 352, 170 ER 1408; *Ferguson v Carrington* (1829) 9 B & C 59, 109 ER 22; *Strutt v Smith* (1834) 1 CM & R 312, 149 ER 1099. These cases were probably precipitated by the greater separation between the count for goods sold and delivered and trover effected in *Bennett v Francis* (1801) 2 Bos & Pul 550, 126 ER 1433. See also *Emanuel v Dane* (1812) 3 Camp 299, 300; 170 ER 1389, 1389.
[20] (1871) LR 7 Ex 26. See also *Re LG Clarke* [1967] Ch 1121 (CA) 1135–36, although the decision in that case appears to have turned on a representation. In Australia, *Hunter BNZ Finance Ltd v CG Maloney Pty Ltd* (1988) 18 NSWLR 420, 433–34, 438.
[21] *Clough v The London and North Western Railway Company* (1871) LR 7 Ex 26, 35.
[22] (1856) 11 Ex 577, 156 ER 960. Approved *Pease v Gloahec* (1866) LR 1 PC 219, 230.

444   V. THIRD PARTIES

20.15 That case involved an action of trover by a defrauded seller of nine casks of acid against the pledgee, to whom the fraudulent purchaser had committed the casks. Pollock CB said that the claimant was 'not in a condition to maintain an action against the defendant, in which they insist upon a right of possession of the acid, until they have paid or tendered to him his demand in respect of the advance to [the pledgor]'.[23] It is implicit in this that once the claimant had satisfied the pledgee's demand, he would gain the right to possess the casks and on this basis would be entitled to maintain trover. It is further implicit that the claimant had effectively avoided the original sale contract and regained the fraudulent purchaser's title, encumbered as it was by the pledgee's right to possess.[24] Pollock CB would also, presumably, have permitted the vendor to have recovered title to any casks that the fraudster had retained, if contrary to fact only some of the nine had been pledged.

20.16 There appear to be no reported cases in which the third party rights bar has been applied in favour of a wrongdoing purchaser in the position of B.[25] All of the cases involve contests between the defrauded vendor A and the innocent third party C. This is perhaps unsurprising because, the asset having been resold, A will usually be satisfied with his damages remedy against B. Nonetheless, in an appropriate case the very existence of the bar must be open to question.

20.17 It is striking that no parallel bar emerged in the law of fraudulent preferences, which is closely analogous. The defendant in *Marks v Feldman*[26] had acquired certain chattels under a bill of sale, which he then sold. The individual from whom he had acquired the bill and the chattels was subsequently made bankrupt, and the bill was avoided as a fraudulent preference. The case involved a claim by the bankrupt's assignee for the proceeds of the intermediate sale as money had and received. This claim succeeded on appeal to the Exchequer Chamber. The defendant was held to have acquired a title which was defeasible. Upon avoidance the assignee was entitled to trace into and claim the proceeds of the intermediate sale. There was no suggestion that the intermediate sale to an innocent purchaser prevented the assignee from avoiding the original transaction.

Discussion

20.18 It is doubtless the case that a claimant would not be entitled to rescind if this would have the effect of divesting an innocent third party purchaser of his property rights. What has not been explained in any decided case is why rescission of the contract between A and B necessarily has this effect.

20.19 Häcker has suggested that the explanation lies in the function of certain sale contracts to pass title in the assets in question.[27] On this view, where title passes by force of a contract, the rescission of that contract removes the basis for the transfer and so title automatically revests in the rescinding party.[28] Where the law prefers the interest of the innocent

---

[23] *Kingsford v Merry* (1856) 11 Ex 577, 579; 156 ER 960, 961.
[24] See also *W Truman (Limited) v Attenborough* (1910) 26 TLR 601.
[25] *Huyton SA v Distribuidora Internacional de Productos Agricolas SA de CV* [2003] 2 Lloyd's Rep 780 (CA) 845–46 was a case of innocent misrepresentation and therefore not a common law case. The passage suggesting that rescission was impossible by reason of the resale of the seeds was arguably *obiter dicta* and is inconsistent with the authorities in equity.
[26] (1870) LR 5 QB 275 (Ex Ch).
[27] B Häcker, 'Rescission and Third Party Rights' [2006] RLR 1, 3–4; Sale of Goods Act 1979, s 17(1).
[28] But see W Swadling, 'Rescission, Property, and the Common Law' (2005) 121 LQR 123.

purchaser C to that of the defrauded vendor A, rescission must be barred otherwise the revesting of title would defeat that preference.

20.20 Häcker's explanation of the thinking behind the bar is open to question, but she herself goes on to argue that this explanation fails to distinguish between two functions that a sale contract of this type performs.[29] These are first, the contractual function of creating and defining the bargain between the parties, and secondly, the proprietary function of passing title. Reflecting this, rescission has both the contractual effect of destroying the bargain and the proprietary effect of revesting title. Häcker argues that there is no necessary conceptual link between these two functions and no good reason why, where third party rights have intervened, the proprietary effect of rescission should not fall away leaving A's right to avoid his bargain with B unaffected. This seems correct in principle.

20.21 Less technically, it is difficult to understand why the protection afforded an innocent third party purchaser should have the incidental effect of protecting a wrongdoer from such relief as may remain available against him by way of rescission. As it is commonly understood, the third party rights bar would protect a wrongdoer even though he still held most of the assets he had acquired under a particular contract, provided only that he had sold some of them to an innocent third party. Equally, if he had sold all of the assets, the bar would entitle him to be undisturbed in his enjoyment of the proceeds, though *Marks v Feldman*[30] indicates that this would not be the case if the transaction were avoided as a fraudulent preference. In many cases A will be satisfied with damages against B, but it will sometimes happen that rescission would offer superior relief.

Conclusion

20.22 In sum, while it is conventionally understood that rescission will be barred where a fraudulent purchaser resells the asset to an innocent third party, and while this finds support in well-known *obiter dicta*, in fact there is no clear authority supporting the bar, and no bar arises where instead the purchaser pledges the asset. In point of principle a bar is unnecessary to the protection of the rights of innocent purchasers, and recognition of a bar would incidentally accord fraudulent purchasers a protection they do not deserve. In an appropriate case it is open to the court to decline to recognize that any bar arises.

(2) The bar in equity

20.23 Although text writers usually express the proposition that the intervention of third party proprietary rights will bar rescission in general terms, in fact it has never applied in equity. Equity is as assiduous as the common law in protecting the property rights of innocent third party purchasers,[31] but it has always managed to achieve this without taking the extreme step of barring rescission.[32]

---

[29] B Häcker, 'Rescission and Third Party Rights' [2006] RLR 1, 16–18.
[30] (1870) LR 5 QB 275 (Ex Ch).
[31] See Chap 21, paras [21.55]–[21.76].
[32] See most recently *Independent Trustee Services Ltd v GP Noble Trustees Ltd* [2013] Ch 91 (CA) [50].

Asset sold

20.24 There are many cases in which contracts have been rescinded in equity even though the asset in question or part of it has been resold to an innocent third party.[33] No distinction appears to be drawn according to the type of asset or the ground for rescission. The claimant will usually be entitled to claim the proceeds of the sale, and if the defendant is holding a traceable exchange product, then the claimant may be entitled to assert a proprietary claim in respect of that.

20.25 The third party's title is sometimes explicitly protected by an undertaking given by the rescinding party and recorded in the order not to dispute or question the intermediate sale,[34] or else to confirm it.[35] It is not necessary that the claimant plead or offer the undertaking, but his willingness to accept the intermediate sale will be a condition of the relief he seeks.[36]

Land encumbered with a lease

20.26 The same approach has been taken in cases where wrongdoing purchasers of land have granted leases to innocent third parties. Thus in *York Buildings Co v Mackenzie*[37] the House of Lords ordered the defendant to reconvey the estates in question subject to leases that had been granted in the interim, and also to account for rent receipts. Again the title of the innocent lessees may be protected by the rescinding claimant confirming the leases as a condition of his relief.[38]

Land encumbered with mortgage

20.27 Older cases indicate that where the wrongdoing purchaser of land has encumbered the land with a mortgage the purchaser is required to pay out the mortgage and reconvey clear title.[39] Where the loan provided the purchase money, counter-restitution of that purchase money should presumably be applied first towards discharge of the security. If the wrongdoing purchaser is impecunious and the purchase money is not sufficient to discharge the security, the rescinding seller will recover the land subject to the charge.[40]

C. Protection of Other Third Party Rights

20.28 There are many ways in which the avoidance of a contract between A and B may prejudice a third party C. If prejudice of any type were to bar rescission, or even prejudice coupled with

---

[33] See Chap 15, paras [15.17]–[15.19]. In *Huyton SA v Distribuidora Internacional de Productos Agricolas SA de CV* [2003] 2 Lloyd's Rep 780 (CA) 845–46 rescission was said to be impossible where the purchaser, who had made an innocent misrepresentation, had resold the seeds in question to an innocent purchaser. The passage in question is arguably *obiter dicta* and is not supported by the earlier authorities.

[34] Eg *Edwards v Browne* (1845) 2 Coll, 63 ER 654. See FM Van Heythuysen, *The Equity Draftsman* (2nd edn, 1828) 99–100.

[35] Eg *Trevelyan v Charter* (1835) 4 LJ (NS) 209, aff'd (1844) 11 Cl & Fin 714. The order is described in *Trevelyan v Charter* (1846) 9 Beav 140, 50 ER 297.

[36] *Jervis v Berridge* (1873) 8 Ch App 351, 357.

[37] (1795) 8 Bro PC 42, 70–71; 3 ER 432, 450.

[38] *Gresley v Mousley* (1859) 4 De G & J 78, 100–02; 45 ER 31, 39–40. Cf *Waters Motors Pty Ltd v Cratchley* (1964) 80 NSW WN 1165, 1177 (contracts).

[39] *Bellamy v Sabine* (1847) 2 Ph 425, 41 ER 1007, further explained (1857) 1 De G & J 566, 44 ER 842; *Reynell v Sprye* (1849) 8 Hare 222, 68 ER 340; aff'd (1852) 1 De G M & G 660, 42 ER 710.

[40] *Bank of Scotland v Hussain* [2010] EWHC 2812 (Ch). Cf *Treadwell v Martin* (1976) 67 DLR (3d) 493, 504–05 (NBSC—App Div), where the claimant was instead given a pecuniary remedy.

reliance, then rescission would only be possible in very few cases. The third party rights bar is more narrowly drawn. It is only engaged where the effect of rescission would be to defeat rights which a third party acquired in reliance on the integrity of the impugned transaction and for which he gave value.[41]

20.29 It is not enough that rescission would render the third party's rights less valuable, as, for example, by shrinking the wrongdoer's resources or increasing the claims on them. This appears to be the effect of *Scholefield v Templer*.[42] Scholefield sought to avoid a release he had granted of Templer's obligations as a surety on grounds of innocent misrepresentation. Templer was himself in financial difficulty and had needed the release to persuade friends to lend him £1000 to be used to effect a compromise with his creditors. Scholefield knew this and specifically wrote to the friends assuring them that he had released Templer, on the faith of which the friends made their advance. The Vice-Chancellor rescinded the release and reinstated Scholefield's rights against Templer, but on condition that Scholefield repaid the friends their advance. On appeal, however, the Lord Chancellor removed the condition. He said he did 'not see any such connection between that advance and the present transaction as to entitle the friends to such relief as has been given to them in this suit to which they are not parties'.[43]

20.30 On this basis it would seem that to activate the bar the effect of rescission must be to destroy or necessarily frustrate the third party's right. It is always open to a third party, who wishes to take substantial steps in reliance on the integrity of a transaction to which he is not party, to approach the parties and negotiate protection.

(1) Multilateral contracts

20.31 Multilateral contracts will generally be incapable of rescission if any of the other parties are innocent, for rescission would have the effect of depriving them of their rights.[44] For example, in *Society of Lloyds v Leighs*[45] the Court of Appeal held on this ground amongst others that the Names in question were not entitled to rescind their contracts of membership in Lloyds. With a view to consolidating and settling an avalanche of unexpected insurance claims, the Society had exercised powers it enjoyed under the Names' membership contracts to commit them to a contract known as Equitas. In seeking to rescind their membership contracts, the real aim of the Names was to avoid the Equitas contract, which obliged them to make substantial premium payments. Perhaps the principal ground on which

---

[41] *Tennent v The City of Glasgow Bank and Liquidators* (1879) 4 App Cas 615 (HL Sc) 620–21; *Hunter BNZ Finance Ltd v CG Maloney Pty Ltd* (1988) 18 NSWLR 420, 433–34, 438.
[42] (1859) 4 De G & J 429, 45 ER 166. See also *Turton v Benson* (1718) 1 P Wms 496, 24 ER 488.
[43] (1859) 4 De G & J 429, 435; 45 ER 166, 168.
[44] *Re Metal Constituents, Limited (Lord Lurgan's case)* [1902] 1 Ch 707, 710; *Senanayake v Cheng* [1966] AC 63 (PC—Singapore) 80; *Alman v Associated Newspaper Group Ltd* (ChD 20 June 1980); *Event Spaces Ltd v Gregg* [2019] EWHC 3447 (Comm) para [40]. In Canada, *Doll v Howard* (1897) 11 Man R 577 (CA); *Mirage Consulting Ltd v Astra Credit Union Ltd* [2017] MBQB 63. In Australia, *Ballantyne v Raphael* (1889) 15 VLR 538. But it would seem that third parties enjoying rights under the Contracts (Rights of Third Parties) Act 1999 are not so protected: see s 3(2), *Moody v Condor Insurance Ltd* [2006] 1 WLR 1847, and HG Beale (ed), *Chitty on Contracts* (33rd edn, 2019) [18-112]. This accords with the rule that the third party rights bar does not apply in favour of volunteers: *Hunter BNZ Finance Ltd v CG Maloney Pty Ltd* (1988) 18 NSWLR 420, 433–34, 438.
[45] [1997] 6 Re LR 289 (CA); followed in *Society of Lloyds v Khan* [1998] 3 FCR 93.

the Court of Appeal upheld the membership contracts, and thus the Equitas contract, was that rescission would prejudice the other Names who had signed up to Equitas because they would ultimately share a greater deficiency or a smaller surplus.

20.32 By contrast, if all of the other parties to a multilateral contract are implicated in the wrongdoer's misconduct then there is no bar to rescission.[46] Following rescission the contract will remain on foot to the extent it involves obligations between the remaining parties,[47] provided those obligations are not frustrated by the withdrawal of the rescinding party. The same consequence occurs if a contract, multilateral in form, in fact comprises separate bargains that are not interdependent. On this principle the claimants in *Taheri v Vitek* were able to set aside the terms of a consent order between themselves and a defendant settling earlier litigation leaving unaffected other parts of the consent order settling claims between that defendant and a third party.[48]

(2) Contracts relating to the subject matter of the voidable transaction

20.33 Third parties may also be affected where the wrongdoer has contracted obligations with them which would become incapable of performance upon avoidance of the wrongdoer's contract with the rescinding party. Thus in *York Buildings Co v Mackenzie*, a contract for the sale of certain estates was avoided 'without prejudice to the title and interests' of third parties who had contracted with the defendant, the defendant being directed to reconvey the estates 'subject to' these contracts.[49] The nature of the contracts is not clear from the report, but they presumably related to the defendant's management and development of the estates.

20.34 An Australian case involved a vendor's claim for the rescission of a sale of a garage business.[50] In the course of operating the business the purchasers had concluded a number of significant contracts with third parties, including franchise and licensing agreements. Those third parties had previously enjoyed similar contracts with the rescinding vendor when he had run the business, and Else-Mitchell J considered that they would not be treated unjustly if similar relations could be recreated. To this end he directed that the purchasers should stand as trustees of the contracts for the rescinding vendor.

20.35 More recently, in *Crystal Palace FC v Dowie* the manager of a football club had, by fraudulent misrepresentations, induced the club to agree to terminate his employment contract early.[51] The club sought to rescind the compromise, which would have revived the employment contract, but its objective was financial compensation rather than securing the manager's services. By the time of trial he was managing another club. Tugendhat J refused to rescind the compromise on the ground that it would not be just to the second club to

---

[46] *Savery v King* (1856) 5 HLC 627, 10 ER 1046; *Dunbar Bank plc v Nadeem* [1998] 3 All ER 876 (CA). In Australia, *Scheuer v Bell* [2004] VSC 71.
[47] *Savery v King* (1856) 5 HLC 627, 10 ER 1046. It may be implicit in *Society of Lloyds v Leighs* [1997] 6 Re LR 289 (CA) that if the Names in question had been entitled to withdraw from the Equitas contract, it would have remained valid as between the remaining Names.
[48] *Taheri v Vitek* (2014) 87 NSWLR 403 (CA) [95]–[104]. Compare *Mirage Consulting Ltd v Astra Credit Union Ltd* [2017] MBQB 63.
[49] *York Buildings Co v Mackenzie* (1795) 8 Bro PC 41, 70–71; 3 ER 432, 450.
[50] *Waters Motors Pty Ltd v Cratchley* (1964) 80 NSW WN 1165.
[51] *Crystal Palace FC (2000) Limited v Dowie* [2007] IRLR 682.

make an order which had the effect of placing its manager under an employee's obligations to the original club.[52]

(3) The winding-up bar

Though it is no longer of great practical importance, it is well established that a shareholder cannot avoid his statutory contract with the company once it has gone into liquidation or is on the verge of doing so.[53] Some judges have explained this as an aspect of the third party rights bar, reasoning that rescission is barred in order to prevent the creditors and innocent shareholders from being prejudiced.[54] This analysis faces a number of difficulties, not least that it cannot explain why the winding-up bar only takes effect upon liquidation. A superior analysis, first articulated by Jessel MR in *Burgess's case*,[55] is that rescission is instead barred because upon liquidation the mutual obligations created by the share allotment contract are superseded by a new scheme of legal relations between the shareholders and the creditors. The bar may also be seen as reflecting the particular allocation of risk and reward that exists between creditors and shareholders in a limited liability company. This is discussed in detail in Chapter 25.

20.36

---

[52] *Crystal Palace FC (2000) Limited v Dowie* [2007] IRLR 682 [216].
[53] *Oakes v Turquand* (1867) LR 2 HL 325.
[54] *Tennent v City of Glasgow Bank* (1879) 4 App Cas 615; *Stone v City and County Bank Limited* (1877) 3 CPD 282 (CA); *Re Scottish Petroleum* (1882) 23 ChD 413 (CA).
[55] *Re Hull and County Bank (Burgess's case)* (1880) 15 ChD 507 (CA) 509, 511–12.

21
Remote Recipients

A.	Introduction	21.01	(2) No avoidance of contract with the remote recipient	21.42
B.	Remote Recipients Vulnerable to Rescission	21.03	(3) Restitution from the original transferee	21.43
	(1) Volunteers	21.04	(4) Counter-restitution to the original transferee	21.45
	(2) Those taking with notice	21.08	(5) Restitution from the remote recipient	21.48
	(3) Assignee of a chose in action	21.22	(6) No counter-restitution to the remote recipient	21.50
	(4) Crossed cheques	21.27	(7) Remote recipient's rights against his transferor	21.54
C.	Nature of the Claim	21.29	E. Protection of Bona Fide Purchasers	21.55
	(1) Basis of the claim against volunteers and those taking with notice	21.29	(1) Common law and equitable doctrines of bona fide purchase	21.55
	(2) Basis of the claim against assignees of a chose in action	21.31	(2) Protection of purchaser of legal title	21.63
	(3) No new claim to rescind upon disposition to remote recipient	21.35	(3) Protection of purchaser of equitable title	21.64
	(4) Need to rescind original transaction	21.36	(4) Onus of proof	21.71
	(5) Remote recipient in no better position than original transferee	21.37		
D.	Consequences of Recovery	21.40		
	(1) Avoidance of original contract	21.41		

A. Introduction

21.01 This chapter is concerned with claims to recover an asset or its exchange product in the hands of a remote recipient. A remote recipient is a purchaser, mortgagee, or other transferee who has acquired his interest from the guilty party to the voidable transaction, or through such a person. The chapter considers the circumstances in which the innocent party may, by rescinding the voidable transaction, obtain title to the asset free from the remote recipient's claim to it. It is therefore fundamentally concerned with the priority between rival claims to property.[1]

21.02 Rescission is available if the remote recipient is a volunteer, takes with notice of the relevant vitiating factor, is the assignee of a chose in action, or is the recipient of a crossed cheque. Each of these four categories is considered in Part B. Part C goes on to consider the nature of the claim against the remote recipient, and Part D examines what occurs when title is recovered free from the remote recipient's claim. Part E outlines the immunity afforded to remote recipients who are bona fide purchasers for value without notice. It notes the special feature of that doctrine as it applies to the equity to rescind (that the law protects even bona

---

[1] For a comparative discussion of English and German law, B Häcker, *Consequences of Impaired Consent Transfers* (2013) chap VI (emphasizing the greater protection of third party purchasers under German law).

fide purchasers of an equitable title) and concludes by considering the surprisingly problematic question of the onus of proof.

B. Remote Recipients Vulnerable to Rescission

Remote recipients of assets disposed of under a voidable transaction are vulnerable to proprietary claims consequent upon rescission when they take no more than the defeasible title initially conferred under the voidable transaction. The main categories of case that arise in practice are: **21.03**

1. volunteers;
2. those taking with notice of the relevant vitiating factor;
3. assignees of a chose in action; and
4. recipients of crossed cheques who are not the named payees.

These categories will be considered in turn.

(1) Volunteers

Equity permits the recovery of assets upon rescission where the remote recipient is a volunteer from one who took a voidable title. That is, recovery is permitted against donees whose donor's title was obtained under a contract or gift procured by fraud, undue influence, or other ground for rescission.[2] The rule is an old one,[3] and encompasses both gifts *inter vivos* and testamentary gifts.[4] **21.04**

The principle is the same at common law. Although there is no clear authority, the rule is implicit in those cases that recognize the indefeasibility of the interest acquired by a subsequent bona fide purchaser for value.[5] The corollary is that a subsequent volunteer obtains only the defeasible interest of his transferor. A similar principle has been applied when a fraudulent buyer becomes bankrupt and his assets pass by operation of law to the trustee in **21.05**

---

[2] *Gould v Okeden* (1731) 4 Brown 198, 2 ER 135, *Bridgeman v Green* (1755) Wilm 58, 64–65; 97 ER 22, 25 (general rule stated; gifts were direct to Green and co-defendants); *Huguenin v Baseley* (1804) 14 Ves Jun 273, 288–90; 33 ER 526, 532–33; *Small v Attwood* (1832) You 407, 535–37; 159 ER 1051, 1103–04 (rev'd on other grounds *Attwood v Small* (1838) 6 Cl & Fin 232, 7 ER 684); *Charter v Trevelyan* (1842, 1844) 11 Cl & Fin 714, 8 ER 1273; *Vane v Vane* (1873) 8 Ch App 383, 397; *Bainbrigge v Browne* (1881) 18 ChD 188, 197 (contract procured by third party treated as donee); *Daly v The Sydney Stock Exchange Limited* (1985) 160 CLR 371, 388; *Twinsectra Limited v Yardley* [1999] Lloyd's Rep Bank 438 (CA) 461–62.
[3] *Joy v Bannister (No 2)* (1617), *Wyatt v Wyatt* (1618–1620) in J Ritchie, *Reports of Cases Decided by Francis Bacon in the High Court of Chancery (1617–1621)* (1932) 36, 126.
[4] *Gould v Okeden* (1731) 4 Brown 198, 2 ER 135; *Charter v Trevelyan* (1842, 1844) 11 Cl & Fin 714, 8 ER 1273.
[5] *Load v Green* (1846) 15 M & W 216, 219; 153 ER 828, 829; *White v Garden* (1851) 10 CB 919, 926–28; 138 ER 364, 367–68; *Stevenson v Newnham* (1853) 13 CB 285, 302; 138 ER 1208, 1215; *Kingsford v Merry* (1856) 11 Ex 577, 579; 156 ER 960, 961 rev'd on other grounds (1856) 1 H & N 503, 156 ER 1299, principle subsequently aff'd *Pease v Gloahec* (1866) LR 1 PC 219, 230; *Cundy v Lindsay* (1878) 3 App Cas 459, 464; *Truman (Limited) v Attenborough* (1910) 26 TLR 601, 603; *Whitehorn Bros v Davison* [1911] 1 KB 463 (CA) 476; *Car and Universal Finance Co Ltd v Caldwell* [1965] 1 QB 525 (CA).

bankruptcy. The trustee obtains only the bankrupt's defeasible title to the goods purchased, and will lose his title when the vendor rescinds the sale.[6]

What counts as value

21.06 To qualify as a volunteer against whom rescission is available the third party must have given no value for the property received. *Inter vivos* and testamentary gifts are straightforward. Beyond these simple cases, authorities concerned with rescission have not much considered what counts as 'value' for the purpose of this rule.[7] The principles established in relation to the general equitable plea of bona fide purchase probably provide some guidance.[8]

21.07 Where section 23 of the Sale of Goods Act 1979 applies, the third party will obtain a good title if there is a 'sale', and he is a bona fide 'buyer' within the meaning of the statute.[9] A 'sale' involves a transfer of property in the goods under a contract of sale, and a 'buyer' is a person who buys or agrees to buy goods.[10] Immunity is therefore given to purchasers who either buy or agree to buy the relevant goods, and it is not necessary for the price to have actually been paid as long as title has passed. A sale on credit is enough.[11]

(2) Those taking with notice

21.08 Rescission in equity is available against a second transferee who had notice of the facts vitiating the transaction under which the original transferee acquired the property.[12] For example, in *Addis v Campbell*,[13] Crook committed a 'gross fraud' on the destitute Addis to purchase his inheritance, a contingent reversionary interest in certain Norfolk lands, at great undervalue. Knowing of the circumstances of the sale to Crook, but wishing to preserve the estates in the family, Addis's relative, Gostling, then purchased Crook's interest. Some years later Addis's successor successfully rescinded the sale and regained the estates.

---

[6] *Load v Green* (1846) 15 M & W 216, 221; 153 ER 828, 830; *Re Eastgate* [1905] 1 KB 465; *Tilley v Bowman* [1910] 1 KB 745 (CA). See also *Hunter BNZ Finance Ltd v CG Maloney Pty Ltd* (1988) 18 NSWLR 420, 434, 437–38 (title to cheques obtained by fraud).

[7] But see *Leask v Scott Brothers* (1877) 2 QBD 376 (CA) 382 (statement *obiter* that past value sufficient); *Babcock v Lawson* (1879) 4 QBD 394, 400 (advances prior to delivery of goods as pledge sufficient).

[8] As to which, see J McGhee and S Elliott (eds), *Snell's Equity* (34th edn, 2020) [4-018]; JD Heydon, MJ Leeming, and PG Turner, *Meagher, Gummow and Lehane's Equity Doctrines and Remedies* (5th edn, 2014) [8-250]; L Tucker *et al* (eds), *Lewin on Trusts* (20th edn, 2020) [44-119]. The point has received detailed treatment in the United States: JN Pomeroy, *A Treatise on Equity Jurisprudence* (5th edn, 1941) vol 3, §§ 746–51; AW Scott and WR Fratcher, *The Law of Trusts* (5th edn, 2013) vol 5, § 29.1.1, § 29.1.2. As to when the question of value is to be assessed, *Independent Trustee Services Ltd v GP Noble Trustees Ltd* [2013] Ch 91 (CA) 115, 116, 126, 129–31 (question to be assessed when the rival equitable interest was asserted, in circumstances where the value had been received under a transaction since rescinded).

[9] '23. Sale under a voidable title. When the seller of goods has a voidable title to them, but his title has not been avoided at the time of the sale, the buyer acquires a good title to the goods, provided he buys them in good faith and without notice of the seller's defect in title.' Cf Uniform Commercial Code, Art 2–403(1).

[10] Sale of Goods Act 1979, ss 2(4), 61(1).

[11] Contrast AW Scott and WR Fratcher, *The Law of Trusts* (4th edn, 1989) vol 5, § 475.1, discussing the position under the Uniform Commercial Code.

[12] *Dunbar v Tredennick* (1813) 1 Ball & Beatty 304, 318–19 (subsequent purchaser of land knew his vendor had bought in breach of fiduciary duty); *Addis v Campbell* (1841) 4 Beav 401, 49 ER 394 (defendant bought an estate without intent to defraud, but knowing that his vendor had been fraudulent when buying); *Re Slater's Trusts* (1879) 11 ChD 227 (assignment of mortgage of reversion to solicitor who knew that the mortgage was a catching bargain); *Twinsectra Limited v Yardley* [1999] Lloyd's Rep Bank 438 (CA) 461–62.

[13] (1841) 4 Beav 401, 49 ER 394.

Gostling acquired a defeasible title because he was aware of the facts that had made Crook's purchase liable to be rescinded.

The same principle is applied when a transaction is voidable at common law. For example, the litigation in *Caldwell's* case[14] was conducted on the agreed basis that the car dealer, Motobella, had notice that the fraudster had wrongfully obtained Caldwell's motor car, so that they obtained only a defeasible legal title when they bought it from him.

21.09

What counts as notice
Relation between notice and bona fides
The cases are clear that notice is distinct from an absence of bona fides. Rescission is available upon proof either that the purchaser had notice or that he lacked bona fides.[15] But both notice and absence of bona fides connote a lack of honesty, and so far cases involving rescission have treated bona fides as being concerned only with an honest lack of notice.[16] A person is a bona fide purchaser only if his lack of notice is both genuine and honest.[17]

21.10

The preferable approach is to focus on what state of mind will cause a subsequent purchaser to acquire a defeasible title; that is, what the law regards as genuine and honest lack of notice. That is considered next.

21.11

Facts causing the purchaser to suspect something is wrong
The title of a remote recipient who gives value is liable to be lost on rescission if he was aware of the circumstances that made his predecessor's title voidable. But it is not necessary for him to know all the details of the earlier transaction. It is enough if the third party suspects that something was wrong. This was established in *Whitehorn Bros v Davison*.[18] Bruford was a jeweller and pearl dealer. He took possession of, and then bought, a pearl necklace from the claimant Whitehorn Bros, another jeweller. Between taking possession and buying the necklace, Bruford pledged it to the defendant pawnbroker, Davison, as security for several advances, both new and old. Whitehorn Bros later disaffirmed the sale to Bruford but the pawnbroker, Davison, refused to give up the necklace. The Court of Appeal held that the trial judge had misdirected the jury as to the onus of proof, and entered judgment for

21.12

---

[14] *Car and Universal Finance Co Ltd v Caldwell* [1965] 1 QB 525 (CA) 527, 533, 552, 556, 559. See also *Whitehorn Bros v Davison* [1911] 1 KB 463 (CA), which turned on whether the pledgee of a pearl necklace had sufficient notice of the defect in title of the pledgor, who had purchased the necklace by fraud.

[15] *Whitehorn Bros v Davison* [1911] 1 KB 463 (CA) 478, 487 (recognizing the distinction); *Percy Edwards (Limited) v Vaughan* (1910) 26 TLR 545 (CA) 546 (notice and good faith left as separate questions for the jury). As to the distinction between notice and want of bona fides in relation to the general doctrine of bona fide purchase, see *Pilcher v Rawlins* (1872) 7 Ch App 259, 269; *Midland Bank Trust Co Ltd v Green* [1985] AC 513, 528 (Lord Wilberforce); JN Pomeroy, *A Treatise on Equity Jurisprudence* (5th edn, 1941) vol 3, §§ 745, 762; cf J McGhee and S Elliott (eds), *Snell's Equity* (34th edn, 2020) [4-021]; L Tucker *et al* (eds), *Lewin on Trusts* (20th edn, 2020) [44-124].

[16] *Whitehorn Bros v Davison* [1911] 1 KB 463 (CA) 487. Section 61(3) of the Sale of Goods Act 1979 provides that '[a] thing is deemed to be done in good faith within the meaning of this Act when it is in fact done honestly, whether it is done negligently or not'. But cf the recent statement that a purchaser may lack bona fides even though he is not dishonest: *Roadchef (Employee Benefits Trustees) Limited v Hill* [2014] EWHC 109 (Ch) [139] ('improper or unconscionable behavior is clearly bad faith, irrespective of dishonesty'; share transfer in breach of trust).

[17] *Midland Bank Trust Co Ltd v Green* [1985] AC 513, 528: 'I think that it would generally be true to say that the words "in good faith" related to the existence of notice. Equity, in other words, required not only absence of notice, but genuine and honest absence of notice', per Lord Wilberforce, speaking of the general equitable doctrine of bona fide purchase.

[18] [1911] 1 KB 463 (CA). Although it was concerned with a claim to rescind for fraud at common law, the principles established should equally apply to rescission on other grounds, and to rescission in equity.

Davison on the basis that there was no evidence on which the jury could have found that he had suspected Bruford's title.

21.13 Vaughan Williams LJ held that it would be enough if Davison knew facts that 'might lead him to wish not to make any further inquiry lest he should find that there was something wrong'.[19] This included 'suspecting' Bruford's title and a failure to inquire 'because he feared the answer he might get'.[20] Kennedy LJ said that it was necessary to show that Davison 'could not have acted honestly in the transaction'.[21]

21.14 The same wide view was adopted in *Car and Universal Finance Co Ltd v Caldwell*,[22] where a different result was reached. There the fraudster had engaged in an earlier dishonest transaction with the car dealer, Motobella. It was common ground between the parties that Motobella had sufficient notice of the fraud in that 'if they did not know the details of the actual fraud they had notice from which they could infer that he had not come by it honestly'.[23] At trial Lord Denning MR said that Motobella 'had had a previous transaction with the rogue which put them on inquiry, or should have done',[24] and the Court of Appeal also accepted that Motobella's prior dealing with the fraudster made its title defeasible.[25]

21.15 In *Gray v Smith*[26] it was emphasized that in assessing the question of notice, close attention should be paid to the ordinary practice in undertaking transactions of the kind sought to be impugned. After considering the documents that would ordinarily be produced and the inquiries that a purchaser would normally undertake, Mr Justice Cooke found that the purchaser of a McLaren F1 motor car had purchased it without notice of an earlier fraud.[27]

21.16 These principles have close similarities to the common law's rules regarding purchases of negotiable instruments. A purchaser will take free from defects in their predecessor's title if they are bona fide purchasers for value.[28] Indeed, in *Whitehorn Bros v Davison*[29] the Court of Appeal cited with approval Lord Blackburn's formulation of those rules in *Jones v Gordon*.[30] Lord Blackburn there said that although it is not enough if the purchaser of a bill of exchange fails to suspect fraud due to carelessness or stupidity, it is different if the inference from the circumstances is that he 'must have had a suspicion that there was something wrong, and that he refrained from asking questions'.[31] This test is very similar to that adopted in *Whitehorn Bros v Davison* and *Caldwell*'s case.

---

[19] *Whitehorn Bros v Davison* [1911] 1 KB 463 (CA) 476.
[20] *Whitehorn Bros v Davison* [1911] 1 KB 463 (CA) 478.
[21] *Whitehorn Bros v Davison* [1911] 1 KB 463 (CA) 487.
[22] [1965] 1 QB 525 (CA).
[23] *Car and Universal Finance Co Ltd v Caldwell* [1965] 1 QB 525 (CA) 527.
[24] *Car and Universal Finance Co Ltd v Caldwell* [1965] 1 QB 525 (CA) 533.
[25] *Car and Universal Finance Co Ltd v Caldwell* [1965] 1 QB 525 (CA) 552, 556, 559.
[26] [2014] 2 All ER (Comm) 359.
[27] *Gray v Smith* [2014] 2 All ER (Comm) 359 [135], [136], [139], [144]–[146], [154].
[28] See para [21.59].
[29] [1911] 1 KB 463 (CA).
[30] (1877) 2 App Cas 616.
[31] *Jones v Gordon* (1877) 2 App Cas 616, 628–29; see also 625–26 (Lord O'Hagan). See also *London Joint Stock Bank v Simmons* [1892] AC 201, 221: 'But regard to the facts of which the taker of such [negotiable] instruments had notice is most material in considering whether he took in good faith. If there be anything which excites the suspicion that there is something wrong in the transaction, the taker of the instrument is not acting in good faith if he shuts his eyes to the facts presented to him and puts the suspicions aside without further inquiry'; Bills of Exchange Act 1882, s 90: 'A thing is deemed to be done in good faith, within the meaning of this Act, where it is in fact done honestly, whether it is done negligently or not.'

If the terms of the third party's contract are uncommercial because of a significantly reduced price, missing or unusual documentation, or any other reason, that is likely to be probative of notice or lack of bona fides.[32] **21.17**

In *Credit Agricole Corporation and Investment Bank v Papadimitriou*[33] the question was whether a bank had notice of the claimant's proprietary interest in funds it had received. The bank raised a plea of bona fide purchase in answer to a claim arising not from an election to rescind but because the funds represented the proceeds of misappropriated property (valuable art deco furniture taken and sold by the fraudster Symes). Upholding the decision of the Gibraltar Court of Appeal, the Privy Council held that given the nature of the transaction, the bank should have inquired into its commercial purpose, and had it done so, it would have concluded that the transaction was improper.[34] The plea of bona fide purchase was therefore not made out. Whilst the case did not involve a voidable transaction the notice test articulated by the Board is very similar to the test established in the context of sales of goods procured by fraud.[35] As discussed earlier, in that context it is enough for facts to be known that 'might lead the third party to wish not to make further inquiry lest he should find that there was something wrong'.[36] **21.18**

Timing of notice

The cases have not considered when notice must be received for rescission to be possible against the remote recipient. The rule for the general doctrine of bona fide purchase is that the plea fails if notice is received before legal title is received, or if notice is received before the full consideration is paid.[37] **21.19**

In principle, that general rule ought to apply in cases of rescission with one qualification. A claim to recover property upon rescission, unlike a vested equitable interest, is defeated by the subsequent bona fide purchase of an equitable interest in the property.[38] Accordingly, **21.20**

---

[32] *Jones v Gordon* (1877) 2 App Cas 616, 632 (bills of exchange); *Heap v Motorists' Advisory Agency Ltd* [1923] 1 KB 577, 590–91 (Factors Act 1889, s 2); *International Alpaca Management Pty Ltd v Ensor* (1995) 133 ALR 561 (Full FCA) 571–72 (re-sale by seller in possession; Sale of Goods Act 1923 (NSW), s 28(1)); *Coutinho & Ferrostaal GmbH v Tracomex (Canada) Ltd* [2015] BCSC 787 [163]–[168] (sale of scrap steel affected by several 'red flags'). See also *Gray v Smith* [2014] 2 All ER (Comm) 359[141]–[153].

[33] [2015] 1 WLR 4265 (PC—Gibraltar).

[34] *Credit Agricole Corporation and Investment Bank v Papadimitriou* [2015] 1 WLR 4265 (PC—Gibraltar) [24], [30], [31], [33] (bank knew that there was no apparent explanation for interposition of Panamanian and Liechtenstein entities unless it was to conceal the origin of the funds; it needed to make inquiries before proceeding as if there was an innocent explanation).

[35] 'The bank must make inquiries if there is a serious possibility of a third party having such a [proprietary] right or, put in another way, if the facts known to the bank would give a reasonable banker in the position of the particular banker serious cause to question the propriety of the transaction': *Credit Agricole Corporation and Investment Bank v Papadimitriou* [2015] 1 WLR 4265 (PC—Gibraltar) [20] (but cf at [33]) following *Sinclair Investments (UK) Ltd v Versailles Trade Finance Ltd* [2012] Ch 453 (CA) [100].

[36] *Whitehorn Bros v Davison* [1911] 1 KB 463 (CA) 476. However, if the claim in *Credit Agricole* had been for rescission, the onus of proof would have rested upon the claimant, and not the bank: Section (4) below. In *Great Investments Ltd v Warner* (2016) 243 FCR 516 (Full Ct) it was said that the dominant view is that any of the five *Baden* levels of knowledge will establish 'notice' for the purpose of what the court described as the 'doctrine of bona fide purchase': at [112], [113], [118].

[37] As to that rule and its qualifications, J McGhee and S Elliott (eds), *Snell's Equity* (34th edn, 2020) [4-027]; JD Heydon, MJ Leeming, and PG Turner, *Meagher, Gummow and Lehane's Equity Doctrines and Remedies* (5th edn, 2014) [8-255]; JN Pomeroy, *A Treatise on Equity Jurisprudence* (5th edn, 1941) vol 3, §§ 753, 755. Cf *Gray v Smith* [2014] 2 All ER (Comm) 359 [129] 'the critical point at which it matters whether the purchaser has such notice is the time at which title passed or valuable considerable was given, whichever is later'.

[38] See para [21.69].

456   V. THIRD PARTIES

where the remote recipient asserts an equitable rather than a legal title, as under an executory purchase of land, if rescission is to be available it should be essential that notice be received before facts occur that give rise to the competing equitable title.

21.21 Notice is a question of fact, and whether a purchaser has notice is to be determined at the time of the acquisition of the relevant title, at the latest.[39]

(3) Assignee of a chose in action

Equitable assignments

21.22 Special rules apply when the remote recipient acquires a chose in action. The general principle is stated in *Mangles v Dixon*, where the Lord Chancellor said that:

> If there is one rule more perfectly established in a court of equity than another, it is, that whoever takes an assignment of a *chose* in action ... takes subject to all the equities of the person who made the assignment.[40]

21.23 One of the 'equities' to which an assignee takes subject under this rule is the entitlement of the debtor or other obligor to rescind the transaction between himself and the assignor by which the chose in action was created. That involves a claim to extinguish the chose in action, and a corresponding defence to actions to enforce it. The principle was first clearly articulated in *Turton v Benson*,[41] and it has since been affirmed and applied on several occasions.[42]

21.24 The pattern just discussed is to be distinguished from the case where a chose in action is properly created, but the creditor or other obligee is induced to assign it by the fraud or other vitiating conduct of the assignee, and that assignee then sub-assigns the chose in action to an innocent third party.[43] Here it is the obligee rather than the obligor who has the

---

[39] *Independent Trustee Services Ltd v GP Noble Trustees Ltd* [2013] Ch 91 (CA) [88] (in the context of a contest between a purchaser and trust beneficiaries).

[40] *Mangles v Dixon* (1852) HLC 702, 731; 10 ER 278, 290 (where the 'equities' consisted of contractual rights entitling a charterer to insist that assignees of a charter party, who took from the shipowner, account for a half share of the freight payable for the relevant voyage). See also, eg *Cavendish v Geaves* (1857) 24 Beav 163, 53 ER 319 (legal right of set-off enforceable against assignees of a bond); *Phipps v Lovegrove* (1873) LR 16 Eq Cas 80, 88 (rule stated); *Banco Santander SA v Banque Paribas* [2000] EWCA Civ 57 (rule restated). For discussion, M Smith and N Leslie, *The Law of Assignment* (3rd edn, 2018) chap 26, section D; G Tolhurst, *The Assignment of Contractual Rights* (2nd edn, 2016) [8.49]–[8.56]; J McGhee and S Elliott (eds), *Snell's Equity* (34th edn, 2020) [3-024], [3-025]; J Starke, *Assignment of Choses in Action in Australia* (1972) 30; O Marshall, *The Assignment of Choses in Action* (1950) 181; M Tudsbery, *The Nature, Requisites and Operation of Equitable Assignments* (1912) chap 7.

[41] (1718) 1 P Wms 496, 24 ER 488.

[42] *Athenaeum Life Assurance Company Society v Pooley* (1858) 3 De G & J 294, 299–302; 44 ER 1281, 1283–84 (Joint Stock Company debentures); *Graham v Johnson* (1869) 8 Eq Cas 36, 43–44 (£1000 bond); *The Wakefield and Barnsley Banking Company v The Normanton Local Board* (1881) 40 LT 697, 699–700 (right to £800 under compromise); *Stoddart v Union Trust Ltd* [1912] 1 KB 181 (CA) 189 (debt). In Australia, *Equuscorp Pty Ltd v Van der Ross* [2005] VSC 110 [38]–[39] (voidable loan assigned). In Canada, *Fleischhaker v Fort Garry Agencies Ltd* (1957) 11 DLR (2d) 599 (Man CA) (contract assigned by wrongdoer to another company in group). See also the discussion in G Tolhurst, *The Assignment of Contractual Rights* (2nd edn, 2016) [8.62].

[43] The distinction is discussed in *Cockell v Taylor* (1852) 15 Beav 103, 118–19; 51 ER 475, 481–82 and *Southern British National Trust Limited v Pither* (1936) 57 CLR 89, 102–04, 108–09. The difference is that between (i) B fraudulently selling goods to A for £50,000, and then B assigning to C his right to receive the £50,000 from A: C takes subject to A's equity to rescind the purchase, and A has a defence to C's claim to enforce the debt, and (ii) B fraudulently purchasing A's right to receive £50,000 from A's debtor, and then assigning the right to that £50,000 on to C: C takes subject to A's equity to rescind his assignment to B, and A may recover the debt from C just as he could recover it from B.

claim to rescind, and what is asserted is not a right to extinguish the chose in action, but a right to recover it from the sub-assignee.

The rule that choses in action are assigned subject to equities is also applied in this context. The second assignee of the chose in action takes it subject to the original assignor's right to rescind the first assignment. The foundational case was *Cockell v Taylor*,[44] where Sir John Romilly MR held that the rule that choses in action are assigned subject to equities extends to an assignor's equity to rescind his assignment. Later cases have confirmed the principle.[45] **21.25**

Statutory assignments

The statutory right to assign choses in action contained in section 136(1) of the Law of Property Act 1925 provides that the assignment is effective 'subject to equities having priority over the right of the assignor'. This proviso catches the equity to rescind.[46] Statutory assignments to third parties may be rescinded in the same way that equitable assignments can be. The availability of rescission against assignees taking under other legislation permitting the assignment of a chose in action depends upon the terms of the relevant statutory provision.[47] **21.26**

(4) Crossed cheques

Section 81 of the Bills of Exchange Act 1882 provides that: 'Where a person takes a crossed cheque which bears on it the words "not negotiable", he shall not have and shall not be capable of giving a better title to the cheque than that which the person from whom he took it had.' **21.27**

The bona fide purchaser of a voidable title to a crossed cheque obtains only a voidable interest in the cheque and its proceeds, and title to the cheque and its traceable proceeds is revested in the rescinding party when rescission occurs.[48] **21.28**

---

[44] (1852) 15 Beav 103, 118–19; 51 ER 475, 481–82.
[45] *Re Slater's Trusts* (1879) 11 ChD 227, 238, 239 (mortgages); *Southern British National Trust Limited v Pither* (1936) 57 CLR 89, 108, 112; cf 102–04 (voidable assignment of right to receive dividends).
[46] *Stoddart v Union Trust Ltd* [1912] 1 KB 181 (CA) 188–89 (referring to the Judicature Act 1873, s 25(1), the predecessor to the Law of Property Act 1925, s 136(1)); *Provident Finance Corporation Pty Ltd v Hammond* [1978] VR 312, 318 (Property Law Act 1958 (Vict), s 134, which is identical to the Law of Property Act 1925, s 136(1)).
[47] See eg *William Pickersgill & Sons Limited v London and Provincial Marine and General Insurance Company Limited* [1912] 3 KB 614, 621 (insurer able to rely on defence of non-disclosure by insured against claim on policy by assignees of the insured, because that defence was one 'arising out of the contract' of insurance within the meaning of the Marine Insurance Act 1906, s 50(2)).
[48] *Fisher v Roberts* (1890) 6 TLR 354; *Great Western Railway Co v London and County Banking Co Ltd* [1901] AC 414, 424; *Radford v Ferguson* (1947) 50 WAR 14, 22; *Hunter BNZ Finance Ltd v CG Maloney Pty Ltd* (1988) 18 NSWLR 420, 437. As to the protection of bankers in such a case: Cheques Act 1957, s 4 (formerly Bills of Exchange Act 1882, s 82).

C. Nature of the Claim

(1) Basis of the claim against volunteers and those taking with notice

21.29 The claim to recover property on rescission is a personal right or power to obtain title to the property when rescission occurs. It is an imperfection in the title of the transferee. *Nemo dat quod non habet* (no one may give a title greater than he has) that imperfection must persist unless and until a subsequent transferee obtains a better title, free from the claim to recover the asset upon rescission. A person taking with notice or as a volunteer from the initial transferee under the voidable transaction does not obtain a better title. They obtain only their predecessor's defeasible title. Rescission crystallizes the imperfection in the title obtained by the remote recipient so as to revest ownership in the rescinding party.

21.30 The right to rescind where property (other than a chose in action) is transferred to a third party therefore derives from an application of the *nemo dat* principle, and is in substance a rule of property law.[49] It is a rule *sui generis*, however, in that the *nemo dat* principle is not being applied in respect of a vested proprietary interest, as is usual, but in respect of a power to alter ownership when a right is exercised.[50]

(2) Basis of the claim against assignees of a chose in action

21.31 Where a chose in action is assigned pursuant to statute, the right to rescind against a subsequent assignee derives from the language of the statute.[51]

21.32 The right to rescind against a subsequent equitable assignee is more complex. Two principles appear to be involved. The first emphasizes the nature of equitable assignment itself. Rescission is available against the subsequent assignee because equitable assignments are only effective to pass what the assignor was 'justly entitled to',[52] and this means the chose in action burdened by the relevant claim to rescind. Thus in *Turton v Benson* Parker LC held that even if Turton's bond was, contrary to the facts, assigned to Benson's creditors for consideration:

> ... yet in truth it was not an assignment, but an agreement only that the assignee should have all the fair and equitable advantage and benefit of the bond that the assignor himself was entitled to (*Hill v Caillove* 1 Ves 123); and if nothing was due, nothing could be assigned over.[53]

---

[49] It is not clear whether the view just expressed is consistent with the reasoning of Lord Hoffmann in *Barclays Bank plc v Boulter* [1999] 1 WLR 1919 (HL) 1924–25. If his Lordship intended to say that an entitlement to recover a title on rescission is not an imperfection in that title, capable of falling within the maxim *nemo dat quod non habet*, it is suggested that this is wrong in principle.

[50] See further Chap 16, paras [16.02]–[16.04], [16.12]–[16.17]. Paras [21.29] to [21.30] of the second edition are the subject of a detailed critique in J Wells, "What is a mere equity?: an investigation of the nature and function of so-called 'mere equities'" (unpublished PhD thesis, January 2019) 111–114. The author rejects the view there set out in favour of an analysis in which the right to recover property upon rescission from a remote recipient springs from the personal equity binding the immediate recipient, being 'imposed afresh' on a successor in title, by reason of their conscience being affected by notice or the absence of value: at 118ff.

[51] Paras [21.31] to [21.34] of the second edition were cited with apparent approval in *Bendigo and Adelaide Bank Ltd v Williamson* [2017] NSWSC 939 [91] (though the point was not fully argued—at [93]).

[52] *Phillips v Phillips* (1861) 4 De GF & J 208, 215; 45 ER 1164, 1166.

[53] *Turton v Benson* (1718) 1 P Wms 496, 499; 24 ER 488, 489. Thus 'if a man does take an assignment of a chose in action he must take his chance as to the exact position in which the party giving it stands': *Mangles v Dixon* (1852) 3 HLC 702, 735; 10 ER 278, 292.

21.33 This reasoning tends to see the right to rescind as an infirmity in the assignor's title, and the right to rescind against equitable assignees as an expression of the *nemo dat* rule: the assignor gives only what he has. Reasoning of this kind has been employed in cases where it is the assigning obligee who asserts the claim to rescind,[54] but is equally applicable where the obligor has the equity to rescind.[55] This approach implies that rescission is available against not only assignees of a chose in action, but also those claiming under any other transaction by which an interest in a chose in action is disposed of, as by declaration of trust or charge.

21.34 The second principle focuses on the distinctive character of choses in action as rights to sue. The principle is that equity will not permit the assigning of a right to sue to deprive the obligor of claims or defences that he could have set up in a suit brought by the original obligee. This assimilates the right to rescind to rights of set-off and other equities. Each is regarded as a personal claim enforceable against the assignee of a chose in action precisely because they were enforceable as against the assignor. This reasoning is confined to rescission by an obligor and cannot apply when it is the obligee who wishes to rescind an assignment of the chose in action. It is also not obvious that this reasoning can apply when a limited interest in a chose in action is conferred, by way of trust or charge.

(3) No new claim to rescind upon disposition to remote recipient

21.35 The disposition to the remote recipient generates no new claim to rescind. Rather, the claim to rescind that arose on completion of the original transaction remains enforceable notwithstanding the asset's subsequent disposal. The imperfection in the title received by the remote recipient is realized upon rescission of the original transaction. This is true of both transfers to volunteers and those taking with notice, and of assignments of choses in action.

(4) Need to rescind original transaction

21.36 The claim to recover property in the hands of a remote recipient derives from rescission of the original transaction. The innocent party rescinds that voidable transaction and an automatic consequence is the recall or, as the case may be, extinction of the assets obtained by the third party. Accordingly, as long as the original transaction remains unrescinded no right to restitution can be asserted against the remote recipient. Where for some reason the right to rescind the original transaction has become barred, the right to recover from the remote recipient is also barred.[56] By the same token, the original transferor cannot assert rights against the other party to the voidable transaction that are founded on the transaction remaining on foot, such as damages for breach of contract, whilst at the same time seeking to recover the subject matter of the transaction in the hands of a remote recipient.[57]

---

[54] *Cockell v Taylor* (1852) 15 Beav 103, 118–19; 51 ER 475, 481–82; *Southern British National Trust Limited v Pither* (1936) 57 CLR 89, 102, 105, 108–10, 112.
[55] *Turton v Benson* (1718) 1 P Wms 496, 499; 24 ER 488, 489.
[56] *Stoddart v Union Trust Limited* [1912] 1 KB 181 (CA) 189 (right to rescind lost by claimant's dealing with property received). That case involved a chose in action. However, the principle is equally applicable to tangible assets received by donees and those taking with notice.
[57] *Stoddart v Union Trust Limited* [1912] 1 KB 181 (CA) 192, 194–95.

(5) Remote recipient in no better position than original transferee

21.37 A remote recipient who is a volunteer or who takes with notice is in no better position than the original transferee.[58] In *Addis v Campbell* Lord Langdale MR explained that:

> Contracting as he did, with Crook [fraudulent purchaser] alone, knowing the fraud which had been practised by Crook ... Gostling [subsequent purchaser] could not place himself in a better situation than Crook alone stood ... by the whole transaction, notwithstanding his payments, he subjected himself, as towards Addis [defrauded vendor], to the same responsibilities to which Crook was already subject ... by the transaction, Gostling placed himself only in the situation in which Crook stood in relation to Addis.[59]

21.38 The principle is the same for the assignment of a voidable chose in action, or a chose in action obtained under a voidable assignment. The assignee is in no better position than the assignor.[60]

21.39 In unusual cases the remote recipient who loses his proprietary interest upon rescission may succeed to proprietary rights that arise in favour of the original transferee as an incident of rescission. The third party succeeds to the restitutionary rights of his predecessor in title. This occurs when a vendor rescinds a sale after his buyer has charged the property to a mortgagee with notice.[61] Upon rescission the purchaser obtains an equitable lien over the subject property for the price paid plus interest, and that lien enures to the benefit of the mortgagee. The equitable lien becomes subject to the charge, presumably by operation of the mortgage itself. The net effect is that the sums lent to the guilty purchaser become secured by a lien over the sale property, but limited to the amount that the rescinding vendor must repay as counter-restitution.[62]

D. Consequences of Recovery

21.40 Rescinding so as to assert a proprietary interest against a remote recipient involves the following:

1. avoidance of the original contract between the rescinding party and the wrongdoer;
2. no avoidance of any contract that may exist between the wrongdoer and the remote recipient, or as between later remote recipients;
3. restitution from the original transferee to the original transferor in respect of benefits conferred under the voidable transaction;

---

[58] '[A] purchaser with notice, is, in Equity, bound to the same extent, and in the same manner, as the person from whom he purchased' and places himself 'in the situation of his predecessor in title': *Dunbar v Tredennick* (1813) 1 Ball & Beatty 304, 319, 320 (interests in land obtained by subsequent purchaser having notice they were acquired in breach of fiduciary duty). Also, *Addis v Campbell* (1841) 4 Beav 401, 415, 416; 49 ER 394, 399, 400.
[59] (1841) 4 Beav 401, 415–16; 49 ER 394, 399, 400.
[60] *Turton v Benson* (1718) 1 P Wms 496, 497; 24 ER 488, 489; *Athenaeum Life Assurance Company Society v Pooley* (1858) 3 De G & J 294, 299–301; 44 ER 1281, 1283–84; *Re Slater's Trusts* (1879) 11 ChD 227, 239; *Southern British National Trust Limited v Pither* (1936) 57 CLR 89, 105, 108, 110, 112.
[61] *Hughes v Macpherson & UBC Home Loans Corporation Limited* [1999] EWCA Civ 1006 (sale of house set aside for undue influence).
[62] *Hughes v Macpherson & UBC Home Loans Corporation Limited* [1999] EWCA Civ 1006.

4. counter-restitution to the original transferee in respect of benefits received under the voidable contract;
5. restitution from the remote recipient;
6. no counter-restitution to the remote recipient;
7. the remote recipient gaining rights against his transferor as a consequence of his loss of title.

Each of these seven consequences will be considered briefly in turn.

(1) Avoidance of original contract

21.41 Rescinding in order to recover or extinguish property received by a remote recipient always involves rescinding the transaction with the original transferee. Where that transaction is a reciprocal contract, that contract must be avoided *ab initio* in order to recover property in the hands of the remote recipient. Likewise a voidable deed of gift must be set aside before property can be recovered from those to whom the donee may have distributed it.

(2) No avoidance of contract with the remote recipient

21.42 On the other hand, a claim to recover the property received by the remote recipient does not require, and nor will it cause, avoidance of the transaction by which the remote recipient acquired it. This point appears not to have been considered in the cases, but it seems to be implicit and to follow as a matter of principle. The circumstances rendering the first transaction voidable will generally not vitiate the later transaction with the remote recipient. That later transaction is not voidable either at the instance of the original transferor, or the remote recipient himself. Instead, there are successive transfers of an asset to which each transferee obtains an imperfect entitlement, and that imperfection is realized when the original transaction is rescinded. Any contract with the remote recipient cannot be avoided by that rescission.

(3) Restitution from the original transferee

21.43 Where the original transferee retains an interest in an asset received from the rescinding party, and disposes of only part of what he took to the remote recipient, that residual interest will be regained by the rescinding party upon rescission.[63]

21.44 Likewise, if benefits such as rent or dividends were derived from the asset between the time it was acquired from the rescinding party and the time it was disposed of to the remote recipient, these must be accounted for upon rescission.[64]

---

[63] See eg *Cockell v Taylor* (1852) 15 Beav 103, 51 ER 475 (sub-mortgage of chose in action). See also Chap 20.
[64] See eg *Dunbar v Tredennick* (1813) 1 Ball & Beatty 304, 322 (rents derived from estates by fraudulent grantee).

(4) Counter-restitution to the original transferee

21.45 Upon rescission, the rescinding transferor is obliged to give counter-restitution of benefits received under the voidable transaction in the ordinary way. The disposition to the remote recipient does not cut back this obligation. The decree in *Addis v Campbell*[65] thus made the normal order for reconveyance to the rescinding claimant upon him repaying the sums that his predecessor, the defrauded vendor, had received from the fraudulent purchaser.

21.46 *Cockell v Taylor*[66] illustrates the principle in the context of a chose in action. The claimant was a bricklayer who had mortgaged his interest in a fund in court to finance his claim to it. The mortgage was in favour of the claimant's solicitors, and was held to be voidable as an unconscionable bargain. The solicitor later granted two sub-mortgages to mortgagees who took bona fide for value. Sir John Romilly MR held that the claimant was entitled to rescind all of the charges on the contested fund, including those asserted by the two sub-mortgagees. Rescission was, however, conditional on the claimant repaying any sums that he had received from the solicitor mortgagee.[67]

21.47 It has been suggested that if the counter-party to the voidable transaction has ceased to exist, or cannot be found, the rescinding party may obtain restitution from the remote recipient upon deducting the amount due to the original transferee.[68] It is doubtful that this is correct. The claim against the remote recipient follows rescission of the original transaction, and whether rescission is possible should not be affected by the extent of that claim. Moreover, the obligation to make counter-restitution is owed to the party entitled to receive it. There is no warrant for treating the obligation as discharged by a notional deduction from the claim against a different party. Where the first party has ceased to exist or cannot be found it will depend upon the particular circumstances of the case whether, by reason of that fact, rescission is barred or not. In the case of a fraudster who has paid a deposit and then absconded, there will be no difficulty in recovering title from a third party who took with notice of the fraud, or as a volunteer. The absence of the fraudster will provide no impediment, for he cannot complain if by his own act he has put it out of the power of the rescinding party to actually repay the deposit, and *a fortiori* the third party cannot complain, for he suffers no prejudice if the deposit remains with the claimant.

(5) Restitution from the remote recipient

21.48 The rescinding party is entitled to recover assets, or their exchange product, remaining in the hands of the remote recipient.[69] *Caldwell*'s case[70] provides a simple illustration. It was

---

[65] (1841) 4 Beav 401, 416; 49 ER 394, 400.
[66] (1852) 15 Beav 103, 51 ER 475.
[67] *Cockell v Taylor* (1852) 15 Beav 103, 116, 126; 51 ER 475, 481, 484. See also *Equuscorp Pty Ltd v Van der Ross* [2005] VSC 110 [39], [42] (rescission of assigned loan would be conditional on repaying outstanding principal).
[68] D Fox, *Property Rights in Money* (2008) [6.52].
[69] See paras [21.03]–[21.28]. As to claims to traceable substitutes received by a remote recipient, *Small v Attwood* (1832) You 407, 535–38; 159 ER 1051 (fraud; money into stock); *El Ajou v Dollar Land Holdings plc* [1993] 3 All ER 717, 735 (fraud; comments *obiter*); *Shalson v Russo* [2005] Ch 281 (fraud; money into yacht).
[70] *Car and Universal Finance Co Ltd v Caldwell* [1965] 1 QB 525 (CA) 527, 533, 552, 556, 559. The contest was in fact over the proceeds of sale of the car, which had been paid into court.

common ground that Motobella, the subsequent purchaser from the fraudster Norris, had notice of his fraud upon Caldwell. Any title in Caldwell's car that they acquired was therefore revested in Caldwell when he disaffirmed the contract with Norris.

If the asset was created under the voidable transaction, as in the case of a loan or share issue, or under the transaction with the remote recipient, as where the wrongdoer has mortgaged the interest received, rescission extinguishes the asset held by the remote recipient. Where the remote recipient has received benefits from the asset received, such as rent or dividends or the benefit of occupation, he must also account for these to the rescinding party.[71]

21.49

(6) No counter-restitution to the remote recipient

If the remote recipient purchases with notice, or buys a chose in action, he is not entitled to counter-restitution from the rescinding party for the price that he paid for the asset. This follows as a matter of principle. It is only the first transaction that is avoided. The subsequent contract with the remote recipient remains intact. The right to retain the consideration passing under that transaction therefore also remains intact, absent some independent claim to recover it.[72]

21.50

In addition, the general rule is that the rescinding party need only return benefits accruing to him under the voidable transaction,[73] and the price paid by the remote recipient is not a benefit that accrued to the rescinding party, either under the voidable transaction or at all. It is rather a benefit that has accrued to the other party to the voidable transaction, and under the separate transaction with the remote recipient.

21.51

The principle is well illustrated by *Addis v Campbell*.[74] There Crook had fraudulently bought Addis's reversionary estate for £650 and then sold it on to Gostling, who knew of the fraud, for £6500. The decree for rescission did not require the rescinding party (Addis's successor) to pay anything in respect of Gostling's £6500 payment to Crook. It required only repayment to Crook of the sums Addis had received from Crook.[75] Subsequent gratuitous payments by Crook to the destitute Addis were also left out of account. The Master of the Rolls emphasized that these were voluntary,[76] and that Gostling's consideration 'all moved to Crook, and no part to Addis, except through the means of Crook... he paid Crook alone'.[77] The rule is the same when rescission occurs at common law.[78]

21.52

A more recent example is *Hughes v Macpherson*.[79] The mortgagee of a house took with notice that the mortgagor had acquired the property by undue influence. When the sale

21.53

---

[71] Eg *Dunbar v Tredennick* (1813) 1 Ball & Beatty 304, 322 (rents derived from estates by purchaser with notice from fraudulent grantee).
[72] Also, para [21.54].
[73] *Logicrose Ltd v Southend United Football Club Ltd* [1988] 1 WLR 1256, 1263–64; Chaps 13, 17.
[74] (1841) 4 Beav 401, 49 ER 394.
[75] *Addis v Campbell* (1841) 4 Beav 401, 416; 49 ER 394, 400.
[76] *Addis v Campbell* (1841) 4 Beav 401, 49 ER 394.
[77] *Addis v Campbell* (1841) 4 Beav 401, 414–15; 49 ER 394, 399.
[78] In *Car and Universal Finance Co Ltd v Caldwell* [1965] 1 QB 525 (CA) there was no suggestion that the rescinding party, Caldwell, was obliged to pay anything in respect of any payments the fraudulent purchaser, Norris, had received from Motobella: who had bought the car from him with notice that he had not come by it honestly.
[79] *Hughes v Macpherson & UBC Home Loans Corporation Limited* [1999] EWCA Civ 1006.

464   V. THIRD PARTIES

was rescinded the vendor was required to repay sums received under the sale, but no payment was required in respect of the sums lent to the purchaser. *Cockell v Taylor*[80] illustrates the rule where there has been a subsequent assignment of a chose in action. There the rescinding party was not obliged to account for any part of the consideration given by the innocent sub-mortgagees to the first mortgagee, although rescission was available against them.[81]

(7) Remote recipient's rights against his transferor

21.54 The remote recipient will ordinarily obtain a right to damages for breach of contract against his transferor, who will have promised a good title but given a bad one. He will also have a claim to restitution if money has been paid and he is able to terminate for breach of condition and show that, having lost title to the asset purchased, there has been a total failure of consideration.

E. Protection of Bona Fide Purchasers

(1) Common law and equitable doctrines of bona fide purchase

Bona fide purchase at law

No general protection to bona fide purchaser

21.55 Unlike equity, the common law gives no general protection to the bona fide purchaser of a legal title.[82] At common law, the general rule is that the bona fide purchaser obtains only that interest held by his vendor. The governing principle is *nemo dat quod non habet*: a man can transfer no more than the title he has.

When the bona fide purchaser is protected

21.56 The common law recognizes certain exceptions to this general rule.[83] Two of the exceptions that remain important today relate to transfers of cash[84] and negotiable instruments.[85] In both instances the common law holds that the bona fide purchaser for value without notice obtains a good title even if his transferor did not, and in both cases the exception is motivated by simple practical imperatives, namely, the need to ensure the proper functioning of money and its equivalent.[86]

---

[80] (1852) 15 Beav 103, 125–26; 51 ER 475, 484.
[81] See further D Fox, *Property Rights in Money* (2008) [6.49].
[82] Eg '*The Shizelle*' [1992] 2 Lloyd's Rep 444, 451 (bona fide purchaser of legal title to ship without notice of encumbrances takes subject to a prior common law mortgage, but not an equitable mortgage).
[83] See further D Browne (ed), *Ashburner's Principles of Equity* (2nd edn, 1983) 50.
[84] *Anon* (1677) 1 Salk 126, 91 ER 119; *Miller v Race* (1758) 1 Burr 452, 97 ER 398; *Sinclair v Brougham* [1914] AC 398, 418; D Fox, 'Bona Fide Purchase and the Currency of Money' [1996] 55 CLJ 547.
[85] *Lickbarrow v Mason* (1787) 2 TR 63, 70; 100 ER 35; *Johnson v Credit Lyonnais Co* (1877) 3 CPD 32, 36 (bill of exchange); *London Joint Stock Bank v Simmons* [1892] AC 201 (negotiable bonds); *Nash v De Freville* [1900] 2 QB 72, 83, 84, 89 (promissory note); *RE Jones Limited v Waring and Gillow Limited* [1926] AC 670, 683 (cheque). See also Bills of Exchange Act 1882, s 59 (bill of exchange), Carriage of Goods by Sea Act 1992, s 2(1)(a), 5(2) (rights to suit of bona fide purchaser of bill of lading).
[86] Money: *Miller v Race* (1758) 1 Burr 452, 457; 97 ER 398; *Sinclair v Brougham* [1914] AC 398, 418. Negotiable instruments: *Fuentes v Montis* (1868) LR 3 CP 268, 276; *Folkes v King* [1923] 1 KB 282 (CA) 300.

Rescission

The common law also recognizes a third exception to the general rule that bona fide purchase cures no defect in title. The exception arises in cases of rescission. A bona fide purchaser for value from one who has received only a voidable title obtains a good title at common law.[87] The innocent purchaser obtains a title superior to that of his transferor. His transferor's title was imperfect because it was liable to be divested by the rescinding party's election to rescind. The title of the innocent third party purchaser is not.

21.57

This rule arose out of contests between defrauded vendors of goods and third party purchasers and pledgees from the fraudster. The foundational case was *White v Garden*.[88] That case and those following it explained the third party's immunity on two grounds. First, it was said that where one of two innocent parties had to suffer from the fraud of a third, the loss should fall on the party whose conduct permitted the fraud or who trusted the fraudster.[89] Secondly, the exception was justified by commercial necessity. In *White v Garden* Jervis CJ said that:

21.58

> The question is one of considerable importance, as affecting the mercantile transactions of this country: for, if the argument urged on the part of the defendants were well founded, goods at all tainted with fraud might be followed through any number of bona fide purchasers—a most inconvenient, and, as it strikes me, a most absurd doctrine. A vendor, who does not choose to avail himself of means of inquiry, would thus, by trusting the vendee, be giving him unlimited means of defrauding the rest of the world.[90]

The same two considerations were relied upon in the parallel group of cases that established the immunity of bona fide purchasers of negotiable instruments.[91]

21.59

White v Garden[92] and the cases following it were also received as having established that if a defrauded vendor could not regain title because the chattels had been on-sold to a bona fide purchaser for value, he could also not rescind the contract of sale. Where property was transferred, rescission was associated with exclusively proprietary claims, and if the right to regain title was lost, so also was the right to rescind. This bar to rescission therefore went

21.60

---

[87] *Load v Green* (1846) 15 M & W 216, 219; 153 ER 828, 829; *White v Garden* (1851) 10 CB 919, 926–28; 138 ER 364, 367–68; *Stevenson v Newnham* (1853) 13 CB 285, 302; 138 ER 1208, 1215; *Kingsford v Merry* (1856) 11 Ex 577, 579; 156 ER 960, 961 (rev'd on other grounds (1856) 1 H & N 503, 156 ER 1299, principle aff'd *Pease v Gloahec* (1866) LR 1 HL 219 (PC) 230); *Fuentes v Montis* (1868) LR 3 CP 268, 276–77; *Cundy v Lindsay* (1878) 3 App Cas 459 (HL) 464; *Truman (Limited) v Attenborough* (1910) 26 TLR 601, 603; *Whitehorn Bros v Davison* [1911] 1 KB 463 (CA) 476; *Car and Universal Finance Co Ltd v Caldwell* [1965] 1 QB 525 (CA).
[88] (1851) 10 CB 919, 138 ER 364.
[89] *White v Garden* (1851) 10 CB 919, 926; 138 ER 364, 367 (Creswell J); *Moyce v Newington* (1878) 4 QBD 32, 35; *Babcock v Lawson* (1879) 4 QBD 394, 400–01; aff'd (1880) 5 QBD 284 (CA) 286. See also the influential decision in *Root v French* (1835) 13 Wendell 570, 572 (Savage CJ in the SCNY), adopted by counsel in *Kingsford v Merry* (1856) 1 H & N 503, 515; 156 ER 1299, 1305, and followed in *Babcock v Lawson* (1879) 4 QBD 394, 395 and *Moyce v Newington* (1878) 4 QBD 32, 35. Also, *Ingram v Little* [1961] 1 QB 31 (CA) 73–74 (Devlin LJ).
[90] (1851) 10 CB 919, 927–28; 138 ER 364, 368. Also, *Root v French* (1835) 13 Wendell 570 (SCNY) 572: 'A contrary principle would endanger the security of commercial transactions, and destroy that confidence upon which what is called the *usual course of trade* materially rests.'
[91] The 'two innocent parties' consideration: *Lickbarrow v Mason* (1787) 2 TR 63, 70; 100 ER 35 (bill of lading); *Johnson v Credit Lyonnais Co* (1877) 3 CPD 32, 36 (bill of exchange); *Nash v De Freville* [1900] 2 QB 72, 76, 83, 84, 89 (promissory note); *RE Jones Limited v Waring and Gillow Limited* [1926] AC 670, 683 (cheque). The 'commercial necessity' consideration: *Fuentes v Montis* (1868) LR 3 CP 268, *Folkes v King* [1923] 1 KB 282, 300. An analogy between the protection of bona fide purchasers of negotiable instruments and those purchasing goods from a fraudulent buyer was drawn in *Root v French* (1835) 13 Wendell 570 (SCNY) 573.
[92] (1851) 10 CB 919, 138 ER 364.

hand in glove with the separate group of cases that denied the defrauded vendor a right to rescind and bring a purely personal claim for the value of goods sold.[93] If the defrauded vendor could not regain title, he could not rescind, but must instead bring a claim for damages in deceit. The true extent of this supposed rule is critically considered in Chapter 20.

Bona fide purchase in equity

21.61 In sharp contrast with the common law, equity has always had a different starting point. The general rule is that the bona fide purchaser for value of a legal title acquires it free from all equitable interests in the property, notwithstanding that they bound the predecessor in title. Equity declines to intervene in such a case on the footing that there are no grounds on which the conscience of the purchaser is affected,[94] and the defence can therefore be lost if the transaction by which value was received is rescinded *ab initio*.[95] Like the common law courts, courts of equity also emphasized the practical considerations behind such an outcome. It was said to further the interest in protecting possession.[96] However, with the whittling away of the requirement that the bona fide purchaser must be in possession before the plea is available,[97] the principle is today best regarded as supporting the interest in the certainty of legal titles.[98]

21.62 The general protection given to the bona fide purchaser of a legal title extends to claims to recover that title upon equitable rescission. The subsequent bona fide purchaser takes free of such claims. He gains an indefeasible title.[99]

(2) Protection of purchaser of legal title

21.63 The remote recipient who obtains legal title in assets transferred under a voidable transaction acquires an indefeasible title if he acquires it bona fide for value and without notice. His ownership is immune to proprietary claims by the original transferor whether founded upon rescission at law[100] or in equity.[101] A remote recipient who obtains legal title via one who is a bona fide purchaser for value should also obtain an indefeasible title, for in that

---

[93] See Chap 14, paras [14.34]–[14.35].
[94] *Pilcher v Rawlins* (1872) LR 7 Ch App 259, 266. See also *Jerrard v Saunders* (1794) 2 Ves Jun 454, 457; 30 ER 721, 723; *AG v Wilkins* (1853) 17 Beav 285, 292; 51 ER 1043, 1046; *Colyer v Finch* (1856) 5 HLC 905, 920; 10 ER 1159, 1165; D O'Sullivan, 'The Rule in *Phillips v Phillips*' (2002) 118 LQR 296.
[95] *Independent Trustee Services Ltd v GP Noble Trustees Ltd* [2013] Ch 91 (CA) [56]–[57], [96], [113].
[96] *Bassett v Nosworthy* (1673) Rep Temp Finch 102, 104, 104; 23 ER 55, 56; DEC Yale, 'Lord Nottingham's Chancery Cases vol 1' (1961) 78 Selden Society 1, 161, 164.
[97] Possession by the purchaser was formerly an essential component of the plea, but it was later held that buying from one in possession was sufficient: *Strode v Blackburne* (1789) 3 Ves 222, 30 ER 979; 1 Ves Jun Supp 366, 34 ER 829; *Wallwyn v Lee* (1803) 9 Ves Jun 24, 32–33; 32 ER 509, 512; *Ogilvie v Jeaffreson* (1860) 2 Giff 353, 379; 66 ER 147, 158; *Pilcher v Rawlins* (1872) LR 7 Ch App 259, 266, 270–71.
[98] The availability of the defence to one who has purchased from a bona fide purchaser has been justified on the basis that it protects the integrity of the first purchaser's legal title: *Independent Trustee Services Ltd v GP Noble Trustees* [2013] Ch 91 (CA) 125.
[99] *Hawes v Wyatt* (1790) 2 Cox 263, 265; 30 ER 122, 123 (rev'd on other grounds (1790) 3 Bro CC 156, 29 ER 463); *Daly v Sydney Stock Exchange* (1985) 160 CLR 371, 388; *Twinsectra Limited v Yardley* [1999] Lloyd's Rep Bank 438 (CA) 461–62.
[100] *White v Garden* (1851) 10 CB 919, 926–28; 138 ER 364, 367–68; note 88 above.
[101] *Hawes v Wyatt* (1790) 2 Cox 263, 265; 30 ER 122, 123; *Daly v Sydney Stock Exchange* (1985) 160 CLR 371, 388; *Twinsectra Limited v Yardley* [1999] Lloyd's Rep Bank 438 (CA) 461–62.

case the claim infecting the title will have been extinguished before the asset reaches his hands.[102]

(3) Protection of purchaser of equitable title

Rescission at common law

Where a legal title is transferred under a transaction voidable at common law, and the original transferee disposes of an equitable interest in the asset to a bona fide purchaser for value, the cases have not considered whether the third party takes an indefeasible interest or not. The answer is not straightforward. Probably the purchaser should be protected, though he would not have been before the Judicature reforms. **21.64**

Before the Judicature reforms the defrauded transferor could regain legal title by electing to disaffirm, and the equitable interest of the remote recipient would not have been protected. That is, a court of Chancery would not have prevented the defrauded party from exercising his right to obtain legal title by disaffirming the contract, or from thereafter recapturing the property, or bringing an action at law, founded upon that title. Legal title could be regained free from an equitable interest asserted by an innocent third party purchaser. **21.65**

That result follows from the limited nature of the protection afforded the bona fide purchaser in a court of Chancery. When successfully made out, a plea of bona fide purchase was a defence that neutralized the other party's claim to equitable relief and left the parties to their rights at common law. It involved no adjudication that the bona fide purchaser obtained a better title, and gave him no equity to relief. The rule was not one of title, but of inaction.[103] For this reason, a plea of bona fide purchase could in principle give a third party purchaser no equity to restrain the exercise of a common law right to rescind, or legal rights founded upon it. **21.66**

There are, however, good reasons for thinking that the position should be different today. If the claim to rescind was equitable rather than legal the remote recipient's equitable title would be protected.[104] But that the claim to rescind is said to arise at law rather than in equity seems an inadequate reason for reversing the outcome, and preferring the title of the original transferor to that of the innocent third party. If the claim to rescind arises at common law, the remote recipient asserting an equitable interest should be protected. The innocent party ought to be allowed to regain legal title in the relevant asset, but burdened by the remote recipient's equitable interest in it.[105] **21.67**

---

[102] If there is an analogy with the law of trusts, an exception should exist where the original transferee under the voidable disposition acquires the asset back after it has passed through the hands of an earlier bona fide purchaser for value. It remains to be seen whether this analogy will be applied.

[103] *Wallwyn v Lee* (1803) 9 Ves Jun 24, 33–34; 32 ER 509, 512–13 (Lord Eldon LC); *Pilcher v Rawlins* (1872) LR 7 Ch App 259, 269; J Pomeroy, *Pomeroy's Equity Jurisprudence and Equitable Remedies* (2nd edn, 1919) vol 2, §§ 735, 739, 743; D O'Sullivan, 'The Rule in *Phillips v Phillips*' (2002) 118 LQR 296.

[104] *Phillips v Phillips* (1861) 4 De GF & J 208, 218–19; 45 ER 1164.

[105] See also Chap 20.

468   V. THIRD PARTIES

Rescission in equity

21.68 The general rule is that the plea of bona fide purchase is only available in favour of one who acquires the legal title.[106] It is unavailable to an innocent purchaser who acquires a purely equitable interest in property. Such a purchaser typically takes subject to all prior equitable interests even though he may have been ignorant of them. That is because the precedence between adverse equitable interests is determined by the equitable priority rules, and the general rule is where the equities are otherwise equal priority in time gives the better equity.[107] The bona fide purchaser of an equitable interest therefore generally takes subject to prior equitable interests.

21.69 But these rules do not apply when the earlier claim is an equitable claim to recover property on rescission. That is an exception to the general principle just noted. A claim to recover property on rescission, along with certain other so-called 'mere equities', such as the equity to rectify an instrument, are said to be defeated by the subsequent bona fide purchase of an equitable interest in the relevant property. This exception is based on statements made *obiter* by Lord Westbury in *Phillips v Phillips*.[108]

21.70 There are two different explanations for the immunity from mere equities that is obtained by the bona fide purchaser of an equitable interest. One group of cases sees this as a principle of equitable priority, and the innocent purchaser as obtaining a superior equity.[109] Another regards the innocent purchaser as obtaining a defence of bona fide purchase.[110] There are technical and practical differences between these two explanations, and the authorities have so far not decided between them.[111]

(4) Onus of proof

21.71 In cases involving the rescission of sales of goods for fraud at common law, the rescinding party has the onus of proving that the remote recipient took with notice or otherwise not in good faith, or that he gave no value, such that his title is vulnerable to rescission.[112] That is also the rule for rescission in equity.[113] A similar rule is applied in Australia when a third

---

[106] *Macmillan Inc v Bishopgate Investment Trust (No 3)* [1995] 1 WLR 978, 999–1000, 1013, 1016 (Millett J). Cf A Reilly, 'Does "equity's darling" need a legal title? Reassessing *Pilcher v Rawlins*' (2016) 10 Journal of Equity 89.

[107] *Rice v Rice* (1853) 2 Drew 73, 78; 61 ER 646; *Macmillan Inc v Bishopgate Investment Trust (No 3)* [1995] 1 WLR 978, 999–1000 (Millett J). Also, an equitable conveyance passes only what the grantor is justly entitled to, and no more: *Phillips v Phillips* (1861) 4 De GF & J 208, 218–19; 45 ER 1164.

[108] (1861) 4 De GF & J 208, 45 ER 1164. Whilst it has been argued that it is doubtful that later cases correctly understood Lord Westbury's true opinion on this point (D O'Sullivan, 'The Rule in *Phillips v Phillips*' (2002) 118 LQR 296), that view is challenged in A Reilly, 'What were Lord Westbury's intentions in *Phillips v Phillips*? Bona fide Purchase of an Equitable Interest' (2021) 80 CLJ 156. For application of the principle in the case of shares, *Crown Master International Trading Co Ltd v China Solar Energy Holdings Ltd* [2015] 4 HKC 505 [60]–[74].

[109] *Tottenham v Green* (1863) 32 LJ Ch (NS) 201, 205; *Re Ffrench's Estate* (1887) 21 IR 283, 312–13; *Scott v Scott* [1924] 1 IR 141, 150–51; A Everton, '"Equitable Interests" and "Equities"—In Search of a Pattern' [1976] Conv 209, 218.

[110] *Ernest v Vivian* (1864) 33 LJ Ch (NS) 513, 519; *Cave v Cave* (1880) 15 ChD 639, 646–47; *Westminster Bank Ltd v Lee* [1956] 1 Ch 7, 19–21; *Latec Investments Limited v Hotel Terrigal Pty Ltd* (1965) 113 CLR 265, 277–78 (Kitto J).

[111] D O'Sullivan, 'The Rule in *Phillips v Phillips*' (2002) 118 LQR 296.

[112] *Whitehorn Bros v Davison* [1911] 1 KB 463 (CA); app'd *Barclays Bank plc v Boulter* [1999] 1 WLR 1919 (HL) 1925.

[113] *Bainbrigge v Browne* (1881) 18 ChD 188, 197 as interpreted *Barclays Bank plc v Boulter* [1999] 1 WLR 1919 (HL) 1925. In *Barclays Bank v Boulter* the statement that the onus rested on the party seeking to rescind appears to have been made in relation to both (i) claims to rescind founded on the vitiating conduct of a third party, of which

party is alleged to have acquired property that is the subject of a constructive as opposed to an express trust.[114]

In contrast, when bona fide purchase is relied on as a defence to a claim for the knowing receipt of trust property,[115] and in the conveyancing context,[116] or to otherwise defeat an existing equitable interest,[117] the rule is different. There the purchaser has the onus of proving that he purchased in good faith and without notice.[118] **21.72**

In *Barclays Bank plc v Boulter*[119] Lord Hoffmann said that this difference turns on whether the plea of bona fide purchase is being used to defeat a vested equitable interest. His Lordship said that in the case of rescission, the claimant retains no proprietary interest in the relevant asset, so that when rescission is asserted against a remote recipient, the plea of bona fide purchase does not operate as a defence. In contrast, it necessarily does operate as a defence when pleaded in order to defeat an existing equitable interest. For this reason, the onus lies with the claimant in a case of rescission, but with the purchaser when the claimant asserts an existing equitable interest.[120] **21.73**

Similar reasoning has been deployed to explain why the onus rule for rescission does not apply when a purchaser relies on the statutory exception to the *nemo dat* rule after having bought bona fide without notice from a mercantile agent who has no title.[121] Lush J explained that the onus is on the purchaser because, but for the statutory title conferred by the legislation, the purchaser has no title at all, whereas the purchaser of a title voidable on rescission obtains a good title save insofar as the injured party can impeach it.[122] **21.74**

---

the other contracting party had notice, and (ii) claims to rescind against a remote recipient of property previously transferred under a voidable transaction. See also D O'Sullivan, 'Developing *O'Brien*' (2002) 118 LQR 337, 342–43.

[114] *United States Surgical Corp v Hospital Products International Pty Ltd* [1983] 2 NSWLR 157 (CA) 258; *Maronis Holdings Ltd v Nippon Credit Australia Pty Ltd* (2001) 38 ACSR 404 (NSWSC) 526; *Southern Cross Mine Management Pty Ltd v Ensham Resources Pty Ltd* [2005] QSC 233 [8].

[115] *GL Baker Ltd v Medway Building and Supplies* [1958] 1 WLR 1216 (CA) 1220–21, 1230, 1237, 1239, 1241–42 (where the Court of Appeal implicitly approved the reasoning of Danckwerts J at first instance on this point). Petition to appeal to the HL dismissed: [1959] 1 WLR 492.

[116] *AG v Biphosphated Guano Co* (1878) 11 ChD 327, 337 (specifically enforceable agreement for a right of way); *Re Nisbet and Potts' Contract* [1905] 1 Ch 391, 402; [1906] 1 Ch 386 (CA) 404, 409, 410 (equitable restrictive covenant); *Wentworth v Rogers* [2004] NSWCA 430 [68].

[117] *Barclays Bank plc v Boulter* [1999] 1 WLR 1919 (HL) 1924; *Royal Bank of Scotland plc v Etridge (No 2)* [2002] 2 AC 773, 838; *Independent Trustee Services Ltd v GP Noble Trustees Ltd* [2013] Ch 91 (CA) [86]; *Roadchef (Employee Benefits Trustees) Limited v Hill* [2014] EWHC 109 (Ch) [137]; *Credit Agricole Corporation and Investment Bank v Papadimitriou* [2015] 1 WLR 4265 (PC—Gibraltar) [21] (proceeds of misappropriated chattels).

[118] Also, J McGhee and S Elliott (eds), *Snell's Equity* (34th edn, 2020) [4-018] (onus of proof on purchaser to prove bona fide purchase and lack of notice). Cf the more complex position in the United States described in JN Pomeroy, *A Treatise on Equity Jurisprudence* (5th edn, 1941) vol 3, § 785.

[119] [1999] 1 WLR 1919 (HL).

[120] *Barclays Bank plc v Boulter* [1999] 1 WLR 1919 (HL) 1924–25.

[121] Factors Act 1889, s 2.

[122] *Heap v Motorists' Advisory Agency Ltd* [1923] 1 KB 577, 590, where Lush J distinguished *Whitehorn Bros v Davison* [1911] 1 KB 463 (CA) and held that the onus of proving bona fide purchase for the purposes of the Factors Act 1889, s 2 was on the purchaser. That conclusion was approved in *Stadium Finance Ltd v Robbins* [1962] 2 QB 664 (CA). The onus is likewise on the third party purchaser who asserts a statutory title after buying from a seller or buyer in possession but without title: *Feuer Leather Corp v Frank Johnstone & Sons* [1981] Com LR 251, 253, app'd *Forsythe International (UK) Ltd v Silver Shipping Co Ltd (The Saetta)* [1994] 1 WLR 1334, 1350 (Sale of Goods Act 1979, ss 24, 25), followed *International Alpaca Management Pty Ltd v Ensor* (1995) 133 ALR 561 (Full FCA) 592–93 (Sale of Goods Act 1923 (NSW), s 28(1)).

21.75 Lord Hoffmann's reasoning is not without difficulty. That the rescinding claimant retains no proprietary interest in the relevant asset does not itself easily explain why the plea of bona fide purchase does not operate as a defence in cases of rescission, but does when the claimant asserts a proprietary interest.[123] The preferable analysis (and which may be implicit in Lord Hoffmann's reasoning), is that the rescinding party has a cause of action against the remote recipient, and notice, or absence of bona fides or value, are elements of that cause of action. It is because of this, and not because the claim is to be characterized as purely personal, that the rescinding party bears the onus of proof.

21.76 But whether or not the reasoning adopted by Lord Hoffmann and Lush J is thought to be persuasive, the onus rules themselves are now well established.

---

[123] Also, an unexercised claim to recover property upon rescission has so many proprietary indicia that the line between it and an equitable interest in property is a fine one: Chap 16, para [16.42].

22

Succeeding to Rights to Rescind

A. Introduction	22.01	C. Settlements	22.08
B. Devolution on Death	22.05	D. Assignment and Conveyance	22.09
(1) Heirs at law	22.05	(1) Assignment	22.09
(2) Beneficiary under a will	22.06	(2) Second conveyance of same	
(3) Executors	22.07	property	22.11

A. Introduction

An unexercised right to recover property on rescission is said to be a personal right in the nature of an equity or mere equity. It only becomes a vested estate or interest in the relevant property when the right to rescind is exercised, either by electing to disaffirm, or by obtaining a court order for rescission.[1] This taxonomy is, however, of relatively recent origin, and it has been long established that an unexercised claim to recover property upon rescission has proprietary features that allow it to persist in favour of a range of third parties.[2] These third parties are entitled to exercise the right to recover the relevant property by rescinding. They effectively succeed to the right to rescind.

22.01

The general principle is that the right to recover property upon rescission passes to a successor of the injured transferor when by his act or by operation of law there is a subsequent assignment, conveyance, devise, or other transfer of the subject matter of the voidable transaction. The right to recover property upon rescission is an inchoate proprietary interest in the hands of the injured party that passes to the successor by force of the second transfer.[3]

22.02

So, for example, if B obtains a conveyance of Blackacre from A by undue influence, C will succeed to the right to regain title to Blackacre by rescission upon perfection of A's later conveyance, devise, or other purported transfer of Blackacre to C. Similarly, C will succeed to a right to rescind a voidable mortgage of Blackacre that A had granted to B, if and when A transfers title to Blackacre to C. Conversely, C may only succeed to the right to rescind by a transfer of A's interest in Blackacre; there is no logical room for a split in A's proprietary interest in Blackacre and the right to rescind a disposition of an interest in it.[4]

22.03

This chapter considers the classes of persons entitled to succeed to a right to recover property upon rescission in this way. Reference is also made to the possibility of assigning rights to rescind that confer purely personal claims.

22.04

---

[1] See Chap 16.
[2] See Chap 3, para [3.42]. For development of the modern taxonomy, see Chap 3, paras [3.43]–[3.51].
[3] *Blacklocks v JB Developments (Godalming) Ltd* [1982] 1 Ch 183, 195–96 and cases there cited.
[4] *Investors Compensation Scheme Ltd v West Bromwich Building Society* [1998] 1 WLR 896 (HL) 916.

B. Devolution on Death

(1) Heirs at law

22.05 There are many old cases in which property was transferred under a tainted conveyance, and following his death the vendor's heir at law rescinded to recover title, though subject always to his predecessor's obligation to make counter-restitution. The heir would succeed to the right to rescind upon devolution of the estate to him. Bills of this kind were familiar in the seventeenth and eighteenth centuries,[5] and there are also reported instances in the nineteenth century.[6] There are, however, no modern examples. The disappearance of succession to estates by rules of primogeniture means that the principle is today largely of historical interest.[7] It remains relevant, however, in indicating that the injured party need not intend to transfer the right to rescind; succession may occur purely by operation of law. The modern analogy is succession under the rules of intestacy.

(2) Beneficiary under a will

22.06 A similar principle is applied in favour of beneficiaries of a deceased estate who take under a will. If after disposing of property under a voidable transaction the testator makes a will devising the whole of his estate to a particular beneficiary, upon the testator's death and administration of the estate,[8] the beneficiary is entitled to rescind and recover the property transferred.[9] The right to sue has a sufficiently proprietary character that it is devised or bequeathed by testamentary language that refers to the property transferred away.[10] The

---

[5] *Lyde or Joyner v Lyde or Joyner* (1616–1617); *Joy v Bannister (No 1)* (1617) in Ritchie, Reports of Cases Decided by Francis Bacon in the High Court of Chancery (1617–1621) (1932) 33; *Long v Long* (1620) in J Ritchie, *Reports of Cases Decided by Francis Bacon in the High Court of Chancery (1617–1621)* (1932) 6, 33, 621; *White v Small* (1682) 2 Cha Ca 103, 22 ER 867; *Coleby v Smith* (1683) 1 Vern 205, 23 ER 416; *Clark v Ward* (1700) Prec Cha 150, 24 ER 72, aff'd 4 Bro PC 70, 2 ER 48; *Clarkson v Hanway* (1723) 2 P Wms 203, 24 ER 700; *Hick v Mors* (1754) Amb 215, 27 ER 143; 3 Keny 117, 96 ER 1329; *Bates v Graves* (1793) 2 Ves Jun 288, 30 ER 637, 1 Ves Jun Supp 264, 34 ER 781.

[6] *Wood v Abrey* (1818) 3 Madd 417, 424; 56 ER 558, 561; *Charter v Trevelyan* (1844) 11 Cl & Fin 714, 8 ER 1273; *Clark v Malpas* (1862) 31 Beav 80, 54 ER 1067, aff'd 4 De GF & J 401, 45 ER 1238.

[7] Administration of Estates Act 1925, s 45.

[8] If the estate is not administered, the beneficiary may still be able to sue if the executor has refused or is unable to join in the action, and is joined as a defendant: A Learmoth, C Ford, J Clark, and J Martyn (eds), *Williams, Mortimer & Sunnucks Executors, Administrators and Probate* (21st edn, 2018) [59-35]; in Australia, *Bridgewater v Leahy* (Qld CA, 14 March 1997) (Fitzgerald P).

[9] *Wilkinson v Brayfield* (1693) 2 Vern 307, 23 ER 799; 1 Eq Ca Abr 258, 21 ER 1031; *Blake v Johnson* (1700) Pre Cha 142, 24 ER 69; *Drew v Merry* (1701) 1 Eq Ca Abr 176, 21 ER 969; C Viner, *A General Abridgment of Law and Equity* (2nd edn, 1793) vol 8, 63 [42]; *Hawes v Wyatt* (1790) 2 Cox 263, 265–67; 30 ER 122, 123–24; *Stump v Gaby* (1852) 2 De M & G 623, 42 ER 1015; *Gresley v Mousley* (1859) 4 De G & J 78, 45 ER 31; *Allcard v Skinner* (1887) LR 36 ChD 145 (CA) 187; see also *Re Sherman dec'd* [1954] 1 ChD 653 (devise of purchaser's entitlements where contract voidable by vendor or representative). Where a will was executed, and the testator subsequently conveyed away estates devised by that will, it was initially thought that the devisee could still sue to rescind the conveyance (*Hawes v Wyatt* (1790) 2 Cox 263, 265; 30 ER 122, 123; (1790) 3 Bro CC 156, 29 ER 463). But it was later held that even a fraudulent conveyance would revoke the earlier will: *Cave v Holford* (1798) 3 Ves 650, 664; 30 ER 1203, 1210; *Harmood v Oglander* (1801) 6 Ves Jun 199, 215; 31 ER 1010, 1018; *Ex p Earl of Illchester* (1803) 7 Ves Jun 348, 373; 32 ER 142, 151; *Simpson v Walker* (1831) 5 Sim 1, 58 ER 238; *Gresley v Mousley* (1859) 4 De G & J 78, 94; 45 ER 31, 37.

[10] See n 9, esp *Blake v Johnson* (1700) Pre Cha 142, 24 ER 69; *Stump v Gaby* (1852) 2 De M & G 623, 42 ER 1015, the reasoning in which is to be read in the light of *Phillips v Phillips* (1861) 4 De G F & J 208, 45 ER 1164.

principle is subject to statutory rules restricting the beneficiaries' right to enforce claims vested in the deceased.[11]

(3) Executors

The executor or personal representative of a deceased estate obtains a right to recover back property that the testator had transferred under a contract voidable by him, as well as the right to set aside purely executory contracts.[12] **22.07**

C. Settlements

There is old authority that a party entitled to succeed to an estate under the terms of a prior settlement may, like an heir at law or beneficiary under a will, rescind a transfer of property made by their predecessor in title to the same extent that the predecessor could have. The cases include instances where the settlement was made by the defrauded party himself,[13] and by one of his predecessors in title.[14] These authorities appear to remain applicable where the settlement provides for the intended beneficiary to succeed to title to the estate in his own name. Where title to the estate was always to remain vested in identified trustees, the beneficiaries' right would seem to be restricted to compelling the trustees to sue to recover it in their name.[15] **22.08**

D. Assignment and Conveyance

(1) Assignment

The right to obtain a proprietary interest in assets upon rescission may be validly assigned. A creditor entitled to rescind and assert an equitable interest in the proceeds of a loan may therefore assign the benefit of the loan to a third party, and thereby confer on that party a **22.09**

---

[11] For example, Succession Act 1981 (Qld), ss 49(1), 66, considered *Bridgewater v Leahy* (Qld CA, 14 March 1997); (1998) 194 CLR 457, 467–68.

[12] *Matthew v Hanbury* (1690) 2 Vern 188, 23 ER 723 (executor rescinded bonds to testator's mistress for undue influence); *Chesterfield v Janssen* (1750) 1 Atk 301, 26 ER 191 (executors rescinded loan as catching bargain); *Nottidge v Prince* (1860) 2 Giff 246, 66 ER 103 (administrator rescinded gifts for undue influence); *Plowright v Lambert* (1885) 52 LT 646 (executor rescinding testator's sale of property for breach of fiduciary duty); see also *Twycross v Grant* (1878) 4 CPD 40 (right to recover price of shares bought on company's fraudulent suppression of facts was transmitted to executor in circumstances where suppression was breach of statute and characterized as a tort). The maxim *actio personalis moritur cum persona* was apparently never thought to restrict the executor's right of suit.

[13] *Earl of Ardglasse v Muschamp* (1684) 1 Vern 237, 23 ER 43 (claimant under settlement made by previous Earl living 'in riot and debauchery in London' rescinded rent-charge of estates procured by fraud); *Hawes v Wyatt* (1790) 2 Cox 263, 266; 30 ER 122, 124; *Dickinson v Burrell* (1866) 1 Eq Cas 337, 342–43.

[14] *Englefeild v Englefeild* (1686–1687) 1 Vern 444, 23 ER 575 (son suing as remainder-man rescinded dispositions of estate by defrauded father); *Browne v Mitton* (1714) 4 Bro CC 167, 2 ER 114 (claimants under a marriage settlement sued to rescind a conveyance by their predecessor in title); *Addis v Campbell* (1841) 4 Beav 401, 49 ER 394 (claimant entitled to estate under an earlier settlement rescinded his predecessor's sale of it).

[15] Cf *Dickinson v Burrell* (1866) 1 Eq Cas 337, 342–43 (beneficiaries of trust declared by vendor in respect of property sold by voidable transfer), discussed D Fox, *Property Rights in Money* (2008) [6.21].

474 V. THIRD PARTIES

right to rescind and assert the proprietary interest himself.[16] A right to rescind may only be assigned if the assignment is made together with the subject matter of the right.[17]

22.10 A right to rescind that confers no proprietary right in the rescinding party, as in the case of an executory contract, is a bare right to sue, and may be assigned only if the assignee can show that the right to rescind is somehow incidental to other property transferred, or that he has a genuine commercial interest in the enforcement of the claim.[18] In principle there ought to be an exception where rescission has occurred at common law, and the only unsatisfied obligation is to repay sums received. That is an obligation enforceable as money had and received. The party entitled to payment should, therefore, be entitled to assign the right as a debt pursuant to section 136 of the Law of Property Act 1925, and notwithstanding that litigation may be necessary to recover the sums due.[19]

(2) Second conveyance of same property

22.11 The principle discussed earlier[20] also finds expression when a party entitled to rescind the transfer of his property later purports to convey the same property to a third party. That third party will become entitled to rescind the first sale and to recover the property transferred by suit brought in his name alone.[21]

22.12 But the position is different if the injured party buys rather than sells under the voidable transaction, and then transfers the property so purchased on to a third party. In that case the third party cannot rescind. He has no right to return to the original vendor the property purchased and recover the price his predecessor paid.[22]

22.13 The reason for this difference lies in the nature of the right held by the party entitled to rescind. In the case of a voidable sale the injured transferor obtains an inchoate proprietary interest in the asset, and a later conveyance of the same asset will pass that interest to the second transferee. The conveyance passes what the vendor has though it may be less than what he says he has.[23] In contrast, the purchaser of property who has a right to rescind obtains what, in his hands, is a complete title, and a conveyance of that property will likewise pass a complete title. The injured purchaser's right to rescind is a wholly personal claim that does not run with the property.[24] He is, accordingly, entitled to rescind even after the

---

[16] *Daly v Sydney Stock Exchange* (1985) 160 CLR 371.
[17] *Investors Compensation Scheme Ltd v West Bromwich Building Society* [1998] 1 WLR 896 (HL) 916, discussed D Fox, *Property Rights in Money* (2008) [6.23].
[18] *Trendtex Trading Corp v Credit Suisse* [1982] 1 AC 679, 702–04.
[19] *Camdex International v Bank of Zambia* [1998] 1 QB 22 (CA) 39 (debt by deposit with bank); D Fox, *Property Rights in Money* (2008) [6.26].
[20] See para [22.09].
[21] *Melbourne Banking Corporation Ltd v Brougham* (1882) 8 App Cas 307, 311; *Fitzroy v Cave* [1905] 2 KB 364 (CA) 371; *Investors Compensation Scheme Ltd v West Bromwich Building Society* [1998] 1 WLR 896 (HL) 916; but cf *Prosser v Edmonds* (1835) 1 Y & C Ex 481, 160 ER 196.
[22] *Re Bank of Hindustan* (1873) LR 16 Eq 417, 431 (shares); *Gross v Lewis Hillman* [1970] 1 Ch 445 (CA) 460–61 (real property); cf *Re Cambrian Mining Co* (1882) 48 LT 114.
[23] Contrast D Fox, *Property Rights in Money* (2008), who argues that the fact pattern must be analysed as one where the assignor alienated his beneficial interest in the real estate to the plaintiffs who were then required to sue the defendants to confirm that it was not in fact subject to the defendants' adverse claim: at [6.25].
[24] *Gross v Lewis Hillman* [1970] 1 Ch 445 (CA) 460 'the right to rescind for misrepresentation does not run with the land in that way'.

conveyance to the third party, if he is able to make counter-restitution by returning a substitute asset.[25] For these reasons a subsequent conveyance of property acquired under a voidable purchase does not ordinarily include the right to rescind that purchase.[26]

This outcome is largely a consequence of the construction of the subsequent conveyance of the property acquired. The third party obtains no right to rescind because, properly construed, the sale to him did not pass his vendor's right to rescind. The position is, therefore, probably different if there is an express attempt to assign the right to rescind a purchase, together with the property itself. In a case of this kind, is the right to rescind to be regarded as a bare right to sue and so assignable only if the assignee can show a genuine commercial interest in enforcing the right, or as a right incidental to the property sold, and therefore freely assignable with it?[27] It is suggested that the latter view is to be preferred.

22.14

---

[25] As to that possibility, see Chap 18, paras [18.52]–[18.62].
[26] The authors are indebted to John McGhee QC for this analysis.
[27] *Trendtex Trading Corp v Credit Suisse* [1982] 1 AC 679, 702–704.

Part VI

OTHER BARS

23

Affirmation

A. Introduction	23.01	(7) Proving knowledge of rights	23.55
B. Nature and Justification	23.04	E. Communication	23.57
(1) Juristic nature	23.04	F. Unequivocal Words or Conduct	23.61
(2) Justification	23.10	(1) General principle	23.61
C. Affirming Party must be Free from the Vitiating Factor	23.14	(2) Application of the general principle	23.64
		(3) Effect of reservation of rights	23.91
(1) Pressure and exploitation	23.14	(4) Possibility of affirming after an election to rescind	23.97
(2) Misrepresentation, mistake, and non-disclosure	23.18	G. Intention to Affirm is not Required	23.98
D. Need for Awareness of Right to Rescind	23.35	(1) General rule	23.98
		(2) Where affirming conduct is not known to other party	23.101
(1) Uncertainty as to whether electing party must know rights	23.35	(3) Relation to awareness of rights	23.102
(2) Awareness of rights required in England	23.40	H. Affirmation is Generally Irrevocable	23.103
		(1) General rule	23.103
(3) Awareness of rights not required in other parts of the Commonwealth	23.42	(2) Exception where subsequent discovery of new ground for rescission	23.104
(4) Whether knowledge of right to rescind should be required	23.51	I. Onus of Proof and Pleading	23.110
(5) What must be known	23.53	(1) Onus of proof	23.110
(6) Deliberately failing to inquire into rights	23.54	(2) Pleading	23.111

A. Introduction

A voidable contract or gift is binding until it is rescinded. The party entitled to rescind is not obliged to do so; he has a choice to either leave the transaction on foot, or to seek to set it aside. In certain circumstances the law regards the making of a choice to leave the transaction on foot, or conduct that has that appearance, as irrevocable, and as causing the right to rescind to be lost. The conduct that leads to loss of the right in these circumstances conveys both the negative choice not to rescind, and also the positive choice to affirm the transaction, and is compendiously described as 'affirmation'.[1] **23.01**

The right to rescind is lost by affirmation when the party entitled to rescind unequivocally manifests an intention to affirm once free from the effects of the vitiating factor. If the transaction is voidable for duress or a similar impairment, the conduct must therefore occur after the impairment has come to an end; and if the transaction is vitiated by misrepresentation, non-disclosure, or mistake, there must be a sufficient awareness of the true facts. Whether the affirming conduct needs to be conveyed to the other party is somewhat unclear, but it probably must be save in exceptional cases. There is also some doubt as to whether the party **23.02**

---

[1] This chapter approved A Burrows, *A Restatement of the English Law of Contract* (2nd edn, 2020) § 34(5)(a).

said to have affirmed must have been aware of his right to rescind. In England he probably does, but not in Australia, New Zealand, or Singapore.

23.03 This chapter outlines the circumstances in which the right to rescind is lost by affirmation. It begins with a discussion of the nature and justification of the principle, then discusses its constituent elements, and concludes by considering certain procedural issues.

B. Nature and Justification

(1) Juristic nature

An election between rights

23.04 The choice to either rescind or affirm a voidable contract is usually described as involving a right of election.[2] It has been emphasized that this involves an application of the doctrine of election,[3] and of the common law rather than the specialized equitable doctrine,[4] and that the election is between rights not remedies.[5]

23.05 The effect of making the choice not to rescind is waiver by election.[6] Although it has been said that the right to rescind is extinguished by the making of the election,[7] this can mislead. The right is waived not extinguished,[8] and may be revived if a fresh ground for rescission is subsequently discovered.[9]

Election and equitable rights to rescind

23.06 Outside the law of rescission, practically all of the instances in which the doctrine of election is said to operate involve alternate and inconsistent rights conferred by the common

---

[2] *Clough v London and North Western Railway Co* (1871) LR 7 Ex 26, 34–35; *Bristol and West Building Society v Mothew* [1998] Ch 1 (CA) 22–23 ('right to elect whether to rescind or affirm'); *Potter v Dyer* [2011] EWCA Civ 1417 [56] ('entitled ... to elect either to affirm or to rescind'). In Australia, *Coastal Estates Pty Ltd v Melevende* [1965] VR 433 (Full Ct) 451 ('affirmation is the determination of an election'); but cf *Hawker Pacific Pty Ltd v Helicopter Charter Pty Ltd* (1991) 22 NSWLR 298 (CA) 304 (rubric of 'affirmation' covers both election and estoppel). As to election generally, KR Handley, *Estoppel by Conduct and Election* (2nd edn, 2016) chap 14.

[3] *Motor Oil Hellas (Corinth) Refineries SA v Shipping Corp of India (The Kanchenjunga)* [1990] 1 Lloyd's Rep 391 (HL) 398.

[4] *Lissenden v CAV Bosch Limited* [1940] AC 412, 418. For the equitable doctrine, J McGhee (ed), *Snell's Equity* (32nd edn, 2010) [6-012]. For discussion of the common law and equitable doctrines of election, see also *Agricultural and Rural Finance Pty Ltd v Gardiner* (2008) 238 CLR 570 [57]–[58].

[5] *Oliver Ashworth (Holdings) Ltd v Ballard (Kent) Ltd* [2000] Ch 12 (CA) 28.

[6] *Johnson v Agnew* [1980] AC 367, 399 (Lord Wilberforce); *Telfair Shipping Corporation v Athos Shipping Co SA (The Athos)* [1981] 2 Lloyd's Rep 74, 87–88; aff'd [1983] 1 Lloyd's Rep 127 (CA); *Motor Oil Hellas (Corinth) Refineries SA v Shipping Corp of India (The Kanchenjunga)* [1990] 1 Lloyd's Rep 391 (HL) 398 'waiver in the sense of abandonment of a right which arises by virtue of a party making an election'; *Bolton Metropolitan BC v Municipal Mutual Insurance Ltd* [2006] 1 WLR 1492 (CA) 1506 'waiver by election'; *SK Shipping Europe plc v Capital VLCC 3 Corp* [2021] 2 Lloyd's Rep 109 'a species of waiver by election'; *SK Shipping Europe plc v Capital VLCC 3 Corp ("Challenger C")* [2022] EWCA Civ 231 [73] 'a form of waiver by election'; cf *Kammins Ballrooms Co Ltd v Zenith Investments (Torquay) Ltd* [1971] AC 850, 883 'this is better categorised as "election" rather than a "waiver"'; *Oliver Ashworth (Holdings) Ltd v Ballard (Kent) Ltd* [2000] Ch 12 (CA) 28, CA 'waiver ... can be used to describe the effect of an election'. Also, KR Handley, *Estoppel by Conduct and Election* (2nd edn, 2016) [14-006].

[7] *Sargent v ASL Developments Ltd* (1974) 131 CLR 634, 640–41 'extinction [of one] confers upon the elector the benefit of enjoying the other [right]'.

[8] As to the effects of waiver, *Banning v Wright* [1972] 1 WLR 972 (HL) 978–79; discussed *Commonwealth of Australia v Verwayen* (1980) 170 CLR 394, 423.

[9] See para [23.104].

law or by statute. But it is well established that a contract voidable for undue influence or other cause recognized only in equity can be irrevocably affirmed,[10] and there is no discernible difference between the rules that regulate the affirmation of transactions voidable in equity and at common law. The origin of the relevant principles is, anyway, to be found in the pronouncements of Lord Blackburn on the eve of and after the Judicature reforms.[11] In rescission, if not elsewhere, the doctrine of election applies as much to equitable claims as it does to those arising at common law.

Election and rescinding gifts

23.07 Before the doctrine of election can become engaged, the electing party must hold alternative rights inconsistent with one another.[12] This is because:

> ... it is this concurrent existence of inconsistent sets of rights which explains the doctrine; because they are inconsistent neither one may be enjoyed without the extinction of the other and that extinction confers upon the elector the benefit of enjoying the other, a benefit denied him so long as both remained in existence.[13]

23.08 But the donor of a voidable gift does not hold alternative rights inconsistent with one another. He has only the right to rescind, and affirming confers the benefit of no other right. In contrast, by affirming a voidable contract the injured party obtains the benefit of rights given by the contract. Affirmation of a voidable gift entails only surrendering the right to rescind it.[14] Waiver is distinct from election precisely because a right may be waived although there is no alternate right inconsistent with it,[15] and the affirmation of a voidable gift involves waiver without election.

23.09 It is for this reason that merely continuing to rely upon a deed of gift will usually not entail a waiver of the right to rescind it. The donor does not thereby gain the benefit of some other legal right. Relying upon the deed will therefore not of itself, without more, import the making of an unequivocal choice to surrender the right to rescind it. This is the preferable explanation of the statement in *Rogge v Rogge*[16] that affirmation does not necessarily bar the right to rescind voluntary dispositions on the grounds established in *Pitt v Holt*.[17] The

---

[10] *Re Cape Breton Company* (1885) 29 ChD 795 (CA) 803, 811 (breach of fiduciary duty); *Goldsworthy v Brickell* [1987] AC 378 (CA) 410 (undue influence). For examples prior to the Judicature reforms, and where the court used the language of 'confirmation' rather than 'acquiescence' or 'laches', *Savery v King* (1856) 5 HLC 627, 663–64; 10 ER 1046; *Wright v Vanderplank* (1856) 8 De G M & G 133, 146–47; 44 ER 340.
[11] The foundation cases are *Clough v London and North Western Railway Co* (1871) LR 7 Ex 26, 34–35 and *Scarfe v Jardine* (1882) 7 App Cas 345, 360–61.
[12] *Kammins Ballrooms Co Ltd v Zenith Investments (Torquay) Ltd* [1971] AC 850, 883; *Bolton Metropolitan BC v Municipal Mutual Insurance Ltd* [2006] 1 WLR 1492 (CA) 1506; cf *Khoury v Government Insurance Office of (NSW)* (1984) 165 CLR 622, 633 'two truly alternative rights or sets of rights'.
[13] *Sargent v ASL Developments Ltd* (1974) 131 CLR 634, 640–41.
[14] As to the affirmation of voidable gifts, *Wright v Vanderplank* (1856) 8 De G M & G 133, 147; 44 ER 340, 345–46; *Mitchell v Homfray* (1881) 8 QBD 587, 591, 593; *Allcard v Skinner* (1887) 36 ChD 145 (CA) 175, 186, 191, 193.
[15] 'The sterilising of a right might, in some circumstances, be attributable to either a waiver or an election, but the doctrines are distinct, for a right may be waived though there is no alternative right inconsistent with it': *Commonwealth of Australia v Verwayen* (1990) 170 CLR 394, 424 (Brennan J). Also, *Agricultural and Rural Finance Pty Ltd v Gardiner* (2008) 238 CLR 570 [60].
[16] [2019] EWHC 1949 (Ch) [162], [166].
[17] [2013] 2 AC 108.

VI. OTHER BARS

equity to rescind a voidable gift is capable of being lost by affirmation if the donor's conduct entails a sufficiently clear waiver of the right.[18]

(2) Justification

23.10 What is the justification for permanently depriving a person of the right to rescind once he has expressed an intention to confirm rather than avoid the transaction?

23.11 A rule that a person irrevocably loses a right simply by intimating that he will not enforce it, or will enforce another instead, is exceptional.[19] It should apply only where required 'in order to do justice to the other party',[20] and election has been said to be based on 'considerations of common sense and equity',[21] in particular upon:

> ... the interests of certainty and because it has been thought to be fair as between the parties that the person affected is entitled to know where he stands and that the person electing should not have the opportunity of changing his election and subjecting his adversary to different obligations.[22]

23.12 But it may be doubted whether this reasoning sufficiently justifies the principles of election as they are applied to voidable contracts, and in particular whether the principles as presently formulated are indeed necessary to do justice to the other party.[23] That is in particular because the law focuses almost exclusively on the quality of the affirming party's conduct, and pays no attention to his subjective intentions or to the effects of his conduct on the other party. As explained later in this chapter, conduct unequivocally evincing an intention to confirm the transaction causes the right to rescind to be lost whether or not the other party relies on that conduct, or would suffer prejudice if the apparent intention was resiled from. The other party may not even need to know of the conduct. Nor is it necessary for any subjective choice to be made; whether or not there has been an affirmation is assessed by objective standards, and the right to rescind may be lost even contrary to the intentions of the electing party. Whether the right to rescind is lost in any given case is also unaffected by the value of the alternate rights obtained when the electing party affirms.

---

[18] See *Wright v Vanderplank* (1856) 8 De G M & G 133, 147; 44 ER 340, 345–46; *Mitchell v Homfray* (1881) 8 QBD 587, 591, 593; *Allcard v Skinner* (1887) 36 ChD 145 (CA) 175, 186, 191, 193.

[19] *O'Connor v SP Bray Limited* (1936) 36 St Rep (NSW) 249, 257 (Jordan CJ). Also, *Agricultural and Rural Finance Pty Ltd v Gardiner* (2008) 238 CLR 570 [95]–[96].

[20] *O'Connor v SP Bray Limited* (1936) 36 St Rep (NSW) 249, 257–58, 262.

[21] 'Election, though the subject of much learning and refinement, is in the end a doctrine based on simply considerations of common sense and equity': *Johnson v Agnew* [1980] AC 367, 398 (Lord Wilberforce). Cf *Craine v Colonial Mutual Fire Insurance Co Ltd* (1920) 28 CLR 305, 326 ' "Waiver" is a doctrine of some arbitrariness introduced by the law to prevent a man in certain circumstances from taking up two inconsistent positions'; *Commonwealth of Australia v Verwayen* (1990) 170 CLR 394, 449 'the somewhat arbitrary doctrine of waiver'.

[22] *Sargent v ASL Developments Ltd* (1974) 131 CLR 634, 656 per Mason J, explaining why a communicated election is irrevocable. See also at 658. Also, *Kosmar Villa Holidays plc v Trustees of Syndicate 1243* [2008] 2 All ER (Comm) 14 (CA) [38], [66], [74] (explaining that the doctrine of election typically arises 'where the parties to a contract have to know where they stand').

[23] See also FMB Reynolds, 'Election Distributed' (1970) 86 LQR 318, 323–24. For further discussion, R Bigwood, 'Fine-Tuning Affirmation of a Contract by Election' [2010] NZLR 37 and 617; Q Liu, 'Rethinking Election: A General Theory' (2013) 35 Syd LR 599.

But although their justification is open to criticism, the rules regarding the affirmation of voidable contracts and gifts are firmly established and regularly applied.[24] The potential for injustice in individual cases tends to be ameliorated by employing flexible notions of what constitutes sufficiently unequivocal conduct,[25] and in England by a rule that the electing party must know of his right to rescind before a binding election can be made.[26]

23.13

C. Affirming Party must be Free from the Vitiating Factor

(1) Pressure and exploitation

Where a contract or gift is voidable for duress or undue influence, the party imposed upon is capable of affirming only after the duress or undue influence has effectively come to an end.[27] The same principle ought to apply in relation to unconscionable bargains, both as a matter of principle and by analogy with the rule that time does not count as laches and acquiescence for so long as the imposition continues.[28]

23.14

Where a contract is voidable because vitiated by mental impairment or drunkenness known to the other, it is capable of being affirmed only once the contracting party has regained his full mental faculties.[29]

23.15

In principle, affirmation of a contract between principal and fiduciary voidable for breach of fiduciary duty is not possible until after the principal is effectively freed from the effects of the breach of duty. That should require awareness of the material facts, and possibly in some cases, appropriate independent advice.[30]

23.16

Particular rules apply to breach of fiduciary duty by directors. Section 177 of the Companies Act 2006 requires a director interested in a transaction by the company to make disclosure

23.17

---

[24] Cf whether affirmation bars a statutory right to rescind depends upon the construction of the relevant provision. In Australia, the court has power to grant an order for rescission pursuant to s 243 of Sched 2 of the Competition and Consumer Act 2010 (formerly s 87 of the Trade Practices Act 1974) even if the injured party has affirmed the transaction, albeit that may well weigh heavily against the exercise of the court's discretion: *Tenji v Henneberry & Associates Pty Ltd* (2000) 98 FCR 324 (Full Ct) [22] ('A positive affirmation of the contract coupled with a demand for compensation might well weigh heavily against the making of such an order'); *Southern Cross Mine Management Pty Ltd v Ensham Resources Pty Ltd* [2005] QSC 233 [639] (rescission still available after affirmation); *Land Enviro Corp Pty Ltd v HTT Huntley Heritage Pty Ltd* [2012] NSWSC 382 [909] (repeated affirmation meant order for rescission ought not be made).
[25] See paras [23.66]–[23.67].
[26] See paras [23.40]–[23.41].
[27] *Savery v King* (1856) 5 HLC 627, 663–64; 10 ER 1046, 1061–62 (presumed undue influence); *Ormes v Beadle* (1860) 2 De GF & J 333, 45 ER 649 (duress); *Moxon v Payne* (1873) LR 8 Ch App 881, 885–86 (undue influence); *Allcard v Skinner* (1887) 36 ChD 145 (CA) 187 (undue influence); *North Ocean Shipping Co Ltd v Hyundai Construction Co Ltd (Atlantic Baron)* [1979] 1 QB 705, 720–21 (duress); *DSND Subsea Limited v Petroleum Geo-Services ASA* [2000] 1 BLR 530, 548 (duress). In Australia, *Hawker Pacific Pty Ltd v Helicopter Charter Pty Ltd* (1991) 22 NSWLR 298 (CA) 304, 306 (duress); *Cockerill v Westpac Banking Corporation* (1996) 142 ALR 227 (FCA) 279 (duress). In NZ, *Haines v Carter* [2001] 2 NZLR 167 (CA) [116] (rev'd in part on another point [2001] 3 NZLR 605 (PC—NZ)).
[28] *Fry v Lane* (1888) 40 ChD 312, 324.
[29] *Matthews v Baxter* (1873) LR 8 Exch 132, 133–134 (drunkenness).
[30] Paras [23.13] and [23.15] of the second edition (paras [23.14] and [23.16] of this edition) were applied in *International Healthway Corp Ltd v The Enterprise Fund III Ltd* [2018] SGHC 246 [80], [81] (contractual payments not affirmatory when made on instructions of directors who caused company to conclude the voidable agreements; statutory right to rescind indirect acquisition of company's own shares in contravention of s 76 of the Companies Act (Sing)).

to the board of directors.[31] Authorities on the predecessors of this provision, which was first introduced in 1929,[32] establish that failure to do so makes the contract voidable.[33] Given that disclosure needs to be made to the board it might have been thought that the board is competent to affirm. But the Act provides that only the shareholders in general meeting may do so, and only in the prescribed manner.[34]

(2) Misrepresentation, mistake, and non-disclosure

General rule: knowledge of material facts required

23.18 Where the right to rescind stems from misrepresentation, mistake, or non-disclosure, no election can be made until the misled party is aware of the true facts.[35] Conduct before that time cannot constitute an irrevocable affirmation,[36] and this is true of electing between rights generally.[37]

23.19 This may be contrasted with the position advocated in the *Restatement of Contracts*. It provides that affirmation occurs in cases of misrepresentation and mistake if the party entitled to avoid 'has reason to know of the mistake or the misrepresentation if it is non-fraudulent or knows of the misrepresentation if it is fraudulent'.[38]

Partial knowledge of truth

23.20 Although it has been said that full knowledge of the true facts is required before a contract voidable for misrepresentation may be affirmed,[39] that is probably too broadly stated. A

---

[31] For transactions that must be disclosed to members, Companies Act 2006, pt 10, chap 4.

[32] *Hely-Hutchinson v Brayhead Ltd* [1968] 1 QB 549 (CA) 589 (Lord Wilberforce).

[33] *Hely-Hutchinson v Brayhead Ltd* [1968] 1 QB 549 (CA) 585–86, 589–90, 594. The Companies Act 2006, s 178 provides that breach of the duty to disclose is regulated by the general law. See also s 180.

[34] Companies Act 2006, s 239. See also *MacPherson v European Strategic Board* [1999] 2 BCLC 203 (company cannot rescind if contract approved by all the shareholders).

[35] *Clough v London and North Western Railway Co* (1871) LR 7 Ex 26, 34, 35 (fraud in sale of goods); *Re Eastgate* [1905] 1 KB 465, 467 (fraud in sale of goods); *Peyman v Lanjani* [1985] Ch 457 (CA) 488–89, 501–03 (ignorance of defect in title permitting 'rescission' for breach); *Occidental Worldwide Investment Corp v Skibs A/S Avanti (The Siboen and Sibotre)* [1976] 1 Lloyd's Rep 293, 325 (misrepresentation as to charterers' financial position); *Fiona Trust & Holding Corporation v Privalov* [2007] 1 All ER (Comm) 81 [36] (alleged fraud as to charterparties); *Banwaitt v Dewji* [2013] EWHC 879 (QB) [74]–[75] (fraudulent misrepresentation; appeal dismissed [2014] EWCA Civ 67). In Australia, *Coastal Estates Pty Ltd v Melevende* [1965] VR 433 (Full Ct) 451–52 (fraud as to sale of land); *Koutsonicolis v Principe (No 2)* (1987) 48 SASR 329 (latent defects in dwelling house). In Canada, *United Shoe Machinery Company of Canada v Brunet* [1909] AC 330 (PC—Canada) 339 (misrepresentation as to goods); *Boulter v Stocks* (1913) 47 SCR 440 (misrepresentation as to size and condition of farm); *Bevan v Anderson and Peace River Sand & Gravel Co* (1957) 12 DLR (2d) 69 (Alta SC) 77 (misrepresentation as to business). In Hong Kong, *Acute Result Holdings Ltd v Lioncap Asia Limited* [2019] HKCFI 1580 [13] (setting aside default judgment in respect of agreement later sought to be rescinded, in circumstances where plaintiff was then unaware of full factual position or right to rescind).

[36] See n 32 and *JAD International Pty Ltd v International Trucks Australia Limited* (1994) 50 FCR 378 (Full Ct) 385–86 (ignorance as to innocent misrepresentation as to truck engine). See also *Greenwood v Leather Shod Wheel Company* [1900] 1 Ch 421 (CA) 437 (affirmation of voidable share allotment; comments *obiter*). In certain circumstances there is an exception if there has been a deliberate failure to inquire: see paras [23.32]–[23.34].

[37] *O'Connor v SP Bray Limited* (1936) St Rep (NSW) 248, 262; *Sargent v ASL Developments Ltd* (1974) 131 CLR 634, 642: 'An elector must at least know of the facts which give rise to those legal rights, as between which an election must be made; without that knowledge the doctrine of election will not be available to make irrevocable his choice of one particular right' (Stephen J).

[38] *Restatement (Second) of Contracts* vol 3, § 380(2) (1981). See also § 381(2), stating the same rule in relation to delay.

[39] *Occidental Worldwide Investment Corp v Skibs A/S Avanti (The Siboen and Sibotre)* [1976] 1 Lloyd's Rep 293, 325 (Kerr J).

contract may be affirmed though the innocent party knows some but not all of the incidents of misrepresentations made,[40] and the same principle seems to apply to contracts voidable for non-disclosure in breach of fiduciary duty.[41]

Similarly, whilst it has been said that an underwriter can affirm a contract of insurance only once he has acquired full knowledge of the material facts,[42] the correct view probably is that he needs to know sufficient of the facts to know that he has the right to rescind, though he is not aware of all aspects or incidents of those facts.[43] **23.21**

The limited authority on the issue indicates that the innocent party's conduct is capable of amounting to affirmation if he knows that he has been defrauded, but does not know all incidents of the fraud;[44] knows facts that would justify rescission for fraud or other cause and is content to bear the risk of further material information coming to light;[45] deliberately and for tactical reasons decides not to acquire definite knowledge of a matter which he believes that he could confirm;[46] or, possibly, evinces an intention to affirm when correctly assuming the falsity of the relevant representations.[47] **23.22**

In some cases where the truth is partially known the affirming party is entitled to revoke the affirmation after discovery of further information, so that it was always only conditional; and in others he is not. The line between the two types of case is not fully developed, and is discussed separately in Part H of this chapter. **23.23**

Immaterial that truth could have been discovered

Unequivocal conduct by a party ignorant of the truth is not a binding affirmation even though he could have discovered the true position. This is well established in the case of voidable policies of insurance,[48] and probably applies to rescission generally.[49] It matches **23.24**

---

[40] *Murray v Palmer* (1805) 2 Sch & Lef 474; *Campbell v Fleming* (1834) 1 Ad & E 40, 41–42; 110 ER 1122; *Coastal Estates Pty Ltd v Melevende* [1965] VR 433 (Full Ct) 442; *Elder's Trustee and Executor Company Limited v Commonwealth Homes and Investment Co Ltd* (1941) 65 CLR 603, 616–17; *JAD International Pty Ltd v International Trucks Australia Limited* (1994) 50 FCR 378 (Full Ct) 389–91; *Insurance Corporation of the Channel Islands Ltd v McHugh and Royal Hotel Limited* [1997] Lloyd's Re Ins LR 94, 127 col 1; *Insurance Corporation of the Channel Islands Ltd v The Royal Hotel Ltd* [1998] 7 Lloyd's Rep IR 151, 161. But cf *Boulter v Stocks* (1913) 47 SCR 440.
[41] *Law v Law* [1905] Ch 140 (CA) 158, although it is unclear whether this reasoning was intended to apply to affirmation other than by entry into a compromise.
[42] *Container Transport International Inc and Reliance Group Inc v Oceanus Mutual Underwriting Association (Bermuda) Ltd* [1984] 1 Lloyd's Rep 476, 498 (Kerr J), foll *Black King Shipping Corporation and Wayang (Panama) SA v Mark Ranald Massie (The Litsion Pride)* [1985] 1 Lloyd's Rep 437, 516 (Hirst J).
[43] *Insurance Corporation of the Channel Islands Ltd v The Royal Hotel Ltd* [1998] 7 Lloyd's Rep IR 151, 161 (Mance J), app'd *Spriggs v Wessington Court Schools Ltd* [2005] 1 Lloyd's Rep IR 474, 489.
[44] *Campbell v Fleming* (1834) 1 Ad & E 40, 41–42; 110 ER 1122; *Insurance Corporation of the Channel Islands Ltd v McHugh and Royal Hotel Limited* [1997] Lloyd's Re Ins LR 94, 127; but cf the narrower interpretation of *Campbell v Fleming* in *Black King Shipping Corporation and Wayang (Panama) SA v Mark Ranald Massie (The Litsion Pride)* [1985] 1 Lloyd's Rep 437, 516–17, construing it as confined to knowledge of evidence rather than facts.
[45] *Law v Law* [1905] Ch 140 (CA) 158; *Elder's Trustee and Executor Company Limited v Commonwealth Homes and Investment Co Ltd* (1941) 65 CLR 603, 616–17.
[46] *Insurance Corporation of the Channel Islands Ltd v The Royal Hotel Ltd* [1998] 7 Lloyd's Rep IR 151, 172.
[47] *Coastal Estates Pty Ltd v Melevende* [1965] VR 433 (Full Ct) 442; but cf *Insurance Corporation of the Channel Islands Ltd v The Royal Hotel Ltd* [1998] 7 Lloyd's Rep IR 151, 162.
[48] *Container Transport International Inc and Reliance Group Inc v Oceanus Mutual Underwriting Association (Bermuda) Ltd* [1984] 1 Lloyd's Rep 476, 498; *The Black King Shipping Corporation and Wayang (Panama) SA v Mark Ranald Massie (The Litsion Pride)* [1985] 1 Lloyd's Rep 437, 516; *Insurance Corporation of the Channel Islands Ltd v The Royal Hotel Ltd* [1998] 7 Lloyd's Rep IR 151, 161.
[49] *Haas Timber & Trading Co Pty Ltd v Wade* (1954) 94 CLR 593, 601–02; *Bevan v Anderson and Peace River Sand & Gravel Co* (1957) 12 DLR (2d) 69 (Alta SC) 75–77.

the principle that on a plea of laches or acquiescence it does not matter that the misled party had the means of discovering the truth; he has no duty to investigate until facts are known that raise suspicion, and delay before that time does not count against him.[50]

23.25 There are statements to the contrary in *Seddon v The North Eastern Salt Company Limited*[51] and in *Leaf v International Galleries*.[52] Both of these decisions involved innocent misrepresentation. But whereas the statements in *Seddon*'s case were generalized, in *Leaf*'s case they were confined to sales of goods. There the notion that the capacity to discover the truth is enough for the right to be lost was connected to the perceived need for congruence between the right of a purchaser of goods to rescind for innocent misrepresentation, and to terminate for breach of condition.

23.26 However, the statements in *Seddon*'s case are anomalous, and the reasoning in *Leaf*'s case has been criticized[53] and may not be consistent with section 1(1) of the Misrepresentation Act 1967.[54] These authorities do not undermine the principle that affirmation requires knowledge, and that having the means of knowledge is not enough.

Suspicion, constructive knowledge, and being put on inquiry

23.27 The general rule is that there can be no affirmation where the party entitled to rescind is merely suspicious, put on inquiry, or has what in other contexts would be constructive knowledge of the true facts.

23.28 The rule is well established for insurance. An underwriter does not affirm if merely put on inquiry as to the existence of the relevant facts;[55] constructive knowledge is also not enough;[56] and nor is suspicion founded on rumour and the like.[57] The principle is also applied outside the insurance context, and seems to apply to rescission generally.[58] In *Aaron's Reefs Ltd v Twiss*[59] inaction during a period where the misled purchaser of shares entertained a 'shrewd suspicion' of what had occurred but had no tangible grounds for rescinding was held to not involve an election to affirm, and that opinion was followed in Australia in *Haas Timber & Trading Co Pty Ltd v Wade*.[60] Similarly, in *Fiona Trust & Holding Corporation v Privalov*[61] Morison J held that the claimants, who alleged that they were the victims of a massive fraud,

---

[50] *Rawlins v Wickham* (1858) 3 De G & J 304, 313–14; 44 ER 1285; *Re The Mount Morgan (West) Gold Mine Limited* (1887) 56 LT 622, 625 col 2; cf also the principle that the ability to discover the truth does not negative misrepresentation: *Directors of the Central Railway Company of Venezuela v Kisch* [1867] LR 2 App Cas 99, 120–21; *Redgrave v Hurd* (1881) 20 ChD 1 (CA) 13–14, 23.
[51] [1905] Ch 326, 334.
[52] [1950] 2 KB 86 (CA) 91, 92.
[53] *Leason Pty Ltd v Princes Farm Pty Ltd* (1983) 2 NSWLR 381, 387.
[54] See *JAD International Pty Ltd v International Trucks Australia Limited* (1994) 50 FCR 378 (Full Ct) 384–85; see further Chap 27, paras [27.51]–[27.54].
[55] *Container Transport International Inc and Reliance Group Inc v Oceanus Mutual Underwriting Association (Bermuda) Ltd* [1984] 1 Lloyd's Rep 476, 498; *Black King Shipping Corporation and Wayang (Panama) SA v Mark Ranald Massie (The Litsion Pride)* [1985] 1 Lloyd's Rep 437, 516.
[56] *Insurance Corporation of the Channel Islands Ltd v The Royal Hotel Ltd* [1998] 7 Lloyd's Rep IR 151, 161.
[57] *The Wakefield and Barnsley Banking Company v The Normanton Local Board* (1881) 40 LT 697, 699 (suspicion of fraud from comments at public house not enough); *Khoury v Government Insurance Office* (1984) 165 CLR 622 (knowledge obtained only when evidence given at trial; earlier awareness of rumours did not count).
[58] *SK Shipping Europe plc v Capital VLCC 3 Corp* [2021] 2 Lloyd's Rep 109 [202](ii) '[t]here must be knowledge, not simply suspicion' decision affirmed *SK Shipping Europe plc v Capital VLCC 3 Corp ("C Challenger")* [2022] EWCA Civ 231.
[59] [1896] AC 273, 290.
[60] (1954) 94 CLR 593, 601–602.
[61] [2007] 1 All ER (Comm) 81 [36].

were entitled to await the outcome of expert investigations before electing to rescind, even though they had previously concluded that the relevant agreements were 'very probably' tainted by fraud.

An Australian authority, *Hoffman v Schilling*,[62] illustrates the principle in the case of a purchase procured by deceit. Hoffman sold Schilling a share in his drilling business without disclosing that he had just been made bankrupt. That was held to be a deceit entitling Schilling to rescind his purchase. Sixteen months later Schilling discovered that Hoffman was an undischarged bankrupt, but at that point made no inquiries as to whether he was also bankrupt at the time of the share sale. Pincus J held that when Schilling discovered Hoffman's bankruptcy he had insufficient knowledge of the material facts for his later actions to amount to an affirmation of the sale. It was not enough if he ought reasonably to have realized that Hoffman had been bankrupted when the sale had occurred.[63] The Full Federal Court dismissed an appeal on this point.[64] **23.29**

A similar principle is applied when delay is said to amount to laches barring rescission. Inaction will count for little if the misled party suspects rather than knows the truth of matters misrepresented or not disclosed.[65] **23.30**

It may be that a lesser degree of knowledge is required for election outside the general law of rescission. In Australia, courts have held in relation to statutory rights to rescind that it is sufficient for the electing party to have a knowledge of circumstances such as will provide information from which the decisive fact giving rise to the legal right is a clear, if not necessary, inference.[66] Those cases have been applied to claims to rescind under the general law,[67] but this runs counter to the authorities, which indicate that it is not enough that the injured party is put on inquiry, or has merely constructive knowledge. **23.31**

Deliberately failing to inquire

There is an exception to the principle just discussed where the person entitled to rescind deliberately and for tactical reasons decides not to acquire definite knowledge of a matter which he believes it likely that he could confirm. It is said that such a person is in effect prepared to take the risk of the position being whatever it is, and is treated as having knowledge of the matter.[68] The exception presupposes that the party entitled to rescind has either personally or through his advisers information that suggests the true position.[69] **23.32**

Whilst this exception was recognized in a case involving voidable contracts of insurance, there seems no reason why it should be restricted to that context. It also seems well arguable **23.33**

---

[62] *Re Hoffman ex p Worrell v Schilling* (1989) 85 ALR 145 (FCA).
[63] *Re Hoffman ex p Worrell v Schilling* (1989) 85 ALR 145 (FCA) 149–50.
[64] *Re Hoffman ex p Worrell v Schilling* (Full FCA, 14 August 1989) [23].
[65] *Directors of the Central Railway Company of Venezuela v Kisch* (1867) LR 2 App Cas 99, 112; *Ogilvie v Currie* (1868) 37 LR Ch (NS) 541, 544–46; *Erlanger v The New Sombrero Phosphate Company* (1878) 3 App Cas 1218, 1249, 1261, 1279.
[66] *Elder's Trustee and Executor Co Ltd v Commonwealth Homes and Investment Co Ltd* (1941) 65 CLR 603, 617 (breach of minimum subscription requirement); see also *Sargent v ASL Developments Ltd* (1974) 131 CLR 634, 642.
[67] *Southern Cross Mine Management Pty Ltd v Ensham Resources Pty Ltd* [2005] QSC 233 [631], citing *Sargent v ASL Developments Ltd* (1974) 131 CLR 634, 642.
[68] *Insurance Corporation of the Channel Islands Ltd v The Royal Hotel Ltd* [1998] 7 Lloyd's Rep IR 151, 172.
[69] *Insurance Corporation of the Channel Islands Ltd v The Royal Hotel Ltd* [1998] 7 Lloyd's Rep IR 151, 162, 172.

that the exception should extend beyond cases where the failure to inquire stems from a tactical decision taken during litigation, and catches any case where the party entitled to affirm deliberately fails to verify matters which he believes could be confirmed.[70] A similar principle exists in relation to knowledge of the right to rescind.[71]

23.34 The line between cases where the injured party is not put to an election even though he is suspicious or put on inquiry, and where he deliberately fails to verify matters that he believes could be confirmed, is one of degree to be judged in the circumstances of the particular case. It may well be difficult to draw in some cases. The distinction would seem to turn both on the degree of knowledge, and the reason for failing to inquire. At a certain point ignorance of the true facts is no excuse; at that point it can fairly be said that the injured party ought to have known.[72]

D. Need for Awareness of Right to Rescind

(1) Uncertainty as to whether electing party must know rights

23.35 The circumstances in which the law requires knowledge of the existence of alternate legal rights before an election between them can occur are notoriously opaque. There are authorities that knowledge of rights is required and also that it is not, and there have also been competing attempts to rationalize the cases. It has been said that the leading decision supporting the view that an awareness of rights is required was wrongly decided,[73] and also that it is correct.[74]

23.36 This uncertainty extends to the law relating to voidable contracts.[75] There are several decisions where rescission has been barred by affirmation without any inquiry into whether the innocent party was aware of their rights,[76] and leading descriptions of the conditions for affirmation make no mention of that requirement, emphasizing only the need for unequivocal conduct.[77]

---

[70] For suggestions that a failure to investigate after suspicion is raised may count against the right to rescind, *Rawlins v Wickham* (1858) 3 De G & J 304, 313–14; 44 ER 1285.
[71] See para [23.54].
[72] 'The loss of the right to elect will, as a matter of law, I think, only arise where the relevant facts are or ought to be known to the party who has such a right': *Fiona Trust & Holding Corporation v Privalov* [2007] 1 All ER (Comm) 81 [36] (Morison J).
[73] *Peyman v Lanjani* [1985] Ch 457 (CA); KR Handley, 'Exploring Election' (2006) 122 LQR 82, 96; KR Handley, *Estoppel by Conduct and Election* (2006) [14-1025].
[74] S Wilken and K Ghaly, *The Law of Waiver, Variation and Estoppel* (3rd edn, 2012) [4.23].
[75] Even in New Zealand, where the principles have largely been codified in s 38 of the Contract and Commercial Law Act 2017 (NZ), probably, knowledge of rights is not necessary,: *Jolly v Palmer* [1985] 1 NZLR 658; *Hughes v Huppert* [1991] 1 NZLR 474; *Crump v Wala* [1994] 2 NZLR 331; *Tawanui Developments Limited v DM Harnett* [2009] NZHC 501 [31]; *AAM Limited v Exotica Enterprise Limited* [2019] NZHC 1482 [103].
[76] *Campbell v Fleming* (1834) 1 Ad & E 40, 110 ER 1122 (fraud); *Ormes v Beadle* (1860) 2 De GF & J 333, 336; 45 ER 649 (duress); *North Ocean Shipping Co Ltd v Hyundai Construction Co Ltd (Atlantic Baron)* [1979] QB 705, 720–21 (duress); *Halifax Building Society v Thomas* [1996] Ch 217 (CA) 226–27 (mortgage fraud). This is also the approach taken in the multitude of false prospectus cases decided in the second half of the nineteenth century. In Australia, *Sargent v Campbell* (1972) Arg LR 708, 711 (misrepresentation).
[77] *Clough v London and North Western Railway Co* (1871) LR 7 Ex 26, 34–35; *Abram Steamship Company Limited (in liq) v Westville Shipping Company Limited* [1923] AC 773, 779, 785–89; *Car and Universal Finance Co Ltd v Caldwell* [1965] 1 QB 525 (CA) 550, 554. In Australia, *Brown v Smitt* (1924) 34 CLR 160, 167–68. In Canada, *United Shoe Machinery Company of Canada v Brunet* [1909] AC 330 (PC—Canada) 339–40; *Kupchak v Dayson Holdings Co Ltd* (1965) 53 DLR (2d) 482 (BCCA) 489–90.

23.37 But there are other decisions where the court did inquire whether the party said to have affirmed knew of his right to rescind,[78] and two cases stand clearly for the proposition that a voidable contract cannot be affirmed without knowledge of the right to rescind it. These are the Australian case of *Coastal Estates Pty Ltd v Melevende*,[79] and the English Court of Appeal's decision in *Peyman v Lanjani*.[80] Each is considered briefly in turn.

23.38 *Coastal Estates v Melevende*[81] concerned a claim by a young man to rescind an executory purchase of eight blocks of vacant land in Westport Bay in Victoria for fraudulent misrepresentations made by the vendor's agent. After noting the divergence in the authorities, the Full Court of the Supreme Court of Victoria held that knowledge of the right to rescind was generally required before a binding election to affirm could be made, and that Mr Melevende had therefore not affirmed.

23.39 *Peyman v Lanjani*[82] came 20 years later, and involved a claim by the purchaser of 'The Creperie' restaurant and associated flats in central London to terminate the uncompleted sale by reason of a defect in the seller's title.[83] The defect arose because the leasehold interest being sold had been obtained by the seller's deception of his landlords. That made the lease voidable at the landlord's option. The Court of Appeal followed *Coastal Estates v Melevende* and held that Mr Peyman, who had come to England from Iran, needed to know of his right to 'rescind' before his conduct could amount to affirmation. Overturning the decision of the trial judge, they held that there had been no such affirmation. The case did not involve a claim to rescind *ab initio* by reason of a prior invalidating cause; Mr Peyman's right was to terminate for breach of condition.[84]

(2) Awareness of rights required in England

23.40 Whilst there can be found appellate decisions in England and Wales since *Peyman v Lanjani* that neither endorse nor reject its approach,[85] the weight of authority supports the conclusion that affirmation requires that the party bound knows of their right to rescind. Colman J has said that *Peyman v Lanjani* is authority binding on the High Court that an election to affirm a voidable contract requires full knowledge of the right to choose to rescind or affirm.[86]

---

[78] *DSND Subsea Limited v Petroleum Geo-Services ASA* [2000] 1 BLR 530, 548 (duress); *Moore Large & Co Ltd v Hermes Credit & Guarantee plc* [2003] 1 Lloyd's Rep IR 315, 334–35 (insurance).

[79] [1965] VR 433 (Full Ct).

[80] [1985] Ch 457 (CA). Older cases can be found suggesting that a knowledge of rights is required; eg *Moxon v Payne* (1873) LR 8 Ch App 881, 885; *Kempson v Ashbee* [1874] LR 10 Ch App 15, 20. In Canada, there is the well-known statement of Riley J in *Bevan v Anderson and Peace River Sand & Gravel Co* (1957) 12 DLR (2d) 69 (Alta SC) 77: 'Innocent people are not deprived of their right of rescission before they had an opportunity of knowing the true facts and of knowing they have a right to rescind.' But this passage was made in the context of a discussion of the effects of the victim's ignorance of the true facts, and it may be doubted whether Riley J meant to say that the victim of misrepresentation must know of his legal right to rescind.

[81] [1965] VR 433 (Full Ct).

[82] [1985] Ch 457 (CA).

[83] *Peyman v Lanjani* [1985] Ch 457 (CA) 482, 496–97.

[84] The claim was to terminate for breach by reason of an undisclosed and irremovable defect in the seller's title. This involves termination *de futuro* not *ab initio* and does not involve 'rescission' in the sense that the term is used here: see Chap 1, paras [1.02], [1.03], [1.31]–[1.32], Chap 5, para [5.65].

[85] *Motor Oil Hellas (Corinth) Refineries SA v Shipping Corp of India (The Kanchenjunga)* [1990] 1 Lloyd's Rep 391 (HL) 398, 399; *Oliver Ashworth (Holdings) Ltd v Ballard (Kent) Ltd* [2000] Ch 12 (CA) 27.

[86] *Moore Large & Co Ltd v Hermes Credit & Guarantee plc* [2003] 1 Lloyd's Rep IR 315, 334, where Colman J referred to, inter alia, *Evans v Bartlam* [1937] AC 473, 479.

That seems to be on the basis that although the Court of Appeal in *Peyman v Lanjani* was concerned with a right to terminate for breach, their Lordships' reasoning indicated that knowledge of rights was also required in the context of rescission for misrepresentation or other prior invalidating cause. In addition, there is a consistent line of first instance authority holding that an underwriter must know of the right to rescind before there can be a binding election to affirm an insurance contract, and it was evidently assumed that this is the rule for rescission generally.[87] The same approach has also been taken outside the insurance context.[88] Moreover, in *Habib Bank Ltd v Tufail*[89] the Court of Appeal regarded it as 'undoubtedly the law' that knowledge of the right to rescind is essential before a misled party may lose the right to rescind for misrepresentation, and in *Ukraine v The Law Debenture Trust Corporation plc*[90] it was accepted in the Court of Appeal that the right to rescind for duress would be lost only if the party imposed upon was aware of their legal rights.[91]

23.41 Although the authorities before *Peyman v Lanjiani* tend to point in the other direction,[92] English law now requires that the innocent party knows of the right to rescind before his conduct will constitute a binding affirmation.

(3) Awareness of rights not required in other parts of the Commonwealth

Australia

23.42 By contrast, and despite the influence of Australian cases in shaping the English position, in Australia the trend has been in the other direction. On several occasions the High Court of Australia has suggested that *Coastal Estates v Melevende* might not be correct,[93] and Handley JA has said that the decision is out of line with the direction of Australian authority

---

[87] *Insurance Corporation of the Channel Islands Ltd v The Royal Hotel Ltd* [1998] 7 Lloyd's Rep IR 151, 161; *Moore Large & Co Ltd v Hermes Credit & Guarantee plc* [2003] 1 Lloyd's Rep IR 315, 334–35; *Spriggs v Wessington Court Schools Ltd* [2005] 1 Lloyd's Rep IR 474, 479; *Involnert Management Inc v Aprilgrange* [2015] 2 Lloyd's Rep 289 [160] (where Leggatt J observed that the rule was difficult to justify in principle, and knowledge was difficult to prove given the constraints imposed by legal professional privilege, whilst noting the presumption discussed in para [23.56] below).

[88] *Donegal International Ltd v Zambia* [2007] 1 Lloyd's Rep 397 [467] ('undoubtedly so' that affirming party must know of facts and right to rescind; alleged misrepresentation); *Gamatronic (UK) Limited v Hamilton* [2016] EWHC 2225 (QB) [226] (knowledge of relevant facts and of the right to rescind; alleged fraudulent misrepresentation of share purchase agreement); *Marme v Inversiones 2007 SL v Natwest Markets plc* [2019] EWHC 366 (Comm) [326] (point agreed by counsel on both sides); *SK Shipping Europe plc v Capital VLCC 3 Corp* [2021] 2 Lloyd's Rep 109 [202](i) (charterparty), affirmed *SK Shipping Europe plc v Capital VLCC 3 Corp ("C Challenger")* [2022] EWCA Civ 231 [73].

[89] [2006] EWCA Civ 374 [15], [20] per Lloyd LJ, with who Longmore LJ and Bennett J agreed. Lloyd LJ did not cite authority for the proposition, which appears to have been accepted by counsel for both parties.

[90] [2019] QB 1121 (CA).

[91] [2019] QB 1121 (CA) [192] (where the point was accepted by counsel and, in not suggesting that the position was otherwise, the court appears to have accepted its correctness).

[92] *Campbell v Fleming* (1834) 1 Ad & E 40, 110 ER 1122; *Ormes v Beadle* (1860) 2 De GF & J 333, 336; 45 ER 649; *Clough v London and North Western Railway Co* (1871) LR 7 Ex 26, 34–35; *United Shoe Machinery Company of Canada v Brunet* [1909] AC 330 (PC—Canada) 339–40; *Abram Steamship Company Limited v Westville Shipping Company Limited* [1923] AC 773, 779, 785–89; *Car and Universal Finance Co Ltd v Caldwell* [1965] 1 QB 525 (CA) 550, 554; *North Ocean Shipping Co Ltd v Hyundai Construction Co Ltd (Atlantic Baron)* [1979] QB 705, 720–21.

[93] *Sargent v ASL Developments Ltd* (1974) 131 CLR 634, 658 (Mason J) (but cf Stephen J at 644–45, with whom McTiernan ACJ agreed); *Turner v Labafox International Pty Ltd* (1974) 131 CLR 660, 670 (Mason J); *Khoury v Government Insurance Office* (1984) 165 CLR 622, 633–34.

since 1920.[94] A Canadian court has likewise declined to follow it in a case not involving fraud.[95]

In *Hoffman v Schilling*[96] Pincus J declined to follow *Coastal Estates v Melevende*. After reviewing the authorities, he concluded that the question remained open; the general rule was that knowledge of the facts giving rise to the right to elect was required, rather than knowledge of the right itself; and that this ought also to apply to the right to rescind for fraud.[97] The analysis of Pincus J was followed by Stevenson J in *Land Enviro Corp Pty Ltd v HTT Huntley Heritage Pty Ltd*.[98] Chesterman J has also said that the question remains open, and that the weight of authority supports the view that knowledge of rights is not necessary.[99] **23.43**

Whether a party having a right to elect must know of his rights in order to make an effective election has also been considered on several occasions in the context of statutory rights. Although that issue turns on the proper construction of the statute,[100] the courts have tended to conclude that the party entitled to elect need not be aware of his legal right to do so,[101] even where the statutory right is a right to rescind.[102] **23.44**

The judgments in *Coastal Estates v Melevende* betray a sympathy for Mr Melevende's plight that may have influenced the court's decision. But the decision is out of step with the weight of Australian authority, and probably does not represent Australian law even in cases involving fraud, save in the State of Victoria, where it continues to have binding effect. **23.45**

---

[94] KR Handley, 'Exploring Election' (2006) 122 LQR 82, 93, referring, in addition to the cases in the previous note, to *Crane v Colonial Mutual Fire Insurance Co* (1920) 28 CLR 305; *O'Connor v SP Bray Limited* (1936) 36 St Rep (NSW) 249; *Elder's Trustee and Executor Co Ltd v Commonwealth Homes and Investment Co Ltd* (1941) 65 CLR 603. But cf *Commonwealth of Australia v Verwayen* (1980) 170 CLR 394, 421 'Election consists in a choice between rights which the person making the election knows he possesses and which are alternative and inconsistent rights' (Brennan J).
[95] *Samson v Lockwood* (1998) 40 OR (3d) 161 (CA for Ontario).
[96] *Re Hoffman, ex p Worrell v Schilling* (1989) 85 ALR 145 (FCA) 151.
[97] His Honour gave three reasons for preferring this approach: it removed the need for awkward examination of what legal advice has been received; it had the virtue of simplicity; and the defrauded party anyway has a right to damages: *Re Hoffman, ex p Worrell v Schilling* (1989) 85 ALR 145 (FCA) 152.
[98] [2012] NSWSC 382 [209] 'I agree with Pincus J that the better view is that that knowledge of a legal right to rescind is not necessary, even in a fraud case, provided that the knowledge of the party otherwise entitled to rescind, of the facts giving rise to that right is so clear that an election not to rescind is manifest' (leave to appeal out of time granted [2014] NSWCA 34).
[99] *Southern Cross Mine Management Pty Ltd v Ensham Resources Pty Ltd* [2005] QSC 233 [632]. Statements to the contrary can be found. For example, in *Aquatic Air Pty Limited v Siewart* [2015] NSWSC 928 [90], Brereton J said that an election to affirm a voidable contract cannot be made unless the right to rescind 'is known to the party entitled to rescind' (claim to rescind under the Australian Consumer Law but expressed as a general principle).
[100] *Ellison v Lutre Pty Ltd* (1999) 88 FCR 116, 129.
[101] See the review in *Ellison v Lutre Pty Ltd* (1999) 88 FCR 116, referring to s 39 of the Business Agents Act 1938 (SA) and similar legislation (*Szep v Blanken* [1969] SASR 65; *Official Receiver v Feldman* (1972) 4 SASR 246); Conveyancing (Vendor Disclosure & Warranty) Regulation 1986 (NSW) and similar regulations (*Molotu Pty Ltd v Solar Power Ltd* (1989) 6 BPR 13 640; *Zucker v Straightlace Pty Ltd* (1987) 11 NSWLR 87); Companies Act 1892 (SA) s 226 (*Commonwealth Homes & Investment Company Ltd v Smith* (1937) 59 CLR 443; *Elder's Trustee and Executor Co Ltd v Commonwealth Homes and Investment Co Ltd* (1941) 65 CLR 603). Contrast Workers Compensation Act 1926 (NSW): *Latter v The Council of the Shire of Musswellbrook* (1936) 56 CLR 422 (knowledge of rights required).
[102] *Tiplady v Gold Coast Carlton* (1984) 8 FCR 438, 451 (rescission under former s 87 of the Trade Practices Act 1974, now s 243 of Sched 2 of the Competition and Consumer Act 2010); *Ellison v Lutre Pty Ltd* (1999) 88 FCR 116, 128, 130 (rescission under investor protection provisions in former s 1073 of the Corporations Law).

Residual relevance of knowledge of rights to election in Australia

23.46 Australian law is, however, complicated by authority suggesting that although knowledge of rights is not necessary to affirm, it nevertheless remains relevant to whether an election has been made in two respects. First, conduct that is otherwise equivocal, rather than unequivocal, may nevertheless be construed as a binding election if the electing party is shown to have been aware of his right to elect, and to have made a conscious choice to do so.[103] Secondly, there is authority that knowledge of the right to elect and a conscious choice to affirm is not required if the acts said to amount to affirmation prejudice or are 'adverse to' the other party; and absent prejudice knowledge of rights is required to make a valid election.[104]

23.47 But it is difficult to see why either of these two principles should have a role in the regulation of voidable contracts. Both add complexity, and are difficult to apply in practice. Nor do they have any convincing basis in principle. The general rule is that a subjective intention to affirm is neither necessary nor sufficient to make a binding election to affirm a voidable contract.[105] It is difficult to reconcile that rule with a principle that an election may be made by equivocal conduct if the electing party was aware of his right to do so.

23.48 The principle that knowledge of rights is needed if the relevant conduct is not adverse to the other party is also anomalous, in that it forms no part of the general doctrine of election. It is fundamental that election does not require the suffering of any prejudice by the party against whom the alternate rights exist. Nor, and despite suggestions to the contrary,[106] can this principle be explained in terms of estoppel, for there may well be no reliance by the party who is the subject of the adverse acts. In addition, although Mason J seems to have equated conduct adverse to the other party with unequivocal conduct,[107] that also is not a fixed equation, and can provide no justification for the rule.

New Zealand

23.49 In New Zealand, in cases involving misrepresentation, where the common law has been replaced by statute,[108] it has also been held that the right to rescind may be lost by affirmation though the affirming party was unaware of their entitlement to rescind.[109]

Singapore

23.50 In *Strait Colonies Pte Ltd v SMRT Alpha Pte Ltd*[110] the Singapore Court of Appeal declined to follow the principle in *Peyman v Lanjiani*. After reviewing decisions in Singapore,

---

[103] *Elder's Trustee and Executor Co Ltd v Commonwealth Homes and Investment Co Ltd* (1941) 65 CLR 603, 618; *Sargent v ASL Developments Ltd* (1974) 131 CLR 634, 646; *Re Hoffman, ex p Worrell v Schilling* (1989) 85 ALR 145 (FCA) 151; *Re Hoffman ex p Worrell v Schilling* (Full FCA, 14 August 1989) [21]; *Wiltrading (WA) Pty Ltd v Lumley General Insurance Ltd* (2005) 30 WAR 290, 304.

[104] *Coastal Estates Pty Ltd v Melevende* [1965] VR 433 (Full Ct) 443, 453; *Khoury v Government Insurance Office* (1984) 165 CLR 622, 633; *Wiltrading (WA) Pty Ltd v Lumley General Insurance Ltd* (2005) 30 WAR 290, 304. See also *Sargent v ASL Developments Ltd* (1974) 131 CLR 634, 657–58 (Mason J); *Turner v Labafox International Pty Ltd* (1974) 131 CLR 660, 670 (Mason J); *Re Hoffman, ex p Worrell v Schilling* (1989) 85 ALR 145 (FCA) 152.

[105] See paras [23.63], [23.99]–[23.101].

[106] *Coastal Estates Pty Ltd v Melevende* [1965] VR 433 (Full Ct) 443 (Sholl J), cf at 453 (Adam J).

[107] *Sargent v ASL Developments Ltd* (1974) 131 CLR 634, 657–58; *Turner v Labafox International Pty Ltd* (1974) 131 CLR 660, 670.

[108] Section 38 of the Contract and Commercial Law Act 2017 provides that 'A party is not entitled to cancel the contract if, with full knowledge of the repudiation, misrepresentation, or breach, the party has affirmed the contract'.

[109] *Overland Development Limited v Ronghuan Dong* [2018] NZHC 2225 [104] (purchase of land subdivision alleged to be affected by misrepresentation; s 38 of the Contract and Commercial Law Act 2017 (NZ)).

[110] [2018] SGCA 36 (Kwang JA, Chong JA, and Loh J).

England, and Australia and considering the applicable policy considerations, the Court of Appeal held that affirmation ought not to require knowledge of the right to rescind.[111] The court also rejected a submission that the position should be different in cases of fraudulent misrepresentation.[112]

(4) Whether knowledge of right to rescind should be required

23.51 Affirmation should not require knowledge of the right to rescind. Ignorance of the law is usually irrelevant to the incidence of civil obligations, and there is no good reason for an exception here.[113] More importantly, there are significant practical difficulties in applying the English rule. It casts on the party alleging affirmation a burden of proof that is very difficult to discharge given the constraints of legal professional privilege.[114] Further, whether affirmation has occurred is judged objectively, and the right to rescind may be lost even contrary to the subjective intentions of the injured party. Accordingly, if an awareness of rights is essential, its function cannot be preservation of the right to rescind until an informed choice is made, for the right may be lost without that.[115]

23.52 The main advantage of the English approach is that it ameliorates the harshness of the principles governing the affirmation of voidable contracts; in particular, that rights may be lost irrespective of intention, and absent any prejudice to the other party. But it is a blunt instrument for that purpose, and similar effects can probably be achieved by employing generous notions of what counts as unequivocal conduct.[116]

(5) What must be known

23.53 If a knowledge of rights is necessary, it seems that the electing party must know that he is entitled to rescind, and also that he has a choice not to. Presumably it is sufficient in this respect if he is aware of the outlines of what each choice entails, as opposed to all the legal consequences. It has been said that there is no requirement for him to know that any choice he may make is irrevocable.[117] In the insurance context it has been held sufficient if the insurer was aware that 'there was at least an arguable point to be taken' in favour of rescission.[118]

---

[111] [2018] SGCA 36 [55], [48]–[64] and agreeing with the analysis at first instance: *SMRT Alpha Pte Ltd v Strait Colonies Pte Ltd* [2017] SGHC 243 [52]–[56]. In that case, the party entitled did in fact know of their right to rescind: see [2018] SGCA 36 [67]–[69].
[112] [2018] SGCA 36 [65], [66].
[113] *Strait Colonies Pte Ltd v SMRT Alpha Pte Ltd* [2018] SGCA 36 [61]; also, *Involnert Management Inc v Aprilgrange* [2015] 2 Lloyd's Rep 289 [160].
[114] *Kammins Ballrooms Co Ltd v Zenith Investments (Torquay) Ltd* [1971] AC 850, 877–78; *Moore Large & Co Ltd v Hermes Credit & Guarantee plc* [2003] 1 Lloyd's Rep IR 315, 335; *Re Hoffman, ex p Worrell v Schilling* (1989) 85 ALR 145 (FCA) 151, 152; *Strait Colonies Pte Ltd v SMRT Alpha Pte Ltd* [2018] SGCA 36 [62], [63]; *Involnert Management Inc v Aprilgrange* [2015] 2 Lloyd's Rep 289 [160]; paras [23.55]–[23.56].
[115] See paras [23.99]–[23.101].
[116] Contra, Q Liu, 'Rethinking Election: A General Theory' (2013) 35 Syd LR 599, 613–14. See also paras [23.13] and [23.66]–[23.67].
[117] *Peyman v Lanjani* [1985] 1 Ch 457 (CA) 486 'it has never been the law that the elector must know also that if he chooses one way or another the law may judge his choice irrevocable'.
[118] *Moore Large & Co Ltd v Hermes Credit & Guarantee plc* [2003] 1 Lloyd's Rep IR 315, 336.

(6) Deliberately failing to inquire into rights

23.54 In *Allcard v Skinner*[119] Lindley and Bowen LJJ emphasized that if the disaffected former novitiate was ignorant of her rights to reclaim the gifts she had made to her holy order, that was only because she had deliberately determined not to inquire into those rights, and her ignorance was therefore no obstacle to a finding of affirmation.[120] This decision implies that in England there is an exception to the rule that the injured party must know of his rights before his conduct amounts to affirmation. The exception arises where there is a deliberate decision to not determine what those rights might be.[121]

(7) Proving knowledge of rights

23.55 The onus of proving that the party entitled to rescind knew of his legal rights is on the party alleging affirmation.[122] That gives rise to evidential difficulties; in particular, because it will usually be necessary to prove that particular legal advice was given, but the party alleged to have received it will be entitled to shelter behind legal professional privilege. These difficulties have been described as a 'powerful objection' to making knowledge of rights a condition of affirmation,[123] and have been advanced as a reason for rejecting the requirement altogether.[124]

23.56 It has been held that in light of these difficulties, the courts will ordinarily infer certain facts and matters in favour of the party alleging affirmation.[125] First, where it is the conduct of solicitors or counsel that is said to constitute affirmation, it will normally be inferred that this conduct has been authorized by the client and has been the subject of legal advice. Secondly, if the evidence indicates that either the legal advisers or their client had knowledge of the facts giving rise to the right to rescind at the time of the affirmatory conduct, there is a further inference that the client has been given legal advice as to his rights arising out of those facts, which may be rebutted by the party seeking to rescind waiving privilege and proving otherwise.[126]

---

[119] (1887) 36 ChD 145 (CA).
[120] *Allcard v Skinner* (1887) 36 ChD 145 (CA) 188, 192.
[121] As to deliberately failing to inquire into the facts surrounding the transaction, see paras [23.32]–[23.34].
[122] *Moore Large & Co Ltd v Hermes Credit & Guarantee plc* [2003] 1 Lloyd's Rep IR 315, 334.
[123] *Moore Large & Co Ltd v Hermes Credit & Guarantee plc* [2003] 1 Lloyd's Rep IR 315, 335.
[124] *Kammins Ballrooms Co Ltd v Zenith Investments (Torquay) Ltd* [1971] AC 850, 877–78, where Lord Pearson described a requirement to prove knowledge of rights as 'an unreasonable burden of proof' given the constraints imposed by legal professional privilege. In Australia, *Re Hoffman, ex p Worrell v Schilling* (1989) 85 ALR 145 (FCA) 151, 152. In Singapore, *Strait Colonies Pte Ltd v SMRT Alpha Pte Ltd* [2018] SGCA 36 [62], [63].
[125] *Moore Large & Co Ltd v Hermes Credit & Guarantee plc* [2003] 1 Lloyd's Rep IR 315, 335–36.
[126] *Moore Large & Co Ltd v Hermes Credit & Guarantee plc* [2003] 1 Lloyd's Rep IR 315; *Involnert Management Inc v Aprilgrange Limited* [2015] 2 Lloyd's Rep 289 [160]; *SK Shipping Europe plc v Capital VLCC 3 Corp* [2021] 2 Lloyd's Rep 109 [202](v), [216](ii) (applying the presumption in the case of a charterparty induced by misrepresentation), decision affirmed *SK Shipping Europe plc v Capital VLCC 3 Corp ("C Challenger")* [2022] EWCA Civ 231.

E. Communication

An election between rights is generally said to be effective or complete only after it is communicated to the party against whom the rights are enforceable.[127] On the other hand, the ratification of a bargain made by an unauthorized agent involves a unilateral manifestation of will, and need not be communicated.[128] **23.57**

There is a difference of opinion as to whether the affirmation of voidable transactions follows the 'election' or 'ratification' model. Some authorities suggest that affirmation must be communicated, particularly those emphasizing that it involves an election between rights.[129] But other statements of the general rule make no mention of a need for communication and emphasize only the need for unequivocal conduct,[130] or imply that communication is unnecessary;[131] and there are cases where a shareholder's right to rescind an allotment for misrepresentation was lost by dealings with the shares apparently not known to the company.[132] An intention to affirm may also be inferred by inaction, though probably only where the inaction conveyed a choice to the other party.[133] Moreover, there do not seem to have been any reported cases where a failure to communicate the affirming conduct was fatal to the defence. **23.58**

The uncertainty exists even in relation to contracts of insurance, where the law tends to be more fully developed. There are indications that an underwriter must communicate to the assured his affirmation of a voidable policy,[134] but also authority that this is not always necessary.[135] **23.59**

---

[127] *Scarfe v Jardine* (1882) 7 App Cas 345, 361; *Sargent v ASL Developments Ltd* (1974) 131 CLR 634, 647, 656; *Khoury v Government Insurance Office* (1984) 165 CLR 622, 633–34; *China National Foreign Trade Transportation Corporation v Evlogia Shipping Co SA of Panama (The Mihalios Xilas)* [1979] 1 WLR 1018 (HL) 1034–35; *Motor Oil Hellas (Corinth) Refineries SA v Shipping Corp of India (The Kanchenjunga)* [1990] 1 Lloyd's Rep 391 (HL) 399.

[128] PG Watts and FMB Reynolds (eds), *Bowstead and Reynolds on Agency* (21st edn, 2018) [2-047], [2-050], [2-074], [2-078].

[129] *Peyman v Lanjani* [1985] Ch 457 (CA) 494 (a case concerning termination for defect in title); *Oliver Ashworth (Holdings) Ltd v Ballard (Kent) Ltd* [2000] Ch 12 (CA) 27–28; *Potter v Dyer* [2011] EWCA Civ 1417 [56]; *SK Shipping Europe plc v Capital VLCC 3 Corp* [2021] 2 Lloyd's Rep 109 [203](i) (summary of principles not challenged on appeal, *SK Shipping Europe plc v Capital VLCC 3 Corp ("C Challenger")* [2022] EWCA Civ 231 [73]). In Australia, *Coastal Estates Pty Ltd v Melevende* [1965] VR 433 (Full Ct) 443; *Russo v Beclar Pty Ltd* (2011) 111 SASR 459 (Full Ct) [11]. In Singapore, *Strait Colonies Ltd v SMRT Alpha Pte Ltd* [2018] SGCA 36 [42] (lease; citing *Jurong Town Corp v Wishing Star Ltd* [2005] 3 SLR(R) 283); *International Healthway Corp Ltd v The Enterprise Fund III Ltd* [2018] SGHC 246 [75] (shares; citing *Aero-Gate Pte Ltd v Engen Marine Engineering Ltd* [2013] 4 SLR 409 [42]).

[130] *Clough v London and North Western Railway Co* (1871) LR 7 Ex 26, 34.

[131] *Car and Universal Finance Co Ltd v Caldwell* [1965] 1 QB 525 (CA) 550.

[132] *Campbell v Fleming* (1834) 1 Ad & E 40, 41–42; 110 ER 1122 (shareholder's dealing with shares purchased after knowledge of the fraud barred rescission by affirmation; decision not put on the basis of *restitutio in integrum* being impossible, though it might have been); *Re Hop and Malt Exchange and Warehouse Company, ex p Briggs* (1866) LR 1 Eq Cas 483 (claimant's instructions to his broker to sell share allotment barred rescission for misstatements in the prospectus, as 'an acquiescence therein').

[133] *North Ocean Shipping Co Ltd v Hyundai Construction Co Ltd (Atlantic Baron)* [1979] 1 QB 705, 721 (delay in seeking rescission coupled with making payments without protest after duress had ended).

[134] *Insurance Corporation of the Channel Islands Ltd v The Royal Hotel Limited* [1998] 7 Lloyd's Rep IR 151, 161, 162 (where Mance J presents the rule as applicable to voidable contracts generally); *Drake Insurance plc v Provident Insurance plc* [2003] 1 Lloyd's Rep IR 781, 789.

[135] *Spriggs v Wessington Court Schools Ltd* [2005] 1 Lloyd's Rep IR 474, 484, where the comments were made *obiter*, and it was held that communication other than to the assured was in that case not enough.

VI. OTHER BARS

23.60 Principle suggests that communication should be required, save perhaps in exceptional cases.[136] That is for two reasons. First, communication is generally required to effectively elect to rescind, and there is no good reason for the rule to be different where the election is the other way.[137] Secondly, communication seems to support the rationale underlying the doctrine. Insofar as one may be detected, the rationale for depriving the affirming party of his right to rescind is that it promotes certainty, and is thought to be fair as between the parties that the person affected is entitled to know where he stands, and that the person electing should not have the opportunity of changing his election and subjecting his adversary to different obligations.[138] Requiring communication aligns with this rationale. Dispensing with communication undermines it.

F. Unequivocal Words or Conduct

(1) General principle

23.61 A voidable transaction may be affirmed either by express words or by unequivocal acts.[139] The conduct must be such that it 'unequivocally manifests an intention to affirm'.[140] It must be unequivocal in the sense of being an act justifiable if an election has been made to affirm and not justifiable if an election had been made to rescind,[141] and it may be that it must be conduct only justifiable on that basis.[142]

23.62 It has been said that either the way in which the election is communicated or the surrounding circumstances must demonstrate objectively that the party affirming is making an informed choice.[143] But it is not necessary that the other subjectively has that

---

[136] For example, in the case of the re-sale of property purchased, or where the other party to the transaction cannot be found. For the contrary view, A Burrows, *A Restatement of the English Law of Contract* (2nd edn, 2020) §19(6) (doubting [23.57] of the second edition, [23.60] of this third edition, in the context of affirmation of a breach of contract, and concluding that communication is not generally necessary).

[137] As to the rule for electing to rescind, see Chap 11, para [11.30].

[138] *Sargent v ASL Developments Ltd* (1974) 131 CLR 634, 656, 658 (Mason J).

[139] *Clough v London and North Western Railway Co* (1871) LR 7 Ex 26, 34; *Abram Steamship Company Limited v Westville Shipping Company Limited* [1923] AC 773, 779, 789; *Peyman v Lanjani* [1985] Ch 457 (CA) 501 'done an unequivocal act, or made an unequivocal statement'; *SK Shipping Europe plc v Capital VLCC 3 Corp* [2021] 2 Lloyd's Rep 109 [203](i) 'unequivocally communicate the decision to exercise (or not to exercise) the right'; *SK Shipping Europe plc v Capital VLCC 3 Corp ('C Challenger')* [2022] EWCA Civ 231 [73] (summary of principles not challenged on appeal). In Australia, *Brown v Smitt* (1924) 34 CLR 160, 167–68; *Coastal Estates Pty Ltd v Melevende* [1965] VR 433 (Full Ct) 443, 452; *Kramer v McMahon* [1970] 1 NSWLR 194, 210. In New Zealand, *Kenny v Fenton* [1971] NZLR 1 (CA) 16–18; in Canada, *Kupchak v Dayson Holdings Co Ltd* (1965) 53 DLR (2d) 482 (BCCA) 489–490. Cf 'manifests to the other party his intention to affirm it or acts with respect to anything what he has received in a manner inconsistent with disaffirmance': *Restatement (Second) of Contracts* vol 3, §§ 380(1), 380(2) (1981).

[140] *Car and Universal Finance Co Ltd v Caldwell* [1965] 1 QB 525 (CA) 550. An election between rights generally requires unequivocal conduct: *Scarfe v Jardine* (1882) 7 App Cas 345, 361; *Tropical Traders Ltd v Goonan* (1964) 111 CLR 41, 55.

[141] *Scarfe v Jardine* (1882) 7 App Cas 345, 361.

[142] Australia: *Tropical Traders Ltd v Goonan* (1964) 111 CLR 41, 55 (right to terminate for late payment); *Sargent v ASL Developments Ltd* (1974) 131 CLR 634, 646 (Stephen J) (election generally); *Champtaloup v Thomas* (1976) 2 NSWLR 264 (CA) 268–69 (contractual right to 'rescind'); *Donau Pty Ltd v ACS AWD Shipbuilder Pty Ltd* (2019) 101 NSWLR 679 (CA) (contractual right to terminate). England: *Strive Shipping Corporation v Hellenic Mutual War Risks Association (The Grecia Express)* [2002] 2 Lloyd's Rep 88, 163. Singapore: *Strait Colonies Ltd v SMRT Alpha Pte Ltd* [2018] SGCA 36 [42] (lease).

[143] *Insurance Corporation of the Channel Islands Ltd v The Royal Hotel Ltd* [1998] 7 Lloyd's Rep IR 151, 162, 163 (Mance J, as his Lordship then was), in the context of voidable contracts of insurance, accepted as stating the law in that context in *Spriggs v Wessington Court Schools Ltd* [2005] 1 Lloyd's Rep IR 474, 479 and in New Zealand in

impression,[144] and the fact that he does is also not determinative.[145] Only the party entitled to rescind may affirm; the wrongdoer has no equivalent right. That is because affirmation involves waiver by election, and only the party who possesses the right to rescind is able to waive it.

Where the transaction is a gift, affirmation requires the manifestation of an intention to confirm the gift.[146] If it is a contract, the intention is to confirm the bargain struck, and this is almost invariably associated with an intention to enforce rights arising under or pursuant to it. In both cases, the affirming party manifests an intention not to rescind, and it has been said that an intention to do so is in substance an intention to affirm.[147]   **23.63**

(2) Application of the general principle

Whether any particular words or actions constitute affirmation is to be assessed in all of the circumstances. Conduct amounting to affirmation in one set of circumstances may well not have that effect in another.   **23.64**

Relevance of the ground for rescission

There seems to be a link between the blameworthiness of the conduct that permits rescission, and the quality of conduct that is sufficient to demonstrate an unequivocal intention to affirm. A certain leniency may be detected in those cases where a person has been induced to purchase property by fraudulent misrepresentation.[148] That probably reflects a natural reluctance to find that an electing party has objectively made an informed choice to affirm rather than repudiate a transaction when it has been procured by active misconduct.[149] Equally, as a matter of principle, the underlying interest in the security of transactions ought to count for less where one of the parties has been guilty of conscious wrongdoing.   **23.65**

Jaggar v Lyttelton Marina Holdings Ltd (in rec) [2006] 2 NZLR 87 [160], and followed also in *Kosmar Villa Holidays plc v Trustees of Syndicate 1243* [2008] 2 All ER (Comm) 14 (CA) [73], [74] (election as to a contractual defence to indemnity). See also *Involnert Management Inc v Aprilgrange Limited* [2015] 2 Lloyd's Rep 289 [161] ('speaks or acts in a way which would reasonably be understood as consistent only with the insurer having made an informed choice to treat the contract as valid'). Difficulties with the principle were identified by Foxton J in *SK Shipping Europe plc v Capital VLCC 3 Corp* [2021] 2 Lloyd's Rep 109 [203](ii), [224], [225] (point not considered on appeal *SK Shipping Europe plc v Capital VLCC 3 Corp ("C Challenger")* [2022] EWCA Civ 231). Cf. also the Australian decision of *Moore v The National Mutual Life Association of Australasia Limited* [2011] NSWSC 416 [77]–[79].

[144] *Insurance Corporation of the Channel Islands Ltd v The Royal Hotel Ltd* [1998] 7 Lloyd's Rep IR 151, 163; *Spriggs v Wessington Court Schools Ltd* [2005] 1 Lloyd's Rep IR 474, 480 (where Stanley Burnton J expressed a preference for this view over that expressed by David Steel J in *Callaghan and Hedges v Thompson* [2000] Lloyd's Rep IR 125, 134); see also *Peyman v Lanjani* [1985] Ch 457 (CA) 502, where Slade LJ applied an objective test.
[145] *Morrison v The Universal Marine Insurance Company* (1873) LR 8 Ex 197, 207: that the assured may have believed that an election had been made is irrelevant if there had in fact been no election as a matter of law.
[146] *Allcard v Skinner* (1887) 36 ChD 145 (CA) 186 (Lindley LJ); cf 'determined to leave the gift where it is ... chose not to disturb the gift' (at 191, 193 per Bowen LJ); 'recognised the gift as her own spontaneous act' (at 175 per Cotton LJ).
[147] *Allcard v Skinner* (1887) 36 ChD 145 (CA) 187, 193.
[148] Eg *Brown v Smitt* (1924) 34 CLR 160, 167–68; *Coastal Estates Pty Ltd v Melevende* [1965] VR 433 (Full Ct) 437.
[149] See also *Baghbadrani v Commercial Union Assurance Co plc* [2000] 1 Lloyd's Rep IR 94, 122 (fraudulent insurance claim) appropriate for insurer to not repudiate liability for fraud without substantial evidence.

498   VI. OTHER BARS

23.66 In cases not involving any significant delay in rescinding, to which different considerations apply,[150] the courts are slow to find that conduct is sufficiently unequivocal to constitute affirmation where the innocent party disputes that he has in fact affirmed. The reports are replete with examples of confirmatory conduct by a party aware of the material facts that has been held to give rise to no binding election.[151] This reflects the justice of the situation. Absent prejudice, which usually triggers other bars, it is a hard thing to irrevocably deprive the innocent party of a right to rescind simply because his conduct evidences the making of a contrary choice.

23.67 The following discussion examines the main categories of affirmatory conduct to have been considered in the authorities.

Invoking or asserting contractual rights

23.68 Invoking or asserting contractual rights is a clear example of electing not to treat a contract as at an end.[152] Continued performance of the substantive terms of the contract, or requesting further performance from the other party, will normally be consistent only with an intention to treat the contract as continuing and will involve an election to affirm.[153] Giving a contractual notice of cancellation may suffice.[154] But the exercise of contractual rights will not always amount to affirmation, and it has been said in Australia that the question must be considered in light of all the circumstances of the particular case, and that 'there is no overriding principle of law that an act done under the contract will always communicate the decision to affirm, regardless of the surrounding circumstances'.[155]

23.69 It has been said that even where contractual rights are positively asserted, that may well not count as affirmation if rescission cannot be effected without the cooperation of the other party, such that the party seeking rescission is, in effect, trapped in the contract.[156]

23.70 In a New Zealand case, it was held that sending a notice to complete an executory contract induced by misrepresentation did not amount to affirmation of the agreement because it was done in the mistaken belief that the notice was required to exercise the statutory right to cancel the agreement.[157]

---

[150] See Chap 24.
[151] *Clough v London and North Western Railway Co* (1871) LR 7 Ex 26, 37–38; *Erlanger v The New Sombrero Phosphate Company* (1878) 3 App Cas 1218, 1282; *Abram Steamship Company Limited v Westville Shipping Company Limited* [1923] AC 773, 779, 789; *Peyman v Lanjani* [1985] Ch 457 (CA) 488–89, 501–03; *Senanayake v Cheng* [1966] AC 63 (PC—Singapore) 78. In Australia, *Brown v Smitt* (1924) 34 CLR 160, 167–68; *Coastal Estates Pty Ltd v Melevende* [1965] VR 433 (Full Ct) 436–37, 443, 452; *Kramer v McMahon* [1970] 1 NSWLR 194, 210; *Re Hoffman ex p Worrell v Schilling* (Full FCA, 14 August 1989); *Cockerill v Westpac Banking Corporation* (1996) 142 ALR 227 (FCA) 281–82; *Scheur v Bell* [2004] VSC 71 [247]–[249]. In New Zealand, *Kenny v Fenton* [1971] NZLR 1 (CA) 16–18. In Canada, *Kupchak v Dayson Holdings Co Ltd* (1965) 53 DLR (2d) 482 (BCCA) 491–95.
[152] *Iron Trades Mutual Insurance Co Ltd v Companhia de Seguros Imperio* [1992] 1 Lloyd's Rep IR 213, 225.
[153] *Strive Shipping Corporation v Hellenic Mutual War Risks Association (The Grecia Express)* [2002] 2 Lloyd's Rep 88, 163.
[154] *WISE (Underwriting Agency) Ltd v Grupo Nacional Provincial SA* [2004] 2 Lloyd's Rep 483 (CA) (insurance); *ZX Group Pty Ltd v LPD Corporation Pty Ltd* [2013] VSC 542 [121]–[123] (purchase of land).
[155] *Champtaloup v Thomas* (1976) 2 NSWLR 264 (CA) 269 (contractual right to 'rescind'), followed *Re Hoffman ex p Worrell v Schilling* (Full FCA, 14 August 1989) [17] (fraud).
[156] *SK Shipping Europe plc v Capital VLCC 3 Corp* [2021] 2 Lloyd's Rep 109 [203](vii); *SK Shipping Europe plc v Capital VLCC 3 Corp ("C Challenger")* [2022] EWCA Civ 231 [73] (principles not challenged on appeal).
[157] *Tapp v Galway* (2007) 8 NZCPR 684 [24], [37]–[40], [54] (rescission for misrepresentation under s 7(3) of the Contractual Remedies Act 1979 (NZ)—see now the Contract and Commercial Law Act 2017); cf *Overland Development Limited v Ronghuan Dong* [2018] NZHC 2225 [111]–[113] (nomination of purchaser was unequivocal affirmation, and distinguishing *Tapp v Galway*).

Remaining in possession

Where premises or a business have been acquired under a voidable contract, and after learning of the material facts the purchaser remains in possession or continues to operate the business, that may constitute affirmation. But it also may not, and much depends on the circumstances surrounding the decision. It has been held that there was no affirmation where the innocent party had a limited choice in the matter,[158] and there is Australian authority that this includes cases where continuing to operate a business is necessary to preserve its value.[159] Nor will it be affirmation if the surrounding circumstances indicate that no election is being made;[160] in particular, if the business is operated or possession maintained following a communicated election to rescind.[161]

23.71

Similar principles have been applied to sales of chattels. In the Canadian case of *Kellogg Brown & Root Inc v Aerotech Herman Nelson Inc*[162] a plea of affirmation was rejected in circumstances where the buyer of portable heaters used them with full knowledge of the misrepresentations, but in circumstances where it had no practical alternative to do otherwise. The heaters in question were urgently needed by American soldiers stationed in Hungary during winter.

23.72

Where these factors are not in play, remaining in possession or continuing to operate a business with full awareness of the misrepresentation or other ground for rescission may constitute affirmation.[163] The position is the same for chattels purchased, and where prompt action is generally required. In the Australian case of *Russo v Beclar Pty Ltd*[164] the retention of a Ferrari motor car for four years following alleged misrepresentations was held to amount to a binding affirmation,[165] and the Full Court observed that '[A]ny rescission must be made within a reasonable time. More than four years is, on any view, grossly unreasonable'.[166] The

23.73

---

[158] *Erlanger v The New Sombrero Phosphate Company* (1878) 3 App Cas 1218, 1261 (purchase of phosphate extraction business procured by breach of fiduciary duty—remaining in possession and working the property 'an inevitable necessity under the circumstances'); *Kupchak v Dayson Holdings Co Ltd* (1965) 53 DLR (2d) 482 (BCCA) 492 (purchasers of motel no practical alternative to continuing to operate it); *Tenji v Henneberry & Associates Pty Ltd* (2000) 98 FCR 324 (Full Ct), 351 ('little choice' but to retain possession of service station purchased; claim to rescind under Trade Practices Act 1974 s 87 (now s 243 of Sched 2 of the Competition and Consumer Act 2010)).

[159] *Alati v Kruger* (1955) 94 CLR 216, 225 (purchaser might lose right to rescind if he vacates premises and unconscientiously allows value to be destroyed); *Evans v Benson & Co* [1961] WAR 12 (Full Ct) 15–16 (preserving leasehold by paying rent); *Coastal Estates Pty Ltd v Melevende* [1965] VR 433 (Full Ct) 436, 445 (paying rates after election to rescind to preserve value of land purchased).

[160] *Kramer v McMahon* [1970] 1 NSWLR 194, 210 (executory purchase of rural bakery induced by misrepresentation) buyer let into possession before completion, and continued possession after becoming aware of truth 'not referable to an election to accept the situation as it emerged at all'.

[161] *Kenny v Fenton* [1971] NZLR 1 (CA) 16–17, 38 (purchase of motel procured by fraud); *Koutsonicolis v Principe (No 2)* (1987) 48 SASR 328, 329 (purchase of dwelling house procured by fraud; buyers remained in possession for six years after proceedings commenced); *Coastal Estates Pty Ltd v Melevende* [1965] VR 433 (Full Ct) 445.

[162] (2004) 238 DLR (4th) 594 (Man CA) 608–13.

[163] *Lagunas Nitrate Company v Lagunas Syndicate* [1899] 2 Ch 392 (CA) 464 (no 'inevitable necessity' in way that company worked mine); *Sargent v Campbell* (1972) Arg LR 708 (HCA) 711 (remaining in possession of boarding house for one month after discovering misrepresentation as to numbers); *Shortt v MacLennan* (1959) SCR 3 (remaining in possession of farm 18 months after discovery of misrepresentation); *Bertrand v Racicot* [1979] 1 SCR 441, 458 (acting for several months as owner involved affirmation of defect in title); *Kupchak v Dayson Holdings Co Ltd* (1965) 53 DLR (2d) 448 (BCCA) 500–501 (continuing to operate motel after discovering truth as to turnover was affirmation—per Sheppard JA, dissenting).

[164] (2011) 111 SASR 459 (Full Ct).

[165] *Russo v Beclar Pty Ltd* (2011) 111 SASR 459 (Full Ct) [11], [19].

[166] *Russo v Beclar Pty Ltd* (2011) 111 SASR 459 (Full Ct) [11]. The purchaser had also made warranty claims under the purchase agreement, and had in addition also failed to establish facts that would entitle him to rescind.

Retaining money repayable upon rescission

23.74 In *Clough v London and North Western Railway Co*[167] the court observed that the jury would have been unlikely to find that the defrauded vendor had affirmed simply by retaining sums repayable on rescission. But it was also said *obiter* that a positive refusal to repay money due upon rescission, when the other party had indicated a willingness to accept it back, might constitute a binding affirmation.[168]

23.75 An insurer's retention of premium income after becoming aware of facts justifying rescission is not itself an affirmation of the contract. But refusal to pay a claim while not electing to rescind and return the premium is evidence of an intent to affirm.[169]

Receiving contractual payments

23.76 An insurer's acceptance of premium income after becoming aware of actionable misrepresentation or non-disclosure is good evidence of affirmation.[170] The acceptance of dividends by a shareholder aware of relevant misstatements has likewise been held to be disentitling affirmation.[171] But passively receiving contractual payments after becoming aware of the material facts may not always involve an election to affirm; and it did not where the sums were instalments automatically credited to the defrauded buyer's account.[172]

Making contractual payments

23.77 In *The Atlantic Baron*[173] Mocatta J held that the purchaser's delay in seeking rescission after the cessation of circumstances involving duress, coupled with the making of final instalment payments without protest, were unequivocal acts of affirmation. In *Marme Inversiones 2007 SL v Natwest Markets plc*[174] it was held that the making of an instalment payment with knowledge of the relevant facts and of the right to rescind involved 'action about as inconsistent with rescission as it is possible to imagine'.[175] Payment of a loss under an insurance policy has been described as 'as clear an affirmation as one could want'.[176] In another case it was held that the mere fact that the party entitled to rescind wished for its own commercial reasons to wait until a new service provider could be engaged, in order to prevent the

---

[167] (1871) LR 7 Ex 26, 37–38.
[168] *Clough v London and North Western Railway Co* (1871) LR 7 Ex 26, 37.
[169] *Spriggs v Wessington Court Schools Ltd* [2005] 1 Lloyd's Rep IR 474, 479. See also N Legh-Jones (ed), *MacGillivray on Insurance Law* (12th edn, 2012) [17-095]–[17-096].
[170] *Spriggs v Wessington Court Schools Ltd* [2005] 1 Lloyd's Rep IR 474. In Australia, *Goodwin v State Government Insurance Office (Qld)* [1994] 2 QdR 15, 22 (Full Ct).
[171] *Scholey v Central Railway Co of Venezuela* (1868) LR 9 Eq 266; 39 LJ Ch 354, approved *Haas Timber & Trading Co Pty Ltd v Wade* (1954) 94 CLR 593, 602.
[172] *Re Hoffman ex p Worrell v Schilling* (Full FCA, 14 August 1989) [13–20] (receipt of monthly payments pursuant to voidable investment in drilling business).
[173] *North Ocean Shipping Co Ltd v Hyundai Construction Co Ltd (The Atlantic Baron)* [1979] 1 QB 705, 721; applied eg *Resorts World v Lee Fook Kheun* [2018] SGHC 173 [57]–[58] (instalment payments of gambling debt over five-year period, signing settlement agreement, and making further payments thereunder).
[174] [2019] EWHC 366 (Comm).
[175] *Marme Inversiones 2007 SL v Natwest Markets plc* [2019] EWHC 366 (Comm) [331] (instalment under swaps contract said to be vitiated by manipulation of LIBOR paid in order to prevent the counterparty terminating the agreement at that point).
[176] *Svenska Handelsbanken v Sun Alliance and London Insurance plc* [1996] 1 Lloyd's Rep 519, 569 (Rix J).

disruption of its business, did not prevent its conduct, in making payments and receiving benefits under the voidable contract, from amounting to an irrevocable election to affirm the contract with the existing service provider.[177]

23.78 The paying of sums other than in accordance with the strict terms of the contract might evince an unequivocal intention to affirm; whether it does so must depend on the circumstances in which the payment was made. In *Peyman v Lanjani*[178] the innocent purchaser paid £10,000 at the vendor's request and not in accordance with the contract. That did not involve affirmation because at the time of payment the purchaser was unaware of the defect in title.[179]

Conduct of litigation

23.79 Affirmation may occur by reason of the way in which litigation is conducted, as where correspondence between solicitors treats the contract as valid and the pleading admits certain contractual obligations,[180] or seeks damages for their breach,[181] or where orders are obtained from the court consistent only with the transaction remaining on foot.[182]

23.80 It is however a prerequisite that the party entitled to rescind is aware of the material facts. Conduct prior to or after proceedings have been commenced will not constitute affirmation if made without that knowledge. A failure to rescind during a period of investigation is therefore usually not evidence of affirmation; nor will it add to a plea of laches or acquiescence. This principle is recognized both in the context of insurance,[183] and in other cases of misrepresentation and non-disclosure.[184]

23.81 In *Erlanger v The New Sombrero Phosphate Company*[185] Lord Blackburn said that a company's voidable purchase of a phosphate-bearing island and works was not affirmed by a resolution that adopted a report by an investigating committee, which had in turn recommended the recovery of damages, but made no mention of rescission. At that point in time, the company had not had the opportunity to properly assess its position or to consult with advisers.

---

[177] *Mototrak Ltd v FCA Australia Pty Ltd* [2018] EWHC 990 (Comm) [81], [82].
[178] [1985] Ch 457 (CA).
[179] *Peyman v Lanjani* [1985] Ch 457 (CA) 502.
[180] *Moore Large & Co Ltd v Hermes Credit & Guarantee plc* [2003] 1 Lloyd's Rep IR 315, 334.
[181] *Insurance Corporation of the Channel Islands Ltd v The Royal Hotel Limited* [1998] 7 Lloyd's Rep IR 151, 161, 174. Cf *Occidental Worldwide Investment Corp v Skibs A/S Avanti (The Siboen and Sibotre)* [1976] 1 Lloyd's Rep 293, 336 (seeking to uphold an agreement in an arbitration and later attempting to rescind it for duress). Contrast *O'Kane v Jones (The Martin P)* [2005] 1 Lloyd's Rep IR 174, 225–26 (conduct of litigation not unequivocal affirmation); *Gamatronic (UK) Limited v Hamilton* [2016] EWHC 2225 (QB) [226] (failure to seek rescission in letter before action or original pleading not consistent only with choice to affirm contract).
[182] *First National Bank plc v Walker* [2001] FLR 21 (CA) (wife recognizing validity of charge in matrimonial proceedings, subsequently seeking to rescind in possession proceedings by mortgagee; barred by election or as abuse of process).
[183] *McCormick v National Motor and Accident Insurance* (1934) 49 Lloyd's Rep 362 (CA) 365 (Scrutton LJ); *Insurance Corporation of the Channel Islands Ltd v McHugh and Royal Hotel Limited* [1997] Lloyd's Re Ins LR 94, 132 (Mance J); *Callaghan and Hedges t/a Stage 3 Discotheque v Syndicate 1049 and Anderson Insurance Services Ltd* [2000] Lloyd's Rep IR 125, 133.
[184] *Erlanger v The New Sombrero Phosphate Company* (1878) LR 3 App Cas 1218, 1251–53, 1258–59; *Lagunas Nitrate Company v Lagunas Syndicate* [1899] 2 Ch 392 (CA) 454; *Senanayake v Cheng* [1966] AC 63 (PC—Singapore) 79; *Fiona Trust & Holding Corporation v Privalov* [2007] 1 All ER (Comm) 81 [36].
[185] (1878) 3 App Cas 1218, 1282.

23.82 Affirmation was not inferred when an insurer had indicated that it had not ascertained the terms of the policy and it was clear that they had not accepted liability.[186] The courts may also be slower to infer an election to affirm if the litigation was part of a reasonable attempt to protect assets purchased under the voidable transaction.[187]

No affirmation from pleading rescission in the alternative

23.83 A claim or pleading that seeks to enforce contractual rights as an alternative to a claim or plea for rescission does not involve affirmation,[188] and this includes pleading a contractual defence by a party free to later plead rescission.[189]

Requesting, consenting to, or undertaking work on property acquired

23.84 Authorities concerned with this fact pattern demonstrate the essentially factual nature of the inquiry as to whether there has been an election to affirm, and the importance of the surrounding circumstances. In *Abram Steamship Company Limited v Westville Shipping Company Limited*[190] the buyer of a ship under construction had sent letters to the yard consenting to certain alterations they had proposed. This was held to be not sufficiently unequivocal in all the circumstances, and the buyers were entitled to rescind for essential error.[191] *Watson v Burton*[192] involved the purchase of a misdescribed property. Wynn-Parry J held that the buyer's requests that the vendor carry out certain work and repairs, including to damage to and leaks in the roof, was when looked at against the whole background, also not an unequivocal election to affirm.[193] In *Evans v Benson & Co*,[194] an Australian case, the buyer's actions in completing improvements to a shed after discovery of the vendor's misrepresentations was held to not amount to affirmation of the purchase.[195]

Instructions as to insured property and rights to inspect

23.85 Giving instructions to an assured concerning the subject matter of the insurance is normally good evidence of the affirmation of a voidable policy,[196] but merely requesting further information or exercising a contractual right to inspect may not be, depending upon the circumstances.[197] It seems that if an underwriter is exercising rights of inspection and it is

---

[186] *Spriggs v Wessington Court Schools Ltd* [2005] 1 Lloyd's Rep IR 474, 488.
[187] *Imperial Ottoman Bank v Trustees, Executors and Securities Investment Corp* [1895] WN 23 (bank participating in action to enforce debentures, subsequently sought to be rescinded).
[188] *Clough v The London and North Western Railway Company* [1871] LR 8 Ex 26, 38; *Coastal Estates Pty Ltd v Melevende* [1965] VR 433 (Full Ct) 440, 450.
[189] *Involnert Management Inc v Aprilgrange Limited* [2015] 2 Lloyd's Rep 289 [179] (underwriters defending claim on insurance policy; contractual defences pleaded whilst investigations into non-disclosure and misrepresentation were ongoing).
[190] [1923] AC 773.
[191] *Abram Steamship Company Limited v Westville Shipping Company Limited* [1923] AC 773, 779, 789.
[192] [1957] 1 WLR 19. The case concerned termination for breach, described as 'rescission'.
[193] *Watson v Burton* [1957] 1 WLR 19, 29–30.
[194] [1961] WAR 12 (Full Ct) 15.
[195] Contrast *Russo v Beclar Pty Ltd* (2011) 111 SASR 459 (Full Ct) [11], [19] where retaining possession of a Ferrari motor vehicle coupled with the making of warranty claims gave rise to a binding affirmation of the purchase, barring any claim for rescission that may have existed.
[196] *Svenska Handelsbanken v Sun Alliance and London Insurance plc* [1996] 1 Lloyd's Rep 519, 569; *Spriggs v Wessington Court Schools Ltd* [2005] 1 Lloyd's Rep IR 474, 479. It may equally be good evidence of waiver of contractual rights in favour of the insurer: *Colonial Mutual Fire Insurance Company Limited* (1920) 28 CLR 305, 325.
[197] *Strive Shipping Corporation v Hellenic Mutual War Risks Association (The Grecia Express)* [2002] 2 Lloyd's Rep 88, 162–63 (exercising rights of inspection not affirmation). This approach is consistent with the principle that an insurer has a reasonable time to undertake investigations, and to make up its mind whether to avoid or not: *McCormick v National Motor and Accident Insurance* (1934) 49 Lloyd's Rep 362 (CA) 365–66. *Strive Shipping*

objectively apparent that this is being done for the purpose of ascertaining the true factual position or to decide what course of action to take, the conduct will ordinarily not be affirmatory. Conversely, if the rights are exercised when the insurer knows the relevant facts and of the right to rescind and has had a reasonable time to decide whether to rescind, exercising rights of inspection may well demonstrate unequivocally that the contract is to be maintained and so cause the right to rescind to be lost.[198]

Reselling and intending or attempting to resell property acquired

The resale of property purchased by the party entitled to rescind, if made with knowledge of the relevant facts and otherwise free of the vitiating factor, will generally amount to an affirmation of the contract.[199] **23.86**

On the other hand, merely intending or attempting to resell may not, even though the true facts are known. In *Brown v Smitt*[200] a letter from the purchaser of a grazing property to his fraudulent vendor indicating an intention to on-sell was, in the circumstances, not sufficiently unequivocal. In another case it was held that the unsuccessful attempts by a defrauded buyer of vacant land to on-sell the land was not a binding affirmation.[201] Rescission was permitted in both cases. **23.87**

These decisions may be contrasted with *Brigg*'s case.[202] There Lord Romilly MR held that a shareholder's instructions to his broker to sell shares in a hop warehousing company, bought on the faith of a misleading prospectus, was 'an acquiescence in' the company's misrepresentation, even though the shares were not in fact sold. The result in *Brigg*'s case reflects the special fragility of the right to rescind voidable allotments of partly paid shares. A shareholder must promptly disaffirm or lose the right. The rule is underpinned by the need to protect the interests of creditors and other shareholders.[203] The contrast between the different results in cases concerning land and shares is best understood as turning on the different policy considerations that are engaged in each type of case. **23.88**

Attempting to rescind in part may be affirmation

An attempt to elect to rescind part and to affirm another part of a contract is ineffective as an election to rescind, unless the part sought to be rescinded is so severable as to be an **23.89**

---

was distinguished in *Involnert Management Inc v Aprilgrange Limited* [2015] 2 Lloyd's Rep 289 [171]–[178] (where Leggatt J said that it was inconsistent with *Iron Trades Mutual v Compania de Seguros Imperio* [1991] 1 Re LR 213, 223–24 which illustrates the true principle: at [171], [178]); see also *SK Shipping Europe plc v Capital VLCC 3 Corp* [2021] 2 Lloyd's Rep 109 [203](viii) (summary of principles not challenged on appeal, *SK Shipping Europe plc v Capital VLCC 3 Corp ('C Challenger')* [2022] EWCA Civ 231 [73]).

[198] *Involnert Management Inc v Aprilgrange Limited* [2015] 2 Lloyd's Rep 289 [171]–[178] and the other authorities in the preceding note. The point is likely to be of less practical importance following the enactment of the Insurance Act 2015, which cuts down an insurer's right to rescind: see Chap 5, paras [5.35]–[5.39].
[199] Eg *Re Cape Breton Company* (1885) 29 ChD 795 (CA) 803, 811 (resale of land purchased by company under a contract voidable for breach of fiduciary duty). As to when a resale bars rescission because it makes *restitutio in integrum* impossible, see Chap 18, para [18.48]ff.
[200] (1924) 34 CLR 160, 167–168.
[201] *Coastal Estates Pty Ltd v Melevende* [1965] VR 433 (Full Ct) 437.
[202] *Re Hop and Malt Exchange and Warehouse Company, ex p Briggs* [1866] LR 1 Eq Cas 483, referred to with apparent approval in *Directors of the Central Railway Company of Venezuela v Kisch* (1867) LR 2 App Cas 99, 112 (Lord Chelmsford LC), and by the High Court of Australia in *Haas Timber & Trading Co Pty Ltd v Wade* (1954) 94 CLR 593, 601 (Dixon CJ, Fullagar and Kitto JJ).
[203] See further Chap 11, paras [11.50]–[11.52], Chap 24, paras [24.88]–[24.90].

independent contract.[204] Where that is not the case, an attempt to rescind part of a contract may amount to a binding affirmation of the whole,[205] and the first *Restatement of Restitution* concludes that this will be so whenever there is conduct inconsistent with rescission of the whole transaction.[206] Whether English law will follow that strict approach remains to be seen, but there are indications that it will.[207]

Affirmation from inaction

23.90 Affirmation said to arise from inaction is subject to special rules. It is discussed separately in Chapter 24.

(3) Effect of reservation of rights

23.91 There is New Zealand authority to the effect that conduct which would otherwise amount to affirmation will not have that effect if made subject to express reservation of rights that follows a communicated election to rescind.[208] This is a sensible result, but remains subject to the general rule that the consequence of a reservation of rights always depends upon the particular circumstances of the case.[209]

23.92 Whether the result is the same if the reservation does not follow an election to rescind is less clear. If the matter is treated as analogous to a landlord's right to waive his right of re-entry following a tenant's acts of forfeiture, a mere reservation of rights should give no protection. Conduct otherwise manifesting an unequivocal intention to affirm will be a binding election irrespective of a prior reservation of the right to rescind.[210] But the strict position applied to election by landlords may well be peculiar to that context,[211] and there seems no unfairness in allowing the injured party to reserve his right to rescind, particularly when the other party is protected by the doctrine of estoppel and other established bars to rescission.

23.93 That is the approach taken in English insurance law. Conduct by an insurer that would otherwise amount to affirmation of a voidable policy will generally not have that effect if the insurer has first reserved its rights; and a failure to reserve is a factor to be taken into account in determining whether he has in fact affirmed.[212] Where a contract is voidable for

---

[204] *United Shoe Machinery Company of Canada v Brunet* [1909] AC 330 (PC—Canada) 340; *Potter v Dyer* [2011] EWCA Civ 1417 [58].

[205] [1909] AC 330 (PC—Canada) 340.

[206] *Restatement (First) of Restitution* 277 (1937): 'A manifestation of an intent to affirm one and to disaffirm another of non-severable parts of the same transaction is abortive ... If there is conduct inconsistent with entire avoidance, the fact that there is an intent not to affirm the entire transaction is ineffective and affirmance takes place.' The point appears not to have been discussed in the *Restatement (Third) of Restitution* (2011); cf at § 54(6) and cmt k (bar described in terms of prejudicial delay rather than affirmation or election).

[207] *Potter v Dyer* [2011] EWCA Civ 1417 [56]–[58]. See also *First National Bank plc v Walker* [2001] FLR 21 (CA).

[208] *Fenton v Kenny* [1969] NZLR 552, 557; *Kenny v Fenton* [1971] NZLR 1 (CA) 16.

[209] *SK Shipping Europe plc v Capital VLCC 3 Corp ('C Challenger')* [2022] EWCA Civ 231 [74]–[75].

[210] *Parker v Smallwood* [1910] 1 Ch 777, 786–87; *Central Estates (Belgravia) Ltd v Woolgar (No 2)* [1972] 1 WLR 1048.

[211] *Oliver Ashworth (Holdings) Ltd v Ballard (Kent) Ltd* [2000] Ch 12 (CA) 30; see also *O'Connor v SP Bray Limited* (1936) St Rep (NSW) 248, 259–60; *Champtaloup v Thomas* (1976) 2 NSWLR 264 (CA) 269; but cf *Craine v The Colonial Mutual Fire Insurance Company Limited* (1920) 28 CLR 305, 324–25; *Sargent v ASL Developments Ltd* (1974) 131 CLR 634, 646, which seem to treat the rule as applicable to election between rights generally.

[212] *Iron Trades Mutual Insurance Co Ltd v Companhia de Seguros Imperio* [1992] 1 Lloyd's Rep IR 213, 227; *Barber v Imperio Reinsurance Co (UK) Ltd* (CA, 15 July 1993); *Svenska Handelsbanken v Sun Alliance and London*

duress, the making of payments without protest after the duress has come to an end has also been held to be evidence of affirmation.[213] In contrast, continuing to trade a business for six weeks after learning of the right to rescind for fraudulent misrepresentation, and which would otherwise have amounted to a binding affirmation, was held to not involve an election when accompanied by a letter before action alleging fraud.[214] A reservation of rights has also been held to be important in determining whether a party entitled to exercise a contractual right to terminate has lost the right by affirmation.[215]

23.94 The principles were considered by Mr Justice Foxton in *SK Shipping Europe plc v Capital VLCC 3 Corp*,[216] whose analysis was affirmed by the Court of Appeal.[217] Charterers sought to rescind a time charterparty for misrepresentations about the vessel's speed and fuel consumption. Foxton J noted the rules applicable to a landlord's right to waive his right of re-entry following a tenant's acts of forfeiture[218] and the authorities to different effect in the English insurance cases,[219] before going on to conclude that some acts are so intrinsically affirmatory that performing them will cause the contract to be affirmed even if they take place under a reservation of rights.[220]

23.95 It was held that whilst a reservation of rights will often have the effect of preventing subsequent conduct constituting an election, this is not an invariable rule.[221] Whether there has been an election requires the court to have regard to all the material, including any reservations that have been communicated. Where conduct is consistent with the reservation of a right to rescind, but also consistent with the continuation of the contract, then an express reservation will preclude the making of an election. This is likely to be the case where there is a reservation of rights accompanying the exercise of a contractual right to obtain information as to a party's rights, or where a party is performing its own obligations while

---

Insurance plc [1996] 1 Lloyd's Rep 519, 568–69; *Strive Shipping Corporation v Hellenic Mutual War Risks Association (The Grecia Express)* [2002] 2 Lloyd's Rep 88, 163. Contrast *Craine v The Colonial Mutual Fire Insurance Company Limited* (1920) 28 CLR 305, 324–25 (reservation of no consequence in assessing whether insurer had waived contractual right, applying the rule applied to forfeiture of leases).

[213] *North Ocean Shipping Co Ltd v Hyundai Construction Co Ltd (The Atlantic Baron)* [1979] 1 QB 705, 721. But in the context of duress, the absence of protest is also relevant to whether there has been any actionable duress: *Occidental Worldwide Investment Corp v Skibs A/S Avanti (The Siboen and Sibotre)* [1976] 1 Lloyd's Rep 293, 336.

[214] *Edwards v Ashik* [2014] EWHC 2454 (Ch); leave to appeal refused [2014] EWCA Civ 1704.

[215] *Champtaloup v Thomas* (1976) 2 NSWLR 264 (CA) 268–69 (requisitions as to title with reservation as to rights not an election to affirm the purchase). See also *QBE Insurance (Australia) Limited v Cape York Airlines Pty Ltd* [2012] 1 QdR 158 (CA) 167–68 (insurer's letters conveying an intention to repair a damaged aircraft subject to conditions is not a binding election to repair rather than pay for the item, because election requires conduct to be 'unqualified' as well as unequivocal).

[216] [2021] 2 Lloyd's Rep 109 [207]–[211].

[217] *SK Shipping Europe plc v Capital VLCC 3 Corp ('C Challenger')* [2022] EWCA Civ 231 [74]–[75].

[218] [2021] 2 Lloyd's Rep 109 [208], [209], and where it was said that these rules may reflect particular features of the landlord and tenant relationship.

[219] ibid at [209] and citing also para [23.88] of the second edition (which argued that a party entitled to rescind should always be able to protect himself against the risk of unintentional affirmation by expressly reserving the right to rescind), and noting also the different approach taken in New York in *McNaught v Equitable Life Insurance* 136 App Div 774, 777 (NY App Div, 1910).

[220] Ibid at [210]–[211], and observing (at [210]) '[t]o put it another way, are there some occasions when, to paraphrase Long Innes J in *Haynes v Hirst* (1927) 27 NSW (SR) 480, 489, a man who eats his cake will find it gone, nonetheless so because he ate it without prejudice?', affirmed *SK Shipping Europe plc v Capital VLCC 3 Corp ("C Challenger")* [2022] EWCA Civ 231 [75].

[221] *SK Shipping Europe plc v Capital VLCC 3 Corp* [2021] 2 Lloyd's Rep 109 [211]; *SK Shipping Europe plc v Capital VLCC 3 Corp ("Challenger C")* [2022] EWCA Civ 231 [74], [75].

506   VI. OTHER BARS

assessing its position. However, where a party makes an unconditional demand for substantial contractual performance of a kind which will lead the counterparty and/or third parties to alter their positions in significant respects, such conduct may be wholly incompatible with the reservation of some kinds of rights, even if the party demanding performance purports at the same time to reserve them. Likewise, delay in exercising a right to rescind is also capable of causing the right to be lost by affirmation notwithstanding a purported reservation of rights.[222]

23.96 It was held that the charterer's actions in fixing the vessel for a long voyage—which required repositioning her from Europe to South East Asia, and would involve the owners in interactions with third parties and exposure to risks as the vessel loaded, carried, and discharged the cargo—involved an unequivocal affirmation of the contract notwithstanding the charterer's reservation of its rights.[223] The charterer's conduct was so inherently affirmatory that it was incompatible with an attempt to reserve a right to set the charterparty aside *ab initio*.[224]

(4) Possibility of affirming after an election to rescind

23.97 Although the authorities are mostly to the contrary, in principle the act of disaffirming a transaction not voidable at common law ought not constitute an irrevocable election to rescind.[225] That is because, as explained in Chapter 11, when a transaction is voidable only in equity, rescission does not automatically follow from the act of disaffirming, and the right to court orders that effect rescission may be lost by subsequent events.[226] If this is correct, in such cases it should be possible for the innocent party to affirm and sue on the transaction after having chosen to rescind it,[227] unless the right to change direction has been lost by estoppel or waived. On the other hand, if rescission is fully effected by an election to disaffirm, that election is necessarily irrevocable. In cases of this kind it is, logically, no longer possible to affirm once there has been an effective election to rescind because the contract has gone.[228]

---

[222] Id., and it being observed that '[t]here are some contexts where actions speak louder than words'.
[223] *SK Shipping Europe plc v Capital VLCC 3 Corp* [2021] 2 Lloyd's Rep 109 [221], [222], [223], affirmed *SK Shipping Europe plc v Capital VLCC 3 Corp ('Challenger C')* [2022] EWCA Civ 231 [76]-[79] (conduct called for significant and prolonged performance of central contractual obligation in order to make a profit, and where any attempt later to rescind *ab initio*—as opposed to terminating *de futuro* without affecting accrued rights—would have given rise to significant difficulties).
[224] *SK Shipping Europe plc v Capital VLCC 3 Corp* [2021] 2 Lloyd's Rep 109 [223], affirmed *SK Shipping Europe plc v Capital VLCC 3 Corp ('Challenger C')* [2022] EWCA Civ 231 [76]-[78]
[225] Cf affirmation, which involves waiver and is necessarily irrevocable: para [23.95].
[226] See Chap 11, paras [11.113]-[11.117].
[227] *Radferry Pty Ltd v Starborne Holdings Pty Ltd*, (Full FCA, 18 December 1998) (purchaser resiled from election to rescind and sought relief on the basis the contract was on foot); *Restatement (First) of Restitution* § 68(2) and cmt thereto at p 282 (1937); also, *Restatement (Third) of Restitution* § 54(6) and cmt k (vol 2, pp 286-87, 294-96) (2011). Cf *Scheur v Bell* [2004] VSC 71 [245], [248].
[228] *Scheur v Bell* [2004] VSC 71 [250], [261] (rescission occurred when an election to rescind made; held that affirmatory conduct must occur before that election). Cf *Clough v London and North Western Railway Co* (1871) LR 7 Ex 26, 37.

G. Intention to Affirm is not Required

(1) General rule

23.98 The doctrine of election between rights generally permits an election to be made irrespective of intention. Unequivocal conduct communicated to the other party effects a binding election 'whether he intended it or not'.[229]

23.99 The right to rescind may likewise be lost by an election to affirm even though that was not intended. The leading descriptions of the bar make no reference to intention,[230] and that intention is not necessary is demonstrated by several cases.[231] In *The Atlantic Baron*,[232] for instance, the right to rescind for duress was lost by conduct amounting to affirmation even though the arbitral tribunal had found that the party imposed upon had never intended to affirm, or to waive any of their rights, and in fact believed that their conduct preserved them. Mocatta J held that this did not matter: 'I do not think that an intention on the part of the owners not to affirm the agreement for the extra payments not indicated to the Yard can avail them in view of their overt acts.'[233]

23.100 Similarly in *Law v Law*[234] the plaintiff had deliberately waited for payments to be made under a contract before commencing proceedings to rescind for breach of fiduciary duty. This was held to bar relief: 'it is now too late for William to repudiate the contract of which he has thus deliberately secured the benefits.'[235] Likewise, the conduct of insurers in connection with protracted litigation has been held to amount to affirmation, even though they and their legal advisers had internally decided to not affirm.[236]

(2) Where affirming conduct is not known to other party

23.101 The conclusion reached earlier is that conduct suggesting an election to affirm should, in general, be communicated if it is to be a binding affirmation.[237] If that is wrong, the law permits the right to rescind to be lost even if the affirming party did not intend to affirm,[238] and the other party was unaware of the affirmatory conduct. Although this seems a highly technical result, and with no obvious justification, there is authority in support of it. In *Brigg's* case[239] Brigg's instructions to his broker to sell the shares that he had been misled into buying, and which the broker was unable to do because dealings in the shares had been

---

[229] *Scarfe v Jardine* (1882) 7 App Cas 345, 361; *Kammins Ballrooms Co Ltd v Zenith Investments (Torquay) Ltd* [1971] AC 850, 883 'the law holds him to his choice even though he was unaware that this would be the legal consequence of what he did' (Lord Diplock). In Australia, *Tropical Traders Ltd v Goonan* (1964) 111 CLR 41, 55 'not that election is a matter of intention. It is an effect which the law annexes to conduct ...'; *Sargent v ASL Developments Ltd* (1974) 131 CLR 634, 646.
[230] *Clough v London and North Western Railway Co* (1871) LR 7 Ex 26, 34.
[231] See also *Champtaloup v Thomas* [1976] 2 NSWLR 264 (CA) 274–75; *Zucker v Straightlace Pty Ltd* (1986) 11 NSWLR 87, 93 (contractual rights to 'rescind').
[232] *North Ocean Shipping Co Ltd v Hyundai Construction Co Ltd (The Atlantic Baron)* [1979] QB 705.
[233] *North Ocean Shipping Co Ltd v Hyundai Construction Co Ltd (The Atlantic Baron)* [1979] QB 705, 721.
[234] [1905] Ch 140 (CA).
[235] *Law v Law* [1905] Ch 140 (CA) 159. This was one of several factors leading to the conclusion that the right to rescind had been lost. It is unclear whether by itself this conduct would have been sufficient.
[236] *Insurance Corporation of the Channel Islands Ltd v The Royal Hotel Ltd* [1998] 7 Lloyd's Rep IR 151, 175.
[237] See para [23.60].
[238] See para [23.99].
[239] *Re Hop and Malt Exchange and Warehouse Company, ex p Briggs* [1866] LR 1 Eq Cas 483.

suspended, was held to be an acquiescence in the allotting company's misrepresentation, notwithstanding that the company was apparently ignorant of Brigg's actions, and there was no indication that he wished to give up the right to rescind if his shares could not be sold.[240] The decision is probably confined to the special case of subscriptions for partly paid shares, where the right to rescind is particularly fragile.

(3) Relation to awareness of rights

23.102 The relationship between the principle that an election may be made without intending to do so and the requirement for an awareness of the right to rescind is problematic. If an awareness of rights is essential its function cannot be to preserve the right to rescind until an informed choice is made, for the right may be lost without that. Rather, and counter-intuitively, the rule simply qualifies what conduct can count as affirmation, but by reference to facts that are exclusively within the knowledge of the electing party. The explanation for this is not obvious. It militates against a requirement that the affirming party must know of his right to rescind.

H. Affirmation is Generally Irrevocable

(1) General rule

23.103 The general rule is that the affirmation of a voidable contract or gift is irrevocable.[241]

(2) Exception where subsequent discovery of new ground for rescission

23.104 To this rule there is an exception where the innocent party discovers a further misrepresentation or non-disclosure justifying rescission. In some cases of this kind the innocent party has been permitted to rescind notwithstanding an earlier affirmation;[242] in others, they have not been.[243]

---

[240] *Re Hop and Malt Exchange and Warehouse Company, ex p Briggs* [1866] LR 1 Eq Cas 483. See also *Spriggs v Wessington Court Schools Ltd* [2005] 1 Lloyd's Rep IR 474, 484.

[241] *Clough v London and North Western Railway Co* (1871) LR 7 Ex 26, 34; *Allcard v Skinner* (1887) 36 ChD 145 (CA) 186–87, 193 (gift); *Johnson v Agnew* [1980] AC 367, 399; *Peyman v Lanjani* [1985] Ch 457 (CA) 494, 500 (comments apparently intended to refer to rescission *ab initio*); *Drake Insurance plc v Provident Insurance plc* [2003] 1 Lloyd's Rep IR 781, 789 (insurance); *SK Shipping Europe plc v Capital VLCC 3 Corp ('Challenger C')* [2022] EWCA Civ 231 [79]. In Australia, *Tropical Traders Ltd v Goonan* (1964) 111 CLR 41, 55 (contractual right to 'rescind'); *Coastal Estates Pty Ltd v Melevende* [1965] VR 433 (Full Ct) 443, 451 (fraud). In New Zealand, *Kenny v Fenton* [1971] NZLR 1 (CA) 16–17.

[242] *Re The London and Provincial Electric Lighting and Power Generating Company Limited; ex p Hale* (1887) 55 LT (NS) 670 (false prospectus case, distinguishing *Whitehouse's case*); *Black King Shipping Corporation and Wayang (Panama) SA v Mark Ranald Massie (The Litsion Pride)* [1985] 1 Lloyd's Rep 437, 517 (insurance); *Involnert Management Inc v Aprilgrange Limited* [2015] 2 Lloyd's Rep 289 [169]. In Australia, *Elder's Trustee and Executor Company Limited v Commonwealth Homes and Investment Co Ltd* (1941) 65 CLR 603, 616–17 (statutory rights to rescind); *Southern Cross Mine Management Pty Ltd v Ensham Resources Pty Ltd* [2005] QSC 233 [631] (breach of fiduciary duty); *Moore v The National Mutual Life Association of Australasia Limited* [2011] NSWSC 416 [81], [83], [95] (insurance). In Canada, *Boulter v Stocks* (1913) 47 SCR 440 (misled buyer of farm discovered third misrepresentation, as to actual acreage, after leasing orchard with knowledge of other misrepresentations, distinguishing *Campbell v Fleming* (1834) 1 Ad & E 40).

[243] *Campbell v Fleming* (1834) 1 Ad & E 40, 110 ER 1122 (new incidents of same fraud); *Re Russian (Vyksounsky) Ironworks Company, Whitehouse's case* [1867] LR 3 Eq 790 (false prospectus case); *Law v Law* [1905] Ch 140 (CA)

New information must provide a ground for rescission

For rescission to be possible in this situation, it seems necessary for the new information 23.105 discovered to provide an independent ground for rescission.[244] If it consists only of new incidents of the fraud known about when the affirmatory conduct occurred, or further corroborative evidence, or immaterial matters, or discovery that the misrepresentation was fraudulent, that is not enough.[245] It has also been said that where there are two misrepresentations, they must not be closely connected.[246]

Causal significance of new information for earlier affirmation

There is some support for the proposition that there can be no rescission if the evidence 23.106 indicates that when the innocent party affirmed, he took the risk that further material information would come to light.[247]

It has also been said that the new information coming to light must, as well as providing a 23.107 separate ground for rescission, be such that had it been known it would have made a material difference to the decision to affirm.[248] That was in the context of a voidable contract of insurance where it had been held that the underwriter was required to know of its right to rescind. Whether new information coming to light would have made a difference to the affirming party's conduct can only sensibly be ascertained if a conscious choice to affirm had previously been made. However, a binding election to affirm a voidable contract is often made without conscious choice. Outside cases where there was a conscious choice, is it necessary to show any causal nexus between the new information and prior affirmatory conduct? There is Australian authority that no causal nexus need be shown. It has been held that an inquiry into whether the new information would have made a difference is appropriate only if the electing party both knew of his right to rescind when the confirmatory

---

158 (breach of fiduciary duty). In Australia, *Coastal Estates Pty Ltd v Melevende* [1965] VR 433 (Full Ct) 442 (fraud).

[244] *Spriggs v Wessington Court Schools Ltd* [2005] 1 Lloyd's Rep IR 474, 489 (insurance). In Australia, *Elder's Trustee and Executor Company Limited v Commonwealth Homes and Investment Co Ltd* (1941) 65 CLR 603, 616–17; *Evans v Benson & Co* [1961] WAR 12 (Full Ct) 15. That is also the view in *Restatement (First) of Restitution* 278–79 (1937). Similarly, in *Boulter v Stocks* (1913) 47 SCR 440, the Supreme Court of Canada emphasized that the information coming to light after the purchaser's affirmatory conduct qualified as a separate ground for rescission.

[245] *Campbell v Fleming* (1834) 1 Ad & E 40, 110 ER 1122; *Black King Shipping Corporation and Wayang (Panama) SA v Mark Ranald Massie (The Litsion Pride)* [1985] 1 Lloyd's Rep 437, 516–17; *Spriggs v Wessington Court Schools Ltd* [2005] 1 Lloyd's Rep IR 474, 489. In Australia, *Evans v Benson & Co* [1961] WAR 12 (Full Ct) 15; *Southern Cross Mine Management Pty Ltd v Ensham Resources Pty Ltd* [2005] QSC 233 [631]. In *Moore v The National Mutual Life Association of Australasia Limited* [2011] NSWSC 416 [85] Ball J said that an insurer should know whether a misrepresentation was innocent or fraudulent before making a choice, but that statement was *obiter* because the insurer in fact lacked knowledge of the misrepresentations when it affirmed the policy (at [83], [93]–[95]), and is contrary to the reasons in *Evans v Benson & Co* [1961] WAR 12 (Full Ct) 15.

[246] *Evans v Benson & Co* [1961] WAR 12 (Full Ct) 15.

[247] *Law v Law* [1905] Ch 140 (CA) 158 (election to affirm by compromise taking risk of further information coming to light). In Australia, *Coastal Estates Pty Ltd v Melevende* [1965] VR 433 (Full Ct) 442 (affirming without full knowledge but correctly assuming the falsity of representations prevents rescission when true facts are discovered); *Elder's Trustee and Executor Company Limited v Commonwealth Homes and Investment Co Ltd* (1941) 65 CLR 603, 616–17. Also, *Restatement (First) of Restitution* 278 (1937): 'A voidable transaction can be affirmed without knowledge of the facts if, and only if, the one affirming assumes the risk of error.'

[248] *Spriggs v Wessington Court Schools Ltd* [2005] 1 Lloyd's Rep IR 474, 489: new non-disclosure must 'make a material difference to the reasonable insurer's decision whether to affirm or to avoid the policy', applied *Involnert Management Inc v Aprilgrange Limited* [2015] 2 Lloyd's Rep 289 [169] (non-disclosure to underwriters of yacht destroyed by fire).

Status of first affirmation

23.108 If the innocent party knows enough to elect, his affirmation is fully effective subject to any right to revoke it when further material information is discovered. The first *Restatement of Restitution* described this situation as one where the innocent party has a right to rescind the affirmation,[250] and there might be some support for this view in the judgment of Rigby LJ in *Lagunas Nitrate Company v Lagunas Syndicate*.[251] However, it seems simpler to regard the initial affirmation as revocable rather than voidable.

Right to rescind arising from totality of conduct

23.109 Where a course of conduct provides several independent grounds for rescission, the right to rescind might equally be preserved in favour of a party who affirms when aware of some but not all of the grounds, if the right to rescind is construed as arising from the totality of the defendant's conduct. When this analysis is adopted, conduct that is clearly affirmatory will not constitute a binding election unless the injured party is aware of all aspects of the wrongful conduct. There is no need to treat the case as one where a prior affirmation is revoked following the discovery of a new ground for rescission.[252]

I. Onus of Proof and Pleading

(1) Onus of proof

23.110 The onus of proving that a right to rescind has been lost by affirmation rests on the party against whom rescission is sought,[253] even if rescission is alleged as a defence rather than a claim.[254] This includes the onus of proving that the party entitled to rescind was aware of the material facts when the affirmatory conduct took place.[255] In those cases where affirmation

---

[249] *Elder's Trustee and Executor Company Limited v Commonwealth Homes and Investment Co Ltd* (1941) 65 CLR 603, 616–17, discussed *JAD International Pty Ltd v International Trucks Australia Limited* (1994) 50 FCR 378 (Full Ct) 389–91.

[250] *Restatement (First) of Restitution* 278–79 (1937). The point is not discussed in the *Restatement (Third) of Restitution* (2011); cf at § 54(6).

[251] [1899] 2 Ch 392 (CA) 452, where Rigby LJ referred to a confirmation being 'voidable' where the confirming party was not fully free of the vitiating factor.

[252] *Southern Cross Mine Management Pty Ltd v Ensham Resources Pty Ltd* [2005] QSC 233 [640]–[642] (breach of fiduciary duty); *Moore v The National Mutual Life Association of Australasia Limited* [2011] NSWSC 416 [81], [83], [93]–[95] (insurance).

[253] *Erlanger v The New Sombrero Phosphate Company* (1878) 3 App Cas 1218, 1283 (delay generally); *Aaron's Reefs Ltd v Twiss* [1896] AC 273, 294; *Peyman v Lanjani* [1985] Ch 457 (CA) 482, 491, 501; *Moore Large & Co Ltd v Hermes Credit & Guarantee plc* [2003] 1 Lloyd's Rep IR 315, 334. In Australia, *Coastal Estates Pty Ltd v Melevende* [1965] VR 433 (Full Ct) 435, 444–45, 454; *Cockerill v Westpac Banking Corporation* (1996) 142 ALR 227 (FCA) 279. In New Zealand, *Kenny v Fenton* [1971] NZLR 1 (CA) 17, 38. In Canada, *Kupchak v Dayson Holdings Co Ltd* (1965) 53 DLR (2d) 448 (BCCA) 489.

[254] *WISE (Underwriting) Agency Ltd v Grupo Nacional Provincial SA* [2004] 2 Lloyd's Rep 483 (CA) 509 (onus on insured resisting defence of rescission).

[255] See the authorities in the previous two notes, and also *Lindsay Petroleum v Hurd* [1874] LR 5 PC 221 (PC—Canada) 241 (in the context of laches and delay); *O'Connor v SP Bray Limited* (1936) St Rep (NSW) 248, 262 (discussing election generally).

requires knowledge of rights as well as awareness of material facts, the onus of proving knowledge of those rights also rests with the party against whom rescission is sought.[256] This gives rise to evidential difficulties. These difficulties, and the rebuttable presumptions of fact that will normally arise to overcome them, were discussed earlier in this chapter.[257]

(2) Pleading

Because the onus of proving affirmation rests on the party against whom rescission is sought, that party must positively plead it as a defence or answer to the claim to rescind. Particulars of when and how the affirmation occurred must be provided.[258] The facts to be particularized include the words or conduct said to constitute affirmation; that the affirming party was free of the alleged vitiating factor when the words were spoken or conduct occurred; and where necessary, details of the knowledge of the right to rescind. **23.111**

It has been held in Canada that a third party to a voidable contract has no standing to plead that the right to rescind the contract was lost by affirmation.[259] **23.112**

---

[256] *Moore Large & Co Ltd v Hermes Credit & Guarantee plc* [2003] 1 Lloyd's Rep IR 315, 334.
[257] See paras [23.55]–[23.56].
[258] *Peyman v Lanjani* [1985] Ch 457 (CA) 500–501.
[259] *Coutinho & Ferrostaal GmbH v Tracomex (Canada) Ltd* [2015] BCSC 787 at [142] (sale of scrap steel procured by fraud; third party with awareness of fraud).

24
Delay and Estoppel

A.	Introduction	24.01	C. When Delay Bars Rescission	24.38
B.	The Different Doctrines Engaged by Delay	24.03	(1) Freedom from the vitiating factor	24.38
			(2) Need for awareness of rights	24.57
	(1) Waiver by affirmation and by acquiescence	24.03	(3) Unreasonable delay after emancipation from the vitiating factor	24.64
	(2) Laches	24.14	(4) What amounts to unreasonable delay	24.71
	(3) Statute of limitations applied directly	24.22		
	(4) Statute of limitations applied by analogy	24.25	(5) The significance of prejudice	24.109
	(5) Mere lapse of time	24.37	D. Estoppel	24.116

A. Introduction

24.01 This chapter considers when and why the right to rescind will be lost by a failure to exercise it. The question is bedevilled by different doctrines doing much the same work, and which tend to be poorly understood. The chapter therefore begins by outlining the different doctrines that are engaged when delay prevents rescission. These are waiver by affirmation and by acquiescence, laches, the statute of limitations applied directly or by analogy, and 'mere delay'. Upon analysis, the different doctrines are probably reducible to three:

1. delay leading to an inference of waiver, which occurs when there is an implied election to affirm, or conduct constituting 'acquiescence';
2. culpable delay that would cause unjustified prejudice if rescission was permitted. This engages the doctrine of laches, and is today probably best regarded as part of the bar '*restitutio in integrum* impossible';
3. delay causing the right to rescind to be lost because the statute of limitations is applied by analogy, or where a sale of goods is induced by innocent misrepresentation.

After outlining the doctrines engaged by delay, the chapter considers when delay will bar rescission. It will be seen that the general rule is that the right to rescind is lost by unreasonable delay in exercising the right, once the innocent party has been emancipated from the effects of the vitiating factor, with prejudice shortening the delay that will be allowed. There is no need for the injured party to be aware of the right to rescind, save where the doctrine of election is to be relied upon.

24.02 Although often accompanied by delay, delay is not essential before rescission will be barred by estoppel. Estoppel is therefore separately considered at the end of this chapter.

B. The Different Doctrines Engaged by Delay

(1) Waiver by affirmation and by acquiescence

Introduction

The term 'waiver' is used in different senses, one of which is the doing of an intentional act **24.03** with knowledge that leads to abandonment of a right. Waiver in this sense looks chiefly at the conduct of the waiving party and differs from estoppel because neither reliance nor detriment need exist.[1] Although the term waiver is also used in other senses, it is waiver in this sense that is relevant here.[2]

The right to rescind a contract or gift is waived in the sense of abandoned when the party **24.04** entitled to rescind affirms the transaction rather than sets it aside.[3] This involves waiver by election, and lapse of time leads to waiver when it causes an election to affirm to be inferred, or to be deemed to have occurred.[4] Lapse of time also leads to waiver outside the rubric of election, in those cases where the waiver or abandonment of an equitable right to rescind is conclusively inferred from long lapse of time.[5] Waiver in this sense involves acquiescence. It is also often described as arising from laches,[6] and that language adds to the substance of the rule in underlining that for waiver to be inferred, the lapse of time must be unexcused in the eyes of the court.

The principles that govern when delay causes waiver by affirmation are largely identical to **24.05** those that determine when waiver is caused by acquiescence, with one important exception. As set out later in this chapter, in England delay leads to an implied election to affirm only if the injured party was aware of his right to rescind, whereas knowledge is unnecessary for the right to be lost by acquiescence.

Waiver by affirmation

Once it arises, a right of election is generally lost after sufficient delay. It is said that the **24.06** electing party:

> ... has in the end to make his election, not as a matter of obligation, but in the sense that, if he does not do so, the time may come when the law takes the decision out of his hands,

---

[1] *Banning v Wright* [1972] 1 WLR 972 (HL) 978–79; *Peyman v Lanjani* [1985] Ch 457 (CA) 494, 500; *Motor Oil Hellas (Corinth) Refineries SA v Shipping Corp of India (The Kanchenjunga)* [1990] 1 Lloyd's Rep 391 (HL) 397; *Oliver Ashworth (Holdings) Ltd v Ballard (Kent) Ltd* [2000] Ch 12 (CA) 28–29. In Australia, *Craine v The Colonial Mutual Fire Insurance Company Limited* (1920) 28 CLR 305, 326–27; *Commonwealth of Australia v Verwayen* (1990) 170 CLR 394, 422–24, 449–50; *Wiltrading (WA) Pty Ltd v Lumley General Insurance Ltd* (2005) 30 WAR 290 (CA) 305–06.

[2] This sense of the term most closely matches its derivation. It has been pointed out that 'waiver' derives from the same root as 'waif'—a thing, or person, abandoned: *Banning v Wright* [1972] 1 WLR 972 (HL) 978–79 (Lord Simon). For other meanings of 'waiver', S Wilken and K Ghaly, *The Law of Waiver, Variation and Estoppel* (3rd edn, 2012) chap 3; *Agricultural and Rural Finance Pty Ltd v Gardiner* (2008) 238 CLR 570 [51]–[56].

[3] See Chap 23, para [23.05].

[4] *Clough v London and North Western Railway Co* (1871) LR 7 Ex 26, 35; *Allcard v Skinner* (1887) 36 ChD 145 (CA) 187; *Aaron's Reefs Limited v Twiss* [1896] AC 273, 294; see para [24.07].

[5] *Gregory v Gregory* (1815) G Coop 201, 204; 35 ER 530 'waived or abandoned'; *Roberts v Tunstall* (1845) 4 Hare 257, 264, 266; 67 ER 645 'the principle of the decisions is that the injured party has waived his right to relief'.

[6] *Roberts v Tunstall* (1845) 4 Hare 257, 67 ER 645; *Lindsay Petroleum Co v Hurd* (1874) LR 5 PC 221 (PC—Canada) 239–40; also *Ross T Smyth & Co Ltd v TD Bailey Son & Co* (1940) 164 LT 102 (HL) 106.

either by holding him to have elected not to exercise the right, or sometimes by holding him to have exercised it.[7]

24.07 The right to elect to rescind or affirm a voidable transaction follows the same pattern. The entitlement to rescind is lost if not exercised within a certain period after the right to elect arises because affirmation is either implied or deemed to have occurred. Implied affirmation occurs where delay either alone or coupled with other factors raises a factual inference that a choice has been made to affirm, and that inference is not rebutted. Affirmation is deemed to have occurred when a choice is conclusively presumed to have been made by reason of the lapse of time.[8] Lapse of time without rescinding will therefore furnish evidence that the party entitled to rescind has determined to affirm,[9] and in some cases is treated as conclusive evidence to that effect.[10] The circumstances in which delay leads to an implied or deemed election to affirm are considered in detail in Part C of this chapter.

Waiver by acquiescence
Two meanings of 'acquiescence'

24.08 'Acquiescence' in the strict or narrow sense refers to an equitable defence arising when a person stands by without objection while a wrong is done to him, so as to induce the other to believe that it is acquiesced in.[11] It is either a species of, or closely resembles, estoppel,[12] and in England requires encouraging or allowing the person doing the act to believe to his detriment that it is acquiesced in,[13] such that it would be dishonest or unconscionable to enforce the right infringed.[14]

24.09 That doctrine has no application where the act complained of has been completed and come to an end without the knowledge or assent of the person whose right is infringed, and gives rise to a vested right of action;[15] there the right is generally not lost absent quite different events.[16] It is this situation that arises when a contract or gift is procured by fraud, undue influence, or other invalidating cause permitting its rescission. When a party entitled to rescind is said to have lost that right by acquiescence, the term refers to a principle distinct

---

[7] *Motor Oil Hellas (Corinth) Refineries SA v Shipping Corp of India (The Kanchenjunga)* [1990] 1 Lloyd's Rep 391 (HL) 398, col 1 (Lord Goff).
[8] See para [24.70].
[9] *Clough v London and North Western Railway Co* (1871) LR 7 Ex 26, 35; *Allcard v Skinner* (1887) 36 ChD 145 (CA) 187; *Aaron's Reefs Limited v Twiss* [1896] AC 273, 294; *Coastal Estates Pty Ltd v Melevende* [1965] VR 433 (Full Ct) 443; *Banwaitt v Dewji* [2013] EWHC 879 (QB) [74].
[10] *Clough v London and North Western Railway Co* (1871) LR 7 Ex 26, 35; *Allcard v Skinner* (1887) 36 ChD 145 (CA) 187 (Lindley LJ).
[11] *Duke of Leeds v Earl of Amherst* (1846) 2 Ph 117, 123; 41 ER 886; *Archbold v Scully* (1861) 9 HLC 360, 383; 11 ER 769; *De Bussche v Alt* (1878) 8 ChD 286 (CA) 314; *Allcard v Skinner* (1887) 36 ChD 145 (CA) 174; *Weld v Petre* [1929] 1 Ch 33 (CA) 51; *Goldsworthy v Brickell* [1987] AC 378 (CA) 410. Cf *Orr v Ford* (1989) 167 CLR 316, 337 ('contemporaneous and informed ("knowing") acceptance or standing by which is treated by equity as "assent" (ie consent)').
[12] *De Bussche v Alt* (1878) 8 ChD 286 (CA) 314 ('no more than an instance of the law of estoppel by words or conduct'); *Holder v Holder* [1968] Ch 353 (CA) 403 ('close resemblance to estoppel'); cf *Goldsworthy v Brickell* [1987] AC 378 (CA) 410. See also *Kammins Ballrooms Co Ltd v Zenith Investments (Torquay) Ltd* [1971] AC 850, 884 describing *Willmott v Barber* (1880) 15 ChD 96 as 'quasi estoppel by acquiescence'.
[13] *Jones v Stones* [1999] 1 WLR 1739 (CA) 1745 (trespass to land).
[14] *Shaw v Applegate* [1977] 1 WLR 970 (CA) 978 (breach of covenant); *Jones v Stones* [1999] 1 WLR 1739 (CA) 1743–44 (trespass to land); see also *Dale v Spurrier* (1802) 7 Ves Jun 232, 235–36; 32 ER 94 (Lord Eldon LC) (improvements to land).
[15] *De Bussche v Alt* (1878) 8 ChD 286 (CA) 314. Cf *Clarke v Hart* (1857) 6 HLC 633, 655–56; 10 ER 1143.
[16] Accord and satisfaction, release under seal, statute of limitations, election if applicable, or exceptionally, laches: *De Bussche v Alt* (1878) 8 ChD 286 (CA) 314; *O'Connor v SP Bray Limited* (1936) 36 St Rep (NSW) 249, 257.

from the strict doctrine of acquiescence.[17] That principle was described by Lord Cottenham LC when dismissing a claim to rescind a mining lease in Ireland:

> The doctrine of carrying equities by acquiescence, I consider to be one of the most important to be attended to; for otherwise, there is great danger of the principles of a Court of Equity, thus improperly exercised, producing great injustice. A man who, with full knowledge of his case, does not complain, but deals with his opponent as if he had no case against him, builds up from day to day a wall of protection for such opponent, which will probably defeat any future attack upon him.[18]

Acquiescence as a bar to rescission
Acquiescence as a bar to rescission describes the knowing acquiescence in the conduct justifying rescission or in the transaction itself,[19] and involves an assent to or implied affirmation of it.[20] It does not require that the other suffers detriment by reason of the acquiescence, and is in this respect quite distinct from estoppel. The term 'acquiescence' (like 'laches') describes the quality of the conduct of the party entitled to rescind, and when conduct characterized as acquiescence bars rescission, it does so because the right to rescind is regarded as having been waived.[21]

24.10

Acquiescence and laches
Loss of the right to rescind by acquiescence in this sense involves 'laches', in that the party entitled to rescind must be guilty of neglect in pursuing his rights,[22] and 'laches' means neglectful delay.[23] Accordingly, laches leading to an inference of waiver entails acquiescence.[24] However, somewhat confusingly, and as explained later, neglectful delay characterized as

24.11

---

[17] *Glasson v Fuller* [1922] SASR 148, 161–62, quoting with approval from JM Lightwood, *The Time Limit on Actions* (1909) 252–53. The court's power to refuse relief by reason of acquiescence or other equitable principles is expressly preserved by s 36(2) of the Limitation Act 1980.
[18] *Vigers v Pike* (1840–1842) 8 Cl & Fin 562, 651–52; 8 ER 220.
[19] *Charter v Trevelyan* (1842, 1844) 11 Cl & Fin 714, 740; 8 ER 1273 'the parties have never, with a knowledge of the facts, done anything which can be considered as an acquiescence in the matter complained of'; *Gresley v Mousley* (1858) 1 Giff 450, 460; 65 ER 995 'acquiescence in the transaction ... [with] a knowledge of the circumstances which would give a right to question the transaction'.
[20] *Earl of Deloraine v Browne* (1792) 3 Bro CC 633, 646; 29 ER 739 and note (4); *Wright v Vanderplank* (1856) 8 De G M & G 133, 149; 44 ER 340 ('there is clear proof of acquiescence. He had full knowledge of all the circumstances, and yet he treated the Defendant as tenant for life up to 1850'); *Gresley v Mousley* (1859) 4 De G & J 78, 90; 45 ER 31 ('confirmed or acquiesced'); *Allcard v Skinner* (1887) 36 ChD 145 (CA) 188 ('she deliberately chose not to attempt to avoid her gifts but to acquiesce in them ... to ratify or confirm them'); *Glasson v Fuller* [1922] SASR 148, 161–62 ('assent'); *Goldsworthy v Brickell* [1987] AC 378 (CA) 410 ('affirmed ... impliedly'). Cf using the term 'acquiescence' to describe affirmation by election (*Orr v Ford* (1989) 167 CLR 316, 338) or as evidencing an election (J Brunyate, *Limitation of Actions in Equity* (1932) 218–19). See also HT Banning and A Brown, *The Law of the Limitation of Actions* (3rd edn, 1906) 231; M Franks, *Limitation of Actions* (1959) 234; *Byrnes v Kendle* (2011) 243 CLR 253, 267, 279–80, 294–95 (different meanings of 'acquiescence' identified).
[21] *Roberts v Tunstall* (1845) 4 Hare 257, 67 ER 645; see also *Wall v Cockerell* (1863) 10 HLC 229, 242–46; 11 ER 1013 (acquiescence used as a synonym for confirmation and waiver); *Pickering v Lord Stamford* (1795) 2 Ves Jun 581, 583; 30 ER 787 (presumption of waiver by reason of delay generally; decree reversed in part (1796–97) 3 Ves Jun 332, 492; 30 ER 1038, 1121); *Life Association of Scotland v Siddal, Cooper v Greene* (1861) 3 De G F & J 58, 72–73, 77; 45 ER 800 (breach of trust).
[22] *Roberts v Tunstall* (1845) 4 Hare 257, 67 ER 645; *Erlanger v The New Sombrero Phosphate Company* (1878) LR 3 App Cas 1218, 1254; *Glasson v Fuller* [1922] SASR 148, 161–62.
[23] *Partridge v Partridge* [1894] 1 Ch 351, 360.
[24] *Fisher v Brooker* [2009] 1 WLR 1764 (HL) [62].

VI. OTHER BARS

laches may also bar rescission in other circumstances, which are not properly described as involving acquiescence, and where the right is not lost by waiver.

Application to rescission at law

24.12 In England and Wales acquiescence probably operates as a bar to rescission at law and in equity.[25] But in Australia there is authority implying that it can only bar a claim to rescind founded on equitable principles,[26] and this approach reflects the position that obtained before the Judicature reforms. But the point is unlikely to make any practical difference, for in Australia the circumstances in which delay leads to acquiescence are substantially the same as those where it causes an implied affirmation, which will cause the loss of a common law right to rescind. There is also Australian authority that neither affirmation nor acquiescence can prevent the court from exercising the statutory power to rescind conferred by section 243 of Schedule 2 of the Competition and Consumer Act 2010 (formerly section 87 of the Australian Trade Practices Act 1974 (Cth)),[27] although it will often cause the statutory discretion to be exercised against making an order for rescission.[28]

24.13 The elements of a defence of acquiescence are considered in more detail in Part C of this chapter.

(2) Laches

24.14 'Laches' is an old French word for slackness or negligence or not doing.[29] The Court of Chancery's reluctance to entertain suits affected by conduct of this kind was explained by Lord Camden in *Smith v Clay*:

> A court of equity which is never active in relief against conscience, or public convenience, has always refused its aid to stale demands, where the party has slept upon his rights and acquiesced for a great length of time. Nothing shall call forth this court into activity, but conscience, good faith, and reasonable diligence; where these are wanting, the Court is passive, and does nothing. Laches and neglect are always discountenanced, and therefore from the beginning of this jurisdiction, there was always a limitation to suits in this court.[30]

24.15 Laches has been described as an equitable defence that requires the defendant to have an equity which, on balance, outweighs the claimant's right taking into account all the

---

[25] *Habib Bank Ltd v Habib Bank AG Zurich* [1981] 1 WRL 1265 (CA) 1285, 1287; *Jones v Stones* [1999] 1 WLR 1739 (CA) 1744, both referring to acquiescence in the strict sense of the term: as to which see para [24.08].

[26] *Orr v Ford* (1989) 167 CLR 316, 340.

[27] *Southern Cross Mine Management Pty Ltd v Ensham Resources Pty Ltd* [2005] QSC 233 [639].

[28] *Tenji v Henneberry & Associates Pty Ltd* (2000) 98 FCR 324 (Full Ct) [22] (affirmation may weigh heavily against discretion to rescind); *Land Enviro Corp Pty Ltd v HTT Huntley Heritage Pty Ltd* [2012] NSWSC 382 [909] (rescission refused following affirmation; leave to appeal out of time granted [2014] NSWCA 34).

[29] *Partridge v Partridge* [1894] 1 Ch 351, 360, citing *Coke on Littleton* 380b; also *Orr v Ford* (1989) 167 CLR 316, 338.

[30] *Smith v Clay* (1767) 3 Bro CC 646, 29 ER 743 (bill of review), said to be of general application in *Gresley v Mousley* (1859) 4 De G & J 78, 95; 45 ER 31 (rescission for breach of fiduciary duty). The court's power to refuse relief by reason of the equitable doctrines of laches is expressly preserved by s 36(2) of the Limitation Act 1980. See further A McGee, *Limitation Periods* (8th edn, 2018) chap 3. In the Cayman Islands, see now *AB Jnr v MB*, 13 August 2012 (Smellie CJ) (Grand Court of the Cayman Islands) [285]–[304].

circumstances affecting those parties.[31] It must be unconscionable or inequitable to enforce the right.[32] The leading exposition of the doctrine is to be found in *Lindsay Petroleum Co v Hurd*.[33] The Privy Council there overturned a decision that the sale of land in Ontario could not be rescinded by reason of delay on the part of the defrauded buyer, and explained the underlying principles as follows:

> Now the doctrine of laches in Courts of Equity is not an arbitrary or a technical doctrine. Where it would be practically unjust to give a remedy, either because the party has, by his conduct, done that which might fairly be regarded as a waiver of it, or where by his conduct and neglect he has, though perhaps not waiving that remedy, yet put the other party in a situation in which it would not be reasonable to place him if the remedy were afterwards to be asserted, in either of these cases, lapse of time is most material... Two circumstances, always important in such cases, are, the length of the delay and the nature of the acts done during the interval, which might affect either party and cause a balance of justice or injustice in taking the one course or the other, so far as relates to the remedy.[34]

It has been observed that the cases provide no more precise definition than this, and that whether rescission is barred by laches is to some degree a matter of judicial impression:

24.16

> I think, from the nature of the inquiry, it must always be a question of more or less, depending on the degree of diligence which might reasonably be required, and the degree of change which has occurred, whether the balance of justice or injustice is in favour of granting the remedy or withholding it. The determination of such a question must largely depend on the turn of mind of those who have to decide, and must therefore be the subject of some uncertainty; but that, I think, is inherent in the nature of the inquiry.[35]

The inquiry in each case focuses upon the particular circumstances before the court.[36] Factors of importance include the period of the delay, the extent to which the defendant's position has been prejudiced by the delay, how far that prejudice has been caused by the claimant's actions, and the claimant's awareness that delay will cause that prejudice.[37]

---

[31] *Nwakobi, The Osha of Obosi v Nzekwu* [1964] 1 WLR 1019 (PC—Nigeria) 1024, 1026. In New Zealand, *O'Connor v Hart* [1983] NZLR 280 (CA) 292–94 (point not considered on appeal: [1985] 1 NZLR 159 (PC—NZ)); *Eastern Service Ltd v No 68 Ltd* [2006] 3 NZLR 335 [13] (SC). In Australia, see *Gillespie v Gillespie* [2013] 2 QdR 440 (CA) 458 (adjudicating the defence of laches 'involves the balancing of equities').

[32] Must be unconscionable to grant relief: *Frawley v Neill, The Times*, 5 April 1999 (CA) (Aldous LJ), foll *Schulman v Hewson* [2002] EWHC 855 (Ch) [45]; *Patel v Shah* [2005] EWCA Civ 157 [32], [39]. Must be inequitable to grant relief: *Goldsworthy v Brickell* [1987] Ch 378 (CA) 416 (Parker LJ) (delay must make it 'inequitable' to rescind); *P&O Nedlloyd BV v Arab Metals Co (No 2)* [2007] 1 WLR 2288 (CA) 2312 ('The question for the court in each case is simply whether, having regard to the delay, its extent, the reasons for it and its consequences, it would be inequitable to grant the relief he seeks', per Moore-Bick LJ, with who Jonathan Parker LJ and Buxton LJ agreed (specific performance)). See also *Nelson v Rye* [1996] 1 WLR 1378, 1388 (account).

[33] (1874) LR 5 PC 221 (PC—Canada), and which also states the law in Australia: *BM Auto Sales Pty Ltd v Budget Rent A Car System Pty Ltd* (1976) 51 ALJR 254, 259; *Orr v Ford* (1989) 167 CLR 316, 341; also *Gillespie v Gillespie* [2013] 2 QdR 440 (CA) 458; *Herrod v Johnston* [2013] 2 QdR 102 (CA) 127–28.

[34] (1874) LR 5 PC 221 (PC—Canada) 239–40, approved *Fisher v Brooker* [2009] 1 WLR 1764 (HL) [64].

[35] *Erlanger v The New Sombrero Phosphate Company* (1878) 3 App Cas 1218, 1279–80 (Lord Blackburn); see also 1230–31 (Lord Penzance).

[36] '[T]he doctrine of laches requires a balancing of equities in relation to the broad span of human conduct. In the abstract, facts and the weight to be given to them are infinitely variable. But in a particular case they have to be identified and weighed for what they are, as a singular exercise': *Eastern Services Ltd v No 68 Ltd* [2006] 3 NZLR 335 (SC) [37] (delay in registration of transfer).

[37] *Nelson v Rye* [1996] 1 WLR 1378, 1392 (claim for account against fiduciary agent); *Fisher v Brooker* [2009] 1 WLR 1764 (HL) [79] (38-year delay caused defendant to obtain benefits exceeding detriment that would flow from enforcing claimant's right; claim for copyright); *Gillespie v Gillespie* [2013] 2 QdR 440 (CA) 462 (the circumstance

'Affirmatory' laches and 'prejudicial' laches

24.17 Laches leading to an inference of waiver entails acquiescence; however, the statements of principle quoted earlier underline that neglectful delay may also bar rescission in other circumstances, where there is no inference of waiver.[38] As a bar to rescission, laches therefore encompasses two distinct circumstances. First, it encompasses conduct that amounts to acquiescence, which entails an inference of waiver. Here the laches is affirmatory. In the second place, laches encompasses circumstances in which the passage of time is coupled with conduct or neglect, the effect of which is that the other party would be placed in an unreasonable situation or the claimant would obtain an unjust advantage, if rescission were to be granted.[39] Here the laches is prejudicial. Laches involving acquiescence may therefore be called 'affirmatory laches', and laches that does not, 'prejudicial laches'.[40]

Common law rights to rescind

24.18 Whether laches will only bar the right to rescind in equity and not at common law has not been decided. In principle it should, because laches only bars equitable relief, not rights arising at law.[41] If this approach is to be adopted, laches only bars equitable claims to rescind. There is some support for this analysis in Australia, where it has been said that a party entitled to rescind simply by repudiating the contract does not lose that right by laches, and that his delay will only count if it amounts to evidence of an election to affirm.[42] It might be thought that today laches should be a defence to a claim to rescind at common law, on the basis that the interest in a uniform approach outweighs the principled objections to it.[43] The juristic basis for that analysis is, however, unclear. Common law rights are generally not lost by mere negligent inaction. The more conventional approach is to test loss of common law rights to rescind by reference to principles of election, and the bar *restitutio in integrum* impossible.

Prejudicial laches and the bar restitutio in integrum impossible

24.19 What is the relationship between laches and the bar usually known as '*restitutio in integrum* impossible'? That bar was developed only in the second half of the nineteenth century, long after the doctrine of laches had become familiar to courts of Chancery. It has been developed in such a way that, today, conduct or neglect that would place the other party in an

---

that the claim was confined to only part of the real property transferred away by undue influence was relevant in weighing charges of prejudice to transferees; eight-year delay no bar); cf *Crossman v Sheahan* (2016) 115 ACSR 130 (NSWCA) 130 [386] (*laches* requires defendant to demonstrate both unreasonable delay and prejudice).

[38] See also J Brunyate, *Limitation of Actions in Equity* (1932) 188–89. As to the different meanings given to the terms acquiescence and laches, *Orr v Ford* (1989) 167 CLR 316, 339.
[39] *Lindsay Petroleum Co v Hurd* (1874) LR 5 PC 221 (PC—Canada) 239–40; *Fysh v Page* (1956) 96 CLR 233, 244.
[40] This division in the operation of laches as a defence to a claim for rescission reflects the doctrine generally, at least in Australia: see eg *Streeter v Western Areas Exploration Pty Ltd* (2011) 278 ALR 291 (WACA) [635] 'The doctrine of laches comprehends two themes. One is delay implying not just quiescence, but rather acquiescence and assent, and the other is delay involving prejudicial change of circumstances' (Murphy JA); *Wright Prospecting Pty Ltd v Hancock Prospecting Pty Ltd* [2013] WASC 248 [59] (applying the analysis in RP Meagher, D Heydon, and M Leeming, *Equity Doctrines and Remedies* (4th edn, 2002) at [36-3005]).
[41] *Fisher v Brooker* [2009] 1 WLR 1764 (HL) [79]. To similar effect, A Burrows, *A Restatement of the English Law of Contract* (2nd edn, 2020) § 34(3), 34(5)(a).
[42] *Re Lucks Limited, Serpell's case* [1928] VLR 466, 472 (Irvine CJ).
[43] The principles of laches were applied to bar a claim not in the nature of equitable relief in *Agbeyegbe v Ikomi* [1953] 1 WLR 263 (PC—Nigeria) (delay in re-listing plaintiff's claim that mortgagee's sale was void for failure to observe formal requirements; delay barred claim).

unreasonable situation or give the claimant an unjust advantage upon rescission will engage the bar *restitutio in integrum* impossible.[44]

24.20 Does this mean that the one set of facts gives rise to two different bars to rescission—what has here been called 'prejudicial laches', and *restitutio in integrum* impossible? Whilst a historical analysis would suggest that this is so, there is a need to simplify this area of law, and one way of doing so is to regard 'prejudicial laches' as now absorbed within the bar *restitutio in integrum* impossible. That seems indeed to be how Lord Blackburn's judgment in *Erlanger*'s case[45] has been understood in England.[46]

24.21 This approach leads to there being no separate work for a bar to rescission called 'laches'. There is instead neglectful delay leading to an inference of waiver, called 'acquiescence', and neglectful delay coupled with prejudice, which causes the right to rescind to be lost because *restitutio in integrum* is regarded as impossible. Although in substance English law has probably adopted this simplified analysis,[47] in practice the nomenclature of laches is regularly employed in cases where the ground for rescission is exclusively equitable. This chapter therefore continues to refer to prejudicial laches as a bar to rescission. The principles discussed may, however, equally be regarded as principles informing the operation of the bar *restitutio in integrum* impossible.

(3) Statute of limitations applied directly

24.22 There is no statutory limitation period within which an election to rescind must be exercised, or for bringing a claim asking the court to order rescission. However, where rescission occurs at common law, vested rights of action accrue after an election to disaffirm is made, and these are subject to the Limitation Act 1980. The claim to recover money paid is a debt imposed by law, a claim for money had and received, and is barred by the six-year time limit in section 5 of the Limitation Act 1980. When title to goods is recovered upon rescission the cause of action for conversion will be lost six years after the conversion occurs, pursuant to sections 2 and 3 of the Act, unless the protection afforded by section 4 can be invoked on the ground that the item was stolen.[48]

24.23 Accordingly, the general rule is that a party who rescinds at common law has six years from the date that he elects to rescind the transaction in which to bring a claim to recover money or property transferred.

24.24 This bar arising from delay differs from all of the others considered in this chapter, because it operates to prevent the enforcement of rights secured by a completed rescission, rather than barring the right to rescind itself.

---

[44] See Chap 18.
[45] *Erlanger v The New Sombrero Phosphate Company* (1878) 3 App Cas 1218, 1279–80.
[46] See Chap 18, para [18.13]. But the position is different in Australia: see Chap 18, para [18.16].
[47] See Chap 18, para [18.13].
[48] Chattels may be stolen although the thief acquires a voidable title to them: *R v Hinks* [2001] 2 AC 241.

(4) Statute of limitations applied by analogy

24.25 The right to rescind is sometimes barred by lapse of time because equity acts by analogy to the statute of limitations.[49] When that occurs the right to rescind is lost automatically by effluxion of the relevant time period after the injured party becomes sufficiently aware of the material facts, and is otherwise free of the vitiating factor.[50]

Not applicable to right to rescind at common law

24.26 The doctrine was developed for claims to equitable relief, which fell outside the old statutes of limitation.[51] Section 36(1) of the Limitation Act 1980 confirms that the statutory time limits continue not to apply to equitable relief, but expressly preserves their application by analogy, pursuant to the equitable doctrine applying before 1 July 1940. The legislation therefore assumes that the doctrine has no application to the exercise of a common law right. There is in any event no evidence that equity ever sought to restrict exercise of the right to rescind at common law for fraud or duress or other ground by applying the statute of limitations by analogy, or would have done so had the issue arisen. The preferable view is that the doctrine has no application to a delay in exercising a right to rescind that arises at common law, and the point was common ground in *IGE USA Investments Limited v The Commissioner for Her Majesty's Revenue and Customs*.[52]

When the analogy is applied
Fraudulent misrepresentation and dishonest breach of fiduciary duty

24.27 Sir George Jessel MR said *obiter* that rescission for fraud is barred by analogy with the statute of limitations.[53] It has been held that a six-year time limit applies to claims to rescind for fraudulent misrepresentation[54] or dishonest non-disclosure in breach of fiduciary duty,[55] so as to recover money or shares, by analogy with the statutory time limit on recovering damages for deceit. The authorities pre-date the Limitation Act 1980 but that should make no difference.[56]

24.28 In *IGE USA Investments Limited v The Commissioner for Her Majesty's Revenue and Customs*[57] the Court of Appeal held that the decision in *Molloy v Mutual Reserve Life Insurance Co*[58] continues to bind and that a six-year time bar applies to claims to rescind for fraudulent misrepresentation in equity whenever the party rescinding could in principle

---

[49] For that general doctrine, *Hovenden v Lord Annesley* (1806) 2 Sch & Lef 607, 630–32; *Knox v Gye* (1872) LR 5 HL 656, 674–75; *P&O Nedlloyd BV v Arab Metals Co (No 2)* [2007] 1 WLR 2288 (CA) 2302–10. Also, Limitation Act 1980, s 36(1).
[50] *Allcard v Skinner* (1887) 36 ChD 145 (CA) 186; *Molloy v Mutual Reserve Life Insurance Co* (1906) 94 LT 756 (CA) 761; *Oelkers v Ellis* [1914] 2 KB 139, 150–51; *Armstrong v Jackson* [1917] 2 KB 822, 830–31.
[51] The most important of which were the Limitation Act 1623 and the Real Property Limitation Act 1833. See further J Brunyate, *Limitation of Actions in Equity* (1932) 2–3.
[52] [2021] Ch 423 (CA) 435 [19], [20].
[53] *Redgrave v Hurd* (1881) 20 ChD 1 (CA) 13, discussed *IGE USA Investments Limited v The Commissioner for Her Majesty's Revenue and Customs* [2021] Ch 423 (CA) 448–49 [67]–[69].
[54] *Molloy v Mutual Reserve Life Insurance Co* (1906) 94 LT 756 (CA); *Armstrong v Jackson* [1917] 2 KB 822, 830–31.
[55] *Oelkers v Ellis* [1914] 2 KB 139, 149–51; *Armstrong v Jackson* [1917] 2 KB 822, 830–31.
[56] Limitation Act 1980, ss 2, 36(1).
[57] [2021] Ch 423 (CA).
[58] (1906) 94 LT 756 (CA).

have relied upon the same facts to bring an action for damages in deceit.[59] The doctrine is applicable whether the contract sought to be set aside is executory or executed, and irrespective of the content of the obligation to make restitution or counter-restitution upon rescission. In each case, the relevant question is instead whether the party seeking to rescind could have relied upon the same facts to bring an action for damages in deceit; where that is so, the six-year time limit applied to the tort of deceit will be applied by analogy.[60]

Recovering an estate or interest in land
The reasoning in the cases just discussed is not expressly restricted to the subject matter of the contract, and on one view implies that a six-year limit will apply to rescind dispositions of any type of property, including real property. But the preferable view is that there is no analogy between the six-year time limit imposed by section 2 of the Limitation Act 1980 for damages in deceit or conversion, and a claim to recover title to land by rescinding for fraud or any other cause.[61]

24.29

If a statutory time limit is to be applied by analogy in such a case it should be the time period applicable to claims to recover possession of land. For unregistered land that is 12 years,[62] unless a reversionary or other future interest was transferred, where different rules apply.[63] The time limits in the Limitation Act 1980 do not apply to registered land save as against a chargee.[64] Adverse possession confers title to registered land after ten years.[65]

24.30

Should a court exercising equitable jurisdiction today regard any of these time limits as applicable by analogy in a claim to recover land upon rescission? There is limited authority on the point. The practice was formerly to regard the statutory period for common law actions to recover possession as a ceiling for bills to regain title to land by rescission. A delay of 20 years after discovery of the fraud was regarded as fatal to a bill to rescind, by analogy with the 20-year statutory limit for possession actions at common law.[66] Likewise, time ran for rescinding reversionary interests only after they fell into possession, by analogy with the statutory rule to that effect.[67]

24.31

It is unclear if the principles articulated in these older cases would be applied today. If they would be, a court should apply the relevant statutory time limit for recovering possession of unregistered and registered land when a claim is brought to recover that title upon rescission. There is however a lack of recent authority, and whether the statute would be applied by analogy must nowadays be considered to be an open question.

24.32

---

[59] [2021] Ch 423 (CA) 446 [59], [60], 452 [84], 456 [98].
[60] [2021] Ch 423 (CA) 436–38 [23], [25], [28], 444 [52], 446–47 [58]–[61], 448 [64], [66], 454 [91].
[61] See also *Hovenden v Lord Annesley* (1806) 2 Sch & Lef 607, 634–35.
[62] Limitation Act 1980, s 15(1).
[63] Limitation Act 1980, s 36(1).
[64] Land Registration Act 2002, s 96.
[65] Land Registration Act 2002, s 97, sched 6.
[66] Limitation Act 1623; Real Property Limitation Act 1833; *Hovenden v Lord Annesley* (1806) 2 Sch & Lef 607, 633–35; see also the submissions in *Charter v Trevelyan* (1842) 11 Cl & Fin 714, 724–28; 8 ER 1273. At that time the statutory limit of 20 years was said to be underpinned by a public policy that 'lands which are the subject of litigation become waste for want of cultivation': *Hovenden v Lord Annesley* (1806) 2 Sch & Lef 607, 630. The period was reduced to 12 years by the Real Property Limitation Act 1874, and remains 12 years today: Limitation Act 1980, s 15.
[67] *Sibbering v Earl of Balcarras* (1850) 3 De G & SM 735, 64 ER 682; *Salter v Bradshaw* (1858) 26 Beav 161, 53 ER 858.

When there is no analogy

Transactions contrary to the self-dealing and fair-dealing rules

24.33 In *Tito v Waddell (No 2)*[68] Sir Robert Megarry held that transactions concluded by fiduciaries in contravention of the fair-dealing and self-dealing rules are not caught by the statutory time limit for breach of trust,[69] and nor will that time limit be applied by analogy, for no sufficient analogy exists.[70] The effect of delay in these cases was said to be governed exclusively by the doctrine of laches.[71] This approach has been considered by the Court of Appeal in the context of determining the limitation period applicable to a claim for an account of profits, and held to be unsound.[72] It therefore appears that a six-year time limit generally applies where a claim is made to rescind transactions contrary to the fair-dealing rules.[73] In cases of self-dealing, no question of rescission should arise.[74]

Undue influence

24.34 In *Allcard v Skinner*[75] Lindley LJ said that the statute of limitations was relevant in assessing the effects of Miss Allcard's delay in seeking to recover the voidable gifts that she had made, and he reasoned as follows:

> This action is not one of those to which the *Statute of Limitations* in terms applies ... But this action very closely resembles an action for money had and received where laches and acquiescence are relied on as a defence: and the question is whether that defence ought to prevail. In my opinion it ought. Taking the statute as a guide ... the lapse of six years becomes a very material element for consideration.[76]

24.35 But the other members of the Court of Appeal did not adopt this reasoning,[77] and there are examples of rescission for undue influence following very long delays. For example, in the Australian case of *Bester v Perpetual Trustee Co Ltd*[78] Street J rescinded a deed of settlement 20 years after its execution, and it was not suggested that the relationship of influence had continued much beyond the time when the claimant had signed the deed as a young woman. More recently, Patten J doubted that there is any limitation by analogy for undue influence.[79]

---

[68] [1977] Ch 106, considering Limitation Act 1939, s 19(2).
[69] Limitation Act 1980, s 21.
[70] [1977] Ch 106, 249–50. 50 (where the discussion included consideration of rescission, though the relevant claim was for equitable compensation).
[71] *Tito v Waddell (No 2)* [1977] Ch 106, 250.
[72] *Gwembe Valley Development Co Ltd v Koshy (No 3)* [2004] 1 BCLC 131 (CA) [104]–[108]. See also, *Vivendi SA v Richards* [2013] BCC 771 [185]–[190]; *Williams v Central Bank of Nigeria* [2014] 2 WLR 355 (SC) [28]–[29], [116]–[118]; *First Subsea Ltd v Balltec Ltd* [2014] EWHC 866 (Ch) [469], [473]; L Tucker et al (eds), *Lewin on Trusts* (20th edn, 2020) [50-083]–[50-085].
[73] *Gwembe Valley Development Co Ltd v Koshy (No 3)* [2004] 1 BCLC 131 (CA) [111] (and noting the exception in cases of fraud and express trust).
[74] See Chap 1, paras [1.72]–[1.76]; also, *JJ Harrison (Properties) Limited v Harrison* [2002] 1 BCLC 162 (CA) (no statutory limitation period in cases of self-dealing; claim for an account against company director constructive trustee).
[75] (1887) 36 ChD 145 (CA).
[76] *Allcard v Skinner* (1887) 36 ChD 145 (CA) 186.
[77] Cotton LJ said that the statute could not be relied on, and Bowen LJ made no mention of the point. Kekewich J had said that no period of delay could be settled on as a definite bar: *Allcard v Skinner* (1887) 36 ChD 145 (CA), 163, 174, 192.
[78] [1970] 3 NSWLR 30, 37–38.
[79] *Clarke v Marlborough Fine Art (London) Ltd*, The Times, 5 July 2001.

The weight of authority is against the application of the statute by analogy in cases of undue influence.[80]

Conclusions

It does seem anomalous that a contract or gift cannot be rescinded in equity for fraudulent misrepresentation after six years have passed, but may be rescinded at law well beyond that.[81] It also seems anomalous that the same contract or gift can be rescinded in equity beyond six years if it is procured by breach of the fair-dealing or self-dealing rules, or by undue influence, even though such conduct often involves much less moral turpitude than fraud. A more rational system would adopt one rule for all grounds of rescission, and for rescission at law and in equity, unless there are compelling reasons for excepting particular grounds, or particular types of property. That is not, however, the law. Whether the statute may be applied by analogy depends on whether the right is legal or equitable, and upon the ground for rescission. The bar is so far only authoritatively recognized in the case of claims to rescind in equity for fraud and fraudulent breaches of fiduciary duty, and there only where the subject matter is an executory transaction, or a completed one involving personal property.

24.36

(5) Mere lapse of time

In England, a lapse of time that does not engage any of the doctrines referred to earlier in this chapter may bar the right to rescind sales of goods induced by innocent misrepresentation.[82] The bar is best regarded as founded on the law's special interest in protecting the security of such transactions.[83] Australian law appears to be different in providing that delay during a period when the buyer of goods is ignorant of the vendor's innocent misrepresentation does not count against him.[84]

24.37

C. When Delay Bars Rescission

(1) Freedom from the vitiating factor

The general principle is that delay only counts against the right to rescind after the innocent party is freed from the effects of the vitiating factor. The application of this principle will be separately considered for each of the different doctrines that delay may engage.

24.38

---

[80] Cf *P&O Nedlloyd BV v Arab Metals Co (No 2)* [2007] 1 WLR 2288 (CA) 2312 (court would not rule out the possibility that a court would regard it as inequitable to allow a claim to be pursued after very long delay, even absent evidence that defendant or third party had altered his position).

[81] Cf *Williams v Central Bank of Nigeria* [2014] 2 WLR 355 (SC) [118], *IGE USA Investments Limited v The Commissioner for Her Majesty's Revenue and Customs* [2021] Ch 423 (CA) 454 [90].

[82] *Leaf v International Galleries* [1950] 2 KB 86 (CA). Cf *P&O Nedlloyd BV v Arab Metals Co (No 2)* [2007] 1 WLR 2288 (CA) 2312 (leaving open the possibility that a court would regard it as inequitable to allow a claim to be pursued after very long delay, even absent evidence that defendant or third party had altered his position).

[83] *Leaf v International Galleries* [1950] 2 KB 86 (CA) 92, 94–95.

[84] *Shuman v Coober Pedy Tours Pty Ltd* (1994) 175 LSJS 159; [1994] SASC 4401 [15]–[16] (King CJ): lapse of four years no bar to rescission of purchase of fossilized 'dinosaur bone', in fact fossilized wood, buyers being unaware of innocent misrepresentation during that period.

Freedom and affirmation

24.39 Delay is evidence of affirmation only if it occurs after the innocent party is put to an election to either rescind or affirm. The innocent party is not put to such an election until after they have been sufficiently freed from the effects of the vitiating factor conferring the right to rescind. Accordingly, in cases of misrepresentation, mistake, and non-disclosure, the only delay material to a defence of affirmation is that which occurs after the affected party is aware of the material facts.[85] Similarly, if the transaction is voidable for duress, undue influence, or like causes, delay begins to count only after the invalidating cause has effectively come to an end.[86]

24.40 The rules that govern what knowledge is required before positive conduct will be treated as an irrevocable affirmation, and which party bears the onus of proof, are discussed in Chapter 23. The same rules ought to apply when affirmation is implied from inaction, and it will be seen that the doctrine of acquiescence is subject to similar principles.

Freedom and acquiescence

24.41 Delay implies acquiescence only if it occurs with knowledge of the facts and freedom of action. The principle was stated by Lord Selborne in *Erlanger v The New Sombrero Phosphate Company*:

> Two things are generally necessary—first, that there should have been sufficient knowledge of the facts on which the equity depends; and, secondly, (when a contract is sought to be rescinded), that there should be substantial freedom of choice and action, independent of the original influence under which the voidable contract was made.[87]

24.42 The principle operates differently where the ground for rescission is founded on misrepresentation, mistake, and non-disclosure, and where it is based on pressure or exploitation. Each will therefore be considered separately.

Misrepresentation, mistake, and non-disclosure

24.43 In cases of misrepresentation, mistake, and non-disclosure, time only counts as evidence of acquiescence after the injured party knows the material facts.[88] It seems that mere suspicion is not enough.[89] Nor does it usually matter that the misled party had the means of

---

[85] *Clough v London and North Western Railway Co* (1871) LR 7 Ex 26, 34–35; *Re Eastgate* [1905] 1 KB 465, 467 (ignorance of fraud by vendor of goods); *Koutsonicolis v Principe (No 2)* (1987) 48 SASR 329 (ignorance of latent defects in dwelling house); *Southern Cross Mine Management Pty Ltd v Ensham Resources Pty Ltd* [2005] QSC 233 [631], [640]–[642], [647]ff (concealed fraud as to agreement for hiring dragline for coal mining); *Fiona Trust & Holding Corporation v Privalov* [2007] 1 All ER (Comm) 81 [36]; see Chap 23, para [23.18].
[86] *Allcard v Skinner* (1887) 36 ChD 145 (CA) 187 (undue influence); *North Ocean Shipping Co Ltd v Hyundai Construction Co Ltd (The Atlantic Baron)* [1979] 1 QB 705, 720–21 (duress); see Chap 23, para [23.14].
[87] (1878) 3 App Cas 1218, 1261.
[88] *Charter v Trevelyan* (1842, 1844) 11 Cl & Fin 714, 740; 8 ER 1273; *Roberts v Tunstall* (1845) 4 Hare 257, 267; 67 ER 645; *Gresley v Mousley* (1858) 1 Giff 450, 460; 65 ER 995; *Wall v Cockerell* (1863) 10 HLC 229, 242–43; 11 ER 1013, 1019; *Erlanger v The New Sombrero Phosphate Company* (1878) 3 App Cas 1218, 1261; *Lagunas Nitrate Company v Lagunas Syndicate* [1899] 2 Ch 392 (CA) 454; *Southern Cross Mine Management Pty Ltd v Ensham Resources Pty Ltd* [2005] QSC 233 [643]–[644].
[89] *Directors of the Central Railway Company of Venezuela v Kisch* (1867) LR 2 App Cas 99, 112; *Ogilvie v Currie* (1868) 37 LR Ch (NS) 541, 544–46; *Erlanger v The New Sombrero Phosphate Company* (1878) 3 App Cas 1218, 1249, 1261, 1279; *Haas Timber & Trading Co Pty Ltd v Wade* (1954) 94 CLR 593, 601–02; *Southern Cross Mine Management Pty Ltd v Ensham Resources Pty Ltd* [2005] QSC 233 [662].

discovering the truth. That the facts could have been discovered is not generally enough;[90] he has no duty to investigate, at least until facts are known that raise suspicion, and delay before that time does not count against him.[91] An exception may exist in the case of voidable share allotments,[92] but there is also authority against this.[93]

Pressure and exploitation
Where a contract or gift is procured by actual or presumed undue influence, the undue influence must have effectively come to an end before acquiescence will be imputed.[94] In cases of presumed undue influence this means that the relationship between the parties giving rise to the presumption of influence must have terminated.[95] Where actual undue influence is exercised the pressure must have effectively ceased.[96] The principle is the same where a contract is voidable as an unconscionable bargain; as long as the imposition continues there is no acquiescence.[97]

24.44

Breach of fiduciary duty
Where a trustee purchases from his beneficiary a long lapse of time may raise a conclusive inference that the right to rescind has been abandoned or waived,[98] and substantial delay will bar relief where a solicitor purchases from his client, unless the client shows that he was not in a position to seek relief.[99] But it is difficult to find examples where the right to rescind was lost by inaction during the continuation of a fiduciary relationship, and it may be that acquiescence is not possible where, though the principal is fully aware of the material facts, he delays whilst the fiduciary relationship continues.[100] The position is otherwise where the breach of duty consists of a director's failure to disclose his interest in a proposed contract by the company, after a resolution on which the director voted. The company's right to rescind may be lost by delay, and it has been said that in such a case the election to rescind must be communicated 'clearly and promptly'.[101]

24.45

---

[90] *Wall v Cockerell* (1863) 10 HLC 229, 11 ER 1013. Cf the similar rules as to disclosure by a fiduciary: *Dunne v English* (1874) LR 18 Eq 524, 535 (Jessell MR).
[91] *Rawlins v Wickham* (1858) 3 De G & J 304, 313–14; 44 ER 1285; *Marquis of Clanricarde v Henning* (1861) 30 Beav 175, 180; 54 ER 855; *Re The Mount Morgan (West) Gold Mine Limited* (1887) 56 LT 622, 625; *Haas Timber & Trading Co Pty Ltd v Wade* (1954) 94 CLR 593, 601–02; *Southern Cross Mine Management Pty Ltd v Ensham Resources Pty Ltd* [2005] QSC 233 [662].
[92] It has been said there that delay with the 'full means of knowledge' is enough (*Peek v Gurney* (1873) 6 App Cas 377, 384), and that after a shareholder hears that misrepresentations may have been made, 'it is his duty in such a case to ascertain for himself whether there is a misrepresentation or not' (*Ashley's case* (1870) LR 9 Eq 263, 269). See also J Brunyate, *Limitation of Actions in Equity* (1932) 255–56.
[93] *Haas Timber & Trading Co Pty Ltd v Wade* (1954) 94 CLR 593, 601–02 where the general rule that the means of knowledge is not enough was stated in the case of a fraudulent allotment of shares. The High Court of Australia also stated that the old rule 'requiring great promptness' in cases of voidable share allotments would not often be applicable today (at 604).
[94] *Allcard v Skinner* (1887) 36 ChD 145 (CA) 187.
[95] *Hatch v Hatch* (1804) 9 Ves Jun 292, 298; 32 ER 615 (Lord Eldon); *Allcard v Skinner* (1887) 36 ChD 145 (CA) 187.
[96] *Purcell v M'Namara* (1806) 14 Ves Jun 91, 120–22; 33 ER 455.
[97] *Fry v Lane* (1888) 40 ChD 312, 324. In New Zealand, *O'Connor v Hart* [1983] NZLR 280 (CA).
[98] *Gregory v Gregory* (1815) G Coop 201, 204; 35 ER 530; aff'd (1821) Jac 631, 37 ER 989 (18 years); *Roberts v Tunstall* (1845) 4 Hare 257, 67 ER 645.
[99] *Champion v Rigby* (1830) Tamlyn 421, 48 ER 168, 1 Russ & M 539, 39 ER 207, aff'd 9 LJ Ch (NS) 211 (18 years); *Marquis of Clanricarde v Henning* (1861) 30 Beav 175, 54 ER 855 (33 years).
[100] *Champion v Rigby* (1840) 9 LJ Ch (NS) 211, 214; *Marquis of Clanricarde v Henning* (1861) 30 Beav 175, 184; 54 ER 855; but cf *Gresley v Mousley* (1859) 4 De G & J 78, 90; 45 ER 31.
[101] *Re Marini Ltd* [2004] BCC 172, 195–96 (Judge Richard Seymour QC, sitting as a Judge of the High Court) (non-compliance with s 317 of the Companies Act 1985; right to rescind lost after four-year delay, if rescission was

Other cases

24.46 If a company is entitled to rescind a purchase that it has made, and the vendors' nominees control the board or the directors are themselves the vendors, delay during the period when that board is in control will generally not count against the claim to rescind, and particularly where the members are misled.[102]

24.47 It has also been held that where one among several objects of a power of appointment sold property to the trustee holding the power to appoint, and the purchase was voidable for breach of fiduciary duty, laches could not be imputed during the time that the trustee remained alive, for during that period the party with the equity to rescind remained 'dependent on the bounty of the purchaser'.[103]

Onus of proof

24.48 The onus of proving the facts necessary to establish a defence of acquiescence is on the party against whom rescission is sought, who seeks to rely upon the defence.[104]

Freedom and laches

24.49 The general rule was stated by Sir James Wigram V-C in *Roberts v Tunstall*:

> Where a transaction of this kind has been brought about by misrepresentation, concealment or undue influence ... the Court considers that the right of the vendor to rescind the sale exists, without the imputation of *laches*, until such time as it is shewn that he was released from the position in which he was placed by those circumstances.[105]

However, the Vice-Chancellor went on to distinguish cases where there is no misrepresentation, concealment, or undue influence, and the right to rescind 'is an equity arising out of the transaction itself, as in the case of the sale of a reversionary interest'.[106] How the running of time affects cases of this kind is less clear. In *Gresley v Mousley* Lord Justice Turner said that lapse of time during the period when a fiduciary relationship continues counts for less than after it comes to an end, but 'I do not say that no weight can be given to it', and left open the question of what effect it would have.[107] But there is other authority that time should only run after the relationship had come to an end,[108] and the point would seem to remain open.

---

otherwise possible). The result would no doubt have been different if the company's delay was explicable by the errant director having control of the board during the period of the delay: see para [24.46].

[102] *Erlanger v The New Sombrero Phosphate Company* (1878) 3 App Cas 1218, 1261, 1281–82; *Lagunas Nitrate Company v Lagunas Syndicate* [1899] 2 Ch 392 (CA) 433, 452, 454.
[103] *Roberts v Tunstall* (1845) 4 Hare 257, 266–67; 67 ER 645.
[104] *Wall v Cockerell* (1863) 10 HLC 229, 243; 11 ER 1013, 1019 (Lord Westbury LC); *Lindsay Petroleum Co v Hurd* (1874) LR 5 PC 221 (PC—Canada) 241 (speaking of laches); *Habib Bank Ltd v Tufail* [2006] EWCA Civ 374 [21]. See also *Life Association of Scotland v Siddal, Cooper v Greene* (1861) 3 De G F & J 58, 77; 45 ER 800 (breach of trust).
[105] (1845) 4 Hare 257, 267; 67 ER 645, cited with approval *Fysh v Page* (1956) 96 CLR 233, 243. In New Zealand, *O'Connor v Hart* [1983] NZLR 280 (CA) 293. More recently, *Humphreys v Humphreys* [2004] EWHC 2201 (Ch) [99] (Rimer J).
[106] *Roberts v Tunstall* (1845) 4 Hare 257, 267; 67 ER 645.
[107] (1859) 4 De G & J 78, 95–96, 99; 45 ER 31.
[108] *Champion v Rigby* (1840) 9 LJ Ch (NS) 211, 214. See also *Lindsay Petroleum Co v Hurd* (1874) LR 5 PC 221 (PC—Canada) 242.

24.50 It is, if not universally, at all events ordinarily necessary that there should be sufficient knowledge of the facts constituting the title to relief.[109] Delay with something less than full knowledge of the facts may count as laches,[110] but it has been said that ignorance of a fraud arising without any fault does not.[111]

24.51 In assessing whether a defence of laches arises, it seems that the knowledge that exists in any particular case is to be weighed alongside other material factors, such as the period of delay, the culpability of the defendant's conduct, and the degree of prejudice on the one side and gain on the other that would accrue upon rescission, by reason of the neglectful delay.[112]

24.52 Delay after notice or knowledge counts more heavily against relief. This was emphasized by Lord Blackburn in *Erlanger*'s case:

> ...a Court of Equity requires that those who come to it to ask its active interposition to give them relief, should use due diligence, after there has been such notice or knowledge as to make it inequitable to lie by. And any change which occurs in the position of the parties or the state of the property after such notice or knowledge should tell much more against the party *in morâ*, than a similar change before he was *in morâ* should do.[113]

Onus of proof
24.53 The onus of proving a defence of laches lies on the party against whom rescission is sought.[114]

Freedom and applying the statute by analogy[115]
24.54 Where the statute of limitations is applied by analogy it has long been established that time begins to run against a claim to rescind for fraud only after the fraud is discovered.[116] Today the statute itself postpones the running of time in certain cases of concealment.[117] Although that provision does not re-enact the old equitable doctrine of concealed fraud, and probably differs in that subsequent concealment postpones the running of time,[118] where the statute is applied by analogy there seems no reason why its provisions as to concealment should not also be applied by analogy.[119]

---

[109] *Champion v Rigby* (1840) 9 LJ Ch (NS) 211, 241.
[110] *Erlanger v The New Sombrero Phosphate Company* (1878) 3 App Cas 1218, 1279, where Lord Blackburn appeared to assume that the bar might arise without knowledge or notice.
[111] *Rolfe v Gregory* (1865) 4 De G J & S 576, 579; 46 ER 1042, 1044.
[112] *Lindsay Petroleum Co v Hurd* (1874) LR 5 PC 221 (PC—Canada) 239–41. In Australia, *Fysh v Page* (1956) 96 CLR 233, 243–44; *JAD International Pty Ltd v International Trucks Australia Limited* (1994) 50 FCR 378 (Full Ct) 388.
[113] *Erlanger v The New Sombrero Phosphate Company* (1878) 3 App Cas 1218, 1279.
[114] *Wall v Cockerell* (1863) 10 HLC 229, 243; 11 ER 1013, 1019 (acquiescence); *Erlanger v The New Sombrero Phosphate Company* (1878) 3 App Cas 1218, 1283 (*restitutio in integrum* impossible); *Lindsay Petroleum Co v Hurd* (1874) LR 5 PC 22 (PC—Canada) 241; *O'Connor v Hart* [1983] NZLR 280 (CA) 294; *Gillespie v Gillespie* [2013] 2 QdR 440 (CA) 460.
[115] The question does not arise in relation to direct application of the statute because the statute only applies to common law rights secured by an antecedent rescission, and for there to have been an effective election to rescind, the injured party must then have been free of the influence of the vitiating factor.
[116] *Hovenden v Lord Annesley* (1806) 2 Sch & Lef 607, 634–36, and cases there discussed.
[117] Limitation Act 1980, s 32; *Newgate Stud Co v Penfold* [2004] EWHC 2993 (ChD) [252]–[256].
[118] *Sheldon v RHM Outhwaite (Underwriting Agencies) Ltd* [1996] AC 102, 144–45, 151.
[119] Sir Robert Megarry V-C seems to have assumed that the predecessor to s 32 of the Limitation Act 1980 would apply if the statutory time limits were applied by analogy: *Tito v Waddell (No 2)* [1977] Ch 106, 244–46.

24.55 The cases indicate that when the statute is applied by analogy, time only begins to run after the party entitled to rescind becomes aware of the material facts,[120] or should with ordinary intelligence have become aware of them.[121]

When lapse of time without knowledge will bar rescission

24.56 It seems that lapse of time without any knowledge of the material facts will bar rescission only in the case of sales of goods induced by innocent misrepresentation.[122]

(2) Need for awareness of rights

Awareness of rights and affirmation

24.57 In England a party entitled to rescind must know of his right to do so before his conduct can amount to an election to affirm.[123] It follows that lapse of time cannot be evidence of affirmation unless the injured party is aware of his right to rescind. This represents an important difference between affirmation and acquiescence. It will be seen that the right to rescind may be lost by acquiescence even though the injured party was always ignorant of his legal rights.

Awareness of rights and acquiescence

24.58 In several of the older cases acquiescence was described in terms that emphasized the need for an awareness of the material facts, but made no mention of any requirement for legal rights to also be known.[124] Lord Selborne described the doctrine in that way in *Erlanger's* case.[125] On the other hand, there are also to be found general statements to the effect that 'acquiescence' requires knowledge of rights,[126] and in *Savery v King*[127] the House of Lords seemed to say that this is true of acquiescence as a bar to a claim to set aside a transaction.[128] This fitted the doctrine applicable to trusts at that time, it being 'quite settled' that the beneficiary of a trust could not be bound by acquiescence absent knowledge of his rights.[129] In *Allcard v Skinner*[130] Cotton LJ said that knowledge of rights was essential,[131] and Lindley LJ

---

[120] *Molloy v Mutual Reserve Life Insurance Co* (1906) 94 LT 756 (CA) 760–63; *Oelkers v Ellis* [1914] 2 KB 139, 149; *Armstrong v Jackson* [1917] 2 KB 822, 830.
[121] *Molloy v Mutual Reserve Life Insurance Co* (1906) 94 LT 756 (CA) 761.
[122] *Leaf v International Galleries* [1950] 2 KB 86 (CA) where the buyer had been acquitted of any laches by the trial judge. Contrast the position in Australia, *Shuman v Coober Pedy Tours Pty Ltd* (1994) 175 LSJS 159; [1994] SASC 4401 [15]–[16].
[123] See Chap 23, para [23.41].
[124] Eg *Vigers v Pike* (1840–1842) 8 Cl & Fin 562, 651–2; 8 ER 220; *Charter v Trevelyan* (1842, 1844) 11 Cl & Fin 714, 740; 8 ER 1273; *Gresley v Mousley* (1858) 1 Giff 450, 460; 65 ER 995 'in cases of this kind, where there is a right to question the transaction, there must be brought home to the person against whom acquiescence is alleged a knowledge of the circumstances that would give a right to question the transaction'.
[125] *Erlanger v The New Sombrero Phosphate Company* (1878) 3 App Cas 1218, 1261; quoted at para [24.41].
[126] *Vyvyan v Vyvyan* (1861) 30 Beav 165, 74; 54 ER 813; aff'd 4 De G F & J 183, 45 ER 1153 (waiver by suit); *Willmott v Barber* (1880) 15 ChD 96, 105 'the doctrine of acquiescence is founded upon conduct with a knowledge of your legal rights' (waiver of covenant).
[127] (1856) 5 HLC 627, 664, 666; 10 ER 1046. The relevant passage has, however, some ambiguities.
[128] See also *Purcell v M'Namara* (1806) 14 Ves Jun 91, 122; 33 ER 455 (Lord Erskine LC). In Australia, *Robinson v Abbott* (1894) 20 VLR 146 (Full Ct).
[129] *Life Association of Scotland v Siddal, Cooper v Greene* (1861) 3 De G F & J 58, 74; 45 ER 800.
[130] (1886) 36 ChD 145 (CA). See also *Champion v Rigby* (1840) 9 LJ Ch (NS) 211, 214 col 2, referring to delay with knowledge of rights.
[131] *Allcard v Skinner* (1887) 36 ChD 145 (CA) 174–75. But the opinion of Cotton LJ in *Evans v Benyon* (1887) 37 ChD 329, 344 was regarded by Wilberforce J in *Re Pauling's Settlement Trusts* [1962] 1 WRL 86, 108 as standing for

and Bowen LJ based their decision on Miss Allcard having deliberately chosen to not inquire into them.[132]

24.59 But despite these statements in the older authorities, and whatever may be the position in relation to the strict or narrow doctrine of acquiescence,[133] the approach today in England is that knowledge of rights is not necessary. This is now the case where a trustee purchases contrary to the fair-dealing rule,[134] and the Court of Appeal in *Goldsworthy v Brickell*[135] said that it is exceedingly doubtful that the position is any different in a case of undue influence. In *Samuel v Wadlow* Toulson LJ, with whom the other members of the Court agreed, said that ignorance of the right to rescind:

> ... was a relevant factor, but there is no hard and fast rule that ignorance of a legal right is a bar to laches or acquiescence. The authorities show that ultimately the court has to look at the whole of the circumstances and decide whether on balance it is just that the agreement should be set aside.[136]

The same principle was applied in *Habib Bank Ltd v Tufail*,[137] which involved a claim to rescind for misrepresentation. It is likely that this principle applies not only to a trustee's purchase from his beneficiary contrary to the fair-dealing rule, and in relation to undue influence and misrepresentation, but to all grounds for rescission in equity. In contrast, in Australia it has been said that in the case of a defence of laches involving only acquiescence or assent, proof of knowledge or belief of rights is a necessary element of the defence, but that the plaintiff's knowledge of its rights will generally be inferred from knowledge of the relevant facts.[138]

24.60 Although knowledge of legal rights may not be necessary for acquiescence, delay after the injured party becomes aware of the right to rescind will usually count for more than an equivalent delay whilst he is ignorant of that right.[139]

Knowledge of rights for affirmation and acquiescence

24.61 Waiver of the right to rescind requires knowledge of the existence of the right if the waiver arises by election, but not if it is founded on the doctrine of acquiescence. Inaction without

---

the contrary proposition in cases of breach of trust. That decision in turn influenced the rule for rescission through *Goldsworthy v Brickell* [1987] 1 Ch 378 (CA) 411–12.

[132] *Allcard v Skinner* (1887) 36 ChD 145 (CA) 188, 192. Lindley LJ also said that the appellant realized it was at least questionable whether the gifts could be reclaimed, and Bowen LJ inclined to think that she was in fact aware of her rights.
[133] *Kammins Ballrooms Co Ltd v Zenith Investments (Torquay) Ltd* [1971] AC 850, 884. See also *Earl of Beauchamp v Winn* (1873) LR 6 HL 223, 234–35; *Re Howlett* [1949] Ch 767, 775. As to the 'strict' doctrine of acquiescence, see para [24.08].
[134] *Holder v Holder* [1968] Ch 353 (CA), following the approach in *Re Pauling's Settlement Trusts* [1962] 1 WRL 86, 108 (unauthorized disposition).
[135] [1987] 1 Ch 378 (CA) 410–12 (Nourse LJ, with whom Parker LJ and Sir John Megaw agreed).
[136] *Samuel v Wadlow* [2007] EWCA Civ 155 [66] (claim to rescind settlement agreement for undue influence).
[137] [2006] EWCA Civ 374 [15]–[22] per Lloyd LJ, with whom Longmore LJ and Bennett J agreed (claim to rescind mortgage for bank's constructive knowledge of misrepresentation as to amount secured).
[138] *Streeter v Western Areas Exploration Pty Ltd* (2011) 278 ALR 291 (WACA) [638]–[639] (Murphy JA, with whom the other members of the court agreed).
[139] Eg *Bullock v Lloyds Bank Ltd* [1955] Ch 317, 327 (four-year delay after becoming aware of right counted for more than nine-year delay before that); *Nutt v Easton* [1899] 1 Ch 873, 879; [1900] 1 Ch 29 (CA) 30 (ten-year delay with knowledge of facts and legal rights made claim to rescind 'hopeless'; 12-year statutory limitation period).

knowledge of the right to rescind may therefore constitute acquiescence, but not an implied election to affirm. However, in the modern English decisions confirming that knowledge of the right to rescind is not required for the defence of acquiescence to be engaged, the reasons indicate that the court considered that the party raising the plea had to demonstrate more than mere inaction implying assent. The party claiming the protection of the defence was also required to demonstrate that it would be inequitable for rescission to be granted.[140] That is not a requirement for waiver by affirmation. It therefore seems that whilst acquiescence operates to cause the right to rescind to be lost by waiver, for the right to be waived there must be a neglect in pursuing the right to rescind[141] that goes beyond what must be established for a finding that an election to affirm is implied or deemed to have occurred.[142] This would provide a logical basis for the different rules for knowledge that apply to the defences of affirmation and acquiescence.[143] The alternative view is that precisely the same inaction without knowledge of the right to rescind may cause waiver by acquiescence but not waiver by election, which would make no sense. The law in this area is probably in need of re-appraisal. For the reasons discussed in Chapter 23, it is suggested that the rules for affirmation should be changed, and the need for a knowledge of rights dispensed with.[144]

Awareness of rights and laches

24.62 To establish a defence of laches not involving acquiescence, which is here called prejudicial laches, it is not necessary to show that the delaying party was aware of their right to rescind. The authoritative formulation in *Lindsay Petroleum Co v Hurd*[145] does not contain any reference to knowledge of rights, and *Samuel v Wadlow*[146] says that it is not necessary. Statements can, however, be found indicating that, absent prejudice, delay counts as laches only if accompanied by knowledge of rights.[147] Certainly it seems that delay after becoming aware of the right to rescind, or the means of knowledge, counts more heavily against the party asserting the right.[148] In an Australian case the complainant's lack of means to enforce their rights, of which advice had been given in general terms, and lack of understanding of what steps needed to be taken, was regarded as counting against a finding of laches.[149]

---

[140] *Goldsworthy v Brickell* [1987] Ch 378 (CA) 409, 411, 416–17 (whole circumstances to be considered to determine if just to permit rescission; must be inequitable to allow rescission); *Habib Bank Ltd v Tufail* [2006] EWCA Civ 374 [20], [25], [38] (rescission must be inequitable); *Samuel v Wadlow* [2007] EWCA Civ 155 [66] (question is whether rescission just in all of the circumstances). These cases also underline that in determining whether rescission would be inequitable the court is to look at all of the circumstances, and retains a broad discretion. Very long and unexplained delay with knowledge of the facts might well suffice, notwithstanding the difficulty of identifying specific prejudice: see *P&O Nedlloyd BV v Arab Metals Co (No 2)* [2007] 1 WLR 2288 (CA) 2312 (court would not rule out the possibility that it might be inequitable to allow a claim to be pursued after very long delay, even absent evidence that defendant or third party had altered his position).
[141] See para [24.11].
[142] See para [24.07].
[143] It would also imply that the waiver of rights arising from election differs from the waiver of rights following acquiescence, and that two different species of 'waiver' are engaged by each doctrine.
[144] See para [23.51].
[145] (1874) LR 5 PC 221 (PC—Canada) 239–41.
[146] [2007] EWCA Civ 155 [66].
[147] *Rees v De Bernardy* [1896] 2 Ch 437, 445. See also JM Lightwood, *The Time Limit on Actions* (1909) 259–60; T Prime and G Scanlan, *The Law of Limitation* (2nd edn, 2001) 306. That the point is one 'on which the decided authorities do not speak with one clear voice' was noted by the Chancellor in *Capcon Holdings plc v Edwards* [2007] EWHC 2662 (Ch) [61], [62] (where it was not necessary to decide the question).
[148] *Turner v Collins* (1871) 7 Ch App 329, 340–42; see also *Bullock v Lloyds Bank Ltd* [1955] Ch 317, 327.
[149] *Gillespie v Gillespie* [2013] 2 QdR 440 (CA) 461 (undue influence as to transfer of house by father to son).

24. DELAY AND ESTOPPEL 531

Awareness of rights and statute of limitations
In *Molloy v Mutual Reserve Life Insurance Co*[150] the Court of Appeal held that there was no **24.63**
need for the party imposed upon to know of his right to rescind before time began to run
for the purposes of applying the statute of limitations by analogy. This appears to continue
to represent the law today.

(3) Unreasonable delay after emancipation from the vitiating factor
Steps to rescind must be taken within a reasonable time
The general rule is that once the party entitled to rescind is aware of the material facts and **24.64**
is otherwise emancipated from the vitiating circumstances, steps to rescind must be taken
within a reasonable time. If there is an unreasonable delay the right to rescind will be lost by
waiver, arising either because an election to affirm is inferred or deemed to have occurred,
or by reason of acquiescence.

The yardstick of reasonable time seems to apply to all grounds for rescission.[151] It is men- **24.65**
tioned in the context of misrepresentation,[152] voidable contracts of insurance,[153] sales
and gifts procured by undue influence,[154] and breach of fiduciary duty by trustees[155] and
directors;[156] and when delay is looked at both in terms of election and acquiescence.[157]
Although there have been suggestions to the contrary,[158] the test of reasonable time seems
universally applicable when assessing whether a right to rescind has been lost by delay.[159]

Unreasonable delay: inference of fact or presumption of law?
Election
In *Clough v London and North Western Railway Co* the Court of Exchequer Chamber de- **24.66**
scribed the effect of delay in the following terms:

---

[150] (1906) 94 LT 756 (CA).
[151] It is also employed in the case of some statutory rights of rescission, such as s 925A of the Australian Corporations Act 2001 (Cth) (unlicensed financial services), as to which, *Bathurst Regional Council v Local Government Financial Services Pty Ltd (No 5)* [2012] FCA 1200 [3293], [3306].
[152] *Re Eastgate* [1905] 1 KB 465, 467 (sale of furniture and other items procured by fraud); *United Shoe Machinery Company of Canada v Brunet* [1909] AC 330 (PC—Canada) 338 (hire of shoe-making machines said to be procured by fraud); *Leaf v International Galleries* [1950] 2 KB 86 (CA) 90, 92 (purchase of painting voidable for innocent misrepresentation); *Haas Timber & Trading Co Pty Ltd v Wade* (1954) 94 CLR 593, 602 (fraudulent share allotment; requirement for rescission within reasonable time described as 'the well-recognized rule in equity'); *SK Shipping Europe plc v Capital VLCC 3 Corp* [2021] 2 Lloyd's Rep 109 [203](v),(vi) (summary of principles not challenged on appeal, [2022] EWCA Civ 231 [73]).
[153] *McCormick v National Motor and Accident Insurance* (1934) 49 Lloyd's Rep 362 (CA) 365–66 (by implication); *Svenska Handelsbanken v Sun Alliance and London Insurance plc* [1996] 1 Lloyd's Rep 519, 569.
[154] *Savery v King* (1856) 5 HLC 627, 666; 10 ER 1046; *Allcard v Skinner* (1887) 36 ChD 145 (CA) 187, 'he ought in my opinion to seek relief within a reasonable time after the removal of the influence under which the gift was made' (Lindley LJ); *Humphreys v Humphreys* [2004] EWHC 2201 (Ch) [99] 'so long as the undue influence persists, claims can be brought whatever the period since the transaction; but that once the complainant is no longer under the defendant's influence, a claim to set the transaction must be brought within a reasonable time' (Rimer J).
[155] *Campbell v Walker* (1800) 5 Ves Jun 678, 680; 31 ER 801.
[156] *Erlanger v The New Sombrero Phosphate Company* (1878) 3 App Cas 1218, 1260.
[157] See nn 148–152.
[158] J Brunyate, *Limitation of Actions in Equity* (1932) 221–25 (no reasonable time requirement where contract voidable for fraud at law, or gift for undue influence in equity). Cf M Franks, *Limitation of Actions* (1959) 251, 254.
[159] This is also the position advocated in *Restatement (Second) of Contracts* vol 3, §§ 381(1), 381(2) (1981).

In such cases the question is, has the person on whom the fraud was practised, having notice of the fraud, elected not to avoid the contract? or has he elected to avoid it? or has he made no election?

We think that so long as he has made no election he retains the right to determine it either way, subject to this...

Lapse of time without rescinding will furnish evidence that he has determined to affirm the contract; and when the lapse of time is great, it probably would in practice be treated as conclusive evidence that he has so determined.[160]

24.67 A very similar opinion was expressed by Lindley LJ in *Allcard v Skinner*, when speaking of a gift voidable for undue influence as opposed to a contract induced by fraud:

... if the donor desires to have his gift declared invalid and set aside, he ought, in my opinion, to seek relief within a reasonable time after the removal of the influence under which the gift was made. If he does not the inference is strong, and if the lapse of time is long the inference becomes inevitable and conclusive, that the donor is content not to call the gift in question, or, in other words, that he elects not to avoid it, or, what is the same thing in effect, that he ratifies and confirms it.[161]

24.68 Both of these statements indicate that once the party entitled to rescind is put to an election, inaction will lead first to a rebuttable inference of fact and then to a conclusive inference that the choice has been made to affirm. Similarly, whilst there are many statements to the effect that delay after an underwriter is put to an election is only evidence of affirmation,[162] there are also indications that an election to affirm will be conclusively inferred after a sufficient lapse of time.[163]

Acquiescence

24.69 On the other hand, when it comes to the rules governing the equitable doctrine of acquiescence the picture appears at first to be different. Since Lord Thurlow's decision in *Earl of Deloraine v Browne*,[164] as explained by Lord Redesdale, it has been accepted that acquiescence is an inference from facts, and that lapse of time is a material fact tending to prove it. For that reason, long delay is not a ground for demurring, unless the statute of limitations applies directly, or by analogy in accordance with settled equitable principle.[165] But the correct view seems to be that the substance of this rule is no different from that just discussed. Long delay may, in appropriate cases, raise a conclusive inference of assent that amounts to a binding acquiescence.[166]

---

[160] (1871) LR 7 Ex 26, 35.
[161] (1887) 36 ChD 145 (CA) 187.
[162] *Allen v Robles* [1969] 1 WLR 1193 (CA) 1196 'delay in itself was of such a length as to evidence that they had in truth decided to accept liability'; *Iron Trades Mutual Insurance Co Ltd v Companhia de Seguros Imperio* [1992] 1 Lloyd's Rep IR 213, 225 'if the delay is such as to evidence that the insurer had in truth decided to accept liability'; *Spriggs v Wessington Court Schools Ltd* [2005] 1 Lloyd's Rep IR 474, 479.
[163] *Liberian Insurance Agency Inc v Mosse* [1977] 2 Lloyd's Rep 560, 565 'deemed to have affirmed the contract if... so much time has elapsed that the necessary inference is one of affirmation'.
[164] *Earl of Deloraine v Browne* (1792) 3 Bro CC 633, 646; 29 ER 739, and Reporter's Notes (1) and (4); *Hovenden v Lord Annesley* (1806) 2 Sch & Lef 607, 637–39.
[165] *Earl of Deloraine v Browne* (1792) 3 Bro CC 633, 29 ER 739.
[166] *Life Association of Scotland v Siddal, Cooper v Greene* (1861) 3 De G F & J 58, 77; 45 ER 800 (breach of trust) 'although the rule be that the onus lies on the party relying on acquiescence to prove the facts from which the consent of the *cestui que trust* is to be inferred, it is easy to conceive cases in which, from great lapse of time, such facts might and ought to be presumed'.

Rebuttable and then conclusive inference of fact
The position therefore appears to be that delay in taking steps to set aside the transaction **24.70** leads to a factual inference that the party entitled to rescind has chosen not to. The legal effect of that is waiver, whether analysed in terms of election between rights or acquiescence in the facts giving rise to the right. In both cases, the longer the delay the stronger is the inference of waiver, and at a certain point in time a court is entitled to conclude that the inference cannot be rebutted. At what point in time a conclusive inference will be drawn is a question of mixed fact and law, and must vary widely from case to case. However, in all cases, the time at which the party seeking relief became aware of the right to do so ought to be of particular importance, for delay thereafter naturally implies that a choice has been made to leave matters where they stand.

(4) What amounts to unreasonable delay

Varies with the circumstances
The degree of delay that will bar a right to rescind varies with the circumstances of the par- **24.71** ticular case. The nature of the contract, and of the property transferred, the presence of prejudice, and the culpability of the conduct permitting rescission are each important.[167] A delay that would bar rescission in one set of circumstances will not do so in another. The context-sensitive nature of the inquiry has been underlined in connection with affirmation,[168] laches,[169] and the effects of delay generally on the right to rescind.[170] The variables that shape the effects of delay are considered in turn.

Unreasonable delay and the type of transaction
An inference of affirmation or acquiescence will be drawn at quite different points in time, **24.72** depending on the type of transaction sought to be set aside.

Ongoing mutual obligations
Where there are ongoing mutual obligations between the parties to the voidable contract, **24.73** an election to affirm is likely to be inferred much earlier.[171] In cases of this kind inaction will more readily lead the party against whom rescission is sought to reasonably conclude that a

---

[167] See paras [24.72]–[24.105]. Cf the rules set out in *Restatement (Second) of Contracts* vol 3, § 381(3) (1981): 'In determining what is a reasonable time, the following circumstances are significant: (a) the extent to which the delay enabled or might have enabled the party with the power of avoidance to speculate at the other party's risk; (b) the extent to which the delay resulted or might have resulted in justifiable reliance by the other party or by third persons; (c) the extent to which the ground for avoidance was the result of any fault by either party; and (d) the extent to which the other party's conduct contributed to the delay'. In Australia, *Haas Timber & Trading Co Pty Ltd v Wade* (1954) 94 CLR 593, 602 (voidable share allotment) 'Delay stands on a somewhat different footing. It is necessarily a matter of degree and must depend on the circumstances of the given case ... The reasonableness of the course taken by the shareholder must be determined by reference not only to the facts affecting his conduct but also to its probable consequences upon the company and others'.
[168] *Aaron's Reefs Limited v Twiss* [1896] AC 273, 294; *Coastal Estates Pty Ltd v Melevende* [1965] VR 433 (Full Ct) 443.
[169] *Allcard v Skinner* (1887) 36 ChD 145 (CA) 163 (Kekewich J).
[170] *Erlanger v The New Sombrero Phosphate Company* (1878) 3 App Cas 1218, 1259 (Lord O'Hagan). In Canada, *Kellogg Brown & Root Inc v Aerotech Herman Nelson Inc* (2004) 238 DLR (4th) 594 (Man CA) [54]. In Australia, *Haas Timber & Trading Co Pty Ltd v Wade* (1954) 94 CLR 593, 602 (Dixon CJ, Fullagar and Kitto JJ).
[171] See also *Restatement (First) of Restitution* 251 (1937): 'mutual rights or duties which would be affected by the rescission, as where the transaction is only partially executed on one side'.

choice not to rescind had been made. This is demonstrated in contracts of insurance, which tend to involve ongoing mutual obligations. A delay of months after discovery of the material facts may cause an underwriter to lose the right to rescind. In *Svenska Handelsbanken v Sun Alliance and London Insurance plc*[172] Rix J accepted that a delay of ten months following discovery of the material facts was sufficient in the circumstances of that case.[173]

Where the contract involves ongoing risk and reward: delay to claim a risk-free reward

24.74 In a series of old cases concerned with mining ventures the courts held that if the subject of a bargain involves property pregnant with risk and that requires an ongoing financial commitment to generate profit, and a claim for a constructive trust or relief from forfeiture is brought by a former participant who had ceased to share in that risk, the claim would be dismissed if not brought promptly after the relevant facts became known.[174] The underlying principle seems to have been that delay in order to claim a risk-free reward defeated the equity to relief, and the cases were subsequently applied on that basis to claims to rescind,[175] and to claims for a constructive trust outside rescission.[176]

Interest in security of the transaction

24.75 Where there is a special interest in upholding the security of a particular type of transaction, a shorter period of time will be allowed. This is the best explanation for *Leaf v International Galleries*,[177] where a delay of five years before rescinding the purchase of a painting was held to be 'much more than a reasonable time'. In so concluding, the Court of Appeal emphasized the need to maintain the security of contracts for the sale of goods.[178]

24.76 Voidable gifts are at the other end of the scale. The only interest protected is the legitimate expectations of the donee. Accordingly, where a voluntary settlement has not been relied upon by the defendant, and rescission would cause no prejudice, it has been permitted after a very long lapse of time,[179] and one text writer has said that less diligence is required when seeking to set aside voluntary dispositions.[180]

---

[172] [1996] 1 Lloyd's Rep 519, 569.
[173] For further, general, observations as to the time to be permitted to an insurer to consider its position, *Kosmar Villa Holidays plc v Trustees of Syndicate 1243* [2008] 2 All ER (Comm) 14 (CA) [78]–[83] per Rix LJ.
[174] *Senhouse v Christian* (1795) 19 Ves Jun 157–59; 34 ER 476–77; 19 Beav 356, 52 ER 387–88 (constructive trust); *Norway v Rowe* (1812) 19 Ves Jun 144, 159; 34 ER 472 (constructive trust); *Prendergast v Turton* (1841) 1 Y & C 98, 110–12; 62 ER 807, aff'd 13 LJ Ch 268 (forfeiture of shares); *Clarke v Hart* (1857) 6 HLC 633, 656; 10 ER 1143 (forfeiture of shares); *Clegg v Edmonson* (1857) 8 De G M & G 787, 808, 814; 44 ER 593 (constructive trust).
[175] *Erlanger v The New Sombrero Phosphate Company* (1878) 3 App Cas 1218, 1281–83 (Lord Blackburn). See also JD Heydon, MJ Leeming, and PG Turner, *Meagher, Gummow and Lehane's Equity Doctrines and Remedies* (5th edn, 2014) [38-3025] and para [24.100] considering the general principle against speculation.
[176] For application of a principle against speculation in cases of constructive trust, *Re Jarvis Dec'd* [1958] 1 WLR 815, 820–21 (small business). In Australia, *Rowe v Oates* (1905) 3 CLR 73 (mine); *Grundt v The Great Boulder Gold Mines Limited* (1937) 59 CLR 641, 679–80 (mine); *Loizou v Derrimut Enterprises Pty Ltd* [2004] VSC 176 [152]–[58] (property development); *Streeter v Western Areas Exploration Pty Ltd* (2011) 278 ALR 291 (WACA) [642]–[646], [663]–[674] (shares in junior mining company; special leave to appeal refused [2011] HCA Trans 330); *Wright Prospecting Pty Ltd v Hancock Prospecting Pty Ltd* [2013] WASC 248 [61] (mining operations). As to resulting trusts, *Patel v Shah* [2005] EWCA Civ 157 (commercial property).
[177] [1950] 2 KB 86 (CA) 90, 92.
[178] *Leaf v International Galleries* [1950] 2 KB 86 (CA) 92, 94–95. See now *Salt v Stratstone Specialist Limited* [2015] EWCA Civ 745 [32]–[35], [47]–[49] (alignment between loss of right to reject for non-conformance, and to rescind for innocent misrepresentation, altered since *Leaf's* case).
[179] *Bester v Perpetual Trustee Co Ltd* [1970] 3 NSWLR 30, 37–38 (settlement by young woman for her own benefit rescinded for undue influence 20 years later; no prejudice to trustee defendant).
[180] M Franks, *Limitation of Actions* (1959) 254.

Unreasonable delay and the type of property

The nature of the property disposed of under the transaction affects what period of delay will bar rescission. **24.77**

Whether produces income

The old authorities drew a distinction between property that did and did not produce income. Lapse of time counted for less where property sought to be regained upon rescission produced no income. Lord Eldon drew this distinction in *Hatch v Hatch*[181] when rescinding a conveyance of the advowson of Sutton from guardian to ward after a 20-year delay, and the notion was subsequently approved in the mid-nineteenth century.[182] The cases offer no explicit explanation for this principle. If the principle continues to have a role today, the asset should neither produce income nor have any use value to be restored upon rescission. A share carrying no right to dividends might qualify. In cases of this kind delay causes less prejudice to the party whose title is impeached because he need not account for income or use value. Complete restitution is made by simply returning title to the asset received. For that reason it may be that a longer delay will be countenanced without imputation of laches. **24.78**

Settlor rescinding settlement for own benefit

There are some indications that the courts take a more generous approach to delay where the claim is to rescind an irrevocable settlement for the benefit of the settlor.[183] In cases of that kind rescission causes limited prejudice; there is none to the trustee, who holds a bare legal title, or to the beneficiary, who is the party seeking to rescind. At most it extinguishes the future claims of any who might take an interest in remainder under the settlement. A right to rescind a settlement of this kind may, nonetheless, be lost by delay. In *Bullock v Lloyds Bank Ltd*[184] Vaisey J held that the claimant's four-year delay after becoming aware of objections to the validity of her settlement did not amount to laches barring her right to rescind, but indicated that the issue was finely balanced.[185] **24.79**

Reversionary interests

The old Chancery courts developed a rule that if a reversionary interest was conveyed, for so long as it remained reversionary, lapse of time counted for little in answer to a claim to rescind.[186] The rule is vividly illustrated by *Salter v Bradshaw*,[187] where Sir John Romilly rescinded the sale of a reversionary estate at Bethnal Green in London on a bill brought 38 years later, underlining that it had been brought only one year after the estate had fallen into possession. The decree was made notwithstanding that the lapse of time had materially prejudiced the defendant by making it much more difficult to prove that full value was given, which he had to do to resist the claim to rescind. **24.80**

---

[181] (1804) 9 Ves Jun 292, 298–99; 32 ER 615.
[182] *Wright v Vanderplank* (1856) 8 De G M & G 133, 150–51; 44 ER 340 (also a case of gift).
[183] *Bester v Perpetual Trustee Co Ltd* [1970] 3 NSWLR 30, 37-38 (irrevocable settlement rescinded for undue influence after a 20-year delay).
[184] [1955] Ch 317, 327.
[185] *Bullock v Lloyds Bank Ltd* [1955] Ch 317, 327, where Vaisey J said 'I have felt a great deal of difficulty about this' and concluded 'with hesitation' that the right to rescind had not been lost.
[186] *Sibbering v Earl of Balcarras* (1850) 3 De G & SM 735, 64 ER 682.
[187] (1858) 26 Beav 161, 53 ER 858.

24.81 The rule is old and its basis unclear. It was said that equity acted by analogy with the statute of limitations.[188] Under both the Limitation Act 1623 and the Real Property Limitation Act 1833 time generally began to run for the recovery of a reversionary estate in land only after it fell into possession, for the right of entry or action was deemed to accrue then.[189] But it was also said that for so long as the property remained reversionary, there continued the state of distress and improvidence underpinning the right to rescind, and that was why time only ran from the moment the interest fell into possession.[190] The rule might also be connected to the notion that a *cestui que trust* whose interest is reversionary is not bound to assert his title until it comes into possession.[191]

24.82 The rules in the Limitation Act 1623 and the Real Property Limitation Act 1833 were concerned only with real property, and it is unclear how far the equitable rule extended to a claim to rescind the transfer of reversionary interests in personal property. It has been applied to an unconscionable bargain involving a reversionary interest in a sum of money,[192] but not where a gift of a reversionary interest in money was voidable for undue influence. Delay was held to bar the right even though the property remained reversionary.[193]

24.83 There seems no reason why the principle should not continue to apply today, at least to transfers of reversionary interests in land, where it is clearly established. If that is correct, the courts should be free to proceed by analogy with the current statutory time bars for recovering possession of reversionary interests in land.[194]

Speculative and fluctuating property

24.84 The party rescinding is not permitted knowingly to speculate on the outcome of the bargain.[195] Once the true facts are known, prompt action is generally required if an investment has been made in speculative assets.[196] Delay will likewise count more heavily if the transaction involves what has been called 'property of a fluctuating nature'.[197]

Unreasonable delay and prejudice

24.85 The significance of prejudice for lapse of time is considered separately later. For present purposes it is to be noted that prompt action is required in at least three types of transaction where it is the risk of prejudice that appears to underpin the need for promptitude.

---

[188] *Sibbering v Earl of Balcarras* (1850) 3 De G & SM 735, 736; 64 ER 682 (counsel's argument).
[189] Real Property Limitation Act 1833, ss 3–4; JM Lightwood, *The Time Limit on Actions* (1909) 52. See now Limitation Act 1980, s 15.
[190] *Beynon v Cook* (1874) 10 Ch App 389, 393 (Jessel MR).
[191] *Life Association of Scotland v Siddal, Cooper v Greene* (1861) 3 De G F & J 58, 73; 45 ER 800; JM Lightwood, *The Time Limit on Actions* (1909) 261. Cf also *Re Blachford* (1884) 27 ChD 676 (reversionary testamentary property).
[192] *Beynon v Cook* (1874) 10 Ch App 389, 393 (sale of reversion by 'distressed' younger son).
[193] *Turner v Collins* (1871) 7 Ch App 329.
[194] Limitation Act 1980, s 15; see paras [24.29]–[24.32].
[195] See para [24.100].
[196] See para [24.100]; see also J Brunyate, *Limitation of Actions in Equity* (1932) 226–27. Also, *Ernest v Vivian* (1863) 33 LJ (Ch) 513, 517 (person entitled to possession of a mine standing by to see whether those wrongfully in possession succeed or are ruined), cited with approval in *Boyns v Lackey* (1958) SR (NSW) 395, 403–04 and in *Streeter v Western Areas Exploration Pty Ltd* (2011) 278 ALR 291 (WACA) [644] (claims for constructive trust rather than rescission).
[197] For that language, eg *Baburin v Baburin (No 2)* [1991] 2 QdR 240 (CA) 258–59 (share sale agreement as to motor garage business in Biloela; 19-year delay; laches established); *Herrod v Johnston* [2013] 2 QdR 102 (CA) 126–27 (grazing partnership; eight-year delay; no laches).

24. DELAY AND ESTOPPEL

The three categories are: voidable gifts that increase the donee's spending; deteriorating assets acquired by the rescinding party; and voidable share allotments. Each of these three categories will be considered in turn.

Gifts that increase the donee's spending

There is some authority that where a gift is of such a nature that it induces the donee to increase his spending in a way that would not otherwise have occurred, there is an obligation to act without undue delay once the vitiating factor has ceased to operate and the donor has the means of knowing of his rights.[198] The notion seems to be founded on the prejudice that rescission could cause, and assumes that the donee is unable to rely on a *pro tanto* defence of change of position. To the extent that he may, this consideration ought logically to fall away, for that defence removes any prejudice that the donee would otherwise suffer upon rescission.

24.86

Deteriorating assets acquired by rescinding party

Where the asset sought to be returned by a rescinding buyer tends by its nature to become less valuable with the passing of time, such as a short lease to extract resources, or an operating mine, there is some authority that an election to rescind should be made promptly after the buyer becomes aware of the material facts, absent which the right will be lost.[199] This seems to be because of the prejudice that would be caused by restoring to the defendant an asset that has deteriorated in a way that has not translated into money or other benefits liable to be restored by the claimant upon rescission. Any such principle ought equally to apply to perishable commodities such as fresh foodstuffs, and ameliorates the harshness of the general rule that rescission is not barred if property deteriorates due to inherent vice.[200]

24.87

Share allotments

Soon after the passing of the Companies Act 1862, the English courts developed a rule that prompt action is required when a shareholder wishes to rescind an allotment of shares in a company incorporated under that Act. Once the shareholder had discovered, or ought to have discovered,[201] the falsity of the company's representations, he would lose the right to rescind unless prompt action was taken.[202] The shareholder had to notify the company of his intention to reject the shares, and to take steps to have his name removed from the share register if the company did not do that itself, at least where he wished to defend liability for a call. Loss of the right was variously put on the basis of laches, election, or simply delay.[203]

24.88

---

[198] *Turner v Collins* (1871) 7 Ch App 329, 341 (gift to family); *Allcard v Skinner* (1887) 36 ChD 145 (CA) 173, 188–89; cf 192 (gift to religious order).

[199] *Erlanger v The New Sombrero Phosphate Company* (1878) 3 App Cas 1218, 1240, 1247–48, 1260–61, 1281; *Lagunas Nitrate Company v Lagunas Syndicate* [1899] 2 Ch 392 (CA) 416, 457, 464.

[200] As to that principle, see Chap 18, para [18.09].

[201] It was said that the right to rescind could be lost by inaction 'with the full means of knowledge' of the truth: *Peek v Gurney* (1873) LR 6 HL 377, 384; see also *Ashley's case* (1870) LR 9 Eq 263, 269.

[202] See further M Franks, *Limitation of Actions* (1959) 252–53; M Arden, D Prentice, and D Richards (eds), *Buckley on the Companies Acts* (15th edn, 2000) [359.114]–[359.128].

[203] *Directors of the Central Railway Company of Venezuela v Kisch* (1867) LR 2 App Cas 99, 125; *Ogilvie v Currie* (1868) 37 LR Ch (NS) 541, 545, 546; *Sharpley v Louth and East Coast Railway Company* (1876) 2 ChD 663, 685; *Aaron's Reefs Limited v Twiss* [1896] AC 273, 294; *First National Reinsurance Company Limited v Greenfield* [1921] 2 KB 260 (CA) 275–79; *Re Southern Woollen-Mills* [1930] 1 NZLR 10, 12.

VI. OTHER BARS

24.89 The rule was developed at a time when equity finance was regularly raised by issuing partly paid shares, and with considerations in mind that were peculiar to that context. Rescission of an allotment of partly paid shares withdraws from the company the asset represented by the shareholder's obligation to contribute. That prejudices the other shareholders and creditors by shrinking the net assets available to satisfy their claims on the company. It also increases the exposure of the remaining shareholders to the company's creditors. In addition, when equity finance is raised in this way, the share register is particularly important as evidence of the company's creditworthiness. The longer the gap is between an election to rescind and removal of the shareholder's name from the register, the greater is the risk that third parties might be misled as to the company's true asset base.

24.90 It was with these considerations in mind that the courts developed the rule that a shareholder must take prompt action or lose his right to rescind, and the allied rule that rescission is wholly barred once winding up commences or is about to commence.[204] The rule requiring prompt action should not apply when fully paid shares are allotted, for the reasons underpinning the rule do not apply with the same force.[205] The High Court of Australia has said that the old rule requiring great promptness on the part of a shareholder seeking to relieve himself from a contract of membership on the ground of fraud 'is one that perhaps can seldom have much reality of application in the course of business as it proceeds at the present time'.[206] It has never been suggested that the principle applies to purchases between shareholders, and the cases are rather to the contrary.[207]

Unreasonable delay and culpability of the conduct permitting rescission

24.91 In general, the claim of a wrongdoer to retain ownership and to uphold his bargain is less deserving of protection than the equivalent claim of an innocent contracting party. This general notion appears to find some expression in the principles applicable to delay.

Laches

24.92 The first *Restatement of Restitution*[208] concludes that the culpability of the defendant is of 'prime importance' in determining the effect of delay on a claim to rescind. In English law, that is always true where the defence is founded on prejudicial laches,[209] which requires that the defendant has an equity that, on balance, outweighs the claimant's right taking into

---

[204] *Oakes v Turquand* (1867) LR 2 HL 325; see Chap 25.
[205] There do not seem to have been any instances where the rule requiring prompt action was applied to allotments of fully paid shares. See also *Coastal Estates Pty Ltd v Melevende* [1965] VR 433 (Full Ct) 443, where Sholl J underlined that the need to rescind share allotments promptly arises 'because the rights of creditors and other shareholders are affected'; and *Kupchak v Dayson Holdings Ltd* (1965) 53 WWR 65, 78 to similar effect.
[206] *Haas Timber & Trading Co Pty Ltd v Wade* (1954) 94 CLR 593, 604, noting that the rule proceeded on the footing that other persons could be expected to enter into engagements with the company on the faith of the membership of the shareholder entitled to rescind (citing *Heymann v European Central Railway Co* (1868) LR 7 Eq 154, 169 per Lord Romilly MR).
[207] Eg *Oelkers v Ellis* [1914] 2 KB 139, 151–52; *Armstrong v Jackson* [1917] 2 KB 822, 830, which both involved brokers selling their own shares. If *Seddon v The North Eastern Salt Company Limited* [1905] 326, 334 suggests otherwise, it ought not to be followed.
[208] *Restatement (First) of Restitution* 251 (1937) 'The degree of culpability of the transferee, if any, is of prime importance; less delay will be permitted against an innocent transferee than against one guilty of fraud or duress'. The point does not appear to be addressed in the *Restatement (Third) of Restitution* (2011); see at §§ 54(6), 70(2) and commentary thereto.
[209] For 'prejudicial laches' see para [24.17].

account all the circumstances affecting them.[210] That necessarily makes the defendant's conduct of prime importance. The point is illustrated by *Fysh v Page*.[211] The High Court of Australia there held that Mrs Fysh was not entitled to rescind the sale of a grazing property in Tasmania, which had devolved to her upon her husband's death, by reason of her laches. In 1942 Mrs Fysh had sold the property to a neighbouring farmer, Page, who was an executor of Mr Fysh's will at the date of the contract but not the conveyance. There was no evidence of unfair dealing, and the claim was brought 12 years after the sale. In dismissing the appeal on the ground that the claim failed for laches, the court emphasized 'the very slender case, if any there be, for equitable relief upon the facts proved as they stood in 1942'.[212] The reasoning indicates that had Page been guilty of active misconduct, Mrs Fysh's delay may not have been fatal to her claim to rescind.[213]

Election
Similarly, where delay is said to evidence an election to affirm, it is generally more difficult for the defendant to prove that a choice to affirm has been made if he has been guilty of active misconduct, rather than mere inadvertence. In *Oelekers v Ellis*[214] Horridge J said that even if the defrauded purchaser of shares had been aware of the material facts, his four-year delay did not amount to an election to affirm.[215] Had the case been one of innocent misrepresentation, that inference would have been far more difficult to resist.

24.93

It has also been said that rejecting liability for fraud is a significant step, and that an insurer should not do so without substantial evidence.[216] In another case the court accepted that full investigations were necessary before solicitors and counsel could properly stand behind a pleading of fraud, and that delay before the investigations were complete was not affirmation.[217] These cases imply that where all other things are equal, a longer period of delay will be permitted if time is being used to determine whether there has been deceit, as opposed to some lesser species of misconduct.

24.94

Delay without knowledge or laches
The quality of the defendant's conduct is also important in the exceptional case where delay without either knowledge or laches bars rescission. This occurred in *Leaf v International Galleries*,[218] where the Court of Appeal held that Mr Leaf was not entitled to rescind his purchase of 'Salisbury Cathedral' for the gallery's innocent misrepresentation that it was a Constable. The claim was brought after five years, and during that time Mr Leaf had been wholly unaware that the attribution was wrong. In dismissing his appeal the court emphasized that Mr Leaf had an opportunity to verify the truth of the representation soon after the

24.95

---

[210] *Nwakobi, The Osha of Obosi v Nzekwu* [1964] 1 WLR 1019 (PC—Nigeria) 1024, 1026. Cf *Goldsworthy v Brickell* [1987] AC 378 (CA) 416 (Parker LJ).
[211] (1956) 96 CLR 233.
[212] *Fysh v Page* (1956) 96 CLR 233, 244.
[213] See also *Lagunas Nitrate Company v Lagunas Syndicate* [1899] 2 Ch 392 (CA) 433–34, where the issue was framed in terms of whether *restitutio in integrum* was possible.
[214] [1913] 2 KB 139.
[215] *Oelekers v Ellis* [1913] 2 KB 139, 151–52.
[216] *Baghbadrani v Commercial Union Assurance Co plc* [2000] 1 Lloyd's Rep IR 94, 122 (fraudulent claim rather than rescission).
[217] *Fiona Trust & Holding Corporation v Privalov* [2007] 1 All ER (Comm) 81 [36].
[218] [1950] 2 KB 86 (CA).

painting was bought, and could not now complain.[219] But that reasoning has been consistently rejected in cases of fraud,[220] and there is little doubt that rescission would have been permitted if the gallery had known that the attribution was wrong.

24.96 The decision can, in this respect, be contrasted with *Charter v Trevelyan*,[221] where the House of Lords confirmed a decree rescinding a conveyance of the manor of Seaton notwithstanding that the bill was brought 37 years after the purchaser had first taken possession, and by the time of the appeal 17 years after that, his grandson was in possession.[222] The buyer, Charter, who was Trevelyan's solicitor and land agent, had practised a deception on him that had remained undiscovered for 37 years. The appeal was dismissed over the objection that the delay exceeded 20 years,[223] and even though the House of Lords accepted that rescission would cause 'great affliction' to the appellant's family.[224] The principles upon which the House of Lords acted have been confirmed since.[225]

24.97 Delay appears to bar rescission without laches or knowledge of the true facts only in cases of innocent misrepresentation, and probably then only if the contract involves a sale of goods.[226]

Delay and duress

24.98 In *Alec Lobb (Garages) Ltd v Total Oil GB Ltd*[227] Deputy Judge Millett QC (as his Lordship then was) said that a plaintiff who seeks to set aside a transaction for economic duress must establish that 'he repudiated the transaction as soon as the pressure was relaxed'. This opinion has been followed by an intermediate appellate court in Australia, in circumstances where the party complaining of economic duress had taken no step to reject the transaction for nine years.[228]

24.99 The position is likely to be otherwise where the duress is not economic, but instead arises from acts of violence or threats of violence. The Hong Kong Court of Appeal confirmed that a deed of gift partly induced by a physical assault had been rescinded notwithstanding that no action was taken to avoid the instrument until some two years had passed, and that during that time the perpetrator had left the country and the victim had confirmed the instrument in correspondence.[229]

---

[219] *Leaf v International Galleries* [1950] 2 KB 86 (CA) 91, 92. Also, *Salt v Stratstone Specialist Limited* [2015] EWCA Civ 745 [32]–[35], [47]–[49].
[220] *Rawlins v Wickham* (1858) 3 De G & J 304, 313–14; 44 ER 1285.
[221] (1842, 1844) 11 Cl & Fin 714, 8 ER 1273.
[222] The appeal was heard 17 years after the bill was filed and 9 years after the making of the first decree for rescission, which had not been complied with.
[223] *Charter v Trevelyan* (1842) 11 Cl & Fin 714, 724–28; 8 ER 1273. For the relevance of 20 years, see para [24.31].
[224] *Charter v Trevelyan* (1842) 11 Cl & Fin 714, 740; 8 ER 1273.
[225] *Savery v King* (1856) 5 HLC 627, 666; 10 ER 1046, 1062–63; *Brown v McLintock* (1873) LR 6 HL 456, 471–72; *Vane v Vane* (1873) 8 Ch App 383, 397.
[226] *Leaf v International Galleries* [1950] 2 KB 86 (CA), and which is now to be read in the light of *Salt v Stratstone Specialist Limited* [2015] EWCA Civ 745. As to the relevance of the contract being for goods, see para [24.75].
[227] [1983] 1 WLR 87, 93; on appeal [1985] 1 WLR 173 (CA).
[228] *Bustfree Pty Ltd v Llewellyn* [2013] QCA 103 [26]–[27] (upholding summary judgment against the plaintiff, and where the court also identified other factors that made the claim hopeless).
[229] *Mir v Mir* [2012] 1 HKLRD 671 (High Court of HK SAR, Ct of First Instance) [74], [93] (Anthony Houghton SC, sitting as a Deputy High Court Judge); appeal dismissed [2013] HKCA 144; [2013] 4 HKC 213 [58]–[89].

Other principles concerning delay
Cannot knowingly speculate on outcome of bargain
Delay with knowledge of the facts in order to see whether the bargain will turn to the advantage of the party entitled to rescind may lead to the right being lost.[230] Lord Blackburn made the point in this well-known passage:

24.100

> If I thought the shareholders had been waiting to see how the market ruled it might have made a difference in my opinion. If no steps to repudiate a lottery ticket were taken till after the ticket came up a blank, so that the purchaser, if it came up a prize, might have kept it, it would surely be inequitable to set aside the contract then. And though not nearly so strong a case, such delay seems to be somewhat of that nature.[231]

The principle has been emphasized in the *Third Restatement of Restitution*, which concludes that 'speculative delay' will bar rescission,[232] for in such a case the claimant seeks, in effect, to obtain 'an unpaid option'.[233] But the mere fact that the contract is inherently speculative is itself no bar. The right to rescind a purchase of land said to contain oil was not barred by laches even though the buyers had drilled a well and found nothing, for at that point they were unaware of the fraud that had been practised,[234] and a similar principle has been applied in old cases involving contingent bargains. That a contingency in favour of the rescinding transferor had occurred was of no consequence if he remained subject to the original vitiating influence.[235]

Time to investigate
Where a contract is voidable for misrepresentation or non-disclosure, the party affected is generally entitled to a reasonable time to investigate in order to ascertain the true facts. This principle is well known in insurance,[236] and seems to apply generally.[237] It was recently

24.101

---

[230] *Ormes v Beadle* (1860) 2 De GF & J 333, 336; 45 ER 649; *Erlanger v The New Sombrero Phosphate Company* (1878) 3 App Cas 1218, 1254, 1281–83; *Lagunas Nitrate Company v Lagunas Syndicate* [1899] 2 Ch 392 (CA) 434. Cf *Southern Cross Mine Management Pty Ltd v Ensham Resources Pty Ltd* [2005] QSC 233 [645]–[646], where an argument of this kind was rejected because the defendant 'ran no real risk' under the agreement sought to be rescinded. See also, JD Heydon, MJ Leeming, and PG Turner, *Meagher, Gummow and Lehane's Equity Doctrines and Remedies* (5th edn, 2014) [38-025] at n 23.

[231] *Erlanger v The New Sombrero Phosphate Company* (1878) 3 App Cas 1218, 1281, also 1282–83. See also R Halson, 'Rescission for Misrepresentation' [1997] 5 RLR 89, 91–92, discussing the allocation of risk when a purchase of assets is rescinded in a falling market; and para [24.74]. For application of the principle in the context of a claim for a constructive trust, *Streeter v Western Areas Exploration Pty Ltd* (2011) 278 ALR 291 (WACA) [674] (six-year delay during which time shares in speculative junior mining company had significantly increased in value after exploration and capital raisings).

[232] *Restatement (Third) of Restitution* § 54(6) (2011).

[233] *Restatement (Third) of Restitution* cmt k at 286 (2011) ('if a claimant were permitted to entertain for any significant period an election between enforcement and avoidance—against a background of potentially fluctuating values—the availability of rescission would give the claimant, in effect, an unpaid option on the defendant's performance. Such a result may be inequitable ...'); also Reporter's Notes at vol 2, 294–96.

[234] *Lindsay Petroleum Co v Hurd* (1874) LR 5 PC 221 (PC—Canada), overturning the decision of the Court of Error and Appeal of Ontario. Contrast *Grymes v Sanders* 93 US 55, 62, 23 Led 798 (1876) (mistaken transfer of land in gold mining area; purchaser lost right to rescind after digging exploratory shafts following discovery of mistake), discussed *Restatement (Third) of Restitution* vol 2, 287, 295 (2011).

[235] *Pickett v Loggon* (1807) 14 Ves Jun 215, 243; 33 ER 503 (Lord Eldon LC).

[236] *McCormick v National Motor and Accident Insurance* (1934) 49 Lloyd's Rep 362 (CA) 365 (Scrutton LJ); *Insurance Corporation of the Channel Islands Ltd v McHugh and Royal Hotel Limited* [1997] Lloyd's Re Ins LR 94, 132 (Mance J); *Callaghan and Hedges t/a Stage 3 Discotheque v Syndicate 1049* [2000] Lloyd's Rep IR 125.

[237] *Erlanger v The New Sombrero Phosphate Company* (1878) LR 3 App Cas 1218, 1251–53, 1258–59; *Lagunas Nitrate Company v Lagunas Syndicate* [1899] 2 Ch 392 (CA) 454; *Senanayake v Cheng* [1966] AC 63 (PC—Singapore) 79; *Fiona Trust & Holding Corporation v Privalov* [2007] 1 All ER (Comm) 81 [36].

applied in *Fiona Trust & Holding Corporation v Privalov*[238] where the claimant ship owners were alleged to have lost their right to rescind certain charter parties by delay amounting to affirmation. Morison J held that the right survived, and that before electing to rescind the claimants were entitled to await the outcome of inquiries of an expert review of the relevant charter parties' terms.

Time to seek a compromise

24.102 Time spent seeking a compromise generally does not amount to laches or evidence affirmation.[239] A different result has been reached in relation to a voidable share allotment.[240] But that authority is probably confined to allotments of partly paid shares, where rescission requires special promptness in order to safeguard the interests of third parties,[241] and there are examples where the general rule has been applied to a voidable allotment of fully paid shares.[242]

Time to remove board of directors

24.103 Where a company has a right to rescind a purchase, but for practical purposes must remove or replace the board before the contract can be disapproved, time spent in doing that does not count against the right to rescind.[243]

Remaining in possession

24.104 Remaining in possession or continuing to operate a business will in some circumstances evidence an intention to affirm. The relevant principles are considered in Chapter 23, and apply equally to conduct said to involve acquiescence.

Delay attributable to wrongful party

24.105 Delay that can be laid at the feet of the wrongful party will generally not constitute an implied election to affirm a voidable contract.[244]

---

[238] [2007] 1 All ER (Comm) 81 [36]. On appeal, [2007] 1 All ER (Comm) 891 (CA); [2007] 2 All ER (Comm) 1053 (HL) (point not considered).

[239] *Erlanger v The New Sombrero Phosphate Company* (1878) LR 3 App Cas 1218, 1252–53 (several months' delay negotiating with vendor); *Kenny v Fenton* [1971] NZLR 1 (CA) 18 (one-year delay following solicitors' letter); *Kramer v McMahon* [1970] 1 NSWLR 194, 210 (negotiations seeking reduced price for bakery not affirmation); *Watson v Burton* [1957] 1 WLR 19, 30 (defect in title; attempts to negotiate a solution not affirmation).

[240] *Ogilvie v Currie* (1868) 37 LR Ch (NS) 541, 547 (inaction when hoping for a compromise).

[241] See paras [24.88]–[24.90].

[242] *Haas Timber & Trading Co Pty Ltd v Wade* (1954) 94 CLR 593, 602 ('A delay which is to be attributed to negotiations between the shareholder complaining and the company cannot be availed of as a ground precluding rescission: see *Neill's case* (1867) 15 WR 894, per Wood VC'; per Dixon CJ, Fullagar and Kitto JJ).

[243] *Erlanger v The New Sombrero Phosphate Company* (1878) LR 3 App Cas 1218, 1281–82. *A fortiori* time does not count where the original board remains in place: *Erlanger's* case at 1281–82; *Lagunas Nitrate Company v Lagunas Syndicate* [1899] 2 Ch 392 (CA) 433, discussed *Streeter v Western Areas Exploration Pty Ltd* (2011) 278 ALR 291 (WACA) [647]–[662], [672] (no restriction existed on removing directors; claim for constructive trust of shares in mining company refused).

[244] *Haas Timber & Trading Co Pty Ltd v Wade* (1954) 94 CLR 593, 604 (company's conduct caused shareholder to delay); *Kellogg Brown & Root Inc v Aerotech Herman Nelson Inc* (2004) 238 DLR (4th) 594 (Man CA) [54]–[57]; *Herrod v Johnston* [2013] 2 QdR 102 (CA) 128 (failure to provide information where inequality of knowledge of transaction).

Unreasonable delay and acting by analogy with the statute

When the statute of limitations is applied by analogy to bar a claim to rescind, time begins to run only after there is an awareness of the material facts, or such notice that a person of ordinary intelligence would have been aware of them. There is no need for the injured party to be aware that he has a right to rescind.[245]

24.106

If the statute is applied by analogy, it provides an upper limit, and the right to rescind may be lost by laches or acquiescence before that time.[246]

24.107

Lord Redesdale said that all equities to relief will be barred after 20 years' delay,[247] but that opinion has not been followed.[248] Accordingly, if the statute of limitations is not applied by analogy, a lapse of time that does not attract a defence of laches or raise an inference of affirmation will not cause the right to rescind to be lost, save in the special case of sales of goods voidable for innocent misrepresentation.[249]

24.108

(5) The significance of prejudice

Prejudice and electing to affirm

Prejudice is neither necessary nor sufficient for conduct to constitute an election between rights. An election to affirm may be inferred from delay, though no prejudice would be suffered by reason of the delay if the contract were subsequently to be rescinded.[250] A principle has, however, been developed in the insurance context to the effect that delay coupled with prejudice will lead to loss of the right to elect. The foundational case is *Allen v Robles*,[251] where the Court of Appeal interpreted passages in *Clough v London and North Western Railway Co*[252] to this effect. *Allen v Robles* concerned an insurer's right of election following the assured's failure to notify a claim within the time specified in the policy. It was therefore not concerned with rescission *ab initio* at all. Nor could it have been referring to the bar *restitutio in integrum* impossible, for that is not a bar to the right to reject a late claim. The case was later treated as applicable to insurance contracts voidable for non-disclosure and misrepresentation,[253] and the High Court of Australia has analysed the doctrine of election between rights in a similar fashion.[254]

24.109

---

[245] *Molloy v Mutual Reserve Life Insurance Co* (1906) 94 LT 756 (CA).

[246] *Sibbering v Earl of Balcarras* (1850) 3 De G & SM 735, 737; 64 ER 682; *Molloy v Mutual Reserve Life Insurance Co* (1906) 94 LT 756 (CA) 762.

[247] *Hovenden v Lord Annesley* (1806) 2 Sch & Lef 607, 636–37. A 20-year limit is also suggested in JM Lightwood, *The Time Limit on Actions* (1909) 256, 262. M Franks, *Limitation of Actions* (1959) 242–43 argues that unexplained delay falling short of 20 years will always bar relief in equity.

[248] *Weld v Petre* [1929] 1 Ch 33 (CA) 55.

[249] *Leaf v International Galleries* [1950] 2 KB 86 (CA).

[250] *Telfair Shipping Corporation v Athos Shipping Co SA (The Athos)* [1981] 2 Lloyd's Rep 74, 88; aff'd [1983] 1 Lloyd's Rep 127 (CA). Reliance is also unnecessary: *Oliver Ashworth (Holdings) Ltd v Ballard (Kent) Ltd* [2000] Ch 12 (CA) 27.

[251] [1969] 1 WLR 1193 (CA) 1196.

[252] (1871) LR 7 Ex 26, 35.

[253] *Liberian Insurance Agency Inc v Mosse* [1977] 2 Lloyd's Rep 560, 565; *Iron Trades Mutual Insurance Co Ltd v Companhia de Seguros Imperio* [1992] 1 Lloyd's Rep IR 213, 225; *Svenska Handelsbanken v Sun Alliance and London Insurance plc* [1996] 1 Lloyd's Rep 519, 569; *Strive Shipping Corporation v Hellenic Mutual War Risks Association (The Grecia Express)* [2002] 2 Lloyd's Rep 88, 162; *Spriggs v Wessington Court Schools Ltd* [2005] 1 Lloyd's Rep IR 474, 479.

[254] *Tropical Traders Ltd v Goonan* (1964) 111 CLR 41, 55 ('rescind' for late payment) 'so long as the respondents' position was not prejudiced in consequence of the delay …'. Cf statements that unequivocal conduct that is 'adverse

544 VI. OTHER BARS

24.110 In substance the principle mirrors the equitable doctrine of prejudicial laches,[255] although the language of laches is used in none of the cases, doubtless because exclusively common law rights were being considered. The principle has been said to involve a deemed affirmation,[256] but that is not compelling because prejudice is not generally necessary or sufficient for the making of an election between rights.

24.111 The authorities have not spelled out what level of prejudice counts,[257] or whether the court retains any discretion once some prejudice is proved. *Clough's* case suggests that the court has no discretion, and the rule is expressed in absolute terms in most of the later cases;[258] though the language in others leaves some room for doubt.[259] The nature and boundaries of this principle have yet to be fully worked out.

Prejudice and acquiescence

24.112 Acquiescence should be more easily inferred if the delay causes or tends to cause prejudice to the party against whom rescission is sought, for delay in those circumstances naturally tends to indicate assent to the conduct complained of.

24.113 Although it is sometimes said that prejudice is necessary for a defence of acquiescence,[260] statements of this kind are best regarded as concerned with the doctrine of laches in the wider sense, which has here been called 'prejudicial laches'. Acquiescence is founded on an inference of waiver, and waiver does not require detriment. There are, moreover, well-known instances of equitable rights to rescind being lost by acquiescence where no material prejudice would have been suffered by reason of the claimant's delay.[261]

Prejudice and laches

24.114 It is well established that if delay causes prejudice, that is material in determining whether a defence of laches is made out. Prejudice to the defendant strengthens the defence,[262] whilst its absence tells against it.[263] It is unclear whether prejudice is essential,[264] and the House of Lords has said whilst it may not be an immutable requirement, 'some sort of detrimental

---

to' or prejudices the other party may be an election though the electing party is ignorant of their rights: *Coastal Estates Pty Ltd v Melevende* [1965] VR 433 (Full Ct) 443, 453; *Khoury v Government Insurance Office* (1984) 165 CLR 622, 633; *Peyman v Lanjani* [1985] Ch 457 (CA) 488–89.

[255] See para [24.17].
[256] *Liberian Insurance Agency Inc v Mosse* [1977] 2 Lloyd's Rep 560, 565 (Donaldson J).
[257] But see *Svenska Handelsbanken v Sun Alliance and London Insurance plc* [1996] 1 Lloyd's Rep 519, 569.
[258] *Liberian Insurance Agency Inc v Mosse* [1977] 2 Lloyd's Rep 560, 565 'he will be deemed to have affirmed' (Donaldson J); *Iron Trades Mutual Insurance Co Ltd v Companhia de Seguros Imperio* [1992] 1 Lloyd's Rep IR 213, 225 'he will lose his right' (Hobhouse J).
[259] *Allen v Robles* [1969] 1 WLR 1193 (CA) 1196 'lapse of time would only operate against them if thereby there was prejudice to Mr Robles'; *Spriggs v Wessington Court Schools Ltd* [2005] 1 Lloyd's Rep IR 474, 479 'mere delay ... will affect the insurer's position if the assured is prejudiced by it'.
[260] *Southern Cross Mine Management Pty Ltd v Evesham Resources Pty Ltd* [2005] QSC 233 [645].
[261] *Gregory v Gregory* (1815) G Coop 201, 204; 35 ER 530; *Roberts v Tunstall* (1845) 4 Hare 257, 67 ER 645.
[262] *Fysh v Page* (1956) 96 CLR 233, 243–44 (significant prejudice from change in relative value of consideration passing to each party under the contract); *Nelson v Rye* [1996] 1 WLR 1378, 1388, 1392, 1395–96 (claim for account against fiduciary agent).
[263] *Lindsay Petroleum Co v Hurd* (1874) LR 5 PC 221 (PC—Canada) 240 (no real prejudice); *Bester v Perpetual Trustee Co Ltd* [1970] 3 NSWLR 30, 37–38 (no prejudice); *Gillespie v Gillespie* [2013] 2 QdR 440 (CA) 462 (prejudice from rescission outweighed by benefits from voidable transaction). Also, *Weld v Petre* [1929] 1 Ch 33 (CA) 56 (claim for redemption, no prejudice).
[264] *Nelson v Rye* [1996] 1 WLR 1378, 1391–92.

reliance is usually an essential element of laches'.[265] In practice, it is difficult to imagine circumstances where the right to rescind could be lost by neglectful delay not amounting to waiver, if the delay would not cause some prejudice upon rescission. The loss of evidence that may have cast a different complexion on the matter may count as relevant prejudice.[266]

Prejudice after an election to rescind has been made
There is Australian authority that the right to rescind may be lost after proceedings for rescission are commenced, if the claimant thereafter acts unconscientiously.[267] This seems to mean careless or intentional conduct that would harm the defendant if rescission were to be granted, as where a rescinding purchaser vacates premises causing a valuable leasehold to be lost.[268] That is consistent with the equitable foundation of a suit for rescission, and in England finds support in cases involving 'rescission' for non-performance.[269]

24.115

D. Estoppel

There are few decided cases in which rights to rescind, or rights secured by a prior rescission, have been lost by estoppel. That is perhaps because in many cases where a plea of estoppel might be available, the defendant will usually have a simpler defence of affirmation, acquiescence, or laches. The lack of authority explains why there appear to be no principles of estoppel peculiar to rescission. The operation of that defence is instead governed by general principles.

24.116

Estoppel may occur with or without delay. In principle the estoppel might arise by a consistent course of dealings, conducted on the footing that a right to rescind would not be exercised, giving rise to an estoppel by convention. But promissory estoppel is more likely. That defence requires words or conduct by the party entitled to rescind, relied on by the other party to the transaction, such that it would be inequitable for rescission afterwards to be granted.

24.117

Where the representation is that the party entitled to rescind would not do so, in England it has been said that the representation must have been (i) clear and unequivocal, (ii) made with the knowledge or intention that it would be acted upon in the way that it was, and (iii) acted on by the other party to his detriment.[270] But other cases express the principle in a

24.118

---

[265] *Fisher v Brooker* [2009] 1 WLR 1764 (HL) 1279 per Lord Neuberger of Abbotsbury, with whom the other members of the House of Lords agreed. This statement should be regarded as describing what is here called 'prejudicial laches' rather than 'affirmatory laches' or acquiescence (see para [24.17]); cf *Streeter v Western Areas Exploration Pty Ltd* (2011) 278 ALR 291 (WACA) [635] per Murphy JA; and cf *Gillespie v Gillespie* [2013] 2 QdR 440 (CA) 458.
[266] *Orr v Ford* (1989) 167 CLR 316, 330; *Baburin v Baburin (No 2)* [1991] 2 QdR 240 (CA) 253–54 (death of witness); *Gillespie v Gillespie* [2013] 2 QdR 440 (CA) 461–62 (not made out on the facts).
[267] *Alati v Kruger* (1955) 94 CLR 216, 225; *Krakowski v Eurolynx Properties Ltd* (1995) 183 CLR 563. Also, *Kramer v McMahon* [1970] 1 NSWLR 194, 210.
[268] *Alati v Kruger* (1955) 94 CLR 216, 225.
[269] *Butler v Croft* (1973) P & CR 1, 11.
[270] *Goldsworthy v Brickell* [1987] 1 Ch 378 (CA) 410–11; see also *Kammins Ballrooms Co Ltd v Zenith Investments (Torquay) Ltd* [1971] AC 850, 884 (intention that representation would affect legal relationship required).

more general way,[271] and more recent statements of principle omit the second requirement altogether.[272] A broader test applies under Australian law.[273]

24.119 An insurer's delay in rescinding an insurance policy after becoming aware of the material facts, which causes the insured not to obtain cover elsewhere, may cause the right to rescind to be lost by estoppel.[274] An estoppel may likewise arise if a donor's delay is so long that it reasonably induces the donee to act upon a belief that the gift would not be disturbed,[275] or where a buyer's representation that a right to rescind a share sale agreement would not be exercised had the effect that the seller was unable to retake control of the company and so prevent the subsequent sale of shares in its subsidiary.[276]

24.120 An estoppel may arise although the party entitled to rescind is unaware of the material facts or his right to rescind, and might in principle merely suspend rather than permanently bar the claim to rescind.[277]

24.121 The law may be moving toward the position where estoppel limits the extent of restitution available upon rescission, whilst not completely barring that remedy, if limited restitution represents 'the minimum equity to do justice' between the parties.[278] However, this possibility of *pro tanto* estoppel, and of estoppel being moulded to fit a recipient's change of position, remains largely unexplored in cases involving rescission.

---

[271] *Telfair Shipping Corporation v Athos Shipping Co SA (The Athos)* [1981] 2 Lloyd's Rep 74, 88; aff'd [1983] 1 Lloyd's Rep 127 (CA) 134–35; *Motor Oil Hellas (Corinth) Refineries SA v Shipping Corp of India (The Kanchenjunga)* [1990] 1 Lloyd's Rep 391 (HL) 399; *Oliver Ashworth (Holdings) Ltd v Ballard (Kent) Ltd* [2000] Ch 12 (CA) 27.

[272] *Capcon Holdings plc v Edwards* [2007] EWHC 2662 (Ch) [35] ('in order to found an estoppel the claimants must prove some representation by the defendants that they have waived their right to rescind and some detriment', per the Chancellor); *Kosmar Villa Holidays plc v Trustees of Syndicate 1243* [2008] 2 All ER (Comm) 14 (CA) [38] ('a representation, in words or conduct, which must be unequivocal and must have been relied upon in circumstances where it would be inequitable for the promise to be withdrawn'; also at [70], per Rix LJ, with whom Jacobs LJ and Forbes J agreed (contractual defence to a claim for indemnity under insurance policy rather than rescission)); *IHC (a firm) v Amtrust Europe* [2015] EWHC 257 (QB) [9]–[14] (rescission of contract of insurance).

[273] *Commonwealth of Australia v Verwayen* (1990) 170 CLR 394; *Giumelli v Giumelli* (1999) 196 CLR 101.

[274] *Morrison v The Universal Marine Insurance Company* (1873) LR 8 Ex 197, 205–06.

[275] *Allcard v Skinner* (1887) 36 ChD 145 (CA) 192.

[276] *Capcon Holdings plc v Edwards* [2007] EWHC 2662 (Ch) [42]–[45] (where the court emphasized also that the effect of the buyer's conduct was that the seller was denied the opportunity to sell the shares elsewhere).

[277] *Motor Oil Hellas (Corinth) Refineries SA v Shipping Corp of India (The Kanchenjunga)* [1990] 1 Lloyd's Rep 391 (HL) 399; *Kosmar Villa Holidays plc v Trustees of Syndicate 1243* [2008] 2 All ER (Comm) 14 (CA) [38] (estoppel may be suspensory only, unlike election which is irrevocable); but contrast JD Heydon, MJ Leeming, and PG Turner, *Meagher, Gummow and Lehane's Equity Doctrines and Remedies* (5th edn, 2014) [17-180] (estoppel by representation generally permanent in effect).

[278] *National Westminster Bank plc v Somer International (UK) Ltd* [2002] QB 1286 (mistaken payment by bank), moving away from *Avon County Council v Howlett* [1983] 1 WLR 605 (CA).

25
Bankruptcy and Winding Up

A. Introduction	25.01	(7) Winding up	25.18
B. Bankruptcy and Winding Up Generally	25.02	C. Winding Up as a Bar to Shareholder's Rescission	25.21
(1) No general bar to rescission	25.02	(1) Introduction	25.21
(2) Supervening bankruptcy: rescinding to assert a proprietary claim	25.04	(2) The bar	25.24
		(3) Rationale	25.31
(3) Supervening bankruptcy: rescinding to assert a personal claim	25.08	(4) Scope	25.42
		(5) When winding up commences	25.62
(4) Rescission as a defence against the trustee in bankruptcy	25.11	(6) Operation of the bar before winding up	25.63
(5) Contracting with an undischarged bankrupt	25.12	(7) Steps to be taken to prevent the bar operating	25.69
(6) Whether right to rescind survives discharge from bankruptcy	25.17	(8) Statutory exceptions	25.77

A. Introduction

25.01 The general rule is that the right to rescind survives the bankruptcy or winding up of the party against whom the right is available. That general rule and its qualifications are considered first. The chapter then considers the special bar that prevents a shareholder in a limited liability company rescinding his statutory contract with the company once it has begun to be wound up.

B. Bankruptcy and Winding Up Generally

(1) No general bar to rescission

25.02 Rescission is not barred simply because it will prejudice unsecured creditors of the guilty party by shrinking the pool of assets available to satisfy their claims. The principle is well illustrated in cases concerning insolvent companies. A voidable share allotment cannot be rescinded after winding up commences, in part because of the prejudice that would cause to creditors and other shareholders. But despite the concern with protecting creditors in this context, a voidable share allotment may still be rescinded before winding up, even though the company is then insolvent. That rescission will prejudice the company's creditors in no way fetters the shareholder's right to rescind.[1]

---

[1] *Re London and Leeds Bank; ex p Carling* (1887) 56 LT (NS) 115; *Elder's Trustee and Executor Co Ltd v Commonwealth Homes and Investment Co Ltd* (1941) 65 CLR 603, 619; paras [25.66]–[25.68].

548   VI. OTHER BARS

25.03 The limited available authority indicates that, with certain exceptions considered later, the bankruptcy or winding up of a contracting party does not bar the other party's right to rescind. There are, however, surprisingly few authorities, and some are difficult to reconcile.

(2) Supervening bankruptcy: rescinding to assert a proprietary claim

Rescinding to recover legal title to goods

25.04 Where a sale of goods is induced by the purchaser's fraud, and the purchaser becomes bankrupt before the vendor elects to rescind, the bankruptcy is no bar to rescission. The trustee in bankruptcy takes only the purchaser's defeasible title to the goods, and by electing to rescind the vendor may recover legal title from the trustee in bankruptcy. This was recognized in *Load v Green*[2] and applied in *Re Eastgate*,[3] and again in *Tilley v Bowman Limited*.[4] Legislative changes since the time of those decisions have not altered the principle.[5] The trustee in bankruptcy continues to take only the bankrupt's imperfect title; or as is sometimes said, a title 'subject to equities'.[6]

Rescinding to assert an equitable proprietary interest

25.05 The rule considered earlier should in principle also apply where an equitable proprietary interest may be asserted by disaffirming the voidable transaction. However, *In the matter of Crown Holdings (London) Limited (in liq)* has decided to the contrary in cases of corporate insolvency.[7] It was held that the statutory scheme for corporate insolvency meant that no right of rescission could be asserted once a voluntary administrator was appointed to a currency exchange business, in circumstances where the defrauded customers could not be said to have a proprietary interest in money paid prior to rescission of their contracts. It was said that the position might, however, be different in the case of bankruptcy.[8]

25.06 This aspect of the decision in *Crown Holdings* has, however, been forcefully criticized.[9]

25.07 The position is also more complicated if no interest may be asserted unless and until a court order for rescission is obtained.[10] By section 285(1) and (2) of the Insolvency Act 1986 the court is empowered to stay legal proceedings against a bankrupt or to allow them to continue on such terms as it thinks fit. On its face this power extends to proceedings to establish a proprietary interest upon rescission. But it may be doubted whether that is what is

---

[2] (1846) 15 M & W 216, 153 ER 828.
[3] [1905] 1 KB 465.
[4] [1910] 1 KB 745 (CA).
[5] Insolvency Act 1986, s 283(5) 'property comprised in a bankrupt's estate is so comprised subject to the rights of any person other than the bankrupt... in relation thereto'.
[6] IF Fletcher, *The Law of Insolvency* (7th edn, 2017) [8-048], [8-049].
[7] [2015] EWHC 1876 (Ch) [1]–[16], [40]–[45].
[8] *In the matter of Crown Holdings (London) Limited (in liq)* [2015] EWHC 1876 (Ch) [1]–[16], [40]–[45].
[9] N Segal, 'The Impact of Insolvency on the Right to Rescind—The Flaw in the Crown' (2016) 29 *Insolvency Intelligence* 27. Parts of the reasoning in *Crown Holdings* arguably receives support from *Angove's Pty Ltd v Bailey* [2016] 1 WLR 3179 (Sup Ct) [25], [26], where the Supreme Court approved the analysis in (1987) 103 LQR 443, 444 in which Professor Goode discountenanced the assertion of a proprietary claim unsupported by a pre-existing 'proprietary base'. However, Mr Segal cites other writings of Professor Goode (*Principles of Corporate Insolvency Law* (4th edn, 2011) 3-305, 6-17) that support a conclusion that the equity to recover property upon rescission should not be barred by insolvency.
[10] See Chap 16.

intended. The legislation expressly preserves third party rights to property forming part of the bankrupt's estate[11] and this arguably includes the equity to a court order for recovering property upon rescission.[12] If that is so, the legislation implicitly authorizes such proceedings, and the court's powers under sections 285(1) and (2) of the Insolvency Act 1986 should arguably be read as excluding such claims. The point has not featured in the reported cases and at present remains open.[13]

(3) Supervening bankruptcy: rescinding to assert a personal claim

25.08 In principle, bankruptcy itself ought not to bar rescission for the purpose of bringing a personal claim against the bankrupt, such as a claim to recover sums paid under the voidable transaction.

25.09 If the innocent party would otherwise be entitled to rescind simply by disaffirming the contract, he should in principle also be able to do so after bankruptcy has occurred, and to prove on that basis as a creditor in respect of the sum paid.[14]

25.10 But if the innocent party is able to rescind only by obtaining a court order for rescission, the position is more uncertain. The court has power to stay proceedings for rescission,[15] and if the innocent party is also regarded as a creditor, no claim for rescission would appear to be possible without leave of the court.[16] Any claim to rescind in order to prove as a creditor in respect of the sums paid seems, therefore, to be subject to judicial control if the innocent party cannot completely effect rescission by his own act.[17]

(4) Rescission as a defence against the trustee in bankruptcy

25.11 As a matter of principle, the trustee in bankruptcy should take the benefit of contracts entered by the bankrupt subject to equities arising by reason of the bankrupt's conduct. A defence of rescission should therefore be available against the trustee in bankruptcy to the same extent that it would have been available as against the bankrupt himself.

---

[11] Insolvency Act 1986, s 283(5).
[12] *In the matter of Crown Holdings (London) Limited (in liq)* [2015] EWHC 1876 (Ch) [43]. See also *Zandfarid v Bank of Credit and Commerce International* [1996] 1 WLR 1420, 1429–30, where Ferris J seemed to accept that an O'Brien counter-claim for rescission of a charge executed by a wife over the matrimonial home may be maintained after the husband has been adjudged bankrupt on petition by the mortgagee bank.
[13] See also *American Sugar Refining Co v Fancher* (1895) NE 206 (SCNY) 208–09 (defrauded vendor of sugar claimed traceable proceeds in hands of assignee for creditors).
[14] The debt generated by rescission will be subject to the normal restrictions imposed by the bankruptcy regime: Insolvency Act 1986, s 285(3).
[15] Insolvency Act 1986, s 285(1), (2).
[16] Insolvency Act 1986, s 285(3).
[17] See also Insolvency Act 1986, s 345 (court's power to discharge contractual obligations on application of other party to the contract). If the innocent party was unable to prove as a creditor in the bankruptcy, there might be some scope for applying the rule in *ex p James* (1874) 9 Ch App 609 so as to restore moneys paid to the party wishing to rescind.

(5) Contracting with an undischarged bankrupt

25.12 An undischarged bankrupt has a limited capacity to contract. A disposition of property before the bankrupt's estate is vested in the trustee in bankruptcy is generally void unless authorized or ratified by the court.[18] Thereafter the bankrupt lacks the title necessary to dispose of what was formerly his property, for ownership has passed to the trustee in bankruptcy.[19]

25.13 Where a bankrupt does seek to contract, and does so by fraudulently concealing his status as a bankrupt, or by other improper conduct that permits the other to rescind, the question arises whether money or property he receives under it may be regained by rescission, or is instead available to the trustee in bankruptcy for the benefit of creditors.[20]

25.14 In principle, the trustee in bankruptcy should obtain no better title than the bankrupt himself, and therefore holds the assets received subject to the rights of the party entitled to rescind. That was the approach adopted in the Australian case of *Hoffman v Schilling*.[21] Mr Hoffman was an undischarged bankrupt, and had fraudulently misrepresented his financial position to Mr Schilling, to whom he sold shares in his drilling business for $25,000. Mr Justice Pincus held that the contract was voidable for fraud.[22] The $25,000 remained separately identified, and the trustee sought a direction as to whether it was property divisible among Mr Hoffman's creditors. The court held that it was not, for Mr Schilling was entitled to rescind and be repaid notwithstanding the bankruptcy. The trustee's appeal was dismissed.[23]

25.15 A different result was reached in *Westpac v Markovic*,[24] another Australian case. The claimant bank sought to rescind a loan to a dishonest bankrupt for fraud, and to assert beneficial title in shares in a petrol station he had bought with the funds. Mr Justice Zelling held that it was too late to rescind once the shares had vested in the Official Receiver pursuant to section 58(1)(b) of the Bankruptcy Act 1966 (Cth),[25] which provides for the automatic vesting of after-acquired property.[26] The decision appears to have proceeded on the basis that the Official Receiver obtained a paramount claim to the shares, notwithstanding that but for the bankruptcy, the dishonest buyer's equitable ownership was defeasible at the instance of the bank. It is doubtful that the decision is correct. The legislation does not purport to give the Official Trustee any title superior to that which the bankrupt himself would, but for the bankruptcy, have enjoyed.

---

[18] Insolvency Act 1986, s 284.
[19] Insolvency Act 1986, s 306.
[20] Insolvency Act 1986, s 307. In Australia, Bankruptcy Act 1966 (Cth), s 58.
[21] *Re Hoffman ex p Worrell v Schilling* (1989) 85 ALR 145 (FCA) 147, 152 (Pincus J), considering the Bankruptcy Act 1966 (Cth).
[22] And also because Mr Hoffman was seeking to sell property that he did not own, the shares having become vested in the trustee in bankruptcy: *Re Hoffman ex p Worrell v Schilling* (1989) 85 ALR 145 (FCA) 147.
[23] *Re Hoffman ex p Worrell v Schilling*, (Full FCA, 14 August 1989).
[24] (1985) 82 FLR 7.
[25] *Westpac v Markovic* (1985) 82 FLR 7, 10. The Official Receiver is now styled the Official Trustee.
[26] Unlike in England and Wales, where vesting occurs when the trustee in bankruptcy gives notice to that effect: Insolvency Act 1986, s 307.

There do not appear to be any English decisions on this question. It is suggested that the approach of Pincus J is to be preferred, and that it should apply as much to section 307 of the Insolvency Act 1986 as to section 58 of the Australian Bankruptcy Act 1966 (Cth).

25.16

(6) Whether right to rescind survives discharge from bankruptcy

It is unclear whether a claim to repayment arising from an unexercised right to rescind is a 'bankruptcy debt' within the meaning of the Insolvency Act 1986.[27] There is authority implying both that the right is[28] and that it is not[29] a bankruptcy debt. If it is a bankruptcy debt, the right will be extinguished by discharge from bankruptcy unless the ground for rescission is deceit,[30] or dishonest breach of trust,[31] which attract the exception in section 281(3) of the Insolvency Act 1986. If it is not a bankruptcy debt, the right to rescind remains enforceable even after discharge from bankruptcy.

25.17

(7) Winding up

Proprietary claims

In *Shalson v Russo* Rimer J doubted whether a proprietary interest could be asserted by seeking to rescind a contract with a company after it had gone into compulsory liquidation:

25.18

> ... if a representor company were to go into compulsory liquidation before any rescission, its assets would cease to be beneficially part of its property and would become subject to the statutory scheme in favour of creditors of the nature discussed in *Ayerst v C & K (Construction) Ltd* [1976] AC 167; and I should be surprised if any subsequent rescission entitled the repesentee to say that the property transferred to the company under the voidable contract must be regarded as having at all times been his property so as to fall outside that scheme.[32]

This was also the conclusion of Murray Rosen QC sitting as a Deputy High Court Judge in *In the matter of Crown Holdings (London) Limited (in liq)*.[33] If this is the law there is an important difference between the right to recover property upon rescission after bankruptcy and that after compulsory winding up. A proprietary interest may be asserted in a bankruptcy, but not in a compulsory liquidation. There seems, however, to be no good reason for this distinction, and the decision in *Crown Holdings* has been criticised on that basis.[34]

---

[27] Insolvency Act 1986, ss 281, 382.
[28] *Mander v Evans* [2001] 1 WLR 2378.
[29] *R (on the application of Steele) v Birmingham City Council* [2005] EWCA Civ 1824.
[30] *Mander v Evans* [2001] 1 WLR 2378.
[31] *Woodland-Ferrari v UCL Group Retirement Scheme* [2003] Ch 115.
[32] *Shalson v Russo* [2005] Ch 281, 324.
[33] [2015] EWHC 1876 (Ch).
[34] N Segal, 'The Impact of Insolvency on the Right to Rescind—The Flaw in the Crown' (2016) 27 *Insolvency Intelligence* 27.

Personal claims

25.19 The cases appear not to have considered whether a creditor is able to rescind his contract with the company after liquidation in order to assert a personal claim to payment, as for funds lent or services provided. That is probably because in most cases the point will not matter, for the creditor is adequately protected by suing on his contract. If rescission does remain available despite the winding up, but a court order is needed before it can occur, proceedings seeking those orders can only be commenced with the court's permission once a winding up order is made.[35]

Rescission as a defence

25.20 In principle a liquidator should take the benefit of contracts entered by the company subject to equities arising from its conduct, including the right of the other party to rescind the contract. A defence of rescission should therefore be available against the liquidator to the same extent that it would have been available against the company itself.

C. Winding Up as a Bar to Shareholder's Rescission

(1) Introduction

25.21 This bar to rescission applies only when a shareholder attempts to rescind the statutory contract between himself and the limited liability company of which he is a member.[36] The bar prevents rescission once winding up begins, or is on the verge of starting. It is usually the original allotee of shares who will wish to rescind, complaining of a misrepresentation made by the company. But the bar also applies in the exceptional case of a subsequent purchaser who proves a right to rescind as against the company. Rescission is barred both for the purpose of avoiding liability as a contributory (in the unusual case where partly paid shares are held), and for the purpose of recovering sums paid to the company as the price for the shares. The bar does not prevent rescission by those who are not shareholders of the company wishing to rescind their statutory contract with the company.[37]

25.22 The bar was developed in 1867 in *Oakes v Turquand*,[38] soon after the passing of the Companies Act 1862. At that time and until the end of the nineteenth century the bar was of great practical importance. Its importance has progressively diminished as equity markets have moved away from partly paid shares, and following the expansion of statutory rights of compensation for investors injured by corporate misrepresentation.

25.23 The bar is rooted in basic notions about the relationship between shareholders and creditors in a limited liability company, and the allocation of risk between them. These notions

---

[35] Insolvency Act 1986, s 130(2).
[36] See generally, G Brian Parker and M Buckley (eds), *Buckley on the Companies Acts* (14th edn, 1981) 326–31 (Companies Act 1862); M Arden, D Prentice, and D Richards (eds), *Buckley on the Companies Acts* (15th edn, 2000) [359.142]–[359.181] (Companies Act 2006).
[37] In Australia, *Southern British National Trust Ltd (in liq) v Pither* (1937) 57 CLR 89 (rule does not apply to debenture holders); *Re York St Mezzanine Pty Ltd (in liq)* (2007) 162 FCR 358 [39]–[40] (rule does not extend to holders of promissory notes); para [25.61].
[38] (1867) LR 2 HL 325.

underpin the Insolvency Act 1986 and the Companies Act 2006, as much as they did the original Companies Act 1862.

(2) The bar

Oakes v Turquand

25.24 The bar originated in *Oakes v Turquand*,[39] which was concerned with the spectacular collapse of an investment house in the City of London. Oakes and Peek were, respectively, the allottee and subsequent purchaser of partly paid shares in Overend, Gurney and Co Limited. It had been established to acquire the well-known partnership of Messrs Overend, Gurney and Co, which carried on substantial business as 'bill brokers and money dealers' in Lombard Street.

25.25 Both Oakes and Peek alleged that they had been induced to purchase by fraudulent misrepresentations in the company's prospectus. It had presented Messrs Overend, Gurney and Co as a profitable business. They alleged that the directors and former partners knew that the business had in fact been posting large losses, and held substantial bad debts for which no provision had been made. After it had been floated, the bank remained in business for only ten months, when it stopped payment. Oakes and Peek each brought a motion to have their name removed from the list of contributories and to stay proceedings for a call made by the liquidators, Turquand and Harding, who had been appointed to wind the company up.[40]

25.26 The issue was whether either Oakes or Peek could avoid liability to contribute to the company's debts during the winding up on the ground that they had been induced to become shareholders by reason of the company's fraudulent misrepresentations. It was held that they could not. The Vice-Chancellor dismissed their motions and the House of Lords dismissed both appeals. Although Oakes might originally have disaffirmed the contract and divested himself of the shares, once the company began to be wound up he lost the right to rescind and was obliged to remain on the list of contributories, and Peek stood in no better position.[41]

25.27 The decision in *Oakes v Turquand* was thereafter applied on numerous occasions. It was confirmed by the House of Lords in *Tennant v City of Glasgow Bank*[42] and in *Houldsworth v City of Glasgow Bank*.[43] The bar was later extended to shareholders seeking to rescind to recover the price paid for shares issued by the company, rather than to simply avoid liability as a contributory.[44]

---

[39] (1867) LR 2 HL 325.
[40] Companies Act 1862, s 35; see now Companies Act 2006, s 125.
[41] *Oakes v Turquand* (1867) LR 2 HL 325, 344, 353, 356, 367, 372, 375.
[42] (1879) 4 App Cas 615 (HL Sc).
[43] (1880) 5 App Cas 317.
[44] *Stone v City and County Bank* (1877) 3 CPD 282 (CA).

The bar today

Bar continues to apply today

25.28 The provisions of the Companies Act 1862 with which *Oakes v Turquand* was concerned are materially reproduced in the Insolvency Act 1986 and the Companies Act 2006, and the reasoning in *Soden v British & Commonwealth Holdings plc*[45] appears to assume that the decision remains relevant today. The rule has been accepted into the law of Australia,[46] New Zealand,[47] and Canada,[48] where the legislation has been modelled on the Companies Act 1862.

Diminished relevance of the bar

25.29 *Oakes v Turquand* was the subject of much litigation in the late nineteenth century.[49] Since that time, however, there have been few reported examples of its application. This is for two principal reasons. The first is that the raising of equity finance by way of partly paid shares has become less and less common. The imperative of avoiding liability for a company's debts was one of the principal motivations for rescinding a share allotment once the company failed, but that liability only exists if partly paid shares have been issued. The second reason is the enactment of the Directors Liability Act 1890 and its successors. The 1890 Act gave the victim of a misleading prospectus rights to damages for innocent misrepresentation. Before then, innocent misrepresentation had been actionable only by way of rescission.[50] The statutory damages conferred by the 1890 Act were also recoverable from the directors after liquidation.[51] The 1890 Act has since been replaced by investor protection legislation that has further expanded the rights of shareholders injured by inaccurate prospectuses and other misleading information provided when securities are issued.[52] In most cases the statutory scheme provides adequate redress and there is no imperative to rescind.

25.30 The twin effects of the decline in partly paid shares and the expansion of alternative forms of relief have diminished the practical importance of the winding-up bar. It does, however,

---

[45] [1998] AC 298, 324.
[46] *Re Lucks Limited (Serpell's case)* [1928] VLR 466; *Southern British National Trust Ltd v Pither* (1937) 57 CLR 89, 113–14; *Elder's Trustee and Executor Co Ltd v Commonwealth Homes and Investment Co Ltd* (1941) 65 CLR 603, 618–19; *Webb Distributors (Aust) Pty Ltd v Victoria* (1993) 179 CLR 15, 30–31; *Sons of Gwalia Ltd v Margaretic* (2007) 231 CLR 160 [54]–[58], [267], [270].
[47] *Re Southern Woollen-Mills* [1930] 1 NZLR 10; *Coupe v JM Coupe Publishing Ltd* [1981] 1 NZLR 275 (CA).
[48] *Re National Stadium Ltd* (1923) 55 OLR 199 (Ont SC) 202; *Milne v Durham Hosiery Mills Ltd* [1925] 3 DLR 725 (Ont SC) 727; *Re Northwestern Trust Co (McAskill's case)* [1926] SCR 412, 419; *Re Blue Range Resource* [2000] AJ 14 (Alta QB).
[49] Well-known examples include *Reese River Silver Mining Company Limited v Smith* (1869) 4 App Cas 64; *Re Hull and County Bank (Burgess's case)* (1880) 15 ChD 507; *Re Scottish Petroleum Company* (1882) 23 ChD 413 (CA). This was in the context of an inundation of claims based upon false prospectuses: *Houldsworth v City of Glasgow Bank* (1880) 5 App Cas 317, 320 ('During the last quarter of a century the courts have been inundated with cases of this kind' per Earl Cairns LC). See further M Lobban, 'Contractual Fraud in Law and Equity c 1750 to c 1850' (1997) 17 OJLS 441.
[50] Save insofar as omissions in the prospectus attracted s 38 of the Companies Act 1867.
[51] *Broome v Speak* [1903] 1 Ch 586 (CA), aff'd *Shepheard v Broome* [1904] AC 342. The right was also additional to any right to rescind: *Greenwood v Leather Shod Wheel Company* [1900] 1 Ch 421. The 1890 Act was apparently enacted to prevent *Derry v Peek* (1889) 14 App Cas 337 applying in this context: *McConnel v Wright* [1903] 1 Ch 546, 558; *Clark v Urquhart* [1930] AC 28, 56. See further *Cadence Asset Management Pty Ltd v Concept Sports Limited* (2005) 55 ACSR 145 (FCA) 148–49 (Finkelstein J) (overturned *Cadence Asset Management Pty Ltd v Concept Sports Limited* (2005) 247 FCR 435 (Full Ct)).
[52] Financial Services and Markets Act 2000, s 90, s 90A. In Australia, Corporations Act 2001, ss 728, 729, 1041H, 1325; Australian Securities and Investments Commission Act 2001, s 12DA; also *York Street Mezzanine Pty Ltd (in liq) v McEvoy* (2007) 162 FCR 358 [42]–[57] (discussing the possibility of statutory rights of rescission conferred by s 601MB and s 925A of the Corporations Act 2001).

have some role to play allocating risk following corporate collapse, principally because it denies misled subscribers the right to rescind so as to prove as creditors for monies paid, with the attendant priority that confers. The following discussion considers the bar's rationale and operation today.

(3) Rationale

Different explanations of the bar

25.31 The explanation for the winding-up bar has changed over time. The differing explanations are considered briefly.

First explanation: statutory language and Henderson's case

25.32 The reasoning in *Oakes v Turquand* itself focused on whether the Companies Act 1862 had displaced the position that had prevailed under the Joint Stock Banks Act 1844, as established in *Henderson v The Royal British Bank*.[53] The House of Lords held that Malins VC was correct in concluding that it had not.[54]

25.33 In coming to this conclusion, close attention was paid to the statutory language in light of the newly accepted doctrine that a contract procured by fraud was valid until rescinded. Oakes and Peek were liable as contributories because the two statutory conditions were met. First, at the date of winding up they had 'agreed' to be members, in that they had a voidable contract with the company which had not been avoided. Secondly, their name was on the register of members.[55] Moreover, the contrary view would undermine the integrity of the register of members, on which creditors may be supposed to have relied.[56]

Second explanation: prejudice to creditors

25.34 Later cases moved away from a focus upon the statutory language toward an explanation that linked the bar to the changes that occurred during winding up. One change emphasized was a change in the rights of creditors upon winding up. Rescission was said to be barred because it would defeat or prejudice creditors' rights. The leading statement of this rationale is *Tennent v City of Glasgow Bank*.[57] It was subsequently adopted in *Stone v The City and County Bank Limited*[58] and *Re Scottish Petroleum*.[59] Australian cases have emphasized the basis of the bar in prejudice to creditors and other shareholders.[60]

25.35 This explanation of the winding-up bar cannot, however, be based solely on the prejudicial effects of rescission for the company's creditors or other shareholders. Creditors and other shareholders are also prejudiced by rescission before winding up, for it shrinks the assets

---

[53] (1857) 7 El & Bl 356, 119 ER 1279.
[54] *Oakes v Turquand* (1867) LR 2 HL 325, 347–48, 353, 362–65.
[55] *Oakes v Turquand* (1867) LR 2 HL 325, 349–50, 353, 365–67, 375.
[56] *Oakes v Turquand* (1867) LR 2 HL 325, 366–67, 376.
[57] (1879) 4 App Cas 615 (HL Sc) 621, 622, adopting the reasoning of the Lord President (who had in turn accepted the submissions of the liquidator): see 618, 621.
[58] (1877) 3 CPD 282 (CA) 308–09 (Bramwell LJ).
[59] (1882) 23 ChD 413 (CA) 439 (Fry LJ).
[60] *Re Lucks Limited (Serpell's case)* [1928] VLR 466, 473; *Crosbie v Naidoo* (2005) 216 ALR 105 (FCA) 110; *Sons of Gwalia Ltd v Margaretic* (2007) 231 CLR 160 [55], [58], cf [270].

available to satisfy their claims on the company. Rescission before winding up is, however, permitted. Equally, an explanation that is based solely upon prejudice to creditors implies that rescission ought to be barred whenever the company is insolvent.[61] But that is also not the law. The bar is engaged only if winding up has commenced or practically commenced, and insolvency is not alone sufficient.[62]

25.36 The explanation based on prejudice to creditors and shareholders is in fact founded on the notion that winding up materially changes the creditors' rights. In place of a claim against the company, creditors have a claim against its assets, which include all funds paid or payable by the shareholders. The real objection is that rescission would impermissibly defeat the claims given to creditors after winding up begins, rather than prejudice to creditors *per se*.[63]

Third explanation: alteration of legal relations

25.37 Neither the statutory language nor prejudice to creditors and shareholders provides a satisfactory explanation for the winding-up bar, and later cases held that winding up bars rescission because the legal rights of all relevant parties are changed such that it would be unjust to permit rescission. This analysis is associated with the reasons of Jessel MR in *Burgess's* case, who offered the following explanation for the bar:

> The doctrine is that after the company is wound up it ceases to exist, and rescission is impossible. There are then only creditors and co-contributories and no company...
>
> As has been pointed out over and over again the position of the parties is altogether changed. Before winding up, the creditor has no right to a personal demand against any one shareholder. He looks to the company ... but after winding up, the company, though it does not technically cease to exist for all purposes, does so for this purpose. The liabilities are no longer the liabilities of the company except to the extent of the assets realised ... but they become liabilities of the shareholders.[64]

The Master of the Rolls went on to say that the rights of shareholders as co-contributories were also to be protected on winding up. Rescission was therefore barred even if the creditors could all be paid in full, because it would have the effect of increasing the contribution due from the remaining shareholders.[65]

25.38 The Supreme Court of Canada has, to like effect, said that the reason for the bar is that 'the winding-up order creates an entirely new situation, by altering the relations, not only between the creditors and the shareholders, but also among the shareholders *inter se*'.[66] Similarly, in Australia, Dixon J said that the bar was the inevitable result of the fact that, upon liquidation, 'an entire change took place in the relation of creditors and shareholders to the assets and of shareholders *inter se*'.[67] *Burgess's* case was also cited with approval by the

---

[61] See *Tennent v City of Glasgow Bank* (1879) 4 App Cas 615 (HL Sc) 622.
[62] *Re London and Leeds Bank; ex p Carling* (1887) 56 LT (NS) 115; *Elder's Trustee and Executor Co Ltd v Commonwealth Homes and Investment Co Ltd* (1941) 65 CLR 603, 619.
[63] *Tennent v City of Glasgow Bank* (1879) 4 App Cas 615 (HL Sc) 621; *Re Hull and County Bank (Burgess's case)* (1880) 15 ChD 507, 512–13; *Re Lucks Limited (Serpell's case)* [1928] VLR 466, 473–74.
[64] *Re Hull and County Bank (Burgess's case)* (1880) 15 ChD 507, 509, 511–12.
[65] See further paras [25.59]–[25.60].
[66] *Re Northwestern Trust Co (McAskill's case)* [1926] SCR 412, 419.
[67] *Southern British National Trust Ltd v Pither* (1937) 57 CLR 89, 114; cited with approval by Crennan J in *Sons of Gwalia Limited v Margaretic* (2007) 231 CLR 160 [270].

High Court of Australia in *Webb Distributors (Aust) Pty Ltd v Victoria*[68] and again by the Federal Court of Australia, where Finkelstein J said as follows:

> The winding up of the company before the contract has been repudiated creates a permanent bar to rescission: *Oakes v Turquand* (1867) LR 2 HL 325. The reasons given in some of the older cases (reasons which may now be stated in somewhat different terms) is that when the company goes into liquidation: (1) the status and relative position of the contracting parties is altered as the shareholder ceases to exist, being converted into a contributory, and the company ceases to exist, being converted into a body of such contributories; (2) the subject matter of the contract is altered there being no longer any shares but only forced contributions of the contributories; and (3) the rights of the creditors have intervened and those creditors are entitled to be paid in priority to all other claimants on the assets of the company, including the capital subscribed by the shareholders: in *Re Hull and County Bank, Burgess's case* (1880) 15 Ch D 507.[69]

This explanation has the advantage of making explicit the wider considerations that underpin the winding-up bar; in particular, its function in preserving the priority of creditors over shareholders as claimants upon the company's assets.

Wider considerations—priority between creditors and shareholders

25.39 The winding-up bar is underpinned by wider considerations peculiar to the limited liability company. The fundamental rule is that claims by members of a limited liability company in their capacity as members are postponed to those of creditors, so that funds contributed by or due from shareholders in that capacity are available to creditors.[70] Rescission after winding up would undermine that fundamental rule. It would allow shareholders to rank as creditors for their equity contribution, and in the case of partly paid shares, would withdraw from creditors the unpaid equity otherwise available to them.

25.40 The principle that shareholder funds are to be available to creditors is in turn a product of the 'dominant and cardinal principle' of limited liability companies, 'that the investor shall purchase immunity from liability beyond a certain limit, on the terms that there shall be and remain a liability up to that point'.[71]

25.41 Looked at from this perspective the rule in *Oakes v Turquand* is a necessary consequence of the allocation of risk and reward between the members and creditors of a limited liability

---

[68] (1993) 179 CLR 15, 30–31.
[69] *Cadence Asset Management Pty Ltd v Concept Sports Limited* (2005) 55 ACSR 145 (FCA) 147 (rev'd on other grounds *Cadence Asset Management Pty Ltd v Concept Sports Limited* (2005) 147 FCR 434 (Full Ct)); also *Sons of Gwalia Limited v Margaretic* (2005) 149 FCR 227 (Full Ct) [13]; but cf *Sons of Gwalia Limited v Margaretic* (2007) 231 CLR 160 [57] (Gummow J).
[70] Insolvency Act 1986, s 74(2)(f). In Australia, Corporations Act 2001, s 563A. On one view, these provisions themselves prohibit rescission on winding up. See also Insolvency Act 1986, ss 88, 127 (prohibiting unauthorized change in status of members after winding up commences). See further *Sons of Gwalia Limited v Margaretic* (2007) 231 CLR 160, which was unsatisfactory because it failed to interpret the Australian Corporations Act 2001, s 563A so as to give effect to a principle that members come last, and was reversed by legislation replacing s 563A of the Corporations Act 2001 (viz the Corporations Amendment (Sons of Gwalia) Act 2010); cf *Re Central Capital Corp* (1996) 132 DLR (4th) 223 (Ont CA); *Re Blue Range Resource* [2000] AJ 14 (Alta QB); *In the Matter of Stirling Homex Corporation* 578 F 2d 206, 211 (1978) (USCA 2d Cir).
[71] *Ooregum Gold Mining of India v Roper* [1892] AC 125, 145; *Soden v British & Commonwealth Holdings plc* [1998] AC 298, 324; see also *Trevor v Whitworth* (1887) 12 App Cas 409. In Australia, *Webb Distributors (Aust) Pty Ltd v Victoria* (1993) 179 CLR 15, 28–29. In Canada, *Re Blue Range Resource* [2000] AJ 14 (Alta QB).

company. That point tends to be obscured by a focus on the particular statutory language, or on the formal changes to the parties' relations that occur after winding up begins.

(4) Scope

Avoiding liability as a contributory

25.42 The bar in *Oakes v Turquand* emerged from claims by shareholders to avoid liability to contribute to the company's debts on winding up, and most of the instances in which it was first applied involved attempts to rescind directed at this end.

25.43 A shareholder has a liability to contribute on a winding up only if partly paid shares are held. The liability is in respect of and limited to sums remaining unpaid on the shares, which upon winding up become a debt payable when calls are made.[72] Liability extends to those who were members within one year of the winding up,[73] and any effective rescission avoids liability in the shareholder's capacity as a current and past member.[74]

25.44 It is now relatively uncommon for partly paid shares to be issued. Equity finance is generally raised by issuing fully paid shares. This feature of the bar is, accordingly, of much less practical importance than it formerly was. Of more importance is whether the bar prevents a subscribing shareholder from rescinding so as to recover the price paid for the shares.

Recovery of the price

25.45 Although *Oakes v Turquand* was concerned with attempts to avoid liability as a contributory, rescission after winding up to recover sums paid to the company also materially affects the balance between creditors and members. It permits a subscribing shareholder to convert himself into a creditor, and thereby to shrink the shareholder funds available to satisfy the claims of other creditors, whilst obtaining a claim to the company's assets in priority to his co-shareholders.

25.46 It is for that reason unsurprising that the rule in *Oakes v Turquand* was in time extended to cases where a subscribing shareholder sought to rescind for the purposes of recovering sums paid for the shares allotted.[75] That was made clear in *Stone v The City and County Bank Limited*.[76] Mr Stone had sought to rescind an allotment of shares in a London bank for fraud, and to recover the £500 he had paid for them. The contract had been disaffirmed when the company was in the process of being voluntarily wound up. Lindley J held that, although but for the winding up Mr Stone would have been entitled to rescind and recover these sums, that right was lost once the winding up began. The Court of Appeal agreed.

25.47 The same approach was taken in the Australian case of *re Lucks Limited*.[77] Mr Serpell had sought to rescind an allotment of preference shares in a drapery business in Melbourne,

---

[72] Companies Act 1862, ss 38, 74, 75; reproduced Insolvency Act 1986, ss 74, 79, 80. In Australia, Corporations Act 2001, ss 515, 516, 520–22, 527.
[73] Companies Act 1862, s 38(1), reproduced Insolvency Act 1986, s 74(1), (2).
[74] *Re London and Mediterranean Bank, (Wright's case)* (1871) 7 Ch App 55, 59, overturning (1871) 12 Eq Cas 331 (cancellation following request from member).
[75] If rescission was possible, the sums paid would be recoverable as money had and received: *In Ruby Consolidated Mining Company (Askew's case)* (1874) 9 Ch App 664, 666.
[76] (1877) 3 CPD 282 (CA).
[77] *Re Lucks Limited (Serpell's case)* [1928] VLR 466.

and to recover the price paid after winding up had in substance commenced. The claim, together with related claims by other shareholders, was dismissed on the ground that the right to rescind had been lost.

Bringing a damages claim
In *Houldsworth v City of Glasgow Bank*[78] the House of Lords held that before a shareholder could recover damages for deceit practised by the company, he had first to rescind the allotment by which he became a shareholder, and that right was lost once winding up commenced.[79]

25.48

The decision was based on the notion that a shareholder's claim for damages is inconsistent with his status as a shareholder. It was said that the shareholder's contract with the company entails a commitment to contribute sums paid toward the debts and liabilities of the company, and a damages claim involves receiving back precisely that sum.[80] Today the rule is explained in terms of protecting creditors from unauthorized reductions of capital.[81]

25.49

This rule has been criticized by scholars, and has been said to be misconceived, and a source of injustice.[82] In England it was partly abolished in 1989 by the addition of section 111A to the Companies Act 1985.[83] On the other hand, in Australia, where the principle in *Houldsworth's* case was formerly applied, no equivalent legislation was enacted until 2010.[84] There corporate collapses led to the bar being considered on a number of occasions; in particular, in determining whether statutory claims for damages may be brought after the right to rescind has become barred by winding up.[85] These cases culminated in *Sons of Gwalia Limited v Margaretic*,[86] where the High Court of Australia held that the principle in *Houldsworth's* case is no longer part of Australian law. Whilst other aspects of that decision have since been reversed by legislation, those legislative changes do not appear to disturb the High Court's decision that the rule in *Houldsworth's* case is not now part of Australian law.[87]

25.50

---

[78] (1880) 5 App Cas 317.
[79] The bar to damages in *Houldsworth's* case applies whether or not the company is in liquidation and irrespective of its solvency.
[80] *Houldsworth v City of Glasgow Bank* (1880) 5 App Cas 317, 325; *Re Addlestone Linoleum Co* (1887) 37 ChD 191, 205–06.
[81] *Webb Distributors (Aust) Pty Ltd v Victoria* (1993) 179 CLR 15, 33; *Soden v British & Commonwealth Holdings plc* [1998] AC 298, 325–26; *Johnson v McGrath* (2005) 195 FLR 101; *Cadence Asset Management Pty Ltd v Concept Sports* (2005) 147 FCR 434 (Full Ct) 446.
[82] *Webb Distributors (Aust) Pty Ltd v Victoria* (1993) 179 CLR 15, 39 (McHugh J, diss).
[83] Companies Act 1989, s 131(1); *Soden v British & Commonwealth Holdings plc* [1998] AC 298, 324, 327; see now s 655 of the Companies Act 2006.
[84] Corporations Act 2001, s 247E (introduced by the Corporations Amendment (Sons of Gwalia) Act 2010). See also *Re Dividend Fund Inc* (1974) VR 451; *Webb Distributors (Aust) Pty Ltd v Victoria* (1993) 179 CLR 15. It had been held that the principle in *Houldsworth's* case received statutory recognition and modification in s 360(1)(k) of the Companies Code and its statutory successors, including s 563A of the Corporations Law (*Webb Distributors (Aust) Pty Ltd v Victoria* (1993) 179 CLR 15, 33–34; *Cadence Asset Management Pty Ltd v Concept Sports Limited* (2005) 147 FCR 434 (Full Ct) 440) but in *Sons of Gwalia Limited v Margaretic* (2007) 231 CLR 160 this view was disapproved. Section 563A was subsequently replaced by the Corporations Amendment (Sons of Gwalia) Act 2010 in order to reverse the effect of the High Court's decision in *Sons of Gwalia*.
[85] *Sons of Gwalia Limited v Margaretic* (2006) 149 FCR 227; *Crosbie v Naidoo* (2005) 216 ALR 105 (Full FCA); *Cadence Asset Management Pty Ltd v Concept Sports Limited* (2005) 147 FCR 434 (Full Ct); *Johnson v McGrath* (2005) 195 FLR 101.
[86] (2007) 231 CLR 160.
[87] Corporations Amendment (Sons of Gwalia) Act 2010. See further, Explanatory Memorandum to the Corporations Amendment (Sons of Gwalia) Bill 2010.

Purchases in the market

Avoiding liability as a contributory

25.51 *Oakes v Turquand*[88] established that the winding-up bar applied equally if the purchaser of shares in the market could show that he was induced to do so by the company's fraud, and was entitled to rescind so as to avoid liability as a contributory. The appeal brought by Peek, who had purchased shares in the market, was accordingly dismissed alongside that of Oakes, who had taken direct from the company.[89] The principle was confirmed in later cases.[90]

Recovery of the price

25.52 A purchase of shares in the market involves a payment to the seller rather than the company. In principle, winding up itself ought not bar any right to rescind the purchase, and to recover sums paid to the vendor, unless it makes counter-restitution impossible.

25.53 It is somewhat unclear when winding up makes counter-restitution impossible. It did not in *Oeklers v Ellis*[91] even though the company there had been dissolved. Dr Oeklers was a doctor in Wiesbaden, who had bought shares in the South Burma Tin mines from a London stockbroker. The broker had failed to disclose that he was in fact selling his own shares. Dr Oeklers was permitted to rescind for breach of fiduciary duty notwithstanding that the company had already gone into liquidation and been dissolved. It was argued that *restitutio in integrum* was impossible,[92] but that was rejected by Horridge J. He granted rescission subject to the buyer giving credit for the sums received on the winding up. In doing so, Horridge J emphasized that, in accordance with the agreement between them, the broker had kept the shares in his own name and never allocated any specific shares to the buyer, though he held sufficient to do so.[93]

25.54 However, simply because Dr Oeklers' interest in the shares in the South Burma Tin mines was merely equitable or inchoate ought not to have made a critical difference to his capacity to make counter-restitution. The right to rescind the purchase of shares in the market after winding up commences remains unclear.

25.55 If counter-restitution is possible, rescission is still not of right. Before the shares can lawfully be returned to the transferor the rescinding party must first obtain either the liquidator's consent (in the case of a voluntary winding up or a winding up by the court) or a court order (when the company is wound up by the court).[94]

Bringing a damages claim

25.56 *Soden v British & Commonwealth Holdings plc*[95] indicates that the rule in *Houldsworth*'s case[96] does not extend to purchasers in the market affected by an actionable misrepresentation

---

[88] (1867) LR 2 HL 325.
[89] For subsequent claims brought by Mr Peek, *Peek v Gurney* (1873) LR 6 HL 377.
[90] In *Tennent v City of Glasgow Bank* (1879) 4 App Cas 615 (HL Sc) 616, 623 Mr Tennent's claim for a reduction (rescission) of his contracts was similarly dismissed, although £5000 of the £6000 of stock he had taken in the City of Glasgow Bank was purchased from existing shareholders. See also *Johnson v McGrath* (2005) 195 FLR 101 [72]–[73].
[91] [1913] 2 KB 139.
[92] *Oeklers v Ellis* [1913] 2 KB 139, 144.
[93] *Oeklers v Ellis* [1913] 2 KB 139, 152.
[94] Insolvency Act 1986, ss 88, 127. In Australia: Corporations Act 2001 ss 493A, 468A.
[95] [1998] AC 298, 325–27.
[96] See para [25.48].

made by the company, for allowing proof of the claim in competition with the general body of creditors does not either directly or indirectly produce a reduction of capital. The reason for the rule therefore does not apply.[97]

Void allotments

It had been said *obiter* in *Oakes v Turquand*[98] that liability as a contributory was conditioned on the shareholder having 'agreed' to be a member, and that although agreement under a voidable contract was enough, the position might be different if the allotment was pursuant to a wholly void contract. Later cases confirmed that there is no liability to contribute after winding up commences if the contract of subscription is void *ab initio*, as where the claimant was fraudulently led to believe that he was acquiring shares in company A but was, in fact, given shares in company B.[99] Presumably a shareholder in such a position is also able to recover sums paid after winding up commences, as money had and received to his use.

25.57

Types of winding up
Voluntary winding up

Stone v City and County Bank[100] decided that the bar in *Oakes v Turquand* applies in the case of a voluntary winding up.[101]

25.58

Winding up a solvent company

The bar applies where the assets of the company are sufficient to pay creditors and the costs of winding up, at least when rescission is sought for the purpose of avoiding liability as a contributory. That is because the statutory obligation to contribute extends to the payment of such sums as are necessary to adjust the rights of contributories among themselves.[102]

25.59

The position is probably the same if the shareholder wishes to rescind in order to recover the price paid for shares. There are comments *obiter* in *Stone v The City and County Bank Limited*[103] that might suggest rescission would be permitted if at the time of repudiation no debts of the company remain unpaid. But it is unlikely that this approach would be followed. Even if the company is solvent, rescission permits a shareholder to become a creditor and thereby to obtain priority over other shareholders, and *Burgess*'s case decided that the bar was intended to protect creditors and shareholders alike.[104]

25.60

---

[97] In Australia, on the other hand, there had been a divergence of views on this point (*Johnson v McGrath* (2005) 195 FLR 101; *Sons of Gwalia Limited v Margaretic* (2006) 149 FCR 227 (Full Ct)), but the issue is now academic following the decision that the bar is not part of Australian law: *Sons of Gwalia Limited v Margaretic* (2007) 231 CLR 160.

[98] (1867) LR 2 HL 325, 346, 375.

[99] *Re International Society of Auctioneers and Valuers, (Baillie's case)* [1898] 1 Ch 110 (Wright J), applying *Cundy v Lindsay* (1878) 3 App Cas 459; see also *Re United Ports and General Insurance Company, (Beck's case)* (1874) 9 Ch App 392 (company amalgamation) 'Mr Beck was put on the register of shareholders without any authority from him. That was a perfectly void act, as utterly unauthorised by him'. In New Zealand, *Re Tobacconists Ltd* [1931] NZLR 289, 302; *Coupe v JM Coupe Publishing Ltd* [1981] 1 NZLR 275 (CA). In Canada, *Re Northwestern Trust Co, (McAskill's case)* [1926] SCR 412, 419–20. For further discussion, M Arden, D Prentice, and D Richards (eds), *Buckley on the Companies Acts* (15th edn, 2000) [359.181].

[100] (1877) 3 CPD 282 (CA).

[101] See also *Milne v Durham Hosiery Mills Ltd* [1925] 3 DLR 725 (Ont SC) 727.

[102] Companies Act 1862, s 38; Insolvency Act 1986, s 74(1); *Re Hull and County Bank (Burgess's case)* (1880) 15 ChD 507.

[103] (1877) 3 CPD 282, 295 (Lindley J).

[104] *Re Hull and County Bank (Burgess's case)* (1880) 15 ChD 507, 512–13.

Persons who are not shareholders

25.61 The rule is confined to shareholders seeking to rescind their contract of membership with the company. In *Southern British National Trust Ltd (in liq) v Pither*[105] the High Court of Australia refused to extend the rule to debenture holders, and in another Australian case the bar was said to not apply to investors who had received interest bearing promissory notes from the company.[106]

(5) When winding up commences

25.62 A voluntary winding up commences from the date of the company's resolution to wind the company up,[107] and winding up by the court begins on the date the winding-up petition is presented.[108] The right to rescind is therefore lost if rescission is attempted after the company's creditors have presented a petition for the compulsory winding up of the company, even if no winding up order has then been made.[109]

(6) Operation of the bar before winding up

25.63 The right to rescind may be lost before winding up actually commences. The leading decision is *Tennent v City of Glasgow Bank* where Earl Cairns LC said as follows:

> The case of *Oakes v Turquand* in this House has established that it is too late, after winding-up has commenced, to rescind a contract for shares on the ground of fraud ... while it decided negatively that a contract could not be rescinded on the ground of fraud after a winding-up commenced, did not decide affirmatively the converse proposition, that up to the time of the commencement of winding-up a contract to take shares could be rescinded on the ground of fraud. Whether it can be so rescinded up to that time must, I think, depend upon the particular circumstances of the case.[110]

The House of Lords held that Mr Tennent was too late to reduce (rescind) his contract with the City of Glasgow Bank, even though his action was commenced the day before the company passed a resolution for its voluntary winding up, and the winding up only began after that.[111] It was emphasized, however, that the facts were 'extremely peculiar' and that no general rule was being laid down.[112]

---

[105] (1937) 57 CLR 89, 113–14.
[106] *York Street Mezzanine Pty Ltd (in liq) v McEvoy* (2007) 162 FCR 358 [39], [40] per Finkelstein J.
[107] Insolvency Act 1986, s 86.
[108] Insolvency Act 1986, s 129(2).
[109] *Kent v Freehold Land and Brickmaking Company* (1868) LR 3 Ch App 493; *Re Lucks Limited (Serpell's case)* [1928] VLR 466, 473–76.
[110] *Tennent v City of Glasgow Bank* (1879) 4 App Cas 615 (HL Sc) 621. Three other members of the court agreed: at 623. See further M Arden, D Prentice, and D Richards (eds), *Buckley on the Companies Acts* (15th edn, 2000) [359.150]–[359.160].
[111] Companies Act 1862, s 130; see now Insolvency Act 1986, s 86.
[112] '[T]he facts are extremely peculiar, and I do not think that your Lordships, in affirming the judgment of the Court of Session, will find it necessary to lay down any general rule extending beyond the peculiar facts of the present case': *Tennent v City of Glasgow Bank* (1879) 4 App Cas 615 (HL Sc) 622.

The facts were unusual because when Mr Tennent brought his action, he and all of the **25.64** other shareholders knew that the company was deeply insolvent and on the verge of being wound up. On 2 October the bank stopped payment, and the court underlined that the directors knew then that the position of the bank was irretrievable and that a winding up was inevitable.

On 5 October the directors issued a notice convening an extraordinary general meeting on **25.65** 22 October, the purpose of which was to consider and, if thought fit, to pass a resolution to wind up the company. The House of Lords held that after this notice it became impossible for any shareholder to repudiate his shares in a manner affecting the rights of creditors.[113] On 18 October a report was sent to Mr Tennent indicating that the bank was deeply insolvent and that large calls were likely to be made, and the next day the report was published in the newspapers. On Monday 21 October Mr Tennent issued and served proceedings for reduction, and the winding up began the next day.

The decision has been distinguished more often than it has been applied. Stirling J distin- **25.66** guished it less than ten years later in *Carling*'s case.[114] That case also concerned an insolvent bank. Mr Carling wrote repudiating his shares and commenced proceedings two days before a winding-up petition was presented, and two weeks after the shares had first been allotted to him. The liquidator testified that at the date of the petition the company had been insolvent for some time. In permitting rescission and allowing Mr Carling to prove in the winding up for the £120 he had paid, Stirling J held that the creditors had no countervailing equity against the claim for rescission. He emphasized that they had no cause to complain given the short time that Mr Carling had been a member, whether or not the company was insolvent at that time.[115]

Tennant's case was also distinguished by the High Court of Australia in *Elder's Trustee and* **25.67** *Executor Co Ltd v Commonwealth Homes and Investment Co Ltd*.[116] The shareholder's writ had been issued six weeks before lodgement of a petition for winding up, and at a time when the company seems to have been insolvent. The court rejected the submission that the principle in *Tennant*'s case applied:

> It is true that the company never had anything but a shadowy business and was in a state almost of inactivity and that its affairs were hopeless, but that is not enough. *Tennent's case* was decided upon peculiar and extreme facts ... the commencement of the actual legal winding up was only a formality; for all practical purposes 'the bank' had gone into liquidation ... The limits of *Tennent's case* are always hard to fix ... But the facts of this case fell well outside the application of the principle.[117]

This decision, and that in *Carling*'s case,[118] underline that the bar is not engaged merely be- **25.68** cause the company is insolvent at the time the shareholder seeks to rescind.[119] Something more is necessary. It is unclear exactly what that is. The limited authority since *Tennant*'s

---

[113] *Tennent v City of Glasgow Bank* (1879) 4 App Cas 615 (HL Sc).
[114] *Re London and Leeds Bank; ex p Carling* (1887) 56 LT (NS) 115.
[115] *Re London and Leeds Bank; ex p Carling* (1887) 56 LT (NS) 115, 117–18.
[116] (1941) 65 CLR 603.
[117] *Elder's Trustee and Executor Co Ltd v Commonwealth Homes and Investment Co Ltd* (1941) 65 CLR 603, 619.
[118] *Re London and Leeds Bank; ex p Carling* (1887) 56 LT (NS) 115.
[119] Cf *Tennent v City of Glasgow Bank* (1879) 4 App Cas 615 (HL Sc) 622.

case betrays an unwillingness to extend the reach of the bar. The case itself implies that the company must at least be insolvent and have stopped business, and that winding up must be imminent. Whether those facts must also be notorious, or known to the rescinding shareholder, is less clear.

(7) Steps to be taken to prevent the bar operating

Rejecting the shares not sufficient

25.69   To rescind the statutory contract between shareholder and company for misrepresentation so as to prevent the winding-up bar from applying, the shareholder must do more than simply notify the company of his election to reject the shares,[120] notwithstanding that the directors are thereafter obliged to rectify the register, and that in default the court is empowered to do so.[121]

Steps required

25.70   Before winding up begins the shareholder must either have procured the removal of his name from the register of members, commenced legal proceedings to do so, or agreed with the company to have the benefit of rectification proceedings taken by another member.[122]

25.71   A court order rescinding an allotment of shares dates from the time when proceedings for rescission were commenced.[123]

Asserting rights short of commencing proceedings

25.72   Taking active steps to assert the right to rescind in legal proceedings but without commencing proceedings for rectification of the register will in some cases prevent the bar from applying.[124]

25.73   The leading decision is *Whiteley's* case.[125] The Court of Appeal there held that the bar did not operate if the shareholder has done all that could reasonably be expected to assert in legal proceedings his right to repudiate the shares.[126] Mr Whiteley had been given unconditional leave to defend a summons to pay a call, on the basis of an affidavit disclosing that he intended to counter-claim for rescission and to have his name removed from the register for misrepresentation. That was held to be enough, even though the counter-claim was not in

---

[120] *Re London and County General Agency Association, (Hare's case)* (1869) 4 Ch App 503, 510–13; *Re Scottish Petroleum Company* (1882) 23 ChD 413 (CA) 434, 436, 439; *Re National Stadium Ltd* (1923) 55 OLR 199 (Ont SC) 205; *Re Southern Woollen-Mills* [1930] 1 NZLR 10, 12–14.
[121] *Reese River Silver Mining Company Limited v Smith* (1869) 4 App Cas 64, 74–75, 77, 81.
[122] *Reese River Silver Mining Company Limited v Smith* (1869) 4 App Cas 64; *Henderson v Lacon* (1867) LR 2 Eq 249, 263; *Re Scottish Petroleum Company* (1882) 23 ChD 413 (CA) 434, 436–37, 439.
[123] *Reese River Silver Mining Company Limited v Smith* (1869) 4 App Cas 64, 73 (Lord Hatherley LC); cf 77–78 (Lord Westbury) (right is to pursue suit to conclusion notwithstanding winding up in interim).
[124] *Re Scottish Petroleum Company* (1882) 23 ChD 413 (CA) 434; *Re London and Leeds Bank; ex p Carling* (1887) 56 LT (NS) 115, 117; *Re General Railway Syndicate (Whiteley's case)* [1900] 1 Ch 365 (CA) 369.
[125] *Re General Railway Syndicate (Whiteley's case)* [1900] 1 Ch 365 (CA).
[126] *Re General Railway Syndicate (Whiteley's case)* [1900] 1 Ch 365 (CA) 369. The court also asked whether what had been done 'was equivalent for all practical purposes, and for all legal purposes, to taking proceedings to have his name removed from the register': at 368.

fact filed until after the winding up had commenced, and that occurred two days after leave to defend had been given.

Had winding up not occurred for some time, any delay in bringing the counter-claim would itself have caused Mr Whiteley to lose the right to rescind. A shareholder who relies on a right to rescind as a defence to calls must promptly take steps to have his name removed from the register, and if he does not do so the right is lost.[127] **25.74**

Whiteley's case was distinguished in New Zealand in *re Southland Woollen-Mills Ltd*.[128] There a notice of intention to defend an action for calls was filed before winding up had commenced. But it was not filed promptly: the shareholders had waited two months after the misrepresentations had been discovered. The notice also did not indicate that the defence was based upon rescission, and was lodged in a court having no jurisdiction to order rescission or rectify the register of members. The notice of intention to defend was held to not be effective to prevent the shareholder being placed on the list of contributories.[129] **25.75**

Failure to sue caused by the company's fraud
In *Whiteley's* case[130] Wright J said *obiter* that winding up would not bar rescission if the company had, by fraud, induced the shareholder to delay bringing an action. The precise content of this principle appears not have been explored in later cases. **25.76**

(8) Statutory exceptions

Some statutory rights to rescind share allotments are expressly said to be exercisable after winding up has begun. The leading example is the right to rescind an irregular share allotment.[131] **25.77**

Australian courts are given certain statutory powers to rescind the contract between shareholder and company in terms that make no reference to winding up one way or the other.[132] Whether these powers permit a court to order rescission after a winding up remains unclear. There are some indications that they do not,[133] and this is the preferable result. A statutory intention to allow rescission after winding up should ordinarily be found only if clear words are used. That is not only because the bar in *Oakes v Turquand* is firmly entrenched, and express words have elsewhere been used to abrogate it.[134] Rescission after winding up distorts **25.78**

---

[127] *First National Reinsurance Company v Greenfield* [1920] 2 KB 260 (CA).
[128] [1930] 1 NZLR 10, 14.
[129] *Re Southland Woollen-Mills Ltd* [1930] 1 NZLR 10, 12–14.
[130] *Re General Railway Syndicate (Whiteley's case)* [1899] 1 Ch 770, 773; rev'd on other grounds [1900] 1 ChD 365 (CA).
[131] Companies Act 2006, s 579(1), (2). In Australia, Corporations Act 2001, s 737(1). See also *Re National Motor Mail-Coach Company Limited* [1908] 2 ChD 228, 234 (considering the predecessors to these provisions).
[132] Competition and Consumer Act 2010, Sched 2, s 243; Corporations Act 2001, s 1325(5). Cf Insolvency Act 1986 (UK), s 186.
[133] *Webb Distributors (Aust) Pty Ltd v Victoria* (1993) 179 CLR 15, 37; *Sons of Gwalia Limited v Margaretic* (2007) 231 CLR 160 [54]–[60] (Gummow J).
[134] Companies Act 2006, s 579(1), (2). In Australia, Corporations Act 2001, s 737(1).

the fundamental rule that claims by members are to be postponed to sums due to creditors, so that funds contributed by or due from shareholders are available to creditors on a winding up.[135] A legislative intention to alter this important balance between shareholders and creditors ought not lightly to be inferred unless that intention is clearly expressed.

---

[135] Insolvency Act 1986, s 74(2)(f). In Australia, Corporations Act 2001, s 563A; also paras [25.39]–[25.41].

26
Contracting Out

A. Introduction	26.01	C. Misrepresentation Act 1967	26.12
B. General Law	26.02	(1) Section 3 of the Misrepresentation Act 1967	26.13
(1) Introduction	26.02		
(2) Types of clauses	26.03	(2) Scope of section 3 of the Misrepresentation Act 1967	26.14
(3) Entire agreement clauses	26.04		
(4) No representation clauses	26.06	(3) Requirement of reasonableness	26.23
(5) Non-reliance clauses	26.09	D. Consumer Protection Legislation	26.34

A. Introduction

This chapter examines the freedom parties have to contract out of rescission for misrepresentation. It first considers the position at general law and then the more far-reaching restrictions that have been introduced through legislation. It is not possible to contract out of the right to rescind for duress.[1]   26.01

B. General Law

(1) Introduction

At general law, the right to rescind for non-fraudulent misrepresentation can be limited or excluded by an express provision of the agreement.[2] One cannot escape such a provision by arguing that it is avoided *ab initio*.[3] However, it is not possible to contract out of a right to rescind for fraudulent misrepresentation. The courts apply the maxim that fraud unravels all: *fraus omnia corrumpit*.[4] As Lord Bingham stated in *HIH Casualty & General*   26.02

---

[1] *Borrelli v Ting* [2010] UKPC 21 (Bermuda) [40].
[2] *Boyd & Forrest v The Glasgow & South-Western Railway Co* [1915] SC 20 (HL) 36; *Toomey v Eagle Star Insurance Co Ltd (No 2)* [1995] 2 Lloyd's Rep 88, 91–92; *HIH Casualty & General Insurance v Chase Manhattan Bank* [2003] 2 Lloyd's Rep 61 (HL) [9].
[3] *Toomey v Eagle Star Insurance Co Ltd (No 2)* [1995] 2 Lloyd's Rep 88, 91; *Pan Atlantic Insurance Ltd v Pine Top Insurance Co* [1993] 1 Lloyd's Rep 496 (CA) 502, on appeal [1994] 2 Lloyd's Rep 427 (HL); *Peekay Intermark Ltd and Harish Pawani v Australia & New Zealand Banking Group Ltd* [2006] EWCA 386 [57]. Cf *Morgan v Pooley* [2010] EWHC 2447 (QB) [114] which surprisingly seems to suggest that exclusion clauses in long contracts drafted by lawyers which parties have not had an opportunity to read beforehand may be treated differently in this regard.
[4] *S Pearson & Son Ltd v Dublin Corporation* [1907] AC 351 (HL) 362, see also 353–54 (non- reliance clauses were held not to apply to a fraudulent misrepresentation; a deceit rather than rescission case but the same principles apply); *Peart Stevenson Associates Ltd v Holland* [2008] EWHC 1868 (QB) (non-reliance clause inapplicable); *Prest v Petrodel Resources Ltd* [2013] 3 WLR 1 (SC) [18]; *Bonhams 1793 Ltd v Cavazzoni* [2014] EWHC 682 (QB).

Insurance v Chase Manhattan Bank '[i]t is clear that the law, on public policy grounds, does not permit a contracting party to exclude liability for his own fraud in inducing the making of the contract.'[5]

(2) Types of clauses

26.03 A clause that purports to bar rescission for non-fraudulent misrepresentation may take a number of forms. It may simply state that rescission for misrepresentation is excluded or that any rights to rescission are waived.[6] For example, a clause stating that '[t]his contract is neither cancellable nor voidable by either party' was held to exclude rescission for innocent misrepresentation, but not negligent misrepresentation.[7] Alternatively it may negate one of the elements of this ground for rescission and thus prevent an entitlement to rescind from ever arising.[8] There appears to be no practical difference between 'agreeing' that an element is not present and 'acknowledging' it.[9] These clauses may take the form of an acknowledgement or agreement that no representations other than those contained in the agreement have been made. Such clauses will be referred to as 'no representation clauses'. Alternatively, the clause may state that the parties do not rely on representations which are not set out in the agreement. Such provisions are commonly known as 'non-reliance clauses'. What statements fall within a particular no representation or non-reliance clause is a question of construction.[10] Both no representation and non-reliance clauses are discussed separately later in this chapter, but first the ineffectiveness of 'entire agreement' clauses in excluding rescission is explained.

(3) Entire agreement clauses

26.04 An entire agreement clause which only states that the written contract represents the whole agreement between the parties protects against the assertion of collateral warranties,[11] but does not exclude the right to rescind for pre-contractual misrepresentation.[12] An entire

---

[5] [2003] 2 Lloyd's Rep 61 (HL) [16], also [76] and [121]. The question as to whether it is possible to contract out of the consequences of an agent's fraud was left open by the majority. See also *Lazarus Estates Ltd v Beasley* [1956] 1 QB 702 (CA) 712; *FoodCo UK LLP (t/a Muffin Break) v Henry Boot Developments Ltd* [2010] EWHC 358 (Ch) [166]; *Wickens v Cheval Property Developments Ltd* [2010] EWHC 2249 (Ch) [19] (non-reliance clause ineffective in case of fraud).
[6] *Walker v Boyle* [1982] 1 WLR 495; *Government of Zanzibar v British Aerospace (Lancaster House) Ltd* [2000] 1 WLR 2333, 2344; *Cleaver v Schyde Investments Ltd* [2011] 2 P & CR 21 [3]; *Bikam OOD v Adria Cable Sarl* [2012] EWHC 621 (Comm) [13]: 'Each party waives its rights against the other in respect of warranties and representations (whether written or oral) not expressly set out in this Agreement.'
[7] *Toomey v Eagle Star Insurance Co Ltd (No 2)* [1995] 2 Lloyd's Rep 88, 91–92.
[8] *AXA Sun Life Services Plc v Campbell Martin Ltd* [2011] 2 Lloyd's Rep 1 (CA) [94]; see examples in *Raiffeisen Zentralbank Osterreich AG v The Royal Bank of Scotland Plc* [2011] 1 Lloyd's Rep 123 [304].
[9] *Springwell Navigation Corp v JP Morgan* [2010] 2 CLC 705 (CA) [170].
[10] *FoodCo UK LLP (t/a Muffin Break) v Henry Boot Developments Ltd* [2010] EWHC 358 (Ch) [166]; *Shill Properties Ltd v Bunch* [2021] EWHC 2142 (Ch) [42]; *Toner v Telford Homes Ltd* [2021] EWHC 516 (QB) [118]–[119].
[11] *Inntrepreneur Pub Co v East Crown Ltd* [2000] 2 Lloyd's Rep 611, 614. Cf *Whitehead Mann Ltd v Cheverny Consulting Ltd* [2006] EWCA 1303. See also *Cassa di Risparmio v Barclays Bank* [2011] 1 CLC 701 [528], [531].
[12] *Deepak Fertilisers and Petrochemicals Corporation v ICI Chemicals & Polymers Ltd* [1999] 1 Lloyd's Rep 387 (CA) 395; *Government of Zanzibar v British Aerospace (Lancaster House) Ltd* [2000] 1 WLR 2333, 2344.

agreement clause which states that the agreement supersedes all prior agreements[13] would be similarly ineffective to bar rescission. The right to rescind is not a right that arises by agreement between the parties but by operation of the law outside the agreement. An entire agreement clause is not engaged because the party seeking to rescind is not asserting the existence of an additional contractual term that is not contained in the contractual document.[14]

In *AXA Sun Life Services Plc v Campbell Martin Ltd*[15] a term headed 'Entire Agreement' stated that 'this Agreement shall supersede any prior promises, agreements, representations, undertakings or implications whether made orally or in writing'.[16] It was agreed that the clause excluded collateral contracts but the issue was whether it also excluded misrepresentations. The Court of Appeal held that it did not. The clause was only concerned with identifying matters agreed, not with inaccurate statements that may have been relied on in entering into the agreement.[17]

26.05

(4) No representation clauses

A 'no representation clause' is an acknowledgement or agreement that (a) no representations other than those embodied in the agreement have been made, or that (b) no representations are made other than those based only on the knowledge or belief of the representor and no further inquiries have been made.[18] Earlier cases suggested that an acknowledgement that no pre-contractual representations had been made could be of limited effect as such clauses could be construed as merely representing the knowledge of the parties at the time the contract was made and consequently not preventing the proof of earlier representations.[19] However, more recent cases suggest that no representation clauses can operate as a contractual estoppel preventing the party seeking to rescind from asserting in proceedings that representations are or were made.[20]

26.06

In the leading case of *Springwell Navigation Corporation v JP Morgan*[21] the Court of Appeal found that there is no legal principle that prevents the parties from agreeing to assume that

26.07

---

[13] *Matchbet Ltd v Openbet Retail Ltd* [2013] EWHC 3067 (Ch) [130]–[132] where such clauses were said to operate because of contractual estoppel.
[14] *RBC Properties Pte Ltd v Defu Furniture Pte Ltd* [2014] SGCA 62 [113].
[15] [2011] 2 Lloyd's Rep 1 (CA).
[16] See also *BSkyB Limited, Sky Subscribers Services Limited v HP Enterprise Services UK Limited, Electronic Data systems LLC* [2010] EWHC 86 (TCC) where a similarly worded clause was also held not to extend to liability for misrepresentation.
[17] *AXA Sun Life Services Plc v Campbell Martin Ltd* [2011] 2 Lloyd's Rep 1 (CA) [36], [38], [80]–[82]; *Mears Ltd v Shoreline Housing Partnership Ltd* [2013] CP Rep 39 (CA) [14]–[17].
[18] *Cremdean Properties Ltd v Nash* (1977) 244 EG 547; *William Sindall Plc v Cambridgeshire CC* [1994] 1 WLR 1016 (CA) 1034; *SAM Business Systems Ltd v Hedley & Co* [2002] EWHC 2733. The *William Sindall* case gave rise to a standard clause which expressly referred to that case and provided that information on a property was given to the best knowledge, information and belief of the seller: *Morgan v Pooley* [2010] EWHC 2447 (QB) [102]–[107]. In *Aquila Wsa Aviation Opportunities II Limited v Onur Air Tasimacilik AS* [2018] EWHC 519 (Comm) no representations were found to have been made in respect of the condition of an aircraft engine which was leased on an expressly stipulated 'as is, where is' basis.
[19] *Thomas Witter Ltd v TBP Industries Ltd* [1996] 2 All ER 573, 597; *EA Grimstead & Son Ltd v McGarrigan* [1999] EWCA (Civ) 3029, 30.
[20] *Trident Turboprop (Dublin) Ltd v First Flight Couriers Ltd* [2008] 2 Lloyd's Rep 581, aff'd [2010] QB 86 (CA); *Raiffeisen Zentralbank Osterreich AG v The Royal Bank of Scotland Plc* [2011] 1 Lloyd's Rep 123 [267].
[21] [2010] 2 CLC 705 (CA).

a certain state of affairs exists or existed, even if that is not the case, so that the contract is made and operates upon that agreed basis.[22] The court emphasized the commercial utility of upholding clauses of this kind so that parties know precisely the basis on which they are entering into their contractual relationship.[23] The court held that the claimant was bound contractually to the acknowledgement contained in the terms that it had signed that no representation or warranty has been made by its counterparty.[24] The application of an estoppel arising from the contract was reaffirmed by the Court of Appeal in *AXA Sun Life Services Plc v Campbell Martin Ltd*.[25]

26.08 Arguments that a 'no representation' clause should be construed restrictively so as not to apply to statements concerning matters within the knowledge of the beneficiary of the clause have been unsuccessful.[26]

(5) Non-reliance clauses

Introduction

26.09 A non-reliance clause usually states that no party to the agreement has entered into it in reliance on any representation of the other party which is not set out in the agreement. Formerly such clauses were thought to operate by raising an evidential estoppel barring the representee from asserting that he had relied on a misrepresentation in entering into the contract; however difficulties in proving the elements of such an estoppel limited their usefulness in practice. As will appear, the ascendance of a 'contractual estoppel' analysis, discussed earlier, has significantly strengthened the effectiveness of non-reliance clauses.[27]

Evidential estoppel

26.10 Formerly non-reliance clauses seemed to operate only by raising an evidential estoppel barring the representee from asserting that he had relied on the misrepresentation in entering into the contract. '[An acknowledgement of non-reliance] is apt to prevent the party who has given the acknowledgement from asserting in subsequent litigation against the party to whom it has been given that it is not true.'[28] To establish an evidential estoppel on the basis of a non-reliance clause the representor had to prove that:

(1) the statement of non-reliance was clear and unequivocal;
(2) the party making it intended that the representor should act on it; and

---

[22] *Springwell Navigation Corporation v JP Morgan* [2010] 2 CLC 705 (CA) [143], [155]–[156]. Affirming More-Bick LJ's statement to this effect in *Peekay Intermark and Harish Pawani v Australia and New Zealand Banking Group Ltd* [2006] EWCA Civ 386 [56]. See also *Cassa di Risparmio v Barclays Bank* [2011] 1 CLC 701 [505]; *Raiffeisen Zentralbank Osterreich AG v The Royal Bank of Scotland Plc* [2011] 1 Lloyd's Rep 123 [230], [250]. Contractual estoppel was endorsed by the Privy Council in *Prime Sight Ltd v Lavarello* [2014] 2 WLR 84 (PC) [47].
[23] *Springwell Navigation Corporation v JP Morgan* [2010] 2 CLC 705 (CA) [144]; *Raiffeisen Zentralbank Osterreich AG v The Royal Bank of Scotland Plc* [2011] 1 Lloyd's Rep 123 [253] 'There is good reason for allowing businessmen to agree with each other the basis of fact (including past fact) upon which they are to do business.'
[24] *Springwell Navigation Corporation v JP Morgan* [2010] 2 CLC 705 (CA) [170].
[25] [2011] 2 Lloyd's Rep 1 (CA) [93]. See also *Bank Leumi (UK) Plc v Wachner* [2011] EWHC 656 (Comm) [184].
[26] *Raiffeisen Zentralbank Osterreich AG v The Royal Bank of Scotland Plc* [2011] 1 Lloyd's Rep 123 [257]–[267].
[27] See A Trukhtanov, 'Misrepresentation: Acknowledgement of Non-reliance as Defence' (2009) 125 LQR 648.
[28] *EA Grimstead & Son Ltd v McGarrigan* [1999] EWCA (Civ) 3029, 31.

(3) the representor believed it to be true and was induced by that belief to enter into the contract.[29] If the representor made the relevant representations in order to persuade the other party to enter into the contract, then he is likely to be found to have known that the representee's acknowledgement of non-reliance did not reflect the true position.[30] In that event no evidential estoppel would arise.

These requirements meant that the parties could not effectively agree on a state of affairs, namely that representations not embodied in the written terms had not been relied on, when they actually knew that this state of affairs did not exist.

Contractual estoppel

26.11 It is now accepted that a non-reliance clause can operate as a contractual estoppel.[31] By entering into an agreement which contains an acknowledgement of non-reliance, the representee may be estopped by the terms of the non-reliance clause from going behind it and raising contrary allegations, even if the representor was aware that the representee was relying on representations not embodied in the contract. In contrast with evidential estoppel, the party relying on contractual estoppel is not required to prove his belief in the truth of the acknowledgement of non-reliance.[32] Contractual estoppel does not require any detriment[33] or reliance[34] to be proved, nor that it would be unconscionable to resile from the agreed statement of fact.[35] Where the parties have wittingly and willingly reached agreement on a particular allocation of risk, they are held to it.[36]

C. Misrepresentation Act 1967

26.12 In England and Wales, Parliament has modified the general law position in relation to non-fraudulent misrepresentation. A term that would otherwise bar rescission for misrepresentation will be rendered ineffective by section 3 of the Misrepresentation Act 1967 if it is

---

[29] *Watford Electronics Ltd v Sanderson CFL Ltd* [2001] BLR 143; [2001] All ER (D) 290 applying *EA Grimstead & Son Ltd v McGarrigan* [1999] EWCA (Civ) 3029 and the principles of evidential estoppel laid down in *Lowe v Lombank Ltd* [1960] 1 WLR 196 (CA).

[30] *EA Grimstead & Son Ltd v McGarrigan* [1999] EWCA (Civ) 3029, 32; *Watford Electronics Ltd v Sanderson CFL Ltd* [2001] BLR 143; [2001] All ER (D) 290 [40]; *Quest 4 Finance Ltd v Maxfield* [2007] 2 CLC 706. It cannot be automatically assumed that the representor relied on a boilerplate clause: *GMAC Commercial Credit Development Ltd v Sandhu* [2004] All ER (D) 589 [118].

[31] *Peekay Intermark Ltd and Harish Pawani v Australia & New Zealand Banking Group Ltd* [2006] EWCA 386 [57] referring to *Colchester Borough Council v Smith* [1992] Ch 421(CA); *Donegal International Limited v Republic of Zambia* [2007] EWHC 197 [465]; *Springwell Navigation Corporation v JP Morgan* [2010] 2 CLC 705 (CA); *Cassa di Risparmio v Barclays Bank* [2011] 1 CLC 701 [510], [514]; *Barclays Bank v Svizera Holdings BV* [2014] EWHC 1020 (Comm) [58]. See also *Bottin (International) Investments Ltd v Venson Group Plc* [2004] EWCA 1368 [66]; *Dorotea Pty Ltd v Christos Doufas Nominees* [1986] 2 Qd R 91.

[32] *FoodCo UK LLP (t/a Muffin Break) v Henry Boot Developments Ltd* [2010] EWHC 358 (Ch) [170]. An argument that contractual estoppel only applied to no representation clauses and evidential estoppel applied to non-reliance clauses was rejected by Lewison J at [171].

[33] *Springwell Navigation Corp v JP Morgan* [2008] EWHC 1186 (Comm) [556]; aff'd [2010] 2 CLC 705 (CA); *Credit Suisse International v Stichting Vestia Groep* [2014] EWHC 3103 (Comm) [309].

[34] *Springwell Navigation Corp v JP Morgan* [2008] EWHC 1186 (Comm) [556]; aff'd [2010] 2 CLC 705 (CA); *First Tower Trustees Ltd v CDS (Superstores International) Ltd* [2019] 1 WLR 637 (CA) [47].

[35] *Springwell Navigation Corporation v JP Morgan* [2010] 2 CLC 705 (CA) [177]; *Re Arboretum Devon (RLH) Ltd* [2021] EWHC 1047 (Ch).

[36] *Aquila Wsa Aviation Opportunities II Limited v Onur Air Tasimacilik AS* [2018] EWHC 519 (Comm).

572   VI. OTHER BARS

not fair and reasonable. The jurisdiction conferred by this section does not extend to international supply contracts.[37]

(1) Section 3 of the Misrepresentation Act 1967

26.13 Section 3 of the Misrepresentation Act 1967 provides:

> If a contract contains a term which would exclude or restrict—
> (a) any liability to which a party to a contract may be subject by reason of any misrepresentation made by him before the contract was made; or
> (b) any remedy available to another party to the contract by reason of such misrepresentation,
> that term shall be of no effect except in so far as it satisfies the requirement of reasonableness as stated in section 11(1) of the Unfair Contract Terms Act 1977; and it is for those claiming that the term satisfies that requirement to show that it does.

The scope of this enactment will now be considered. The requirement of reasonableness will be examined thereafter.

(2) Scope of section 3 of the Misrepresentation Act 1967

Clauses falling within section 3 of the Misrepresentation Act 1967

26.14 The exclusion clause must be a 'term' of the contract for section 3 to be applicable. If it is a non-contractual disclaimer then it will fall outside the scope of this section.[38] Secondly, the term must 'exclude or restrict any liability ... or remedy'. The courts have generally looked at substance rather than form to ascertain whether clauses are attempts to exclude or restrict liability or remedies for misrepresentation so as to engage section 3. The section has been applied to direct denials of the right to rescind. For example, a condition of a contract of sale which stated that 'no error, mis-statement or omission in any preliminary answer concerning the property ... shall annul the sale' was struck down on the basis of that section.[39] It has also been applied to a term which asserted that no representations had been made. The clause stated: '[n]otwithstanding any statement of fact included in these particulars the vendor shall be conclusively deemed to have made no representation within the meaning of the Misrepresentation Act 1967.' The court held that this was only a form of words the intended and actual effect of which was to exclude or restrict liability.[40]

26.15 Section 3 was held to be applicable to a covenant not to sue whereby each party agreed that 'it shall not commence any lawsuit or assert any claim, whether known or unknown,

---

[37] See para [26.32].
[38] *Cremdean Properties Ltd v Nash* (1977) 244 EG 547 (CA); *McGrath v Shah* (1989) 57 P & CR 452, 460–61; *Collins v Howell-Jones* [1981] EGD 207 (CA) 212–23; *Walker v Boyle* [1982] 1 WLR 495, 501; *IFE Fund SA v Goldman Sachs International* [2006] EWHC 2887 [65].
[39] *Walker v Boyle* [1982] 1 WLR 495.
[40] *Cremdean Properties Ltd v Nash* (1977) 244 EG 547 (CA) 551.

against the other party ... based on actions, discussions or agreements ... which occurred prior to the signing of this Agreement'.[41] The section has also been applied to terms which attempted to shift the onus onto the representee to verify the correctness of all representations.[42] Thus a clause which provided that 'any intending purchaser must satisfy himself by inspection or otherwise as to the correctness of each statement contained in the particulars' fell within the section.[43] Section 3 also applied to a clause which stated that a charterer's acceptance of a vessel was conclusive proof that it had examined the vessel and found her to be in all respects seaworthy and satisfactory.[44]

Clauses not falling within section 3 of the Misrepresentation Act 1967

Clauses within consumer contracts were taken outside of section 3 of the Misrepresentation Act 1967 by the Consumer Rights Act 2015.[45] Thus section 3 only applies to contracts entered into between traders themselves and contracts entered into between consumers themselves. **26.16**

Section 3 has been held not to apply to a clause that merely limited the authority of agents to make representations.[46] It has also been said that section 3 does not extend to terms which go to the question whether the alleged representation of fact was made at all.[47] Section 3 does not affect the question whether, having regard to the agreed terms, a supposed representee would have understood the supposed representor to be making representations at all and what representations, if any, were impliedly made.[48] There is a distinction between clauses which exclude liability and duty-defining clauses which set out the terms on which parties conduct their business.[49] In *IFE Fund SA v Goldman Sachs International* this point was illustrated as follows: **26.17**

> If a seller of a car said to a buyer 'I have serviced the car since it was new, it has had only one owner and the clock reading is accurate', those statements would be representations, and they would still have that character even if the seller added the words 'but those statements are not representations on which you can rely' ... If, however, the seller of the car said 'The clock reading is 20,000 miles, but I have no knowledge whether the reading is true or false', the position would be different, because the qualifying words could not fairly be regarded as an attempt to exclude liability for a false representation arising from the first half of the sentence.[50]

---

[41] *Six Continents Hotels Inc v Event Hotels GmbH* [2006] EWHC 2317.
[42] *Cremdean Properties Ltd v Nash* (1977) 244 EG 547 (CA).
[43] *South Western General Property Co Ltd v Marton* [1982] EGD 113, 120–21.
[44] *Howard Marine and Dredging Co Ltd v A Ogden & Sons (Excavations) Ltd* [1978] QB 574 (CA).
[45] Consumer Rights Act 2015, Sched 4, para 1. However, provision is made to apply a test of unfairness to such terms in consumer contracts: para [26.35].
[46] *Overbrooke Estates Ltd v Glencombe Properties Ltd* [1974] 1 WLR 1335 (a statement in conditions of sale that the vendors did not make representations and that the vendor's agents (the auctioneers) had no authority to make representations was held not to be an exclusion or restriction on liability to which s 3 applied but only a limitation of the ostensible authority of the agent). See also *Collins v Howell-Jones* [1981] EGD 207 (CA) 210–11.
[47] *William Sindall Plc v Cambridgeshire CC* [1994] 1 WLR 1016 (CA) 1034.
[48] *Raiffeisen Zentralbank Osterreich AG v The Royal Bank of Scotland Plc* [2011] 1 Lloyd's Rep 123 [273], [287]. Applied in *Springwell Navigation Corp v JP Morgan* [2010] 2 CLC 705 (CA) [180].
[49] *Raiffeisen Zentralbank Osterreich AG v The Royal Bank of Scotland Plc* [2011] 1 Lloyd's Rep 123 [297], [310]–[317].
[50] *IFE Fund SA v Goldman Sachs International* [2006] EWHC 2887 [68]–[69].

In that decision statements regarding non-verification of information, and non-acceptance of responsibility for reviewing the information, were found to go to the scope of the representations being made and not to be attempts to exclude liability for misrepresentation so as to bring them within the section.[51]

26.18 Thus not every disclaimer will fall within section 3. Clauses which on a proper construction only refine the extent of any representations made may fall outside it. In *Raiffeisen Zentralbank Osterreich AG v The Royal Bank of Scotland Plc*[52] disclaimers agreeing the ambit of what was represented were construed as saying that the information passed on 'was believed to be true but that no warranty or representation is being given as to the accuracy or completeness of the contents (or the reasonableness of that belief).'[53] The result was that the information provider would only be liable if he did not believe the information to be true; but not otherwise.[54] The disclaimers were not construed as clauses seeking to exclude liability. In *Brown v InnovatorOne Plc*[55] disclaimers made it clear that no representation was made that the information provided was complete. Those provisions qualified representations of fact actually made and indicated that the recipient should not rely on the completeness or accuracy of those representations. The court held that they fell outside of section 3 since they did not exclude or restrict liability in respect of representations actually made nor did they attempt to re-write history or, in other words, part from reality.[56] In *First Tower Trustees Ltd v CDS (Superstores International) Ltd*[57] the Court of Appeal held that where in a non-consumer contract the term in question, as a matter of interpretation, does no more than describe the relevant party's primary obligations, section 3 will not apply.

26.19 Even if a clause does not fall within section 3 of the Misrepresentation Act 1967, it could still potentially be subject to section 3(2)(b)(i) of the Unfair Contract Terms Act 1977. Section 3(2)(b)(i) of that Act controls terms in contracts where a party is dealing on its standard terms allowing a party to claim to be entitled to render a contractual performance substantially different from that which was reasonably expected of him, or to render no performance at all. In *AXA Sun Life Services Plc v Campbell Martin Ltd* it was suggested *obiter* that 'in appropriate circumstances a pre-contractual representation or promise may affect the performance that is reasonably expected of a party'.[58]

---

[51] *IFE Fund SA v Goldman Sachs International* [2006] EWHC 2887 [65]–[70] relying on *William Sindall Plc v Cambridgeshire CC* [1994] 1 WLR 1016 (CA). But note that in *Cremdean Properties Ltd v Nash* (1977) 244 EG 547 (CA) s 3 was applied to a clause which, *inter alia*, stated that: 'These particulars are prepared for the convenience of an intending purchaser or tenant and although they are believed to be correct their accuracy is not guaranteed.' Similarly in *Morgan v Pooley* [2010] EWHC 2447 (QB), s 3 was applied to a clause which appeared only to define the extent of the representations made which stated that 'it is agreed and declared that the reply to any enquiry or information supplied in any property information form is given to the best knowledge, information and belief of the Seller, and that neither the Seller nor his legal representative has made any further enquiries into such matters'.
[52] [2011] 1 Lloyd's Rep 123.
[53] *Raiffeisen Zentralbank Osterreich AG v The Royal Bank of Scotland Plc* [2011] 1 Lloyd's Rep 123 [317].
[54] *Raiffeisen Zentralbank Osterreich AG v The Royal Bank of Scotland Plc* [2011] 1 Lloyd's Rep 123 [317].
[55] [2012] EWHC 1321 (Comm).
[56] *Brown v InnovatorOne Plc* [2012] EWHC 1321 (Comm) [899] applying *Raiffeisen Zentralbank Osterreich AG v The Royal Bank of Scotland Plc* [2011] 1 Lloyd's Rep 123 [314].
[57] [2019] 1 WLR 637 (CA) [43]; see also *Impact Funding Solutions Ltd v Barrington Support Services Ltd* [2017] AC 73 (Sup Ct) [36].
[58] [2011] 2 Lloyd's Rep 1 (CA) [50].

No representation and non-reliance clauses

26.20 It is a matter of construction of the terms of the relevant clause in the context of the transaction whether section 3 of the Misrepresentation Act 1967 applies to a particular no representation or non-reliance clause.[59] There is an argument that all such clauses do not on their face 'exclude or restrict liability' for misrepresentation;[60] rather, they only acknowledge that one of the elements necessary to establish this ground for rescission is not present. In *Watford Electronics Ltd v Sanderson CFL Ltd*[61] Chadwick LJ appeared to doubt that an acknowledgement of non-reliance is in substance an exclusion clause to which section 3 of the Misrepresentation Act is applicable.[62] However, this argument places too much emphasis on the form of the term at the expense of its substance.[63] If a clause has 'the purported effect' of excluding liability or remedies for misrepresentation, it engages section 3 of the Act.[64] In *Government of Zanzibar v British Aerospace (Lancaster House) Ltd* Judge Raymond Jack QC expressed the view that section 3 would cover a non-reliance clause, adding:

> A term which negates a reliance which in fact existed is a term which excludes a liability which the representor would otherwise be subject to by reason of the representation. If that were wrong, it would mean that section 3 could always be defeated by including an appropriate non-reliance clause in the contract, however unreasonable that might be.[65]

26.21 In *Raiffeisen Zentralbank Osterreich AG v The Royal Bank of Scotland Plc* Christopher Clarke J concluded that parties could agree not to treat certain statements as representations upon which reliance could be placed and this agreement would fall outside of section 3, but added that:

> ... to tell the man in the street that the car you are selling him is perfect and then agree that the basis of your contract is that no representations have been made or relied on, may be nothing more than an attempt retrospectively to alter the character and effect of what has gone before and in substance [be] an attempt to exclude or restrict liability.[66]

This statement was approved by the Court of Appeal in *Springwell Navigation Corporation v JP Morgan*.[67]

---

[59] For discussion of 'non representation' and 'non-reliance' clauses, see paras [26-06]–[26.09].

[60] Peel points out that the Misrepresentation Act 1967 does not contain a provision similar to s 13 of the Unfair Contract Terms Act 1977 which states that 'excluding or restricting liability' includes 'excluding or restricting liability by reference to terms and notices which exclude or restrict the relevant obligation or duty': E Peel (2001) 117 LQR 545, 548.

[61] [2001] BLR 143 [40].

[62] See also *Titan Steel Wheels Ltd v Royal Bank of Scotland* [2010] 2 Lloyd's Rep 92 [98]; *Crestsign Ltd v National Westminster Bank Plc* [2015] 2 All ER (Comm) 133 [112]–[119] (permission to appeal given on other grounds: [2015] EWCA Civ 986); *Thornbridge Ltd v Barclays Bank Plc* [2015] EWHC 3430 (QB); *Sears v Minco Plc* [2016] EWHC 433 (Ch) [80]. In these three cases the court accepted that the 1977 Act did not apply to the clauses in question because they were 'basis clauses' and not exclusion clauses. However the latter two decisions were disapproved in *First Tower Trustees Ltd v CDS (Superstores International) Ltd* [2019] 1 WLR 637 (CA).

[63] In *AXA Sun Life Services Plc v Campbell Martin Ltd* [2011] 2 Lloyd's Rep 1 (CA) [51] Stanley Burnton LJ rejected such an argument as 'too formalistic'.

[64] *Thomas Witter Limited v TBP Industries Limited* [1996] 2 All ER 573, 597.

[65] *Government of Zanzibar v British Aerospace (Lancaster House) Ltd* [2000] 1 WLR 2333, 2347. See also *Shaftsbury House (Developments) Limited v Lee* [2010] EWHC 1484 (Ch) [67].

[66] [2011] 1 Lloyd's Rep 123 [315].

[67] [2010] 2 CLC 705 (CA) [181]–[182].

26.22 There is little doubt that as a matter of substance, the effect of non-reliance clauses is to 'exclude or restrict liability' if representations had been made and were in fact relied on. Giving section 3 a purposive interpretation, clauses operating in this way ought to be treated as falling within its ambit. 'No representation' clauses should be treated similarly if they deem representations actually made not to have been made. Recent decisions have made it clear that section 3 does apply to such clauses.[68] However. if the relevant provision merely refines the extent of any representations made, it will fall outside of section 3 for the reasons discussed earlier in this chapter.[69]

(3) Requirement of reasonableness

Onus of proof

26.23 The party who wishes to rely on a term to which section 3 of the Misrepresentation Act 1967 applies must prove that it was reasonable. The party seeking rescission does not need to prove that it was unreasonable. This is made clear by the words of section 3 itself.

Requirement of reasonableness

26.24 The 'requirement of reasonableness' is defined in section 11(1) of the Unfair Contract Terms Act 1977 as follows:

> In relation to a contract term, the requirement of reasonableness for the purposes of ... section 3 of the Misrepresentation Act 1967 ... is that the term shall have been a fair and reasonable one to be included having regard to the circumstances which were, or ought reasonably to have been, known to or in the contemplation of the parties when the contract was made.

26.25 Schedule 2 to the Act sets out a number of non-exhaustive guidelines for the application of the reasonableness test. These guidelines include matters such as the relative strength of the bargaining positions of the parties, whether the representee received an inducement for the term or could have entered into a contract without the term with someone else, and whether the representee knew or ought to have known about the term.[70] On a literal construction, and for reasons that are not self-evident, these guidelines are not applied by the statute to section 11(1).[71] However, they are so applied by the courts. The guidelines are considered to be of general application in relation to the question of reasonableness.[72]

26.26 An additional factor not listed in Schedule 2 that has been taken into account in applying the reasonableness test was that the exclusion clause expressly permitted reliance on information obtained through particular channels.[73] A different additional factor has been

---

[68] *Hardy v Griffiths* [2015] Ch 417; *First Tower Trustees Ltd v CDS (Superstores International) Ltd* [2019] 1 WLR 637 (CA); *Toner v Telford Homes Ltd* [2021] EWHC 516 (QB).
[69] See paras [26.16]ff.
[70] Particular emphasis was placed on the knowledge of the term in *Morgan v Pooley* [2010] EWHC 2447 (QB) [110]–[115].
[71] Unfair Contract Terms Act 1977, s 11(2).
[72] *Stewart Gill Limited v Horatio Meyer & Co Limited* [1992] 1 QB 600 (CA) 608; *Overseas Medical Supplies Ltd v Orient Transport Services Ltd* [1999] 2 Lloyd's Rep 273 (CA) 10; *Avrora Fine Arts Investment Ltd v Christie, Manson & Woods Ltd* [2012] PNLR 35 [149].
[73] *FoodCo UK LLP (t/a Muffin Break) v Henry Boot Developments Ltd* [2010] EWHC 358 (Ch) [177]; *Hardy v Griffiths* [2015] Ch 417 [74].

whether the claimant would be left without a remedy if the exclusion clause were upheld or whether he would be able to recover something through a different cause of action.[74] The clarity of the term in question has also been treated as a relevant factor in determining reasonableness.[75] Other factors that have also been found to be relevant in a mis-selling case involving a financial product included the complexity of the derivative product that was sold, the 'hard sell' of the product, the unavailability of impartial expert advice, and adverse findings that had been made by the financial regulator ('poor disclosure of exit costs …; failure to ascertain the customer's understanding of risk; non-advised sales straying into advice; a mismatch between the duration of the hedge product and the underlying loan; and rewards and incentives being a driver of such practices').[76]

Each element of an exclusion clause is tested separately but by reference to all the terms of the contract. **26.27**

> [T]he reasonableness of each term to which the 1977 Act applies must be considered separately even to the extent of looking to see whether each clause contains one term or more than one, 'although, of course, in considering whether that requirement is satisfied in relation to each term, the existence of the other term in the contract is relevant'.[77]

The test is retrospective; the court must determine whether the term was reasonable at the time that the contract was entered into.[78]

In the *Thomas Witter* case it was held that an exclusion clause that does not distinguish between fraudulent and non-fraudulent misrepresentation, and hence attempts to exclude liability for fraudulent misrepresentation, cannot be reasonable and is therefore ineffective.[79] However, in *Government of Zanzibar v British Aerospace (Lancaster House) Ltd*[80] the court took a different view holding that clauses dealing with representations are not intended by the parties to apply where a representation has been fraudulently made. Such clauses would not automatically contravene the legislation merely because they do not expressly exclude fraud. This view seems preferable as a matter of principle. **26.28**

A term is not necessarily reasonable because of the fact that both parties were represented by solicitors or because it takes a common or standard form.[81] But in *Cleaver v Schyde Investments Ltd* these two factors, together with the fact that the well-established conveyancing term endorsed by a professional body had a long history and was contained in a contract that had been negotiated by the parties, weighed in favour of upholding the autonomy **26.29**

---

[74] *Avrora Fine Arts Investment Ltd v Christie, Manson & Woods Ltd* [2012] PNLR 35 [152].
[75] *Camerata Property Inc v Credit Suisse Securities (Europe) Ltd* [2011] EWHC 479 (Comm) [187].
[76] *Crestsign Ltd v National Westminster Bank Plc* [2015] 2 All ER (Comm) 133 [119]–[121] (permission to appeal given on other grounds: [2015] EWCA Civ 986). Cf *Titan Steel Wheels Ltd v Royal Bank of Scotland* [2010] 2 Lloyd's Rep 92 [105]–[108].
[77] *SAM Business Systems Ltd v Hedley & Co* [2002] EWHC 2733 [62] quoting *Watford Electronics Ltd v Sanderson CFL Ltd* [2001] BLR 143 16. Cf *Stewart Gill Ltd v Horatio Myer & Co Ltd* [1992] 2 QB 600 (CA) 608–609 ('term' to be taken 'as whole term or clause as drafted').
[78] *Thomas Witter Limited v TBP Industries Limited* [1996] 2 All ER 573, 598.
[79] [1996] 2 All ER 573, 598.
[80] [2000] 1 WLR 2333, 2346–47; *Six Continents Hotels Inc v Event Hotels GmbH* [2006] EWHC 2317 [53]; *FoodCo UK LLP (t/a Muffin Break) v Henry Boot Developments Ltd* [2010] EWHC 358 (Ch) [166]–[167].
[81] *Walker v Boyle* [1982] 1 WLR 495, 507–08.h

of the contracting parties to agree restrictions on the purchaser's right to rescind.[82] The case concerned a standard conveyancing term which restricted a purchaser's right to 'rescind' to cases of fraud or recklessness or where the property differed substantially from what the purchaser had been led to expect, and confined the purchaser to recovering damages in all other situations. Etherton LJ considered it to be 'a perfectly rational and commercially justifiable apportionment of risk in the interests of certainty and the avoidance of litigation'.[83] However, the court refused to overturn the trial judge's findings that the clause was not fair and reasonable in the particular case.[84] In *Lloyd v Browning*,[85] the Court of Appeal held that a commonly used conveyancing clause excluding liability for misrepresentation was reasonable for reasons similar to those in *Cleaver v Schyde Investments Ltd*. In *First Tower Trustees Ltd v CDS (Superstores International) Ltd*[86] on the other hand, a term in a lease that sought to exclude reliance on written answers that had been given to formal pre-contractual enquiries was held to be unreasonable.

26.30   In *EA Grimstead & Son Ltd v McGarrigan*[87] Chadwick LJ explained the policies which favour upholding acknowledgements of non-reliance in commercial contracts between experienced parties of equal bargaining power, particularly where both parties had the benefit of legal advice. The first was commercial certainty. The parties ought to be able to order their affairs on the basis that the agreement, irrespective of what was said before it was signed, regulates their relationship. The second was that the price payable reflected the risks that each of the parties accepted. The greater the representations that the purchaser could rely upon, the higher the price that he could be expected to pay. This rationale was thought to be equally applicable to a covenant not to sue.[88]

26.31   In *Watford Electronics Ltd v Sanderson CFL Ltd* Chadwick LJ further articulated his views as to the application of the fair and reasonable test in a commercial context:

> Where experienced businessmen representing substantial companies of equal bargaining power negotiate an agreement ... they should in my view be taken to be the best judge of the commercial fairness of the agreement which they have made; including the fairness of each of the terms in that agreement. They should be taken to be the best judge on the question whether the terms of the agreement are reasonable.[89]

The application of the test is clearly context-specific and all relevant factors are to be taken into account including matters such as the relative bargaining power of the parties, their levels of sophistication, the possibility of negotiation, and the presence or absence of

---

[82] [2011] 2 P & CR 21 (CA) [38], [54]. See also *Hardy v Griffiths* [2015] Ch 417 [74]. In *Standard Chartered Bank v Ceylon Petroleum Corp* [2011] EWHC 1785 (Comm) [569] a non-reliance clause contained in a standard form ISDA Master Agreement was found to satisfy the reasonableness requirement.

[83] [2011] 2 P & CR 21 (CA) [38]. Similarly in *AXA Sun Life Services Plc v Campbell Martin Ltd* [2011] 2 Lloyd's Rep 1 (CA) [59]–[63] Stanley Burnton LJ emphasized the usefulness of the clauses in question in providing certainty.

[84] In *First Tower Trustees Ltd v CDS (Superstores International) Ltd* [2019] 1 WLR 637 (CA) [75] it was also held that an appeal court should not interfere with the trial judge's evaluation of reasonableness.

[85] [2013] EWCA Civ 1637; [2014] 1 P&CR 11.

[86] [2019] 1 WLR 637 (CA).

[87] [1999] EWCA (Civ) 3029, 34; *National Westminster Bank plc v Utrecht-America Finance Co* [2001] 3 All ER 733 (CA), cited with approval by Clarke LJ at [60]–[61]; *Raiffeisen Zentralbank Osterreich AG v The Royal Bank of Scotland Plc* [2011] 1 Lloyd's Rep 123 [321]–[323].

[88] *Six Continents Hotels Inc v Event Hotels GmbH* [2006] EWHC 2317 [54].

[89] [2001] BLR 143 [55].

legal advice.[90] But it must be kept in mind that the statutory test is not whether the parties acted reasonably, whether they subjectively considered what they agreed to be reasonable, nor whether reliance on the term is reasonable,[91] but—reflecting a more paternalistic approach—whether objectively the term was a fair and reasonable one at the time the contract was made. Any development of a general rule that terms in commercial contracts between experienced and equally strong parties are always fair and reasonable would be contrary to the wording of section 11. As that provision is drafted, the test must be applied to the facts of each particular case.

International supply contracts

The court does not have jurisdiction under section 3 of the Misrepresentation Act 1967 to review a term that would otherwise bar rescission for misrepresentation if the contract in question is an international supply contract as defined in section 26 of the Unfair Contract Terms Act 1977.[92] A contract is an international supply contract if (a) it is a contract for the sale of goods (or one under which possession or ownership of goods passes) made between parties whose places of business are in different states; and (b) one of the following conditions is satisfied: the goods will be carried from the territory of one state to another; the acts constituting offer and acceptance are done in the territories of different states; or the contract provides for the goods to be delivered to the territory of a state other than that within whose territory those acts were done.

26.32

Choice of law provisions

Section 27 of the Unfair Contract Terms Act 1977 provides that where the law applicable to a contract is the law of any part of the United Kingdom only by choice of the parties (and apart from that choice would be the law of some country outside the United Kingdom) sections 2 to 7 and 16 to 21 of the 1977 Act do not operate as part of the law applicable to the contract. This section ought not to limit the court's jurisdiction under section 3 of the Misrepresentation Act 1967 because it is section 8 of the Unfair Contract Terms Act 1977 that inserts the current section 3 into the Misrepresentation Act 1967; and hence it falls outside of the field of operation of section 27.

26.33

D. Consumer Protection Legislation

Prior to the commencement of the Consumer Rights Act 2015, an exclusion clause purporting to bar rescission for misrepresentation was potentially rendered ineffective by the Unfair Terms in Consumer Contracts Regulations 1999[93] if it was unfair and it was a contractual term to which the Regulations applied. The Regulations applied to contractual

26.34

---

[90] *FoodCo UK LLP (t/a Muffin Break) v Henry Boot Developments Ltd* [2010] EWHC 358 (Ch) [177]; *Lloyd v Browning* [2013] EWCA Civ 1637; [2014] 1 P&CR 11 [34]; *First Tower Trustees Ltd v CDS (Superstores International) Ltd* [2019] 1 WLR 637 (CA) [69]ff. See also A Burrows *A Restatement of the English Law of Contract* (2016) 97, 101.

[91] Contrast the wording of s 3 of the Misrepresentation Act 1967 before its amendment in 1977: the term 'shall be of no effect except to the extent that ... the court or arbitrator may allow reliance on it as being fair and reasonable in the circumstances of the case'.

[92] *Trident Turboprop (Dublin) Ltd v First Flight Couriers Ltd* [2010] QB 86 (CA).

[93] SI 1999/2083.

terms that had not been individually negotiated and were in contracts between a person acting for purposes relating to his trade, business, or profession and a consumer. A term was regarded as unfair if, contrary to the requirement of good faith, it caused a significant imbalance in the parties' rights and obligations arising under the contract, to the detriment of the consumer.

26.35 The Consumer Rights Act 2015 revoked the Unfair Terms in Consumer Contracts Regulations. Instead provision is made in section 62 of the Act to apply a test of unfairness to such terms in consumer contracts; that is, contracts between a trader and a consumer. A term is unfair if, contrary to the requirement of good faith, it causes a significant imbalance in the parties' rights and obligations under the contract to the detriment of the consumer.[94] Whether a term is fair is to be determined (a) by taking into account the nature of the subject matter of the contract; and (b) by reference to all the circumstances existing when the term was agreed and to all of the other terms of the contract, or of any other contract on which it depends.[95] A term of a consumer contract may not be assessed for fairness under section 62 to the extent that (a) it specifies the main subject matter of the contract; or (b) the assessment is of the appropriateness of the price payable under the contract by comparison with the goods, digital content, or services supplied under it,[96] provided that in each case, the term is expressed in plain and intelligible language and is brought to the consumer's attention in such a way that an average consumer would be aware of the term.[97] Schedule 2 of the Act contains an indicative and non-exhaustive list of terms of consumer contracts that may be regarded as unfair. Terms not found on the list in the Schedule may be found by a court to be unfair by application of the fairness test.[98]

---

[94] Section 62(4).
[95] Section 62(5).
[96] Section 64(1).
[97] Section 64(2)–(5).
[98] Consumer Rights Bill 2013, Explanatory Notes [288].

27

Bars for Non-Fraudulent Misrepresentation

A. Introduction	27.01	(4) New Zealand	27.31
B. Transfer of Title to Real Property	27.05	(5) Canada	27.32
(1) Nature of the bar	27.05	(6) Hong Kong and Singapore	27.34
(2) Abolition of the bar in England and Wales	27.10	D. Incorporation as a Contractual Term	27.36
		(1) Nature of the bar	27.36
(3) Partial abolition of the bar in Australia	27.12	(2) Abolition of the bar in England and Wales	27.39
(4) Abolition of the bar in New Zealand	27.13	(3) Australia	27.40
(5) Canada	27.14	(4) New Zealand	27.44
(6) Hong Kong and Singapore	27.16	(5) Canada	27.45
C. Transfer of Title to Personal Property	27.18	(6) Hong Kong and Singapore	27.46
(1) Nature of the bar	27.18	E. Contracts for the Sale of Goods	27.48
(2) Abolition of the bar in England and Wales	27.28	(1) Bar on rescinding all sales of goods	27.48
(3) Australia	27.29	(2) Rescission barred when contractual right to reject is lost	27.54

A. Introduction

This chapter considers four bars to rescission that are peculiar to contracts procured by non-fraudulent misrepresentation. A representation is not made fraudulently if the party making it honestly believed it to be true; that is, he did not know it to be false, and nor was he recklessly indifferent to its truth. 27.01

Innocent misrepresentation became clearly recognized as a ground for rescission only in the late nineteenth century.[1] Rescission on this ground has a special potential to cause prejudice, and to disrupt settled expectations, in a manner that is disproportionate to the blameworthiness of the conduct complained of. That asymmetry explains the development of the bars considered in this chapter.[2] The three bars considered in Parts B, C, and D were developed by the English courts in the late nineteenth and first part of the twentieth centuries, but then replaced in England and Wales by the scheme established by the Misrepresentation Act 1967.[3] Before that occurred, however, each of these bars had come to be accepted to varying degrees by the courts in Australia, New Zealand, and Canada. In 27.02

---

[1] The seminal decision was *Redgrave v Hurd* (1881) 20 ChD 1 (CA).
[2] Cf E Bant, 'Seddon's Case: Sense or Nonsense?' [2013] 77 Conv 33, 46 (arguing that the bar is justified by the interest in the finality of transactions, but not explaining why that interest is paramount in cases of innocent misrepresentation but not where other grounds for rescission are engaged).
[3] The 1967 Act replaced the common law bars with a statutory power to refuse rescission for non-fraudulent misrepresentation, and to award damages in lieu. This is discussed in Chap 28.

582 VI. OTHER BARS

some of those jurisdictions the bars have not been removed by statute, and continue to be of significant practical importance.

27.03 The last bar considered, in Part E, was in part a product of early New Zealand case law, and in part derived from decisions of the English courts. It appears to have been wholly abolished either by statute or subsequent decisions, save in the State of Victoria in Australia, and perhaps in parts of Canada.

27.04 This chapter is different from the others in the book because it considers the law in New Zealand, Australia, Canada, Hong Kong and Singapore in some detail. That is because, unlike most of the topics considered in the book, there is no uniformity in the principles applied in England and those three related jurisdictions.

B. Transfer of Title to Real Property

(1) Nature of the bar

27.05 During the nineteenth century the English courts developed a rule that a completed contract for transferring an estate in land could not be rescinded for non-fraudulent misrepresentation.[4] The bar caught both sales[5] and leases.[6] The cases involved attempts to rescind by purchasers or lessees dissatisfied with the title that they had received, and who complained that it was less than what was represented. However, the bar became associated with all completed transactions involving the sale of land,[7] and was probably understood also to apply in the event that the purchaser or lessee had made any actionable misrepresentation, whether relating to title or not.[8] Although there was one instance where the bar was not applied in England,[9] that decision was later reinterpreted[10] and disapproved.[11]

Rationale

27.06 The rule was justified on the twin bases that the purchaser of land had an opportunity to fully investigate title, and the law's special interest in protecting the finality of completed transactions involving land.[12]

---

[4] The foundational case was the decision of Lord Manners, Lord Chancellor of Ireland, in *Legge v Croker* (1811) 1 Ball & Beaty 506. For earlier traces of the bar, *Thomas v Powell* (1794) 2 Cox 394, 30 ER 182 as interpreted in *M'Culloch v Gregory* (1855) 1 K & J 286, 291; 69 ER 466 (cf counsel's submissions at (1855) 1 K & J 286, 289).
[5] *Edwards v M'Leay* (1818) 2 Swan 287, 289; 36 ER 625, 626; *Wilde v Gibson* (1848) 1 HLC 605, 633; 9 ER 897, 909; *Brownlie v Campbell* (1880) 5 App Cas 925 (HL Sc) 938.
[6] *Legge v Croker* (1811) 1 Ball & Beaty 506, 514–15; *Angel v Jay* [1911] 1 KB 666, 671–72, 673; *Elder v Auerbach* [1949] 2 All ER 692 (CA) 699; *Hill v Harris* [1965] 1 QB 601; *Laurence v Lexcourt Holdings* [1978] 1 WLR 1128 (CA) 1134.
[7] *May v Platt* [1900] 1 Ch 616, 623; *The Public Trustee v The Chancellor of the Duchy of Lancaster* [1927] 1 KB 516 (CA) 528–29; *Long v Lloyd* [1958] 1 WLR 773 (CA) 756; *Shortt v MacLennan* [1959] SCR 3, 4.
[8] Cf *Goldsmith v Rodger* [1968] 2 Lloyd's Rep 249 (CA).
[9] *Hart v Swaine* (1877) 7 ChD 42, 47 (conveyance of copyhold innocently represented to be freehold).
[10] *Brownlie v Campbell* (1880) 5 App Cas 925 (HL Sc) 937.
[11] *Soper v Arnold* (1887) 37 ChD 96 (CA) 102.
[12] *Clare v Lamb* (1875) LR 10 CP 334, 338–39; *Svanasio v McNamara* (1956) 96 CLR 186, 199, 206–07; *Redican v Nesbitt* [1923] SCR 135, 146; C Grunfeld, 'Note to *Long v Lloyd* [1958] 1 WLR 753' (1958) 21 MLR 550; MG Bridge, 'Misrepresentation and Merger: Sale of Land Principles and Sale of Goods Contracts' (1986) 20 UBCLR 53, 80–84; Tenth Report of the Law Reform Committee (Innocent Misrepresentation) 1967 [6]. In the United States, *Restatement (Third) of Restitution* § 37, cmt e, vol 2, 620–22 (2011).

27.07 Instead of allowing the bar to rest upon policy alone, theoretical explanations have also been invented. It has been said that *restitutio in integrum* is impossible after completion,[13] and also that the rule is there to ensure consistency between the common law and equity, for a vendor's contractual misstatement does not allow the purchaser to revest title once it has passed.[14] Neither explanation is persuasive. Completion does not make *restitutio in integrum* impossible in cases of fraud, undue influence, or other ground for rescission, and there is no reason why it should for non-fraudulent misrepresentation. Likewise, the explanation based on the need to ensure consistent outcomes at law and in equity lacks force because it is uncontroversial that a fraudulent misrepresentation permits a conveyance to be rescinded in equity, and notwithstanding that the misrepresentation may be a term of the contract and confers no common law right to revest title.

27.08 Several cases also invested explanatory force in the merger of contract and conveyance upon completion of a sale of land, or simply in the notion of completion itself.[15] But neither merger nor completion prevent rescission for fraud, undue influence, or other ground for rescission, and for that reason statements of this kind are better regarded as describing the conditions for the bar's operation, rather than the reason why it exists. This form of reasoning has, however, been important in practice, because it helped to permit the completion bar to migrate to cases that did not involve land, as explained later in this chapter.

Registered land

27.09 The bar was developed in connection with conveyances and leases of unregistered or old system land. Unless the applicable system of land registration provides otherwise, the bar should apply as much to registered as unregistered land.[16]

(2) Abolition of the bar in England and Wales

27.10 The bar was removed by section 1(b) of the Misrepresentation Act 1967, which provides as follows:

> Where a person has entered into a contract after a misrepresentation has been made to him, and ... (b) the contract has been performed ... then, if otherwise he would be entitled to rescind the contract without alleging fraud, he shall be so entitled, subject to the provisions of this Act, notwithstanding the matters mentioned in paragraphs ... (b) of this section.

---

[13] *Angel v Jay* [1911] 1 KB 666, 671; HA Hammelmann, 'Seddon v North Eastern Salt Co' (1939) 91 LQR 91, 96.
[14] MG Bridge, 'Misrepresentation and Merger: Sale of Land Principles and Sale of Goods Contracts' (1986) 20 UBCLR 53, 81–82 and notes thereto; see also *Redican v Nesbitt* [1923] SCR 135, 152 (Anglin J).
[15] *Angel v Jay* [1911] 1 KB 666, 671–72 (completion); *Svanasio v McNamara* (1956) 96 CLR 186, 206–207 (merger); *Montgomery and Rennie v Continental Bags (NZ) Limited* [1972] NZLR 884, 891, 893 (completion and merger); *Baird v BCE Holdings Pty Ltd* (1996) 40 NSWLR 374, 379, 380; *Redican v Nesbitt* [1923] SCR 135, 152 (merger as one explanation for rule).
[16] *Montgomery and Rennie v Continental Bags (NZ) Limited* [1972] NZLR 884, 891–93; but contrast *Baird v BCE Holdings Pty Ltd* (1996) 40 NSWLR 374, 380. For discussion, E Bant, 'Seddon's Case: Sense or Nonsense?' [2013] 77 Conv 33, 43–46.

27.11 The provision was introduced in this form against the recommendations of the Law Reform Committee whose report provided the background to the 1967 Act. It had concluded that there were compelling reasons why finality should be the predominant consideration in sales and long leases of land, and that both types of transaction should be excluded.[17] But section 1(b) appears not to have attracted any particular criticism for upsetting the finality of sales of land or long leases. That is perhaps because the power to award damages in lieu of rescission will be triggered if finality would be improperly upset,[18] and this counterbalances the otherwise destabilizing effects of section 1(b) of the 1967 Act.

(3) Partial abolition of the bar in Australia

27.12 The High Court of Australia acknowledged the bar on rescinding completed dispositions of land for non-fraudulent misrepresentation in *Svanasio v McNamara*,[19] and it has been applied[20] and affirmed since.[21] Two of the Australian States and Territories have removed it by statute.[22] Where it remains, the rigour of the restriction is tempered by the rule that rescission[23] or relief analogous to rectification[24] will be permitted if sufficiently serious mistakes have been made when conveying an interest in land. In addition, in those cases where the injured party is entitled to relief in the nature of rescission, under section 243 of Schedule 2 of the Competition and Consumer Act 2010, the court retains a discretion to order rescission after conveyance, and the bar does not apply.

(4) Abolition of the bar in New Zealand

27.13 The bar was accepted in New Zealand in *Montgomery and Rennie v Continental Bags (NZ) Limited*.[25] However, the Contract and Commercial Law Act 2017 (NZ) has abolished this limitation, and replaced it with a judicial discretion to permit rescission after title to land has been conveyed.[26]

---

[17] Tenth Report of the Law Reform Committee (Innocent Misrepresentation) 1962 [6]–[7].
[18] Eg *William Sindall plc v Cambridgeshire County Council* [1994] 1 WLR 1016 (CA) 1038, 1045.
[19] (1956) 96 CLR 186, 198, 200, 207, 209.
[20] *Dean v Gibson* [1958] VR 563, 568–70.
[21] *Krakowski v Eurolynx Properties Ltd* (1995) 183 CLR 563, 585; *Baird v BCE Holdings Pty Ltd* (1996) 40 NSWLR 374, 380.
[22] South Australia: Misrepresentation Act 1972 (SA), s 6(1)(b); Australian Capital Territory: Civil Law (Wrongs) Act 2002 (ACT), s 173(2).
[23] *Svanasio v McNamara* (1956) 96 CLR 186; see also *Watson v Cullen* (1886) 5 NZLR 17. See further Chap 7, paras [7.31]–[7.32].
[24] *Lukacs v Wood* (1978) 19 SASR 520 (order that wrong block be exchanged for correct one); *Tutt v Doyle* (1997) 42 NSWLR 10 (CA) (purchasers ordered to reconvey land equivalent to extra they had gained by reason of vendor's unilateral conveyancing error).
[25] [1972] NZLR 884, 889.
[26] Contract and Commercial Law Act 2017 (NZ), ss 28 (mistake), 37 (misrepresentation), 42 (effect of cancelling), 43–49 (discretionary relief upon cancellation) (formerly the Contractual Remedies Act 1979 (NZ)).

(5) Canada

27.14 The rule is well established in Canada. It has been re-stated by the Supreme Court of Canada on several occasions[27] and is regularly applied,[28] save in New Brunswick, where it has been abrogated by legislation.[29] The rule has been held to extend to rights in the nature of a *profit a prendre*.[30]

27.15 However, in Canada the rigour of the bar is ameliorated by the doctrine of 'error in *substantialibus*', which allows a completed conveyance of land to be rescinded if there is a sufficiently significant discrepancy between the thing promised and that actually received.[31]

(6) Hong Kong and Singapore

27.16 Section 2(b) of the Misrepresentation Ordinance (Cap 284) mirrors the language of section 1(b) of the Misrepresentation Act 1967 and so abolishes the bar in Hong Kong.

27.17 In Singapore, section 1(b) of the Misrepresentation Act (Cap 390) has incorporated the provisions of section 1(b) of the Misrepresentation Act 1967 into the law of Singapore. The bar has therefore been abolished there as well.

C. Transfer of Title to Personal Property

(1) Nature of the bar

27.18 In the early twentieth century the bar discussed in Part B of this chapter migrated from contracts involving land to contracts for personal property. It came to be thought that completion would bar rescission for non-fraudulent misrepresentation, even if the contract involved personal rather than real property. The key decision was *Seddon v The North Eastern Salt Company Limited*.[32] Mr Seddon had sought to rescind his purchase of shares in the London Salt Company, alleging that he had been the victim of gross, but not fraudulent, misrepresentations as to the company's trading losses. Mr Justice Joyce dismissed the claim for several reasons. One was the nature of the transaction itself. It was an 'executed' rather than 'executory' contract 'for the sale of property',[33] and Joyce J said that agreements of this kind could not be rescinded where the misrepresentation was not fraudulent.

---

[27] *Cole v Pope* (1898) 29 SCR 3; *Redican v Nesbitt* [1923] SCR 135; *Shortt v MacLennan* [1959] SCR 3; see also *Kingu v Walmar Ventures Ltd* (1986) 10 BCLR (2d) 15 (BCCA) 20–21 (McLachlin JA).
[28] Eg *Intrawest Corp v No 2002 Taurus Ventures Ltd* (2006) 54 BCLR (4th) 173 [66] (non-fraudulent misrepresentations as to land for a ski-lodge at Whistler).
[29] Law Reform Act (New Brunswick) 2011, s 6(1). It provides that execution of a contract is not a bar to rescission, but a matter that the court may take into account in deciding whether to rescind.
[30] *Houle v Knelsen Sand and Gravel Ltd* (2015) ABQB 659 [65], [66] (contract to sell license to extract gravel from land; bar not applied because misrepresentation involved error *in substantialibus*—[68]–[73]).
[31] See Chap 7, paras [7.34]–[7.37].
[32] [1905] 1 Ch 326.
[33] *Seddon v The North Eastern Salt Company Limited* [1905] 1 Ch 326, 332.

27.19 In coming to this decision Joyce J referred to cases concerned with the rescission of conveyances of land for innocent misrepresentation, and to one older common law case.[34] These were regarded as applicable notwithstanding that Mr Seddon had bought shares rather than an estate in land, the common law had never permitted rescission for non-fraudulent misrepresentation, and equity had not previously regarded completion as a bar outside cases involving land.[35]

27.20 Although Joyce J's judgment contained no statement of general principle, the head-note to the report did. It was in the following terms:

> The Court will not grant rescission of an executed contract for the sale of a chattel or chose in action on the ground of innocent misrepresentation. In order for the plaintiff to succeed in such a case fraud must be proved.[36]

Reception of the bar

27.21 Over the next 60 years the principle set out in the head-note to *Seddon's* case was repeatedly affirmed and treated as correct in England and Ireland.[37] But at the same time, English courts exhibited a marked reluctance to apply it, and *Seddon's* case was distinguished on at least three occasions.[38]

27.22 Moreover, the existence of the bar appeared to be undermined by statements in other cases indicating that a contract for the sale of goods could be rescinded for innocent misrepresentation.[39] The bar was also repeatedly attacked by Lord Denning, who viewed it as mistaken;[40] although the Court of Appeal later concluded that Lord Denning had not carried the day.[41] On the occasions when the Privy Council[42] and House of Lords[43] had the opportunity to reject the rule, they did not do so. Commentators also attacked the rule, saying that Joyce J had not understood that the cases he relied on were concerned with contracts

---

[34] *Kennedy v The Panama, New Zealand, and Australian Royal Mail Company Limited* (1867) LR 2 QB 580.
[35] *Whurr v Devenish* (1904) 20 TLR 385 (goods); see also *Redgrave v Hurd* (1881) 20 ChD 1 (CA) 14 (discussing rescission of share allotments for innocent misrepresentation); *AG v Ray* (1874) 9 Ch App 397 (annuity).
[36] *Seddon v The North Eastern Salt Company Limited* [1905] 1 Ch 326.
[37] Aff'd in *Hindle v Brown* (1904) 20 TLR 385 and *Armstrong v Jackson* [1917] 2 KB 822, 825, and distinguished in a manner that seemed to affirm the rule in *Compagnie Française des Chemins de fer Paris-Orleans v Leeston Shipping Company Ltd* [1919] Lloyd's Rep 235, 238; *First National Reinsurance Company v Greenfield* [1921] 2 KB 260 (CA) 272. The rule was applied in *Lecky v Walter* [1914] IR 378 (Ch) 386, 389 (purchase of eight bonds issued by a company interested in oil fields in Wyoming) and in *Angel v Jay* [1911] 1 KB 666 (lease), although the latter case could equally have been based on the principle applied to land, discussed in Part B of this chapter.
[38] *Compagnie Française des Chemins de fer Paris-Orleans v Leeston Shipping Company Ltd* [1919] Lloyd's Rep 235, 238; *First National Reinsurance Company v Greenfield* [1921] 2 KB 260 (CA) 272; *Senanayake v Cheng* [1966] AC 63 (PC—Singapore) 81–83.
[39] *T & J Harrison v Knowles & Foster* [1918] 1 KB 608 (CA) 609; *L'Estrange v F Graucob Limited* [1934] 2 KB 394 (CA) 403–04, 407. Cf *Goldsmith v Rodger* [1968] 2 Lloyd's Rep 249 (CA) 251 'still ... an open question in this Court'.
[40] *Solle v Butcher* [1950] 1 KB 671 (CA) 695–96 cf 703 (Jenkins LJ); *Leaf v International Galleries* [1950] 2 KB 86 (CA) 90 cf 95 (Evershed LJ); *Curtis v Chemical Cleaning and Dyeing Co* [1951] 1 KB 805 (CA) 810; *Frederick E Rose (London) Ltd v William H Pim Jnr & Co Ltd* [1953] 2 QB 450 (CA) 461.
[41] *Long v Lloyd* [1958] 1 WLR 753 (CA) 756–58. But his views were taken up in Canada: *Ennis v Klassen* (1990) 70 DLR (4th) 321 (Man CA) [46].
[42] *Senanayake v Cheng* [1966] AC 63 (PC—Singapore) 81–83 of which one commentator said that the court should have been 'bold enough to declare that *Seddon's* case and *Angel v Jay* were wrong': LS Sealy, 'Note to *Senanayake v Cheng* [1965] 3 WLR 715' [1966] CLJ 11, 14.
[43] *Bell v Lever Bros* [1932] AC 161. Scrutton LJ had cast doubts on the rule in *Lever Bros v Bell* [1931] 1 KB 577 (CA) 578.

involving land, that their rationale did not apply to sales of goods, and that the rule had the potential to cause injustice.[44]

Whether the bar truly formed part of English law prior to its abolition by statute was never authoritatively established. Probably it did, because by that point *Seddon*'s case had stood for some 60 years without being overruled.[45] **27.23**

Scope of the bar

The scope of the bar is uncertain. On some occasions it has been described as being concerned with contracts involving chattels and choses in action, in keeping with the head-note to the report of *Seddon*'s case.[46] Other cases have simply said that there can be no rescission for innocent misrepresentation if a contract has been executed, performed, or completed;[47] whilst a third group has focused on its application to contracts involving shares.[48] **27.24**

In the jurisdictions where it continues to exist, the bar probably applies to completed contracts involving personal property when rescission is sought for non-fraudulent misrepresentation, save to the extent that specific exceptions have been recognized in the authorities that have distinguished *Seddon*'s case.[49] **27.25**

Rationale

No rationale for the bar was provided in the reasoning in *Seddon*'s case, and none has been suggested by subsequent authorities. The principle turns on the proposition that the remedy of rescission is confined to contracts, not conveyances.[50] But both equity and the common law have long rescinded completed contracts for the transfer of property, and this notion provides no real rationale for the rule. **27.26**

The bar is only defensible on the ground that the interest in protecting the security of contracts increases once completion has occurred, and after that happens it is not displaced **27.27**

---

[44] See eg HA Hammelmann, 'Seddon v North Eastern Salt Co' (1939) 91 LQR 91; C Grunfeld, 'Note to *Long v Lloyd* [1958] 1 WLR 753' (1958) 21 MLR 550, 550–52; MG Bridge, 'Misrepresentation and Merger: Sale of Land Principles and Sale of Goods Contracts' (1986) 20 UBCLR 53, 101–02; Tenth Report of the Law Reform Committee (Innocent Misrepresentation) 1962 [10]. This criticism has been noted by the courts; see eg *Vimig Pty Ltd v Contract Tooling Pty Ltd* (1987) 9 NSWLR 731, 734; *Baird v BCE Holdings Pty Ltd* (1996) 40 NSWLR 374, 379–80. See also *Ennis v Klassen* (1990) 70 DLR (4th) 321 (Man CA) [33], [34] observing that the reasons for barring rescission after a conveyance of land do not apply to chattels.
[45] *Leaf v International Galleries* [1950] 2 KB 86 (CA) 95 (Lord Evershed MR). The same reasoning has been applied in Australia: *Vimig Pty Ltd v Contract Tooling* (1987) 9 NSWLR 731, 735, 736.
[46] *Lecky v Walter* [1914] IR 378 (Ch) 386; *Armstrong v Jackson* [1917] 2 KB 822, 825; *Grogan v 'The Astor' Limited* (1925) 25 St Rep (NSW) 409, 410.
[47] *Compagnie Française des Chemins de fer Paris-Orleans v Leeston Shipping Company Ltd* [1919] Lloyd's Rep 235, 238; *Wilson v Brisbane City Council* [1931] St R Qd 360, 384; *Root v Badley* [1960] NZLR 757; *Vimig Pty Ltd v Contract Tooling Pty Ltd* (1987) 9 NSWLR 731, 737; *Bathurst Regional Council v Local Government Financial Services Pty Ltd (No 5)* [2012] FCA 1200 [3117].
[48] *First National Reinsurance v Greenfield* [1921] 2 KB 260 (CA) 272; *Senanayake v Cheng* [1966] AC 63 (PC—Singapore) 81–83; *Baird v BCE Holdings Pty Ltd* (1996) 40 NSWLR 374, 379.
[49] Allotments of shares (*First National Reinsurance Company v Greenfield* [1921] 2 KB 260 (CA); *Grogan v 'The Astor' Limited* (1925) 25 St Rep (NSW) 409); interests in a partnership (*Senanayake v Cheng* [1966] AC 63 (PC—Singapore) 81–83; hire purchase contract where goods used but no title received from financier (*Mihaljevic v Eiffel Tower Motors Pty Ltd and General Credits Ltd* [1973] VR 545).
[50] *Westdeutsche Landesbank Girozentrale v Islington London Borough Council; Kleinwort Benson Ltd v Sandwell Borough Council* [1994] 4 All ER 890, 923, where Hobhouse J referred in passing to the 'now discredited doctrine in *Seddon v North Eastern Salt Co Ltd* [1905] 1 Ch 326 [1904–7] All ER Rep 817, which turned upon a proposition that the remedy of rescission was confined to the rescission of contracts, not conveyances'.

where the only ground for complaint is non-fraudulent misrepresentation. Fundamentally, the bar articulates a policy decision about the sanctity of completed bargains.

(2) Abolition of the bar in England and Wales

27.28 The rule in *Seddon*'s case was removed by section 1(b) of the Misrepresentation Act 1967.[51] This followed recommendations of the Law Reform Committee, which concluded that it 'can work serious injustice'.[52]

(3) Australia

27.29 The rule has been accepted in Australian State courts on several occasions;[53] distinguished;[54] applied at least once;[55] and considered and deliberately rejected at least twice.[56] The High Court has so far decided to leave an assessment of *Seddon*'s case for another day,[57] and its place in Australian law remains uncertain.[58] It certainly seems well arguable that the bar does form part of Australian law.

27.30 Some parts of Australia have, however, abolished the rule, either entirely,[59] or in its application to certain kinds of contract.[60] The bar should not apply to limit orders otherwise available under section 243 of Schedule 2 of the Competition and Consumer Act 2010. Where the injured party is entitled to relief in the nature of rescission under that provision, the court has a discretion to order rescission notwithstanding that the transaction has been completed.

---

[51] Reproduced at para [27.10].
[52] Tenth Report of the Law Reform Committee (Innocent Misrepresentation) 1962 [3]. A principal cause of the injustice was that in many cases the purchaser of goods had no opportunity to inspect them in advance, and the right to rescind would be lost before the defect was discovered. That problem was dealt with by abolishing the rule in *Seddon*'s case, and also by s 4(1) of the Misrepresentation Act 1967, which prolonged the right to reject non-conforming goods by liberalizing the rules that regulate when they are accepted. Section 4 was later repealed. The relevant provisions are now found in ss 35 and 35A of the Sale of Goods Act 1979 and Consumer Rights Act 2015, ss 20–22.
[53] *Grogan v 'The Astor' Limited* (1925) 25 St Rep (NSW) 409, 410; *Kramer v Duggan* (1955) 55 St Rep (NSW) 385, 389; *Wilson v Brisbane City Council* [1931] St R Qd 360, 384; *Bathurst Regional Council v Local Government Financial Services Pty Ltd (No 5)* [2012] FCA 1200 [3117]; see also *Krakowski v Eurolynx Properties Ltd* (1995) 183 CLR 563, 585.
[54] *Grogan v 'The Astor' Limited* (1925) 25 St Rep (NSW) 409, 411; *Mihaljevic v Eiffel Tower Motors Pty Ltd and General Credits Ltd* [1973] VR 545, 564–65.
[55] *Vimig Pty Ltd v Contract Tooling Pty Ltd* (1987) 9 NSWLR 731, 736.
[56] *Leason Pty Ltd v Princes Farm Pty Ltd* [1983] 2 NSWLR 381, 387 (sale of thoroughbred colt); *Baird v BCE Holdings Pty Ltd* (1996) 40 NSWLR 374, 380. Also, *Vitek v Taheri* [2013] NSWSC 589 [79]–[81] (comments *obiter* doubting the bar).
[57] *Svanasio v McNamara* (1956) 96 CLR 186, 198, 209.
[58] It was described as a 'live issue' in *Akron Securities v Illife* (1994) 41 NSWLR 353, 366, 369. See also AJ Duggan, 'Misrepresentation' in P Parkinson (ed), *The Principles of Equity* (2nd edn, 2002) 187–88, P MacFarlane and L Willmott, 'Rescission of an Executed Contract at Common Law for an Innocent Misrepresentation' (1998) 10 Bond LR 58.
[59] South Australia: Misrepresentation Act 1972 (SA), s 6(1)(b); Australian Capital Territory: Civil Law (Wrongs) Act 2002, s 173(2).
[60] In NSW the rule has been abolished for sales of goods: Sale of Goods Act 1923 (NSW), s 4(2A)(b). In Victoria the rule has been abolished for supplies of goods: Australian Consumer Law and Fair Trading Act 2012 (Vict), s 24.

(4) New Zealand

27.31 The bar was accepted in New Zealand in *Root v Badley*.[61] However, the Contract and Commercial Law Act 2017 (NZ) has effectively abolished it, and conferred a judicial discretion to permit rescission in those cases where the bar would otherwise apply.[62]

(5) Canada

27.32 In Canada, as in Australia, the rule has been accepted by some courts and rejected by others.[63] The Supreme Court has not ruled on the point.[64] The dominant modern view is that:

> ... execution or performance of a contract is a relevant, but not decisive, factor to be considered when deciding whether the remedy of rescission should be denied because of the plaintiff's undue delay in seeking a remedy or because rescission might affect third parties, or would otherwise be inequitable.[65]

27.33 In Canada the principle is ameliorated by the doctrine of error *in substantialibus*, under which a completed contract may be rescinded if there is a sufficiently significant discrepancy between what was contracted for and received.[66]

(6) Hong Kong and Singapore

27.34 Section 2(b) of the Misrepresentation Ordinance (Cap 284) mirrors the language of section 1(b) of the Misrepresentation Act 1967 and so abolishes the bar in Hong Kong.

27.35 In Singapore, section 1(b) of the Misrepresentation Act (Cap 390) incorporates the provisions of section 1(b) of the Misrepresentation Act 1967 into the law of Singapore. The bar has therefore been abolished there as well.

---

[61] [1960] NZLR 757.
[62] Contract and Commercial Law Act 2017 (NZ), ss 28 (mistake), 37 (misrepresentation), 42 (effect of cancelling), 43–49 (discretionary relief upon cancellation).
[63] *Northern & Central Gas Corp Ltd v Hillcrest Collieries Ltd* (1975) 59 DLR (3d) 533 (Alta SC), 600 (accepting the rule); *Bevan v Anderson and Peace River Sand & Gravel Co* (1957) 12 DLR (2d) 69 (Alta SC) (rejecting the rule); *Ennis v Klassen* (1990) 70 DLR (4th) 321 (Man CA) [46] (rejecting the rule). See also the cases cited in MG Bridge, 'Misrepresentation and Merger: Sale of Land Principles and Sale of Goods Contracts' (1986) 20 UBCLR 53, 95 notes 183–84; S Waddams, *The Law of Contracts* (7th edn, 2017) [4-24].
[64] But see *Shortt v MacLennan* [1959] SCR 3, where there are some indications of approval of the rule.
[65] *S-244 Holdings Ltd v Seymour Building Systems Ltd* (1994) 93 BCLR (2d) 34, adopting the position suggested in S Waddams, *The Law of Contracts* (3rd edn, 1993); see now (7th edn, 2017) [4-24].
[66] For that doctrine, see Chap 7, paras [7.34]–[7.37].

D. Incorporation as a Contractual Term

(1) Nature of the bar

27.36 This bar is founded on *Pennsylvania Shipping Co v Compagnie Nationale de Navigation*.[67] It was there decided that once an innocent misrepresentation becomes a contractual term, it ceases to operate as a ground for rescission. Two reasons were given. First, incorporation was said to 'merge' the representation into a 'higher contractual right' that extinguishes the claim to rescind; and secondly, equity was said to only supplement the common law in this field.[68]

27.37 The first ground for the decision is difficult to understand, and seems not to have been followed save in Canada.[69] On the other hand, the second ground has been further developed by scholars and courts, who have said that when an innocent misrepresentation becomes a contractual term the common law and statute provide sufficient relief, and allocate risk more appropriately, and for this reason the equitable right to rescind should be excluded.[70]

27.38 There is, however, some doubt as to how far this bar was ever part of English law. Twenty years before Branson J's decision, Roche J had come to the opposite conclusion in *Compagnie Française des Chemins de fer Paris-Orleans v Leeston Shipping Company Ltd*.[71] In that case a charter-party was rescinded for innocent misrepresentation, and Roche J rejected a submission that incorporation of the representation coupled with partial performance prevented rescission.[72] His Lordship held that a pre-contractual representation 'does not cease to be a representation because it is also made in the contract',[73] a point subsequently underlined in Australian courts,[74] but rejected in Canada.[75] *Leeston Shipping* appears not to have been brought to the attention of Branson J in the *Pennsylvania Shipping* case.

---

[67] [1936] 2 All ER 1167.
[68] *Pennsylvania Shipping Co v Compagnie Nationale de Navigation* [1936] 2 All ER 1167, 1171.
[69] *Zien v Field* (1963) 41 DLR (2d) 394 (BCCA) 408–409; rev'd on another point [1963] SCR 632.
[70] MG Bridge, 'Misrepresentation and Merger: Sale of Land Principles and Sale of Goods Contracts' (1986) 20 UBCLR 53, 109–10; *Leaf v International Galleries* [1950] 2 KB 86 (CA) 95 (Lord Evershed MR); see also LCB Gower, 'Note to *Leaf v International Galleries* [1950] 1 All ER 693' (1950) 13 MLR 362, 367, suggesting that rescission should be permitted only if the misrepresentation would permit the contract to be terminated for breach.
[71] [1919] Lloyd's Rep 235.
[72] *Compagnie Française des Chemins de fer Paris-Orleans v Leeston Shipping Company Ltd* [1919] Lloyd's Rep 235, 237.
[73] *Compagnie Française des Chemins de fer Paris-Orleans v Leeston Shipping Company Ltd* [1919] Lloyd's Rep 235, 238.
[74] *Alati v Kruger* (1955) 94 CLR 216, 220, 222; *Mihaljevic v Eiffel Tower Motors Pty Ltd and General Credits Ltd* [1973] VR 545, 566; *Kramer v McMahon* [1970] NSWLR 194, 204 (fraudulent misrepresentation) 'a statement in a contract may constitute a term of it and also act as a representation of fact ... at one and the same time'. These cases make clear that when an actionable misrepresentation is also a term of the contract, the representee may either sue for breach of contract, or rescind *ab initio*.
[75] '[A] representation to induce a contract loses all force and effect as a representation inducing the contract once it is embodied in the contract as a term thereof': *Zien v Field* (1963) 41 DLR (2d) 394 (BCCA) 409 rev'd on another point [1963] SCR 632; see para [27.45].

(2) Abolition of the bar in England and Wales

27.39 If it ever did exist, the bar was removed in England and Wales by section 1(a) of the Misrepresentation Act 1967, which provides as follows:

> Where a person has entered into a contract after a misrepresentation has been made to him, and (a) the misrepresentation has become a term of the contract ... then, if otherwise he would be entitled to rescind the contract without alleging fraud, he shall be so entitled, subject to the provisions of this Act, notwithstanding the matters mentioned in paragraphs (a) ... of this section.

The section was introduced following a recommendation from the Law Reform Committee, which concluded that 'it is clearly desirable that the same remedies be available to a purchaser whether or not the false statement is incorporated in the contract'.[76]

(3) Australia

27.40 It is doubtful that Australian law recognizes this bar, but the point is not unarguable if it can be shown that the party seeking to rescind has adequate remedies at common law, such that rescission ought not be allowed.

27.41 The strongest authority in favour of the bar is *Academy of Health and Fitness Pty Ltd v Power*.[77] Crockett J there held that that rescission was not prevented when an innocent misrepresentation that a health club sauna would be available daily became incorporated as a contractual warranty. However, Crockett J's reasons seemed to leave open the possibility that rescission might be barred if the representation was a condition of the contract, permitting it to be terminated for breach.[78] Although the bar was also not applied in *Mihaljevic v Eiffel Tower Motors*,[79] there too the court seemed to accept that it might in other circumstances, if the claimant had adequate remedies at law.

27.42 On the other hand, the incorporation bar has been squarely rejected in New South Wales, first in *Kramer v McMahon*,[80] then in *Simons v Zartom Investments Pty Ltd*,[81] and again in *Leason Pty Ltd v Princes Farm Pty Ltd*.[82] In *Leason's* case Helsham CJ explained that 'the basis for the remedy of rescission for misrepresentation is that the contract was entered into as a result of a false inducement ... I do not think the terms of the contract itself have anything to do with the equitable doctrine or remedy'.[83]

---

[76] Tenth Report of the Law Reform Committee (Innocent Misrepresentation) 1962 [16]. See further M Bridge (ed), *Benjamin's Sale of Goods* (11th edn, 2020) [12-073]–[12-074].
[77] [1973] VR 254, 264–66. In *Homes v Burgess* [1975] 2 NZLR 311, 317 Casey J said *obiter* that 'it may be doubtful' whether the decision would be followed in New Zealand.
[78] *Academy of Health and Fitness Pty Ltd v Power* [1973] VR 254, 265–66.
[79] *Mihaljevic v Eiffel Tower Motors Pty Ltd and General Credits Ltd* [1973] VR 545, 564–65.
[80] [1970] 1 NSWLR 194, 204 (Helsham J) (sale of rural bakery).
[81] [1975] 2 NSWLR 30, 36 (rescission of sale of home unit).
[82] [1983] 2 NSWLR 381 (innocent misrepresentations about blood-line of colt).
[83] *Leason Pty Ltd v Princes Farm Pty Ltd* [1983] 2 NSWLR 381, 388; also JD Heydon, MJ Leeming, and PG Turner, *Meagher, Gummow and Lehane's Equity Doctrines and Remedies* (5th edn, 2014) [13-060]–[13-070]; AJ Duggan 'Misrepresentation' in P Parkinson (ed), *The Principles of Equity* (2nd edn, 2002) 185–86. Contrast MG Bridge, 'Misrepresentation and Merger: Sale of Land Principles and Sale of Goods Contracts' (1986) 20 UBCLR 53, 110.

27.43 The bar has been abolished by statute in two of the Australian States and Territories,[84] and in others in the context of sales or supplies of goods.[85] In those cases where the injured party is entitled to relief in the nature of rescission under section 243 of Schedule 2 of the Competition and Consumer Act 2010, the court has a discretion to order rescission notwithstanding that the misrepresentation is also a contractual term.[86]

(4) New Zealand

27.44 There were formerly suggestions that the incorporation of an innocent misrepresentation into a contract was a bar to rescission in New Zealand.[87] However, the Contract and Commercial Law Act 2017 (NZ) has abolished any limit that did exist, and now confers a judicial discretion to permit rescission.[88]

(5) Canada

27.45 In *Zien v Field*[89] the British Columbia Court of Appeal followed the decision of Branson J in the *Pennsylvania Shipping* case[90] to hold that rescission was unavailable where an alleged misrepresentation about the working capital of a business had become a contractual term.[91] The Supreme Court allowed an appeal against the decision on other grounds, but did not specifically consider this point.[92] Later cases in other Provinces have followed the British Columbia Court of Appeal's decision,[93] or assumed that it was correct.[94] The bar therefore appears to be established in Canada.

(6) Hong Kong and Singapore

27.46 Section 2(a) of the Misrepresentation Ordinance (Cap 284) mirrors the language of section 1(a) of the Misrepresentation Act 1967 and so abolishes the bar in Hong Kong.

27.47 In Singapore, section 1(a) of the Misrepresentation Act (Cap 390) incorporates the provisions of section 1(a) of the Misrepresentation Act 1967 into the law of Singapore. The bar has therefore been abolished there as well.

---

[84] Misrepresentation Act 1972 (SA), s 6(1) (a); Civil Law (Wrongs) Act 2002 (ACT), s 173(2).
[85] Sale of Goods Act 1923 (NSW), s 4(2A)(a); Australian Consumer Law and Fair Trading Act 2012 (Vict), s 24(2).
[86] Eg *Bantic v Boss Properties Pty Ltd* [2000] VSC 121 [223]–[224] (discussing the predecessor provision, s 87 of the Trade Practices Act 1974).
[87] *Holmes v Burgess* [1975] 2 NZLR 311, 317.
[88] Contract and Commercial Law Act 2017 (NZ), ss 28 (mistake), 37 (misrepresentation), 42 (effect of cancelling), 43–49 (discretionary relief upon cancellation).
[89] (1963) 41 DLR (2d) 394 (BCCA).
[90] *Pennsylvania Shipping Co v Compagnie Nationale de Navigation* [1936] 2 All ER 1167.
[91] (1963) 41 DLR (2d) 394 (BCCA) 408–09 per Tysoe JA, with whom Wilson JA agreed. Davey JA, who dissented, also agreed with the opinion of Tysoe JA in this respect: at 396.
[92] *Field v Zien* [1963] SCR 632, deciding that the term breached was a warranty, not a condition entitling the buyer to terminate.
[93] *Renner v Racz* (1972) 22 DLR (3d) 443 (Alta SC, App Div) [31]–[32].
[94] *Abraham v Wingate Properties Limited* [1986] 1 WWR 568 (Man CA) [5] (statement *obiter*).

E. Contracts for the Sale of Goods

(1) Bar on rescinding all sales of goods

In New Zealand and the State of Victoria in Australia the courts developed a rule that sales of goods could not be rescinded for non-fraudulent misrepresentation unless there was also a fundamental difference between the article contracted for and received.[95] The restriction rested on an interpretation of the provision in the relevant Sale of Goods Act[96] providing for a general saving of 'common law' rules.[97] It was thought that this implicitly excluded equitable rights to rescind.[98]

27.48

New Zealand
In New Zealand, this bar has now been abolished and replaced by the statutory scheme established in the Contract and Commercial Law Act 2017 (NZ).

27.49

Australia
The bar was recognized by the Full Court of the Supreme Court of Victoria in *Watt v Westhoven*.[99] But other Australian State courts have subsequently rejected this bar, and rescinded contracts for the sale of goods for innocent misrepresentation.[100] Some States have amended their sales of goods legislation so as to abolish any such limitation.[101]

27.50

The rationale for this bar was never sound, for the saving provisions in the Sale of Goods Act 1893 and its equivalents in Australia and New Zealand were plainly not intended to abrogate equitable rights and remedies.[102] The preferable view is that this bar is not part of Australian law save in Victoria, for *Watt v Westhoven*[103] has not been overturned or abrogated by legislation, and therefore remains binding authority in that State.[104]

27.51

---

[95] *Riddiford v Warren* (1901) 20 NZLR 572 (CA) (lambs); *Watt v Westhoven* [1933] VLR 458 (Full Ct) (Hillman motor car); *Holmes v Burgess* [1975] 2 NZLR 311, 317 (racing colt 'sound as a bell').

[96] In New Zealand, the former Sale of Goods Act 1895 (NZ) (re-enacted s 61(2), Sale of Goods Act 1908 (NZ), s 60(2), now s 200(2) of the Contract and Commercial Law Act 2017). In Australia, Sale of Goods Act 1923 (Vict), s 4(2).

[97] 'The rules of the common law, including the law merchant, save in so far as they are inconsistent with the express provisions of this Act, and in particular ... the effect of fraud, misrepresentation, duress or coercion, mistake or other invalidating cause, shall continue to apply to contracts for the sale of goods.'

[98] *Riddiford v Warren* (1901) 20 NZLR 572 (CA) 577, 583–84 per Williams J with whom Connolly, Edwards, and Cooper JJ agreed; but cf the reasons of Denniston J; *Watt v Westhoven* [1933] VLR 458 (Full Ct) 462, 465, 467; see also at 466, 468.

[99] [1933] VLR 458 (Full Ct).

[100] *Graham v Freer* (1980) 35 SASR 424, 435–36 (criticizing and rejecting the rule); *Leason Pty Ltd v Princes Farm Pty Ltd* [1983] 2 NSWLR 381, 387 (thoroughbred colt); *JAD International Pty Ltd v International Trucks Australia Limited* (1994) 50 FCR 378 (Full Ct).

[101] Sale of Goods Act 1923 (NSW), s 4(2A); Sale of Goods Act 1954 (ACT), s 62(1), (2).

[102] In *Thomas Borthwick & Sons (Australasia) Ltd v South Otago Freezing Co Ltd* [1978] 1 NZLR 538 (CA) 545 the Court of Appeal read down the language in *Riddiford v Warren* (1901) 20 NZLR 572 (CA).

[103] [1933] VLR 458 (Full Ct).

[104] For further discussion of the bar, R Lawson, 'Innocent Misrepresentation and the Sale of Goods' (1976) NZLJ 76; DW McLauchlan, 'Rescission for Innocent Misrepresentation' (1976) NZLJ 252; C Turner, 'Rescission of a Contract for the Sale of Goods for Innocent Misrepresentation: *Graham v Freer*' (1982) 8 Adelaide LJ 197; MG Bridge, 'Misrepresentation and Merger: Sale of Land Principles and Sale of Goods Contracts' (1986) 20 UBCLR 53, 91–93; AJ Duggan, 'Misrepresentation' in P Parkinson (ed), *The Principles of Equity* (2nd edn, 2002) 184–85.

Canada

27.52 This limitation has not been adopted in Canada, although it has been argued that it should be.[105]

England and Wales

27.53 The bar has never been thought to apply in England and Wales. It has been accepted there that contracts for the sale of goods are subject to equitable rights and obligations,[106] and that sales of goods may be rescinded for non-fraudulent misrepresentation.[107]

(2) Rescission barred when contractual right to reject is lost

27.54 In the 1950s the English courts, led by Lord Denning, developed a principle that the right to rescind a purchase of goods for non-fraudulent misrepresentation was lost once the purchaser lost his contractual right to reject; that is, he had accepted them within the meaning of the Sale of Goods Act 1893.[108] The bar appeared to apply irrespective of whether the representation was a term of the contract.[109]

England and Wales

27.55 Section 1 of the Misrepresentation Act 1967 makes no mention of this supposed limitation, and the Law Reform Committee appeared to assume that it did not exist.[110]

27.56 But it may be that section 1(b) of the 1967 Act, which was directed at the rule in *Seddon's* case, has also had the effect of abolishing this limitation. This is suggested by an Australian case, which considered section 6(1)(b) of the Misrepresentation Act 1972 of South Australia, a provision equivalent to section 1(b) of the 1967 Act. It was held that section 6(1)(b) abolishes this bar too, because the reference in section 6(1)(b) to the contract being 'performed' includes acts of acceptance sufficient to extinguish the right to reject.[111]

27.57 This reasoning may well be followed in England and Wales if the issue were ever to arise. But the point is today of limited practical importance. That is because the right to reject non-conforming goods has been so extended over time, that in most cases where goods have been accepted such that the right to reject is lost,[112] the misled party will have affirmed the contract and thereby also lost the right to rescind.

---

[105] For the argument that Canada should adopt this limitation, MG Bridge, 'Misrepresentation and Merger: Sale of Land Principles and Sale of Goods Contracts' (1986) 20 UBCLR 53, 89–94, 116–17.
[106] See eg *Re Wait* [1927] 1 Ch 606 (CA) (equitable proprietary interest).
[107] *Goldsmith v Rodger* [1968] 2 Lloyd's Rep 249 (sale of fishing vessel rescinded for innocent misrepresentation). See also *Whurr v Devenish* (1904) 20 TLR 385; *T & J Harrison v Knowles & Foster* [1918] 1 KB 608 (CA); *Leaf v International Galleries* [1950] 2 KB 86 (CA); *Long v Lloyd* [1958] 1 WLR 753 (CA). But cf the bar discussed in Chap 28.
[108] Since replaced by the Sale of Goods Act 1979.
[109] *Leaf v International Galleries* [1950] 2 KB 86 (CA) 90–91; *Long v Lloyd* [1958] 1 WLR 753 (CA) 760–61; *Frederick E Rose (London) Ltd v William H Pim Jnr & Co Ltd* [1953] 2 QB 450 (CA) 461; discussed FJ Odgers, 'Note to *Long v Lloyd* [1958] 1 WLR 753' [1958] CLJ 166, 166–67; C Grunfeld, 'Note to *Long v Lloyd* [1958] 1 WLR 753' (1958) 21 MLR 550, 553; PS Atiyah, 'Rescission of a Contract of Sale of Goods' (1959) 22 MLR 76, 79; R Lawson, 'Innocent Misrepresentation and the Sale of Goods' (1976) NZLJ 76; MG Bridge, 'Misrepresentation and Merger: Sale of Land Principles and Sale of Goods Contracts' (1986) 20 UBCLR 53, 110–14.
[110] Tenth Report of Law Reform Committee (Innocent Misrepresentation) 1962 [15].
[111] *JAD International Pty Ltd v International Trucks Australia Limited* (1994) 50 FCR 378 (Full Ct) 384–85.
[112] Sale of Goods Act 1979, ss 35, 35A; Consumer Rights Act 2015, ss 20–22.

Australia

This limitation seems never to have been accepted in Australia. It has been said to be 'not correct', and that affirmation of the contract rather than acceptance of the goods bought bars the right to rescind a contract for the sale of goods.[113]

27.58

New Zealand

In New Zealand, if the bar was ever accepted, it has been abolished and replaced by the statutory scheme contained in the Contract and Commercial Law Act 2017 (NZ).[114]

27.59

Canada

Opinions for[115] and against[116] this bar may be found in Canadian cases, but the trend seems to be against it.[117] It has been said that the issue is of limited practical importance because the buyer's right to reject is so prolonged that by the time it is lost, the right to rescind is likely to have also been lost by reason of affirmation or delay.[118]

27.60

---

[113] *Leason Pty Ltd v Princes Farm Pty Ltd* [1983] 2 NSWLR 381, 387.

[114] Contract and Commercial Law Act 2017 (NZ), ss 28 (mistake), 37 (misrepresentation), 42 (effect of cancelling), 43–49 (discretionary relief upon cancellation), and replacing the equivalent provisions in the Contractual Remedies Act 1979 (NZ).

[115] *Diamond v British Columbia Thoroughbred Breeders' Society* (1965) 52 DLR (2d) 146 (BCSC) [69]–[70].

[116] *Ennis v Klassen* (1990) 70 DLR (4th) 321 (Man CA) [46].

[117] *Ennis v Klassen* (1990) 70 DLR (4th) 321 (Man CA); *S-244 Holdings Ltd v Seymour Building Systems Ltd* (1994) 93 BCLR (2d) 34.

[118] MG Bridge, 'Misrepresentation and Merger: Sale of Land Principles and Sale of Goods Contracts' (1986) 20 UBCLR 53, 111.

28

Disproportionate Effect: Section 2(2) of the Misrepresentation Act 1967

A. Introduction	28.01	D. Measure of Damages		28.15
B. Conditions to the Exercise of the Power	28.06	(1) Consequential loss		28.22
		(2) Two mistaken theories		28.25
C. Grounds on which the Power may be Exercised	28.10	E. Disproportionate Effect and the Fair-dealing Rule		28.36

A. Introduction

28.01 Section 2(2) of the Misrepresentation Act 1967 confers on judges and arbitrators a discretionary power, where rescission is claimed for non-fraudulent misrepresentation, to 'declare the contract subsisting and award damages in lieu of rescission'.[1]

28.02 This new power was introduced at the same time that a number of bars that had developed to rescission for non-fraudulent misrepresentation were removed, as discussed in the previous chapter. The combined effect was to rebalance the availability of rescission for non-fraudulent misrepresentation, stripping away limitations perceived to be irrational while still keeping the right within defensible bounds.

28.03 The power introduced in section 2(2) was intended to be used where the consequences for the defendant of rescission would be disproportionately hard compared to the injury suffered, particularly where the misrepresentation relates to a fact of minor importance.[2] Section 2(2) in effect creates a discretionary bar to rescission in these circumstances.[3] But while the provision was intended to protect defendants, a claimant who proves his title to rescind may nonetheless invite the court to award damages in lieu.

28.04 Before the middle part of the twentieth century only fraudulent misrepresentations sounded in damages. In the 1960s, however, a cause of action in damages for negligent misrepresentation came to be recognized at common law,[4] and section 2(1) of the 1967 Act

[1] Singapore and Hong Kong have identical legislation: Misrepresentation Act, s 2(2); Misrepresentation Ordinance, s 3(2). There is parallel though differently worded legislation in South Australia and in the Australian Capital Territory: Misrepresentation Act 1972 (SA), s 7(3)–(5) and Civil Law (Wrongs) Act 2002 (ACT), s 175.
[2] See Law Reform Committee, 'Innocent Misrepresentation' (Cmnd 1782, 1962) [11]–[13]. See *SK Shipping Europe plc v Capital VLCC 3 Corp* [2021] 2 Lloyd's Rep 109 [237], [244].
[3] The South Australian Misrepresentation Act 1972, s 7(4) expressly provides that such a declaration 'is a bar to rescission'.
[4] *Hedley Byrne & Co Ltd v Heller & Partners Ltd* [1964] AC 465.

created a statutory right to damages where there has been a misrepresentation preceding a contract, it being a defence to such a claim that the defendant acted honestly and reasonably in saying what he did. If this can be established then there is no damages claim at common law or under s 2(1). In creating a power to give damages for the loss occasioned by a purely innocent misrepresentation that is reasonably believed to be true, section 2(2) is without precedent or parallel.

Section 2(2) purports to apply both where the claim is that the contract 'ought to be' rescinded and also where the claim is that the contract 'has been' rescinded, in other words whether the power to rescind lies with the court or the claimant. Given the exclusion of claims founded on fraudulent misrepresentation, however, the provision can only apply in cases where rescission lies in the power of the court.[5] This is fortunate because, as Mustill J observed in *The Lucy*, 'formidable difficulties' might follow where a court declared a contract subsisting which had already been effectively rescinded.[6]

B. Conditions to the Exercise of the Power

The power to award damages in lieu of rescission may only be exercised where:

> ... a person has entered into a contract after a misrepresentation has been made to him otherwise than fraudulently, and he would be entitled, by reason of the misrepresentation, to rescind the contract...

Since the power may be exercised in relation to any non-fraudulent misrepresentation, damages may be awarded under section 2(2) in a wider class of cases than under section 2(1), there being no defence under section 2(2) that the misrepresentation was made honestly and was reasonably believed to be true. Moreover, while the power conferred by the provision is to 'declare the contract subsisting and award damages in lieu of rescission', a contract may be declared subsisting even though there is no relevant loss to support an award of damages.[7] The power may not be exercised in a case of mere non-disclosure.[8]

The second of the two conditions contained in the passage excerpted in paragraph 28.06 gave rise to a question whether the power can be exercised where the claimant's right to rescind has become barred, for example on the ground that *restitutio in integrum* is no longer possible.[9] In *Thomas Witter Ltd v TBP Industries Ltd*,[10] Jacob J reasoned that a requirement

---

[5] See Chap 11. This point is explored in PG Turner, 'Rescission and Damages "in lieu" thereof under the Misrepresentation Act 1967' (2016) 132 LQR 388.

[6] *Atlantic Lines & Navigation Co Inc v Hallam Ltd (The Lucy)* [1983] 1 Lloyd's Rep 188, 202; *SK Shipping Europe plc v Capital VLCC 3 Corp* [2021] 2 Lloyd's Rep 109 [235]ff and also [2022] EWCA Civ 231 [87], querying whether the power is available where on any view the contract has come to an end by the time the court adjudicates. The equivalent legislation in South Australia, the Misrepresentation Act 1972, expressly provides in s 7(5) that: 'Where a contract has been rescinded but is subsequently declared to be subsisting under section (3), the respective rights and liabilities of the contracting parties will be determined in all respects as if the contract had never been rescinded.' That legislation applies equally where the misrepresentation was fraudulent.

[7] *Bank Negara Indonesia 1946 v Taylor* [1995] CLC 255; *Huyton SA v Distribuidora Internacional de Productos Agricolas SA de CV* [2003] 2 Lloyd's Rep 780 (CA) 846; *UCB Corporate Services Ltd v Thomason* [2004] 2 All ER (Comm) 774, aff'd [2005] 1 All ER (Comm) 601 (CA).

[8] *Ramphul v Toole* (unreported CA, 17 March 1989). See, however, para [28.28].

[9] This question was first noted by P Atiyah and G Treitel, 'Misrepresentation Act 1967' (1967) 30 MLR 369.

[10] [1996] 2 All ER 573, 589.

VI. OTHER BARS

that the right to rescind persist at the time of judgment would be unattractive because persistence depends 'on a host of factors which have nothing to do with the behaviour of either party'. However, these *obiter* remarks were not followed in subsequent cases, most notably in *Government of Zanzibar v British Aerospace Ltd*.[11] Eventually, the Court of Appeal resolved the issue in *Salt v Stratstone Specialist Limited*,[12] ruling that damages can only be awarded under section 2(2) where 'rescission is available (or was available at the time the contract was rescinded)'.

28.09 The reasons are essentially twofold. First, the plain language of the statute 'supposes that rescission is an option open to the court'.[13] This follows from the reference to the claimant being otherwise 'entitled ... to rescind the contract'; the reference to damages being given 'in lieu of rescission'; and the fact that the balancing exercise the provision contemplates only makes sense on the basis rescission is a possibility. Secondly, the mischief at which section 2(2) is directed does not obtain where rescission has been barred, because the court is not in these circumstances otherwise obliged to grant a remedy that is disproportionately hard on the defendant. The claimant may still of course be entitled to damages under section 2(1) of the Misrepresentation Act 1967, and so he is not necessarily left without a remedy.

C. Grounds on which the Power may be Exercised

28.10 The power to award damages in lieu of rescission is discretionary and so damages cannot be claimed under section 2(2) as of right. It is for the party seeking to persuade the court to exercise the discretion to establish the case for that exercise.[14] Section 2(2) states that, provided the other stipulated conditions are satisfied, the court 'may' declare the contract subsisting and award damages:

> ... if of the opinion that it would be equitable to do so, having regard to the nature of the misrepresentation and the loss that would be caused by it if the contract were upheld, as well as to the loss that rescission could cause to the other party.

28.11 The Jenkins Committee, which proposed the legislation, considered that the power might be exercised where the consequences of rescission would be out of all proportion to the injury suffered, provided that damages would give adequate compensation.[15] The Court of Appeal has emphasized, however, that the adequacy of damages should not be lightly assumed and rescission remains the normal remedy.[16] That case involved a Cadillac CTS

---

[11] [2000] 1 WLR 2333; *Floods of Queensferry Ltd v Shand Construction Ltd (No 3)* [2000] Building LR 81; *Pankhania v London Borough of Hackney* [2002] EWHC 2441 (Ch). Mustill J's earlier *obiter dictum* in *Atlantic Lines & Navigation Co Inc v Hallam Ltd (The Lucy)* [1983] 1 Lloyd's Rep 188, 202 seems also to have proceeded on this basis. See also *Jaggard v Sawyer* [1995] 1 WLR 269 (CA) 284–85 and 290, where Millett LJ took a like view in relation to damages in lieu of injunctive relief.
[12] [2016] RTR 17 (CA) [17], noted on this point by T Foxton [2016] LMCLQ 489.
[13] *Government of Zanzibar v British Aerospace (Lancaster House) Ltd* [2000] 1 WLR 2333, 2342.
[14] *British & Commonwealth Holdings plc v Quadrex Holdings Inc* [1995] CLR 1169 (CA) 1200. It has been held in Hong Kong that it is not necessary to plead reliance on the statute: *Green Park Properties Ltd v Dorku Ltd* [2000] 4 HKC 538 (CA). The Singapore Court of Appeal had held that the court may operate s 2(2) of its own motion: *RBC Properties Pte Ltd v Defu Furniture Pte Ltd* [2015] 1 SLR 997 (CA) [130].
[15] Law Reform Committee, 'Innocent Misrepresentation' (Cmnd 1782, 1962) [12]–[13].
[16] *Salt v Stratstone Specialist Limited* [2016] RTR 17 (CA) [31]. See also *SK Shipping Europe Limited v Capital VLCC 3 Corp* [2022] EWCA Civ 231 [86] ('a strong starting point').

wrongly sold as new. Damages had been assessed at £3000, being the difference between the actual value of the car at the time of purchase and its value as new, plus £250 for the inconvenience caused by defects needing repair. Longmore LJ thought this was not sufficient compensation for the wrong suffered.

28.12 The factors identified in section 2(2) are not exhaustive,[17] but they are the ones to which the court will usually give most weight.[18] Principally the language of the provision contemplates 'a balancing exercise between the situation if damages are awarded and that if rescission were granted'.[19] The court should have regard to 'the nature of the misrepresentation', including the comparative importance of the misrepresented fact to the overall transaction, and whether and to what extent the defendant can be faulted for having made the misrepresentation.[20]

28.13 So far as the importance of the misrepresentation is concerned, the court will consider whether in its absence the claimant would have negotiated substantially better terms.[21] It may be helpful to ask whether the misrepresentation went to the root of the bargain.[22] The power to declare a contract subsisting may be exercised even where the claimant would not have contracted at all if that would have left him in a position not substantially better than his position under the contract.[23] The question in both cases is whether the claimant was substantially prejudiced by reason of his reliance on the misrepresentation.

28.14 The statutory discretion is unlikely to be exercised in relation to contracts of insurance, in part because of the 'policing' function of rescission.[24]

D. Measure of Damages

28.15 Notwithstanding that it has been in force for more than half a century, very few reported cases have raised questions concerning the measure of damages under section 2(2). However, it is clear that damages under this provision are damages for the 'loss that would

---

[17] Eg, the court may also take into account the claimant's delay in rescinding (*Harsten Developments Limited v Bleaken* [2012] EWHC 2704 (Ch) [151]); the extent to which the claimant failed to properly protect his own interests when entering the contract (*Odyssey Cinemas Limited v Village Theatres Three Limited* [2010] NICA 25 at [24]); and whether the contract is still capable of being performed (*Green Park Limited v Dorku Ltd* [2000] 4 HKC 538 (CA)). In *TSB Bank plc v Camfield* [1995] 1 WLR 430 (CA) 439, Roch LJ said it would have been wrong to declare the contract subsisting because damages would have been an empty remedy.
[18] *William Sindall plc v Cambridgeshire CC* [1994] 1 WLR 1016 (CA) 1042–43.
[19] *Government of Zanzibar v British Aerospace (Lancaster House) Ltd* [2000] 1 WLR 2333, 2342. See also *Northcote Housing Association v Dixon* [2001] All ER 452.
[20] *William Sindall plc v Cambridgeshire CC* [1994] 1 WLR 1016 (CA) 1036 and 1043; *Atlantic Lines & Navigation Co Inc v Hallam Ltd (The Lucy)* [1983] 1 Lloyd's Rep 188, 202; *SK Shipping Europe plc v Capital VLCC 3 Corp* [2021] 2 Lloyd's Rep 109 [234]. The Court of Appeal in that last case noted that the measure of damages available to compensate the representee can itself be a factor affecting the exercise of the discretion to award damages in lieu: [2022] EWCA Civ 231 [82].
[21] *Huyton SA v Distribuidora Internacional de Productos Agricolas SA de CV* [2003] 2 Lloyd's Rep 780 (CA) 846.
[22] *Atlantic Lines & Navigation Co Inc v Hallam Ltd (The Lucy)* [1983] 1 Lloyd's Rep 188, 202; *SK Shipping Europe plc v Capital VLCC 3 Corp* [2021] 2 Lloyd's Rep 109 [234](i). In Singapore, *RBC Properties Pte Ltd v Defu Furniture Pte Ltd* [2015] 1 SLR 997 (CA) [131]; *Tiong Swee Eng v Yeo Khee Siang* [2015] SGHC 116 at [74]–[77].
[23] *UCB Corporate Services Ltd v Thomason* [2004] 2 All ER (Comm) 774, aff'd [2005] 1 All ER (Comm) 601 (CA); *SK Shipping Europe plc v Capital VLCC 3 Corp* [2021] 2 Lloyd's Rep 109 [234](v)–(vi).
[24] *Ramphul v Toole* (unreported CA, 17 March 1989); *Highlands Insurance Co v Continental Insurance Co* [1987] 1 Lloyd's Rep 109, 118.

be caused by [the misrepresentation] if the contract were upheld'.[25] The reference to the loss 'caused by' the misrepresentation indicates that it is necessary to compare the claimant's current financial position, as a party to a subsisting contract, with the financial position he would have occupied if the misrepresentation had not been made, and to measure damages by the difference. That points to the ordinary reliance measure of damages applicable, for example, to damages for negligent misrepresentation at common law. This is the measure an untutored reading of section 2(2) would suggest, and it seems to have been the Court of Appeal's starting point in the only two cases in which that court has addressed the measure of damages.[26]

28.16 Accordingly, where absent the misrepresentation the claimant would still have entered the contract but at a different price or on different terms, the measure of damages under section 2(2) should usually be the extent or value of this difference.[27] Where instead the claimant would not have entered the contract at all, the measure of damages should usually be the difference between the position he in fact occupies and the position he would have occupied had the contract not been made. If absent the misrepresentation the claimant would have ended up in no better position, then there will be no loss and damages will be nil. That was the situation in *UCB Corporate Services*.[28]

28.17 More complex is the situation where, absent the misrepresentation, the claimant would not have entered the contract and would thereby have avoided a considerable loss occurring for reasons unrelated to the falsity of the misrepresentation. Those were the assumed facts of *William Sindall*,[29] and both Hoffmann and Evans LJJ made clear that in this type of case one cannot simply measure damages by the difference between the claimant's actual financial position and the position he would have occupied had the misrepresentation not been made.

28.18 The contract in that case was one for the sale of a parcel of land, which, after the sale, declined very substantially in value along with the rest of the market. The vendor had made a minor misrepresentation in relation to certain drains running across the property, which would cost very little to divert. To allow rescission in circumstances such as these would allow the purchaser to escape from what turned out to be a bad bargain, and to shift the consequences of the market decline back onto the vendor, where the loss attributable to the existence of the drains was very small by comparison.

28.19 Hoffmann LJ said that 'section 2(2) is concerned with damage caused by the property not being what it was represented to be' and that those damages 'should never exceed the sum

---

[25] *William Sindall plc v Cambridgeshire CC* [1994] 1 WLR 1016 (CA) 1036–37 and 1043. While the cited words are used in the statute to identify factors to be taken into account in deciding whether to rescind or to award damages in lieu, Hoffmann and Evans LJJ agreed that it is clear from the statute that it is this loss that is to be compensated if the contract is upheld.

[26] *William Sindall plc v Cambridgeshire CC* [1994] 1 WLR 1016 (CA) and *UCB Corporate Services Ltd v Thomason* [2004] 2 All ER (Comm) 774, aff'd [2005] 1 All ER (Comm) 601 (CA). In Singapore, *Tiong Swee Eng v Yeo Khee Siang* [2015] SGHC 116 [77].

[27] *SK Shipping Europe plc v Capital VLCC 3 Corp* [2021] 2 Lloyd's Rep 109 [253] (citing and applying this sentence).

[28] [2004] 2 All ER (Comm) 774, aff'd [2005] 1 All ER (Comm) 601 (CA). In Singapore, *Tiong Swee Eng v Yeo Khee Siang* [2015] SGHC 116 [77].

[29] *William Sindall plc v Cambridgeshire CC* [1994] 1 WLR 1016 (CA).

which would have been awarded if the representation had been a warranty'.[30] Tettenborn has pointed out that Hoffmann LJ was essentially contemplating an exercise similar to that required by *South Australia Asset Management Corporation v York Montague Ltd*,[31] namely one of identifying the part of the loss the claimant suffered by entering the transaction that flowed from the falsity of the statement.[32]

28.20 It has been suggested that the ordinary reliance measure of damages may not have been intended because of section 2(3) of the Misrepresentation Act 1967.[33] That provision requires that any damages awarded under section 2(2) be taken into account when calculating damages under section 2(1). It is therefore argued that it must at least be possible that damages awarded under section 2(2) could differ from, and be less than, damages awarded under section 2(1) in respect of the same misrepresentation. This is taken to indicate that the reliance measure in tort cannot be applicable both to section 2(1) and to section 2(2).

28.21 This argument overlooks that the reliance measure comes in more and less expansive variants. Damages under section 2(1) are awarded on the same basis as damages for deceit,[34] which is unusually expansive. This would be inappropriate for damages under section 2(2), as those damages may be given in respect of wholly innocent misrepresentations. If damages under section 2(2) are understood as being given on the ordinary, less expansive reliance measure, then one can see how they may in some cases be less extensive than damages under section 2(1).

(1) Consequential loss

28.22 What limited judicial authority there is, all *obiter dicta*, indicates that some consequential losses may be awarded under section 2(2).[35] It has, however, been suggested by several commentators that consequential losses should not be recoverable at all,[36] and it has also been suggested that consequential losses should only be recoverable to the extent the claimant would avoid those losses if the contract were rescinded.[37] The idea seems to be that if consequential loss were generally available, the damages awarded under section 2(2) might put the claimant in a better position than if the contract were rescinded.

---

[30] These remarks cannot be read as a complete analysis of s 2(2) because not all potentially relevant representations concern the state of property being transferred under a contract. Cf the facts of *UCB Corporate Services Ltd v Thomason* [2004] 2 All ER (Comm) 774.
[31] [1997] AC 191.
[32] A Tettenborn, *The Law of Damages* (2nd edn, 2010) [17.58].
[33] P Atiyah and G Treitel, 'Misrepresentation Act 1967' (1967) 30 MLR 369; J Edelman et al, *McGregor on Damages* (21st edn, 2020) [49-074].
[34] *Royscott Trust Ltd v Rogerson* [1991] 2 QB 297 (CA). In South Australia, *Copping and Perball Pty Ltd v ANZ McCaughan Ltd* (1997) 67 SASR 525 (Full Ct) [82] and [348].
[35] *William Sindall plc v Cambridgeshire CC* [1994] 1 WLR 1016 (CA) 1044 (wasted transaction expenses); *SK Shipping Europe plc v Capital VLCC 3 Corp* [2021] 2 Lloyd's Rep 109 [256].
[36] E Peel, *Treitel: The Law of Contract* (15th edn, 2020) [9-088]; HG Beale (ed), *Chitty on Contracts* (33rd edn, 2018) [7-109]; J Edelman et al, *McGregor on Damages* (21st edn, 2020) [49-078]; and H Beale, 'Damages in Lieu of Rescission for Misrepresentation' (1995) 111 LQR 60, 63. The Jenkins Committee seems to have intended that, 'The measure of damages should be the loss directly and naturally resulting in the ordinary course of events from the misrepresentation': 'Conclusions reached at Seventh Meeting on 16th May, 1961' (National Archives).
[37] A Tettenborn, *The Law of Damages* (2nd edn, 2010) [17.60]–[17.61].

28.23 While the comparatively generous remoteness criteria applicable in a case of deceit do not apply, there is no indication in the statute that the claimant should not be entitled to recover in accordance with the usual criteria applicable in a case of non-fraudulent misrepresentation. It is true that in some cases damages under section 2(2) might as a result be more advantageous to a claimant than rescission would be. There is no reason, however, why the measure of damages should be artificially restricted to ensure that this does not occur.

28.24 This is for two reasons. First, where the losses the claimant has suffered by relying on the representation (including consequential losses) are considerable, it will not often be the case that the representation is sufficiently minor in importance as to justify the application of section 2(2). Secondly, and more fundamentally, where the claimant's reliance losses (including consequential losses) are such that an award of damages would place him in a financial position superior to the position if instead the contract were rescinded, it will necessarily be the case that rescission would not be disproportionately hard on the defendant as compared with the loss the claimant would suffer if the contract were upheld. Rescission would in such a case be attractive to the defendant compared with compensating the claimant for the full extent of his losses. That is not the sort of case in which the statutory power was intended to be exercised.

(2) Two mistaken theories

28.25 First, while damages are given 'in lieu of rescission', they are not designed to place the claimant in the financial position he would have occupied if the contract had been rescinded.[38] That is unlikely to be right because it would defeat the purpose of the provision, which is to protect the defendant from the potentially disproportionate consequences of rescission. For example, where an asset has declined sharply in value for reasons unrelated to the misrepresentation,[39] damages designed to put the claimant purchaser in the same position as if the contract were rescinded would be just as hard on the defendant as rescission itself.[40] There would have been no purpose in introducing section 2(2) if the court's only power was to give a pecuniary remedy tantamount to rescission. The statutory phrase 'damages in lieu of rescission' simply means damages instead of rescission, as one would expect, and does not signal any special measure of damages.[41]

28.26 Birks supported a pecuniary rescission approach, arguing that Parliament cannot have intended to reverse the established rule that innocent misrepresentations do not sound in damages.[42] It appears from the legislation, however, that Parliament intended to do just that in the limited class of cases where an award of damages would be less hard on the defendant

---

[38] An idea advanced in J Edelman et al, *McGregor on Damages* (21st edn, 2020) [49–076] and J Cartwright, *Misrepresentation, Mistake and Non-disclosure* (5th edn, 2019) [4–73].
[39] As in *William Sindall plc v Cambridgeshire CC* [1994] 1 WLR 1016 (CA).
[40] The editors of *McGregor on Damages* contends that this is not so because, they assert, in a case of innocent misrepresentation rescission is barred, or an adjustment is made, where assets passing under a contract have depreciated in value: J Edelman et al, *McGregor on Damages* (21st edn, 2020) [49–083]. This is not supported by the authorities, although there are good reasons for thinking that the law should develop in this direction. See Chapter 18, paras [18.95]–[18.97].
[41] Cf *Pavlovic v Commonwealth Bank of Australia* (1992) 56 SASR 587, 590.
[42] PBH Birks, 'Unjust Factors and Wrongs: Pecuniary Rescission for Undue Influence' [1997] RLR 72.

than rescission. The use of the word 'damages' in the provision, and the connection with 'loss', is decisive, for those words are not apt to describe the relief given upon rescission, which is essentially bilateral and restitutionary.[43] Birks argued in favour of an expansive interpretation of the word 'damages', but the authority on which he relied has since been doubted by the House of Lords.[44]

Proponents of a pecuniary rescission approach to the measure of damages under section 2(2) have gained support from research conducted by Niranjan Venkatesan and presented in his unpublished doctoral thesis, *Damages for Misrepresentation*.[45] He found in the National Archives fascinating notes of deliberations on the legislation in Standing Committee which indicate that the author of the notes believed that damages under section 2(2) would compensate for loss suffered by reason of rescission being refused.[46]

28.27

Enticing as this material is, there are five reasons why it should be disregarded. First, as noted above the language used in the provision is more consistent with conventional compensatory damages than a restitutionary measure and certainly does not compel a restitutionary measure.

28.28

Secondly, the author's analysis leaves a paradox, for, as noted above, the whole purpose of the statutory innovation was to empower the court to ameliorate the drastic character of the rescission remedy, which an equivalent pecuniary remedy would not achieve. Dr Venkatesan argues that the Jenkins Committee's concern was with the drastic character of the specific consequences of rescission, as opposed to the monetary unwinding of the transaction. That is difficult to tease out of the Jenkins Committee's report and, more fundamentally, it is difficult to see how the one is any more onerous than the other, as Dr Venkatesan recognizes.

28.29

Thirdly, the author of the Standing Committee notes relied on a comparison with the measure of damages awarded under Lord Cairns' Act in substitution for an injunction. Citing *Leeds Industrial Cooperative Society Ltd v Slack*,[47] the author asserted that the measure in that context is the 'loss (including prospective loss) suffered by the plaintiff by reason of his not obtaining the injunction to which he would otherwise have been entitled'. The suggestion is that damages under section 2(2) should likewise compensate the claimant for the refusal of rescission.

28.30

This misunderstands the decision in *Slack*. It is true that Viscount Finlay said at one point in his speech that the damages should give an 'equivalent for what is lost by the refusal of the injunction', but he made clear elsewhere that the damages are given as compensation for the injury that would be caused by the tort.[48] Lord Dunedin spoke to the same effect,[49] and

28.31

---

[43] See Chap 13, para [13.03].
[44] Birks relied on *Friends Provident Life Office v Hillier Parker May & Rowden (a firm)* [1997] QB 85 (CA), which was subsequently doubted on this point in *Royal Brompton Hospital NHS Trust v Hammond* [2002] 1 WLR 1397 (HL) [33].
[45] N Venkatesan, 'Damages for Misrepresentation' (DPhil thesis, 2015) 300–19.
[46] 'Notes on Amendment Nos 26 and 29' in *Misrepresentation Bill: Notes on Amendments [Commons] Committee Stage*, LCO 2/7378 (National Archives).
[47] [1924] AC 851.
[48] Cf 859 and 857: 'damages ... must necessarily cover not only injury already sustained but also injury that would be inflicted in the future by the commission of the act threatened'.
[49] See 865: 'a pecuniary payment equalling the loss to be occasioned by the act against which, but for the provision in question, an injunction would have been obtained'.

so did Bingham MR and Millett LJ in passages in *Jaggard v Sawyer* that were subsequently endorsed by the Supreme Court.[50] That an injunction would have prevented the injury from occurring does not entail that damages should be measured as the difference between the claimant's position with and without an injunction. Consistently with this, damages under section 2(2) compensate for the injury caused by the misrepresentation on the basis that the contract is upheld, not whatever injury would be caused by the refusal of rescission.

28.32 Fourthly, the apparent views of the author of the notes on the deliberations of the Standing Committee fall a long way short of a clear statement given in Parliament by a minister or the promoter of a bill such as might be an admissible aide to construction within the *Pepper v Hart*[51] exception.[52]

28.33 Finally, whatever views may have been expressed in Standing Committee, the cases in which the measure of damages under section 2(2) has been considered give no support to a pecuniary rescission measure. Most importantly, in *William Sindall plc v Cambridgeshire CC*,[53] the Court of Appeal effectively refused an invitation to adopt that approach. In *SK Shipping Europe*,[54] Foxton J considered that he was bound to accept that section 2(2) is not concerned with awarding the monetary equivalent of rescission. He considered this conclusion to be intrinsically right approaching the problem purposively because if the remedy of rescission would have disproportionate consequences, it would be wrong in principle to assess damages on a basis that would replicate those consequences.

28.34 A second theory favours the contractual measure of damages. But although Evans LJ expressed a preference for this measure in *William Sindall plc v Cambridgeshire CC*,[55] that is difficult to reconcile with principle. To award a contractual measure of damages would involve treating the representation as if it were a warranty in circumstances where the claimant did not bargain for a warranty.[56] Moreover, a contract measure might lead to a claimant purchaser recovering damages under section 2(2) greater than the damages that might be recovered in an action for deceit. This may be illustrated by postulating a purchase at £50,000 of an asset in fact worth £40,000 but that would have been worth £75,000 had the representation been true.[57] Damages in contract would be £35,000—the difference between the value as represented less the value as is—whereas damages in deceit would be only £10,000.

28.35 Moreover, the Court of Appeal made no attempt to apply the contract measure (or the pecuniary rescission measure) in its more recent decision in *UCB Corporate Services Ltd v*

---

[50] *Jaggard v Sawyer* [1995] 1 WLR 269 (CA) 276H ('to compensate the plaintiff for future unlawful conduct') and 286A ('to compensate for those future wrongs which an injunction would have prevented'), endorsed in *One Step (Support) Ltd v Morris-Garner* [2019] AC 649 at [44]. Lord Reed's remarks at [47] should not be taken to indicate a different view, as to which see J McGhee and S Elliott (eds), *Snell's Equity* (34th edn, 2020) as supplemented [20-063] and A Burrows, *Remedies for Torts, Breach of Contract, and Equitable Wrongs* (4th edn, 2019) 317.
[51] [1993] AC 593.
[52] The 'experience of those who have trawled Hansard for guidance as to the meaning of the 1967 Act has not been a wholly happy one': *SK Shipping Europe plc v Capital VLCC 3 Corp* [2021] 2 Lloyd's Rep 109 [236].
[53] [1994] 1 WLR 1016 (CA) 1037–38 (Hoffmann LJ) and 1044–45 (Evans LJ).
[54] *SK Shipping Europe plc v Capital VLCC 3 Corp* [2021] 2 Lloyd's Rep 109 [237].
[55] [1994] 1 WLR 1016 (CA) 1045. See also *Floods of Queensferry Ltd v Shand Constructions Ltd (No 3)* [2000] Building LR 81 [34].
[56] See H Beale, 'Damages in Lieu of Rescission for Misrepresentation' (1995) 111 LQR 60, 63.
[57] The illustration is borrowed from J Edelman et al, *McGregor on Damages* (21st edn, 2020) [49-081].

Thomason.[58] Given the nature of the representation in that case, which did not relate to the nature or quality of the performance the defendant was to give, a contract measure would have been conceptually inapposite. For these reasons the contract measure is unlikely to be correct.

E. Disproportionate Effect and the Fair-dealing Rule

Section 2(2) of the 1967 Act was introduced because it was believed that rescission on grounds of innocent misrepresentation could have a disproportionate effect and that, following the abolition of certain bars, the general law would not contain the resources necessary to ameliorate this effect. More recently, however, the courts have asserted an 'undoubted discretion'[59] to refuse rescission for disproportionate effect under the general law in a limited class of cases where a fiduciary has not complied with the requirements of the fair-dealing rule. This power was exercised in *Hurstanger Ltd v Wilson* where the clients knew their fiduciary loan broker might receive a commission but did not give informed consent.[60] The discretionary power does not appear to extend to other grounds for rescission, so that in the case of a bribe or an entirely secret commission rescission is available as of right.[61]

28.36

---

[58] [2005] 1 All ER (Comm) 601 (CA).
[59] *UBS AG v Kommunale Wasserwerke Leipzig GmbH* [2017] 2 Lloyd's Rep 621 (CA) [162].
[60] [2008] Bus LR 216 (CA) [45]–[51].
[61] *Ross River Ltd v Cambridge City Football Club Ltd* [2008] 1 All ER 1004 [203] (Briggs J); *UBS AG v Kommunale Wasserwerke Leipzig GmbH* [2017] 2 Lloyd's Rep 621 (CA) [371] (Gloster LJ in a dissenting judgment); *Wood v Commercial First Business Limited* [2020] CTLC 1 [129](2) and on appeal [2022] Ch 123 (CA) [83], [101].

Part VII

GIFTS AND DEEDS

29

Gifts and Deeds

A. Introduction	29.01	(7) Gifts made by deed	29.40
B. Gifts	29.02	(8) Dispositions of another's assets: powers of appointment	29.52
(1) How gifts are made	29.02	(9) Gifts and theft	29.55
(2) Void gifts	29.08	(10) Assimilation of gifts to disadvantageous contracts	29.56
(3) Discretion to reject and to reclaim a gift	29.13	C. Deeds	29.63
(4) Special vulnerability of gifts to rescission	29.15	(1) Introduction	29.64
(5) Significance of how the gift is made and what is given	29.24	(2) Duress	29.68
		(3) Fraud	29.72
(6) Gifts made by conduct	29.27	(4) Cancellation of deeds	29.83

A. Introduction

This chapter considers the right to rescind gifts and transactions effected by deed. Gifts are more vulnerable to rescission than are simple contracts and the rules peculiar to them are considered in Part B. Part C considers the view that a transaction effected by deed cannot be rescinded at common law save for duress, and that resort must otherwise be had to equity. The conclusion is that this opinion is wrong and that deeds may be rescinded at law to the same extent that a simple contract can be. 29.01

B. Gifts

(1) How gifts are made

Gifts are customarily divided into three categories: *donationes mortis causa*; testamentary gifts; and gifts *inter vivos*. This discussion is only concerned with gifts *inter vivos*. It is, however, as well to distinguish these from the first two categories before going further. 29.02

Donationes mortis causa are gifts made in contemplation of death. The gift is intended to take full effect only when the donor dies. When the donor does die, title vests automatically in the donee insofar as possible, and not in the donor's personal representative. If title cannot be fully vested without some further step, a trust is raised by which the court will compel the personal representative to assist in transferring title to the donee.[1] 29.03

---

[1] See further JD Heydon, MJ Leeming, and PG Turner, *Meagher, Gummow and Lehane's Equity Doctrines and Remedies* (5th edn, 2014) chap 31; G Virgo (ed), 'Gifts', in *Halsbury's Laws of England* (5th edn, 2020) vol 52, [272].

610   VII. GIFTS AND DEEDS

29.04 In contrast, testamentary gifts have no effect at all before the donor's death, and upon death the assets gifted vest in the donor's personal representative, and are distributed pursuant to the terms of the will. After the testator's death the beneficiary enjoys no vested equitable interest in the relevant property. His right is rather to compel due administration of the deceased estate.

29.05 Gifts *inter vivos* are gifts between living persons, and typically take effect immediately, although the donor may attach conditions. They are the subject of discussion here. As explained later, the right to rescind gifts of this kind appears to be affected by the way in which they are made. It is therefore necessary to briefly consider how gifts *inter vivos* may be made.[2]

29.06 The making of a gift *inter vivos* is the act of the donor. It involves the donor in forming the intention to give and then acting on that intention by doing whatever it is necessary for him to do to transfer the relevant asset to the donee.[3] What must be done depends on what is to be given. Provided that the necessary donative intention exists, money may be given by delivery of cash or payment into a bank account,[4] and chattels may generally be given by delivering possession.[5] But other interests require more formal acts. A deed is generally required to make a gift of legal title to unregistered land;[6] a gift of the legal (statutory) estate in registered land must be by registered transfer;[7] and transferring legal title to shares generally requires that the holder's name is recorded in the register of members.[8] Writing is required to transfer certain types of property.[9]

29.07 In unusual cases a gift that is not effective to pass legal title because the requisite formal steps have not been complied with will nonetheless be effective to pass equitable title.[10] The cases are unusual because the general rule is that equity will not perfect an imperfect gift. Assets may also be gifted by transferring them to trustees to hold on trust, or by the donor himself making a declaration of trust in respect of them.[11]

---

[2] See further G Virgo (ed), 'Gifts', in *Halsbury's Laws of England* (5th edn, 2020) vol 52, [201], [202], [231]–[248].
[3] *R v Hinks* [2001] 2 AC 241, 266.
[4] *R v Hinks* [2001] 2 AC 241; cf gift by delivery of a cheque, which is different: *Re Swinburne* [1926] Ch 38.
[5] *R v Hinks* [2001] 2 AC 241, 266; *Cochrane v Moore* (1890) 25 QB 57 (CA) 72–73. As to what amounts to delivery, and constructive delivery, in the context of gifts, G Virgo (ed), 'Gifts', in *Halsbury's Laws of England* (5th edn, 2020) vol 52, [237]–[239]; F Pollock, 'Gifts of Chattels Without Delivery' (1890) 24 LQR 446. Exceptions exist, as in the case of a British ship: Merchant Shipping Act 1995, s 16 (registered bill of sale required).
[6] Law of Property Act 1925, s 52(1); see also the exceptions in s 52(2).
[7] Land Registration Act 2002, s 27(2); Land Registration Rules 2003, r 58.
[8] Companies Act 2006, ss 554, 770–772; see also Stock Transfer Act 1963. It is generally only registered holders who enjoy the full complement of statutory and contractual rights that comprise a share. Registration is also treated as legal title in equity. A gift of shares not perfected by registration may be effective in equity in certain circumstances: *Milroy v Lord* (1862) 4 De GF & J 264, 45 ER 1185; *Re Rose, Midland Bank Executor and Trustee Co v Rose* [1949] Ch 78; *Re Rose, Rose v IRC* [1952] Ch 499 (CA); *Pennington v Waine* [2002] 1 WLR 2075 (CA).
[9] Such as equitable interests in land: Law of Property Act 1925, s 53.
[10] See JD Heydon, MJ Leeming, and PG Turner, *Meagher, Gummow and Lehane's Equity Doctrines and Remedies* (5th edn, 2014) [6-075]–[6-155]; also *Pascoe v Turner* [1979] 1 WLR 431 (CA) (oral gift of house relied on by donee to her detriment, acquiesced in by donor, enforced by proprietary estoppel compelling donor to execute conveyance).
[11] *Milroy v Lord* (1862) 4 De GF & J 264, 45 ER 1185.

(2) Void gifts

29.08 Before considering the right to rescind a gift, it is appropriate to first identify the principal contexts in which impaired consent will make a gift void rather than voidable.

29.09 A mistake founding a plea of *non est factum* will make a deed of gift void. Where a gift is effected by conduct alone, a sufficient mistake may negative the necessary donative intention, such that there is no valid gift of property, or probably, of money.[12] Mental impairment will also probably[13] make a gift void, and the degree of impairment that is necessary depends upon the circumstances of the gift, in particular, its size relative to the donor's other assets.[14]

29.10 There is a difference of opinion as to whether a gift made by a minor of money, or property he is able to own,[15] is valid and indefeasible, or ineffective unless ratified when the minor reaches the age of majority.[16] Neither possibility involves rescission, and the point therefore is not considered here.

29.11 A gift may also be rendered ineffective in equity because a presumption of resulting trust arises and is not rebutted. Whether a presumption arises depends on the relationship between the donor and donee and the nature of the assets sought to be transferred, and these factors therefore affect whether a gift has validly been made in any particular case.[17]

29.12 When a gift is rendered void for any of these reasons the rights that arise as between the parties fall outside the scope of the law of rescission, which is concerned only with gifts that are valid until rescinded.

(3) Discretion to reject and to reclaim a gift

Donee's right to reject an unwanted gift

29.13 A gift may be made even if the donee is ignorant of it. If, after discovering the gift, the donee decides that he does not want it, he has an absolute discretion to reject the gift.[18] A

---

[12] *R v Hinks* [2001] 2 AC 241, 262, referring to the 'distinction between a fully effective gift and one which is vitiated by incapacity, fraud or some other feature which would lead both the man in the street and the law to say that the transfer was not a true gift resulting from an actual intention of the donor to give'. See also at 265. Cf *United Enterprises Pty Ltd v Fryer* [2005] 1 QdR 337 (mistake causing allotment of new shares instead of conversion of existing shares; allotment declared to be void *ab initio*).

[13] Following a review of the authorities, Mr Christopher Nugee QC (as his Lordship then was) determined that 'there is real doubt whether as a matter of law incapacity makes a voluntary transaction such as a gift void rather than voidable', and expressed the view that it would be preferable if equitable defences were clearly available, which would be the case if the transaction were merely voidable: *Sutton v Sutton* [2009] EWHC 2576 (Ch) [46], [51]. But cf the authorities in n 15.

[14] *Re Beaney Dec'd* [1978] 1 WLR 771 (house); *The Special Trustees for Great Ormond Street Hospital for Children v Rushin* [2003] All ER (D) 598 (money to buy cars); *Williams v Williams* [2003] EWHC 742 (house); *Qutb v Hussain* [2005] EWHC 157 (Ch) (money and house at undervalue).

[15] A minor cannot hold a legal estate in land: Law of Property Act 1925, s 1(6).

[16] See G Virgo (ed), 'Gifts', in *Halsbury's Laws of England* (5th edn, 2020) vol 52, [211] (gifts by minors 'voidable'); 'Report of the Committee on the Age of Majority' (1967) Cmnd 3342, 98 (gifts by minors indefeasible), doubted A Burrows, *The Law of Restitution* (3rd edn, 2011) 314. Also, *Sutton v Sutton* [2009] EWHC 2576 (Ch) [51] (gifts by minors probably voidable).

[17] See generally L Tucker et al (eds), *Lewin on Trusts* (20th edn, 2020) [10-002]–[10-016].

[18] *Butler and Baker's case* (1591) 3 Co Rep 25, 26 b to 27 a; 76 ER 684, 689; *Standing v Bowring* (1885) 31 ChD 282 (CA); *Re Paradise Motor Co Ltd* [1968] 1 WLR 1225 (CA); *R v Hinks* [2001] 2 AC 241, 266–67. See also *Dewar v Dewar* [1975] 1 WLR 1532, 1538 (gift though donee treated as loan).

disclaimer is irrevocable, and revests title in the donor.[19] If the donee is not able to revest legal title by simply rejecting the gift, as where it comprises shares registered in the donee's name, he is entitled to the court's assistance to do so.[20] It is doubtful that a donee aware of the gift at the time and who consents to it retains the same power to disclaim, but the point seems not to have been decided. The donee's right of rejection has some similarities to a right to rescind.[21]

Donor has no right to reclaim a completed gift

29.14 Although a donee has a complete discretion to reject a gift of which he is ignorant, a donor enjoys no general right to reclaim a completed gift, and may do so only if the gift is expressed to be revocable, or is otherwise conditional.[22] In order to recover an absolute and effective gift the donor must show that his consent was vitiated in some way.[23] His *animus donandi* must have been impaired.[24]

(4) Special vulnerability of gifts to rescission

Grounds for rescinding gifts

29.15 Most of the reported cases concerning the rescission of gifts fall into one of two categories. The first is gifts of money or property tainted by undue influence. Many of the recent cases involve gifts by the elderly. The second category arises in the context of trusts and settlements, and is concerned with claims to rescind voluntary deeds by reason of the donor's mistake as to its effects, often following mistaken legal advice. However, although these are the main categories, in principle any ground that would permit a contract to be rescinded should permit the rescission of a completed gift.

29.16 *Langton v Langton*[25] had decided that an exception exists in relation to unconscionable bargains.[26] Deputy Judge Charles QC there held that a gift cannot be rescinded as an unconscionable bargain. Factors that would make a contract voidable as an unconscionable bargain are, in the context of a gift, indicia of undue influence. The possibly of rescission for 'equitable fraud' not amounting to undue influence was left open, but without discussing

---

[19] *Standing v Bowring* (1885) 31 ChD 282 (CA) 286 citing with approval *Butler and Baker's case* (1591) 3 Co Rep 25, 26 b; 76 ER 684; *Re Paradise Motor Co Ltd* [1968] 1 WLR 1125 (CA) 1143.
[20] *Standing v Bowring* (1885) 31 ChD 282 (CA).
[21] For further analysis of a donee's power to reject an unwanted gift, J Hill, 'The Role of the Donee's Consent in the Law of Gift' (2001) 117 LQR 127.
[22] *Standing v Bowring* (1885) 31 ChD 282 (CA); *Ogilvie v Littleboy* (1897) 13 TLR 399 (CA) 400; aff'd *Ogilvie v Allen* (1899) 15 TLR 294 (HL). The Law Reform (Miscellaneous Provisions) Act 1970, s 3(2) has changed the common law rules as to engagement rings. They are now presumed to have been given absolutely, and not conditionally upon marriage, unless the contrary is shown.
[23] *Allcard v Skinner* (1887) 36 ChD 145 (CA) 182–83; *Ogilvie v Littleboy* (1897) 13 TLR 399 (CA) 400; aff'd *Ogilvie v Allen* (1899) 15 TLR 294 (HL); *Brusewitz v Brown* (1923) NZLR 1106, 1109 (Salmond J); *Louth v Diprose* (1992) 175 CLR 621, 631–32.
[24] PBH Birks, 'Undue Influence as Wrongful Exploitation' (2004) 120 LQR 34, 37.
[25] [1995] 2 FLR 890, 907–10, rejecting the view in *Snell's Principles of Equity* (29th edn, 1991) 551, and approved in *Randall v Randall* [2004] EWHC 2258 (Ch) [94] ('For my part, if I may be allowed to say so, I see no reason, despite Mr Warner's submissions to the contrary, to question the reasoning in *Langton v Langton*. However, the point does not arise for decision.')
[26] As to this ground for rescission, see Chap 7.

what this meant.[27] It is suggested that this opinion is wrong.[28] In *Evans v Lloyd*[29] Judge Keyser QC[30] rightly declined to follow *Langton v Langton*. A gift may be rescinded as an 'unconscionable bargain'. The reference to 'bargain' does not delimit the scope of the doctrine. It may be better if this ground for rescission was called 'unconscionable conduct', as it is in Australia, and where it is uncontroversial that the doctrine applies as much to gifts as it does to contracts.[31]

Special vulnerability of gifts to rescission

29.17 Gifts *inter vivos* are more vulnerable than contracts to rescission in the following respects.

29.18 Undue influence is more easily proved in the case of a gift, for a gift is more readily construed as a transaction that 'calls for explanation'. Gifts also tend to be made between parties whose relationship is one of trust and confidence, so that a presumption of undue influence will arise if the gift is not trivial.[32] It remains unclear whether the test to be applied is itself different from that applied in the contractual context.[33] There would appear to be sound reasons why the test should be more relaxed in relation to actual undue influence, for the law has a correspondingly weaker interest in protecting the integrity of the transaction.[34]

29.19 A serious unilateral mistake as to the effects of a deed of gift that is not known to the donee will permit the gift to be rescinded, if it would be unjust to allow it to stand,[35] but the same mistake will have no effect on the validity of a contract. The other contracting party must know of the mistake, and be guilty of some sharp practice before rescission is available.[36] In addition, it has been held that the law requires less exact *restitutio in integrum* where a voluntary disposition is set aside, that partial rescission is possible notwithstanding the bar on the partial rescission of contracts, and that the affirmation bar is applied less strictly.[37]

29.20 Where a donor is induced to make a gift by undue influence, misrepresentation, breach of fiduciary duty, or other vitiating conduct by a third party, as opposed to the donee himself,

---

[27] [1995] 2 FLR 890, 909. Cf *Hart v O'Connor* [1985] AC 1000 (PC—NZ) 1024: '"Fraud" in its equitable context ... is victimisation, which can consist either of the active extortion of a benefit or the passive acceptance of a benefit in unconscionable circumstances.'

[28] Also, D Capper, 'Unconscionable Bargains and Unconscionable Gifts' [1996] Conv 308 (doubting the reasoning in *Langton v Langton*).

[29] [2013] EWHC 1725 (Ch) [52] (dismissal of claim for rescission of gift of agricultural holdings made by farm-worker).

[30] Sitting as a Judge of the High Court.

[31] *Wilton v Farnworth* (1948) 76 CLR 646 (partly deaf and simple gold miner); *Louth v Diprose* (1992) 175 CLR 621, 626–28, 630, 637–38 (infatuation); also, *Kakavas v Crown Melbourne Ltd* (2013) 250 CLR 392; 298 ALR 35 (HCA) (lawful gambling; claim failed on facts).

[32] *Royal Bank of Scotland plc v Etridge (No 2)* [2002] 2 AC 773. See eg *Re Craig, Dec'd* [1971] Ch 95, 121 (substantial gift by elderly man to secretary-companion). But the question must be considered in all of the circumstances: *Evans v Lloyd* [2013] EWHC 1725 (Ch) [59]–[65] (gift by farm worker of all of his property; no relationship of trust and confidence and gift explicable by normal human motivations, in the particular circumstances).

[33] There are some suggestions that equity takes a stricter approach in cases of gifts: eg *Wright v Carter* [1903] 1 Ch 27 (CA) 50. But in *Royal Bank of Scotland plc v Etridge (No 2)* [2002] 2 AC 773 no particular distinction seems to have been drawn between the test in relation to gifts and contracts. Cf *Louth v Diprose* (1992) 175 CLR 621, 628.

[34] For the argument that the test should be different for gifts, D Nolan, 'The Classical Legacy and Modern English Contract Law' (1996) 59 MLR 603, 611. The test for testamentary gifts is stricter than for gifts *inter vivos* and for contracts: *Craig v Lamoureux* [1920] AC 349 (PC—Canada) 356–57, critically discussed in P Ridge, 'Equitable Undue Influence and Wills' (2004) 120 LQR 617.

[35] *Ogilvie v Littleboy* (1897) 13 TLR 399 (CA) 400 col 1; aff'd *Ogilvie v Allen* (1899) 15 TLR 294 (HL); *Pitt v Holt* [2013] 2 AC 108.

[36] *Riverlate Properties Ltd v Paul* [1975] 1 Ch 133 (CA) 140–45; *Taylor v Johnson* (1983) 151 CLR 422.

[37] *Rogge v Rogge* [2019] EWHC 1949 (Ch) [162]–[168], [172], [175] (rescission relying upon *Pitt v Holt*).

the gift may be set aside whether or not the donee was aware of the relevant conduct.[38] By contrast, before a contract agreed in this situation may be set aside, the other contracting party must (at least) know of the relevant vitiating circumstance.[39]

29.21 Similarly, where a person suffers from impaired understanding by reason of age, mental infirmity, or illness, that will render a gift by him void irrespective of the donee's awareness of the condition, but the same impairment will make his contract merely voidable, and then only if the other party was sufficiently aware of it.[40] Reason for special vulnerability of gifts to rescission

29.22 It is apparent from the foregoing survey that vitiated consent permits the rescission of gifts when unaccompanied by the additional factors that must be present in order to render a contract voidable. The reason is that the law's interest in protecting bargains, and in the security of contracts, is not engaged in the case of a gift, even if made by deed.[41] The principle of *pacta sunt servanda* (pacts are to be respected)[42] does not apply where there is no binding agreement.[43] For this reason a gift may be rescinded if the donor's consent was sufficiently vitiated, even though the donee bore no responsibility for the impairment and was ignorant of it.

29.23 The position is in this respect similar to a payment made in the mistaken belief that it was due, the paradigm case of a mistaken payment. A right to restitution arises if the payer makes a causative mistake, and there is no need to show that the payee contributed to or was even aware of the error.[44] In that case, and the case of a gift, recovery is permitted for mistakes that would not upset a contract because the law's interest in protecting bargains is not engaged. But the analogy between mistaken payments and vitiated gifts must not be pressed

---

[38] Undue influence: eg *Bridgeman v Green* (1755) Wilm 58, 62, 64–65; 97 ER 22 (HL); *Huguenin v Baseley* (1807) 14 Ves Jun 273, 288–90, 301; 33 ER 526; *Bullock v Lloyds Bank Ltd* [1955] 2 Ch 317. Misrepresentation: *Scholefield v Templer* (1859) 4 De G & J 429, 433–34; 45 ER 166. Breach of fiduciary duty: eg *Liles v Terry* [1895] QB 679 (CA) 686; *Barron v Willis* [1900] 2 Ch 121 (CA) 133.

[39] Undue influence: eg *Bainbrigge v Browne* (1881) 28 ChD 188, 197–99; *Credit Lyonnais Bank Nederland NV v Burch* [1997] 1 All ER 144 (CA) 152; *Royal Bank of Scotland plc v Etridge (No 2)* [2002] 2 AC 773. Misrepresentation: *Sturge v Starr* (1833) 2 My & K 195, 196; 39 ER 918. Breach of fiduciary duty: *Logicrose Ltd v Southend United Football Club Ltd* [1988] 1 WLR 1256, 1261; *Rolled Steel Products (Holdings) Ltd v British Steel Corporation* [1986] 1 Ch 246 (CA) 298, 303, 306, 307; *Heinl v Jyske Bank (Gibraltar) Ltd* [1999] Lloyd's Rep Bank 511 (CA) 521, 533. See further Chap 9.

[40] *Imperial Loan Company Limited v Stone* [1892] 1 QB 599 (CA) (contract); *Baldwyn v Smith* [1900] 1 Ch 588 (contract); *Gibbons v Wright* (1954) 91 CLR 423 (conveyance for value); *Re Beaney Dec'd* [1978] 1 WLR 771 (gift); *Hart v O'Connor* [1985] AC 1000 (PC—NZ) (contract); *The Special Trustees for Great Ormond Street Hospital for Children v Rushin* [2003] All ER (D) 598 (contract and gift distinguished); *Williams v Williams* [2003] EWHC 742 (gift); but cf *Sutton v Sutton* [2009] EWHC 2576 (Ch) [46] (concluding that it remains open whether a gift by a person lacking capacity is void or voidable). See further Chap 7.

[41] This passage was cited with apparent approval in *Pitt v Holt* [2013] 2 AC 108 [114]. See further PBH Birks, *Unjust Enrichment* (2nd edn, 2005) 149 (no risk allocation by contract, no risk taking); J Cartwright, *Unequal Bargaining: A Study of Vitiating Factors in the Formation of Contracts* (1991) (interest in integrity of bargaining process not engaged); D Nolan, 'The Classical Legacy and Modern English Contract Law' (1996) 59 MLR 603, 610–11; cf HW Tang, 'Restitution for Mistaken Gifts' (2004) 20 JCL 1, arguing that there are moral and social factors that speak in favour of the sanctity of gifts, and see also P Ridge, 'Third Party Volunteers and Undue Influence' (2014) 130 LQR 112, 117–19 (discussing different explanations for the vulnerability of gifts to rescission, and noting that gifts sit between contracts and mistaken payments in the 'hierarchy of transactions' that the law will undo); S Zogg, *Proprietary Consequences in Defective Transfers of Ownership* (2020) 122, 464–65, 472–76.

[42] 'Contract law is built on the principle that bargains freely entered into should be enforced': *Samuel v Wadlow* [2007] EWCA Civ 155 [47].

[43] Cf in earlier times this maxim probably extended to any form of 'pact'; the Canon law rule was 'pacts, however naked, must be kept'.

[44] *Barclays Bank Ltd v WJ Simms Son & Cooke (Southern) Ltd* [1980] 1 QB 677.

too far. Although in both cases the law's interest in protecting bargains is not engaged, its other interest, in protecting legitimate expectations or reliance, is different.[45]

(5) Significance of how the gift is made and what is given

29.24 In considering when a gift may be rescinded and what rights are conferred upon rescission it is necessary to consider both how the gift is made, and what precisely is given. There appear to be relevant differences between the right to rescind gifts effected by deed and by conduct, and gifts of money and property.[46] These differences are summarized in what follows.

Gifts effected by conduct and by deed

29.25 When a gift is made by conduct alone the donee's right to retain the asset given cannot rest on the existence of a deed of transfer and, conversely, there is no need to set aside a deed as a condition of restoring what was given. It is suggested later that the obligation to make restitution of money donated by simple payment arises from the moment of receipt, whilst money gifted by deed need not be returned until the deed is set aside. The former accordingly falls outside the reach of the law of rescission, while the latter is squarely within it. Further, as also set out later in this chapter, there might be differences between the types of mistake that count when money is given by deed and by simple payment.

Gifts of money and of property

29.26 Rescission of a gift of money confers a personal claim to repayment. In some cases, it may also generate a proprietary claim. On the other hand, where property is given, the cases so far indicate that rescission generates a purely proprietary claim. The rescission of gifts of money and property are therefore also considered separately.

(6) Gifts made by conduct

Gifts of money made by conduct

Grounds for recovery

29.27 A gift made by payment of money may be reclaimed if induced by fraud,[47] undue influence,[48] or innocent misrepresentation,[49] and, it would appear, any other ground permitting the rescission of a contract.

29.28 The effect of mistake has been controversial. If there is a relevant analogy with the rules concerning mistaken payments, a right to restitution should arise whenever a gift of money is vitiated by a causative mistake. That was the view of Brennan J in *David Securities Pty*

---

[45] See para [29.29].
[46] Gifts of services are put to one side because there do not appear to be any cases that have considered a claim for restitution in respect of a gift of services impaired by fraud, mistake, or like cause.
[47] *Booth v Warrington* (1714) 4 Brown 164, 2 ER 111 (gift of 1000 guineas induced by fraud ordered to be repaid).
[48] *Morley v Loughnan* [1893] 1 Ch 736; *Hammond v Osborn* [2002] EWCA Civ 885.
[49] *Re Glubb* [1900] 1 Ch 354 (CA) 362, 364.

Ltd v Commonwealth Bank of Australia,[50] and it has been endorsed by some scholars.[51] But statements made *obiter* by Sir Wilfred Green MR in *Morgan v Ashcroft*[52] are against that conclusion, and other scholars have argued that a gift of money is not recoverable for a mere causative mistake; the mistake must also be serious.[53]

29.29 It is true that the opinion of Sir Wilfred Green was probably shaped by contemporary conceptions as to what mistakes permit the recovery of non-contractual payments, and that these have since been abandoned.[54] But notwithstanding that English law does not recognize the Civilian concept of a 'contract of gift',[55] a gift remains a form of consensual transaction in a sense that a mere mistaken payment is not, at least in the usual case where both parties appreciate that a gift is intended and has been made.[56] Zogg argues that a 'gift' by deed or by conduct provides a 'legal basis' for the retention of benefits received, and so that rescission is always required before a claim for restitution may be made.[57] There do, moreover, seem to be material differences between the interests that are in play when a gift is impaired by a unilateral mistake, and where there is a mistaken overpayment of a debt or other form of liability mistake. As Meier has observed, a donee may legitimately rely on an executed gift affected by a causative, pre-donative mistake, in a manner that, intuitively, deserves some protection. But there can be no corresponding legitimate reliance on the security of a sum paid in the mistaken belief that it was due, or paid twice by accident.[58] Lord Scott has added strong support to the view that a gift of money cannot be recovered for a merely causative mistake, and that something more is required.[59] The analysis of the Supreme Court in *Pitt v Holt* is expressed in terms that are not confined to voluntary dispositions made by deed, and seems to indicate that in all cases where a 'voluntary disposition' is sought to be rescinded there must be a causative mistake that is also sufficiently serious to attract the intervention of equity.[60] If this is correct, in England the test of 'serious

---

[50] (1992) 175 CLR 353, 392–93, where Brennan J also noted that there was authority to the contrary. In the Isle of Man, *Clarkson v Barclays Private Bank and Trust (Isle of Man) Ltd* [2007] WTLR 1703 [41] (if mistake was causative of the gift that is sufficient for it to be unjust to allow the gift to stand); see further paras [29.40]–[29.47].

[51] G Virgo, *The Principles of the Law of Restitution* (3rd edn, 2015) 182–83; B Häcker, *Consequences of Impaired Consent Transfers* (2013) 118, 328.

[52] [1938] 1 KB 49 (CA) 66: 'If a father, believing that his son has suffered a financial loss, gives him a sum of money he surely could not claim repayment if he afterwards discovered that no such loss had occurred'; cf Scott LJ at 74.

[53] S Meier and R Zimmermann, 'Judicial Development of the Law, *Error Iuris*, and the Law of Unjustified Enrichment—A View from Germany' (1999) 115 LQR 556, 562–63, critically considered A Burrows, *The Law of Restitution* (3rd edn, 2011) 218–19, further developed S Meier, 'Unjust Factors and Legal Grounds' in D Johnson and R Zimmermann (eds), *Unjustified Enrichment: Key Issues in a Comparative Perspective* (2002) 44, 47–48, 52–53.

[54] PBH Birks, *Introduction to the Law of Restitution* (1989) 154–55.

[55] B Häcker, *Consequences of Impaired Consent Transfers* (2013) 19.

[56] A gift may, technically, be made without the knowledge or consent of the donee: see para [29.13].

[57] S Zogg, *Proprietary Consequences in Defective Transfers of Ownership* (2020) 122, 464–65, 472–73, 477–81, 501 (and considering separately the case of a gift effected by deed and conduct). The notion finds some support also in *Deutsche Morgan Grenfell v IRC* [2007] 1 AC 558 [21], where Lord Hoffmann remarked that 'unlike civilian systems, English law has no general principle that to retain money paid without any legal basis (such as debt, gift, compromise, etc) is unjust enrichment'.

[58] S Meier, 'Unjust Factors and Legal Grounds' in D Johnson and R Zimmerman (eds), *Unjustified Enrichment: Key Issues in a Comparative Perspective* (2002) 47–48, 52–53. Also, S Zogg, *Proprietary Consequences in Defective Transfers of Ownership* (2020) 453, 455–56, 500 (property rights have at least same sanctity and contractual rights).

[59] *Deutsche Morgan Grenfell Group plc v Inland Revenue* [2007] 1 AC 558 [87].

[60] *Pitt v Holt* [2013] 2 AC 108 [114], [121], [122], [126], [128], [142]. See also *Van der Merwe v Goldman* [2016] 4 WLR 71 [31] and *Rogge v Rogge* [2019] EWHC 1949 (Ch) (*Pitt v Holt* applied in claim to set aside of payments); also, S Zogg, *Proprietary Consequences in Defective Transfers of Ownership* (2020) 122.

mistake' articulated in *Pitt v Holt* governs all payments of money that are intended as gifts, irrespective of whether the gift is made by deed or by conduct.

For these reasons, it is suggested that the restrictive rule for mistakes in deeds of gift also apply to gifts of money effected by simple payment. The mistake must be of so serious a character as to render it unjust on the part of the donee to retain the money given.[61] A causative mistake is not sufficient.   **29.30**

Nature of right to restitution that arises
When a gift of money is vitiated by fraud, misrepresentation, or other vitiating cause the donor is entitled to orders for an account and repayment as against the donee,[62] and, at least in cases of undue influence, also against volunteers to whom the donee has distributed the sums gifted.[63] Although both involved the unauthorized taking of money rather than a vitiated gift, *Bank Belge Pour L'Etranger v Hambrouck*[64] and *Lipkin Gorman v Karpnale Ltd*[65] imply that, apart from an equitable claim to account, an action for money had and received might also be available against volunteers to whom the donee has distributed the money, if it is traceably identifiable in their hands.   **29.31**

Interim injunctive relief has been granted where gifts of money were alleged to have been procured by undue influence, but in both cases additional factors were present that supported the injunction.[66] In Australia, where a gift of money to purchase an interest in a house was procured by unconscionable conduct, the court declared that the donee held the interest in the house on trust for the donor.[67] There was no challenge to that form of the order, but on appeal it was asked whether the appropriate order would have been for repayment of the sum given.[68] Statements *obiter* and decisions in connection with mistaken payments may provide support for the assertion of a proprietary claim over money where the donee knows that it has been paid to him by mistake or other factor vitiating the donor's consent.[69]   **29.32**

---

[61] *Ogilvie v Littleboy* (1897) 13 TLR 399 (CA) 400 col 1; aff'd *Ogilvie v Allen* (1899) 15 TLR 294 (HL); *Pitt v Holt* [2013] 2 AC 108; see paras [29.42]–[29.43].
[62] *Morley v Loughnan* [1893] 1 Ch 736, 757–58 (order for account and repayment of gifts of £140,000 received by donee's undue influence); *Re Glubb* [1900] 1 Ch 354 (CA) 362, 364 (gifts of money to a charity vitiated by innocent misrepresentation; payments voidable and recoverable in equity); *Jennings v Cairns* [2003] EWCA 1935 (gift of £171,000 ordered to be repaid as procured by undue influence; trial judge's description as 'equitable compensation' apparently a misnomer); *Hammond v Osborne* [2002] EWCA Civ 885 [16], [33] (gift of £297,000 proceeds of investments set aside for undue influence).
[63] *Morley v Loughnan* [1893] 1 Ch 736, 757–58 (order for account and repayment of that part of gifts of £140,000 received by donee's brothers); *Hammond v Osborne* [2002] EWCA Civ 885 [9] (donee's son obliged to refund money received from donee).
[64] [1921] 1 KB 321 (CA).
[65] [1991] 2 AC 548, 560, 565, 566, 575, 577, where it was emphasized that the payments to the third party (a gambling club) took effect as gifts, and were recoverable because no consideration was given.
[66] *Morley v Loughnan* [1893] 1 Ch 736, 746, 748, 757 (undue influence): interim injunction granted in respect of £50,000 given for certain objects, but applied by the donee for his own purposes; *Hammond v Osborne* [2002] EWCA Civ 885 [12] (undue influence): freezing order obtained, but claimants had also alleged sums were received for first defendant to manage, not as a gift.
[67] *Diprose v Louth (No 1)* (1990) SASR 438.
[68] *Louth v Diprose* (1992) 175 CLR 621, 638–39 (Deane J).
[69] In the case of mistaken payments not intended as gifts, it has been said *obiter* that a trust might be imposed if the recipient realizes the mistake prior to dissipation of the funds: *Westdeutsche Landesbank Girozentrale v Islington LBC* [1996] AC 669, 715. A trust will arise if the recipient appreciates that the payer's mistake was the product of a fraud: *Bank of America v Arnell* [1999] Lloyd's Rep Bank 399.

29.33 Claimants typically seek an order 'setting aside' gifts of money procured by undue influence, and the courts usually make that form of order.[70] The authorities have not considered how far this reflects the underlying obligations of the donee, and whether an immediate obligation to make restitution is owed, or whether the obligation arises only if and when the gift is set aside. This may be material to when and how the right to restitution is lost by affirmation.

29.34 On one view, it is necessary to set aside the gift before any right to restitution can arise. But the Civilian 'contract of gift' is unknown in English law, and it is not obvious what exactly there is to set aside when a gift of money is made by payment. Although the contrary is well arguable, the right to be repaid should probably arise immediately. The donee's conscience is affected as from the moment of receipt, and no instrument or agreement exists that is *prima facie* inconsistent with an obligation to make restitution. By analogy with the rule for mistaken payments, the obligation to repay should arise from the moment the sums are received.

29.35 If this is correct, gifts of money made by conduct rather than deed are not to be assimilated to the doctrine of rescission at all. There is no need for the donor to elect to set aside the gift, or to seek an order for rescission, and the bars to rescission do not apply in their ordinary form. In the eyes of the law the transaction is ineffective as from the outset, and the donor's right is to enforce a claim to repayment that vested at the moment the moneys were paid. That right may be lost or cut down if the donee can establish a defence of change of position,[71] and probably also by later disentitling conduct on the part of the donor, such as laches or acquiescence, or if the donor ratifies the gift after emancipation from the vitiating factor.

Gifts of property made by conduct
Grounds for restitution

29.36 A sufficiently serious mistake will negative the donative intention necessary to pass legal title to chattels gifted by delivery.[72] If title to chattels does pass, authorities in analogous contexts might suggest that a defrauded donor is entitled to regain legal title by electing to disaffirm the gift, if it was induced by fraud, or possibly also on other grounds.[73] That would align gifts with contracts procured by fraud. Save for this possibility, where title to property is transferred by conduct alone, the donor must commence proceedings for rescission, and

---

[70] *Hammond v Osborn* [2002] EWCA Civ 885 [16], [33] (Nourse LJ) ('set aside' gift of money for undue influence).

[71] *Pitt v Holt* [2013] 2 AC 108 [125], [126], [142].

[72] *RE Jones Ltd v Waring & Gillow* [1926] AC 670, 696 (example of tradesman delivering goods to wrong person); *Cundy v Lindsay* (1878) 3 App Cas 459 and *Ingram v Little* [1961] 1 QB 31 (CA) where no title passed to goods delivered under a contract void for mistake; see also *Citibank NA v Brown Shipley & Co Ltd* [1991] 2 All ER 690, 699–700; *Shogun Finance Ltd v Hudson* [2004] 1 AC 919. But cf C MacMillan, 'Rogues, Swindlers and Cheats: The Development of Mistake of Identity in English Contract Law' [2005] 64 CLJ 711, 730. F Pollock and R Wright, *An Essay on Possession in the Common Law* (1888) 100–14, considers the effect of different mistakes on the delivery of chattels.

[73] *Hunter BNZ Finance Ltd v CG Maloney Pty Ltd* (1988) 18 NSWLR 420, 433–34, 437; foll *Orix Australia Corporation Ltd v M Wright Hotel Refrigeration Pty Ltd* (2000) 15 FLR 267, 272–73. Those cases are authority that when party A transfers legal title in a cheque to party B by reason of C's fraudulent misrepresentations, and there is no contract between A and B and no representation by B, B obtains a voidable title that A is able to regain by disaffirming the transfer to B.

obtain a court order for revesting title in the property gifted,[74] and if necessary an account of income derived from it.[75]

There is no clear English authority on whether mistake permits the rescission of a gift of property effected by conduct, and if so what kinds of mistake count. One view is that if the mistake does not prevent legal title from passing, the gift may be recovered at the election of the donor whenever induced by a causative mistake. This aligns with the rule for the recovery of mistaken payments, and has been adopted in New Zealand.[76] But there is no equivalence between mistaken payments and the mistaken transfer of title to property by conduct. The law has always treated the transfer and recovery of money and property quite differently. Further, rescission of a gift of property under a deed is not permitted simply because a causative mistake is made; the mistake must be of so serious a character as to render it unjust on the part of the donee to retain the property given.[77] Although there is room for doubt, it is suggested that the same rule should apply to property gifted by conduct.[78]

29.37

Nature of the right to restitution arising
Cases concerning voidable deeds of gift indicate that a donor rescinding a gift of property is able to assert an equitable proprietary interest in exchange substitutes held by the donee.[79] The position should be the same where property is gifted other than by deed.

29.38

When property is gifted by conduct rather than deed in circumstances allowing the gift to be set aside, it is unclear whether beneficial title passes pending rescission, or is immediately revested in the donor when the transfer is completed. Beneficial title always passes defeasibly under a voidable contract, and the majority judgments in *Allcard v Skinner* indicate that this is also true of a gift of property induced by presumed undue influence.[80] It establishes that in cases of presumed undue influence beneficial title does pass, but defeasibly. But it is notable that Cotton LJ disagreed, and said that a trust exists from the outset,[81] and this seems to have been the view of the trial judge, Kekewich J.[82] Where a gift had been obtained by the donee's dishonesty or actual undue influence, or perhaps by that of a third party to the knowledge of the donee, there is an argument that the law should automatically impose a constructive trust. The point appears not to have been directly considered.[83]

29.39

---

[74] Eg *Nottidge v Prince* (1860) 2 Giff 246, 271; 66 ER 103, 113 (rescission for undue influence; gift of £5,728 of annuities effected by donor's instructions to broker to transfer into name of donee; order that stock transferred into name of donor's representative).
[75] *Allcard v Skinner* (1887) 36 ChD 145 (CA) 175 (Cotton LJ) dissenting from the conclusion that the claim was barred by delay (dividends from shares received since commencement of the action).
[76] *University of Canterbury v Attorney-General* [1995] 1 NZLR 78, 85–86.
[77] *Ogilvie v Littleboy* (1897) 13 TLR 399 (CA) 400 col 1; aff'd *Ogilvie v Allen* (1899) 15 TLR 294 (HL); *Pitt v Holt* [2013] 2 AC 108; see paras [29.42]–[29.43].
[78] See further para [29.29].
[79] *Pesticcio v Huet* (2003) 73 BMLR 57; aff'd [2004] EWCA Civ 372.
[80] (1887) 36 ChD 145 (CA) 184, 186–87, 191 (gifts of railway stock transferred into donee's name; also, *Hammond v Osborn* [2002] EWCA Civ 885 [60] (Ward LJ)).
[81] *Allcard v Skinner* (1887) 36 ChD 145 (CA) 173, 175.
[82] *Allcard v Skinner* (1887) 36 ChD 145 (CA) 164–65.
[83] The reasoning in *Bank of America v Arnell* [1999] Lloyd's Rep Bank 399 may imply that a trust is imposed automatically in a case of this kind.

(7) Gifts made by deed

Rescinding deeds of gift for mistake

29.40 A deed of gift is voidable on the same grounds that permit the rescission of a simple contract.[84] But a gift effected by deed differs from a simple contract because the donor may rescind it for mistakes that will not allow a contract to be set aside.

29.41 It was formerly thought that a donor could rescind a deed of gift if he executed it under a unilateral misconception as to its effects but not its consequences. That principle was associated with the decision of Millett J in *Gibbon v Mitchell*.[85]

29.42 In *Pitt v Holt*[86] the Supreme Court has, however, now approved the different and wider test enunciated by the Court of Appeal in *Ogilvie v Littleboy*,[87] and confirmed on appeal by the House of Lords.[88] It was there held that the mistake must be 'of so serious a character as to render it unjust on the part of the donee to retain the property given'.[89] In *Pitt v Holt* the Supreme Court underlined that to rescind a voluntary disposition for mistake, it must be shown that there was an actual mistake, of a relevant type, and that was sufficiently serious to satisfy the *Ogilvie v Littleboy* test.[90] The Supreme Court provided valuable guidance in relation to each of these three matters and subsequent cases have provided further elucidation of the propositions to be derived from *Pitt v Holt*.[91]

29.43 As to the first point, what counts as a 'mistake', *Pitt v Holt* decides that a mistake is to be distinguished from mere ignorance, inadvertence, or misprediction, each of which does not permit rescission. What is needed is proof that the disponer made an actual mistake about some past or present matter of fact or law.[92] In addition, there will be no operative mistake if it is found that the disponer deliberately ran the risk of being wrong about the relevant point, or is to be taken to have run that risk.[93]

29.44 In relation to the second issue (the mistake must be of a relevant type), in *Gibbon v Mitchell*[94] Millett J had said *obiter* that a mistake as to the consequences or advantages to be gained from the transaction, as opposed to its effect, is not enough, and this was subsequently held

---

[84] Save that in England it has been said that the doctrine of unconscionable bargains does not apply: *Langton v Langton* [1995] 2 FLR 890; cf *Evans v Lloyd* [2013] EWHC 1725 (Ch) [52], and in Australia, *Louth v Diprose* (1992) 175 CLR 621. See para [29.16].

[85] [1990] 1 WLR 1304, 1309 (rescission of deed purporting to surrender life interest under marriage settlement so as to vest fund exclusively in two named children, which had a wholly different effect); *Woolf v Woolf* [2004] STC 1633 (rescission of reversionary lease for mistake). See also, *Sieff v Fox* [2005] 1 WLR 3811, 3841–46.

[86] [2013] 2 AC 108.

[87] (1897) 13 TLR 399 (CA).

[88] *Ogilvie v Allen* (1899) 15 TLR 294 (HL).

[89] (1897) 13 TLR 399 (CA) 400 col 1. In Australia, *Jenys v Public Curator of Queensland* (1953) 90 CLR 113, 134 'the finding that she did not sufficiently understand the transaction ... is not enough by itself to invalidate the gift'. The test in *Ogilvie v Littleboy* is quite different from the principle expressed in *Gibbon v Mitchell*, as was noted by Lloyd LJ in *Sieff v Fox* [2005] 1 WLR 3811, 3845. *Ogilvie v Littleboy* appears not to have been brought to the court's attention in *Gibbon v Mitchell* [1990] 1 WLR 1304.

[90] *Pitt v Holt* [2013] 2 AC 108 [103] (adopting the analysis of Lloyd LJ).

[91] The principles to be derived from *Pitt v Holt* were set out in eleven propositions in *Van der Merwe v Goldman* [2016] 4 WLR 71 [26] (Morgan J), applied eg *Re Clarke* [2019] EWHC 1193 (Ch), and in four propositions in *Kennedy v Kennedy* [2015] WTLR [36] (Sir Terence Etherton), applied eg *Rogge v Rogge* [2019] EWHC 1949 (Ch) [43]. See also, *JTC Employer Solutions Trustees Limited v Khadem* [2021] EWHC 2929 (Ch) [32]–[33].

[92] *Pitt v Holt* [2013] 2 AC 108 [104], [105], [108], [109].

[93] *Pitt v Holt* [2013] 2 AC 108 [114].

[94] [1990] 1 WLR 1304, 1309.

to include the gift's fiscal consequences.[95] That distinction, and the version of it explained by Lloyd LJ in the Court of Appeal,[96] was disapproved by the Supreme Court in *Pitt v Holt*.[97] What is required is simply proof of a causative mistake of sufficient gravity.[98] A mistake of law that is basic to the transaction may therefore suffice, even if it does not involve a mistake about the legal effect or nature of the transaction.[99] However, the Supreme Court also observed that cases of this kind will be rare, and that 'the test will normally be satisfied only when there is a mistake either as to the legal character or nature of the transaction, or as to some matter of fact or law which is basic to the transaction'.[100] It is clear, however, that a mistake about the consequences of a transaction may also provide a ground for its rescission, and that in an appropriate case this can include the transaction's fiscal consequences.[101] Indeed, the appeal in *Pitt v Holt* was just such a case.

In addition to comprising an actual mistake (as distinct from mere ignorance, inadvertence, or misprediction), and being causative, in order to confer a right to rescind a voluntary disposition, the mistake must also be 'of so serious a character as to render it unjust on the part of the donee to retain the property given'.[102] 'Unjust' means against conscience, and whether the mistake is so serious that it would be unconscionable to allow the disposition to stand is to be evaluated objectively.[103] A close assessment of the particular facts in the case before the court is required. Of importance is the circumstances of the mistake and its consequences for the donor, and whether there has been any relevant change of position on the part of the donee.[104] The assessment is to be made in the round, with a focus on the importance of the mistake to the transaction, and the seriousness of its consequences. The court is required to form an assessment of the justice of the case; that is, to evaluate whether in all of the circumstances it would be unconscionable or unjust to leave the mistake uncorrected.[105]

29.45

---

[95] *Anker-Petersen v Christensen* [2002] WTLR 313, 330–31; *Woolf v Woolf* [2004] STC 1633 [25]; *Sieff v Fox* [2005] 1 WLR 3811, 3845; *Pitt v Holt* [2012] Ch 132 (CA) [209]. See also *AMP (UK) plc v Barker* [2001] PLR 77 [70] (distinction between effects and consequence is to ensure relief kept within reasonable bounds, so parties cannot resile simply because mistaken about commercial effects or change their mind).
[96] *Pitt v Holt* [2012] Ch 132 (CA) [209]–[210].
[97] *Pitt v Holt* [2013] 2 AC 108 [121]–[123], [132]–[134], [142].
[98] *Pitt v Holt* [2013] 2 AC 108 [122].
[99] *Pitt v Holt* [2013] 2 AC 108 [119], [121]–[122], and clarifying that the 'effect' of the transaction means its legal nature or character.
[100] *Pitt v Holt* [2013] 2 AC 108 [122].
[101] *Pitt v Holt* [2013] 2 AC 108 [132]–[134], [142]; but cf the observations at [135] (in cases where the principal aim of the transaction is avoiding tax mistake might be negatived if the disponer is taken to have run the risk of the scheme failing, or it may be that in such a case the court will have a discretion to refuse rescission on policy grounds). See also *Kennedy v Kennedy* [2015] WTLR [36], [39], [46], [47] (setting aside one clause of an instrument of appointment by trustees affected by a mistake as to fiscal consequences, and noting that the transaction was not an artificial tax avoidance arrangement or part of one); *Van der Merwe v Goldman* [2016] 4 WLR 71 [48] (rescission of transfer and settlement for mistake as to fiscal consequences); *JTC Employer Solutions Trustees Limited v Khadem* [2021] EWHC 2929 (Ch) [9]–[11], [33]–[36], [57] (rescission of escrow agreement for mistake as to fiscal consequence, and considering whether facts proved and jurisdiction to be exercised notwithstanding HMRC did not appear).
[102] *Pitt v Holt* [2013] 2 AC 108 [103]; that is, the test articulated by Lindley LJ in *Ogilvie v Littleboy* (1897) 13 TLR 399 (CA) 400, col 1.
[103] *Pitt v Holt* [2013] 2 AC 108 [125].
[104] *Pitt v Holt* [2013] 2 AC 108 [126].
[105] *Pitt v Holt* [2013] 2 AC 108 [128].

Jersey and the Isle of Man

29.46 The Royal Court of Jersey has adopted a similar test. In *re S Trust*[106] Commissioner Bailhache held that transfers of assets to a trustee and then subsequently by that trustee were voidable at the instance of the settlor following mistaken legal advice about the taxation consequences of the transfers.[107] In permitting the transfers to be rescinded by the settlor the Commissioner followed earlier decisions of the Royal Court to reject the distinction between mistakes as to effects and as to consequences developed in *Gibbon v Mitchell* and approved by the Court of Appeal in *Pitt v Holt*, in favour of the test expressed in *Ogilvie v Littleboy*.[108]

29.47 The Jersey courts are likely to be more willing than English courts to permit voluntary dispositions by and to trustees to be rescinded for a mistake as to the taxation consequences of the disposition.[109] It seems that rescission will generally be permitted in such a case if the mistake was causative, as long as the scheme adopted was lawful and the consequences of the mistake are serious.[110] The law of the Isle of Man appears to be the same in this respect, although there are indications there that any causative mistake will be regarded as sufficiently serious to permit the disposition to be set aside.[111]

Restitution of money and property

29.48 Upon the rescission of a deed of gift, any executory obligations created by the deed are extinguished *ab initio*, and the donor is entitled to have the subject matter of the gift restored.

29.49 The donor of money under a deed should be entitled to an account and repayment as against the donee, and where appropriate against volunteers to whom the donee has distributed the sums gifted. But a donor who pays pursuant to a deed of gift cannot obtain a right to restitution unless and until the deed is set aside. In contrast, for the reasons set out earlier, the donor who gives by simple payment should automatically become entitled to restitution.

29.50 There is a dearth of authority as to whether title to an asset transferred pursuant to a deed of gift becomes immediately subject to a constructive trust, or behaves like title under a voidable contract, passing subject to an equity to regain it upon rescission. In principle the structure should be the same as for simple contracts. Certainly vitiated deeds of gift are generally described as 'voidable', and as liable to be set aside at the suit of the claimant, although the language cannot be decisive.[112] The equity may be exercised against subsequent donees and those who take with notice,[113] and rescission permits a proprietary claim to the

---

[106] [2011] JLR 375.
[107] *In re S Trust* [2011] JLR 375 [51].
[108] At [19]–[21], citing *Re the A Trust* [2009] JLR 447; *In re First Conferences Limited 2003 Employee Benefit Trust* [2010] JRC 055A and *In re the Lochmore Trust* [2010] JRC 068. The Commissioner declined to follow the decision of the Court of Appeal in *Pitt v Holt*: at [27]–[43]. The decision in *Re S Trust* was approved in *CC Ltd v Apex Trust Ltd* [2012] JLR 314 [30]–[31] (mistake as to ability to access assets placed into trust).
[109] Compare the observations in *In re S Trust* [2011] JLR 375 [39] with those of the Supreme Court in *Pitt v Holt* [2013] 2 AC 108 [135].
[110] *Re the A Trust* [2009] JLR 447; *In re S Trust* [2011] JLR 375 [39], [44]–[51].
[111] *Clarkson v Barclays Private Bank and Trust (Isle of Man) Ltd* [2007] WTLR 1703 [41]; *Re Betsam Trust* [2009] WTLR 1489 [28]–[29], [37]–[38].
[112] *Gibbon v Mitchell* [1990] 1 WLR 1304, 1310; *Goldsworthy v Brickell* [1987] Ch 378 (CA) 401; see also 409, 417; *Re the Estate of Brocklehurst Dec'd v Roberts* [1978] Ch 14, 31; *Re Craig Dec'd* [1971] Ch 95, 100; *Inche Noriah v Shaik Allie Bin Omar* [1927] AC 127 (PC—Singapore) 136.
[113] This general rule has mostly been articulated in cases where undue influence by a third party caused the donor to make a gift to the donee, but so as to make clear that recovery is also available against subsequent recipients from the donee who are volunteers or take with notice: *Bridgeman v Green* (1755) Wilm 58, 97 ER 22;

traceable product of the gift retained in the donee's hands;[114] though whether the interest is a charge to the extent of the value of the asset initially transferred, or full beneficial title, may depend upon the quality of the donee's conduct.[115]

Rescission of part of a deed of gift
Where a single deed contains multiple gifts, and only one gift is tainted by undue influence, **29.51** the court may set aside the deed only to the extent of the vitiated portion.[116] The courts have sometimes declared such gifts to be 'void as against' the affected party,[117] but this appears to be shorthand for an order that the gift is rescinded as against that party.

(8) Dispositions of another's assets: powers of appointment

Although the effect of an appointment made in fraud on the power remains uncertain,[118] it **29.52** is now established that the defective exercise of a power of appointment by trustees which enlivens the rule in *re Hastings-Bass*,[119] is merely voidable and not void.[120]

The kinds of errors that count for this purpose are wider than those that would justify set- **29.53** ting aside a gift of the donor's own property; in particular, it is established that a sufficiently significant mistake as to the fiscal consequences of the appointment will suffice.[121]

A mistake in the exercise of a power of appointment may trigger either the rule in *re* **29.54** *Hastings-Bass*, or if the mistake is sufficiently serious, a right to rescind for mistake.[122]

(9) Gifts and theft

In English law a donee may be guilty of theft even though the gift is fully effective and the **29.55** donor has no right to rescind it.[123] In practice, however, it seems likely that if a donee could

---

Bainbrigge v Browne (1881) 28 ChD 188, 197, 199; *Barron v Willis* [1900] 2 Ch 121 (CA) 133, aff'd [1902] AC 271. No claim is available against bona fide purchases from the donee: *Pesticcio v Huet* (2003) 73 BMLR 57.

[114] *Pesticcio v Huet* (2003) 73 BMLR 57 (interim orders founded on claim to traceable substitute for house donee had acquired by undue influence).
[115] *Pesticcio v Huet* (2003) 73 BMLR 57 [134].
[116] *Niersmans v Pesticcio* [2004] EWCA Civ 372; *Wright v Carter* [1903] 1 Ch 27 (CA) 54, 56, 59–60, 62–64 (deed of gift set aside as against solicitor, but not wife and children). Cf *Bainbrigge v Browne* (1881) 28 ChD 188 (grant of security to father's creditors set aside as against father only); *Turner v Collins* (1871) 7 Ch App 329 (son's deed of gift voidable in respect of share deriving from mother; right lost by delay).
[117] *Niersmans v Pesticco* [2004] EWCA Civ 372 [5]; *Wright v Carter* [1903] 1 Ch 27 (CA) 64.
[118] *Pitt v Holt* [2013] 2 AC 108 [62]; cf suggestions that the appointment will be void in such a case: *Topham v Duke of Portland* (1869) LR 5 Ch App 40; *Cloutte v Storey* [1911] 1 Ch 18 (CA) 30; *Sieff v Fox* [2005] 1 WLR 3811, 3836–37; *Roadchef (Employee Benefits Trustees) Limited v Hill* [2014] EWHC 109 (Ch) [131].
[119] *Re Hastings-Bass, Dec'd* [1975] Ch 25 (CA); *Pitt v Holt* [2013] 2 AC 108, 126–47.
[120] *Pitt v Holt* [2013] 2 AC 108 [93]. As to powers of appointment generally, *Schmidt v Rosewood Trust Ltd* [2003] 2 AC 709 (PC—Manx) 725-27 (Lord Walker, giving the advice of the Board).
[121] *Pitt v Holt* [2013] 2 AC 108 [65]; *Sieff v Fox* [2005] 1 WLR 3811, 3845–46, 3848.
[122] *Pitt v Holt* [2013] 2 AC 108 [7], [12]; *Abacus Trust Co (Isle of Man) v Barr* [2003] Ch 409, 414–15, where Lightman J referred to *Anker-Petersen v Christensen* [2002] WTLR 313, in which deeds for re-settling a will trust were rescinded for mistake. See also R Walker, 'The Limits of the Principle in Re Hastings-Bass' (2002) PCB 226, 239–40.
[123] *R v Hinks* [2001] 2 AC 241, rejecting the criticism of Professor Sir John Smith QC and other scholars. See also the dissenting opinion of Lord Hobhouse. Contrast *Police v Dronjak* [1990] 3 NZLR 75.

be convicted of theft, the donor would almost always have a right to rescind for fraud, mistake, undue influence, or some other vitiating factor.[124]

(10) Assimilation of gifts to disadvantageous contracts

Introduction

29.56 Where a transaction is in substance a gift rather than a reciprocal bargain, equity will treat it as such, looking at the substance rather than the form of the transaction.[125] Conversely, where the transaction is plainly a reciprocal contract, that it may be a bad bargain for one party will not make the transaction a gift for the purposes of determining whether it may be rescinded. The fundamental rule is that, subject to narrow exceptions, a person is bound by contracts that they have entered, irrespective of their understanding or the fairness of the terms.[126] That is not so for gifts. A sufficient lack of understanding as to the effect of the instrument is a ground for rescinding it. The special principles applicable to the rescission of gifts therefore do not apply to contracts.[127]

29.57 The distinction between gifts and disadvantageous contracts has, however, tended to be confused in relation to guarantees and like transactions. Whilst the earlier confusion has been dispelled in English law, in Australia it has become entrenched in the jurisprudence relating to surety wives.

Securing the debts of another

29.58 Where security is given for another's debts, and the security transaction is voidable because undue influence is exercised by that other to the creditor's knowledge, a series of cases in the nineteenth century described the party providing security as a 'volunteer' and the transaction as 'voluntary'.[128] The idea that the security was akin to a gift formed part of the explanation of the right to rescind it. That approach was later abandoned in England,[129] and

---

[124] In *R v Hinks* [2001] 2 AC 241 the donor would appear to have had a right to rescind the gifts for the donee's undue influence. In *R v Lawrence* [1972] AC 626, even if there had been a contract to pay a fare of £7, it would have been voidable for fraud. In *R v Gomez* [1993] AC 442 the court found that the contract was voidable. See also *R v Hinks* [2001] 2 AC 241, 276.

[125] *Huguenin v Baseley* (1807) 14 Ves Jun 273, 301; 33 ER 526. In *Van der Merwe v Goldman* [2016] 4 WLR 71 [31] Morgan J held that the distinction rested upon whether consideration had been given for the benefit conferred by the transaction.

[126] *L'Estrange v F Graucob Ltd* [1934] 2 KB 394 (CA); *Saunders v Anglia Building Society* [1971] AC 1004, 1016; *Hart v O'Connor* [1985] AC 1000 (PC—NZ); also, *Wilton v Farnworth* (1948) 76 CLR 646, 649.

[127] Thus in *Ellis v Ellis* (1909) 26 TLR 166, 167, in rescinding a settlement vitiated by mistake as to its effects, Warrington J specifically noted that the case involved a gift, not a contract, and in *Baird v BCE Holdings Pty Ltd* (1996) 40 NSWLR 374, 382 Young J correctly declined to rescind a contract for mistake as to its effects, holding that authorities concerned with the rescission of gifts were inapposite. See also, *Jones v Moss* [2007] NSWSC 969 [51] (consideration for deed of conveyance not appearing on face of the instrument). The importance of confining the special rules concerned with rescission for mistake to voluntary dispositions was underlined also by Sir Andrew Park in *Smithson v Hamilton* [2008] 1 WLR 1453 [111], [119], [120] (pension scheme; discussed B Häcker, 'Mistakes in the Execution of Documents: Recent Cases on Rectification and Related Doctrines' (2008) 19 KLJ 293, 330).

[128] Examples include *Archer v Hudson* (1844) 7 Beav 551, 560; 49 ER 1180; (1846) 15 LJ Ch 211, 211, col 2; *Maitland v Irving* (1846) 15 Sim 437, 443; 60 ER 688; *Blackie v Clarke* (1852) 15 Beav 595, 600–01; 51 ER 669. See further S Gardner, 'A Confused Wife's Equity' (1982) 2 OJLS 130, 133–34.

[129] *Bainbrigge v Browne* (1881) 28 ChD 188, 197–99.

forms no part of the rules governing the right of a wife or unmarried partner to rescind a guarantee or mortgage given to secure their partner's debts.[130]

The old approach has, however, become entrenched in Australia, where classification of the surety wife as a 'volunteer' has been used to explain why rescission is available if she does not understand the transaction, and the lending institution does not *inter alia* take steps to explain it.[131] A wife is said to be a 'volunteer' in this context if she obtained no financial benefit from the loan provided,[132] and it appears to be a condition to rescission for lack of understanding that she was a 'volunteer' in this sense.[133]   **29.59**

Criticism

It is wrong in principle to assimilate gifts with security transactions when the surety or mortgagor obtains no financial benefit from the loan. Gifts are more easily rescinded than reciprocal contracts because the law's interest in protecting bargains, and in the security of contracts, is not engaged in the case of a gift, even if made by deed. The maxim *pacta sunt servanda* does not apply to a mere gift. Those principles do not cease to apply if one party to a contract obtains no financial benefit from it. Guarantees and mortgages are contracts not gifts, irrespective of a court's assessments of the financial advantage obtained by the surety. That a bargain is a bad one is relevant to the right to rescind only insofar as it may be probative of the existence of undue influence, unconscionable conduct, or other vitiating factor.[134] It does not turn a contract into a gift so as to attract the rules applicable to the rescission of donations.   **29.60**

The special rules developed in Australia to protect wives securing their husbands' debts are driven by judicial policy. The analysis of the disposition as 'voluntary' obscures this, and wrongly suggests that it has a basis in established principle. The rule in fact places those providing security for their partner's debts on the same footing as persons of unsound mind,[135] and is driven by the same kinds of outcome-driven analysis that formerly disabled heirs and reversioners from contracting when a different judicial policy held sway.   **29.61**

The requirement that the transaction must have been of no financial benefit to the wife has no basis in principle, and the application of this test in a relationship between husband and wife raises factual questions that a court is ill-equipped to decide. Moreover, given that the rules are policy driven, they should be judged by reference to how far they give effect to the law's objective. The policy justification for requiring that a wife obtain no financial benefit as   **29.62**

---

[130] *Royal Bank of Scotland plc v Etridge (No 2)* [2002] 2 AC 773; D O'Sullivan, 'Developing O'Brien' (2002) 118 LQR 337.
[131] *Yerkey v Jones* (1939) 63 CLR 649, 685; *Garcia v National Australia Bank* (1998) 194 CLR 395, 408–09, 411, 412.
[132] *Garcia v National Australia Bank* (1998) 194 CLR 395, 409, 411, 412. This has since been construed to mean a direct or immediate benefit: *Agripay Pty Ltd v Byrne* [2011] 2 QdR 501 (CA) [11], also [62], [78].
[133] *Garcia v National Australia Bank* (1998) 194 CLR 395, 409; applied, eg *Dowdle v Pay Now for Business Pty Ltd* [2012] QSC 272 [101], [103], [107].
[134] *Huguenin v Baseley* (1807) 14 Ves Jun 273, 296; 33 ER 526; *Zamet v Hyman* [1961] 1 WLR 1142 (CA) 1149 ('extravagantly one-sided', 'astonishing' document); *Alec Lobb (Garages) Ltd v Total Oil Great Britain Ltd* [1983] 1 WLR 87, 94–95; [1985] 1 WLR 173 (CA) 181–83.
[135] *Imperial Loan Company Limited v Stone* [1892] 1 QB 599 (CA); *Baldwyn v Smith* [1900] 1 Ch 588; *Gibbons v Wright* (1954) 91 CLR 423; *Hart v O'Connor* [1985] AC 1000 (PC—NZ); *The Special Trustees for Great Ormond Street Hospital for Children v Rushin* [2003] All ER (D) 598; see Chap 7, para [7.45], [7.51].

a condition of permitting her to rescind by reason of her own misunderstanding is difficult to understand.[136]

C. Deeds

29.63 The discussion here considers and rejects the view that deeds cannot generally be rescinded at common law and that resort must be had to equitable principles. It also discusses the principles applicable to the cancellation of deeds.

(1) Introduction

29.64 At common law, special rules concerning the effects of forgery, interlineation and erasure, and mistake (the plea of *non est factum*) did much of the work that might have been done by rescission. Beyond these cases the sanctity of deeds in the early common law admitted few instances in which an instrument regular on its face would not be enforced. The special status of deeds at common law led the courts of Chancery to develop a jurisdiction to set aside deeds procured by improper means, and historically one of the foundations for that jurisdiction was the absence of any defence at common law. In time the sanctity of deeds at common law was whittled away. Its remnants today are that contracts by deed do not have to be supported by consideration, and the rule that a deed raises a range of common law evidentiary estoppels.[137] These do not however prevent duress or fraud from being averred.[138]

29.65 Despite this whittling away, it is still often thought that deeds are rescinded only in equity, not at common law. That is also the impression from the literature, which indicates that the common law confines itself to specific rules concerning the effects of interlineation, erasure, forgery, and the plea of *non est factum*. The only exception is said to be duress.[139] The older works present a similar picture.[140] In the United States there appears to be no recognized common law jurisdiction to rescind deeds; that is done in equity.[141]

---

[136] Cf Canadian law also regards lack of benefit as material: *North West Life Assurance Co of Canada v Shannon Height Developments Ltd* (1987) 4 ACWS (3d) 246 (BCCA). See also *Bank of Montreal v Collum* (2004) 242 DLR (4th) 510, 29 BCLR (4th) 18 (BCCA) [37]–[45]. Cf MH Ogilvie 'The Reception of Etridge (No 2) in Canada' [2008] JBL 191, 201.

[137] T Chitty, A Denning, and C Harvey, *A Selection of Leading Cases on the Various Branches of the Law: With Notes by John William Smith* (13th edn, 1929) vol 2, 754–65; J Morrison and H Goolden, *A Treatise on Deeds by Robert F Norton* (2nd edn, 1928) 151; H Beale (ed), *Chitty on Contracts* (34th edn, 2021) vol 1, [1-039], [1-043], [1-047].

[138] J Morrison and H Goolden, *A Treatise on Deeds by Robert F Norton* (2nd edn, 1928) 151; H Beale (ed), *Chitty on Contracts* (34th edn, 2021) vol 1, [1-047].

[139] J Morrison and H Goolden, *A Treatise on Deeds by Robert F Norton* (2nd edn, 1928) 4–5, 151; G Dworkin, *Odgers' Construction of Deeds and Statutes* (5th edn, 1967) 3–5; D McDonnell and J Monroe (eds), *Kerr on the Law of Fraud and Mistake* (7th edn, 1952) 443–48.

[140] E Coke, *The First Part of the Institutes of the Law of England or a Commentary upon Littleton* (17th edn, 1817) vol 1, [35b]; C Viner, *A General Abridgment of Law and Equity* (2nd edn, 1793) vol 8 'Faits', 36–42, 45, 57–59, 90, 91; R Preston (ed), *Sheppard's Touchstone of Common Assurances* (7th edn, 1820) 61, 70.

[141] J Dawson and G Palmer, *Cases on Restitution* (2nd edn, 1969) 311. See also H Black, *A Treatise on the Rescission of Contracts and Cancellation of Written Instruments* (1916) 25–27, 30–60, 131–33, 592–94, 1031–36, 1554–56.

29. GIFTS AND DEEDS   627

In fact, however, the common law has long recognized that duress provides a defence to an action on a deed, and in the mid-nineteenth century it developed an equivalent rule for fraud. Despite this, the subject is almost completely neglected in the literature, and this has promoted the misconception that deeds must always be rescinded in equity. **29.66**

The point is unlikely to matter in most cases. However, it might where the party to a contract under seal wishes to obtain the advantages that rescission at common law confers, such as the automatic extinction of the contract and the immediate recovery of legal title. **29.67**

(2) Duress

It is an ancient rule of the common law that duress is an independent defence to an action upon a deed regular on its face, and which is signed, sealed, and delivered.[142] The rule might have been founded on some forgotten statute.[143] The leading authority remains *Whelpdale's case*,[144] notwithstanding that it was decided by the Court of King's Bench as long ago as 1604. It established that duress made a deed 'voidable' not void, did not provide the basis for a plea of *non est factum*, and was to be specially pleaded as a defence. It was later said that evidence of duress was only admissible if a defence of duress was specially pleaded, and could not be led under a plea of *non est factum*,[145] underlining its status as a defence separate from that plea. **29.68**

There is some uncertainty whether it is duress itself that provides the defence, or whether duress permits the party imposed to elect to rescind, and it is the rescission that gives rise to a defence. Although the rule today for simple contracts is that it is rescission, and not the ground for rescission, that provides a defence, the principles regarding deeds obtained by duress were established in a quite different era. In particular, they well preceded the now familiar distinction between void and voidable contracts. Some support for the view that duress itself makes a deed unenforceable is to be found in *Barton v Armstrong*.[146] The Privy Council there held that a deed was 'void' as against the plaintiff because procured by duress.[147] **29.69**

But the preferable view is that a deed procured by duress remains valid and enforceable unless and until it is set aside. That was the opinion of Holmes J in *Fairbanks v Snow*,[148] who held that the court in *Whelpdale's case*[149] meant what it said when it described a deed procured by duress as 'voidable', and noted that the position was different if the duress went 'to **29.70**

---

[142] J Ames, *Lectures on Legal History and Miscellaneous Legal Essays* (1913) 113, fn 1. For Year Book authority, W Holdsworth, *A History of English Law* (A Goodhart et al, ed) (7th edn, 1956) vol 8, 51; see also D Ibbetson, *A Historical Introduction to the Law of Obligations* (1999) 71–72. For the formal requirements of deeds today, Law of Property (Miscellaneous Provisions) Act 1989, s 1; Companies Act 2006, s 46.
[143] J Ames, *Lectures on Legal History and Miscellaneous Legal Essays* (1913) 113.
[144] (1604) 5 Co Rep 119a, 119a; 77 ER 239, 240.
[145] 'And yet, where duress or threats are the defence, there is authority upon authority that they cannot be given in evidence upon non est factum, but must be pleaded specially': *Edwards v Brown, Harries and Stephens* (1831) 1 C & J 307, 313; 148 ER 1436, 1439.
[146] [1976] AC 104 (PC — Aust).
[147] *Barton v Armstrong* [1976] AC 104 (PC — Aust) 120 'the appeal should be allowed and a declaration made that the deeds in question were executed by Barton under duress and are void so far as concerns him'.
[148] 13 NE 596 (1887).
[149] (1604) 5 Co Rep 119a, 77 ER 239.

the height of such bodily compulsion as turns the ostensible party into a mere machine'.[150] In that event, the deed would be of no effect at all. After reviewing Year Book authority, Holmes J held that threats by a stranger made without the knowledge or privity of the obligee provided no ground for avoiding a promissory note, which was therefore enforceable notwithstanding that the threats had caused the obligor to execute it in fear for her husband's life.[151]

29.71 Although there is no authority on the point, by analogy with the rules for fraud, the transaction should be avoided if and when the party imposed upon elects to disaffirm it.

(3) Fraud

29.72 Although it has been said that the common law affords no defence to one induced to enter a deed by fraud of a kind that does not fall within one of the common law's special rules as to forgery, interlineation, erasure, and *non est factum,* and this is the law in parts of the United States, it was probably English law only prior to the middle of the nineteenth century. The preferable view is that today deeds can be rescinded at common law for fraud, and that it is not necessary to have resort to equitable principles to do so.

The view that fraud provides no defence to a deed at common law

29.73 Professor Ames successfully promoted the idea that, unlike duress, fraud does not provide an independent legal defence to a deed in English law; the defrauded party must in such a case turn to equity.[152] Ames concludes that fraud only became a defence to an action on a deed in courts of law when section 83 of the Common Law Procedure Act 1854 permitted the equitable defence of fraud to be raised. English scholars followed Ames' view.[153] It probably influenced the rule in the United States, which is that fraud inducing entry into a deed (as distinct from fraud in its execution) provides no defence at law to an action to enforce a deed.[154] Ames' view implies that fraud also provides no ground for rescinding a transaction under seal in order to recover money or property transferred. The claimant must turn to equity for this.

The authorities

29.74 Ames' view of English law is principally founded on Lord Abinger's opinion in *Mason v Ditchbourne and Sarson*,[155] and on *Wright v Campbell*.[156] Looked at in isolation, these cases

---

[150] *Fairbanks v Snow* 13 NE 596, 598 (1887). Holmes J said that duress renders a contract voidable for the same reason that fraud does; in both cases 'the party has been subjected to an improper motive'. This part of his reasoning was adopted by the Privy Council in *Barton v Armstrong* [1976] AC 104 (PC—Aust) 118.
[151] *Fairbanks v Snow* 13 NE 596, 599 (1887).
[152] J Ames, *Lectures on Legal History and Miscellaneous Legal Essays* (1913) 106.
[153] W Barbour, 'A History of Contract in Early English Equity' in P Vinogradoff (ed), *Oxford Studies in Social and Legal History Volume 4* (1914) 1, 23. To similar effect, but discussing the early law, D Ibbetson, *A Historical Introduction to the Law of Obligations* (1999) 72.
[154] J Ames, *Lectures on Legal History and Miscellaneous Legal Essays* (1913) 106, fn 4; E Abbott, 'Fraud as a Defence at Law in the Federal Courts' (1915) 15 Columbia LR 489; J Dawson and G Palmer, *Cases on Restitution* (2nd edn, 1969) 311.
[155] (1835) 1 M & Rob 460, 174 ER 158.
[156] (1861) 2 F & F 393, 175 ER 1111.

29. GIFTS AND DEEDS 629

provide strong support for his analysis. But both decisions were overtaken by subsequent developments that Ames does not address.

Mason v Ditchbourne and Sarson[157] was an action on a bond to secure an obligation to pay for a legal practice purchased by the defendants, who pleaded *non est factum* and also that the bond was obtained by fraud and covin. Lord Abinger held that the defendants could not lead evidence that the bond was obtained by fraudulent misrepresentations about the extent of the legal practice they had bought, for the following reason:

29.75

> My opinion is, that the defence which you rely upon, is not open to you on this record. The old books tell us that the plea of fraud and covin is a kind of special *non est factum*, and it ends 'and so the defendant says it is not his deed.' Such a plea would, I admit, let in evidence of fraud in the execution of the instrument declared upon: as if its contents were misread, or a different deed were substituted for that which the party intended to execute. You may perhaps be relieved in equity, but in a Court of Law it has always been my opinion that such a defence is unavailing, when once it is shewn that the party knew perfectly well the nature of the deed he was executing.[158]

Ames does not, however, mention the proceedings that followed *Mason v Ditchbourne and Sarson*, reported by way of notes.[159] These indicate that on proceedings for a new trial Lord Abinger's opinion was rejected, and that evidence of fraud was held to be admissible as a defence to the bond sued upon, although it is unclear whether the evidence was admitted as proof of a plea of *non est factum*, or in support of a separate defence of fraud. The latter is more likely.[160]

29.76

Despite the fact that Lord Abinger's decision was effectively reversed on appeal, his views in *Mason v Ditchbourne* were accepted in *Wright v Campbell*[161] in 1861. The plaintiff sued to enforce a deed whereby the defendant covenanted to repay the plaintiff sums he had advanced to a third person. The defendant pleaded first, *non est factum*, and second, fraud. Byles J stated at the outset of the case:

29.77

> The defendants having read it, and executed it, knowing its contents, surely, though you showed the transaction out of which it arose to have been fraudulent, yet in an action at law, on the deed, that would not be available as a legal defence.[162]

After argument in which *Mason v Ditchbourne* was cited by counsel, the report continued:

> Byles J, having read the case, declared that he should rule in accordance with it; that the plea of fraud, in an action on a specialty, was a kind of special plea of *non est factum*, and

---

[157] (1835) 1 M & Rob 460, 174 ER 158.
[158] *Mason v Ditchbourne and Sarson* (1835) 1 M & Rob 460, 460–61; 174 ER 158, 158.
[159] *Connop v Holmes* (1835) 2 CM & R 719, 720; 150 ER 304, 305, note (a); *Mason v Ditchbourne and Sarson* (1835) 1 M & Rob 460, 462; 174 ER 158, 159 (end note).
[160] That is because this view was consistent with the decision in *Edwards v Brown, Harries and Stephens* (1831) 1 C & J 307, 148 ER 1436 four years previously, which decided that evidence of fraud could not be led to substantiate a plea of *non est factum*, but implied that it could to support a defence of fraud specially pleaded. That was also consistent with the rule for duress, which also did not support a plea of *non est factum*, but provided an independent defence that was to be specially pleaded. See also CG Addison, *Treatise on the Law of Contracts* (1847) 1, 2, 5; D Ibbetson, *A Historical Introduction to the Law of Obligations* (1999) 72.
[161] (1861) 2 F & F 393, 175 ER 1111.
[162] *Wright v Campbell* (1861) 2 F & F 393, 175 ER 1111.

would let in evidence of fraud in regard to the actual execution of the deed, as its contents being misread or misrepresented; but that no other defence, founded on the nature of the transaction, out of which it arose, was admissible or available. Verdict for the plaintiff.[163]

29.78 To the extent that *Wright v Campbell* is founded on Lord Abinger's decision in *Mason v Ditchbourne* it rests on unstable ground because, although this was apparently not brought to the attention of Byles J, his decision had been overturned. Neither case provides convincing support for Ames' view.

29.79 More importantly, a group of other cases indicate fairly clearly that by the middle of the nineteenth century, courts of law did recognize fraud as an independent defence to an action on a deed. This followed, and seems to have been a part of, the progressive expansion of what could be averred as a defence to an action on a deed.[164] The early cases were *Edwards v Brown, Harries and Stephens*,[165] *D'Aranda v Houston*[166] (which Lord Abinger declined to follow in *Mason v Ditchbourne*) and *Connop v Holmes*.[167] In *Spencer v Handley and Burges*[168] the court clearly indicated that it was a defence to a claim on a deed that the underlying transaction was procured by the obligee's fraud, although it seems to have recognized that new ground was being broken.[169] This approach was confirmed in *Evans v Edmonds*[170] in 1853, and two years later *Canham v Barry*[171] decided that fraud could be raised as a special plea in defence to an action upon a deed, wholly separate from *non est factum*.

Fraud as a defence to action on a deed

29.80 The decisions just discussed indicate that fraud does provide an independent defence to a claim upon a deed at common law. This mirrors the rule for duress. The difference between the two was, however, that whilst the duress rule was long established, the law concerning fraud only emerged during the first half of the nineteenth century.

Fraud as a ground for rescinding a deed

29.81 In *Grenville v Da Costa*[172] the court held that an agreement could be 'rescinded' to bring money had and received 'although the contract be under seal'. Although that case involved rescission for repudiation, at the time it was decided the courts drew no relevant distinction between rescission for subsequent repudiation and pre-contractual fraud.[173] The leading text on vendor and purchaser cited the case as authority for the general proposition that 'although the contract is under seal, yet the purchaser may, if he have a right to rescind the contract, bring an action for money had and received, to recover back his purchase-money'.[174]

---

[163] (1861) 2 F & F 393, 394; 175 ER 1111, 1112.
[164] Obligor of a bond could aver its illegal consideration as a defence: *Collins v Blantern* (1765) 2 Wils KB 341, 95 ER 847, plea of *non est factum* being inappropriate: 2 Wils KB 341, 352; 95 ER 847, 853. Absence of the bargained for consideration for a deed (patented devices for net making) also a good defence where buyer 'cheated and imposed upon': *Hayne v Maltby* (1789) 3 TR 438, 100 ER 665.
[165] (1831) 1 C & J 307, 148 ER 1436.
[166] (1834) 6 Car & P 511, 172 ER 1342.
[167] (1835) 2 CM & R 719, 150 ER 304.
[168] (1842) 4 Man & G 414, 134 ER 169.
[169] (1842) 4 Man & G 414, 419–20; 134 ER 169, 172 (Maule J and Tindal CJ).
[170] (1853) 13 CB 777, 138 ER 1407.
[171] (1855) 15 CB 597, 139 ER 558.
[172] (1797) Peake Add Cas 113, 170 ER 213.
[173] See Chap 3, para [3.27].
[174] E Sugden, *A Concise and Practical Treatise of the Law of Vendors and Purchasers of Estates* (14th edn, 1862) 237. See also S Williston, 'Repudiation of Contracts' (1901) 14 HLR 317, 328.

There is also a range of other suggestions that deeds may be set aside for fraud at common law.[175]

The cases imply that fraud provides a right to rescind a deed at common law, and that re‑ **29.82** scission, not the fraud itself, provides the defence, mirroring the position as to the effect of fraud on contracts not under seal.[176]

(4) Cancellation of deeds

Source of power to cancel

Before the Judicature reforms the business of cancelling deeds was dominated by courts **29.83** of Chancery, and on one view that was because the common law courts lacked power to do so.[177] If this is correct, the court's power to make orders for cancellation today is purely equitable, and to be exercised in accordance with equitable principles.

But the business of cancelling deeds improperly procured was probably domin‑ **29.84** ated by Chancery before the Judicature reforms not because courts of law had no power at all to cancel, but because in many cases of fraud and imposition the common law's procedures were regarded as inadequate to do justice.[178] The old common law courts did exercise a power to order the cancellation of deeds where they had been used for fraudulent purposes; in particular, where releases were executed to defeat a bona fide legal claim.[179] There were also other discrete situations where the common law courts would try the question of whether a transaction was tainted by fraud, and upon proof of fraud, act to deny effect to the transaction. The two principal ex‑ amples were devises, which were always dealt with at law,[180] and conveyances by way of

---

[175] *Pilbrow v Pilbrow's Atmospheric Railway and Canal Propulsion Company* (1848) 5 CB 440, 453; 136 ER 950, 955, '[i]t is not true, that a deed that is obtained by fraud is therefore void. The rule is, that the party defrauded may, at his election, treat it as void'; *Stump v Gaby* (1852) 2 De M & G 623, 630; 42 ER 1015, 1018 'I do not deny that a deed may be so fraudulent as to be set aside at law; this however is not such a case; but I will assume that the con‑ veyance might have been set aside in equity for fraud'. See also *Saunders v Anglia Building Society* [1971] AC 1004, 1026; H Ballow and J Fonblanque, *A Treatise of Equity* (1793) (first pub anon 1737 and attrib Henry Ballow) vol 1, 61; J Willis, *Pleadings in Equity* (1820) 118 note (a); J Hill, *A Practical Treatise on the Law Relating to Trustees* (1845) 116; G Spence, *The Equitable Jurisdiction of the Court of Chancery* (1846) vol 1, 622.

[176] *Dawes v Harness* (1875) LR 10 CP 166, 167–68; *United Shoe Machinery Company of Canada v Brunet* [1909] AC 330 (PC—Canada) 338; *Coastal Estates Pty Ltd v Melevende* [1965] VR 433 (Full Ct) 441; see also *Gordon v Street* [1899] 2 QB 641 (CA) 644, 650–51.

[177] G Spence, *The Equitable Jurisdiction of the Court of Chancery* (1846) vol 1, 624 'we find bills seeking relief on the ground of the inability of the Courts of Law to afford the specific relief which the case required, as the cancella‑ tion of a deed'; *Duncan v Worrall* (1822) 10 Price 31, 44; 147 ER 232, 236 (insurance policy vitiated by misrepresen‑ tation) 'if ... I could have decided that the Defendant's possession of it was the effect of misrepresentation on the part of the person who obtained it, and claimed to avail himself of it, I must have ordered the paper to be delivered up to be cancelled. A jury or Court of Law could not make any such order ...'.

[178] J Mitford, *A Treatise on the Pleadings in Suits in the Court of Chancery by English Bill* (2nd edn, 1787) 116; G Spence, *Equitable Jurisdiction of the Court of Chancery* (1846) vol 1, 622–26; *Bright v Enyon* (1757) 1 Burr 390, 395– 96; 97 ER 365, 367–68, where Lord Mansfield refers to the concurrent jurisdiction of courts of law and equity in cases of fraud, and notes that procedures in Chancery allow 'the better investigating truth, and ... more compleat redress'.

[179] *Payne v Rogers* (1780) 1 Dougl 407, 99 ER 261; *Legh v Legh* (1799) 1 B & P 447, 126 ER 1002; *Barker and Owen v Richardson* (1827) 1 Y & J 362, 148 ER 710.

[180] Testamentary dispositions of real estate tainted by fraud were always dealt with in proceedings at law, on an issue *devisavit vel non* (*Bates v Graves* (1793) 2 Ves Jun 287, 30 ER 637 esp Reporter's Note; 1 Ves Jun Supp 264, 34 ER 781), and proof of fraud ended in a verdict of *non devisavit*—he did not devise: see *Wyndham v Chetwynd* (1755) unreported, cited *Bright v Eynon* (1757) 1 Burr 390, 397; 97 ER 365, 369, where it was said 'the court dir‑ ected the jury to find "non devisavit", though there was a devise in fact; but it was obtained by fraud, and therefore

fine.[181] There is no reason to doubt that a court of law could order a deed to be cancelled upon proof that it had been avoided for duress or fraud, if sufficient cause to make such an order was shown.

29.85 The correct view is that deeds are voidable for duress and fraud both at common law and in equity, and that the court's power to cancel a deed incidental to its rescission also derives from both common law and equitable principles.

Effect of orders for cancellation

29.86 In earlier times an order for cancelling a deed provided for the instrument to be defaced in a manner that prevented or inhibited action on it at law.[182] Following the withering away of the old rules concerning proof of deeds, orders for delivery up and cancellation now have a purely evidential function, and serve to protect the rescinding party and the public by, in the case of delivery up, removing the instrument from the defendant's possession, and in the case of cancellation, advertising its invalidity. Accordingly, if a deed is cancelled as part of an order for rescission, as by the signatures being cut off or the words 'cancelled' written across it, an appeal court effectively reinstates the former position by declaring that the instrument is unaffected by the cutting or writing.[183]

---

considered as no devise at all'. For subsequent proceedings, *Wyndham v Chetwynd* (1756) 1 Keny 253, 96 ER 984; (1757) 2 Keny 122, 96 ER 121, 1 Bl W 95, 96 ER 53, 1 Burr 414, 97 ER 377 (where the jury verdict of 'no devise' is reported). See also JN Pomeory, *A Treatise on Equity Jurisprudence* (5th edn, 1941) vol 3, [913].

[181] The courts of common law would deny effect to fines on proof of fraud: W Cruise, *An Essay on the Nature and Operation of Fines and Recoveries* (2nd edn, 1786) vol 1, ch 15 (discussing proceeding by writ of error, writ of deceit, motion, pleas and acts in pais; fraud is discussed at 311–15). Warrants of attorney confessing judgment might also have been open to attack at law on the ground of fraud: see *Barnesly v Powel* (1749) 1 Ves Sen 284, 288; 27 ER 1034, 1036.

[182] See further Chap 3, para [3.37].

[183] *Bonyton v Boynton*, 19 June 1878 (CA) reproduced in A Ingpen, F Bloxam, and H Garrett (eds), *Seton on Decrees* (7th edn, 1912) vol 3, 2234.

Index

affirmation
  awareness of rights
    in Australia 23.02, 23.42–23.48
    deliberate failure to inquire 23.54
    electing party, knowledge of rights 23.35–23.39
    in England 23.02, 23.40–23.41
    intention, relation to 23.102
    in New Zealand 23.02, 23.49
    not required in other parts of Commonwealth 23.42–23.50
    proof of 23.55–23.56
    in Singapore 23.02, 23.50
    what must be known 23.53
  communication
    insurance contract 23.59
    rationale, supporting 23.60
    requirement for 23.57, 23.58, 23.60
  delay causing waiver by *see* **delay**
  election between rights 23.04–23.05
  general principles 23.01–23.02
  generally irrevocable 23.103–23.109
  gifts, voidable 23.08–23.09
  from inaction 23.90
  inconsistent rights, electing party holding 23.07
  intention, no requirement of
    awareness of rights, relation to 23.102
    conduct not known to other party 23.101
    general rule 23.98–23.100
  irrevocable, being
    general rule 23.103
    subsequent discovery of new grounds, exception where 23.104–23.109
  juristic nature 23.04–23.09
  justification 23.10–23.13
  loss of right to rescind 23.02
  onus of proof 23.110
  pleading 23.111–23.112
  pleading rescission in the alternative, effect of 23.83
  remaining in possession as evidence of intention 24.104
  reservation of rights, effect of 23.91–23.96
  rules, application of 23.13
  subsequent discovery of new grounds, exception where 23.104–23.109
    causal significance 23.106–23.107
    new information providing 23.105
    revocability of earlier affirmation 23.104–23.109
    status of first affirmation 23.108
    totality of conduct, right to rescind arising from 23.109
  unequivocal words of conduct, by
    application of principle 23.64–23.90
    attempted resale of property acquired 23.86–23.88
    attempting to rescind in part 23.89
    blameworthiness of conduct causing rescission 23.65
    contractual rights, invoking or asserting 23.68–23.70
    general principle 23.61–23.63
    ground of rescission, relevance 23.65–23.67
    insured property, instructions as to 23.85
    of intention to confirm gift 23.63
    litigation, conduct of 23.79–23.82
    making contractual payments 23.77–23.78
    money payable on rescission, retaining 23.74–23.75
    receiving contractual payments 23.76
    remaining in possession 23.71–23.73
    working on property acquired 23.84
  vitiating factor, affirming party free from
    breach of fiduciary duty 23.16–23.17
    drunkenness 23.15
    duress 23.14
    mental impairment 23.15
    misrepresentation 23.18–23.34
    mistake 23.18–23.34
    non-disclosure 23.18–23.34
    see also **non-disclosure**
    undue influence 23.14
    see also **mistake**
agent
  bribery *see* **bribery**
  conflict of interest *see* **conflict of interest**; **fiduciaries, transactions with**
assumpsit
  breach of warranty, pleading 3.19
  general assumpsit
    nature of 3.20
    relationship with special assumpsit 3.22–3.23, 3.29
    rescission, plea requiring 3.24–3.26
    value of services under repudiated contract, claim for 14.42–14.43
  indebitatus assumpsit 3.21
  nature of 3.19
  special assumpsit
    relationship with general assumpsit 3.22–3.23, 3.29
Australia, law in
  affirmation
    awareness of rights 23.02, 23.42–23.48

634   INDEX

Australia, law in (*cont.*)
  residual knowledge of rights to
    election   23.46–23.48
  breach of fiduciary duty   16.52
  chattels, non-contractual transfer   14.11
  compensation for improvements and
    repairs   17.52–17.54
  constructive trust   16.21
  election to rescind   11.97–11.101
  equitable compensation   2.11
  financial adjustments, equitable interest   17.20
  guarantees   5.49–5.50, 5.55
  innocent misrepresentation
    where contractual right to reject lost   27.58
    contractual term, incorporation as   27.40–27.43
    sale of goods, bar to rescission of   27.48,
      27.50–27.51
    transfer of title to personal property, bar to
      rescission for   27.29–27.30
    transfer of title to real property, bar to rescission
      for   27.12
  mental infirmity   7.60
  mistake
    common   7.10
    rescission for   7.31–7.32
    unilateral   7.20–7.22
  mortgages   19.26, 19.27, 19.38
  property rights   13.30
  representation   4.23
  rescission on terms   19.26–19.30, 19.36–19.37
  third party wrongdoers, rescission
    against   19.11–19.12
  unconscionable bargain   7.103

bankruptcy
  discharge from, whether right to rescind
    surviving   25.17
  right to rescind not barred by, general rule   25.01
  supervening bankruptcy
    rescission to assert personal interest   25.08–25.10
    rescission to assert proprietary
      claim   25.04–25.07
    rescission to assert proprietary
      interest   25.05–25.07
  trustee in
    no better title than bankrupt, obtaining   25.14
    rescission as defence against   25.11
    undischarged bankrupt, contract
      with   25.12–25.16
bars to rescission
  affirmation *see* **affirmation**
  common law and equity, bars peculiar
    to   10.30–10.33
  contracting out *see under* **misrepresentation**
  delay *see* **delay**
  disproportionate effect
    general law   28.30
    statutory bar for   28.01–28.14
  estoppel   24.116–24.121
  impossibility of *restitutio in integrum see*
    impossibility of *restitutio in integrum*
  for non-fraudulent misrepresentation *see* **innocent
    misrepresentation**
  third party rights *see* **third party rights**
  winding-up *see* **winding-up**
bona fide purchaser
  common law and equitable doctrines of bona fide
    purchase   21.55–21.62
  of equitable title
    'mere equities'   21.69
    rescission at common law   21.64–21.67
    rescission in equity   21.68–21.70
  in equity   21.61–21.62
  of legal title   21.63
  no general protection   21.55
  onus of proof   21.71–21.76
  rescission   21.57–21.60
  when protected   21.56
breach of trust
  dispositions ineffective in   1.67–1.68
bribery   8.49–8.71
  agent
    bribe paid by   8.65–8.66
    character of   8.53
    remedies against   8.49
  benefits constituting   8.59–8.60
  conflict of interest, need for   8.54–8.55
  contract procured by, rescission
    at law and equity   8.51
    as void   8.50
  counterparty, implication of   8.61–8.64
  elements of   8.52–8.60
  fiduciary, meaning   8.53
  meaning   8.52
  money paid, proprietary claim to   16.55
  secrecy, element of   8.56–8.58
  third party, bribe paid by   8.67–8.71
  transactions ineffective for   1.87–1.89
buildings
  compensation for improvements and repairs   17.35
business sale agreements
  rescission, substitutive counter-restitution   18.60

Canada, law in
  affirmation   23.72, 23.112
  compensation   17.65
  election to rescind   11.104
  error in *substantialibus*   7.11, 7.34–7.37, 27.33
  guarantees   5.52, 5.54, 5.55
  innocent misrepresentation
    where contractual right to reject lost   27.60
    contractual term, incorporation as   27.45
    sale of goods, bar to rescission of   27.52
    transfer of title to personal property, bar to
      rescission for   27.32–27.33
    transfer of title to real property, bar to rescission
      for   27.14–27.15
  mistake, rescission for   7.34–7.37

proprietary claims 16.52
representation 4.23, 4.24
rescission on terms 19.32
unconscionable bargain 7.103
cancellation
  historical function 3.37
  modern function 12.08
causation
  duress
    but for test 6.67
    economic duress 6.65–6.68
    goods, duress to 6.65–6.68
    illegitimate pressure as 6.61
    independent advice, relevance of complainant taking 6.72
    lack of practical choice, separation of 6.58–6.60
    person, duress to 6.63–6.64
    proof of 6.07
    protest at time of transaction 6.70–6.71
    as question of fact 6.69
    relevant factors 6.69–6.73
    removal of pressure, steps to avoid transaction on 6.73
    subjective nature of 6.62
  fiduciaries, transactions with 8.72
  misrepresentation
    fraudulent misrepresentation 4.104, 4.109
    innocent misrepresentation 4.105–4.108
    reliance on representation 4.100–4.102
chattels
  benefits derived from
    accounting for 17.03, 17.06
    actual use or compensation, payment for 17.05–17.06
    assets not used, measure where 17.10–17.12
    joint acquisitions 17.14
    monetary receipt 17.42
    rescission in equity, available on 17.01
    use value, measure of 17.07–17.09
  counter-restitution 14.53–14.55
  mutual restitution (in equity) 15.12
cheques
  chattels 14.11, 14.12
  communication 11.31
  crossed 21.02, 21.03, 21.27, 21.28
  exchange product 14.33
  fraud 1.46, 1.98, 5.47, 14.12, 14.13, 21.05
  mental infirmity 7.53
  need to return to tender of benefits 14.60
  non-contractual payments 16.08
  non-disclosure 5.47
  pleading, disaffirming by 11.21
  proprietary claims 16.43
  restitution grounds 29.36
  retrospective title 16.44
  tracing into substitutes 16.11
choses in action
  basis of claim against assignee 21.34
  equitable assignments 21.25
  no new claim to rescind 21.35
  property not recoverable at law 14.21
  statutory assignments 21.26
  transfer of title 27.24
common law, rescission at
  absence of action for rescission 3.33
  bars to rescission at common law 10.32
  common law action, absence of 3.33
  contexts 10.22
  election to rescind at 11.53–11.56
  extinction of contract *see* **extinction of contract**
  fusion with equitable principles
    absence of 10.03–10.09
    equity rules prevailing 10.10–10.14
    reform 10.15–10.19
  grounds for rescission 10.23–10.24
  historical development 3.04
  insurance *see* **insurance**
  interaction between common law and equitable doctrines
    classes of case 10.39
    transactions voidable at law 10.43–10.46
  mutual restitution *see* **mutual restitution (at law)**
  proprietary claims *see* **proprietary claims**
  rescission in equity, distinctions with 10.34–10.38
  restitutio in integrum impossible *see* **impossibility of restitutio in integrum**
  transactions voidable at law
  supervening event barring rescission at law before election to rescind 10.43–10.46
  at time of election to rescind 10.40–10.42
  unilateral mistake 7.12
common mistake
  Commonwealth jurisdictions, approach in 7.10–7.11
  meaning 7.02
  as not ground for rescission 7.03, 7.07–7.09
compensation
  in Canada 17.65
  for deterioration and depreciation
    adjustment, not calling for 17.55
    inherent vice, due to 17.56
    measure of 17.60
    purchaser's claims 17.55–17.58
    purchaser's fault, arising from 17.56
    vendor's claims 17.59–17.60
  discretion in fixing 17.33
  equitable *see* **equitable compensation**
  for improvements and repairs
    in Australia 17.52–17.54
    defect in title, purchaser knowing of 17.39
    against fiduciary 17.41
    against fraudster 17.40, 17.51
    at instance of party in possession 17.36
    to land and buildings 17.35
    market value, equivalent improvement in 17.43–17.47
    measure of 17.43
    necessary 17.49

compensation (*cont.*)
  non-necessary 17.50
  purchaser's claims 17.48–17.54
  substantial, permanent or lasting 17.42
  tort, damages in 17.54
  undue influence, in case of 17.41
  vendor's claims 17.38–17.47
 insurance policies, cost 17.63
 for intervening improvements or
      deterioration 17.33
 irrelevant detriments 17.61–17.66
 meaning 17.34
 for serious detriment 17.66
 transaction expenses 17.62
 for wasted expenses 17.64
compromises
 entry into, duty of disclosure 5.59–6.64
   family arrangements 5.59
   general 5.59
   general releases 5.63–5.64
   releases unsupported by consideration 5.60–5.62
 family arrangements
   disclosure, duty of 5.59
   mistake 7.38–7.39
 time to seek 24.102
conflict of interest
 adverse duty clouding loyalty of fiduciary 8.01
 adverse interest, consent to 8.18–8.20
 bribery *see* **bribery**
 causation irrelevant 8.72–8.73
 company and director, transaction
      between 8.19–8.20
 complete disclosure, fiduciary making 8.21–8.25
 disinterested advice, obtaining
   independent advice 8.30–8.31, 8.40
   requirement 8.29
   scope of 8.32–8.33
 double employment 8.34–8.48
   adverse duty or interest, principal giving consent
      to 8.38–8.41
   breach of rule 8.34
   counterparty, fiduciary having interest in 8.35
   disclosure and advice, duty of
      fiduciary 8.42–8.44
   fair-dealing rule, meeting requirements of 8.36
   implication of counterparty 8.46–8.48
   substantive fairness 8.45
 fair-dealing rule *see* **fiduciaries, transactions with**
 substantive fairness requirement 8.26–8.28
 termination of relationship, transactions
      on 8.14–8.15
constructive trust
 in Australia 16.21
 equitable rescission, interest arising on 16.61,
      16.63–16.64
consumer insurance contracts
 disclosure, duty of 5.35
 statutory modification of common law for insurance
      premiums 14.82–14.84

consumer protection legislation
 rescission for misrepresentation 26.34–26.35
conversion
 legal title required for 14.17
 no retrospective liability for 14.15–14.16
 property transferred, claim for 14.14
 retrospective liability for 13.30
counter-restitution
 ability to make, impossibility of *restitutio in
      integrum* 18.33
 by accounting 15.57–15.59
 where asset changed
   delay in return 18.86
   deterioration 18.85
   interest in business 18.89
   in nature 18.87–18.90
   repairs and alterations enhancing value 18.90
   restrictive common law rules 18.91–18.92
 common law and equity compared 10.38
 by conditional relief
   effects 15.50–15.51
   'he who seeks equity must do equity'
      maxim 15.47
   nature of relief 15.46
 contrary authority 14.61–14.62
 financial adjustments *see* **financial adjustments**
 impossible
   asset recovered after sale 18.50–18.51
   basic rule 18.48
   some assets available and some not 18.49
 intangible benefits 18.100
 market decline, depreciation of assets owing
      to 18.93–18.98
 money, receipt of 18.103–18.105
 nature of obligation to make 14.45–14.51
 no need to offer 15.60–15.61
 where not required
   where assets and services worthless 18.46
   benefits obtained other than under
      contract 18.34–18.35
   costless benefits, in case of 18.39
   where defendant bound to confer
      benefits 18.43–18.45
   where inability to return asset or benefit as
      defendant's fault 18.36
   insurance fraud, in case of 18.40–18.42
   loss of asset following tender 18.37–18.38
   set-off 18.47
 to original transferee 21.45–21.47
 possession, occupation and use of asset
   of chattels 18.84
   general rule 18.77–18.78
   of land 18.80–18.83
   letting out 18.78
   restrictive common law rules 18.79–18.84
 rescission at law, benefits received by
      rescinding party
   categories of case 14.49–14.50
   chattels 14.53–14.55, 14.69–14.71

clarity of law, lack of 14.51
conditional relief, absence of 14.46
general rule 14.45
instruments, execution of 14.75
limits on 14.47
money 14.56–14.58, 14.76–14.85
nature of obligation to make
    counter-restitution 14.45–14.51
non-money benefits 14.60
practical considerations 14.75
principle 14.45–14.48
property able to be revested 14.69–14.71
property not able to be revested 14.72–14.75
return or tender, need for 14.52–14.65
security for counter-restitution 14.66–14.68
for services 14.86
shares, exception for 14.59, 14.72–14.73
strict approach to 14.68
tender rule 14.64–14.65
unilateral act, revesting title by 14.74
United States, position in 14.63–14.65
rescission in equity, benefits received by rescinding
    party 15.44–15.68
by accounting 15.57–15.59
by conditional relief 15.46–15.56
on equitable rescission by election 15.73–15.76
failure to satisfy conditions 15.52–15.55
general rule 15.44
independently enforceable right, lack of 15.62
lien 15.56
money 15.65–15.66
nature of obligation to make 15.45–15.62
offer, no need for 15.60–15.61
property 15.63–15.64
right limited to insisting on proper
    allowances 15.59
for services received 15.67–15.68
security for 14.66–14.68
services performed under contract
general rule 18.99
of salvage 18.100
self-help basis, rescission on 18.101
substitutive 18.52–18.76
where asset unavailable 18.70–18.71
business sale agreements, rescission of 18.60
Canadian law 18.58
cases on 18.57
disguised loans 18.59
in equity 18.55–18.61
flexibility, lack of 18.56
of fungibles 18.63–18.65
future of 18.62–18.76
no general bar 18.62
individual characteristics, unavailable asset
    having 18.71
law, not possible at 18.54
measure of 18.74–18.76
of non-fungibles 18.66–18.73
non-money benefits 18.68

where parties expecting resale 18.61
pecuniary 18.52
possibility of 18.52–18.53
for services 18.67
unique characteristics, asset with 18.73
value not reliably estimated, effect of 18.72

damages
claims in, circumstances of rescission giving rise
    to 2.01
compensatory 13.24–13.25
double recovery, principle against 2.06
equitable compensation, indistinguishable
    from 2.11
financial position of parties, adjusting 13.06
for innocent misrepresentation *see* **innocent
    misrepresentation**
measure of, equivalent to restitution 2.06
and relief on rescission 13.04
restitutio in integrum as object of 13.03
right to rescission, independent of 2.03–2.09
deceit
action in 4.09
claims to rescission and damages, giving rise to 2.03
purchase procured by 23.29
third party, of 8.67
tort of 4.08
deed, transaction effected by
cancellation
    effect of order 29.86
    source of power 29.83–29.85
common law, sanctity of deeds at 29.64
duress as defence to action on 29.66, 29.68–29.71
equity, rescission in 29.01, 29.65
fraud
    defence at common law 29.72–29.82
    rescission at common law 29.81–29.82
    United States, law in 29.72
gifts *see* **gifts**
void and voidable gifts 1.38
delay
after emancipation from vitiating factor
    inference of fact or presumption of
        law 24.66–24.70
    reasonable time, steps to rescind
        within 24.64–24.65
awareness of rights
    acquiescence and affirmation contrasted 24.61
    and laches 24.62
    statute of limitations, application of 24.63
    waiver by acquiescence 24.58–24.60
    waiver by affirmation 24.57
barring rescission, freedom from vitiating
    factors 24.38–24.56
board of directors, time to remove 24.103
compromise, time to seek 24.102
culpable 24.01
deterioration of asset, causing 18.55
doctrines of 24.01

delay (cont.)
  and duress 24.98–24.99
  effect of 24.66
  and estoppel 24.02
  general principles 24.01–24.02
  impossibility of *restitutio in integrum* 18.12–18.16
  inference of waiver, leading to 24.01
  investigation, time for 24.101
  knowledge, lapse of time without 24.56
  laches
    and acquiescence 24.11
    affirmatory 24.17
    amounting to 23.30
    awareness of rights 24.62
    and common law rights to rescind 24.18
    conduct permitting rescission, culpability of 24.92
    as equitable defence 24.15
    meaning 24.14
    onus of proof 24.53–24.56
    prejudice, significance of 24.114
    prejudicial 24.17, 24.19–24.21
    rescission barred by 24.16
    restitutio in integrum impossible, where 24.19–24.21
    vitiating factor, freedom from 24.49–24.53
  mere lapse of time 24.37
  prejudice, significance of 18.13, 24.01, 24.16, 24.71, 24.78, 24.80, 24.85–24.97
    as to acquiescence 24.112–24.113
    after election to rescind 24.115
    as to election to affirm 24.109–24.111
    laches 24.114
  prejudicial change of circumstances, rescission after 18.117
  speculating on outcome of bargain 24.100
  sale of goods 24.97
  statute of limitations, application of
    analogy, applying statute by 24.25–24.36, 24.54–24.55
    awareness of rights 24.63
    breach of statutory duty 24.27–24.28
    direct application of the statute 24.22–24.24
    estate or interest in land, recovery of 24.29–24.32
    fraud 24.27–24.28
    self-dealing and fair-dealing rules, transaction contrary to 24.33
    undue influence 24.34–24.35
    unreasonable delay 24.106–24.108
    vitiating factor, freedom from 24.54–24.55
  unreasonable
    circumstances of 24.71
    conduct permitting rescission, culpability of 24.91–24.97
    deteriorating assets, in case of 24.87
    donee's spending, gift increasing 24.86
    income, property producing 24.78
    interest in security of transaction 24.75–24.76
    ongoing mutual obligations, in case of 24.73
    ongoing risk and reward, contract involving 24.74
    prejudice, causing 24.85–24.90
    property, type of 24.77–24.84
    reversionary interests, in case of 24.80–24.83
    settlor rescinding settlement for own benefit 24.79
    share allotments, in case of 24.88–24.90
    speculative property, in case of 24.84
    statute of limitations, acting by analogy of 24.106–24.108
    transaction, type of 24.72
    without knowledge or laches 24.95–24.97
  vitiating factor, freedom from
    acquiescence 24.41–24.48
    affirmation 24.39–24.40
    general principle 24.38
    laches 24.49–24.53
    statute of limitations, application of 24.54–24.55
  waiver by acquiescence
    abandonment 24.04
    awareness of rights 24.58–24.61
    bar to rescission, as 24.10
    breach of fiduciary duty, in case of 24.45
    company, vendors' nominees controlling 24.46
    emancipation from vitiating factor, after 24.69
    and laches 24.11
    meanings 24.08–24.09
    misrepresentation, mistake or non-disclosure 24.43
    onus of proof 24.48
    prejudice, significance of 24.112–24.113
    pressure and exploitation, in case of 24.44
    principles 24.05
    rescission at law, application to 24.12–24.13
    trustee, sale of property to 24.47
    vitiating factor, freedom from 24.41–24.48
  waiver by affirmation
    awareness of rights 24.57, 24.61
    conduct permitting rescission, culpability of 24.93–24.94
    meaning 24.03
    prejudice, significance of 24.109–24.115
    principles 24.05
    remaining in possession as evidence of intention 24.104
    right of election, loss of 24.06–24.07
    vitiating factor, freedom from 24.39–24.40
    wrongful party, attributable to 24.105
directors
  misuse of powers by, to alienate company property 1.78
discretion
  in Australia 27.12, 27.30, 27.31
  application to rescission at law 24.12
  compensation 17.33
  conflict of interest 8.57
  counter-restitution 15.67
  disproportionate effect 28.03, 28.10, 28.36

INDEX 639

election to rescind 11.66, 11.86, 11.87, 11.92, 11.93–11.95, 11.102, 11.107
executory contracts 12.17
extinction of contract 12.06, 12.15, 12.17, 12.19, 12.22
fair-dealing rule 1.70, 28.36
grant of rescission 12.22–12.24
insurer's right to rescind 10.29
and misrepresentation 4.16, 4.69
New Zealand 11.102, 27.13, 27.31, 27.44
partial rescission 19.04
prejudice 24.111
proprietary claims 16.15, 16.69–16.70
rejection or reclaiming a gift 29.13–29.14
repayment and account 15.37
and rescission as defence 11.43
restitutio in integrum 13.07, 13.13, 13.15, 13.16, 13.23, 16.70, 17.20, 17.30, 17.31, 17.33, 18.25, 18.123
  where impossible 18.27, 18.31
separating spouses 5.20
voidable transactions 11.66
dishonest assistance
  elements 8.71
  liability 16.65–16.68
  retrospectivity 16.66
drunkenness
  affirmation, conditions for 23.15
  and unsoundness of mind 7.58
duress
  absence of practical choice or alternative *see* coercion requirement *below*
  acquiescence, evidence of 24.44
  affirmation, conditions for 23.14
  categories of 6.06
  causation
    but for test 6.67
    economic duress 6.65–6.68
    goods, duress to 6.65–6.68
    illegitimate pressure as 6.61
    independent advice, relevance of complainant taking 6.72
    lack of practical choice, separation of 6.58–6.60
    person, duress to 6.63–6.64
    proof of 6.07
    protest at time of transaction 6.70–6.71
    as question of fact 6.69
    relevant factors 6.69–6.73
    removal of pressure, steps to avoid transaction on 6.73
    requirement 6.71–6.74
    subjective nature of 6.62
  chattels, mutual restitution 14.07–14.09
  coercion requirement
    development 6.46–6.47
    lack of practical choice and causation, separation of 6.58–6.60
    legal action, alternative of 6.55–6.56
    monopoly supplier, alternative to 6.54
    practical alternatives, factors in determining 6.50–6.57
    practical or real choice, absence of 6.48–6.49
    proof of 6.07
    test of 6.48–6.49
    urgency, in case of 6.57
  commercial pressure, legitimacy of 6.38
  as defence to action on deed 29.66, 29.68–29.71
  and delay 24.98–24.99
  doctrine of 6.01
  economic
    causation 6.65–6.68
    examples 6.26
    nature 6.25
  of goods *see* of property, *below*
  illegitimate pressure
    assessment of illegitimacy 6.28
    causation *see* causation *above*
    causing entry into transaction 6.05
    coercion *see* coercion requirement *above*
    demand, nature of 6.10
    good faith, claim in 6.29
    lawful act, threat of 6.41–6.45
    nature of 6.09
    nature of illegitimacy 6.27–6.45
    removal of, steps to avoid transaction on 6.73
    requirement for 6.27–6.29
    threat *see* threat *below*
    unlawful act, threat of 6.30–6.36
  lack of procedural fairness 6.05
  non-contractual payments, recovery 6.08
  to person
    causation 6.63–6.64
    threat 6.20
  of property
    causation 6.65–6.68
    current position 6.22–6.24
    examples 6.24
    former law 6.21
  rescission for, requirements 6.07
  scope of 6.02
  threat
    blackmail 6.44
    breach of contract, to commit 6.32–6.36
    core feature 6.18
    by counterparty to transaction 6.12
    criminal prosecution, to instigate 6.45
    direct or indirect 6.13
    against economic interests 6.25–6.26
    of enforcement of legal rights through civil proceedings 6.39
    general principles 6.11–6.13
    of lawful act 6.37–6.45
    leased goods, to take possession of 6.40
    meaning 6.11
    offer distinguished 6.11, 6.17–6.18
    against person 6.20
    person at whom aimed 6.12
    against property 6.21–6.24

duress *(cont.)*
   stricken vessel, not to help 6.45
   tort or crime, to commit 6.31
   types 6.19–6.45
     of unlawful act 6.30–6.36
     warning distinguished 6.11, 6.14–6.16
   as threat and demand 6.05
   voluntary conduct 6.74
   as wrong 6.03

election to rescind
   abolition, question of 10.16
   affirmation after, possibility of 23.97
   automatic operation of 13.07
   being irrevocable 11.57–11.58
   Caldwell's case
     details of case 11.35–11.36
     effect 11.40
     prior to 11.31–11.34
     scope of rule 11.37–11.40
   call on shares, defending 11.50–11.52
   choice of entitled parties 11.01
   common law, transactions voidable at
     extinction of contract after election 12.04–12.06
     mutual restitution after election 14.36, 14.46, 14.69–14.70, 14.74, 14.76
     overview 11.53–11.58
     restitution of benefits transferred 14.02–14.20
   communication conditions 11.36–11.40
   defence, rescission as 11.45–11.46
   delay, loss after 24.06–24.07
   dispensing with
     former application of rule for 11.31–11.34
     fraud, contract procured by 11.31–11.40
     general rule requiring 11.30
     to other party 11.35
   and equitable rights 23.06
   equity, transactions voidable in
     in Australia 11.97–11.101
     in Canada 11.104
     equitable interest in assets transferred 11.60
     foundational cases 11.67–11.79
     gift, in context of 11.90
     historical context 3.53–3.54, 11.62–11.66
     in Hong Kong 11.105
     irrevocability 11.113–11.117
     in Jersey 11.106
     lack of clear picture as to effects 11.107
     mutual restitution 15.69–15.76
     in New Zealand 11.102–11.103
     reappraisal, need for 11.59, 11.111
     recent decisions 11.80–11.84
     reconciliation of authorities 11.112
     'rescission by court order' line of authority 11.85–11.95
     'rescission by election' line of authority 11.67–11.84, 11.108–11.110
     summary of law 11.59–11.61
     United States, position in 11.64–11.65, 11.115
   expansion, question of 10.16
   extinction of contract *see* **extinction of contract**
   facts not known at the time, justified by 11.10
   general principles 11.03
   how an election made 11.03–11.52
   keeping open 11.08–11.09
   Law Commission on 11.38
   oral submission in court, disaffirming by 11.29
   part of transaction only 11.18
   pleading, disaffirming by
     alternative, rescission as plea in 11.28
     amendment to pleading 11.24
     by defence and counterclaim 11.23
     equitable rescission, application to 11.25–11.26
     form of plea 11.27
     general rule 11.19–11.22
     by reply 11.23
     types of pleading 11.23
   prejudice, significance of 24.115
   questions arising 11.02
   'rescission by election' line of authority 11.67–11.84
     difficulties with 11.108–11.110
   rescission used as defence, supposed limitations 11.44–11.47
     that disaffirmance prior to proceeding necessary 11.45–11.46
     that no benefit must have been received 11.47
   supervening event barring rescission at law prior to 10.43–10.46
   tender or return of benefits, requirement 11.48–11.49
   transactions voidable at law at time of 10.40–10.42
   by unequivocal conduct 11.15–11.18
     attempting to rescind part only 11.18
     requirement 11.15
     subsequent acts, effect of 11.16–11.17
   unequivocal intention to disaffirm, communicating 11.03–11.14
     general rule 11.03
     justified by facts not known at the time 11.10
     keeping open 11.08–11.09
     knowledge of rescinding party 11.11
     by mere non-performance 11.07
     overlapping claims to rescind *ab initio* and terminate for breach 11.12–11.14
     possession, retaking 11.05–11.06
     by words or conduct 11.04

equitable compensation
   affirmation of contract, effect of 2.11
   claim to 2.10
   damages, indistinguishable from 2.11
   restitution and counter-restitution rules, governed by 2.13
   senses of 2.12

equity, rescission in
   bars to rescission 10.33
   executed and partly executed transactions, historical 3.38
   extinction of contract *see* **extinction of contract**

following election 12.12–12.13
fusion of principles with common law
  absence of 10.03–10.09
  equity rules prevailing 10.10–10.14
  reform 10.15–10.19
  grounds for rescission 10.25–10.26
  insurance *see* **insurance**
  limited interference, policy of 3.59–3.62
  mutual restitution *see* **mutual restitution (in equity)**
  proprietary claims *see* **proprietary claims**
  rescission at law, overview of distinctions with 10.34–10.38
historical development 3.34
interaction between common law and equitable doctrines
  classes of case 10.39
  transactions voidable at law 10.43–10.46
origins 10.20
persistence of distinction between rescission at law and in equity 10.03–10.19
rules prevailing over common law 10.10–10.14
transactions voidable at law
  supervening event barring rescission at law
    before election to rescind 10.43–10.46
  at time of election to rescind 10.40–10.42
transactions wholly ineffective in equity
  bribes 1.87–1.89
  categories 1.66
  where claimant as party 1.70–1.86
  where claimant not a party 1.67–1.69
  distinguished from voidable transactions 1.58–1.59
  failure of basis 1.92
  fair-dealing rule 1.70–1.71
  fraud, contracts as instruments of 1.83–1.86
  identity fraud 1.79–1.82
  mistaken payments 1.93
  misuse of powers by directors to alienate company property 1.78
  overview 1.65–1.66
  ratification 1.63–1.64
  resulting trust, apparent gift made ineffective by 1.90
  self-dealing rule 1.72–1.76
  trust, imposed 1.90
  unauthorized agent, contract procured by 1.77–1.78
  and void contracts 1.57
  and voidable transactions 1.58

estoppel
contractual 26.11
and delay 24.02
delay, with or without 24.117
evidential 26.10
extent of restitution, limiting 24.121
insurance policy, delay in rescinding 24.119
loss of rights to rescind, cases on 24.116
material facts, party unaware of 24.120
pro tanto 24.121
representations 24.118

executor
succession to rights of rescission 22.07

executory contracts
extinction 12.17–12.19

exploitation of weakness *see* **unconscionable bargain**

extinction of contract
of accrued rights 13.27
common law, rescission at
  effect of 12.05
  election, communicating 12.04
  repudiation for breach of condition 12.04
  well-settled 12.02
court order, set aside by
  contractual claim, defence to 12.10
  delivery up and cancellation 12.08
  general rule 12.07
  injunction 12.09
election, contract set aside by
  at common law 12.04
  in equity 12.11–12.21
election to rescind not causing 12.14–12.16
in equity
  court order, set aside by 12.07–12.10
  discretion to grant rescission 12.22–12.24
  election, contract set aside by 12.21
  financial consequences, working out 12.24
  treatment as 12.20
executory contracts 12.17–12.19
rescission, as feature of 1.02, 1.06–1.34, 12.01
United States, law in 1.10–1.13

fair-dealing rule
discretion 1.70, 28.36
disproportionate effect, and 28.36
equitable compensation 2.10
family arrangements 8.36
fiduciaries, and *see* **fiduciaries, transactions with**
rescission in equity 1.70–1.71
trustees 1.70–1.71
undue influence, and 8.07–8.08

family arrangements
adversarial relationships 5.19
compromise involving 5.59, 7.38–7.39
disclosure, requirement of 5.09, 5.14–5.20
double employment
  adverse duty or interest, principal giving consent to 8.38–8.41
  breach of rule 8.35
  counterparty, fiduciary having interest in 8.35
  disclosure and advice, duty of fiduciary 8.42–8.44
  fair-dealing rule, meeting requirements of 8.36
  implication of counterparty 8.46–8.48
  substantive fairness 8.45
prospective partnerships 5.58
separating spouses, disclosure between 5.20

642 INDEX

fiduciaries, transactions with
  abuse of confidence 8.04
  bribery *see* **bribery**
  causation irrelevant 8.72–8.73
  fair-dealing rule
    adverse interest, consent to 8.18–8.20
    basis of 8.05–8.06
    complete disclosure, fiduciary making 8.21–8.25
    compliance with 8.17–8.33
    conflict, transaction as 8.13
    contracts of sale, transactions involving 8.16
    as contractual disability 8.09–8.10
    disinterested advice, obtaining 8.29–8.33
    regulation by 8.03
    relationships to which applying 8.11
    scope of 8.11–8.16
    substantive fairness requirement 8.26–8.28
    termination of relationship, transactions on 8.14–8.15
    transactions outside scope of relationship 8.12–8.13
  fairness, proof of 8.17
  presumed undue influence, relationship with 8.07–8.08
  upholding, onus of proof 8.03, 8.06
fiduciary relationship
  disclosure, requirement of 5.12–5.13
financial adjustments
  compensation *see* **compensation**
  on counter-restitution *see* **counter-restitution**
  equitable interest
    compounded 17.19
    date from which running 17.18
    discretionary 17.18
    law in Australia 17.20
    principle 17.16–17.17
  equivalent benefits, offsetting 17.30–17.31
  indemnity 17.23–17.29
    see also **indemnity**
  interest 17.15–17.22
    at common law 17.21–17.22
    in equity 17.16–17.20
    see also equitable interest *above*
  land and chattels, benefits derived from
    accounting for 17.03, 17.06
    actual use or compensation, payment for 17.05–17.06
    assets not used, measure where 17.10–17.12
    joint acquisitions 17.14
    monetary receipt 17.42
    rescission in equity, available on 17.01
    use value, measure of 17.07–17.09
fraud
  bribery by way of 8.67
  chattels, restitution 14.03–14.06
  cheques 1.46, 1.98, 5.47, 14.12, 14.13, 21.05
  civil standard of proof 4.07
  concurrent jurisdiction 2.04–2.05
  constructive 7.69
  contract of sale, defrauded seller disaffirming 3.16
  contracting out of 26.02
  contracts as instruments of 1.83–1.86
  defence, rescission as
    difference between law and equity 11.42
    general rule 11.41
    limitations on 11.44–11.47
    loss of 11.43
  as defence to action on deed
    bond, action on 29.75
    at common law 29.73, 29.80
    English authorities 29.74–29.79
    recognition as 29.79
    rescission, as ground for 29.81–29.82
    United States, law in 29.72
  by dishonest bankrupt 25.15
  effect on contract
    at common law 3.05
  effect on title
    at common law 3.06–3.15
    in equity 3.42–3.52
  election to rescind contract *see* **election to rescind**
  equitable 4.10, 7.69
    effect on contract 3.40–3.41
  fraus omnia corrumpit (fraud unravels all) 26.02
  as ground for rescission 3.27
  identity 1.79–1.82
  lease procured by 13.31
  misrepresentation *see* **fraudulent misrepresentation**
  money paid, proprietary claim to 16.49–16.50
  non-contractual payments
    procured by 1.94–1.98
  property other than money taken by 1.99
  proving 4.05
  restitutio in integrum
    judicial discretion 13.13
    restitutio in integrum bar, application of 18.10
  sale of goods 14.57, 18.20, 25.04
  termination *ab initio* 12.06
  vulnerability of contracts to rescission for 4.13–4.16
fraudulent misrepresentation
  allotment of shares following 11.68–11.74
  Australia, election to rescind in 11.97–11.101
  causation 4.104, 4.109
  concurrent jurisdiction 4.11
  contracting out of 26.02
  damages for 28.04
  equity, action in 4.10
  ignorance of falsehood 4.06
  intention of representor 4.08
  materiality 4.65
  meaning 4.04
  mechanism 4.15
  nature of 4.05–4.08
  opportunity to discover truth, effect 4.120
  statute of limitations, application of 24.27–24.28
  victims, advantages given to 4.12

vulnerability of contracts to rescission for
        fraud 4.13–4.16
fusion
    absence of 10.02, 10.03–10.09
    of principles of common law and equity 10.01,
        10.15, 18.24
    weak evidence of 10.04

gifts
    affirmation of voidable 23.08–23.09
        see also **affirmation**
    apparent, made ineffective by resulting trust 1.90
    categories
        donationes mortis causa 29.03
        inter vivos 29.05, 29.06
        testamentary 29.04
    completed, donor having no right to reclaim 29.14
    conduct, effected by
        of money 29.27–29.35
        of property 29.36–29.39
        significance 29.25
    contract of 29.34
    deed, made by
        mistake, rescission for 29.40–29.45
        money and property, restitution of 29.48–29.50
        rescission of part of deed of gift 29.51
        significance of 29.25
    disadvantageous contracts, assimilation
            to 29.56–29.62
        another's debts, securing 29.58–29.59
        criticism 29.60–29.62
        distinction 29.57
        fundamental rule 29.56
    dispositions of another's assets 29.52–29.54
    impaired mental capacity 7.46, 29.21
    intention to confirm 23.63
    inter vivos
        living persons between 29.05
        making 29.06
    in Isle of Man 29.47
    in Jersey 29.46–29.47
    legal title, not effective to pass 29.07
    by minor 29.10
    mistake *see* **mistake**
    of money
        conduct, effected by 29.27–29.35
        recovery, grounds for 29.27–29.30
        repayment, claim to 29.26
        restitution, nature of right to 29.31–29.35
    of property
        claim to return 29.26
        conduct, effected by 29.36–29.39
        recovery, grounds for 29.36–29.37
        restitution, nature of right to 29.38–29.39
    rescission
        grounds for 29.15–29.16
        impaired understanding, donor having 29.21
        for mistake 29.19, 29.23
        of part of deed 29.51

    for undue influence 29.18, 29.20
    vitiated consent, due to 29.22–29.23
    vulnerability to 29.01, 29.17–29.23
resulting trust, presumption of 29.11
significance of how made 29.24–29.26
theft by donee 29.55
third party wrongdoing, effect 9.21
unconscionable bargain 7.74, 7.86, 29.16
undue influence 29.15
unwanted, discretion to reject 29.13
void 29.08–29.12
voidable 1.05
voidable instruments 1.38
grounds for rescission
    at common law 10.23–10.24
    conflict of interest *see* **conflict of interest**;
        fiduciaries, transactions with
    duress *see* **duress**
    in equity 3.35, 10.08, 10.25–10.26
    exploitation of weakness *see* **unconscionable
        bargain**
    gifts 29.15–29.23
    guarantees
        'accommodation sureties' 5.54
        ambit of duty of disclosure 5.44
        in Australia 5.49–5.50, 5.55
        in Canada 5.52, 5.54, 5.55
        circumstances, according to 5.53–5.54
        credit, matters relating to 5.45–5.48
        duty to disclose unusual features 5.43–5.48
        fidelity bonds 5.53
        inducement or reliance 5.56–5.57
        materiality 5.55, 5.57
        no general duty to disclose 5.41–5.42
        in New Zealand 5.51
    impaired capacity *see* **impaired capacity;
        intoxication; mental infirmity**
    misrepresentation *see* **misrepresentation**
    mistake *see* **mistake**
    non-disclosure *see* **non-disclosure**
    of past indebtedness 13.19
    third party wrongdoing *see* **third party wrongdoing**
    uberrimae fides, not being 5.41
    unconscionable bargain *see* **unconscionable
        bargain**
    undue influence *see* **undue influence**
    of unusual features 4.36, 5.43–5.48

heir
    succession to rights of rescission 22.05
historical foundations of rescission
    at common law 3.04–3.33
    contracts of insurance, special status 3.55–3.63
    in equity 3.34–3.54
Hong Kong, law in
    election to rescind 11.105
    innocent misrepresentation, contractual term
        and 27.46
    rescission on terms 19.33

644 INDEX

Hong Kong, law in (*cont.*)
  transfer of title to personal property, bar to rescission for 27.34
  transfer of title to real property, bar to rescission for 27.16

identity fraud
  beneficial title, absence of intention to transfer 1.79
  rescission and transactions ineffective in equity 1.79–1.82

impaired capacity
  availability of rescission for 7.42
  drunkenness *see* **drunkenness**
  intoxication *see* **intoxication**
  mental infirmity *see* **mental infirmity**
  versus other types of disability 7.43
  versus rescission as an unconscionable bargain 7.42
  versus unilateral mistake 7.44

impossibility of *restitutio in integrum*
  assessment, date of 18.121–18.123
  where asset changed
    delay in return 18.86
    deterioration 18.85
    interest in business 18.89
    in nature 18.87–18.90
    repairs and alterations enhancing value 18.90
    restrictive common law rules 18.91–18.92
  basic principles 18.01–18.16
  where counter-restitution impossible
    asset recovered after sale 18.50–18.51
    basic rule 18.48
    some assets available and some not 18.49
  where counter-restitution not required
    assets and services worthless 18.46
    benefits obtained other than under contract 18.34–18.35
    costless benefits, in case of 18.39
    where defendant bound to confer benefits 18.43–18.45
    general rule 18.33
    inability to return asset or benefit as defendant's fault 18.36
    insurance fraud, in case of 18.40–18.42
    loss of asset following tender 18.37–18.38
    set-off 18.47
  and defence of change of position 18.07–18.08
  delay, role of 18.12–18.16
  distinction between law and equity, persistence of 18.30–18.32
  equity, bar in 18.27–18.29
  of executed contract 18.26
  fault, role of 18.09–18.11
  intangible benefits 18.102
  at law 18.18–18.26
  market decline, depreciation of assets owing to 18.93–18.98
  onus of proof 18.124
  possession, occupation and use of asset of chattels 18.84
    general rule 18.77–18.78
    of land 18.80–18.83
    letting out 18.78
    restrictive common law rules 18.79–18.84
  possession of land, claimant enjoying 18.23
  prejudicial change of circumstances
    comparatively blameless misconduct 18.112–18.116
    conscious wrongdoing 18.108–18.111
    delay, effect of 18.117
    general rule 18.106
    joint purposes, money committed to 18.118
    reversible 18.119–18.120
    unjustified 18.107–18.117
  and prejudicial laches 24.19–24.21
  purpose of bar
    defendant, protection of 18.03–18.04
    unjust enrichment, prevention 18.05–18.06
  scope of bar 18.17
  services performed under contract
    general rule 18.99
    of salvage 18.100
    self-help basis, rescission on 18.101
  substitutive counter-restitution *see* **counter-restitution**

indemnity
  declaratory relief, disadvantage of 17.29
  financial adjustment for 17.23–17.29
  necessary consequence of contract, outlays as 17.26
  rescinding claimant, right of 17.27
  scope of 17.25
  third party
    benefit conferred on 17.24
    sums paid to 17.28
  for undischarged or contingent future liabilities 17.28

information
  passing on as not a representation 4.28

injunction
  contract set aside 12.09

innocent misrepresentation
  bars for
    Commonwealth law 27.04
    contractual terms, incorporation as *see* contractual term, incorporation as *below*
    development 27.02–27.03
    sale of goods *see* sale of goods, bar to rescission of *below*
    transfer of title to personal property *see* transfer of title to personal property, bar to rescission for *below*
  causation 4.105–4.108
  claim of rescission, discretion to declare contract subsisting and award damages
    application of provision 28.05
    barred, right to rescission having become 28.08
    conditions for exercise of 28.06–28.09
    for consequential loss 28.22–28.24
    contractual measure 28.17–28.18

disproportionate effect and fair dealing
  rule 28.36
grounds for exercise of 28.10–28.14
High Court, views in 28.08–28.09
importance of misrepresentation 28.12
introduction of 28.01–28.03
loss, measure of 28.15–28.21
measure of damages 28.15–28.35
mischief of 28.09
mistaken theories 28.25–28.35
reliance measure 28.20–28.21
rescission as option open to the court 28.09
use, intended 28.03
communication of election to rescind, need
  for 11.39
contractual term, incorporation as
  Australia, rule in 27.40–27.43
  Canada, rule in 27.45, 27.60
  England and Wales, abolition of bar in 27.39
  Hong Kong, rule in 27.46
  nature of bar 27.36–27.38
  New Zealand, rule in 27.44
  Singapore, rule in 27.47
damages for 4.09, 28.04
fraud principles, application of 18.116
general law 26.12
as ground for rescission in equity 4.10
materiality
  requirement 4.67–4.71
  special case where not required 4.72–4.73
meaning 4.04
mechanism 4.15
recognition as ground for rescission 27.02
restitution 2.07
sales of goods, bar to rescission of all 27.48–27.53
  Australia, rule in 27.48, 27.50–27.51
  Canada, rule in 27.52
  England and Wales, no application in 27.53
  New Zealand, rule in 27.48–27.49, 27.59
sales of goods, rescission barred where contractual
  right to reject lost 27.54–27.60
  Australia, rule in 27.58
  Canada, rule in 27.60
  England and Wales 27.54, 27.55–27.57
  New Zealand, rule in 27.59
transfer of title to personal property, bar to
  rescission for
  Australia, rule in 27.29–27.30
  Canada, rule in 27.32–27.33
  England and Wales, abolition of the bar in 27.28
  Hong Kong, rule in 27.34
  nature of 27.18–27.27
  New Zealand, rule in 27.31
  rationale 27.26–27.27
  reception of 27.21–27.23
  scope of 27.24–27.25
  Singapore, rule in 27.35
transfer of title to real property *see* transfer of title to
  real property, bar to rescission for *below*

transfer of title to real property, bar to rescission for
  Australia, partial abolition in 27.12
  Canada, rule in 27.14–27.15
  England and Wales, abolition in 27.10–27.11
  Hong Kong, abolition in 27.16
  nature of 27.05–27.09
  New Zealand, abolition in 27.13
  rationale 27.06–27.08
  registered land 27.09
  Singapore, abolition in 27.17
insurance
affirmation, conditions for 23.28
affirmation of contract, communication 23.59
common law and equity, special relationship
  of 3.56–3.58
consumer insurance contracts 5.35
contract
  election to disaffirm for
    non-disclosure 11.16–11.17
  non-disclosure after entry into contract 5.32
  right to rescind, source of 10.27–10.29
  uberrimae fides, being 5.25
delay in rescinding policy, estoppel arising 24.119
deliberately failing to inquire 23.32–23.34
disclosure, duty of 5.24–5.40
  common law 5.25–5.27
  in Commonwealth jurisdictions 5.40
  consumer insurance contracts 5.35
  exceptions 5.30
  inducement 5.33
  under general law 5.26
  of insurer 5.31
  non-consumer insurance contracts 5.36–5.39
  non-disclosure after entry into contract 5.32
  onus of proof 5.34–5.39
  of proposing assured 5.28–5.30
  special nature of bargain 5.25–5.27
  wilful ignorance 5.29
facts relevant to risk, full disclosure of 3.55
fraud, counter-restitution of premium not
  required 14.80–14.81, 18.41–18.42
historical, rescission of 3.55–3.63
marine *see* **marine insurance**
misrepresentation neither deliberate or
  reckless 19.09
non-consumer insurance contracts 5.36–5.39
partial rescission of insurance contracts 19.09
premium, counter-restitution 14.79
rescission at law, grounds for 10.23, 16.03
intellectual property rights
rescinded contract, transferred under 15.13
inter-bank payments
proprietary claims 16.45
interest
financial adjustments *see* **financial adjustments**
intoxication
degree of 7.66
knowledge of 7.67–7.68
as not ground for rescission alone 7.58

646 INDEX

intoxication (*cont.*)
    requisite 7.66
    see also **drunkenness**
Isle of Man
    gifts 29.47

Jersey, law in
    election to rescind 11.106
    gifts 29.46–29.47

land
    benefits derived from
        accounting for 17.03, 17.06
        actual use or compensation, payment for 17.05–17.06
        assets not used, measure where 17.10–17.12
        joint acquisitions 17.14
        monetary receipt 17.42
        rescission in equity, available on 17.01
        use value, measure of 17.07–17.09
    compensation for improvements and repairs 17.35
    completed conveyances
        Australia, law in 7.31–7.32
        early English authorities 7.28
        England and Wales 7.29–7.30
        New Zealand, law in 7.33
    estate or interest in, recovery of 24.29–24.32
    lease, encumbered by 20.26
    mortgage, encumbered with 20.27
    obtaining possession 15.10
    possession, occupation and use 18.80–18.83
    possession of, claimant enjoying 18.23
    registered *see* **registered land**
    sale *see* **sale of land**
    unregistered *see* **unregistered land**
lien
    right to repayment, securing 15.38, 15.56
limitation of actions
    application of
        by analogy 24.25–24.36, 24.54–24.55
        anomalies 24.36
        breach of fiduciary duty 24.27–24.28
        directly 24.22–24.24
        estate or interest in land, recovery of 24.29–24.32
        fraud, rescission for 24.27–24.28
        self-dealing and fair-dealing rules, transaction contrary to 24.33
        undue influence 24.34–24.35
    awareness of rights 24.63
    right to rescind at common law, not applying to 24.26
    unreasonable delay 24.106–24.108
    vitiating factor, freedom from 24.54–24.55

marine insurance
    duty of disclosure 5.29, 5.30
    fraud
        counter-restitution not required 18.41–18.42
        premium not recoverable on 14.80–14.81
    representation, materiality and substantial falsity of 4.87
    restitutio in integrum 13.33
mental infirmity 7.45–7.64
    actual knowledge 7.61–7.62
    affirmation, conditions for 23.15
    Australia, law in 7.60
    complete lack of mental capacity rendering transaction void 7.45
    constructive knowledge 7.62
    court protection, those under 7.58–7.60
    development of requirements 7.47–7.50
    gifts made with 7.46, 29.21
    knowledge of 7.61–7.64
    previous episodes of disorder, evidence of 7.56
    requisite mental infirmity 7.51–7.57
        cheque signing 7.53
        transfer of home 7.54
    unsoundness of mind *per se* 7.47
misrepresentation
    acquiescence, evidence of 24.43
    affirmation, conditions for
        constructive knowledge 23.27–23.31
        immaterial that truth could have been discovered 23.24–23.26
        inquiry, being put on 23.27–23.31
        material facts, knowledge of 23.18–23.19
        partial knowledge 23.20–23.23
        suspicion 23.27–23.31
    construction or meaning
        document to be read as a whole 4.42
        intention, role 4.41, 4.43
        test to be applied 4.39–4.43
    continuing representation
        of fact 4.93
        treatment as 4.90
    contracting out of rescission for
        choice of law provisions 26.33
        consumer protection legislation 26.34–26.35
        entire agreement clauses 26.04–26.05
        general law 26.02–26.11
        international supply contracts 26.32
        Misrepresentation Act 1967 26.12–26.33
        non-reliance clauses 26.09–26.11
        onus of proof 26.33
        reasonableness requirement 26.23–26.33
        representation clauses, lack of 26.06–26.08
        types of clauses 26.03
    damages in lieu of rescission 4.16, 28.01–28.29
    distinctions between types, importance
        outside rescission 4.09
        in relation to rescission 4.10–4.12
    elements of 4.02
    falsity of representation
        changes of circumstances 4.90–4.99
        continuing representation 4.90–4.99
        forecasts or projections 4.94
        intention, representations of 4.94–4.99
        knowledge that representation false 4.114

INDEX 647

representor's knowledge of 4.113
requirement 4.81
statements as to the future 4.94–4.99
substantial correctness 4.83–4.87
at time of reliance 4.88–4.89
fraudulent *see* **fraudulent misrepresentation**
future, statements as to
   intention or promise honestly held or believed 4.60–4.61
   statement of fact, not generally a 4.57–4.59
at general law 26.02–26.11
as ground for rescission 7.03
implied representation
   concealment, implied from 4.38
   conduct giving rise to 4.26–4.27
   context of 4.31
   from express statements 4.33–4.35
   market in which item offered 4.37
   nature of transaction, implied from 4.36
   partial disclosure 4.33–4.35
   statement of opinion 4.34
innocent *see* **innocent misrepresentation**
materiality
   definition 4.63
   effect 4.111
   of non-fraudulent misrepresentation 4.67–4.71
   onus of proof 4.110–4.113
   onus of proving reliance, shifting 4.64
   requirement 4.62, 4.64–4.73
matters not being representation
   categories 4.44
   fraud, effect of 4.44
   future, statements as to 4.57–4.61
   mere puff (sales talk) 4.45–4.47
   statement of opinion or belief 4.48–4.49
   see also statement of opinion *below*
meaning 4.01
Misrepresentation Act 1967 26.12–26.33
   clauses falling within Section 3 26.14–26.15
   clauses not falling within Section 3 26.16–26.19
   provisions of Section 3 26.13
   scope of Section 3 26.14–26.22
and mistake 4.01, 7.02, 7.04
negligent *see* **negligent misrepresentation**
no representation clauses 26.06–26.08, 26.20–26.22
non-fraudulent, meaning 27.01
see also **innocent misrepresentation; negligent misrepresentation**
non-reliance clauses 26.09–26.11
   contractual estoppel 26.11
   evidential estoppel 26.10
   general rule 26.09
   lack of 26.20–26.22
   reasonableness, requirement of 26.24–26.31
   statutory provisions 26.12–26.33
recovery of compensation, avenue and scope 4.09
reliance on representation
   ambiguous statements or conduct 4.103
   causation, question of 4.100–4.102

circumstances 4.102
claimant unaware of 4.115
non-reliance, examples 4.114–4.118
onus of proof 4.110–4.113
opportunity to discover truth, effect 4.119–4.120
presumption of 4.110–4.113
representee not influenced by 4.117–4.118
representee's conduct, link with 4.100
subsequent transactions in 4.121–4.124
representation
   ambiguous statements or conduct 4.103
   being contractual term 4.20–4.25
   changes of circumstances 4.90–4.99
   conduct giving rise to 4.26–4.27
   continuing 4.90–4.99
   definition 4.20, 4.21
   in document 4.24
   document to be read as a whole 4.42
   of existing fact 4.17–4.19
   express or implied 4.26–4.27
   falsity *see* falsity of representation *above*
   implied *see* implied representation *above*
   intention of maker 4.43
   of law 4.17–4.19
   materiality *see* materiality *above*
   passing on information generally not a representation 4.28
   persons making 4.74–4.75
   persons to whom made 4.76–4.80
   pre-contractual 4.21, 4.23
   reliance on *see* reliance on representation *above*
   repeated, deemed by contract to be 4.25
   silence, effect of 4.29–4.31
   subject matter of 4.39–4.43
   substantial correctness 4.83–4.87
   unilateral mistake as to 4.41
   warranty distinguished 4.22
rescission for, contracting out of
   avoidance *ab initio*, argument for 26.02
   categories of clauses 26.03
   entire agreement clauses 26.04–26.05
sale of shares induced by, damages for 2.08
by silence 5.10–5.11
state of mind of representor 4.03
statement of opinion
   indicia of 4.48
   involving representation of fact 4.50–4.56
   as not representation of fact 4.48
   reasonable grounds for holding opinion 4.53–4.56
   state of mind, misrepresenting 4.50–4.51
types 4.04
unfair terms 26.35
mistake 7.02–7.40
affirmation, conditions for
   constructive knowledge 23.27–23.31
   deliberately failing to inquire 23.32–23.34
   immaterial that truth could have been discovered 23.24–23.26

648　INDEX

mistake (*cont.*)
    inquiry, being put on 23.27–23.31
    material facts, knowledge of 23.18–23.19
    partial knowledge 23.20–23.23
    suspicion 23.27–23.31
  Canada, error in *substantialibus* 7.11, 7.34–7.37, 27.33
  common
    Commonwealth jurisdictions, approach in 7.10–7.11
    meaning 7.02
    as not ground for rescission 7.03, 7.07–7.09
  compromise and family arrangements 7.38–7.39
  contracts vulnerable to rescission for 7.06
  deed of gift, rescission of 29.19, 29.40–29.45
  error in *substantialibus*, Canadian doctrine 7.34–7.37
  gifts made under 1.38, 7.40, 29.19, 29.23, 29.28–29.30, 29.36–29.37, 29.40–29.45
  land, completed conveyances 7.28–7.33
  and misrepresentation 4.01, 7.02, 7.04
  special cases 7.06
  special doctrine of rescission for 7.27–7.40
  unilateral 7.12–7.26
    in Australia 7.20–7.22
    common law 7.12
    Commonwealth jurisdictions 7.20–7.23
    England and Wales 7.13–7.20
    impaired capacity, versus 7.44
    machine-generated contracts 7.24–7.26
    meaning 7.02
    in New Zealand 7.23
    and non-disclosure 5.11
    rectification, compared to 7.19
    in Singapore 7.22
    subject matter of contract 7.12, 7.17
    terms of contract, as to 7.12, 7.17
    third party wrongdoing, relationship with 9.06
mortgages
  Australia 19.26, 19.27, 19.38
  bargains 19.05
  bona fide purchase 21.55
  conditional relief 15.51
  consent to adverse duties or interest 8.41
  as contracts, not gifts 29.60
  counter-restitution 21.46
  description of interest 16.62
  exploitation of weakness 7.86
  irrelevant detriments 17.63
  land encumbered with 20.27
  remote recipient 21.39, 21.49, 21.53
  sub-mortgage of chose in action 21.43
  unregistered land 15.07
  void/voidable 15.09, 15.53, 15.74, 22.03
mutual mistake *see* **common mistake**
mutual restitution (at law)
  benefits transferred by rescinding party 14.14
    money paid 14.36–14.40
    nature of right 14.02
    property 14.03–14.28
    proprietary claims 16.02–16.11
    services provided 14.41–14.44
    substitute assets 14.29–14.35, 16.10–16.11
  of chattels
    in Australia 14.11
    counter-restitution 14.53–14.55, 14.69–14.71
    duress, effect of 14.07–14.09
    fraud, effect of 14.03–14.06
    identity, mistake as to 14.12
    non-contractual transfer 14.10–14.12
    personal claims to value of 14.34–14.35
    rescinding transferee in possession, position of 14.71
    revesting title to by disaffirming 14.69–14.70
  counter-restitution 14.56–14.58, 14.76–14.85
    failure of consideration 14.37, 14.77
    goods sold, sums received for 14.85
    insurance premiums 14.79
    marine insurance, fraud exception for 14.80–14.81
    money had and received 14.36, 14.76
    non-contractual payments 14.39
    obligation, when arising 14.36, 14.78
    proprietary claims 16.05–16.09
    restitution 14.36–14.40
    unconditionally accruing rights 14.38
  general principles 13.01–13.06, 14.02, 14.45
  of property transferred
    chattels 14.03–14.12
    conversion, remedy of 14.14–14.17
    disposal to purchaser with notice 14.29–14.30
    exchange product 14.33
    innocent purchaser, disposal to 14.31–14.32
    intangible legal, not recoverable 14.21–14.22
    not recoverable 14.21–14.28
    proceeds of sale 14.29–14.32
    recaption 14.18–14.20
    registered land, position of 14.28
    remedies once legal title regained 14.14–14.20
    substitutive restitution 14.29–14.35, 16.11
    tangible legal personal 14.12
    unregistered land, position of 14.23–14.27
    value of chattels, personal claims to 14.34–14.35
    voidable preferences 14.32
  rights to 14.01
  for services provided
    general assumpsit, claim in 14.42–14.43
    value, right to 14.41–14.44
  statutory modification of common law for insurance premiums 14.82–14.84
  value of asset, payment of sum representing 14.34–14.35
mutual restitution (in equity)
  benefits transferred by rescinding party
    money paid 15.33–15.38
    nature of right 15.03
    property 15.04–15.13 *see also* property transferred *below*

proprietary claims 16.12–16.70
for services provided 15.39–15.43
counter-restitution *see* **counter-restitution**
equitable rescission by election
  contingent claims to restitution 15.72
  counter-restitution 15.73–15.76
  personal claims 15.71
  proprietary claims 15.69–15.70
general principles 13.01–13.06, 15.03, 15.45
general rule 15.35
of money paid
  counter-restitution 15.65–15.66
  lien to secure right to repayment 15.38
  not money had and received 15.36
  personal or proprietary right 15.33
  repayment and account 15.37
  types of payment 15.34
of property transferred
  chattels 15.12
  counter-restitution 15.63–15.64
  exchange product 15.19
  intellectual property rights 15.13
  original passing of title 15.05
  possession of land, obtaining 15.10
  proceeds of sale 15.17–15.18
  property created, effect on 15.06
  registered land 15.08–15.09
  replacement asset, purchase of 15.16
  revesting of title, order for 15.04
  shares 15.11
  substitutive restitution 15.14–15.32, 16.44
  unregistered land 15.07
  value of assets transferred 15.20–15.32
for services provided
  amount payable 15.41, 15.43
  counter-restitution 15.67–15.68
  principles 15.39
  true value, distortion of 15.43
  types 15.42
value of asset, payment of sum representing
  authorities for 15.21–15.24
  measure 15.25–15.26
  as pecuniary rescission 15.28
  pecuniary rescission 15.20
  prejudice to defendant, avoiding 15.30–15.31
  and proceeds of sale 15.29
  property law principles, re-modelling 15.32
workings of equitable rescission, difficulties in describing 15.02

negligent misrepresentation
communication of election to rescind, need for 11.39
damages for 28.04
meaning 4.04
New Zealand, law in
affirmation 23.02, 23.49, 23.70
breach of fiduciary duty 16.52
guarantees 5.51

innocent misrepresentation
  where contractual right to reject lost 27.59
  contractual term, incorporation as 27.44
  sale of goods, bar to rescission of 27.48, 27.49
  transfer of title to personal property, bar to rescission for 27.31
  transfer of title to real property, bar to rescission for 27.13
mistake 7.12
  rescission for 7.03
  unilateral 7.23
rescission
  misrepresentation, for 11.102–11.103
  on **terms** 19.31
  unconscionable bargain 7.103
  unilateral mistake 7.23
non est factum plea
void contract 1.36
non-contractual payments
counter-restitution 14.39
fraud, procured by 1.94–1.98
proprietary claims 16.08–16.09
non-disclosure
affirmation, conditions for
  constructive knowledge 23.27–23.31
  deliberately failing to inquire 23.32–23.34
  immaterial that truth could have been discovered 23.24–23.26
  inquiry, being put on 23.27–23.31
  material facts, knowledge of 23.18–23.19
  partial knowledge 23.20–23.23
  suspicion 23.27–23.31
compromise, entry into *see* **compromise**
delay *see* **delay**
course of dealings where disclosure required 5.10–5.11
family arrangements 5.09, 5.14–5.20
fiduciary and principal, transactions between 5.07
in fiduciary relationship 5.12–5.13
general duty of disclosure, absence 5.02–5.09
guarantees *see* **guarantees**
of material facts 5.01, 5.03
misrepresentation by silence 5.10–5.11
mistake, shifting risk of 5.04
nature of transaction leading to unfairness 5.08
in pre-contractual dealings 5.06
relationship of parties, categories 5.05–5.08
relationships of trust and confidence 5.21–5.23
relationships where disclosure required 5.12–5.23
rescission, permitting 5.04–5.09
rescission for 10.29
sales of land, contract for 5.65–5.66
unilateral mistake, leading to 5.11

partial rescission
as affirmation 23.89
bargains, rule applied to 19.05–19.07
justice of 19.35
meaning 19.01

partial rescission (*cont.*)
  processes 19.01
  of properly severable part 19.02
  rationale 19.03–19.04
  on terms *see* **rescission on terms**
  against third party wrongdoers 19.10–19.16
    see also **third party wrongdoers**
  unilateral dispositions 19.08
  use of term 19.01
prejudice
  and acquiescence 24.112–24.115
  affirmation 23.46, 23.48
  Australia 23.46, 23.48
  bankruptcy and winding up 20.36, 25.02
  bargains 19.06
  change of circumstances, prejudicial 18.106–18.120
  costless benefits 18.39
  counter-restitution 21.47
  to creditors 25.34–25.36, 25.37
  delay 18.13, 24.01, 24.16, 24.71, 24.78, 24.80, 24.85–24.97
  disclosure and advice 8.42
  discretion to grant rescission 12.24
  election to affirm 24.109–24.111
  following election to rescind 24.115
  grounds for rescission 23.66
  interest in security of transaction 24.76
  judicial discretion 13.12
  whether knowledge of right to rescind should be required 23.51–23.52
  multilateral contracts 20.31
  protection of third party rights, other 20.28
  significance 24.109–24.115
  uncertainty, resolving 16.40
  unfair 18.25, 18.27, 18.31
  unjustifiable/unjustified 15.30, 15.72, 18.02, 18.06, 18.08, 18.71, 18.107–18.117
  value of asset 15.29
  vendor's claims 17.46
  voidable transactions 20.33
profits
  account of
    not restitutionary remedy 2.17
    purpose 2.17
  assets with definite market value, sale of 2.39
  Re Cape Breton Company, rule in 2.29–2.35
    exceptions to 2.36–2.39
  cases in which rule applying 2.32
  claiming a pecuniary accounting and payment of net profit 2.27
  contractual regime, priority of 2.25
  disgorgement of 2.14–2.39
    assets with definite market value, sale of 2.39
    Re Cape Breton Company, rule in 2.29–2.35
    distinction between profit-based remedies and rescission 2.16–2.23
    exceptions to *Re Cape Breton Company* rule 2.36–2.39
  personal accountability for profits absent rescission 2.27–2.39
  proprietary relief absent rescission 2.24–2.26
  regular trade supplies, sales of 2.38
  sale of principal's own property 2.37
  dissenting judgment 2.33–2.35
  exceptions to rule 2.36–2.39
  fiduciary, accountability of 2.14–2.15
  measurement of profit 2.31, 2.34
  personal accountability for profits absent rescission 2.27–2.39
  principal's own property, sale of 2.37
  proprietary relief absent rescission 2.24–2.26
  regular trade supplies, sales of 2.38
  remedies based on profit-based remedies, and rescission
    basis of remedy 2.18
    conflation of 2.21
    distinction between 2.16–2.23
    independence of 2.16, 2.20
    overlap 2.19–2.20
  rule, establishment 2.28
  secret, recovery of 2.33
proprietary claims
  asserting 16.01
  Canadian law 16.50
  disaffirmation conferring equitable interest
    authorities 16.31–16.36
    beneficial interest, when arising 16.34
    confusion as to 16.37–16.38
    on fraud 16.25–16.29
    other than fraud, cases on 16.30–16.40
    purchase of shares under voidable contract 16.33
    uncertainty, resolving 16.39–16.40
  England and Wales 16.53–16.54
  on equitable rescission 16.45–16.58
    bankruptcy 25.04–25.07
    constructive trust, interest as 16.61, 16.63–16.64
    description of interest 16.60–16.62
    disaffirmation conferring equitable interest 16.25–16.40
    entitlement, discretion as to 16.69–16.70
    equitable title, recovery of 16.21–16.24
    fiduciary duty, interest arising 16.63–16.64
    knowing receipt and dishonest assistance, liability 16.65–16.68
    legal title, recovery of 16.20
    money paid, claims to 16.45–16.58
    nature of interest arising 16.59–16.70
    property 15.04–15.13
    prospective and retrospective interests 16.59
    recovering title 16.19–16.24
    retrospective equitable title 16.41–16.44
    title passing pending 16.12–16.18
  fraud, in case of 16.51
  grounds other than fraud or breach of fiduciary duty 16.56–16.58
  ineffective transactions 1.57–1.99
  interest, nature of 16.48

INDEX 651

to money 16.49–16.50
to money paid
  breach of fiduciary duty 16.52–16.54
  bribes 1.87–1.89, 16.55
on rescission at law
  for money 16.05–16.09
  non-contractual payments 16.08–16.09
  for property 14.03–14.13, 16.02–16.04
retrospective equitable title 16.41–16.44
  conferring right to trace 16.42–16.43
  creating no retrospective liabilities 16.44
substitutes, tracing into 16.10–16.11
to traceable substitute 16.45–16.47
void contracts 1.54

quantum meruit 1.30
quasi-contract
  general assumpsit, origin of claims in 3.20

recaption
  remedy of 14.18–14.20
  risks 14.19
recovery of benefits
  void and voidable contracts 1.49–1.56
registered land
  rescission of contract to transfer
    register, rectification of 15.08
    registrable transfer, execution of 15.09
  title to, regaining 14.28
remote recipient
  bona fide purchaser *see* **bona fide purchaser**
  bona fide purchaser, protection 21.55–21.76
  chose in action, assignee of
    basis of claim against 21.31–21.34
    counter-restitution to original transferee 21.46
    equitable assignment 21.22–21.25
    nemo dat principle 21.33
    original transferor, no better position than 21.38
    rescission available against 21.02
    rights to sue 21.34
    statutory assignment 21.26
    subsequent equitable assignee, right against 21.32
  consequences of recovery against
    counter-restitution to original transferee 21.45–21.47
    list of 21.40
    no avoidance of contract with remote recipient 21.42
    no counter-restitution to remote recipient 21.50–21.53
    original contract, avoidance 21.41
    remote recipient's rights against transferor 21.54
    restitution from original transferee 21.43–21.44
    restitution from remote recipient 21.48–21.49
  of crossed cheque
    rescission available against 21.02
    statutory provision 21.27
    voidable interest, acquiring 21.28

disposition to, new claim to rescind on 21.35
meaning 21.01
notice of vitiating factor with
  and absence of bona fides 21.10–21.11
  basis of claim against 21.29–21.30
  common law, transaction voidable at 21.09
  documents ordinarily produced 21.15
  fraud, inferring 21.14
  negotiable instruments, purchasers 21.16
  nemo dat principle 21.30
  purchaser suspecting wrong 21.12–21.18
  rescission against 21.08–21.09
  rescission available against 21.02
  timing of notice 21.19–21.21
  trust property, knowing receipt of 21.18
  uncommercial terms, contract on 21.17
  unregistered land, interests in 21.18
original transferor, no better position than 21.37–21.39
proprietary rights 21.39
recovery from deriving from rescission of original transaction 21.36
recovery of asset or exchange product in hands of 21.01
voidable transaction, receipt under 21.03
volunteer *see* **volunteer**
vulnerable to rescission 21.03–21.28
  assignee of chose in action 21.22–21.26
  crossed cheques 21.27–21.28
  those taking with notice 21.08–21.21
  volunteers 21.04–21.07
rescission
  as action of electing to reject contract or gift 1.33
  administration by court 10.19
  claims in damages, giving rise to 2.01
  common law *see* **common law**
  concept 1.01
  defect, based on 1.02, 1.28
  development of principles, judicature reforms halting 10.21
  as discharge of contract for post-contractual breach 1.32
  discretion to grant 12.22–12.24
  by election 3.53
  election for *see* **election to rescind**
  in equity *see* **equity**
  extinction *see* **extinction of contract**
  financial adjustments *see* **financial adjustments**
  financially better position than award of damages, claimant in 2.08
  forms 1.02
  grounds for *see* **grounds for rescission**
  independence from concurrent claims 2.01
  by innocent party 3.02
  insurance market 10.18
  legal process of 1.34
  legal title to goods, recovering 25.04
  loss of right 23.01
    on failure to exercise 24.01

rescission (*cont.*)
  for mistake 7.27–7.40
  neighbouring concepts distinguished 1.01
  no general bar to 25.02–25.03
  not compensation for loss 2.09
  orders for reconveyance upon 3.52
  original position
    object of returning parties to 13.01–13.06, 13.24
    restoring parties to 2.09
  overview of distinction at law and in equity 10.20–10.47
  partial *see* **partial rescission**
  proprietary claims *see* **proprietary claims**
  radical consequences 10.17
  relief, object of 13.04
  separate origins 10.01
  structure at common law 10.20
  succession to rights
    assignment 22.09–22.10
    by beneficiary under will 22.06
    classes of persons entitled 22.04
    devolution in death 22.05–22.07
    example 22.03
    of executor 22.07
    general principle 22.02
    by heirs at law 22.05
    on second conveyance of same property 22.11–22.14
    under settlement 22.08
  termination *ab initio see* **termination *ab initio***
  terminology 1.02, 1.31–1.34
  unexercised right to, nature 22.01
  windfalls 13.05
rescission on terms
  alternative analysis 19.39
  application, scope of 19.24
  in Australia 19.26–19.30, 19.36–19.37
  in Canada, not considered 19.32
  comment on 19.34–19.46
  compensatory remedy, treatment as 19.36
  contradictions 19.37–19.38
  guarantees 19.40–19.46
  in Hong Kong 19.33
  mistaken dispositions of real property 19.22–19.25
  in New Zealand 19.31
  principle 19.17
  restitutio in integrum, necessary to ensure challenge to 19.18–19.21
  unjust enrichment 19.43
  wife, legal charge by to secure husband's loan 19.19–19.21
restitutio in integrum
  award in damages, object of 13.03
  contractual rights on accrued, extinguishment of 13.27
  and damages 2.08
  equivalent benefits, offsetting 17.31
  fiscal consequences 13.32
  heretical approaches 13.14–13.25
  impossible *see* **impossibility of** *restitutio in integrum*
  interest and income, payment of 13.34
  judicial discretion
    changed circumstances, effect of 13.12
    detail, court working out 13.10
    equity, rescission in 13.08
    fraud, in case of 13.13
    law, rescission in 13.07
    rescinding claimant, terms imposed on 13.11
    settled principles 13.09
  justice of case, requirement of 13.16
  meaning 13.02
  objective 13.01–13.06
  practical justice, to achieve 13.15–13.25
  profit-based remedies and rescission 2.21, 2.23
  retrospective effects 16.25, 16.27, 16.29, 16.34, 16.35, 16.36
    on contractual rights 13.27–13.31
    conversion, liability for 13.30
    fiscal consequences 13.32
    interest and income, payment of 13.34
    lease, voidable 13.31
    property rights 13.29–13.31
    theory 13.26
  rules of equity prevailing principle 10.11
  Scots law, term borrowed from 18.02
  in simple case 13.08
  substantial 13.08
restitution
  and claim in damages 2.06
  counter-restitution *see* **counter-restitution**
  estoppel, effect of 24.121
  fragility of right to 1.56
  on innocent misrepresentation 2.07
  money, gift of
    conduct, effected by 29.31–29.35
    deed, made by 29.48–29.50
  mutual *see* **mutual restitution (at law); mutual restitution (in equity)**
  property, gift of
    conduct, effected by 29.38–29.39
    deed, made by 29.48–29.50
  rescission, as consequence of 2.08
  rescission as condition to 3.16–3.29
  restitutio in integrum see restitutio in integrum
  termination *ab initio*, in case of 1.23–1.30
  termination *de futuro*, in case of 1.23–1.30
resulting trust
  apparent gifts made ineffective by 1.90
  gift, presumption arising on 29.11
retrospectivity
  bars 26.21
  contracts ineffective until ratified 1.40
  conversion, no liability for 14.15–14.16
  creating no retrospective liability 16.44
  equitable title 16.41–16.44
  exchange product 15.19
  fiduciary duties 16.63

fusion of principles of common law and
    equity 10.01, 10.15, 18.24
grounds for rescission 4.57
knowing receipt and dishonest assistance 16.66
non-disclosure 5.32
property rights 13.29, 13.30
proprietary relief absent rescission 2.24
prospective and retrospective interests 16.59
restitutio in integrum 16.25, 16.27, 16.29, 16.34,
    16.35, 16.36
retrospective effects 13.26
trace, right to 16.42–16.43
undue influence 6.91, 11.81

sale of goods
    delay 24.97
    distinction between rescission at law and in
        equity 10.22
    England and Wales 27.53
    failure of consideration 14.77
    fraud 14.57, 18.20, 25.04
    innocent representation 24.01, 27.53
    interest in security of transactions 24.75
    international supply contracts 26.32
    transfer of title to personal property 27.22
sale of land
    disclosure, duty of 5.65–5.66
    rescission at law, not possible 14.23–14.28
    rescission in equity, how effected 15.07–15.10
separability, doctrine of 1.16
set-off
    against separate obligation owed by
        counter-party 18.47
settlement
    success to rights of rescission 22.08
severable transactions
    undue influence 6.120
shareholder
    company in liquidation, no avoidance of statutory
        contract with 20.36
    winding up as bar to rescission *see* **winding-up**
shares
    allotment, unreasonable delay 24.88–24.90
    call on, defending 11.50–11.52
    counter-restitution at law 14.59, 14.72–14.73
    fraudulent misrepresentation, rescission of
        allotment following 11.68–11.74
    legal title to 14.22
    partly paid, issue of 11.52
    reassignment of 15.11
Singapore
    affirmation 23.02, 23.50
    innocent misrepresentation, contractual term
        and 27.46
    mistake, unilateral 7.22
    transfer of title to personal property, bar to
        rescission for 27.34
    transfer of title to real property, bar to rescission
        for 27.17

surety contracts
    business debts, guarantee by wife
        avoidance, vulnerable to 9.10
        constructive notice to creditor 9.08–9.13
        husband as agent of creditor 9.09
        influence, husband taking advantage of 9.07
    measures immunizing security 9.18–9.20
    non-commercial relationship, special circumstances
        of 9.15
    safeguards 9.20
    special measures requirement 9.14–9.20
    transaction not to surety's financial
        advantage 9.16–9.17

termination *ab initio*
    conditionally transferred property or money,
        dissolution of obligations 1.17
    contractual rights and obligations, effects
        on 1.14–1.19
    development of rules 3.32
    effect of 12.05
    election, communicating 12.04
    equitable relief, basis of 1.19
    fraud, contract procured by 12.06
    money paid, recovery of 1.29
    performance of obligation, effect of 1.18
    property transferred or created 1.24–1.28
    rescission, as synonym for 1.03
    revesting of title 1.25–1.28
    services rendered, payment for 1.29
    termination *de futuro* distinguished
        character of terminating event, turning on 1.09
        at common law 3.30–3.32
        extra-judicial explanation 1.08
        justification for rescission, in US 1.11
        nature and basis of distinction 1.07–1.13
        restitution, rights to 1.23–1.30
        terminology 1.31–1.34
        United States, law in 1.10–1.13
    unperformed or executory obligations,
        extinguishing 1.14–1.15
termination *de futuro*
    character of terminating event, turning on 1.09
    conditionally transferred property or money,
        dissolution of obligation 1.21
    contractual damages, surviving rights 1.22
    contractual rights and obligations, effects
        on 1.20–1.22
    development of rules 3.32
    extra-judicial explanation 1.08
    money paid, recovery of 1.29
    property transferred or created 1.24–1.28
    restitution, rights to 1.23–1.30
    services rendered, payment for 1.30
    termination *ab initio* distinguished
        character of terminating event, turning on 1.09
        at common law 3.30–3.32
        extra-judicial explanation 1.08
        justification for rescission, in US 1.11

termination *de futuro* (*cont.*)
    nature and basis of distinction 1.07–1.13
    restitution, rights to 1.23–1.30
    terminology 1.31–1.34
    United States, law in 1.10–1.13
    terminology 1.31–1.34

third party rights
    bona fide purchaser *see* **bona fide purchaser**
    defeating, effect of rescission 20.28
    as defence to claim to rescind 20.04
    destruction or frustration of 20.30
    intervention
        as bar to rescission 20.02
        as impossibility of *restitutio in integrum* 20.03
    jurisdictional limits 20.01
    at law 20.09–20.22
    lease, land encumbered by 20.26
    less valuable, rendered 20.29
    mortgage, land encumbered with 20.27
    multilateral contracts 20.31–20.32
    pledges, cases involving 20.14–20.15, 20.22
    property rights, protection
        asset sold 20.24–20.25
        authorities 20.10–20.17
        in equity 20.23–20.27
        fraudulent preferences compared 20.17
        indefeasible title, acquisition of 20.06
        innocent claimant, acquired from 20.08
        innocent third party, position of 20.18, 20.21, 20.23–20.27
    protection 20.06–20.27
        bar at law 20.09–20.22
        bar in equity 20.23–20.27
        other rights 20.28–20.36
        property rights *see above* property rights, protection
    purchaser's fraud, goods procured by 20.10–20.13
    remote recipient *see* **remote recipient**
    rescission of original sale, barring 20.07
    on sale 21.07
    subject matter of voidable transaction, contracts relating to 20.33–20.35
    title, function of passing 20.19–20.20
    winding-up bar 20.36
    wrongdoing purchaser 20.16

third party wrongdoers
    contracts
        agency 9.04
        basic rule precluding rescission 9.03
        knowledge of misconduct 9.05
        unilateral mistake, relationship with 9.06
    rescission against
        Australia, rule in 19.11–19.12
        bank 19.13–19.16
        comment on 19.34–19.46
        of contract 9.03–9.06
        gratuitous dispositions 9.21
        Irish case 19.13–19.16
        level of implication for 9.01
        as partial rescission 19.10–19.16
        as surety contract 9.07–9.20 *see also* **surety contracts**
        wife, security given by 9.02 *see also* **surety contracts**
    surety contract *see also* **surety contracts**
    surety contracts 9.07–9.20
    unilateral mistake 9.06

tracing
    retrospective equitable title conferring right to 16.42–16.43
    into substitutes 15.19, 16.10–16.11

trust
    constructive trust upon rescission 16.59–16.70
    payments of money, imposed on 1.91–1.98
    property other than money taken by fraud 1.99

trustees
    fair-dealing rule 1.70–1.71
    self-dealing rule 1.72–1.76, 8.02
    trust estate, title to 1.67

unconscionable bargains 7.69–7.103
    Commonwealth jurisdictions, approach in 7.103
    and conduct 7.01
    counterparty to show that transaction was fair, just and reasonable 7.93–7.96
    court interpretation 7.72
    defence possible 7.93–7.96
    England and Wales 7.70, 7.72
    examples 7.75
    'expectant heirs' 7.76
    exploitation 7.69–7.103
    fraud, and 7.69
    general principle 7.80–7.88
        applications of 7.84–7.88
    gifts 7.74, 7.86, 29.16
    gifts, doctrine not applied to 7.74, 29.16
    and impaired capacity 7.42
    independent advice 7.97–7.100
    and mistake 7.17
    poverty and ignorance, relevance 7.77, 7.78
    requirements as ground for rescission 7.70, 7.71
    serious disadvantage, relative to counterparty 7.75–7.79
    transaction overreaching and oppressive 7.89–7.92
    versus undue influence 7.73
    weakness exploited in morally culpable manner 7.80–7.88
        character of conduct 7.81
        general principle 7.80–7.83
        stronger party, conduct of 7.81, 7.82
        unequal bargaining power 7.81
        victimization 7.80

undue influence
    acquiescence, evidence of 24.44
    actual
        causation 6.89–6.92
        as equitable wrong 6.83
        examples 6.84–6.86
        exercise of 6.80–6.88

irrelevant matters 6.93
meaning 6.76
proof of 6.77, 6.87–6.93
substitute contract, avoidance 6.87–6.93
affirmation, conditions for 23.14
all surrounding circumstances 6.98
delay in seeking to rescind after 24.34–24.35
doctrine of 6.01
gift made under 1.38, 29.18, 29.20
gifts 29.15
ordinary motives, transaction not explicable by reference to 6.107
presumed
   arising without presumption of undue influence 6.100–6.101
   effect of 6.03
   establishment of case, tool in 6.96
   evidential burden 6.77
   exercise of free will, proof that transaction was result of 6.114
   explanation, transaction calling for 6.105–6.111
   fair-dealing rule, relationship with 8.07–8.08
   independent advice, effect 6.87, 6.115–6.119
   irrebuttably presumed relationship of influence 6.102–6.104
   manifest disadvantage 6.109
   meaning 6.76
   nature and effect of transaction, complainant understanding 6.115
   nature of 6.94–6.96
   onus of proof, shift in 6.78, 6.112
   proved or presumed relationships 6.97–6.99
proof of 6.76–6.79
rebuttal, failure 6.112–6.119
relationship of influence, proof of 6.95, 6.97–6.104
relationship of trust and confidence pre-dating impugned transaction 6.99
relationship proved or presumed 6.97–6.99
right to rescind as 'equitable right' 10.07
right to rescind, equitable nature of 10.07
scope of 6.02, 6.75
severable transactions 6.120
types 6.76, 6.79
versus unconscionable bargain 7.73
as wrong 6.03
unilateral mistake 7.12–7.26
in Australia 7.20–7.22
common law 7.12
Commonwealth jurisdictions 7.20–7.23
England and Wales 7.13–7.20
gifts 7.05
impaired capacity, versus 7.44
machine-generated contracts 7.24–7.26
meaning 7.02
in New Zealand 7.23
and non-disclosure 5.11
rectification, compared to 7.19
in Singapore 7.22
subject matter of contract 7.11, 7.17

terms of contract, as to 7.12, 7.17
third party wrongdoing, relationship with 9.06
United States, law in
counter-restitution 14.63–14.65
equity, transactions voidable in 11.64–11.65, 11.115
extinction of contract 1.10–1.13
fraud 29.72
unjust enrichment
prevention 18.05–18.06
rescission on terms 19.43
unregistered land
remote recipient 21.18
rescission of contract to transfer
   at law 14.23–14.27
   re-conveyance, execution 15.07

void contract
bribery 8.50
drunkenness 7.65
equitable title, location of 1.54
factors causing voidness 1.36
ineffective until ratified
   contrast with valid until rescinded 1.42–1.44
   meaning 1.40–1.41
meaning 1.04, 1.36
recovery of benefits 1.49–1.56
restitution, right to 1.49–1.56
for sale of land 1.47
transfer of title under 1.45–1.48
valid and binding 1.39
voidable
dispositions 1.59
meaning 1.60–1.62
principles of rescission, application 1.62
voidable contract
affirmation *see* **affirmation**
change from 'void' to 'voidable' 3.63
at common law 12.02
defence to claim on 1.43
drunkenness 7.65
effect of rescission 1.14
equitable title, location of 1.54
equity to rescind 16.16–16.18
historical development 3.05, 3.40–3.41, 3.63
intoxication 7.66
legal and beneficial title to property, passing 1.05
meaning 1.04, 1.35
mortgages 15.09, 15.53, 15.74, 22.03
parties' rights, governing until brought to an end 1.51
purchase of shares under 16.33
ratification 1.40–1.41
recovery of benefits 1.49–1.56
relationships of trust and confidence 5.21, 5.22
rescission *ab initio* 1.37
restitution, fragility of right to 1.56
serious disadvantage 7.79
third party rights 20.33–20.35
title passing under 16.12–16.15

voidable contract (*cont.*)
   transactions calling for explanation 6.108
   transfer of title under 1.45, 1.48
   valid until rescinded 1.39

volunteer, as remote recipient
   basis of claim against 21.29–21.30
   defeasible interest of transferor, receiving 21.05
   no value for property, giving 21.06–21.07
   original transferor, no better position than 21.37
   rescission available against 21.02
   voidable title, receipt from person taking 21.04

warranties
   and representations 4.22

will
   beneficiary, succession to rights of rescission 22.06

winding up
   commencement of 25.62
   defence, rescission as 25.20
   personal claims, assertion of 25.19
   proprietary claims, assertion of 25.18
   right to rescind not barred by 25.01
   shareholder's rescission, as bar to 25.21–25.78
      application of 25.21
      assertion of rights short of commencement of proceedings 25.72–25.75
      basic notions 25.23
      commencement of winding up, timing 25.62
      continuing representation of bar 25.28
      creditors, prejudice to 25.34–25.36, 25.37
      damages claim, bringing 25.48–25.50, 25.56
      development 25.22
      diminished relevance 25.29–25.30
      explanations for 25.31–25.41
      fraud, failure to sue caused by 25.76
      legal relations, alteration of 25.37–25.38
      liability as contributory, avoiding 25.42–25.44, 25.51
      market purchases 25.51–25.56
      operation before winding up 25.63–25.68
      origin of 25.22, 25.24–25.27
      persons who are not shareholders 25.61
      price, recovery of 25.45–25.47, 25.52–25.55
      rationale 25.31–25.41
      scope of 25.42–25.61
      shares, rejection of 25.69
      solvent company, winding up 25.59–25.60
      statutory exceptions 25.77–25.78
      steps to prevent operation of 25.69–25.76
      void allotments 25.57
      voluntary winding up 25.58
      wider considerations underpinning 25.39–25.41